CASES AND MATERIALS

CORPORATIONS AND OTHER BUSINESS ORGANIZATIONS

NINTH EDITION—UNABRIDGED

by

MELVIN ARON EISENBERG
Koret Professor of Law,
University of California at Berkeley

FOUNDATION PRESS

NEW YORK, NEW YORK

2005

© 1940, 1950, 1951, 1958, 1959, 1969, 1980, 1988, 1995, 2000 FOUNDATION PRESS
© 2005 By FOUNDATION PRESS
        395 Hudson Street
        New York, NY 10014
        Phone Toll Free 1–877–888–1330
        Fax (212) 367–6799
        fdpress.com
Printed in the United States of America

ISBN 1–58778–878–0

TEXT IS PRINTED ON 10% POST
CONSUMER RECYCLED PAPER

PREFACE

In many areas of corporate law, it is difficult to fully understand the issues and the legal rules without some background knowledge of basic accounting and financial concepts. Accordingly, this casebook includes introductory materials on such topics as financial statements, the present-value rule, diversification, valuation, the efficient capital market hypothesis, and dividend policy. These materials have been chosen and edited with an eye to ensuring that they are accessible to students who don't have an accounting and financial background. The materials are introduced gradually, at relevant points throughout the book, so that students are not faced with an onslaught of unfamiliar concepts.

Because of the importance of statutes in corporation law, students should refer to the Statutory Supplement whenever a cross-reference to that Supplement appears. When a cross-referenced statutory provision includes an Official Comment, the Comment should be read as well. Other cross-references to the Statutory Supplement (for example, references to excerpts from the Restatement (Second) of Agency) should be treated the same way.

In the preparation of this casebook, the following conventions have been used: Where a portion of the text of an original source (such as a case) has been omitted, the omission is indicated by ellipses. The omission of footnotes from original sources is not indicated, but the original footnote numbers are used for those footnotes that are retained.

The American Law Institute's Principles of Corporate Governance: Analysis and Recommendations (1994) is cited simply as ALI, Principles of Corporate Governance.

I thank Shawn Bayern and Joel Willard for outstanding work as research assistants; Steve Vercelloni for exceeding skill and diligence in preparing the manuscript for publication; and Elizabeth Erdinger, Marlene Harmon, Ginny Irving, Janice Kelly, Michael Levy, and Alice Youmans, Reference Librarians at the Law School at the University of California at Berkeley, and Kathleen Vanden Heuvel, the Library's Associate Director, for their thorough, accurate, fast, unflagging, and marvelous responses to the innumerable problems I sent them.

MELVIN A. EISENBERG

*

SUMMARY OF CONTENTS

ANALYTICAL TABLE OF CONTENTS

CHAPTER XII Structural Changes: Corporate Combina-

CHAPTER XIV The Public Distribution of Securities ---- 1263

*

TABLE OF CASES

Principal cases are in bold type. Non-principal cases are in roman type. References are to Pages.

*

CASES AND MATERIALS

CORPORATIONS AND OTHER BUSINESS ORGANIZATIONS

*

CHAPTER I

AGENCY

SECTION 1. INTRODUCTION

Courses in corporations or business associations are, in large part, courses in organizational law. The most common forms of business organization in this country are sole proprietorships, corporations, general and limited partnerships, and limited liability companies. Based on tax filings, as of 2001 there were 18,328,000 sole proprietorships in the United States (exclusive of farms), 5,136,000 corporations, and 2,132,000 unincorporated associations. U.S. Bureau of the Census, Statistical Abstract of the United States 483 (2004).

A *sole proprietorship* is a business organization that is owned by a single individual, and is not cast in a special legal form of organization, such as a corporation, that can be utilized only by filing an organic document with the state pursuant to an authorizing statute.

The term *business organization* may seem to be an inappropriate characterization of a form that involves only a single owner. That terminology can, however, be justified on at least two grounds.

First, a business enterprise that is owned by an individual is likely to have a degree of psychological and sociological identity separate from that of the individual. This separateness of a sole proprietor's enterprise is often expressed by giving the enterprise its own name, like "Acme Shoe Company." Furthermore, a sole proprietor usually will consider only a certain portion of her property and cash as invested in the business, and will keep a separate set of financial records for the enterprise, as if the enterprise's finances were separate from her own.

Thus, if Alice Adams begins a new business in 2005—say, Acme Shoe Company—she is likely to issue a balance sheet for the business that does not show all of her assets and liabilities, but only those assets dedicated to, and those liabilities arising out of, the enterprise's operations. (See Section 4, An Introduction to Financial Statements, infra.) In short, as a psychological matter Adams and those who deal with her are likely to regard Acme Shoe Company as an enterprise or firm that has a certain degree of separateness from Adams herself, and a certain amount of capital. As a matter of law, however, a sole proprietorship has no separate identity from its owner. If Adams takes no special legal step, like incorporating the enterprise, all of her wealth will be effectively committed to the enterprise, because an individual who owns a sole proprietorship has unlimited personal liability for obligations incurred in the conduct of the business.

[handwritten margin note: Small Business. sole proprieter is not separate from owner.]

The second reason for calling a sole proprietorship an organization is that a sole proprietor typically will not conduct the business by herself, but will engage various people—salespersons, mechanics, managers—to act on her behalf, and subject to her control, in conducting the business. The employment by one person, *P*, of another, *A*, to act on *P*'s behalf, and subject to her control, brings us to the most elementary form of organizational law, known as the law of agency. An *agent* is a person who by mutual assent acts on behalf of another and subject to the other's control. The person for whom the agent acts is a *principal.* Agency law governs: (1) The relationship between agents and principals. (2) The relationship between agents and third persons with whom an agent deals, or purports to deal, on a principal's behalf. (3) The relationship between principals and third persons when an agent deals, or purports to deal, with a third person on the principal's behalf.

Although agency is a consensual relationship, whether an agency relationship has been created does not turn on whether the parties *think of themselves* as or *intend* to be agent and principal. "Agency is the fiduciary relationship that arises when one person (a 'principal') manifests assent to another person (an 'agent') that the agent shall act on the principal's behalf and subject to the principal's control, and the agent manifests assent or otherwise consents so to act." Restatement (Third) of Agency § 1.01. "Whether a relationship is one of agency is a legal conclusion made after an assessment of the facts of the relationship and the application of the law of agency to those facts. Although agency is a consensual relationship, how the parties to any given relationship label it is not dispositive." Id. § 1.02, Comment *a*.

SECTION 2. AUTHORITY

Morris Oil Co. v. Rainbow Oilfield Trucking, Inc.

New Mexico Court of Appeals, 1987.
106 N.M. 237, 741 P.2d 840.

■ GARCIA, JUDGE. . . .

Defendant Dawn appeals from the judgment rendered against it in favor of Morris Oil Company, Inc. (Morris), based upon a determination that Rainbow Oilfield Trucking, Inc. (Rainbow) was Dawn's agent when it incurred indebtedness with Morris. We affirm the trial court.

FACTS

Appellant Dawn, the holder of a certificate of public convenience and necessity, is engaged in the oilfield trucking business in the Farmington area. Rainbow was a New Mexico corporation established for the purpose of operating an oilfield trucking business in the Hobbs area. Defendant corporations entered into several contracts whereby Rainbow would be permitted to use Dawn's certificate of public convenience and necessity in operating a trucking enterprise in Hobbs. Dawn reserved the right to full and complete control over the operations of Rainbow in New Mexico. Dawn was to collect all charges due and owing for transportation conducted by Rainbow and, after deducting a $1,000 per month "clerical fee" and a percentage of the gross receipts, was to remit the balance to Rainbow. Under a subcontract entered into by defendants, Rainbow was to be responsible for payment of operating expenses, including fuel; further, the subcontract provides that all operations utilizing fuel were to be under the direct control and supervision of Dawn. All billing for services rendered by Rainbow would be made under Dawn's name, with all monies to be collected by Dawn.

Defendants also entered into a terminal management agreement which provided that Dawn was to have complete control over Rainbow's Hobbs operation. The agreement further recited that Rainbow was not to become the agent of Dawn and was not empowered to incur or create any debt or liability of Dawn "other than in the ordinary course of business relative to terminal management." The agreement recited that Rainbow was to be an independent contractor and not an employee, and that liability on the part of Rainbow for creating charges in violation of the agreement would survive the termination of the agreement. Dawn was to notify Rainbow of any claim of such charges whereby Rainbow would assume the defense, compromise or payment of such claims.

Rainbow operated the oilfield trucking enterprise under these contractual documents, during which time Rainbow established a relationship with plaintiff Morris, whereby Morris installed a bulk dispenser at the Rainbow terminal and periodically delivered diesel fuel for use in the trucking operation. The enterprise proved unprofitable, however, and Rainbow ceased its operations and ultimately declared bankruptcy, owing Morris approximately $25,000 on an open account.

When Morris began its collection efforts against Rainbow, it determined that Rainbow had ceased its operations, everyone associated with Rainbow had moved back to Texas and it did not appear likely that the account would be paid. Morris was directed by Rainbow's representative in Texas to Dawn for payment of the account.

When Rainbow ceased its operations, Dawn was holding some $73,000 in receipts from the Hobbs operation. Dawn established an escrow account through its Roswell attorneys to settle claims arising from Rainbow's Hobbs operation. When Morris contacted Dawn with regard to the outstanding account, it was notified of the existence of the escrow account and was asked to forbear upon collection efforts, indicting that payment would be forthcoming from the escrow account. Dawn's representatives indicated that it was necessary to wait for authorization from Rainbow's parent Texas corporation before paying the account. At no time did Rainbow or Dawn question the amount or legitimacy of Morris' open account balance.

Dawn's principal [owner] further testified that the subcontract and terminal management agreement were cancelled by Dawn when he learned that Rainbow was incurring debts in Dawn's name. The charges owing to Morris, however, were incurred in the name of Rainbow and not Dawn.

Although some claims were paid from the attorneys' escrow account established by Dawn, there was no explanation at trial why the Morris claim was not paid. When Morris learned that the escrow funds had been disbursed without payment of its charges, it instituted this action and also sought to garnish the remaining $13,000 held by Dawn from the impounded funds. Rainbow did not defend, and the trial court entered a default judgment against Rainbow, from which it does not appeal.

DISCUSSION

The trial court found that Dawn retained the right to direct control and supervision of Rainbow's New Mexico operations, and that in the course of those operations, Rainbow incurred a balance of almost $25,000 on an open account with Morris for fuel used in the New Mexico operations. The trial court further found that when Rainbow defaulted on payments on Morris' account, Dawn made representations over a period of time concerning the existence of a fund held by Dawn to settle indebtedness created by Rainbow operating under the subcontract. The court determined that Morris delayed its collection efforts pending disbursement of the funds, and that Dawn was aware that Morris was relying upon Dawn's representations that payment would be made from the impounded fund. The trial court concluded that Rainbow was at all times in its dealings with Morris the agent of Dawn and, therefore, Dawn was responsible for the account balance.

Dawn urges one point of error on appeal; that the trial court erred in finding liability based on a principal-agent relationship between the defendants. Dawn relies upon the language in the terminal management agreement which states:

>   4. Rainbow is not appointed and shall not become the agent of Dawn and is not empowered to incur or create any debt or liability of Dawn other than in the ordinary course of business relative to terminal management. Rainbow shall not enter into or cause Dawn to become a party to any agreement without the express written consent of Dawn.

>   5. Rainbow shall be considered an independent contractor and not an employee of Dawn.

Dawn's reliance upon these paragraphs of the agreement is unpersuasive for two reasons. First, the agreement specifically states that Rainbow may create liabilities of Dawn in the ordinary course of business of operating the terminal. There is no question that the liability to Morris was incurred in the ordinary course of operating the trucking business. Second, the recitation of the parties in their contractual documents need not bind third parties who deal with one of them in ignorance of those instructions. See South Second Livestock Auction, Inc. v. Roberts, 69 N.M. 155, 364 P.2d 859 (1961); see also Great Northern R.R. Co. v. O'Connor, 232 U.S. 508, 34 S.Ct. 380, 58 L.Ed. 703 (1914).

While Dawn argues from cases discussing apparent authority, we view this as a case of undisclosed agency. Rainbow contracted in its own name and not in the name of Dawn Enterprises, Inc. Thus, this case involves concepts relating to undisclosed agency rather than to apparent authority, and is governed by principles of undisclosed principal-agent contracts. See, e.g., 3 Am.Jur.2d Agency § 316 (1986).

It is well established that an agent for an undisclosed principal subjects the principal to liability for acts done on his account if they are usual or necessary in such transactions. Restatement (Second) of Agency § 194 (1958). This is true even if the principal has previously forbidden the agent to incur such debts so long as the transaction is in the usual course of business engaged in by the agent. Id.

The indebtedness in the instant case is squarely governed by well-established principles of agency where an undisclosed principal entrusts the agent with the management of his business. The undisclosed principal is subject to liability to third parties with whom the agent contracts where such transactions are usual in the business conducted by the agent, even if the contract is contrary to the express directions of the principal. Restatement (Second) of Agency § 195 (1958).

Dawn's reliance upon Bloodgood v. Woman's Ben. Ass'n, 36 N.M. 228, 13 P.2d 412 (1932) is misplaced. Indeed, the case stands for the proposition that a principal may limit an agent's authority, and further, that the limitation will be binding upon a third party dealing with the agent if the third party has knowledge of the limitation of authority. Here there is no evidence that Morris had any actual knowledge of the existence of the Rainbow–Dawn agency, let alone any claimed limitations by Dawn on Rainbow's authority. It is undisputed that Morris thought it was dealing solely with Rainbow when it sold fuel.

Morris correctly observes that secret instructions or limitations placed upon the authority of an agent must be known to the party dealing with the agent, or the principal is bound as if the limitations had not been made. Chevron Oil Co. v. Sutton, 85 N.M. 679, 515 P.2d 1283 (1973)....

Moreover, assuming arguendo that Dawn was not responsible for the indebtedness to Morris for the reasons urged on appeal, it is clear that Dawn ratified the open account after learning of its existence when Morris contacted Dawn regarding payment. A principal may be held liable for the unauthorized acts of his agent if the principal ratifies the transaction after acquiring knowledge of the material facts concerning the transaction. Ulibarri Landscaping Material, Inc. v. Colony Materials, Inc., 97 N.M. 266, 639 P.2d 75 (Ct.App.1981).

It was undisputed that in several telephone conversations between the principals of Dawn and Morris, the material facts of the Morris open account were disclosed to Dawn. At no time did Dawn dispute the legitimacy or amount of the open account, and indeed assured Morris that payment would be forthcoming from the funds retained from Rainbow's revenues. Despite this, Dawn used the fund to pay itself a $1,000 per month clerical fee, to pay legal fees incurred as a result of its agency with Rainbow and to settle other claims arising from the Rainbow operations. Where the principal retains the benefits or proceeds of its business relations with an agent with knowledge of the material facts, the principal is deemed to have ratified the methods employed by the agent in generating the proceeds. See id. See also 3 Am.Jur.2d Agency § 194 (1986). The diesel fuel provided by Morris was used in Rainbow's trucking operation. Dawn collected the receipts due to Rainbow. Dawn seeks to retain the benefits of the agency with Rainbow, and yet at the same time disclaims responsibility for the business of the agent by which the benefits were generated. This it cannot do. Ulibarri Landscaping Material, Inc. v. Colony Materials, Inc.

In sum, for the foregoing reasons, we affirm.

IT IS SO ORDERED. . . .

■ BIVINS and MINZNER, JJ., concur.

NOTE ON THE RESTATEMENTS OF AGENCY

Restatement (Second) of Agency was completed in 1958. Since the late 1990s, the American Law Institute has been working on Restatement (Third) of Agency. As of the date this Casebook went to press, it seems highly likely that the new Restatement will be adopted at the 2005 meeting of the ALI, and published some time thereafter. Since it will be some time before the cases begin utilizing Restatement (Third) of Agency extensively, and since Restatement (Second) of Agency plays an important role in many existing decisions, this Chapter refers to both Restatements.

For ease of exposition, in the balance of this chapter the two Restatements will sometimes be referred to as Restatement Second and Restatement Third, respectively.

———

RESTATEMENT (SECOND) OF AGENCY §§ 8A, 8B, 26, 27, 32, 33, 35, 39, 42, 43, 49, 82–85, 87–90, 93, 94, 97–100A, 113, 144, 154, 161, 186

[See Statutory Supplement]*

———

* References in the Casebook to the *Statutory Supplement* are to *Corporations and Other Business Organizations—Statutes,* *Rules, Materials, and Forms* (M. Eisenberg ed., Foundation Press; revised annually).

RESTATEMENT (THIRD) OF AGENCY §§ 2.01–2.03, 2.05, 3.01, 3.03, 3.06, 4.01–4.02, 6.01–6.03, 6.10, 8.14

[See Statutory Supplement]

———

NOTE ON AUTHORITY

1. *Terminology*. An *agent* is a person who by mutual assent acts on behalf and subject to the control of another—the principal. For some purposes, agents are classified as general or special. A *general agent* is an agent who is authorized to conduct a series of transactions involving continuity of service. A *special agent* is an agent who is authorized to conduct only a single transaction, or only a series of transactions not involving continuity of service. Restatement Second § 3.

A *principal* is a person on whose behalf and subject to whose control an agent acts. Principals are conventionally divided into three classes: disclosed, partially disclosed or unidentified, and undisclosed.

A principal is *disclosed* if, when an agent and a third party interact, the third party has notice that the agent is acting for a principal and has notice of the principal's identity.

A principal is *partially disclosed* or *unidentified* if, when an agent and a third party interact, the third party has notice that the agent is acting for a principal but does not have notice of the principal's identity.

A principal is *undisclosed* if, when an agent and a third party interact, the third party has no notice that the agent is acting for a principal.

In the case of vicarious liability for *torts* committed by an agent, a principal is traditionally referred to as a master and an agent is traditionally referred to as a servant. A *master* is a principal who controls, or has the right to control, the *physical conduct* of an agent in the performance of the agent's services. A *servant* is an agent whose physical conduct in the performance of services for the principal is subject to the control of the principal. Restatement Second § 2. Both terms are purely technical, and "do not denote menial or manual service. Many servants perform exacting work requiring intelligence rather than muscle. Thus the officers of a corporation or a ship, [and the interns] in a hospital ... are servants...." Id., Comment c.

Restatement Third adopts a different approach to a principal's vicarious liability for an agent's torts. Rather than using the terms *master* and *servant*, Restatement Third uses the terms *principal* and *employee*. And rather than using a test based on whether the principal has the right to control the physical activity of the agent, Restatement

Third defines an employee, for the purposes of the principal's vicarious liability in tort, as an agent whose principal "controls or has the right to control the manner and means of the agent's performance of work." Id. § 7.07(3)(a).

Against the background of this terminology, Restatement Third adopts the following rule to govern the principal's vicarious tort liability:

> (1) An employer is subject to vicarious liability for a tort committed by its employee acting within the scope of employment.
>
> (2) An employee acts within the scope of employment when performing work assigned by the employer or engaging in a course of conduct subject to the employer's control. An employee's act is not within the scope of employment when it occurs within an independent course of conduct not intended by the employee to serve any purpose of the employer.

Id. § 7.07(1), (2).

The vicarious liability of a master or principal for the tort of a servant or employee is referred to as liability in *respondeat superior.* The rationale of respondeat superior has been well-summarized by Professor Fishman as follows:

> The adoption of enterprise liability under respondeat superior is justified on several policy grounds. First, the ability of the enterprise to spread the risk from losses is important. The enterprise is in a better position than . . . the injured third person to spread the risk of loss, either through insurance or the ability to factor the potential losses into the price for the goods produced. A second reason suggests that proper allocation of resources is promoted by requiring an enterprise to include in the price of its goods the costs of the accidents which are closely associated with the enterprise's operations. A third reason . . . is that the [principal] is in a position to control the employee and placing the risk of loss here could lead to greater safety. A fourth reason is that it is considered more equitable to place the liability on the [principal], because it provides greater assurance that the accident victim will be paid, or because there is a societal preference to make certain losses costs of doing business rather than losses to be borne by individual households.

Fishman, Inherent Agency Power—Should Enterprise Liability Apply to Agents' Unauthorized Contracts?, 19 Rutgers L.J. 1, 48–49 (1987).

A variety of problems can arise out of an actual or alleged principal-agency relationship. Perhaps the most common problem is, what liabilities arise out of a given transaction between the agent and a third person? Most of the issues implicated by that question are addressed by the legal rules governing *authority.* This Note will emphasize the liability of the principal to the third person (Section 2), but will also consider the liability of the third person to the principal (Section 3), the liability of the agent to the third person (Section 4), and the duties and liabilities of the agent and the principal to each other (Sections 5 and 6). Although the law of agency encompasses liabilities in tort as well as in contract, for the most part the balance of this Note will address only issues that relate to contractual transactions.

2. *Liability of Principal to Third Person.* Under the law of agency, a principal becomes liable to a third person as a result of an act or transaction by another, A, on the principal's behalf, if A had actual, apparent, or (traditionally) inherent authority to act on the principal's behalf in the way that he did, or was an agent by estoppel, or if the principal ratified the act or transaction.

a. *Actual authority.* An agent has *actual authority* to act in a given way on a principal's behalf if the principal's words or conduct would lead a reasonable person in the agent's position to believe that the principal wishes the agent so act. If an agent has actual authority and acts within the scope of that authority, the principal is bound.

> *Illustration 1:* P goes to an office where, as he knows, several brokers have desks, and leaves upon the desk of A, thinking it to be the desk of X, a note signed by him, which states: "I authorize you to contract in my name for the purchase of 100 shares of Western Union stock at today's market." A comes in, finds the note and, not knowing of the mistake, immediately makes a contract with T in P's name for the purchase of the shares. A had actual authority to make the contract.[1]

Actual authority may be either *express* or *implied:* "It is possible for a principal to specify minutely what the agent is to do. To the extent that he does this, the agent may be said to have express authority. But most authority is created by implication. Thus, in the authorization to 'sell my automobile', the only fully expressed power is to transfer title in exchange for money or a promise to give money. In fact, under some circumstances ... there may ... be power to take or give possession of the automobile or to extend credit or to accept something in partial exchange. These powers are all implied or inferred from the words used, from customs and from the relations of the parties. They are described as 'implied authority.' " Restatement Second § 7, Comment c; see also Restatement Third § 2.02, Comment *b*.

A common type of implied actual authority is *incidental authority,* which is the authority to do incidental acts that are reasonably necessary to accomplish an actually authorized transaction, or that usually accompany a transaction of that type. If the principal has authorized the agent to engage in a given transaction, and certain acts are reasonably necessary to accomplish the transaction, or usually accompany it, a reasonable person in the agent's position would believe that the authority to engage in the transaction also conferred

---

1. All the Illustrations in this Note are either literal or slightly modified versions of Illustrations in Restatement Second and Restatement Third.

authority to engage in those acts. Here are two examples of implied actual authority:

> *Illustration 2:* P directs A to sell goods by auction at a time and place at which, as P and A know, a statute forbids anyone but a licensed auctioneer to conduct sales by auction. Nothing to the contrary appearing, A's actual authority includes [implied] actual authority to employ a licensed auctioneer.

> *Illustration 3:* P authorizes A, a local broker, to sell and convey land. At the time and place it is the custom to make such sales with a warranty of title. A has implied actual authority to execute and deliver a proper deed to the purchaser and to insert in the deed the usual covenants as to title.

If an agent has actual authority, the principal is bound even if the third person did not know that the agent had actual authority, and indeed even if the third person thought the agent was herself the principal, not merely an agent. Accordingly, an undisclosed principal is bound by her agent's authorized transaction even though the agent purports to act strictly on his own behalf. One reason the undisclosed principal is liable is that she set the transaction in motion and stood to gain from it. A second reason is this: Even if the undisclosed principal was not directly liable to the third person, the agent would be. Therefore, the third person could sue the agent. If he did so, the agent could then sue the principal for indemnification of the damages he had to pay the third person. (See Section 6 of this Note, infra.) Accordingly, allowing the third person to sue the undisclosed principal does not materially enlarge the principal's liability, and collapses two lawsuits into one.

b. *Apparent authority.* An agent has *apparent authority* to act in a given way on a principal's behalf in relation to a third person, T, if manifestations of the principal to T (or manifestations by the agent to T that the principal authorized the agent to employ) would lead a reasonable person in T's position to believe that the principal had authorized the agent to so act. If an agent has apparent authority and acts within the scope of that authority, the principal is bound. Here are four examples:

> *Illustration 4:* P writes to A directing him to act as his agent for the sale of Blackacre. P sends a copy of this letter to T, a prospective purchaser. A has actual authority to sell Blackacre and, as to T, apparent authority.

> *Illustration 5:* Same facts as in Illustration 4, except that in the letter to A, P adds a postscript, not included in the copy to T, telling A to make no sale until after communication with P. A has no actual authority to sell Blackacre but, as to T, he has apparent authority.

> *Illustration 6:* Same facts as in Illustration 4, except that after A and T have received the letters, P telegraphs a revocation to A. A has no actual authority but, as to T, he has apparent authority to sell Blackacre.

Illustration 7: P owns a granary and employs A to manage it. A's employment agreement with P states that A's authority to purchase grain is limited to transactions that do not exceed $5000; larger purchases require P's express approval. This limit is unusual in the granary business. P directs A to tell T, a seller of grain, that A's unilateral authority to purchase is unlimited because P believes this will induce T to give priority to orders placed by A. A represents to T that A's authority to purchase is unlimited and enters into a contract on P's behalf with T to buy $10,000 of grain. P is bound by the contract with T. A has actual authority to make the representation to T. A has apparent authority to enter into the contract with T because T reasonably believes A has authority to bind P to a contract to buy the grain.

In most cases, actual and apparent authority go hand in hand, as Illustration 4 suggests. For example, if P Bank appoints A as cashier, and nothing more is said, A will reasonably believe he has the authority that cashiers normally have, and third persons who deal with A will reasonably believe the same thing. Apparent authority becomes salient in such a case if P Bank does not actually give A all the authority that cashiers usually have, and a customer deals with A knowing that A is a cashier, but not knowing that P Bank has placed special limits on A's authority.

The apparent authority of A in the cashier hypothetical is a special type of apparent authority known as *power of position.* "[A]pparent authority can be created by appointing a person to a position, such as that of manager or treasurer, which carries with it generally recognized duties; to those who know of the appointment there is apparent authority to do the things ordinarily entrusted to one occupying such a position, regardless of unknown limitations which are imposed upon the particular agent. . . . If a principal puts an agent into, or knowingly permits him to occupy, a position in which according to the ordinary habits of persons in the locality, trade or profession, it is usual for such an agent to have a particular kind of authority, anyone dealing with him is justified in inferring that he has such authority, in the absence of reason to know otherwise." Restatement Second § 27, Comment a and § 49, Comment c.

Illustration 8: P bank appoints A as an information clerk, with authority only to answer questions of depositors. During alterations, however, the bank directs A to occupy the space normally occupied by one of the receiving tellers, [with] a sign indicating that it is the "information" window. The sign becomes displaced and T, a depositor in the bank, makes a cash deposit with A, believing that he is a teller. P is bound by this transaction.

c. *Agency by estoppel.* Still another type of authority is known as "agency by estoppel." The core of agency by estoppel is described as follows in Restatement Third § 2.05:

A person who has not made a manifestation that an actor has authority as an agent and who is not otherwise liable as a party to a transaction purportedly done by the actor on that person's account is liable to a third party who is induced to make a detrimental change in position because the transcription is believed to be on the person's account, if

>   (1) the person intentionally or carelessly caused such belief, or

>   (2) having notice of such a belief and that it might induce others to change their positions, the person did not take reasonable steps to notify them of the facts.

The concept of agency by estoppel is so close to the concept of apparent authority that for most practical purposes the former concept can be subsumed in the latter.

d. *Inherent authority.* Under the doctrine of *inherent authority*, an agent may bind a principal in certain cases even when the agent had neither actual nor apparent authority. Although the doctrine of inherent authority is relatively well established, its exact contours are not always clear, and Restatement Third drops or at least reconceptualizes the doctrine.

Section 161 of Restatement Second concerns the inherent authority of general agents of disclosed or partially disclosed principals. Under Section 161, a disclosed or partially disclosed principal is liable for an act done on his behalf by a general agent, even if the principal had forbidden the agent to do the act, if (i) the act usually accompanies or is incidental to transactions that the agent is authorized to conduct, and (ii) the third person reasonably believes the agent is authorized to do the act. Section 194 of Restatement Second concerns the inherent authority of agents for undisclosed principals. It provides that "A general agent for an undisclosed principal authorized to conduct transactions subjects his principal to liability for acts done on his account, if usual or necessary in such transactions, although forbidden by the principal to do them." Unlike Section 161, Section 194 does not require that the third person reasonably believes the agent is authorized to act. Indeed, such a requirement could not be imposed, because in the case of an undisclosed principal the third person will not know that he is dealing with an agent.

A major rationale of inherent authority in Restatement Second is based on an analogy to the doctrine of respondeat superior in torts:

>   ... It is inevitable that in doing their work, either through negligence or excess of zeal, agents will harm third persons or will deal with them in unauthorized ways. It would be unfair for an enterprise to have the benefit of the work of its agents without making it responsible to some extent for their excesses and failures to act carefully. The answer of the common law has been the creation of special agency powers or, to phrase it otherwise, the imposition of liability upon the principal because of unauthorized or negligent acts of his servants and other agents....*

* Recall that the terms "master" and "servant" have technical meanings in agency law. (Footnote by ed.)

... [The principal's liability under the doctrine of inherent authority] is based primarily upon the theory that, if one appoints an agent to conduct a series of transactions over a period of time, it is fair that he should bear losses which are incurred when such an agent, although without authority to do so, does something which is usually done in connection with the transactions he is employed to conduct. Such agents can properly be regarded as part of the principal's organization in much the same way as a servant is normally part of the master's business enterprise.... The basis of [inherent authority] is comparable to the liability of a master for the torts of his servant.... In the case of the master, it is thought fair that one who benefits from the enterprise and has a right to control the physical activities of those who make the enterprise profitable, should pay for the physical harm resulting from the errors and derelictions of the servants while doing the kind of thing which makes the enterprise successful. The rules imposing liability upon the principal for some of the contracts and conveyances of a general agent, whether or not a servant, which he is neither authorized nor apparently authorized to make, are based upon a similar public policy. Commercial convenience requires that the principal should not escape liability where there have been deviations from the usually granted authority by persons who are such essential parts of his business enterprise. In the long run it is of advantage to business, and hence to employers as a class, that third persons should not be required to scrutinize too carefully the mandates of permanent or semipermanent agents who do no more than what is usually done by agents in similar positions.

Restatement Second § 89, Comment *a*, § 161, Comment b.

An alternative rationale for the doctrine of inherent authority is based on the principal's reasonable expectations. In a world with perfect information, faithful agents will follow all instructions impeccably. In the real world, however, agents acting in good faith will not infrequently deviate from their instructions. Agents, like everyone else, will make mistakes, which may take the form of misinterpreting their instructions or forgetting one of numerous instructions. Furthermore, an agent may reasonably believe that his principal's objective is best served by violating a particular instruction. A principal's instructions to her agent are necessarily given in the present to govern the future. The future, however, may develop in such a way that the agent reasonably believes that if the principal knew all the facts, she would not want the agent to follow a given instruction. Of course, the agent could go back to the principal for further instructions, but often it is infeasible to take that course of action—for example, because a valuable opportunity must be taken immediately or not at all. These real-world facts are reflected in a passage in the Comment to Restatement Second § 8A: "It is inevitable that in doing their work, either through negligence or excess of zeal, agents will harm third persons or will deal with them in unauthorized ways. It would be unfair for an enterprise to have the benefit of the work of its agents without making it responsible to some extent for their excesses and failures to act carefully.''

Given these realities, the doctrine of inherent authority can be justified on the ground that it is or should be foreseeable to a principal, when he appoints an agent, that as a practical matter the agent, acting in good faith for the benefit of the principal, is likely to deviate occasionally from instructions. As between the principal, who appointed the agent, who benefits from the agent's activities, and who could or should have foreseen a certain range of deviations from instructions, on the one hand, and the third person who contracts with the agent, on the other, a loss that results from a foreseeable deviation is better placed on the principal.

Restatement Third does not use the term ''inherent agency power,'' because ''[o]ther doctrines stated in this Restatement encompasses the justifications underpinning [the concept of inherent agency] including the importance of interpretation by the agent in the agent's relationship with the principle....'' Id. § 2.01, Comment b. In keeping with this Comment, Restatement Third § 2.02 defines the scope of actual authority in an expansive manner:

> (1) An agent has actual authority to take action designated or implied in the principal's manifestations and acts necessary or incidental to achieving the principal's objectives, as the agent reasonably understands them when the agent determines how to act.

> (2) An agent's interpretation of the principal's manifestations is reasonable if it reflects any meaning by the agent to be ascribed by the principal and, in the absence of any meaning known to the agent, as a reasonable person in the agent's position would interpret the manifestations in light of the context, including circumstances of which the agent has notice....

The Comment to Section 2.02 makes clear that in determining an agent's actual authority, a literal interpretation of the principal's manifestations does not always govern:

> An agent's understanding of the principal's interests and objectives is an element of the agent's reasonable interpretation of the principal's conduct. If a literal interpretation of a principal's communication to the agent would authorize an act inconsistent with the principal's interests or objectives known to the agent, it is open to question whether the agent's literal interpretation is reasonable.

Id. at Comment b. Correspondingly, the Comment recognizes that an agent may properly act in a way that is knowingly at variance with the principal's original instructions if the agent believes that (i) circumstances have changed since the initial instructions, (ii) were the principal to reconsider the matter, different instructions would have been given, and (iii) it is impracticable to communicate with the principal for further clarification before action needs to be taken:

... *Illustration 9:* P owns and operates a golf course on land that almost entirely surrounds Blackacre. P retains A, directing A to buy Blackacre but to offer no more than $250,000. Blackacre is to be sold at an auction in which the successful bidder will be required to deposit a check in an amount equal to 10 percent of the bid. P gives A a blank check to use in making the deposit. A has notice of P's long-term business plan to enhance the aesthetic and athletic qualities of the course and thereby make it more profitable. At the auction of Blackacre, A learns for the first time that there will be one other bidder, B. A also learns that B's plan for using Blackacre is to construct a cement factory on it. A is unable to contact P to relay this information and receive further instructions. A succeeds in purchasing Blackacre for P by bidding $260,000. A acted with actual authority.*

e. *Ratification.* Even if an agent has neither actual, apparent, nor inherent authority, the principal will be bound to the third person if the agent purported to act on the principal's behalf, and the principal, with knowledge of the material facts, either (1) affirms the agent's conduct by manifesting an intention to treat the agent's conduct as authorized, or (2) engages in conduct that is justifiable only if he has such an intention.

Manifesting an intention to treat the agent's conduct as authorized is sometimes known as *express ratification.* Here is an example:

Illustration 10: Without power to bind P, A purports to represent him in buying a horse from T. P affirms. P is now a party to the transaction.

Engaging in conduct that is justifiable only if the principal intends to treat the agent's conduct as authorized is sometimes known as *implied ratification.* The most common example is the case where, as a result of the purported agent's transaction, the principal, with knowledge of the facts, receives or retains something to which he would otherwise not be entitled. Here is an example:

Illustration 11: P owns an advertising agency and employs A to service existing accounts by purchasing space in advertising media. A does not have authority to set terms with clients. A executes an agreement with T that commits P to develop a new advertising campaign for T. P learns of the agreement and then retains advance payment made by T for the new advertising campaign. By accepting and retaining the payment, P has ratified the unauthorized agreement made by A.

Ratification need not be communicated to the third person to be effective, although it must be objectively manifested. Restatement Third § 4.01, Comment d. However, to be effective a ratification must occur before either the third person has withdrawn, or there has been a material change in circumstances that would make it inequitable to bind the third party unless the third party chooses to be bound. See Restatement Third § 4.05.

---

* Illustration 9 is based on Restatement Third § 2.02, Illustrations 20–22.

As the Comment to Restatement (Second) of Agency § 52 points out, "The concept of ratification . . . is unique. It does not conform to the rules of contracts, since it can be accomplished without consideration to or manifestation by the purported principal and without fresh consent by the other party." The justification of the concept lies in its functionality. The Comment to Restatement Third provides the following rationale:

> Ratification often serves the function of clarifying situations of ambiguous or uncertain authority. A principal's ratification confirms of validates the agent's right to have acted as the agent did. That is, an agent's action may have been effective to bind the principal to the third party, and the third party to the principal, because the agent acted with apparent authority. See § 2.03. If the principal ratifies the agent's act, it is thereafter not necessary to establish that the agent acted with apparent authority. Moreover, by replicating the effects of actual authority, the principal's ratification eliminates claims the principal would otherwise have against the agent for acting without actual authority. . . . The principal's ratification may also eliminate claims that third parties could assert against the agent when the agent has purported to have authority to bind the principal but the principal is not bound. . . .

A related but different rationale for the concept of ratification was stated by Judge Posner in *Goldstick v. ICM Realty*, 788 F.2d 456, 460 (7th Cir.1986):

> . . . The best explanation [of the concept of ratification] may be that the principal would not have ratified the contract unless he had seen a commercial advantage in doing so, and that the advantage would be less if the ratification had no binding effect. Ordinarily a principal ratifies an agent's unauthorized transaction in order to protect the principal's relationship with the other party to the transaction, usually a customer or supplier: and for ratification to have this protective effect it has to be more than an idle gesture, signifying nothing because unenforceable.

f. *Acquiescence.* A concept that is comparable to but different from ratification is authority by *acquiescence.* "[I]f the agent performs a series of acts of a similar nature, the failure of the principal to object to them is an indication that he consents to the performance of similar acts in the future under similar conditions." Restatement Second § 43, Comment b. Suppose, for example, an agent engages in a series of comparable purchases on the principal's behalf. Prior to the first purchase, a reasonable person in the agent's position would not have thought he had authority to enter into such a transaction. Nevertheless, the principal did not object either to that purchase or to later such purchases when she learned of them. At that point, a reasonable person in the agent's position would assume that the principal approved the agent's engaging in such purchases. Accordingly, the principal's acquiescence gives rise to actual authority. As to third persons who know of the acquiescence, the acquiescence also gives rise to apparent authority.

g. *Termination of agent's authority.* As a general rule, a principal has the *power* to terminate an agent's authority at any time, even if doing so violates a contract between the principal and the agent, and even if it had been agreed that the agent's authority was irrevocable. This rule rests largely on the ground that contracts relating to personal services will not be specifically enforced. (There is an important but limited exception to this rule, which applies to a type of relationship known as an *agency (or power) coupled with an interest.* This exception will be discussed in Chapter 6, infra.) However, such a contract is effective to create *liability* (damages) for wrongful termination. Here is an example:

> *Illustration 12:* In consideration of A's agreement to advertise and give his best energies to the sale of Blackacre, its owner, P, grants to A "a power of attorney, irrevocable for one year" to sell it. A advertises and spends time trying to sell Blackacre. At the end of three months P informs A that he revokes. A's authority is terminated, but A has a right to damages for breach of contract.

3. *Liability of Third Person to Principal.* Section 2 considered the liability of a principal to a third person. What is the liability of the third person to the principal? The general rule is that if an agent and a third person enter into a contract, and the agent's principal is liable to the third person under the contract, then the third person is liable to the principal. Restatement Second § 292; Restatement Third §§ 6.01–6.03. The major exception is that the third person is not liable to an undisclosed principal if the agent or the principal knew that the third person would not have dealt with the principal if he had known the principal's identity. See Restatement Second § 292, Comment c; Restatement Third § 6.03, Comment d.

4. *Liability of Agent to Third Person.*

Where an agent has entered into a contract with a third person on behalf of a principal, whether the agent will be liable to the third person turns in the first instance on whether the principal is bound under the contract.

a. *Where the principal is bound.* Where the agent has actual, apparent, or inherent authority, so that the principal is bound to the third person, the agent's liability to the third person largely depends on whether the principal was disclosed, undisclosed, or partially disclosed (or unidentified).

(i) *Disclosed principal.* Assume that the principal was disclosed (that is, at the time of the transaction the third person had notice that the agent was acting on behalf of a principal, and had notice of the principal's identity). If the principal is bound by the agent's act because the agent had actual, apparent, or inherent authority, or because the principal ratified the act, the general rule is that the agent is not bound to the third person. Restatement Second § 320; Restatement Third § 6.01. The theory is that in such a case the third person did not expect the agent to be bound; he did expect the principal to be bound; and he gets just what he expects.

(ii) *Undisclosed principal.* If the principal was undisclosed (that is, if at the time of the transaction the agent purported to act on his own behalf), the general rule is that the agent is bound even though the principal is bound too. Restatement Second § 322; Restatement Third § 6.03. The theory is that the third person must have expected the agent to be a party to the contract, because that is how the agent presented the transaction. However, there has been a quirk in the law here. Under the majority rule, if the third person, after learning of an undisclosed principal's identity, obtains a judgment against the principal, the agent is discharged from liability even if the judgment is not satisfied. Similarly, the undisclosed principal is discharged if the third person obtains a judgment against the agent. Under the minority rule, which is sounder, neither the agent nor the principal is discharged by a judgment against the other, but only by satisfaction of the judgment. That rule is adopted in Restatement Third § 6.09.

(iii) *Partially disclosed (or unidentified) principal.* If the principal was partially disclosed (or unidentified)—that is, if at the time of the transaction the third person had notice that the agent was acting on behalf of a principal, but did not have notice of the principal's identity—the general rule is that the agent as well as the principal is bound to the third person. Restatement Second § 321; Restatement Third § 6.02. The theory is that if the third person did not know the identity of the principal, and therefore could not investigate the principal's credit or reliability, he probably expected that the agent would be liable, either solely or as a co-promisor or surety.

b. *Where the principal is not bound.* If the principal is *not* bound by the agent's act, because the agent did not have actual, apparent, or inherent authority, the general rule is that the agent is liable to the third person. The agent's liability is usually based on the theory that an agent makes an implied warranty of authority to the third person. However, a few authorities have adopted a theory that the agent can be held liable on the contract itself. In principle, the difference between the two theories might lead to a difference in the measure of damages. Under the liability-on-the-contract theory, the third person will recover the gains that he would have derived under the contract—essentially, expectation damages. In contrast, under the implied-warranty theory it might seem that the third person would recover only the losses he suffered by having entered into the transaction—essentially, reliance damages. However, both Restatement Second and Restatement Third, while adopting the implied-warranty theory, provide for an expectation measure of damages, just as if the contract theory had been adopted. See Restatement Second § 329; Restatement Third § 6.10.

5. *Liability of Agent to Principal.* If an agent takes an action that he has no actual authority to perform, but the principal is nevertheless bound because the agent had apparent authority, the agent is liable to the principal for any resulting damages to the principal. Restatement

Second § 383, Comment e; Restatement Third § 8.09, Comment b. Whether an agent is liable to the principal for an act that binds the principal by virtue of the agent's inherent but not actual authority is an unsettled point.

6. *Liability of Principal to Agent.* If an agent has acted within his actual authority, the principal is under a duty to indemnify the agent for payments the agent made that were authorized or made necessary in executing the principal's affairs. This includes (i) authorized payments made by the agent on the principal's behalf; (ii) payments made by the agent to a third person under contracts on which the agent was authorized to make himself liable (for example, where the agent acted on behalf of a partially disclosed or undisclosed principal); (iii) payments of damages to third parties that the agent incurs because of an authorized act that constituted a breach of contract for which the agent was liable to the third person; and (iv) expenses in defending actions brought against the agent by third persons because of the agent's authorized conduct. See Restatement Second §§ 438–440; Restatement Third § 8.14.

SECTION 3.   THE AGENT'S DUTY OF LOYALTY

Tarnowski v. Resop

Supreme Court of Minnesota, 1952.
236 Minn. 33, 51 N.W.2d 801.

■ KNUTSON, JUSTICE.

Plaintiff desired to make a business investment. He engaged defendant as his agent to investigate and negotiate for the purchase of a route of coin-operated music machines. On June 2, 1947, relying upon the advice of defendant and the investigation he had made, plaintiff purchased such a business from Phillip Loechler and Lyle Mayer of Rochester, Minnesota, who will be referred to hereinafter as the sellers. The business was located at LaCrosse, Wisconsin, and throughout the surrounding territory. Plaintiff alleges that defendant represented to him that he had made a thorough investigation of the route; that it had 75 locations in operation; that one or more machines were at each location; that the equipment at each location was not more than six months old; and that the gross income from all locations amounted to more than $3,000 per month. As a matter of fact, defendant had made only a superficial investigation and had investigated only five of the locations. Other than that, he had adopted false representations of the sellers as to the other locations and had passed them on to plaintiff as his own. Plaintiff was to pay $30,620 for the business. He paid $11,000 down. About six weeks after the purchase, plaintiff discovered that the representations made to him by defendant were false, in that there were not more than 47 locations;

that at some of the locations there were no machines and at others there were machines more than six months old, some of them being seven years old; and that the gross income was far less than $3,000 per month. Upon discovering the falsity of defendant's representations and those of the sellers, plaintiff rescinded the sale. He offered to return what he had received, and he demanded the return of his money. The sellers refused to comply, and he brought suit against them in the district court of Olmsted county. The action was tried, resulting in a verdict of $10,000 for plaintiff. Thereafter, the sellers paid plaintiff $9,500, after which the action was dismissed with prejudice pursuant to a stipulation of the parties.

In this action, brought in Hennepin county, plaintiff alleges that defendant, while acting as agent for him, collected a secret commission from the sellers for consummating the sale, which plaintiff seeks to recover under his first cause of action. In his second cause of action, he seeks to recover damages for [losses caused by defendant's wrong].

1.   With respect to plaintiff's first cause of action, the principle that all profits made by an agent in the course of an agency belonging to the principal, whether they are the fruits of performance or the violation of an agent's duty, is firmly established and universally recognized. Smitz v. Leopold, 51 Minn. 455, 53 N.W. 719. . . .

It matters not that the principal has suffered no damage or even that the transaction has been profitable to him. Raymond Farmers Elevator Co. v. American Surety Co., 207 Minn. 117, 290 N.W. 231, 126 A.L.R. 1351.

The rule and the basis therefor are well stated in Lum v. Clark, 56 Minn. 278, 282, 57 N.W. 662, where, speaking through Mr. Justice Mitchell, we said: "Actual injury is not the principle the law proceeds on, in holding such transactions void. Fidelity in the agent is what is aimed at, and, as a means of securing it, the law will not permit him to place himself in a position in which he may be tempted by his own private interests to disregard those of his principal. . . . It is not material that no actual injury to the company [principal] resulted, or that the policy recommended may have been for its best interest. Courts will not inquire into these matters. It is enough to know that the agent in fact placed himself in such relations that he might be tempted by his own interests to disregard those of his principal. The transaction was nothing more or less than the acceptance by the agent of a bribe to perform his duties in the manner desired by the person who gave the bribe. Such a contract is void. This doctrine rests on such plain principles of law, as well as common business honesty, that the citation of authorities is unnecessary."

The right to recover profits made by the agent in the course of the agency is not affected by the fact that the principal, upon discovering a fraud, has rescinded the contract and recovered that with which he parted. Restatement, Agency, § 407(2). Comment e on Subsection (2) reads: "If an agent has violated a duty of loyalty to the principal so that the principal is entitled to profits which the agent has thereby made, the fact that the principal has brought an action against a third person and has been made whole by such action does not prevent the principal from recovering from the agent the profits which the agent has made. Thus, if the other contracting party has given a bribe to the agent to make a contract with him on behalf of the principal, the principal can rescind the transaction, recovering from the other party anything received by him, or he can maintain an action for damages against him; in either event the principal may recover from the agent the amount of the bribe."

It follows that, insofar as the secret commission of $2,000 received by the agent is concerned, plaintiff had an absolute right thereto, irrespective of any recovery resulting from the action against the sellers for rescission.

2.   Plaintiff's second cause of action is brought to recover damages for (1) losses suffered in the operation of the business prior to rescission; (2) loss of time devoted to operation; (3) expenses in connection with rescission of the sale and investigation therewith; (4) nontaxable expenses in connection with the prosecution of the suit against the sellers; and (5) attorneys' fees in connection with the suit.

The case comes to us on a bill of exceptions. No part of the testimony of the witnesses is included, so we must assume that the evidence establishes the items of damage claimed by plaintiff. Our inquiry is limited to a consideration of the question whether a principal may recover of an agent who has breached his trust the items of damage mentioned after a successful prosecution of an action for rescission against the third parties with whom the agent dealt for his principal.

The general rule is stated in Restatement, Agency, § 407(1), as follows: "If an agent has received a benefit as a result of violating his duty of loyalty, the principal is entitled to recover from him what he has so received, its value, or its proceeds, and also the amount of damage thereby caused, except that if the violation consists of the wrongful disposal of the principal's property, the principal cannot recover its value and also what the agent received in exchange therefor."

In Comment a on Subsection (1) we find the following: ". . . In either event, whether or not the principal elects to get back the thing improperly dealt with or to recover from the agent its value or the amount of benefit which the agent has improperly received, he is, in addition, entitled to be indemnified by the agent for any loss which has been caused to his interest by the improper transaction. Thus, if the purchasing agent for a restaurant purchases with the principal's money defective food, receiving a bonus therefor, and the use of the food in the restaurant damages the business, the principal can recover from the agent the amount of money improperly expended by him, the bonus which the agent received, and the amount which will compensate for the injury to the business."

The general rule with respect to damages for a tortious act is that "The wrong-doer is answerable for all the injurious consequences of his tortious act, which according to the usual course of events and the general experience were likely to ensue, and which, therefore, when the act was committed, he may reasonably be supposed to have foreseen and anticipated." 1 Sutherland, Damages (4 ed.) § 45, quoted with approval in Sargent v. Mason, 101 Minn. 319, 323, 112 N.W. 255, 257. . . .

Bergquist v. Kreidler, 158 Minn. 127, 196 N.W. 964, involved an action to recover attorneys' fees expended by plaintiffs in an action seeking to enforce and protect their right to the possession of real estate. Defendant, acting as the owner's agent, had falsely represented to plaintiffs that they could have possession on August 1, 1920. It developed after plaintiffs had purchased the premises that a tenant had a lease running to August 1, 1922, on a rental much lower than the actual value of the premises. Defendant (the agent) conceded that plaintiffs were entitled to recover the loss in rent, but contended that attorneys' fees and disbursements expended by plaintiffs in testing the validity of the tenant's lease were not recoverable. In affirming plaintiffs' right to recover we said, 158 Minn. 132, 196 N.W. 966: ". . . the litigation in which plaintiffs became involved was the direct, legitimate, and a to be expected result of appellant's misrepresentation. The loss sustained by plaintiffs in conducting that litigation 'is plainly traceable' to appellant's wrong and he should make compensation accordingly."

So far as the right to recover attorneys' fees is concerned, the same may be said in this case. Plaintiff sought to return what had been received and demanded a return of his down payment. The sellers refused. He thereupon sued to accomplish this purpose, as he had a right to do, and was successful. His attorneys' fees and expenses of suit were directly traceable to the harm caused by defendant's wrongful act. As such, they are recoverable.

. . . The general rule applicable here is stated in 15 Am.Jur., Damages, § 144, as follows: "It is generally held that where the wrongful act of the defendant has involved the plaintiff in litigation with others or placed him in such relation with others as makes it necessary to incur expense to protect his interest, such costs and expenses, including attorneys' fees, should be treated as the legal consequences of the original wrongful act and may be recovered as damages."

The same is true of the other elements of damage involved. . . .

Affirmed.

———

RESTATEMENT (THIRD) OF AGENCY § 8.05, ILLUSTRATION 1. "P, who owns a stable of horses, employs A to take care of them.

While P is absent for a month, and without P's consent, A rents the horses [for his own personal gain] to persons who ride them. Although being ridden is beneficial to the horses, A is subject to liability to P for the amount A receives for the rentals.''

————

READING v. ATTORNEY–GENERAL, [1951] App.Cas. 507 (H.L.). Reading was a sergeant in the Royal Army Medical Corps during World War II, stationed in Cairo. In 1943, an unidentified man asked Reading whether he would assist in selling cases of whisky and brandy in Cairo, for which he would be paid a few pounds. About a month later Reading was met by a man named Manole, who told Reading that a truck, which Reading was to board, would come at a specified time and place. Reading, dressed in uniform, boarded the truck and conducted it through Cairo. By arrangement he met Manole later on the same day, and received an envelope which contained £2,000. This process was repeated on a number of occasions. In all, Reading was paid around £20,000. The Crown (that is, the English Government) later seized these amounts, on the ground that they had been paid to Reading "for accompanying . . . a loaded lorry in and about Cairo whilst dressed in uniform and thereby falsely representing himself as acting in the course of his military duties . . . in order to avoid police inspection of the said lorry." Reading brought suit to recover the seized amount. Justice Denning, at trial, dismissed Reading's complaint:

> In my judgment, it is a principle of law that if a servant, in violation of his duty of honesty and good faith, takes advantage of his service to make a profit for himself, in this sense, that the assets of which he has control, or the facilities which he enjoys, or the position which he occupies, are the real cause of his obtaining the money, as distinct from being the mere opportunity for getting it, that is to say, if they play the predominant part in his obtaining the money, then he is accountable for it to the master. It matters not that the master has not lost any profit, nor suffered any damage. Nor does it matter that the master could not have done the act himself. It is a case where the servant has unjustly enriched himself by virtue of his service without his master's sanction. It is money which the servant ought not to be allowed to keep, and the law says it shall be taken from him and given to his master, because he got it solely by reason of the position which he occupied as a servant of his master.... [Reading] ... was using his position as a sergeant in His Majesty's Army and the uniform to which his rank entitled him to obtain the money which he received. In my opinion any official position, whether marked by a uniform or not, which enables the holder to earn money by its use gives his master a right to receive the money so earned even though it was earned by a criminal act. "You have earned", the master can say, "money by the use of your position as my servant. It is not for you, who have gained this advantage, to set up your own wrong as a defence to my claim."

The House of Lords affirmed.

———

RESTATEMENT (SECOND) OF AGENCY
§§ 13, 387–396, 401, 403, 404, 407

[See Statutory Supplement]

———

RESTATEMENT (THIRD) OF AGENCY §§ 8.01–8.05

[See Statutory Supplement]

———

Jensen & Meckling, Theory of the Firm: Managerial Behavior, Agency Costs and Ownership Structure

3 J. Financial Economics 305, 308 (1976).

We define an agency relationship as a contract under which one or more persons (the principal(s)) engage another person (the agent) to perform some service on their behalf which involves delegating some decision making authority to the agent. If both parties to the relationship are utility maximizers there is good reason to believe that the agent will not always act in the best interests of the principal. The *principal* can limit divergences from his interest by establishing appropriate incentives for the agent and by incurring monitoring costs designed to limit the aberrant activities of the agent. In addition in some situations it will pay the *agent* to expend resources (bonding costs) to guarantee that he will not take certain actions which would harm the principal or to ensure that the principal will be compensated if he does take such actions. However, it is generally impossible for the principal or the agent at zero cost to ensure that the agent will make optimal decisions from the principal's viewpoint. In most agency relationships the principal and the agent will incur positive monitoring and bonding costs (non-pecuniary as well as pecuniary), and in addition there will be some divergence between the agent's decisions and those decisions which would maximize the welfare of the principal. The dollar equivalent of the reduction in welfare experienced by the principal due to this divergence is also a cost of the agency relationship, and we refer to this latter cost as the "residual loss". We define *agency costs* as the sum of:

(1) the monitoring expenditures by the principal,

(2) the bonding expenditures by the agent,

(3) the residual loss.

SECTION 4.   AN INTRODUCTION TO FINANCIAL STATEMENTS

The law of business associations is about enterprises that are organized for profit. Accordingly, issues concerning such matters as accounting, valuation, and portfolio theory often lurk behind the legal rules and the cases in this area, and sometimes take center stage. It would be impossible to fully develop these issues in a book like this, which is primarily devoted to explicitly legal materials. However, from time to time in this book, beginning here, materials will be set out that at least provide a vocabulary concerning these issues.

———

Lawrence A. Cunningham, Introductory Accounting, Financing and Auditing 31–32

(4th ed. 2004).

The Fundamental Equation

There is one governing law that enables accountants to prepare the financial statements from the underlying bookkeeping records in a form that reliably states the entity's financial condition at a point in time and its financial performance over a period of time. It is called the *fundamental equation* and is written as follows:

$$\text{Assets} = \text{Liabilities} + \text{Owners' Equity} \ldots$$

Double-Entry Bookkeeping.

By definition, the fundamental equation is of course an equation. That means the left side of the equation must always equal the right side of the equation. In other words, the amounts on the left must balance with the amounts on the right. And here we can see the meaning of the term "balance sheet." The fundamental equation is simply the balance sheet in its most elementary form. The intuition should be obvious: the rights and claims an entity holds against others (its assets) must equal the rights and claims others hold against it (its creditors with respect to its liabilities and the owners as residual claimants with respect to the equity).

To keep the fundamental equation always in balance at every moment in time, accountants developed an ingenious system called double-entry bookkeeping. Here is another point of linguistic purity: the idea behind double-entry bookkeeping is that, to keep the fundamental equation in balance, there will be *two entries* for every transaction to be accounted for.

Debits and credits.

Double-entry bookkeeping is implemented by two mechanisms whose labels are not only of no use to us but whose very names have been the source of endless agonizing by students new to the art of the project. The terms are *"debits"* and *"credits."* Before your anxiety heightens, let us put out into the open what continues to be to many a secret. When used to describe accounting steps in double-entry bookkeeping . . . these terms have no other meaning except the following: **debit means the left-side entry** and **credit means right-side entry**. That is the secret. They have absolutely no other meaning. . . .

D. Herwitz, Materials on Accounting for Lawyers 1–3, 11–12

1980.

. . . THE BALANCE SHEET

The object of bookkeeping is to make it as easy as possible for anyone who understands the language to get a clear and accurate summary of how well a business is doing. Suppose we want a financial picture of E. Tutt, who recently graduated from law school. Certainly one important facet is how much he owns. Since we really are concerned with his business and not his personal affairs, we forget his car, his clothes, and other personal property, and we look to see what he has in his office:

(a) Office furniture

(b) Office equipment

(c) Stationery and supplies

(d) Library

(e) Cash in the bank [of $1,000]

All of these would be understood by laymen to be what the accountant calls them: *assets.*

We would also want some measurement of these assets; i.e., we would want to put a dollar figure on them. And since the price at which the property was bought is ordinarily much easier to ascertain and less subjective than the "present value" of the property, it would make sense to record E. Tutt's assets at *cost.*

If E. Tutt bought all his property out of his own funds and has not yet earned anything, we could simply add up the assets to find out how E. Tutt stands in his business. But if he has borrowed money from a bank to buy some of his assets or, perhaps more likely, has bought some on credit, E. Tutt's personal "stake" in the business would not be as large as if he had bought everything from his own funds. In order to give a true picture of his financial position, we would want to know where the money came from to buy the assets. Suppose we find that he acquired the assets as follows:

(a) Office furniture: bought on credit from Frank Co. for $400;

(b) Office equipment: bought on credit from Elmer Co. for $300;

(c) Stationery and supplies: bought from Stanley for $100 on a promissory note;

(d) Library: purchased for $200 cash, out of Tutt's original "stake" of $1,000;

(e) $800 cash: balance of Tutt's original "stake" remaining.

We could then list, in parallel columns, the assets and their sources:

Assets		Sources	
(a) Office furniture	$ 400	Frank Co.	$ 400 (a)
(b) Office equipment	300	Elmer Co.	300 (b)
(c) Stationery and supplies	100	Stanley	100 (c)
(d) Library	200		
(e) Cash (balance remaining)	800	E. Tutt	1,000 (d, e)
	$1,800		$1,800

This parallel listing of assets and their sources is what the accountant calls a *balance sheet*. It shows, at any point in time, what assets the business now has and where the money came from to acquire them. Since that is all it is, no matter how complicated the business or how long its history the totals of the two columns are always equal.

To give a somewhat clearer picture of how well off E. Tutt himself is, we can separate the sources of assets into two groups: "outside" sources, or here, money owed by the business to outsiders; and "inside" sources, here, what Tutt himself has put into the business. The outside sources, which are usually called "*Liabilities*", may be money owed on open account, usually called an "account payable;" another "outside" source is money advanced on a note, a "note payable". The "inside" source here is E. Tutt's contribution (his "stake" or equity in the business) which is often called "*Proprietorship*". We might also rearrange the assets, listing them in the order in which they are likely to be used up. The result would be a somewhat more refined balance sheet that might look like this:

Assets		Liabilities & Proprietorship	
		Liabilities:	
(e) Cash	$ 800	Accounts Payable	
(c) Supplies	100	Frank Co.	$ 400 (a)
(a) Furniture	400	Elmer Co.	300 (b)
(b) Equipment	300	Notes Payable	
		Stanley	100 (c)
(d) Library	200	Proprietorship	1,000 (d, e)
	$1,800		$1,800

Note that no change has been made except a change in presentation. The essential meaning is the same. But because clear disclosure is one of the accountant's main concerns, matters of presentation are important. . . .

. . . THE INCOME STATEMENT

The balance sheet shows the present status of the assets and the "sources of assets" resulting from all transactions since the business was formed. It is drawn up at regular intervals which will vary with the needs of the business. There is another, and increasingly more important, basic financial statement: the *income statement.* The income statement is a statement for a period of time, giving a summary of earnings between balance sheet dates. A fundamental distinction between the two is that the balance sheet speaks as of a particular date, while the income statement covers a period of time between successive balance sheet dates. . . .

It may be easiest to start by drawing up an income statement for E. Tutt, say for the month of June. Suppose that during the month he receives legal fees of $600 and $400.

(1)	Professional Income	$600
(2)	Professional Income	$400

To find his net income, we have to subtract his expenses for the month. Suppose that the operating expenses were as follows:

(3)	Rent	$200
(4)	Secretary	$230
(5)	Telephone	$ 15
(6)	Heat & Light	$ 5
(7)	Miscellaneous	$ 5

In addition, during the month Tutt suffered a loss when a thief broke into his office and stole $20 cash. This loss is treated as just another expense:

(8)	Theft loss	$ 20

There is no particular form required for an income statement, so long as it is a clear and fair statement of the information. An acceptable one might look like this:

INCOME STATEMENT—E. TUTT, JUNE

(1 & 2)	Professional Income		$1,000
	Less: Expenses		
(3)	Rent	$200	
(4)	Secretary	230	
(5)	Telephone	15	
(6)	Heat & Light	5	
(7)	Miscellaneous	5	
(8)	Theft Loss	20	
	Total Expenses		475
	NET INCOME		$525

To get started on seeing how the income statement fits into the balance sheet we might ask where "net income" shows up on a balance sheet. In lay terms, it is an increase in the owner's stake in the business, which we call "Proprietorship". Hence, if no other change in Proprietorship occurs, the balance sheet figure for Proprietorship on June 30 should be $525 larger than on June 1.

R. Hamilton, Fundamentals of Modern Business 154–55

1989.

. . . *[E]very transaction entered into by a business must be recorded in at least two ways if the balance sheet is to continue to balance.* This last point underlies the concept of that mysterious subject, *double entry bookkeeping*, and is the cornerstone on which modern accounting is built.

Assume that we have a new business, just starting out, in which the owner has invested $10,000 in cash. . . . The opening balance sheet will look like this:

Assets:		Liabilities	–0–
Cash	10,000	Owner's Equity	10,000

Now let us assume that the owner buys a used truck for $3,000 cash. The effect of this transaction is to reduce cash by $3,000 and create a new asset on the balance sheet:

Assets:		Liabilities	–0–
Cash	7,000	Owner's Equity	10,000
Used Truck	3,000		
	10,000		10,000

Voila! The balance sheet still balances. Let us assume next that the owner goes down to the bank and borrows an additional $1,000. This also has a dual effect: it increases cash by $1,000 (since the business is receiving the proceeds of the loan) and increases liabilities by $1,000 (since the business thereafter has to repay the loan). Yet another balance sheet can be created showing the additional effect of this second transaction:

4

Assets:		Liabilities	
Cash	8,000	Debt to Bank	1,000
Used Truck	3,000	Owner's Equity	10,000
	11,000		11,000

NOTE ON BALANCE SHEETS

In evaluating a balance sheet, it must be borne in mind that the entries on a balance sheet do not necessarily reflect real or market values. Instead, the entries are (or should be) constructed according to generally accepted accounting principles ("GAAP"), and typically reflect only "book value," that is, the value (more precisely, the amount) at which various assets and liabilities are recorded or "booked" on the financial statements. Thus, under generally accepted accounting principles a building is normally shown on the balance sheet at the original cost of the asset, minus depreciation (that is, the assumed loss of value of the asset over its useful life). Depreciation, in turn, is determined by a formula, rather than by actual loss in value. For example, under "straight-line" depreciation, a plant built at a cost of $1 million might be depreciated by deducting 5% of that cost every year during a projected twenty-year life. After four years, therefore, the value of the plant shown on the books (the "book value") would be $800,000 ($1 million cost minus $50,000 annual depreciation for each of four years), even though the fair market value of the plant—the price the owner could get for the plant if he sold it—was, say, $1.4 million. Because balance-sheet net worth is simply balance-sheet assets minus balance-sheet liabilities, actual net worth may be much higher or much lower than the figure for owner's equity recorded on the balance sheet.

CHAPTER II

PARTNERSHIP

————

INTRODUCTORY NOTE

This chapter will consider the basic partnership form, general partnerships. Two special partnership forms, limited partnerships and limited liability partnerships, will be considered in Chapter 7, infra. Although partnership had a rich history under the common law, it has long been governed by statute. Until recently, the relevant statute was the Uniform Partnership Act (the UPA), which was promulgated by the National Conference of Commissioners on Uniform State Laws (NCCUSL) in 1914 and was adopted in every state except Louisiana.

In 1994, NCCUSL adopted the Revised Uniform Partnership Act (RUPA), which is intended to supersede the UPA. Under RUPA § 1006, RUPA applies to all partnerships formed after RUPA is adopted in any given state and, after a transition period, to partnerships formed even before RUPA was adopted. As of the time this casebook was written, about two-thirds of the states had adopted RUPA, and one-third had not. Some of the largest and most commercially important states, such as New York, Ohio, and Pennsylvania, are among the states that have not made the switch. The cases in this Chapter are for the most part (although not exclusively) based on the UPA. That is partly because as of this writing, the UPA is still in effect in many states; partly because RUPA is so new that it has not yet spawned much case law; and partly because RUPA continues many of the rules of the UPA. In general, however, the Text Notes will discuss both the UPA and RUPA, especially where RUPA makes a material change in a relevant UPA.

————

As of 2002, there were 780,000 general partnerships in the United States, with an average of 4 partners in each partnership. Tim Wheeler and Maureen Parsons, Partnership Returns, 2002, 24 Statistics of Income Bulletin No. 2, at 46–57 (2004).

————

SECTION 1. PARTNERSHIP FORMATION

————

HILCO PROPERTY SERVICES, INC. v. UNITED STATES, 929 F.Supp. 526 (D.N.H. 1996). "The conduct of the parties and the circumstances surrounding their relationship and transactions control the factual question of whether a partnership existed in cases where the parties have not documented their intentions in a written agreement.... [A]lthough the question of intent is a crucial part of the calculus, 'the only necessary intent ... is an intent to do those things which constitute a partnership.' Id. Thus,

> [t]he key factor is not the subjective intent of the parties to form a partnership.... It is immaterial that the parties do not call their relationship, or believe it to be, a partnership, especially where the rights of third parties are concerned."

UNIFORM PARTNERSHIP ACT §§ 6, 7

REVISED UNIFORM PARTNERSHIP ACT §§ 101(6), 202

[See Statutory Supplement]

Martin v. Peyton

New York Court of Appeals, 1927.
246 N.Y. 213, 158 N.E. 77.

Appeal from Supreme Court, Appellate Division, First Department.

Action by Charles S. Martin against William C. Peyton and others. A judgment of the Special Term, entered on the report of a referee in favor of the defendants was affirmed by the Appellate Division (219 App.Div. 297, 220 N.Y.S. 29), and plaintiff appeals. Affirmed.

ANDREWS, J. Much ancient learning as to partnership is obsolete. Today only those who are partners between themselves may be charged for partnership debts by others. (Partnership Law [Cons. Laws, ch. 39], sec. 11.) There is one exception. Now and then a recovery is allowed where in truth such relationship is absent. This is because the debtor may not deny the claim. (Sec. 27.)

Partnership results from contract, express or implied. If denied it may be proved by the production of some written instrument; by testimony as to some conversation; by circumstantial evidence. If nothing else appears the receipt by the defendant of a share of the profits of the business is enough. (Sec. 11.)

Assuming some written contract between the parties the question may arise whether it creates a partnership. If it be complete; if it expresses in good faith the full understanding and obligation of the parties, then it is for the court to say whether a partnership exists. It may, however, be a mere sham intended to hide the real relationship. Then other results follow. In passing upon it effect is to be given to each provision. Mere words will not blind us to realities. Statements that no partnership is intended are not conclusive. If as a whole a contract contemplates an association of two or more persons to carry on as co-owners a business for profit a partnership there is. (Sec. 10.) On the other hand, if it be less than this no partnership exists. Passing on the contract as a whole, an arrangement for sharing profits is to be considered. It is to be given its due weight. But it is to be weighed in connection with all the rest. It is not decisive. It may be merely the method adopted to pay a debt or wages, as interest on a loan or for other reasons.

An existing contract may be modified later by subsequent agreement, oral or written. A partnership may be so created where there was none before. And again, that the original agreement has been so modified may be proved by circumstantial evidence—by showing the conduct of the parties.

In the case before us the claim that the defendants became partners in the firm of Knauth, Nachod & Kuhne, doing business as bankers and brokers, depends upon the interpretation of certain instruments. There is nothing in their subsequent acts determinative of or indeed material upon this question. And we are relieved of questions that sometimes arise. "The plaintiff's position is not," we are told, "that the agreements of June 4, 1921, were a false expression or incomplete expression of the intention of the parties. We say that they express defendants' intention and that that intention was to create a relationship which as a matter of law constitutes a partnership." Nor may the claim of the plaintiff be rested on any question of estoppel. "The plaintiff's claim," he stipulates, "is a claim of actual partnership, not of partnership by estoppel. . . ."

Remitted then, as we are, to the documents themselves, we refer to circumstances surrounding their execution only so far as is necessary to make them intelligible. And we are to remember that although the intention of the parties to avoid liability as partners is clear, although in language precise and definite they deny any design to then join the firm of K.N. & K.; although they say their interests in profits should be construed merely as a measure of compensation for loans, not an interest in profits as such; although they provide that they shall not be liable for any losses or treated as partners, the question still remains whether in fact they agree to so associate themselves with the firm as to "carry on as co-owners a business for profit."

In the spring of 1921 the firm of K.N. & K. found itself in financial difficulties. John R. Hall was one of the partners. He was a friend of Mr. Peyton. From him he obtained the loan of almost $500,000 of Liberty bonds, which K.N. & K. might use as collateral to secure bank advances. This, however, was not sufficient. The firm and its members had engaged in unwise speculations, and it was deeply involved. Mr. Hall was also intimately acquainted with George W. Perkins, Jr., and with Edward W. Freeman. He also knew Mrs. Peyton and Mrs. Perkins and Mrs. Freeman. All were anxious to help him. He, therefore, representing K.N. & K., entered into negotiations with them. While they were pending a proposition was made that Mr. Peyton, Mr.

Perkins and Mr. Freeman or some of them should become partners. It met a decided refusal. Finally an agreement was reached. It is expressed in three documents, executed on the same day, all a part of the one transaction. They were drawn with care and are unambiguous. We shall refer to them as "the agreement," "the indenture" and "the option."

We have no doubt as to their general purpose. The respondents were to loan K.N. & K. $2,500,000 worth of liquid securities, which were to be returned to them on or before April 15, 1923. The firm might hypothecate them to secure loans totaling $2,000,000, using the proceeds as its business necessities required. To insure respondents against loss K.N. & K. were to turn over to them a large number of their own securities which may have been valuable, but which were of so speculative a nature that they could not be used as collateral for bank loans. In compensation for the loan the respondents were to receive 40 per cent of the profits of the firm until the return was made, not exceeding, however, $500,000 and not less than $100,000. Merely because the transaction involved the transfer of securities and not of cash does not prevent its being a loan within the meaning of section 11. The respondents also were given an option to join the firm if they or any of them expressed a desire to do so before June 4, 1923.

Many other detailed agreements are contained in the papers. Are they such as may be properly inserted to protect the lenders? Or do they go further? Whatever their purpose, did they in truth associate the respondents with the firm so that they and it together thereafter carried on as co-owners a business for profit? The answer depends upon an analysis of these various provisions.

As representing the lenders, Mr. Peyton and Mr. Freeman are called "trustees." The loaned securities when used as collateral are not to be mingled with other securities of K.N. & K., and the trustees at all times are to be kept informed of all transactions affecting them. To them shall be paid all dividends and income accruing therefrom. They may also substitute for any of the securities loaned securities of equal value. With their consent the firm may sell any of its securities held by the respondents, the proceeds to go, however, to the trustees. In other similar ways the trustees may deal with these same securities, but the securities loaned shall always be sufficient in value to permit of their hypothecation for $2,000,000. If they rise in price the excess may be withdrawn by the defendants. If they fall they shall make good the deficiency.

So far there is no hint that the transaction is not a loan of securities with a provision for compensation. Later a somewhat closer connection with the firm appears. Until the securities are returned the directing management of the firm is to be in the hands of John R. Hall, and his life is to be insured for $1,000,000, and the policies are to be assigned as further collateral security to the trustees. These requirements are not unnatural. Hall was the one known and trusted by the defendants. Their acquaintance with the other members of the firm was of the slightest. These others had brought an old and established business to the verge of bankruptcy. As the respondents knew, they also had engaged in unsafe speculation. The respondents were about to loan $2,500,000 of good securities. As collateral they were to receive others of problematical value. What they required seems but ordinary caution. Nor does it imply an association in the business.

The trustees are to be kept advised as to the conduct of the business and consulted as to important matters. They may inspect the firm books and are entitled to any information they think important. Finally they may veto any business they think highly speculative or injurious. Again we hold this but a proper precaution to safeguard the loan. The trustees may not initiate any transaction as a partner may do. They may not bind the firm by any action of their own. Under the circumstances the safety of the loan depended upon the business success of K.N. & K. This success was likely to be compromised by the inclination of its members to engage in speculation. No longer, if the respondents were to be protected, should it be allowed. The trustees, therefore, might prohibit it, and that their prohibition might be effective, information was to be furnished them. Not dissimilar agreements have been held proper to guard the interests of the lender.

As further security each member of K.N. & K. is to assign to the trustees their interest in the firm. No loan by the firm to any member is permitted and the amount each may draw is fixed. No other distribution of profits is to be made. So that realized profits may be calculated the existing capital is stated to be $700,000, and profits are to be realized as promptly as good business practice will permit. In case the trustees think this is not done, the question is left to them and to Mr. Hall, and if they differ then to an arbitrator. There is no obligation that the firm shall continue the business. It may dissolve at any time. Again we conclude there is nothing here not properly adapted to secure the interest of the respondents as lenders. If their compensation is dependent on a percentage of the profits still provision must be made to define what these profits shall be.

The "indenture" is substantially a mortgage of the collateral delivered by K.N. & K. to the trustees to secure the performance of the "agreement." It certainly does not strengthen the claim that the respondents were partners.

Finally we have the "option." It permits the respondents or any of them or their assignees or nominees to enter the firm at a later date if they desire to do so by buying 50 per cent or less of the interests therein of all or any of the members at a stated price. Or a corporation may, if the respondents and the members agree, be formed in place of the firm. Meanwhile, apparently with the design of protecting the firm business against improper or ill-judged action which might render the option valueless, each member of the firm is to place his resignation in the hands of Mr. Hall. If at any time he and the trustees agree that such resignation should be accepted, that member shall then retire, receiving the value of his interest calculated as of the date of such retirement.

This last provision is somewhat unusual, yet it is not enough in itself to show that on June 4, 1921, a present partnership was created nor taking these various papers as a whole do we reach such a result. It is quite true that even if one or two or three like provisions contained in such a contract do not require this conclusion, yet it is also true that when taken together a point may come where stipulations immaterial separately cover so wide a field that we should hold a partnership exists. As in other branches of the law a question of degree is often the determining factor. Here that point has not been reached. . . .

The judgment appealed from should be affirmed, with costs.

■ CARDOZO, CH. J., POUND, CRANE, LEHMAN, KELLOGG and O'BRIEN, JJ., concur.

Judgment affirmed, etc.

————

Lupien v. Malsbenden

Supreme Judicial Court of Maine, 1984.
477 A.2d 746.

■ Before McKUSICK, C.J., and NICHOLS, ROBERTS, WATHEN, GLASSMAN and SCHOLNIK, JJ.

■ McKUSICK, CHIEF JUSTICE.

Defendant Frederick Malsbenden appeals a judgment of the Superior Court (York County) holding him to partnership liability on a written contract entered into between plaintiff Robert Lupien and one Stephen Cragin doing business as York Motor Mart.[1] The sole issue asserted on appeal is whether the Superior Court erred in its finding that Malsbenden and Cragin were partners in the pertinent part of York Motor Mart's business. We affirm.

On March 5, 1980, plaintiff entered into a written agreement with Stephen Cragin, doing business in the town of York as York Motor Mart, for the construction of a Bradley automobile.[2] Plaintiff made a deposit of $500 towards the purchase price of $8,020 upon signing the contract, and made a further payment of $3,950 one week later on March 12. Both the purchase order of March 5, 1980, and a later bill of sale, though signed by Cragin, identified the seller as York Motor Mart. At the jury-waived trial, plaintiff testified that after he signed the contract he made visits to York Motor Mart on an average of once or twice a week to check on the progress being made on his car. During those visits plaintiff generally dealt with Malsbenden because Cragin was seldom present. On one such visit in April, Malsbenden told plaintiff that it was necessary for the latter to sign over ownership of his pickup truck, which would constitute the balance of the consider-

---

1. Cragin "disappeared" several months before this action was commenced. Plaintiff Lupien originally named Cragin as a co-defendant. However, since Cragin was never served with process, the Superior Court at the behest of both Lupien and defendant Malsbenden dismissed the claim against Cragin.

2. A Bradley automobile is a "kit car" constructed on a Volkswagen chassis.

ation under the contract, so that the proceeds from the sale of the truck could be used to complete construction of the Bradley. When plaintiff complied, Malsbenden provided plaintiff with a rental car, and later with a "demo" model of the Bradley, for his use pending the completion of the vehicle he had ordered. When it was discovered that the "demo" actually belonged to a third person who had entrusted it to York Motor Mart for resale, Malsbenden purchased the vehicle for plaintiff's use. Plaintiff never received the Bradley he had contracted to purchase.

In his trial testimony, defendant Malsbenden asserted that his interest in the Bradley operation of York Motor Mart was only that of a banker. He stated that he had loaned $85,000 to Cragin, without interest, to finance the Bradley portion of York Motor Mart's business.[3] The loan was to be repaid from the proceeds of each car sold. Malsbenden acknowledged that Bradley kits were purchased with his personal checks and that he had also purchased equipment for York Motor Mart. He also stated that after Cragin disappeared sometime late in May 1980, he had physical control of the premises of York Motor Mart and that he continued to dispose of assets there even to the time of trial in 1983.

The Uniform Partnership Act, adopted in Maine at 31 M.R.S.A. §§ 281–323 (1978 & Supp.1983–1984), defines a partnership as "an association of 2 or more persons ... to carry on as co-owners[4] a business for profit." 31 M.R.S.A. § 286 (1978). Whether a partnership exists is an inference of law based on established facts. *See Dalton v. Austin,* 432 A.2d 774, 777 (Me.1981); *Roux v. Lawand,* 131 Me. 215, 219, 160 A. 756, 757 (1932); *James Bailey Co. v. Darling,* 119 Me. 326, 328, 111 A. 410, 411 (1920). A finding that the relationship between two persons constitutes a partnership may be based upon evidence of an agreement, either express or implied,

> to place their money, effects, labor, and skill, or some or all of them, in lawful commerce or business with the understanding that a community of profits will be shared.... No one factor is alone determinative of the existence of a partnership....

Dalton v. Austin, 432 A.2d at 777; *Cumberland County Power & Light Co. v. Gordon,* 136 Me. 213, 218, 7 A.2d 619, 622 (1939). *See James Bailey Co. v. Darling,* 119 Me. at 328, 111 A. at 411. If the arrangement between the parties otherwise qualifies as a partnership, it is of no matter that the parties did not expressly agree to form a partnership or did not even intend to form one:

> It is possible for parties to intend no partnership and yet to form one. If they agree upon an arrangement which is a partnership in

---

3. Malsbenden's testimony indicated that Cragin carried on an automotive repair business at the York Motor Mart that was unrelated to the Bradley operation. Malsbenden testified, without contradiction, that he had no involvement with that other business.

4. As we made clear in *Dalton v. Austin,* 432 A.2d 774, 777 (Me.1981), the term "co-owners" as used in the statute does not necessarily mean joint title to all assets. On the contrary, "the right to participate in control of the business is the essence of co-ownership." *Id.*

fact, it is of no importance that they call it something else, or that they even expressly declare that they are not to be partners. The law must declare what is the legal import of their agreements, and names go for nothing when the substance of the arrangement shows them to be inapplicable.

James Bailey Co. v. Darling, 119 Me. at 328, 111 A. at 411 (quoting *Beecher v. Bush,* 45 Mich. 188, 193–94, 7 N.W. 785, 785–86 (1881)).

Here the trial justice concluded that, notwithstanding Malsbenden's assertion that he was only a "banker," his "total involvement" in the Bradley operation was that of a partner. The testimony at trial, both respecting Malsbenden's financial interest in the enterprise and his involvement in day-to-day business operations, amply supported the Superior Court's conclusion. Malsbenden had a financial interest of $85,000 in the Bradley portion of York Motor Mart's operations. Although Malsbenden termed the investment a loan, significantly he conceded that the "loan" carried no interest. His "loan" was not made in the form of a fixed payment or payments, but was made to the business, at least in substantial part, in the form of day-to-day purchases of Bradley kits, other parts and equipment, and in the payment of wages. Furthermore, the "loan" was not to be repaid in fixed amounts or at fixed times, but rather only upon the sale of Bradley automobiles.

The evidence also showed that, unlike a banker, Malsbenden had the right to participate in control of the business and in fact did so on a day-to-day basis.[5] According to Urbin Savaria, who worked at York Motor Mart from late April through June 1980, Malsbenden during that time opened the business establishment each morning, remained present through part of every day, had final say on the ordering of parts, paid for parts and equipment, and paid Savaria's salary. On plaintiff's frequent visits to York Motor Mart, he generally dealt with Malsbenden because Cragin was not present. It was Malsbenden who insisted that plaintiff trade in his truck prior to the completion of the Bradley because the proceeds from the sale of the truck were needed to complete the Bradley. When it was discovered that the "demo" Bradley given to plaintiff while he awaited completion of his car actually belonged to a third party, it was Malsbenden who bought the car for plaintiff's use. As of three years after the making of the contract now in litigation, Malsbenden was still doing business at York Motor Mart, "just disposing of property."

Malsbenden and Cragin may well have viewed their relationship to be that of creditor-borrower, rather than a partnership. At trial Malsbenden so asserts, and Cragin's departure from the scene in the spring of 1980 deprives us of the benefit of his view of his business arrangement with Malsbenden. In any event, whatever the intent of these two men as to their respective involvements in the business of

---

5. Thus its facts clearly distinguish the case at bar from *James Bailey Co. v. Darling,* 119 Me. 326, 332, 111 A. 410, 413 (1920), where although the defendant advanced money for the purchase of automobiles that was to be repaid upon the sale of individual automobiles, the defendant had no control over the business.

making and selling Bradley cars, there is no clear error in the Superior Court's finding that the Bradley car operation represented a pooling of Malsbenden's capital and Cragin's automotive skills, with joint control over the business and intent to share the fruits of the enterprise. As a matter of law, that arrangement amounted to a partnership under 31 M.R.S.A. § 286.

The entry is:

Judgment affirmed.

All concurring.

———

NOTE ON THE FORMATION OF PARTNERSHIPS

1. *Formalities.* Corporations, limited partnerships, limited liability partnerships, and limited liability companies can be organized (formed) only if certain formalities are complied with and a filing is made with the state. In contrast, general partnerships can be organized with no formalities and no filing. The absence of a filing requirement reflects in part a conception that partnership status depends on the factual characteristics of a relationship between two or more persons, not on whether the persons think of themselves as having entered into a partnership.

Although no filings are *required* under either the UPA or RUPA, RUPA *permits* certain filings. See, e.g., Note on the Authority of Partners, Section 4, infra.

2. *The Four–Element Test, Mutual Right of Control, and Loss–Sharing.* It is sometimes said that where there is no express partnership agreement, a relationship will be considered a partnership only if four elements are present—an agreement to share profits, an agreement to share losses, a mutual right of control or management of the business, and a community of interest in the venture. See, e.g., Weingart v. C & W Taylor Partnership, 248 Mont. 76, 809 P.2d 576 (1991); Corpus Christi v. Bayfront Associates, Ltd., 814 S.W.2d 98 (Tex.App.1991). This four-element test departs from the statutory test of both UPA § 6(a) and RUPA § 202, which provide simply that with certain exceptions a partnership is "an association of two or more persons to carry on as co-owners a business for profit," and say nothing about control or loss-sharing.

Although the Comments to both UPA § 6(a) and RUPA § 202 say that "to state that partners are co-owners of a business is to state that they each have the power of ultimate control," in fact even explicit partnership agreements frequently do not involve either ultimate control or loss-sharing for every partner. For example, many partnership agreements vest control in only one or more managing partners, or create elaborate allocations of voting power in which some partners do not share. Similarly, not every partnership agreement provides for loss sharing by every partner. If *explicit* partnership agreements do not always include control and loss-sharing as elements of the partnership relation, why should courts require those elements as a condition to finding an *implicit* partnership?

A better approach is that the presence or absence of the four specified elements, including mutual control and loss-sharing, is evidence, but not a requirement, of a partnership relation. This approach was taken, for example, in Beckman v. Farmer, 579 A.2d 618, 627 (D.C.App.1990), where the court said that "[t]he customary attributes of partnership, such as loss sharing and joint control of decisionmaking are necessary guideposts of inquiry, but none is conclusive." Other cases have held that once profit-sharing has been shown, it is not essential to show that there was an agreement to share in the losses. See Hansford v. Maplewood Station Business Park, 621 N.E.2d 347 (Ind.App.1993); Endsley v. Game–Show Placements, Ltd., 401 N.E.2d 768 (Ind.App.1980).

SECTION 2.   THE LEGAL NATURE OF A PARTNERSHIP

———

UNIFORM PARTNERSHIP ACT § 6

———

REVISED UNIFORM PARTNERSHIP ACT §§ 101(6), 201

[See Statutory Supplement]

———

NOTE ON THE LEGAL NATURE OF A PARTNERSHIP: ENTITY OR AGGREGATE STATUS

1. *Entity v. Aggregate.* Individuals may associate in a wide variety of forms. The issue often arises whether a given form of association has a legal status separate from that of its members, or is simply an aggregate of its members. Frequently, this issue is stated in terms of whether a particular form of association is or is not a "separate legal entity" or a "legal person" (as opposed to a natural person, that is, an individual). A variety of issues may turn on the answer to this question—for example, whether the association can sue and be sued in its own name, and whether it can hold property in its own right.

In the history of English and American law this issue arose in the context of many different kinds of associations, such as universities, charitable institutions, and even municipalities. In most cases the issue was eventually resolved in a straightforward way, but in the case of partnerships it continued to be vexing. The predominant although not exclusive view under the common law was that a partnership was not an entity, but merely an aggregate of its members, or, as it was sometimes put, that a partnership was no more a legal entity than was a friendship.

2. *The UPA.* In 1902, when the National Conference of Commissioners on Uniform State Laws determined to promulgate a Uniform Partnership Act, Dean James Barr Ames of Harvard Law School was appointed to draft the Act. Subsequently, the Commissioners instructed Dean Ames, at his own urging, to draft the Act on the theory that a partnership is a legal entity. Accordingly, in the drafts submitted by Dean Ames a partnership was defined as "*a legal person* formed by the association of two or more individuals for the purpose of carrying on business with a view to profit," and various provisions of the drafts reflected the entity theory. Dean Ames died before the work was completed, however, and his successor, Dean William Draper Lewis of the University of Pennsylvania Law School, was distinctly unfriendly to the entity view. Ultimately, Dean Lewis convinced the Commissioners to instruct him to draft the Act on the aggregate theory. UPA Section 6 therefore provides simply that "A partnership is an association of two or more persons to carry on as co-owners a business for profit." Although the language of this provision does not in itself render the issue free from doubt (since an association can be either an aggregate or an entity), it is pretty clear that the Act was intended to adopt the aggregate rather than the entity theory of partnership.

However, that is not the end of the story. Having adopted the aggregate theory in principle, in practice the UPA deals with a number of specific issues (such as the ownership of partnership property) *as if* a partnership is an entity. For many purposes, this approach works pretty well. Generally speaking, however, the entity theory of partnership works much better than the aggregate theory. In cases where the UPA treats the partnership as if it is an entity, despite the aggregate theory, the results are good but the manner in which the statute reaches those results involves needlessly complex mechanics. In cases where the UPA does not treat the partnership as if it is an entity, the results tend to be bad and in need of legislative revision.

3. *Other Statutes in UPA jurisdictions.* The question often arises whether a partnership that operates in a UPA jurisdiction is to be treated as an aggregate or an entity for the purpose of statutes *other* than the UPA. See, e.g., United States v. A & P Trucking Co., 358 U.S. 121 (1958). This question is a matter of legislative intent under the relevant statute. As in all such matters, the answer will depend on the language employed and the purposes manifested in the statute. The fact that the UPA adopts the aggregate theory will be relevant, but not dispositive, in answering that question. A legislature may choose to treat a partnership as an entity for purposes of another statute, even though a partnership is defined as an association under the UPA. See, e.g., United States v. A & P Trucking Co., 358 U.S. 121, 79 S.Ct. 203, 3 L.Ed.2d 165 (1958).

4. *RUPA.* In contrast to the UPA, RUPA confers entity status on partnerships. RUPA § 101, like UPA § 6, defines a partnership as "an association of two or more persons to carry on as co-owners a

business for profit." However, RUPA § 201 then squarely provides that "A partnership is an entity."

By conferring entity status on partnerships, RUPA was able to drastically simplify many partnership rules, such as those dealing with partnership property and partnership litigation. Nevertheless, entity status does not inherently resolve every issue to which it is relevant. Just as the drafters of the UPA, having denied entity status to partnerships, remained free to (and did) craft rules to reach entity-like results on certain issues, so the drafters of RUPA, having conferred entity status on partnerships, remained free to (and did) craft rules to reach aggregate-like results on certain issues.

To put this differently, no result on any specific partnership-law issue can be "derived" or follows "logically" or "by necessity" from a partnership's legal-entity status under RUPA, any more than any result on any specific issue can be derived, or follows "logically" or "by necessity" from the UPA's denial of that status. Having declared that a partnership is an entity, the drafters of RUPA still had to make policy choices on such issues as whether the partnership could hold property, could sue and be sued in its own name, and so forth. It is true that generally speaking the best rule in many of these areas is one that is consistent with entity status, but it is important not to forget that an independent policy choice must still be made on each issue. The adoption of legal-entity status for partnerships at most simplified the drafting of RUPA and gave a slight push toward certain results. Thus in one or two areas RUPA itself reaches an aggregate-like result. For example, under RUPA, as under the UPA, a partner is individually liable for partnership debts. Under RUPA § 404(b), a partner has a duty of loyalty and care not only to the partnership but to the other partners. Under RUPA § 404(d), a partner's duty of good faith and fair dealing extends both to the partnership and to the other partners.

SECTION 3.   THE ONGOING OPERATION OF PARTNERSHIPS

———

(a) MANAGEMENT

———

UNIFORM PARTNERSHIP ACT §§ 18(e), (g), (h), 19, 20

———

**REVISED UNIFORM PARTNERSHIP
ACT §§ 103, 401(f), (i), (j), 403**

[See Statutory Supplement]

———

Summers v. Dooley

Supreme Court of Idaho, 1971.
94 Idaho 87, 481 P.2d 318.

■ DONALDSON, JUSTICE.

This lawsuit, tried in the district court, involves a claim by one partner against the other for $6,000. The complaining partner asserts that he has been required to pay out more than $11,000 in expenses without any reimbursement from either the partnership funds or his partner. The expenditure in question was incurred by the complaining partner (John Summers, plaintiff-appellant) for the purpose of hiring an additional employee. The trial court denied him any relief except for ordering that he be entitled to one half $966.72 which it found to be a legitimate partnership expense.

The pertinent facts leading to this lawsuit are as follows. Summers entered a partnership agreement with Dooley (defendant-respondent) in 1958 for the purpose of operating a trash collection business. The business was operated by the two men and when either was unable to work, the non-working partner provided a replacement at his own expense. In 1962, Dooley became unable to work and, at his own expense, hired an employee to take his place. In July, 1966, Summers approached his partner Dooley regarding the hiring of an additional employee but Dooley refused. Nevertheless, on his own initiative, Summers hired the man and paid him out of his own pocket. Dooley, upon discovering that Summers had hired an additional man, objected, stating that he did not feel additional labor was necessary and refused to pay for the new employee out of the partnership funds. Summers continued to operate the business using the third man and in October of 1967 instituted suit in the district court for $6,000 against his partner, the gravamen of the complaint being that Summers has been required to pay out more than $11,000 in expenses, incurred in the hiring of the additional man, without any reimbursement from either the partnership funds or his partner. After trial before the court, sitting without a jury, Summers was granted only partial relief[1] and he has appealed. He urges in essence that the trial court erred by failing to conclude that he should be reimbursed for expenses and costs connected in the employment of extra help in the partnership business.

The principal thrust of appellant's contention is that in spite of the fact that one of the two partners refused to consent to the hiring of additional help, nonetheless, the non-consenting partner retained profits earned by the labors of the third man and therefore the non-consenting partner should be estopped from denying the need and value of the employee, and has by his behavior ratified the act of the other partner who hired the additional man.

---

1. The trial court did award Summers one half of $966.72 which it found to be a legitimate partnership expense.

The issue presented for decision by this appeal is whether an equal partner in a two man partnership has the authority to hire a new employee in disregard of the objection of the other partner and then attempt to charge the dissenting partner with the costs incurred as a result of his unilateral decision.

The State of Idaho has enacted specific statutes with respect to the legal concept known as "partnership." Therefore any solution of partnership problems should logically begin with an application of the relevant code provision.

In the instant case the record indicates that although Summers requested his partner Dooley to agree to the hiring of a third man, such requests were not honored. In fact Dooley made it clear that he was "voting no" with regard to the hiring of an additional employee.

An application of the relevant statutory provisions and pertinent case law to the factual situation presented by the instant case indicates that the trial court was correct in its disposal of the issue since a majority of the partners did not consent to the hiring of the third man. I.C. § 53–318(8) provides:

> "Any difference arising as to ordinary matters connected with the partnership business may be decided by a *majority of the partners....*" (emphasis supplied) . . .

The intent of the legislature may be implied from the language used, or inferred on grounds of policy or reasonableness.... A careful reading of the statutory provision indicates that subsection 5 bestows *equal rights in the management and conduct of the partnership business* upon all of the partners. The concept of equality between partners with respect to management of business affairs is a central theme and recurs throughout the Uniform Partnership law, I.C. § 53–301 et seq., which has been enacted in this jurisdiction. Thus the only reasonable interpretation of I.C. § 53–318(8) is that business differences must be decided by a majority of the partners provided no other agreement between the partners speaks to the issues....

In the case at bar one of the partners continually voiced objection to the hiring of the third man. He did not sit idly by and acquiesce in the actions of his partner. Under these circumstances it is manifestly unjust to permit recovery of an expense which was incurred individually and not for the benefit of the partnership but rather for the benefit of one partner.

Judgment affirmed. Costs to respondent.

■ McQuade, C.J., and McFadden, Shepard and Spear, JJ., concur.

————

SANCHEZ v. SAYLOR, 129 N.M. 742, 13 P.3d 960 (2000). Sanchez and Saylor were partners. A third party was considering lending money to the partnership to finance a proposed restructuring of the partnership's debt, but the potential lender required Sanchez to provide his personal financial statements as a condition to granting the loan. Sanchez refused to furnish the statements that the potential lender required. Saylor brought suit against Sanchez on the ground that Sanchez's refusal to provide his financial statements to the potential lender violated his fiduciary obligations. Held, for Sanchez:

> ... We turn to *Covalt v. High*, 100 N.M. 700, 675 P.2d 999 (Ct.App.1983) ... Covalt and High formed an oral partnership which owned and rented an office to a corporation, CSI, in which Covalt owned 25 percent of the corporate stock and High owned 75 percent.... After resigning from CSI, Covalt demanded that the partnership increase CSI's rent, but High took no action. See *id.* The increase in rent would benefit the partnership, but it was detrimental to High. The district court found that CSI could afford the rent increase and High had breached his fiduciary duty. See *id*.

> In reversing, this Court stated that "all partners have equal rights in the management and conduct of the business of the partnership," that Covalt therefore "was legally invested with an equal voice in the management of the partnership affairs," and that "neither partner had the right to impose his will or decision concerning the operation of the partnership business upon the other." *Id*. at 703, 675 P.2d at 1002. The fact that a proposal benefitted the partnership did not require High to agree. See id. As authority for its decision, *Covalt* cited UPA, Section 54–1–18(H), stating "any difference arising as to ordinary matters connected with the partnership business may be decided by a majority of the partners." Further, the Court relied on the interpretation of the UPA language by the Idaho Supreme Court in *Summers v. Dooley*, 94 Idaho 87, 481 P.2d 318 (1971) that the language is mandatory rather than permissive in nature and means that business differences must be decided by a majority, not by one of two equal partners when the other objects. *See Summers*, 481 P.2d at 320–21.

> Simply stated, *Covalt* says that, absent an enforceable agreement covering such circumstances of disagreement, when both partners in a two-partner partnership disagree on an advantageous prospective business transaction, it is dissolution, not an action for breach of fiduciary duty, that is the appropriate avenue of relief....

> ... Without [the *Covalt*] rule, virtually each instance in which one partner for personal reasons does not agree with a proposed transaction that will benefit the partnership can result in a claim for breach of his or her partnership or fiduciary duty. Absent an enforceable contractual duty to agree, if the two partners cannot agree and do not want to (or cannot) continue their partnership, under *Covalt* the remedy is dissolution....

QUESTION

Suppose that A, B, and C form a partnership. A contributes 90% of the capital, and by agreement is entitled to 90% of any profits and is responsible for 90% of any losses. B and C each contribute 5% of the capital and by agreement each is entitled to 5% of any profits, and responsible for 5% of any losses. Nothing is said in the agreement concerning how decisions will be made. If A votes one way on an ordinary matter connected with the partnership, and B and C vote another way, who prevails?

———

NOTE ON THE MANAGEMENT OF PARTNERSHIPS

1. *Voting.* The cases and authorities are divided on the issue raised in Summers v. Dooley. In accord with *Summers* is Covalt v. High, 100 N.M. 700, 675 P.2d 999 (App.1983). But see National Biscuit Co. v. Stroud, 249 N.C. 467, 106 S.E.2d 692 (1959).

The rule of UPA § 18(h), that any difference arising as to ordinary matters connected with the partnership business may be decided by a majority of the partners, is "subject to any agreement between them." Partnership agreements often contain provisions vesting management in a managing partner, a managing committee, "senior partners," or some other group composed of less than all the partners, and such agreements override Section 18(h). The same result may be reached even without explicit agreement—for example on the basis of a course of conduct:

> [I]t is ... well settled ... that an agreement for exclusive control of the management of the business by one partner may be implied from the course of conduct of the parties. Here, it was fairly [inferable] from the course of conduct of Parks and Patterson that there was an implied agreement that Parks should be the managing partner.

Parks v. Riverside Ins. Co. of Am., 308 F.2d 175, 180 (10th Cir.1962). Such an implied agreement, if found, would pretty clearly block the nonmanaging partners from objecting to a decision of the managing partners relating to ordinary matters connected with the partnership business solely on the ground that the decision was not arrived at by a majority vote.

RUPA § 401(j) generally follows the voting rules of UPA § 18(h), although there are several differences between the sections. Under UPA § 18(h):

> Any difference arising as to ordinary matters connected with the partnership business may be decided by a majority of the partners; but no act in contravention of any agreement between the partners may be done rightfully without the consent of all the partners.

Under RUPA § 401(j):

A difference arising as to a matter in the ordinary course of business of a partnership may be decided by a majority of the partners. An act outside the ordinary course of business of a partnership and an amendment to the partnership agreement may be undertaken only with the consent of all of the partners.

RUPA § 401(j) must be read in conjunction with RUPA § 101(5), which defines the term "partnership agreement" to mean "the agreement, written or oral, among the partners concerning the partnership." The Comment to § 101(5) adds:

> The definition of "partnership agreement".... is intended to include any agreement among the partners ... concerning either the affairs of the partnership or the conduct of its business.... [T]he agreement may be inferred from the conduct of the parties.

> In many partnerships, there is no single document—or no document at all—called a "Partnership Agreement," either because the partnership is itself implicit rather than explicit, or because the partners lack either the inclination or the funds to make a formal agreement. In such cases, under RUPA § 101(5) the "partnership agreement" consists of the fragmentary explicit and implicit agreements that are made from time to time as the partnership relation evolves. Furthermore, even when a partnership does have an explicit and formal "Partnership Agreement," under RUPA § 401(j) unanimity is required not only to depart from this formal agreement, but to depart from any further fragmentary agreement or course of conduct that gives rise to an implied agreement. Thus changes in the way the partnership is actually conducted, not just changes in the way in which it has been explicitly agreed that the partnership will be conducted, may constitute amendments of the partnership agreement for purposes of § 401(j).

2. *Participation*. Because UPA Section 18(h) provides that partnership action requires a majority vote, what is added by UPA Section 18(e), which provides that all partners have equal rights in the management and conduct of the partnership business? Presumably, the effect of this Section is that absent contrary agreement, every partner must be *consulted* in partnership decisions.

> For a majority of partners to say; We do not care what one partner may say, we, being the majority, will do what we please, is, I apprehend, what this Court will not allow. So, again, with respect to making Mr. *Robertson* the treasurer, Mr. *Const* had a right to be consulted; his opinion might be overruled, and honestly overruled, but he ought to have had the question put to him and discussed: In all partnerships ... the partners are bound to be true and faithful to each other: They are to act upon the joint opinion of all, and the discretion and judgment of anyone cannot be excluded: What weight is to be given to it is another question....

Const v. Harris, 37 Eng.Rep. 1191, 1202 (Ch.1824) (Lord Chancellor Eldon). Accordingly, absent contrary agreement a majority of partners who made decisions without consulting a minority partner would violate § 18(e), even though the majority could have overridden the minority partner if he had been consulted.

RUPA § 401(f) continues the rule of UPA § 18(e), by conferring on each partner the right to participate in management. The Comment to § 401(f) notes that UPA § 18(e) "has been interpreted broadly to mean that, absent contrary agreement, each partner has a continuing right to participate in the management of the partnership and to be informed about the partnership business, even if his assent . . . is not required."

———

NOTE ON WHAT LAW GOVERNS THE INTERNAL AFFAIRS OF PARTNERSHIPS

Legal rules that concern business organizations fall into two general categories: (i) rules that deal with the organization's internal affairs—such as the powers, rights, and duties of the owners, managers, and organs of the organization as among themselves; and (ii) rules that deal with the obligations of the owners, managers, and organs of the organization, and of the organization itself, to third persons.

Often, the laws of more than one state might in theory be applied to determine what rules govern an organization's internal affairs. In such cases, the body of law known as *conflict of laws* or *choice of law* determines which state's law governs. In the case of corporations, limited partnerships, and limited liability companies, which are formed by filing organizational documents in a given state, the general choice-of-law rule is that internal affairs are governed by the law of the state in which the corporation is incorporated or in which the limited partnership or limited liability company is organized. In contrast, the formation of a general partnership does not require the filing of organizational documents. Accordingly, the choice-of-law rule to determine what law governs the internal affairs of general partnerships must depend on other factors. The UPA does not include a provision governing the choice of law for the internal affairs of a general partnership. However, RUPA § 106 provides that a general partnership's internal affairs are governed by the law of the state in which the partnership has its chief executive office.

———

(b) INDEMNIFICATION AND CONTRIBUTION

———

UNIFORM PARTNERSHIP ACT §§ 18(a), (b), (c), (d), (f)

———

REVISED UNIFORM PARTNERSHIP ACT §§ 401(a)–(e), (h)

[See Statutory Supplement]

———

NOTE ON INDEMNIFICATION AND CONTRIBUTION

As discussed in Section 5, infra, partners are individually liable to partnership creditors for partnership obligations. As between the partners, however, each partner is liable only for his share of partnership obligations. Thus if one partner pays off a partnership obligation in full (or, for that matter, if he simply pays more than his share), he is entitled to indemnification from the partnership for the difference between what he paid and his share of the liability.

Indemnification should be distinguished from contribution. In a proper case, a *partner* has a right to be *indemnified* by the *partnership*. In contrast, in a proper case the *partnership* has a right to require *contribution* from one or more *partners*. Thus the obligation to indemnify a partner is a partnership liability, and the obligation to make contribution is a liability of a partner. Partners may, for example, be required to make contribution to the partnership to fund a partnership obligation to indemnify another partner, so that all partners share a burden that was initially placed on only one. Contribution may also be required for other purposes—in particular, paying off partnership creditors and equalizing capital losses.

"Indemnification resolves the apparent conflict between a partner's joint or joint and several liability, whereby a partner may be called upon to pay the entire amount of partnership debt to third parties under UPA § 15 and RUPA § 306 and the proportionate sharing of profits and losses among the partners under UPA § 18(a) and RUPA § 401(b). A partner who pays or incurs a personal liability to a third party on behalf of the partnership becomes a creditor of the partnership in the amount of the payment or liability, in effect subrogated to the rights of the creditor.... If a going partnership indemnifies the partner, all partners incur a detriment in proportion to their profit shares if the business is profitable, or otherwise according to their loss shares. If the partnership is unable to pay, all partners must contribute to make up the resulting deficit under UPA §§ 18(a) and 40(b)(11) and (d) and RUPA §§ 401(b) and 807(b) according to their loss shares. If the partners are unable to contribute or cannot be sued, the paying partner, rather than the third party, bears the loss." Bromberg & Ribstein on Partnership § 6.02(f).

———

(c) DISTRIBUTIONS, REMUNERATION, AND CAPITAL CONTRIBUTIONS

――――

UNIFORM PARTNERSHIP ACT §§ 18(a), (b), (c), (d), (f)

――――

REVISED UNIFORM PARTNERSHIP ACT § 401(a)–(e), (h)

[See Statutory Supplement]

――――

QUESTION

Suppose A, B, and C form a partnership. A contributes 90% of the capital, and B and C each contribute 5%. All work full-time in the partnership business, with roughly equal responsibilities. Nothing is said in the partnership agreement concerning how partnership profits will be divided. If the partnership makes a profit in a given year, how is it to be divided?

――――

(d) CAPITAL ACCOUNTS AND DRAWS

――――

W. Klein & J. Coffee, Business Organization and Finance 80–84

Ninth ed., 2004.

. . . CONTRIBUTIONS, ACCOUNTS, AND RETURNS

A.   CAPITAL ACCOUNTS

Suppose that Abe, Bill, Pamela and Morris have formed a partnership for the acquisition and operation of a grocery store. Abe and Bill each are to contribute $15,000 and Pamela $20,000, in cash or in property to be used in the business. Morris will contribute neither cash nor property but will agree to manage the store for five years and will receive a salary slightly lower than what he might earn elsewhere. If the partnership follows customary bookkeeping patterns, its books will show the following information under a heading that is likely to be called "Capital Accounts":

Abe	$15,000
Bill	15,000
Pamela	20,000
Morris	0
Total	$50,000

. . . In the absence of an agreement to the contrary, if the business were sold for cash, each partner would be entitled to receive an amount equal to his or her capital account, if available. Any excess or deficit would be shared in accordance with each partner's share of gain and loss (a point to be illustrated below).

Capital contribution does not necessarily control the sharing of gain and loss, and shares of gain may differ from shares of loss. For example, our four partners could agree that each will be entitled to an equal 25 percent share of any profits, despite the difference in initial contribution. Indeed, this is the result that will be provided by the Uniform Partnership Act (Sec. 18(a)) in the absence of an agreement to the contrary. At the same time, and again in the absence of an agreement to the contrary, no partner will be entitled to interest on his or her capital account. Losses might be allocated equally among the partners (again, the result in the absence of express agreement) or might be allocated first pro rata among the contributors of initial capital, to the extent of such capital, and then, perhaps, equally among all partners. . . .

Suppose that all profits and losses are to be shared equally, and suppose that at the end of the first year of operation the profit (after the payment of Morris's salary) is $20,000, or $5,000 per partner. One way of recording this outcome would be to adjust the capital accounts, which would then appear as follows:

Abe	$20,000 *
Bill	20,000
Pamela	25,000
Morris	5,000
Total	$70,000

*$15,000 initial capital plus $5,000 profit share.

If, on the other hand, the firm experienced a loss of $20,000 in its first year of operations, the capital accounts would be:

Abe	$10,000
Bill	10,000
Pamela	15,000
Morris	(5,000)
Total	$30,000

(Parentheses around a number indicate that it is a negative amount.) If, at this point, the business were sold for exactly the amount of the total capital accounts, $30,000, Morris would be required to contribute $5,000 and the resulting total, $35,000, would then be distributed $10,000 each to Abe and Bill and $15,000 to Pamela. This result may seem to be hard on Morris, and there is some legal authority for relieving him of the debt, at least to the extent that he contributed services without adequate compensation. The issue is one that the partners should think about at the outset. They might well agree that losses are to be shared by the partners in accordance with their initial capital contributions. . . .

B. DRAW

Thus far we have referred to profits and losses, which are book-keeping concepts. It is vital to note that profit does not necessarily generate any spare cash. For example, a new retail store may be highly profitable but may need all its profits to expand its inventory. And even if a firm has had profits and does have spare cash, the partners are not automatically entitled to receive a cash payment. There is a separate term—called "draw"—that is used to describe cash distributions to partners. The amount of the draw of each partner is determined by majority vote of the partners (again, in the absence of some other express agreement) and may be more or less than the profit. . . .

Returning now to the bookkeeping effects of a draw, suppose that our grocery store partnership generates an accounting profit of $20,000 in the first year of its operations. . . . We have just seen how this net profit figure can be translated into adjustments to partner capital accounts. Now suppose that there is a draw. Suppose, for example, that the partners agree that each is to be paid $3,000 from partnership funds. The $3,000 would reduce the capital accounts, so they would then be:

Abe	$17,000 *
Bill	17,000
Pamela	22,000
Morris	2,000
Total	$58,000

*$15,000 initial capital account, plus $5,000 profit share, minus $3,000 draw.

Next, assume that there is a loss of $20,000 in the first year, instead of a profit; that the partnership agreement allocates this loss equally among all the partners; and that despite the loss, there is a cash distribution (draw) of $3,000 to each partner. The partnership capital accounts would then be as follows:

Abe	$ 7,000*
Bill	7,000
Pamela	12,000
Morris	(8,000)
Total	$18,000

* $15,000 initial capital account, minus $5,000 loss share, minus $3,000 draw.

All of this makes sense if you think about it for a few moments. Bear in mind that the capital accounts are not expected to correspond to values in the firm but instead are merely intended to reflect the relative claims of the partners to the assets of the partnership, which is of importance mostly in the case of withdrawal of a partner or liquidation of the partnership. A partner's share of profit can be thought of as something that he or she has earned and reinvested in the firm. The draw can be thought of as earnings or capital taken out of the firm. The capital account allows us to keep track of relative claims where initial contributions and profit shares differ. The same function is served where, for one reason or another, partners do not draw from the firm amounts strictly in proportion to their profit shares.

C.   CAPITAL ACCOUNTS AND VALUE OF A PARTNER'S INTEREST

To illustrate the difference between capital account and value, and the role of the capital account, suppose that the partnership capital accounts stand as follows:

Abe	$17,000
Bill	17,000
Pamela	22,000
Morris	2,000
Total	$58,000

Suppose that the business has increased in value because of the construction of a large housing development nearby. This is the kind of gain that [under the principles of accounting] ordinarily would not be reflected on the partnership books as long as the firm continues to operate with the same owners. Now suppose that the business is sold for $78,000 cash, net of all debts or other obligations. There is a surplus of $20,000 above the amount in the capital accounts (that is, above the amount of the initial contributions increased by profits and decreased by distributions to the partners). This $20,000 can be thought of as previously unrecorded profit; it would be allocated equally among the partners ($5,000 apiece), so that each partner would receive the following amount:

Abe	$22,000 *
Bill	22,000
Pamela	27,000
Morris	7,000
Total	$78,000

*$17,000 current capital account, plus $5,000 share of profit on sale of business.

Finally, assume that the store is sold for less than the amount in the capital accounts—for example, for $38,000. Here there is a previously unrecognized loss of $20,000. In the absence of an agreement to the contrary, the loss would be borne equally by all the partners (again, $5,000 apiece). The relative claims of the partners would therefore be as follows:

Abe	$12,000
Bill	12,000
Pamela	17,000
Morris	(3,000)
Total	$38,000

SECTION 4.   THE AUTHORITY OF A PARTNER

———

UNIFORM PARTNERSHIP ACT §§ 3, 4(3), 9, 10, 11, 12, 13, 14

———

REVISED UNIFORM PARTNERSHIP ACT
§§ 301, 302, 303, 304, 305, 306, 308

[See Statutory Supplement]

———

RNR Investments Limited Partnership v. Peoples First Community Bank

District Court of Appeal of Florida, First District, 2002.
812 So.2d 561.

■ VAN NORTWICK, J. . . . .

Factual and Procedural History

RNR is a Florida limited partnership formed pursuant to chapter 620, Florida Statutes, to purchase vacant land in Destin, Florida, and to construct a house on the land for resale. Bernard Roeger was RNR's general partner and Heinz Rapp, Claus North, and S.E. Waltz, Inc., were limited partners. The agreement of limited partnership provides for various restrictions on the authority of the general partner. Paragraph 4.1 of the agreement required the general partner to prepare a budget covering the cost of acquisition and construction of the project (defined as the "Approved Budget") and further provided, in pertinent part, as follows:

> The Approved Budget for the Partnership is attached hereto as Exhibit "C" and is approved by evidence of the signatures of the Partners on the signature pages of this Agreement. . . . In no event, without Limited Partner Consent, shall the Approved Budget be exceeded by more than five percent (5%), nor shall any line item thereof be exceeded by more than ten percent (10%), . . .

Paragraph 4.3 restricted the general partner's ability to borrow, spend partnership funds and encumber partnership assets, if not specifically provided for in the Approved Budget. Finally, with respect to the development of the partnership project, paragraph 2.2(b) provided:

> The General Partner shall not incur debts, liabilities or obligations of the Partnership which will cause any line item in the Approved Budget to be exceeded by more than ten percent (10%) or which will cause the aggregate Approved Budget to be exceed by more

than five percent (5%) unless the General Partner shall receive the prior written consent of the Limited Partner.

In June 1998, RNR, through its general partner, entered into a construction loan agreement, note and mortgage in the principal amount of $990,000. From June 25, 1998 through Mar. 13, 2000, the bank disbursed the aggregate sum of $952,699, by transfers into RNR's bank account. All draws were approved by an architect, who certified that the work had progressed as indicated and that the quality of the work was in accordance with the construction contract. No representative of RNR objected to any draw of funds or asserted that the amounts disbursed were not associated with the construction of the house.

RNR defaulted under the terms of the note and mortgage by failing to make payments due in July 2000 and all monthly payments due thereafter. The Bank filed a complaint seeking foreclosure. RNR filed an answer and affirmative defenses. In its first affirmative defense, RNR alleged that the Bank had failed to review the limitations on the general partner's authority in RNR's limited partnership agreement. RNR asserted that the Bank had negligently failed to investigate and to realize that the general partner had no authority to execute notes, a mortgage and a construction loan agreement and was estopped from foreclosing. The Bank filed a motion for summary judgment with supporting affidavits attesting to the amounts due and owing and the amount of disbursements under the loan.

In opposition to the summary judgment motion, RNR filed the affidavit of Stephen E. Waltz, the president one of RNR's limited partners, S.E. Waltz, Inc. In that affidavit, Mr. Waltz stated that the partners anticipated that RNR would need to finance the construction of the residence, but that paragraph 2.2(b) of the partnership agreement limited the amount of any loan the general partner could obtain on behalf of RNR to an amount that would not exceed by more than 10% the approved budget on any one line item or exceed the aggregate approved budget by more than 5%, unless the general partner received the prior written consent of the limited partners. Waltz alleged that the limited partners understood and orally agreed that the general partner would seek financing in the approximate amount of $650,000. Further, Waltz stated:

> Even though the limited partners had orally agreed to this amount, a written consent was never memorialized, and to my surprise, the [Bank], either through its employees or attorney, . . . never requested the same from any of the limited partners at any time prior to [or] after the closing on the loan from the [Bank] to RNR.

Waltz alleged that the partners learned in the spring of 2000 that, instead of obtaining a loan for $650,000, Roeger had obtained a loan for $990,000, which was secured by RNR's property. He stated that the limited partners did not consent to Roeger obtaining a loan from the Bank in the amount of $990,000 either orally or in writing and that the limited partners were never contacted by the Bank as to whether they had consented to a loan amount of $990,000.

RNR asserts that a copy of the limited partnership agreement was maintained at its offices. Nevertheless, the record contains no copy of an Approved Budget of the partnership or any evidence that would show that a copy of RNR's partnership agreement or any partnership budget was given to the Bank or that any notice of the general partner's restricted authority was provided to the Bank.

... [T]he trial court entered a summary final judgment of foreclosure in favor of the Bank. The foreclosure sale has been stayed pending the outcome of this appeal.. . .

Apparent Authority of the General Partner

Although the agency concept of apparent authority was applied to partnerships under the common law, see, e.g., *Taylor v. Cummer Lumber Co.*, 59 Fla. 638, 52 So. 614, 616 (1910), in Florida the extent to which the partnership is bound by the acts of a partner acting within the apparent authority is now governed by statute. Section 620.8301(1), Florida Statutes (2000),[7] a part of the Florida Revised Uniform Partnership Act (FRUPA), provides:

> Each partner is an agent of the partnership for the purpose of its business. An act of a partner, including the execution of an instrument in the partnership name, for apparently carrying on in the ordinary scope of partnership business or business of the kind carried on by the partnership, in the geographic area in which the partnership operates, binds the partnership unless the partner had no authority to act for the partnership in the particular manner and the person with whom the partner was dealing knew or had received notification that the partner lacked authority.

Thus, even if a general partner's actual authority is restricted by the terms of the partnership agreement, the general partner possesses the apparent authority to bind the partnership in the ordinary course of partnership business or in the business of the kind carried on by the partnership, unless the third party "knew or had received a notification that the partner lacked authority." Id. "Knowledge" and "notice" under FRUPA are defined in section 620.8102. That section provides that "[a] person knows a fact if the person has actual knowledge of the fact." § 620.8102(1), Fla. Stat. (2000). Further, a third party has notice of a fact if that party "(a) [k]nows of the fact; (b) [h]as received notification of the fact; or (c) [h]as reason to know the fact exists from all other facts known to the person at the time in question." § 620.8102(2), Fla. Stat. (2000). Finally, under section 620.8303 a partnership may file a statement of partnership authority setting forth any restrictions in a general partner's authority.

---

7. RNR mistakenly argues that section 620.8301(1) has no application to a limited partnership because that section is part of the Florida Revised Uniform Partnership Act, not the Florida Revised Uniform Limited Partnership Act. Section 620.186, however, provides, as follows:

In any case not provided for in this act, the provisions of the Uniform Partnership Act or the Revised Uniform Partnership Act of 1995, as applicable, and the rules of law and equity shall govern.

Commentators have described the purpose of these knowledge and notice provisions, as follows:

> Under RUPA, the term knew is confined to actual knowledge, which is cognitive awareness. . . . Therefore, despite the similarity in language, RUPA provides greater protection [than the Uniform Partnership Act (UPA)] to third persons dealing with partners, who may rely on the partner's apparent authority absent actual knowledge or notification of a restriction in this regard. RUPA effects a slight reallocation of the risk of unauthorized agency power in favor of third parties. That is consistent with notions of the expanded liability of principals since the UPA was drafted.

> RUPA attempts to balance its shift toward greater protection of third parties by providing several new ways for partners to protect themselves against unauthorized actions by a rogue partner. First, the partnership may notify a third party of a partner's lack of authority. Such notification is effective upon receipt, whether or not the third party actually learns of it. More significantly, the partnership may file a statement of partnership authority restricting a partner's authority.

Donald J. Weidner & John W. Larson, *The Revised Uniform Partnership Act: The Reporters' Overview*, 49 BUS. LAW 1, 31–32 (1993) (footnotes omitted). "Absent actual knowledge, third parties have no duty to inspect the partnership agreement or inquire otherwise to ascertain the extent of a partner's actual authority in the ordinary course of business, . . . even if they have some reason to question it." Id. at 32 n. 200. The apparent authority provisions of section 620.8301(1), reflect a policy by the drafters that "the risk of loss from partner misconduct more appropriately belongs on the partnership than on third parties who do not knowingly participate in or take advantage of the misconduct . . ." J. Dennis [Hynes], *Notice and Notification Under the Revised Uniform Partnership Act: Some Suggested Changes*, 2 J. SMALL & EMERGING BUS. L. 299, 308 (1998).

Analysis

Under section 620.8301(1), the determination of whether a partner is acting with authority to bind the partnership involves a two-step analysis. The first step is to determine whether the partner purporting to bind the partnership apparently is carrying on the partnership business in the usual way or a business of the kind carried on by the partnership. An affirmative answer on this step ends the inquiry, unless it is shown that the person with whom the partner is dealing actually knew or had received a notification that the partner lacked authority. See *Kristerin Dev. Co. v. Granson Inv.*, 394 N.W.2d 325, 330 (Iowa 1986) (applying Iowa version of UPA). Here, it is undisputed that, in entering into the loan, the general partner was carrying on the business of RNR in the usual way. The dispositive question in this appeal is whether there are issues of material fact as to whether the Bank had actual knowledge or notice of restrictions on the general partner's authority.

RNR argues that, as a result of the restrictions on the general partner's authority in the partnership agreement, the Bank had constructive knowledge of the restrictions and was obligated to inquire as to the general partner's specific authority to bind RNR in the construction loan. We cannot agree. Under section 620.8301, the Bank could rely on the general partner's apparent authority, unless it had actual knowledge or notice of restrictions on that authority. While the RNR partners may have agreed upon restrictions that would limit the general partner to borrowing no more than $650,000 on behalf of the partnership, RNR does not contend and nothing before us would show that the Bank had actual knowledge or notice of any restrictions on the general partner's authority. Here, the partnership could have protected itself by filing a statement pursuant to section 620.8303 or by providing notice to the Bank of the specific restrictions on the authority of the general partner. . . .

Because there is no disputed issue of fact concerning whether the Bank had actual knowledge or notice of restrictions on the general partner's authority to borrow, summary judgment was proper.

AFFIRMED.

■ MINER AND WOLF, JJ, concur.

———

Northmon Investment Company v. Milford Plaza Associates

Supreme Court, Appellate Division, New York, 2001.
284 A.D.2d 250, 727 N.Y.S.2d 419.

■ SULLIVAN, P.J., ELLERIN, WALLACH, RUBIN and BUCKLEY, JJ.

Supreme Court, New York County . . . in a dispute between partners concerning appellants' [defendants'] authority to enter into a 99–year lease of real property constituting the partnership's only asset, found in respondents' favor that appellants lack such authority. . . . [The decision is] unanimously affirmed, with costs.

Appellants lack authority to enter into the contemplated 99–year lease even if such lease were to be deemed in the ordinary course of the partnership's business. A partner's authority to bind the partnership to transactions apparently in the ordinary course of the partnership's business (*see,* Partnership Law § 20[1]) does not affect the right of partners as between themselves to prevent contemplated transactions with third parties, or otherwise to assert their "equal rights in the management and conduct of the partnership business" (*see,* Partnership Law § 40[5]). Appellants cannot impose their decision to enter into this lease upon respondents (*see, Riley v. Maran,* 82 Misc.2d 702, 706–707, 370 N.Y.S.2d 302; *see also,* Partnership Law § 40[8]), and, indeed, respondents' right to interfere with this or any other contract or prospective contract involving the partnership is "absolute" and "privileged, excusable and justified" (*Braden v. Perkins,* 174 Misc. 885, 22 N.Y.S.2d 144). Nor do the newly discovered partnership agreements avail appellants. Assuming such agreements . . . can be fairly construed to preclude respondents' interference with a contemplated or consummated long-term lease, it remains that the agreements, on their face, terminate the partnership in 2075, many years before the contemplated 99–year lease would expire. Since such a lease cannot be deemed ordinary, respondents would not be bound by it (*see,* Partnership Law § 40[2],[3][b],[c]) . . . .

––––––––

NOTE ON THE AUTHORITY OF PARTNERS

1. *UPA.* The basic default rule governing a partner's *actual* authority under the UPA is that each partner is an agent of the partnership for the purpose of its business. However, the UPA's rule on a partner's *apparent* authority is somewhat ambiguous and controversial. Under the UPA, a partner has authority to bind the partnership by any act "for apparently carrying on in the usual way the business of the partnership of which he is a member." There is controversy whether this means an act within the apparent course of business as carried on by *the partner's firm* or the course of business of *other firms* in the same locality engaged in the same general line of business. In Burns v. Gonzalez, 439 S.W.2d 128 (Tex.Civ.App.1969), the court adopted the latter view.

2. *RUPA.* RUPA § 301(1) makes clear, as the UPA did not, that a partnership is bound by an act of the partner for apparently carrying on in the usual way (i) the partnership business or (ii) business *of the kind* carried on by the partnership. The Comment to § 301(1) states:

> Section 301(1). . . . clarifies that a partner's apparent authority includes acts for carrying on in the ordinary course "business of the kind carried on by the partnership," not just the business of the particular partnership in question. The UPA is ambiguous on this point, but there is some authority for an expanded construction. . . . See, e.g., Burns v. Gonzalez, 439 S.W.2d 128, 131 (Tex.Civ.App.1969) (dictum) . . . .

The treatment of authority under RUPA also differs from the UPA in certain other respects. For example, RUPA § 302 provides elaborate rules concerning when a transfer of partnership property is binding. In addition:

1. RUPA § 301 makes subtle shifts in determining when the knowledge or notice of T, a third person, of a restriction on the authority of a partner, P, will prevent partnership liability from arising out of a transaction between T and P, who purports to act on the partnership's behalf. "Under UPA section 9(1), the partnership was not bound by the unauthorized actions of a partner if the third party had '*knowledge*' of the partner's lack of authority. Under UPA section 9(1), a third party had knowledge when he or she had actual knowledge or '*when he has knowledge of such other facts as in the circumstances shows bad faith.*' This latter language creates an implied or inquiry

notice, the exact parameters of which are ill-defined. Under RUPA, the third party will not be placed under a duty of inquiry or be deemed to have notice from the facts and circumstances. *Only actual knowledge or receipt of a notification of a partner's lack of authority will meet the standard.*" Merrill, Partnership Property and Partnership Authority Under the Revised Uniform Partnership Act, 49 Bus.Law. 83, 88–89 (1993) (emphasis added.)

2. RUPA § 303 enables a partnership to file a "Statement of Partnership Authority." Under § 303, a *grant* of authority in such a Statement is normally conclusive in favor of third persons, even if they have no actual knowledge of the Statement, unless they have actual knowledge that the partner has no such authority. However, a *limitation* on a partner's authority in such a Statement—other than a limitation on the partner's authority to transfer real property—will not be effective unless the third party *knows* of the limitation or the Statement has been delivered to him. In contrast, a limitation in a Statement of Partnership Authority of a partner's authority to transfer partnership *real property* is effective against all third persons if a certified copy of the Statement is filed in the real-property recording office.

Why would a partnership want to file a Statement that can *expand* a partner's authority simply because it is filed, but normally will not *limit* a partner's authority unless it is not only filed but also delivered? One answer is that persons who deal with a partnership may require such a Statement to ensure themselves that the partnership will be bound. Furthermore, "[in] the process of searching for the grant of authority, the third party will acquire actual knowledge of any restriction on authority in a filed statement. [Furthermore,] the ... partners may protect themselves by delivering the statement to all known creditors, actual or potential." Merrill, supra, at 89.

———

BROMBERG & RIBSTEIN ON PARTNERSHIP § 4.02(a)(4). "It is not clear what is meant by the inclusion of 'apparently' in U.P.A. § 9(1) and R.U.P.A. § 301.... 'Apparently' does probably *expand* liability to include transactions that were not in the usual course but appeared to the plaintiff to be so...."

———

SECTION 5. LIABILITY FOR PARTNERSHIP OBLIGATIONS

———

UNIFORM PARTNERSHIP ACT §§ 9, 13, 14, 15, 16, 17, 36

———

REVISED UNIFORM PARTNERSHIP ACT §§ 305, 306, 307, 308

[See Statutory Supplement]

DAVIS V. LOFTUS, 334 Ill.App.3d 761, 778 N.E.2d 1144 (Ill. App. 2002). Davis claimed that two lawyers, Loftus and Engel, at the law firm of Gottlieb & Schwartz, had committed malpractice in connection with a real estate transaction that Davis had engaged in. Davis sued all the partners of the firm for damages. Some of the partners of the firm, including Frink, were denominated "income partners," as opposed to "equity partners." According to the partnership agreement, the firm paid each income partner a fixed level of compensation, determined on an annual basis by the Executive Committee, plus a bonus. The partnership agreement added that: "Income Partners will not share in Partnership Net Profit or Loss." Each income partner made a "capital contribution" of $10,000 to the firm. If an income partner withdrew from the firm, or upon dissolution of the firm, the firm would return the $10,000 capital contribution to the income partner without any adjustment for the growth or profits of the firm from the time of the capital contribution. Income partners had no voting rights and were not eligible to serve on the executive committee.

Held, the "income partners" were not partners with the meaning of the liability provisions of the Uniform Partnership Act:

> Section 13 of the Uniform Partnership Act (the Act) (805 ILCS 205/13 (West 1992)) provides that a partnership is liable for any wrongful act of any partner acting in the course of partnership business. Section 15 makes all partners liable for any such acts. 805 ILCS 205/15 (West 1992). The trial court found Frink and others not liable for the acts of Loftus and Engel based on its finding that the income partners of Gottlieb & Schwartz are not "partners" within the meaning of the Act.

> The substance and not the form of a business relationship determines whether the relationship qualifies as a partnership. *Koestner v. Wease & Koestner Jewelers, Inc.*, 63 Ill.App.3d 1047, 1050–51, 21 Ill.Dec. 76, 381 N.E.2d 11 (1978). Thus, we must decide whether the provisions of the partnership agreement pertaining to "Income Partners" make them partners within the meaning of the Act.

> *Cook v. Lauten*, 1 Ill.App.2d 255, 117 N.E.2d 414 (1954), controls our disposition of this appeal. In that case the plaintiff and the defendant signed an "agreement for junior partnership." *Cook*, 1 Ill.App.2d at 258, 117 N.E.2d 414. The agreement named the plaintiff as the managing partner and sole owner of the firm's assets, and established the defendant's compensation as a fixed annual salary plus a bonus. While the defendant could advance money to the firm, the firm would only return the same amount

later. The defendant, as a junior partner, had no right to participate in the firm's profits or losses. The court held:

> "[T]he agreement for a 'junior partnership' negatives every
> one of the elements essential to constitute a partnership
> relation. * * * Defendant's salary is fixed regardless of profits
> or losses of the alleged partnership and plaintiff as managing
> partner may by unilateral action alter defendant's share of the
> profit at will. * * * In short, defendant was to have no
> interest in the so-called 'partnership' except his unpaid salary
> and one month's bonus." *Cook*, 1 Ill.App.2d at 259, 117
> N.E.2d 414.

Here, too, the agreement established that income partners, including Frink, received a fixed salary plus a bonus, and the
income partners took no share of the partnership's profit or loss.
While income partners paid a "capital contribution" to the firm,
the firm would repay the same amount, without regard to the
firm's profit or loss from the time of the "capital contribution."
The executive committee, like the managing partner in *Cook*, set
the level of compensation for all income partners. Moreover, the
income partners had no right to vote on the management or
conduct of the partnership business. See 805 ILCS 205/18(e)
(West 1992). Following *Cook*, we find that income partners under
Gottlieb & Schwartz' partnership agreement do not qualify as
partners within the meaning of the Act, and therefore the Act
provides no basis for holding income partners liable for the acts
of Loftus and Engel.

NOTE ON LIABILITY FOR PARTNERSHIP OBLIGATIONS

1. *UPA.* The provisions of the Uniform Partnership Act governing
liability for partnership obligations reflect an amalgam of the entity
and aggregate theories. On the one hand, UPA §§ 9, 13, and 14 make
"the partnership" liable for defined acts of the partners. It might seem
to follow that this liability could be enforced by a suit against the
partnership. However, the UPA does not authorize such a suit, because
it does not recognize a partnership as an entity, and unless authorized
by statute, suit normally cannot be brought against an association that
is not an entity. Indeed, the UPA goes to the opposite extreme. Under
UPA § 15(a), partners are *jointly and severally* liable for wrongful acts
and omissions of the partnership such as torts, and breaches of trust.
Under UPA § 15(b), however, partners are only *jointly* liable "for all
other debts and obligations of the partnership," such as breaches of
contract. At common law, if an obligation is "joint and several" the
obligors can be sued either jointly or separately. If, however, an
obligation is only "joint" the obligee must join all the obligors in the
same suit (subject to a few exceptions where jurisdiction over all the
obligors cannot be obtained). See C. Clark, Handbook of the Law of
Code Pleading 373–74 (2d ed. 1947). Thus under the UPA, an action

on a partnership's contractual obligation must be brought against all the partners, and if even one partner is not joined, the action can be dismissed on motion by the partners who were joined.

The inability of a UPA partnership contract creditor to sue a partnership in its own name is obviously undesirable, and many states have statutorily patched up the UPA rule. Some states achieved this objective by adopting a Common Name Statute, which explicitly allows a partnership to be sued in its own name. An example is N.Y.Civ. Prac.L. & R. § 1025: "Two or more persons conducting a business as a partnership may sue or be sued in the partnership name...." Under such statutes, a judgment is binding on the partnership property and on the individual property of all partners who are served. Other states patched up the UPA by changing the rule that a contract creditor of a partnership needs to join all the partners in a suit to establish liability on the contract claim. Some states make *all* partnership liabilities joint and several, not just wrongful acts or omissions and breaches of trust. Other states adopted Joint Debtor Statutes, which provide that a suit against joint obligors can proceed even if some of the obligors are not joined. See, e.g., Cal.Civ.Proc.Code § 410.70. Under such statutes, a judgment is binding on both the joint (partnership) property and on the property of those partners who are served.

2. *RUPA.* Unlike the UPA, RUPA § 307(a) specifically provides that a partnership may both sue and be sued in its own name. Furthermore, RUPA § 306 provides that partners are jointly and severally liable for all obligations of the partnership. However, RUPA adds a new barrier to *collecting* against an individual partner. Under RUPA § 307, a judgment against a *partner* based on a claim against the *partnership* normally cannot be satisfied against the partner's individual assets unless and until a judgment on the same claim has been rendered against the partnership, and a writ of execution on that judgment has been returned unsatisfied. To put this differently, RUPA § 307 adopts an exhaustion rule, under which in a suit against a partner based on a claim against the partnership, partnership assets must be exhausted before a partner's individual assets can be reached. (This exhaustion rule is made subject to certain exceptions, one of which is that the rule does not apply if the partnership is in bankruptcy.) As the Comment to RUPA § 306 points out, "Joint and several liability under RUPA differs ... from the classic model [of joint and several liability outside RUPA], which permits a judgment creditor to proceed immediately against any of the joint and several judgment debtors." In effect, therefore, RUPA takes an aggregate-like approach to a partner's *liability*, but an entity-like approach to *collecting judgments* based on that liability. RUPA § 307 also provides that, subject to certain exceptions, a judgment against a partnership is not by itself a judgment against a partner, and cannot be satisfied from a partner's assets unless there is also a judgment against the partner.

SECTION 6.   PARTNERSHIP INTERESTS AND PARTNERSHIP PROPERTY

UNIFORM PARTNERSHIP ACT §§ 8, 18(g), 24, 25, 26, 27, 28

REVISED UNIFORM PARTNERSHIP ACT §§ 203, 204, 501, 502, 503, 504

[See Statutory Supplement]

Rapoport v. 55 Perry Co.

New York Supreme Court, Appellate Division, 1975.
50 A.D.2d 54, 376 N.Y.S.2d 147.

Cross appeals from an order of the Supreme Court (HILDA G. SCHWARTZ, J.), entered July 16, 1975 in New York County, which denied a motion by plaintiffs for summary judgment and a cross motion by defendants for summary judgment dismissing the complaint. . . .

■ TILZER, J. In 1969, Simon, Genia and Ury Rapoport entered into a partnership agreement with Morton, Jerome and Burton Parnes, forming the partnership known as 55 Perry Company. Pursuant to the agreement, each of the families owned 50% of the partnership interests. In December of 1974 Simon and Genia Rapoport assigned a 10% interest of their share in the partnership to their adult children, Daniel and Kalia. The Parnes defendants were advised of the assignment and an amended partnership certificate was filed in the County Clerk's office indicating the addition of Daniel and Kalia as partners. However, when the plaintiffs, thereafter, requested the Parnes defendants to execute an amended partnership agreement to reflect the above changes in the partnership, the Parnes refused, taking the position that the partnership agreement did not permit the introduction of new partners without consent of all the existing partners. Thereafter, the plaintiffs Rapoport brought this action seeking a declaration that Simon and Genia Rapoport had an absolute right to assign their interests to their adult children without consent of the defendants and that such assignment was authorized pursuant to paragraph 12 of the partnership agreement. The plaintiffs further sought to have Daniel and Kalia be declared partners in 55 Perry Company and have their names entered upon the books of the partnership as partners. The defendants Parnes interposed an answer, taking the position that the partnership agreement did not permit admission of additional partners without consent of all the existing partners and that the filing of the amended certificate of partnership was unauthorized. After joinder of issue plaintiffs moved for summary judgment and although the defendants did not cross-move for similar relief, such was, nevertheless, requested in their answering papers.

On the motion for summary judgment both parties agreed that there were no issues of fact and that there was only a question of the interpretation of the written documents which should be disposed of as a matter of law by the court. Nevertheless, the court below found that the agreement was ambiguous and that there was a triable issue with respect to the intent of the parties. We disagree and conclude that the agreement is without ambiguity and that pursuant to the terms of the agreement and of the Partnership Law, consent of the Parnes defendants was required in order to admit Daniel Rapoport and Kalia Shalleck to the partnership.

Plaintiffs, in support of their contention that they have an absolute right to assign their interests in the partnership to their adult children and that the children must be admitted to the partnership as partners rely on paragraph 12 of the partnership agreement which provides as follows: "No partner or partners shall have the authority to transfer, sell . . . assign or in any way dispose of the partnership realty and/or personalty and shall not have the authority to sell, transfer, assign . . . his or their share in this firm, nor enter into any agreement as a result of which any person shall become interested with him in this firm, unless the same is agreed to in writing by a majority of the partners as determined by the percentage of ownership . . . except for members of his immediate family who have attained majority, in which case no such consent shall be required." As indicated, plaintiffs argue that the above provision expressly authorizes entry of their adult children into the partnership. Defendants, on the other hand, maintain that paragraph 12 provides only for the right of a partner to assign or transfer a share of the profits in the partnership. We agree with that construction of the agreement.

A reading of the partnership agreement indicates that the parties intended to observe the differences, as set forth in the Partnership Law, between assignees of a partnership interest and the admission into the partnership itself of new partners. The Partnership Law provides that subject to any contrary agreement between the partners, "[n]o person can become a member of a partnership without the consent of all the partners." (Partnership Law, § 40, subd 7.)[2] Subdivision 1 of section 53 of the Partnership Law provides that an assignee of an interest in the partnership is not entitled "to interfere in the management or administration of the partnership business" but is merely entitled to receive "the profits to which the assigning partner would otherwise be entitled." Additionally, section 50 of the Partnership Law indicates the differences between the rights of an assignee and a new partner. That section states that the "property rights of a partner are (a) his rights in specific partnership property, (b) his interest in the partnership, and (c) his right to participate in the

---

2. The Partnership Law is New York's version of the UPA. (footnote by ed.)

management." On the other hand, as already indicated above, an assignee is excluded in the absence of agreement from interfering in the management of the partnership business and from access to the partnership books and information about partnership transactions. (Partnership Law, § 53.)

The effect, therefore, of the various provisions of the Partnership Law, above discussed, is that unless the parties have agreed otherwise, a person cannot become a member of a partnership without consent of all the partners whereas an assignment of a partnership interest may be made without consent, but the assignee is entitled only to receive the profits of the assigning partner. And, as already stated, the partnership agreement herein clearly took cognizance of the differences between an assignment of an interest in the partnership as compared to the full rights of a partner as set forth in section 50 of the Partnership Law. Paragraph 12 of the agreement by its language has reference to section 53 of the Partnership Law dealing with an "assignment of partner's interest." It (par 12) refers to assignments, encumbrances and agreements "as a result of which any person shall become interested with (the assignor) in this firm." That paragraph does not contain language with respect to admitting a partner to the partnership with all rights to participate in the management of its affairs. Moreover, interpretation of paragraph 12 in this manner is consistent with other provisions of the partnership agreement. For example, in paragraph 15 of the agreement, the following is provided:

> "In the event of the death of any partner the business of this firm shall continue with the heir, or distributee providing he has reached majority, or fiduciary of the deceased partner having the right to succeed the deceased partner with the same rights and privileges and the same obligations, pursuant to all of the terms hereof."

In that paragraph, therefore, there is specific provision to succeed to all the privileges and obligations of a partner—language which is completely absent from paragraph 12.

Accordingly, it appears that contrary to plaintiffs' contention that paragraph 12 was intended to give the parties the right to transfer a full partnership interest to adult children, without consent of all other partners (an agreement which would vary the rights otherwise existing pursuant to Partnership Law, § 40, subd 7) that paragraph was instead intended to limit a partner with respect to his right to assign a partnership interest as provided for under section 53 of the Partnership Law (i.e., the right to profits)—to the extent of prohibiting such assignments without consent of other partners except to children of the existing partners who have reached majority. Therefore, it must be concluded that pursuant to the terms of the partnership agreement, the plaintiffs could not transfer a full partnership interest to their children and that the children only have the rights as assignees to receive a share of the partnership income and profits of their assignors.

Accordingly, the order entered July 16, 1975 should be modified on the law to grant summary judgment in favor of the defendants to the extent of declaring that the partnership agreement does not permit entry into the partnership of new partners, including adult children of the partners who have reached their majority, without consent of all the partners; [and] that the plaintiffs, pursuant to the terms of the agreement, had the right to assign their interests to their adult children but that such children, i.e., Daniel Rapoport and Kalia Shalleck, have not become partners but only have the rights of assignees to receive a share of the partnership income and profits of their assignors. . . .

■ NUNEZ, J. (dissenting). I agree with Special Term that the written partnership agreement providing for the assignment of partners' shares to members of their immediate families without the consent of the other partners is ambiguous and that there is a triable issue as to intent. The agreement being ambiguous, construction is a mixed question of law and fact and resolution thereof to determine the parties' intent should await a trial. . . .

■ STEVENS, P.J., KUPFERMAN and MURPHY, JJ., concur with TILZER, J.; NUNEZ, J., dissents in an opinion. . . .

———

NOTE ON PARTNERSHIP PROPERTY

1. *UPA.* Property that is used by a partnership may be either partnership property or the property of a partner that is loaned by the partner to the partnership. The issue whether property used by the partnership is partnership property or the property of an individual partner may be important for several different reasons. First, the issue may be important for purposes of determining who has the power to transfer the property. Property owned by the partnership can be transferred by the partnership. Property loaned to the partnership cannot be. Second, the issue may be important if creditors of the partnership are competing with creditors of an individual partner, and the question arises whether any given property is owned by the partnership or owned by the partner and loaned to the partnership. Third, the issue may be important if the partnership is dissolved: If property used by the partnership is partnership property, on dissolution the property must be sold or valued along with other partnership assets, and the proceeds of the sale or the value of the asset must be distributed among the partners. In contrast, if property used by the partnership is the individual property of a partner, on dissolution the property must normally be returned directly to that partner, rather than sold or valued for the account of all the partners.[1] This third issue may be especially important if the property is crucial to the partner-

---

1. But see Pav–Saver Corp. v. Vasso Corp., 143 Ill.App.3d 1013, 97 Ill.Dec. 760, 493 N.E.2d 423 (1986) (wrongfully dissolving partner held not entitled to return of property).

ship's business, so that as a practical matter whoever owns the property has the ability to continue the business.

If the aggregate theory of the UPA was strictly applied, a partnership could not own property. Rather, the property that the partners think of as partnership property would as a matter of law be held by the individual partners as joint tenants or tenants in common. For a variety of reasons, such a regime would be wholly impracticable. Accordingly, in the matter of partnership property, as in several other matters, the UPA lays down rules that effectively treat the partnership *as if* it were an entity.

This objective is accomplished largely with smoke and mirrors. UPA § 8 recognizes the concept of "partnership property," and explicitly permits real property to be held in the partnership's name. (Even before the UPA, it was well settled that personal property could be so held.) UPA § 25(1) provides that "partnership property" is owned by the *partners,* under the ingenuous nomenclature *tenancy in partnership.* However, UPA § 25(2) then systematically strips from the individual partners every incident normally associated with ownership. Under § 25(2)(a), a partner has no right to possess partnership property as an individual. Under § 25(2)(b), a partner cannot individually assign his rights in specific partnership property. Under § 25(2)(c), a partner's rights in specific partnership property cannot be subject to attachment or execution by a creditor of the partner in the latter's individual capacity. Under § 25(2)(d), when a partner dies his right in specific partnership property does not devolve on his heirs or legatees. Under § 25(2)(e), widows, heirs, and next of kin cannot claim dower, curtesy, or allowances in a partner's right to specific partnership property. In short, under the UPA individual partners own the partnership property in theory, but in practice all the incidents of ownership are vested in the partnership, so that the "tenan[cy] in partnership" rule of the UPA has no real-world significance.

2. *RUPA.* RUPA, which confers entity status on partnerships, drops the elaborate tenancy-in-partnership apparatus of the UPA. RUPA § 203 provides that "Property acquired by a partnership is property of the partnership and not the partners individually." RUPA § 204 then sets out a series of rules and presumptions concerning whether any given property is partnership property or the separate property of a partner. These provisions are supplemented by § 501, which provides that "A partner is not a co-owner of partnership property and has no interest in partnership property which can be transferred, either voluntarily or involuntarily." The purpose of § 501 is to explicitly abolish the UPA concept of tenancy in partnership.

——————

NOTE ON PARTNERSHIP INTERESTS

1. *The Partner's Interest in the Partnership.* Although a partner does not own partnership property under the UPA, except in a metaphysical sense, he does own his *interest* in the partnership, that

is, his share of the partnership. The net result is a functional two-level ownership structure that is somewhat comparable to the two-level ownership structure in a corporation. In the case of a corporation, the corporation owns the corporate property, and the shareholder owns her shares in the corporation. In the case of a partnership the partnership owns the partnership property—either in practice (under the UPA) or full out (under RUPA)—and the partner owns her interest in the partnership.

2. *Assignment.* As compared to ordinary property interests, a partnership interest is conditioned in one very important respect. Normally, the owner of a property interest can freely sell it, and a creditor can freely levy on it. In contrast, although a partnership interest is assignable, a partner cannot make an assignment of her partnership interest that would substitute the transferee as a partner in the transferor's place, because it is a rule of partnership law that no person can become a partner without the consent of all the partners. Accordingly, when a partnership interest is assigned, the assignment normally is not a full transfer of the interest. Instead, it is a transfer to secure a debt that the assignor-partner owes to the assignee-creditor. The assignee-creditor cannot levy on a partnership interest in such a way as to be substituted as a partner, nor can the creditor recover his debt by selling the partnership interest to a third party who will be substituted as a partner. Accordingly, as pointed out in *Rapoport,* the assignee of a partnership interest does not become a partner (unless all the other partners consent), and has no right to information about the partnership and no right to inspect the partnership books. However, as long as the partnership continues in existence, the assignee of a partnership interest does have a right to receive the distributions to which the assigning partner would otherwise be entitled, and on dissolution the assignee has a right to receive the assigning partner's interest. In practice, despite the limitations on the assignor's rights, partnership interests have a fairly high degree of assignability. See A. Bromberg, Enforcement of Partnership Obligations—Who is Sued for The Partnership?, 71 Neb. L. Rev. 143, 240 (1992).

A partner who has assigned her partnership interest remains a partner. However, RUPA § 601(4)(ii) explicitly permits the nonassigning partners to expel the assignor from the partnership, and UPA § 31(c) permits the nonassigning partners to dissolve the partnership as of right even if the partnership is not at will.

3. *Partnership Creditors.*

a. *UPA.* A partner's *separate creditor* (that is a creditor who has extended credit to a partner as an individual, rather than extending credit to a partnership) is in a position somewhat comparable to the assignee of a partnership interest. Under UPA § 28, if such a creditor obtains a judgment, he can get a *charging order* on the partner's partnership interest. Such an order will effectively give the creditor the right to be paid the partnership distributions to which the debtor-partner would be otherwise entitled. The creditor can foreclose on the partnership interest under UPA § 28, and thereby cause its sale. In that case, the buyer of the interest has the right to compel dissolution if (i) the term of the partnership has expired, or (ii) the partnership is at will. Alternatively, the creditor may put the individual partner into bankruptcy, which will result in dissolution of the partnership under UPA § 31(5).

Bromberg & Ribstein on Partnership § 3.05(d)(3)(4) comment as follows on charging orders:

> After [a charging order is entered, the debtor partner] continues to be a partner in all respects except distributions and withdrawals from the firm. Moreover, the charging creditor is not yet in the position even of an assignee of the interest. This is apparent because UPA § 28(2) and RUPA § 504 refer to the further step of foreclosure on the debtor partner's partnership interest, which would be necessary only if the interest had not already been assigned to the creditor. By foreclosing, the creditor can obtain a sale of the interest at which the interest is purchased by the creditor or a third party. . . .

> Even after foreclosure and sale, the creditor may be far from collecting the debt. At the foreclosure sale only the partner's interest, not specific assets of the partnership, is sold. . . . It is unlikely that the interest will bring a high price from third parties, because of the limited role to which the purchaser is relegated. If the creditor is the purchaser, it will still be entitled only to receive the charged partner's cash flow. Moreover, until dissolution the creditor has no right to an accounting.

> One change in the creditor's current status as a result of the foreclosure and sale is that the creditor now owns the partner's entire financial interest in the partnership, including all amounts ultimately due the partner on dissolution after settlement of liabilities. Another is that the purchaser can exercise the assignee's power to seek a judicial dissolution under UPA § 32(2) or RUPA § 801(6) . . . On dissolution, the creditor or other purchaser of the interest at foreclosure can finally obtain whatever share would have come to the debtor partner after payment of all partnership creditors and claims of co-partners.

b. *RUPA*. RUPA § 504 continues UPA § 28 largely unchanged in substance. RUPA § 504 does add some details that are not found in UPA § 28, but for the most part these details are consistent with the case law under § 28. Like the UPA, RUPA § 801(a) provides that a transferee of a partner's transferable interest is entitled to judicial dissolution on the partnership (i) at any time in a partnership at will, and (ii) after the expiration of the partnership's term or the completion of the undertaking in a partnership for a particular undertaking.

4. *Priorities*.

a. *UPA*. A major problem in partnership law concerns the relative priorities of creditors of the partnership (*partnership creditors*) and creditors of a partner in the partner's individual capacity (*separate creditors*). UPA § 40(h) provides that: (i) partnership creditors have priority over separate creditors as to partnership assets, and (ii) separate creditors have priority over partnership creditors as to the individual assets of the partners. See also UPA § 36(4). This rule, which was also in the Bankruptcy Act prior to 1978, is known as the "dual priorities" or "jingle" rule. The rule was widely criticized on the ground that it kept partnership creditors from getting the full benefit of personal liability of the individual partners. The Bankruptcy Reform Act of 1978 responded to that criticism. Under Chapter 7 of the Bankruptcy Code, in a partnership bankruptcy the partnership creditors have priority over separate creditors as to partnership assets, and if debts to partnership creditors remain unpaid after partnership assets are exhausted, partnership creditors are put on a parity with separate creditors in dividing up the partner's individual assets. 11 U.S.C. § 723(c). Thus in the usual case, the UPA jingle rule is preempted by the Bankruptcy Code.

b. *RUPA*. RUPA drops the dual priorities rule of the UPA to reflect the abolition of the jingle rule in the Bankruptcy Code.

SECTION 7. THE PARTNER'S DUTY OF LOYALTY

UNIFORM PARTNERSHIP ACT § 21

REVISED UNIFORM PARTNERSHIP ACT §§ 103(a), (b) (3), (5), 104, 403, 404, 405

[See Statutory Supplement]

Meinhard v. Salmon

New York Court of Appeals, 1928.
249 N.Y. 458, 164 N.E. 545.

Appeal from a judgment of the Appellate Division of the Supreme Court in the first judicial department, entered June 28, 1928, modifying and affirming as modified a judgment in favor of plaintiff entered upon the report of a referee.

■ CARDOZO, CH. J. On April 10, 1902, Louisa M. Gerry leased to the defendant Walter J. Salmon the premises known as the Hotel Bristol at the northwest corner of Forty-second street and Fifth avenue in the city of New York. The lease was for a term of twenty years, commencing May 1, 1902, and ending April 30, 1922. The lessee undertook to change the hotel building for use as shops and offices at a cost of $200,000. Alterations and additions were to be accretions to the land.

Salmon, while in course of treaty with the lessor as to the execution of the lease, was in course of treaty with Meinhard, the plaintiff, for the necessary funds. The result was a joint venture with terms embodied in a writing. Meinhard was to pay to Salmon half of the moneys requisite to reconstruct, alter, manage and operate the property. Salmon was to pay to Meinhard 40 per cent of the net profits for the first five years of the lease and 50 per cent for the years thereafter. If there were losses, each party was to bear them equally. Salmon, however, was to have sole power to "manage, lease, underlet and operate" the building. There were to be certain pre-emptive rights for each in the contingency of death.

The two were coadventurers, subject to fiduciary duties akin to those of partners (King v. Barnes, 109 N.Y. 267). As to this we are all agreed. The heavier weight of duty rested, however, upon Salmon. He was a coadventurer with Meinhard, but he was manager as well. During the early years of the enterprise, the building, reconstructed, was operated at a loss. If the relation had then ended, Meinhard as well as Salmon would have carried a heavy burden. Later the profits became large with the result that for each of the investors there came a rich return. For each, the venture had its phases of fair weather and of foul. The two were in it jointly, for better or for worse.

When the lease was near its end, Elbridge T. Gerry had become the owner of the reversion. He owned much other property in the neighborhood, one lot adjoining the Bristol Building on Fifth avenue and four lots on Forty-second street. He had a plan to lease the entire tract for a long term to some one who would destroy the buildings then existing, and put up another in their place. In the latter part of 1921, he submitted such a project to several capitalists and dealers. He was unable to carry it through with any of them. Then, in January, 1922, with less than four months of the lease to run, he approached the defendant Salmon. The result was a new lease to the Midpoint Realty Company, which is owned and controlled by Salmon, a lease covering the whole tract, and involving a huge outlay. The term is to be twenty years, but successive covenants for renewal will extend it to a maximum of eighty years at the will of either party. The existing buildings may remain unchanged for seven years. They are then to be torn down, and a new building to cost $3,000,000 is to be placed upon the site. The rental, which under the Bristol lease was only $55,000, is to be from $350,000 to $475,000 for the properties so combined. Salmon personally guaranteed the performance by the lessee of the covenants of the new lease until such time as the new building had been completed and fully paid for.

The lease between Gerry and the Midpoint Realty Company was signed and delivered on January 25, 1922. Salmon had not told Meinhard anything about it. Whatever his motive may have been, he had kept the negotiations to himself. Meinhard was not informed even of the bare existence of a project. The first that he knew of it was in February when the lease was an accomplished fact. He then made demand on the defendants that the lease be held in trust as an asset of the venture, making offer upon the trial to share the personal obligations incidental to the guaranty. The demand was followed by refusal, and later by this suit. A referee gave judgment for the plaintiff, limiting the plaintiff's interest in the lease, however, to 25 per cent. The limitation was on the theory that the plaintiff's equity was to be restricted to one-half of so much of the value of the lease as was contributed or represented by the occupation of the Bristol site. Upon cross-appeals to the Appellate Division, the judgment was modified so as to enlarge the equitable interest to one-half of the whole lease. With this enlargement of plaintiff's interest, there went, of course, a corresponding enlargement of his attendant obligations. The case is now here on an appeal by the defendants.

Joint adventurers, like copartners, owe to one another, while the enterprise continues, the duty of the finest loyalty. Many forms of conduct permissible in a workaday world for those acting at arm's length, are forbidden to those bound by fiduciary ties. A trustee is held to something stricter than the morals of the market place. Not honesty alone, but the punctilio of an honor the most sensitive, is then the standard of behavior. As to this there has developed a tradition that is unbending and inveterate. Uncompromising rigidity has been the attitude of courts of equity when petitioned to undermine the rule of undivided loyalty by the "disintegrating erosion" of particular exceptions (Wendt v. Fischer, 243 N.Y. 439, 444). Only thus has the level of conduct for fiduciaries been kept at a level higher than that trodden by the crowd. It will not consciously be lowered by any judgment of this court.

The owner of the reversion, Mr. Gerry, had vainly striven to find a tenant who would favor his ambitious scheme of demolition and construction. Baffled in the search, he turned to the defendant Salmon in possession of the Bristol, the keystone of the project. He figured to himself beyond a doubt that the man in possession would prove a likely customer. To the eye of an observer, Salmon held the lease as owner in his own right, for himself and no one else. In fact he held it as a fiduciary, for himself and another, sharers in a common venture. If this fact had been proclaimed, if the lease by its terms had run in favor of a partnership, Mr. Gerry, we may fairly assume, would have laid before the partners, and not merely before one of them, his plan of reconstruction. The pre-emptive privilege, or, better, the pre-emptive opportunity, that was thus an incident of the enterprise, Salmon appropriated to himself in secrecy and silence. He might have warned Meinhard that the plan had been submitted, and that either would be free to compete for the award. If he had done this, we do not need to say whether he would have been under a duty, if successful in the competition, to hold the lease so acquired for the benefit of a venture then about to end, and thus prolong by indirection its responsibilities and duties. The trouble about his conduct is that he excluded his coadventurer from any chance to compete, from any chance to enjoy the opportunity for benefit that had come to him alone by virtue of his agency. This chance, if nothing more, he was under a duty to concede.

The price of its denial is an extension of the trust at the option and for the benefit of the one whom he excluded.

No answer is it to say that the chance would have been of little value even if seasonably offered. Such a calculus of probabilities is beyond the science of the chancery. Salmon, the real estate operator, might have been preferred to Meinhard, the woolen merchant. On the other hand, Meinhard might have offered better terms, or reinforced his offer by alliance with the wealth of others. Perhaps he might even have persuaded the lessor to renew the Bristol lease alone, postponing for a time, in return for higher rentals, the improvement of adjoining lots. We know that even under the lease as made the time for the enlargement of the building was delayed for seven years. All these opportunities were cut away from him through another's intervention. He knew that Salmon was the manager. As the time drew near for the expiration of the lease, he would naturally assume from silence, if from nothing else, that the lessor was willing to extend it for a term of years, or at least to let it stand as a lease from year to year. Not impossibly the lessor would have done so, whatever his protestations of unwillingness, if Salmon had not given assent to a project more attractive. At all events, notice of termination, even if not necessary, might seem, not unreasonably, to be something to be looked for, if the business was over and another tenant was to enter. In the absence of such notice, the matter of an extension was one that would naturally be attended to by the manager of the enterprise, and not neglected altogether. At least, there was nothing in the situation to give warning to any one that while the lease was still in being, there had come to the manager an offer of extension which he had locked within his breast to be utilized by himself alone. The very fact that Salmon was in control with exclusive powers of direction charged him the more obviously with the duty of disclosure, since only through disclosure could opportunity be equalized. If he might cut off renewal by a purchase for his own benefit when four months were to pass before the lease would have an end, he might do so with equal right while there remained as many years (cf. Mitchell v. Reed, 61 N.Y. 123, 127). He might steal a march on his comrade under cover of the darkness, and then hold the captured ground. Loyalty and comradeship are not so easily abjured....

We have no thought to hold that Salmon was guilty of a conscious purpose to defraud. Very likely he assumed in all good faith that with the approaching end of the venture he might ignore his coadventurer and take the extension for himself. He had given to the enterprise time and labor as well as money. He had made it a success. Meinhard, who had given money, but neither time nor labor, had already been richly paid. There might seem to be something grasping in his insistence upon more. Such recriminations are not unusual when coadventurers fall out. They are not without their force if conduct is to be judged by the common standards of competitors. That is not to say that they have pertinency here. Salmon had put himself in a position in which thought of self was to be renounced, however hard the abnegation. He was much more than a coadventurer. He was a managing coadventurer (Clegg v. Edmondson, 8 D.M. & G. 787, 807). For him and for those like him, the rule of undivided loyalty is relentless and supreme (Wendt v. Fischer, supra; Munson v. Syracuse, etc., R.R. Co., 103 N.Y. 58, 74). A different question would be here if there were lacking any nexus of relation between the business conducted by the manager and the opportunity brought to him as an incident of management (Dean v. MacDowell, 8 Ch.D. 345, 354; Aas v. Benham, 1891, 2 Ch. 244, 258; Latta v. Kilbourn, 150 U.S. 524). For this problem, as for most, there are distinctions of degree. If Salmon had received from Gerry a proposition to lease a building at a location far removed, he might have held for himself the privilege thus acquired, or so we shall assume. Here the subject-matter of the new lease was an extension and enlargement of the subject-matter of the old one. A managing coadventurer appropriating the benefit of such a lease without warning to his partner might fairly expect to be reproached with conduct that was underhand, or lacking, to say the least, in reasonable candor, if the partner were to surprise him in the act of signing the new instrument. Conduct subject to that reproach does not receive from equity a healing benediction.

A question remains as to the form and extent of the equitable interest to be allotted to the plaintiff. The trust as declared has been held to attach to the lease which was in the name of the defendant corporation. We think it ought to attach at the option of the defendant Salmon to the shares of stock which were owned by him or were under his control. The difference may be important if the lessee shall wish to execute an assignment of the lease, as it ought to be free to do with the consent of the lessor. On the other hand, an equal division of the shares might lead to other hardships. It might take away from Salmon the power of control and management which under the plan of the joint venture he was to have from first to last. The number of shares to be allotted to the plaintiff should, therefore, be reduced to such an extent as may be necessary to preserve to the defendant Salmon the expected measure of dominion. To that end an extra share should be added to his half.

Subject to this adjustment, we agree with the Appellate Division that the plaintiff's equitable interest is to be measured by the value of half of the entire lease, and not merely by half of some undivided part. A single building covers the whole area. Physical division is impracticable along the lines of the Bristol site, the keystone of the whole. Division of interests and burdens is equally impracticable. Salmon, as tenant under the new lease, or as guarantor of the performance of the tenant's obligations, might well protest if Meinhard, claiming an equitable interest, had offered to assume a liability not equal to Salmon's, but only half as great. He might justly insist that the lease must be accepted by his coadventurer in such form as it had been given, and not constructively divided into imaginary fragments. What must be yielded to the one may be demanded by the other. The lease as it has been executed is single and entire. If confusion has resulted from the union of adjoining parcels, the trustee who consented to the union must bear the inconvenience (Hart v. Ten Eyck, 2 Johns. Ch. 62). . . .

[Three judges dissented. Andrews, J., who wrote the dissenting opinion, agreed that "(w)ere this a general partnership I should have little doubt as to the correctness of this result assuming the new lease to be an offshoot of the old," but concluded that the parties' joint venture "had in view a very limited object and was to end at a limited time."]

———

LATTA v. KILBOURN, 150 U.S. 524, 541 (1893). It is "well settled that one partner cannot, directly or indirectly use partnership assets for his own benefit; that he cannot in conducting the business of a partnership, take any profit clandestinely for himself; that he cannot carry on the business of the partnership for his private advantage; that he cannot carry on another business in competition or rivalry with that of the firm, thereby depriving it of the benefit of his time, skill, and fidelity, without being accountable to his copartners for any profit that may accrue to him therefrom; that he cannot be permitted to secure for himself that which it is his duty to obtain, if at all, for the firm of which he is a member; nor can he avail himself of knowledge or information which may be properly regarded as the property of the partnership, in the sense that it is available or useful to the firm for any purpose within the scope of the partnership business."

———

NOTE ON SUITS BY A PARTNER AGAINST A PARTNERSHIP

One method by which a partner can vindicate her rights against other partners is by a suit for an accounting. UPA § 22 provides a right to an accounting: (1) when a partner is wrongfully excluded from the business (§ 22(a)); (2) if the right is granted under the partnership agreement (§ 22(b)); (3) for appropriation of an unauthorized benefit in violation of § 21 (§ 22(c)); or (4) or whenever other circumstances render it just and reasonable (§ 22(d)).

However, "cases involving such actions are rare. An action for an accounting . . . usually indicates that an atmosphere of mistrust exists in the partnership. In this situation, the easy dissolution permitted under the UPA will often be the appropriate course to follow, particularly if there is no uncompleted term or undertaking." Bromberg & Ribstein on Partnership § 6.08(b).

What about simply suing for the alleged wrong? UPA § 13 provides that "[w]here, by any wrongful conduct or omission of any partner acting in the ordinary course of business of the partnership or with the authority of his co-partners, loss or injury is caused to any person, *not being a partner in the partnership* . . . the partnership is liable therefor. . . ." (Emphasis added.) By reason of the italicized phrase, this section is commonly interpreted not to authorize a suit by a partner against a partnership. As a result, the courts have often limited a partner's remedies against the partnership to suits for dissolution or for an accounting. See Beckman v. Farmer, 579 A.2d 618, 649 (D.C.App.1990); Hubbard, Alternative Remedies in Minority Partners' Suits on Partnership Causes of Action, 39 Sw.L.J. 1022 (1986). In *Beckman,* the court justified the rule on the ground that:

> [P]ractical difficulties commend the settlement of accounts before an action at law between partners can be maintained. The value of partners' respective interests cannot be determined while accounts are in flux, but only after partnership liabilities are satisfied, all assets are marshalled, the partners' capital accounts adjusted, and the amount of any surplus ascertained.

Id. at 649–50. This justification is unconvincing. It may be true that the complete settlement of accounts is easier at the termination of the partnership, but a partner who wants to make a claim against the partnership is not asking for a complete settlement of accounts.

Given the weak or nonexistent justification of the traditional rule, it is not surprising that the rule is subject to inconsistent and important exceptions:

> The general rule is subject to several exceptions ... [For example, an accounting in] equity may not be necessary when breach of the partnership agreement, wrongful dissolution, fraudulent breach of trust, or misappropriation of money clearly belonging to another partner is charged. . . .

Id. at 650.

2. *RUPA.* RUPA § 305, which is the counterpart of UPA § 13, drops the phrase "not being a partner in the partnership." The Comment states that this change "is intended to permit a partner to sue the partnership on a tort or other theory during the term of the partnership, rather than being limited to the remedies of dissolution and accounting."

SECTION 8.   DISSOLUTION (I): DISSOLUTION BY RIGHTFUL ELECTION

UNIFORM PARTNERSHIP ACT §§ 29, 30, 31(1), 38(1), 40

REVISED UNIFORM PARTNERSHIP ACT §§ 601, 602, 603, 701, 801, 802, 803, 804, 807

[See Statutory Supplement]

GIRARD BANK v. HALEY, 460 Pa. 237, 332 A.2d 443 (1975). Mrs. Reid, a partner in an at-will UPA partnership, had sent the following letter to the other three partners: "I am terminating the partnership which the four of us entered into on the 28th day of September, 1958." The issue was whether this letter caused a dissolution of the partnership. The chancellor, at trial, held that it did not, because neither in the letter nor at trial did Mrs. Reid offer evidence to justify a termination of the partnership. Reversed.

In supposing that justification was necessary the learned court below fell into error. Dissolution of a partnership is caused, under § 31 of the [UPA], "by the express will of any partner." The expression of that will need not be supported by any justification. If no "definite term or particular undertaking [is] specified in the partnership agreement," such an at-will dissolution does not violate the agreement between the partners; indeed, an expression of a will to dissolve is effective as a dissolution even if in contravention of the agreement. Ibid. We have recognized the generality of a dissolution at will. If the dissolution results in breach of contract, the aggrieved partners may recover damages for the breach and, if they meet certain conditions, may continue the firm business for the duration of the agreed term or until the particular undertaking is completed. See § 38 of the Act....

The remaining question is whether or not the unilateral dissolution made by Mrs. Reid violated the partnership agreement. The agreement contains no provision fixing a definite term, and the sole "undertaking" to which it refers is that of maintaining and leasing real property. This statement is merely one of general purpose, however, and cannot be said to set forth a "particular undertaking" within the meaning of that phrase as it is used in the Act. A "particular undertaking" under the statute must be capable of accomplishment at some time, although the exact time may be unknown and unascertainable at the date of the agreement. Leasing property, like many other trades or businesses, involves entering into a business relationship which may continue indefinitely; there is nothing "particular" about it. We thus conclude, on the record before us, that the dissolution of the partnership was not in contravention of the agreement.

———

Creel v. Lilly

Court of Appeals of Maryland, 1999.
354 Md. 77, 729 A.2d 385.

■ Bell, C.J., and Eldridge, Rodowsky, Chasanow, Raker, Wilner and Cathell JJ.

■ Chasanow, Judge....

I. BACKGROUND

On approximately June 1, 1993, Joseph Creel began a retail business selling NASCAR racing memorabilia. His business was originally located in a section of his wife Anne's florist shop, but after about a year and a half he decided to raise capital from partners so that he could expand and move into his own space. On September 20, 1994, Mr. Creel entered into a partnership agreement—apparently prepared without the assistance of counsel—with Arnold Lilly and Roy Altizer to form a general partnership called "Joe's Racing." . . .

The three-man partnership operated a retail store in the St. Charles Towne Center Mall in Waldorf, Maryland. For their initial investment in Joe's Racing, Mr. Lilly and Mr. Altizer each paid $6,666 in capital contributions, with Mr. Creel contributing his inventory and supplies valued at $15,000. Pursuant to the partnership agreement, Mr. Lilly and Mr. Altizer also paid $6,666 to Mr. Creel ($3,333 each) "for the use and rights to the business known as Joe's Racing Collectables." . . .

Joe's Racing had been in existence for almost nine months when Mr. Creel died on June 14, 1995. Mrs. Creel was appointed personal representative of his estate. . . .

In accordance with [UPA] § 9–602(4),[10] Joe's Racing was automatically dissolved upon Mr. Creel's death and because the partnership agreement did not expressly provide for continuation of the partnership nor did his estate consent to its continuation, the surviving partners were required under UPA to wind up the business. *See* [UPA] § 9–601 and § 9–609(a) . . . . We adopt the following procedural history of the case [from the opinion of the Court of Special Appeals]:

> ". . . [Mrs. Creel] filed in the circuit court a complaint seeking an accounting and a declaratory judgment against Messrs. Lilly and Altizer, individually and doing business under the name 'Good Ole Boys Racing.' She asserted that, instead of winding up the affairs of Joe's Racing in accordance with her demand, Lilly and Altizer continued the partnership business under a new name, using the assets of the partnership. . . .

> . . . [After a four-day trial, the trial court] determined that Joseph Creel had a 52% interest in the partnership. . . .

> The court also found that the surviving partners sought to wind up and close out the partnership and took all reasonable steps to do so, and that there was no breach by them of any fiduciary duty to the Estate. The lease on the store premises occupied by the partnership expired on 31 August 1995, and on that date Mr. Lilly conducted an inventory of all merchandise in the store. Based on that inventory, an accountant computed the value of the partnership business; Mrs. Creel was invited to review

---

10. Section 9–602 states in pertinent part:

"Dissolution is caused:

* * *

(4) By the death of any partner[.]"

the books and records and retain her own accountant or appraiser if she questioned [Mr. Lilly or Mr. Altizer's] figures. *She declined to do so. After 31 August 1995, Messrs. Lilly and Altizer ceased doing business as Joe's Racing and began doing business together under the name 'Good Ole Boys Racing.'*

The court accepted the valuation prepared by [Mr. Lilly and Mr. Altizer's] accountant as the correct value of the partnership assets as of 31 August 1995, and found that the surviving partners fully disclosed and delivered to the Estate all records of the financial affairs of the Joe's Racing partnership up to 31 August 1995, which the court took to be the end of the winding up period. Rejecting [Mrs. Creel's] assertions . . . that [Mr. Lilly and Mr. Altizer] were obligated to liquidate the partnership assets in order to wind up the partnership. . . . the court declared that the estate was entitled to a total of $21,631 [representing the Estate's 52% interest in the value of the partnership as determined by the audit] valuation. . . ." [Emphasis added by the Court of Appeals.]

The Court of Special Appeals affirmed the judgment of the [trial court], finding that under UPA "winding up" does not always mean "liquidate;" therefore, Joe's Racing had no duty to sell off all of its assets in a liquidation sale. . . . Mrs. Creel filed a petition for certiorari in May 1998, which we granted.

II. DISCUSSION AND ANALYSIS

A.

We begin our analysis by reviewing the law of partnership as it pertains to the issues in this case. Maryland enacted UPA in 1916. *Shafer Bros. v. Kite,* 43 Md.App. 601, 607, 406 A.2d 673, 677 (1979). . . .

A partnership is either (1) for a definite term or a particular undertaking or (2) at will, which means the business has no definite term or particular undertaking. 59A AM.JUR.2D *Partnership* §§ 89 & 90 (1987). *See also* § 9A–101(k). An at-will partnership continues indefinitely and can be dissolved by the express will of any partner or automatically by the happening of a specific event as mandated by UPA, such as the death of a partner. 59A AM.JUR.2D *Partnership* § 89 (1987). *See also* § 9–602(4). Under UPA, partners may avoid the automatic dissolution of the business upon the death of a partner by providing for its continuation in their partnership agreement. *See Gerding v. Baier,* 143 Md. 520, 524, 122 A. 675, 677 (1923). Sophisticated partnerships virtually always use carefully drafted partnership agreements to protect the various partners' interests by providing for the continuation of the business, the distribution of partnership assets, etc., in the face of various contingencies such as death. *See* JUDSON A. CRANE & ALAN R. BROMBERG, LAW OF PARTNERSHIP § 73, at 417–19 (1968). Less sophisticated partnerships, however, are often operating under oral terms or a "homemade" agreement that does not contain protections for the partners or the business.

While the death of a partner automatically dissolves the partnership unless there is an agreement stating otherwise, the partnership is not terminated until the winding-up process is complete.... The winding-up procedure that applies in this case is found in § 9–609(a), which states in pertinent part: "When dissolution is caused in any way ... each partner ... unless otherwise agreed, may have the partnership property applied to discharge its liabilities, and the surplus applied to pay in cash the net amount owing to the respective partners."

Historically, under many courts and commentators' interpretation of UPA, when a partner died and the partnership automatically dissolved because there was no consent by the estate to continue the business nor was there a written agreement allowing for continuation, the estate had the right to compel liquidation of the partnership assets.... Reducing all of the partnership assets to cash through a liquidation was seen as the only way to obtain the true value of the business. *Dreifuerst v. Dreifuerst,* 90 Wis.2d 566, 280 N.W.2d 335, 338 (Ct.App.1979). However, while winding up has often traditionally been regarded as synonymous with liquidation, this "fire sale" of assets has been viewed by many courts and commentators as a harsh and destructive measure. Consequently, to avoid the drastic result of a forced liquidation, many courts have adopted judicial alternatives to this potentially harmful measure. *See Fortugno v. Hudson Manure Company,* 51 N.J.Super. 482, 144 A.2d 207, 219 (App.Div.1958)(court approved an alternative proposal to the complete liquidation of the partnership, stating that it "recogniz[ed] that a forced sale of the partnership will destroy a great part of the value of the business...."). *See also* full discussion on judicial alternatives to liquidation in Part II.B., *infra.*

Over time, the UPA rule requiring automatic dissolution of the partnership upon the death of a partner, in the absence of consent by the estate to continue the business or an agreement providing for continuation, with the possible result of a forced sale of all partnership assets was viewed as outmoded by many jurisdictions including Maryland. The development and adoption of RUPA by the National Conference of Commissioners on Uniform State Laws (NCCUSL) mitigated this harsh UPA provision of automatic dissolution and compelled liquidation.

RUPA's underlying philosophy differs radically from UPA's, thus laying the foundation for many of its innovative measures. RUPA adopts the "entity" theory of partnership as opposed to the "aggregate" theory that the UPA espouses. Thomas R. Hurst, *Will the Revised Uniform Partnership Act (1994) Ever Be Uniformly Adopted?,* 48 FLA. L.REV. 575, 579 (1996). Under the aggregate theory, a partnership is characterized by the collection of its individual members, with the result being that if one of the partners dies or withdraws, the partnership ceases to exist. *See* Joan E. Branch, Note, *The Revised Uniform Partnership Act Breakup Provisions: Should They Be Adopted?,* 25 CREIGHTON L.REV. 701, 701 (1992). On the other hand, RUPA's entity theory allows for the partnership to continue even with the departure of a member because it views the partnership as "an entity distinct from its partners." Section 9A–201.

This adoption of the entity theory, which permits continuity of the partnership upon changes in partner identity, allows for several significant changes in RUPA. Of particular importance to the instant case is that under RUPA "a partnership no longer automatically dissolves due to a change in its membership, but rather *the existing partnership may be continued if the remaining partners elect to buy out the dissociating partner.*"[11] *Will the Revised Uniform Partnership Act (1994) Ever Be Uniformly Adopted?*, 48 FLA. L.REV. at 579 (emphasis added)(footnote omitted). In contrast to UPA, RUPA's "buy-out" option does not have to be expressly included in a written partnership agreement in order for it to be exercised; however, the surviving partners must still actively choose to exercise the option, as "continuation is not automatic as with a corporation." *Will the Revised Uniform Partnership Act (1994) Ever Be Uniformly Adopted?*, 48 FLA. L.REV. at 579–80 (footnote omitted). This major RUPA innovation therefore delineates two possible paths for a partnership to follow when a partner dies or withdraws: "[o]ne leads to the winding up and termination of the partnership and the other to continuation of the partnership and purchase of the departing partner's share." *Will the Revised Uniform Partnership Act (1994) Ever Be Uniformly Adopted?*, 48 FLA. L.REV. at 583 (footnote omitted). Critically, under RUPA the estate of the deceased partner no longer has to consent in order for the business to be continued nor does the estate have the right to compel liquidation.

B.

As discussed earlier, the traditional manner in which UPA allows for the continuation of the partnership upon the death of a partner is to either obtain the consent of the deceased partner's estate or include a continuation clause in the partnership agreement. *Gianakos,* 238 Md. at 183, 208 A.2d at 721. There have been several cases in other jurisdictions, however, where neither of these conditions was met and the court elected another option under UPA instead of a "fire sale" of all the partnership assets to ensure that the deceased partner's estate received its fair share of the partnership. . . . These jurisdictions have recognized the unfairness and harshness of a compelled liquidation and found other judicially acceptable means of winding up a partnership under UPA, such as ordering an in-kind distribution of the assets

---

11. RUPA uses the term "dissociation" rather than dissolution. "Dissociation" is viewed as having a less significant impact on the partnership than dissolution, which is in line with RUPA's entity theory of partnership of continuing the business whenever possible. John W. Larson et al., *Revised Uniform Partnership Act Reflects a Number of Significant Changes,* 10 J. PARTNERSHIP TAX'N 232, 236 (1993). *See also* § 9A–601, which describes the events causing a partner's dissociation, including death. Under RUPA, a dissociation may result in dissolution and a winding up of partnership business. *See* §§ 9A–801 through 9A–807, which provide for the winding up of partnership business. Even after a dissociation leads to a dissolution, RUPA offers a final opportunity for the partners to continue the partnership if they so choose. *See* § 9A–802(b). . . .

or allowing the remaining partners to buy out the withdrawing partner's share of the partnership. . . .

C.

In applying the law discussed in Part II.A. and B. to the facts of this case, we want to clarify that while UPA is the governing act, our holding is also consistent with RUPA and its underlying policies. The legislature's recent adoption of RUPA indicates that it views with disfavor the compelled liquidation of businesses and that it has elected to follow the trend in partnership law to allow the continuation of business without disruption, in either the original or successor form, if the surviving partners choose to do so through buying out the deceased partner's share.

In this appeal, however, we would arrive at the same holding regardless of whether UPA or RUPA governs. Although our holding departs from the general UPA rule that the representative of the deceased partner's estate has a right to demand liquidation of the partnership, as we discuss in this subsection, *infra,* our position of "no forced sale" hardly represents a radical departure from traditional partnership law. . . .

1. Compelled Liquidation Issue

The first issue is whether the Creel estate has the right to demand liquidation of Joe's Racing where its partnership agreement does not expressly provide for continuation of the partnership and where the estate does not consent to continuation. . . . [We find] that Good Ole Boys is a successor partnership, rather than a continuation of Joe's Racing, [but that finding] does not negate the need for a complete discussion of this issue. Unless there is consent to continue the business or an agreement providing for continuation, upon the death of a partner the accurate value of the partnership must be ascertained as of the date of dissolution and the proportionate share paid to the deceased partner's estate, no matter if we are dealing with a subsequent new partnership or a continuation of the original business. If a compelled liquidation of all partnership assets is seen as the only way to arrive at its true value, then property from the original partnership will have to be sold whether the present business is a continuation or a successor business; regardless, the potential harm of such a "fire sale" affects both equally. . . .

We find it is sound public policy to permit a partnership to continue either under the same name or as a successor partnership without all of the assets being liquidated. Liquidation can be a harmful and destructive measure, especially to a small business like Joe's Racing, and is often unnecessary to determining the true value of the partnership. *See Arnold v. Burgess,* 113 Idaho 786, 747 P.2d 1315, 1322 (Ct.App.1987)("A forced sale of partnership assets will often destroy a great part of the value of the business and may prevent the continuation of a valuable source of livelihood for former partners.''). We now explore the "true value of the partnership" issue and whether liquidation is the only way to obtain it. . . .

In accordance with . . . [the] UPA, Lilly and Altizer provided Mrs. Creel with an accounting, which was based on the valuation performed by the accountant they hired. Mrs. Creel contends that this accounting did not reflect the true value of Joe's Racing, and as a result the estate did not receive its proportionate share of the partnership. . . .

. . . [We] disagree as to Mrs. Creel's argument that the accountant's valuation was in error and that the trial court subsequently arrived at an incorrect distribution of Mr. Creel's interest in the partnership. . . .

[W]e hold that Maryland's UPA—particularly in light of the legislature's recent adoption of RUPA—does not grant the estate of a deceased partner the right to demand liquidation of a partnership where the partnership agreement does not expressly provide for continuation of the partnership and where the estate does not consent to continuation. To hold otherwise vests excessive power and control in the estate of the deceased partner, to the extreme disadvantage of the surviving partners. We further hold that where the surviving partners have in good faith wound up the business and the deceased partner's estate is provided with an accurate accounting allowing for payment of a proportionate share of the business, then a forced sale of all partnership assets is unwarranted.

2.   Damages Issue

The second issue is whether the Creel estate is entitled to its partnership percentage share of the profits generated by the surviving partners' alleged continued use of the partnership assets. Mrs. Creel argues that because Lilly and Altizer did not liquidate the partnership as she demanded, they continued the partnership with the use of partnership property and inventory. For this reason . . . Mrs. Creel claims she is entitled to damages from this continued use. Her contention can be quickly dispensed with due to the trial judge's implicit finding that Joe's Racing was not continued, but instead was properly wound up on August 31, 1995. Therefore, as Good Ole Boys is a successor partnership to Joe's Racing and not a continuation business, there are no "continuation" damages at issue. . . .

JUDGMENT OF THE COURT OF SPECIAL APPEALS AFFIRMED. . . .

———

NOTE ON DISTRIBUTIONS IN DISSOLUTION, AND ON "SERVICES PARTNERS"

1.   *Distributions in Dissolution.* a. *UPA.* UPA § 40(b) sets out the rules for the distribution of assets after a partnership is dissolved. The

first priority is to pay off creditors other than partners. The second priority is to pay off partners for obligations other than capital or profits (for example, a loan that a partner made to the partnership). The third priority is to pay off partners in respect of capital. The fourth priority is to pay off partners in respect of profits. All of these priorities, even those in respect of partnership capital and profits, are defined as "liabilities"—an unusual meaning of that term, which normally refers to debts, not to ownership or equity claims.

Under UPA § 40(d), the partners must contribute the amount necessary to satisfy liabilities as provided in § 18(a). Section 18(a), in turn, provides that each partner shall contribute toward the losses sustained by the partnership, according to his share in the profits. "Losses" in § 18(a) is defined, like "liabilities" in § 40(b), to include losses to capital.

Now suppose that C and S form Partnership P. By agreement, Capital Partner C contributes $100,000 capital, but will not be actively engaged in running the business, while Service Partner S contributes no capital but will spend his full time running the business. Profits are to be shared 50–50, but nothing is said about sharing losses. S performs services of a value of $100,000, which causes an increase in the value of P's gross assets by that amount. After three years, the partnership is dissolved. During these three years, no distribution had been made to either partner and no salary has been paid to S. On dissolution, the partnership's gross assets are worth $200,000, and the partnership owes $100,000 to creditors. C's capital account remains at $100,000. If the value of S's services are not deemed to augment S's capital account, on liquidation the creditors will get $100,000 and C will get $100,000 in respect of his capital account. S will get nothing.

Alternatively, suppose that after all debts to creditors are paid, Partnership P is worth only $50,000; the capital account of Capital Partner C has shrunk from $100,000 to $50,000; and the capital account of Services Partner S is $0. If UPA Section 18(a) is read in a relatively straightforward way, so that S must contribute toward losses of capital according to his share in the profits, then S must contribute $25,000 to equalize the capital loss—that is, to reduce C's capital loss. See Richert v. Handly, 53 Wash.2d 121, 330 P.2d 1079 (1958). The result is that S loses $125,000 ($100,000 in the value of his services, and the $25,000 payment to C). In contrast, C loses $25,000 ($100,000 capital, offset by the $50,000 return of capital and S's $25,000 contribution).

These results seem inappropriate. In Schymanski v. Conventz, 674 P.2d 281, 284 (Alaska 1983), the court said, in such a case, that although "[t]he general rule is that, in the absence of an agreement to such effect, a partner contributing only personal services is ordinarily *not* entitled to any share of partnership capital pursuant to dissolution," nevertheless "[p]ersonal services may qualify as capital contributions to a partnership where an express or implied agreement to such effect exists." (Emphasis in original.) This exception makes it easy for a court to get around the general rule, by finding an implied agreement when necessary to avoid a particularly unfair result. See also Parker v. Northern Mixing Co., 756 P.2d 881 (Alaska 1988).

Similarly, in Thompson v. Beth, 14 Wis.2d 271, 111 N.W.2d 171, 175 (1961), the court distinguished between cases in which a partner contributes services only on a "day-to-day" basis, and cases in which "the skill and labor of the partner are his contribution to the capital assets of the partnership." In the former type of case, the court said, the partner's services would not augment his capital account. In the latter type of case, however, the partner's services would augment his capital account. This distinction also leaves a lot of room for a court to get around the general rule by finding that a partner's services were in the latter category rather than the former.

Some cases hold that a special rule applies to joint ventures, and then conclude that the relationship in question was a joint venture rather than a partnership. In Kovacik v. Reed, 49 Cal.2d 166, 169–70, 315 P.2d 314, 315–16 (1957), the court came to the same result by a different path:

> . . . Where . . . as in the present case, one partner . . . contributes the money capital as against the other's skill and labor . . . upon loss of the money the party who contributed it is not entitled to recover any part of it from the party who contributed only services. . . . The rationale . . . is that where one party contributes money and the other contributes services, then in the event of a loss each would lose his own capital—the one his money and the other his labor. Another view would be that in such a situation the parties have, by their agreement to share equally in profits, agreed that the values of their contributions—the money on the one hand and the labor on the other—were likewise equal; it would follow that upon the loss, as here, of both money and labor, the parties have shared equally in the losses.

Accord: Becker v. Killarney, 177 Ill.App.3d 793, 127 Ill.Dec. 102, 532 N.E.2d 931 (1988); Snellbaker v. Herrmann, 315 Pa.Super. 520, 462 A.2d 713 (1983) *Kovacik* has been distinguished where the services partner received compensation for his services. See Century Universal Enterprises, Inc. v. Triana Development Corp., 158 Ill.App.3d 182, 110 Ill.Dec. 229, 510 N.E.2d 1260 (1987).

The approach taken in *Kovacik* is sound. If a services-only partner has been fully compensated for his services, it is hard to see why he should not be required to contribute toward making up a capital loss. Otherwise, a capital partner would bear all the partnership's loss and the services-only partner would bear none. But if a services-only partner has not been compensated for his services, then if he must contribute toward the capital loss, he would lose all the value of his services while the capital partner would lose only part of the value of his capital. It is unlikely that the parties would have agreed to this result if they had negotiated on the issue when the partnership was formed. As *Kovacik* suggests, therefore, where a services-only partner has not been compensated for her services, the partners should normally be deemed to have impliedly agreed that she need not contribute to a capital loss.

b. *RUPA.* RUPA § 401(h) continues the rule of UPA § 18. The Comment to § 401(h) makes clear that the rule is intended to apply in the capital-loss context, and provides the following justification for applying the rule to services partners:

> The default rules [of § 401(h)] apply, as does UPA Section 18(a), where one or more of the partners contribute no capital, although there is case law to the contrary. See, e.g., Kovacik v. Reed, 49 Cal.2d 166, 315 P.2d 314 (1957); Becker v. Killarney, 177 Ill.App.3d 793, 532 N.E.2d 931 (1988). It may seem unfair that the contributor of services, who contributes little or no capital, should be obligated to contribute toward the capital loss of the large contributor who contributed no services. In entering a partnership with such a capital structure, the partners should foresee that application of the default rule may bring about unusual results and take advantage of their power to vary by agreement the allocation of capital losses.

This attempt at justification does more to show why RUPA § 401(h) is wrong than why it is right. The Comment begins by frankly recognizing that the result "may seem unfair." It then states that even if the rule is unfair the partners can contract around it. Of course, any rule of partnership law, no matter how foolish, could be "justified" by the argument that it can be contracted around. The point of partnership law, however, should be to make good rules that the parties probably would have agreed to if they had addressed the issue, not to make bad rules that the partners can contract around. Furthermore, many partners don't know partnership law, and therefore won't realize they need to contract around any given rule. Indeed, because persons can be partners without an intention to form a partnership, many partners don't even realize that they are partners, let alone realize that they should consider contracting around any given rule of partnership law.

NOTE ON JOINT VENTURES

As pointed out in the Note on Distributions in Dissolution and on Services Partners, supra, some courts have held that a services partner need not contribute toward a capital loss where the enterprise is a "joint venture" rather than a partnership. The line between a joint venture and a partnership is exceedingly thin. "[M]ost courts have [distinguished] between isolated transactions and continuing enterprises by classifying the former as joint ventures." 1 A. Bromberg & L. Ribstein, Partnership 2:42–2:43 (1994).

Some authorities take the position that joint ventures are generally governed by partnership law. See, e.g., id. at 192 ("Whether a [joint venture] is considered a partnership or merely analogized to one, the venturers are governed by the rules applicable to partners"); Comment, The Joint Venture: Problem Child of Partnership, 38 Calif.L.Rev. 860 (1950). In contrast, other commentators argue that joint ventures are not merely a form of partnership, and not entirely subject to partnership rules. See, e.g., Jaeger, Partnership or Joint Venture?, 37 Notre Dame Law. 138 (1961). The same split is found in the cases. Some cases suggest that it makes no legal difference whether an enterprise is characterized as a partnership or a joint venture, while others suggest that special rules apply to joint ventures.

As a realistic matter, what seems to be involved is this: Certain rules of the UPA, such as Section 18(a), produce unsatisfactory results in certain kinds of cases. Courts that want to avoid these results will sometimes do so, if they plausibly can, by holding that a "special rule" applies to joint ventures, and that the enterprise in the case at hand falls within the special rule. In many or most such cases, the desired result could probably be reached, without applying special rules to joint ventures, by finding that the parties had an implied agreement that overrides the relevant rule of the UPA.

The Comment to RUPA § 202 states that "relationships that are called 'joint ventures' are partnerships if they otherwise fit the definition of a partnership. An association is not classified as a partnership, however, simply because it is called a 'joint venture.' "

Page v. Page

Supreme Court of California, 1961.
55 Cal.2d 192, 10 Cal.Rptr. 643, 359 P.2d 41.

■ Traynor, J.—Plaintiff and defendant are partners in a linen supply business in Santa Maria, California. Plaintiff appeals from a judgment declaring the partnership to be for a term rather than at will.

The partners entered into an oral partnership agreement in 1949. Within the first two years each partner contributed approximately $43,000 for the purchase of land, machinery, and linen needed to begin the business. From 1949 to 1957 the enterprise was unprofitable, losing approximately $62,000. The partnership's major creditor is a corporation, wholly owned by plaintiff, that supplies the linen and machinery necessary for the day-to-day operation of the business. This corporation holds a $47,000 demand note of the partnership. The partnership operations began to improve in 1958. The partnership earned $3,824.41 in that year and $2,282.30 in the first three months of 1959. Despite this improvement plaintiff wishes to terminate the partnership.

The Uniform Partnership Act provides that a partnership may be dissolved "By the express will of any partner when no definite term or particular undertaking is specified." (Corp.Code, § 15031, subd. (1)(b).) The trial court found that the partnership is for a term, namely, "such reasonable time as is necessary to enable said partnership to repay from partnership profits, indebtedness incurred for the purchase of land, buildings, laundry and delivery equipment and linen for the operation of such business. . . .'' Plaintiff correctly contends that this finding is without support in the evidence.

Defendant testified that the terms of the partnership were to be similar to former partnerships of plaintiff and defendant, and that the understanding of these partnerships was that "we went into partnership to start the business and let the business operation pay for itself,—put in so much money, and let the business pay itself out." There was also testimony that one of the former partnership agreements provided in writing that the profits were to be retained until all obligations were paid. . . .

Viewing this evidence most [favorably] for defendant, it proves only that the partners expected to meet current expenses from current income and to recoup their investment if the business were successful.

Defendant contends that such an expectation is sufficient to create a partnership for a term under the rule of Owen v. Cohen, 19 Cal.2d 147, 150 [119 P.2d 713]. In that case. . . . the partners borrowed substantial amounts of money to launch the enterprise and there was an understanding that the loans would be repaid from partnership profits. . . . [T]he court properly held that the partners impliedly promised to continue the partnership for a term reasonably required to allow the partnership to earn sufficient money to accomplish the understood objective. . . .

In the instant case, however, defendant failed to prove any facts from which an agreement to continue the partnership for a term may be implied. The understanding to which defendant testified was no more than a common hope that the partnership earnings would pay for all the necessary expenses. Such a hope does not establish even by implication a "definite term or particular undertaking" as required by section 15031, subdivision (1)(b), of the Corporations Code.

All partnerships are ordinarily entered into with the hope that they will be profitable, but that alone does not make them all partnerships for a term and obligate the partners to continue in the partnerships until all of the losses over a period of many years have been recovered.

Defendant contends that plaintiff is acting in bad faith and is attempting to use his superior financial position to appropriate the now profitable business of the partnership. Defendant has invested $43,000 in the firm, and owing to the long period of losses his interest in the partnership assets is very small. The fact that plaintiff's wholly owned corporation holds a $47,000 demand note of the partnership may make it difficult to sell the business as a going concern. Defendant fears that upon dissolution he will receive very little and that plaintiff, who is the managing partner and knows how to conduct the operations of the partnership, will receive a business that has become very profitable because of the establishment of Vandenberg Air Force Base in its vicinity. Defendant charges that plaintiff has been content to share the losses but now that the business has become profitable he wishes to keep all the gains.

There is no showing in the record of bad faith or that the improved profit situation is more than temporary. In any event these contentions are irrelevant to the issue whether the partnership is for a term or at will. Since, however, this action is for a declaratory judgment and will be the basis for future action by the parties, it is appropriate to point out that defendant is amply protected by the fiduciary duties of copartners.

Even though the Uniform Partnership Act provides that a partnership at will may be dissolved by the express will of any partner (Corp.Code, § 15031, subd. (1)(b)), this power, like any other power held by a fiduciary, must be exercised in good faith.

We have often stated that "Partners are trustees for each other, and in all proceedings connected with the conduct of the partnership every partner is bound to act in the highest good faith to his copartner and may not obtain any advantage over him in the partnership affairs by the slightest misrepresentation, concealment, threat or adverse pressure of any kind." (Llewelyn v. Levi, 157 Cal. 31, 37 [106 P. 219]; Richards v. Fraser, 122 Cal. 456, 460 [55 P. 246]; Yeomans v. Lysfjord, 162 Cal.App.2d 357, 361–362 [327 P.2d 957]; cf. MacIsaac v. Pozzo, 26 Cal.2d 809, 813 [161 P.2d 449]; Corp.Code, § 15021.) . . . .

A partner at will is not bound to remain in a partnership, regardless of whether the business is profitable or unprofitable. A partner may not, however, by use of adverse pressure "freeze out" a copartner and appropriate the business to his own use. A partner may not dissolve a partnership to gain the benefits of the business for himself, unless he fully compensates his copartner for his share of the prospective business opportunity. In this regard his fiduciary duties are at least as great as those of a shareholder of a corporation.

In the case of In re Security Finance Co., 49 Cal.2d 370, 376–377 [317 P.2d 1], we stated that although shareholders representing 50 per cent of the voting power have a right under Corporations Code, section 4600, to dissolve a corporation, they may not exercise such right in order "to defraud the other shareholders [citation], to 'freeze out' minority shareholders [citation], or to sell the assets of the dissolved corporation at an inadequate price. [Citation.]"

Likewise in the instant case, plaintiff has the power to dissolve the partnership by express notice to defendant. If, however, it is proved that plaintiff acted in bad faith and violated his fiduciary duties by attempting to appropriate to his own use the new prosperity of the partnership without adequate compensation to his copartner, the dissolution would be wrongful and the plaintiff would be liable as provided by subdivision (2)(a) of Corporations Code, section 15038 (rights of partners upon wrongful dissolution) for violation of the implied agreement not to exclude defendant wrongfully from the partnership business opportunity.*

The judgment is reversed.

■ GIBSON, C.J., McCOMB, J., PETERS, J., WHITE, J., DOOLING, J., and WOOD (PARKER), J. pro tem., concurred.

———

LEFF v. GUNTER, 33 Cal.3d 508, 189 Cal.Rptr. 377, 658 P.2d 740 (1983). "There is an obvious and essential unfairness in one partner's attempted exploitation of a partnership opportunity for his own personal benefit and to the resulting detriment of his copartners. It may be assumed, although perhaps not always easily proven, that such competition with one's own partnership is greatly facilitated by access to relevant information available only to partners. Moreover, it is equally obvious that a formal disassociation of oneself from a partnership does not change this situation unless the interested parties specifically agree otherwise. It is no less a violation of the trust imposed between partners to permit the exploitation of that partnership information and opportunity to the prejudice of one's former associates by the simple expedient of withdrawal from the partnership."

———

ROSENFELD, MEYER & SUSMAN V. COHEN, 146 Cal.App.3d 200, 194 Cal.Rptr. 180 (1983). "[The lower court's] holding that a partner may dissolve a partnership at will in bad faith is not only contrary to *Page v. Page* . . . and other cases heretofore cited, but is also contrary to the established principle that even non-fiduciaries must exercise their rights in good faith, deal fairly with each other and refrain from injuring the right of another party to receive the benefits of an agreement or relationship. . . .

"Moreover, the law and motion department's ruling that as a matter of law a partner has the absolute right to dissolve a partnership at will without regard to breach of fiduciary consequences is contrary to the principle that a person may be estopped from exercising rights in bad faith."

———

NOTE ON PARTNERSHIP BREAKUP UNDER THE UPA

One of the most difficult issues in partnership law is how to treat cases in which a person's status as a partner is terminated, the partnership is to be terminated as a going concern, or both. (The complexity of these issues is illustrated by the fact that they occupy

———

* The consequences of wrongful dissolution are considered in Section 9, infra. [Footnote by ed.]

about a third of the text and comment of RUPA.) The difficult substantive issues raised by these issues have been made even more complex by the nomenclature that partnership law has employed. The UPA and RUPA take different strategies toward both the underlying substantive issues and the nomenclature. This Note will focus on dissolution under the UPA. A Note in Section 9, infra, will concern partnership breakup under RUPA.

Before getting directly into the legal issues, it is useful to outline the business economics involved.

Assume that a partnership is to be terminated as a going concern. Typically, the termination process will fall into three phases.

(i) The first phase consists of an event—which may be a decision of a partner or a court—that sets the termination in motion. Under the UPA, this phase is referred to as "dissolution."

The principal draftsman of the UPA explained the manner in which that statute uses the term "dissolution" as follows:

> [The term "dissolution" is used in the UPA to designate] a change in the relation of the partners caused by any partner ceasing to be associated in the carrying on of the business. As thus used "dissolution" does not terminate the partnership, it merely ends the carrying on of the business in that partnership. The partnership continues until the winding up of partnership affairs is completed.

Lewis, The Uniform Partnership Act, 24 Yale L.J. 617, 626–27 (1915).

(ii) The second phase consists of the process of actually terminating the partnership's business. Inevitably, some period of time must elapse between (A) the moment at which the event that sets termination of the business in motion occurs and (B) the time at which termination of the business is completed. For example, if the partnership is in the manufacturing business, to terminate the business the partnership will need to pay off its debts, settle its contracts with employees and suppliers, find a purchaser for the factory, and so forth. Under the UPA, this phrase is referred to as "winding up."

(iii) The final phase consists of the completion of the second phase and an end to the partnership as a going concern. Under the UPA, this phase is referred to as "termination."

To put all of this somewhat differently, the term "dissolution" is used in the UPA to describe a change in the *legal status* of the partners and the partnership. The term "winding-up" is used to describe the *economic* event of liquidation that follows dissolution.

Under the UPA, any termination of a person's status as a partner effects a dissolution of the partnership. It's not easy to see why this should be so when, as often happens, the remaining partners rightfully carry on the partnership's business after one partner has departed. Basically, the UPA's treatment of this issue seems to have been driven by conceptualism. The UPA treats a partnership as an aggregate of persons to carry on business for profit as co-owners, rather than as an entity. Because the UPA treats a partnership as an aggregate, the drafters seemed to have believed that it followed "logically" that any change in the identity of the partners "necessarily" worked a dissolution of the partnership. If a partnership is conceptualized as an aggregate of the partners, and if the partners in Partnership P are A, B, C, and D, then it may have seemed to the drafters of the UPA that if D ceases to be a partner, Partnership P "must be" dissolved, because there is no longer an aggregate of A, B, C, and D. Following this line, UPA § 29 defines dissolution as "the change in the relation of partners caused by any partner ceasing to be associated in the carrying on" of the partnership's business.

The law, however, should not be built on deductive logic, but on policy, morality, and experience. We make legal rules because they are desirable, not because they are deducible. If a person ceases to be a partner, the law can treat the partnership as either dissolved or not dissolved. Which course the law takes should depend on which treatment better protects expectations and best reflects social policy. This, in turn, depends on what consequences the law should and does attach to dissolution.

Broadly speaking, dissolution may carry consequences (1) among the partners, (2) between the partners as a group and third persons, such as individuals or firms with whom the partnership has contracted, and (3) for tax purposes. The remainder of this Note will consider each of these areas.

1. *Consequences Among the Partners.* Under the UPA, upon the occurrence of dissolution—which, remember, under the UPA means simply that any partner ceases to be a partner—then unless otherwise agreed, either the partnership must sell its assets for cash and distribute the proceeds of the sale among all the partners or, under cases like *Creel*, must make either a cash payment of the value of a partner's share of the partnership or an in-kind distribution. (If, however, a partner, *W*, *wrongfully* causes dissolution, UPA § 38(2)(b) provides that although the *partnership* is dissolved, the remaining partners can continue the partnership's *business*. To do so, the remaining partners must either: (i) Pay *W* the value of her partnership interest (but without counting the value of the partnership's good will), minus any damages caused by the dissolution; or (ii) Put up a bond to secure such a payment, and indemnify *W* against present and future partnership liabilities. See Section 9, infra.)

UPA § 38(1) provides that "[w]hen dissolution is [rightfully] caused ... each partner ... *unless otherwise agreed*, may have the partnership property applied to discharge its liabilities, and the surplus applied to pay in cash the net amount owing to the respective partners." (Emphasis added.) It is well accepted that under the "unless" clause, the partnership agreement can provide that after the termination of a person's status as a partner (and, therefore, after dissolution of the partnership under the UPA) the remaining partners can continue the partnership *business*, even if the partnership has been dissolved and the dissolution is rightfully caused. See, e.g.,

Meehan v. Shaughnessy, 404 Mass. 419, 535 N.E.2d 1255 (1989); Adams v. Jarvis, 23 Wis.2d 453, 127 N.W.2d 400 (1964).

Agreements that enable remaining partners to continue the partnership's business after dissolution are common, especially in large partnerships, such as law partnerships. Such agreements are usually known as business-continuation agreements or, more simply, continuation agreements. Typically, continuation agreements include not only the right of the remaining partners to continue the partnership's business, but also the terms on which the partner who causes dissolution (or his estate) will be compensated for his partnership interest.

2. *Effect of Dissolution on the Relationship Between the Partnership and Third Parties.* As among the partners, it often won't matter very much whether the withdrawal of a partner does or does not cause dissolution, because as among the partners a continuation agreement can override the substantive effects that dissolution would otherwise have. However, dissolution may also affect the relationship of the partnership to third persons.

For example, suppose that Partnership P, consisting of partners A, B, C, and D, is dissolved by the withdrawal of D, but the business of the partnership is continued by A, B, and C under a continuation agreement. Because P has been dissolved, the partnership of A, B, and C may be deemed a "new" partnership for legal purposes, so that P's assets and agreements, such as leases, licenses, or franchises, must be "transferred" to the new partnership. See Report of the ABA Subcommittee on the Revision of the U.P.A., 43 Bus.Law. 121, 160–62 (1987). In a much remarked-on case, Fairway Development Co. v. Title Insurance Co., 621 F.Supp. 120 (N.D.Ohio 1985), Fairway, a partnership, sued Title Insurance Co. under a title guarantee policy. The policy had been issued at a time when the partners in Fairway were B, S, and W. Subsequently, B and S transferred their partnership interests to W and a third party, X. W and X apparently continued Fairway's business under the Fairway name. The court nevertheless held that Title Insurance Co. was not bound under its policy because the partnership to which it had issued the policy had been legally dissolved.

A debated point under the UPA is whether a partnership agreement can provide not only that the partnership business may be continued after dissolution, but also that the withdrawal of a partner will not cause dissolution, so that the partnership's relation with third parties will not be affected by a partner's withdrawal, as happened in the *Fairway* case. The prevailing (but not unanimous) answer is no, on the ground that UPA § 31 expressly states that "[d]issolution is caused" by the withdrawal of a partner.

3. *Tax Consequences.* The tax-law treatment of dissolution is relatively straightforward, and largely unimpeded by conceptualism. Internal Revenue Code § 708 provides that a partnership's existence does not terminate for tax purposes until either "(A) no part of any business, financial operation, or venture of the partnership continues to be carried on by any of [the] partners in a partnership, or (B) within a twelve-month period there is a sale or exchange of fifty

percent or more of the total interest in partnership capital and profits." Accordingly, dissolution under partnership law is normally a non-event for federal income tax purposes. (Warning: Despite IRC § 708, dissolution may have tax effects on a non-continuing partner or his estate. Even these effects, however, can normally be avoided by a continuation agreement.)

SECTION 9. DISSOLUTION (II): DISSOLUTION BY JUDICIAL DECREE AND WRONGFUL DISSOLUTION

UNIFORM PARTNERSHIP ACT §§ 31(2), 32, 38(2)

REVISED UNIFORM PARTNERSHIP ACT §§ 601, 602, 603, 701, 801, 802, 803, 804, 807

[See Statutory Supplement]

Drashner v. Sorenson

Supreme Court of South Dakota, 1954.
75 S.D. 247, 63 N.W.2d 255.

■ SMITH, P.J. In January 1951 the plaintiff, C.H. Drashner, and defendants, A.D. Sorenson and Jacob P. Deis, associated themselves as co-owners in the real estate, loan and insurance business at Rapid City. For a consideration of $7500 they purchased the real estate and insurance agency known as J. Schumacher Co. located in an office room on the ground floor of the Alex Johnson Hotel building. The entire purchase price was advanced for the partnership by the defendants, but at the time of trial $3,000 of that sum had been repaid to them by the partnership. Although, as will appear from facts presently to be outlined, their operations were not unsuccessful, differences arose and on June 15, 1951 plaintiff commenced this action in which he sought an accounting, dissolution and winding up of the partnership. The answer and counterclaim of defendants prayed for like relief.

The cause came on for trial September 4, 1951. The court among others made the following findings. VII. "That thereafter the plaintiff violated the terms of said partnership agreement, in that he demanded a larger share of the income of the said partnership than he was entitled to receive under the terms of said partnership agreement; that the plaintiff was arrested for reckless driving and served a term in jail for said offense; that the plaintiff demanded that the defendants permit him to draw money for his own personal use out of the moneys held in escrow by the partnership; that the plaintiff spent a large amount of time during business hours in the Brass Rail Bar in Rapid City, South Dakota, and other bars, and neglected his duties in connection with the business of the said partnership.... That the plaintiff, by his actions hereinbefore set forth, has made it impossible to carry on the partnership." The conclusions adopted read as follows: I "That the defendants are entitled to continue the partnership and have the value of the plaintiff's interest in the partnership business determined, upon the filing and approval of a good and sufficient bond, conditioned upon the release of the plaintiff from any liability arising out of the said partnership, and further conditioned upon the payment by the defendants to the plaintiff of the value of plaintiffs' interest in the partnership as determined by the Court." II "That in computing the value of the plaintiff's interest in the said partnership, the value of the good will of the business shall not be considered." III "That the value of the partnership shall be finally determined upon a hearing before this Court, ..." and IV "That the plaintiff shall be entitled to receive one-third of the value of the partnership property owned by the partnership on the 12th day of September, 1951, not including the good will of the business, after the payment of the liabilities of the partnership and the payment to the defendants of the invested capital in the sum of $4,500.00." Judgment was accordingly entered dissolving the partnership as of September 12, 1951.

After hearing at a later date the court found: I "That the value of the said partnership property on the 12th day of September, 1951, was the sum of Four Thousand Four Hundred Ninety-eight and 90/100 Dollars ($4498.90), and on said date there was due and owing by the partnership for accountant's services the sum of Four Hundred Eighty Dollars ($480.00), and that on said date the sum of Four Thousand Five Hundred Dollars ($4500.00) of the capital invested by the defendants had not been returned to the defendants." and II "That there is not sufficient partnership property to reimburse the defendants for their invested capital." Thereupon the court decreed "that the plaintiff had no interest in the property of the said partnership", and that the defendants were the sole owners thereof.

The assignments of error are predicated upon insufficiency of the evidence to support the findings and conclusions. Of these assignments, only those which question whether the court was warranted in finding that (a) the plaintiff caused the dissolution wrongfully, and (b) the value of the partnership property, exclusive of good will, was $4498.90 on the 12th day of September, 1951, merit discussion. A preliminary statement is necessary to place these issues in their framework.

The agreement of the parties contemplated an association which would continue at least until the $7500 advance of defendants had been repaid from the gross earnings of the business. Hence, it was not a partnership at will. Vangel v. Vangel, 116 Cal.App.2d 615, 254 P.2d 919; Zeibak v. Nasser, 12 Cal.2d 1, 82 P.2d 375. In apparent recognition of that fact, both plaintiff and defendants sought dissolution in contravention of the partnership agreement, see SDC 49.0603(2) under SDC 49.0604(1)(d) on the ground that the adverse party had caused the dissolution wrongfully by willfully and persistently committing a breach of the partnership agreement, and by so conducting himself in matters relating to the partnership business as to render impracticable the carrying on of the business in partnership with him.

[The court here quoted U.P.A. Section 38(2)].

From this background we turn to a consideration of the evidence from which the trial court inferred that plaintiff caused the dissolution wrongfully.

The breach between the parties resulted from a continuing controversy over the right of plaintiff to withdraw sufficient money from the partnership to defray his living expenses. Plaintiff was dependent upon his earnings for the support of his family. The defendants had other resources. Plaintiff claimed that he was to be permitted to draw from the earnings of the partnership a sufficient amount to support himself and family. The defendants asserted that there was a definite arrangement for the allocation of the income of the partnership and there was no agreement for withdrawal by plaintiff of more than his allotment under that plan. Defendants' version of the facts was corroborated by a written admission of plaintiff offered in evidence. From evidence thus sharply in conflict, the trial court made a finding, reading as follows: "That the oral partnership agreement between the parties provided that each of the three partners were to draw as compensation one-third of one-half of the commissions earned upon sales made by the partners; that the other one-half of the commissions earned on sales made by the partners and one-half of the commissions earned upon sales made by salesmen employed by the partnership, together with the earnings from the insurance business carried on by the partnership, was to be placed in a fund to be used for the payment of the operating expenses of the partnership, and after the payment of such operating expenses to be used to reimburse the defendants for the capital advanced in the purchase of the Julius Schumacher business and the capital advanced in the sum of Eight Hundred Dollars ($800.00) for the operating expenses of the business."

As an outgrowth of this crucial difference, there was evidence from which a court could reasonably believe that plaintiff neglected the business and spent too much time in a nearby bar during business hours. At a time when plaintiff had overdrawn his partners and was also indebted to one of defendants for personal advances, he requested $100 and his request was refused. In substance he then said, according to the testimony of the defendant Deis, that he would see that he "gets some money to run on", if they "didn't give it to him he was going to dissolve the partnership and see that he got it." Thereafter plaintiff pressed his claims through counsel, and eventually brought this action to dissolve the partnership. The claim so persistently asserted was contrary to the partnership agreement found by the court.

The foregoing picture of the widening breach between the parties is drawn almost entirely from the evidence of defendants. Of course, plaintiff's version of the agreement of the parties, and of the ensuing differences, if believed, would have supported findings of a different order by the trier of the fact. It cannot be said, we think, that the trial court acted unreasonably in believing defendants, and we think it equally clear the court could reasonably conclude that the insistent and continuing demands of the plaintiff and his attendant conduct rendered it reasonably impracticable to carry on the business in partnership with him. It follows, we are of the opinion, the evidence supports the finding that plaintiff caused the dissolution wrongfully. Zeibak v. Nasser, 12 Cal.2d 1, 82 P.2d 375; Owen v. Cohen, 19 Cal.2d 147, 119 P.2d 713; Meherin v. Meherin, 93 Cal.App.2d 459, 209 P.2d 36; and Vangel v. Vangel, 116 Cal.App.2d 615, 254 P.2d 919.

This brings us to a consideration of the sufficiency of the evidence to support the finding of the court that the property of the partnership was of the value of $4498.90 as of the date of dissolution.

Bitter complaint is made because the trial court refused to consider the good will of this business in arriving at its conclusion. The feeling of plaintiff is understandable. These partners must have placed a very high estimate upon the value of the good will of this agency because they paid Mr. Schumacher $7500 to turn over that office with its very moderate fixtures and its listing of property, together with an agreement that he would not engage in the business in Rapid City for at least two years. No doubt they attached some of this good will value to the location of the business which was under only a month to month letting. Cf. 38 C.J.S., Good Will, § 3, page 951; In re Brown's Will, 242 N.Y. 1, 150 N.E. 581, 44 A.L.R. 510, at page 513. Their estimate of value was borne out by the subsequent history of the business. Its real estate commissions, earned but only partly received, grossed $21,528.25 and its insurance commissions grossed $661.21 in the period January 15 to August 31, 1951. In that period the received commissions paid all expenses, including the commissions of salesmen, retired $3,000 of the $7500 purchase price advanced by defendants, and all of $800 of working capital so advanced, allowed the parties to withdraw $1453.02 each, and accumulated a cash balance of $2221.43. In addition the partnership has commissions due.... Notwithstanding this indication of the great value of the good will of this business, the statute does not require the court to take it into consideration in valuing the property of the business in these circumstances. The statute provides such a sanction for causing the dissolution of a partnership wrongfully. SDC 49.0610(2)(c)(2) quoted supra. The court applied the statute....

That the $1500 value placed on [the assets other than good will] was conservative we do not question. However, after mature study and reflection we have concluded that the court's finding is not against the clear weight of the evidence appearing in this record. Hence we are not at liberty to disturb it.

The brief of plaintiff includes some discussion of his right to a share in the profits from the date of the dissolution until the final judgment. It does not appear from the record that this claim was presented to the trial court, or that the net profit of the business during that period was evidenced. Because that issue was not presented below, it is not before us.

The judgment of the trial court is affirmed.

All the Judges concur.

––––––

NOTE ON WRONGFUL DISSOLUTION

Drashner v. Sorenson illustrates that drastic consequences can befall a wrongfully dissolving partner under the UPA, in the form of (i) damages; (ii) a valuation of his interest that does not reflect the real value of the interest because goodwill is not taken into account; and (iii) a continuation of the business without him. These consequences may have a special impact in a partnership without an expressly specified term—that is, without an expressly specified duration. Suppose one of the partners, *A*, elects to dissolve such a partnership on the theory that the partnership is at will. If the court finds that despite the absence of a specified duration, the partnership is for a term as a matter of implication, *A* will have dissolved the partnership in contravention of the partnership agreement. The penalties for guessing wrong on whether the court will make such a finding "may act as significant disincentives to dissolution [and may therefore] tend to stabilize the partnership." Hillman, The Dissatisfied Participant in the Solvent Business Venture: A Consideration of the Relative Permanence of Partnerships and Close Corporations, 67 Minn.L.Rev. 1, 34 (1982). For comparable reasons, a partner who believes that other partners have engaged in wrongful conduct is taking a risk if she tries to dissolve a partnership through a self-help election, as opposed to going to court for a decree under UPA Section 32. The other side of the coin, of course, is that judicial proceedings entail delay.

––––––

NOTE ON THE EXPULSION OF A PARTNER

The expulsion of a partner prior to the end of the partnership term *without good cause* is ordinarily a wrongful violation of the partnership agreement, and the wrongfully expelled partner ordinarily has a right to have the partnership dissolved and liquidated. See UPA §§ 31(1)(d); 32(1)(d), 38(1). In contrast, UPA § 38(1) provides that "if dissolution is caused by the expulsion of a partner, *bona fide under the partnership agreement* and if the expelled partner is discharged from all partnership liabilities, either by payment or agreement . . . , he shall receive in cash only the net amount due him from the partnership." (Emphasis added.) Under this section, a partnership agreement may lawfully provide that a partner can be expelled without cause upon a designated vote of the remaining partners. See Lawlis v.

Kightlinger & Gray, 562 N.E.2d 435 (Ind.App.1990); Miller v. Foulston, Siefkin, Powers & Eberhardt, 246 Kan. 450, 790 P.2d 404 (1990).

To fall within UPA § 31(1)(d), an expulsion must be "bona fide." In *Lawlis,* supra, the court stated that "if the power to involuntarily expel partners granted by a partnership agreement is exercised in bad faith or for a 'predatory purpose,' . . . the partnership agreement is violated, giving rise to an action for damages the affected partner has suffered as a result of his expulsion." Id. at 440.

What does "bona fide" or "good faith" mean in this context? It cannot mean that a partner may be expelled only for cause: under such an interpretation, the power to expel a partner under an expulsion provision of a partnership agreement would be no greater than the power to expel a partner even in the absence of an expulsion provision. In *Lawlis,* the court said, "the expelling partners act in 'good faith' regardless of motivation if [the expulsion] does not cause a wrongful withholding of money or property legally due the expelled partner at the time he is expelled." Id. at 443. This seems too restrictive. In Winston & Strawn v. Nosal, 279 Ill.App.3d 231, 664 N.E.2d 239 (1996), Nosal was expelled from a law firm, Winston & Strawn. The expulsion followed (1) Nosal's request for partnership information concerning actions of the partnership's executive committee—in particular, concerning actions of Fairchild, the managing partner—in increasing the compensation and ownership interests of the committee members, and (2) Nosal's threat to sue if his request for information was not granted. Winston & Strawn then brought an action for a declaratory judgment that the expulsion was valid under the partnership agreement. The trial court granted summary judgment for Winston & Strawn. Reversed:

> It is well-established that a fiduciary relationship exists between partners and that each partner is bound to exercise the utmost good faith and honesty in all matters relating to the partnership business. . . . *Labovitz v. Dolan*, 189 Ill.App.3d 403, 136 Ill.Dec. 780, 545 N.E.2d 304 (1989) . . . .

> Illinois has yet to address the extent of the duty of good faith in the context of partner outplacement or expulsion. Courts in other jurisdictions, however, have concluded that partners owe one another a duty of good faith in the context of expulsion, even where the partnership agreement permits expulsion without cause. . . .

> In this case, there is no dispute that the partnership agreement places no restriction upon the expulsion of a partner other than approval by the requisite majority. However, the agreement also grants all partners unrestricted access "to the books and records of the partnership." Access to partnership books is also guaranteed under section 19 of the Act. . . .

> Nosal claims that the documents he sought would have revealed the executive committee's plan to retain much of the firm's wealth and management power in the hands of its mem-

bers. Specifically, the documents would have proven that upon assuming control, and without generally notifying the remaining capital partners, the executive committee dramatically increased the total number of partnership "points," or portions of ownership interest in the firm, and then awarded themselves large increases.

Indeed, the record substantiates that in 1990, the executive committee voted its members considerable increases in individual points which were not given to the remaining capital partners. Nosal's evidence indicates that other capital partners were never notified about this action, and that when Nosal ... sought to learn about it, [he was] repeatedly denied documents expressly guaranteed [to him] under the partnership agreement. We recognize ... testimony that the executive committee had the prerogative to designate the number of points for each capital partner; however, we find nothing in the agreement permitting such self-promoting action as was taken here without the full awareness of the remaining capital partners.

Nosal also alleges that Fairchild intentionally kept such data from him because Nosal could have uncovered evidence of Fairchild's ongoing fraudulent billing scheme subsequently discovered by the firm.

... We note that among the documents sought by Nosal was a firm auditor's internal control report, which arguably could have disclosed questionable billing practices by Fairchild. It cannot be ignored that Nosal's [expulsion] immediately succeeded his ongoing requests for sensitive firm information, and came just days after he presented Fairchild with a draft complaint threatening to sue the firm to enforce his right to examine books and records. The evidence further indicates that it was Fairchild, in his discretion, who was largely instrument in the sudden decision to outplace Nosal despite the fact that just a week before, Nosal was given a favorable review, a compensation increase, and assurances ... that he was not among those to be outplaced.

Fairchild's steadfast refusal of Nosal's access to records, his role in the outplacement, and the fact that it occurred just after Nosal's threatened lawsuit, raise an inference that Nosal was expelled solely because he persisted in invoking rights belonging to him under the partnership agreement and that the reasons advanced by the firm were pretextual. Regardless of the discretion conferred upon partners under a partnership agreement, this does not abrogate their high duty to exercise good faith and fair dealing in the execution of such discretion. Labovitz, 189 Ill. App.3d at 412, 136 Ill.Dec. 780, 545 N.E.2d 304. Nosal has sufficiently raised a triable issue that his expulsion occurred in breach of this duty.

———

LEVY v. NASSAU QUEENS MEDICAL GROUP, 102 A.D.2d 845, 476 N.Y.S.2d 613, 614 (1984). "While [an expulsion in] bad faith may be actionable, there must be some showing that the partnership acted out of a desire to gain a business or property advantage for the remaining partners.... Policy disagreements do not constitute bad faith 'since at the heart of the partnership concept is the principle that partners may choose with whom they wish to be associated.'"

CRUTCHER v. SMITH, 209 B.R. 347 (Bankr. Ct. E.D. Pa. 1997). "The threshold issue is a factual question of whether the Debtor [Partner] was wrongfully expelled by the Defendants from the partnership, or whether the Debtor caused his own termination from the partnership by failing to fulfill his duties as a partner.... [The Defendants claim] that the Debtor himself breached the oral partnership agreement and subsequently disassociated himself from the Business, and therefore that his own acts caused dissolution of the partnership in January 1996. In particular, the Defendants claim that the Debtor failed to replace the $500 bad check which he gave to Smith [, one of the partners, and used $110 of partnership funds]....

"However, ... we conclude that the Debtor's alleged wrongful acts were insufficient to trigger a dissolution of the partnership.... '"[I]t is not for every trivial departure from duty or violation of the articles of partnership, or for every trifling fault or misconduct that courts of equity will interfere and decree a dissolution.'" [Potter v. Brown, 328 Pa. 554, 562, 195 A. 901, 904 (1938)], (quoting Story on Partnership, § 287). Although the Debtor's misuse of $110 in partnership funds was technically 'misconduct,' the sum at issue was minimal. The failure to reimburse Smith for [a] $500 bad check was more of a personal wrongful act against Smith than an act against the Business, but arguably was also 'misconduct' inter se the partners. However, the amounts, even when put together, are relatively inconsequential in light of the Business's 1996 gross income of over $200,000. Certainly a $610 offset could have been effected in any future distributions to the partners. We believe that these minor infractions are insufficient to trigger a dissolution of the partnership....

"The Debtor's argument in support of his wrongful expulsion by the Defendants, on the other hand, more logically explains his disassociation from the Business. In essence, the Debtor argues that the Defendants engaged in several definitive steps to ensure his exclusion from the partnership....

"... First, the Defendants refused to allow the Debtor to participate in the daily operation of the Business after his hospitalization. Second, upon discovering the Debtor's hospitalization, the Defendants immediately notified [the bank] that there were problems in the partnership and placed an 'alert' on the account which was operative only upon an attempt by the Debtor to withdraw funds from the account. The defendants then proceeded to open a new account bearing only their names. Thus, the Debtor was excluded from all financial matters related to the Business and the partnership in general. . . . Most notably, [the Defendants] did not obtain the Debtor's consent for, nor give him notice of, their purchase of an investment property . . . with partnership funds, thereby depriving the Debtor of any managerial and decision-making authority as a partner.

"These events indicate that the Defendants took unequivocal measures to strip the Debtor of all of his rights as a partner, thereby excluding him from the operation and management of the partnership. The debtor thus has sufficiently established that he was wrongfully expelled from the partnership by the Defendants."

––––––––

NOTE ON PARTNERSHIP BREAKUP UNDER RUPA

RUPA's provisions on partnership breakup are even more complex than those of the UPA. To begin with nomenclature, RUPA continues to use the terms "dissolution," "winding up," and "termination." However, RUPA adds a new term, "dissociation," to describe the termination of a person's status as a partner.

1. *Events of Dissociation.* Although the term "dissociation" is new, the concept is not. Even under the UPA, a variety of events result in the termination of a person's status as a partner, and there is a very substantial overlap between the UPA and RUPA concerning the description of those events. For example, RUPA § 602(a) continues the rule of the UPA that every partner has the right to withdraw (dissociate) from the partnership at any time, rightfully or wrongfully, by express will. RUPA § 602(c) provides that a partner who wrongfully dissociates is liable to the partnership and to the other partners for damages caused by the dissociation. Furthermore, if a partner wrongfully dissociates, the partnership can continue without him.

2. *Rightful and Wrongful Dissociation.* RUPA § 602 distinguishes between events of dissociation that involve rightful conduct by the dissociated partner and events of dissociation that involve wrongful conduct. An event of dissociation is rightful unless it is specified as wrongful in § 602(b). The major types of wrongful dissociation are: (i) A dissociation that is in breach of an express provision of the partnership agreement. (ii) A withdrawal of a partner by the partner's express will before the expiration of the partnership term or the completion of an undertaking for which the partnership was formed. (iii) A partner has engaged in wrongful conduct that adversely and materially affected the partnership business. (iv) A partner has willfully or persistently committed a material breach of the partnership agreement or of a duty of care, loyalty, good faith, and fair dealing owed to the partnership or the other partners under § 404.

The Comment to RUPA § 602 states:

> [Under 602(a)] . . . a partner has the power to dissociate at any time by expressing a will to withdraw, even in contravention

of the partnership agreement. The phrase "rightfully or wrongful-ly" reflects the distinction between a partner's *power* to withdraw in contravention of the partnership agreement and a partner's *right* to do so. In this context, although a partner can not be enjoined from exercising the power to dissociate, the dissociation may be wrongful under subsection (b)....

... The significance of a wrongful dissociation is that it may give rise to damages under subsection (c) and, if it results in the dissolution of the partnership, the wrongfully dissociating partner is not entitled to participate in winding up the business....

3.   *Consequences of Dissociation.* The partnership-breakup provisions of RUPA are driven by functional considerations, rather than by the "nature" of a partnership (although the Comments occasionally lapse into conceptual justifications based on the entity theory). Along these lines, RUPA, unlike the UPA, does not provide that every termination of a person's status as a partner—every dissociation—causes dissolution. Instead, the key issue is whether dissociation has occurred, and what are the consequences of the *kind* of dissociation that occurred.

There is an important distinction here between the partnership and the partnership's business. Under the UPA, if the partnership status of one or more partners is terminated, the partnership is dissolved but the remaining partners might continue the business, albeit as a new partnership. For example, the remaining partners might agree on a buyout price with the departing partners, or might buy the partnership business at an auction pursuant to winding up, or might continue the business under a continuation agreement. Under RUPA, however, the dissociation of a partner does not necessarily cause dissolution at all. For example, upon a wrongful dissociation, or a dissociation by death, the partnership is not dissolved—and there-fore the partnership's business continues—unless within ninety days a majority of the remaining partners dissociate or agree to wind up. Under RUPA, dissociation, rather than necessarily causing dissolution, leads to two forks in the statutory road: winding up under Article 8 or mandatory buyout under Article 7. Which fork must be taken under RUPA depends on the nature of the event of dissociation.

First Fork: Winding Up. The events of dissociation that require the partnership to be wound up under RUPA are described in § 801. These events include notice of a partner's express will to withdraw in a partnership at will; the expiration of the partnership's term in a partnership for a term; and an uncured event that makes it unlawful for all or substantially all of the partnership's business to be contin-ued. The Official Comment states:

... Under RUPA, not every partner dissociation causes a dissolution of the partnership. Only certain departures trigger a dissolution. The basic rule is that a partnership is dissolved, and its business must be wound up, only upon the occurrence of one of the events listed in Section 801. All other dissociations result in a buyout of the partner's interest under Article 7 and a continuation of the partnership entity and business by the remaining partners.

Section 801 continues two basic rules from the UPA. First, it continues the rule that any member of an *at-will* partnership has the right to force a liquidation. Second, by negative implication, it continues the rule that the partners who wish to continue the business of a *term* partnership can not be forced to liquidate the business by a partner who withdraws prematurely in violation of the partnership agreement.

Second Fork: Buyout. If, upon the dissociation of a partner, winding up is not required under § 801, then RUPA § 701 requires a mandatory buyout of the dissociated partner's interest by the partnership. However, if the dissociation was wrongfully caused by the dissociated partner, § 701(c) provides that the buyout price under § 701(b) is to be reduced by damages for the wrongful dissociation. Furthermore, under § 701(h) a partner who wrongfully dissociates before the expiration of a definite term, or the completion of a particular undertaking, is not entitled to payment of any portion of the buyout price until the expiration of the term or completion of the undertaking, unless the partner establishes to the satisfaction of the court that earlier payment will not cause undue hardship to the business of the partnership. A deferred payment must be adequately secured and bear interest. Under § 701(b), the buyout price of a dissociated partner's interest is the amount that would have been distributable to the dissociating partner if, on the date of dissociation, the assets of the partnership were sold at a price equal to the greater of the liquidation value or the value based on a sale of the entire business as a going concern, without the dissociated partner, and the partnership was wound up as of that date.

CHAPTER III

THE CORPORATE FORM

SECTION 1. THE CHARACTERISTICS OF THE CORPORATION

1. *Publicly Held Enterprises.* The corporation has traditionally been the preferred choice of form for business enterprises that are to be publicly held (that is, whose ownership interests are to be held by members of the public, as opposed to owner-managers). This preference results from five central attributes of the corporate form.

a. Limited liability. Shareholders are not personally liable for corporate obligations. This legal rule is conventionally expressed by the statement that shareholders have *limited liability.* The *managers* of a corporation are also normally not personally liable for corporate obligations: As long as corporate managers act on the corporation's behalf and within their authority, they are treated like agents, not principals, for liability purposes.

b. Free Transferability of Ownership Interests. Ownership (or "equity") interests in corporations—represented by shares of stock—are freely transferable.

c. Continuity of existence. The legal existence of a corporation is perpetual, unless a shorter term is stated in the certificate of incorporation. As a result, a corporation is relatively secure against early termination. This may have a beneficial impact on long-term planning. See Rock & Wachter, *Waiting for the Omelet to Set,* 24 J. Corp. L. 913 (1999).

d. Centralized management. Under the corporate statutes, a corporation is normally managed by or under the direction of a board of directors, and a shareholder as such has no right to participate in management.

e. Entity status. A corporation is a "legal person" or "legal entity." As a result, a corporation can exercise power and have rights in its own name. For example, a corporation can sue or be sued, and can hold property.

2. *Privately Held Enterprises.* If an enterprise is not to be publicly held, the choice of form is much more complex. Today, such a firm might be either a close corporation, a general partnership, a limited liability partnership, a limited partnership, or a limited liability company. The general-partnership form has been considered in Chapter 2. Close corporations will be considered in Chapter 6. The remaining forms will be considered in Chapter 7.

SECTION 2. SELECTING A STATE OF INCORPORATION

Under traditional choice-of-law rules, a firm can incorporate wherever it chooses, and a corporation's internal affairs are governed by the law of its state of incorporation—even if the corporation has no business contacts with that state.

A corporation with only a few owners—a "close corporation"—will almost invariably incorporate locally, that is, in the state where it has its principal place of business. Partly this is for tax reasons. If a corporation *does business* in a state, the state will impose a doing-business tax on the corporation on a basis that reflects the amount of that business. If a corporation is *incorporated* in a state, the state will impose a franchise tax for the privilege of incorporation, even if the corporation does not do business in that state. Elements of the doing-business and franchise taxes may overlap, so that if a corporation is doing business mainly in one state, its total tax bill usually will be less if it is also incorporated in that state. Furthermore, local attorneys, familiar with local corporate law, may be hesitant about rendering formal opinions on the laws of other states, and are likely to recommend local incorporation.

In the case of a publicly held corporation, a different calculus prevails. Publicly held corporations usually do business in a great number of states. For reasons that will be discussed in Chapter 4, a majority of large publicly held corporations are incorporated in Delaware. Many others are incorporated in states that have adopted the Model Business Corporation Act, promulgated by the Committee on Corporate Laws of the ABA's Section of Business Law. Because the law of the state of incorporation normally governs internal corporate affairs, and because Delaware is preeminent for publicly held corporations, the Delaware statute provides a major axis of this book. A second major axis is provided by the Model Act. Although the Model Act itself has no official status, it serves as the basis for the statutes of many states. Recurring reference will also be made to the California and New York statutes, because these states account for a significant portion of total corporations as a result of the size of their populations and their commercial significance.

SECTION 3. ORGANIZING A CORPORATION

Once a decision has been made to incorporate, and the state of incorporation has been selected, the next step is to create or *organize* the corporation. To begin this process, an *incorporator* files a *certificate of incorporation, articles of incorporation,* or *charter* (the nomenclature varies from state to state) with a designated state office—usually the office of the Secretary of State.

DEL. GEN. CORP. LAW §§ 101, 102, 103, 106, 107, 108, 109

[See Statutory Supplement]*

REV. MODEL BUS. CORP. ACT §§ 2.01, 2.02, 2.03, 2.05, 2.06

[See Statutory Supplement]

FORM OF CERTIFICATE OF INCORPORATION

[See Statutory Supplement]

NOTE ON AUTHORIZED AND ISSUED STOCK AND ON PREEMPTIVE RIGHTS

An important function of a certificate of incorporation is to designate the classes of stock, and the number of shares of each class, that the corporation is *authorized* to issue. If the corporation's authorized stock consists of one class of common stock, the certificate need only designate the number of authorized shares. If there is to be more than one class of stock, and particularly if there is to be one or more classes of preferred stock (that is, stock that carries a preference as to dividends, on liquidation, or both, over common stock), the certificate of incorporation must either (i) designate the terms of each class or (ii) authorize the board to issue portions of the authorized class in series from time to time and to designate the terms of each series as it is issued. A sale of stock by the corporation is known as an *issuance of stock*. Only stock that has been authorized in the certificate of incorporation can be issued. Authorized stock that has not yet been issued is known as *authorized but unissued* stock. Authorized stock that has been issued is known as *issued stock* or *outstanding stock*. Sometimes a corporation repurchases stock that it has previously issued. Such stock may sometimes be referred to as *treasury stock* or *authorized and issued but not outstanding stock*.

The power to issue authorized but unissued stock, and the price at which the stock will be issued, is in the hands of the board, subject only to certain very limited constraints. At common law, one of these constraints was that each existing shareholder had the right to sub-

---

* References in this book to the "Statutory Supplement" are to Corporations and Business Associations; Statutes, Rules, Materials, and Forms (M. Eisenberg ed.).

scribe to her proportionate part of a new issue of stock of the class she held. This is known as the *preemptive right*. The right was riddled with exceptions—for example, it did not apply to stock that was issued for property rather than cash. Modern statutes provide that shareholders have no preemptive rights unless the certificate of incorporation provides such a right. Few do.

Even where shareholders have no preemptive rights, the board may not issue stock for the purpose of reallocating or perpetuating control. See, e.g., Note on Condec v. Lunkenheimer, Chapter 4, section 2, infra; Schwartz v. Marien, 37 N.Y.2d 487, 373 N.Y.S.2d 122, 335 N.E.2d 334 (1975). The right to prohibit a non-pro-rata stock issuance for an improper purpose is sometimes referred to as the "quasi-preemptive right." And under basic fiduciary principles, the board cannot issue stock to directors at an unfairly low price.

———

NOTE ON THE BASIC MODES OF CORPORATE FINANCE

An initial question for a corporation is how to finance its business. The three major modes of corporate finance are common stock, debt, and preferred stock.

1. *Common Stock.* Traditionally, shares of common stock are conceived as ownership or *equity* interests in the corporation, so that the body of common shareholders are the corporation's owners. Normally, but not invariably, common stock carries the right to vote in the election of directors and certain other matters. Typically, or at least often, dividends are paid on common stock, but many corporations do not pay dividends, and in any event whether dividends are paid, and if so in what amount, is generally in the discretion of the board. As a result, common stock has no fixed claim on the corporation. Partly for this reason, modern financial theory often conceives of common stock as ultimate or *residual* ownership. "Common shareholders are often thought of as the owners of the firm or as the holders of the *equity* interest in the firm. . . . The equity interest is sometimes usefully thought of as the *residual* interest—the claim to what is left after all senior claimants have been satisfied." W. Klein & J. Coffee, Business Organization and Finance 2003 (9th ed. 2004) (emphasis added). The "senior claimants" to which Coffee & Klein refer are debt and preferred stock.

2. *Debt.* Debt is a fixed claim against the corporation for principal and interest. The major types of corporate debt are *trade debt, bank debt, bonds, debentures*, and *notes.*

(a) *Trade debt.* When a business purchases goods or services, payment is typically not due for thirty, sixty, or ninety days. Trade debt consists principally of amounts that a corporation owes for such goods and services at any point in time. Trade debt appears on a corporation's balance sheet as Accounts Payable.

(b) *Bank debt*. A business will often be financed in significant part by commercial-bank loans. Bank loans appear on a corporation's balance sheet under captions such as Loans Payable.

(c) *Bonds and debentures*. Another method of financing a corporation is to issue bonds or debentures. Essentially, bonds and debentures are promises, embodied in an instrument, to repay amounts that the firm has borrowed on a long-term basis, typically by selling the bonds on the general market or on some special market. Bonds appear on a corporation's balance sheet under captions such as Bonds Payable, or under a caption that describes specific bond issues, such as 7.5% Senior Debentures. Unlike bank loans, bonds and debentures normally represent money borrowed from the public, or at least from a significant group of lenders or investors. "As a matter of historical practice, bonds and debentures are long term obligations issued under indentures, bonds generally being secured obligations and debentures being unsecured obligations." W. Bratton, Corporate Finance—Cases and Materials 175 (5th ed. 2003).

> A bond [or] debenture . . . is simply a promise by the borrower to pay a specified amount on a specified date, together with interest at specified times, on the terms and subject to the conditions spelled out in a governing indenture. . . . Bonds [and] debentures . . . are, then . . . promissory notes issued pursuant to and governed by longer contracts [known as indentures]. Some of the governing terms and conditions will be set out on the face of the [bond or debenture]. Most terms, however, will be in the [indenture] that governs the instrument and will be merely referred to on its face. The note incorporates the contract by reference. . . .
>
> It is the practice in both financial and legal writing to use "bond" as a generic term for all long term debt securities. . . .

Id. at 175–76.

Bratton describes an *indenture* as follows:

> An indenture is a contract entered into between the borrowing corporation and a trustee. The trustee administers the payments of interest and principal, and monitors and enforces compliance with other obligations on behalf of the bondholders as a group. The indenture defines the assorted obligations of the borrower, the rights and remedies of the holders of the bonds, and the role of the trustee.
>
> The borrower contracts with a trustee rather than directly with the holders of the bonds so as to permit the bonds to be sold in small denominations to large numbers of scattered investors. Given widespread ownership in small amounts, unilateral monitoring and enforcement by each holder is not cost effective. The device of the trust solves this problem. . . .
>
> The "bonds" and the "indenture" need to be conceptually distinguished. The bonds set out a promise to pay that runs to the holders of the bonds. The indenture is a bundle of additional

promises (including a backup promise to pay) that run to the trustee. The holders of the bonds are third party beneficiaries of the promises in the indenture. Even though the promises in the bonds run directly to the holders, the bonds are subject to the indenture, and therefore may be enforced directly by the holders only to the extent that the indenture allows. Indentures generally constrain the unilateral enforcement rights of small holders, channeling enforcement through the central agency of the trustee. The device of the trust indenture, then, not only facilitates enforcement by the widely scattered holders, but also restrains such enforcement. It facilitates borrowing in small amounts from large numbers of widely scattered lenders not only by constraining the issuer as against the holders, but by protecting the issuer from the holders.

Id. at 176.

(d) *Notes*. There is no legally recognized distinction between bonds and debentures, on the one hand, and notes, on the other. However, "Under the historical practice, notes may be long term or short term obligations, but in either case are not issued pursuant to an indenture. Recent practice has changed this. Today, 'notes' often are issued pursuant to indentures as unsecured long term obligations. But they tend to be intermediate term securities, coming due in ten years or less, where 'debentures' tend to mature in ten years or more." Id. at 175.

3. *Preferred Stock.* Preferred stock is a hybrid that combines the ownership element of common stock and the senior nature of debt. The basic elements of preferred stock are described as follows in Hunt, Williams & Donaldson, Basic Business Finance 358–61 (5th ed. 1974):

> From the purely legal point of view ... preferred stock is a type of ownership and thus takes a classification similar to that of the common stock.... Unlike [a] bond, ... preferred stock does not contain any promise of repayment of the original investment; and as far as the shareholders are concerned, this must be considered as a permanent investment for the life of the company. Further, there is no legal obligation to pay a fixed rate of return on the investment.
>
> The special character of the preferred stock lies in its relationship to the common stock. When a preferred stock is used as a part of the corporate capital structure, the rights and responsibilities of the owners as the residual claimants to the asset values and earning power of the business no longer apply equally to all shareholders. Two types of owners emerge, representing a voluntary subdivision of the overall ownership privileges. Specifically, the common shareholders agree that the preferred shareholder shall have "preference" or first claim in the event that the directors are able and willing to pay a dividend. In the case of what is termed a nonparticipating or *straight preferred stock*, which is the most frequent type, the extent of this priority is a

fixed percentage of the par value of the stock or a fixed number of dollars per share in the case of stock without a nominal or par value. . . .

In most cases the prior position of preferred stock also extends to the disposition of assets in the event of liquidation of the business. Again, the priority is only with reference to the common stock and does not affect the senior position of creditors in any way. . . . *

Typically, preferred stock carries a dividend that is payable period-ically—often, quarterly—in the board's discretion. Thus the most obvious difference between debt and preferred stock is that debthold-ers have a fixed claim on the corporation for interest and principal, while preferred shareholders normally have no fixed claims for distri-butions. Instead, the claims of preferred stock for distributions are only contingent: *If* the corporation proposes to pay a dividend on common, *then* it must first pay a designated dividend to the preferred. *If* the corporation liquidates, *then* before it distributes anything to the common it must satisfy the preferred's liquidation preference.

Often, the preferred's dividend preference is "cumulative"—that is, no dividend can be paid on common unless all prior dividends on the preferred have been paid. (If a preferred is noncumulative, a dividend can be paid on common as long as the current dividend on the preferred is paid.) Often too, preferred is given the right to vote on the election of directors if, but only if, preferred dividends are in default for a designated number of periods.

4. *Convertibles, Classified Stock, and Derivatives.* In the mod-ern world, the basic elements of common stock, preferred stock, and debt are often disaggregated, and their fragments are combined to design more exotic corporate securities. For example, preferred stock is often issued in several classes, and common stock may be issued in several classes as well (*classified common*). In such cases, each class enjoys somewhat different rights than the others in respect of voting, dividend, or liquidation rights, or all three. Many preferred stocks, and some bonds, are made convertible into common stock at the option of the holder, on specified terms. Furthermore, new types of securities may be "derived" from common stock, in the sense that although the securities are not themselves common stock, their value largely de-pends on the value of a corporation's common stock and on the terms of their relationship to the common stock. The simplest example is a "right" or "warrant," which is a security issued by the corporation that gives the holder a right or option to purchase common stock on specified terms.

———

* As quoted in V. Brudney & W. Bratton, Corporate Finance—Cases and Material 335–36 (4th ed. 1993).

NOTE ON INITIAL DIRECTORS

Once a corporation is under way, its board of directors is elected by the shareholders. However, a corporation has no shareholders until stock is issued, and the function of issuing stock is normally vested in the board. Accordingly, there must be a mechanism either for naming initial directors before stock is issued, or for issuing stock before directors are elected by the shareholders. There are two basic mechanisms to solve this problem. Under the law of some states, like New York, the corporation's incorporators have the powers of shareholders until stock is issued, and the powers of directors until directors are elected. N.Y.Bus.Corp.Law §§ 404(a), 615(c). Under such a statute, the incorporators will typically adopt by-laws, fix the number of directors, and elect initial directors to serve until the first annual meeting of shareholders. See N.Y.Bus.Corp.Law § 404(a). Under the law of other states, the initial directors can be named in the corporation's certificate of incorporation. Del.Gen.Corp.Law §§ 107, 108. If the initial directors are named in the certificate of incorporation, the functions of the incorporators pass to the directors when the certificate is filed and recorded. Del.Gen.Corp.Law §§ 107, 108(a).

Once the initial directors are named, either by the incorporators or by the certificate of incorporation, they will hold an organization meeting. A typical agenda for such a meeting is reflected in the Form of Minutes of Organization Meeting that follows.

FORM OF MINUTES OF ORGANIZATION MEETING

[See Statutory Supplement]

NOTE ON SUBSCRIPTIONS FOR SHARES

Normally, stock is issued by a corporation in a simultaneous exchange for cash or property. In some cases, however, a would-be shareholder enters into a "subscription agreement," under which he agrees to purchase a corporation's stock when it is issued to him at some future date. Typically, in such cases, the corporation has not yet been formed. (The agreement is then made on the would-be corporation's behalf by incorporators, agents, or trustees.) Agreements of this type are called pre-incorporation subscription agreements.

There is a good deal of old law on various aspects of such agreements. The old general rule was that a pre-incorporation subscription was only a continuing offer by the subscriber, and that a subscriber therefore was not bound if he made a timely revocation. Under this rule, a subscriber could revoke his agreement until the moment of incorporation or, in the alternative, until the corporation, once formed, issued stock to the subscriber. There was an exception where the mutual promises of subscribers were expressed as consideration for each other. In that case, a contract was deemed to be formed immediately. In addition, subscription agreements entered into *after* the corporation was formed were treated as ordinary contracts, and raised no special problems of enforceability.

This treatment of pre-incorporation subscription agreements has been changed by the modern corporate statutes. Most statutes now provide that pre-incorporation subscriptions are irrevocable for a specified period of time unless all the subscribers consent to a revocation or the agreement otherwise provides. See, e.g., Del.Gen. Corp.Law § 165 (preincorporation subscription agreements irrevocable for six months except with the consent of all other subscribers); Model Act § 6.20(a) (same). Because of these statutory changes, the law relating to subscriptions is of greatly diminished importance, and current cases on the subject are rare.

FORM OF BY–LAWS

[See Statutory Supplement]

FORM OF STOCK CERTIFICATE

[See Statutory Supplement]

DEL. GEN. CORP. LAW § 109

[See Statutory Supplement]

MODEL BUS. CORP. ACT §§ 2.06, 10.20–10.21

[See Statutory Supplement]

SECTION 4.   PREINCORPORATION TRANSACTIONS BY PROMOTERS

A *promoter* is a person who transforms an idea into a business by bringing together the needed persons and assets, and superintending the various steps required to bring the new business into existence. Often, a promoter of a corporation makes contracts for the benefit of the corporation even before the corporation has been formed. If, as is usually the case, the corporation is later formed, and benefits from such a contract, issues may arise regarding who is liable under the contract.

(a) *Liability of the promoter.* The general rule is that when a promoter makes a contract for the benefit of a contemplated corporation, the promoter is personally liable on the contract and remains liable even after the corporation is formed.

An exception to the general rule is that if the party who contracted with the promoter knew that the corporation was not in existence at the time of contracting, and nevertheless agreed to look solely to the corporation for performance, the promoter is not deemed a party to the contract. Such an agreement may be express or implied. As a practical matter, it is often difficult to predict whether a court will or will not find an implied contract of this sort.

For example, in Goodman v. Darden, Doman & Stafford Associates, 100 Wash.2d 476, 670 P.2d 648 (1983), Goodman had proposed to renovate an apartment building owned by Darden, Doman & Stafford Associates (DDS). During the course of negotiations, Goodman informed DDS that he would be forming a corporation to limit his personal liability. In August 1979, a contract was made between DDS and "BUILDING DESIGN AND DEVELOPMENT INC. (In Formation) John A. Goodman, President." DDS knew that the Building Design corporation was not yet in existence. On November 1, Goodman filed articles of incorporation. Between August and December 1979 DDS made five progress payments on the contract. The first check was made out to "Building Design and Development Inc.—John Goodman." Goodman struck out his name and endorsed the check "Bldg. Design & Dev. Inc., John A. Goodman, Pres." He instructed DDS to make further payments to the corporation only, and DDS did so. The court held that Goodman was liable on the contract:

> ... The fact that a contracting party knows that the corporation is nonexistent does not indicate any agreement to release the promoter. To the contrary, such knowledge alone would seem to indicate that the members of DDS intended to make Goodman a party to the contract. They could not hold the corporation, a nonexistent entity, responsible and of course they would expect to have recourse against someone (Goodman) if default occurred....

> The only other evidence of the parties' intent to make the corporation the sole party to the contract is that the progress payments were made payable to the corporation. However, they were so written only at the instruction of Goodman and in fact the first check written by DDS after the signing of the contract was written to the corporation *and* Goodman as an individual. This evidence does not show by reasonable certainty that DDS intended to contract only with the corporation....

In contrast, in Company Stores Development Corp. v. Pottery Warehouse, Inc., 733 S.W.2d 886 (Tenn.App.1987), Company Stores leased a store to Pottery Warehouse, Inc., for five years. Pottery

Warehouse was not incorporated at the time of the lease. The lease recited that the corporation was to be organized, and was signed as follows:

THE POTTERY WAREHOUSE, INC.

a corporation to be formed under the laws of the State of Tennessee

BY *Jane M. Vosseller*

> *Its President*. . . .

The court held that the promoter was not liable:

> In the instant case, the stipulations of fact establish the plaintiff intended to look solely to Pottery Warehouse, Inc., for satisfaction of the obligation arising under the lease at the time of execution. At the time the lease was signed, plaintiff was aware of the nonexistence of the corporate entity and did not require Vosseller to sign the agreement in an individual capacity but as a president of a future corporate entity. The lease imputes no intention on the part of Vosseller to be bound personally.

(b) *Liability of the corporation.* A corporation that is formed after a promoter has entered into a contract on its behalf is not bound by the contract, without more. The reason is that the corporation was not in existence when the contract was made, and therefore did not authorize—and indeed could not have authorized—the promoter to enter into the contract on its behalf. However, after the corporation has been formed it may become bound in one of several ways. "The usual grounds that have been suggested are ratification, adoption, novation, and that the proposition made to the promoters is a continuing offer to be accepted or rejected by the corporation when it comes into being, and upon acceptance becomes an original contract on its part; and the liability has also been sustained on the ground that the corporation, by accepting the benefits of a contract, takes it cum onere, and is estopped to deny its liability on the contract." Clifton v. Tomb, 21 F.2d 893 (4th Cir.1927). In Illinois Controls, Inc. v. Langham, 70 Ohio St.3d 512, 639 N.E.2d 771 (1994), the court held that if a promoter is liable under a contract under the law of promoter's liability, the fact that the corporation also becomes liable on the contract, by adopting it, does not relieve the promoter of liability. Instead, in such a case the promoter and the corporation are jointly and severally liable.

———

RESTATEMENT (SECOND) OF AGENCY § 326

[See Statutory Supplement]

———

RESTATEMENT (THIRD) OF CONTRACTS § 6.04

[See Statutory Supplement]

————

SECTION 5. CONSEQUENCES OF DEFECTIVE INCORPORATION

————

MODEL BUS. CORP. ACT §§ 2.03, 2.04

[See Statutory Supplement]

————

DEL. GEN. CORP. LAW §§ 106, 329

[See Statutory Supplement]

————

NOTE ON DEFECTIVE INCORPORATION

Sometimes there is a defect in the process of forming a corporation. For example, the certificate of incorporation may fail to include a required provision in proper form, or may not be properly filed. The issue then arises, what is the effect of the defect on the corporation's status. This issue is usually put in terms of whether a corporation exists de jure, de facto, by estoppel, or not at all. The problem arises most commonly when a third party seeks to hold the would-be shareholders personally liable on the ground that corporate status was not attained, and therefore neither was limited liability. The problem may also arise in a quo warranto proceeding brought by the state to test the validity of corporate statutes. Most states provide by statute for such proceedings, often without using the term "quo warranto." See, e.g., N.Y. Bus. Corp. Law § 109; Cal. Corp. Code § 180(a). This form of proceeding derives from an ancient prerogative writ issued on behalf of the King against one who falsely claimed an office or franchise.

1. *De Jure Corporation.* A de jure corporation is a corporation organized in compliance with the requirements of the state of incorporation. A de jure corporation's status cannot be attacked by either private parties or the state. People v. Ford, 128 N.E. 479 (Ill. 1920). Most courts hold that perfect compliance with the statutory requirements for incorporation is not required to attain de jure status. Instead, *substantial compliance* will suffice. Therefore, an enterprise that fails to meet all the requirements for incorporation may nevertheless be a de jure corporation if the noncompliance is insubstantial. What constitutes substantial compliance is determined on a case-by-case basis, according to the nature of the unsatisfied requirement and the extent to which compliance has been attempted. For example, if

the certificate of incorporation was properly filed except that the address for the corporation's principal place of business inadvertently stated the wrong street number, there would undoubtedly be substantial compliance. Also, some courts hold that for a corporation to attain de jure status there must be exact compliance with all *mandatory* statutory requirements, but that failure to comply with requirements that are only *directory* will not will not preclude de jure status. See, e.g., J.W. Butler Paper Co. v. Cleveland, 77 N.E. 99 (Ill. 1906). Whether a particular requirement is mandatory or directory for this purpose is a matter of statutory interpretation. For example, in People v. Ford, supra, the Illinois attorney general filed a proceeding, in the nature of a quo warranto, against three incorporators who had failed to comply with a statutory requirement that the certificate of incorporation be sealed. The incorporators had used incorporation forms provided by the office of the Illinois secretary of state. These forms neither contained nor mentioned a seal. The court concluded that the corporation had de jure status. The provision for a seal was only directory, the court said, because the purpose of the statute was to make a public record and a seal did not further that purpose.

2. *De facto Corporation.* A *de facto* corporation is said to exist when there is insufficient compliance to constitute a de jure corporation vis-a-vis a challenge by *the state*, but the steps taken toward formation of a corporation are sufficient to treat the enterprise as a corporation with respect to *third parties*. In such cases, the corporate status can be invalidated by the state through quo warranto proceedings, but not by creditors or other persons who have had dealings with the enterprise. A de facto corporation requires a colorable attempt to incorporate and some actual use or exercise of corporate privileges. For example, in Cantor v. Sunshine Greenery, Inc., 398 A.2d 571 (N.J. 1979), on November 21, B reserved the corporate name, "Sunshine Greenery, Inc." with the secretary of state. On December 3, B and C executed a certificate of incorporation and sent it by mail to the secretary of state, along with a check for the filing fee. On December 16, Sunshine Greenery entered into a lease. For some unexplained reason, the certificate of incorporation was not officially filed until December 18, two days after the execution of a lease by Sunshine Greenery. The court held that Sunshine greenery was a de facto corporation prior to December 18, and therefore B and C were not personally liable on the lease. (Note that quo warranto proceedings can be maintained against a de facto corporation, because de facto theory is a defense only against a "collateral attack" on corporate status—in effect, only against a challenge raised by private actors—not against a challenge by the state itself.)

3. *Estoppel.* In many cases in which neither a de jure nor a de facto corporation has been formed, the courts have held that a party who has dealt with an enterprise on the basis that it is a corporation is estopped from denying the enterprise's corporate status. Neither the precise contours of the estoppel theory nor its relationship to the de facto theory has ever been entirely clear. It is sometimes said that the estoppel theory differs from the de facto theory in that estoppel is

effective for only a specific transaction. However, the de facto theory also may be effective only for a specific transaction: A decision in one suit that a corporation has de facto status will normally not be res judicata in a suit brought by an unrelated plaintiff on an unrelated transaction.

As a practical matter, however, there is likely to be a difference between the *precedential* effect of decisions based on estoppel theory and decisions based on de facto theory. Because a decision based on estoppel theory will normally turn heavily on the plaintiff's conduct, it may have only a limited precedential effect on future cases involving other plaintiffs and other transactions. In contrast, a decision based on de facto theory will normally turn on the defendant's conduct in attempting to organize a corporation. Because that conduct will be the focus of any future de facto case involving those defendants, a decision that a de facto corporation was formed by the conduct may have a significant precedential effect.

A problem with the estoppel theory is that in fact it is not a single theory, but a cluster of very different rules covering cases that fall into very different categories, only one of which involves a true estoppel, that is, reliance by one party on the other's representation.

   (i)   *Denial of corporate status by the would-be shareholders*. In one kind of estoppel case, an enterprise and its owners, who engage in a transaction with a third party, T, claim at the time that the enterprise is a corporation. Later, T brings suit against the purported corporation and the enterprise, and its owners deny that the enterprise is a corporation. This is a true estoppel case, at least if T relied on the initial claim of corporate status.

   (ii)   *Technical contexts*. In another kind of estoppel case, the question of corporate status is raised in a technical, procedural context. For example, in a suit brought by a would-be corporation, the defendant may seek to raise the defense that the plaintiff is not really a corporation and therefore cannot sue in a corporate name. The courts tend to regard such defenses as nonmeritorious and to brush them off, using "estoppel" as a handy tool to do so.

   (iii)   *Liability of would-be shareholders*. In the most important category of estoppel cases, a third party who has dealt with an enterprise on the basis that it is a corporation seeks to impose personal liability on the would-be shareholders, who in turn raise estoppel as a defense. Here the issue is whether, as a matter of equity, the claimant, having dealt with the enterprise as if it were a corporation, should be prevented—"estopped"—from treating it as anything else. A leading case in this category is Cranson v. International Business Mach. Corp., 234 Md. 477, 200 A.2d 33 (1964). I.B.M. had sold typewriters to Real Estate Service Bureau on credit. I.B.M. dealt with Bureau as if Bureau were a corporation. In fact it wasn't, because, without the knowledge of the would-be shareholders, their attorney had negligently failed to file the certificate of incorporation before the transaction with the third party. The court held that the estoppel doctrine can be applied to shield the would-be shareholders from personal liability even when a would-be corporation does not have de facto existence. Although the organizational defects in the case might have prevented the Bureau from being a de facto corporation, "we think that I.B.M. having dealt with the Bureau as if it were a corporation and relied on its credit rather than that of [the would-be shareholders], is estopped to assert that the Bureau was not incorporated at the time the typewriters were purchased."

In this third category of cases, estoppel theory is comparable in its function to de facto theory. However, the two theories differ in two important ways in their application:

First, the nub of estoppel theory in such cases is that the third party has dealt with the business as if it were a corporation. Presumably, therefore, the theory would not apply to a tort claimant or other involuntary creditor who was a stranger to the business before his claim arose. In contrast, the de facto theory can be applied to such claimants.

Second, the would-be shareholders would not need to resort to the estoppel theory if they could establish that their business had de facto corporate status. Presumably, therefore, less in the way of corporateness must be shown to establish a corporation by estoppel than to establish a de facto corporation. (Thus in Cranson v. International Business Mach., supra, the court applied the estoppel theory only after observing that because the certificate of incorporation had not been filed at the time of the transaction, the de facto theory might not be applicable.)

There is an obvious relationship between the first and second points. A tort claimant or other involuntary creditor has a stronger claim against would-be shareholders than a contract creditor, because a contract creditor who transacts with a would-be corporation expects only limited liability, while the expectation of a typical tort or other involuntary creditor is usually not so limited. Accordingly, it should be easier for would-be shareholders to assert limited liability against a contact creditor than against a tort creditor. This result is accomplished by estoppel theory, which allows easier assertion of limited liability than does de facto theory, but is effectively limited to contract creditors.

4. *Who May Be Held Liable.* If a would-be corporation is neither a de jure nor a de facto corporation, nor a corporation by estoppel, the courts have divided on which would-be shareholders may be held personally liable for debts incurred in the corporation's name. Older decisions imposed personal liability against all of the would-be shareholders, on the theory that if the enterprise is not a corporation, it is a partnership, and therefore the would-be shareholders are general partners. Harrill v. Davis, 168 F. 187 (8th Cir. 1909). The modern trend, however, imposes personal liability only against those owners who actively participated in the management of the business. Those owners who actively participated are held personally liable as if they were partners, but passive investors are not. Baker v. Bates–Street

Shirt Co., 6 F.2d 854 (1st Cir. 1925). Model Business Corporation Act § 2.04 takes a different approach. Under that provision, only persons acting as or on behalf of a corporation who *know* there was no incorporation are jointly and severally liable for the would-be corporation's liabilities. This provision protects would-be shareholders of defectively formed corporations in cases where the would-be shareholders honestly and reasonably, although erroneously, believed that a corporation had been properly formed. Model Act § 2.04 eliminates much but not necessarily all of the need for estoppel doctrine. According to the Comment to section 2.04:

> While no special provision is made in section 2.04, the section does not foreclose the possibility that persons who urge defendants to execute contracts in the corporate name knowing that no steps to incorporate have been taken may be estopped to impose personal liability on individual defendants. This estoppel may be based on the inequity perceived when persons, unwilling or reluctant to enter into a commitment under their own name, are persuaded to use the name of a nonexistent corporation, and then are sought to be held personally liable under section 2.04 by the party advocating that form of execution. By contrast, persons who knowingly participate in a business under a corporate name are jointly and severally liable on ''corporate'' obligations under section 2.04 and may not argue that plaintiffs are ''estopped'' from holding them personally liable because all transactions were conducted on a corporate basis.

McCHESNEY, DOCTRINAL ANALYSIS AND STATISTICAL MODELING IN LAW: THE CASE OF DEFECTIVE INCORPORATION, 71 Wash. U. L.Q. 493, 498–99 (1993). ''Three requirements are typically cited for application of the de facto corporation doctrine. There must have been: (1) a statute in existence by which incorporation was legally possible; (2) a 'colorable' attempt to comply with the statute; and (3) some actual use or exercise of corporate privileges. Because every state has a corporation statute and defendants ordinarily have been acting under the aegis of a supposed corporation, the three factors typically dissolve into one: whether defendants' attempts to incorporate had gone far enough to be deemed 'colorable compliance.' For example, an attempt to file the articles of incorporation, albeit unsuccessful, has frequently sufficed as the necessary attempt at statutory compliance. 'In addition, some cases and commentators have added good faith of corporation or associates as a fourth element. [The good faith requirement] is often omitted, however, because a colorable compliance with the incorporation statute usually encompasses a good faith attempt to incorporate.' ''

SECTION 6.   THE CLASSICAL ULTRA VIRES DOCTRINE

INTRODUCTORY NOTE

1. *The Classical Ultra Vires Doctrine*. Under the classical theory of corporate existence, the corporation is regarded as a fictitious person, endowed with life and capacity only insofar as provided in its charter. Early corporate charters tended to narrowly circumscribe the activities in which a corporation could permissibly engage. Transactions outside that sphere were characterized by the courts as *ultra vires* (beyond the corporation's power) and unenforceable—unenforceable *against* the corporation because beyond the corporation's powers, and unenforceable *by* the corporation on the ground of lack of mutuality. A leading example is Ashbury Railway Carriage & Iron Co. v. Riche, 7 L.R.–Eng. & Ir.App. 653, 33 L.T.R. 450 (1875). Ashbury was authorized by its charter "to make and sell, or lend on hire, railway-carriages and wagons, and all kinds of railway plant, fittings, machinery, and rolling-stock; to carry on the business of mechanical engineers and general contractors; to purchase and sell, as merchants, timber, coal, metals, or other materials; and to buy and sell any such materials on commission, or as agents." 7 L.R.–Eng. & Ir.App. at 654. Ashbury purchased a concession to construct and operate a railway line in Belgium, and Riche contracted to do the construction. After Riche had done some of the work, Ashbury repudiated the contract. Riche brought suit. The House of Lords held for Ashbury on the ground that it lacked the power under its charter to build a railroad, and therefore lacked the power to contract for that purpose.

The original purpose of the ultra vires doctrine seems to have been to protect the public or the state from unsanctioned corporate activity. Accordingly, under classical English law even unanimous shareholder ratification would not be a bar to an ultra vires defense if the transaction was outside the objects of the corporation. See *Ashbury*, supra; Frommel, Reform of the Ultra Vires Rule: A Personal View, 8 The Company Lawyer 11 (1987).

2. *Powers and Purposes*. In theory, the classical ultra vires doctrine was applicable to two somewhat different kinds of questions. The first question was whether a corporation had acted beyond its *purposes*, that is, had engaged in a type of business activity not permitted under its certificate. The second question was whether the corporation had exercised a *power* not specified in its certificate. In practice, the two questions tended to merge. For example, certificates of incorporation commonly contained clauses that described the corporation's various purposes and powers as both purposes and powers.

3. *Recurring Problems*. A number of problems concerning specific types of corporate transactions tended to recur under the classical vires doctrine. One of these recurring problems concerned the power of a corporation to guarantee a third party's debts. Early cases often held that such guarantees were ultra vires in the absence of a provision in the certificate of incorporation that explicitly conferred the power to guarantee. See, e.g., Brinson v. Mill Supply Co., 219 N.C. 498, 14 S.E.2d 505 (1941). Present-day statutes make this problem

moot by explicitly empowering corporations to make guarantees. See, e.g., Del. Gen. Corp. Law § 123.

Another recurring problem concerned the power of a corporation to be a general partner. Early cases often held that a corporation had no power to enter into a partnership unless that power was explicitly granted by a statute or by the certificate of incorporation. See, e.g., Whittenton Mills v. Upton, 76 Mass. (10 Gray) 582 (1858); Central R.R. Co. v. Collins, 40 Ga. 582 (1869). The concern was that a corporate partner would be bound by the acts and decisions of copartners who were not its duly appointed officers, thereby improperly impinging on the board's power and duty to manage the corporation. (The cases did permit corporations to enter into joint ventures, which are usually temporary in nature and created for a limited purpose.) Present-day statutes make this problem moot by explicitly empowering corporations to become partners. See, e.g., Del. Gen. Corp. Law § 122(11); N.Y.Bus.Corp.Law § 202(15); Model Bus. Corp. Act § 3.02(9).

4. *Limitations on the Ultra Vires Doctrine.* Ultra vires was always regarded by the commentators as an unsound doctrine. For example, Ballantine, writing in 1927, argued that "in general the objects and purposes clause of the articles should operate simply like by-laws or articles of partnership, as limitations on the actual authority of the directors and officers to bind the corporation, but not upon their ostensible or apparent authority, unless reasonably to be inferred or actually known." Ballantine, Proposed Revision of the Ultra Vires Doctrine, 12 Cornell L.Q. 453, 455 (1927). Neither the courts nor, for the most part, the legislatures, ever went quite that far, but the history of the doctrine is one of steady erosion by the courts and the bar, resulting in large part from the widespread view that the doctrine was unsound. This erosion proceeded along a variety of fronts:

(i) It was established even in early cases that corporate powers could be implied as well as explicit. See Sutton's Hospital Case, 10 Coke 23a (1613). The courts eventually became very liberal in finding implied powers, including implied powers to enter into business activities not specified in the certificate. Thus in Jacksonville, Mayport, Pablo Ry. & Navigation Co. v. Hooper, 160 U.S. 514, 526, 16 S.Ct. 379, 40 L.Ed. 515 (1896), the Supreme Court held that a Florida company whose purpose, under its charter, was to run a railroad, could also engage in leasing and running a resort hotel. "Undoubtedly the main business of a corporation is to be confined to that class of operations which properly appertain to the general purposes for which its charter was granted. But it may also enter into and engage in transactions which are auxiliary or incidental to its main business." Similarly, in John B. Waldbillig, Inc. v. Gottfried, 22 A.D.2d 997, 254 N.Y.S.2d 924 (1964), aff'd 16 N.Y.2d 773, 209 N.E.2d 818, 262 N.Y.S.2d 498 (1965), the court held that a corporation organized to "engage in the business of building, construction, and contracting" could have incidental or implied power to practice engineering.

(ii) Generally speaking, ultra vires was not a defense to corporate tort or criminal liability. Furthermore, even in areas where ultra vires was a defense, it could not be used to reverse completed transactions. Accordingly, the major impact of the doctrine was confined to executory contracts.

(iii) Even as applied to executory contracts, the ambit of the doctrine was limited. The difficult case occurred where only one party had performed under the contract, and the nonperforming party then sought to assert ultra vires as a defense for its nonperformance. Under the majority view, the nonperforming party, having received a benefit under the contract, was "estopped" from asserting the ultra vires defense. See, e.g., Joseph Schlitz Brewing Co. v. Missouri Poultry & Game Co., 287 Mo. 400, 229 S.W. 813 (1921). Under the minority view—known as the "federal rule"—part performance did not have an estoppel effect, on the theory that an ultra vires contract was prohibited by law and therefore void. Even the cases taking this view, however, usually permitted the performing party to recover in restitution for the value of any benefit conferred. See Central Transportation Co. v. Pullman's Palace Car Co., 139 U.S. 24, 11 S.Ct. 478, 35 L.Ed. 55 (1891).

(iv) Under American law, unanimous shareholder approval barred the ultra vires defense unless creditors would be injured. See Note, 83 U.Pa.L.Rev. 479, 488–92 (1935).

(v) The final source of erosion of the ultra vires doctrine was the decreasing significance of the certificate of incorporation as a limit on the corporation's purposes and powers. Draftsmen began writing endless and crushingly boring certificate-of-incorporation provisions that enumerated every possible business purpose and power imaginable. Eventually, most statutes made this kind of draftsmanship unnecessary, by stating that the certificate of incorporation could provide simply that the corporation could engage in any lawful business, and by setting out a laundry list of powers that are conferred on every corporation even without enumeration in the certificate.

(vi) The next step, going beyond mere erosion, was the adoption in modern statutes of provisions that almost (but not quite) abolish the ultra vires doctrine. The Delaware and Model Act provisions in the following cross-references are examples. Similar statutes have been adopted in all but a few states. See Schaeftler, Ultra Vires–Ultra Useless: The Myth of State Interest in Ultra Vires Acts of Business Corporations, 9 J.Corp.Law 81, 81–83 & n. 6 (1983).

———

DEL. GEN. CORP. LAW §§ 101(b), 102(a)(3), 121, 122, 124

[See Statutory Supplement]

———

MODEL BUS. CORP. ACT §§ 3.01(a), 3.02, 3.04

[See Statutory Supplement]

———

Goodman v. Ladd Estate Co.

Supreme Court of Oregon, 1967.
246 Or. 621, 427 P.2d 102.

■ Before McAllister, C.J., and Sloan, Goomwin, Holman[2] and Lusk, JJ.

■ Lusk, Justice.

Plaintiffs brought this suit to enjoin the defendant Ladd Estate Company, a Washington corporation, from enforcing a guaranty agreement executed by Westover Tower, Inc., a corporation, in favor of Ladd Estate. From a decree dismissing the suit plaintiffs appeal.

In 1961 the defendant Walter T. Liles[1] held all the common shares of Westover and he, Dr. Edmond F. Wheatley and Samuel H. Martin were its directors.

On September 8, 1961, Dr. Wheatley borrowed $10,000 from Citizens Bank of Oregon and gave his promissory note therefor, which was endorsed by Ladd Estate. Contemporaneously with this transaction Liles, individually, and Westover, by Liles as president, and Martin, as secretary, executed an agreement in writing by which they unconditionally guaranteed Ladd Estate against loss arising out of the latter's endorsement of the Wheatley note to Citizens Bank. The agreement was also signed by Ladd Estate. It recited that it was made at the request of Liles and Westover and that Ladd Estate would not have guaranteed payment of the Wheatley note without the guarantee of Liles and Westover to Ladd Estate.

Wheatley defaulted on his note, Ladd Estate paid to Citizens Bank the amount owing thereon, $9,583.61, and demanded reimbursement from Westover. Upon the latter's rejection of the demand Ladd filed an action at law upon the guaranty agreement against Liles and Westover.

The plaintiffs Morton J. Goodman and Edith Goodman, husband and wife, came into the case in this manner: On September 27, 1963, plaintiffs purchased all the common shares of Westover from a receiver appointed by the Circuit Court for Multnomah County who was duly authorized to make such sale. At the time of such purchase, plaintiffs were fully aware of the guaranty agreement given by Westover and Liles to Ladd Estate. It is conceded that the guaranty agreement was ultra vires the corporation. Plaintiffs, as stockholders, brought this suit pursuant to the provisions of ORS 57.040. [ORS 57.040 is comparable to Del.G.C.L. § 124, supra] . . . .

It will be noticed that the court may set aside and enjoin the performance of the ultra vires contract if it deems such a course equitable. Plaintiffs argue that to deny them the relief they seek would be "shocking," because Westover executed the guaranty agreement in order to enable one of its directors, Wheatley, to obtain a loan of money to be used for purposes entirely foreign to any corporate

2. Did not participate in this decision. (Footnote by the court.)

1. Pursuant to stipulation, the suit was dismissed as to Liles and Westover. The stipulation provided that "this suit may proceed in the same manner as if the said Walter T. Liles and Westover Tower, Inc. were parties hereto."

purpose. We see nothing shocking or even inequitable about it. The corporation was organized for the purposes, among others, to engage in the business of providing housing for rent or sale and to obtain contracts of mortgage insurance from the Federal Housing Commissioner, pursuant to the provisions of the National Housing Act, 12 U.S.C.A. § 1701 et seq. Authorized capital stock comprised 30,100 shares of which 100 shares, having a par value of $1 per share and designated preferred stock, were issued to the Commissioner, pursuant to § 1743(b)(1), U.S.C.A. and 30,000 shares, having a par value of $1 per share and designated common stock, were issued to Liles. Voting rights of the shareholders were vested exclusively in the holders of the common stock. The guaranty agreement recites that, at the request of Liles and Westover, Ladd Estate guaranteed payment of the Wheatley note. Ladd Estate made good on its endorsement when Wheatley defaulted and now calls upon Westover to honor its obligation. The agent of the plaintiffs, who purchased the shares for them, testified that he considered the question whether the guaranty was a valid obligation of the corporation before making the purchase and concluded that it was not. The fact that he guessed wrong does not in any way enhance plaintiffs' claim to equitable consideration.

Neither would it be inequitable to enforce the agreement because of the purpose which the guaranty was intended to serve. Even before the enactment of ORS 57.040 a corporation might properly enter into a guaranty agreement in the legitimate furtherance of its business or purposes: Depot R. Syndicate v. Enterprise B. Co., 87 Or. 560, 562, 170 P. 294, 171 P. 223, L.R.A. 1918C, 1001; 19 Am.Jur.2d 493, Corporations § 1030; that the agreement does not further such purposes is what makes it ultra vires. But the statute says the agreement is enforceable even though ultra vires, and to accept the plaintiffs' argument would be to say that because it is ultra vires the agreement is inequitable and, therefore, unenforceable. This would effectually emasculate the statute.

Moreover, plaintiffs are in no position to invoke the aid of a court of equity. Liles, the former holder of their shares—all the voting shares of Westover—induced Ladd Estate to endorse Wheatley's note by procuring Westover to execute the guaranty agreement. If a shareholder himself has participated in the ultra vires act he cannot thereafter attack it as ultra vires: 7 Fletcher, Cyc. of Corporations (perm. ed., 1964 rev.) 613, § 3453. This would seem to be emphatically so of a shareholder who exercises the entire voting power of the corporation. Plaintiffs, as purchasers of Liles' shares, are in no better position than he would have been to raise the question: McCampbell v. Fountain Head R. Co., 111 Tenn. 55, 75, 77 S.W. 1070, 102 Am.St.Rep. 731; 7 Fletcher, op. cit. 614, § 3456.

It should be added that no rights of creditors of Westover are involved and there is nothing to indicate that the security of any mortgage guaranteed by the Federal Housing Commissioner would be impaired by enforcement of the agreement here in question....

We are of the opinion that plaintiffs are not entitled to equitable relief. The decree is affirmed.

———

INTER–CONTINENTAL CORP. v. MOODY, 411 S.W.2d 578 (Tex. Civ.App.1966). Inter–Continental Corp., a Texas corporation, guaranteed a note given by Shively, Inter–Continental's president, to Moody. Moody knew or should have known that Inter–Continental's guarantee was given for Shively's personal benefit. Subsequently, Shively lost control of Inter–Continental, and Inter–Continental refused to pay the note. Moody then brought suit on the guarantee. Texas had a statute comparable to Del.Gen.Corp.Law § 124. Inter–Continental defended against Moody on the ground that the note was ultra vires. It also arranged for a minority shareholder to intervene to enjoin payment of the note on the same ground. Inter–Continental's attorney drafted the shareholder's petition and promised to pay his legal expenses. The court held that the defense of ultra vires by Inter–Continental was barred under the statute, even if the third party actually knew that the corporation lacked authority to enter into the transaction. However, the court continued, a shareholder can intervene to enjoin an ultra vires act even if he has been solicited to do so by the corporation, provided the shareholder is not the corporation's agent.

———

711 KINGS HIGHWAY CORP. v. F.I.M.'S MARINE REPAIR SERV. INC., 51 Misc.2d 373, 273 N.Y.S.2d 299 (Spec.Term 1966). Kings Highway leased a motion-picture theater to Marine Repair for fifteen years, beginning July 1, 1966. Before July 1, Kings Highway brought an action for a declaratory judgment to invalidate the lease on the ground that it was void because it would be ultra vires for Marine Repair to conduct a motion-picture theater business. The New York statute, Bus.Corp.Law § 203, was comparable to Del.Gen.Corp.Law § 124. Held, for Marine Repair. "It is undisputed that the present case does not fall within the stated exceptions contained in Section 203.... Neither is there merit to the plaintiff's contention that Section 203 applies only where ultra vires is raised as a defense. Notwithstanding the fact that this section is entitled 'Defense of ultra vires' it seems that except in the three stated situations set forth in the section, which are not applicable to the instant case, ultra vires may not be invoked as a sword in support of a cause of action any more than it can be utilized as a defense...."

SECTION 7.   THE OBJECTIVE AND CONDUCT OF THE CORPORATION

The question considered in this Section is, to what extent may a corporation act in a manner that is not intended to maximize corporate profits. This question is often put in terms of whether a given act would be "ultra vires," but it penetrates much more deeply into the nature of the corporate institution, and its place in society, than does the classical ultra vires issue.

―――――

(a) THE SHAREHOLDERS' INTERESTS, THE PRESENT-VALUE RULE, AND DIVERSIFICATION

―――――

Richard A. Brealey & Stewart C. Myers Principles of Corporate Finance
Seventh ed., 2003.*

INTRODUCTION TO PRESENT VALUE ...

Your apartment house has burned down, fortunately without injury to you or your employees, leaving you with a vacant lot worth $50,000 and a check for $200,000 from the fire insurance company. You consider rebuilding, but your real estate adviser suggests putting up an office building instead. The construction cost would be $300,000, and there would also be the cost of the land, which might otherwise be sold for $50,000. On the other hand, your adviser foresees a shortage of office space and predicts that a year from now the new building would fetch $400,000 if you sold it. Thus you would be investing $350,000 now in the expectation of realizing $400,000 a year hence. You should go ahead if the **present value (PV)** of the expected $400,000 payoff is greater than the investment of $350,000. Therefore, you need to ask yourself, "What is the value today of $400,000 to be received one year from now, and is that present value greater than $350,000?"

Calculating Present Value

The present value of $400,000 one year from now must be less than $400,000. After all, *a dollar today is worth more than a dollar tomorrow,* because the dollar today can be invested to start earning interest immediately. This is the first basic principle of finance. Thus, the present value of a delayed payoff may be found by multiplying the payoff by a discount factor which is less than 1. (If the discount factor were more than 1, a dollar today would be worth *less* than a dollar tomorrow.) If C_1 denotes the expected payoff at time period 1 (1 year hence), then

$$\text{Present value (PV)} = \text{discount factor} \times C_1$$

This discount factor is expressed as the reciprocal of 1 plus a *rate of return:*

$$\text{Discount factor} = \frac{1}{1 + r}$$

The rate of return r is the reward that investors demand for accepting delayed payment.

Now we can value the real estate investment, assuming for the moment that the $400,000 payoff is a sure thing. The office building is not the only way to obtain $400,000 a year from now. You could invest in United States government securities maturing in a year. Suppose these securities yield 7 percent interest. How much would you have to invest in them in order to receive $400,000 at the end of the year? That's easy: you would have to invest $400,000/1.07, which is $373,832. Therefore, at an interest rate of 7 percent, the present value of $400,000 1 year from now is $373,832.

Let's assume that, as soon as you've committed the land and begun construction on the building, you decide to sell your project. How much could you sell it for? That's another easy question. Since the property produces $400,000, investors would be willing to pay $373,832 for it today. That's what it would cost them to get a $400,000 payoff from investing in government securities. Of course you could always sell your property for less, but why sell for less than the market will bear? The $373,832 present value is the only feasible price that satisfies both buyer and seller. Therefore, the present value of the property is also its market price.

To calculate present value, we discount expected future payoffs by the rate of return offered by comparable investment alternatives in the capital markets. This rate of return is often referred to as the **discount rate, hurdle rate,** or **opportunity cost of capital.** It is called the *opportunity cost* because it is the return forgone by investing in the project rather than investing in securities. In our example the opportunity cost was 7 percent. Present value was obtained by dividing $400,000 by 1.07:

$$\text{PV} = \text{discount factor} \times C_1 = \frac{1}{1 + r} \times C_1 = \frac{400,000}{1.07} = \$373,832$$

Net Present Value

The building is worth $373,832, but this does not mean that you are $373,832 better off. You committed $350,000, and therefore your **net present value (NPV)** is $23,832. Net present value (**NPV**) is found by subtracting the required investment:

$$\text{NPV} = \text{PV} \times \text{required investment} = 373,832 - 350,000 = \$23,832$$

In other words, your office development is worth more than it costs— it makes a *net* contribution to value. The formula for calculating NPV can be written as

$$\text{NPV} = C_0 + \frac{C_1}{1 + r}$$

remembering that C_0, the cash flow at time period 0 (that is, today) will usually be a negative number. In other words, C_0 is an investment and therefore a cash *outflow.* In our example, $C_0 = -\$350,000$.

A Comment on Present Value

We made one unrealistic assumption in our discussion of the office development: Your real estate adviser cannot be *certain* about future values of office buildings. The $400,000 figure represents the best *forecast,* but it is not a sure thing.

If the future value of the building is risky, our calculation of NPV is wrong. Investors could achieve $400,000 with certainty by buying $373,832 worth of United States government securities, so they would not buy your building for that amount. You would have to cut your asking price to attract investors' interest.

Here we can invoke a second basic financial principle: *A safe dollar is worth more than a risky one.* Most investors avoid risk when they can do so without sacrificing return. However, the concepts of present value and the opportunity cost of capital still make sense for risky investments. It is still proper to discount the payoff by the rate of return offered by a comparable investment. But we have to think of *expected* payoffs and the *expected* rates of return on other investments.

Not all investments are equally risky. The office development is riskier than a government security but is probably less risky than a start-up biotech venture. Suppose you believe the project is as risky as investment in the stock market and that stock market investments are forecasted to return 12 percent. Then 12 percent becomes the appropriate opportunity cost of capital. That is what you are giving up by not investing in comparable securities. You can now recompute NPV:

$$PV = \frac{400,000}{1.12} = \$357,143$$

$$NPV = PV - 350,000 = \$7143$$

If other investors agree with your forecast of a $400,000 payoff and your assessment of a its risk, then your property ought to be worth $357,143 once construction is under way. If you tried to sell it for more than that, there would be no takers, because the property would then offer an expected rate of return lower than the 12 percent available in the stock market. The office building still makes a net contribution to value, but it is much smaller than our earlier calculations indicated.

The value of the office building depends on the timing of the cash flows and their uncertainty. The $400,000 payoff would be worth exactly that if it could be realized instantaneously. If the office building is as risk-free as government securities, the one–year delay reduces value to $373,382. If the office building is as risky as investment in the stock market, then uncertainty reduces value by a further $16,689 to $357,143....

Present Values and Rates of Return

We have decided that construction of the office building is a smart thing to do, since it is worth more than it costs—it has a positive net present value. To calculate how much it is worth, we worked out how much one would have to pay to achieve the same income by investing directly in securities. The project's present value is equal to its future income discounted at the rate of return offered by these securities.

We can say this in another way: Our property venture is worth undertaking because its rate of return exceeds the cost of capital. The return on the capital invested is simply the profit as a proportion of the initial outlay:

$$\text{Return} = \frac{\text{profit}}{\text{investment}} = \frac{400{,}000 - 350{,}000}{350{,}000} = .14 \text{ or } 14\%$$

The cost of capital is once again the return forgone by *not* investing in securities. In our present case, if the office building is as risky as investing in the stock market, the return forgone is 12 percent. Since the 14 percent return on the office building exceeds the 12 percent cost, you should go ahead with the project.

Here then we have two equivalent decision rules for capital investment.

1. *Net present value rule.* Accept investments that have positive net present values.

2. *Rate-of-return rule.* Accept investments that offer rates of return in excess of their opportunity costs of capital. . . .

A FUNDAMENTAL RESULT

Our justification of the present value rule was restricted to two periods and to a certain cash flow. However, the rule also makes sense for uncertain cash flows that extend far into the future. The argument goes like this:

1. A financial manager should act in the interest of the firm's owners, its stockholders. Each stockholder wants three things:

    (*a*)   To be as rich as possible, that is, to maximize current wealth.

    (*b*)   To transform that wealth into whatever time pattern of consumption he or she desires.

    (*c*)   To choose the risk characteristics of that consumption plan.

2. But stockholders do not need the financial manager's help to reach the best time pattern of consumption. They can do that on their own, providing they have free access to competitive capital markets. They can also choose the risk characteristics of their consumption plan by investing in more or less risky securities.

3. How then can the financial manager help the firm's stockholders? There is only one way: increasing the market value of each stockholder's stake in the firm. The way to do that is to seize all investment opportunities that have a positive net present value.

Despite the fact that shareholders have different preferences, they are unanimous in the amount that they want to invest in real assets. This means that they can cooperate in the same enterprise and can safely delegate operation of that enterprise to professional managers. These managers do not need to know anything about the tastes of their shareholders and should not consult their own tastes. Their task is to maximize net present value. If they succeed, they can rest assured that they have acted in the best interest of their shareholders.

This gives us the fundamental condition for successful operation of a modern capitalist economy. Separation of ownership and control is essential for most corporations, so authority to manage has to be delegated. It is good to know that managers can all be given one simple instruction: Maximize net present value.

Hu, New Financial Products, The Modern Process of Financial Innovation, and the Puzzle of Shareholder Welfare

69 Tex.L.Rev. 1273, 1278–1283 (1991).

The most basic principle of corporate law is that a corporation is to be primarily run for the pecuniary benefit of its shareholders. Apart from the impact of nonstockholder constituency statutes and notions of social responsibility generally, few would disagree with this principle as a general matter.

But what does this principle mean in the usual day-to-day operation of publicly held corporations? . . .

The traditional conception of the basic pecuniary goals of a corporation is based on the simple premise that what is good for the corporation is good for the shareholder. If corporate welfare is furthered, as through the maximization of earnings or earnings per share, shareholder welfare is presumed to be furthered as well. . . .

The traditional conception is based on two related assumptions. First, accounting-based measures such as earnings or earnings per share are appropriate indicators of corporate performance. Second, the welfare of a shareholder is largely coincident with the welfare of the corporation.

Unfortunately, both of these classic assumptions are of limited validity. Financial theorists have long argued—and corporate managers are starting to realize—that maximization of total corporate earnings or even earnings per share does not necessarily maximize shareholder wealth. Earnings growth as a sole measure of corporate performance fails to measure the risk characteristics of corporate investments, the extent of investments in working and fixed capital needed to sustain the firm, dividend policy, and the time value of money. . . .

The second assumption underlying the traditional conception, that the welfare of the corporation is coincident with the welfare of its shareholder, is also fundamentally flawed. For example, there may be a conflict of interest concerning risk between the corporation and its shareholders.... [M]odern financial theory suggests that corporations concerned about the well-being of shareholders will generally take more risks than corporations concerned about the entity's own well-being; shareholders can, by holding a portfolio of stocks, diversify away much of the risk that a corporation might itself find daunting. Similarly, there may be a conflict of interest as to time. For example, from the point of view of shareholders, the best thing to do with the typical company in a dying industry may be to liquidate the company immediately, pay the net proceeds to shareholders, and allow shareholders to put the money to better use. From the point of view of the company itself—and its managers and employees—long-term decline may be preferable.

[A second, competing] conception of the pecuniary goals of a corporation is directly focused on the welfare of the shareholder. Under this view, shareholder wealth maximization is sought directly, rather than as a by-product of corporate welfare. Managers should seek to take those actions that maximize the wealth of shareholders through a combination of maximizing the actual short-or long-term trading price of each share of common stock and the dividends they actually receive. There is no focus on measures of corporate performance like accounting earnings and no concern for the corporation independent of the welfare of its shareholders.

The shift to this second conception has been gradual but discernible. Most academics now believe that shareholder wealth maximization is the basic pecuniary objective of the modern publicly held corporation. Judges have typically subscribed to this standard only in the most limited of circumstances, typically in the context of a sale of the entire company.

Hu, Risk, Time, and Fiduciary Principles in Corporate Investment

38 U.C.L.A. L.Rev. 277, 291–94, 299–300 (1990).

... *The Paramount Importance of Nondiversifiable Risk*

Assume that ... a corporation is trying to decide between Project B and Project C. [Project B has a projected return of 10%. Project C has a projected return of 15%.] The variability of returns on the two projects suggests that Project C is riskier than Project B. Thus, it follows that management should choose Project C only if it believes that the additional return [on Project C] is somehow worth the additional risk.

This view ignores diversification effects. If a shareholder invests exclusively in one corporation and that corporation invests in Project C, the shareholder would be intensely interested in what happens in a year; the one "flip of the coin" would determine whether the shareholder makes money or loses it. In a close corporation setting, the shareholder may well have all or a substantial part of his wealth in shares of one corporation. That corporation's financial welfare can be equated to the shareholder's; if the corporation does badly, the shareholder does badly.

In the typical publicly held corporation setting, however, a shareholder is usually able to avoid keeping all his eggs in one basket. Assume that the publicly held corporation ("Corporation I") invests in Project C and the economy has other publicly held corporations (Corporations II, III, IV, and so forth), each of which also invests in projects with risks and returns similar to Project C. If the shareholder can invest half his funds in Corporation I and half his funds in Corporation II, and if the economic forces affecting Corporation I and those affecting Corporation II are completely unrelated, then the chances of both such companies ending up with a loss is only 25%, not 50%; there are two flips of the coin, and there is only a 25% chance both coins would end up tails. By the simple act of investing in two companies, the investor will cut in half the possibility of disaster.

The investor could extend this diversification further. Intuition and statistics suggest that the investor who invests in 100 such corporations that in turn invest in projects with characteristics like Project C (all with flips of the coin which are completely independent of each other) is virtually certain to receive a return very close to 15%. Under these circumstances, because of diversification, Project C is really no riskier than Project B. Thus, if all of the risk associated with Projects B and C can be diversified away—if both have zero "systematic" or "nondiversifiable" risk—a corporation should invest in Project C because it provides a higher expected return than Project B.

What does this first type of diversification effect suggest to managers dedicated to maximizing shareholder wealth? If shareholders are diversified and the risk associated with a project can be diversified away, managers can concentrate on expected returns and pay relatively little attention to such "diversifiable," "unique," or "unsystematic" risk. Stated more generally, if shareholders hold diversified portfolios (as is usually presumed for publicly held corporations), corporate managers dedicated to acting consistently with shareholder optimality should pay relatively little attention to unsystematic risk in judging among investment alternatives. . . .

————

(b) INTERESTS OTHER THAN MAXIMIZATION OF THE SHAREHOLDERS' ECONOMIC WEALTH

NOTE ON DODGE v. FORD MOTOR CO.

One of the most famous of all corporation-law cases is Dodge v. Ford Motor Co., 204 Mich. 459, 170 N.W. 668 (1919). The case is unusual in its early consideration of the issue (or at least one aspect of the issue) that is now known as corporate social responsibility.

Ford Motor had been incorporated in 1903. Henry Ford owned 58% of Ford Motor's stock and controlled the board. Two Dodge brothers owned 10%, and five other shareholders owned the balance. From 1908 on, Ford Motor had paid a regular annual dividend of $1.2 million, and between December 1911 and October 1915 it paid special dividends totaling $41 million. At the close of its July 31, 1916, fiscal year, Henry Ford, who controlled the board, declared it to be the settled policy of the company not to pay in the future any special dividends, but to put back into the business for the future all of the earnings of the company, other than the regular dividend of $1.2 million. "My ambition," declared Mr. Ford, "is to employ still more men; to spread the benefits of this industrial system to the greatest possible number, to help them build up their lives and their homes. To do this, we are putting the greatest share of our profits back into the business." At the time of the announcement, Ford Motor had a surplus of $112 million, including $52.5 million in cash and $1.3 million in municipal bonds.

The Dodge brothers then brought a suit whose objects included compelling a dividend equal to 75% of the accumulated cash surplus. The trial court ordered Ford Motor to declare a dividend of $19.3 million—equal to half of its cash surplus as of July 31, 1916, minus special dividends paid between the time the complaint was filed and July 31, 1917. The Michigan Supreme Court affirmed this portion of the trial court's decree:

> When plaintiffs made their complaint and demand for further dividends the Ford Motor Company had concluded its most prosperous year of business. The demand for its cars at the price of the preceding year continued.... [I]t reasonably might have expected a profit for the year [beginning August 1, 1916], of upwards of $60,000,000.... Considering [the facts of this case] a refusal to declare and pay further dividends appears to be not an exercise of discretion on the part of the directors, but an arbitrary refusal to do what the circumstances required to be done. These facts and others call upon the directors to justify their action, or failure or refusal to act. In justification, the defendants have offered testimony [proving that: Ford Motor had a general policy to reduce the price of its cars every year while maintaining or improving quality. It could have produced 600,000 cars in the year beginning August 1, 1916, and sold them for $440 each. However, the policy of reducing prices called for the cars to be sold at $360 each, a difference of $48 million.]

> The plan, as affecting the profits of the business for the year beginning August 1, 1916, and thereafter, calls for a reduction in the selling price of the cars.... In short, the plan does not call for and is not intended to produce immediately a more profitable business but a less profitable one; not only less profitable than formerly but less profitable than it is admitted it might be made.

The apparent immediate effect will be to diminish the value of shares and the returns to shareholders.

It is the contention of plaintiffs that the apparent effect of the plan is intended . . . to continue the corporation henceforth as a semieleemosynary institution and not as a business institution. In support of this contention they point to the attitude and to the expressions of Mr. Henry Ford. . . .

. . . [Mr. Ford's] testimony creates the impression, also, that he thinks the Ford Motor Company has made too much money, has had too large profits, and that although large profits might be still earned, a sharing of them with the public, by reducing the price of the output of the company, ought to be undertaken. We have no doubt that certain sentiments, philanthropic and altruistic, creditable to Mr. Ford, had large influence in determining the policy to be pursued by the Ford Motor Company—the policy which has been herein referred to.

It is said by his counsel that—

> "Although a manufacturing corporation cannot engage in humanitarian works as its principal business, the fact that it is organized for profit does not prevent the existence of implied powers to carry on with humanitarian motives such charitable works as are incidental to the main business of the corporation." . . .

The difference between an incidental humanitarian expenditure of corporate funds for the benefit of the employees, like the building of a hospital for their use and the employment of agencies for the betterment of their condition, and a general purpose and plan to benefit mankind at the expense of others, is obvious. There should be no confusion (of which there is evidence) of the duties which Mr. Ford conceives that he and the stockholders owe to the general public and the duties which in law he and his codirectors owe to protesting, minority stockholders. A business corporation is organized and carried on primarily for the profit of the stockholders. The powers of the directors are to be employed for that end. The discretion of directors is to be exercised in the choice of means to attain that end and does not extend to a change in the end itself, to the reduction of profits or to the nondistribution of profits among stockholders in order to devote them to other purposes.

. . . As we have pointed out, and the proposition does not require argument to sustain it, it is not within the lawful powers of a board of directors to shape and conduct the affairs of a corporation for the merely incidental benefit of shareholders and for the primary purpose of benefitting others, and no one will contend that if the avowed purpose of the defendant directors was to sacrifice the interests of shareholders it would not be the duty of the courts to interfere.

A.P. Smith Mfg. Co. v. Barlow

Supreme Court of New Jersey, 1953.
13 N.J. 145, 98 A.2d 581, appeal dismissed, 346 U.S. 861, 74 S.Ct. 107, 98 L.Ed. 373 (1953).

■ JACOBS, J. The Chancery Division, in a well-reasoned opinion by Judge Stein, determined that a donation by the plaintiff The A.P. Smith Manufacturing Company to Princeton University was *intra vires*. Because of the public importance of the issues presented, the appeal duly taken to the Appellate Division has been certified directly to this court under Rule 1:5–1(*a*).

The company was incorporated in 1896 and is engaged in the manufacture and sale of valves, fire hydrants and special equipment, mainly for water and gas industries. Its plant is located in East Orange and Bloomfield and it has approximately 300 employees. Over the years the company has contributed regularly to the local community chest and on occasions to Upsala College in East Orange and Newark University, now part of Rutgers, the State University. On July 24, 1951 the board of directors adopted a resolution which set forth that it was in the corporation's best interests to join with others in the 1951 Annual Giving to Princeton University, and appropriated the sum of $1,500 to be transferred by the corporation's treasurer to the university as a contribution towards its maintenance. When this action was questioned by stockholders the corporation instituted a declaratory judgment action in the Chancery Division and trial was had in due course.

Mr. Hubert F. O'Brien, the president of the company, testified that he considered the contribution to be a sound investment, that the public expects corporations to aid philanthropic and benevolent institutions, that they obtain good will in the community by so doing, and that their charitable donations create favorable environment for their business operations. In addition, he expressed the thought that in contributing to liberal arts institutions, corporations were furthering their self-interest in assuring the free flow of properly trained personnel for administrative and other corporate employment. Mr. Frank W. Abrams, chairman of the board of the Standard Oil Company of New Jersey, testified that corporations are expected to acknowledge their public responsibilities in support of the essential elements of our free enterprise system. He indicated that it was not "good business" to disappoint "this reasonable and justified public expectation," nor was it good business for corporations "to take substantial benefits from their membership in the economic community while avoiding the normally accepted obligations of citizenship in the social community." Mr. Irving S. Olds, former chairman of the board of the United States Steel Corporation, pointed out that corporations have a self-interest in the maintenance of liberal education as the bulwark of good government. He stated that "Capitalism and free enterprise owe their survival in no small degree to the existence of our private, independent universities" and that if American business does not aid in their maintenance it is not "properly protecting the long-range interest of its stockholders, its employees and its customers." Similarly, Dr.

Harold W. Dodds, President of Princeton University, suggested that if private institutions of higher learning were replaced by governmental institutions our society would be vastly different and private enterprise in other fields would fade out rather promptly. Further on he stated that "democratic society will not long endure if it does not nourish within itself strong centers of non-governmental fountains of knowledge, opinions of all sorts not governmentally or politically originated. If the time comes when all these centers are absorbed into government, then freedom as we know it, I submit, is at an end."

The objecting stockholders have not disputed any of the foregoing testimony nor the showing of great need by Princeton and other private institutions of higher learning and the important public service being rendered by them for democratic government and industry alike. Similarly, they have acknowledged that for over two decades there has been state legislation on our books which expresses a strong public policy in favor of corporate contributions such as that being questioned by them. Nevertheless, they have taken the position that (1) the plaintiff's certificate of incorporation does not expressly authorize the contribution and under common-law principles the company does not possess any implied or incidental power to make it, and (2) the New Jersey statutes which expressly authorize the contribution may not constitutionally be applied to the plaintiff, a corporation created long before their enactment. See *R.S.* 14:3–13; *R.S.* 14:3–13.1 *et seq.*

In his discussion of the early history of business corporations Professor Williston refers to a 1702 publication where the author stated flatly that "The general intent and end of all civil incorporations is for better government." And he points out that the early corporate charters, particularly their recitals, furnish additional support for the notion that the corporate object was the public one of managing and ordering the trade as well as the private one of profit for the members. See 3 *Select Essays on Anglo–American Legal History* 201 (1909); 1 *Fletcher, Corporations (rev. ed.* 1931), 6.... However, with later economic and social developments and the free availability of the corporate device for all trades, the end of private profit became generally accepted as the controlling one in all businesses other than those classed broadly as public utilities. *Cf. Dodd, For Whom Are Corporate Managers Trustees?*, 45 Harv.L.Rev. 1145, 1148 (1932). As a concomitant the common-law rule developed that those who managed the corporation could not disburse any corporate funds for philanthropic or other worthy public cause unless the expenditure would benefit the corporation. *Hutton v. West Cork Railway Company*, 23 Ch.D. 654 (1883); *Dodge v. Ford Motor Co.*, 204 Mich. 459, 170 N.W. 668, 3 A.L.R. 413 (Sup.Ct.1919).... During the 19th Century when corporations were relatively few and small and did not dominate the country's wealth, the common-law rule did not significantly interfere with the public interest. But the 20th Century has presented a different climate. *Berle and Means, The Modern Corporation and Private Property* (1948). Control of economic wealth has passed largely from individual entrepreneurs to dominating corporations, and calls upon the corporations for reasonable philanthropic donations have come to be made with increased public support. In many instances such contributions have been sustained by the courts within the common-law doctrine upon liberal findings that the donations tended reasonably to promote the corporate objectives. . . .

. . . [C]ourts, while adhering to the terms of the common-law rule, have applied it very broadly to enable worthy corporate donations with indirect benefits to the corporations. In *State ex rel. Sorensen v. Chicago B. & Q.R. Co.*, 112 *Neb.* 248, 199 *N.W.* 534, 537 (1924), the Supreme Court of Nebraska, through Justice Letton, went even further and without referring to any limitation based on economic benefits to the corporation said that it saw . . . "no reason why a railroad corporation may not, to a reasonable extent, donate funds or services to aid in good works." . . .

When the wealth of the nation was primarily in the hands of individuals they discharged their responsibilities as citizens by donating freely for charitable purposes. With the transfer of most of the wealth to corporate hands and the imposition of heavy burdens of individual taxation, they have been unable to keep pace with increased philanthropic needs. They have therefore, with justification, turned to corporations to assume the modern obligations of good citizenship in the same manner as humans do. Congress and state legislatures have enacted laws which encourage corporate contributions, and much has recently been written to indicate the crying need and adequate legal basis therefor. . . . In actual practice corporate giving has correspondingly increased. Thus, it is estimated that annual corporate contributions throughout the nation aggregate over 300 million dollars with over 60 million dollars thereof going to universities and other educational institutions. Similarly, it is estimated that local community chests receive well over 40% of their contributions from corporations; these contributions and those made by corporations to the American Red Cross, to Boy Scouts and Girl Scouts, to 4–H Clubs and similar organizations have almost invariably been unquestioned.

During the first world war corporations loaned their personnel and contributed substantial corporate funds in order to insure survival; during the depression of the '30s they made contributions to alleviate the desperate hardships of the millions of unemployed; and during the second world war they again contributed to insure survival. They now recognize that we are faced with other, though nonetheless vicious, threats from abroad which must be withstood without impairing the vigor of our democratic institutions at home and that otherwise victory will be pyrrhic indeed. More and more they have come to recognize that their salvation rests upon sound economic and social environment which in turn rests in no insignificant part upon free and vigorous nongovernmental institutions of learning. It seems to us that just as the conditions prevailing when corporations were originally created required that they serve public as well as private interests, modern conditions require that corporations acknowledge and discharge social as well as private responsibilities as members of the communities within which they operate. Within this broad concept there is no difficulty in sustaining, as incidental to their proper objects and in aid of the public welfare, the power of corporations to contribute corporate funds within reasonable limits in support of academic institutions. But even if we confine ourselves to the terms of the common-law-rule in its application to current conditions, such expenditures may likewise readily be justified as being for the benefit of the corporation; indeed, if need be the matter may be viewed strictly in terms of actual survival of the corporation in a free enterprise system. . . .

In 1930 a statute was enacted in our State which expressly provided that any corporation could cooperate with other corporations and natural persons in the creation and maintenance of community funds and charitable, philanthropic or benevolent instrumentalities conducive to public welfare, and could for such purposes expend such corporate sums as the directors "deem expedient and as in their judgment will contribute to the protection of the corporate interests." . . . In 1950 a more comprehensive statute was enacted. *L.* 1950, *c.* 220; *N.J.S.A.* 14:3–13.1 *et seq.* In this enactment the Legislature declared that it shall be the public policy of our State and in furtherance of the public interest and welfare that encouragement be given to the creation and maintenance of institutions engaged in community fund, hospital, charitable, philanthropic, educational, scientific or benevolent activities or patriotic or civic activities conducive to the betterment of social and economic conditions; and it expressly empowered corporations acting singly or with others to contribute reasonable sums to such institutions, provided, however, that the contribution shall not be permissible if the donee institution owns more than 10% of the voting stock of the donor and provided, further, that the contribution shall not exceed 1% of capital and surplus unless the excess is authorized by the stockholders at a regular or special meeting. To insure that the grant of express power in the 1950 statute would not displace preexisting power at common law or otherwise, the Legislature provided that the "act shall not be construed as directly or indirectly minimizing or interpreting the rights and powers of corporations, as heretofore existing, with reference to appropriations, expenditures or contributions of the nature above specified." *N.J.S.A.* 14:3–13.3. It may be noted that statutes relating to charitable contributions by corporations have now been passed in 29 states. See *Andrews, supra,* 235.

The appellants contend that the foregoing New Jersey statutes may not be applied to corporations created before their passage. Fifty years before the incorporation of The A.P. Smith Manufacturing Company our Legislature provided that every corporate charter thereafter granted "shall be subject to alteration, suspension and repeal, in the discretion of the legislature." L.1846, p. 16; *R.S.* 14:2–9. A similar reserved power was placed into our State Constitution in 1875 (Art. IV, Sec. VII, par. 11), and is found in our present Constitution. . . .

. . . We are entirely satisfied that within the orbit of above authorities the legislative enactments found in *R.S.* 14:3–13 and

N.J.S.A. 14:3–13.1 *et seq.* and applied to pre-existing corporations do not violate any constitutional guarantees afforded to their stockholders.

... And since in our view the corporate power to make reasonable charitable contributions exists under modern conditions, even apart from express statutory provision, its enactments simply constitute helpful and confirmatory declarations of such power, accompanied by limiting safeguards.

In the light of all of the foregoing we have no hesitancy in sustaining the validity of the donation by the plaintiff. There is no suggestion that it was made indiscriminately or to a pet charity of the corporate directors in furtherance of personal rather than corporate ends. On the contrary, it was made to a preeminent institution of higher learning, was modest in amount and well within the limitations imposed by the statutory enactments, and was voluntarily made in the reasonable belief that it would aid the public welfare and advance the interests of the plaintiff as a private corporation and as part of the community in which it operates. We find that it was a lawful exercise of the corporation's implied and incidental powers under common-law principles and that it came within the express authority of the pertinent state legislation. As has been indicated, there is now widespread belief throughout the nation that free and vigorous non-governmental institutions of learning are vital to our democracy and the system of free enterprise and that withdrawal of corporate authority to make such contributions within reasonable limits would seriously threaten their continuance. Corporations have come to recognize this and with their enlightenment have sought in varying measures, as has the plaintiff by its contribution, to insure and strengthen the society which gives them existence and the means of aiding themselves and their fellow citizens. Clearly then, the appellants, as individual stockholders whose private interests rest entirely upon the well-being of the plaintiff corporation, ought not be permitted to close their eyes to present-day realities and thwart the long-visioned corporate action in recognizing and voluntarily discharging its high obligations as a constituent of our modern social structure.

The judgment entered in the Chancery Division is in all respects

Affirmed.

■ *For affirmance*—CHIEF JUSTICE VANDERBILT, and JUSTICES HEHER, OLIPHANT, WACHENFELD, BURLING and JACOBS—6.

For reversal—None.

———

DEL. GEN. CORP. LAW § 122(9), (12)

[See Statutory Supplement]

———

MODEL BUS. CORP. ACT § 3.02(12)–(14)

[See Statutory Supplement]

NOTE ON THE CONDUCT OF THE CORPORATION

1.   Virtually all states have now adopted statutory provisions relating to corporate contributions that are comparable to Del.Gen. Corp.Law § 122(9) and Model Bus.Corp.Act § 3.02(13). Although typically these provisions do not explicitly incorporate a limit of reasonableness, the commentators generally agree that such a limit is to be implied. Of particular significance is the commentary of Ray Garrett, a principal figure in the drafting history of the Model Act:

> Donations should be reasonable in amount in the light of the corporation's financial condition, bear some reasonable relation to the corporation's interest, and not be so "remote and fanciful" as to excite the opposition of shareholders whose property is being used. Direct corporate benefit is no longer necessary, but corporate interest remains as a motive.

Garrett, Corporate Donations, 22 Bus.Law. 297, 301 (1967).

2.   There is very little direct authority on the permissibility of taking ethical considerations into account in framing corporate action where doing so might not enhance profits. However, statutory provisions like Model Bus.Corp.Act § 3.02(13) provide indirect support for doing so, since it would be anomalous to permit the corporation to donate money it has already earned for public welfare or charitable purposes, while prohibiting the corporation from forgoing a limited amount of profits in the service of generally recognized ethical principles.

3.   The Conference Board regularly surveys corporations to determine the level of charitable giving. In 2003, the Conference Board surveyed 231 corporations in 2003, and found that the median level of charitable giving by the corporations (and charitable foundations that the corporations had created) was 1.68% of the corporations' pretax income. This was about the same as the median in 2002, but was a jump from the period 1999–2001, when the median was around 1% to 1.2%. About half of the contributions were in cash; the other half were in goods, services, or other non-cash donations. The Conference Board, The 2004 Corporate Contributions Report 7 (2004).

––––––

MILTON FRIEDMAN, THE SOCIAL RESPONSIBILITY OF BUSINESS IS TO INCREASE ITS PROFITS, N.Y. Times, Sept. 13, 1970, § 6 (magazine) at 32. "In a free-enterprise, private-property system, a corporate executive is an employee of the owners of the business. He has direct responsibility to his employers. That responsibility is to conduct the business in accordance with their desires, which generally will be to make as much money as possible while conforming to the basic rules of the society, both those embodied in law and those embodied in ethical custom.''

―――――

AMERICAN LAW INSTITUTE, PRINCIPLES OF CORPORATE GOVERNANCE §§ 2.01, 6.02

[See Statutory Supplement]

―――――

CONN. GEN. STATS. ANN. §§ 33–756

[See Statutory Supplement]

―――――

INDIANA CODE ANN. § 23–1–35–1

[See Statutory Supplement]

―――――

N.Y. BUS. CORP. LAW § 717

[See Statutory Supplement]

―――――

PENNSYLVANIA CONSOL. STATS. ANN. TITLE 15, §§ 1711, 1715, 1716, 1717, 2502

[See Statutory Supplement]

―――――

NOTE ON "OTHER CONSTITUENCIES" UNDER DELAWARE LAW

Delaware does not have an other-constituency statute like the statutes that are cross-referenced above. However, the Delaware Supreme Court has made a number of pronouncements—not all of which are necessarily consistent—on the overall obligations of management. Most of these pronouncements have occurred in takeover cases, and have addressed the board's power to take an action whose effect is to block a takeover. The seminal Delaware case on that issue is Unocal Corp. v. Mesa Petroleum Co., 493 A.2d 946, 955 (Del.1985). There the court said:

In [determining] the board's exercise of corporate power to forestall a takeover bid our analysis begins with the basic principle that corporate directors have a fiduciary duty to act in the best interests of the corporation's stockholders. . . .

* * *

An aspect of review [of a board action to block a tender offer] is the element of balance. If a defensive measure is to come within the ambit of the business judgement rule, it must be reasonable in relation to the threat posed. This entails an analysis by the directors of the nature of the takeover bid and its effect on the corporate enterprise. Examples of such concerns may include: inadequacy of the price offered, nature and timing of the offer, questions of illegality, the impact on the "constituencies" other than shareholders (i.e., creditors, customers, employees, and perhaps even the community generally), the risk of nonconsummation, and the quality of securities being offered in the exchange. . . .

The two quoted passages seem to pull in opposite directions: the first focuses only on the shareholders; the second refers to other constituencies as well. However, in a later case, Revlon, Inc. v. MacAndrews & Forbes Holdings, Inc., 506 A.2d 173, 176 (Del.1985), the Delaware Court put an important limit on the second passage in *Unocal:*

   . . . [W]hile concern for various corporate constituencies is proper when addressing a takeover threat, that principle is limited by the requirement that there be some rationally related benefit accruing to the stockholders.

   The Revlon board argued that it acted in good faith in protecting the noteholders because *Unocal* permits consideration of other corporate constituencies. Although such considerations may be permissible, there are fundamental limitations upon that prerogative. A board may have regard of various constituencies in discharging its responsibilities, provided there are rationally related benefits accruing to the stockholders.

In subsequent opinions, the Delaware Supreme Court repeated the *Unocal* litany, sometimes explicitly including the *Revlon* qualification, see, e.g., Mills Acquisition Co. v. Macmillan, Inc., 559 A.2d 1261, 1282 n. 29 (Del.1989), and sometimes not, see, e.g., Ivanhoe Partners v. Newmont Mining Corp., 535 A.2d 1334, 1341–42 (Del.1987).

The Delaware cases also suggest that a board can act against threats to "corporate policy" or "corporate policy and effectiveness." See *Unocal,* supra, *Ivanhoe Partners*, supra. These suggestions leave open whether "corporate policy" is an autonomous goal, which the board can choose to further independent of the concept of maximizing shareholder interests. Some passages in Paramount Communications, Inc. v. Time Inc., 571 A.2d 1140 (Del.1989), seem to suggest this possibility. For example, in that case the court mentioned, with apparent approval, that the board was motivated by a desire to see "to the preservation of Time's 'culture,' i.e., its perceived editorial integrity in journalism. . . ." Other language in the case, however, seems to focus on a threat to the shareholder's interests.

———

KATZ v. OAK INDUS., INC., 508 A.2d 873, 879 (Del.Ch.1986). (Allen, Ch.) "It is the obligation for directors to attempt, within the law, to maximize the long-run interests of the corporation's stockholders; that they may sometimes do so 'at the expense' of others . . . does not for that reason constitute a breach of duty. It seems likely that corporate restructurings designed to maximize shareholder values may in some instances have the effect of requiring bondholders to bear greater risk of loss and thus in effect transfer economic value from bondholders to stockholders. . . . But if courts are to provide protection against such enhanced risk, they will require either legislative direction to do so or the negotiation of indenture provisions designed to afford such protection."

———

CREDIT LYONNAIS BANK NEDERLAND, N.V. v. PATHE COM-MUNICATIONS CORP., 1991 WL 277613 (Del.Ch.1991). In this case, Chancellor Allen stated that "At least where a corporation is operating in the vicinity of insolvency, a board of directors is not merely the agent of the residual risk bearers [that is, the shareholders], but owes its duty to the corporate enterprise." He elaborated on this observation as follows:

The possibility of insolvency can do curious things to incentives, exposing creditors to risks of opportunistic behavior and creating complexities for directors. Consider, for example, a solvent corporation having a single asset, a judgment for $51 million against a solvent debtor. The judgment is on appeal and thus subject to modification or reversal. Assume that the only liabilities of the company are to bondholders in the amount of $12 million. Assume that the array of probable outcomes of the appeal is as follows:

	Expected Value
25% chance of affirmance ($51mm)	$12.75
70% chance of modification ($4mm)	$2.8
5% chance of reversal ($0)	0
Expected Value of Judgment on Appeal	$15.55

Thus, the best evaluation is that the current value of the equity is $3.55 million. ($15.55 million expected value of judgment on appeal [minus] $12 million liability to bondholders). Now assume an offer to settle at $12.5 million (also consider one at $17.5 million). By what standard do the directors of the company evaluate the fairness of these offers? The creditors of this solvent company would be in favor of accepting either a $12.5

million offer or a $17.5 million offer. In either event they will avoid the 75% risk of insolvency and default. The stockholders, however, will plainly be opposed to acceptance of a $12.5 million settlement (under which they get practically nothing). More importantly, they very well may be opposed to acceptance of the $17.5 million offer under which the residual value of the corporation would increase from $3.5 to $5.5 million. This is so because the litigation alternative, with its 25% probability of a $39 million outcome to them ($51 million—$12 million [=] $39 million) has an expected value to the residual risk bearer of $9.75 million ($39 million – 25% chance of affirmance), substantially greater than the $5.5 million available to them in the settlement. While in fact the stockholders' preference would reflect their appetite for risk, it is possible (and with diversified shareholders likely) that shareholders would prefer rejection of both settlement offers.

But if we consider the community of interests that the corporation represents it seems apparent that one should in this hypothetical accept the best settlement offer available providing it is greater than $15.55 million, and one below that amount should be rejected. But that result will not be reached by a director who thinks he owes duties directly to shareholders only. It will be reached by directors who are capable of conceiving of the corporation as a legal and economic entity. Such directors will recognize that in managing the business affairs of a solvent corporation in the vicinity of insolvency, circumstances may arise when the right (both the efficient and the fair) course to follow for the corporation may diverge from the choice that the stockholders (or the creditors, or the employees, or any single group interested in the corporation) would make if given the opportunity to act.

Id. at 31, n. 55.

SECTION 8.   THE NATURE OF CORPORATE LAW

———

M. EISENBERG, THE STRUCTURE OF THE CORPORATION 1 (1976). "Corporate law is constitutional law; that is, its dominant function is to regulate the manner in which the corporate institution is constituted, to define the relative rights and duties of those participating in the institution, and to delimit the powers of the institution vis-à-vis the external world."

———

Melvin A. Eisenberg, The Conception that the Corporation is a Nexus of Contracts, and the Dual Nature of the Firm

24 J. Corp. Law 819 (1998).

I. INTRODUCTION

In 1976 by Michael Jensen and William Meckling formulated the conception that the corporation is a nexus of contracts in their famous article *The Theory of the Firm: Managerial Behavior, Agency Costs, and Ownership Structure.*[1] Since that time, the conception has dominated the law-and-economics literature in corporate law. The validity of this conception, however, cannot be established by economic analysis. That does not make the conception invalid, but it does mean that its validity must be examined along other dimensions....

II. A BRIEF INTELLECTUAL HISTORY

It is useful to begin by developing the intellectual history of the Jensen and Meckling article. That history begins with Ronald Coase's landmark paper, *The Nature of the Firm.*[2] In that paper, Coase characterized the boundaries of the firm as the range of exchanges over which the market system was superseded and resource allocation was accomplished instead by authority and direction:

> [I]n economic theory we find that the allocation of factors of production between different uses is determined by the price mechanism. The price of factor *A* becomes higher in *X* than in *Y*. As a result, *A* moves from *Y* to *X* until the difference between the prices in *X* and *Y*, except insofar as it compensates for other differential advantages, disappears. Yet in the real world, we find that there are many areas where this does not apply. If a workman moves from department *Y* to department *X*, he does not go because of a change in relative prices, but because he is ordered to do so.
>
> .... Outside the firm, price movements direct production, which is co-ordinated through a series of exchange transactions on the market. Within a firm, these market transactions are eliminated and in place of the complicated market structure with exchange transactions is substituted the entrepreneur-coordinator, who directs production.

Coase argued that activities will be included within a firm when the costs of using markets—that is, contracts—are greater than the costs of direction by authority. The essential issue in the theory of the firm, therefore, was why some economic activity takes place within firms, so that the activity is directed by authority, while other economic activity takes place across markets, so that the activity is determined by contract.

1. Michael C. Jensen & William H. Meckling, *The Theory of the Firm: Managerial Behavior, Agency Costs, and Ownership Structure*, 3 J. Fin. Econ. 305 (1976).

2. Ronald H. Coase, *The Nature of the Firm*, 4 Economica 386 (1937).

Coase did not explicitly define the firm in this paper. Implicitly, however, he defined the firm to consist of the activities under the direction of the entrepreneur, who in turn was defined as the person or persons who take the place of the price mechanism in the direction of resources. Coase stated that the question what constitutes a firm can be approached in practice by considering the relationship of employer and employee. One of the essentials of this relationship, he said, is that the employer must have the right to control the work of the employee.[4] "We thus see," he concluded, "that it is the fact of direction which is the essence of the legal concept of employer and employee"—and, by extension, of the firm.

In their paper *Production, Information Costs, and Economic Organization*,[10] Alchian and Harold Demsetz objected to the Coasian conception of the firm, and emphasized instead the role of team production within the firm and the role of agreement and monitoring in team production. It is a "delusion," they said, "to see the firm characterized by the power to settle issues by fiat, by authority, or by disciplinary action superior to that available in the conventional market."[11] Rather,

[The firm] has no power of fiat, no authority, no disciplinary action any different in the slightest degree from ordinary market contracting between any two people. [In the case of a contract between me and you,] I can "punish" you only by withholding future business or by seeking redress in the courts for any failure to honor our exchange agreement. That is exactly all that any employer can do. He can fire or sue, just as I can fire my grocer by stopping purchases from him or sue him for delivering faulty products. What then is the content of the presumed power to manage and assign workers to various tasks? Exactly the same as one little consumer's power to manage and assign his grocer to various tasks. The single consumer can assign his grocer to the task of obtaining whatever the customer can induce the grocer to provide at a price acceptable to both parties. That is precisely all that an employer can do to an employee. To speak of managing, directing, or assigning workers to various tasks is a deceptive way of noting that the employer continually is involved in renegotiation of contracts on terms that must be acceptable to both parties. Telling an employee to type this letter rather than to file that document is like my telling a grocer to sell me this brand of tuna rather than that brand of bread.... Wherein then is the relationship between a grocer and his employee different from that between a grocer and his customers? It is in a *team* use of inputs and a centralized position of some party in the contractual arrangements of *all* other inputs. It is the *centralized contractual*

4. *Id.* at 404–05.

10. Armen A. Alchian and Harold Demsetz, Production, Information Costs, and Eco- nomic Organization, 62 AM. ECON. REV. 777 (1972).

11. Id. at 777.

agent in a team productive process—not some superior authoritarian directive or disciplinary power.[12]

Jensen and Meckling applauded Alchian and Demsetz's objection to Coase's theory of the firm, but concluded that Alchian and Demsetz had not gone far enough in rejecting Coase:

Alchian and Demsetz . . . object to the notion that activities within the firm are governed by authority, and correctly emphasize the role of contracts as a vehicle for voluntary exchange. They emphasize the role of monitoring in situations in which there is joint input or team production. We sympathize with the importance they attach to monitoring, but we believe the emphasis which Alchian–Demsetz place on joint input production is too narrow and therefore misleading. Contractual relations are the essence of the firm, not only with employees but with suppliers, customers, creditors, etc.

Jensen and Meckling therefore substituted, for Coase's conception of the firm, the competing conception that the firm was a nexus of contracts—and, more particularly, "that most organizations are simply *legal fictions which serve as a nexus for a set of contracting relationships among individuals*...."[14]

Before proceeding further, it is necessary to clarify the meaning of the nexus-of-contracts conception. The conception neither can nor does mean what it literally says. In ordinary language, the term *contract* means an agreement. In law, the term means a legally enforceable promise. Pretty clearly, however, the nexus-of-contracts conception does not mean either that the corporation is a nexus of agreements or that it is a nexus of legally enforceable promises. Instead, the conception means that the corporation is a nexus of reciprocal arrangements. But then why is the term *contracts*, rather than the term *reciprocal arrangements*, used in the nexus-of-contracts conception?

One possible explanation is that the term *nexus of contracts* was coined by economists, and "[e]conomists tend to view contracts as relationships characterized by reciprocal relations and behavior."[15] ... Whatever the explanation, ... I will use the term *nexus of contracts* in the way it is meant, that is, a nexus of reciprocal arrangements....

IV.   THE PROBLEM OF MANDATORY LEGAL RULES

A central issue raised by the nexus-of-contracts conception is how to deal with the rules of corporate law. Clearly, these rules are basic to the constitution of the corporation. Equally clearly, they are not reciprocal arrangements; in particular, some important rules of corpo-

12. *Id.* at 777–78 (emphasis in original).

14. [Jensen and Meckling, *supra* note 1] at 310–11 (emphasis in original).

15. Oliver Hart, An Economist's Perspective on The Theory of the Firm, 89 Co-lum.L.Rev. 1757, 1764 n.30. Hart builds here on Jeffrey N. Gordon, The Mandatory Structure of Corporate Law, 89 Colum.L.Rev. 1549 (1989).

ration law, such as the federal laws that govern insider trading and tender offers, are mandatory.

Some commentators deal with this issue by taking the position that none of the rules of corporation law are really mandatory. . . .

The strategy of denying that there are mandatory rules of corporate law is not only untenable; it is unnecessary. Nothing in the nexus-of-contracts conception requires a denial that there are mandatory corporate rules. After all, even real contracts are governed by a number of mandatory rules, such as the rules that concern consideration, unconscionability, and good faith. Accordingly, the nexus-of-contracts conception could easily be interpreted to mean that the corporation is a nexus of reciprocal arrangements made within a framework of mandatory legal rules, just as many other reciprocal arrangements, like contracts, trusts, and marriages, are made within a framework of mandatory legal rules.

Unfortunately, it has proved tempting to confuse the positive proposition the corporation is a nexus of reciprocal arrangements with the normative proposition that the persons who constitute a corporation should be free to make whatever reciprocal arrangements they choose, without the constraints of any mandatory legal rules. For example, Stephen Bainbridge states that "The nexus of contracts model has important implications for a range of corporate law topics, the most obvious of which is the debate over the proper role of mandatory legal rules."[20] However, insofar as the nexus of contracts is a positive conception, it has no implications for the proper role of mandatory legal rules. To reason from the nexus-of-contracts conception to a rejection of mandatory legal rules is to mistakenly reason from *is* to *ought*.

Whether any rules of corporation law should be mandatory, and if so, what those rules should be, are important and difficult questions. Contracts—real contracts—should normally be respected and legally enforced. Under appropriate conditions, so should certain other forms of private ordering. In the corporate context, however, contracts and other forms of private ordering are subject to special problems. For example, there are a number of potential limits on the force of shareholder consent to corporate actions. The consent may be fictitious—as where the approval is given in part by nonshareholders with power to vote, like brokers who hold stock in street name. The consent may be tainted by a conflict of interest—as where a majority of the approving shareholders benefit from the approval in a way that other shareholders do not. The consent may be coerced—as where the shareholders are threatened that unless they approve a proposal, management will refuse to take some action that is in the shareholders' interests, like the payment of dividends. The consent may be impoverished—as where shareholders approve an action they deem second best because management's control of the agenda prevents

---

20. Stephen M. Bainbridge, Community and Statism: A Conservative Contractarian Critique of Progressive Corporate Law Scholarship, 82 Cornell L.Rev. 856, 860 (1997). . . .

them from voting on an action they deem first best, or where the shareholders have only a weak, incomplete, or nonexistent idea of a proposal for which they vote.

Furthermore, the respect that is normally due to contracts and other forms of private ordering is significantly diminished when the contract or private ordering creates adverse third-party effects—negative externalities. The possibility of such effects is especially salient in the corporate context, because of the interdependence of individuals and groups who are interested in the corporation but may not be parties to a given arrangement. For example, a shareholders' agreement between two of three shareholders in a close corporation may have a significant negative effect on the third shareholder. A contract between the board and the chief executive officer may have a significant negative effects on the shareholders as a group. A restructuring of the corporation initiated by the board and approved by the shareholders may have a significant negative effect on bondholders.

Given the special problems of contract and private ordering in the corporate context, whether any particular rule of corporate law should be mandatory must be examined on a rule-by-rule basis in light of the extent, if any, to which the power to contract around the given rule may implicate these problems. One of the defects of the nexus-of-contracts conception is that it too easily leads to a substitution of conclusory thinking for careful rule-by-rule analysis of these issues.

VI.   THE DUAL NATURE OF THE FIRM

Recall that Coase's conception of the firm turned on the entrepreneur's *authority* (that is, his power) to direct his subordinates through rules and orders. Recall too that in contrast, Alchian and Demsetz argued that the concept of authority in the firm was a delusion. "The firm," they said, "has no power of fiat, no authority, no disciplinary action any different in the slightest degree from ordinary market contracting between any two people." Accordingly, they said, there is no difference between the employer-employee relationship and the grocer-customer relationship:

> To speak of managing, directing, or assigning workers to various tasks is a deceptive way of noting that the employer continually is involved in renegotiation of contracts on terms that must be acceptable to both parties. Telling an employee to type this letter rather than to file that document is like my telling a grocer to sell me this brand of tuna rather than that brand of bread.[32]

This analysis, in turn, is a lynchpin of Jensen and Meckling's nexus-of-contracts conception.

This analysis is not exactly wrong. But neither is it exactly right. It catches half the truth, but only half. To begin with, many or most of the contracts in a corporation are sticky. It is usually easy to switch grocers, but it is usually not easy to quit jobs. Consider, for example,

---

32. Alchian and Demsetz, supra note 10, at 777.

an employee with firm-specific skills, or with great seniority, unvested stock options, or other benefits that will be lost if he resigns.

Much more important, the position that there is no difference between contracting to do an act and being ordered or directed to do an act lacks all correspondence with reality. Corporations are hierarchical organizations. Anyone who has worked in a hierarchical organization knows that the way in which directions are experienced by supervisors and subordinates is entirely different from the way in which contracts are experienced by contracting parties. To use Alchian and Demsetz's example, both employer and employee experience employer's direction to type a letter in a very different way than customer and grocer experience grocer's trying to sell tuna rather than bread.

This difference is qualitative, not merely quantitative. When a consumer needs to decide whether to buy bread or tuna, his decision will be based on whether bread or tuna is the best choice (by whatever metric of best he employs), all things considered—that is, considering, on the merits, all the reasons for and against each alternative. In contrast, when a subordinate is given a direction by a superior, the fact of the direction normally excludes the subordinate from considering any reason for action except the direction. Thus a subordinate normally follows a direction more or less reflexively, whether he likes the direction or not, and whether or not he considers the direction best, all things considered. As Bainbridge has observed, "there is a sharp disconnect between Alchian and Demsetz's argument and the real world of work. Command-and-control is the norm in most workplaces. Workers generally accept hierarchical authority and perceive obedience to authority as an integral part of their job: 'for the majority, disobedience is unthinkable.' "[35] . . .

All this is of great psychological and sociological importance, because most people work in hierarchical organizations. But it is of economic importance as well, just because it is of psychological and sociological importance. Just as a subordinate experiences getting a direction differently than making a real contract, so too does a superior experience giving a direction differently than making a real contract. There are costs to inducing action by making real contracts, and there are costs to inducing action by giving directions. Firms exist in part when the cost of inducing action through giving directions is less than the cost of inducing action through making real contracts.

Furthermore, a corporation—or more generally, a firm—is not only a hierarchical organization; it is a *bureaucratic* hierarchical organization. That means, among other things, that much of the activity in a corporation is organized by established bureaucratic rules that are not open to continued re-examination, let alone negotiation. To paraphrase a remark of Benjamin Klein, an organization is embedded in its human capital, but is greater than the sum of its parts.

35. Bainbridge, Participatory Management Within a Theory of the Firm, 21 J. Corp. L. 657, 663–64 (1996) (quoting John F. Witte, Democracy, Authority, and Alienation in Work: Workers' Participation in an American Corporation 38 (1980)). . . .

Employees come and go, but the organization maintains the memory of how things are done.[38]

More generally, an organization consists not only of assets, persons, and relationships among persons, but of the rules that organize those assets, persons, and relationships. Some of those rules are contractual, but most are bureaucratic in the sense that they are hierarchically adopted and persist over time as persons, assets, and relationships come and go.

To put this differently, the corporation has a dual nature. In the first quarter of the twentieth century, it was discovered that light, theretofore described and understood as a wave (a portion of the electromagnetic spectrum), can alternatively be described and understood as a particle (a photon) and that, correspondingly, the building-blocks of atoms, such as electrons, theretofore described and understood as particles, can alternatively be described and understood as waves. So too the firm can be described and understood either as a set of reciprocal arrangements or as a bureaucratic hierarchical organization. To describe and understand firms purely as bureaucratic hierarchical organizations misses the voluntary element of many of the arrangements that constitute a firm. To describe firms purely as a set of reciprocal arrangements misses the extent to which firms are organized by bureaucratic rules and operate by hierarchical directions issued by superiors to subordinates. . . .

---

38. See Klein, Vertical Integration as Organizational Ownership: The Fisher Body– General Motors Relationship Revisited, 4 J.L. ECON. & ORGANIZATION 199; 208 (1988).

CHAPTER IV

CORPORATE STRUCTURE

SECTION 1. SHAREHOLDERSHIP IN PUBLICLY HELD CORPORATIONS

NOTE ON SHAREHOLDERSHIP IN PUBLICLY HELD CORPORATIONS

At one time, corporation law reflected what might be called a traditional, or inverted-pyramid, model of corporate governance. Under this model, at the top of the inverted pyramid were the shareholders, who own the corporation, who elect the board of directors, and whose approval is required for major or fundamental corporate actions. At the next level down were the board, which manages the corporation's business, makes business policy, and selects the officers. At the bottom of the inverted pyramid were the officers, who under this model act as agents of the board and execute its policies and decisions.

The traditional model was called into drastic question in 1932, with the publication of Berle & Means's classic work, *The Modern Corporation and Private Property*. One of this book's principal conclusions, almost revolutionary at the time, was that in publicly held corporations *control* had come to be divorced from *ownership*. The modern publicly held corporation has thousands or even hundreds of thousands of shareholders. When Berle & Means wrote in 1932, corporate ownership was marked not only by large *numbers* of *shareholders*, but by *dispersal of shareholdings*, that is, patterns of shareholdings in which no single individual, firm, or compact group owns more than a tiny fraction of a corporation's stock. Where shareholdership is highly dispersed, the corporation will be controlled not by the shareholders, but by management; that is what Berle & Means meant by the separation of *ownership*, which still lay with the shareholders, and *control*, which had shifted to management.

As a result of this separation of ownership and control, the inherent conflict between principal and agent—the agency-cost problem—is compounded, because when the principal consists of a highly dispersed group, it faces not only an agency-cost problem but a collective-action problem, that is, a problem of coordinating the decisions of the members of the group. There are two basic reasons why dispersion of shareholdings presents a severe collective-action problem.

First, if a shareholder owns only a tiny amount of a corporation's stock it is not cost-effective for her to spend a significant amount of time on the corporation's affairs. Such a shareholder will be "rationally apathetic," that is, it will be rational for the shareholder not to invest her time in reviewing the corporation's affairs in any real depth. If all shareholders in a corporation own only tiny percentages of the corporation's stock, then all the corporation's shareholders will be rationally apathetic.

Second, when a corporation's stock is held by thousands of shareholders living across the country, voting must be done by proxy rather than in person. Typically, in such a corporation, management controls, and has cost-free access to, the corporate proxy machinery. In contrast, shareholders who want to oppose a management action must find a way to coordinate, which will be difficult enough, and then must pay the expense of a proxy contest out of their own pockets. If a proxy contest does occur, management has in its favor both cost-free access to the corporate proxy machinery and the legitimacy that goes with incumbency. Moreover, a shareholder who is extremely dissatisfied with management will often prefer *exit* to *voice*, that is, will often prefer to sell her stock rather than to vote against management. As a result, the market siphons off many potential anti-management shareholders. That is a major reason why in a corporation with a great number of shareholders and highly dispersed shareholdings, management, rather than shareholders, will normally have control.

Since the time at which Berle & Means wrote, however, there has been a major shift in the pattern of shareholdings, from highly dispersed to partially concentrated, because a very large and increasing proportion of equities (shares) in American corporations have come to be held by institutional investors.

In the U.S., almost all institutional shareholders fall into six basic categories:

1. *Private Pension Plans.* Private pension plans are normally established by private (usually corporate) employers, to provide retirement income for the employer's employees. The most important provisions of these plans, for present purposes, concern decisionmaking power over (i) the acquisition and disposition of the plan's portfolio assets (portfolio decisions) and (ii) how to vote portfolio stocks (voting decisions). Portfolio and voting decisions are often delegated by the employer to fiduciaries, such as banks, who are hired to administer the plan. Particularly among larger corporate employers, however, part or all of the decisionmaking power may be retained by the employer's own management. In such cases, the employer usually exercises portfolio and voting decisionmaking powers through portfolio managers on its own payroll.

2. *Public Pension Plans.* Public pension plans are established by governmental employers, such as states and cities, to assure retirement income for public employees. As in the case of private pension plans, decisionmaking powers may be either retained or delegated to fiducia-

ries. Often, portfolio decisions are delegated while voting decisions are retained.

3. *Banks*. Bank trust departments often manage the funds of pension plans, and commonly serve as trustees for individuals and estates.

4. *Investment Companies*. Investment companies manage money on behalf of individuals or, less commonly, other entities. The most common type of investment company is the mutual fund, which is an open-ended company, in the sense that investors can withdraw their investment at any time, based on the value of the mutual fund's assets at the time of demand. The other major type of investment company is a closed-end company. A closed-end company is a corporation that raises funds for investment in which the owners of the company's shares have no right to withdraw their investments, although they can sell their shares in the company on the open market.

5. *Insurance Companies*. Insurance companies accumulate huge liquid funds based on the premiums paid by their insureds. These funds are invested by the insurance companies in portfolios that include equities.

6. *Foundations*. Foundations, including universities and religious institutions, typically have endowments, which they invest either through outside professional managers or on their own behalf.

Table 1 shows the percentage of total equity (that is, total value of U.S. stock of all corporations) held by institutional investors as of 2001:

TABLE 1
2001 ($billions)

TYPE OF INSTITUTION	EQUITY HOLDINGS	% TOTAL EQUITY MARKET
Pension Funds	$4,001.3	26.3%
Private Trusteed	1,902.3	12.5%
Private Insured	883.3	5.8%
State & Local	1,215.7	8.0%
Investment Companies	2,865.1	18.8%
Open–End Mutual Funds	2,836.1	18.7%
Closed–End	29.0	0.2%
Insurance Companies	1,076.3	7.1%
Life Insurance	905.2	6.0%
Property & Casualty	171.1	1.1%
Bank & Trust Companies	253.8	1.7%
Foundations	285.8	1.9%
All Institutions	8,482.3	55.8%

Source: The Conference Board, Institutional Investment Report 32, Table 14.

As this table shows, institutional investor holdings now account for about 56% of all equities. Furthermore, institutions tend to invest more heavily in larger companies. As a result, U.S. institutional investors held 61.4 percent of the stock of the largest 1,000 U.S. corporations in 2001. Id. at 7.[1]

The growth of equity holdings by institutional investors has fundamental implications for American corporate governance. Unlike individual shareholdings, institutional shareholdings tend to be very large in absolute terms, so that an investment in governance can be cost-justified. Moreover, institutional shareholdings tend to be *concentrated* rather than dispersed. As a result, coordination becomes substantially easier.

The increased concentration of shareholdings in publicly held corporations, due to the dramatic increase of shareholdings by institutional investors, has set the stage for a dramatic increase in the shareholder role in the modern publicly held corporation. As shareholders get more sophisticated, the costs of playing an active shareholder role decreases. As shareholdings get larger, the cost-benefit ratio for investing time in playing that role improves. As shareholdings become more concentrated, coordination between shareholders becomes easier.

However, setting the stage is one thing; putting on the play is another. A number of social and legal forces affect the role of institutional investors in corporate governance in the United States. Some of these forces point in very different directions.

Paramount among the *social* forces is the problem of conflicts of interest. Many institutional investors have ties to management that inhibit voting against management's wishes. Take for example, *banks*. If the trust department of Bank *B* holds the stock of Corporation C in a pension portfolio, and C is also a client of Bank B's commercial department, a trust officer of Bank B will think long and hard before voting against a proposal made by C's management, or in favor of a proposal that C's management opposes. *Insurance companies*, like banks, often have extensive commercial contacts with corporations whose stock they hold in their investment portfolios. *Mutual funds* may want to stay on management's good side to keep open their lines of access for getting information about a corporation's business. Corporate managers of *corporate pension funds* will be uncomfortable voting against other corporate managers, and external managers of

1. There is a difference between assets "held" and assets "managed" by the various types of institutional investors. For example, in 2001 pension funds "held" 41.5 percent of all institutional-investor assets (including both stocks and other kinds of investments such as bonds) but "managed" only 21.1 percent of total institutional investor assets. This means that pension funds internally managed only 50.6 percent of their own assets, while the remaining 49.4 percent is allocated to other institutional investors to be managed for them. Some of this money is allocated by pension funds to banks, so that while banks hold 11.5 percent of total 2001 institutional investor assets, they managed 18.9 percent of total 2001 institutional-investor assets. Similarly, investment companies managed 32.3 percent of total institutional assets, although they held only 22.5 percent. Id. at 11, 35.

corporate pension funds may fear that if they vote against management positions, the sponsors will switch to other external managers.

In addition, at least until about 15 years ago there was a cultural norm, shared by many institutional investors, under which voting against management "wasn't done." A governing rule was the so-called Wall Street Rule—If you don't like management, sell. The corollary of that Rule was, if you don't sell, support management. In addition, prior to 1992 the SEC's Proxy Rules made it very difficult for institutional shareholders to communicate with each other to determine whether it was in their mutual interests to combine forces in connection with voting on a management proposal or initiating a proposal of their own.

In 1992, The SEC revised the Proxy Rules to remove most of the constraints on communication on institutional investors that had been imposed by these rules. Another federal agency, the U.S. Department of Labor ("DOL"), has been a major agent of change. One of the DOL's responsibilities is the administration of the Employee Retirement Income Security Act ("ERISA"). Pension plans are the dominant kinds of institutional investors, and among other things, ERISA imposes certain fiduciary obligations of the managers of pension plans. Under ERISA, whoever exercises discretion over plan assets must manage those assets "solely in the interest of the participants and beneficiaries and for the exclusive purpose of providing benefits to participants and their beneficiaries." This is known as the "exclusive benefit rule." In 1988, the DOL issued a well-publicized letter which stated that the fiduciary duties of managing pension-plan assets included not only portfolio decisions but voting decisions.

Under ERISA, therefore, a private pension-plan trustee must take voting decisions seriously, and cannot simply follow the Wall Street Rule. Well-informed observers believe that, partly as result of the DOL's activities and partly for other reasons, the institutional-investor community has come to accept and practice the idea that voting is important. The result has been a significant shift from a passivity norm to an activity norm.

Much of the current institutional-shareholder activism in the United States has been led by public-pension funds. In part this is because public-pension funds have fewer ties to management than other types of institutional investors, and are therefore not as subject to conflict-of-interest problems. In part too, this activism is related to the fact that public-pension funds often follow an indexing strategy. An investment fund that uses an indexing strategy essentially mimics the market, in the sense that the fund contains the same proportion of each equity on a given market as does the market itself. There are two ideas behind indexing: (1) Under a postulate of financial economics, known as the efficient-capital-markets hypothesis, it is difficult and perhaps not possible to outguess the market, or at least to outguess the market by a margin sufficient to cover the costs of analysis and trading. (2) Under another postulate, known as the theory of diversification, a diversified portfolio eliminates important risks. Under an indexation strategy, an institutional shareholder who disapproves of the management of a corporation cannot simply sell its stock (because that would defeat the concept of indexation), and therefore has a greater incentive to become active in voting and monitoring.

Although public-pension plans and, to a lesser extent, unions have taken the lead in institutional investor activity, other institutional investors seem to be stepping up their activities as well. Partly this is because there has been an increased perception that some level of activism can increase the value of a portfolio; partly it is because there has been a shift in the culture of institutional investors; and partly it is because once public-pension plans take a position that is clearly proper, it is not easy for other institutional investors to hide.

Despite these legal and cultural shifts, there remain important constraints on the extent to which institutional investors can be expected to be active monitors of the corporations in which they hold stock. One of these constraints consists of limits on holdings. Under modern portfolio theory, an institutional investor should diversify its portfolio. That objective will normally prevent any given institutional investor from putting too many eggs in any single corporate basket, particularly in light of the huge capitalization of many large American publicly held corporations. In addition, certain kinds of institutional investors are statutorily forbidden to hold more than a fixed percentage of the stock of any given corporation. As a result of these economic and legal constraints, typically any one institutional investor will have limited holdings in any one corporation.

The significance of limited holdings by any given institutional investor in any given portfolio corporation is that it reduces the investor's cost-benefit ratio for active involvement, and leads to a free-rider problem. Any expenses the institutional investor incurs for beyond-the-ordinary-course shareholder activities will benefit the other shareholders more than itself. Suppose, for example, Institution S holds 1% of Corporation C's stock. Corporation C has a governance rule that diminishes C's value. A proxy contest to repeal the rule, and thereby increase the value of C stock, would cost $500,000. Assume that if S mounts such a contest, it will derive no economic benefit except the increased value of its C stock. In that case, if S does mount the contest, in effect it will spend $5,000 on itself and $495,000 on behalf of the other shareholders, who will free ride at S's expense.

The free-rider problem shows that institutional investors are not likely to engage in monitoring or voting activity that (i) goes beyond the monitoring and voting activity in which the investor can be expected to engage in the normal course of its shareholding capacity; (ii) would require significant expenditures; (iii) would increase the value of the institution's holding in its portfolio companies by less than the costs of the activity; and (iv) would result in no private economic benefit to the investor beyond the increased value of that holding. However, if all of these conditions are *not* satisfied, monitoring and voting activity may be engaged in. In fact, all of these conditions frequently aren't satisfied, for a variety of reasons.

First. Much voting activity requires very little effort. Furthermore, in many cases the same issue recurs in a number of corporations—for example, how to deal with anti-takeover provisions of various kinds—so that the investor need only make a one-time expenditure of effort to determine its general position, and can then amortize the expenditure over a number of votes.

Second. A vote on a recurring issue, like a certain type of corporate-governance rule, may send a message to all portfolio corporations, and may therefore have an economic benefit to the investor beyond its impact on the immediate portfolio corporation.

Third. Unless an investor has adopted an indexing strategy, it must monitor its portfolio corporations in any event, to determine whether to hold or sell.

Fourth. The costs of playing a shareholder role have been dramatically reduced by the development of firms like Institutional Shareholders Services. These firms analyze a huge number of proxy materials, and report those analyses in bulletins that are distributed regularly to institutional-investor clients. In effect, the clients of these services form a sort of *research coalition*, by pooling their funds through the subscription prices they pay for the costs of the services' analyses.

Fifth. In many cases, a voting decision has a very obvious and dramatic effect on the value of a portfolio stock, as where the vote concerns a merger or a value-decreasing anti-takeover provision. In such cases, beyond-the-normal-course voting activity will often be cost-justified.

Sixth. Even in less dramatic cases, there has been an increasing acceptance of the idea that changes in a corporation's governance rules, and often in its management, can increase the value of the corporation's stock, so that it may be more cost-effective to hold and vote than to sell.

Seventh. Under ERISA, as interpreted by the DOL, many institutional investors are legally obliged to vote in a way that maximizes the value of their shares. Institutional investors that don't fall within the coverage of ERISA may be under a comparable fiduciary obligation.

The bottom line is that institutional investors have grown increasingly activist. The question then arises, what is the competence of institutional shareholders as shareholders? Certainly, institutional shareholders are not equipped to make, or even meaningfully assesses, individual business decisions in the ordinary course. There are, however, several areas in which institutional shareholders can play a meaningful role.

● Institutional shareholders can meaningfully assess the corporation's governance structure—for example, its rules concerning takeover defenses, or the conduct of elections. Managers are usually self-interested as to governance rules, because such rules typically bear on the preservation and enhancement of managerial positions. Even apart from the problem of managerial self-interest, institutional shareholders may have special competence in this area because they can review such rules across corporations as a class.

• Institutional shareholders can meaningfully assess proposed structural changes, like mergers. Again, managers will often be self-interested in such proposals, if only because structural changes will normally threaten to reduce or promise to enhance managerial positions. Even apart from the problem of managerial self-interest, institutional shareholders may have special competence to assess such proposals, because managers are typically trained in making operational business decisions, while institutional shareholders specialize in making financial decisions. Moreover, often the market will react to such proposals, and institutional shareholders can use the market's reaction as strong evidence of the proposal's merit.

• Institutional shareholders can meaningfully assess overall management performance, both by comparing the financial results of management's performance with the performance of managers in like corporations, and by taking into account the evaluation of a particular management by the business community as a whole.

• Finally, institutional investors may play a role in corporate business and policy and in the dismissal of chief executive officers. For example, institutional investors have induced various corporations to restructure their operations by spinning off some businesses to focus on core businesses. In other cases, pressures from institutional investors have helped lead boards to dismiss chief executive officers who were viewed as ineffective.

The next issue is the *forms* that institutional involvement in corporate governance may take.

1.   The simplest form of institutional involvement is taking an active posture in voting on management or shareholder proposals.

2.   A more aggressive form of involvement is not only to *vote* on shareholder proposals, but to *make* shareholder proposals. The most common types of proposals made by institutional investors concern the *structure* or *rules* of corporate governance—for example, a requirement of a majority of independent directors, or the deletion of an anti-takeover rule.

3.   Another possible form of institutional activity is the election of individuals as directors to represent institutional investors. In general, institutional investors in the United States have not followed this path, perhaps partly because of concerns that trading in a corporation's stock by an investor with a representative on the corporation's board might be deemed insider trading. However, institutions sometimes have joined movements begun by others to oust directors and replace them with new directors. In such cases, the new directors would not be representatives of, or even selected by, the institutional investors, so that the insider-trading problem is not salient.

4.   An extremely important process through which the concerns of institutional investors are expressed is that of consultation. Many large institutional investors get their points across, without voting, by

consultation with management. Consultation can concern either specific issues, such as a proposed merger, or general corporate policies. As a practical matter, institutional investors probably get more done through consultation than through voting on management or shareholder proposals. However, there is an important interrelation between the consultation process and the voting process, because the implied or actual threat that an institutional investor will bring an issue to a vote (either on a shareholder proposal or in the election of directors) is an important incentive for managers to take seriously the concerns expressed by institutional investors in the consultation process.

SECTION 2. THE ALLOCATION OF LEGAL POWER BETWEEN MANAGEMENT AND SHAREHOLDERS

DEL. GEN. CORP. LAW § 141(a)

[See Statutory Supplement]

REV. MODEL BUS. CORP. ACT § 8.01(b)

[See Statutory Supplement]

Charlestown Boot & Shoe Co. v. Dunsmore

New Hampshire Supreme Court, 1880.
60 N.H. 85.

CASE. Demurrer to the declaration in which the following facts were alleged:—The plaintiffs are a manufacturing corporation having for its object a dividend of profits, and commenced business in 1871. Dunsmore was elected director in 1871 and Willard in 1873, and entered upon the discharge of their duties, and have continued so to act by virtue of successive elections until the present time. December 10, 1874, the corporation[1] voted to choose a committee to act with the directors to close up its affairs, and chose one Osgood for such committee. Osgood tendered his services, but the defendants refused to act with him, and contracted new debts to a larger extent than allowed by law. By their negligence, debts due to the corporation to the amount of $2,161.23 have been wholly lost. By their negligence in disposing of the goods of the corporation, a loss has accrued of $3,300.40. By their neglect to sell the buildings and machinery of the

---

1. By "the corporation," in this phrase and some others, the court seems to mean the body of shareholders. (Footnote by ed.)

corporation when they might and ought, and were urged by Osgood to sell, the same depreciated in value to the extent of $20,000.

Also for that the plaintiffs owned and possessed a certain shop of the value of $10,000, and a large amount of machinery and fixtures of the value of $10,000; "and whereas it was the duty of said defendants, directors as aforesaid, to procure sufficient and proper insurance against fire to be made on said property, and keep the same so sufficiently insured, of all which the said defendants had notice, yet they did not and would not keep the said property so insured, and afterwards, to wit, on the 28th day of April, 1878, while the said property was so remaining without insurance, the same was wholly consumed by fire and wholly lost to the plaintiff, whereby the plaintiff suffered great loss and damage, to wit, $20,000."

■ SMITH, J. The provision of the statute is, that the business of a dividend paying corporation shall be managed by the directors. The statute reads, "The business of every such corporation shall be managed by the directors thereof, subject to the by-laws and votes of the corporation, and under their direction by such officers and agents as shall be duly appointed by the directors or by the corporation." G.L., c. 148, s. 3; Gen.Stats., c. 134, s. 3. The only limitation upon the judgment or discretion of the directors is such as the corporation by its by-laws and votes shall impose. It may define its business, its nature and extent, prescribe rules and regulations for the government of its officers and members, and determine whether its business shall be wound up or continued; but when it has thus acted, the business as thus defined and limited is to be managed by its directors, and by such officers and agents under their direction as the directors or the corporation shall appoint. The statute does not authorize a corporation to join another officer with the directors, nor compel the directors to act with one who is not a director. They are bound to use ordinary care and diligence in the care and management of the business of the corporation, and are answerable for ordinary negligence. *March v. Railroad,* 43 N.H. 516, 529; *Scott v. Depeyster,* 1 Edw. Ch. 513, 543; Ang. & Ames Corp., s. 314. There is no difference in this respect between the agents of corporations and those of natural persons, unless expressly made by the charter or by-laws. *Id., s.* 315. It would be unreasonable to hold them responsible for the management of the affairs of the corporation if compelled to act with one who to a greater or less extent could control their acts. The statute not only entrusts the management of the business of the corporation to the directors, but places its other officers and agents under their direction. When a statute provides that powers granted to a corporation shall be exercised by any set of officers or any particular agents, such powers can be exercised only by such officers or agents, although they are required to be chosen by the whole corporation; and if the whole corporation attempts to exercise powers which by the charter are lodged elsewhere, its action upon the subject is void. *Insurance Co. v. Keyser,* 32 N.H. 313, 315. The vote choosing Osgood a committee to act with the directors in closing up the affairs of the plaintiff corporation was inoperative and void.

The declaration also alleges that it was the duty of the defendants, as directors, to keep the property of the corporation insured. There is no statute that makes it the duty of the directors of a corporation to keep its property insured, and there are no facts alleged from which we can say, as matter of law, that it was the duty of the defendants to insure the property of the corporation.

Demurrer sustained.

■ STANLEY, J., did not sit: the others concurred.

———

PEOPLE EX REL. MANICE v. POWELL, 201 N.Y. 194, 200–01, 94 N.E. 634, 637 (1911). "The board of directors of a corporation do not stand in the same relation to the corporate body which a private agent holds towards his principal. . . . In corporate bodies the powers of the board of directors are, in a very important sense, original and undelegated.' (*Hoyt v. Thompson's Executors,* 19 N.Y. 207, 216; *Beveridge v. N.Y.E.R.R. Co.,* 112 N.Y. 1, 22, 23.)

"While the ordinary rules of law relating to an agent are applicable in considering the acts of a board of directors in behalf of a corporation when dealing with third persons, the individual directors making up the board are not mere employees, but a part of an elected body of officers constituting the executive agents of the corporation. They hold such office charged with the duty to act for the corporation according to their best judgment, and in so doing they cannot be controlled in the reasonable exercise and performance of such duty. As a general rule the stockholders cannot act in relation to the ordinary business of the corporation, nor can they control the directors in the exercise of the judgment vested in them by virtue of their office.

"The relation of the directors to the stockholders is essentially that of trustee and *cestui que trust.* The peculiar relation that they bear to the corporation and the owners of its stock grows out of the inability of the corporation to act except through such managing officers and agents. The corporation is the owner of the property, but the directors in the performance of their duty possess it, and act in every way as if they owned it."

———

DEL. GEN. CORP. LAW § 141(k)

[See Statutory Supplement]

———

CAL. CORP. CODE §§ 303, 304

[See Statutory Supplement]

———

N.Y. BUS. CORP. LAW § 706

[See Statutory Supplement]

––––––––

NOTE ON REMOVAL OF DIRECTORS

1. *Removed by the Shareholders.* Shareholders can remove a director for cause, even in the absence of a statute that so provides. See, e.g., Auer v. Dressel, 306 N.Y. 427, 118 N.E.2d 590 (1954); Campbell v. Loew's, Inc., 36 Del.Ch. 563, 134 A.2d 852 (1957). Shareholders cannot remove a director without cause, in the absence of specific authority to do so under the statute, the certificate of incorporation, or the by-laws. See, e.g., Frank v. Anthony, 107 So.2d 136 (Fla.App.1958). Some statutes permit the shareholders to remove a director without cause. See, e.g., Cal.Corp.Code § 303(a); Model Bus.Corp.Act § 8.08. A few statutes permit the shareholders to remove a director without cause if the certificate or by-laws so provide. See, e.g., N.Y.Bus.Corp.Law § 706(b). A certificate or by-law provision can permit removal without cause only of directors elected after the provision has been adopted. See, e.g., Everett v. Transnation Development Corp., 267 A.2d 627 (Del.Ch.1970).

2. *Removal by the Board.* In the absence of statute, the board cannot remove a director, with or without cause. See, e.g., Bruch v. National Guarantee Credit Corp., 13 Del.Ch. 180, 116 A. 738 (1922). Whether the certificate of incorporation can change this rule is uncertain. See Dillon v. Berg, 326 F.Supp. 1214 (D.Del.1971), aff'd 453 F.2d 876 (3d Cir.); Bruch v. National Guarantee Credit Corp., supra. However, some statutes permit the board to remove a director for cause, see, e.g., Mass.Gen.Laws ch. 156B, § 51(c), or for specified reasons, such as conviction of a felony, see, e.g., Calif.Corp.Code § 302. A few statutes permit the board to remove a director for cause or for specified reasons if the certificate of incorporation so provides. See, e.g., N.J.Stat.Ann. § 14A:6–6.

3. *Removal by the Court.* The cases are split on whether a court can remove directors for cause. Compare Webber v. Webber Oil Co., 495 A.2d 1215 (Me.1985) (courts do not have power to remove directors) with Ross v. 311 North Central Avenue Building Corp., 130 Ill.App.2d 336, 264 N.E.2d 406 (1970) (courts have power to remove directors, at least for fraud or the like). However, some statutes permit the courts to remove a director for specified reasons, such as fraudulent or dishonest acts. These statutes usually provide that a petition for such removal can be brought only by a designated percentage of the shareholders (most commonly 10%), by the attorney general, or in some cases, by either. See, e.g., Calif.Corp.Code § 304; N.Y.Bus.Corp. Law § 706(d).

––––––––

Schnell v. Chris–Craft Industries, Inc.

Supreme Court of Delaware, 1971.
285 A.2d 437.

■ HERRMANN, JUSTICE (for the majority of the court):

This is an appeal from the denial by the Court of Chancery of the petition of dissident stockholders for injunctive relief to prevent management[1] from advancing the date of the annual stockholders' meeting from January 11, 1972, as previously set by the by-laws, to December 8, 1971.

The opinion below is reported at 285 A.2d 430. This opinion is confined to the frame of reference of the opinion below for the sake of brevity and because of the strictures of time imposed by the circumstances of the case.

It will be seen that the Chancery Court considered all of the reasons stated by management as business reasons for changing the date of the meeting; but that those reasons were rejected by the Court below in making the following findings:

"I am satisfied, however, in a situation in which present management has disingenuously resisted the production of a list of its stockholders to plaintiffs or their confederates and has otherwise turned a deaf ear to plaintiffs' demands about a change in management designed to lift defendant from its present business doldrums, management has seized on a relatively new section of the Delaware Corporation Law for the purpose of cutting down on the amount of time which would otherwise have been available to plaintiffs and others for the waging of a proxy battle. Management thus enlarged the scope of its scheduled October 18 directors' meeting to include the by-law amendment in controversy after the stockholders committee had filed with the S.E.C. its intention to wage a proxy fight on October 16.

"Thus plaintiffs reasonably contend that because of the tactics employed by management (which involve the hiring of two established proxy solicitors as well as a refusal to produce a list of its stockholders, coupled with its use of an amendment to the Delaware Corporation Law to limit the time for contest), they are given little chance, because of the exigencies of time, including that required to clear material at the S.E.C., to wage a successful proxy fight between now and December 8. . . ."

In our view, those conclusions amount to a finding that management has attempted to utilize the corporate machinery and the Delaware Law for the purpose of perpetuating itself in office; and, to that end, for the purpose of obstructing the legitimate efforts of dissident stockholders in the exercise of their rights to undertake a proxy contest against management. These are inequitable purposes, contrary to established principles of corporate democracy. The advancement by directors of the by-law date of a stockholders' meeting, for such

---

1. We use this word as meaning "managing directors".

purposes, may not be permitted to stand. Compare Condec Corporation v. Lunkenheimer Company, Del.Ch., 230 A.2d 769 (1967).

When the by-laws of a corporation designate the date of the annual meeting of stockholders, it is to be expected that those who intend to contest the reelection of incumbent management will gear their campaign to the by-law date. It is not to be expected that management will attempt to advance that date in order to obtain an inequitable advantage in the contest.

Management contends that it has complied strictly with the provisions of the new Delaware Corporation Law in changing the by-law date. The answer to that contention, of course, is that inequitable action does not become permissible simply because it is legally possible....

We are unable to agree with the conclusion of the Chancery Court that the stockholders' application for injunctive relief here was tardy and came too late....

Accordingly, the judgment below must be reversed and the cause remanded, with instructions to nullify the December 8 date as a meeting date for stockholders; to reinstate January 11, 1972 as the sole date of the next annual meeting of the stockholders of the corporation; and to take such other proceedings and action as may be consistent herewith regarding the stock record closing date and any other related matters.

[The dissenting opinion of Chief Justice Wolcott is omitted.]

A.A. BERLE & G. MEANS, THE MODERN CORPORATION AND PRIVATE PROPERTY 220 (rev. ed. 1967). "[A]n underlying thesis in corporation law ... could be applied to each and every power in the whole corporate galaxy. Succinctly stated, the thesis [is] that all powers granted to a corporation or to the management of a corporation, or to any group within the corporation, whether derived from statute or charter or both, are necessarily and at all times exercisable only for the ratable benefit of all the shareholders as their interest appears. That, in consequence, the *use* of the power is subject to equitable limitation when the power has been exercised to the detriment of their interest, however absolute the grant of power may be in terms, and however correct the technical exercise of it may have been."

Blasius Industries, Inc. v. Atlas Corp.

Court of Chancery of Delaware, 1988.
564 A.2d 651.

OPINION

■ ALLEN, CHANCELLOR.

Two cases pitting the directors of Atlas Corporation against that company's largest (9.1%) shareholder, Blasius Industries, have been consolidated and tried together. Together, these cases ultimately require the court to determine who is entitled to sit on Atlas' board of directors. . . .

The first of the cases was filed on December 30, 1987. As amended, it challenges the validity of board action taken at a telephone meeting of December 31, 1987 that added two new members to Atlas' seven member board. That action was taken as an immediate response to the delivery to Atlas by Blasius the previous day of a form of stockholder consent that, if joined in by holders of a majority of Atlas' stock, would have increased the board of Atlas from seven to fifteen members and would have elected eight new members nominated by Blasius.

As I find the facts of this first case, they present the question whether a board acts consistently with its fiduciary duty when it acts, in good faith and with appropriate care, for the primary purpose of preventing or impeding an unaffiliated majority of shareholders from expanding the board and electing a new majority. For the reasons that follow, I conclude that, even though defendants here acted on their view of the corporation's interest and not selfishly, their December 31 action constituted an offense to the relationship between corporate directors and shareholders that has traditionally been protected in courts of equity. As a consequence, I conclude that the board action taken on December 31 was invalid and must be voided. . . .

The facts set forth below represent findings based upon a preponderance of the admissible evidence, as I evaluate it.

I.

Blasius Acquires a 9% Stake in Atlas.

Blasius is a new stockholder of Atlas. It began to accumulate Atlas shares for the first time in July, 1987. On October 29, it filed a Schedule 13D with the Securities Exchange Commission disclosing that, with affiliates, it then [owned] 9.1% of Atlas' common stock. It stated in that filing that it intended to encourage management of Atlas to consider a restructuring of the Company or other transaction to enhance shareholder values. It also disclosed that Blasius was exploring the feasibility of obtaining control of Atlas, including instituting a tender offer or seeking "appropriate" representation on the Atlas board of directors.

Blasius has recently come under the control of two individuals, Michael Lubin and Warren Delano, who after experience in the commercial banking industry, had, for a short time, run a venture capital operation for a small investment banking firm. Now on their own, they apparently came to control Blasius with the assistance of Drexel Burnham's well noted junk bond mechanism. Since then, they have made several attempts to effect leveraged buyouts, but without success. . . .

The prospect of Messrs. Lubin and Delano involving themselves in Atlas' affairs, was not a development welcomed by Atlas' management. Atlas had a new CEO, defendant Weaver, who had, over the course of the past year or so, overseen a business restructuring of a sort. Atlas had sold three of its five divisions. It had just announced (September 1, 1987) that it would close its once important domestic uranium operation. The goal was to focus the Company on its gold mining business. By October, 1987, the structural changes to do this had been largely accomplished. Mr. Weaver was perhaps thinking that the restructuring that had occurred should be given a chance to produce benefit before another restructuring (such as Blasius had alluded to in its Schedule 13D filing) was attempted, when he wrote in his diary on October 30, 1987:

> 13D by Delano & Lubin came in today. Had long conversation w/MAH & Mark Golden [of Goldman Sachs] on issue. All agree we must dilute these people down by the acquisition of another Co. w/stock, or merger or something else.

The Blasius Proposal of A Leverage Recapitalization Or Sale.

Immediately after filing its 13D on October 29, Blasius' representatives sought a meeting with the Atlas management. Atlas dragged its feet. A meeting was arranged for December 2, 1987 following the regular meeting of the Atlas board. Attending that meeting were Messrs. Lubin and Delano for Blasius, and, for Atlas, Messrs. Weaver, Devaney (Atlas' CFO), Masinter (legal counsel and director) and Czajkowski (a representative of Atlas' investment banker, Goldman Sachs).

At that meeting, Messrs. Lubin and Delano suggested that Atlas engage in a leveraged restructuring and distribute cash to shareholders. In such a transaction, which is by this date a commonplace form of transaction, a corporation typically raises cash by sale of assets and significant borrowings and makes a large one time cash distribution to shareholders. The shareholders are typically left with cash and an equity interest in a smaller, more highly leveraged enterprise. Lubin and Delano gave the outline of a leveraged recapitalization for Atlas as they saw it.

Immediately following the meeting, the Atlas representatives expressed among themselves an initial reaction that the proposal was infeasible. On December 7, Mr. Lubin sent a letter detailing the proposal. In general, it proposed the following: (1) an initial special cash dividend to Atlas' stockholders in an aggregate amount equal to (a) $35 million, (b) the aggregate proceeds to Atlas from the exercise of option warrants and stock options, and (c) the proceeds from the sale or disposal of all of Atlas' operations that are not related to its continuing minerals operations; and (2) a special non-cash dividend to Atlas' stockholders of an aggregate $125 million principal amount of 7% Secured Subordinated Gold–Indexed Debentures. The funds necessary to pay the initial cash dividend were to principally come from (i) a "gold loan" in the amount of $35,625,000, repayable over a three to five year period and secured by 75,000 ounces of gold at a price of $475 per ounce, (ii) the proceeds from the sale of the discontinued

Brockton Sole and Plastics and Ready–Mix Concrete businesses, and (iii) a then expected January, 1988 sale of uranium to the Public Service Electric & Gas Company. . . .

The proposal met with a cool reception from management. . . .

On December 30, 1987, Blasius caused Cede & Co. (the registered owner of its Atlas stock) to deliver to Atlas a signed written consent (1) adopting a precatory resolution recommending that the board develop and implement a restructuring proposal, (2) amending the Atlas bylaws to, among other things, expand the size of the board from seven to fifteen members—the maximum number under Atlas' charter, and (3) electing eight named persons to fill the new directorships. . . .

The reaction was immediate. Mr. Weaver conferred with Mr. Masinter, the Company's outside counsel and a director, who viewed the consent as an attempt to take control of the Company. They decided to call an emergency meeting of the board, even though a regularly scheduled meeting was to occur only one week hence, on January 6, 1988. The point of the emergency meeting was to act on their conclusion (or to seek to have the board act on their conclusion) "that we should add at least one and probably two directors to the board . . ." (Tr. 85, Vol. II). A quorum of directors, however, could not be arranged for a telephone meeting that day. A telephone meeting was held the next day. At that meeting, the board voted to amend the bylaws to increase the size of the board from seven to nine and appointed John M. Devaney and Harry J. Winters, Jr. to fill those newly created positions. Atlas' Certificate of Incorporation creates staggered terms for directors; the terms to which Messrs. Devaney and Winters were appointed would expire in 1988 and 1990, respectively.

The Motivation of the Incumbent Board In Expanding the Board and Appointing New Members.

In increasing the size of Atlas' board by two and filling the newly created positions, the members of the board realized that they were thereby precluding the holders of a majority of the Company's shares from placing a majority of new directors on the board through Blasius' consent solicitation, should they want to do so. Indeed the evidence establishes that that was the principal motivation in so acting.

The conclusion that, in creating two new board positions on December 31 and electing Messrs. Devaney and Winters to fill those positions the board was principally motivated to prevent or delay the shareholders from possibly placing a majority of new members on the board, is critical to my analysis of the central issue posed by the first filed of the two pending cases. If the board in fact was not so motivated, but rather had taken action completely independently of the consent solicitation, which merely had an incidental impact upon the possible effectuation of any action authorized by the shareholders, it is very unlikely that such action would be subject to judicial nullification. See, e.g., Frantz Manufacturing Company v. EAC Industries, Del.Supr., 501 A.2d 401, 407 (1985); Moran v. Household International, Inc., Del.Ch., 490 A.2d 1059, 1080, aff'd, Del.Supr., 500

A.2d 1346 (1985). The board, as a general matter, is under no fiduciary obligation to suspend its active management of the firm while the consent solicitation process goes forward. . . .

. . . I conclude that, while the addition of these qualified men would, under other circumstances, be clearly appropriate as an independent step, such a step was in fact taken in order to impede or preclude a majority of the shareholders from effectively adopting the course proposed by Blasius. . . .

II.

Plaintiff attacks the December 31 board action as a selfishly motivated effort to protect the incumbent board from a perceived threat to its control of Atlas. Their conduct is said to constitute a violation of the principle, applied in such cases as Schnell v. Chris–Craft Industries, Del.Supr., 285 A.2d 437 (1971), that directors hold legal powers [subject] to a supervening duty to exercise such powers in good faith pursuit of what they reasonably believe to be in the corporation's interest. The December 31 action is also said to have been taken in a grossly negligent manner, since it was designed to preclude the recapitalization from being pursued, and the board had no basis at that time to make a prudent determination about the wisdom of that proposal, nor was there any emergency that required it to act in any respect regarding that proposal before putting itself in a position to do so advisedly.

Defendants, of course, contest every aspect of plaintiffs' claims. They claim the formidable protections of the business judgment rule. See, e.g., Aronson v. Lewis, Del.Supr., 473 A.2d 805 (1984); Grobow v. Perot, Del.Supr., 539 A.2d 180 (1988); In re J.P. Stevens & Co., Inc. Shareholders Litigation, Del.Ch.,542 A.2d 770 (1988).

They say that, in creating two new board positions and filling them on December 31, they acted without a conflicting interest (since the Blasius proposal did not, in any event, challenge *their* places on the board), they acted with due care (since they well knew the persons they put on the board and did not thereby preclude later consideration of the recapitalization), and they acted in good faith (since they were motivated, they say, to protect the shareholders from the threat of having an impractical, indeed a dangerous, recapitalization program foisted upon them). Accordingly, defendants assert there is no basis to conclude that their December 31 action constituted any violation of the duty of the fidelity that a director owes by reason of his office to the corporation and its shareholders.

Moreover, defendants say that their action was fair, measured and appropriate, in light of the circumstances. Therefore, even should the court conclude that some level of substantive review of it is appropriate under a legal test of fairness, or under the intermediate level of review authorized by *Unocal Corp. v. Mesa Petroleum Co.,* Del.Supr., 493 A.2d 946 (1985), defendants assert that the board's decision must be sustained as valid in both law and equity.

III. . . .

On balance, I cannot conclude that the board was acting out of a self-interested motive in any important respect on December 31. I conclude rather that the board saw the "threat" of the Blasius recapitalization proposal as posing vital policy differences between itself and Blasius. It acted, I conclude, in a good faith effort to protect its incumbency, not selfishly, but in order to thwart implementation of the recapitalization that it feared, reasonably, would cause great injury to the Company.

The real question the case presents, to my mind, is whether, in these circumstances, the board, even if it *is* acting with subjective good faith (which will typically, if not always, be a contestable or debatable judicial conclusion), may validly act for the principal purpose of preventing the shareholders from electing a majority of new directors. The question thus posed is not one of intentional wrong (or even negligence), but one of authority *as between the fiduciary and the beneficiary* (not simply legal authority, *i.e.,* as between the fiduciary and the world at large).

IV.

It is established in our law that a board may take certain steps—such as the purchase by the corporation of its own stock—that have the effect of defeating a threatened change in corporate control, when those steps are taken advisedly, in good faith pursuit of a corporate interest, and are reasonable in relation to a threat to legitimate corporate interests posed by the proposed change in control. See Unocal Corp. v. Mesa Petroleum Co., Del.Supr., 493 A.2d 946 (1985); Kors v. Carey, Del.Ch., 158 A.2d 136 (1960); Cheff v. Mathes, Del. Supr., 199 A.2d 548 (1964); Kaplan v. Goldsamt, Del.Ch., 380 A.2d 556 (1977). Does this rule—that the reasonable exercise of good faith and due care generally validates, in equity, the exercise of legal authority even if the act has an entrenchment effect—apply to action designed for the primary purpose of interfering with the effectiveness of a stockholder vote? Our authorities, as well as sound principles, suggest that the central importance of the franchise to the scheme of corporate governance, requires that, in this setting, that rule not be applied and that closer scrutiny be accorded to such transaction.

1. *Why the deferential business judgment rule does not apply to board acts taken for the primary purpose of interfering with a stockholder's vote, even if taken advisedly and in good faith.*

A. The question of legitimacy.

The shareholder franchise is the ideological underpinning upon which the legitimacy of directorial power rests. Generally, shareholders have only two protections against perceived inadequate business performance. They may sell their stock (which, if done in sufficient numbers, may so affect security prices as to create an incentive for altered managerial performance), or they may vote to replace incumbent board members.

It has, for a long time, been conventional to dismiss the stock-holder vote as a vestige or ritual of little practical importance. It may be that we are now witnessing the emergence of new institutional voices and arrangements that will make the stockholder vote a less predictable affair than it has been. Be that as it may, however, whether the vote is seen functionally as an unimportant formalism, or as an important tool of discipline, it is clear that it is critical to the theory that legitimates the exercise of power by some (directors and officers) over vast aggregations of property that they do not own. Thus, when viewed from a broad, institutional perspective, it can be seen that matters involving the integrity of the shareholder voting process involve [considerations] not present in any other context in which directors exercise delegated power.

B. Questions of this type raise issues of the allocation of authority as between the board and the shareholders.

The distinctive nature of the shareholder franchise context also appears when the matter is viewed from a less generalized, doctrinal point of view. From this point of view, as well, it appears that the ordinary considerations to which the business judgment rule originally responded are simply not present in the shareholder voting context. That is, a decision by the board to act for the primary purpose of preventing the effectiveness of a shareholder vote inevitably involves the question who, as between the principal and the agent, has authority with respect to a matter of internal corporate governance. That, of course, is true in a very specific way in this case which deals with the question who should constitute the board of directors of the corporation, but it will be true in every instance in which an incumbent board seeks to thwart a shareholder majority. A board's decision to act to prevent the shareholders from creating a majority of new board positions and filling them does not involve the exercise of *the corporation's power* over its property, or with respect to *its* rights or obligations; rather, it involves allocation, between shareholders as a class and the board, of effective power with respect to governance of the corporation. This need not be the case with respect to other forms of corporate action that may have an entrenchment effect—such as the stock buybacks present in *Unocal, Cheff* or *Kors v. Carey.* Action designed principally to interfere with the effectiveness of a vote inevitably involves a conflict between the board and a shareholder majority. Judicial review of such action involves a determination of the legal and equitable obligations of an agent towards his principal. This is not, in my opinion, a question that a court may leave to the agent finally to decide so long as he does so honestly and competently; that is, it may not be left to the agent's business judgment.

2. *What rule does apply: per se invalidity of corporate acts intended primarily to thwart effective exercise of the franchise or is there an intermediate standard?*

Plaintiff argues for a rule of *per se* invalidity once a plaintiff has established that a board has acted for the primary purpose of thwarting the exercise of a shareholder vote. Our opinions in Canada

Southern Oils, Ltd. v. Manabi Exploration Co., Del.Ch., 96 A.2d 810 (1953) and Condec Corporation v. Lunkenheimer Company, Del.Ch., 230 A.2d 769 (1967) could be read as support for such a rule of *per se* invalidity. . . .

. . . A *per se* rule that would strike down, in equity, any board action taken for the primary purpose of interfering with the effectiveness of a corporate vote would have the advantage of relative clarity and predictability.[4] It also has the advantage of most vigorously enforcing the concept of corporate democracy. The disadvantage it brings along is, of course, the disadvantage a *per se* rule always has: it may sweep too broadly. In two recent cases dealing with shareholder votes, this court struck down board acts done for the primary purpose of impeding the exercise of stockholder voting power. In doing so, a per se rule was not applied. Rather, it was said that, in such a case, the board bears the heavy burden of demonstrating a compelling justification for such action. [Aprahamian v. HBO & Co., 531 A.2d 1204 (1987) (Del.Ch.1987); Phillips v. Insituform, 1987 WL 16285 (Del.Ch. 1987).]

In my view, our inability to foresee now all of the future settings in which a board might, in good faith, paternalistically seek to thwart a shareholder vote, counsels against the adoption of a *per se* rule invalidating, in equity, every board action taken for the sole or primary purpose of thwarting a shareholder vote, even though I recognize the transcending significance of the franchise to the claims to legitimacy of our scheme of corporate governance. It may be that some set of facts would justify such extreme action. This, however, is not such a case.

3. *Defendants have demonstrated no sufficient justification for the action of December 31 which was intended to prevent an unaffiliated majority of shareholders from effectively exercising their right to elect eight new directors.*

The board was not faced with a coercive action taken by a powerful shareholder against the interests of a distinct shareholder constituency (such as a public minority). It was presented with a consent solicitation by a 9% shareholder. Moreover, here it had time (and understood that it had time) to inform the shareholders of its views on the merits of the proposal subject to stockholder vote. The only justification that can, in such a situation, be offered for the action taken is that the board knows better than do the shareholders what is in the corporation's best interest. While that premise is no doubt true for any number of matters, it is irrelevant (except insofar as the shareholders wish to be guided by the board's recommendation) when the question is who should comprise the board of directors. The theory of our corporation law confers power upon directors as the agents of the shareholders; it does not create Platonic masters. It may be that the Blasius restructuring proposal was or is unrealistic and would lead to injury to the corporation and its shareholders if

---

4. While it must be admitted that any rule that requires for its invocation the finding of a subjective mental state (*i.e.,* a primary purpose) necessarily will lead to controversy concerning whether it applies or not, nevertheless, once it is determined to apply, this *per se* rule would be clearer than the alternative discussed below.

pursued. Having heard the evidence, I am inclined to think it was not a sound proposal. The board certainly viewed it that way, and that view, held in good faith, entitled the board to take certain steps to evade the risk it perceived. It could, for example, expend corporate funds to inform shareholders and seek to bring them to a similar point of view. See, e.g. Hall v. Trans–Lux Daylight Picture Screen Corporation, Del.Ch., 171 A. 226, 227 (1934); Hibbert v. Hollywood Park, Inc., Del.Supr., 457 A.2d 339 (1983). But there is a vast difference between expending corporate funds to inform the electorate and exercising power for the primary purpose of foreclosing effective shareholder action. A majority of the shareholders, who were not dominated in any respect, could view the matter differently than did the board. If they do, or did, they are entitled to employ the mechanisms provided by the corporation law and the Atlas certificate of incorporation to advance that view. They are also entitled, in my opinion, to restrain their agents, the board, from acting for the principal purpose of thwarting that action.

I therefore conclude that, even finding the action was taken in good faith, it constituted an unintended violation of the duty of loyalty that the board owed to the shareholders. I note parenthetically that the concept of an unintended breach of the duty of loyalty is unusual but not novel. . . . That action will, therefore, be set aside by order of this court. . . .

[During the pendency of the case involving Blasius's attack on the action of the directors in adding two members to the board, Blasius presented Atlas with shareholder consents purporting to show that a majority of Atlas's shareholders had adopted Blasius's proposals to enlarge the board from seven to fifteen, elect eight new directors nominated by Blasius, and take certain other actions. Atlas appointed Manufacturers Hanover Trust Company to act as judge of the shareholders' "vote." Manufacturers reported that the vote had been extremely close, but that none of Blasius's proposals had succeeded. Blasius then brought a second case, in which it challenged certain of Manufacturers' determinations. That case was consolidated with Blasius's attack on the action of the directors in adding two members to the board. The court upheld most of Manufacturers' determinations and Manufacturers' conclusion that Blasius had lost the vote, and rendered judgment in the second case for the defendants.]

––––––

NOTE ON CONDEC CORP. v. LUNKENHEIMER CO.

In Condec Corp. v. Lunkenheimer Co., 43 Del.Ch. 353, 230 A.2d 769 (1967), referred to in *Blasius,* Condec wanted to merge with Lunkenheimer, but Lunkenheimer resisted. Condec then acquired some Lunkenheimer shares through a tender offer, and made a second tender offer which if successful would have given Condec slightly more than half of Lunkenheimer's 410,000 shares. Lunkenheimer's board then caused Lunkenheimer to swap 75,000 shares of its stock for 75,000 shares of a wholly owned subsidiary of U.S. Industries, which would dilute Condec's interest to a minority. Condec attacked the transaction. Held, for Condec:

[S]hares may not be issued for an improper purpose such as a take-over of voting control from others. As stated in Yasik v. Wachtel, 25 Del.Ch. 247, 17 A.2d 309:

"It is fundamental that directors stand in a fiduciary relation to the corporation and its shareholders, and that their primary duty is to deal fairly and justly. It is a breach of this duty, wholly apart from any consideration of pre-emptive rights, for directors to make use of the issuance of shares to accomplish an improper purpose, such as to enable a particular person or group to maintain or obtain voting control, against the objection of shareholders from whom control is thereby wrested...."

This does not mean that stock issued to raise money to eliminate a deficit is to be invalidated merely because defendant directors thereby fairly avail themselves of an opportunity to acquire additional shares to fortify their natural desire to remain in control, Aldridge v. Franco–Wyoming, 28 Del.Ch. 320, 326, 42 A.2d 879. Where, however, the objective sought in the issuance of stock is not merely the pursual of a business purpose but also to retain control, it has been held to be a mockery to suggest that the "control" effect of an agreement in litigation is merely incidental to its primary business objective. In Matter of Seminole Oil and Gas Corporation, 38 Del.Ch. 246, 150 A.2d 20. . . .

Finally, we are not here concerned with the need of proving corporate injury as has been held to be the case when a stockholder attacks derivatively the spending of corporate funds for the purchase of his corporation's own stock, Kors v. Carey, 39 Del.Ch. 47, 158 A.2d 136. This rather is a case of a stockholder with a contractual right to assert voting control being deprived of such control by what is virtually a corporate legerdemain. Manipulation of this type is not permissible, Canada Southern Oils v. Manabi Exploration Co., 33 Del.Ch. 537, 96 A.2d 810.

NOTE ON THE BUSINESS JUDGMENT RULE

Corporate law employs a number of different standards of judicial review of the conduct of directors and officers, depending on the type of conduct involved. The most lenient standard—the standard that is easiest for officers and directors to satisfy—is the business judgment rule, referred to in *Blasius*. The meaning and application of this rule will be considered in depth in Chapter VIII, The Duty of Care. At this point, suffice to say that under the business judgment rule, if certain conditions are satisfied a director or officer will not be liable for the consequences of a decision unless the decision was irrational. In

Blasius, Chancellor Allen in effect concluded that conduct that interferes with shareholder voting is not reviewed under the business judgment rule. Instead, a much more stringent standard of review—the standard of compelling justification—should be applied.

———

NOTE ON TAKEOVERS

Until around the mid–1960s, it was very difficult to oust an incumbent management of a publicly held corporation. In principle, such an ouster could be achieved through a proxy fight, in which insurgents mobilized support among other shareholders to vote the incumbents out of office. However, for a variety of reasons proxy fights were not often launched, and were only intermittently successful. Correspondingly, it was difficult to acquire a corporation against the objections of its managers, because the principal forms of acquisitions, such as mergers and the purchase of a corporation's assets, require approval by the board of the corporation proposed to be acquired.

In the mid–1960s, however, hostile takeovers came to be an important way to both oust incumbent managements and effect acquisitions. In a hostile takeover, Corporation A makes a public offer—called a *bid* or *tender offer*—to purchase stock in Corporation B, up to a stated amount and subject to certain conditions. The tender offer is made to B's shareholders, not to B. The tender-offer price is almost invariably well above the prevailing market price for B's stock.

Because a tender offer is made to B's shareholders, rather than to B, the approval of B's board is not required. Nevertheless, despite the fact that a tender offer is made to shareholders rather than to the corporation, incumbent managers tend to resist takeovers by causing the corporation to take defensive actions to stymie a bid. The law governing tender offers is complex, and will be considered in depth in Chapter 12. At the risk of oversimplification, the most fundamental rule in this body of law—at least in Delaware, where most takeover cases arise—is the test laid down in Unocal Corp. v. Mesa Petroleum Co., 493 A.2d 946 (Del. 1985), as supplemented in Unitrin, Inc. v. American General Corp., 651 A.2d 1361 (Del. 1995).

Under the *Unocal* test, if the board wants to take defensive actions against takeover, it must satisfy what is sometimes called an *enhanced business judgment rule* or *intermediate standard of review* (intermediate, that is, between the standard of review of director action that is embodied in the business judgment rule, which is relatively easy to satisfy, and the standards of review under the duty of loyalty, which are harder to satisfy). To meet this standard of review, a board must first show that it had reasonable grounds for believing that the tender offer presented a danger to corporate policy and effectiveness. That burden is met by showing good faith and reasonable investigation—presumably, a more thorough investigation than would be required for most other business decisions. The board must then satisfy a proportionality test: the defensive action must be reasonable in relation to the threat posed. Under *Unitrin*, in applying the proportionality test the court should first direct its attention to whether the board's defensive action was "draconian," because "either preclusive or coercive." Even if the defensive action was not preclusive or coercive, it must be "within a range of reasonable responses to the threat" posed by the tender offer.

Although the *law* of tender offers will be considered in Chapter 12, the *phenomenon* of tender offers has shaped much of present corporate law and practice. For example, the potential ability of management to block takeover bids has led to renewed emphasis on proxy fights or—as in *Blasius*—consent solicitations. This, in turn, has led to attempts by incumbent managers to take various kinds of actions—again as in *Blasius*—to prevent their removal by shareholder vote or shareholder consent.

———

NOTE ON WEIGHTED VOTING IN PUBLICLY HELD CORPORATIONS

In the majority of publicly held corporations, only common shareholders have voting rights, and each share of common stock carries one vote. However, voting rights can be conferred on preferred stock, or even on bonds. Furthermore, a corporation may have two or more classes of common stock, each with different voting rights. When there are two or more classes of common stock, often one class has voting power all out of proportion to its equity interests. Such structures are sometimes referred to as dual-class common, super-voting stock, or weighted voting. Although not new, the incidence of such structures increased during the takeover movement in the 1980s, when they were often installed as an anti-takeover defense.

In theory, the creation of such a structure affects only the relative rights of different shareholders, not the allocation of power between managers and shareholders. As the use of such structures to defend against takeovers suggests, however, in practice these structures usually involve the issuance of super-voting stock to members of a control group with the objective of allowing control to be maintained with a minimum investment.

In Stroh v. Blackhawk Holding Corp., 48 Ill.2d 471, 272 N.E.2d 1 (1971), noted, 85 Harv.L.Rev. 1676 (1972), 26 Sw.L.J. 618 (1972), Blackhawk's certificate authorized a Class A and a Class B stock. Class B voted share for share with Class A, but was entitled neither to dividends nor to participate in the proceeds of liquidation. After Blackhawk's formation, its promoters purchased 500,000 shares of Class B at a quarter of a cent per share, and 87,868 shares of Class A at $3.40 per share, and thereafter sold Class A stock to the public at $4 per share. As of June 1968, Blackhawk had outstanding 1,237,681 Class A shares and 500,000 Class B shares, the latter representing an investment of $1250 but carrying 28.78% of the total vote. The court upheld the validity of the B stock:

> ... Section 14 of the Business Corporation Act ... provides that shares of stock in an Illinois corporation may be divided into classes,
>
>> "with such designations, preferences, qualifications, limitations, restrictions and such special or relative rights as shall be stated in the articles of incorporation. The articles of incorporation shall not limit or deny the voting power of the shares of any class...."
>
> Section 14 ... clearly expresses the intent of the legislature to be that parties to a corporate entity may create whatever restrictions and limitations they may want with regard to their corporate stock by expressing such restrictions and limitations in the articles of incorporation....
>
> ... It has long been the common practice in Illinois to classify shares of stock such that one may invest less than another in a corporation, and yet have control. One of two shareholders may purchase ten shares of a class of stock issued at its par value of $1,000 per share, and his business partner may purchase 100 shares of another class of the corporate stock issued at its par value of $10 per share. The parties, for varying reasons, may be very willing that the party investing the $1,000 have control of the management of the corporation, as opposed to the party having the investment of $10,000....
>
> In this case the parties went one step further than is customary. The stock which could be bought cheaper, and yet carry the same voting power per share, was not permitted to share at all in the dividends or assets of the corporation. This additional step did not invalidate the stock.

In Providence & Worcester Co. v. Baker, 378 A.2d 121 (Del.1977), a form of weighted voting was achieved by limiting the number of votes that could be cast by any one shareholder. P & W's certificate provided that each holder of common stock had one vote per share for his first 50 shares, but only one vote per 20 shares for all shares over 50. The validity of these limitations was challenged by the trustees in bankruptcy of Penn Central, who held 28% of P & W's stock, but were effectively restricted to 3% of the total voting power. The court upheld the restrictions under Del. § 212(a), which states that "[u]nless otherwise provided in the certificate of incorporation ... each stockholder shall be entitled to 1 vote for each share of capital stock held by such stockholder." The court concluded that "if the General Assembly intended to bar the type of restriction on stockholders' voting rights here under review, such prohibition would appear in § 212.... Under § 212(a), voting rights of stockholders may be varied from the 'one share-one vote' standard by the certificate of incorporation. . . ." See also Lacos Land Co. v. Arden Group, Inc., 517 A.2d 271 (Del.Ch.1986); 1 F.H. O'Neal & R. Thompson, O'Neal's Close Corporations § 3.16 (3d ed. 1992).

In several situations, Congress has acted to prevent abuses in this area. For example, § 18 of the Investment Company Act of 1940, 15 U.S.C.A. § 80a–18, forbids the issuance of nonvoting stock by companies subject to that Act, except in a few special cases.

The rules of the New York Stock Exchange, the American Stock Exchange and NASDAQ, set certain limits on weighted voting in listed corporations.

See generally Gordon, Ties that Bond: Dual Class Common Stock and the Problem of Shareholder Choice, 76 Calif.L.Rev. 1 (1988); Gilson, Evaluating Dual Class Common Stock: The Relevance of Substitutes, 73 Va.L.Rev. 807 (1987).

––––––

**NEW YORK STOCK EXCHANGE, LISTED
COMPANY MANUAL § 313.00**

[See Statutory Supplement]

––––––

International Brotherhood of Teamsters v. Fleming Companies, Inc.

Supreme Court of Oklahoma, 1999.
975 P.2d 907.

■ . . . SIMMS. J:

The United States Court of Appeals, Tenth Circuit, John C. Porfilio, Presiding Judge, pursuant to 20 O.S. [Oklahoma Statutes] 1991, § 1601, certified to the Oklahoma Supreme Court the following question of law:

> Does Oklahoma law [A] restrict the authority to create and implement shareholder rights plans exclusively to the board of directors, or [B] may shareholders propose resolutions requiring that shareholder rights plans be submitted to the shareholders for vote at the succeeding annual meeting?

We answer the first part of the question in the negative and the second part affirmatively. We hold under Oklahoma law there is no exclusive authority granted boards of directors to create and implement shareholder rights plans, where shareholder objection is brought and passed through official channels of corporate governance. We find no Oklahoma law which gives exclusive authority to a corporation's board of directors for the formulation of shareholder rights plans and no authority which precludes shareholders from proposing resolutions or bylaw amendments regarding shareholder rights plans. We hold shareholders may propose bylaws which restrict board implementation of shareholder rights plans, assuming the certificate of incorporation does not provide otherwise.

The International Brotherhood of the Teamsters General Fund [Teamsters] owns sixty-five shares of Fleming Companies, Inc. [Fleming or the company] stock. In 1986, Fleming implemented a shareholder's rights plan with the term of the plan to expire in 1996. The rights plan implemented by Fleming is an anti-takeover mechanism. Such plans give boards of directors authority to adopt and execute discriminatory shareholder rights upon the occurrence of some triggering event, usually when a certain percentage of shares has been amassed by a single shareholder. A board can place "restrictions or conditions on the exercise, transfer or receipt of" shareholder rights which can severely dilute the shareholding power of one seeking control of a company.[1] The defensive plans usually result in entrenching existing management, making a takeover without the approval of incumbent management more difficult. These rights plans can make it far more expensive to effect a takeover. Because the rights plans make the merger of companies more painful for the suitor and assist incumbent management in maintaining control, the plans are often called "poison pill rights plans" or "poison pills."

From a target company's perspective, rights plans can often buy valuable time to implement [a] merger strategy or even secure more lucrative offers from other suitors. In this context, a rights plan might serve not only the protectionist objectives of an existing management, but also the company's overall interests in the event of takeover, including the interests of shareholders.

However, rights plans can often stifle mergers, causing some shareholder groups to view them with increasing skepticism, because ... company mergers can be financially lucrative for shareholders who own stock in a target company. A poison pill not only makes many mergers cost prohibitive and therefore might prevent a merger altogether, but it can decrease the profits in those mergers which do ultimately occur. As a result, poison pills have the ability to strip shareholders of financial benefit which might normally be associated with a takeover.

The stock market has had a long history of shareholder passivity, but this is likely a thing of the past. The rise of the institutional investor and the increased knowledge of stockholders as a whole is forcing an increased accountability to shareholders for many boards of directors. As a result, the demands of the Teamsters in its case against Fleming is something courts may encounter with increasing frequency in the years to come.

The trial court, which ruled in the Teamsters' (shareholders) favor, expressed concern with Fleming's position, stating that it effectively removed corporate authority regarding share marketability from the shareholders and vested it exclusively in a board of directors,

---

1. John H. Matheson & Brent A. Olson, Shareholder Rights and Legislative Wrongs; Toward Balanced Takeover Legislation, 59 Geo.Wash.L.Rev. 1425, 1450 (1990).

which might view the situation from the most self-interested point of view.

Teamsters were critical of Fleming's rights plan, seeing it as a means of entrenching the current Fleming board of directors in the event Fleming became the target of a takeover. In 1996, the Teamsters organized and introduced a non-binding resolution for the annual shareholders meeting. The 1996 resolution called on the Fleming board to redeem the existing rights plan. The then current rights plan had been in effect since 1986 and was scheduled for renewal. The Teamsters proposal was met with apparent hostility from Fleming's board and the rights plan remained intact, despite a majority shareholder vote in agreement with the Teamsters' resolution to redeem it.

The following year, 1997, Teamsters mounted a more organized effort to change the continued implementation of the rights plan. Teamsters prepared a proxy statement for inclusion in the proxy materials for the 1997 annual shareholder's meeting. With the proxy effort, the Teamsters proposed an amendment to the company's bylaws which would require any rights plan implemented by the board of directors to be put to the shareholders for a majority vote.[3] The proposal was essentially a ratification procedure wherein the shareholders would force the board to formulate a rights plan both the board and shareholders could agree on or do away with such a plan altogether.

Fleming refused to include the resolution in its 1997 proxy statement, declaring the proposal was not a subject for shareholder action under Oklahoma law. Teamsters then brought an action in the Federal District Court for the Western District of Oklahoma. The district court ruled in favor of the Teamsters, the court finding that "shareholders, through the device of bylaws, have a right of review."[4] Fleming appealed to the 10th Circuit Court of Appeals, which submitted the certified question to this Court.

Fleming sought to postpone any shareholder vote on the 1997 proxy issue until after the resolution of this case. But the U.S. District

---

3. The 1997 proxy proposal provided:

Resolved, That shareholders hereby exercise their right under 18 O.S.A. Sec. 1013 to amend the bylaws of Fleming Companies, Inc. to add the following Article:

Article X Poison Pills (Shareholder Rights Plans)

A. The Corporation shall not adopt or maintain a poison pill, shareholder rights plan, rights agreement or any other form of "poison pill" which is designed to or has the effect of making acquisition of large holdings of the Corporation's shares of stock more difficult or expensive (such as the 1986 "Rights Agreement"), unless such plan is first approved by a majority shareholder vote. The Company shall redeem any such rights now in effect. The affirmative vote of a majority of shares voted shall suffice to approve such a plan.

B. This article shall be effective immediately and automatically as of the date it is approved by the affirmative vote of the holders of a majority of the shares, present, in person or by proxy at a regular or special meeting of shareholders.

C. Notwithstanding any other provision of these bylaws, this Article may not be amended, altered, deleted or modified in any way by the Board of Directors without prior shareholder approval.

4. Transcript of Oral Arguments, District Court's oral ruling, January 14, 1997, p. 31.

Court and later the 10th Circuit denied Fleming's motion to suspend the injunction. Fleming was then forced to allow its shareholders to vote on the Teamsters' proxy. The Teamsters' resolution passed with approximately 60% of the voted shares.

Fleming's position is that 18 O.S.1991 § 1038 gives the board of directors authority to create and issue shareholder rights plans, subject only to limits which might exist in the corporation's certificate of incorporation; and that shareholders cannot through bylaws restrict the board's powers to implement a rights plan.[5] The Teamsters' position is that 18 O.S.1991 § 1013 gives shareholders of a publicly traded corporation, such as Fleming, the authority to adopt bylaws addressing a broad range of topics from a corporation's business, corporate affairs, and rights and powers of shareholders and directors.[6] It is this apparent conflict which brings this federal certified question to this Court.

This is a case of first impression in Oklahoma and there is little guidance from other states. Oklahoma and Delaware have substantially similar corporation acts, especially with regard to Title 18, §§ 1013 & 1038 which are of primary concern here. 8 Del.C. § 109(a) & (b); 8

---

5. 18 O.S.1991 § 1038:

Rights and options respecting stock. Subject to any provisions in the certificate of incorporation, every corporation may create and issue, whether or not in connection with the issue and sale of any shares of stock or other securities of the corporation, rights or options entitling the holders thereof to purchase from the corporation any shares of its capital stock of any class or classes, such rights or options to be evidenced by or in such instrument or instruments as shall be approved by the board of directors. The terms upon which, including the time or times, which may be limited or unlimited in duration, at or within which, and the price or prices at which any such shares may be purchased from the corporation upon the exercise of any such right or option, shall be such as shall be stated in the certificate of incorporation, or in a resolution adopted by the board of directors providing for the creation and issue of such rights or options, and, in every case, shall be set forth or incorporated by reference in the instrument or instruments evidencing such rights or options. In the absence of actual fraud in the transaction, the judgment of the directors as to the consideration for the issuance of such rights or options and the sufficiency thereof shall be conclusive. In case the shares of stock of the corporation to be issued upon the exercise of such rights or options shall be shares having a par value, the price or prices so to be received therefor shall not be less than the par value thereof. In case the shares of stock so to be issued shall be shares of stock without par value, the consideration therefor shall be determined in the manner provided for in Section 34 of this act.

6. 18 O.S.1991 § 1013(A) & (B): Bylaws

A. The original or other bylaws of a corporation may be adopted, amended or repealed by the incorporators, by the initial directors if they were named in the certificate of incorporation, or, before a corporation has received any payment for any of its stock, by its board of directors. After a corporation has received any payment for any of its stock, the power to adopt, amend or repeal bylaws shall be in the shareholders entitled to vote, or, in the case of a nonstock corporation, in its members entitled to vote; provided, however, any corporation, in its certificate of incorporation, may confer the power to adopt, amend or repeal bylaws upon the directors or, in the case of a nonstock corporation, upon its governing body by whatever name designated. The fact that such power has been so conferred upon the directors or governing body, as the case may be, shall not divest the shareholders or members of the power, nor limit their power to adopt, amend or repeal bylaws.

B. The bylaws may contain any provision, not inconsistent with law or with the certificate of incorporation, relating to the business of the corporation, the conduct of its affairs, and its rights or powers or the rights or powers of its shareholders, directors, officers or employees.

Del.C. § 157. However, a review of Delaware decisions revealed no comparable case from that state.

The 10th Circuit's question is ultimately one of corporate governance and what degree of control shareholders can exact upon the corporations in which they own stock.

In the scheme of corporate governance the role of shareholders has been purposefully indirect. Shareholders' direct authority is limited. State ex rel. Oklahoma Employment Sec. Comm'n v. First Nat'l Bank of Texhoma, 197 Okla. 652, 174 P.2d 259 (1946); State ex rel. Oklahoma Employment Sec. Comm'n v. Tulsa Flower Exch., 192 Okla. 293, 135 P.2d 46 (1943); Sumner Coal–Mining Co. v. Pleasant, 127 Okla. 174, 259 P. 1055 (1926); Oberly v. Kirby, 592 A.2d 445, 458 (Del.1991). This is true for obvious reasons. Large corporations with perhaps thousands of stockholders could not function if the daily running of the corporation was subject to the approval of so many relatively attenuated people. However, the authority given a board of directors under the Oklahoma General Corporation Act, 18 O.S.1991 § 1027, is not without shareholder oversight, 18 O.S.1991 § 1013(B).

Fleming's argument relies on this passage, 18 O.S.1991 § 1038 (emphasis added):

> Subject to any provisions in the certificate of incorporation, every corporation may create and issue ... rights or options entitling the holders thereof to purchase from the corporation any shares of its capital stock of any class or classes, such rights or options to be evidenced by or in such instrument or instruments as shall be approved by the board of directors.

In making its argument, Fleming asserts that the word "corporation" is synonymous with "board of directors" as the term is used in 18 § 1038. Therefore, according to Fleming, "every corporation may create and issue ... rights and options[.]", can actually be read to say "[every corporation's board of directors] may create and issue ... rights and options[.]" However, in light of the fact that both terms, "corporation" and "board of directors", are used distinctly throughout the General Corporation Act and within the text of 18 § 1038 itself, this assertion is flawed. Further, the Former Business Corporation Act, 18 § 1.2(1) and (23), defines "corporation" and "director" differently. The statutes indicate our legislature has an understanding of the distinct definitions it assigns to these terms, and we find it unlikely the legislature would interchange them as Fleming contends.

While this Court would agree with Fleming that a corporation may create and issue rights and options within the grant of authority given it in 18 § 1038, it does not automatically translate that the board of directors of that corporation has in itself the same breadth of authority.

A shareholder rights plan is essentially a variety of stock option plan. Its use as an anti-takeover mechanism does not change its essential character. While shareholder ratification of poison pills has not been tested in the courts, the same cannot be said for stock option plans as a whole. There is authority supporting shareholder ratification of stock option plans.

For example, in Michelson v. Duncan, 407 A.2d 211, 218–20 (Del.1979), shareholders ratified a stock option package, curing a voidable act of the corporation's board of directors. Unlike the instant case, *Michelson* does not focus on whether shareholders have the authority to ratify the stock option plan, but rather explains that shareholder approval can cure the invalidity of an otherwise voidable act of the company's board. Despite this distinction, however, the case does reveal that stock option plans themselves can be subject to shareholder approval....

Further authority for shareholder approval of stock option plans is found in the Internal Revenue Code. 26 U.S.C §§ 422(b)(1) & 423(b)(2) (emphasis added).

422(b) Incentive stock option....

(1) the option is granted pursuant to a plan which includes the aggregate number of shares which may be issued under option and the employees (or class of employees) eligible to receive options, and which is approved by the stockholders of the granting corporation within 12 months before or after the date such plan is adopted[.]

423(b) Employee stock purchase plan....

(2) such plan is approved by the stockholders of the granting corporation within 12 months before or after the date such plan is adopted[.]

Although the option plans referred to in the revenue code are not shareholder rights plans, the revenue code's recognition of shareholder approval of stock options is similar to *Michelson*, in that it reveals stock option plans are not exempt from shareholder approval or ratification.

We find nothing in the Oklahoma General Corporation Act, 18 O.S.1991 § 1001 et seq., or existing case law which indicates the shareholder rights plan is somehow exempt from shareholder adopted bylaws. Fleming argues that only the certificate of incorporation can limit the board's authority to implement such a plan, relying on § 1038. While this Court might agree that a certificate of incorporation, which somehow precludes bylaw amendments directed at shareholder rights plans, could preclude the Teamsters from seeking the bylaw changes which are proposed in this case, neither party has indicated Fleming's certificate speaks in any way to the board's authority or shareholder constraints regarding shareholder rights plans. We find no authority to support the contention that a certificate of incorporation which is silent with regard to shareholder rights plans precludes shareholder enacted bylaws regarding the implementation of rights plans.

A number of states have taken affirmative steps to ensure their domestic corporations, and in many instances the board of directors itself, are able to implement shareholder rights plans to protect the company from takeover. The legislation is typically called a shareholders rights plan endorsement statute. However, the Oklahoma legislature has not passed such legislation. There are at least twenty-four states with these share rights plan endorsement statutes.

Some examples of shareholders rights plan endorsement statutes which give explicit authority to directors of the corporation read as follows:

> Nothing contained in this chapter is intended or shall be construed in any way to limit, modify or restrict an issuing public corporation's authority to take any action which the directors may appropriately determine to be in furtherance of the protection of the interests of the corporation and its shareholders, including without limitation the authority to adopt or enter into plans, arrangements or instruments that deny rights, privileges, power or authority to the holder or holders of at least a specified number of shares or percentage of share ownership or voting power in certain circumstances. Id. St. § 30–1706(1) (emphasis added).

> [E]xcept as otherwise provided in the articles of incorporation, a corporation may create and issue, whether or not in connection with the issue and sale of its shares or bonds, rights or options entitling the holders thereof to purchase from the corporation, upon such consideration, terms and conditions as may be fixed by the board, shares of any class or series, whether authorized but unissued shares, treasury shares or shares to be purchased or acquired, notes of the corporation or assets of the corporation. The terms and conditions of such rights or options may include, without limitation, restrictions or conditions that preclude or limit the exercise, transfer or receipt of such rights or options by any person or persons owning or offering to acquire a specified number or percentage of the outstanding common shares or other securities of the corporation, or any transferee or transferees of any such person or persons, or that invalidate or void such rights or options held by any such person or persons or any such transferee or transferees. Il.St. Ch. 805 § 5/6.05(f) (emphasis added) . . . .

These examples illustrate how a board of directors can operate with relative autonomy when a rights plan endorsement statute applies. This does not suggest the absence of a share rights plan endorsement statute in Oklahoma precludes the implementation of such a takeover defense. We merely find that without the authority granted in such an endorsement statute, the board may well be subject to the general procedures of corporate governance, including the enactment of bylaws which limit the board's authority to implement shareholder rights plans. . . .

In answering this certified question, we do not suggest all shareholder rights plans are required to submit to shareholder approval, ratification or review; this is not the question presented to us. Instead, we find shareholders may, through the proper channels of corporate governance, restrict the board of directors authority to implement shareholder rights plans.

CERTIFIED QUESTION ANSWERED.

■ SUMMERS, C.J., HARGRAVE, V.C.J., LAVENDER, OPALA, WILSON, KAUGER, and WATT, JJ., concur.

■ HODGES, J., no vote.

————

MM Companies, Inc. v. Liquid Audio, Inc.

Supreme Court of Delaware, 2003.
813 A.2d 1118.

■ Before: HOLLAND, BERGER, and STEELE, JUSTICES.

■ HOLLAND, JUSTICE:

This is an expedited appeal from a final judgment entered by the Court of Chancery. That final judgment permitted an incumbent board of directors to adopt defense measures which changed the size and composition of the board's membership. The record reflects that those defensive actions were taken for the primary purpose of impeding the shareholders' right to vote effectively in an impending election for successor directors. We have concluded that the judgment of the Court of Chancery must be reversed. This matter is remanded for further proceedings in accordance with this opinion.

Procedural Background

On August 26, 2002, MM Companies, Inc. ("MM") filed its original complaint in this action in the Court of Chancery against Liquid Audio, Inc. ("Liquid Audio"), as well as Raymond A. Doig, Gerald W. Kearby, Robert G. Flynn, Stephen V. Imbler and Ann Winblad (the "Director Defendants"). The original complaint sought injunctive relief against the August 22, 2002 action taken by the board of directors of Liquid Audio ("Board") to expand from five to seven members, and the purported effects that expansion might have on Liquid Audio's 2002 annual meeting that was scheduled for September 26, 2002. MM alleged that the Director Defendants' decision to expand the Board violated the principles established by the decision of the Court of Chancery in *Blasius*[10] and the decision of this Court in *Unocal.*[11] . . . .

Chancery Court Denies Relief

. . . [A] trial was held on October 21, 2002. At the conclusion of the trial, the Court of Chancery ruled in favor of the defendants, holding that the Board expansion did not violate Delaware law under either *Blasius* or *Unocal.* The Court of Chancery rejected the plaintiff's independent *Blasius* claim on the basis that the addition of two new directors "did not impact the shareholder vote or the shareholder

10. *Blasius Indus., Inc. v. Atlas Corp.,* 564 A.2d 651 (Del.Ch.1988).

11. *Unocal Corp. v. Mesa Petroleum Co.,* 493 A.2d 946 (Del.1985).

choices in any significant way." The Court of Chancery rejected the plaintiff's *Unocal* claim, on the basis that: plaintiff did "not contend that the board expansion was coercive," the expansion was not "preclusive," because the "choices that the shareholders had before the board action was taken were the same as they had after," and the plaintiff failed to make a showing that "the action that the board took falls outside a range of reasonable responses."

Following the entry of the final judgment, MM filed a Notice of Appeal and a Motion for Expedited Scheduling. The motion was granted by this Court. Oral argument was held on December 3, 2002.

Issues on Appeal

MM has raised two issues on appeal. First, it contends that the Court of Chancery erred in ruling that the "compelling justification" standard, as enunciated in *Blasius,* was not applicable to the Board's action. In support of that argument, MM relies upon the finding by the Court of Chancery that the Director Defendants manipulated the size and composition of the Liquid Audio board during a contested election for directors *primarily* to interfere with and impede the success of MM's ability to gain two-of-five directorships on the Board, and, thus, to diminish the influence of MM's nominees on the Board.

Second, MM argues that the Court of Chancery erred in ruling that the precepts of this Court's holding in *Unocal* and its progeny were not violated by the Board's defensive action. According to MM, the Director Defendants never identified a legally cognizable threat to the corporate policy and effectiveness of Liquid Audio and, to the extent that a threat existed, never demonstrated that the "manipulation of the size and composition" of the Liquid Audio board was a reasonable response in relation to such threat. Based upon that asserted lack of record evidence, MM submits the Court of Chancery erred in concluding that this Court's holding in *Unocal* was not violated.

Background Facts

Liquid Audio is a publicly traded Delaware corporation, with its principal place of business in Redwood City, California. Liquid Audio's primary business consists of providing software and services for the digital transmission of music over the Internet. MM is a publicly traded Delaware corporation with its principal place of business in New York, New York. As of October 2002, MM was part of a group that collectively held slightly over 7% of Liquid Audio's common stock.

For more than a year, MM has sought to obtain control of Liquid Audio. On October 26, 2001, MM sent a letter to the Liquid Audio board of directors indicating its willingness to acquire the company at approximately $3 per share. Liquid Audio's board rejected MM's offer as inadequate, after an analysis of the offer and consultation with its investment banker, Broadview International LLC ("Broadview").

Liquid Audio's bylaws provide for a staggered board of directors that is divided into three classes. Only one class of directors is up for election in any given year. The effect is to prevent an insurgent from obtaining control of the company in under two years.[12]

From November 2001, until August 2002, the Liquid Audio board of directors consisted of five members divided into three classes. Class I had two members (defendants Flynn and Imbler), whose terms expire in 2003; Class II had one member (defendant Winblad), whose term expires in 2004; and Class III had two members (defendants Kearby and Doig), whose terms expired in 2002. Defendants Flynn, Doig and Imbler were not elected to the Board by the stockholders of Liquid Auido. They were appointed to the Board by the directors of Liquid Audio to fill vacancies on the Board.

In October 2001, prior to the appointment of defendants Doig and Imbler to the Board, MM requested the Liquid Audio board to call a special meeting of the company's stockholders to consider filling the existing vacancies on the Board and to consider other proposals to be presented to the stockholders. On October 24, 2001, the Liquid Audio board issued a press release which stated that it had denied MM's request to call a special meeting because the Board believed that under the Liquid Audio bylaws stockholders are not permitted to call special meetings. Thereafter, the Board appointed defendants Doig and Imbler to the Liquid Audio board of directors.

MM's Various Actions

On November 13, 2001, MM announced its intention to nominate its own candidates for the two seats on Liquid Audio's board of directors that were up for election at the next annual meeting. On December 18, 2001, MM delivered a formal notice to Liquid Audio stating that it intended to nominate Seymour Holtzman and James Mitarotonda as directors to fill the two seats on the Board then held by the individuals designated as Class III directors whose terms expired at the next annual meeting. The December 18, 2001 notice also requested that the Board adopt resolutions declaring certain amendments to the certificate of incorporation and bylaws advisable and that such amendments be submitted to the stockholders.

On December 20, 2001, MM sent notice to Liquid Audio informing the Board of its intention to bring before the annual meeting a proposal that would amend the bylaws and increase the size of the Board by four members. The December 20, 2001 notice also informed the Board of MM's intention to nominate four individuals as directors to fill those four newly created directorships. MM subsequently demanded that the Board commit to fixing an annual meeting date by February 22, 2002.

On February 22, 2002, MM renewed its October 2001 offer to acquire Liquid Audio. That offer, however, was at the reduced price of

12. *See* Lucian Arye Bebchuk, John C. Coates, IV & Guhan Subramanian, *The Powerful Antitakeover Force of Staggered Boards:* *Theory, Evidence, and Policy,* 54 Stanford L.Rev. 887 (2002).

$2.50 per share. The Liquid Audio board rejected that offer as inadequate.

On May 17, 2002, MM forwarded a written demand to Liquid Audio under Section 220, which requested a list of stockholders of Liquid Audio and related materials. Liquid Audio did not respond to the demand letter. On May 30, 2002, MM filed an action under Section 220 seeking, among other things, an order of the Court of Chancery directing that Liquid Audio forward to MM the information identified in the demand letter. A hearing before the Court of Chancery with respect to the Section 220 complaint was scheduled to be held on June 14, 2002.

On June 10, 2002, MM filed proxy materials with the Securities and Exchange Commission ("SEC") and commenced soliciting proxies for a shareholder meeting Liquid Audio planned to have on July 1, 2002. In addition to proposing two nominees for the Board, MM's proxy statement included a takeover proposal to increase the size of the Board by an additional four directors and to fill those positions with its nominees. As outlined in its initial proxy materials, MM's takeover proposal sought to expand the Board from five members to nine. If MM's two directors were elected and its four proposed directors were also placed on the Board, MM would control a majority of the Board.

Alliance Merger

On June 13, 2002, Liquid Audio announced a stock-for-stock merger transaction with Alliance Entertainment Corp. ("Alliance"). This announcement came three days after MM mailed its proxy statement and other materials to the stockholders of Liquid Audio, and one day before the scheduled Court of Chancery hearing in connection with the Section 220 complaint. In addition to announcing the merger, the Liquid Audio board also announced that: the July 1, 2002 meeting would be postponed; a special meeting of stockholders of Liquid Audio would be held sometime in the future to vote upon the merger; and, if the merger received the requisite stockholder and regulatory approval, the merger would "close in the Fall of 2002." Based upon this announcement, the annual meeting was postponed indefinitely by the Liquid Audio board.

The merger with Alliance that was announced to the stockholders of Liquid Audio on June 13, 2002 and the merger agreement executed by Liquid Audio and Alliance in connection therewith were not approved unanimously by the Board. The record reflects that at a meeting of the Board held to vote upon the merger and the merger agreement, defendants Kearby, Flynn, Imbler and Doig voted for the merger and the merger agreement and defendant Winblad voted against the merger and the merger agreement.

After Liquid Audio announced that the annual meeting would be postponed indefinitely, MM filed an amended complaint, seeking an order of the Court of Chancery directing Liquid Audio to hold the annual meeting as soon as possible, and a motion for expedited and summary proceedings. On June 20, 2002, the Court of Chancery granted MM's motion for expedited and summary proceedings and directed that a trial in connection with MM's application for relief be held on July 15, 2002.

Shortly, before that trial took place, the Liquid Audio board announced that certain terms of the merger agreement had been modified to permit Liquid Audio to conduct a self-tender offer under which Liquid would acquire up to 10 million shares of its common stock at $3.00 per share in cash, if the merger was approved by the stockholders of Liquid Audio. Upon consummation of the merger and a fully subscribed self-tender offer, Liquid Audio's stockholders would own 26% and Alliance stockholders would own 74% of the combined enterprise. The Liquid Audio board also announced that certain senior officers of Liquid Audio committed not to tender their shares in the self-tender offer. Finally, the Liquid Audio board announced that the Director Defendants reduced the "trigger" of Liquid Audio's shareholders rights plan or "poison pill" to 10% from 15%. The modified merger agreement was approved unanimously by the Board at a meeting held on July 14, 2002.

After expedited discovery, a trial was held on July 15, 2002. The Court of Chancery ordered that the annual meeting of Liquid Audio's shareholders occur on September 26, 2002. The record date for the meeting was August 12, 2002.

Board Adds Two Directors

By the middle of August 2002, it was apparent that MM's nominees, Holtzman and Mitarotonda, would be elected at the annual meeting, to serve in place of the two incumbent nominees, as members of the Liquid Audio board. On August 23, 2002, Liquid Audio announced that the Board had amended the bylaws to increase the size of the Board to seven members from five members. The Board also announced that defendants James D. Somes and Judith N. Frank had been appointed to fill the newly created directorships. Defendant Somes was appointed to serve as a Class II member of the Board and defendant Frank was appointed to serve as a Class I member of the Board. After the Board expanded from five directors to seven, MM revised its proxy statement to note that its proposal to add four directors, if successful, would have resulted in a board with eleven directors, instead of nine.

MM Challenges Board Expansion

On August 26, 2002, MM filed its initial lawsuit challenging the Board's decision to add two directors. In the initial complaint, MM alleged that the Board expansion interfered with MM's ability to solicit proxies in favor of its two nominees for election to the Liquid Audio board at the annual meeting. In support of this claim, MM alleged that "some stockholders would believe that electing two members of a seven-member board, rather than two members of a five-member board, would not be worthwhile, and, thus, such stockholders simply would not vote."

At the September 26, 2002 annual meeting, the two directors proposed by MM, Holtzman and Mitarotonda, were elected to serve as directors of the Board. Liquid Audio's stockholders, however, did not approve MM's takeover proposals that would have expanded the Board and placed MM's four nominees on the Board. The stockholders' vote on both issues was consistent with the recommendation of Institutional Investor Services ("ISS"), a proxy voting advisory service, which had recommended that the stockholders vote in favor of MM's two nominees, but recommended against stockholders voting to give MM outright and immediate control of the Board.

Following the election of MM's two nominees to the Liquid Audio board of directors at the annual meeting, MM filed an amended lawsuit, challenging the Board's appointment of directors Somes and Frank. In the amended complaint, MM alleged that the expansion of the Liquid Audio board, its timing, and the Board's appointment of two new directors violated the principles of *Blasius* and *Unocal*. According to MM, that action frustrated MM's attempt to gain a "substantial presence" on the Board for at least one year and guaranteed that Liquid Audio's management will have control of, or a substantial presence on, the Board for at least two years.

Board's Primary Purpose: Impede Effective Vote

The expedited trial was held by the Court of Chancery, as scheduled. During pretrial discovery, the Director Defendants identified the primary purpose of their action in expanding the Liquid Audio board from five to seven members. Their response to the following interrogatory request is illustrative:

> 6. Summarize the complete reasons that support the decision of the Board to amend the Bylaws or to approve the Bylaw Amendment.
>
> *Response:* Subject to and without waiving the General Objections stated above, Defendants state that the Board of Directors, after receiving legal advice regarding their fiduciary duties, voted to expand the size of the board after a thorough and deliberate evaluation of the qualifications and expected contributions of Judith N. Frank and James D. Somes to Liquid's current operations and business plans. Furthermore, the Board of Directors believed that the Company would benefit from having seven directors instead of only five directors. In particular, the Company believed that it would benefit from creating new directorships and placing two additional outside directors on the board in light of the potential difficulties that may result from the addition of MM's nominees on the Board and in light of the possibility that one or more directors would decide to resign for a variety of reasons including, but not limited to, a reluctance to serve alongside a slate of directors proposed by MM. . . .

When defendant Doig was asked to elaborate upon this response to the interrogatory request, he testified:

> There was concern that if the MM slate won and then it did become too acrimonious and that Ms. Winblad and Mr. Imbler decided to resign, that ran an undue risk to the shareholders by giving MM the ability to control the company.

The testimony of each other member of the Board also reflects that the Director Defendants were concerned that incumbent directors Winblad and Imbler would resign from the Liquid Audio board if MM's nominees were elected to the board at the annual meeting, which would result in MM gaining control of the Board. The record also reflects that the timing of the Director Defendants' decision to expand the Board was to accomplish its primary purpose: to minimize the impact of the election of MM's nominees to the Board. The Court of Chancery's post-trial ruling from the bench states:

> The board's concern was that given the past acrimonious relationship between MM and Liquid Audio, a relationship characterized by litigation, if MM's two nominees were elected, the possibility of continued acrimony might cause one or more of the current board members to resign. If one director resigned, that would deadlock the board two-to-two; and if two directors resigned, then MM would gain control on a two-to-one basis. Either scenario could jeopardize the pending merger, which the incumbent board favored. That was the *primary* reason. (emphasis added).

After making that factual determination, the Court of Chancery recognized the effect of the Board's action in changing the size and composition of its membership immediately prior to the election of directors at the annual meeting:

> By adding two additional directors, the board foreclosed the result that it feared: The possibility of a deadlock or of MM taking control of the board. The reason is that even if MM's two nominees were elected at the 2002 annual meeting, the current directors would still constitute a majority of five. The result of the board's action was to *diminish the influence of any nominees of MM* that were elected, at least in numerical terms.

Thus, based upon the evidence presented at trial, including an assessment of the witnesses' credibility, the Court of Chancery concluded that the Director Defendants amended the bylaws to expand the Board from five to seven, appointed two additional members of the Board, and timed those actions for the *primary purpose* of diminishing the influence of MM's nominees, if they were elected at the annual meeting.

Corporate Governance Principles

The most fundamental principles of corporate governance are a function of the allocation of power within a corporation between its stockholders and its board of directors. The stockholders' power is the right to vote on specific matters, in particular, in an election of directors. The power of managing the corporate enterprise is vested in the shareholders' duly elected board representatives. Accordingly, while these "fundamental tenets of Delaware corporate law provide for a separation of control and ownership,"[13] the stockholder franchise has been characterized as the "ideological underpinning" upon which the legitimacy of the directors managerial power rests.[14]

Maintaining a proper balance in the allocation of power between the stockholders' right to elect directors and the board of directors' right to manage the corporation is dependent upon the stockholders' unimpeded right to vote effectively in an election of directors. This Court has repeatedly stated that, if the stockholders are not satisfied with the management or actions of their elected representatives on the board of directors, the power of corporate democracy is available to the stockholders to replace the incumbent directors when they stand for re-election. Consequently, two decades ago, this Court held:

> The Courts of this State will not allow the wrongful subversion of corporate democracy by manipulation of the corporate machinery or by machinations under the cloak of Delaware law. Accordingly, careful judicial scrutiny will be given a situation in which the right to vote for the election of successor directors has been *effectively frustrated* and denied.[15]

This Court and the Court of Chancery have remained assiduous in carefully reviewing any board actions designed to interfere with or impede the effective exercise of corporate democracy by shareholders, especially in an election of directors.

Corporate Governance Review Standards

The "defining tension" in corporate governance today has been characterized as "the tension between deference to directors' decisions and the scope of judicial review."[16] The appropriate standard of judicial review is dispositive of which party has the burden of proof as any litigation proceeds from stage to stage until there is a substantive determination on the merits. Accordingly, identification of the correct analytical framework is essential to a proper judicial review of challenges to the decision-making process of a corporation's board of directors.

The business judgment rule, as a standard of judicial review, is a common-law recognition of the statutory authority to manage a corporation that is vested in the board of directors. The business judgment rule is a "presumption that in making a business decision the directors of a corporation acted on an informed basis, in good faith and in the honest belief that the action taken was in the best interests of the company."[17] An application of the traditional business judgment rule

13. *Malone v. Brincat,* 722 A.2d 5, 9 (Del.1998).

14. *Blasius Indus., Inc. v. Atlas Corp.,* 564 A.2d 651, 659 (Del.Ch.1988).

15. *Giuricich v. Emtrol Corp.,* 449 A.2d 232, 239 (Del.1982).

16. E. Norman Veasey, *The Defining Tension in Corporate Governance in America,* 52 Bus. Law. 393 (1997).

17. *Unitrin, Inc. v. American Gen. Corp.,* 651 A.2d at 1373 quoting *Aronson v. Lewis,* 473 A.2d 805, 811 (Del.1984).

places the burden on the "party challenging the [board's] decision to establish facts rebutting the presumption."[18] The effect of a proper invocation of the business judgment rule, as a standard of judicial review, is powerful because it operates deferentially. If the business judgment rule is not rebutted, a "court will not substitute its judgment for that of the board if the [board's] decision can be 'attributed to any rational business purpose.' "[19]

In *Blasius,* Chancellor Allen set forth a cogent explanation of why judicial review under the deferential traditional business judgment rule standard is inappropriate when a board of directors acts for the *primary* purpose of impeding or interfering with the effectiveness of a shareholder vote, especially in the specific context presented in *Blasius* of a contested election for directors . . . :

In *Blasius,* the Chancellor did not adopt a rule of *per se* invalidity once a plaintiff has established that a board of directors has acted for the primary purpose of interfering with or impeding the effective exercise of a shareholder vote. Instead, the Chancellor concluded that such situations required enhanced judicial scrutiny, pursuant to which the board of directors "bears the heavy burden of demonstrating a compelling justification for such action" . . .

In *Blasius,* the Chancellor set aside the board's action to expand the size of its membership for the primary purpose of impeding and interfering with the effectiveness of a shareholder vote in a contested election for directors. In this case, not only did the Liquid Audio board of directors take similar action in expanding the size of its membership and appointing two new directors to fill those positions, but it took that action for the same *primary* purpose. . . .

. . . [T]his Court has noted that the non-deferential *Blasius* standard of enhanced judicial review, which imposes upon a board of directors the burden of demonstrating a compelling justification for such actions, is rarely applied. . . .

In this case, however, the Court of Chancery was presented with the ultimate defensive measure touching upon an issue of control. It was a defensive action taken by an incumbent board of directors for the primary purpose of interfering with and impeding the effectiveness of the shareholder franchise in electing successor directors. Accordingly, the incumbent board of directors had the burden of demonstrating a compelling justification for that action to withstand enhanced judicial scrutiny *within* the *Unocal* standard of reasonableness and proportionality.

Unocal Required Compelling Justification

This case presents a paragon of when the compelling justification standard of *Blasius* must be applied within *Unocal*'s requirement that any defensive measure be proportionate and reasonable in relation to

18. *Id.*

19. *Id.,* quoting *Unocal Corp. v. Mesa Petroleum Co.,* 493 A.2d 946, 954 (Del.1985) (citation omitted).

the threat posed. The *Unocal* standard of review applies because the Liquid Audio board's action was a "defensive measure taken in response to some threat to corporate policy and effectiveness which touches upon issues of control."[30] The compelling justification standard of *Blasius* also had to be applied *within* an application of the *Unocal* standard to that specific defensive measure because the primary purpose of the Board's action was to interfere with or impede the effective exercise of the shareholder franchise in a contested election for directors.

The Court of Chancery properly decided to examine the Board's defensive action to expand from five to seven members and to appoint two new members in accordance with the *Unocal* standard of enhanced judicial review. Initially, the Court of Chancery concluded that defensive action was not preclusive or coercive. If a defensive measure is not draconian, because it is neither coercive nor preclusive, proportionality review under *Unocal* requires the focus of enhanced judicial scrutiny to shift to the range of reasonableness.[31]

After the Court of Chancery determined that the Board's action was not preclusive or coercive, it properly proceeded to determine whether the Board's action was reasonable and proportionate in relation to the threat posed.[32] Under the circumstances presented in this case, however, the Court of Chancery did not "recognize the special [importance] of protecting the shareholder's franchise within *Unocal*'s requirement that any defensive measure be proportionate and reasonable in relation to the threat posed."[33] Since the Court of Chancery had already concluded that the *primary* purpose of the Liquid Audio board's defensive measure was to interfere with or impede an effective exercise of the shareholder's franchise in a contested election of directors, the Board had the burden of demonstrating a compelling justification for that action.

When the *primary purpose* of a board of directors' defensive measure is to interfere with or impede the effective exercise of the shareholder franchise in a contested election for directors, the board must first demonstrate a compelling justification for such action as a condition precedent to any judicial consideration of reasonableness and proportionately. As this case illustrates, such defensive actions by a board need not actually prevent the shareholders from attaining any success in seating one or more nominees in a contested election for directors and the election contest need not involve a challenge for outright control of the board of directors. To invoke the *Blasius* compelling justification standard of review *within* an application of the *Unocal* standard of review, the defensive actions of the board only need to be taken for the primary purpose of interfering with or

---

30. *Gilbert v. El Paso Co.,* 575 A.2d 1131, 1144 (Del.1990).

31. *Unitrin, Inc. v. American Gen. Corp.,* 651 A.2d 1361, 1387–88 (Del.1995).

32. In our review of the Court of Chancery's *Unocal* analysis, we have assumed

without deciding that the Board was independent and had reasonable grounds for believing that there was a danger to corporate policy.

33. *Stroud v. Grace,* 606 A.2d at 92 n. 3.

impeding the effectiveness of the stockholder vote in a contested election for directors.

Board Expansion Invalid

The record reflects that the primary purpose of the Director Defendants' action was to interfere with and impede the effective exercise of the stockholder franchise in a contested election for directors. The Court of Chancery concluded that the Director Defendants amended the bylaws to provide for a board of seven and appointed two additional members of the Board for the primary purpose of diminishing the influence of MM's two nominees on a five-member Board by eliminating either the possibility of a deadlock on the board or of MM controlling the Board, if one or two Director Defendants resigned from the Board. That defensive action by the Director Defendants compromised the essential role of corporate democracy in maintaining the proper allocation of power between the shareholders and the Board, because that action was taken in the context of a contested election for successor directors. Since the Director Defendants did not demonstrate a compelling justification for that defensive action, the bylaw amendment that expanded the size of the Liquid Audio board, and permitted the appointment of two new members on the eve of a contested election, should have been invalidated by the Court of Chancery.

One of the most venerable precepts of Delaware's common law corporate jurisprudence is the principle that "inequitable action does not become permissible simply because it is legally possible."[34] At issue in this case is not the validity generally of either a bylaw that permits a board of directors to expand the size of its membership or a board's power to appoint successor members to fill board vacancies. In this case, however, the incumbent Board timed its utilization of these otherwise valid powers to expand the size and composition of the Liquid Audio board for the primary purpose of impeding and interfering with the efforts of the stockholders' power to effectively exercise their voting rights in a contested election for directors. As this Court held more than three decades ago, "these are inequitable purposes, contrary to established principles of corporate democracy . . . and may not be permitted to stand."[35]

Conclusion

The judgment of the Court of Chancery is reversed. This matter is remanded for further proceedings in accordance with this opinion.

SECTION 3. THE LEGAL STRUCTURE OF MANAGEMENT

---

34. *Schnell v. Chris–Craft Indus., Inc.,* 285 A.2d 437, 439 (Del.1971).

35. *Id.*

NOTE ON THE STRUCTURE OF THE CORPORATION

1. *Modern Corporate Practice.* In the traditional model of corporate structure, the board managed the business of the corporation. The board still has a central legal role in the corporation, but today it is widely understood that the traditional *managing model* of the board is no longer descriptive, if it ever was. Under modern corporate practice in publicly held corporations, the management function is ordinarily located not in the board, but in the executives, and the central figure in the corporation is not the board, but the chief executive officer (CEO). The limited role of the board in managing the corporation is the result of several critical constraints imposed by modern board practice.

a. *Constraints of time.* A recent survey of 158 large corporations found that the directors spent a median of eight days—presumably, around 64 hours—a year on fulfilling their responsibilities for regular board service. Directors serving on committees of the board spent additional time on corporate affairs—six days for members of the audit committee, five days for members of the compensation committee, and four days for members of other committees. Mercer Human Resource Consulting, Trends in Outside Director Compensation 18 (2004). Counting in committee time would bring the average number of hours a year spent by the directors on corporate affairs to around 100. That's still not very much, and in any event board committees deal with special issues, not general corporate welfare. A survey of a number of directors by Korn/Ferry International found reported that they spent an average of 18 hours per month on board matters, including travel time. Korn/Ferry International, 31st Annual Board of Directors Study 26 (2004). If travel time averages a few hours per month, that would bring the total of actual working time to about 180 hours a year. It's not clear what accounts for the difference between the results in the two surveys, but even 180 hours a year is far short of the amount of time that would be required to manage the business of a large publicly held corporation in the normal sense of that term: Such businesses are far too complex to be managed by directors who are very much part-time.

b. *Constraints of information.* The distribution of information in the corporation is highly asymmetrical: the officers typically not only have much more information than the board, but control much of the flow of information to the board. By controlling the information that the board receives, the officers heavily shape the decisions that the board makes.

c. *Constraints of composition.* The typical board includes a number of directors who are economically or psychologically tied to the corporation's executives, particularly to the CEO. Indeed, a number of seats on a board are usually held by inside directors, that is, by the corporation's own executives. The inside director, dependent on the CEO for both retention and promotion, and on other executives for day-to-day support, is highly unlikely to dissent at a board meeting from the inside line determined by the CEO prior to the meeting. At least until recently, and still today to varying extents, outside directors often have economic ties to the corporation, and ties of friendship, colleagueship, or both, to the CEO.

3. *The Monitoring Board.* Because of the unrealistic nature of the managing model, in the last twenty-five years there has been a shift from a managing model to a *monitoring model.* The monitoring model of the board recognizes that in a publicly held corporation the management function is exercised not by the board, but by the senior executives. Under the monitoring model, therefore, the primary although not exclusive function of the board of a publicly held corporation is, not to manage the business of the corporation, but to select, regularly evaluate, fix the compensation of, and, where appropriate, replace the senior executives; to monitor the conduct of the corporation's business to evaluate whether the business is being properly managed; and to review and, where appropriate, approve, major corporate plans and policies.

This functional component of the monitoring model is complemented by a structural component. If the board has the function of monitoring the senior executives, it must be structured to effectuate that function. Effectuating that function requires that the board consist of at least a majority of directors who are independent of the senior executives. The composition of boards is strongly moving in that direction. A survey of the 100 largest American corporations found that in 81 of the corporations, independent directors comprised 75% or more of the boards.[37] New rules of the New York Stock Exchange and NASDAQ require listed corporations to have a majority of independent directors. The rules also require the boards of such corporations to have audit, nominating, and compensation committees, composed exclusively of such independent directors, to aid in implementing the monitoring function. The Korn/Ferry study found that all of corporations represented in its survey had audit and compensation committees, and 96% had nominating committees. Id. at 13. The average number of inside directors on each of these committees was zero. The average number of audit committee meetings per year was eight; of compensation committees, five; and of nominating committees, four. Id. at 14–15.

Another structural feature that has emerged recently to reinforce the independence of directors is the designation of a lead director in cases where the CEO is also Chairman of the Board. The Korn/Ferry study reported, "Once considered controversial and divisive, a lead director is now seen as integral in fostering a positive working relationship with the CEO, maintaining independence of the board from management, and stimulating open discourse among outside directors by serving as an impartial sounding board. Four of five (80 percent) of the . . . respondents have an elected or appointed lead director who presides at executive sessions and evaluates the CEO.

---

37. Sherman & Sterling LLP, Corporate Governance Practices of the 100 Largest U.S. Public Companies 2 (2004).

This practice has been integrated with astounding speed: only 32 percent of respondents' boards had formalized the lead director role in 2002." Id. at 27.

Today, the monitoring model of the board has been almost universally accepted and adopted in large publicly held corporations and indeed is required for all corporations listed on the New York Stock Exchange or NASDAQ. Ultimately, the utility of the monitoring model of the board rests on its economic advantage in providing an additional system to monitor the efficiency of management—in particular, of the CEO. The monitoring board, taken alone, is an imperfect mechanism to achieve that end, but because all systems to monitor the efficiency of the management of publicly held corporations are imperfect, it is important to construct a web of overlapping and even redundant monitoring systems. The monitoring board is one important part of that web.

AMERICAN LAW INSTITUTE, PRINCIPLES OF CORPORATE GOVERNANCE §§ 3.01, 3.02, 3.05, 3A.01–3A.05

[See Statutory Supplement]

NEW YORK STOCK EXCHANGE

Listed Company Manual ¶ 303A

[See Statutory Supplement]

SARBANES–OXLEY ACT OF 2002

[See Statutory Supplement]

NOTE ON THE SARBANES–OXLEY ACT

[See Appendix]

NOTE ON THE ARCHITECTURE OF CORPORATE LAW

Corporation law is often conceived of as state law, but this conception is much too narrow. Corporate law serves various functions. It enables corporations to be organized. It provides corporations with certain endowments—most prominently, entity status, limited liability, perpetual existence, the right to own property and make contracts, and the power to sue and be sued. It sets the level of care required of directors and officers. It provides a special remedial structure to resolve claims by shareholders. It facilitates various transactions and conduct in which a corporation may choose to engage. It addresses various kinds of conflict of interest. (These may be either *traditional conflicts*, which typically involve self-interested transactions between managers and their corporations, or *positional conflicts*, which involve actions by managers to maintain and enhance their positions.) Any body of rules that addresses one or more of these functions is part of the body of corporate law.

Viewed from this perspective, corporate law consists of four major modules: state statutory law; state judge-made law; federal law, such as Sarbanes–Oxley and the Securities Acts; and private ordering or "soft law," such as the New York Stock Exchange listing rules. Each of these modules serves a distinct function. Essentially—State statutory law enables corporations to be organized, provides corporations with various endowments, and facilitates corporate transactions. State judge-made law sets the level of care required of officers and directors, regulates traditional conflicts of interest, and gives content to remedial structures to protect shareholder rights and resolve shareholder claims. Federal law regulates traditional conflicts directly, through rules on insider training, and regulates positional conflicts of interest indirectly, through rules that govern the proxy voting system and by regulating the flow of information concerning management's performance. The rules of the major stock exchanges regulate positional conflicts directly, by requiring an independent board and committees to monitor the corporation's executives.

NOTE ON THE CHOICE OF THE STATE OF INCORPORATION

Under traditional choice of law rules: (1) a corporation's internal affairs are governed by the law of its state of incorporation; and (2) a firm can incorporate in whatever state it chooses—even a state in which the corporation does no business.

A corporation with only a few owners—a "close corporation"—will almost invariably incorporate locally, that is, in the state in which it has its principal place of business. Partly this is for tax reasons. If a corporation *does business* in a state, the state will impose a *doing-business tax* on the corporation, measured by the amount of that business. If a corporation is *incorporated* in a state, the state will impose a *franchise tax* for the privilege of incorporation, even if the corporation does not do business in that state. Elements of the doing-business and franchise taxes may overlap, so that if a corporation is doing business mainly in one state, its total tax bill usually will be lower if it is incorporated in that state. Furthermore, a local attorney, familiar with local corporate law, may be hesitant about rendering formal opinions on the law of another state, and is therefore likely to recommend local incorporation so that he can confidently give legal advice to the corporation after it is organized.

In the case of a publicly held corporation, a different calculus prevails. For such a corporation, the franchise tax is likely to be inconsequential in comparison with the corporation's total revenues, so that tax consequences are unlikely to figure heavily in the choice of the state of incorporation. On the state's side of the equation, franchise-tax revenues may represent a potentially enormous source of revenue to a state with a small fiscal base. The legislature of a small state therefore has a great economic incentive to design a corporate statute that will attract incorporation—or reincorporation from other states—particularly by large publicly held corporations, which will pay larger franchise taxes. If the state is successful in attracting incorporations and reincorporations, the resulting franchise-tax revenues can subsidize a large portion of the state's budget, because the out-of-pocket cost of maintaining the statute will be negligible. Even a large state has an incentive to design a statute that will attract incorporation, because the revenues of the local corporate bar may depend in part on the extent of local incorporation.

Delaware is by far the most successful state in attracting incorporation, and especially reincorporation, by publicly held corporations. More than 500,000 business entities have their legal home in Delaware, including more than 50% of all U.S. publicly-traded companies and 58% of the Fortune 500, even though very few of these corporations do much or any business in Delaware. (In contrast, Delaware's share of total incorporations—that is, publicly and privately held corporations—is less than 3.5%. Thompson & Thomas, The Public and Private Face of Derivative Lawsuits, Vanderbilt University Law School Law and Economics Working Paper No. 04–14.) Because of Delaware's huge share of the "charter market," on the one hand, and its small size on the other, franchise taxes account for about 20 percent of all taxes collected in Delaware. In contrast, in most states franchise taxes are probably well under 1% of total tax revenues—often, probably under 0.1%. See R. Romano, The Genius of American Law 6–11 (Tables 1–1, 1–2) (1993).

Although shareholder approval is nominally required for determining a corporation's state of incorporation, for all practical purposes a decision to reincorporate is almost invariably made by the corporation's managers. The reason why Delaware is so successful in attracting managers to cause their corporations to incorporate there—or more accurately, to reincorporate there from other states—is hotly contested. One position, known as the *race to the bottom*, is most closely associated with William Cary's seminal article, Federalism and Corporate Law: Reflections Upon Delaware, 83 Yale L.J. 663 (1974). This position is as follows: Corporate law is a product that states sell. Suppose a principal is represented by an agent, A, whom the principal cannot closely monitor. A third party who wishes to sell a product to the principal through A will have an incentive to give A a side payment—a bribe—to induce A to purchase the product on the principal's behalf. In the market for corporate law, the shareholders are in the position of the principals, managers are in the position of A, and the legislature is in the position of the third party. Under basic agency-cost theory, a state legislature therefore has an incentive to give managers side payments to induce them to cause their corporations to incorporate or reincorporate in the legislature's state. For a variety of reasons, the side payments cannot be paid in money. Instead, the side payments take the form of a suboptimal, hands-off approach to regulating traditional and positional conflicts.

A counter position, known as *race-to-the-top*, has been formulated by Ralph Winter and others. See Winter, State Law, Shareholder Protection, and the Theory of the Corporation, 6 J. Leg. Stud. 271 (1977). Winter argued that if Delaware law unduly favored managers, shareholders in Delaware corporations would earn lower-than-normal returns, and Delaware corporations would therefore have a higher cost of capital. This would either bankrupt Delaware corporations in the product markets, or cause the ouster of management through takeover bids. Therefore, managers would avoid incorporating in Delaware if its law unduly favored managers. Since Delaware is in fact by far the most popular state of incorporation for large publicly held corporations, the race-to-the-bottom analysis, Winter said, must be wrong. Indeed, Winter argued, the incentive for states to sell corporate law must lead Delaware (and other states) to produce an optimal statutory corporate law regime, because a state that offers the optimal, value maximizing statutory regime will attract the most incorporations.

This argument has only limited power, both because it runs counter to agency-cost theory and because it depends on a drastic overstatement of the power of the product market, the capital market, and the takeover market in this context. Begin with the product market. The costs to the corporation of suboptimal state legislative rules are likely to be relatively small when compared to the corporation's income. Small costs will seldom if ever bankrupt corporations in imperfectly competitive product markets, because publicly held corporations operating in such markets usually have the capacity to absorb huge losses and still stay solvent.

The cost of raising equity capital is also unlikely to have a significant effect on manager's choice of the state of incorporation. First, publicly held corporations don't raise much capital by issuing new equity in the capital markets. Second, even if a corporation does raise capital by issuing new equity, the impact of a suboptimal legal regime will fall on shareholders, not managers. For example, suppose that C Corporation is incorporated in a state, S, with a suboptimal corporate statute. C Corporation wants to raise $500,000 in equity in the capital market. If not for the adverse impact of S's suboptimal legal regime, C could raise $500,000 by issuing 10,000 shares at $50 per share. Given the adverse impact of S's legal regime, to raise $500,000 C must sell 11,111 shares at $45 per share. This dilutes the value of C's stock, and that dilution is a cost. However, that cost will be borne by C's shareholders rather than by its managers. If the managers own stock or stock options, they will suffer some loss in the value of the stock or options. However, that loss will normally be miniscule compared to the gain the managers can reap from engaging in the traditional and positional conflicts that S's suboptimal legal regime fails to properly regulate.

The market for corporate control—or more accurately, the hostile-takeover market—also has only limited impact in this context. A hostile takeover bid cannot succeed unless it includes a premium that is significantly above the market price of the target's stock. Partly this is because most existing shareholders of the target will value their stock at a price higher than the market price, or they would already have sold. Mostly it is because the target's managers can create formidable obstacles to a takeover that often result in bidding contests and that normally can be overcome, if at all, only by paying shareholders a substantial premium over the pre-tender market price. Accordingly, to complete a successful hostile takeover, a bidder normally must pay a premium of about 40% above the market price of the target's stock. In addition, a hostile bidder must also pay very large fees to investment bankers, lawyers, and other professionals. Since the suboptimality of a state's statutory-law regime is highly unlikely to reduce the value of a corporation by more than a few percentage points, these huge premiums and fees will almost never be economically justified if the bidder's only strategy is to replace a suboptimal legal regime with an optimal legal regime.

Several commentators have attempted to resolve differences between the race-to-the-bottom and race-to-the-top arguments through the generation and analysis of data, but the studies are inconclusive. For example, in an article published in 2001, Rob Daines calculated that based on stock-market valuations, Delaware firms were worth more than non-Delaware firms in twelve out of the sixteen years during the period 1981–1996—5% more, on average. Daines, Does Delaware Law improve Firm Value?, 62 J. Financial Econ. 559–71. In a more recent article, however, Guhan Subrahmanian recalculated the value of Delaware firms during the period 1991–1996, and extended the analysis to the period 1997–2001. Subrahmanian concluded that Delaware firms were worth approximately 3% more than non-Delaware firms during the period 1991–1993, and approximately 2% more than non-Delaware firms during the period 1994–1996. Furthermore, after 1996 the value of Delaware firms did not differ in a statistically different way from the value of non-Delaware firms. Subrahmanian, The Disappearing Delaware Effect, 20 J. Law., Econ. & Org. 32 (2004).

The inconclusive nature of the data is not surprising. There are a number of reasons why it is difficult if not impossible to assess the optimality of Delaware's corporate statute by analyzing stock-market valuations.

1. Delaware law consists of judge-made law as well as legislative law. Delaware's judge-made law is vastly richer than the judge-made law of any other state, and Delaware judges are extremely skilled at corporation law. Therefore, even if Delaware's statutory law is suboptimal, that defect might be more than offset by the advantages of Delaware's judge-made law.

2. If a corporation is incorporated in a given state, it is often necessary to get opinions from counsel in that state—as opposed to a corporation's regular counsel—on a legal issue affecting a proposed corporate transaction or course of conduct. In addition to a judiciary that is skilled in corporate law, Delaware has a high-quality bar that is

skilled in corporate law, and to whom regular corporate counsel located in other states can turn with confidence. Of course, most states with large cities also have high-quality corporate bars, but few if any very small states could offer a corporate bar that matches Delaware's. Furthermore, the Delaware corporate bar puts in a lot of effort to make sure that the Delaware statute is technically up to speed. Even if the Delaware statute was suboptimal, its cost could be offset by these advantages.

3. As Michael Klausner has pointed out, because so many corporations are incorporated in Delaware, incorporation in Delaware brings in its train a type of benefit known as a network externality. Just as it may be desirable to use certain software, such as Microsoft Windows, whether or not it is better than other software, just because so many other people use it and are familiar with it, so it may be better to incorporate in Delaware, whether or not Delaware law is better than other state law, just because so many other corporations use and are familiar with it. See Klausner, Corporations, Corporate Law, and Network of Contract, 81 Va. L. Rev. 757 (1995). Furthermore, because so many corporations have incorporated in Delaware, it has become a good corporate address, like Park Avenue in New York City, or Boardwalk in Monopoly. Again, even if the Delaware statute was suboptimal, its cost could be offset by the network-externality and good-corporate-address benefits that Delaware incorporation brings.

4. Today, there isn't that much significant difference between the Delaware statute and most other state corporate-law statutes. That's not surprising. If all states are competing for management favor, their statutes are likely to converge. But if the state statutes converge, then the state statutes as a group may be suboptimal, but the Delaware statute might not be more suboptimal than other statutes.

5. As Kahan and Kamar have put it, the race is over and Delaware has won. Kahan and Kamar, The Myth of State Competition in Corporate Law, 55 Stan. L. Rev. 679 (2002). Now that Delaware has won the race, and holds a kind of monopoly position, the Delaware legislature has a special incentive *not* to lead in the adoption of innovative suboptimal rules. This special incentive is to avoid massive federal intervention in corporate law. Unlike the states, the federal government has an interest in the efficiency of national securities markets and, partly because its revenues depend heavily on corporate income, on the efficiency of the corporate system. However, for various reasons, the federal government does not intervene to correct every suboptimal state corporation–law rule. However, as state statutory corporate law becomes highly suboptimal, the risk of federal intervention increases. A state that has had little success in the charter market has much to gain and little to lose by offering innovative suboptimal rules to managers. If the rules attract incorporation, the state comes out ahead; if the rules stimulate federal intervention, the state is no worse off. In contrast, if comprehensive national corporate-law rules were established for publicly held corporations, over time Delaware could lose its leading position, because there would be less incentive to incorporate in one state rather than the other. Therefore, precisely because of its historical success in the charter market, Delaware is more threatened by the possibility of comprehensive

federal intervention than any other state. Furthermore, because of Delaware's massive market share, innovative suboptimal rules in Delaware are more likely to provoke federal intervention than innovative suboptimal rules any other state. Accordingly, having achieved a monopoly position in significant part because of its past leadership in offering suboptimal rules, Delaware now has an incentive not to lead in the adoption of innovative suboptimal rules.[1]

6. Finally, a comparison between the Delaware statute and other state statutes has limited significance not only because the difference between state statutes tends to be small, but also because of the limited significance of state statutory corporation law. Much of the real action in corporation law is not in state statutory law, but in the other three modules of corporation law described in previous Note—state judge-made law, federal law, and private ordering or soft law. The effect of small differences between state statutes tend to be swamped by the overriding significance of the law in those other modules. Of course, it is the general social interest that state statutory law be optimal, but suboptimal state statutory law can be, and is, compensated for in many respects by the law in the other three modules.

NOTE ON DIRECTORS' INFORMATIONAL RIGHTS

Under the common law, a director has a wide-ranging right to information concerning the corporation, which may be exercised through inspection of books, records, and documents. Although the right is often characterized as "absolute," the cases are split on whether the director's intent is relevant to exercise of the right.

Under one line of authority, which finds its fullest expression in the New York cases, the director's intent is deemed irrelevant, on the theory that a director must have unqualified access to information if he is to perform his directorial duties. For example, in Cohen v. Cocoline Products, Inc., 309 N.Y. 119, 127 N.E.2d 906 (1955), the court said that, "In order properly to perform his directing duties, a corporate director must . . . keep himself informed as to the policies, business and affairs of the corporation, and as to the acts of its officers. He owes a stewardship obligation to the corporation and its stockholders, and he may be subjected to liability for improper management during his term of office. Because of these positive duties and potential liabilities, the courts of this State have accorded to corporate directors an absolute, unqualified right . . . to inspect their corporate books and records." 309 N.Y. at 123, 127 N.E.2d at 907–08.

Under a competing line of authority, the director's intent is deemed relevant, on the theory that his right to information presupposes that he is not hostile to the corporation. For example, in State v. Seiberling Rubber Co., 53 Del. 295, 298, 168 A.2d 310, 312 (1961), the

---

1. See Melvin A. Eisenberg, The Structure of Corporation Law, 89 COLUM. L. REV. 461 (1989).

Delaware Superior Court said that "if it can be established that [the director's] motives are improper, or that they are in derogation to the interest of the corporation, then his right to inspect ceases to exist."

Several cases have coupled the principle that a director has an absolute right to information with the principle that the order granting the right can impose protective terms and conditions on its exercise. See, e.g., State ex rel. Moore v. State Bank, 561 S.W.2d 722 (Mo.App. 1978).

AMERICAN LAW INSTITUTE, PRINCIPLES OF CORPORATE GOVERNANCE § 3.03

[See Statutory Supplement]

SECTION 4.   FORMALITIES REQUIRED FOR ACTION BY THE BOARD

DEL. GEN. CORP. LAW §§ 141(b), (f), (i), 229

[See Statutory Supplement]

MODEL BUS. CORP. ACT §§ 8.20, 8.21, 8.22, 8.23, 8.24

[See Statutory Supplement]

NOTE ON FORMALITIES REQUIRED FOR ACTION BY THE BOARD

The validity of an action by the board of directors involves rules concerning the requirements for meeting, notice, quorum, and voting. These rules can be considered at two levels. At the first level are rules that set out the formalities for board action. At the second level are rules concerning the consequence of noncompliance with the first-level rules.

Level 1: The Governing Rules. Unless otherwise indicated, the following account is based on predominant statutory patterns.

(i) *Meetings.* A single director, as such, normally has no power. Instead, directors can act only as a body. Usually, directors must act at a duly convened meeting at which a quorum is present. Most statutes provide that a meeting of the board can be conducted by conference telephone, or by any other means of communication through which all participating directors can simultaneously hear each other. In addition, most statutes also permit the board to act by unanimous written consent without a meeting of any kind.

(ii) *Notice.* Formal notice is not required for a regular board meeting: If the meeting is a regular one, the directors are already on notice of its date, time, and place. In the case of a special meeting, notice of date, time, and place must be given to every director. The notice need not state the purpose of a meeting unless the certificate of incorporation or the bylaws otherwise provide. The statutes usually provide that notice must be given a stated number of days in advance of the meeting, but then add that the stated period may be made shorter or longer by the certificate of incorporation or by-laws. Most statutes provide that notice can be waived in writing before or after a meeting, and that attendance at a meeting constitutes a waiver unless the director attends merely to protest against holding the meeting.

(iii) *Quorum.* A quorum of a board consists of a majority of the *full board,* that is, a majority of the authorized number of directors (not simply a majority of the directors then in office, which may be less than the authorized number because of board vacancies). A majority of statutes permit the certificate of incorporation or bylaws to require a greater number for a quorum than a majority of the full board. A substantial minority of the statutes, including the Delaware statute and the Model Act, permit the certificate or bylaws to set a lower number, but usually no less than one-third of the full board.

(iv) *Voting.* Assuming that a quorum is present when a vote is taken, the affirmative vote of a majority of those present (not simply a majority of those voting) is required for action. Most statutes provide that the articles or bylaws can require a greater-than-majority vote for board action.

Level 2: Consequences of Noncompliance. The consequences of noncompliance with the rules that govern the formalities required for board action are not always clear. In publicly held corporations, where bureaucratic order usually prevails, lack of a quorum, lack of the requisite affirmative vote, or an uncured defect of notice, will usually render board action ineffective. However, in closely held corporations, where formalities are seldom followed, the results of a failure to observe proper formalities are much less clear-cut. Unless otherwise indicated, the balance of this Note concerns cases involving closely held corporations.

(i) *Unanimous explicit, but informal, approval.* Some cases, most of which are quite old, have held that informal approval by directors—that is, approval without following the requisite formalities—is ineffective, even if the approval is explicit and unanimous. A leading case was Baldwin v. Canfield, 26 Minn. 43, 54, 1 N.W. 261, 270 (1879). Cases like *Baldwin* are of doubtful validity today. More characteristic of modern authority is Gerard v. Empire Square Realty Co., 195 App.Div. 244, 187 N.Y.S. 306 (1921). Plaintiff brought an action against several related corporations to recover damages for breach of an employment contract. The corporations' shares were owned by five persons, all of whom were directors. Owing to dissension, no shareholders' or directors' meetings were held, but there was evidence that each director had separately agreed to the hiring of the plaintiff. The court held that on these facts the corporations would be bound:

> I think that under the circumstances of the case we are considering, where the directors own all the capital stock of the corporations, where they are members of the same family but so at variance that directors' and stockholders' meetings are not held, their action, concurred in by all, although separately and not as a body, binds the corporation. We must recognize the fact that [corporations] are, in perhaps the majority of instances, conducted by officers and directors little informed in the law of corporations, who often act informally, sometimes without meetings or even by-laws. To hold that in all instances technical conformity to the requirements of the law of corporations is a condition to a valid action by the directors, would be to lay down a rule of law which could be used as a trap for the unwary who deal with corporations, and to permit corporations sometimes to escape liability to which an individual in the same circumstances would be subjected.

The results in this area are too disparate to be captured by a single clear rule. In general, however, it is fair to say that most modern courts would hold that explicit but informal approval by all the directors is effective where a person who has contracted with a corporate officer has been led to regard his transaction with the corporation as valid, and all the shareholders either are directors or have acquiesced in the transaction or in a past practice of informal board action. See Anderson v. K.G. Moore, Inc., 6 Mass.App.Ct. 386, 376 N.E.2d 1238 (1978), cert. denied 439 U.S. 1116, 99 S.Ct. 1020, 59 L.Ed.2d 74 (1979).

Indeed, today cases involving unanimous explicit although informal approval would probably be analogized to the modern statutory rule that the board can act by written consent even without a meeting. It might be argued that the negative implication of these statutes is that no effect should be given to informal unanimous approval unless it is in writing. Thus, in Village of Brown Deer v. City of Milwaukee, 16 Wis.2d 206, 114 N.W.2d 493 (1962), cert. denied 371 U.S. 902, 83 S.Ct. 205, 9 L.Ed.2d 164, the court stated that, "The legislature has said that the corporation could act informally, without a meeting, by obtaining the consent in writing of all of the directors. In our opinion, this pronouncement has preempted the field and prohibits corporations from acting informally without complying with the statute." In *Brown Deer*, however, apparently only a majority of the directors knew of the transaction in question, so there was no unanimous approval, formal or informal. Other cases decided in jurisdictions that have unanimous-written-consent statutes have held that the corporation was bound by unanimous oral consent. See Note, Corporations: When Informal Action by Corporate Directors Will Be Permitted to Bind the Corporation, 53 B.U.L.Rev. 101, 120 (1973).

(ii) *Explicit approval by a majority coupled with acquiescence by remaining directors.* In the type of case just considered, all the directors informally but explicitly approve a transaction. Suppose that a majority of the directors explicitly approve a transaction, while the remaining directors knew of the transaction and took no action to disavow it, so that they may be said to have acquiesced in the transaction. The difference between this case and the case in which all the directors explicitly but informally approve is not very significant. Accordingly, the courts will normally treat cases alike. See, e.g., Winchell v. Plywood Corp., 324 Mass. 171, 85 N.E.2d 313 (1949). The same result will normally follow even if there is no explicit approval by a majority of the directors, but all the directors acquiesce. See e.g., Juergens v. Venture Capital Corp., 1 Mass.App.Ct. 274, 295 N.E.2d 398 (1973); Pierce v. Astoria Fish Factors, Inc., 31 Wash.App. 214, 640 P.2d 40 (1982).

(iii) *Majority approval or acquiescence.* Suppose, finally, that a majority of the directors of a closely held corporation approve a transaction, explicitly or by acquiescence, but the remaining directors lack knowledge of the transaction. Some courts have refused to hold the corporation liable under these circumstances. See, e.g., Hurley v. Ornsteen, 311 Mass. 477, 42 N.E.2d 273 (1942). Other courts have held the corporation liable if the *shareholders* acquiesced in the transaction, or the shareholders or the remaining directors acquiesced in a practice of informal action by the directors. One theory is that the remaining directors would have known of the transaction if they had been properly active. Another is that the shareholders, if they have tolerated informal action by the directors over a period of time, have by that acquiescence authorized the directors to act in that manner. See, e.g., Holy Cross Gold Mining & Milling Co. v. Goodwin, 74 Colo. 532, 223 P. 58 (1924).

NOTE ON COMMITTEES

The boards of publicly held corporations often accomplish much of their work through committees. Committees can be advisory to the board, but alternatively the board may delegate to a committee the power to make decisions about specific matters or a range of matters. Most statutes contain a short list of matters that cannot be delegated, but generally speaking there is very little that cannot be delegated. In general, the rules governing board procedures—such as the rules concerning notice, quorum, and voting—are applicable to committees as well.

DEL. GEN. CORP. LAW § 141(c)

[See Statutory Supplement]

MODEL BUS. CORP. ACT § 8.25

[See Statutory Supplement]

SECTION 5. AUTHORITY OF CORPORATE OFFICERS

DEL. GEN. CORP. LAW § 142

[See Statutory Supplement]

MODEL BUS. CORP. ACT §§ 8.40, 8.41

[See Statutory Supplement]

NOTE ON AUTHORITY

[See Chapter 1, supra]

NOTE ON THE AUTHORITY OF CORPORATE OFFICERS

Legal questions concerning the authority of a corporate officer typically arise in the context of a transaction between a third person and the corporation in which an officer, rather than the board, acted on the corporation's behalf. The application of the principle of apparent authority in such cases may rest on the officer's position, that is, his title.

1. *President.* There are a great number of cases concerning the apparent authority of a president by virtue of his title. Some cases hold that a president does not have any apparent authority by virtue of his position—that instead, he has only the actual authority that the board has conferred upon him. For example, in Federal Services Finance Corp. v. Bishop Nat. Bank of Hawaii at Honolulu, 190 F.2d 442 (9th Cir.1951), supplemented 205 F.2d 11 (9th Cir.1953), the court held that the president had no presumed power, by virtue of his office, to cash checks payable to the company's order.

However, the prevalent modern rule is that the president has apparent authority to bind his company to contracts in the usual and regular course of business, but not to contracts of an "extraordinary" nature. See, e.g., Lee v. Jenkins Bros., 268 F.2d 357 (2d Cir.1959), cert. denied 361 U.S. 913, 80 S.Ct. 257, 4 L.Ed.2d 183. The difficulty lies in drawing a line between what is "ordinary" and what is "extraordinary." Some cases have been restrictive in determining the apparent authority of a president, perhaps influenced by statutory language that the business of the corporation shall be managed by the board. See, e.g., Liebermann v. Princeway Realty Corp., 17 A.D.2d 258, 233 N.Y.S.2d 1001 (1962), aff'd 13 N.Y.2d 999, 245 N.Y.S.2d 390, 195 N.E.2d 57 (1963). Other cases, such as Lee v. Jenkins Brothers, supra, determine the president's apparent authority in a more expansive manner. An expansive interpretation reflects both the reality that the management of the business of the corporation is normally conducted by or under the supervision of its executives rather than its board, and a sound understanding of the normal expectations of third persons in such cases.

Any attempt at precision in determining the apparent authority of a president would almost certainly be futile, because the issue is highly dependent on the context in which it arises, and the types of business transactions that may arise are endlessly variable. Nevertheless, certain boundaries can be identified. To begin with, some matters, such as the declaration of dividends, are required by statute to be decided by the board. Typically, the statutes also enumerate certain matters that the board cannot delegate to a committee, such as approval of an action that requires approval by both the board and the shareholders pursuant to statute. By analogy, it would normally not be within the apparent authority of the president to take binding action on these matters.

Beyond these boundaries, among the elements to be taken into account for purposes of determining what constitutes an "extraordinary" action, that would normally be outside the apparent authority of the president, are the economic magnitude of the action in relation to corporate assets and earnings, the extent of risk involved, the time-span of the action's effect, and the cost of reversing the action. Examples of extraordinary acts for these purposes include the creation of long-term or other significant debt, the reacquisition of equity or debt securities, significant capital investments, significant business combinations, the disposition of significant businesses, entry into important new lines of business, significant acquisitions of stock in other corporations, and actions that would foreseeably expose the corporation to significant litigation or significant new regulatory problems. A useful generalization is that decisions that would make a significant change in the structure of the business enterprise, or in the structure of control over the enterprise, are extraordinary corporate actions and therefore normally outside the president's apparent authority.

Of course, the president, or any other officer, may have actual authority that is greater than his apparent authority. The president's actual authority may be found in the certificate of incorporation, the by-laws, or board resolutions, or may derive from a pattern of past acquiescence by the board, or from the board's ratification of a specific transaction.

2. *CEO.* The terminology employed in the traditional rules concerning the apparent authority of a corporate officer has become somewhat archaic. When these rules were formulated, the top officer in the corporation had the title of president, the number-two officer had the title of executive vice-president, and the top financial officer had the title of treasurer. Today, matters are much different. The title that signifies the top officer is not president, but chief executive officer, or CEO. (The CEO usually holds a second title, which may be either chairman of the board, president, or both.) The title that usually signifies the number-two officer is Chief Operating Officer, or COO. Often the COO title is held by the president, so that today often the president is the number-two rather than the number-one executive.

It remains to be seen how the apparent authority of corporate officers will be adapted to this shift in terminology.

3. *Chairman of the Board.* There is little case-law on the apparent authority of a chairman of the board by virtue of his position, in part because the actual authority of the chairman varies significantly. Often, but not always, the chairmanship title is simply piled on to the CEO title. However, "In some [corporations, the chairman's office] is held by a chief executive officer who has relinquished day-by-day operations to a younger man while still holding the reins of power; in others it is held by a retired chief executive officer whose counsel and advice are still valued; in still others it provides a formula for dividing up between two relatively equal principals the control of the corporation." American Express Co. v. Lopez, 72 Misc.2d 648, 340 N.Y.S.2d 82 (Civ.Ct.1973).

4. *Vice-Presidents.* The case-law on the apparent authority of vice-presidents is also sparse. Under the relatively strict outlook of the earlier cases, a vice-president, as such, had little or no apparent authority. See James F. Monaghan, Inc. v. M. Lowenstein & Sons, 290 Mass. 331, 195 N.E. 101 (1935). There is some indication that courts today may follow a more expansive approach to the authority of a vice-president, at least if the vice-president has the appearance of standing close to the top of the corporate hierarchy. See Kanavos v. Hancock Bank & Trust Co., 14 Mass.App.Ct. 326, 439 N.E.2d 311 (1982).

5. *Secretary.* The secretary of a corporation has apparent authority to certify the records of the corporation, including resolutions of the board. A secretary's certificate that a given resolution was duly adopted by the board is therefore conclusive in favor of third party relying on the certificate. See, e.g., Diamond Paint Co. of Houston v. Embry, 525 S.W.2d 529 (Tex.Civ.App.1975). The significance of the secretary's power of certification is demonstrated in In re Drive–In Development Corp., 371 F.2d 215, 219–20 (7th Cir.1966), cert. denied Creditors' Committee of Drive–In Development Corp. v. National Boulevard Bank of Chicago, 387 U.S. 909, 87 S.Ct. 1691, 18 L.Ed.2d 626 (1967), which involved the question whether a corporation was bound by a guaranty:

> ... [T]he referee found that Drive In's minute book did not show that a resolution authorizing Maranz to sign the guaranty

was adopted by the directors and that Dick [the corporate secretary] could not recall a specific directors' meeting at which such a resolution was approved. From these findings, the referee concluded that Maranz, who signed the guaranty on behalf of Drive In, had no authority, "either actual or implied or apparent," to bind Drive In. This conclusion was erroneous. Drive In was estopped to deny Maranz' express authority to sign the guaranty because of the certified copy of a resolution of Drive In's board of directors purporting to grant such authority furnished to the bank by Dick, whether or not such a resolution was in fact formally adopted.

Other than the very important power of certification, a secretary's apparent authority, by virtue of his position, is close to nil. See, e.g., Ideal Foods, Inc. v. Action Leasing Corp., 413 So.2d 416, 417 (Fla.App. 1982) ("The secretary of a corporation, merely as such, is a ministerial officer, without authority to transact the business of the corporation upon his volition and judgment").

6. *Treasurer.* The apparent authority of the treasurer, under the case-law, is also close to nil. See, e.g., Ideal Foods, Inc. v. Action Leasing Corp., 413 So.2d 416 (Fla.App.1982).

7. *Closely Held Corporations.* In the context of closely held corporations, some cases hold that if the president has been exercising absolute authority over the corporation's affairs, and the board has never questioned, altered, or rejected his decisions, the president will have extremely wide actual and apparent authority. See, e.g., Allen v. France Packing Co., 170 Pa.Super. 632, 90 A.2d 289 (1952); Blasingame v. American Materials, Inc., 654 S.W.2d 659 (Tenn.1983). More generally, it has been said that:

> Although the same broad principles of corporation and agency law determine the powers of officers in both close and publicly held corporations, the factual differences in the patterns of operation of the two kinds of corporations lead to wide disparities in the powers the courts actually recognize in corporate officers. In a close corporation, ownership and management normally coalesce; and the participants often conduct their enterprise internally much as if it were a partnership. The courts have seldom articulated a difference in the rules governing officers' powers in close and publicly held corporations; yet they appear in fact to have often cut through the technical legal form of close corporations to reach the results that would be reached if the enterprises were conducted as partnerships. In other words, the courts frequently, and perhaps usually, recognize in officers of a close corporation the same powers that are possessed by partners in a firm under the general rule of partnership law which makes each partner an agent of the firm for the purposes of its business and empowers each partner to bind the firm by acts apparently carried on to further the usual business of the partnership.

Zimmerman v. Hogg & Allen, 286 N.C. 24, 33, 209 S.E.2d 795, 801 (1974).

8. *Ratification.* Even if an officer lacks both actual and apparent authority, the corporation may be bound by the officer's act in entering into a contract or other transaction on its behalf, if the board later ratifies the officer's act. Ratification may occur where a corporation, knowing all of the facts, accepts and uses the proceeds of an unauthorized contract executed on its behalf. Western American Life Ins. Co. v. Hicks, 135 Ga.App. 90, 217 S.E.2d 323 (1975).

————

SCHOONEJONGEN v. CURTISS WRIGHT CORP., 143 F.3d 120 (3d Cir.1998). "Beyond the board of directors, the corporation may validly act through its ... officers as authorized corporate agents. In general, an officer's powers stem from the organic law of the corporation, or a board delegation of authority which maybe express or implied.... Express authority to act on behalf of the corporation is usually manifested through a statute, the certificate of corporation, the by-laws, or a board or shareholder action.... Implied actual authority, which is express authority circumstantially proved, may be found through evidence as to the manner in which the business has operated in the past, the facts attending the transaction in question, circumstantial evidence of board declarations surrounding the given transaction, or the habitual usage or course of dealing common to the company.... Similarly, authority will be implied when it is reasonably necessary and proper to effectuate the purpose of the office or the main authority conferred."

SECTION 6. FORMALITIES REQUIRED FOR SHAREHOLDER ACTION

————

DEL. GEN. CORP. LAW §§ 211, 213, 214, 216, 222, 228

[See Statutory Supplement]

————

REV. MODEL BUS. CORP. ACT §§ 7.01, 7.02, 7.03–7.07, 7.21, 7.25–7.28

[See Statutory Supplement]

————

NOTE ON FORMALITIES REQUIRED FOR SHAREHOLDER ACTION

1. *Meeting and Notice.* Notice of place, time, and date is required for the annual meeting of shareholders and for any special

meeting. The notice of a *special* meeting must describe the purpose for which the meeting is called. Under most state statutes, the notice of an annual meeting must describe the matters to be acted upon only in certain cases—for example, when it is proposed to amend the certificate of incorporation, sell substantially all of the corporation's assets, engage in a merger, or dissolve. Some state statutes, and the federal Proxy Rules, also require a description of purpose in the notice of an annual meeting. However, the Proxy Rules do not apply to all corporations.

Because the identity of the shareholders in a publicly held corporation constantly undergoes change, normally notice of a meeting is given to those persons who are shareholders of record on a designated *record date* prior to the meeting, not to those persons who are beneficial owners of stock on the date of the meeting. Correspondingly, only those persons who were record holders on the record date are entitled to vote at the meeting. The record date is normally fixed in the by-laws, or by the board, within prescribed statutory limits. If a record date is not fixed in this manner, the statutes usually provide that the record date will be the day of, or the business day preceding, the day on which the notice of meeting is sent. (Under an older, alternative procedure that is still sanctioned in many statutes, but is generally regarded as archaic, the corporation can close its share-transfer books as of a given date, and give notice only to those persons who were record holders at the time the transfer books were closed.)

2. *Quorum.* Under most of the statutes, a majority of the shares entitled to vote is necessary for a quorum, unless the certificate of incorporation sets a higher or lower figure. A substantial majority of the statutes provide that the certificate cannot set a quorum lower than one-third of the shares entitled to vote. Most of the remaining statutes set no minimum.

3. *Voting.* (i) *Ordinary matters.* Under most statutes, the affirmative vote of a majority of the shares represented at a meeting is required for shareholder action on ordinary matters. Under some statutes, however, only the affirmative vote of a majority of those voting is required. If a statute requires the affirmative vote of a majority of those present, an abstention effectively counts as a negative vote.

Virtually all the statutes permit the certificate of incorporation to set a higher vote than would otherwise be required. Under some of the statutes, a certificate amendment that adds a provision requiring a higher-than-normal vote may be adopted only by the same vote as that required under the amendment.

(ii) *Fundamental changes.* A group of actions known as *fundamental changes*, which consists of amendments of the certificate of incorporation, merger, sale of substantially all assets, and dissolution, often require approval by a majority (or sometimes two-thirds) or two-thirds of the outstanding voting shares, rather than a majority of those present or voting at the meeting. However, the Model Act requires only a majority of the shares voting on such matters, provided a majority of the outstanding shares are present at the meeting.

(iii) *Election of directors.* The election of directors requires only a plurality vote—that is, those candidates who receive the highest number of votes are elected, up to the maximum number to be chosen at the election, even if they receive less than a majority of the votes present at the meeting. Cumulative voting for directors is required by some states, and is sometimes voluntarily adopted even when not required. The mechanics of cumulative voting are described in the next Section.

(iv) *Written consent.* The statutes typically permit the shareholders to act by written consent in lieu of a meeting. Many or most of the statutes permit shareholder action by written consent only if the consent is unanimous.

SECTION 7.   CUMULATIVE VOTING

NOTE ON CUMULATIVE VOTING

1. *Straight Voting and Cumulative Voting.* In the normal regime for voting on directors—what is sometimes called a "straight" voting regime—a shareholder can cast, for each candidate for election to the board, a number of votes equal to her number of shares. For example, assume that shareholder S owns 100 shares in Blue Corporation, that Blue's board consists of seven directors, and that all seven directorship positions are up for election. Under straight voting, S can cast a total of 700 votes, but cannot cast more than 100 votes for any one candidate.

In contrast, under a cumulative-voting regime a shareholder can cast for any single candidate, or for two or more candidates, as she chooses, a number of votes equal to the number of shares she holds times the number of directors to be elected. Thus in the Blue corporation example, under cumulative voting S can cast 700 votes for one candidate, or 350 votes for each of two candidates, or 300 shares for each of two candidates and 100 shares for a third candidate, and so forth.

Under straight voting, a minority shareholder or faction can never elect a director to the board over the opposition of the majority. For example, suppose that Blue corporation has 300 shares, 100 of which are held by S, and 200 of which are held by T. Recall that Blue has seven directors, all of which are up for election. Under straight voting, S can cast no more than 100 votes for any of her candidates. Since T can cast 200 votes for each of his seven candidates, T can elect all the directors.

In contrast, if cumulative voting is in effect, S can distribute her 700 votes among one or more candidates. Similarly, T can cast a total of 1400 votes, which he can distribute among one or more candidates.

Suppose that S casts 350 votes for each of two candidates. If T distributes his 1400 votes among seven candidates, each of his candidates will receive 200 votes. Accordingly, S will elect her two candidates, because they will each receive more votes (350) than any of T's candidates (200). T will elect five candidates.

Suppose that T casts 351 votes for each of two candidates. In that case, T can cast only 698 votes for his other five candidates. Accordingly, some of T's candidates will receive less than 350 votes, and S will still elect her two candidates to the board.

2. *Mathematics*. Aranow & Einhorn, Proxy Contests for Corporate Control 10.04[B] (3d ed. 1998) discusses the mathematics of cumulative voting, as follows:

> The mathematics of cumulative voting can become a very involved subject which we will not undertake to discuss in all its aspects. There are two basic formulas, both of which are relatively simple. The first formula is used to determine the minimum number of shares needed to elect a particular number of directors:

$$X = \frac{(S \times N)}{D + 1} + 1$$

X = minimum number of shares needed
S = total number of shares that will be voted at meeting
N = number of directors desired to elect
D = total number of directors to be elected

> For example, assume there exists a corporation with 1,000 shares outstanding and seven directors to be elected. A minority stockholders' group wishes to elect two directors. It is estimated that 800 shares will be voted at the meeting. Applying these figures to the formula, the resulting calculation is:

$$\frac{(800 \times 2)}{7 + 1} + 1 = 201$$

> The stockholders' group knows that it must have ownership or control of at least 201 shares in order to elect two directors.

> The second formula can be used to determine how many directors can be elected by a group controlling a particular number of shares:

$$N = \frac{(X) \times (D + 1)}{S}$$

N = number of directors that can be elected
X = number of shares controlled
D = total number of directors to be elected

S = total number of shares that will be voted at meeting

In the example above, assume that the stockholders' group knows it will control 201 shares. Applying the figures to this formula, the resulting calculation is:

$$\frac{201 \times 8}{800} = 2.01$$

Thus, cumulation will result in the election of two directors. There are several other formulas that can be applied to more complicated questions.*

3. *Mandatory Cumulative Voting*. The percentage of stock that minority shareholders must hold to elect at least one director under cumulative voting varies inversely with the number of directors to be elected. Accordingly, a 12% minority (for example) can elect one director if nine directors are to be elected, but cannot elect any directors if three directors are to be elected. This can give rise to various problems when cumulative voting is mandatory.

One problem is whether, when cumulative voting is mandatory, a corporation can have a classified board, in which the directors are divided into classes and each class serves for a term of years. Where a board is classified the minority must hold more stock to elect a single director than if a board of the same size was unclassified. In Wolfson v. Avery, 6 Ill.2d 78, 126 N.E.2d 701 (1955), the Illinois court held that an Illinois constitutional requirement of cumulative voting prohibited classified boards. The Illinois Constitution was later amended to eliminate this requirement. In Bohannan v. Corporation Commission, 82 Ariz. 299, 313 P.2d 379 (1957), the Arizona court held to the contrary of Wolfson v. Avery. Subsequently, the Arizona legislature enacted a statutory provision that permitted classification if a board had nine or more directors.

Still another issue concerns the removal of directors: Cumulative voting could be undercut if a director who is elected by a minority under cumulative voting could then be removed by majority. Accordingly, some statutes provide that under cumulative voting, a director

---

* Jesse Fried points out that:

The standard formula for determining the minimum number of shares necessary to elect a particular number of directors yields an easily interpretable result only when the expression (S x N)/(D + 1) is a whole number.

Suppose, as in the Aranow and Einhorn example, that there is a corporation with seven directors to be elected and a minority group wishes to elect two directors. However, 803 shares (rather than the 800 shares used in their example) will be voted at the meeting. The standard formula indicates that the number of shares needed to elect two directors is now:

[(803 x 2)/(7 + 1)] + 1 = 201.75

If there are only whole shares, does this mean that the minority group needs 201 to elect two directors, or 202 shares? The answer is, surprisingly, 201—if the standard formula does not yield a whole number you must round down to determine the number of whole shares needed.

If there are fractional shares, then the standard formula yields the wrong result.

A more useful formula for determining the minimum number of shares needed (X), is X > (S x N)/(D + 1)

If there are fractional shares, then any fraction greater than the righthandside expression will allow you to elect N directors. If there are whole shares, then you round up to the next whole number.

cannot be removed if the number of shares voting against her removal would be sufficient to elect her. See, e.g., Cal.Corp. Code § 303(a)(1).

SECTION 8. LIMITED LIABILITY

———

DEL. GEN. CORP. LAW § 102(b)(6)

[See Statutory Supplement]

———

REV. MODEL BUS. CORP. ACT § 6.22(b)

[See Statutory Supplement]

———

INTRODUCTORY NOTE ON LIMITED LIABILITY

It is commonly said that shareholders ordinarily have limited liability for corporation obligations. Actually, shareholders ordinarily have *no* liability for corporate obligations: Under modern statutes, a shareholder's risk is ordinarily limited to her *investment*—that is, the most a shareholder stands to lose, even if the corporation fails, is the amount that she paid for her shares.

Nevertheless, the term "limited liability" is universally used to refer to the no-liability rule, and it will therefore be used in this casebook as well.

It is also sometimes said that shareholders are not liable for corporate obligations because corporations are separate legal entities. In fact, however, the entity status of corporations has almost nothing to do with shareholder limited liability. For example, English law conferred entity status on corporations long before shareholders were afforded limited liability. Similarly, the Revised Uniform Partnership Act (RUPA) confers entity status on partnerships, but also provides that the partners are individually liable for all partnership obligations once the partnership's assets are exhausted. Accordingly, although cases in which liability is imposed on shareholders despite the ordinary rules are commonly said to involve "disregard of the corporate entity" or "piercing the corporate veil," really these cases involve only a conclusion that under given kinds of circumstances there are good reasons why the normal statutory rule of limited liability should not be applied.

It should also be borne in mind that corporate managers, as well as corporate shareholders, are ordinarily not liable for corporate obligations. Shareholders are not liable for corporate obligations by statute. In contrast, managers are not liable for corporate obligations on straightforward agency principles: In the case of a contract that is made by an agent within his authority, the agent is not liable as long as she purported to act in that capacity and the identity of her principal was disclosed. Similarly, in the case of a tort by a corporate employee that injures a third party, a manager normally will not be *vicariously* liable to the third party even if the employee was a subordinate of the manager. (However, a corporate manager may be liable to a third party if he either personally commits or directs the commission of the tortious action. The liability of corporate managers to third parties is considered in more detail in the Note on Civil Liabilities of Directors and Officers in Chapter 8, Section 1.)

———

Fletcher v. Atex, Inc.

United States Court of Appeals, Second Circuit, 1995.
68 F.3d 1451.

■ Before: KEARSE, CALABRESI, and CABRANES, CIRCUIT JUDGES.

■ JOSE A. CABRANES, CIRCUIT JUDGE:

This is a consolidated appeal from a final judgment of the United States District Court for the Southern District of New York (Morris E. Lasker, Judge), granting defendant-appellee Eastman Kodak Company's motion for summary judgment and dismissing all claims against it in two actions, Fletcher v. Atex, Inc., 92 Civ. 8758 and Hermanson v. 805 Middlesex Corp., Inc., 94 Civ. 1272. Fletcher v. Atex, Inc., 861 F.Supp. 242 (S.D.N.Y.1994). The plaintiffs-appellants filed suit against Atex, Inc. ("Atex") and its parent, Eastman Kodak Company ("Kodak"), to recover for repetitive stress injuries that they claim were caused by their use of computer keyboards manufactured by Atex.

Plaintiffs-appellants argue that the district court erred in granting summary judgment in favor of Kodak on the ground that Kodak could be held liable for the plaintiffs' alleged injuries. They contend that summary judgment was inappropriate because genuine issues of material fact existed regarding Kodak's liability as a defendant. . . .

I.   BACKGROUND

The Fletcher and Hermanson plaintiffs filed their respective complaints on December 4, 1992, and February 25, 1994, seeking recovery from Atex and Kodak, among others, for repetitive stress injuries that they claim were caused by their use of Atex computer keyboards. From 1981 until December 1992, Atex was a wholly-owned subsidiary of Kodak. In 1987, Atex's name was changed to Electronic Pre–Press Systems, Inc., ("EPPS"), but its name was changed back to Atex in 1990. In December 1992, Atex sold substantially all of its assets to an independent third party and again changed its name to 805 Middlesex Corp., which holds the proceeds from the sale. Kodak continues to be the sole shareholder of 805 Middlesex Corp.

After extensive discovery, Kodak moved for summary judgment in Fletcher on April 21, 1994, and in Hermanson on April 28, 1994. The plaintiffs opposed Kodak's motion, arguing that genuine issues of material fact existed as to Kodak's liability under any number of theories, including (1) that Atex was merely Kodak's alter ego or instrumentality; (2) that Atex was Kodak's agent in the manufacture and marketing of the keyboards; (3) that Kodak was the "apparent manufacturer" of the Atex keyboards; and (4) that Kodak acted in tortious concert with Atex in manufacturing and marketing the allegedly defective keyboards.

In support of their first theory, the plaintiffs argued that Kodak "dominated and controlled" Atex by maintaining significant overlap between the boards of directors of the two companies, "siphoning" off funds from Atex through use of a cash management system, requiring Kodak's approval for major expenditures, stock sales, and real estate acquisitions, participating in negotiations involving the sale of Atex to a third party, and including references to Atex as a "division" of Kodak and to the "merger" between Atex and Kodak in Atex's promotional literature and Kodak's Annual Report....

On August 17, 1994, the district court rejected each of the plaintiffs' theories of Kodak's liability and granted Kodak's motion for summary judgment in both actions. In its opinion, the court referred to, but did not rely upon, an identical suit filed against Atex and Kodak in New York state court, King v. Eastman Kodak Co., No. 23439/92 (N.Y.Sup.Ct. June 9, 1994), in which Kodak's motion for summary judgment was granted on similar grounds. Fletcher, 861 F.Supp. at 243.

.... [T]he district court found that Kodak and Atex observed all corporate formalities and maintained separate corporate existences. It held that Atex's participation in Kodak's cash management system and Kodak's control over Atex's major expenditures and asset sales were insufficient to raise an issue of material fact regarding Kodak's liability under an alter ego theory. Id. at 244–45.... This appeal followed.

II. DISCUSSION ...

The plaintiffs claim that the district court erred in granting Kodak's motion for summary judgment on their alter ego theory of liability. The plaintiffs ... argue that ... genuine issues of material fact remain that preclude a grant of summary judgment in favor of Kodak.

The district court correctly noted that "[u]nder New York choice of law principles, '[t]he law of the state of incorporation determines when the corporate form will be disregarded and liability will be imposed on shareholders.' " Fletcher, 861 F.Supp. at 244 (quoting Kalb, Voorhis & Co. v. American Fin. Corp., 8 F.3d 130, 132 (2d Cir.1993)). Because Atex was a Delaware corporation, Delaware law determines whether the corporate veil can be pierced in this instance.

Delaware law permits a court to pierce the corporate veil of a company "where there is fraud or where [it] is in fact a mere instrumentality or alter ego of its owner." Geyer v. Ingersoll Publications Co., 621 A.2d 784, 793 (Del.Ch.1992). Although the Delaware Supreme Court has never explicitly adopted an alter ego theory of parent liability for its subsidiaries, lower Delaware courts have applied the doctrine on several occasions, as has the United States District Court for the District of Delaware. See Geyer, 621 A.2d at 793; Mabon, Nugent & Co. v. Texas Am. Energy Corp., No. CIV.A. 8578, 1990 WL 44267, at *5, (Del.Ch. Apr.12, 1990); Harper v. Delaware Valley Broadcasters, Inc., 743 F.Supp. 1076, 1085 (D.Del.1990), aff'd, 932 F.2d 959 (3d Cir.1991). Thus, under an alter ego theory, there is no requirement of a showing of fraud. Id. at 1085. To prevail on an alter ego claim under Delaware law, a plaintiff must show (1) that the parent and the subsidiary "operated as a single economic entity" and (2) that an "overall element of injustice or unfairness . . . [is] present." Id. (internal quotation marks omitted); see also Mabon, 1990 WL 44267, at *5; Harco Nat'l Ins. Co. v. Green Farms, Inc., No. CIV.A. 1331, 1989 WL 110537, at *5, (Del.Ch. Sept.19, 1989).

In the New York state action of King v. Eastman, the court granted Kodak's motion for summary judgment, relying on an erroneous interpretation of Delaware's alter ego doctrine. The court noted that although the plaintiffs had raised "ample questions of fact regarding the first element of the piercing theory—domination," they made "no showing that Kodak used whatever dominance it had over Atex to perpetrate a fraud or other wrong that proximately cause[d] injury to them." This was an error; under Delaware law, the alter ego theory of liability does not require any showing of fraud. . . .

b. Summary Judgment on the Alter Ego Theory

To prevail on an alter ego theory of liability, a plaintiff must show that the two corporations " 'operated as a single economic entity such that it would be inequitable . . . to uphold a legal distinction between them.' " Harper, 743 F.Supp. at 1085 (quoting Mabon, 1990 WL 44267, at * 5). Among the factors to be considered in determining whether a subsidiary and parent operate as a "single economic entity" are:

> "[W]hether the corporation was adequately capitalized for the corporate undertaking; whether the corporation was solvent; whether dividends were paid, corporate records kept, officers and directors functioned properly, and other corporate formalities were observed; whether the dominant shareholder siphoned corporate funds; and whether, in general, the corporation simply functioned as a facade for the dominant shareholder."

Harco, 1989 WL 110537, at *4 (quoting United States v. Golden Acres, Inc., 702 F.Supp. 1097, 1104 (D.Del.1988)). As noted above, a showing of fraud or wrongdoing is not necessary under an alter ego theory, but the plaintiff must demonstrate an overall element of injustice or unfairness. Harco, 1989 WL 110537, at *5.

A plaintiff seeking to persuade a Delaware court to disregard the corporate structure faces "a difficult task." Harco, 1989 WL 110537, at *4. Courts have made it clear that "[t]he legal entity of a corporation will not be disturbed until sufficient reason appears." Id. Although the question of domination is generally one of fact, courts have granted motions to dismiss as well as motions for summary judgment in favor of defendant parent companies where there has been a lack of sufficient evidence to place the alter ego issue in dispute. See, e.g., Akzona, Inc. v. Du Pont, 607 F.Supp. 227, 237 (D.Del.1984) (rejecting plaintiffs' alter ego theory of liability on a motion to dismiss); Nelson v. International Paint Co., 734 F.2d 1084, 1092 (5th Cir.1984) ("[I]n the lack of sufficient evidence to place the alter ego issue in dispute, a corporate defendant may be entitled to summary judgment."); see also Japan Petroleum Co. (Nigeria) v. Ashland Oil Inc., 456 F.Supp. 831, 838, 846 (D.Del.1978) (finding that subsidiary was not instrumentality of parent on a motion for summary judgment).

Kodak has shown that Atex followed corporate formalities, and the plaintiffs have offered no evidence to the contrary. Significantly, the plaintiffs have not challenged Kodak's assertions that Atex's board of directors held regular meetings, that minutes from those meetings were routinely prepared and maintained in corporate minute books, that appropriate financial records and other files were maintained by Atex, that Atex filed its own tax returns and paid its own taxes, and that Atex had its own employees and management executives who were responsible for the corporation's day-to-day business. The plaintiffs' primary arguments regarding domination concern (1) the defendant's use of a cash management system; (2) Kodak's exertion of control over Atex's major expenditures, stock sales, and the sale of Atex's assets to a third party; (3) Kodak's "dominating presence" on Atex's board of directors; (4) descriptions of the relationship between Atex and Kodak in the corporations' advertising, promotional literature, and annual reports; and (5) Atex's assignment of one of its former officer's mortgage to Kodak in order to close Atex's asset-purchase agreement with a third party. The plaintiffs argue that each of these raises a genuine issue of material fact about Kodak's domination of Atex, and that the district court therefore erred in granting summary judgment to Kodak on the plaintiffs' alter ego theory. We find that the district court correctly held that, in light of the undisputed factors of independence cited by Kodak, "the elements identified by the plaintiffs ... [were] insufficient as a matter of law to establish the degree of domination necessary to disregard Atex's corporate identity." Fletcher, 861 F.Supp. at 245.

First, the district court correctly held that "Atex's participation in Kodak's cash management system is consistent with sound business practice and does not show undue domination or control." Id. at 244. The parties do not dispute the mechanics of Kodak's cash management system. Essentially, all of Kodak's domestic subsidiaries participate in the system and maintain zero-balance bank accounts. All funds transferred from the subsidiary accounts are recorded as credits to the subsidiary, and when a subsidiary is in need of funds, a transfer is made. At all times, a strict accounting is kept of each subsidiary's funds.

Courts have generally declined to find alter ego liability based on a parent corporation's use of a cash management system. See, e.g., In re Acushnet River & New Bedford Harbor Proceedings, 675 F.Supp. 22, 34 (D.Mass.1987) (Without "considerably more," "a centralized cash management system ... where the accounting records always reflect the indebtedness of one entity to another, is not the equivalent of intermingling funds" and is insufficient to justify disregarding the corporate form.); United States v. Bliss, 108 F.R.D. 127, 132 (E.D.Mo. 1985) (cash management system indicative of the "usual parent-subsidiary relationship"); Japan Petrol., 456 F.Supp. at 846 (finding segregation of subsidiary's accounts within parent's cash management system to be "a function of administrative convenience and economy, rather than a manifestation of control"). The plaintiffs offer no facts to support their speculation that Kodak's centralized cash management system was actually a "complete commingling" of funds or a means by which Kodak sought to "siphon[ ] all of Atex's revenues into its own account."

Second, the district court correctly concluded that it could find no domination based on the plaintiffs' evidence that Kodak's approval was required for Atex's real estate leases, major capital expenditures, negotiations for a sale of minority stock ownership to IBM, or the fact that Kodak played a significant role in the ultimate sale of Atex's assets to a third party. Again, the parties do not dispute that Kodak required Atex to seek its approval and/or participation for the above transactions. However, this evidence, viewed in the light most favorable to the plaintiffs, does not raise an issue of material fact about whether the two corporations constituted "a single economic entity." Indeed, this type of conduct is typical of a majority shareholder or parent corporation. See Phoenix Canada Oil Co. v. Texaco, 842 F.2d 1466, 1476 (3d Cir.1988) (declining to pierce the corporate veil where subsidiary required to secure approval from parent for "large investments and acquisitions or disposals of major assets"), cert. denied, 488 U.S. 908, 109 S.Ct. 259, 102 L.Ed.2d 247 (1988); *Akzona*, 607 F.Supp. at 237 (same, where parent approval required for expenditures exceeding $850,000); Japan Petrol., 456 F.Supp. at 843 (finding no parent liability where parent approval required for expenditures exceeding $250,000). In *Akzona*, the Delaware district court noted that a parent's "general executive responsibilities" for its subsidiary's operations included approval over major policy decisions and guaranteeing bank loans, and that that type of oversight was insufficient to demonstrate domination and control. *Akzona*, 607 F.Supp. at 238 (internal quotation marks omitted). Similarly, the district court in the instant case properly found that the presence of Kodak employees at periodic meetings with Atex's chief financial officer and comptroller to be "entirely appropriate." Fletcher, 861 F.Supp. at 245 (citing *Akzona*, 607 F.Supp. at 238); see *Acushnet*, 675 F.Supp. at 34 ("The quarterly and annual reports made [to the parent] do not represent an untoward intrusion by the owner into the corporate enterprise. The right of shareholders to remain informed is similarly recognized in many public and closely held corporations.'').

The plaintiffs' third argument, that Kodak dominated the Atex board of directors, also fails. Although a number of Kodak employees have sat on the Atex board, it is undisputed that between 1981 and 1988, only one director of Atex was also a director of Kodak. Between 1989 and 1992, Atex and Kodak had no directors in common. Parents and subsidiaries frequently have overlapping boards of directors while maintaining separate business operations. In Japan Petroleum, the Delaware district court held that the fact that a parent and a subsidiary have common officers and directors does not necessarily demonstrate that the parent corporation dominates the activities of the subsidiary. 456 F.Supp. at 841; see Scott–Douglas Corp. v. Greyhound Corp., 304 A.2d 309, 314 (Del.Super.Ct.1973) (same). Since the overlap is negligible here, we find this evidence to be entirely insufficient to raise a question of fact on the issue of domination.

Fourth, the district court properly rejected the plaintiffs' argument that the descriptions of the relationship between Atex and Kodak and the presence of the Kodak logo in Atex's promotional literature justify piercing the corporate veil. Fletcher, 861 F.Supp. at 245. The plaintiffs point to several statements in both Kodak's and Atex's literature to evidence Kodak's domination of its subsidiary. For example, plaintiffs refer to (1) a promotional pamphlet produced by EPPS (a/k/a Atex) describing Atex as a business unit of EPPS and noting that EPPS was an "agent" of Kodak; (2) a document produced by Atex entitled "An Introduction to Atex Systems," which describes a "merger" between Kodak and Atex; (3) a statement in Kodak's 1985 and 1986 annual reports describing Atex as a "recent acquisition[ ]" and a "subsidiar[y] . . . combined in a new division"; and (4) a statement in an Atex/EPPS document, "Setting Up TPE 6000 on the Sun 3 Workstation," describing Atex as "an unincorporated division of Electronic Pre–Press Systems, Inc., a Kodak company." They also refer generally to the fact that Atex's paperwork and packaging materials frequently displayed the Kodak logo.

It is clear from the record that Atex never merged with Kodak or operated as a Kodak division. The plaintiffs offer no evidence to the contrary, apart from these statements in Atex and Kodak documents that they claim are indicative of the true relationship between the two companies. Viewed in the light most favorable to the plaintiffs, these statements and the use of the Kodak logo are not evidence that the two companies operated as a "single economic entity." See Coleman v. Corning Glass Works, 619 F.Supp. 950, 956 (W.D.N.Y.1985) (upholding corporate form despite "loose language" in annual report about "merger" and parent's reference to subsidiary as a "division"), aff'd, 818 F.2d 874 (1987); Japan Petrol., 456 F.Supp. at 846 (noting that representations made by parent in its annual reports that subsidiary serves as an agent "may result from public relations motives or an attempt at simplification"); American Trading & Prod. Corp. v. Fischbach & Moore, Inc., 311 F.Supp. 412, 416 (N.D.Ill.1970) ("boastful" advertising and consideration of subsidiaries as "family" do not prove that corporate identities were ignored).

Fifth, the plaintiffs contend that Atex's assignment of its former CEO's mortgage to Kodak in order to close the sale of Atex's assets to a third party is evidence of Kodak's domination of Atex. We reject this argument as well. The evidence is undisputed that Kodak paid Atex the book value of the note and entered into a formal repayment agreement with the former CEO. Formal contracts were executed, and the two companies observed all corporate formalities.

Finally, even if the plaintiffs did raise a factual question about Kodak's domination of Atex, summary judgment would still be appropriate because the plaintiffs offer no evidence on the second prong of the alter ego analysis. The plaintiffs have failed to present evidence of an "overall element of injustice or unfairness" that would result from respecting the two companies' corporate separateness. See Harper, 743 F.Supp. at 1085 (holding that plaintiff cannot prevail on alter ego theory "because he has failed to allege any unfairness or injustice which would justify the court in disregarding the [companies'] separate legal existences"). In the instant case, the plaintiffs offer nothing more than the bare assertion that Kodak "exploited" Atex "to generate profits but not to safeguard safety." There is no indication that Kodak sought to defraud creditors and consumers or to siphon funds from its subsidiary. The plaintiffs' conclusory assertions, without more, are not evidence, see Quinn, 613 F.2d at 445, and are completely inadequate to support a finding that it would be unjust to respect Atex's corporate form.

For all of the foregoing reasons, the district court's order entering summary judgment on the plaintiffs' alter ego theory of liability is affirmed. . . .

[The court also granted summary judgment for Kodak on the plaintiffs' other theories.]

———

Walkovszky v. Carlton

Court of Appeals of New York, 1966.
18 N.Y.2d 414, 276 N.Y.S.2d 585, 223 N.E.2d 6.

■ FULD, JUDGE. This case involves what appears to be a rather common practice in the taxicab industry of vesting the ownership of a taxi fleet in many corporations, each owning only one or two cabs.

The complaint alleges that the plaintiff was severely injured four years ago in New York City when he was run down by a taxicab owned by the defendant Seon Cab Corporation and negligently operated at the time by the defendant Marchese. The individual defendant, Carlton, is claimed to be a stockholder of 10 corporations, including Seon, each of which has but two cabs registered in its name, and it is implied that only the minimum automobile liability insurance required by law (in the amount of $10,000) is carried on any one cab. Although seemingly independent of one another, these corporations are alleged to be "operated . . . as a single entity, unit and enterprise" with regard to financing, supplies, repairs, employees and garaging, and all are named as defendants.[1] The plaintiff asserts that he is also entitled to hold their stockholders personally liable for the damages sought because the multiple corporate structure constitutes an unlawful attempt "to defraud members of the general public" who might be injured by the cabs.

The defendant Carlton has moved, pursuant to CPLR 3211(a)7, to dismiss the complaint on the ground that as to him it "fails to state a cause of action". The court at Special Term granted the motion but the Appellate Division, by a divided vote, reversed, holding that a valid cause of action was sufficiently stated. The defendant Carlton appeals to us, from the nonfinal order, by leave of the Appellate Division on a certified question.

The law permits the incorporation of a business for the very purpose of enabling its proprietors to escape personal liability (see, e.g., Bartle v. Home Owners Co-op., 309 N.Y. 103, 106, 127 N.E.2d 832, 833) but, manifestly, the privilege is not without its limits. Broadly speaking, the courts will disregard the corporate form, or, to use accepted terminology, "pierce the corporate veil", whenever necessary "to prevent fraud or to achieve equity". (International Aircraft Trading Co. v. Manufacturers Trust Co., 297 N.Y. 285, 292, 79 N.E.2d 249, 252.) In determining whether liability should be extended to reach assets beyond those belonging to the corporation, we are guided, as Judge Cardozo noted, by "general rules of agency". (Berkey v. Third Ave. Ry. Co., 244 N.Y. 84, 95, 155 N.E. 58, 61, 50 A.L.R. 599.) In other words, whenever anyone uses control of the corporation to further his own rather than the corporation's business, he will be liable for the corporation's acts "upon the principle of *respondeat superior* applicable even where the agent is a natural person". . . . Such liability, moreover, extends not only to the corporation's commercial dealings . . . but to its negligent acts as well. . . .

In [Mangan v. Terminal Transp. System, 247 App.Div. 853, 286 N.Y.S. 666, mot. for lv. to app. den. 272 N.Y. 676, 286 N.Y.S. 666,] the plaintiff was injured as a result of the negligent operation of a cab owned and operated by one of four corporations affiliated with the defendant Terminal. Although the defendant was not a stockholder of any of the operating companies, both the defendant and the operating companies were owned, for the most part, by the same parties. The defendant's name (Terminal) was conspicuously displayed on the sides of all of the taxis used in the enterprise and, in point of fact, the defendant actually serviced, inspected, repaired and dispatched them. These facts were deemed to provide sufficient cause for piercing the corporate veil of the operating company—the nominal owner of the cab which injured the plaintiff—and holding the defendant liable. The operating companies were simply instrumentalities for carrying on the business of the defendant without imposing upon it financial and

---

1. The corporate owner of a garage is also included as a defendant.

other liabilities incident to the actual ownership and operation of the cabs. . . .

In the case before us, the plaintiff has explicitly alleged that none of the corporations "had a separate existence of their own" and, as indicated above, all are named as defendants. However, it is one thing to assert that a corporation is a fragment of a larger corporate combine which actually conducts the business. (See Berle, The Theory of Enterprise Entity, 47 Col.L.Rev. 343, 348–350.) It is quite another to claim that the corporation is a "dummy" for its individual stockholders who are in reality carrying on the business in their personal capacities for purely personal rather than corporate ends. (See African Metals Corp. v. Bullowa, 288 N.Y. 78, 85, 41 N.E.2d 466, 469.) Either circumstance would justify treating the corporation as an agent and piercing the corporate veil to reach the principal but a different result would follow in each case. In the first, only a larger *corporate* entity would be held financially responsible . . . while, in the other, the stockholder would be personally liable. . . . Either the stockholder is conducting the business in his individual capacity or he is not. If he is, he will be liable; if he is not, then it does not matter—insofar as his personal liability is concerned—that the enterprise is actually being carried on by a larger "enterprise entity". (See Berle, The Theory of Enterprise Entity, 47 Col.L.Rev. 343.)

At this stage in the present litigation, we are concerned only with the pleadings and, since CPLR 3014 permits causes of action to be stated "alternatively or hypothetically", it is possible for the plaintiff to allege both theories as the basis for his demand for judgment. In ascertaining whether he has done so, we must consider the entire pleading, educing therefrom " 'whatever can be imputed from its statements by fair and reasonable intendment.' " (Condon v. Associated Hosp. Serv., 287 N.Y. 411, 414, 40 N.E.2d 230, 231. . . .) Reading the complaint in this case most favorably and liberally, we do not believe that there can be gathered from its averments the allegations required to spell out a valid cause of action against the defendant Carlton.

The individual defendant is charged with having "organized, managed, dominated and controlled" a fragmented corporate entity but there are no allegations that he was conducting business in his individual capacity. Had the taxicab fleet been owned by a single corporation, it would be readily apparent that the plaintiff would face formidable barriers in attempting to establish personal liability on the part of the corporation's stockholders. The fact that the fleet ownership has been deliberately split up among many corporations does not ease the plaintiff's burden in that respect. The corporate form may not be disregarded merely because the assets of the corporation, together with the mandatory insurance coverage of the vehicle which struck the plaintiff, are insufficient to assure him the recovery sought. If Carlton were to be held individually liable on those facts alone, the decision would apply equally to the thousands of cabs which are owned by their individual drivers who conduct their businesses through corporations organized pursuant to section 401 of the Business Corporation Law, Consol.Laws, c. 4 and carry the minimum insurance required by subdivision 1 (par. [a]) of section 370 of the Vehicle and Traffic Law, Consol.Laws, c. 71. These taxi owner-operators are entitled to form such corporations (cf. Elenkrieg v. Siebrecht, 238 N.Y. 254, 144 N.E. 519, 34 A.L.R. 592), and we agree with the court at Special Term that, if the insurance coverage required by statute "is inadequate for the protection of the public, the remedy lies not with the courts but with the Legislature." It may very well be sound policy to require that certain corporations must take out liability insurance which will afford adequate compensation to their potential tort victims. However, the responsibility for imposing conditions on the privilege of incorporation has been committed by the Constitution to the Legislature (N.Y. Const., art. X, 1) and it may not be fairly implied, from any statute, that the Legislature intended, without the slightest discussion or debate, to require of taxi corporations that they carry automobile liability insurance over and above that mandated by the Vehicle and Traffic Law.

This is not to say that it is impossible for the plaintiff to state a valid cause of action against the defendant Carlton. However, the simple fact is that the plaintiff has just not done so here. While the complaint alleges that the separate corporations were undercapitalized and that their assets have been intermingled, it is barren of any "sufficiently particular[ized] statements" (CPLR 3013; see 3 Weinstein–Korn–Miller, N.Y.Civ.Prac., par. 3013.01 et seq., pp. 30–142 et seq.) that the defendant Carlton and his associates are actually doing business in their individual capacities, shuttling their personal funds in and out of the corporations "without regard to formality and to suit their immediate convenience." (Weisser v. Mursam Shoe Corp., 2 Cir., 127 F.2d 344, 345, 145 A.L.R. 467, supra.) Such a "perversion of the privilege to do business in a corporate form" (Berkey v. Third Ave. Ry. Co., 244 N.Y. 84, 95, 155 N.E. 58, 61, 50 A.L.R. 599, supra) would justify imposing personal liability on the individual stockholders. (See African Metals Corp. v. Bullowa, 288 N.Y. 78, 41 N.E.2d 466, supra.) Nothing of the sort has in fact been charged, and it cannot reasonably or logically be inferred from the happenstance that the business of Seon Cab Corporation may actually be carried on by a larger corporate entity composed of many corporations which, under general principles of agency, would be liable to each other's creditors in contract and in tort.[2]

In point of fact, the principle relied upon in the complaint to sustain the imposition of personal liability is not agency but fraud. Such a cause of action cannot withstand analysis. If it is not fraudulent

2. In his affidavit in opposition to the motion to dismiss, the plaintiff's counsel claimed that corporate assets had been "milked out" of, and "siphoned off" from the enterprise. Quite apart from the fact that these allegations are far too vague and conclusory, the charge is premature. If the plaintiff succeeds in his action and becomes a judgment creditor of the corporation, he may then sue and attempt to hold the individual defendants accountable for any dividends and property that were wrongfully distributed (Business Corporation Law, §§ 510, 719, 720).

for the owner-operator of a single cab corporation to take out only the minimum required liability insurance, the enterprise does not become either illicit or fraudulent merely because it consists of many such corporations. The plaintiff's injuries are the same regardless of whether the cab which strikes him is owned by a single corporation or part of a fleet with ownership fragmented among many corporations. Whatever rights he may be able to assert against parties other than the registered owner of the vehicle come into being not because he has been defrauded but because, under the principle of *respondeat superior,* he is entitled to hold the whole enterprise responsible for the acts of its agents.

In sum, then, the complaint falls short of adequately stating a cause of action against the defendant Carlton in his individual capacity.

The order of the Appellate Division should be reversed, with costs in this court and in the Appellate Division, the certified question answered in the negative and the order of the Supreme Court, Richmond County, reinstated, with leave to serve an amended complaint.

■ KEATING, JUDGE (dissenting).

The defendant Carlton, the shareholder here sought to be held for the negligence of the driver of a taxicab, was a principal shareholder and organizer of the defendant corporation which owned the taxicab. The corporation was one of 10 organized by the defendant, each containing two cabs and each cab having the "minimum liability" insurance coverage mandated by section 370 of the Vehicle and Traffic Law. The sole assets of these operating corporations are the vehicles themselves and they are apparently subject to mortgages.[1]

From their inception these corporations were intentionally undercapitalized for the purpose of avoiding responsibility for acts which were bound to arise as a result of the operation of a large taxi fleet having cars out on the street 24 hours a day and engaged in public transportation. And during the course of the corporations' existence all income was continually drained out of the corporations for the same purpose.

The issue presented by this action is whether the policy of this State, which affords those desiring to engage in a business enterprise the privilege of limited liability through the use of the corporate devise, is so strong that it will permit that privilege to continue no matter how much it is abused, no matter how irresponsibly the corporation is operated, no matter what the cost to the public. I do not believe that it is.

Under the circumstances of this case the shareholders should all be held individually liable to this plaintiff for the injuries he suffered. (See Mull v. Colt Co., D.C., 31 F.R.D. 154, 156; Teller v. Clear Service

---

1. It appears that the medallions, which are of considerable value, are judgment proof. (Administrative Code of City of New York, § 436–2.0.) [Footnote by the court.]

Corporation, 9 Misc.2d 495, 173 N.Y.S.2d 183.) At least, the matter should not be disposed of on the pleadings by a dismissal of the complaint. "If a corporation is organized and carries on business without substantial capital in such a way that the corporation is likely to have no sufficient assets available to meet its debts, it is inequitable that shareholders should set up such a flimsy organization to escape personal liability. The attempt to do corporate business without providing any sufficient basis of financial responsibility to creditors is an abuse of the separate entity and will be ineffectual to exempt the shareholders from corporate debts. It is coming to be recognized as the policy of law that shareholders should in good faith put at the risk of the business unencumbered capital reasonably adequate for its prospective liabilities. If capital is illusory or trifling compared with the business to be done and the risks of loss, this is a ground for denying the separate entity privilege." (Ballantine, Corporations [rev. ed., 1946], § 129, pp. 302–303.) . . .

■ DESMOND, C.J., and VAN VOORHIS, BURKE and SCILEPPI, JJ., concur with FULD, J.

■ KEATING, J., dissents and votes to affirm in an opinion in which BERGAN, J., concurs.

Order reversed, etc.

NOTE ON FURTHER PROCEEDINGS IN WALKOVSZKY v. CARLTON

Following the decision in *Walkovszky*, the plaintiff amended his complaint. The Appellate Division held that "the amended complaint sufficiently alleges a cause of action against appellant, i.e., that he and the other individual defendants were conducting the business of the taxicab fleet in their individual capacities." Walkovszky v. Carlton, 29 A.D.2d 763, 287 N.Y.S.2d 546 (1968). That decision was affirmed by the Court of Appeals, 23 N.Y.2d 714, 296 N.Y.S.2d 362, 244 N.E.2d 55 (1968), noting that the amended complaint "now meets the pleading requirements set forth in [our prior] opinion and states a valid cause of action." Neither opinion stated the particulars in which the amended complaint differed from the original.

Berle, The Theory of Enterprise Entity

47 Columbia Law Rev. 343 (1947).

As the scale of business enterprises enlarged, the process of subdivision began; hence subsidiary corporations wholly-owned or partly-owned; or holding companies combined into a series of corporations constituting a combined economic enterprise; and so forth. More often than not, a single large-scale business is conducted, not by a single corporation, but by a constellation of corporations controlled by a central holding company, the various sectors being separately incorporated, either because they were once independent and have been acquired, or because the central concern, entering new fields, created new corporations to develop them, or for tax reasons. In some instances, departments of the business are separately incorporated and operated as separate legal units....

This is far from the original conception of a corporation. The legal doctrine of corporate personality was built around the idea of a sovereign grant of certain attributes of personality to a definable group, engaged in an enterprise. The so-called "artificial personality" was designed to be the enterpriser of a project. Multiplicity of artificial personalities within an enterprise unit would probably have been impossible under most early corporation laws....

It is the thesis of this essay:

That the entity commonly known as "corporate entity" takes its being from the reality of the underlying enterprise, formed or in formation;

That the state's approval of the corporate form sets up a prima facie case that the assets, liabilities and operations of the corporation are those of the enterprise;

But that where the corporate entity is defective, or otherwise challenged, its existence, extent and consequences may be determined by the actual existence and extent and operations of the underlying enterprise, which by these very qualities acquires an entity of its own, recognized by law.

For brevity, this hypothesis is hereafter referred to as the theory of "enterprise entity." ...

[An] illustration of judicial erection of a new entity occurs in situations where the corporate personality (as embodied in its charter, books and so forth) does not correspond to the actual enterprise, but merely to a fragment of it. The result is to construct a new aggregate of assets and liabilities. Typical cases appear where a partnership or a central corporation owns the controlling interest in one or more other corporations, but has so handled them that they have ceased to represent a separate enterprise and have become, as a business matter, more or less indistinguishable parts of a larger enterprise. The decisions disregard the paper corporate personalities and base liability on the assets of the enterprise....

This category of cases stands [most] squarely on the foundation of economic enterprise-fact. The courts disregard the corporate fiction specifically because it has parted company with the enterprise-fact, for whose furtherance the corporation was created; and, having got that far, they then take the further step of ascertaining what is the actual enterprise-fact and attach the consequences of the acts of the component individuals or corporations to that enterprise entity, to the extent that the economic outlines of the situation warrant or require.

NOTE ON LIMITED LIABILITY AGAINST TORT CLAIMANTS

1. *The problem.* What justifies the rule that shareholders are not liable for the obligations of their corporation? In addressing this question, a distinction must be drawn between obligations to voluntary creditors and to involuntary creditors. The paradigm case of the voluntary creditor is a person who has made a contract with the corporation, which the corporation has broken. The paradigm case of the involuntary creditor is a person who has been injured by the corporation's tortious conduct.

In the case of contract creditors, limited liability is often easy to justify. Most non-lawyers don't know much law, but they do know some. One legal rule that is probably known to most businesspersons is that shareholders have limited liability. Therefore, when a businessperson contracts with a corporation, she is likely to know that she cannot hold the shareholders liable if the corporation defaults. And at least in theory, a contract creditor who deals with a corporation can contract around limited liability by tailoring her contract to reflect the shareholders' limited liability. So, for example, the creditor might require personal guarantees from the corporation's shareholders, might require covenants (promises) that the corporation will not take designated steps that could impair its financial condition, or might charge a price that impounds (reflects) the cost of the extra risk entailed in dealing with an enterprise whose owners are not liable for its obligations.

This justification of limited liability, however, completely fails in the case of a tort creditor, such as a pedestrian who is run over by a corporation's taxi. Furthermore, at least in the case of a publicly held corporation, the large body of shareholders may be better risk-bearers than an injured tort victim. See Leebron, Limited Liability, Tort Victims, and Creditors, 91 Colum.L.Rev. 1565, at 1601–02 (1992).

Moreover, in most or all tort contexts limited liability seems to be inefficient. Modern conceptions of policy suggest that an enterprise should internalize—should be made to bear—the costs that the enterprise entails, including costs from injuries to third persons. Limited liability therefore seems to provide exactly the *wrong* incentive. Under a regime of limited liability, the owners of a corporation will reap all the benefits of the risks the corporation takes, but will not suffer all the costs of those risks. Accordingly, limited liability provides corporations with an incentive to take risks that are economically undue in the sense that managers who desire to advance the interests of their shareholders may make investments that would be inefficient if all externalities had to be taken into account. As Henry Hansmann and Reinier Kraakman put it:

> The most familiar inefficiency created by limited liability is the incentive it provides for the shareholder to direct the corporation to spend too little on precautions to avoid accidents. In contrast, a rule of unlimited liability induces the socially efficient level of

expenditure on precautions by making the shareholder personally liable for any tort damages that the corporation cannot pay.

Further, limited liability encourages overinvestment in hazardous industries. Since limited liability permits cost externalization, a corporation engaged in highly risky activities can have positive value for its shareholder, and thus can be an attractive investment, even when its net present value to society as a whole is negative. Consequently, limited liability encourages excessive entry and aggregate overinvestment in unusually hazardous industries.

Hansmann & Kraakman, Toward Unlimited Shareholder Liability for Corporate Torts, 100 Yale L.J. 1879, 1882–83 (1991).

An efficiency argument *for* limited liability, even in the tort context, is that in the absence of limited liability, the market for publicly held stock would be less efficient. The essential points of this argument, made by Halpern, Trebilcock & Turnbull, An Economic Analysis of Limited Liability in Corporation Law, 30 U. Toronto L.J. 117 (1980) and by F. Easterbrook & D. Fischel, The Economic Structure of Corporate Law 40–44 (1991), are as follows: A requirement of an efficient capital market is that the relevant capital assets (here, corporate stock) can be quickly and easily converted into cash. This characteristic is known as liquidity. A condition necessary to achieve liquidity is that the asset be worth the same amount to all potential investors. However, if shareholders had unlimited liability for tort claims, tort creditors would sue only very wealthy shareholders, like banks and pension funds, because non-wealthy shareholders would be unable to satisfy a judgment. As a result, the market for stock would not function efficiently, because the value of shares would vary inversely with the wealth of the shareholder. If, under such a regime, a tort creditor sued, say, only one wealthy shareholder, and collected the entire amount of his claim from that shareholder, that shareholder would seek contribution from other shareholders. However, because of transaction costs she would seek contribution only from other wealthy shareholders. Since the right of contribution therefore would be very important under such a regime, wealthy shareholders would need to continually incur costs to monitor the wealth of other shareholders. The need to incur those costs would make the market even less efficient.

However, the stock-market-efficiency argument does not apply to either closely held corporations or wholly owned subsidiaries, neither of which have publicly traded stock. Even in the case of publicly held corporations, the real-world weight of the stock-market-efficiency argument is difficult to judge. A rule that shareholders were liable to tort creditors would presumably be coupled with a rule, similar to that of the Revised Uniform Partnership Act, that required exhaustion of corporate assets before suit was brought against a shareholder. Based on past history, the likelihood that any shareholder in a publicly held corporation would be required to make any payments to tort creditors under an exhaustion regime would be only slightly more than zero, because very few publicly held corporations have faced tort claims that exceeded their ability to pay.

Moreover, under a rule of shareholder liability for tort claims, wealthy shareholders would avoid investment in corporations that did not make adequate provision for tort claims through insurance. This would be a powerful incentive to corporations to adequately insure. That, in turn, would not only be a socially desirable result, but would further minimize the likelihood that liability would actually be imposed on shareholders. Leebron concludes that the market effects of making shareholders of publicly held corporations liable to tort creditors would probably be too small to affect the efficiency of stock markets.

The analysis of limited liability against tort creditors was moved forward in 1991, when both Leebron and Hansmann & Kraakman made notable contributions to the debate (in their articles cited above) by developing the concept that shareholders should be liable to tort creditors, but only on a pro rata basis, rather than on a joint and several basis. Under *joint and several* shareholder liability, each shareholder would be unlimitedly liable for all of a corporation's debts to tort creditors. Thus a shareholder who held only one share in a publicly held corporation could in theory be liable for the corporation's entire tort debts—in the worst case, hundreds of millions of dollars or more. In contrast, under *pro rata* shareholder liability each shareholder would be liable to a corporation's tort creditors only for that portion of the creditors' claims that equaled the shareholder's pro rata holding of the corporation's shares. In short, shareholders would have *individual* liability to tort creditors, but not *unlimited* liability.

> To see how these rules differ, suppose that a wealthy investor holds five percent of a hotel company, while two impecunious hoteliers hold the remaining ninety-five percent. If a fire causes tort damages that exceed the company's assets by $200 million, the wealthy investor is potentially liable for $200 million under the joint and several rule but only $10 million under the pro rata rule.

Hansmann & Kraakman, supra, at 1892–93.

Pro rata shareholder liability would largely undercut the argument that limited liability is required for stock-market efficiency. Because each shareholder would bear only her own pro rata portion of liability, differences in wealth would not normally cause different shareholders to value the same shares differently. Furthermore, under a regime of pro rata liability a shareholder would have no need to monitor the wealth of other shareholders, because there would be no need for, and therefore no right to, contribution.

Some objections can be made to pro rata liability. Janet Cooper Alexander has shown that for jurisdictional reasons grounded on due process concerns, pro rata liability for tort claims could be effectively imposed only under the law of the state of incorporation or by the federal government. Alexander, Unlimited Shareholder Liability

Through a Procedural Lens, 106 Harv.L.Rev. 387 (1992). However, that is not an argument against imposing such liability, but only an argument concerning how such liability should be imposed. Joe Grundfest has argued that capital markets would undercut a regime of pro rata liability by generating a clientele of investors, such as offshore shareholders, who would be de facto attachment-proof. Grundfest, The Limited Future of Unlimited Liability: A Capital Markets Perspective, 102 Yale L.J. 387 (1992). However, this objection is inapplicable to closely held corporations and wholly owned subsidiaries. Furthermore, the discounted risk of liability might be too small to make it worthwhile for investors to allocate their resources on that basis, so that whether the risk of pro rata liability would produce a clientele effect is highly speculative.

A somewhat different problem with pro rata liability is that such liability might lead investors to purchase smaller shareholdings in individual corporations than they otherwise would, partly to reduce and diversify their exposure to tort claims, and partly because the smaller the shareholder's exposure, the higher are the transaction costs of bringing suit against the shareholder. This might lead to an inefficient degree of diversification, and might also reduce the likelihood of shareholder monitoring of corporate management, because the likelihood of such monitoring is partly a function of the size of a shareholder's holding.

2. *The Current State of Play.* The efficiency arguments for making shareholders liable to tort creditors at least on a pro rata basis seem to be very strong, particularly in the case of close corporations and wholly-owned subsidiaries. Nevertheless, the legislative trend is not only to preserve but to *extend* limited liability, as evidenced by the recent, rapid, and widespread adoption of statutes authorizing limited liability companies and limited liability partnerships. See Chapter 7. How is this to be explained?

To begin with, there is a question whether individual shareholder liability, pro rata or otherwise, is really a salient issue as regards publicly held corporations. As a practical matter, piercing is normally important only where the corporation lacks sufficient assets to pay the creditor's claims. That is not a frequent occurrence in the case of publicly held corporations—although it does happen, and in a handful of cases, tort claims themselves have resulted in the bankruptcy of such corporations.

More important, in the case of publicly held corporations the policy reasons for limiting shareholder liability, even as to tort creditors, are not insubstantial. The efficiency-of-the-market argument has already been explored. In addition, under the law of agency the normal predicate for making a principal vicariously liable for a tort committed by his agent is that the principal stood to benefit from those activities *and* had control over the agent's activities. In the context of publicly held corporations, however, management is vested in the board and the officers, not in the shareholders. In that context, therefore, the control predicate of vicarious liability is missing.

The lack-of-control problem is exacerbated by another issue: This issue is *which* shareholders will be subject to liability for corporate torts—those who were shareholders at the time the harm occurred, those who were shareholders when the harm became known, or those who are shareholders when there is a judgment against or a settlement with the corporation. Hansmann & Kraakman essentially conclude that those persons who were shareholders at the time the harm became known should be liable. However, those persons not only lacked control over the harmful activity, but lacked even the possibility of control, unless they coincidentally happened to be shareholders when harm occurred. Furthermore, making those shareholders liable seems inconsistent with the argument that the objective of shareholder liability is to make the corporation internalize the cost of its wrongs. Given the turnover of shareholdings in publicly held corporations, under the Hansmann & Kraakman approach the impact of the wrong would often not fall on, and therefore will not be fully internalized by, shareholders who benefit from the wrong.

In corporations that are *not* publicly held, the story is much different. In such corporations, control and ownership are usually intertwined. Two classes of corporations normally fall into this category: corporations whose shares are owned by only a few shareholders (close corporations), and subsidiary corporations that are wholly or mostly owned by a single parent corporation. However, if limited liability is granted to publicly held corporations, the legislatures may not want to get into the difficult game of drawing lines between close corporations and publicly held corporations, or between wholly owned subsidiaries and subsidiaries that have some public ownership.

Another possible explanation for granting limited liability, even to close corporations, is that generally speaking, legislatures seem much more willing to require *firms* to bear risks they were not at fault for creating than to require *individuals* to bear such risks. Even in the case of close corporations, therefore, the legislatures might believe that liability should not be imposed on shareholders who played no role in planning, authorizing, or executing tortious conduct.

Still another explanation of the persistence and expansion of limited liability to tort creditors is that legislatures often seem to put a low weight on requiring businesses to internalize negative externalities. For example, legislatures have only recently required firms to internalize environmental costs. State legislatures, in particular, often seem to put much more weight on promoting local business-formation than on requiring the internalization of externalities.

It must also be recognized that the inefficiency of providing limited liability against the claims of tort creditors may be virtually irrelevant to a state legislature whose only concern is the citizens of its own state. Assume, for example, that a national corporation is incorporated in State A, which has 1% of the national population. State A will reap all the benefits of the franchise tax that a corporation must pay for the privilege of incorporating in that state. In contrast, the citizens of State A will bear only 1% of the costs inefficiently imposed on tort victims; the other 99% of these costs will fall on the citizens of other states. Furthermore, once State A adopts and maintains a rule of limited liability to tort creditors, there is little or no incentive for other states to adopt a different rule, even if they wanted to do so, because corporations could avoid the rule by migrating to State A.

Finally, the doctrine of piercing the corporate veil allows courts to impose liability on shareholders in appropriate cases, notwithstanding the limited-liability rule. Although in theory this doctrine can be applied to any corporation, in practice it is only applied to close corporations and subsidiaries. Thus Professor Presser observes that there seems "to be an increasing trend toward the imposition of liability on corporate shareholders in the tort area, particularly in the area of toxic torts, and particularly by federal courts. This increased tort liability activity seems most often to have occurred in the parent-subsidiary context...." S. Presser, Piercing the Corporate Veil 1–67 (1994). As a practical matter, therefore, the piercing doctrine may act as a safety valve that takes some of the pressure off the limited-liability rule in those cases where the efficiency of the rule is in question.

Minton v. Cavaney

Supreme Court of California, 1961.
56 Cal.2d 576, 15 Cal.Rptr. 641, 364 P.2d 473.

■ TRAYNOR, JUSTICE. The Seminole Hot Springs Corporation, hereinafter referred to as Seminole, was duly incorporated in California on March 8, 1954. It conducted a public swimming pool that it leased from its owner. On June 24, 1954 plaintiffs' daughter drowned in the pool, and plaintiffs recovered a judgment for $10,000 against Seminole for her wrongful death. The judgment remains unsatisfied.

On January 30, 1957, plaintiffs brought the present action to hold defendant Cavaney personally liable for the judgment against Seminole. Cavaney died on May 28, 1958 and his widow, the executrix of his estate, was substituted as defendant. The trial court entered judgment for plaintiffs for $10,000. Defendant appeals.

Plaintiffs introduced evidence that Cavaney was a director and secretary and treasurer of Seminole and that on November 15, 1954, about five months after the drowning, Cavaney as secretary of Seminole and Edwin A. Kraft as president of Seminole applied for permission to issue three shares of Seminole stock, one share to be issued to Kraft, another to F.J. Wettrick and the third to Cavaney. The commissioner of corporations refused permission to issue these shares unless additional information was furnished. The application was then abandoned and no shares were ever issued. There was also evidence that for a time Seminole used Cavaney's office to keep records and to receive mail. Before his death Cavaney answered certain interrogatories. He was asked if Seminole "ever had any assets?" He stated that "insofar as my own personal knowledge and belief is concerned said corporation did not have any assets." Cavaney also stated in the return to an attempted execution that "[I]nsofar as I know, this corporation had no assets of any kind or character. The corporation was duly organized but never functioned as a corporation."

Defendant introduced evidence that Cavaney was an attorney at law, that he was approached by Kraft and Wettrick to form Seminole, and that he was the attorney for Seminole. Plaintiffs introduced Cavaney's answer to several interrogatories that he held the post of secretary and treasurer and director in a temporary capacity and as an accommodation to his client.

Defendant contends that the evidence does not support the court's determination that Cavaney is personally liable for Seminole's debts and that the "alter ego" doctrine is inapplicable because plaintiffs failed to show that there was " '(1) . . . such unity of interest and ownership that the separate personalities of the corporation and the individual no longer exist and (2) that, if the acts are treated as those of the corporation alone, an inequitable result will follow.' " Riddle v. Leuschner, 51 Cal.2d 574, 580, 335 P.2d 107, 110; Automotriz Del Golfo De California S.A. De C.V. v. Resnick, 47 Cal.2d 792, 796, 306 P.2d 1, 63 A.L.R.2d 1042; Minifie v. Rowley, 187 Cal. 481, 487, 202 P. 673.

The figurative terminology "alter ego" and "disregard of the corporate entity" is generally used to refer to the various situations that are an abuse of the corporate privilege. . . . The equitable owners of a corporation, for example, are personally liable when they treat the assets of the corporation as their own and add or withdraw capital from the corporation at will . . . ; when they hold themselves out as being personally liable for the debts of the corporation . . . ; or when they provide inadequate capitalization and actively participate in the conduct of corporate affairs. . . .

In the instant case the evidence is undisputed that there was no attempt to provide adequate capitalization. Seminole never had any substantial assets. It leased the pool that it operated, and the lease was forfeited for failure to pay the rent. Its capital was " 'trifling compared with the business to be done and the risks of loss . . .' " Automotriz Del Golfo De California S.A. De C.V. v. Resnick, supra, 47 Cal.2d 792, 797, 306 P.2d 1, 4. The evidence is also undisputed that Cavaney was not only the secretary and treasurer of the corporation but was also a director. The evidence that Cavaney was to receive one-third of the shares to be issued supports an inference that he was an equitable owner (see Riddle v. Leuschner, supra, 51 Cal.2d 574, 580, 335 P.2d 107), and the evidence that for a time the records of the corporation were kept in Cavaney's office supports an inference that he actively participated in the conduct of the business. The trial court was not required to believe his statement that he was only a "temporary" director and officer "for accommodation." In any event it merely raised a conflict in the evidence that was resolved adversely to defendant. Moreover, section 800 of the Corporations Code provides that ". . . the business and affairs of every corporation shall be controlled by a board of not less than three directors." Defendant does not claim that Cavaney was a director with specialized duties (see 5 U.Chi.L.Rev. 668). It is immaterial whether or not he accepted the office of director as an "accommodation" with the understanding that he would not exercise any of the duties of a director. A person may not in this manner divorce the responsibilities of a director from the statutory duties and powers of that office....

In this action to hold defendant personally liable upon the judgment against Seminole plaintiffs did not allege or present any evidence on the issue of Seminole's negligence or on the amount of damages sustained by plaintiffs. They relied solely on the judgment against Seminole. Defendant correctly contends that Cavaney or his estate cannot be held liable for the debts of Seminole without an opportunity to relitigate these issues.... Cavaney was not a party to the action against the corporation, and the judgment in that action is therefore not binding upon him unless he controlled the litigation leading to the judgment....

The judgment is reversed.

■ Gibson, C.J., and Peters, White and Dooling, JJ., concur.

■ [The opinion of Justice Schauer, concurring and dissenting, is omitted. Justice McComb concurred without opinion.]

ARNOLD v. BROWNE, 27 Cal.App.3d 386, 396, 103 Cal.Rptr. 775, 783 (1972). "Evidence of inadequate capitalization is, at best, merely a factor to be considered by the trial court in deciding whether or not to pierce the corporate veil (Harris v. Curtis, 8 Cal.App.3d 837, 841, 87 Cal.Rptr. 614). To be sure, it is an important factor, but no case has been cited, nor have any been found, where it has been held that this factor alone *requires* invoking the equitable doctrine prayed for in the instant case."

SLOTTOW FIDELITY FEDERAL BANK v. AMERICAN CASUALTY CO., 10 F.3d 1355 (9th Cir. 1993). "[T]he plaintiffs ... had an excellent argument under an alter ego theory for piercing the corporate veil. To begin with, [the] initial capitalization of $500,000 was woefully inadequate for a corporation that handled trust agreements of the magnitude involved here. The investors claimed damages [against the corporation] in the range of $10,000,000; the case settled for nearly half that. Under California law, inadequate capitalization of a subsidiary may alone be a basis for holding the parent corporation liable for acts of the subsidiary. See, e.g., Nilsson, Robbins, Dalgarn, Berliner, Carson & Wurst v. Louisiana Hydrolec, 854 F.2d 1538, 1544 (9th Cir.1988)...."

TRUCKWELD EQUIPMENT CO., INC. v. OLSON, 26 Wash.App. 638, 645, 618 P.2d 1017, 1022 (1980) "Although there may be situations in which a corporation is so thinly capitalized that it manifests a fraudulent intent, we do not find such to be true in the case at bar.... Olson acquired Aztec when it was financially troubled; he was not the original incorporator and he sought only to improve Aztec's profit picture. Despite gross sales of over $800,000 it appears a combination of unfortunate timing and persistent working capital problems sounded Aztec's death knell. We know of no rule of law requiring a corporate stockholder to commit additional private funds to an already faltering corporation."

———

RADASZEWSKI v. TELECOM CORP., 981 F.2d 305 (8th Cir. 1992). "... In order to pierce the corporate veil, a plaintiff must show, among other things, that the defendant's control of a subsidiary has

> been used by the defendant to commit fraud or wrong, to perpetrate the violation of a statutory or other positive legal duty, or dishonest and unjust act in contravention of plaintiff's legal rights...."

Collet [v. American National Stores, Inc., 708 S.W.2d 273, 284 Mo.App. 1986]. To satisfy this ... element, plaintiff cites no direct evidence of improper motivation or violation of law on Telecom's part. He argues, instead, that Contrux was undercapitalized.

"... [T]he creation of an undercapitalized subsidiary justifies an inference that the parent is either deliberately or recklessly creating a business that will not be able to pay its bills or satisfy judgments against it. This point has been made clear by the Supreme Court of Missouri....

"Here, the District Court held, and we assume, that Contrux [the subsidiary] was undercapitalized in the accounting sense. Most of the money contributed to its operation by Telecom [the parent] was in the form of loans, not equity, and, when Contrux first went into business, Telecom did not pay for all of the stock that was issued to it.... Telecom in effect concedes that Contrux's balance sheet was anemic, and that, from the point of view of generally accepted accounting principles, Contrux was inadequately capitalized. Telecom says, however, that this doesn't matter, because Contrux had $11,000,000 worth of liability insurance available to pay judgments like the one that Radaszewski hopes to obtain. No one can say, therefore, the argument runs, that Telecom was improperly motivated in setting up Contrux, in the sense of either knowingly or recklessly establishing it without the ability to pay tort judgments.

"In fact, Contrux did have $1,000,000 in basic liability coverage, plus $10,000,000 in excess coverage. This coverage was bound on March 1, 1984, about five and one-half months before the accident involving Radaszewski. Unhappily, Contrux's insurance carrier became insolvent two years after the accident and is now in receivership. . . .

"The District Court rejected this argument. Undercapitalization is undercapitalization, it reasoned, regardless of insurance. The Court said:

> The federal regulation does not speak to what constitutes a properly capitalized motor carrier company. Rather, the regulation speaks to what constitutes an appropriate level of *financial responsibility.*

. . . This distinction escapes us. The whole purpose of asking whether a subsidiary is 'properly capitalized,' is precisely to determine its 'financial responsibility.' If the subsidiary is financially responsible, whether by means of insurance or otherwise, the policy behind . . . the *Collet* test is met. Insurance meets this policy just as well, perhaps even better, than a healthy balance sheet."

————

Sea–Land Services, Inc. v. Pepper Source

United States Court of Appeals, Seventh Circuit, 1993.
993 F.2d 1309.

■ Before BAUER, CHIEF JUDGE, ROVNER, CIRCUIT JUDGE, and TIMBERS, SENIOR CIRCUIT JUDGE.[1]

■ TIMBERS, SENIOR CIRCUIT JUDGE.

Appellants appeal from a judgment entered after a bench trial in the Northern District of Illinois, James F. Holderman, *District Judge,* piercing the corporate veil and awarding appellee $118,132.61 in damages. . . .

[Appellee Sea–Land Services, Inc. ("Sea–Land"), an ocean carrier, shipped peppers on behalf of The Pepper Source ("PS"), one of the appellants here. PS then stiffed Sea–Land on the freight bill, which was rather substantial. Sea–Land filed a federal diversity action for the money it was owed. On December 2, 1987, the district court entered a default judgment in favor of Sea–Land and against PS in the amount of $86,767.70. But PS was nowhere to be found; it had been "dissolved" in mid–1987 for failure to pay the annual state franchise tax. Worse yet for Sea–Land, even had it not been dissolved, PS apparently had no assets. With the well empty, Sea–Land could not recover its judgment against PS. Hence the instant lawsuit.

[In June 1988, Sea–Land brought this action against Gerald J. Marchese and five business entities he owns: PS, Caribe Crown, Inc., Jamar Corp., Salescaster Distributors, Inc., and Marchese Fegan Associates. Marchese also was named individually. Sea–Land sought by this suit to pierce PS's corporate veil and render Marchese personally liable for the judgment owed to Sea–Land, and then "reverse pierce"

---

1. The Honorable William H. Timbers, Senior Circuit Judge, United States Court of   Appeals for the Second Circuit, sitting by designation.

Marchese's other corporations so that they, too, would be on the hook for the $87,000. Thus, Sea–Land alleged in its complaint that all of these corporations "are alter egos of each other and hide behind the veils of alleged separate corporate existence for the purpose of defrauding plaintiff and other creditors." Count I, § 11. Not only are the corporations alter egos of each other, alleged Sea–Land, but also they are alter egos of Marchese, who should be held individually liable for the judgment because he created and manipulated these corporations and their assets for his own personal uses. Count III, § § 9–10. (Hot on the heels of the filing of Sea–Land's complaint, PS took the necessary steps to be reinstated as a corporation in Illinois.)

[In an order dated June 22, 1990, the trial court earlier ... court discussed and applied the test for corporate veil-piercing explicated in *Van Dorn Co. v. Future Chemical and Oil Corp.*, 753 F.2d 565 (7th Cir.1985). Analyzing Illinois law, we held in *Van Dorn* that

a corporate entity will be disregarded and the veil of limited liability pierced when two requirements are met:

[F]irst, there must be such unity of interest and ownership that the separate personalities of the corporation and the individual [or other corporation] no longer exist; and second, circumstances must be such that adherence to the fiction of separate corporate existence would sanction a fraud or promote injustice.

753 F.2d at 569–70. As for determining whether a corporation is so controlled by another to justify disregarding their separate identities, the Illinois cases, as we summarized them in *Van Dorn*, focus on four factors: "(1) the failure to maintain adequate corporate records or to comply with corporate formalities, (2) the commingling of funds or assets, (3) undercapitalization, and (4) one corporation treating the assets of another corporation as its own."

[The first and most striking feature that emerges from our examination of the record is that these corporate defendants are, indeed, little but Marchese's playthings. Marchese is the sole shareholder of PS, Caribe Crown, Jamar, and Salescaster. None of the corporations ever held a single corporate meeting. During his deposition, Marchese did not remember any of these corporations ever passing articles of incorporation, bylaws, or other agreements. As for physical facilities, Marchese runs all of these corporations out of the same, single office, with the same phone line, the same expense accounts, and the like. And how he does "run" the expense accounts! When he fancies to, Marchese "borrows" substantial sums of money from these corporations—interest free, of course. The corporations also "borrow" money from each other when need be, which left at least PS completely out of capital when the Sea–Land bills came due. What's more, Marchese has used the bank accounts of these corporations to pay all kinds of personal expenses, including alimony and child support payments to his ex-wife, education expenses for his children, maintenance of his personal automobiles, health care for his pet—the list goes on and on. Marchese did not even have a personal bank account!]*

. . . The issues raised by the second prong of *Van Dorn* were tried on July 6 and 7, 1992. On July 9, 1992, the [district] court entered judgment for Sea–Land, awarding it $118,132.61 in damages. The court concluded that Sea–Land satisfied the second prong of *Van Dorn* by establishing wrongs beyond its inability to collect on its judgment.

On the instant appeal, appellants contend that the evidence presented by Sea–Land at trial was insufficient to satisfy the second prong of *Van Dorn*. They also assert that the court misapplied Illinois law in reaching its decision. . . .

. . . Sea–Land adduced sufficient evidence at trial to establish additional wrongs to justify piercing the corporate veil. First, Sea–Land demonstrated that Marchese and his corporations were unjustly enriched. We have defined "unjust enrichment" as the receipt of money or its equivalent under circumstances that, in equity and good conscience, suggest that it ought not to be retained because it belongs to someone else. *Midcoast Aviation, Inc. v. General Elec. Credit Corp.,* 907 F.2d 732, 737 (7th Cir.1990). At trial, Sea–Land demonstrated that Marchese obtained countless benefits at the expense of not only Sea–Land, but the Internal Revenue Service (IRS) and other creditors as well. Indeed, Marchese used PS funds to pay his personal expenses as well as expenses incurred by his other corporations. As a result, PS was left without sufficient funds to satisfy Sea–Land or PS's other creditors. *American Trade Partners v. A-1 Int'l Importing Enter.,* 770 F.Supp. 273, 278 (E.D.Pa.1991) (corporate veil pierced on basis of unjust enrichment where managing shareholder, with knowledge of debt to creditor, used corporation's funds to pay personal expenses). Since Marchese was enriched unjustly by his intentional manipulation and diversion of funds from his corporate entities, to allow him to use these same entities to avoid liability "would be to sanction an injustice." *Gromer, Wittenstrom & Meyer, P.C. v. Strom,* 140 Ill.App.3d 349, 354, 489 N.E.2d 370, 374 (1986).

Sea–Land also satisfied the second prong of *Van Dorn* by demonstrating at trial that Marchese used his corporate entities as "playthings" to avoid his responsibilities to creditors. An accountant testified that Marchese's payment of personal expenses with corporate funds enabled those corporations to avoid their monetary obligations to vendors, creditors, and federal and state tax authorities. One example was Marchese's withdrawal of $19,000 as salary from Jamar Corporation. This withdrawal rendered Jamar insolvent and thus unable to satisfy liabilities in excess of $450,000. Marchese also frequently took "shareholder loans" from the corporations to pay personal expenses, leaving the corporations with insufficient funds to satisfy liabilities as they became due. Further, a tax accountant testified that Marchese's business practices were replete with illegal transactions.

* The bracketed paragraphs are adapted from a prior appeal in this case, 941 F.2d 519 (7th Cir. 1991).

Indeed, as we previously recognized, "for years Marchese flagrantly has disregarded the tax code concerning the treatment of corporate funds." *Sea–Land, supra,* 941 F.2d at 522 n. 2.

Marchese's practice of avoiding liability to Sea–Land and other creditors by insuring that his corporations had insufficient funds with which to pay their debts, is ground for piercing the corporate veil. *Van Dorn, supra,* 753 F.2d at 572–73 (piercing of corporate veil allowed where subsidiary was stripped by parent corporation of its assets and rendered insolvent to the prejudice of creditor). Further, as the district court here properly recognized, Marchese was the "dominant force" behind all of the corporations and was responsible for the manipulation and diversion of corporate funds without regard for creditors or the law. *B. Kreisman & Co. v. First Arlington Nat'l Bank,* 91 Ill.App.3d 847, 415 N.E.2d 1070 (1980) (piercing corporate veil proper where defendant was the dominant force behind corporation). On the basis of the facts adduced at trial, the court properly concluded that Sea–Land satisfied the second-prong of *Van Dorn* and therefore was entitled to pierce the corporate veil. . . .

Appellants further assert that Sea–Land fails to satisfy the requirement that a nexus exist between its injuries and the fraud or injustice committed by appellants. *South Side Bank v. T.S.B. Corp.,* 94 Ill. App.3d 1006, 419 N.E.2d 477 (1981). This claim fails, however, in view of the fact that Marchese assured Sea–Land in 1987 that it would receive payment from PS as long as there were sufficient funds. The court's findings that Marchese knew at that time that he would manipulate the funds of PS so as to insure that Sea–Land would not be paid, and that he eventually did manipulate those funds, were not clearly erroneous. Since Marchese's intentional and improper financial maneuvering caused Sea–Land's inability to collect on its default judgment, the required nexus existed here. . . .

Affirmed.

Eisenberg, Corporate Groups, in The Law Relating to Corporate Groups

(M. Gillooly ed. 1993).

... With few if any exceptions, wholly owned [subsidiaries] exist only as a response to legal rules. It is very difficult to find economic reasons for wholly owned [subsidiaries], because almost any economic goal that can be achieved by the creation of a wholly owned subsidiary can be equally well-achieved by the creation of a division [that is, a business owned by a corporation and operated in a relatively autonomous manner]. A corporate enterprise may find it desirable to organize itself in such a manner as to provide autonomy, or considerable autonomy, to one or more of its businesses or functions, but ... this goal can be served perfectly well through the use of divisions ... If Corporation A chooses to run its wholly owned Business B as an autonomous business, it is economically irrelevant whether Business B is run as a division or as a subsidiary. If Corporation A acquires all the stock of Corporation C, it is economically irrelevant whether C is thereafter maintained as a subsidiary or run as a division. In fact, a corporation that puts some of its business units into subsidiary form is likely to treat those units in exactly the same way that it treats other businesses that are divisions. . . .

The kinds of legal rules that prompt the formation of wholly owned groups are endless. In some cases, a special legal rule may require the formation of a subsidiary. For example, in the case of multinational corporations, a host country might require a local business to be locally incorporated. Alternatively, a special legal rule may invite the formation of a subsidiary. For example, the creation of a subsidiary may confer some tax advantage. In other cases, however, the purpose of a wholly owned group is not to comply with or take the invitation of legal rules, but to circumvent [the rights of corporate creditors or shareholders].

wholly owned has reasons other than control

BERKEY v. THIRD AVE. RY. CO., 244 N.Y. 84, 155 N.E. 58 (1926) (Cardozo, J.). "The whole problem of the relation between parent and subsidiary corporations is one that is still enveloped in the mists of metaphor. Metaphors in law are to be narrowly watched, for starting as devices to liberate thought, they end often by enslaving it. We say at times that the corporate entity will be ignored when the parent corporation operates a business through a subsidiary which is characterized as an 'alias' or a 'dummy.' All this is well enough if the picturesqueness of the epithets does not lead us to forget that the essential term to be defined is the act of operation. Dominion may be so complete, interference so obtrusive, that by the general rules of agency the parent will be a principal and the subsidiary an agent. Where control is less than this, we are remitted to the tests of honesty and justice. Ballentine, Parent and Subsidiary Corporations, 14 Cal. Law Review, 12, 18, 19, 20. The logical consistency of a juridical conception will indeed be sacrificed at times, when the sacrifice is essential to the end that some accepted public policy may be defended or upheld. This is so, for illustration, though agency in any proper sense is lacking, where the attempted separation between parent and subsidiary will work a fraud upon the law. . . . At such times unity is ascribed to parts which, at least for many purposes, retain an independent life, for the reason that only thus can we overcome a perversion of the privilege to do business in a corporate form."

CARTE BLANCHE (SINGAPORE) PTE., LTD. v. DINERS CLUB INTERNATIONAL, INC., 2 F.3d 24 (2d Cir.1993). "Ultimately, the question in any particular case is whether, in light of the circumstances, 'the policy behind the presumption of corporate independence and limited shareholder liability—encouragement of business development—is outweighed by the policy justifying disregarding the corporate form—the need to protect those who deal with the corporation.' "

NOTE ON THE APPLICATION OF THE PIERCING–THE–VEIL DOCTRINE

Although the tests announced by the courts for piercing the corporate veil are often similar from state to state, the manner in which those tests are applied, and therefore the incidence of piercing, may vary considerably across jurisdictions. For example, Epperson & Canny examined the operation of the piercing doctrine in three neighboring jurisdictions—the District of Columbia, Maryland, and Virginia. Epperson & Canny, The Capital Shareholder's Ultimate Calamity: Pierced Corporate Veils and Shareholder Liability in the District of Columbia, Maryland, and Virginia, 37 Cath.U.L.Rev. 605 (1988). They concluded that in the District of Columbia, a disregard of corporate formalities, without more, may constitute prima facie evidence of unfairness or inequity. In contrast, Maryland courts accord the corporate entity "an extraordinary measure of deference, apparently relaxed only in instances of proven common law fraud." Virginia courts commonly resorted to a more fluid analysis which endeavors to take into account the "totality of the circumstances." Id. at 614–18, 621, 626.

NOTE ON AN EMPIRICAL ANALYSIS OF PIERCING CASES

Professor Robert Thompson conducted an exhaustive empirical analysis of piercing cases that has yielded much valuable information. Thompson, Piercing The Corporate Veil: An Empirical Study, 76 Cornell L.Rev. 1036 (1991). Thompson considered 2,000 piercing cases, mostly decided between the mid–1950s and the mid–1980s. Courts pierced the corporate veil in approximately 40% of the cases, although there were often noticeable differences in the rate of plaintiffs' success according to the category of case and the state in which the case was decided. The corporate veil was pierced more often in contract cases (42%) than in tort cases (31%). In no case was the corporate veil of a publicly held corporation pierced to impose liability on public shareholders, although many cases apparently involved piercing the veil of a subsidiary of a publicly held corporation to make the publicly held parent liable.

Not covered in Class   *(to end)* ✓

NOTE ON UNITED STATES v. BESTFOODS AND DIRECT LIABILITY

Closely related to piercing-the-veil cases in a parent-subsidiary context are cases in which a parent is sought to be held liable *without* piercing the subsidiary's veil, on the ground that the parent directed the subsidiary's operations, or some relevant portion of those operations, and is therefore *directly* liable as a primary wrongdoer for wrongs that were committed in the course of those operations. A leading exemplar of this kind of case is United States v. Bestfoods, 524 U.S. 51, 118 S.Ct. 1876, 141 L.Ed.2d 43 (1998).

This case arose under the Comprehensive Environmental Response, Compensation, and Liability Act of 1980 (CERCLA). Under that Act, the federal government may, under certain conditions: (1) use the Hazardous Substance Superfund to finance efforts to clean up pollution from hazardous substances, and then (2) replenish the Fund by bringing suit against "any person who at the time of disposal of any hazardous substance owned or operated any facility" involved in the pollution. The term "owner or operator" is defined as "any person owning or operating" a facility.

Ott Chemical Co.—referred to in the Court's opinion as Ott II—manufactured chemicals at a plant near Muskegon, Michigan, and significantly polluted the soil and the ground water by both intentionally and unintentionally dumping hazardous materials over a long period of time. From 1956 to 1972, Ott II was a wholly owned subsidiary of CPC International. The United States sued CPC under CERCLA. (Ott II was by this time defunct.) The District Court held CPC liable, but the Sixth Circuit reversed on the ground that CPC and Ott II maintained separate personalities, and CPC did not utilize the subsidiary's corporate form to perpetuate fraud or subvert justice. The Supreme Court vacated the Sixth Circuit's opinion, and remanded the case to the District Court for further proceedings pursuant to the Court's opinion. The relevant portions of the Court's opinion follow:

It is a general principle of corporate law deeply "ingrained in our economic and legal systems" that a parent corporation (so-called because of control through ownership of another corporation's stock) is not liable for the acts of its subsidiaries. Douglas & Shanks, Insulation from Liability Through Subsidiary Corporations, 39 *Yale L.J.* 193 (1929) (hereinafter Douglas).... Thus it is hornbook law that "the exercise of the 'control' which stock ownership gives to the stockholders ... will not create liability beyond the assets of the subsidiary. That 'control' includes the election of directors, the making of by-laws ... and the doing of all other acts incident to the legal status of stockholders. Nor will a duplication of some or all of the directors or executive officers be fatal." Douglas 196....

If [CERCLA] rested liability entirely on ownership of a polluting facility, this opinion might end here [because Ott II owned the facility]; but CERCLA liability may turn on operation as well as ownership, and nothing in the statute's terms bars a parent corporation from direct liability for its *own* actions in operating a facility owned by its subsidiary. As Justice (then-Professor) Douglas noted almost 70 years ago, derivative liability cases are to be distinguished from those in which "the alleged wrong can seemingly be traced to the parent through the conduit of its own personnel and management" and "the parent is directly a participant in the wrong complained of." Douglas 207, 208. In such instances, the parent is directly liable for its own actions. The fact that a corporate subsidiary happens to own a polluting facility operated by its parent does nothing, then, to displace the rule that the parent "corporation is [itself] responsible for the wrongs committed by its agents in the course of its business," *Mine Workers v. Coronado Coal Co.*, 259 U.S. 344, 395, 42 S.Ct. 570, 577, 66 L.Ed. 975 (1922), and whereas the rules of veil-piercing limit derivative liability for the actions of another corporation, CERCLA's "operator" provision is concerned primarily with direct liability for one's own actions. . . .

This much is easy to say; the difficulty comes in defining actions sufficient to constitute direct parental "operation." . . .

. . . If . . . direct liability for the parent's operation of the facility is to be kept distinct from derivative liability for the subsidiary's own operation, the focus of the enquiry must necessarily be different under the two tests. "The question is not whether the parent operates the subsidiary, but rather whether it operates the facility, and that operation is evidenced by participation in the activities of the facility, not the subsidiary. . . ." Oswald [, Bifurcation of the Owner and Operator Analysis Under CERCLA, 72 Wash. U.L.Q. 223, 269 (1994)]. . . .

. . . [T]he District Court wrongly assumed that the actions of the joint officers and directors are necessarily attributable to CPC. The District Court emphasized the facts that CPC placed its own high-level officials on Ott II's board of directors and in key management positions at Ott II, and that those individuals made major policy decisions and conducted day-to-day operations at the facility: "Although Ott II corporate officers set the day-to-day operating policies for the company without any need to obtain formal approval from CPC, CPC actively participated in this decision-making because high-ranking CPC officers served in Ott II management positions." *Id.*, at 559. . . .

In imposing direct liability on these grounds, the District Court failed to recognize that "it is entirely appropriate for directors of a parent corporation to serve as directors of its subsidiary, and that fact alone may not serve to expose the parent corporation to liability for its subsidiary's acts." *American Protein Corp. v. AB Volvo*, 844 F.2d 56, 57(C.A.2), cert. denied, 488 U.S. 852, 109 S.Ct. 136, 102 L.Ed.2d 109 (1988). . . .

This recognition that the corporate personalities remain distinct has its corollary in the "well established principle [of corporate law] that directors and officers holding positions with a parent and its subsidiary can and do 'change hats' to represent the two corporations separately, despite their common ownership." *Lusk v. Foxmeyer Health Corp.*, 129 F.3d 773, 779 (C.A.5 1997). . . . Since courts generally presume "that the directors are wearing their 'subsidiary hats' and not their 'parent hats' when acting for the subsidiary," P. Blumberg, *Law of Corporate Groups: Procedural Problems in the Law of Parent and Subsidiary Corporations* S 1.02.1, at 12 (1983), it cannot be enough to establish liability here that dual officers and directors made policy decisions and supervised activities at the facility. The Government would have to show that, despite the general presumption to the contrary, the officers and directors were acting in their capacities as CPC officers and directors, and not as Ott II officers and directors, when they committed those acts.[13] The District Court made no such enquiry here, however, disregarding entirely this time-honored common law rule. . . .

We accordingly agree with the Court of Appeals that a participation-and-control test looking to the parent's supervision over the subsidiary, especially one that assumes that dual officers always act on behalf of the parent, cannot be used to identify operation of a facility resulting in direct parental liability. Nonetheless, a return to the ordinary meaning of the word "operate" in the organizational sense will indicate why we think that the Sixth Circuit stopped short when it confined its examples of direct parental operation to exclusive or joint ventures, and declined to find at least the possibility of direct operation by CPC in this case.

In our enquiry into the meaning Congress presumably had in mind when it used the verb "to operate," we recognized that the statute obviously meant something more than mere mechanical activation of pumps and valves, and must be read to contemplate "operation" as including the exercise of direction over the facility's activities. . . . The Court of Appeals recognized this by indicating that a parent can be held directly liable when the parent operates the facility in the stead of its subsidiary or alongside the subsidiary in some sort of a joint venture. *See* 113 F.3d, at 579. We anticipated a further possibility above, however, when we observed that a dual officer or director might depart so far from the norms of parental influence exercised through dual office-holding as to serve the parent, even when ostensibly acting on behalf of the subsidiary in operating the facility. *See* n. 13, *supra.* Yet another possibility, suggested by the facts of this case, is that an agent of the parent with no hat to wear but the parent's hat might manage or direct activities at the facility.

Identifying such an occurrence calls for line drawing yet again, since the acts of direct operation that give rise to parental liability must necessarily be distinguished from the interference that stems from the normal relationship between parent and

13. We do not attempt to recite the ways in which the Government could show that dual officers or directors were in fact acting on behalf of the parent. Here, it is prudent to say only that the presumption that an act is taken on behalf of the corporation for whom the officer claims to act is strongest when the act is perfectly consistent with the norms of corporate behavior, but wanes as the distance from those accepted norms approaches the point of action by a dual officer plainly contrary to the interests of the subsidiary yet nonetheless advantageous to the parent.

subsidiary. Again norms of corporate behavior (undisturbed by any CERCLA provision) are crucial reference points. Just as we may look to such norms in identifying the limits of the presumption that a dual officeholder acts in his ostensible capacity, so here we may refer to them in distinguishing a parental officer's oversight of a subsidiary from such an officer's control over the operation of the subsidiary's facility. "[A]ctivities that involve the facility but which are consistent with the parent's investor status, such as monitoring of the subsidiary's performance, supervision of the subsidiary's finance and capital budget decisions, and articulation of general policies and procedures, should not give rise to direct liability." Oswald 282. The critical question is whether, in degree and detail, actions directed to the facility by an agent of the parent alone are eccentric under accepted norms of parental oversight of a subsidiary's facility.

There is, in fact, some evidence that CPC engaged in just this type and degree of activity at the Muskegon plant. The District Court's opinion speaks of an agent of CPC alone who played a conspicuous part in dealing with the toxic risks emanating from the operation of the plant. G.R.D. Williams worked only for CPC; he was not an employee, officer, or director of Ott II, see Tr. of Oral Arg. 7, and thus, his actions were of necessity taken only on behalf of CPC. The District Court found that "CPC became directly involved in environmental and regulatory matters through the work of ... Williams, CPC's governmental and environmental affairs director. Williams ... became heavily involved in environmental issues at Ott II." 777 F.Supp., at 561. He "actively participated in and exerted control over a variety of Ott II environmental matters," *ibid.*, and he "issued directives regarding Ott II's responses to regulatory inquiries," *id.*, at 575.

We think that these findings are enough to raise an issue of CPC's operation of the facility through Williams's actions ... [14] (Emphasis added.)

SECTION 9.   EQUITABLE SUBORDINATION OF SHAREHOLDER CLAIMS

NOTE ON EQUITABLE SUBORDINATION OF SHAREHOLDER CLAIMS

1. *Equitable Subordination.* Under the doctrine of equitable subordination, when a corporation is in bankruptcy, debt claims that a controlling shareholder has against the corporation may be subordi-

---

14. ... [T]he Government is, of course, [also] free on remand to point to any additional evidence ... that would tend to establish that Ott II's decisionmakers acted on specific orders from CPC.

nated to the claims of other persons, including the claims of preferred shareholders, on various equitable grounds. The doctrine of equitable subordination is often referred to as the ''Deep Rock'' doctrine, named after the corporation—a subsidiary—in the seminal case of Taylor v. Standard Gas & Electric Co., 306 U.S. 307, 59 S.Ct. 543, 83 L.Ed. 669 (1939). The Court in that case subordinated the parent's claim, as a creditor of the subsidiary, to the claims of other creditors and preferred stockholders of the subsidiary, because of the parent's improper management of the subsidiary for the parent's benefit, and because the subsidiary had been inadequately capitalized. See also Pepper v. Litton, 308 U.S. 295, 310, 60 S.Ct. 238, 246, 84 L.Ed. 281 (1939); Hackney & Benson, Shareholder Liability for Inadequate Capital, 43 U.Pitt.L.Rev. 837 (1982).

In Gannett Co. v. Larry, 221 F.2d 269 (2d Cir.1955), Gannett Company was in the newspaper-publishing business. Berwin Paper was also in the business of publishing a newspaper. To ensure a supply of newsprint in view of a threatened shortage, Gannett purchased all the stock of Berwin Paper, and converted Berwin from a publisher to a newsprint supplier. Gannett lent substantial sums to Berwin for that purpose. The threatened newsprint shortage never materialized. As a result, by 1952 the newsprint market had changed completely, and Berwin was operating at a loss. In 1953, Berwin became insolvent, and a trustee in bankruptcy was appointed. The court subordinated Gannett's claim for the sums it had loaned to Berwin to the claims of other creditors. ''[T]he losses suffered by Berwin were suffered, not in an attempt by Gannett primarily to make the subsidiary a financially profitable proposition, but to turn it into a source of newsprint, of no interest to the other creditors—unless financially profitable—but of distinct interest to Gannett, whether or not financially profitable, because of Gannett's newsprint shortage. Because of this factor. . . . 'It would be unfair to allow the claim of Gannett on a parity with other creditors who lacked the interest which Gannett had in Berwin's disastrous experiment in the newsprint field.' In such circumstances, proof of fraud or illegality is not necessary''.

2. *Comparison With Piercing.* Hackney & Benson comment that ''As compared with denying to a shareholder his privilege of limited liability, the equitable remedy of subordination is much less drastic: it simply takes an investment already made, and denies it the status of a creditor's claim on a parity with outside creditors, whereas imposing liability for corporate debts undermines the essential premise of limited liability—that a shareholder's risk is limited to the amount of his investment. . . . It is logical, therefore, for the courts to have found it fair to subordinate a controlling person's claim based upon a lesser evidence of misuse of the corporate form than what is required to impose affirmative personal liability for all corporate obligations. Furthermore, if actual shareholder capital were so small as to result in treating a shareholder loan as equity, then the equity as supplemented by the subordinated loan may be deemed an adequate cushion to support limited liability. Accordingly, inadequate capitalization may

result in subordination when it does not necessarily require imposition of affirmative liability." Hackney & Benson, supra, at 882.

3. *Undercapitalization*. Undercapitalization plays an important role in equitable subordination, as it does in piercing the corporate veil. In Arnold v. Phillips, 117 F.2d 497 (5th Cir.1941), cert. denied 313 U.S. 583, 61 S.Ct. 1102, 85 L.Ed. 1539 (1941), Arnold formed a brewery company with capital stock of $50,000, paid for in cash. He then lent the brewery $75,000, so that it would have enough to start operations. The business began to lose heavily, and Arnold advanced large additional sums. Eventually, the brewery went into bankruptcy liquidation. In the bankruptcy proceedings, a mortgage held by Arnold to secure his loans was held invalid on the ground of inadequate capitalization insofar as the mortgage represented money Arnold loaned the brewery to build and equip its plant, but valid as to subsequent advances made after the brewery became a going concern. The court said:

> The two series of advances differ materially as respects their nature and purpose. Those made before the enterprise was launched were, as the district court found, really capital. Although the charter provided for no more capital than $50,000, what it took to build the plant and equip it was a permanent investment, in its nature capital.... There can be little doubt that what he contributed to the plant was actually intended to be capital, notwithstanding the charter was not amended and demand notes were taken....

> After two years of prosperity, with the original capital thus enlarged demonstrated to be sufficient, with a book surplus of nearly $100,000 after payment of large salaries and dividends in the form of interest, there arose a situation very different from that in the beginning. Adversity then occurring raised a problem not different from that which commonly faces a corporation having losses. It may borrow to meet its needs. Had this corporation borrowed of a bank upon the security of the plant, the debt would no doubt be valid. What would render it invalid when Arnold furnished the money? ...

> ... It would be hard to say in this case that $50,000 was not a substantial capital, and impossible so to say after holding that the real capital was $125,500, though some was irregularly paid in [as a purported loan].

4. *Common Pool*. If a parent and a subsidiary, or two affiliated corporations, are both bankrupt, the courts sometimes consolidate the assets and liabilities of the several corporations into a common pool. See In re Seatrade Corp., 255 F.Supp. 696 (S.D.N.Y.1966), aff'd sub nom. Chemical Bank New York Trust Co. v. Kheel, 369 F.2d 845 (2d Cir.); Landers, A Unified Approach to Parent, Subsidiary, and Affiliate Questions in Bankruptcy, 42 U.Chi.L.Rev. 589, 629–51 (1975).

BENJAMIN v. DIAMOND, 563 F.2d 692, 699–702 (5th Cir.1977). "[T]hree conditions must be satisfied before exercise of the power of equitable subordination is appropriate. (i) The claimant [who may be an owner, director, or officer of the bankrupt corporation] must have engaged in some type of inequitable conduct.... (ii) The misconduct must have resulted in injury to the creditors of the bankrupt or conferred an unfair advantage on the claimant.... (iii) Equitable subordination of the claim must not be inconsistent with the provisions of the Bankruptcy Act....

"In determining whether these three conditions are satisfied three principles must be kept in mind. The first is that inequitable conduct directed against the bankrupt or its creditors may be sufficient to warrant subordination of a claim irrespective of whether it was related to the acquisition or assertion of that claim....

"The second principle is that a claim or claims should be subordinated only to the extent necessary to offset the harm which the bankrupt and its creditors suffered on account of the inequitable conduct. For example, if a claimant guilty of misconduct asserts two claims, each worth $10,000, and the injury he inflicted on the bankrupt or its creditors amounted to $10,000, only one of his claims should be subordinated. Since the exercise of the subordination power is governed by equitable principles, ... subordination of the other claim would be improper.

"The third guiding principle relates to allocation of the burden of proof....

"... To constitute the type of challenge contemplated by the Court, an objection resting on equitable grounds cannot be merely formal, but rather must contain some substantial factual basis to support its allegation of impropriety.... The proper rule is that

> the claimant's verified proof of claim obliges the objecting trustee to come forward with enough substantiations to overcome the claimant's *prima facie* case and thus compel [the claimant] to actually prove the validity and honesty of his claim.

3A J. Moore & L. King, Collier on Bankruptcy, § 63.06, at 1785 (14th ed. 1976) ...

UNIFORM FRAUDULENT TRANSFER ACT § 4(a)

[See Statutory Supplement]

BANKRUPTCY CODE § 548

[See Statutory Supplement]

NOTE ON TRANSFERS MADE BY A CORPORATION WITHOUT AN EQUIVALENT EXCHANGE

Under the Bankruptcy Code, a transfer by a corporation to its shareholders without an equivalent exchange—for example, a dividend—can be recovered on the corporation's behalf, even if the corporation was solvent at the time of the transfer, if the corporation "was engaged in business or a transaction, or was about to engage in business or a transaction, for which any property remaining with the debtor was an unreasonably small capital." Similarly, under the Uniform Fraudulent Transfer Act (UFTA) a transfer without an equivalent exchange can be recovered if the corporation "was engaged or was about to engage in a business or a transaction for which the remaining assets of the debtor were unreasonably small in relation to the business or transaction." The Reporter's Note to UFTA § 4 states that the term "assets," rather than the term "capital," was used in § 4 to avoid confusing the concept of working capital with the legal concept of capital under corporate law.

SECTION 10. THE CORPORATE ENTITY AND THE INTERPRETATION OF STATUTES AND CONTRACTS

The following two issues often arise:

(1) Does a statute or contract that applies to a corporation also apply by implication to the corporation's shareholders? For example, if Corporation A agrees with X not to compete with X, may A's sole shareholder compete with X?

(2) Does a statute or contract that applies to an individual also apply by implication to a corporation that the individual owns? For example, if a statute prohibits non-citizens from owning ships that ply the U.S. coastal trade, does the statute also prohibit a corporation from owning ships if all of the corporation's stock is held by noncitizens?

These issues do not concern whether liability should be imposed on the corporation's shareholders despite the general rule of limited liability. Rather, they are questions of interpretation. In making such interpretations, it must be borne in mind that on the one hand, the law normally treats a corporation and its shareholders as distinct, but on the other hand, the legislature or the contracting parties may not intend to treat a corporation and its shareholders as distinct for all purposes.

Two of the leading cases in this area are United States v. Milwaukee Refrigerator Transit Co., 142 Fed. 247, 255 (E.D.Wis.1905), and Anderson v. Abbott, 321 U.S. 349, 64 S.Ct. 531, 88 L.Ed. 793 (1944). In the *Milwaukee* case, a statute prohibited railroads from giving rebates to shippers. The statute was held applicable to a corporation that was not itself a shipper, but had been formed by a shipper's officers and principal shareholders for the purpose of obtaining what were in substance rebates. "[A] corporation will be looked upon as a legal entity as a general rule, and until sufficient reason to the contrary appears; but, when the notion of legal entity is used to defeat public convenience . . . the law will regard the corporation as an association of persons." In the *Anderson* case, a statute made a shareholder in a national bank liable for the debts of the bank "to the amount of his stock therein, at the par value thereof in addition to the amount invested in such stock." The question was whether this statute applied to shareholders of a parent corporation with a national bank subsidiary, even though technically only the parent was a shareholder in the bank. The Supreme Court concluded that the parent's shareholders would be deemed shareholders of the bank for the purpose of the statute, on the ground that to hold otherwise would permit that purpose to be undercut:

> It has often been held that the interposition of a corporation will not be allowed to defeat a legislative policy, whether that was the aim or only the result of the arrangement. . . .
>
> To allow this holding company device to succeed would be to put the policy of double liability at the mercy of corporation finance.

321 U.S. at 362–63, 64 S.Ct. at 537–38. See also Reich v. Gateway Press, Inc., 13 F.3d 685 (3d Cir.1994); Kavanaugh v. Ford Motor Co., 353 F.2d 710, 716–17 (7th Cir.1965); Note, Efficacy of the Corporate Entity in Evasion of Statutes, 26 Iowa L.Rev. 350 (1941).

CHAPTER V

SHAREHOLDER INFORMATIONAL RIGHTS AND PROXY VOTING

SECTION 1. SHAREHOLDER INFORMATIONAL RIGHTS UNDER STATE LAW

(a) INSPECTION OF BOOKS AND RECORDS

DEL. GEN. CORP. LAW §§ 219, 220

[See Statutory Supplement]

REV. MODEL BUS. CORP. ACT §§ 7.20, 16.01–16.04

[See Statutory Supplement]

CAL. CORP. CODE §§ 1600, 1601

[See Statutory Supplement]

N.Y. BUS. CORP. LAW § 624

[See Statutory Supplement]

Saito v. McKesson HBOC, Inc.

Supreme Court of Delaware, 2002.
806 A.2d 113.

■ Before VEASEY, CHIEF JUSTICE, WALSH, HOLLAND, BERGER, JUSTICES and HARTNETT, JUSTICE (Retired), constituting the Court en Banc.

■ BERGER, JUSTICE.

In this appeal, we consider the limitations on a stockholder's statutory right to inspect corporate books and records. The statute, 8 Del.C. § 220, enables stockholders to investigate matters "reasonably related to [their] interest as [stockholders]" including, among other things, possible corporate wrongdoing. It does not open the door to the wide ranging discovery that would be available in support of litigation. For this statutory tool to be meaningful, however, it cannot be read narrowly to deprive a stockholder of necessary documents solely because the documents were prepared by third parties or because the documents predate the stockholder's first investment in the corporation. A stockholder who demands inspection for a proper purpose should be given access to all of the documents in the corporation's possession, custody or control, that are necessary to satisfy that proper purpose. Thus, where a § 220 claim is based on alleged corporate wrongdoing, and assuming the allegation is meritorious, the stockholder should be given enough information to effectively address the problem, either through derivative litigation or through direct contact with the corporation's directors and/or stockholders.

Factual and Procedural Background

On October 17, 1998, McKesson Corporation entered into a stock-for-stock merger agreement with HBO & Company ("HBOC"). On October 20, 1998, appellant, Noel Saito, purchased McKesson stock. The merger was consummated in January 1999 and the combined company was renamed McKesson HBOC, Incorporated. HBOC continued its separate corporate existence as a wholly-owned subsidiary of McKesson HBOC.

Starting in April and continuing through July 1999, McKesson HBOC announced a series of financial restatements triggered by its year-end audit process. During that four month period, McKesson HBOC reduced its revenues by $327.4 million for the three prior fiscal years. The restatements all were attributed to HBOC accounting irregularities. The first announcement precipitated several lawsuits, including a derivative action pending in the Court of Chancery, captioned *Ash v. McCall*, Civil Action No. 17132. Saito was one of four plaintiffs in the *Ash* complaint, which alleged that: (i) McKesson's directors breached their duty of care by failing to discover the HBOC accounting irregularities before the merger; (ii) McKesson's directors committed corporate waste by entering into the merger with HBOC; (iii)HBOC's directors breached their fiduciary duties by failing to monitor the company's compliance with financial reporting requirements prior to the merger; and (iv) McKesson HBOC's directors failed in the same respect during the three months following the merger. Although the Court of Chancery granted defendants' motion to dismiss the complaint, the dismissal was without prejudice as to the pre-merger and post-merger oversight claims.

In its decision on the motion to dismiss, the Court of Chancery specifically suggested that Saito and the other plaintiffs "use the 'tools at hand,' most prominently § 220 books and records actions, to obtain information necessary to sue derivatively."[1] Saito was the only Ash plaintiff to follow that advice. The stated purpose of Saito's demand was:

> (1) to further investigate breaches of fiduciary duties by the boards of directors of HBO & Co., Inc., McKesson, Inc., and/or McKesson HBOC, Inc. related to their oversight of their respective company's accounting procedures and financial reporting; (2) to investigate potential claims against advisors engaged by McKesson, Inc. and HBO & Co., Inc. to the acquisition of HBO & Co., Inc. by McKesson, Inc.; and (3) to gather information relating to the above in order to supplement the complaint in *Ash v. McCall*, et al., . . . in accordance with the September 15, 2000 Opinion of the Court of Chancery.

Saito demanded access to eleven categories of documents, including those relating to Arthur Andersen's pre-merger review and verification of HBOC's financial condition; communications between or among HBOC, McKesson, and their investment bankers and accountants concerning HBOC's accounting practices; and discussions among members of the Boards of Directors of HBOC, McKesson, and/or McKesson HBOC concerning reports published in April 1997 and thereafter about HBOC's accounting practices or financial condition.

After trial, the Court of Chancery found that Saito stated a proper purpose for the inspection of books and records—to ferret out possible wrongdoing in connection with the merger of HBOC and McKesson. But the court held that Saito's proper purpose only extended to potential wrongdoing after the date on which Saito acquired his McKesson stock. The court also held that Saito did not have a proper purpose to inspect documents relating to potential claims against third party advisors who counseled the boards in connection with the merger. Finally, the court held that Saito was not entitled to HBOC documents because Saito was not a stockholder of pre-merger HBOC, and, with respect to post-merger HBOC, he did not establish a basis on which to disregard the separate existence of the wholly-owned subsidiary.

DISCUSSION

Stockholders of Delaware corporations enjoy a qualified common law and statutory right to inspect the corporation's books and records.[2] Inspection rights were recognized at common law because, "[a]s a matter of self-protection, the stockholder was entitled to know how his agents were conducting the affairs of the corporation of which he or she was a part owner."[3] The common law right is codified in 8 Del.C. § 220, which provides in relevant part:

---

1. Ash v. McCall, 2000 WL 1370341, *15 (Del.Ch.).

2. Shaw v. Agri–Mark, Inc., 663 A.2d 464 (Del.1995).

3. Id. at 467.

(b) Any stockholder ... shall, upon written demand under oath stating the purpose thereof, have the right ... to inspect for any proper purpose the corporation's stock ledger, a list of its stockholders, and its other books and records, and to make copies or extracts therefrom. A proper purpose shall mean a purpose reasonably related to such person's interest as a stockholder.

Once a stockholder establishes a proper purpose under § 220, the right to relief will not be defeated by the fact that the stockholder may have secondary purposes that are improper. The scope of a stockholder's inspection, however, is limited to those books and records that are necessary and essential to accomplish the stated, proper purpose.

After trial, the Court of Chancery found "credible evidence of possible wrongdoing," which satisfied Saito's burden of establishing a proper purpose for the inspection of corporate books and records. But the Court of Chancery limited Saito's access to relevant documents in three respects. First, it held that, since Saito would not have standing to bring an action challenging actions that occurred before he purchased McKesson stock, Saito could not obtain documents created before October 20, 1998. Second, the court concluded that Saito was not entitled to documents relating to possible wrongdoing by the financial advisors to the merging companies. Third, the court denied Saito access to any HBOC documents, since Saito never was a stockholder of HBOC. We will consider each of these rulings in turn.

A. *The Standing Limitation*

By statute, stockholders who bring derivative suits must allege that they were stockholders of the corporation "at the time of the transaction of which such stockholder complains...." The Court of Chancery decided that this limitation on Saito's ability to maintain a derivative suit controlled the scope of his inspection rights. As a result, the court held that Saito was "effectively limited to examining conduct of McKesson and McKesson HBOC's boards following the negotiation and public announcement of the merger agreement."

Although we recognize that there may be some interplay between the two statutes, we do not read § 327 as defining the temporal scope of a stockholder's inspection rights under § 220. The books and records statute requires that a stockholder's purpose be one that is "reasonably related" to his or her interest as a stockholder. The standing statute, § 327, bars a stockholder from bringing a derivative action unless the stockholder owned the corporation's stock at the time of the alleged wrong. If a stockholder wanted to investigate alleged wrongdoing that substantially predated his or her stock ownership, there could be a question as to whether the stockholder's purpose was reasonably related to his or her interest as a stockholder, especially if the stockholder's only purpose was to institute derivative litigation. But stockholders may use information about corporate mismanagement in other ways, as well. They may seek an audience with the board to discuss proposed reforms or, failing in that, they may prepare a stockholder resolution for the next annual meeting, or mount a proxy fight to elect new directors. None of those activities would be prohibited by § 327.

Even where a stockholder's only purpose is to gather information for a derivative suit, the date of his or her stock purchase should not be used as an automatic "cut-off" date in a § 220 action. First, the potential derivative claim may involve a continuing wrong that both predates and postdates the stockholder's purchase date. In such a case, books and records from the inception of the alleged wrongdoing could be necessary and essential to the stockholder's purpose. Second, the alleged post-purchase date wrongs may have their foundation in events that transpired earlier. In this case, for example, Saito wants to investigate McKesson's apparent failure to learn of HBOC's accounting irregularities until months after the merger was consummated. Due diligence documents generated before the merger agreement was signed may be essential to that investigation. In sum, the date on which a stockholder first acquired the corporation's stock does not control the scope of records available under § 220. If activities that occurred before the purchase date are "reasonably related" to the stockholder's interest as a stockholder, then the stockholder should be given access to records necessary to an understanding of those activities.[4]

B.   *The Financial Advisors' Documents*

The Court of Chancery denied Saito access to documents in McKesson–HBOC's possession that the corporation obtained from financial and accounting advisors, on the ground that Saito could not use § 220 to develop potential claims against third parties. On appeal, Saito argues that he is seeking third party documents for the same reason he is seeking McKesson HBOC documents—to investigate possible wrongdoing by McKesson and McKesson HBOC. Since the trial court found that to be a proper purpose, Saito argues that he should not be precluded from seeing documents that are necessary to his purpose, and in McKesson HBOC's possession, simply because the documents were prepared by third party advisors.

We agree that, generally, the source of the documents in a corporation's possession should not control a stockholder's right to inspection under § 220. It is not entirely clear, however, that the trial court restricted Saito's access on that basis. The Court of Chancery decided that Saito's interest in pursuing claims against McKesson HBOC's advisors was not a proper purpose. It recognized that a secondary improper purpose usually is irrelevant if the stockholder establishes his need for the same documents to support a proper

---

4. As noted ... above, a Section 220 proceeding does not open the door to wide ranging discovery. See *Brehm v. Eisner*, 746 A.2d 244, 266–67 (Del.2000) (Plaintiffs "bear the burden of showing a proper purpose and [must] make specific and discrete identification, with rifled precision ... [to] establish that each category of books and records is essential to the accomplishment of their articulated purpose ..."); *Security First Corp. v. U.S. Die Casting and Dev. Co.*, 687 A.2d 563, 568, 570 (Del.1997) ("mere curiosity or desire for a fishing expedition" is insufficient.).

purpose. But the court apparently concluded that the categories of third party documents that Saito demanded did not support the proper purpose of investigating possible wrongdoing by McKesson and McKesson HBOC.

We cannot determine from the present record whether the Court of Chancery intended to exclude all third party documents, but such a blanket exclusion would be improper. The source of the documents and the manner in which they were obtained by the corporation have little or no bearing on a stockholder's inspection rights. The issue is whether the documents are necessary and essential to satisfy the stockholder's proper purpose. In this case, Saito wants to investigate possible wrongdoing relating to McKesson and McKesson HBOC's failure to discover HBOC's accounting irregularities. Since McKesson and McKesson HBOC relied on financial and accounting advisors to evaluate HBOC's financial condition and reporting, those advisors' reports and correspondence would be critical to Saito's investigation.

C. *HBOC Documents*

Finally, the Court of Chancery held that Saito was not entitled to any HBOC documents because he was not a stockholder of HBOC before or after the merger. Although Saito is a stockholder of HBOC's parent, McKesson HBOC, stockholders of a parent corporation are not entitled to inspect a subsidiary's books and records, "[a]bsent a showing of a fraud or that a subsidiary is in fact the mere alter ego of the parent...."[5] The Court of Chancery found no basis to disregard HBOC's separate existence and, therefore, denied access to its records.

We reaffirm this settled principle, which applies to those HBOC books and records that were never provided to McKesson or McKesson HBOC. But it does not apply to relevant documents that HBOC gave to McKesson before the merger, or to McKesson HBOC after the merger. We assume that HBOC provided financial and accounting information to its proposed merger partner and, later, to its parent company. As with the third party advisors' documents, Saito would need access to relevant HBOC documents in order to understand what his company's directors knew and why they failed to recognize HBOC's accounting irregularities.

Conclusion

Based on the foregoing, the decision of the Court of Chancery is AFFIRMED in part and REVERSED in part, and this matter is REMANDED for further action in accordance with this decision. Jurisdiction is not retained.

———

NOTE ON SHAREHOLDERS' INSPECTION RIGHTS

1. *Common Law; Interpretation of the Statutes.* At common law, a shareholder "acting in good faith for the purpose of advancing the

---

5. *Skouras v. Admiralty Enterprises, Inc.*, 386 A.2d 674, 681 (Del.Ch.1978).

interests of the corporation and protecting his own interest as a stockholder" has a right to examine the corporate books and records at reasonable times. Albee v. Lamson & Hubbard Corp., 320 Mass. 421, 424, 69 N.E.2d 811, 813 (1946). The general rule is that the shareholder has the burden of alleging and proving good faith and proper purpose. Id. But see Bennett v. Mack's Supermarkets, Inc., 602 S.W.2d 143 (Ky.1979).

Many or most legislatures have now enacted statutes governing the right of inspection. Many of these statutes are more limited in their coverage than the common law rule. For example, a statute may apply only to certain kinds of shareholders (such as those who are record holders of at least 5% of the corporation's stock or who have been record holders for at least six months) or only to certain kinds of books and records. A common problem of interpretation is whether the statutes: (i) Preserve the common law rule that the shareholder must prove a proper purpose. (ii) Discard the proper-purpose test. (iii) Preserve the proper-purpose test, but place on the corporation the burden of proving that the shareholder's purpose is improper. Generally, the last interpretation is followed, at least if the language is ambiguous. See, e.g., Crane Co. v. Anaconda Co., 39 N.Y.2d 14, 382 N.Y.S.2d 707, 346 N.E.2d 507 (1976). A second common problem of interpretation is whether the statutes replace or supplement the common law. The general answer is that the statutes supplement the common law, so that a suit for inspection that does not fall within the relevant statute can still be brought under the common law. See, e.g., Bank of Heflin v. Miles, 294 Ala. 462, 318 So.2d 697 (1975).

2. *"Proper Purpose."* Among the purposes the courts have recognized as "proper," for purposes of exercising the shareholder's inspection right, are to determine the financial condition of the corporation and to ascertain the value of the petitioner's shares.

3. *Mixed Purposes.* Suppose the shareholder has mixed purposes, one proper and one not. In Helmsman Management Services, Inc. v. A & S Consultants, Inc., 525 A.2d 160, 164, 166 (Del.Ch.1987), the court held that "Once it is determined that a shareholder has a proper purpose that is primary, any secondary purpose or ulterior motive that the stockholder might have is irrelevant." Accordingly, "even if [the shareholder] does have an ulterior (*i.e.*, a non-shareholder-related) purpose, it would still not be barred from relief under [Del.Gen.Corp.Law] § 220, unless the ulterior purpose is also its primary purpose."

4. *The Pillsbury Case.* In State ex rel. Pillsbury v. Honeywell, Inc., 291 Minn. 322, 191 N.W.2d 406 (1971), Pillsbury was a shareholder of Honeywell, Inc. Pillsbury opposed the Vietnam war, and asked Honeywell to produce its shareholder ledger and all corporate records dealing with weapons and munitions manufacture. Pillsbury admitted that his sole motive in purchasing Honeywell stock was to persuade Honeywell to cease producing munitions, but argued that the desire to communicate with fellow shareholders was per se a proper purpose. Honeywell argued that a proper purpose contem-

plates a concern with investment return. The Minnesota court held for Honeywell:

> Several courts agree with petitioner's contention that a mere desire to communicate with other shareholders is, per se, a proper purpose.... This would seem to confer an almost absolute right to inspection. We believe that a better rule would allow inspections only if the shareholder has a proper purpose for such communication....
>
> Petitioner had utterly no interest in the affairs of Honeywell before he learned of Honeywell's production of fragmentation bombs. Immediately after obtaining this knowledge, he purchased stock in Honeywell for the sole purpose of asserting ownership privileges in an effort to force Honeywell to cease such production.... Such a motivation can hardly be deemed a proper purpose germane to his economic interest as a shareholder.

Honeywell was a Delaware corporation, and the Minnesota Court apparently assumed for purposes of the case that Delaware law applied, or in any event was no different than Minnesota law insofar as relevant. In Credit Bureau Reports, Inc. v. Credit Bureau of St. Paul, Inc., 290 A.2d 691 (Del.1972), however, the Delaware Supreme Court repudiated the *Pillsbury* case insofar as it applied to requests for stockholder lists:

> [In] General Time Corporation v. Talley Industries, Inc., Del. Supr., 240 A.2d 755 (1968).... we stated that, under [Del.Gen. Corp.Law] § 220, "the desire to solicit proxies for a slate of directors in opposition to management is a purpose reasonably related to the stockholder's interest as a stockholder"; and we held that "any further or secondary purpose in seeking the list is irrelevant." Those rulings are dispositive.... The defendant corporation ... relies upon Pillsbury v. Honeywell, Inc., Minn., 191 N.W.2d 406 (1971). Insofar as the *Pillsbury* case is inconsistent herewith, it is inconsistent with [§ 220] as properly applied.

See also The Conservative Caucus Research, Analysis & Education Foundation, Inc. v. Chevron Corp., 525 A.2d 569 (Del.Ch.1987).

5. *Stockholder Lists*. As a practical matter, the courts are understandably much readier to grant access to stockholder lists and the like than to grant access to otherwise-confidential financial and business information, such as internal data and contracts. In the case of business and financial information, the shareholder will normally have to show the court a specific and plausible reason why the information is needed. In contrast, in the case of stockholder lists a statement by a shareholder that he wants the list to communicate with other shareholders will usually, although not always, suffice. This distinction is understandable. Requiring the production of a stockholder list is almost invariably a necessary step for shareholders to exercise their role in corporate governance, imposes only a minimum burden on the corporation, and usually cannot injure the business of the corporation. In contrast, other kinds of information may be costly to produce, may

have the potential to injure the corporation's business if misused, and (depending on the information) may not be necessary for the normal exercise of the shareholder's role.

In some cases, the statutes themselves distinguish between different types of corporate books and records. See, e.g., Del.Gen.Corp.Law § 220; see also Model Act §§ 7.20(b), 16.02.

––––––

NOTE ON RECORD OWNERSHIP AND THE RECORD DATE

The persons who are listed as shareholders on the corporation's records are known as *record owners*. For a variety of reasons, the persons who actually own shares—the *beneficial* owners—often differ from the record owners. For example, the stock of individual and even institutional shareholders is often held in "street name," that is, in the name of a broker or a bank. Brokers, banks, and others, in turn, often deposit the stock they hold in regional stock depositories (described below), which place the stock under still another name.

To promote certainty, in various contexts corporation law confers rights on record owners, rather than beneficial owners. One of these contexts is voting: normally, only record owners have the right to notice of a meeting and the right to vote.

When a corporation proposes to hold a meeting at which a shareholder vote will be taken, it must give notice of the meeting. To comply with the disclosure requirements of federal law, the notice frequently must be given a month or so before the meeting will take place. Because shares in publicly held corporations are constantly changing hands, the group of persons who are record owners on the date notice is given will differ from the persons who are record owners on the meeting date. Accordingly, if the shareholders entitled to vote at the meeting were the record holders as of the meeting date, then some shareholders entitled to vote would not have received notice of the meeting (because they purchased their shares after the notice was given), and the vote would be invalid.

To resolve this dilemma, the law permits corporations to set a *record date*—which is typically on or around the date that notice of the relevant meeting is given—for determining the shareholders who will be entitled to vote at the meeting. As a result, those persons, and only those persons, who are record shareholders on the record date are entitled to vote, even though the record date is a month or so before the meeting date, and many of the persons who were record holders on the record date are not record holders on the meeting date. (Under an older procedure, which is now little used, in lieu of setting a record date the corporation could close its transfer books, that is, could refuse to record transfers of stock between the time of the close of the books and the time of the meeting. As a result, all persons who were record holders when the transfer books were closed would still be record holders on the meeting date.)

J. Heard & H. Sherman, Conflicts of Interest in the Proxy Voting System 74–78

(1987).

The Owner Identification Problem . . .

As many companies have discovered during their proxy solicitations, in today's securities markets it is difficult to identify just who a company's beneficial owners are, and even more difficult to determine who has voting authority for their shares. The problem of identifying beneficial owners exists because many individual shareholders, and most institutional investors, register their shares in so-called "street name" (. . . shares registered in the name of a bank or broker) or "nominee name" (registered in the name of a bank nominee account).

Stockholders register their shares in street name for a variety of reasons. Active traders do so to expedite stock transfers and subsequent reregistration. Individuals who do not want to store stock certificates themselves leave their shares with a broker, who usually registers the shares in the broker's name. . . . Other shareholders are required to register in street name. For example, individuals who purchase stock on margin must leave their shares with their broker, and since they do not truly own the shares until they are paid for in full, their brokers register the shares in street name. . . .

Roughly 70 percent of all corporate stock is now held in street name. Of this amount, approximately 30 percent is held in broker name and 70 percent in bank nominee name.

Street name registration makes it difficult for companies to identify who their beneficial owners are. The identification problem is further complicated by the use of depositories. Shares registered in the name of a bank or broker rarely are held by the bank or broker any more. Instead, most banks and brokers hold their shares at one of the four regional depositories, the largest of which is the Depository Trust Co. in New York (nominee name Cede and Co.). When a bank or a broker holds its shares at a depository, the depository becomes the official holder of record for the shares. Thus, a company soliciting proxies is likely to find that "Cede and Co." and the other depositories are the registered owners of a majority of its shares.

One problem for companies soliciting proxy votes is that the depositories have no "beneficial interest" in the shares registered in their name; they are merely custodians of the physical securities. Companies wishing to identify who their beneficial owners are must obtain security listings from a depository telling them who "owns" the shares held at the depository. But this list only tells a company which banks and brokers hold shares registered in their name at the depository, not who the ultimate beneficial owners (the brokers' and banks' own customers) really are. . . .

. . . [T]he problem became critical in the early 1980s when some companies, unable to identify their beneficial owners and unable to guarantee that their proxy material was being received by owners in time to vote, if at all, were forced to postpone annual meetings because they failed to reach a quorum. To remedy the situation, the SEC passed its "NOBO" rules for brokers in 1985. Under the NOBO requirements, brokers must report to issuer companies the name, address and security position of clients holding the company's shares in broker name, as long as the client does not object (hence NOBO, for non-objecting beneficial owner).

The Depositories

. . . The holders of record for the majority of shares in the market today are the four major depositories: Depository Trust Co. [DTC] (nominee name—Cede and Co.), Midwest Securities Depository Trust Co. (Kray and Co.), Pacific Securities Depository Trust Co. (Pacific and Co.) and Philadelphia Depository Trust Co. (Philadep and Co.). Of the four, Depository Trust is by far the largest, followed by Midwest Depository. . . .

. . . The number of shares held by the four depositories combined represents more than 70 percent of all shares outstanding in the United States. . . .

————

F. BALOTTI & J. FINKELSTEIN, **THE DELAWARE LAW OF CORPORATIONS AND BUSINESS ASSOCIATIONS** § 7.45 (3d ed. 2005 Supp.). "A 'stocklist' for most public corporations consists of far more than simply a list of stockholders with their addresses and numbers of shares. A stockholder with a proper purpose has a right to obtain subsidiary information available to the corporation including magnetic tape compilations, breakdowns of stockholdings by depository nominees, and (where appropriate) lists of beneficial owners of stock available to the issuer pursuant to [SEC] Rule 14b–1(c) (the 'NOBO list'). Similarly, a shareholder is ordinarily entitled to transfer sheets from the date of the list provided to him to the meeting date, expiration of the tender offer, or other relevant date.

"However, the corporation is not required to manufacture such items for the convenience of the stockholder if the corporation does not already have access to them. In *R.B. Associates of New Jersey, L.P. v. The Gilette Co.,* [C.A. No. 9711 (Del.Ch. Mar.22, 1988)], a stockholder sought to require a corporation to obtain a NOBO list which it did not already have in its possession in order to produce it to the stockholder seeking inspection. The Court of Chancery held:

> Neither broad concepts of fairness, nor the words of Section 220, in my opinion, require that a corporation be forced, in each instance, to exercise the option created by the applicable SEC

rules at the behest of a shareholder. What fairness does require, and what our opinions repeatedly return to, is the principle that relief in a Section 220 case should afford to a shareholder the same information as the corporation has in its books, records, and other papers.''

(b) REPORTING UNDER STATE LAW

MODEL BUS. CORP. ACT §§ 16.20

[See Statutory Supplement]

CAL. CORP. CODE § 1501

[See Statutory Supplement]

N.Y. BUS. CORP. LAW § 624(e)

[See Statutory Supplement]

NOTE ON REPORTING UNDER STATE LAW

The inspection right requires a shareholder to take affirmative action and incur costs to obtain information, and may be defeated in litigation. In contrast, the Securities Exchange Act, which is applicable to corporations that have at least 500 record holders of a class of equity securities and meet certain other conditions, requires the corporation to report certain information to all shareholders without specific shareholder requests. However, a corporation that has less than 500 shares may be publicly held in the sense that its shareholders are scattered and not directly involved either in managing the corporation or in monitoring management. Accordingly, there is a need to require corporations that have significant public ownership, but are not covered by the Securities Exchange Act, to report to their shareholders information on at least some subjects, such as financial results and material conflict-of-interest transactions.

The Model Business Corporation Act partially addresses that need. For example, § 16.20 requires that every corporation must furnish to its shareholders annual financial statements, including a balance sheet and an income statement. The statements must be prepared on the basis of generally accepted accounting principles if the corporation prepares its financial statements on that basis. Many statutes, such as

N.J.Stat.Ann. § 14A:5–28, simply provide that a corporation must furnish "its balance sheet as at the end of the preceding fiscal year, and its profit and loss and surplus statements for such fiscal year" upon a shareholder's written request. Some statutes, like that of Delaware, don't require corporations to furnish financial statements to shareholders even on written request.

SECTION 2. SHAREHOLDER INFORMATIONAL RIGHTS UNDER FEDERAL LAW AND STOCK EXCHANGE RULES

INTRODUCTORY NOTE

Given the limitations on the shareholder's inspection right, and the limited obligations to report under state law, it was probably inevitable that corrective action would be taken to ensure that shareholders are provided with adequate information at the corporation's expense. Two major bodies of rules evolved to alleviate the deficiencies in the inspection right: the Securities Exchange Act of 1934 and the regulations promulgated thereunder, and the rules for listed companies promulgated by various stock exchanges. To put these rules in context, this Section will begin with overviews of the Securities Exchange Act and the stock markets.

(a) AN OVERVIEW OF THE STOCK MARKETS

S. Ross, R. Westerfield & B. Jordan, Fundamentals of Corporate Finance

Sixth ed. 2003.*

Capital Markets and the Corporation

[Two] primary advantages of the corporate form of organization are that ownership can be transferred more quickly and easily than with other forms and that money can be raised more readily. Both of these advantages are significantly enhanced by the existence of financial markets and financial markets play an extremely important role in corporate finance....

A financial market, like any market, is just a way of bringing buyers and sellers together. In financial markets, it is debt and equity securities that are bought and sold. Financial markets differ in detail, however. The most important differences concern the types of securi-

* Copyright, and reprinted with the permission of, The McGraw–Hill Companies.

ties that are traded, how trading is conducted, and who the buyers and sellers are. Some of these differences are discussed next.

Primary versus Secondary Markets

Financial markets function as both primary and secondary markets for debt and equity securities. The term *primary market* refers to the original sale of securities by governments and corporations. The *secondary markets* are those in which these securities are bought and sold after the original sale. Equities are, of course, issued solely by corporations. Debt securities are issued by both governments and corporations. In the discussion that follows, we focus on corporate securities only.

Primary Markets. In a primary market transaction, the corporation is the seller, and the transaction raises money for the corporation. Corporations engage in two types of primary market transactions: public offerings and private placements. A public offering, as the name suggests, involves selling securities to the general public, whereas a private placement is a negotiated sale involving a specific buyer.

By law, public offerings of debt and equity must be registered with the Securities and Exchange Commission (SEC). Registration requires the firm to disclose a great deal of information before selling any securities. The accounting, legal, and selling costs of public offerings can be considerable.

Partly to avoid the various regulatory requirements and the expense of public offerings, debt and equity are often sold privately to large financial institutions such as life insurance companies or mutual funds. Such private placements do not have to be registered with the SEC and do not require the involvement of underwriters (investment banks that specialize in selling securities to the public).

Secondary Markets. A secondary market transaction involves one owner or creditor selling to another. It is therefore the secondary markets that provide the means for transferring ownership of corporate securities. Although a corporation is only directly involved in a primary market transaction (when it sells securities to raise cash), the secondary markets are still critical to large corporations. The reason is that investors are much more willing to purchase securities in a primary market transaction when they know that those securities can later be resold if desired.

Dealer versus Auction Markets. There are two kinds of secondary markets: *auction* markets and *dealer* markets. Generally speaking. dealers buy and sell for themselves, at their own risk. A car dealer, for example. buys and sells automobiles. In contrast, brokers and agents match buyers and sellers, but they do not actually own the commodity that is bought or sold. A real estate agent, for example, does not normally buy and sell houses.

Dealer markets in stocks and long-term debt are called *over-the-counter* (OTC) markets. Most trading in debt securities takes place over the counter. The expression *over the counter* refers to days of old when securities were literally bought and sold at counters in offices around the country. Today, a significant fraction of the market for stocks and almost all of the market for long-term debt have no central location; the many dealers are connected electronically.

Auction markets differ from dealer markets in two ways. First, an auction market or exchange has a physical location (like Wall Street). Second, in a dealer market, most of the buying and selling is done by the dealer. The primary purpose of an auction market, on the other hand, is to match those who wish to sell with those who wish to buy. Dealers play a limited role.

Trading in Corporate Securities. The equity shares of most of the large firms in the United States trade in organized auction markets. The largest such market is the New York Stock Exchange (NYSE), which accounts for more than 85 percent of all the shares traded in auction markets. Other auction exchanges include the American Stock Exchange (AMEX) and regional exchanges such as the Pacific Stock Exchange.

In addition to the stock exchanges, there is a large OTC market for stocks. In 1971, the National Association of Securities Dealers (NASD) made available to dealers and brokers an electronic quotation system called NASDAQ (NASD Automated Quotation system, pronounced "naz-dak" and now spelled "Nasdaq"). There are roughly two times as many companies on Nasdaq as there are on NYSE, but they tend to be much smaller in size and trade less actively. There are exceptions, of course. Both Microsoft and Intel trade OTC, for example....

Listing. Stocks that trade on organized exchange are said to be *listed* on that exchange. In order to be listed, firms must meet certain minimum criteria concerning, for example, asset size and number of shareholders. These criteria differ from one exchange to another.

NYSE has the most stringent requirements of the exchanges in the United States. For example, to be listed on NYSE, a company is expected to have a market value for its publicly held shares of at least $100 million and a total of at least 2,000 shareholders with at least 100 shares each. There are additional minimums on earnings, assets, and number of shares outstanding.

(b) AN OVERVIEW OF THE SEC AND THE SECURITIES EXCHANGE ACT

Securities and Exchange Commission, How the SEC Protects Investors and Maintains Market Integrity
2004 rev.

Securities Exchange Act of 1934.

With this Act, Congress created the Securities and Exchange Commission. The Act empowers the SEC with broad authority over all aspects of the securities industry. This includes the power to register, regulate, and oversee brokerage firms, transfer agents, and clearing agencies as well as the nation's securities self regulatory organizations (SROs). The various stock exchanges, such as the New York Stock Exchange, and American Stock Exchange are SROs. The National Association of Securities Dealers, which operates the NASDAQ system, is also an SRO.

The Act also identifies and prohibits certain types of conduct in the markets and provides the Commission with disciplinary powers over regulated entities and persons associated with them.

The Act also empowers the SEC to require periodic reporting of information by companies with publicly traded securities.

Corporate Reporting

Companies with more than $10 million in assets whose securities are held by more than 500 owners must file annual and other periodic reports. These reports are available to the public through the SEC's EDGAR database.

Proxy Solicitations

The Securities Exchange Act also governs the disclosure in materials used to solicit shareholders' votes in annual or special meetings held for the election of directors and the approval of other corporate action. This information, contained in proxy materials, must be filed with the Commission in advance of any solicitation to ensure compliance with the disclosure rules. Solicitations, whether by management or shareholder groups, must disclose all important facts concerning the issues on which holders are asked to vote.

_____

SECURITIES EXCHANGE ACT § 12(a), (b), (g)

[See Statutory Supplement]

_____

SECURITIES EXCHANGE ACT RULE 12g–1

[See Statutory Supplement]

_____

(c) PERIODIC DISCLOSURE UNDER THE SECURITIES EXCHANGE ACT

_____

SECURITIES EXCHANGE ACT § 13(a)

[See Statutory Supplement]

————

SECURITIES EXCHANGE ACT RULES 13a–1, 13a–11, 13a–13

————

SECURITIES EXCHANGE ACT FORMS 8–K, 10–K, 10–Q

[See Statutory Supplement]

————

NOTE ON PERIODIC REPORTING BY REGISTERED CORPORATIONS

The Securities Exchange Act addresses the informational deficiencies in state law by imposing periodic-reporting requirements on corporations with a security registered under section 12. Section 13 of the Act, and the rules promulgated thereunder, requires such corporations to file a Form 10–K annually, a Form 10–Q quarterly, and a Form 8–K within four business days after the occurrence of certain specified events. Among the matters that trigger an 8–K Report are a change in control of the corporation, the acquisition or disposition of a significant amount of assets, a change of accountants, the termination of a material definitive agreement, the departure of a director or principal officer (CEO, president, chief operating officer, chief financial officer, chief accounting officer, or any person performing similar functions), amendments to the articles or bylaws, amendments to the corporation's code of ethics, and waivers of a provision of the corporation's code of ethics. The Form 10–K must include audited financial statements; management's discussion of the corporation's financial condition and results of operations; and disclosure concerning legal proceedings, developments in the corporation's business, executive compensation, conflict-of-interest transactions, and other specified issues. The Form 10–Q must include quarterly financial data prepared in accordance with generally accepted accounting principles; a management report; and disclosures concerning legal proceedings, defaults on senior securities, and other specified issues. Periodic reporting is also required under the Proxy Rules in connection with the corporation's annual meeting.

The disclosure required by the Securities Exchange Act's periodic reporting requirements is sometimes called *structured* disclosure, because what must be disclosed and how it must be disclosed is structured by the relevant SEC rules. Another example of structured disclosure is the disclosure required under the Securities Act when a corporation makes a public offering of its securities.

Of course, a corporation may make voluntary timely disclosure of material corporate developments even if not required to do so by law. Furthermore, the rules of the major stock exchanges often require listed corporations to make timely disclosure of material developments.

———

(d) DISCLOSURE UNDER STOCK EXCHANGE RULES

———

NEW YORK STOCK EXCHANGE, LISTED COMPANY MANUAL §§ 202.01, 202.03, 202.05, 202.06[1]

[See Statutory Supplement]

SECTION 3.   THE PROXY RULES (I): AN INTRODUCTION

———

NOTE ON TERMINOLOGY

This and the next two Sections concern the Proxy Rules, which are promulgated by the SEC. The following terms are important in considering these Rules:

Proxy holder. A person authorized to vote shares on a shareholder's behalf.

Proxy, form of proxy, or *proxy form.* The written instrument in which such an authorization is embodied. (The term proxy is also sometimes used to mean a proxy holder, but for purposes of clarity that usage will be avoided in this Chapter.)

Proxy solicitation. The process by which shareholders are asked to give their proxies.

Proxy Statement. A written statement sent to shareholders as a means of proxy solicitation.

Proxy materials. The proxy statement and form of proxy.

———

SECURITIES EXCHANGE ACT § 14(a), (c)

———

1. For similar rules, see American Stock Exchange, AMEX Company Guide, §§ 401–405 (Disclosure Policies), 2 CCH, American Stock Exchange Guide § 10,121– 10,125; Nat'l Ass'n Sec. Dealers Manual (CCH) § 5, Schedule D, Part II, § 1806A, at 1571–72.

**SECURITIES EXCHANGE ACT RULES 14a–1–14a–
6, 14c–2, 14c–3, Schedule 14A, Schedule 14C**

[See Statutory Supplement]

———

NOTE—AN OVERVIEW OF THE PROXY RULES

1. *Background.* Proxy voting is the dominant mode of share-holder decisionmaking in publicly held corporations. There are two basic reasons for this. First, shareholders in such corporations are often geographically dispersed, so that a given shareholder may not live near the site of the meeting. Second, a given shareholding will normally represent only a small fraction of a shareholder's total wealth. Accordingly, physical attendance at a shareholders's meeting is normally an uneconomical use of a shareholder's time when he can vote by proxy.

A natural outgrowth of the preference for proxy voting is proxy solicitation—the process of systematically contacting shareholders, and urging them to execute and return proxy forms that authorize named proxyholders to cast the shareholder's votes, either in a manner designated in the proxy form or according to the proxyholder's discretion.

Despite this state of affairs, as of the 1930's state law hardly regulated proxy voting, except in the extreme case in which proxies had been fraudulently solicited. Abuses were notorious and wide-spread. Accordingly, Congress entered the field in 1934 through Section 14(a) of the Securities Exchange Act. In itself, Section 14(a) has no effect on private conduct: its only effect was to authorize the SEC to promulgate rules that will govern private conduct. Pursuant to Section 14(a), the SEC has promulgated a set of Proxy Rules that serve a variety of purposes.

2. *Coverage.* Rule 14a–2 provides that the Proxy Rules "apply to every solicitation of a proxy with respect to securities registered pursuant to section 12 of the Act," with certain exceptions such as "[a]ny solicitation made otherwise than on behalf of the registrant where the total number of persons solicited is not more than ten." The definitions of "proxy" and "solicitation" are extremely broad. Under Rule 14a–1(f), the term "proxy" means "every proxy, consent, or authorization within the meaning of section 14(a) of the Act. The consent or authorization may take the form of failure to object or to dissent." Under Rule 14a–1(l)(1), the term "solicitation" includes "(i) [a]ny request for a proxy . . .; (ii) [a]ny request to execute or not to execute, or to revoke, a proxy; or (iii) [t]he furnishing of a form of proxy or other communication to security holders under circumstances reasonably calculated to result in the procurement, withholding or revocation of a proxy." This language has been given a very expansive interpretation. For example, in Studebaker Corp. v. Gittlin, 360 F.2d 692 (2d Cir.1966), Gittlin, a shareholder in Studebaker, had

solicited authorizations from other Studebaker shareholders to inspect Studebaker's stockholder list for the purpose of meeting the five percent test under the relevant New York inspection statute. Judge Friendly stated:

> ... The assistant general counsel of the SEC ... stated at the argument that the Commission believes § 14(a) should be construed, in all its literal breadth, to include authorizations to inspect stockholders lists, even in cases where obtaining the authorizations was not a step in a planned solicitation of proxies.
>
> We need not go that far to uphold the order of the district court. In SEC v. Okin, 132 F.2d 784 (2d Cir.1943), this court ruled that a letter which did not request the giving of any authorization was subject to the Proxy Rules if it was part of "a continuous plan" intended to end in solicitation and to prepare the way for success. This was the avowed purpose of Gittlin's demand for inspection of the stockholders list. . . .

Id. at 695–96.

3. *Transactional Disclosure.* One purpose of the Proxy Rules is to require full disclosure in connection with transactions that shareholders are being asked to approve, such as mergers, certificate amendments, or election of directors. This purpose is accomplished in the first instance by Rule 14a–3 and Schedule 14A. Rule 14a–3 provides that no solicitation of proxies that is subject to the Proxy Rules shall be made unless the person being solicited "is concurrently furnished or has previously been furnished with a written proxy statement containing the information specified in Schedule 14A." Schedule 14A, in turn, lists in detail the information that must be furnished when specified types of transactions are to be acted upon by the shareholders. Rule 14a–3 and Schedule 14A are backed up by Rule 14a–9, which provides that no solicitation subject to the Proxy Rules shall contain any statement that is false or misleading with respect to any material fact or omits a material fact.

4. *Periodic Disclosure.* The Proxy Rules also require certain forms of annual disclosure. Much of this disclosure is only very loosely related to any specific action the shareholders are asked to vote upon. For example, Rule 14a–3 provides that the proxy statement for an annual meeting at which directors are to be elected must be accompanied by an annual report that includes audited balance sheets for each of the corporation's two most recent fiscal years, audited income statements for its three most recent fiscal years, and certain other information. Under Items 7 and 8 of Schedule 14A, the proxy statement for an annual meeting at which directors are being elected must disclose the compensation of the five most highly paid executives and the executive officers as a group (including not only salary, but bonuses, deferred compensation, stock options, and the like), and significant conflict-of-interest transactions during the corporation's last fiscal year involving, among others, directors, executive officers, and five percent beneficial owners. Under Item 7, the proxy statement for such a meeting must also disclose whether the corporation has audit,

nominating, and compensation committees, and if so, the number of meetings each committee held during the last fiscal year and the functions it performs. Furthermore, if a corporation's stock is registered under section 12, and the corporation proposes to take an action that requires shareholder approval, or to hold an annual meeting at which directors are to be elected, then even if the corporation is not soliciting proxies it must distribute essentially the same information that would be required if it was soliciting proxies. See § 14(c), Regulation 14C, and Schedule 14C. This set of rules has its principal bite where the corporation has a controlling shareholder who can take actions at the shareholder level without soliciting proxies.

5. *Proxy Contests.* Proxy Rule 14a–11 regulates proxy contests, in which insurgents try to oust incumbent directors. Basically, Rule 14a–11 is an adaptation of the salient concepts of other Proxy Rules to the special circumstances of a proxy fight. Its main bite is to require the filing of certain information by insurgents.

6. *Access to the Body of Shareholders.* Proxy Rules 14a–7 and 14a–8 provide mechanisms through which shareholders can communicate with each other. See Section 5, infra.

7. *Mechanics of Proxy Voting.* Still another purpose of the Proxy Rules is to regulate the mechanics of proxy voting itself. This is done, somewhat indirectly, through Rule 14a–4, which governs the form of proxy.

FORM OF PROXY

[See Statutory Supplement]

NOTE ON THE ANNUAL REPORT TO SHAREHOLDERS

When proxies for the election of directors are solicited on behalf of a corporation that is subject to the Proxy Rules, the corporation must send an Annual Report to its shareholders, either in advance of or concurrently with the proxy statement. This Annual Report to shareholders must be distinguished from the annual report on Form 10–K that the corporation must file with the SEC.

[The] annual report to security holders is one of the most widely read disclosure documents, and potentially the best suited for communicating information in an informative, readable and understandable form to security holders and potential investors. The detailed disclosure required in annual reports on Form 10–K is of significant value to securities analysts. Many analysts have ready access to such reports and are able to analyze their contents. Form 10–K reports, however, are of little direct value to the average security holder who ... [does] not have such access and may not have the necessary background and expertise to analyze the contents. The Commission believes that it is necessary to recognize the varying information[al] needs of different users of financial disclosure documents. The Commission considers it essential, therefore, that the annual report to security holders contain meaningful information about the company.

Notice of Proposed Amendments to Rules 14a–3 and 14c–3 Under the Securities Exchange Act of 1934, Exchange Act Release No. 10,591 (Jan. 10, 1974).

The contents of the Annual Report to shareholders are governed by Rule 14a–3. The Report must include, among other things, the corporation's financial statements; selected financial data; and management's discussion and analysis of the corporation's financial condition and results of operations (MD & A). Either the Annual Report or the Proxy Statement must prominently feature an undertaking to furnish a copy of the Form 10–K to any shareholder, without charge, upon written request.

To encourage informality and directness in the Annual Report to shareholders, Rule 146–3(c) provides that the Report is not to be deemed either soliciting material within the Proxy Rules or a "filing" under Securities Exchange Act § 18, which concerns express civil liabilities under that Act. (However, if the Annual Report to shareholders contains a material misstatement or omission, it can serve as the basis for a suit under Rule 10b–5. See Chapter 10, infra.)

————

Randall S. Thomas & Catherine T. Dixon, Aranow & Einhorn's Proxy Contests for Corporate Control*
(3d ed. 1998).

§ 5.03[A][1], [3] 603[A], [D].

Exemption for Unilateral Voting Announcements

As part of the 1992 proxy amendments, the SEC established a new exception to the "solicitation" definition for published or broadcast announcements by stockholders who otherwise are *not* soliciting proxies, of how they plan to vote on any matter submitted for stockholder approval. [Rule 14a–1(*l*)(2)]. This regulatory safe harbor extends to a stockholder's announced reasons for his or her decision to vote, abstain, or withhold proxies....

The new exemption for broadcast or published statements of voting position appears to have lent impetus to recent "Just Vote No" campaigns waged by large public pension funds and other institutional investors to express disapproval of incumbent management's policies. During the proxy seasons immediately following the 1992 adoption of the new safe harbor rule, several stockholder activists relied on its safeguards to publicize their decisions to withhold authority from all or part of the registrant's board slate as a signal of their dissatisfaction with poor corporate performance. These campaigns by large, influential holders have been effective in focusing management attention on shareholder concerns, even where such action is only threatened....

.... *Ten–Person Exemption for Solicitations by Non–Registrants*

Rule 14a–2(b)(2) provides a qualified exemption permitting non-registrant solicitations of up to 10 stockholders to be made without incurring proxy filing and disclosure obligations. Originally adopted in 1942, this exemption has continuing utility for those who wish to "test the waters" by consulting with a few key stockholders prior to deciding whether to launch a regulated solicitation. Where the ownership of a large amount of a public company's common stock is concentrated in the portfolios of 10 or fewer institutional stockholders, proxies representing a substantial proportion of the total voting power may be secured by an insurgent without conforming to any proxy rule except Rule 14a–9....

An insurgent's preliminary discussions with target company shareholders protected by Rule 14a–2(b)(2) nonetheless may constitute "group" activities requiring the filing of a group Schedule 13D. Communications among putative dissidents about whether to initiate a proxy fight similarly may implicate the Section 13(d) "group" concept....

Rules Governing the Delivery and Filing of the Proxy (Or Information) Statement and Other Soliciting Materials

... [A]ll soliciting materials *except* the proxy statement and form of proxy may be filed with (or mailed for filing to) the SEC in final or "definitive" form at the time they are first published, sent, or given to shareholders, whether such use occurs prior or subsequent to the circulation of the definitive proxy statement [but need not be filed with the Commission for review before being disseminated]....

Any person soliciting proxies from holders of Section 12–registered securities must furnish, to each shareholder solicited, a written proxy statement setting forth the information prescribed by the line-item requirement of Schedule 14A. [Normally,] the proxy statement must be delivered to each solicitee prior to or contemporaneously with the solicitation. If the solicitation is conducted on behalf of the registrant and relates to the annual meeting or, respectively, to a special meeting or action sought to be taken by written consent in lieu of the annual meeting, each proxy statement must be accompanied or preceded by the annual report to shareholders....

Unless eligible for the "plain-vanilla" exclusion discussed ... [infra,] five copies of both the proxy statement and form of proxy must be filed in preliminary form with the SEC at least ten calendar days in advance of the date on which the definitive version is first circulated to shareholders. During this 10–day period, the staff of the Division of

Corporation Finance may review the preliminary materials (along with any other soliciting materials on file) for compliance with the disclosure requirements of Schedule 14A, Rule 14a–9 (proxy antifraud rule) and Rule 14a–4 (form of proxy; scope of discretionary voting authority) . . . .

Filing Requirements for Preliminary and Definitive Proxy Statements and Forms of Proxy–Exclusion for "Plain–Vanilla" Solicitations

In late 1987, the SEC created an exclusion for specified "plain-vanilla" proxy or information statements "to relieve registrants and the SEC of unnecessary administrative burdens and preparation and processing costs associated with the filing and processing of proxy materials . . . subject to selective [staff] review procedures, but ordinarily . . . not selected for review in preliminary form." Under Rule 14a–6(a), the registrant is compelled to file its proxy (or information) statements solely in definitive form [but not in preliminary form] for solicitations in the following subject-matter categories: (a) the election of directors; (b) the election, approval, or ratification of accountants; (c) a shareholder proposal carried in the registrant's proxy statement pursuant to Rule 14a–8; and/or (d) the approval or ratification of a registrant's executive or director compensation plan, or amendments thereto . . . .

SECTION 4. THE PROXY RULES (II): PRIVATE ACTIONS UNDER THE PROXY RULES

SECURITIES EXCHANGE ACT RULE 14a–9

[See Statutory Supplement]

NOTE ON J.I. CASE CO. v. BORAK

In J.I. Case Co. v. Borak, 377 U.S. 426, 84 S.Ct. 1555, 12 L.Ed.2d 423 (1964), the Supreme Court held that a shareholder could bring a private action for violation of the Proxy Rules, although neither the 1934 Act nor the Proxy Rules themselves explicitly provide for such an action. The rationale in *Borak* was as follows:

> . . . Private enforcement of the proxy rules provides a necessary supplement to Commission action. As in antitrust treble damage litigation, the possibility of civil damages or injunctive relief serves as a most effective weapon in the enforcement of the proxy requirements. The Commission advises that it examines over 2,000 proxy statements annually and each of them must necessarily be expedited. Time does not permit an independent examination of the facts set out in the proxy material and this

results in the Commission's acceptance of the representations contained therein at their face value, unless contrary to other material on file with it. Indeed, on the allegations of respondent's complaint, the proxy material failed to disclose alleged unlawful market manipulation of the stock of ATC, and this unlawful manipulation would not have been apparent to the Commission until after the merger.

We, therefore, believe that under the circumstances here it is the duty of the courts to be alert to provide such remedies as are necessary to make effective the congressional purpose.

Id. at 432–33, 84 S.Ct. at 1560.

————

WYANDOTTE v. U.S., 389 U.S. 191, 202, 88 S.Ct. 379, 19 L.Ed.2d 407 (1967). "In [J.I. Case Co. v. Borak] we concluded that criminal liability was inadequate to ensure the full effectiveness of the statute which Congress had intended. Because the interest of the plaintiffs in those cases fell within the class that the statute was intended to protect, and because the harm that had occurred was of the type that the statute was intended to protect, and because the harm that had occurred was of the type that the statute was intended to forestall, we held that civil actions were proper. That conclusion was in accordance with a general rule of the law of torts. See Restatement (Second) of Torts § 286."

————

CORT v. ASH, 422 U.S. 66, 95 S.Ct. 2080, 45 L.Ed.2d 26 (1975). "In determining whether a private remedy is implicit in a statute not expressly providing one, several factors are relevant. First, is the plaintiff 'one of the class for whose *especial* benefit the statute was enacted,' Texas & Pacific R. Co. v. Rigsby, 241 U.S. 33, 39, 36 S.Ct. 482, 484, 60 L.Ed. 874 (1916) (emphasis supplied)—that is, does the statute create a federal right in favor of the plaintiff? Second, is there any indication of legislative intent, explicit or implicit, either to create such a remedy or to deny one? . . . Third, is it consistent with the underlying purposes of the legislative scheme to imply such a remedy for the plaintiff? . . . And finally, is the cause of action one traditionally relegated to state law, in an area basically the concern of the States, so that it would be inappropriate to infer a cause of action based solely on federal law?"

[handwritten margin note: Factors for whether private remedy is implicit in a statute not providing one.]

————

[handwritten: see casenotes]

Mills v. Electric Auto–Lite Co.

Supreme Court of the United States, 1970.
396 U.S. 375, 90 S.Ct. 616, 24 L.Ed.2d 593.

■ Mr. JUSTICE HARLAN delivered the opinion of the Court.

This case requires us to consider a basic aspect of the implied private right of action for violation of § 14(a) of the Securities Exchange Act of 1934,[1] recognized by this Court in J.I. Case Co. v. Borak, 377 U.S. 426, 84 S.Ct. 1555, 12 L.Ed.2d 423 (1964). As in *Borak* the asserted wrong is that a corporate merger was accomplished through the use of a proxy statement that was materially false or misleading. The question with which we deal is what causal relationship must be shown between such a statement and the merger to establish a cause of action based on the violation of the Act.

I

Petitioners were shareholders of the Electric Auto–Lite Company until 1963, when it was merged into Mergenthaler Linotype Company. They brought suit on the day before the shareholders' meeting at which the vote was to take place on the merger, against Auto–Lite, Mergenthaler, and a third company, American Manufacturing Company, Inc. The complaint sought an injunction against the voting by Auto–Lite's management of all proxies obtained by means of an allegedly misleading proxy solicitation; however, it did not seek a temporary restraining order, and the voting went ahead as scheduled the following day. Several months later petitioners filed an amended complaint, seeking to have the merger set aside and to obtain such other relief as might be proper.

In Count II of the amended complaint, which is the only count before us,[5] petitioners predicated jurisdiction on § 27 of the 1934 Act, 15 U.S.C. § 78aa. They alleged that the proxy statement sent out by the Auto–Lite management to solicit shareholders' votes in favor of the merger was misleading, in violation of § 14(a) of the Act and SEC Rule 14a–9 thereunder. (17 CFR § 240.14a–9.) Petitioners recited that before the merger Mergenthaler owned over 50% of the outstanding shares of Auto–Lite common stock, and had been in control of Auto–Lite for two years. American Manufacturing in turn owned about one-third of the outstanding shares of Mergenthaler, and for two years had been in voting control of Mergenthaler and, through it, of Auto–Lite. Petitioners charged that in light of these circumstances the proxy statement was misleading in that it told Auto–Lite shareholders that their board of directors recommended approval of the merger without also informing them that all 11 of Auto–Lite's directors were nominees of Mergenthaler and were under the "control and domination of Mergenthaler." Petitioners asserted the right to complain of this alleged violation both derivatively on behalf of Auto–Lite and as representatives of the class of all its minority shareholders.

On petitioners' motion for summary judgment with respect to Count II, the District Court for the Northern District of Illinois ruled as a matter of law that the claimed defect in the proxy statement was, in light of the circumstances in which the statement was made, a material

1. 48 Stat. 895, as amended, 15 U.S.C. § 78n(a).

5. In the other two counts, petitioners alleged common-law fraud and that the merger was *ultra vires* under Ohio law.

omission. The District Court concluded, from its reading of the *Borak* opinion, that it had to hold a hearing on the issue whether there was "a causal connection between the finding that there has been a violation of the disclosure requirements of § 14(a) and the alleged injury to the plaintiffs" before it could consider what remedies would be appropriate. (Unreported opinion dated February 14, 1966.)

After holding such a hearing, the court found that under the terms of the merger agreement, an affirmative vote of two-thirds of the Auto–Lite shares was required for approval of the merger, and that the respondent companies owned and controlled about 54% of the outstanding shares. Therefore, to obtain authorization of the merger, respondents had to secure the approval of a substantial number of the minority shareholders. At the stockholders' meeting, approximately 950,000 shares, out of 1,160,000 shares outstanding, were voted in favor of the merger. This included 317,000 votes obtained by proxy from the minority shareholders, votes that were "necessary and indispensable to the approval of the merger." The District Court concluded that a causal relationship had thus been shown, and it granted an interlocutory judgment in favor of petitioners on the issue of liability, referring the case to a master for consideration of appropriate relief. (Unreported findings and conclusions dated Sept. 26, 1967; opinion reported at 281 F.Supp. 826 (1967)).

The District Court made the certification required by 28 U.S.C. § 1292(b), and respondents took an interlocutory appeal to the Court of Appeals for the Seventh Circuit. That court affirmed the District Court's conclusion that the proxy statement was materially deficient, but reversed on the question of causation. The court acknowledged that, if an injunction had been sought a sufficient time before the stockholders' meeting, "corrective measures would have been appropriate." 403 F.2d 429, 435 (1968). However, since this suit was brought too late for preventive action, the courts had to determine "whether the misleading statement and omission caused the submission of sufficient proxies," as a prerequisite to a determination of liability under the Act. If the respondents could show, "by a preponderance of probabilities, that the merger would have received a sufficient vote even if the proxy statement had not been misleading in the respect found," petitioners would be entitled to no relief of any kind. *Id.,* at 436.

The Court of Appeals acknowledged that this test corresponds to the common-law fraud test of whether the injured party relied on the misrepresentation. However, rightly concluding that "[r]eliance by thousands of individuals, as here, can scarcely be inquired into" (*id.,* at 436 n. 10), the court ruled that the issue was to be determined by proof of the fairness of the terms of the merger. If respondents could show that the merger had merit and was fair to the minority shareholders, the trial court would be justified in concluding that a sufficient number of shareholders would have approved the merger had there been no deficiency in the proxy statement. In that case respondents would be entitled to a judgment in their favor.

Claiming that the Court of Appeals has construed this Court's decision in *Borak* in a manner that frustrates the statute's policy of enforcement through private litigation, the petitioners then sought review in this Court. We granted certiorari, 394 U.S. 971, 89 S.Ct. 1470, 22 L.Ed.2d 752 (1969), believing that resolution of this basic issue should be made at this stage of the litigation and not postponed until after a trial under the Court of Appeals' decision.

II

As we stressed in *Borak,* § 14(a) stemmed from a congressional belief that "[f]air corporate suffrage is an important right that should attach to every equity security bought on a public exchange." H.R.Rep. No. 1383, 73d Cong., 2d Sess., 13. The provision was intended to promote "the free exercise of the voting rights of stockholders" by ensuring that proxies would be solicited with "explanation to the stockholder of the real nature of the questions for which authority to cast his vote is sought." *Id.,* at 14; S.Rep. No. 792, 73d Cong., 2d Sess., 12; see 377 U.S., at 431, 377 U.S. 426, 84 S.Ct. 1555, 1559, 12 L.Ed.2d 423. The decision below, by permitting all liability to be foreclosed on the basis of a finding that the merger was fair, would allow the stockholders to be bypassed, at least where the only legal challenge to the merger is a suit for retrospective relief after the meeting has been held. A judicial appraisal of the merger's merits could be substituted for the actual and informed vote of the stockholders.

The result would be to insulate from private redress an entire category of proxy violations—those relating to matters other than the terms of the merger. Even outrageous misrepresentations in a proxy solicitation, if they did not relate to the terms of the transaction, would give rise to no cause of action under § 14(a). Particularly if carried over to enforcement actions by the Securities and Exchange Commission itself, such a result would subvert the congressional purpose of ensuring full and fair disclosure to shareholders.

Further, recognition of the fairness of the merger as a complete defense would confront small shareholders with an additional obstacle to making a successful challenge to a proposal recommended through a defective proxy statement. The risk that they would be unable to rebut the corporation's evidence of the fairness of the proposal, and thus to establish their cause of action, would be bound to discourage such shareholders from the private enforcement of the proxy rules that "provides a necessary supplement to Commission action." J.I. Case Co. v. Borak, 377 U.S., at 432, 84 S.Ct. at 1560.[9]

---

9. The Court of Appeals' ruling that "causation" may be negated by proof of the fairness of the merger also rests on a dubious behavioral assumption. There is no justification for presuming that the shareholders of every corporation are willing to accept any and every fair merger offer put before them; yet such a presumption is implicit in the opinion of the Court of Appeals. That court gave no indication of what evidence petitioners might adduce, once respondents had established that the merger proposal was equitable, in order to show that the shareholders would nevertheless have rejected it if the solicitation had not been misleading. Proof of actual reliance by thousands of individuals would, as the court acknowledged, not be feasible, see R. Jennings & H. Marsh, Securi-

Such a frustration of the congressional policy is not required by anything in the wording of the statute or in our opinion in the *Borak* case. Section 14(a) declares it "unlawful" to solicit proxies in contravention of Commission rules, and SEC Rule 14a–9 prohibits solicitations "containing any statement which . . . is false or misleading with respect to any material fact, or which omits to state any material fact necessary in order to make the statements therein not false or misleading. . . ." Use of a solicitation that is materially misleading is itself a violation of law, as the Court of Appeals recognized in stating that injunctive relief would be available to remedy such a defect if sought prior to the stockholders' meeting. In *Borak,* which came to this Court on a dismissal of the complaint, the Court limited its inquiry to whether a violation of § 14(a) gives rise to "a federal cause of action for rescission or damages," 377 U.S., at 428, 84 S.Ct. at 1558. Referring to the argument made by petitioners there "that the merger can be dissolved only if it was fraudulent or non-beneficial, issues upon which the proxy material would not bear," the Court stated: "But the causal relationship of the proxy material and the merger are questions of fact to be resolved at trial, not here. We therefore do not discuss this point further." *Id.,* at 431, 84 S.Ct. at 1559. In the present case there has been a hearing specifically directed to the causation problem. The question before the Court is whether the facts found on the basis of that hearing are sufficient in law to establish petitioners' cause of action, and we conclude that they are.

Where the misstatement or omission in a proxy statement has been shown to be "material," as it was found to be here, that determination itself indubitably embodies a conclusion that the defect was of such a character that it might have been considered important by a reasonable shareholder who was in the process of deciding how to vote.[10] This requirement that the defect have a significant *propensity* to affect the voting process is found in the express terms of Rule 14a–9, and it adequately serves the purpose of ensuring that a cause of action cannot be established by proof of a defect so trivial, or so unrelated to the transaction for which approval is sought, that correc-

---

ties Regulation, Cases and Materials 1001 (2d ed. 1968); and reliance on the *nondisclosure* of a fact is a particularly difficult matter to define or prove, see 3 L. Loss, Securities Regulation, 1766 (2d ed. 1961). In practice, therefore, the objective fairness of the proposal would seemingly be determinative of liability. But, in view of the many other factors that might lead shareholders to prefer their current position to that of owners of a larger, combined enterprise, it is pure conjecture to assume that the fairness of the proposal will always be determinative of their vote. Cf. Wirtz v. Hotel, Motel & Club Employees Union, 391 U.S. 492, 508, 88 S.Ct. 1743, 1752, 20 L.Ed.2d 763 (1968).

10. . . . In this case, where the misleading aspect of the solicitation involved failure to reveal a serious conflict of interest on the part of the directors, the Court of Appeals concluded that the crucial question in determining materiality was "whether the minority shareholders were sufficiently alerted to the board's relationship to their adversary to be on their guard." 403 F.2d at 434. An adequate disclosure of this relationship would have warned the stockholders to give more careful scrutiny to the terms of the merger than they might to one recommended by an entirely disinterested board. Thus, the failure to make such a disclosure was found to be a material defect "as a matter of law," thwarting the informed decision at which the statute aims, regardless of whether the terms of the merger were such that a reasonable stockholder would have approved the transaction after more careful analysis. See also Swanson v. American Consumer Industries, Inc., 415 F.2d 1326 (C.A.7th Cir.1969).

tion of the defect or imposition of liability would not further the interests protected by § 14(a).

There is no need to supplement this requirement, as did the Court of Appeals, with a requirement of proof of whether the defect actually had a decisive effect on the voting. Where there has been a finding of materiality, a shareholder has made a sufficient showing of causal relationship between the violation and the injury for which he seeks redress if, as here, he proves that the proxy solicitation itself, rather than the particular defect in the solicitation materials, was an essential link in the accomplishment of the transaction. This objective test will avoid the impracticalities of determining how many votes were affected, and, by resolving doubts in favor of those the statute is designed to protect, will effectuate the congressional policy of ensuring that the shareholders are able to make an informed choice when they are consulted on corporate transactions. . . .

III

Our conclusion that petitioners have established their case by showing that proxies necessary to approval of the merger were obtained by means of a materially misleading solicitation implies nothing about the form of relief to which they may be entitled. We held in *Borak* that upon finding a violation the courts were "to be alert to provide such remedies as are necessary to make effective the congressional purpose," noting specifically that such remedies are not to be limited to prospective relief. 377 U.S., at 433, 434, 84 S.Ct. at 1560. In devising retrospective relief for violation of the proxy rules, the federal courts should consider the same factors that would govern the relief granted for any similar illegality or fraud. One important factor may be the fairness of the terms of the merger. Possible forms of relief will include setting aside the merger or granting other equitable relief, but, as the Court of Appeals below noted, nothing in the statutory policy "requires the court to unscramble a corporate transaction merely because a violation occurred." 403 F.2d at 436. In selecting a remedy the lower courts should exercise " 'the sound discretion which guides the determinations of courts of equity,' " keeping in mind the role of equity as "the instrument for nice adjustment and reconciliation between the public interest and private needs as well as between competing private claims." Hecht Co. v. Bowles, 321 U.S. 321, 329–330, 64 S.Ct. 587, 591–592, 88 L.Ed. 754 (1944), quoting from Meredith v. Winter Haven, 320 U.S. 228, 235, 64 S.Ct. 7, 11, 88 L.Ed. 9 (1943). . . .

. . . [A] determination of what relief should be granted in Auto-Lite's name must hinge on whether setting aside the merger would be in the best interests of the shareholders as a whole. In short, in the context of a suit such as this one, § 29(b) leaves the matter of relief where it would be under *Borak* without specific statutory language— the merger should be set aside only if a court of equity concludes, from all the circumstances, that it would be equitable to do so. Cf. SEC

v. National Securities, Inc., 393 U.S. 453, 456, 463–464, 89 S.Ct. 564, 566, 570, 21 L.Ed.2d 668 (1969).

Monetary relief will, of course, also be a possibility. Where the defect in the proxy solicitation relates to the specific terms of the merger, the district court might appropriately order an accounting to ensure that the shareholders receive the value that was represented as coming to them. On the other hand, where, as here, the misleading aspect of the solicitation did not relate to terms of the merger, monetary relief might be afforded to the shareholders only if the merger resulted in a reduction of the earnings or earnings potential of their holdings. In short, damages should be recoverable only to the extent that they can be shown. If commingling of the assets and operations of the merged companies makes it impossible to establish direct injury from the merger, relief might be predicated on a determination of the fairness of the terms of the merger at the time it was approved. These questions, of course, are for decision in the first instance by the District Court on remand, and our singling out of some of the possibilities is not intended to exclude others. . . .

For the foregoing reasons we conclude that the judgment of the Court of Appeals should be vacated and the case remanded to that court for further proceedings consistent with this opinion.

It is so ordered.

[The opinion of Justice Black, concurring in part and dissenting in part, is omitted.]

NOTE ON FURTHER PROCEEDINGS IN MILLS v. ELECTRIC AUTO–LITE

On remand, the District Court held the exchange to be unfair and awarded damages of $1,233,918.35, as well as approximately $740,000 in pre-judgment interest. The Seventh Circuit reversed, concluding that the merger terms were fair and the plaintiff was therefore not entitled to damages. 552 F.2d 1239 (7th Cir.1977), cert. denied, 434 U.S. 922, 98 S.Ct. 398, 54 L.Ed.2d 279.

NOTE ON TSC INDUSTRIES v. NORTHWAY, INC.

In TSC Industries, Inc. v. Northway, Inc., 426 U.S. 438, 96 S.Ct. 2126, 48 L.Ed.2d 757 (1976), the Supreme Court addressed the issue of how materiality was to be defined, as follows:

> . . . [I]n *Mills,* . . . we held that there was no need to demonstrate that the alleged defect in the proxy statement actually had a decisive effect on the voting. So long as the misstatement or omission was material, the causal relation between violation and injury is sufficiently established, we concluded, if "the proxy solicitation itself . . . was an essential link in the accomplishment

of the transaction." 396 U.S., at 385, 90 S.Ct., at 622. After *Mills*, then, the content given to the notion of materiality assumes heightened significance. . . .

The question of materiality, it is universally agreed, is an objective one, involving the significance of an omitted or misrepresented fact to a reasonable investor. Variations in the formulation of a general test of materiality occur in the articulation of just how significant a fact must be or, put another way, how certain it must be that the fact would affect a reasonable investor's judgment. . . .

What is Material?

The Court of Appeals in this case concluded that material facts include "all facts which a reasonable shareholder *might* consider important." 512 F.2d, at 330 (emphasis added). This formulation of the test of materiality has been explicitly rejected by at least two courts as setting too low a threshold for the imposition of liability under Rule 14a–9. Gerstle v. Gamble-Skogmo, Inc., 478 F.2d 1281, 1301–1302 (C.A.2 1973); Smallwood v. Pearl Brewing Co., 489 F.2d 579, 603–604 (C.A.5 1974). . . .

Rejected Test

. . . [T]he disclosure policy embodied in the proxy regulations is not without limit. See id., at 384, 90 S.Ct., at 621. Some information is of such dubious significance that insistence on its disclosure may accomplish more harm than good. The potential liability for a Rule 14a–9 violation can be great indeed, and if the standard of materiality is unnecessarily low, not only may the corporation and its management be subjected to liability for insignificant omissions or misstatements, but also management's fear of exposing itself to substantial liability may cause it simply to bury the shareholder in an avalanche of trivial information—a result that is hardly conducive to informed decisionmaking. Precisely these dangers are presented, we think, by the definition of a material fact adopted by the Court of Appeals in this case—a fact which a reasonable shareholder *might* consider important. We agree with Judge Friendly, speaking for the Court of Appeals in *Gerstle*, that the "might" formulation is "too suggestive of mere possibility, however unlikely." 478 F.2d, at 1302.

The general standard of materiality that we think best comports with the policies of Rule 14a–9 is as follows: an omitted fact is material if there is a substantial likelihood that a reasonable shareholder would consider it important in deciding how to vote. This standard is fully consistent with *Mills* general description of materiality as a requirement that "the defect have a significant *propensity* to affect the voting process." It does not require proof of a substantial likelihood that disclosure of the omitted fact would have caused the reasonable investor to change his vote. What the standard does contemplate is a showing of a substantial likelihood that, under all the circumstances, the omitted fact would have assumed actual significance in the deliberations of the reasonable shareholder. Put another way, there must be a substantial likelihood that the disclosure of the omitted fact would have

Test

been viewed by the reasonable investor as having significantly altered the "total mix" of information made available.

Virginia Bankshares, Inc. v. Sandberg

Supreme Court of the United States, 1991.
501 U.S. 1083, 111 S.Ct. 2749, 115 L.Ed.2d 929.

See Casebriefs

■ . . . JUSTICE SOUTER delivered the opinion of the Court.

Section 14(a) of the Securities Exchange Act of 1934, 48 Stat. 895, 15 U.S.C. § 78n(a), authorizes the Securities and Exchange Commission to adopt rules for the solicitation of proxies, and prohibits their violation. In J.I. Case Co. v. Borak, 377 U.S. 426, 84 S.Ct. 1555, 12 L.Ed.2d 423 (1964), we first recognized an implied private right of action for the breach of § 14(a) as implemented by SEC Rule 14a–9, which prohibits the solicitation of proxies by means of materially false or misleading statements.[2]

The questions before us are whether a statement couched in conclusory or qualitative terms purporting to explain directors' reasons for recommending certain corporate action can be materially misleading within the meaning of Rule 14a–9, and whether causation of damages compensable under § 14(a) can be shown by a member of a class of minority shareholders whose votes are not required by law or corporate bylaw to authorize the corporate action subject to the proxy solicitation. We hold that knowingly false statements of reasons may be actionable even though conclusory in form, but that respondents have failed to demonstrate the equitable basis required to extend the § 14(a) private action to such shareholders when any indication of congressional intent to do so is lacking.

I

In December 1986, First American Bankshares, Inc., (FABI), a bank holding company, began a "freeze-out" merger, in which the First American Bank of Virginia (Bank) eventually merged into Virginia Bankshares, Inc., (VBI), a wholly owned subsidiary of FABI. VBI owned 85% of the Bank's shares, the remaining 15% being in the hands of some 2,000 minority shareholders. FABI hired the investment banking firm of Keefe, Bruyette & Woods (KBW) to give an opinion on the appropriate price for shares of the minority holders, who would lose their interests in the Bank as a result of the merger. Based on market quotations and unverified information from FABI, KBW gave the Bank's executive committee an opinion that $42 a share would be a

---

2. . . .

The Federal Deposit Insurance Corporation (FDIC) administers and enforces the securities laws with respect to the activities of federally insured and regulated banks. See Section 12(i) of the Exchange Act, 15 U.S.C. § 78*l*(i). An FDIC rule also prohibits materially misleading statements in the solicitation of proxies, 12 CFR § 335.206 (1991), and is essentially identical to Rule 14a–9. See generally Brief for SEC et al. as Amici Curiae 4, n. 5.

fair price for the minority stock. The executive committee approved the merger proposal at that price, and the full board followed suit.

Although Virginia law required only that such a merger proposal be submitted to a vote at a shareholders' meeting, and that the meeting be preceded by circulation of a statement of information to the shareholders, the directors nevertheless solicited proxies for voting on the proposal at the annual meeting set for April 21, 1987.[3] In their solicitation, the directors urged the proposal's adoption and stated they had approved the plan because of its opportunity for the minority shareholders to achieve a "high" value, which they elsewhere described as a "fair" price, for their stock.

Although most minority shareholders gave the proxies requested, respondent Sandberg did not, and after approval of the merger she sought damages in the United States District Court for the Eastern District of Virginia from VBI, FABI, and the directors of the Bank. She pleaded two counts, one for soliciting proxies in violation of § 14(a) and Rule 14a–9, and the other for breaching fiduciary duties owed to the minority shareholders under state law. Under the first count, Sandberg alleged, among other things, that the directors had not believed that the price offered was high or that the terms of the merger were fair, but had recommended the merger only because they believed they had no alternative if they wished to remain on the board. At trial, Sandberg invoked language from this Court's opinion in Mills v. Electric Auto–Lite Co., 396 U.S. 375, 385, 90 S.Ct. 616, 622, 24 L.Ed.2d 593 (1970), to obtain an instruction that the jury could find for her without a showing of her own reliance on the alleged misstatements, so long as they were material and the proxy solicitation was an "essential link" in the merger process.

The jury's verdicts were for Sandberg on both counts, after finding violations of Rule 14a–9 by all defendants and a breach of fiduciary duties by the Bank's directors. The jury awarded Sandberg $18 a share, having found that she would have received $60 if her stock had been valued adequately....

On appeal, the United States Court of Appeals for the Fourth Circuit affirmed ..., holding that certain statements in the proxy solicitation were materially misleading for purposes of the Rule, and that respondents could maintain their action even though their votes had not been needed to effectuate the merger. 891 F.2d 1112 (1989).[4] We granted certiorari because of the importance of the issues presented. 495 U.S. 903, 110 S.Ct. 1921, 109 L.Ed.2d 285 (1990).

II

The Court of Appeals affirmed petitioners' liability for two statements found to have been materially misleading in violation of § 14(a)

---

3. Had the directors chosen to issue a statement instead of a proxy solicitation, they would have been subject to an SEC antifraud provision analogous to Rule 14a–9. See 17 CFR 240.14c–6 (1990). See also 15 U.S.C. § 78n(c).

4. The Court of Appeals reversed the District Court, however, on its refusal to certify a class of all minority shareholders in Sandberg's action. Consequently, it ruled that petitioners were liable to all of the Bank's former minority shareholders for $18 per share. 891 F.2d, at 1119.

of the Act, one of which was that "The Plan of Merger has been approved by the Board of Directors because it provides an opportunity for the Bank's public shareholders to achieve a high value for their shares." App. to Pet. for Cert. 53a. Petitioners argue that statements of opinion or belief incorporating indefinite and unverifiable expressions cannot be actionable as misstatements of material fact within the meaning of Rule 14a–9, and that such a declaration of opinion or belief should never be actionable when placed in a proxy solicitation incorporating statements of fact sufficient to enable readers to draw their own, independent conclusions.

A

We consider first the actionability per se of statements of reasons, opinion or belief. Because such a statement by definition purports to express what is consciously on the speaker's mind, we interpret the jury verdict as finding that the directors' statements of belief and opinion were made with knowledge that the directors did not hold the beliefs or opinions expressed, and we confine our discussion to statements so made.[5] That such statements may be materially significant raises no serious question. The meaning of the materiality requirement for liability under § 14(a) was discussed at some length in TSC Industries, Inc. v. Northway, Inc., 426 U.S. 438, 96 S.Ct. 2126, 48 L.Ed.2d 757 (1976), where we held a fact to be material "if there is a substantial likelihood that a reasonable shareholder would consider it important in deciding how to vote." Id., at 449, 96 S.Ct., at 2132. We think there is no room to deny that a statement of belief by corporate directors about a recommended course of action, or an explanation of their reasons for recommending it, can take on just that importance. Shareholders know that directors usually have knowledge and expertness far exceeding the normal investor's resources, and the directors' perceived superiority is magnified even further by the common knowledge that state law customarily obliges them to exercise their judgment in the shareholders' interest. Cf. Day v. Avery, 179 U.S.App.D.C. 63, 71, 548 F.2d 1018, 1026 (1976) (action for misrepresentation). Naturally, then, the share owner faced with a proxy request will think it important to know the directors' beliefs about the course they recommend, and their specific reasons for urging the stockholders to embrace it.

B

1

But, assuming materiality, the question remains whether statements of reasons, opinions, or beliefs are statements "with respect to ... material fact[s]" so as to fall within the strictures of the Rule. Petitioners argue that we would invite wasteful litigation of amorphous issues outside the readily provable realm of fact if we were to

---

5. In TSC Industries, Inc. v. Northway, Inc., 426 U.S. 438, 444, n. 7, 96 S.Ct. 2126, 2130, n. 7, 48 L.Ed.2d 757 (1976), we reserved the question whether scienter was necessary for liability generally under § 14(a). We reserve it still.

recognize liability here on proof that the directors did not recommend the merger for the stated reason. . . .

Attacks on the truth of directors' statements of reasons or belief, however, need carry no such threats. Such statements are factual in two senses: as statements that the directors do act for the reasons given or hold the belief stated and as statements about the subject matter of the reason or belief expressed. In neither sense does the proof or disproof of such statements implicate the concerns expressed in Blue Chip Stamps [v. Manor Drug Stores, 421 U.S. 723, 95 S.Ct. 1917, 44 L.Ed. 539 (1975)]. The root of those concerns was a plaintiff's capacity to manufacture claims of hypothetical action, unconstrained by independent evidence. Reasons for directors' recommendations or statements of belief are, in contrast, characteristically matters of corporate record subject to documentation, to be supported or attacked by evidence of historical fact outside a plaintiff's control. Such evidence would include not only corporate minutes and other statements of the directors themselves, but circumstantial evidence bearing on the facts that would reasonably underlie the reasons claimed and the honesty of any statement that those reasons are the basis for a recommendation or other action, a point that becomes especially clear when the reasons or beliefs go to valuations in dollars and cents.

It is no answer to argue, as petitioners do, that the quoted statement on which liability was predicated did not express a reason in dollars and cents, but focused instead on the "indefinite and unverifiable" term, "high," value, much like the similar claim that the merger's terms were "fair" to shareholders. The objection ignores the fact that such conclusory terms in a commercial context are reasonably understood to rest on a factual basis that justifies them as accurate, the absence of which renders them misleading. Provable facts either furnish good reasons to make a conclusory commercial judgment, or they count against it, and expressions of such judgments can be uttered with knowledge of truth or falsity just like more definite statements, and defended or attacked through the orthodox evidentiary process that either substantiates their underlying justifications or tends to disprove their existence. . . . In this case, whether $42 was "high," and the proposal "fair" to the minority shareholders depended on whether provable facts about the Bank's assets, and about actual and potential levels of operation, substantiated a value that was above, below, or more or less at the $42 figure, when assessed in accordance with recognized methods of valuation.

Respondents adduced evidence for just such facts in proving that the statement was misleading about its subject matter and a false expression of the directors' reasons. Whereas the proxy statement described the $42 price as offering a premium above both book value and market price, the evidence indicated that a calculation of the book figure based on the appreciated value of the Bank's real estate holdings eliminated any such premium. The evidence on the significance of market price showed that KBW had conceded that the market was closed, thin and dominated by FABI, facts omitted from the statement. There was, indeed, evidence of a "going concern" value for the Bank in excess of $60 per share of common stock, another fact never disclosed. However conclusory the directors' statement may have been, then, it was open to attack by garden-variety evidence, subject neither to a plaintiff's control nor ready manufacture, and there was no undue risk of open-ended liability or uncontrollable litigation in allowing respondents the opportunity for recovery on the allegation that it was misleading to call $42 "high."

This analysis comports with the holding that marked our nearest prior approach to the issue faced here, in *TSC Industries,* 426 U.S., at 454–55, 96 S.Ct., at 2135. There, to be sure, we reversed summary judgment for a *Borak* plaintiff who had sued on a description of proposed compensation for minority shareholders as offering a "substantial premium over current market values." But we held only that on the case's undisputed facts the conclusory adjective "substantial" was not materially misleading as a necessary matter of law, and our remand for trial assumed that such a description could be both materially misleading within the meaning of Rule 14a–9 and actionable under § 14(a). See *TSC Industries,* supra, at 458–460, 463–464, 96 S.Ct., at 2136–2138, 2139.

2

Under § 14(a), then, a plaintiff is permitted to prove a specific statement of reason knowingly false or misleadingly incomplete, even when stated in conclusory terms. In reaching this conclusion we have considered statements of reasons of the sort exemplified here, which misstate the speaker's reasons and also mislead about the stated subject matter (e.g., the value of the shares). A statement of belief may be open to objection only in the former respect, however, solely as a misstatement of the psychological fact of the speaker's belief in what he says. In this case, for example, the Court of Appeals alluded to just such limited falsity in observing that "the jury was certainly justified in believing that the directors did not believe a merger at $42 per share was in the minority stockholders' interest but, rather, that they voted as they did for other reasons, e.g., retaining their seats on the board." 891 F.2d, at 1121.

The question arises, then, whether disbelief, or undisclosed belief or motivation, standing alone, should be a sufficient basis to sustain an action under § 14(a), absent proof by the sort of objective evidence described above that the statement also expressly or impliedly asserted something false or misleading about its subject matter. We think that proof of mere disbelief or belief undisclosed should not suffice for liability under § 14(a), and if nothing more had been required or proven in this case we would reverse for that reason.

On the one hand, it would be rare to find a case with evidence solely of disbelief or undisclosed motivation without further proof that the statement was defective as to its subject matter. While we certainly would not hold a director's naked admission of disbelief incompetent evidence of a proxy statement's false or misleading character, such an unusual admission will not very often stand alone, and we do not substantially narrow the cause of action by requiring a plaintiff to demonstrate something false or misleading in what the statement expressly or impliedly declared about its subject.

On the other hand, to recognize liability on mere disbelief or undisclosed motive without any demonstration that the proxy statement was false or misleading about its subject would authorize § 14(a) litigation confined solely to what one skeptical court spoke of as the "impurities" of a director's "unclean heart." Stedman v. Storer, 308 F.Supp. 881, 887 (S.D.N.Y.1969) (dealing with § 10(b)). This, we think, would cross the line that *Blue Chip Stamps* sought to draw. While it is true that the liability, if recognized, would rest on an actual, not hypothetical, psychological fact, the temptation to rest an otherwise nonexistent § 14(a) action on psychological enquiry alone would threaten just the sort of strike suits and attrition by discovery that *Blue Chip Stamps* sought to discourage. We therefore hold disbelief or undisclosed motivation, standing alone, insufficient to satisfy the element of fact that must be established under § 14(a).

C

Petitioners' fall-back position assumes the same relationship between a conclusory judgment and its underlying facts that we described in Part II–B–1, supra. Thus, citing Radol v. Thomas, 534 F.Supp. 1302, 1315, 1316 (S.D.Ohio 1982), petitioners argue that even if conclusory statements of reason or belief can be actionable under § 14(a), we should confine liability to instances where the proxy material fails to disclose the offending statement's factual basis. There would be no justification for holding the shareholders entitled to judicial relief, that is, when they were given evidence that a stated reason for a proxy recommendation was misleading, and an opportunity to draw that conclusion themselves.

The answer to this argument rests on the difference between a merely misleading statement and one that is materially so. While a misleading statement will not always lose its deceptive edge simply by joinder with others that are true, the true statements may discredit the other one so obviously that the risk of real deception drops to nil. Since liability under § 14(a) must rest not only on deceptiveness but materiality as well (i.e., it has to be significant enough to be important to a reasonable investor deciding how to vote, see *TSC Industries*, 426 U.S., at 449, 96 S.Ct., at 2132), petitioners are on perfectly firm ground insofar as they argue that publishing accurate facts in a proxy statement can render a misleading proposition too unimportant to ground liability.

But not every mixture with the true will neutralize the deceptive. If it would take a financial analyst to spot the tension between the one and the other, whatever is misleading will remain materially so, and liability should follow. Gerstle v. Gamble–Skogmo, Inc., 478 F.2d 1281, 1297 (C.A.2 1973) ("[I]t is not sufficient that overtones might have been picked up by the sensitive antennae of investment analysts"). Cf. Milkovich v. Lorain Journal Co., ... 110 S.Ct. 2695, 2708, 111 L.Ed.2d 1 (1990) (a defamatory assessment of facts can be actionable even if the facts underlying the assessment are accurately presented). The point of a proxy statement, after all, should be to inform, not to challenge the reader's critical wits. Only when the inconsistency would exhaust the misleading conclusion's capacity to influence the reasonable shareholder would a § 14(a) action fail on the element of materiality.

Suffice it to say that the evidence invoked by petitioners in the instant case fell short of compelling the jury to find the facial materiality of the misleading statement neutralized. The directors claim, for example, to have made an explanatory disclosure of further reasons for their recommendation when they said they would keep their seats following the merger, but they failed to mention what at least one of them admitted in testimony, that they would have had no expectation of doing so without supporting the proposal, App. at 281–82. And although the proxy statement did speak factually about the merger price in describing it as higher than share prices in recent sales, it failed even to mention the closed market dominated by FABI. None of these disclosures that the directors point to was, then, anything more than a half-truth, and the record shows that another fact statement they invoke was arguably even worse. The claim that the merger price exceeded book value was controverted, as we have seen already, by evidence of a higher book value than the directors conceded, reflecting appreciation in the Bank's real estate portfolio. Finally, the solicitation omitted any mention of the Bank's value as a going concern at more than $60 a share, as against the merger price of $42. There was, in sum, no more of a compelling case for the statement's immateriality than for its accuracy.

III

The second issue before us, left open in Mills v. Electric Auto–Lite Co., 396 U.S., at 385, n. 7, 90 S.Ct., at 622, n. 7, is whether causation of damages compensable through the implied private right of action under § 14(a) can be demonstrated by a member of a class of minority shareholders whose votes are not required by law or corporate bylaw to authorize the transaction giving rise to the claim.

[The Court held that the answer to this question was, no. The plaintiffs argued that such a claim could be supported by two theories: that the proxy statement was an essential link between the director's proposal and the merger (1) because VBI and FABI would have been unwilling to proceed with the merger unless the minority approved, and (2) because the vote of the minority was the means to satisfy a state statutory requirement of minority shareholder approval as a condition for saving the merger from voidability resulting from a conflict of interest. The court rejected the first theory on the ground that acceptance of the concept would give rise to speculative claims. As to the second theory, the court said:]

This case does not ... require us to decide whether § 14(a) provides a cause of action for lost state remedies, since there is no indication in the law or facts before us that the proxy solicitation resulted in any such loss. The contrary appears to be the case. Assuming the soundness of respondents' characterization of the proxy statement as materially misleading, the very terms of the Virginia statute indicate that a favorable minority vote induced by the solicitation would not suffice to render the merger invulnerable to later attack on the ground of the conflict. The statute bars a shareholder from seeking to avoid a transaction tainted by a director's conflict if, inter alia, the minority shareholders ratified the transaction following disclosure of the material facts of the transaction and the conflict. Va.Code § 13.1–691(A)(2) (1989). Assuming that the material facts about the merger and Beddow's interests were not accurately disclosed, the minority votes were inadequate to ratify the merger under state law, and there was no loss of state remedy to connect the proxy solicitation with harm to minority shareholders irredressable under state law. Nor is there a claim here that the statement misled respondents into entertaining a false belief that they had no chance to upset the merger, until the time for bringing suit had run out.[14]

IV

The judgment of the Court of Appeals is reversed.

It is so ordered.

■ JUSTICE SCALIA, concurring in part and concurring in the judgment....

I recognize that the Court's disallowance (in Part II–B–2) of an action for misrepresentation of belief is entirely contrary to the modern law of torts, as authorities cited by the Court make plain. See Vulcan Metals Co. v. Simmons Mfg. Co., 248 F. 853, 856 (C.A.2 1918); W. Keeton, D. Dobbs, R. Keeton, & D. Owen, Prosser and Keeton on Law of Torts § 109 (5th ed. 1984), cited ante, at 2759. I have no problem with departing from modern tort law in this regard, because I think the federal cause of action at issue here was never enacted by Congress, see Thompson v. Thompson, 484 U.S. 174, 190–192, 108 S.Ct. 513, 521–523, 98 L.Ed.2d 512 (1988) (SCALIA, J., concurring in judgment), and hence the more narrow we make it (within the bounds of rationality) the more faithful we are to our task....

I concur in the judgment of the Court, and join all of its opinion except Part II.

■ JUSTICE STEVENS, with whom JUSTICE MARSHALL joins, concurring in part and dissenting in part.

While I agree in substance with Parts I and II of the Court's opinion, I do not agree with the reasoning in Part III....

---

14. Respondents do not claim that any other application of a theory of lost state remedies would avail them here. It is clear, for example, that no state appraisal remedy was lost through a § 14(a) violation in this case....

The case before us today involves a merger that has been found by a jury to be unfair, not fair. The interest in providing a remedy to the injured minority shareholders therefore is stronger, not weaker, than in *Mills*. The interest in avoiding speculative controversy about the actual importance of the proxy solicitation is the same as in *Mills*. Moreover, as in *Mills*, these matters can be taken into account at the remedy stage in appropriate cases. Accordingly, I do not believe that it constitutes an unwarranted extension of the rationale of *Mills* to conclude that because management found it necessary—whether for "legal or practical reasons"—to solicit proxies from minority shareholders to obtain their approval of the merger, that solicitation "was an essential link in the accomplishment of the transaction." Id., at 385, and n. 7, 90 S.Ct., at 622, and n. 7. In my opinion, shareholders may bring an action for damages under § 14(a) of the Securities Exchange Act of 1934, 48 Stat. 895, 15 U.S.C. § 78n(a), whenever materially false or misleading statements are made in proxy statements. That the solicitation of proxies is not required by law or by the bylaws of a corporation does not authorize corporate officers, once they have decided for whatever reason to solicit proxies, to avoid the constraints of the statute. I would therefore affirm the judgment of the Court of Appeals.

■ JUSTICE KENNEDY, with whom JUSTICE MARSHALL, JUSTICE BLACKMUN, and JUSTICE STEVENS join, concurring in part and dissenting in part.

I am in general agreement with Parts I and II of the majority opinion, but do not agree with the views expressed in Part III regarding the proof of causation required to establish a violation of § 14(a). With respect, I dissent from Part III of the Court's opinion. . . .

II . . .

The Court seems to assume, based upon [footnote 7] in *Mills* reserving the question, that Sandberg bears a special burden to demonstrate causation because the public shareholders held only 15 percent of the Bank's stock. Justice STEVENS is right to reject this theory. Here, First American Bankshares, Inc. (FABI) and Virginia Bankshares, Inc. (VBI) retained the option to back out of the transaction if dissatisfied with the reaction of the minority shareholders, or if concerned that the merger would result in liability for violation of duties to the minority shareholders. The merger agreement was conditioned upon approval by two-thirds of the shareholders, App. 463, and VBI could have voted its shares against the merger if it so decided. To this extent, the Court's distinction between cases where the "minority" shareholders could have voted down the transaction and those where causation must be proved by nonvoting theories is suspect. Minority shareholders are identified only by a *post hoc* inquiry. The real question ought to be whether an injury was shown by the effect the nondisclosure had on the entire merger process, including the period before votes are cast.

The Court's distinction presumes that a majority shareholder will vote in favor of management's proposal even if proxy disclosure suggests that the transaction is unfair to minority shareholders or that the board of directors or majority shareholder are in breach of fiduciary duties to the minority. If the majority shareholder votes against the transaction in order to comply with its state law duties, or out of fear of liability, or upon concluding that the transaction will injure the reputation of the business, this ought not to be characterized as nonvoting causation. Of course, when the majority shareholder dominates the voting process, as was the case here, it may prefer to avoid the embarrassment of voting against its own proposal and so may cancel the meeting of shareholders at which the vote was to have been taken. For practical purposes, the result is the same: because of full disclosure the transaction does not go forward and the resulting injury to minority shareholders is avoided. The Court's distinction between voting and nonvoting causation does not create clear legal categories.

III . . .

There is no authority whatsoever for limiting § 14(a) to protecting those minority shareholders whose numerical strength could permit them to vote down a proposal. One of Section 14(a)'s "chief purposes is 'the protection of investors.' " J.I. Case Co. v. Borak, 377 U.S., at 432, 1559–1560. Those who lack the strength to vote down a proposal have all the more need of disclosure. The voting process involves not only casting ballots but also the formulation and withdrawal of proposals, the minority's right to block a vote through court action or the threat of adverse consequences, or the negotiation of an increase in price. The proxy rules support this deliberative process. These practicalities can result in causation sufficient to support recovery.

The facts in the case before us prove this point. Sandberg argues that had all the material facts been disclosed, FABI or the Bank likely would have withdrawn or revised the merger proposal. The evidence in the record, and more that might be available upon remand, see infra, . . . meets any reasonable requirement of specific and nonspeculative proof.

FABI wanted a "friendly transaction" with a price viewed as "so high that any reasonable shareholder will accept it." App. 99. Management expressed concern that the transaction result in "no loss of support for the bank out in the community, which was important." Id., at 109. Although FABI had the votes to push through any proposal, it wanted a favorable response from the minority shareholders. Id., at 192. Because of the "human element involved in a transaction of this nature," FABI attempted to "show those minority shareholders that [it was] being fair." Id., at 347. . . .

[The evidence supports the] theory that FABI would not have pursued the transaction if full disclosure had been proved and the shareholders had realized the inadequacy of the price. . . .

I would affirm the judgment of the Court of Appeals.

———

WILSON v. GREAT AMERICAN INDUSTRIES, INC., 979 F.2d 924 (2d Cir.1992). Chenango engaged in a merger with Great American. Plaintiffs, who had been minority shareholders in Chenango, alleged that material misstatements in the Proxy Statement caused them to exchange their shares of Chenango common stock for new preferred stock in Great American. At the time of the merger, the defendants (Great American, Chenango, and various officers, directors, and attorneys connected with those two corporations) owned 73 percent of Chenango's stock, which was well over the two-thirds necessary under New York law to approve a merger. New York law required that Chenango have a shareholders' meeting to approve the merger, but the only informational requirement under the New York statute was that each shareholder be given notice of the meeting accompanied by a "copy of the plan of merger." Because Chenango stock was registered under § 12(g) of the Securities Exchange Act, Chenango was also required to provide shareholders with an Information Statement pursuant to § 14(c) of the Act. However Chenango went further, and sought approval of the merger by Chenango's minority shareholders. The Second Circuit held that *Virginia Bankshares* did not bar the plaintiffs' action if, as a result of false statements in the Proxy Statement, the plaintiffs had lost their appraisal right or some other state remedy. See also Howing Co. v. Nationwide Corp., 972 F.2d 700, 709–710 (6th Cir.1992), *cert. denied* 507 U.S. 1004, 113 S.Ct. 1645, 123 L.Ed.2d 266 (1993); cf. Scattergood v. Perelman, 945 F.2d 618 (3d Cir.1991).

———

NOTE ON CAUSATION, RELIANCE, AND STANDING IN PRIVATE ACTIONS UNDER THE PROXY RULES

1. Mills v. Electric Auto–Lite Co., supra, leaves no doubt that a materially false or misleading proxy statement must be deemed to be the cause of a shareholder vote that the proxy statement solicits. Accordingly, where a shareholder seeks to set aside or enjoin a transaction approved by the shareholders on the ground that the approval was solicited by a proxy statement that involved misstatements or omissions, he need do nothing more to prove causation than to prove materiality. See Gaines v. Haughton, 645 F.2d 761, 773–74 (9th Cir.1981), cert. denied 454 U.S. 1145, 102 S.Ct. 1006, 71 L.Ed.2d 297 (1982); Weisberg v. Coastal States Gas Corp., 609 F.2d 650, 653 (2d Cir.1979), cert. denied 445 U.S. 951, 100 S.Ct. 1600, 63 L.Ed.2d 786 (1980).

2. If a proxy statement is materially misleading or omits to state a material fact, and a majority of shareholders vote in favor of the action proposed in the proxy statement, does a shareholder who did

not grant a proxy in reliance on the Proxy Statement have standing under Rule 14a–9? In Cowin v. Bresler, 741 F.2d 410, 427 (D.C.Cir. 1984), the court held that the answer is, yes:

> ... *Borak* itself identifies the injury section 14(a) sought to prevent:

>> The injury which a stockholder suffers from corporate action pursuant to a deceptive proxy solicitation ordinarily flows from the damage done the corporation, rather than from the damage inflicted directly upon the stockholder. The damage suffered results not from the deceit practiced on him alone but rather from the deceit practiced on the stockholders as a group.

> 377 U.S. at 432, 84 S.Ct. at 1560.

> The injury [the shareholder-plaintiff] alleges was not caused by his individual reliance on deceptive proxy solicitations. Rather, his claim is that other shareholders elected appellees as directors because they were misled by the proxy materials. The installation of ... directors [so elected] has injured [the shareholder]. This injury is totally divorced from any reliance, or lack of reliance, on [the shareholder's] part and falls precisely into the scope of injury Congress sought to protect. *Borak,* 377 U.S. at 432, 84 S.Ct. at 1559. Requiring reliance in these circumstances would serve no legitimate policy and we decline to do so. *See Hershfang v. Knotter,* 562 F.Supp. 393, 397–98 (E.D.Va.1983), *aff'd mem.,* 725 F.2d 675 (4th Cir.1984) (plaintiff has standing under section 14(a) despite his lack of reliance because injury suffered has no connection to his individual reliance).

> We think sentiment expressed in a recent district court opinion persuasive.

>> It is abundantly clear that Congress' intent to protect the investing public would be seriously hampered if one who misuses the proxy process cannot be brought to task by those shareholders who have from the outset recognized his deceptions, but has only to fear that the other shareholders whom he has successfully beguiled will belatedly become enlightened and seek redress for the damage he has done them.

> *Lynch v. Fulks,* [1981 Transfer Binder] Fed.Sec.L.Rep. (CCH) § 97,831, at 90,134 (D.Kan. Dec. 12, 1980).

See also Palumbo v. Deposit Bank, 758 F.2d 113, 116 (3d Cir.1985); Dann v. Studebaker–Packard Corp., 288 F.2d 201, 209 (6th Cir.1961).

––––––

NOTE ON THE STANDARD OF FAULT IN PRIVATE ACTIONS UNDER THE PROXY RULES

Under *Borak* and *Mills,* shareholders have standing to bring an action under Rule 14a–9, which prohibits false or misleading proxy statements. Does a plaintiff-shareholder prevail in such an action if he shows that a proxy statement was false or misleading by virtue of a material misstatement or omission, or must he also show that the misstatement or omission resulted from the defendant's fault? If the plaintiff must show fault, does negligence suffice?

In the leading case of Gerstle v. Gamble–Skogmo, Inc., 478 F.2d 1281 (2d Cir.1973), the Second Circuit, in an opinion written by Judge Friendly, held that negligence sufficed to establish liability under Rule 14a–9:

> We thus hold that in a case like this, where the plaintiffs represent the very class who were asked to approve a merger on the basis of a misleading proxy statement and are seeking compensation from the beneficiary who is responsible for the preparation of the statement, they are not required to establish any evil motive or even reckless disregard of the facts. Whether in situations other than that here presented "the liability of the corporation issuing a materially false or misleading proxy statement is virtually absolute, as under Section 11 of the 1933 Act with respect to a registration statement," Jennings & Marsh, Securities Regulation: Cases and Materials 1358 (3d ed. 1972), we leave to another day. 478 F.2d at 1298–1301. Accord: Herskowitz v. Nutri/System, Inc., 857 F.2d 179 (3d Cir.1988), cert. denied 489 U.S. 1054, 109 S.Ct. 1315, 103 L.Ed.2d 584 (1989); Gould v. American–Hawaiian Steamship Co., 535 F.2d 761 (3d Cir.1976).

But see Adams v. Standard Knitting Mills, Inc., 623 F.2d 422 (6th Cir.1980), cert. denied 449 U.S. 1067, 101 S.Ct. 795, 66 L.Ed.2d 611. ("scienter should be an element of liability in private suits under the proxy provisions as they apply to outside accountants").

In Shidler v. All American Life & Financial Corp., 775 F.2d 917, 927 (8th Cir.1985), the Eighth Circuit addressed the issue that Judge Friendly left to another day in *Gerstle,* and held there was no liability without fault in an action under Section 14(a):

> The purpose of section 14(a) is "to prevent management or others from obtaining authorization for corporate action by means of deceptive or inadequate disclosure in proxy solicitation." J.I. Case Co. v. Borak, 377 U.S. 426, 431, 84 S.Ct. 1555, 1559, 12 L.Ed.2d 423 (1964). A strict liability rule would impose liability for fully innocent misstatements. It is too blunt a tool to ferret out the kind of deceptive practices Congress sought to prevent in enacting section 14(a).

The Supreme Court has several times explicitly taken note of the position taken in *Gerstle* and other cases that scienter is not an element of liability under § 14(a), and has each time declined to address the issue. See Ernst & Ernst v. Hochfelder, 425 U.S. 185, 209 n. 28, 96 S.Ct. 1375, 1388 n. 28, 47 L.Ed.2d 668 (1976); TSC Indus., Inc. v. Northway, 426 U.S. 438, 444 n. 7, 96 S.Ct. 2126, 2130 n. 7, 48 L.Ed.2d 757 (1976); *Virginia Bankshares,* supra, at note 5.

———

NOTE ON STATE LAW

Perhaps as a result of experience under the Proxy Rules, the standards applied by state courts today, in reviewing the adequacy of disclosure to shareholders under state law in connection with a matter proposed for a shareholder vote, is likely to be close to the standards under the Proxy Rules. See Chapter 10, Section 5, infra.

SECTION 5.   THE PROXY RULES (III): SHAREHOLDER PROPOSALS

––––––

SECURITIES EXCHANGE ACT RULE 14a–7

[See Statutory Supplement]

––––––

SECURITIES EXCHANGE ACT RULE 14a–8

[See Statutory Supplement]

––––––

NOTE ON NO–ACTION LETTERS INTERPRETING RULE 14a–8

Rule 14a–8 provides that if management believes a shareholder proposal may properly be excluded from the corporation's proxy statement under Rule 14a–8, it must submit to the SEC staff a statement of the reasons why it deems omission of the proposal to be proper. If the staff agrees with management's statement, it sends management a "no-action letter"—that is, a letter stating that if the shareholder proposal is omitted, no action will be taken by the SEC. If the staff disagrees with management's statement, it sends a letter stating why the proposal should be included. Such letters are also referred to as no-action letters, although in fact they are just the opposite—that is, they implicitly threaten legal proceedings if management omits the shareholder proposal. In such cases management may still omit the shareholder proposal, and run the risk of legal proceedings by the SEC, but that option is seldom if ever exercised.

––––––

AMERICAN TELEPHONE AND TELEGRAPH CO., SEC Division of Corporation Finance, Fed.Sec.L.Rep. (CCH) ¶ 76,820 (1994). [SEC No–Action letter.] "The [shareholder] proposal requests that the Company implement a policy that, as the Company continues or expands its business in Mexico, it will evaluate the environmental and human rights context in which the Company operates. The proposal then sets forth four specific elements of the proposed policy.

"... [Rule 14a–8(i)(5)] ... permits the omission of a proposal if it relates to operations which account for less than 5% of the registrant's total assets and is not otherwise significantly related to the registrant's business. The staff is of the view that the proposal is 'otherwise significantly related' to the Company's business. Accordingly, the staff does not believe the Company may rely on Rule 14a–8(c)(5) as a basis for omitting the proposal from its proxy materials."

———

Aon Corporation

[SEC NO–ACTION LETTER].
March 6, 1997.

The proposal requests that the board initiate a policy mandating no further purchases of tobacco equities and that the Company divest itself of all tobacco stocks by January 1, 1998.

The [SEC Division of Corporate Finance] is unable to concur in your view that the proposal may be omitted from the Company's proxy materials under Rule 14a–8(i)(5). That provision permits the omission of a proposal if it relates to operations which account for less than 5% of the registrant's total assets, net earnings and gross sales, and is not otherwise significantly related to the registrant's business. The staff is of the view that the proposal is "otherwise significantly related" to the Company's business. Accordingly, the Division does not believe the Company may rely on Rule 14a–8(i)(5) as a basis for omitting the proposal from its proxy materials.

The Division is unable to concur in your view that the proposal may be omitted from the Company's proxy materials under Rule 14a–8(i)(7) as a matter relating to ordinary business operations. Accordingly, the Division does not believe that the Company may rely on Rule 14a–8(i)(7) as a basis for omitting the proposal from its proxy materials....

———

Division of Corporation Finance: Staff Legal Bulletin No. 14A Shareholder Proposals

July 12, 2002.

Rule 14a–8 provides an opportunity for a shareholder owning a relatively small amount of a company's securities to have his or her proposal placed alongside management's proposals in that company's proxy materials for presentation to a vote at an annual or special meeting of shareholders. The rule generally requires the company to include the proposal unless the shareholder has not complied with the rule's procedural requirements or the proposal falls within one of the rule's 13 substantive bases for exclusion.

Rule 14a–8(i)(7) is one of the substantive bases for exclusion in rule 14a–8. It provides a basis for excluding a proposal that deals with a matter relating to the company's ordinary business operations. The fact that a proposal relates to ordinary business matters does not conclusively establish that a company may exclude the proposal from its proxy materials. As the Commission stated in Exchange Act Release No. 40018, proposals that relate to ordinary business matters but that focus on "sufficiently significant social policy issues . . . would not be considered to be excludable because the proposals would transcend the day-to-day business matters."

In the 2001–2002 proxy season, shareholders submitted proposals to several companies relating to equity compensation plans. Some of these proposals requested that the companies submit for shareholder approval all equity compensation plans that potentially would result in material dilution to existing shareholders. We received four no-action requests from companies seeking to exclude these proposals from their proxy materials in reliance on rule 14a–8(i)(7). In each instance, we took the view that the proposal could be excluded in reliance on rule 14a–8(i)(7) because the proposal related to general employee compensation, an ordinary business matter.

The Commission has stated that proposals involving "the management of the workforce, such as the hiring, promotion, and termination of employees," relate to ordinary business matters. Our position to date with respect to equity compensation proposals is consistent with this guidance and the Division's historical approach to compensation proposals. Since 1992, we have applied a bright-line analysis to proposals concerning equity or cash compensation:

- We agree with the view of companies that they may exclude proposals that relate to general employee compensation matters in reliance on rule 14a–8(i)(7); and

- We do not agree with the view of companies that they may exclude proposals that concern only senior executive and director compensation in reliance on rule 14a–8(i)(7).

The Commission has previously taken the position that proposals relating to ordinary business matters "but focusing on sufficiently significant social policy issues . . . generally would not be considered to be excludable, because the proposals would transcend the day-to-day business matters and raise policy issues so significant that it would be appropriate for a shareholder vote." The Division has noted many times that the presence of widespread public debate regarding an issue is among the factors to be considered in determining whether proposals concerning that issue "transcend the day-to-day business matters."

We believe that the public debate regarding shareholder approval of equity compensation plans has become significant in recent months. Consequently, in view of the widespread public debate regarding shareholder approval of equity compensation plans and consistent with our historical analysis of the "ordinary business" exclusion, we are modifying our treatment of proposals relating to this topic. Going forward, we will take the following approach to rule 14a–8(i)(7) submissions concerning proposals that relate to shareholder approval of equity compensation plans:

- *Proposals that focus on equity compensation plans that may be used to compensate only senior executive officers and directors.* As has been our position since 1992, companies may not rely on rule 14a–8(i)(7) to omit these proposals from their proxy materials.

- *Proposals that focus on equity compensation plans that may be used to compensate senior executive officers, directors and the general workforce.* If the proposal seeks to obtain shareholder approval of all such equity compensation plans, without regard to their potential dilutive effect, a company may rely on rule 14a–8(i)(7) to omit the proposal from its proxy materials. If the proposal seeks to obtain shareholder approval of all such equity compensation plans that potentially would result in material dilution to existing shareholders, a company may not rely on rule 14a–8(i)(7) to omit the proposal from its proxy materials.

- *Proposals that focus on equity compensation plans that may be used to compensate the general workforce only, with no senior executive officer or director participation.* If the proposal seeks to obtain shareholder approval of all such equity compensation plans, without regard to their potential dilutive effect, a company may rely on rule 14a–8(i)(7) to omit the proposal from its proxy materials. If the proposal seeks to obtain shareholder approval of all such equity compensation plans that potentially would result in material dilution to existing shareholders, a company may not rely on rule 14a–8(i)(7) to omit the proposal from its proxy materials. . . .

Roosevelt v. E.I. Du Pont de Nemours & Co.

United States Court of Appeals, District of Columbia Circuit, 1992.
958 F.2d 416.

■ Before EDWARDS, RUTH BADER GINSBURG, and SENTELLE, CIRCUIT JUDGES.

■ Opinion for the Court filed by CIRCUIT JUDGE RUTH BADER GINSBURG.

■ RUTH BADER GINSBURG, CIRCUIT JUDGE.

Amelia Roosevelt appeals the district court's judgment that E.I. Du Pont de Nemours & Co. ("Du Pont") could omit her shareholder proposal from its proxy materials for the 1992 annual meeting. The district court concluded that Roosevelt's proposal "deals with a matter relating to the conduct of [Du Pont's] ordinary business operations," and is therefore excludable under Securities and Exchange Commission ("SEC") Rule 14a–8(c)(7), 17 C.F.R. § 240.14a–8(c)(7). We affirm the district court's judgment and deal first with a threshold question. Consistent with congressional intent and Supreme Court case law, we hold, a private right of action is properly implied from section 14(a) of the Securities Exchange Act of 1934 (the "Act"), 15 U.S.C. § 78n(a), to enforce a company's obligation to include shareholder proposals in annual meeting proxy materials. Reaching the merits, we uphold the district court's determination that Roosevelt's two-part proposal is excludable under Rule 14a–8(c)(7).

I. Background

Prior to Du Pont's 1991 annual shareholder meeting, Friends of the Earth Oceanic Society ("Friends of the Earth") submitted a proposal, on behalf of Roosevelt, regarding: (1) the timing of Du Pont's phase out of the production of chlorofluorocarbons ("CFCs") and halons; and (2) the presentation to shareholders of a report detailing (a) research and development efforts to find environmentally sound substitutes, and (b) marketing plans to sell those substitutes.[1] Du Pont opposed inclusion of the proposal in its proxy materials; as required by SEC rule, see 17 C.F.R. § 240.14a–8(d), the company notified the SEC staff of its intention to omit the proposal and its reasons for believing the omission proper. Friends of the Earth filed with the staff a countersubmission on Roosevelt's behalf urging that the proposal was not excludable.

The SEC staff issued a "no-action letter"; citing the Rule 14a–8(c)(7) exception for matters "relating to the conduct of the [company's] ordinary business operations," the staff stated that it would not recommend Commission enforcement action against Du Pont if the company excluded the proposal. Du Pont, SEC No–Action Letter

---

1. Roosevelt's proposal consists of twelve "whereas" clauses followed by two resolutions. In relevant part, the proposal states:

Whereas, The international scientific community has determined that synthetic chemicals—including chlorofluorocarbons (CFCs), halons, carbon tetrachloride, methyl chloroform, and hydrochlorofluorocarbons (HCFCs)—are destroying the Earth's protective ozone layer at an alarming rate;

* * *

Whereas, Many governments are taking action beyond the Montreal Protocol [the international ozone protection treaty, including an agreement to stop CFC production in the year 2000]; for example, Germany plans to stop CFC and halon production in 1995, and German CFC producers Hoechst AG and Kali-Chemie have announced they will stop making CFCs in 1995;

* * *

Resolved, That the shareholders of the Du Pont Company, assembled in annual meeting in person and by proxy, request that the Board of Directors:

1. Rapidly accelerate plans to phase out CFC and halon production, surpassing our global competitors which have set a 1995 target date;

2. Present a report to shareholders within six months detailing (a) research and development program expenditures which dramatically increase efforts to find CFC and halon substitutes which do not harm the ozone layer or contribute significantly to global warning; and (b) a marketing plan to sell those environmentally safe alternatives to present customers.

(available March 8, 1991). Roosevelt did not seek Commission review of the staff's disposition.

Instead, with the 1991 meeting weeks away, Roosevelt filed a complaint and a motion for a temporary restraining order in federal district court. Denying the motion, the motions judge stated preliminarily that "[t]he Supreme Court has recognized an implied private right of action for alleged violations of Rule 14a–8." She found, however, that Roosevelt had not shown the requisite irreparable harm. If Du Pont mailed its proxy materials on March 18, as scheduled, without Roosevelt's proposal, the motions judge observed, a supplemental mailing containing the proposal could still be made in advance of the April 24 annual meeting date. C.A. No. 91–556, Memorandum Order (March 18, 1991) at 1, 3. The trial judge held an expedited trial on the morning of April 2, 1991; in a Memorandum Opinion filed two days later, he ruled that, based on the "ordinary business operations" exception in Rule 14a–8(c)(7), Du Point could omit Roosevelt's proposal. C.A. No. 91–556, Memorandum Opinion (April 4, 1991) ("Mem. Op.").

We expedited Roosevelt's appeal when she informed us that she sought inclusion of her proposal in the proxy materials for Du Pont's 1992 annual meeting. C.A. No. 91–5087, Order (April 9, 1991) (per curiam). Before the appeal was heard, Du Pont had again advised the SEC that it intended to exclude the proposal, and the SEC staff had issued a second no-action letter, once more concluding that "[t]here appears to be some basis for [Du Pont's] view that the proposal may be excluded ... pursuant to rule 14a–8(c)(7)." Du Pont, SEC No-Action Letter (available Sept. 11, 1991).[3] Neither Roosevelt nor the SEC staff requested the Commission's view on the applicability of the "ordinary business operations" exception to Roosevelt's proposal.

II.   The Implied Private Right of Action and Shareholder Proposals

Before reviewing the district court's application of Rule 14a–8(c)(7), we resolve a preliminary question: Does a shareholder have an implied right of action under section 14(a) of the Act and Commission Rule 14a–8 when a company refuses to include the shareholder's proposal in proxy materials? ...

[The court held that a shareholder did have such a right of action.]

III.   Roosevelt's Proposals and the Rule 14a–8(c)(7)
Exception for "Ordinary Business Operations"

Reaching the merits, we restate the district court's ruling: "Roosevelt's proposal deals with matters relating to the conduct of the ordinary business operations of Du Pont. Therefore, [under Rule 14a–8(c)(7)], Du Pont properly omitted her proposal from its proxy

---

3. The staff reasoned in September 1991, as it had the previous March, that "the thrust of the proposal appears directed at those questions concerning the timing, re- search and marketing decisions that involve matters relating to the conduct of the Company's ordinary business operations." Id.

statement." Mem.Op. at 1. In reviewing this ruling, we emphasize that Roosevelt's disagreement with Du Pont's current policy is not about whether to eliminate CFC production or even whether to do so at once. The former is an end to which Du Pont is committed, and immediate cessation, before environmentally safe alternatives are available, is not what Roosevelt proposes.

Roosevelt differs with Du Pont on a less fundamental matter—the rapidity with which the near-term phase out should occur. Roosevelt seeks a target no later than 1995 ("surpassing [Du Pont's] global competitors which have set a 1995 target date"). In contrast, when this litigation began, Du Pont had set a target of "as soon as possible, but at least by the year 2000." Mem.Op. at 4.

In recent months and days, the "at least by" year has moved ever closer to Roosevelt's target. Prior to oral argument, Roosevelt informed the court, pursuant to Fed.R.App.P. 28(j) and D.C.Cir.R. 11(h), that Du Pont had issued a press release reiterating its "as soon as possible" policy, but "advancing the end point to year-end 1994 for Halons and 1996 for CFCs." Du Pont Corporate News, Oct. 22, 1991, at 1 (citing "scientific data released today by the United Nations Environment Programme ... and World Meteorological Organization"). Following oral argument, Du Pont informed the court that, "[i]n response to an announcement issued by the White House today regarding an accelerated phaseout of CFCs and Halons," the company "will accelerate its CFC end date to no later than December 31, 1995 in developed countries." Du Pont Statement on Accelerated CFC Phaseout, Feb. 12, 1992.

Although the regulation necessary to give effect to the President's announcement has not yet been adopted, Du Pont immediately reported that it "supports the Administration's position," id., and that it will phase out CFC production by December 31, 1995. We accept that public statement as the company's current timetable. While the SEC staff and the district court considered Roosevelt's proposal with the company's year—2000 end point in view, we think it proper to take account of the current reality: Roosevelt's proposal would have Du Pont surpass its global competitors' target of 1995; Du Pont projects completion of the phase out "as soon as possible," but no later than year-end 1995.

Roosevelt has confirmed that the first, or phase-out portion of her proposal is the "core issue" and that, if necessary, she would withdraw the second, or report-to-shareholders portion, so that the first portion could be included in Du Pont's 1992 proxy materials. Plaintiff–Appellant's Reply to Brief of the Securities and Exchange Commission, Amicus Curiae, at 4–5. We therefore consider separately the two portions of Roosevelt's proposal.

Because both parts of Roosevelt's proposal must be measured against the Rule 14a–8(c)(7) "ordinary business operations" exception, we set out here the Commission's general understanding of that phrase. When the Commission adopted the current version of the "ordinary business operations" exception, it announced its intention to interpret the phrase both "more restrictive[ly]" and "more flexibly than in the past." *Adoption of Amendments Relating to Proposals by Security Holders,* Exchange Act Release No. 12,999, 41 Fed.Reg. 52,-994, 52,998 (Dec. 3, 1976) ("*1976 Rule 14a–8 Amendments*"). Specifically, the Commission explained:

> [T]he term "ordinary business operations" has been deemed on occasion to include certain matters which have significant policy, economic or other implications inherent in them. For instance, a proposal that a utility company not construct a proposed nuclear power plant has in the past been considered excludable under [the predecessor of (c)(7)]. In retrospect, however, it seems apparent that the economic and safety considerations attendant to nuclear power plants are of such magnitude that a determination whether to construct one is not an "ordinary" business matter. Accordingly, proposals of that nature, as well as others that have major implications, will in the future be considered beyond the realm of an issuer's ordinary business operations. . . .

Id.; see *Grimes,* 909 F.2d at 531 (observing that, "[u]nfortunately, the phrase [ordinary business operations] has no precise definition"). The Commission contrasted with matters of such moment as a decision not to build a nuclear power plant, "matters . . . mundane in nature [that] do not involve any substantial policy . . . considerations." *1976 Rule 14a–8 Amendments,* 41 Fed.Reg. at 52,998. Proposals of that genre, the Commission said, may be safely omitted from proxy materials.

In its brief as amicus curiae, the SEC stated that it regarded the first portion of Roosevelt's proposal, on the timing of the CFC phase out, as not excludable under Rule 14a–8(c)(7), but the second part, on research and development programs and marketing plans, as fitting within the "ordinary business operations" exception. Brief of the Securities and Exchange Commission, Amicus Curiae, at 31. The Commission noted that "[its] staff, in contrast, viewed the timing of the phase-out as an ordinary business matter." Id. at 32 n. 23. We agree with the Commission on the second part of Roosevelt's proposal but not on the first.

A.   The Phase Out Target Date

It is not debated in this case that CFCs contribute intolerably to depletion of the ozone layer and that their manufacture has caused a grave environmental hazard. However, Roosevelt's proposal, we emphasize again, relates not to *whether* CFC production should be phased out, but *when* the phase out should be completed. Cf. Loews Corporation, SEC No–Action Letter (available Feb. 22, 1990) (shareholder proposal for eventual cessation of manufacture of tobacco products; company unsuccessfully urged that what products it makes is a matter of "ordinary business operations").

Timing questions no doubt reflect "significant policy" when large differences are at stake. That would be the case, for example, if Du Pont projected a phase-out period extending into the new century. On the other hand, were Roosevelt seeking to move up Du Pont's target date by barely a season, the matter would appear much more of an "ordinary" than an extraordinary business judgment. In evaluating the Commission's classification of the timing question here as extraordinary, *i.e.*, one involving "fundamental business strategy" or "long-term goals," see Brief of the Securities and Exchange Commission, Amicus Curiae, at 31, we are mindful that the SEC focused on a five-year interval, see id. at 32 n. 25, not an interval cut down to one year. See supra pp. 425–26.[19]

We are furthermore mindful that we sit in this case as a court of review and owe respect to the findings made by the district court. The trial judge concluded from the record that "Du Pont's 'as soon as possible' policy," contrary to Roosevelt's argument, "does not lack definition." Mem.Op. at 5. The judge found the policy genuine based on evidence that Du Pont had already spent more than $240 million developing alternatives to CFCs and had just announced the shutdown of the facility that had been the largest CFC plant in the world. Id. Du Pont, the district court also observed, continues to work "toward a global policy of phasing out CFCs" and "with CFC consumers to phase out their use of CFCs." Id.

Stressing the undisputed need for the responsible development of safe substitutes, and the acknowledged irresponsibility of suddenly cutting off all CFC production, the trial judge highlighted the essential difference between this case and the nuclear power plant in the Commission's *1976 Rule 14a–8 Amendments* example. See supra p. 426. Phasing out CFC production is not a go/no go matter. Cf. *Medical Comm.*, 432 F.2d at 663 (proposal to halt immediately all production of napalm). The phase out takes work "day-to-day . . . with equipment manufacturers to help develop the technology needed for alternative compounds." Mem.Op. at 6. It takes careful planning "in sensitive areas, such as the storage of perishable food and medical products (like vaccines and transfusable blood)," and expertise "in technical fields, such as the sterilization of temperature-sensitive surgical instruments." Id.

We recognize that "ordinary business operations" ordinarily do not attract the interest of both the executive and legislative branches of the federal government. See supra notes 15, 18. But government regulation of the CFC phase out, even the President's headline-attracting decision to accelerate the schedule initially set by Congress, does not automatically elevate shareholder proposals on timing to the status of "significant policy." See supra p. 427. What the President and Congress have said about CFCs is not the subject of our closest look. Instead, Rule 14a–8(c)(7) requires us to home in on Roosevelt's proposal, to determine whether her request dominantly implicates ordinary business matters. The gap between her proposal and the

---

19. As Roosevelt correctly points out, the principle of deference described in Chevron U.S.A. Inc. v. NRDC, Inc., 467 U.S. 837, 104 S.Ct. 2778, 81 L.Ed.2d 694 (1984), is not applicable here, for neither the staff's no-action letter nor the Commission's brief ranks as an agency adjudication or rulemaking. See Reply Brief at 12–14. Nonetheless, we value the SEC's presentation; the Commission's brief has clarified several points and thereby aided our analysis considerably.

company's schedule is now one year, not five. The steps to be taken to accomplish the phase out are complex; as the district court found, the company, having agreed on the essential policy, must carry it out safely, using "business and technical skills" day-to-day that are not meant for "shareholder debate and participation." Mem.Op. at 5, 6.

In sum, the parties agree that CFC production must be phased out, that substitutes must be developed, and that both should be achieved sooner rather than later. Du Pont has undertaken to eliminate the products in question by year-end 1995, and has pledged to do so sooner if "possible." The trial judge has found Du Pont's "as soon as possible" pledge credible. In these circumstances, we conclude that what is at stake is the "implementation of a policy," "the timing for an agreed-upon action," see Brief of the Securities and Exchange Commission, Amicus Curiae, at 31, and we therefore hold the target date for the phase out a matter excludable under Rule 14a–8(c)(7).

B.   The Report to Shareholders

The second part of Roosevelt's proposal solicits a report from management within six months detailing research and development efforts on environmentally safe substitutes and a marketing plan to sell those substitutes. See supra note 1. This portion of the proposal, the SEC concluded in agreement with its staff, "requires detailed information about the company's day-to-day business operations [and] is subject to exclusion pursuant to [Rule 14a–8(c)(7)]." Brief of the Securities and Exchange Commission, Amicus Curiae, at 31. Roosevelt concedes that the report is not central to her proposal, see supra p. 426, and we find no cause to place the matter outside the "ordinary business operations" exception.

For a time, the Commission staff "ha[d] taken the position that proposals requesting issuers to prepare reports on specific aspects of their business or to form [study committees] would not be excludable under Rule 14a–8(c)(7)." *Amendments to Rule 14a–8 Under the Securities Exchange Act of 1934 Relating to Proposals by Security Holders,* Exchange Act Release No. 20,091, 48 Fed.Reg. 38,218, 38,221 (Aug. 23, 1983). The Commission has changed that position. Pointing out that the staff's interpretation "raise[d] form over substance," the Commission instructed the staff to "consider whether the subject matter of the [requested] report or [study] committee involves a matter of ordinary business: where it does, the proposal [is] excludable under Rule 14a–8(c)(7)." Id.

We need not linger over the report issue. The staff's no-action letters in this respect are unremarkable and entirely in keeping with current practice. See, e.g., Carolina Power & Light Co., SEC No–Action Letter (available Mar. 8, 1990) (shareholder proposal requesting preparation of a report on specific aspects of company's nuclear operations, covering, *inter alia,* safety, regulatory compliance, emissions problems, hazardous waste disposal and related cost information, may be omitted as relating to ordinary business operations).

Just as the Commission has clarified that requests for special reports or committee studies are not automatically includable in proxy materials, we caution that such requests are not inevitably excludable. But Roosevelt has not shown that the detailed research and development or marketing information she seeks implicates significant policy issues, and not merely implementation arrangements. She does not, for example, suggest that Du Pont is developing or planning to market hazardous substitutes. Cf. Lovenheim v. Iroquois Brands, Ltd., 618 F.Supp. 554, 556, 561 (D.D.C.1985) (in light of "ethical and social significance" of proposal, court granted preliminary injunction barring corporation from excluding from its proxy materials shareholder proposal that requested formation of committee to study, and submission of report to shareholders about, whether company's supplier produced pate de foie gras in a manner involving undue pain or suffering to animals and whether distribution of product should be discontinued pending development of a more humane method).

In agreement with the district judge, the Commission, and the staff, we hold that the second part of Roosevelt's proposal falls within the "ordinary business operations" exception.

Conclusion

A private right of action is properly implied from section 14(a) of the Act, and Commission Rule 14a–8 thereunder, to enforce a registrant's obligation to include a shareholder's proposal in proxy materials mailed out in advance of the annual meeting. Roosevelt's proposal, however, may be excluded by Du Pont because, in both of its parts, the proposal falls within the exception furnished by Rule 14a–8(c)(7) for matters relating to "ordinary business operations." Accordingly, the judgment of the district court is

Affirmed.

NOTE ON CORPORATE–GOVERNANCE SHAREHOLDER PROPOSALS

Shareholder resolutions are conventionally divided into social-policy resolutions and corporate-governance resolutions. Georgeson Shareholder Communications, Inc., a well-known proxy solicitation firm, regularly surveys corporate-governance proposals made during the annual proxy season (normally, the first six months of the year, when most annual meetings occur). In the 2004 proxy season, 776 corporate-governance proposals were submitted. Of these, 414 were withdrawn for a variety of factors, including legal or regulatory action (such as SEC rulings that the proposals did not qualify under Rule 14a–8); negotiations between the proposing shareholder and the corporation; or capitulation by one or the other. Forty-seven percent of the proposals were made by individual shareholders, 43% were made by labor unions, 3% were made by public pensions, 2% by religious groups, and 5% by other shareholder groups.

A number of the governance proposals received a majority vote in favor. In fact, certain kinds of proposals received an *average* majority vote in favor. These included proposals to expense options at the time of grant, to rescind poison pills, to repeal classified boards, and to require approval of future golden parachutes. Some other kinds of proposals received an average vote of between 25% and 39%. These included proposals that shareholder approval be required for supplemental retirement plans, that there should be an independent board chairman, that there should be a majority of independent directors, and that stock options should be performance based.

Georgeson commented as follows on the 2004 proxy season:

> An increasingly common view is that the Sarbanes–Oxley Act (SOX) has made companies less inclined to fight against shareholder proposals relating to governance policy. Another more controversial view is that companies have "got religion" and are willingly accepting shareholders' governance mandates. We see a trend for companies not to fight as hard to maintain governance policies that are opposed by majority shareholder votes.

Georgeson Shareholder Annual Corporate Governance Review—2004, at ii.

An important aspect of the 2004 Proxy Season was the flowering of "exempt," "withhold," and "just-vote-no" campaigns. As described by Georgeson

> Exempt campaigns had a true emergence in 2004. Our research indicates that votes of at least 15% (measured as a percentage of votes cast) were withheld from 468 directors at 258 companies in the S & P 1500 that held meetings during the first seven month of 2004. In addition, eleven companies were the subject of exempt solicitations for which Form 14a–103 filings (Notice of Exempt Solicitation) were made under Rule 14a–6(g). In past years we have not collected data on *withhold*, *just-vote-no* or *just-vote-yes* (in support of shareholder resolutions opposed by management) solicitations. 2004 marks the start of our efforts to compile a new set of exempt-campaign statistics for our annual review. Our assumption is that these campaigns will increase in the future regardless of the fate of the access rule.

> "Full-blown" proxy contests declined in 2004. There were 27 contests during the period January through September 2004 versus 37 in 2003—a substantial 24% decline. This statistic measures only full-fledged proxy contests. i.e., those in which the competing parties both sought proxy voting authority. It does not include the withhold and just-vote-no campaigns that are exempt from filing requirements under SEC Rule 14a–2(b) (1) because the dissident is not seeking proxy voting authority. The two most prominent battles in the U.S. this year—the campaign against directors at the Walt Disney Company and the proposed takeover of PeopleSoft by Oracle—did not involve actual contested solicitations. This year's proxy fights generally involved small and mid-

cap companies where dissidents could take significant ownership positions that increase the odds of winning. Closed-ended funds remained a popular target for dissidents, particularly funds with high "institutional" ownership, which is also believed to improve the likelihood of dissident success. Few U.S. domestic contests involved change of control, although unsuccessful control contests were waged in Korea and Japan. We believe that in 2004 the pending SEC access rule caused dissidents to be less interested in proxy contests as well as shareholder proposals, while encouraging greater use of exempt solicitations, particularly withhold campaigns specifically designated as a trigger mechanism by the access proposal. . . .

Id. at i–ii.

NOTE ON SHAREHOLDER SOCIAL–POLICY PROPOSALS

In the 2003 proxy season, 299 social-policy shareholder resolutions were filed. Of these, 145 came to a vote. Some of these were withdrawn because they were headed for defeat at the SEC, but most of the withdrawals came as a result of agreements between the proponents and the corporations. For example, New York City led a campaign to amend Equal Employment Opportunity statements to prohibit anti-gay discrimination. Of nineteen such proposals, 13 were withdrawn when the corporations agreed in full to the action requested.

Among the 299 social-policy resolutions that were filed in 2003, 59 concerned environmental issues, 31 concerned global-labor issues, 31 concerned equal-employment, 24 concerned tobacco, and 23 concerned health issues. In the case of social-policy proposals, any vote over 15 percent is considered high. Of the proposals that were voted on in 2003, the votes on two were in the 40 percent range, the votes on five fell in the 30 percent range, and the votes on eighteen fell in the 20 percent range. IRRC, Social Policy Shareholder Resolutions in 2003 (2004).

SECTION 6.   PROXY CONTESTS

Rosenfeld v. Fairchild Engine and Airplane Corp.

Court of Appeals of New York, 1955.
309 N.Y. 168, 128 N.E.2d 291.

■ FROSSEL, JUDGE. In a stockholder's derivative action brought by plaintiff, an attorney, who owns 25 out of the company's over 2,300,000 shares, he seeks to compel the return of $261,522, paid out of the corporate treasury to reimburse both sides in a proxy contest for their expenses. The Appellate Division, 284 App.Div. 201, 132 N.Y.S.2d 273, has unanimously affirmed a judgment of an Official Referee, Sup., 116 N.Y.S.2d 840, dismissing plaintiff's complaint on the merits, and we agree. Exhaustive opinions were written by both courts below, and it will serve no useful purpose to review the facts again.

Of the amount in controversy $106,000 was spent out of corporate funds by the old board of directors while still in office in defense of their position in said contest; $28,000 [was] paid to the old board by the new board after the change of management following the proxy contest, to compensate the former directors for such of the remaining expenses of their unsuccessful defense as the new board found was fair and reasonable; payment of $127,000, representing reimbursement of expenses to members of the prevailing group, was expressly ratified by a 16 to 1 majority vote of the stockholders.

The essential facts are not in dispute, and, since the determinations below are amply supported by the evidence, we are bound by the findings affirmed by the Appellate Division. The Appellate Division found that the difference between plaintiff's group and the old board "went deep into the policies of the company", and that among these Ward's contract was one of the "main points of contention". The Official Referee found that the controversy "was based on an understandable difference in policy between the two groups, at the very bottom of which was the Ward employment contract".

By way of contrast with the findings here, in Lawyers' Advertising Co. v. Consolidated Ry., Lighting & Refrigerating Co., 187 N.Y. 395, at page 399, 80 N.E. 199, at page 200, which was an action to recover for the cost of publishing newspaper notices not authorized by the board of directors, it was expressly found that the proxy contest there involved was "by one faction in its contest with another for the control of the corporation ... a contest for the perpetuation of their offices and control." We there said by way of *dicta* that under *such* circumstances the publication of certain notices on behalf of the management faction was not a corporate expenditure which the directors had the power to authorize.

Other jurisdictions and our own lower courts have held that management may look to the corporate treasury for the reasonable expenses of soliciting proxies to defend its position in a bona fide policy contest. . . .

It should be noted that plaintiff does not argue that the aforementioned sums were fraudulently extracted from the corporation; indeed, his counsel conceded that "the charges were fair and reasonable", but denied "they were legal charges which may be reimbursed for". This is therefore not a case where a stockholder challenges specific items, which, on examination, the trial court may find unwarranted, excessive or otherwise improper. Had plaintiff made such objections here, the trial court would have been required to examine the items challenged.

If directors of a corporation may not in good faith incur reasonable and proper expenses in soliciting proxies in these days of giant corporations with vast numbers of stockholders, the corporate business might be seriously interfered with because of stockholder indifference and the difficulty of procuring a quorum, where there is no contest. In the event of a proxy contest, if the directors may not freely answer the challenges of outside groups and in good faith defend their actions with respect to corporate policy for the information of the stockholders, they and the corporation may be at the mercy of persons seeking to wrest control for their own purposes, so long as such persons have ample funds to conduct a proxy contest. The test is clear. When the directors act in good faith in a contest over policy, they have the right to incur reasonable and proper expenses for solicitation of proxies and in defense of their corporate policies, and are not obliged to sit idly by. The courts are entirely competent to pass upon their *bona fides* in any given case, as well as the nature of their expenditures when duly challenged.

It is also our view that the members of the so-called new group could be reimbursed by the corporation for their expenditures in this contest by affirmative vote of the stockholders. With regard to these ultimately successful contestants, as the Appellate Division below has noted, there was, of course, "no duty . . . to set forth the facts, with corresponding obligation of the corporation to pay for such expense". However, where a majority of the stockholders chose—in this case by a vote of 16 to 1—to reimburse the successful contestants for achieving the very end sought and voted for by them as owners of the corporation, we see no reason to deny the effect of their ratification nor to hold the corporate body powerless to determine how its own moneys shall be spent.

The rule then which we adopt is simply this: In a contest over policy, as compared to a purely personal power contest, corporate directors have the right to make reasonable and proper expenditures, subject to the scrutiny of the courts when duly challenged, from the corporate treasury for the purpose of persuading the stockholders of the correctness of their position and soliciting their support for policies which the directors believe, in all good faith, are in the best interests of the corporation. The stockholders, moreover, have the right to reimburse successful contestants for the reasonable and bona fide expenses incurred by them in any such policy contest, subject to like court scrutiny. That is not to say, however, that corporate directors can, under any circumstances, disport themselves in a proxy contest with the corporation's moneys to an unlimited extent. Where it is established that such moneys have been spent for personal power, individual gain or private advantage, and not in the belief that such expenditures are in the best interests of the stockholders and the corporation, or where the fairness and reasonableness of the amounts allegedly expended are duly and successfully challenged, the courts will not hesitate to disallow them.

The judgment of the Appellate Division should be affirmed, without costs.

■ DESMOND, JUDGE (concurring). We granted leave to appeal in an effort to pass, and in the expectation of passing, on this question, highly important in modern-day corporation law: is it lawful for a corporation, on consent of a majority of its stockholders, to pay, out of its funds, the expenses of a "proxy fight", incurred by competing candidates for election as directors? Now that the appeal has been argued, I doubt that the question is presented by this record....

... The reason why that important question is, perhaps, not directly before us in this lawsuit is because, as the Appellate Division properly held, [284 App.Div. 201, 132 N.Y.S.2d 273] plaintiff failed "to urge liability as to specific expenditures". The cost of giving routinely necessary notice is, of course, chargeable to the corporation. It is just as clear, we think, that payment by a corporation of the expense of "proceedings by one faction in its contest with another for the control of the corporation" is *ultra vires,* and unlawful. Lawyers' Advertising Co. v. Consolidated Ry., Lighting & Refrigerating Co., 187 N.Y. 395, 399, 80 N.E. 199, 200. Approval by directors or by a majority stock vote could not validate such gratuitous expenditures. Continental Securities Co. v. Belmont, 206 N.Y. 7, 99 N.E. 138, 51 L.R.A.,N.S., 112. Some of the payments attacked in this suit were, on their face, for lawful purposes and apparently reasonable in amount but, as to others, the record simply does not contain evidentiary bases for a determination as to either lawfulness or reasonableness. Surely, the burden was on plaintiff to go forward to some extent with such particularization and proof. It failed to do so, and so failed to make out a prima facie case.

We are, therefore, reaching the same result as did the Appellate Division but on one only of the grounds listed by that court, that is, failure of proof. We think it not inappropriate, however, to state our general views on the question of law principally argued by the parties, that is, as to the validity of corporate payments for proxy solicitations and similar activities in addition to giving notice of the meeting, and of the questions to be voted on. For an answer to that problem we could not do better than quote from this court's opinion in the Lawyers' Advertising Co. case, 187 N.Y. 395, 399, 80 N.E. 199, 200, supra: "The remaining notices were not legally authorized and were not legitimately incidental to the meeting or necessary for the protection of the stockholders. They rather were proceedings by one faction in its contest with another for the control of the corporation, and the expense thereof, as such, is not properly chargeable to the latter.... [I]t would be altogether too dangerous a rule to permit directors in control of a corporation and engaged in a contest for the perpetuation of their offices and control, to impose upon the corporation the unusual expense of publishing advertisements or, by analogy, of dispatching special messengers for the purpose of procuring proxies in their behalf." ...

The judgment should be affirmed, without costs.

■ VAN VOORHIS, JUDGE (dissenting)....

No resolution was passed by the stockholders approving payment to the management group. It has been recognized that not all of the $133,966 in obligations paid or incurred by the management group was designed merely for information of stockholders. This outlay included payment for all of the activities of a strenuous campaign to persuade and cajole in a hard-fought contest for control of this corporation. It included, for example, expenses for entertainment, chartered airplanes and limousines, public relations counsel and proxy solicitors. However legitimate such measures may be on behalf of stockholders themselves in such a controversy, most of them do not pertain to a corporate function but are part of the familiar apparatus of aggressive factions in corporate contests. . . .

The Appellate Division acknowledged in the instant case that "It is obvious that the management group here incurred a substantial amount of needless expense which was charged to the corporation," but this conclusion should have led to a direction that those defendants who were incumbent directors should be required to come forward with an explanation of their expenditures under the familiar rule that where it has been established that directors have expended corporate money for their own purposes, the burden of going forward with evidence of the propriety and reasonableness of specific items rests upon the directors. . . . The complaint should not have been dismissed as against incumbent directors due to failure of plaintiff to segregate the specific expenditures which are *ultra vires,* but, once plaintiff had proved facts from which an inference of impropriety might be drawn, the duty of making an explanation was laid upon the directors to explain and justify their conduct. . . .

There is no doubt that the management was entitled and under a duty to take reasonable steps to acquaint the stockholders with essential facts concerning the management of the corporation, and it may well be that the existence of a contest warranted them in circularizing the stockholders with more than ordinarily detailed information. . . .

What expenses of the incumbent group should be allowed and what should be disallowed should be remitted to the trial court to ascertain, after taking evidence, in accordance with the rule that the incumbent directors were required to assume the burden of going forward in the first instance with evidence explaining and justifying their expenditures. Only such as were reasonably related to informing the stockholders fully and fairly concerning the corporate affairs should be allowed. The concession by plaintiff that such expenditures as were made were reasonable in amount does not decide this question. By way of illustration, the costs of entertainment for stockholders may have been, and it is stipulated that they were, at the going rates for providing similar entertainment. That does not signify that entertaining stockholders is reasonably related to the purposes of the corporation. The Appellate Division, as above stated, found that the management group incurred a substantial amount of needless expense. That fact being established, it became the duty of the incumbent directors to unravel and explain these payments.

Regarding the $127,556 paid by the new management to the insurgent group for their campaign expenditures, the question immediately arises whether that was for a corporate purpose....

... The case most frequently cited and principally relied upon from among [the] Delaware decisions is Hall v. Trans–Lux Daylight Picture Screen Corp. [20 Del.Ch. 78]. There the English case was followed of Peel v. London & North Western Ry. Co.... which distinguished between expenses merely for the purpose of maintaining control, and contests over policy questions of the corporation. In the Hall case the issues concerned a proposed merger, and a proposed sale of stock of a subsidiary corporation. These were held to be policy questions, and payment of the management campaign expenses was upheld.

In our view, the impracticability [of distinguishing between expenses incurred merely for the purpose of maintaining control, and expenses in contests over policy questions] is illustrated by the statement in the Hall case, supra, 20 Del.Ch. at page 85, 171 A. at page 229, that "It is impossible in many cases of intracorporate contests over directors, to sever questions of policy from those of persons". This circumstance is stressed in Judge Rifkind's opinion in [Steinberg v. Adams, 90 F.Supp. 604] at page 608: "The simple fact, of course, is that generally policy and personnel do not exist in separate compartments. A change in personnel is sometimes indispensable to a change of policy. A new board may be the symbol of the shift in policy as well as the means of obtaining it."

... [I]nasmuch as it is generally impossible to distinguish whether "policy" or "personnel" is the dominant factor, any averments must be accepted at their face value that questions of policy are dominant. Nowhere do these opinions mention that the converse is equally true and more pervasive, that neither the "ins" nor the "outs" ever say that they have no program to offer to the shareholders, but just want to acquire or to retain control, as the case may be. In common experience, this distinction is unreal....

The main question of "policy" in the instant corporate election, as is stated in the opinions below and frankly admitted, concerns the long-term contract with pension rights of a former officer and director, Mr. J. Carlton Ward, Jr. The insurgents' chief claim of benefit to the corporation from their victory consists in the termination of that agreement, resulting in an alleged actuarial saving of $350,000 to $825,000 to the corporation, and the reduction of other salaries and rent by more than $300,000 per year. The insurgents had contended in the proxy contest that these payments should be substantially reduced so that members of the incumbent group would not continue to profit personally at the expense of the corporation. If these charges were true, which appear to have been believed by a majority of the shareholders, then the disbursements by the management group in the proxy contest fall under the condemnation of the English and the Delaware rule.

These circumstances are mentioned primarily to illustrate how impossible it is to distinguish between "policy" and "personnel", ... but they also indicate that personal factors are deeply rooted in this contest. That is certainly true insofar as the former management group is concerned. . . .

Some expenditures may concededly be made by a corporation represented by its management so as to inform the stockholders, but there is a clear distinction between such expenditures by management and by mere groups of stockholders. The latter are under no legal obligation to assume duties of managing the corporation. They may endeavor to supersede the management for any reason, regardless of whether it be advantageous or detrimental to the corporation but, if they succeed, that is not a determination that the company was previously mismanaged or that it may not be mismanaged in the future. A change in control is in no sense analogous to an adjudication that the former directors have been guilty of misconduct. The analogy of allowing expenses of suit to minority stockholders who have been successful in a derivative action based on misconduct of officers or directors, is entirely without foundation.

Insofar as a management group is concerned, it may charge the corporation with any expenses within reasonable limits incurred in giving widespread notice to stockholders of questions affecting the welfare of the corporation. . . . Expenditures in excess of these limits are *ultra vires.* The corporation lacks power to defray them. The corporation lacks power to defray the expenses of the insurgents in their entirety. The insurgents were not charged with responsibility for operating the company. No appellate court case is cited from any jurisdiction holding otherwise. No contention is made that such disbursements could be made, in any event, without stockholder ratification; they could not be ratified except by unanimous vote if they were *ultra vires.* The insurgents, in this instance, repeatedly announced to the stockholders in their campaign literature that their proxy contest was being waged at their own personal expense. If reimbursement of such items were permitted upon majority stockholder ratification, no court or other tribunal could pass upon which types of expenditures were "needless", to employ the characterization of the Appellate Division in this case. Whether the insurgents should be paid would be made to depend upon whether they win the stockholders election and obtain control of the corporation. It would be entirely irrelevant whether the corporation is "benefitted" by their efforts or by the outcome of such an election. The courts could not indulge in a speculative inquiry into that issue. That would truly be a matter of business judgment. In some instances corporations are better governed by the existing management and in others by some other group which supersedes the existing management. Courts of law have no jurisdiction to decide such questions, and successful insurgent stockholders may confidently be relied upon to reimburse themselves whatever may be the real merits of the controversy. The losers in a proxy fight may understand the interests of the corporation more accurately than their successful adversaries, and agitation of this character may ultimately result in corporate advantage even if there be no change in management. Nevertheless, under the judgment which is appealed from, success in a proxy contest is the indispensable condition upon which reimbursement of the insurgents depends. Adventurers are not infrequent who are ready to take advantage of economic recessions, reduction of dividends or failure to increase them, or other sources of stockholder discontent to wage contests in order to obtain control of well-managed corporations, so as to divert their funds through legal channels into other corporations in which they may be interested, or to discharge former officers and employees to make room for favored newcomers according to the fashion of political patronage, or for other objectives that are unrelated to the sound prosperity of the enterprise. The way is open and will be kept open for stockholders and groups of stockholders to contest corporate elections, but if the promoters of such movements choose to employ the costly modern media of mass persuasion, they should look for reimbursement to themselves and to the stockholders who are aligned with them. If the law be that they can be recompensed by the corporation in case of success, and only in that event, it will operate as a powerful incentive to persons accustomed to taking calculated risks to increase this form of high-powered salesmanship to such a degree that, action provoking reaction, stockholders' meetings will be very costly. To the financial advantages promised by control of a prosperous corporation, would be added the knowledge that the winner takes all insofar as the campaign expenses are concerned. To the victor, indeed, would belong the spoils. . . .

■ CONWAY, C.J., and BURKE, J., concur with FROESSEL, J.; DESMOND, J., concurs in part in a separate opinion; VAN VOORHIS, J., dissents in an opinion in which DYE and FULD JJ., concur.

Judgment affirmed.

———

J. Heard & H. Sherman Conflicts of Interest in the Proxy Voting System 84–85

(1987).

Very few contested elections are run without the aid of professional proxy solicitors. Because of their experience and personal contacts in the investment community and at proxy departments of brokerage houses and banks, professional solicitors usually are able to generate a higher vote turnout than issuer companies can do by themselves. For this reason, both management and the dissident side usually engage their own solicitors during contested elections. Even for uncontested elections, companies that are worried about not reaching a quorum count employ the services of a solicitor to guarantee a high turnout. Companies also use solicitors when they expect significant opposition to uncontested management proposals, such as antitakeover charter amendments or defensive recapitalizations.

The leading proxy solicitation firms include Georgeson and Co., the Carter Organization, D.F. King and Co., Morrow and Co. and the Kissel–Blake Organization.

By virtue of their years of experience in the business, solicitors often know how a particular shareholder, or a particular type of shareholder, will vote on different issues. For this reason, firms trying to pass proposals that they fear will be met with strong opposition often engage solicitors to determine whether or not the proposal should even be included on the ballot. For example, Georgeson and Co. prepares a best case/worst case voting scenario for clients on various types of proposals. If the likely outcome seems to be a defeat for management, based on Georgeson's analysis, the issuer company will often decide to exclude the proposal from its ballot. John Wilcox, a principal at Georgeson, told IRRC that this explains why so few antitakeover proposals are defeated. According to Wilcox, most antitakeover proposals that are likely to be defeated, based on Georgeson's or another solicitor's analysis, are never put on a ballot in the first place.

When engaged by management or a dissident during a contested election, a solicitor's services are invaluable. The solicitor handles all the physical requirements of the proxy campaign. It identifies beneficial owners, mails the proxy material to recordholders, makes sure that beneficial owners have received proxy material from the recordholder bank or broker, rounds up late votes with phone calls or follow-up mailings, and tabulates the vote for management or the dissident.

The first of these functions, identifying beneficial owners, is among the most important services a solicitor can offer. . . . [R]egistration in bank nominee name often enables a beneficial owner to hide its identity and security position from the issuer company. When votes come in to a solicitor from a bank client, the proxy is signed by the bank, and the owner is identified only by an account number assigned to the client by his bank. The owner's name does not appear on the proxy card. When such votes are cast against management or a dissident, the interested party has no way of knowing who is behind the shares being voted against him. But proxy solicitors have developed their own data bases over the years that match bank account numbers with the identity of their owners. This enables a solicitor to tell a client who is behind the bank votes being cast during the proxy campaign. When the proxy vote is going against the solicitor's client, this ability becomes very important, for it allows the solicitor or the solicitor's client to contact the shareowner and ask him to reconsider his vote.

During a proxy campaign, a solicitor keeps in close contact with the proxy clerks at brokerage firms and with appropriate bank officers to make sure that their client's proxy material is being forwarded to beneficial owners. A solicitor can therefore decide if a second mailing is necessary. Such contact also enables a solicitor to tell his client how the vote is progressing, since brokers and banks usually tally votes as they are received but wait until shortly before a meeting to submit their proxies. If a solicitor determines that the final voting results may go against its client, advance information gives the solicitor's client time to exert more pressure on important shareholders to influence their vote, to resolicit shareholders who may have voted against the client, or to redouble efforts to reach shareholders who have not responded.

When final proxies arrive, the solicitor checks them to make sure that they are valid proxies, that they have been signed correctly, that they represent the appropriate number of shares, and that they are not duplicate or replacement proxies. Once done, the solicitor usually also participates in the actual tabulation at the annual meeting. The solicitor's experience can save a company much time when counting the vote, since the solicitor knows which way of sorting and collating the proxies will be the most expedient. When proxy votes are challenged by the opposing side in a proxy contest, the solicitor's knowledge of the technical requirements of valid proxies can prove invaluable. . . .

———

HEINEMAN v. DATAPOINT CORP., 611 A.2d 950 (Del.1992). "The complaint alleges a successful contest for corporate control, with the victors in that contest using their newly acquired positions to cause the corporation to reimburse the costs of waging that contest. Proof of these facts at trial would represent a *prima facie* case of director self-dealing."

CHAPTER VI

THE SPECIAL PROBLEMS OF CLOSE CORPORATIONS

SECTION 1. INTRODUCTION

(a) A BRIEF LOOK BACK AT PARTNERSHIP

NOTE ON PARTNERSHIP LAW AND CORPORATE LAW

Corporations can be divided into three classes: (1) *Publicly held corporations*, which typically have a large number of shareholders, and whose shares are publicly traded. (2) *Private corporations*, whose shares are not publicly traded, although they may have more than a small number of shareholders, and (3) *Close corporations*, a subset of private corporations Close corporations have only a small number of shareholders, and are often characterized by owner-management and restrictions on the transferability of ownership interests. In important respects, close corporations resemble partnerships, which are also typically characterized by a small number of owners, owner-manage-ment, and restrictions on the transferability of ownership interests. Indeed, certain aspects of partnership law form an important backdrop to the study of close corporations, because in the last forty or so years, years legislators and courts have looked to partnership-law norms in solving close-corporation-law problems.

1. *Basic Partnership–Law Norms.* The most striking aspect of partnership law is its heavily contractual nature. For many purposes, both the Uniform Partnership Act (the "UPA") and the Revised Uni-form Partnership Act ("RUPA") operate only in the absence of an agreement by the partners on a given issue. The following is a highly generalized summary of the partnership-law rules most salient to the ongoing conduct of the firm:

a. *Internal governance.* As concerns internal governance, part-nership law is facilitative rather than mandatory. Both the UPA and RUPA provide default rules to govern situations that the partners' arrangements fail to cover, but allow the owners to contract for different rules. The basic governance rules are:

(i) Absent contrary agreement, all partners have equal rights in the management and conduct of the partnership business.

(ii) Absent contrary agreement, differences among the partners "as to ordinary matters connected with the partnership business" are determined by a majority of the partners, but matters that are outside the scope of the partnership business, or that would be in conflict with the partnership agreement, require unanimous approval.

b. *Authority.* Any partner has power to bind the partnership on a matter in the ordinary course of business. This is the case even if by virtue of the partnership's internal arrangements the partner lacks actual authority, unless the third party with whom the partner deals knows that the partner lacks actual authority.

c. *Distributive shares.* Absent contrary agreement, partnership profits are shared per capita, and no partner is entitled to a salary.

d. *Transferability.* Absent contrary agreement, no person can become a member of a partnership without the consent of all the partners.

e. *Term.* Partnerships are normally created for a limited term— frequently a relatively short term—and dissolution is easy. If the partnership is not for a specified term (express or implied), any partner may cause dissolution at any time. If the partnership is for a specified term, dissolution occurs at the end of the term and under certain other circumstances.

f. *Fiduciary duties.* Partners stand in a fiduciary relationship to each other.

g. *Liability.* Partners in a general partnership are individually liable for the partnership's obligations.

2. *Basic Corporation–Law Norms.* Traditional corporation-law norms were diametrically opposed to almost every one of these partnership-law norms:

a. *Internal governance.* As to many aspects of internal governance, the traditional corporate statutes were mandatory. For example, under traditional corporate-law norms, shareholders, as such, have no right to participate in the management of the corporation's business.

b. *Authority.* Because shareholders, as such, have no right to participate in the management of the corporation's business, they also have no apparent authority to bind the corporation.

c. *Distributive shares.* Corporate distributions are not shared per capita, but in proportion to stock ownership.

d. *Transferability.* Shares of stock, and the shareholder status they carry, are freely transferable.

e. *Term.* Corporations are normally created for a perpetual term, and dissolution is relatively difficult.

f. *Fiduciary duties.* The traditional view was that shareholders do not stand in a direct fiduciary relationship to each other, although that view has now changed in material respects. See chapters 9 and 10, infra.

g. *Liability.* Shareholders are not individually liable for a corporation's obligations.

Most of these basic corporate-laws norms were designed with an eye to the publicly held corporation. As will be seen in this Chapter, the application of these norms in the close-corporation context often leads to the frustration of legitimate expectations. As a result, under modern law, in close corporations many of these traditional norms can be overridden by agreement.

(b) An Introduction to the Close Corporation

Donahue v. Rodd Electrotype Co.

Supreme Judicial Court of Massachusetts, 1975.
367 Mass. 578, 328 N.E.2d 505.

■ Tauro, Chief Justice.

The plaintiff, Euphemia Donahue, a minority stockholder in the Rodd Electrotype Company of New England, Inc. (Rodd Electrotype), a Massachusetts corporation, brings this suit against the directors of Rodd Electrotype, Charles H. Rodd, Frederick I. Rodd and Mr. Harold E. Magnuson, against Harry C. Rodd, a former director, officer, and controlling stockholder of Rodd Electrotype and against Rodd Electrotype (hereinafter called defendants). The plaintiff seeks to rescind Rodd Electrotype's purchase of Harry Rodd's shares in Rodd Electrotype and to compel Harry Rodd "to repay to the corporation the purchase price of said shares, $36,000, together with interest from the date of purchase." The plaintiff alleges that the defendants caused the corporation to purchase the shares in violation of their fiduciary duty to her, a minority stockholder of Rodd Electrotype.[4]

The trial judge, after hearing oral testimony, dismissed the plaintiff's bill on the merits. He found that the purchase was without prejudice to the plaintiff and implicitly found that the transaction had been carried out in good faith and with inherent fairness. The Appeals Court affirmed with costs. Donahue v. Rodd Electrotype Co. of New England, Inc., 1 Mass.App. 876, 307 N.E.2d 8 (1974). The case is before us on the plaintiff's application for further appellate review....

[Briefly, the facts were as follows: In the mid–1930's Harry Rodd and Joseph Donahue had become employees of Royal Electrotype (the predecessor of Rodd Electrotype). Donahue's duties were confined to

4. In form, the plaintiff's bill of complaint presents, at least in part, a derivative action, brought on behalf of the corporation, and, in the words of the bill, "on behalf of ... [the] stockholders" of Rodd Electrotype. Yet ... the plaintiff's bill, in substance, was one seeking redress because of alleged breaches of the fiduciary duty owed *to her*, a minority stockholder, by the controlling stockholders.

We treat the bill of complaint (as have the parties) as presenting a proper cause of suit in the personal right of the plaintiff....

operational matters within the plants, and he never participated in the management aspect of the business. In contrast, Rodd's advancement within the company was rapid, and in 1946 he became general manager and treasurer. Subsequently Rodd acquired 200 of the corporation's 1000 shares and Donahue (at Rodd's suggestion) acquired 50 shares. In 1955 Rodd became president and general manager, and later that year Royal itself purchased the remaining 750 shares, so that Rodd and Donahue became Royal's sole shareholders, owning 80% and 20% of its stock, respectively. In 1960 the corporation was renamed Rodd Electrotype, and in the early 60's Harry Rodd's two sons, Charles and Frederick, took important positions with the company. In 1965 Charles succeeded his father as president and general manager.

In 1970 Harry Rodd was seventy-seven years old and not in good health, and his sons wished him to retire. Prior to 1967 Harry had distributed 117 of his 200 shares equally among his sons and his daughter, and had returned 2 shares to the corporate treasury. Harry insisted that as a condition to his retirement some financial arrangement be made with respect to his remaining 81 shares. Accordingly, Charles, acting on the corporation's behalf, negotiated for the purchase of 45 of Harry's shares for $800/share—a price which, Charles testified, reflected book and liquidating value. At a special board meeting in July 1970, the corporation's board (then consisting of Charles and Frederick Rodd and a lawyer) voted to have the corporation make the purchase at this price. Subsequently Harry Rodd sold 2 shares to each of his three children at $800/share, and gave each child 10 shares as a gift.[7] Meanwhile Donahue had died and his 50 shares had passed to his wife and son. When the Donahues learned that the corporation had purchased Harry Rodd's shares, they offered their shares to the corporation on the terms given to Harry but the offer was rejected.[10] This suit followed.]

In her argument before this court, the plaintiff has characterized the corporate purchase of Harry Rodd's shares as an unlawful distribution of corporate assets to controlling stockholders. She urges that the distribution constitutes a breach of the fiduciary duty owed by the Rodds, as controlling stockholders, to her, a minority stockholder in the enterprise, because the Rodds failed to accord her an equal opportunity to sell her shares to the corporation. The defendants reply that the stock purchase was within the powers of the corporation and met the requirements of good faith and inherent fairness imposed on a fiduciary in his dealings with the corporation. They assert that there is no right to equal opportunity in corporate stock purchases for the corporate treasury. For the reasons hereinafter noted, we agree with the plaintiff and reverse the decree of the Superior Court. However, we limit the applicability of our holding to "close corporations," as

7. An inference is permissible that the "gift" of these shares was a part of the "deal" for the stock purchase.

10. Between 1965 and 1969, the company offered to purchase the Donahue shares for amounts between $2,000 and $10,000 ($40 to $200 a share). The Donahues rejected these offers.

hereinafter defined. Whether the holding should apply to other corporations is left for decision in another case, on a proper record.

A. *Close Corporations.* In previous opinions, we have alluded to the distinctive nature of the close corporation ... but have never defined precisely what is meant by a close corporation. There is no single, generally accepted definition. Some commentators emphasize an "integration of ownership and management" (Note, Statutory Assistance for Closely Held Corporations, 71 Harv.L.Rev. 1498 [1958]), in which the stockholders occupy most management positions.... Others focus on the number of stockholders and the nature of the market for the stock. In this view, close corporations have few stockholders; there is little market for corporate stock. The Supreme Court of Illinois adopted this latter view in Galler v. Galler, 32 Ill.2d 16, 203 N.E.2d 577 (1964).... We accept aspects of both definitions. We deem a close corporation to be typified by: (1) a small number of stockholders; (2) no ready market for the corporate stock; and (3) substantial majority stockholder participation in the management, direction and operations of the corporation.

As thus defined, the close corporation bears striking resemblance to a partnership.... Just as in a partnership, the relationship among the stockholders must be one of trust, confidence and absolute loyalty if the enterprise is to succeed....

In Helms v. Duckworth, 101 U.S.App.D.C. 390, 249 F.2d 482 (1957) ... Judge Burger, now Chief Justice Burger, writing for the court, emphasized the resemblance of the two-man close corporation to a partnership: "In an intimate business venture such as this, stockholders of a close corporation occupy a position similar to that of joint adventurers and partners. While courts have sometimes declared stockholders 'do not bear toward each other that same relation of trust and confidence which prevails in partnerships,' this view ignores the practical realities of the organization and functioning of a small 'two-man' corporation organized to carry on a small business enterprise in which the stockholders, directors, and managers are the same persons" (footnotes omitted). Id. at 486.

Although the corporate form provides ... advantages for the stockholders (limited liability, perpetuity, and so forth), it also supplies an opportunity for the majority stockholders to oppress or disadvantage minority stockholders. The minority is vulnerable to a variety of oppressive devices, termed "freeze-outs," which the majority may employ.... An authoritative study of such "freeze-outs" enumerates some of the possibilities: "The squeezers ... may refuse to declare dividends; they may drain off the corporation's earnings in the form of exorbitant salaries and bonuses to the majority shareholder-officers and perhaps to their relatives, or in the form of high rent by the corporation for property leased from majority shareholders ...; they may deprive minority shareholders of corporate offices and of employment by the company...."

The minority can, of course, initiate suit against the majority and their directors. Self-serving conduct by directors is proscribed by the director's fiduciary obligation to the corporation.... However, in practice, the plaintiff will find difficulty in challenging dividend or employment policies. Such policies are considered to be within the judgment of the directors ... [G]enerally, plaintiffs who seek judicial assistance against corporate dividend or employment policies do not prevail....

Thus, when these types of "freeze-outs" are attempted by the majority stockholders, the minority stockholders, cut off from all corporation-related revenues, must either suffer their losses or seek a buyer for their shares. Many minority stockholders will be unwilling or unable to wait for an alteration in majority policy. Typically, the minority stockholder in a close corporation has a substantial percentage of his personal assets invested in the corporation. The stockholder may have anticipated that his salary from his position with the corporation would be his livelihood. Thus, he cannot afford to wait passively. He must liquidate his investment in the close corporation in order to reinvest the funds in income-producing enterprises.

At this point, the true plight of the minority stockholder in a close corporation becomes manifest. He cannot easily reclaim his capital. In a large public corporation, the oppressed or dissident minority stockholder could sell his stock in order to extricate some of his invested capital. By definition, this market is not available for shares in the close corporation. In a partnership, a partner who feels abused by his fellow partners may cause dissolution by his "express will ... at any time" ... and recover his share of partnership assets and accumulated profits.... By contrast, the stockholder in the close corporation or "incorporated partnership" may achieve dissolution and recovery of his share of the enterprise assets only by compliance with the rigorous terms of the applicable chapter of the General Laws....

Thus, in a close corporation, the minority stockholders may be trapped in a disadvantageous situation. No outsider would knowingly assume the position of the disadvantaged minority. The outsider would have the same difficulties. To cut losses, the minority stockholder may be compelled to deal with the majority. This is the capstone of the majority plan. Majority "freeze-out" schemes which withhold dividends are designed to compel the minority to relinquish stock at inadequate prices.... When the minority stockholder agrees to sell out at less than fair value, the majority has won.

Because of the fundamental resemblance of the close corporation to the partnership, the trust and confidence which are essential to this scale and manner of enterprise, and the inherent danger to minority interests in the close corporation, we hold that stockholders[17] in the close corporation owe one another substantially the same fiduciary duty in the operation of the enterprise[18] that partners owe to one

---

17. We do not limit our holding to majority stockholders. In the close corporation, the minority may do equal damage through unscrupulous and improper "sharp dealings" with an unsuspecting majority. See Helms v. Duckworth, 101 U.S.App.D.C. 390, 249 F.2d 482 (1957).

18. We stress that the strict fiduciary duty which we apply to stockholders in a close corporation in this opinion governs *only*

another. In our previous decisions, we have defined the standard of duty owed by partners to one another as the "utmost good faith and loyalty." Cardullo v. Landau, 329 Mass. 5, 8, 105 N.E.2d 843 (1952); DeCotis v. D'Antona, 350 Mass. 165, 168, 214 N.E.2d 21 (1966). Stockholders in close corporations must discharge their management and stockholder responsibilities in conformity with this strict good faith standard. They may not act out of avarice, expediency or self-interest in derogation of their duty of loyalty to the other stockholders and to the corporation.

We contrast this strict good faith standard with the somewhat less stringent standard of fiduciary duty to which directors and stockholders of all corporations must adhere in the discharge of their corporate responsibilities. Corporate directors are held to a good faith and inherent fairness standard of conduct (Winchell v. Plywood Corp., 324 Mass. 171, 177, 85 N.E.2d 313 [1949]) and are not "permitted to serve two masters whose interests are antagonistic." Spiegel v. Beacon Participations, 297 Mass. 398, 411, 8 N.E.2d 895, 904 (1937). "Their paramount duty is to the corporation, and their personal pecuniary interests are subordinate to that duty." Durfee v. Durfee & Canning, Inc., 323 Mass. 187, 196, 80 N.E.2d 522, 527 (1948).

The more rigorous duty of partners and participants in a joint adventure, here extended to stockholders in a close corporation, was described by then Chief Judge Cardozo of the New York Court of Appeals in Meinhard v. Salmon, 249 N.Y. 458, 164 N.E. 545 (1928): "Joint adventurers, like co-partners, owe to one another, while the enterprise continues, the duty of the finest loyalty. Many forms of conduct permissible in a workaday world for those acting at arm's length, are forbidden to those bound by fiduciary ties. . . . Not honesty alone, but the punctilio of an honor the most sensitive, is then the standard of behavior." Id. at 463–464, 164 N.E. at 546. . . .

B. *Equal Opportunity in a Close Corporation.* Under settled Massachusetts law, a domestic corporation, unless forbidden by statute, has the power to purchase its own shares. . . . An agreement to reacquire stock "[is] enforceable, subject, at least, to the limitations that the purchase must be made in good faith and without prejudice to creditors and stockholders." . . . When the corporation reacquiring its own stock is a close corporation, the purchase is subject to the additional requirement, in the light of our holding in this opinion, that the stockholders, who, as directors or controlling stockholders, caused the corporation to enter into the stock purchase agreement, must have acted with the utmost good faith and loyalty to the other stockholders.

To meet this test, if the stockholder whose shares were purchased was a member of the controlling group, the controlling stockholders

their actions relative to the operations of the enterprise and the effects of that operation on the rights and investments of other stockholders. We express no opinion as to the standard of duty applicable to transactions in the shares of the close corporation when the corporation is not a party to the transaction. Cf. Andrews, The Stockholder's Right to Equal Opportunity in the Sale of Shares, 78 Harv.L.Rev. 505 (1965). Compare Perlman v. Feldmann, 219 F.2d 173 (2d Cir.), cert. den. 349 U.S. 952, 75 S.Ct. 880, 99 L.Ed. 1277 (1955) with Zahn v. Transamerica Corp., 162 F.2d 36 (3d Cir.1947).

must cause the corporation to offer each stockholder an equal opportunity to sell a ratable number of his shares to the corporation at an identical price. Purchase by the corporation confers substantial benefits on the members of the controlling group whose shares were purchased. These benefits are not available to the minority stockholders if the corporation does not also offer them an opportunity to sell their shares. The controlling group may not, consistent with its strict duty to the minority, utilize its control of the corporation to obtain special advantages and disproportionate benefit from its share ownership. See Jones v. H.F. Ahmanson & Co., 1 Cal.3d 93, 108, 81 Cal.Rptr. 592, 460 P.2d 464 (1969); Note, 83 Harv.L.Rev. 1904, 1908 (1970). Cf. Brudney and Chirelstein, Fair Shares in Corporate Mergers and Takeovers, 88 Harv.L.Rev. 297, 334 (1974).

The benefits conferred by the purchase are twofold: (1) provision of a market for shares; (2) access to corporate assets for personal use. By definition, there is no ready market for shares of a close corporation. The purchase creates a market for shares which previously had been unmarketable. It transforms a previously illiquid investment into a liquid one. If the close corporation purchases shares only from a member of the controlling group, the controlling stockholder can convert his shares into cash at a time when none of the other stockholders can. Consistent with its strict fiduciary duty, the controlling group may not utilize its control of the corporation to establish an exclusive market in previously unmarketable shares from which the minority stockholders are excluded. See Jones v. H.F. Ahmanson & Co. . . . .

The purchase also distributes corporate assets to the stockholder whose shares were purchased. Unless an equal opportunity is given to all stockholders, the purchase of shares from a member of the controlling group operates as a *preferential* distribution of assets. In exchange for his shares, he receives a percentage of the contributed capital and accumulated profits of the enterprise. The funds he so receives are available for his personal use. The other stockholders benefit from no such access to corporate property and cannot withdraw their shares of the corporate profits and capital in this manner unless the controlling group acquiesces. Although the purchase price for the controlling stockholder's shares may seem fair to the corporation and other stockholders under the tests established in the prior case law (see Spiegel v. Beacon Participations, 297 Mass. 398, 429, 8 N.E.2d 895 [1937]; Winchell v. Plywood Corp., 324 Mass. 171, 178, 85 N.E.2d 313 [1949]), the controlling stockholder whose stock has been purchased has still received a relative advantage over his fellow stockholders, inconsistent with his strict fiduciary duty—an opportunity to turn corporate funds to personal use.

The rule of equal opportunity in stock purchases by close corporations provides equal access to these benefits for all stockholders. We hold that, in any case in which the controlling stockholders have exercised their power over the corporation to deny the minority such equal opportunity, the minority shall be entitled to appropriate relief.

To the extent that language in Spiegel v. Beacon Participations, 297 Mass. 398, 431, 8 N.E.2d 895 (1937), and other cases suggests that there is no requirement of equal opportunity for minority stockholders when a close corporation purchases shares from a controlling stockholder, it is not to be followed.

C. *Application of the Law to this Case.* We turn now to the application of the learning set forth above to the facts of the instant case.

The strict standard of duty is plainly applicable to the stockholders in Rodd Electrotype. Rodd Electrotype is a close corporation [under the test set out above]. . . .

. . . In testing the stock purchase from Harry Rodd against the applicable strict fiduciary standard, we treat the Rodd family as a single controlling group. . . . From the evidence, it is clear that the Rodd family was a close-knit one with strong community of interest. . . .

Moreover, a strong motive of interest requires that the Rodds be considered a controlling group. When Charles Rodd and Frederick Rodd were called on to represent the corporation in its dealings with their father, they must have known that further advancement within the corporation and benefits would follow their father's retirement and the purchase of his stock. . . .

On its face, then, the purchase of Harry Rodd's shares by the corporation is a breach of the duty which the controlling stockholders, the Rodds, owed to the minority stockholders, the plaintiff and her son. The purchaser distributed a portion of the corporate assets to Harry Rodd, a member of the controlling group, in exchange for his shares. The plaintiff and her son were not offered an equal opportunity to sell their shares to the corporation. In fact, their efforts to obtain an equal opportunity were rebuffed by the corporate representative. As the trial judge found, they did not, in any manner, ratify the transaction with Harry Rodd.

Because of the foregoing, we hold that the plaintiff is entitled to relief. Two forms of suitable relief are set out hereinafter. The judge below is to enter an appropriate judgment. The judgment may require Harry Rodd to remit $36,000 with interest at the legal rate from July 15, 1970, to Rodd Electrotype in exchange for forty-five shares of Rodd Electrotype treasury stock. This, in substance, is the specific relief requested in the plaintiff's bill of complaint. Interest is manifestly appropriate. A stockholder, who, in violation of his fiduciary duty to the other stockholders, has obtained assets from his corporation and has had those assets available for his own use, must pay for that use. See Silversmith v. Sydeman, 305 Mass. 65, 74, 25 N.E.2d 215 (1940). Cf. Spiegel v. Beacon Participations, 297 Mass. 398, 420, 8 N.E.2d 895 (1937). In the alternative, the judgment may require Rodd Electrotype to purchase all of the plaintiff's shares for $36,000 without interest. In the circumstances of this case, we view this as the equal opportunity which the plaintiff should have received. Harry Rodd's retention of thirty-six shares, which were to be sold and given to his children within a year of the Rodd Electrotype purchase, cannot disguise the fact that the corporation acquired one hundred per cent of that portion of his holdings (forty-five shares) which he did not intend his children to own. The plaintiff is entitled to have one hundred per cent of her forty-five shares similarly purchased.[30]

The final decree, in so far as it dismissed the bill as to Harry C. Rodd, Frederick I. Rodd, Charles H. Rodd, Mr. Harold E. Magnuson and Rodd Electrotype Company of New England, Inc., and awarded costs, is reversed. The case is remanded to the Superior Court for entry of judgment in conformity with this opinion.

So ordered.*

■ WILKINS, JUSTICE (concurring).

I agree with much of what the Chief Justice says in support of granting relief to the plaintiff. However, I do not join in any implication (see, e.g., footnote 18 and the associated text) that the rule concerning a close corporation's purchase of a controlling stockholder's shares applies to all operations of the corporation as they affect minority stockholders. That broader issue, which is apt to arise in connection with salaries and dividend policy, is not involved in this case. The analogy to partnerships may not be a complete one.

NOTE ON NIXON v. BLACKWELL

In Nixon v. Blackwell, 626 A.2d 1366 (Del.Supr.1993), E.C. Barton & Co. had two classes of stock outstanding: Class A Voting Common Stock and Class B Nonvoting Common Stock. All the Class A stock and most of the Class B stock was held by or for the benefit of corporate employees. The plaintiffs, who were not employees, owned 25% of the Class B.

There was no public market for, or trading in, either class of the corporation's stock. This created a liquidity problem for the shareholders—that is, the shareholders could not readily convert the stock into cash by selling it. Over the years, the corporation addressed the liquidity problem in several ways:

(i) The Corporation established an Employee Stock Ownership Plan (ESOP) designed to hold Class B stock for the benefit of eligible employees of the Corporation. Under the plan, terminating and retiring employees were entitled to receive their interest in the ESOP by taking either Class B stock or cash in lieu of stock. Most terminating employees and retirees elected to receive cash in lieu of stock. Thus,

---

30. If there has been a significant change in corporate circumstances since this case was argued, this is a matter which can be brought to the attention of the court below and may be considered by the judge in granting appropriate relief in the form of a judgment.

* See also Comolli v. Comolli, 241 Ga. 471, 246 S.E.2d 278 (1978); cf. Schwartz v. Marien, 37 N.Y.2d 487, 335 N.E.2d 334, 373 N.Y.S.2d 122 (1975). For additional cases and materials on the fiduciary obligations of shareholders in close corporations, see Section 7(a), infra. (Footnote by ed.)

the ESOP provided employee-shareholders with a substantial measure of liquidity that was not available to non-employee shareholders.

(ii) The corporation also purchased "key man" life-insurance policies on certain employees, with death benefits payable to the corporation. The corporation, in turn, agreed to use a portion of these benefits to repurchase its stock from the employee-shareholders' estates.

(iii) Occasionally, the corporation offered to purchase the Class B stock of the non-employee stockholders through self-tender offers.

There was a suggestion, at least, that the programs for providing liquidity to employee-shareholders reflected the plan of the founder of the corporation, from whom the plaintiffs had inherited their stock, concerning employee management and benefits.

The plaintiffs, who were non-employee shareholders, argued that the corporation's directors, all of whom were employees, were improperly pursuing a discriminatory liquidity policy that favored employee-shareholders over non-employee shareholders through the ESOP plan and key-man life-insurance policies. At trial, the Vice Chancellor found for the plaintiffs on the ground that the defendants breached their fiduciary duty as directors, and treated the plaintiffs unfairly, by providing no means through which non-employee shareholders could liquidate their stock at fair value, while providing liquidity for terminating and retiring employees. The Delaware Supreme Court reversed:

> The trial court in this case ... appears to have adopted the novel legal principle that Class B stockholders had a right to "liquidity" equal to that which the court found to be available to the defendants. It is well established in [Delaware] jurisprudence that stockholders need not always be treated equally for all purposes. . . . To hold that fairness necessarily requires precise equality is to beg the question. . . .
>
> . . . [The] holding of the trial court overlooks the significant facts that the minority stockholders were not: (a) employees of the Corporation; (b) entitled to share in an ESOP; (c) qualified for key man insurance; or (d) protected by specific provisions in the certificate of incorporation, by-laws, or a stockholders' agreement.
>
> There is support in this record for the fact that the ESOP is a corporate benefit and was established, at least in part, to benefit the Corporation. Generally speaking, the creation of ESOPs is a normal corporate practice and is generally thought to benefit the corporation. The same is true generally with respect to key man insurance programs. . . .
>
> Accordingly, we hold that the Vice Chancellor erred as a matter of law in concluding that the liquidity afforded to the employee stockholders by the ESOP and the key man insurance required substantially equal treatment for the non-employee stockholders. Moreover, the Vice Chancellor failed to evaluate and articulate, for example, whether or not and to what extent (a)

corporate benefits flowed from the ESOP and the key man insurance; (b) the ESOP and key man insurance plans are novel, extraordinary, or relatively routine business practices; (c) [the founder's] plan for employee management and benefits should be honored; and (d) the self-tenders showed defendants' willingness to provide an exit opportunity for the plaintiffs. . . .

We hold on this record that defendants have met their burden of establishing the entire fairness of their dealings with the non-employee Class B stockholders, and are entitled to judgment. The record is sufficient to conclude that plaintiffs' claim that the defendant directors have maintained a discriminatory policy of favoring Class A employee stockholders over Class B non-employee stockholders is without merit. The directors have followed a consistent policy originally established by . . . the founder of the Corporation. . . .

NOTE

One response to the kinds of problems described in Donahue v. Rodd Electrotype Co. is to plan around them in advance, by making special arrangements designed to suit the needs of the parties. In a partnership, this would be a relatively simple matter. As regards internal governance, partnership law is highly contractual in nature—that is, it gives the parties wide scope to determine the rules by which their relationship will be governed. In contrast, corporation law traditionally was not as attuned to contractualization, and in the corporate context there was often serious question whether such arrangements would be deemed valid. Today, however courts and legislatures have shown themselves increasingly ready to enforce contractual arrangements in close corporations, leading to what might be called the contractualization of the close corporation.

Accordingly, the materials in Sections 2, 3, 4, 7, and 11, infra, will be concerned to a large extent with the role of *advance planning* in the close corporation. Sections 5, 8, 9, and 10 will consider the remedies available when advance planning has been inadequate or the problems are of a kind that resist advance solution.

NOTE ON LEGISLATIVE STRATEGIES TOWARD THE CLOSE CORPORATION

Many of the problems raised by the early close-corporation case law reflects the fact that traditional statutory rules were drafted with publicly held corporations in mind. Accordingly, one of the major responses to these problems has been the enactment of new statutory provisions aimed primarily or exclusively at close corporations. The substantive content of such provisions will be considered throughout this chapter. The purpose of this Note is to lay the groundwork for that consideration by examining several different legislative strategies toward the close corporation. The principal strategies to be examined are those exemplified by Delaware, New York, and the Model Act. Almost all other close-corporation legislation either derives from or closely parallels one of these statutes.

1. *Unified Strategies.* One legislative strategy is to make no special provision for close corporations as such, but to modify traditional statutory norms so that they will meet the needs of close corporations, although applicable to publicly held corporations as well.

2. *The New York and the Model Act Strategies.* A second legislative strategy is to follow the unified approach up to a point, but to add one or two important provisions that are applicable only to those corporations with defined shareholding characteristics. Thus N.Y.Bus. Corp.Law § 620(c) authorizes certain kinds of certificate provisions "so long as no shares of the corporation are listed on a national securities exchange or regularly quoted in an over-the-counter market by one or more members of a national or affiliated securities association." Similarly, Model Act § 7.32 authorizes certain kinds of shareholder agreements in corporations that are not listed on a national securities exchange or traded in a market maintained by one or more members of a national securities association.

3. *Statutory Close Corporations.*

a. *Delaware.* A third legislative strategy follows the unified approach up to a point, but adds an integrated set of provisions that are explicitly made applicable *only* to corporations that both qualify for, and formally elect, statutory close-corporation status. In effect, therefore, the statute contemplates a special subclass of close corporations, which may be called *statutory close corporations.* Under Del. Gen. Corp. Law § 342, a corporation can *qualify* for statutory close-corporation status if its certificate provides that:

> (1) All of the corporation's issued stock of all classes . . . shall be represented by certificates and shall be held of record by not more than a specified number of persons, not exceeding 30; and

> (2) All of the issued stock of all classes shall be subject to one or more of the restrictions on transfer permitted by § 202 of this title; and

> (3) The corporation shall make no offering of any of its stock of any class which would constitute a "public offering" within the meaning of the United States Securities Act of 1933. . . .

Under § 343, a corporation that qualifies for statutory close-corporation status can *elect* such status by adopting a heading in its certificate that states the name of the corporation and the fact that it is a close corporation.

Most of the substantive provisions of Del.Gen.Corp.Law Subchapter XIV are enabling—that is, most of the provisions do not regulate the conduct of the shareholders or managers of such corporations, but simply authorize shareholders in statutory close corporations to enter into arrangements that might otherwise be unenforceable or of doubtful validity. Subchapter XIV provides enormous flexibility—so much so, that for a well-advised corporation that elects to qualify under this Subchapter, many or most governance issues will turn on the lawyer's drafting, rather than on corporate law. On the other hand, the remaining provisions of the Delaware General Corporation Law are sufficiently flexible so that much the same is true even for close corporations that are not statutory close corporations under Subchapter XIV.

b. *Significance of statutory close corporations.* The data shows that only a tiny fraction of newly formed corporations elect to become statutory close corporations. 1 O'Neal and Thompson's Close Corporations and LLCs § 1.20 (rev. 3d ed. 2004). The result is that for practical purposes, statutory close corporation provisions are much ado about very little. For example, O'Neal & Thompson found that Wisconsin reported 5,101 statutory close corporations out of 98,602 total incorporations. Alabama reported 5,324 statutory close corporations out of 155,198 total corporations. Pennsylvania reported approximately 24,000 statutory close corporations out of approximately 580,-000 total corporations. The Kansas Secretary of State's office reported less than 5 percent statutory close corporations and "probably a lot less," adding that observations of attorneys and experienced people indicate that the number has been declining. Delaware reported 16,684 statutory close corporations in 1985. Four other states enacting statutory close-corporation supplements reported even smaller numbers—863 statutory close corporations out of 82,694 total corporations in Missouri; 828 statutory close corporations out of 97,009 total corporations in Montana; 742 statutory close corporations out of 63,172 in Nevada; and 753 statutory close corporations out of 12,422 total corporations in Wyoming. In Texas, about 6% of filing corporations elected close corporation status.

"The greatest use of statutory close corporation status appears to be in California. A 1978 survey of 300 articles of incorporation filed in California showed 28 percent filed as statutory close corporations. A 1985 survey of 200 California incorporations found 19 percent to be statutory close corporations. The attorney who conducted the California surveys suggests, however, that the number is 'entirely misleading' because many corporations electing to become statutory close corporations are organized by nonlawyers using printed forms who do not understand the reasons they are electing statutory close corporation status. He states further that many lawyers mistakenly believe they have to elect close corporation status to be eligible to elect the tax status provided by Subchapter S of the Internal Revenue Code or believe they have to elect such status to come within the 'short form' exemption of the California securities law. After excluding corporations formed by nonlawyers, those formed by lawyers under erroneous beliefs, and one-person corporations seeking to avoid corporate formalities while retaining corporate limited liability, the attorney conducting the surveys concluded that "the number of 'real' situations for the use of the statutory close corporation would be extremely small but also undeterminable"." Id.

NOTE ON NON–ELECTING CORPORATIONS

Recall that some statutes define a class of statutory close corporations, and provide that only those corporations that explicitly opt in to the statutory-close corporation provisions are covered by those provisions. A difficult issue arises under such statutes concerning the effect of the statute on close corporations that do not opt in to become statutory close corporations. This issue is especially important because so few close corporations elect statutory close-corporation status. In Ramos v. Estrada, 8 Cal.App.4th 1070, 10 Cal.Rptr.2d 833 (1992), Broadcast Corp. was owned by two groups. Under an agreement, each group was required to vote for the directors upon whom a majority of the group had agreed. The Estradas, who were members of one group, wanted to vote in a different way from the majority of their group. The issue was whether the voting agreement was enforceable. Section 706 of the California Corporation Code provided as follows:

(a) Notwithstanding any other provision of this division, an agreement between two or more shareholders of a close corporation [defined under section 158(a) as "a corporation whose articles contain . . . a provision that all of the corporation's issued shares of all classes shall be held of record by not more than a specified number of persons, not exceeding 35, and a statement 'This corporation is a close corporation.'], if in writing and signed by the parties thereto, may provide that in exercising any voting rights the shares held by them shall be voted as provided by the agreement, or as the parties may agree or as determined in accordance with a procedure agreed upon by them. . . .

(d) This section shall not invalidate any voting or other agreement among shareholders . . . which agreement . . . is not otherwise illegal.

Although Broadcast Corp. was not a statutory close corporation, the court held that the voting agreement was enforceable:

Even though this corporation does not qualify as a close corporation, this agreement is valid and binding on the Estradas. . . .

The Legislative Committee comment regarding section 706, subdivision (d) states that "[t]his subdivision is intended to preserve any agreements which would be upheld under court decisions even though they do not comply with one or more of the requirements of this section, including voting agreements of corporations other than close corporations." . . .

The instant agreement is valid, enforceable and supported by consideration.

A much different position was taken by the Delaware court in Nixon v. Blackwell, 626 A.2d 1366 (Del.1993):

> We wish to address ... [w]hether there should be any special, judicially-created rules to "protect" minority stockholders of closely-held Delaware corporations.
>
> The case at bar points up the basic dilemma of minority stockholders in receiving fair value for their stock as to which there is no market and no market valuation. It is not difficult to be sympathetic, in the abstract, to a stockholder who finds himself or herself in that position. A stockholder who bargains for stock in a closely-held corporation and who pays for those shares ... can make a business judgment whether to buy into such a minority position, and if so on what terms. One could bargain for definitive provisions of self-ordering permitted to a Delaware corporation through the certificate of incorporation or by-laws by reason of the provisions in 8 Del.C. §§ 102, 109, and 141(a). Moreover, in addition to such mechanisms, a stockholder intending to buy into a minority position in a Delaware corporation may enter into definitive stockholder agreements, and such agreements may provide for elaborate earnings tests, buy-out provisions, voting trusts, or other voting agreements. See, e.g., 8 Del.C. § 218; Sonitrol Holding Co. v. Marceau Investissements, Del.Supr., 607 A.2d 1177 (1992).
>
> The tools of good corporate practice are designed to give a purchasing minority stockholder the opportunity to bargain for protection before parting with consideration. It would do violence to normal corporate practice and our corporation law to fashion [a] ruling which would result in a court-imposed stockholder buy-out for which the parties had not contracted.
>
> In 1967, when the Delaware General Corporation Law was significantly revised, a new Subchapter XIV entitled "Close Corporations; Special Provisions," became a part of that law for the first time.... [S]ubchapter XIV applies only to "close corporations," as defined in section 342. "Unless a corporation elects to become a close corporation under this subchapter in the manner prescribed in this subchapter, it shall be subject in all respects to this chapter, except this subchapter." 8 Del.C. § 341. The corporation before the Court in this matter, is not a "close corporation." Therefore it is not governed by the provisions of Subchapter XIV.
>
> One cannot read into the situation presented in the case at bar any special relief for the minority stockholders in this closely-held, but not statutory "close corporation" because the provisions of Subchapter XIV relating to close corporations and other statutory schemes preempt the field in their respective areas. It would run counter to the spirit of the doctrine of independent legal significance, and would be inappropriate judicial legislation for this Court to fashion a special judicially-created rule for minority investors when the entity does not fall within those statutes, or when there are no negotiated special provisions in the certificate

of incorporation, by-laws, or stockholder agreements. The entire fairness test, correctly applied and articulated, is the proper judicial approach....

See also Sundberg v. Lampert Lumber Co., 390 N.W.2d 352 (Minn. App.1986); Hunt v. Data Management Resources, Inc., 26 Kan. App.2d 405, 985 P.2d 730 (1999).

SECTION 2.   SPECIAL VOTING ARRANGEMENTS AT THE SHAREHOLDER LEVEL

———

(a) VOTING AGREEMENTS

———

DEL. GEN. CORP. LAW §§ 212(e), 218(c)

[See Statutory Supplement]

———

MODEL BUS. CORP. ACT §§ 7.22(d), 7.31

[See Statutory Supplement]

———

CAL. CORP. CODE §§ 158(a), 705(e), 706

[See Statutory Supplement]

———

N.Y. BUS. CORP. LAW §§ 609(f), 620

[See Statutory Supplement]

———

Ringling Bros.–Barnum & Bailey Combined Shows v. Ringling

Supreme Court of Delaware, 1947.
29 Del.Ch. 610, 53 A.2d 441.

Suit by Edith Conway Ringling against Ringling Brothers–Barnum & Bailey Circus Combined Shows, Inc., and others to determine the right of individual defendants to hold office as directors or officers of the corporation and to determine the validity of election of directors at the 1946 annual stockholders' meeting. From a decree for complainant entered in conformity with opinion of the Vice Chancellor, 49 A.2d 603, the defendants appeal. . . .

■ PEARSON, JUDGE.

The Court of Chancery was called upon to review an attempted election of directors at the 1946 annual stockholders meeting of the corporate defendant. The pivotal questions concern an agreement between two of the three present stockholders, and particularly the effect of this agreement with relation to the exercise of voting rights by these two stockholders. At the time of the meeting, the corporation had outstanding 1000 shares of capital stock held as follows: 315 by petitioner Edith Conway Ringling; 315 by defendant Aubrey B. Ringling Haley (individually or as executrix and legatee of a deceased husband); and 370 by defendant John Ringling North. The purpose of the meeting was to elect the entire board of seven directors. The shares could be voted cumulatively. Mrs. Ringling asserts that by virtue of the operation of an agreement between her and Mrs. Haley, the latter was bound to vote her shares for an adjournment of the meeting, or in the alternative, for a certain slate of directors. Mrs. Haley contends that she was not so bound for reason that the agreement was invalid, or at least revocable.

The two ladies entered into the agreement in 1941. It makes like provisions concerning stock of the corporate defendant and of another corporation, but in this case, we are concerned solely with the agreement as it affects the voting of stock of the corporate defendant. The agreement recites that each party was the owner "subject only to possible claims of creditors of the estates of Charles Ringling and Richard Ringling, respectively" (deceased husbands of the parties), of 300 shares of the capital stock of the defendant corporation; that in 1938 these shares had been deposited under a voting trust agreement which would terminate in 1947, or earlier, upon the elimination of certain liability of the corporation; that each party also owned 15 shares individually; that the parties had "entered into an agreement in April 1934 providing for joint action by them in matters affecting their ownership of stock and interest in" the corporate defendant; that the parties desired "to continue to act jointly in all matters relating to their stock ownership or interest in" the corporate defendant (and the other corporation). The agreement then provides as follows:

"Now, Therefore, in consideration of the mutual covenants and agreements hereinafter contained the parties hereto agree as follows:

"1. Neither party will sell any shares of stock or any voting trust certificates in either of said corporations to any other person whosoever, without first making a written offer to the other party hereto of all of the shares or voting trust certificates proposed to be sold, for the same price and upon the same terms and conditions as in such proposed sale, and allowing such other party a time of not less than 180 days from the date of such written offer within which to accept same.

"2. In exercising any voting rights to which either party may be entitled by virtue of ownership of stock or voting trust certificates held by them in either of said corporation, each party will consult and confer with the other and the parties will act jointly in exercising such voting rights in accordance with such agreement as they may reach with respect to any matter calling for the exercise of such voting rights.

"3. In the event the parties fail to agree with respect to any matter covered by paragraph 2 above, the question in disagreement shall be submitted for arbitration to Karl D. Loos, of Washington, D.C. as arbitrator and his decision thereon shall be binding upon the parties hereto. Such arbitration shall be exercised to the end of assuring for the respective corporations good management and such participation therein by the members of the Ringling family as the experience, capacity and ability of each may warrant. The parties may at any time by written agreement designate any other individual to act as arbitrator in lieu of said Loos.

"4. Each of the parties hereto will enter into and execute such voting trust agreement or agreements and such other instruments as, from time to time they may deem advisable and as they may be advised by counsel are appropriate to effectuate the purposes and objects of this agreement.

"5. This agreement shall be in effect from the date hereof and shall continue in effect for a period of ten years unless sooner terminated by mutual agreement in writing by the parties hereto.

"6. The agreement of April 1934 is hereby terminated.

"7. This agreement shall be binding upon and inure to the benefit of the heirs, executors, administrators and assigns of the parties hereto respectively."

The Mr. Loos mentioned in the agreement is an attorney and has represented both parties since 1937, and, before and after the voting trust was terminated in late 1942, advised them with respect to the exercise of their voting rights. At the annual meetings in 1943 and the two following years, the parties voted their shares in accordance with mutual understandings arrived at as a result of discussions. In each of these years, they elected five of the seven directors. Mrs. Ringling and Mrs. Haley each had sufficient votes, independently of the other, to elect two of the seven directors. By both voting for an additional candidate, they could be sure of his election regardless of how Mr. North, the remaining stockholder, might vote.[1]

---

1. Each lady was entitled to cast 2205 votes (since each had the cumulative voting rights of 315 shares, and there were 7 vacancies in the directorate). The sum of the votes of both is 4410, which is sufficient to allow 882 votes for each of 5 persons. Mr. North, holding 370 shares, was entitled to cast 2590 votes, which obviously cannot be divided so as to give to more than two candidates as many as 882 votes each. It will be observed that in order for Mrs. Ringling and Mrs. Haley to be sure to elect five directors (regardless of how Mr. North might vote) they must act together in the sense that their combined votes must be divided among five different candidates and at least one of the five must be voted for by both Mrs. Ringling and Mrs. Haley.

Some weeks before the 1946 meeting, they discussed with Mr. Loos the matter of voting for directors. They were in accord that Mrs. Ringling should cast sufficient votes to elect herself and her son; and that Mrs. Haley should elect herself and her husband; but they did not agree upon a fifth director. The day before the meeting, the discussions were continued, Mrs. Haley being represented by her husband since she could not be present because of illness. In a conversation with Mr. Loos, Mr. Haley indicated that he would make a motion for an adjournment of the meeting for sixty days, in order to give the ladies additional time to come to an agreement about their voting. On the morning of the meeting, however, he stated that because of something Mrs. Ringling had done, he would not consent to a postponement. Mrs. Ringling then made a demand upon Mr. Loos to act under the third paragraph of the agreement "to arbitrate the disagreement" between her and Mrs. Haley in connection with the manner in which the stock of the two ladies should be voted. At the opening of the meeting, Mr. Loos read the written demand and stated that he determined and directed that the stock of both ladies be voted for an adjournment of sixty days. Mrs. Ringling then made a motion for adjournment and voted for it. Mr. Haley, as proxy for his wife, and Mr. North voted against the motion. Mrs. Ringling (herself or through her attorney, it is immaterial which), objected to the voting of Mrs. Haley's stock in any manner other than in accordance with Mr. Loos' direction. The chairman ruled that the stock could not be voted contrary to such direction, and declared the motion for adjournment had carried. Nevertheless, the meeting proceeded to the election of directors. Mrs. Ringling stated that she would continue in the meeting "but without prejudice to her position with respect to the voting of the stock and the fact that adjournment had not been taken." Mr. Loos directed Mrs. Ringling to cast her votes 882 for Mrs. Ringling, 882 for her son, Robert, and 441 for a Mr. Dunn, who had been a member of the board for several years. She complied. Mr. Loos directed that Mrs. Haley's votes be cast 882 for Mrs. Haley, 882 for Mr. Haley, and 441 for Mr. Dunn. Instead of complying, Mr. Haley attempted to vote his wife's shares 1103 for Mrs. Haley, and 1102 for Mr. Haley. Mr. North voted his shares 864 for a Mr. Woods, 863 for a Mr. Griffin, and 863 for Mr. North. The chairman ruled that the five candidates proposed by Mr. Loos, together with Messrs. Woods and North, were elected. The Haley–North group disputed this ruling insofar as it declared the election of Mr. Dunn; and insisted that Mr. Griffin, instead, had been elected. A directors' meeting followed in which Mrs. Ringling participated after stating that she would do so "without prejudice to her position that the stockholders' meeting had been adjourned and that the directors' meeting was not properly held." Mr. Dunn and Mr. Griffin, although each was challenged by an opposing faction, attempted to join in voting as directors for different slates of officers. Soon after the meeting, Mrs. Ringling instituted this proceeding.

The Vice Chancellor determined that the agreement to vote in accordance with the direction of Mr. Loos was valid as a "stock pooling agreement" with lawful objects and purposes, and that it was not in violation of any public policy of this state. He held that where the arbitrator acts under the agreement and one party refuses to comply with his direction, "the Agreement constitutes the willing party . . . an implied agent possessing the irrevocable proxy of the recalcitrant party for the purpose of casting the particular vote." It was ordered that a new election be held before a master, with the direction that the master should recognize and give effect to the agreement if its terms were properly invoked. [In reaching this result, Vice Chancellor Seitz stated, "Here an implied agency based on an irrevocable proxy is fully justified to implement the Agreement without doing violence to its terms. Moreover, the provisions of the Agreement make it clear that the proxy may be treated as one coupled with an interest so as to render it irrevocable under the circumstances. . . . Obviously, to deny specific performance here would be tantamount to declaring the Agreement invalid. Since petitioner's rights in this respect were properly preserved at the stockholders' meeting, the meeting was a nullity to the extent that it failed to give effect to the provisions of the Agreement here involved. However, I believe it preferable to hold a new election rather than attempt to reconstruct the contested meeting. In this way the parties will be acting with explicit knowledge of their rights."]

Before taking up defendants' objections to the agreement, let us analyze particularly what it attempts to provide with respect to voting, including what functions and powers it attempts to repose in Mr. Loos, the "arbitrator". The agreement recites that the parties desired "to continue to act jointly in all matters relating to their stock ownership or interest in" the corporation. The parties agreed to consult and confer with each other in exercising their voting rights and to act jointly—that is, concertedly; unitedly; towards unified courses of action—in accordance with such agreement as they might reach. Thus, so long as the parties agree for whom or for what their shares shall be voted, the agreement provides no function for the arbitrator. His role is limited to situations where the parties fail to agree upon a course of action. In such cases, the agreement directs that "the question in disagreement shall be submitted for arbitration" to Mr. Loos "as arbitrator and his decision thereon shall be binding upon the parties". These provisions are designed to operate in aid of what appears to be a primary purpose of the parties, "to act jointly" in exercising their voting rights, by providing a means for fixing a course of action whenever they themselves might reach a stalemate.

Should the agreement be interpreted as attempting to empower the arbitrator to carry his directions into effect? Certainly there is no express delegation or grant of power to do so, either by authorizing him to vote the shares or to compel either party to vote them in accordance with his directions. The agreement expresses no other function of the arbitrator than that of deciding questions in disagreement which prevent the effectuation of the purpose "to act jointly". The power to enforce a decision does not seem a necessary or usual incident of such a function. Mr. Loos is not a party to the agreement. It does not contemplate the transfer of any shares or interest in shares to him, or that he should undertake any duties which the parties might compel him to perform. They provided that they might designate any other individual to act instead of Mr. Loos. The agreement does not attempt to make the arbitrator a trustee of an express trust. What the arbitrator is to do is for the benefit of the parties, not for his own benefit. Whether the parties accept or reject his decision is no concern of his, so far as the agreement or the surrounding circumstances reveal. We think the parties sought to bind each other, but to be bound only to each other, and not to empower the arbitrator to enforce decisions he might make.

From this conclusion, it follows necessarily that no decision of the arbitrator could ever be enforced if both parties to the agreement were unwilling that it be enforced, for the obvious reason that there would be no one to enforce it. Under the agreement, something more is required after the arbitrator has given his decision in order that it should become compulsory: at least one of the parties must determine that such decision shall be carried into effect. Thus, any "control" of the voting of the shares, which is reposed in the arbitrator, is substantially limited in action under the agreement in that it is subject to the overriding power of the parties themselves.

The agreement does not describe the undertaking of each party with respect to a decision of the arbitrator other than to provide that it "shall be binding upon the parties". It seems to us that this language, considered with relation to its context and the situations to which it is applicable, means that each party promised the other to exercise her own voting rights in accordance with the arbitrator's decision. The agreement is silent about any exercise of the voting rights of one party by the other. The language with reference to situations where the parties arrive at an understanding as to voting plainly suggests "action" by each, and "exercising" voting rights by each, rather than by one for the other. There is no intimation that this method should be different where the arbitrator's decision is to be carried into effect.

Assuming that a power in each party to exercise the voting rights of the other might be a relatively more effective or convenient means of enforcing a decision of the arbitrator than would be available without the power, this would not justify implying a delegation of the power in the absence of some indication that the parties bargained for that means. The method of voting actually employed by the parties tends to show that they did not construe the agreement as creating powers to vote each other's shares; for at meetings prior to 1946 each party apparently exercised her own voting rights, and at the 1946 meeting, Mrs. Ringling, who wished to enforce the agreement, did not attempt to cast a ballot in exercise of any voting rights of Mrs. Haley. We do not find enough in the agreement or in the circumstances to justify a construction that either party was empowered to exercise voting rights of the other.

Having examined what the parties sought to provide by the agreement, we come now to defendants' contention that the voting provisions are illegal and revocable. They say that the courts of this state have definitely established the doctrine "that there can be no agreement, or any device whatsoever, by which the voting power of stock of a Delaware corporation may be irrevocably separated from the ownership of the stock, except by an agreement which complies with Section 18 of the Corporation Law [concerning voting trusts] and except by a proxy coupled with an interest...."

[Section 18] authorizes, among other things, the deposit or transfer of stock in trust for a specified purpose, namely, "vesting" in the transferee "the right to vote thereon" for a limited period; and prescribes numerous requirements in this connection. Accordingly, it seems reasonable to infer that to establish the relationship and accomplish the purpose which the statute authorizes, its requirements must be complied with.

But the statute does not purport to deal with agreements whereby shareholders attempt to bind each other as to how they shall vote their shares. Various forms of such pooling agreements, as they are sometimes called, have been held valid and have been distinguished from voting trusts.... We think the particular agreement before us does not violate Section 18 or constitute an attempted evasion of its requirements, and is not illegal for any other reason.

Generally speaking, a shareholder may exercise wide liberality of judgment in the matter of voting, and it is not objectionable that his motives may be for personal profit, or determined by whims or caprice, so long as he violates no duty owed his fellow shareholders. Heil v. Standard G. & E. Co., 17 Del.Ch. 214, 151 A. 303. The ownership of voting stock imposes no legal duty to vote at all. A group of shareholders may, without impropriety, vote their respective shares so as to obtain advantages of concerted action. They may lawfully contract with each other to vote in the future in such way as they, or a majority of their group, from time to time determine.

Reasonable provisions for cases of failure of the group to reach a determination because of an even division in their ranks seem unobjectionable. The provision here for submission to the arbitrator is plainly designed as a deadlock-breaking measure, and the arbitrator's decision cannot be enforced unless at least one of the parties (entitled to cast one-half of their combined votes) is willing that it be enforced. We find the provision reasonable. It does not appear that the agreement enables the parties to take any unlawful advantage of the outside shareholder, or of any other person. It offends no rule of law or public policy of this state of which we are aware.

Legal consideration for the promises of each party is supplied by the mutual promises of the other party. The undertaking to vote in accordance with the arbitrator's decision is a valid contract. The good faith of the arbitrator's action has not been challenged and, indeed, the record indicates that no such challenge could be supported.

Accordingly, the failure of Mrs. Haley to exercise her voting rights in accordance with his decision was a breach of her contract....

. . . The Court of Chancery may, in a review of an election, reject votes of a registered shareholder where his voting of them is found to be in violation of rights of another person. Compare: In re Giant Portland Cement Co., 26 Del.Ch. 32, 21 A.2d 697; In re Canal Construction Co., 21 Del.Ch. 155, 182 A. 545. It seems to us that upon the application of Mrs. Ringling, the injured party, the votes representing Mrs. Haley's shares should not be counted. Since no infirmity in Mr. North's voting has been demonstrated, his right to recognition of what he did at the meeting should be considered in granting any relief to Mrs. Ringling; for her rights arose under a contract to which Mr. North was not a party.

With this in mind, we have concluded that the election should not be declared invalid, but that effect should be given to a rejection of the votes representing Mrs. Haley's shares. No other relief seems appropriate in this proceeding. Mr. North's vote against the motion for adjournment was sufficient to defeat it. With respect to the election of directors, the return of the inspectors should be corrected to show a rejection of Mrs. Haley's votes, and to declare the election of the six persons for whom Mr. North and Mrs. Ringling voted.

This leaves one vacancy in the directorate. The question of what to do about such a vacancy was not considered by the court below and has not been argued here. For this reason, and because an election of directors at the 1947 annual meeting (which presumably will be held in the near future) may make a determination of the question unimportant, we shall not decide it on this appeal. If a decision of the point appears important to the parties, any of them may apply to raise it in the Court of Chancery, after the mandate of this court is received there.

An order should be entered directing a modification of the order of the Court of Chancery in accordance with this opinion.

NOTE ON VOTING AGREEMENTS AND IRREVOCABLE PROXIES

Contracts among shareholders concerning the manner in which their shares will be voted—usually known as voting or pooling agreements—are of two general types. In one type, the parties agree in advance on the exact way in which they will vote their shares during the term of the contract: for example, they may agree to vote for each other as directors. In a second type, the parties do not agree in advance on the exact way in which they will vote their shares, but instead agree that during the term of the contract they will vote their shares as a unit, in a way to be decided by agreement, ballot, or other means. In dealing with both types of voting agreement the courts have been confronted with two questions: (i) Are such agreements valid? (ii) Assuming they are valid, how can their effectiveness be assured?

1. *Validity of Voting Agreements.* A number of older cases held shareholder voting agreements either invalid or revocable at will, but

the modern rule is that shareholder voting agreements are normally valid. However, a voting agreement is invalid if it is based on a "private benefit"—that is, a side payment—given by one party to the other in exchange for his vote. A typical case is Palmbaum v. Magulsky, 217 Mass. 306, 104 N.E. 746 (1914). P and D were two of the three shareholders in American Biscuit Company. P held D's promissory note, and agreed to surrender the note if D would vote his stock in favor of a proposal to sell American Biscuit's assets to another corporation. D voted for the proposal, but P refused to surrender the note, and brought suit upon it. D set up the agreement as a defense, but the court held that the agreement was illegal and therefore unenforceable. "It is the duty of a stockholder of a corporation, in attendance at meetings of the stockholders, to act fairly and in good faith. He is not justified in entering into any agreement to vote so as to perpetrate a fraud upon any other stockholder. The defendant's vote to dispose of all the assets of the corporation was in consideration of the surrender of the note to him by the plaintiff. This was illegal and the agreement was void as against public policy.... The contract in the case now before us operated as a fraud upon [the third shareholder]."

The rule that a voting agreement based on a private benefit is invalid is an application of the broader principle, well-established in corporate law, that a shareholder may not sell his vote. See, e.g., Chew v. Inverness Management Corp., 352 A.2d 426 (Del.Ch.1976).

2. *Enforcement of Voting Agreements; Irrevocable Proxies; Proxies Coupled with an Interest.*

a. *Damages and specific enforcement.* Money damages are normally an inadequate remedy for breach of a voting agreement. Nevertheless, in the past, courts that upheld such agreements split on whether they will be specifically enforced. The modern trend, however, is strongly in favor of granting that remedy. For example, in Weil v. Beresth, 154 Conn. 12, 220 A.2d 456 (1966), A, B, C, and D, majority shareholders of Sales Corporation, entered into a voting agreement in 1954 under which they agreed, among other things: (i) to vote for the election of each other as directors; (ii) to vote to amend the by-laws by decreasing the number of directors from five to four; and (iii) not thereafter to vote to amend the new by-laws without the consent of all parties. The agreement was complied with until a shareholders' meeting in 1965, at which B, C, and D voted to adopt a new by-law increasing the number of directors to five, and to elect five directors, including A, B, C, D, and B's son. A then filed suit seeking specific enforcement of the voting agreement and restoration of the old by-law. Recognizing that money damages would be an inadequate remedy, the Connecticut court held that A was entitled to an injunction requiring the defendants to repeal the new by-law and re-enact the original bylaw. The court also approved an injunction compelling B's son to resign if the trial court deemed such relief appropriate. See also Galler v. Galler, Section 3, infra; Beresovski v. Warszawski, 28 N.Y.2d 419, 322 N.Y.S.2d 673, 271 N.E.2d 520 (1971). But see Chayes,

Madame Wagner and the Close Corporation, 73 Harv.L.Rev. 1532, 1535 (1960):

The question of the relief to be granted for violation [of agreements among shareholders in the closely held corporation] raises problems more vexing, difficult, and real than ever were to be found on the validity side. What is in issue is the specific enforcement of an ongoing, intimate, personal, consensual relation. This is something the Anglo–American legal system has—wisely it may be supposed—not lightly granted as a matter of course.

b. *Proxies.* To the extent the courts are reluctant to grant specific enforcement of voting agreements, the parties may expressly or impliedly substitute a self-executing remedy, such as giving each other proxies. In Smith v. San Francisco & N.P. Ry. Co., 115 Cal. 584, 47 P. 582 (1897) three shareholders agreed to vote their shares together as determined by ballot. The court held that the agreement impliedly gave the two shareholders in the majority on any ballot an irrevocable proxy to vote the shares of the third. In *Ringling,* the Chancellor similarly held that the arbitrator had an implied proxy to vote the parties' shares as he determined, but the Delaware Supreme Court reversed on this issue.[1]

c. *Proxy coupled with an interest.* Even if a proxy is expressly conferred in connection with a voting agreement, a further problem remains. Classically a proxy has been treated as an agency relationship, in which the shareholder is the principal and the proxyholder is the agent. It is a rule of agency law, however, that a principal can terminate an agent's authority at will, even if the termination is in breach of contract (although in such cases the principal may be liable to the agent in damages). See Restatement, Second, of Agency § 118. There is an exception to this rule in cases where the agent holds a "power coupled with an interest," or, as the Restatements of Agency call it, a "power given as security." See Restatement (Second) of Agency §§ 138, 139; Restatement (Third) of Agency §§ 3.12, 3.13. Generally speaking, this exception is applicable to arrangements in which it is understood that the "agent" or power-holder has an interest in the subject-matter to which the power relates, and is therefore not expected to execute the power solely on the power-giver's behalf—the crux of the normal agency relationship—but on his own behalf as well. Accordingly, the safest way to insure that a proxy will be irrevocable is to confer it upon a proxyholder who has an "interest" *in the shares to which the proxy relates.* Relatively clear examples are cases where the proxyholder is a pledgee of the shares, or has agreed to purchase the shares. See N.Y.Bus.Corp.Law § 609(f)(1), (2).

---

1. Compare Me.Bus.Corp.Law § 617(2):

2. When [a written voting] agreement specifies how the shares shall be voted, or provides a clear formula for ascertaining how the shares shall be voted, in case of a breach or anticipatory breach thereof by one or more parties thereto, the agreement shall, unless it specifically provides otherwise, be deemed to constitute an irrevocable proxy to the parties not in breach to vote all shares subject to the agreement in accordance with the terms of the agreement.

Where a proxy is given pursuant to a voting agreement, however, normally the proxyholder is either an arbitrator, who has no proprietary interest in the shares or the corporation, or a shareholder, who has a proprietary interest *in the corporation* but not in the shares that are the subject-matter of the proxy. In In re Chilson, 19 Del.Ch. 398, 409, 168 A. 82, 86 (1933), the court held that where a proxyholder has only "an interest in the corporation generally," or "an interest in the bare voting power or the results to be accomplished by the use of" the proxy, the proxy is revocable. On the other hand, in Deibler v. Chas. H. Elliott Co., 368 Pa. 267, 81 A.2d 557 (1951), the Supreme Court of Pennsylvania, construing Delaware law, upheld the irrevocability of a proxy given to secure payment of the purchase price of stock in a Delaware corporation and the seller's continued employment by the corporation. This issue is now often addressed by the statutes. For example, Del. Gen. Corp. Law § 212(e) provide that "A proxy may be made irrevocable regardless of whether the interest with which it is coupled is an interest in the stock itself or an interest in the corporation generally."

––––––

HAFT v. HAFT, 671 A.2d 413 (Del.Ch.1995) (Allen, Ch.). Herbert Haft, the founder and CEO of Dart Group Corporation, transferred 172,730 shares of Dart Class B common stock to his son, Ronald Haft. Class B was Dart's sole class of voting stock. The transferred shares constituted 57% of the outstanding Class B, and therefore carried the power to elect the Dart board. In exchange for the stock, Roland gave Herbert a promissory note and granted Herbert a lifetime irrevocable proxy to vote the stock.

Subsequently, Ronald sought to revoke the proxy. The court held that Herbert Haft's interests in Dart by virtue of his position was sufficient to render specifically enforceable Ronald's contractual undertaking to not revoke the proxy:

1. The Applicable Statute

The Delaware General Corporation Law states that a proxy may be made irrevocable "if, and only as long as, it is coupled with an interest sufficient in law to support an irrevocable power." 8 Del.Ch. § 212(e) (1991)....

Under the Delaware corporation law (§ 212(e)) an interest sufficient to support an irrevocable proxy must be either "an interest in the stock itself or an interest in the corporation generally." 8 Del.Ch. § 212(e) (1991). Do Herbert Haft's interests, other than as a secured creditor, qualify under the statute? As I now explain, in my opinion they do.

2. Relevant Legal Precedents

The predecessor of Section 212 was amended as part of the general revision of the Delaware General Corporation Law in

1967. The language in question ("an interest in the corporation generally") was introduced into our statute at that time. The apparent purpose for doing so was to erase the implication arising from dicta in a 1933 Master's Report, which had been confirmed by this court. The report was in the case of In re *Chilson*, Del.Ch., 168 A. 82 (1933). The *Chilson* dicta was to the effect that in order to support irrevocability of a proxy, the holder had to have an interest in the stock itself. . . .

Prior to the 1967 revision the question whether the interest of a CEO in his position was such an interest as, standing alone, would support the enforceability of the agreed-upon irrevocable proxy according to its terms had occasionally been addressed by courts in other jurisdictions. In Deibler v. Chas. H. Elliott Co., 368 Pa. 267, 81 A.2d 557 (1951), the Pennsylvania Supreme Court, applying Delaware law, held that an irrevocable proxy given to the seller of corporate stock both to secure payment for the stock and to protect his on-going contract of employment with the corporation, remained irrevocable after the note had been paid. The court accepted the argument that the on-going employment contract constituted a sufficient interest to specifically enforce the agreement made. A similar result had been reached by the Supreme Court of Michigan in 1947: Ecclestone v. Indialantic, Inc., 319 Mich. 248, 29 N.W.2d 679 (1947).

3. Policy Considerations

No Delaware court has been required to address this question under the language of amended Section 212. In now doing so, it is appropriate to acknowledge that the corporate law has tended to distrust and discourage the separation of the shareholder claim as equity investor (i.e., the right to enjoy distributions on stock if, as, and when declared) from the right to vote stock. For example there was for many years a rather clear rule against the sale of a corporate vote unattached to the sale of the underlying stock. A powerful argument can be advanced that generally the congruence of the right to vote and the residual rights of ownership will tend towards efficient wealth production.

A proxy is, of course, a means temporarily to split the power to vote from the residual ownership claim of the stockholder. In the vast number of instances in which proxies to vote stock are used, however, this split occasions no significant divergence between the interests of the proxy holder and the holder of the residual corporate interest because the proxy is of relatively short duration and in all events is revocable unilaterally. Thus, in effect, the grant of the proxy represented a judgment (which may be enforced through revocation) that the holder of the proxy will exercise it in the economic interest of the residual owner. A potentially inefficient split between the interests of the voter and the interests of the residual owners may, however, develop when the proxy is irrevocable. Such a holder is free from the unilateral control of the grantor and may be expected to be inclined to exercise voting rights in a way that benefits himself. There is of course, as a general matter, nothing legally suspect in contracting parties exercising contracted for rights in a self-interested manner. Yet the exercise of voting control over corporations by persons whose interest in them is not chiefly or solely as a residual owner will create circumstances in which the corporation will be less than optimally efficient in the selection of risky investment projects.(A simple, if gross, example: the holder of an irrevocable proxy with voting control might simply refuse to elect a board that will accept the best investment projects (those with the highest risk adjusted rate of return) unless some side payment to him is arranged). The special additional costs associated with such a divorce between ownership and voting (the costs being expressed either as an otherwise unnecessary expense or as the selection of non-optimizing investment projects) will of course tend to diminish as the voter's interest becomes aligned with the residual owners interest.

In this light, the dicta of *In re Chilson* may be thought to offer a means of limiting the agency costs that irrevocable proxies occasion. By recognizing only an interest in the stock itself as an interest that will support the irrevocability of a proxy, the rule of *Chilson* would eliminate a class of cases in which the incentives of the proxy holder to exploit the corporation would be greatest, that is, those in which she simply has no economic interest at all in the residual equity of the firm. . . .

4.   Fashioning a Rule of Judicial Decision. . . .

. . . I confess to the view that a corporation law rule allowing for the specific enforceability of an irrevocable proxy that is coupled only with the holder's interest in maintaining a salaried office seems mischievous in terms of its possible efficiency effects. But in light of the 1967 amendment to the Delaware statutory law . . . and the absence of contrary precedent, I am required to express the opinion that such an interest—the interest that Herbert Haft had and retains as the senior executive officer of Dart— is sufficient under our law to render specifically enforceable the express contract for an irrevocable proxy. . . .

———

(b) Voting Trusts

———

DEL. GEN. CORP. LAW § 218

[See Statutory Supplement]

———

MODEL BUS. CORP. ACT § 7.30

[See Statutory Supplement]

CAL. CORP. CODE § 706

[See Statutory Supplement]

NOTE ON VOTING TRUSTS

1. *In General.* A voting trust is a device by which shareholders separate (i) the voting rights in, and the legal title to, their shares from (ii) the beneficial ownership of the shares. This is accomplished by conferring the voting rights and legal title on one or more voting trustees, while retaining the ultimate right to distributions and appreciation. Usually, two or more shareholders are involved, so that the voting trust is a type of pooling agreement. Sometimes, however, only one shareholder is involved—for example, where a sole shareholder creates a voting trust to satisfy creditors, or to vest control of his business in managers. The creation of a voting trust normally requires (i) the execution of a written trust agreement between participating shareholders and the voting trustees, and (ii) a transfer to the trustee, for a specified period, of the shareholders' stock certificates and the legal title to their stock. The voting trustee then registers the transfer on the corporation's books, so that during the term of the trust the trustee is the record owner of the shares, entitled to vote in the election of directors and often on other matters as well. Dividends are paid by the corporation to the trustee, but are almost invariably then paid over by the trustee to the beneficial owners. Several statutes require the trustee to issue certificates of beneficial interest to participating shareholders, and frequently such certificates are issued, even where not statutorily required, to facilitate trading in the beneficial interests.

Voting trusts are an effective and a moderately simple way to separate control and beneficial ownership for a limited period of time. The separation is self-executing, because the trustee is the legal owner and is registered as such on the corporation's books. The separation survives transfers by the beneficial owners, since they can transfer only their retained equitable interests (essentially, most ownership rights except the right to vote during the term of the trust). Upon termination of the voting trust, the beneficial owners receive stock certificates which reinstate them as complete owners, registered as such on the corporation's books.

2. *Validity.* The early attitude of some courts toward voting trusts was highly unfavorable. See, e.g., Warren v. Pim, 66 N.J.Eq. 353, 375, 59 A. 773, 789 (1904) ("[a]ny arrangement that permanently separates the voting power from stock ownership nullifies, to the

extent of the stock involved, the annual submission of the question of the management of the company to the stockholders''). The majority of courts, however, either declared voting trusts to be valid or held that the plaintiff was not in a position to attack them. See, e.g., Massa v. Stone, 346 Mass. 67, 190 N.E.2d 217 (1963).

Today, statutes both explicitly validate voting trusts and regulate their creation and their content. Among the most common forms of regulation are a maximum time period (usually ten years), and a requirement that the voting-trust agreement be filed with the corporation and open to inspection. Such statutes are normally deemed to preempt the common law rules governing the validity of voting trusts. The cases are not entirely uniform in dealing with the consequences of failure to comply with the statutory requirements. Some cases have held that such a failure invalidates the voting trust. See, e.g., Abercrombie v. Davies, discussed below. Smith v. Biggs Boiler Works Co., 32 Del. Ch. 147, 82 A.2d 372 (1951) (voting trust held invalid where no provision was made for deposit of stock with trustees); Christopher v. Richardson, 394 Pa. 425, 147 A.2d 375 (1959) (voting trust held invalid where under its terms it might have exceeded statutory ten-year period). Other cases have been considerably more tolerant. For example, in De Marco v. Paramount Ice Corp., 30 Misc.2d 158, 102 N.Y.S.2d 692 (1950), a voting trust was attacked on the ground that a copy of the trust agreement had not been filed in the office of the corporation, as required by the statute. The answer stated that the agreement had been filed after the plaintiff's suit was brought. The court held that "the failure to file merely means that the trust agreement is not invalid but merely inoperative to permit the trustees to exercise the voting rights granted thereby until it is so filed."

3. *Overlap of Voting Trusts and Shareholders' Voting Agreements*. In the context of close corporations, voting trusts may sometimes be used, like voting agreements, to allocate voting control in other than a pro rata manner, or to preserve the solidarity of a faction consisting of less than all the shareholders. Because voting trusts and voting agreements may have substantially overlapping purposes, the substantive legal rules applicable to one of these two legal forms have sometimes been applied to an arrangement that was nominally cast in the other form. Thus in Abercrombie v. Davies, 36 Del.Ch. 371, 130 A.2d 338 (1957), the Delaware Supreme Court held that an "Agent's Agreement" that was in form a voting agreement was in substance a voting trust, and therefore had to comply with the statutory voting-trust provisions:

> A review of the Delaware decisions upon the subject of voting trusts shows that our courts have indicated that one essential feature that characterizes a voting trust is the separation of the voting rights of the stock from the other attributes of ownership....

> When we apply these tests to the Agents' Agreement we find: (1) that the voting rights of the pooled stock have been divorced from the beneficial ownership, which is retained by the stockhold-

ers; (2) that the voting rights have been transferred to fiduciaries denominated Agents; (3) that the transfer of such rights is, through the medium of irrevocable proxies, effective for a period of ten years; (4) that all voting rights in respect of all the stock are pooled in the Agents as a group, through the device of proxies running to the agents jointly and severally, and no stockholder retains the right to vote his or its shares; and (5) that on its face the agreement has for its principal object voting control of American.

These elements, under our decisions, are the elements of a voting trust.

Because the statutory provisions governing voting trusts had not been complied with, the court held that the Agreement was unenforceable.

Conversely, in Oceanic Exploration Co. v. Grynberg, 428 A.2d 1 (Del.1981), the Delaware Supreme Court held that an agreement that was denominated a "voting trust" was not a voting trust for purposes of the voting-trust statute, and therefore was enforceable despite a failure to comply with the statute:

> ... [T]he voting trust statute was not intended to be all inclusive in the sense that it was designed to apply to every set of facts in which voting rights are transferred to trustees incident to or as part of the assignment of other stockholder rights. Rather, a voting trust is a stockholder pooling arrangement with the criteria that voting rights are separated out and irrevocably assigned for a definite period of time to voting trustees for control purposes while other attributes of ownership are retained by the depositing stockholders.... [W]e ... find that the final contract in issue here, with its multifaceted aspects including a stock purchase option agreement running from an already unified majority shareholder group to the corporation may be so foreign to the stockholder voting trust agreement to which the language used by the General Assembly was directed that it is beyond the contemplated scope of the statute. Given the scope of this agreement it may be that the voting rights are not separated from the other retained attributes of ownership. In short, the agreement here may not be a voting trust as that term is used in our law.

———

(c)   CLASSIFIED STOCK AND WEIGHTED VOTING

———

DEL. GEN. CORP. LAW §§ 102(a)(6), 212(a)

[See Statutory Supplement]

———

MODEL BUS. CORP. ACT §§ 6.01, 7.21, 8.04

[See Statutory Supplement]

––––––

NOTE ON CLASSIFIED STOCK AND WEIGHTED VOTING

"One of the simplest and most effective ways of assuring that all the participants or that particular minority shareholders will have representation on the board of directors is to set up two or more classes of stock, provide that each class is to vote for and elect a specified number or a stated percentage of the directors, and then issue each class or a majority of shares in each class to a different shareholder or faction of shareholders.... Class A common stock might be given power, for instance, to elect three directors and Class B common stock power to elect two." 1 F.H. O'Neal & R. Thompson, O'Neal's Close Corporations § 3.19 (3d ed.). A few statutes validate this technique explicitly (e.g., N.Y.Bus.Corp.Law § 703), and most of the remaining statutes validate it implicitly by providing that a corporation may have one or more classes of stock with such voting powers as shall be stated in the certificate (e.g., Del.Gen.Corp.Law § 151(a)). In its simplest version, the use of classified common does not necessarily involve voting power for any class that is disproportionate to the investment made by that class. Often, however, separate classes carry voting power whose weight differs considerably from the relative investment made by their holders. At the extreme, a class of stock may have proprietary rights but no voting power, or voting power but no proprietary rights.

In Lehrman v. Cohen, 43 Del.Ch. 222, 222 A.2d 800 (1966), the Cohen and Lehrman families each owned equal quantities of the voting stock of Giant Food, Inc., designated Class AC and Class AL common stock, respectively. Each class of stock was entitled to elect two members of Giant Food's four-member board of directors. Over the years, there were differences of opinion between the Cohen and Lehrman families as to operating policies of the Company. At a certain point, an arrangement was made which provided for the establishment of a fifth directorship to obviate the risk of deadlock. Under the arrangement, Giant Food's certificate of incorporation was amended to create a third class of stock, designated Class AD common stock, consisting of one share of $10 par value stock. The Class AD stock had the right to elect one director, but essentially had no right to distributions and could be called (redeemed) for $10 by a vote of the other four directors. The share of the Class AD stock was issued to Food Giant's long-time counsel, Joseph Danzansky, who, by prearrangement, voted the share for himself as the fifth director.

Subsequently, the plaintiff, a member of the Lehrman family who at that point owned all the AL stock, claimed that the Class AD stock was illegal on the ground that in substance it was a voting trust and did not comply with the voting trust statute. The court rejected this argument:

The criteria of a voting trust under our decisions have been summarized by this Court in Abercrombie v. Davies, 36 Del.Ch. 371, 130 A.2d 338 (1957). The tests there set forth, accepted by both sides of this cause as being applicable, are as follows: (1) the voting rights of the stock are separated from the other attributes of ownership; (2) the voting rights granted are intended to be irrevocable for a definite period of time; and (3) the principal purpose of the grant of voting rights is to acquire voting control of the corporation. . . .

. . . The AD arrangement did not separate the voting rights of the AC or the AL stock from the other attributes of ownership of those classes of stock. Each AC and AL stockholder retains complete control over the voting of his stock; each can vote his stock directly; no AL or AC stockholder is divested of his right to vote his stock as he sees fit; no AL or AC stock can be voted against the shareholder's wishes; and the AL and AC stock continue to elect two directors each.

The court also held that it was not illegal to create a class of stock having voting rights but no proprietary rights.

SECTION 3.   AGREEMENTS CONTROLLING MATTERS WITHIN THE BOARD'S DISCRETION

Voting arrangements of the kind discussed in Section 2, supra, control only those matters that are decided on a shareholder level. Typically, however, the issues that are most important to shareholders in a close corporation are determined on a board level—for example, managerial positions, managerial compensation, and dividends. If the shareholders attempt to also control these matters by agreement, the problem arises whether (or under what conditions) such an agreement is valid, in the face of the normal statutory provision that the business of the corporation shall be managed by or under the direction of the board. That question is addressed by the materials in this section.

McQuade v. Stoneham

Court of Appeals of New York, 1934.
263 N.Y. 323, 189 N.E. 234.

Appeal, by permission of Court of Appeals, from judgment of Appellate Division, First Department, unanimously affirming judgment for plaintiff for $42,827.38 and other relief.

■ POUND, CH. J. The action is brought to compel specific performance of an agreement between the parties, entered into to secure the control of National Exhibition Company, also called the baseball club (New York Nationals or "Giants"). This was one of Stoneham's enterprises which used the New York Polo Grounds for its home games. McGraw was manager of the Giants. McQuade was, at the time the contract was entered into, a city magistrate. He resigned December 8, 1930.

Defendant Stoneham became the owner of 1,306 shares, or a majority of the stock of National Exhibition Company (there being then 2,500 shares outstanding). Plaintiff and defendant McGraw each purchased seventy shares of his stock. Plaintiff paid Stoneham $50,338.10 for the stock he purchased. As a part of the transaction the agreement in question was entered into. It was dated May 21, 1919. Some of its pertinent provisions are:

"VIII. The parties hereto will use their best endeavors for the purpose of continuing as directors of said company and as officers thereof the following:

"Directors: Charles A. Stoneham, John J. McGraw, Francis X. McQuade, with right to the party of the first part (Stoneham) to name all additional directors as he sees fit.

"Officers: Charles A. Stoneham, president; John J. McGraw, vice-president; Francis X. McQuade, treasurer.

"IX. No salaries are to be paid to any of the above officers or directors, except as follows: President, $45,000; vice-president, $7,500; treasurer, $7,500.

"X. There shall be no change in said salaries, no change in the amount of capital, or the number of shares, no change or amendment of the by-laws of the corporation or any matters regarding the policy of the business of the corporation or any matters which may in anywise affect, endanger or interfere with the rights of minority stockholders, excepting upon the mutual and unanimous consent of all . . . of the parties hereto.

"XIV. This agreement shall continue and remain in force so long as the parties or any of them or the representative of any own the stock referred to in this agreement, to wit, the party of the first part, 1,166 shares, the party of the second part 70 shares and the party of the third part 70 shares, except as may otherwise appear by this agreement. . . ."

In pursuance of this contract Stoneham became president and McGraw vice-president of the corporation. McQuade became treasurer. In June, 1925, his salary was increased to $10,000 a year. He continued to act until May 2, 1928, when Leo J. Bondy was elected to succeed him. The board of directors consisted of seven men. The four outside of the parties hereto were selected by Stoneham and he had complete control over them. At the meeting of May 2, 1928, Stoneham and McGraw refrained from voting, McQuade voted for himself and the other four voted for Bondy. Defendants did not keep their agreement with McQuade to use their best efforts to continue him as treasurer. On the contrary, he was dropped with their entire acquiescence. At the next stockholders' meeting he was dropped as a director, although they might have elected him.

The courts below have refused to order the reinstatement of McQuade, but have given him damages for wrongful discharge, with a right to sue for future damages.

The cause for dropping McQuade was due to the falling out of friends. McQuade and Stoneham had disagreed. The trial court has found in substance that their numerous quarrels and disputes did not affect the orderly and efficient administration of the business of the corporation; that plaintiff was removed because he had antagonized the dominant Stoneham by persisting in challenging his power over the corporate treasury and for no misconduct on his part. The court also finds that plaintiff was removed by Stoneham for protecting the corporation and its minority stockholders. We will assume that Stoneham put him out when he might have retained him, merely in order to get rid of him.

Defendants say that the contract in suit was void because the directors held their office charged with the duty to act for the corporation according to their best judgment and that any contract which compels a director to vote to keep any particular person in office and at a stated salary is illegal. Directors are the exclusive executive representatives of the corporation, charged with administration of its internal affairs and the management and use of its assets. They manage the business of the corporation (Gen.Corp.Law, Cons. Laws, c. 23, sec. 27). "An agreement to continue a man as president is dependent upon his continued loyalty to the interests of the corporation" (Fells v. Katz, 256 N.Y. 67, 72, 175 N.E. 516, 517). So much is undisputed.

Plaintiff contends that the converse of this proposition is true and that an agreement among directors to continue a man as an officer of a corporation is not to be broken so long as such officer is loyal to the interests of the corporation and that, as plaintiff has been found loyal to the corporation, the agreement of defendants is enforceable.

Although it has been held that an agreement among stockholders whereby it is attempted to divest the directors of their power to discharge an unfaithful employee of the corporation is illegal as against public policy (Fells v. Katz, supra), it must be equally true that the stockholders may not, by agreement among themselves, control the directors in the exercise of the judgment vested in them by virtue of their office to elect officers and fix salaries. Their motives may not be questioned so long as their acts are legal. The bad faith or the improper motives of the parties does not change this rule (Manson v. Curtis, 223 N.Y. 313, 324, 119 N.E. 559). Directors may not by agreements entered into by stockholders abrogate their independent judgment (Creed v. Copps, 103 Vt. 164, 71 A.L.R.Ann. 1287).

Stockholders may, of course, combine to elect directors. That rule is well settled. As Holmes, Ch. J., pointedly said (Brightman v. Bates, 175 Mass. 105, 110, 55 N.E. 809, 811): "If stockholders want to make their power felt, they must unite. There is no reason why a majority should not agree to keep together." The power to unite is, however, limited to the election of directors and is not extended to contracts whereby limitations are placed on the power of directors to manage the business of the corporation by the selection of agents at defined salaries.

The minority shareholders whose interests McQuade says he has been punished for protecting, are not, aside from himself, complaining about his discharge. He is not acting for the corporation or for them in this action. It is impossible to see how the corporation has been injured by the substitution of Bondy as treasurer in place of McQuade. As McQuade represents himself in this action and seeks redress for his own wrongs, "we prefer to listen to [the corporation and the minority stockholders] before any decision as to their wrongs" (Faulds v. Yates, 57 Ill. 416).

It is urged that we should pay heed to the morals and manners of the market place to sustain this agreement, and that we should hold that its violation gives rise to a cause of action for damages, rather than base our decision on any outworn notions of public policy. Public policy is a dangerous guide in determining the validity of a contract, and courts should not interfere lightly with the freedom of competent parties to make their own contracts. We do not close our eyes to the fact that such agreements, tacitly or openly arrived at, are not uncommon, especially in close corporations where the stockholders are doing business for convenience under a corporate organization. We know that majority stockholders, united in voting trusts, effectively manage the business of a corporation by choosing trustworthy directors to reflect their policies in the corporate management. Nor are we unmindful that McQuade has, so the court has found, been shabbily treated as a purchaser of stock from Stoneham. We have said: "A trustee is held to something stricter than the morals of the market place" (Meinhard v. Salmon, 249 N.Y. 458, 464, 164 N.E. 545, 546), but Stoneham and McGraw were not trustees for McQuade as an individual. Their duty was to the corporation and its stockholders, to be exercised according to their unrestricted lawful judgment. They were under no legal obligation to deal righteously with McQuade if it was against public policy to do so.

The courts do not enforce mere moral obligations, nor legal ones either, unless someone seeks to establish rights which may be waived by custom and for convenience. We are constrained by authority to hold that a contract is illegal and void so far as it precludes the board of directors, at the risk of incurring legal liability, from changing officers, salaries or policies or retaining individuals in office, except by consent of the contracting parties. On the whole, such a holding is probably preferable to one which would open the courts to pass on the motives of directors in the lawful exercise of their trust. . . .

The judgment of the Appellate Division and that of the Trial Term should be reversed and the complaint dismissed, with costs in all courts.

[The court also held that the agreement violated the Inferior Criminal Courts Act, which provided that "[n]o city magistrate shall engage in any other business or profession . . . , but each of said justices and magistrates shall devote his whole time and capacity, so far as the public interest demands, to the duties of his office...." At the date of the agreement McQuade was a city magistrate, and he did not resign his position until after commencement of the action.]

■ [The opinion of LEHMAN, J., concurring in the result, is omitted.]

NOTE ON CLARK v. DODGE

In Clark v. Dodge, 269 N.Y. 410, 199 N.E. 641 (1936), two corporations manufactured medicinal preparations under secret formulas. Clark owned 25%, and Dodge owned 75%, of the stock of each corporation. Clark and Dodge entered into an agreement which provided that (1) Dodge would vote for Clark as a director. (2) Dodge, acting in his directorial capacity, would continue Clark as general manager as long as Clark proved faithful, efficient, and competent. (3) Clark would always receive as salary or dividends one-fourth of the corporation's net income. (4) No salaries to other officers would be unreasonable in amount or incommensurate with the services rendered by those officers. The court held that the agreement was valid:

> Except for the broad dicta in the *McQuade* opinion, we think there can be no doubt that the agreement here in question was legal and that the complaint states a cause of action. There was no attempt to sterilize the board of directors as in [*McQuade*]....
>
> If there was any invasion of the powers of the directorate under that agreement it is so slight as to be negligible; and certainly there is no damage suffered by or threatened to anybody. The broad statements in the *McQuade* opinion, applicable to the facts there, should be confined to those facts.

Galler v. Galler

Supreme Court of Illinois, 1964, reh. denied 1964.
32 Ill.2d 16, 203 N.E.2d 577.

■ UNDERWOOD, JUSTICE. Plaintiff, Emma Galler, sued in equity for an accounting and for specific performance of an agreement made in July, 1955, between plaintiff and her husband, of one part, and defendants, Isadore A. Galler and his wife, Rose, of the other. Defendants appealed from a decree of the superior court of Cook County granting the relief prayed. The First District Appellate Court reversed the decree and denied specific performance, affirming in part the order for an accounting, and modifying the order awarding master's fees. (45 Ill. App.2d 452, 196 N.E.2d 5.) That decision is appealed here on a certificate of importance.

There is no substantial dispute as to the facts in this case. From 1919 to 1924, Benjamin and Isadore Galler, brothers, were equal partners in the Galler Drug Company, a wholesale drug concern. In

1924 the business was incorporated under the Illinois Business Corporation Act, each owning one half of the outstanding 220 shares of stock. In 1945 each contracted to sell 6 shares to an employee, Rosenberg, at a price of $10,500 for each block of 6 shares, payable within 10 years. They guaranteed to repurchase the shares if Rosenberg's employment were terminated, and further agreed that if they sold their shares, Rosenberg would receive the same price per share as that paid for the brothers' shares. Rosenberg was still indebted for the 12 shares in July, 1955, and continued to make payments on account even after Benjamin Galler died in 1957 and after the institution of this action by Emma Galler in 1959. Rosenberg was not involved in this litigation either as a party or as a witness, and in July of 1961, prior to the time that the master in chancery hearings were concluded, defendants Isadore and Rose Galler purchased the 12 shares from Rosenberg. A supplemental complaint was filed by the plaintiff, Emma Galler, asserting an equitable right to have 6 of the 12 shares transferred to her and offering to pay the defendants one half of the amount that the defendants paid Rosenberg. The parties have stipulated that pending disposition of the instant case, these shares will not be voted or transferred. For approximately one year prior to the entry of the decree by the chancellor in July of 1962, there were no outstanding minority shareholder interests.

In March, 1954, Benjamin and Isadore, on the advice of their accountant, decided to enter into an agreement for the financial protection of their immediate families and to assure their families, after the death of either brother, equal control of the corporation. [The agreement was executed in July 1955, after Benjamin had fallen ill. In September 1956, Emma agreed to permit Isadore's son Aaron to become president for one year and agreed that she would not interfere with the business during that year. In December 1957, Benjamin died.] The evidence is undisputed that defendants had decided prior to Benjamin's death they would not honor the agreement, but never disclosed their intention to plaintiff or her husband. . . .

Shortly after Benjamin's death, Emma went to the office and demanded the terms of the 1955 agreement be carried out. Isadore told her that anything she had to say could be said to Aaron, who then told her that his father would not abide by the agreement. He offered a modification of the agreement by proposing the salary continuation payment but without her becoming a director. When Emma refused to modify the agreement and sought enforcement of its terms, defendants refused and this suit followed.

During the last few years of Benjamin's life both brothers drew an annual salary of $42,000. Aaron, whose salary was $15,000 as manager of the warehouse prior to September, 1956, has since the time that Emma agreed to his acting as president drawn an annual salary of $20,000. In 1957, 1958, and 1959 a $40,000 annual dividend was paid. Plaintiff has received her proportionate share of the dividend.

The July, 1955, agreement in question here, entered into between Benjamin, Emma, Isadore and Rose, recites that Benjamin and Isadore each own 47½% of the issued and outstanding shares of the Galler Drug Company, an Illinois corporation, and that Benjamin and Isadore desired to provide income for the support and maintenance of their immediate families. No reference is made to the shares then being purchased by Rosenberg. The essential features of the contested portions of the agreement are substantially as set forth in the opinion of the Appellate Court: (2) that the bylaws of the corporation will be amended to provide for a board of four directors; that the necessary quorum shall be three directors; and that no directors' meeting shall be held without giving ten days notice to all directors. (3) The shareholders will cast their votes for the above named persons (Isadore, Rose, Benjamin and Emma) as directors at said special meeting and at any other meeting held for the purpose of electing directors. (4, 5) In the event of the death of either brother his wife shall have the right to nominate a director in place of the decedent. (6) Certain annual dividends will be declared by the corporation. The dividend shall be $50,000 payable out of the accumulated earned surplus in excess of $500,000. If 50% of the annual net profits after taxes exceeds the minimum $50,000 then the directors shall have discretion to declare a dividend up to 50% of the annual net profits. If the net profits are less than $50,000 nevertheless the minimum $50,000 annual dividend shall be declared, providing the $500,000 surplus is maintained. Earned surplus is defined. (9) The certificates evidencing the said shares of Benjamin Galler and Isadore Galler shall bear a legend that the shares are subject to the terms of this agreement. (10) A salary continuation agreement shall be entered into by the corporation which shall authorize the corporation upon the death of Benjamin Galler or Isadore Galler, or both, to pay a sum equal to twice the salary of such officer, payable monthly over a five-year period. Said sum shall be paid to the widow during her widowhood, but should be paid to such widow's children if the widow remarries within the five-year period. (11, 12) The parties to this agreement further agree and hereby grant to the corporation the authority to purchase, in the event of the death of either Benjamin or Isadore, so much of the stock of Galler Drug Company held by the estate as is necessary to provide sufficient funds to pay the federal estate tax, the Illinois inheritance tax and other administrative expenses of the estate. If as a result of such purchase from the estate of the decedent the amount of dividends to be received by the heirs is reduced, the parties shall nevertheless vote for directors so as to give the estate and heirs the same representation as before (2 directors out of 4, even though they own less stock), and also that the corporation pay an additional benefit payment equal to the diminution of the dividends. In the event either Benjamin or Isadore decides to sell his shares he is required to offer them first to the remaining shareholders and then to the corporation at book value, according each six months to accept the offer.

The Appellate Court found the 1955 agreement void because "the undue duration, stated purpose and substantial disregard of the provisions of the Corporation Act outweigh any considerations which might call for divisibility" and held that "the public policy of this state demands voiding this entire agreement".

While the conduct of defendants towards plaintiff was clearly inequitable, the basically controlling factor is the absence of an objecting minority interest, together with the absence of public detriment. . . .

At this juncture it should be emphasized that we deal here with a so-called close corporation. . . . For our purposes, a close corporation is one in which the stock is held in a few hands, or in a few families, and wherein it is not at all, or only rarely, dealt in by buying or selling. (Brooks v. Willcuts, 8th Cir.1935, 78 F.2d 270, 273.) Moreover, it should be recognized that shareholder agreements similar to that in question here are often, as a practical consideration, quite necessary for the protection of those financially interested in the close corporation. While the shareholder of a public-issue corporation may readily sell his shares on the open market should management fail to use, in his opinion, sound business judgment, his counterpart of the close corporation often has a large total of his entire capital invested in the business and has no ready market for his shares should he desire to sell. He feels, understandably, that he is more than a mere investor and that his voice should be heard concerning all corporate activity. Without a shareholder agreement, specifically enforceable by the courts, insuring him a modicum of control, a large minority shareholder might find himself at the mercy of an oppressive or unknowledgeable majority. Moreover, as in the case at bar, the shareholders of a close corporation are often also the directors and officers thereof. With substantial shareholding interests abiding in each member of the board of directors, it is often quite impossible to secure, as in the large public-issue corporation, independent board judgment free from personal motivations concerning corporate policy. For these and other reasons too voluminous to enumerate here, often the only sound basis for protection is afforded by a lengthy, detailed shareholder agreement securing the rights and obligations of all concerned. For a discussion of these and other considerations, see Note, "A Plea for Separate Statutory Treatment of the Close Corporation", 33 N.Y.U.L.Rev. 700 (1958).

As the preceding review of the applicable decisions of this court points out, there has been a definite, albeit inarticulate, trend toward eventual judicial treatment of the close corporation as *sui generis*. Several shareholder-director agreements that have technically "violated" the letter of the Business Corporation Act have nevertheless been upheld in the light of the existing practical circumstances, i.e., no apparent public injury, the absence of a complaining minority interest, and no apparent prejudice to creditors. However, we have thus far not attempted to limit these decisions as applicable only to close corporations and have seemingly implied that general considerations regarding judicial supervision of all corporate behavior apply.

The practical result of this series of cases, while liberally giving legal efficacy to particular agreements in special circumstances notwithstanding literal "violations" of statutory corporate law, has been to inject much doubt and uncertainty into the thinking of the bench and corporate bar of Illinois concerning shareholder agreements. See e.g., Cary, "How Illinois Corporations May Enjoy Partnership Advantages: Planning for the Closely Held Firm." 48 N.W.U.L.Rev. 427; Note, "The Validity of Stockholders' Voting Agreements in Illinois," 3 U.Chi. L.Rev. 640.

It is therefore necessary, we feel, to discuss the instant case with the problems peculiar to the close corporation particularly in mind. . . .

This court has recognized, albeit *sub silentio,* the significant conceptual differences between the close corporation and its public-issue counterpart in, among other cases, Kantzler v. Benzinger, 214 Ill. 589, 73 N.E. 874, where an agreement quite similar to the one under attack here was upheld. Where, as in *Kantzler* and here, no complaining minority interest appears, no fraud or apparent injury to the public or creditors is present, and no clearly prohibitory statutory language is violated, we can see no valid reason for precluding the parties from reaching any arrangements concerning the management of the corporation which are agreeable to all. . . .

Since the question as to the duration of the agreement is a principal source of controversy, we shall consider it first. The parties provided no specific termination date, and while the agreement concludes with a paragraph that its terms "shall be binding upon and shall inure to the benefits of" the legal representatives, heirs and assigns of the parties, this clause is, we believe, intended to be operative only as long as one of the parties is living. It further provides that it shall be so construed as to carry out its purposes, and we believe these must be determined from a consideration of the agreement as a whole. Thus viewed, a fair construction is that its purposes were accomplished at the death of the survivor of the parties. While these life spans are not precisely ascertainable, and the Appellate Court noted Emma Galler's life expectancy at her husband's death was 26.9 years, we are aware of no statutory or public policy provision against stockholders' agreements which would invalidate this agreement on that ground. . . . While defendants argue that the public policy evinced by the legislative restrictions upon the duration of voting trust agreements (Ill.Rev.Stat.1963, chap. 32, par. 157.30a) should be applied here, this agreement is not a voting trust, but as pointed out by the dissenting justice in the Appellate Court, is a straight contractual voting control agreement which does not divorce voting rights from stock ownership. That the policy against agreements in which stock ownership and voting rights are separated, indicated in Luthy v. Ream, 270 Ill. 170, 110 N.E. 373, is inapplicable to voting control agreements was emphasized in Thompson wherein a control agreement was upheld as not attempting to separate ownership and voting power. While limiting voting trusts in 1947 to a maximum duration of 10 years, the legislature has indicated no similar policy regarding straight voting agreements although these have been common since prior to 1870. In view of the history of decisions of this court generally upholding, in the absence of fraud or prejudice to minority interests or public policy, the right of stockholders to agree among themselves as to the manner in which their stock will be voted, we do not regard the period of time within which this agreement may remain effective as rendering the agreement unenforceable.

The clause that provides for the election of certain persons to specified offices for a period of years likewise does not require invalidation. In Kantzler v. Bensinger, 214 Ill. 589, 73 N.E. 874, this court upheld an agreement entered into by all the stockholders providing that certain parties would be elected to the offices of the corporation for a fixed period. In Faulds v. Yates, 57 Ill. 416, we upheld a similar agreement among the majority stockholders of a corporation, notwithstanding the existence of a minority which was not before the court complaining thereof. See also Hornstein, "Judicial Tolerance of the Incorporated Partnership," 18 Law and Contemporary Problems 435 at page 444.

We turn next to a consideration of the effect of the stated purpose of the agreement upon its validity. The pertinent provision is: "The said Benjamin A. Galler and Isadore A. Galler desire to provide income for the support and maintenance of their immediate families." Obviously, there is no evil inherent in a contract entered into for the reason that the persons originating the terms desired to so arrange their property as to provide post-death support for those dependent upon them. Nor does the fact that the subject property is corporate stock alter the situation so long as there exists no detriment to minority stock interests, creditors or other public injury. It is, however, contended by defendants that the methods provided by the agreement for implementation of the stated purpose are, as a whole, violative of the Business Corporation Act (Ill.Rev.Stat.1963, chap. 32, pars. 157.28, 157.30a, 157.33, 157.34, 157.41) to such an extent as to render it void *in toto*.

The terms of the dividend agreement require a minimum annual dividend of $50,000, but this duty is limited by the subsequent provision that it shall be operative only so long as an earned surplus of $500,000 is maintained. It may be noted that in 1958, the year prior to commencement of this litigation, the corporation's net earnings after taxes amounted to $202,759 while its earned surplus was $1,543,270, and this was increased in 1958 to $1,680,079 while earnings were $172,964. The minimum earned surplus requirement is designed for the protection of the corporation and its creditors, and we take no exception to the contractual dividend requirements as thus restricted. Kantzler v. Benzinger, 214 Ill. 589, 73 N.E. 874.

The salary continuation agreement is a common feature, in one form or another, of corporate executive employment. It requires that the widow should receive a total benefit, payable monthly over a five-year period, aggregating twice the amount paid her deceased husband in one year. This requirement was likewise limited for the protection of the corporation by being contingent upon the payments being income tax-deductible by the corporation. The charge made in those cases which have considered the validity of payments to the widow of an officer and shareholder in a corporation is that a gift of its property by a noncharitable corporation is in violation of the rights of its shareholders and *ultra vires*. Since there are no shareholders here other than the parties to the contract, this objection is not here applicable, and its effect, as limited, upon the corporation is not so prejudicial as to require its invalidation.

Having concluded that the agreement, under the circumstances here present, is not vulnerable to the attack made on it, we must consider the accounting feature of this action. The trial court allowed the relief prayed, an action we deem proper except as to the master's fees which were modified by the Appellate Court. Since no question is here raised regarding them, we affirm the action of that court in this respect. The questions as to salary which the Appellate Court correctly held were improperly increased became ones of fact to be determined by the trial court.

We hold defendants must account for all monies received by them from the corporation since September 25, 1956, in excess of that theretofore authorized.

Accordingly, the judgment of the Appellate Court is reversed except insofar as it relates to fees, and is, as to them affirmed. The cause is remanded to the circuit court of Cook County with directions to proceed in accordance herewith.

Affirmed in part and reversed in part, and remanded with directions.

NOTE ON FURTHER PROCEEDINGS IN GALLER v. GALLER

The decree in *Galler* ordered Isadore and Rose to "account for all monies received by them from the company since September 25, 1956 [up to the time of the decree], in excess of that theretofore authorized," but provided that Isadore and Aaron be allowed "fair compensation . . . for services rendered by them to the corporation during said period." On remand, defendants argued that the salaries of Aaron and Isadore during the relevant period represented the fair market value of their services, and in any event since Isadore's $42,000 salary after Benjamin's death was a continuation of his salary under the agreement, it had been "theretofore authorized" within the meaning of the decree. The appellate court rejected both arguments. As to the former issue, the court adopted the findings of a master who valued Isadore's services at $10,000/year and Aaron's at $15,000/year. As to whether continuation of Isadore's $42,000 salary was authorized by the agreement, the court said

    . . . Isadore's continued receipt of the same salary upon the death of Benjamin without the *quid pro quo* for his brother's family, is an alteration of the past arrangement, and was without authorization.

Furthermore, the clear import of the 1955 shareholders' agreement is that the partnership-like arrangement was intended to remain after the death of either Benjamin or Isadore. While not specifically addressing itself to salaries, the agreement provides that upon the death of either Benjamin or Isadore, four directors are to be elected; two from Isadore's family and two from Benjamin's family. The officers and their salaries are voted upon by the directors. Dividends are required to be paid provided $500,000 earned surplus is maintained. It may be inferred that this agreement sought to replace a deceased brother's position as an officer with members of his family, thereby permitting them to share equally in the company's earnings, including salaries, a significant means of distributing the corporate profits. This inference is not negated by the fact that no provision in the 1955 agreement requires equality of salaries between the family branches.

For other disputes among the Gallers after the Supreme Court's decree, see Galler v. Galler, 69 Ill.App.2d 397, 217 N.E.2d 111 (1966); Galler v. Galler, 95 Ill.App.2d 340, 238 N.E.2d 274 (1968).

————

WASSERMAN v. ROSENGARDEN, 84 Ill.App.3d 713, 40 Ill.Dec. 430, 406 N.E.2d 131 (1980). Joseph and Ralph Rosengarden each owned 40% of the stock of Autohaus Corporation. Leonard Wasserman owned the remaining 20%. Wasserman claimed that the Rosengardens had breached an oral agreement under which all three parties would continue to vote for one another as directors and officers, and all three would receive equal salaries and share equally in any distributed profits. The trial court granted the Rosengardens' motion for judgment on the pleadings, in part on the ground the alleged agreement was ultra vires and unenforceable. Reversed.

"Like the court in *Galler,* we see no reason for precluding the parties from reaching arrangements concerning the management of the closely held corporation which were agreeable to the three shareholders. Fraud, injury to the public, or harm to creditors have not been suggested. Nor is a minority interest complaining about the terms of the oral shareholder's agreement. Defendants protest that, under the alleged agreement, plaintiff has received a disproportionately large return for his investment, but the economic consequences of the agreement do not govern its validity."

————

DEL. GEN. CORP. LAW §§ 102(b)(1), 141(a), 142(b), 350, 351, 354

[See Statutory Supplement]

————

MODEL BUS. CORP. ACT §§ 2.02(b), 2.06, 7.32, 8.01(b)

N.Y. BUS. CORP. LAW § 620

[See Statutory Supplement]

CAL. CORP. CODE §§ 158, 186, 300, 312

[See Statutory Supplement]

ADLER v. SVINGOS, 80 A.D.2d 764, 436 N.Y.S.2d 719 (1981). Adler, Shaw, and Svingos each owned 33⅓% of the shares of 891 First Ave. Corp., a New York corporation that operated a restaurant. The corporation's certificate of incorporation was filed in November 1978. In December 1978, Adler, Shaw, and Svingos executed a Stockholders' Agreement. Paragraph 8 of the Agreement provided that all corporate operations, including changes in corporate structure, would require unanimous consent of the three signatories. Subsequently, when Adler and Shaw sought to sell the business, Svingos objected, relying upon the Stockholders' Agreement. Adler and Shaw then brought an action seeking to strike paragraph 8 of the Agreement as void under New York B.C.L. § 620(b), on the ground that under section 620(b) a provision that restricts the board in the management of the business of the corporation must be located in the certificate of incorporation. Svingos counterclaimed, and asked for reformation of the certificate of incorporation to reflect Paragraph 8 of the Stockholders' Agreement. The trial court granted summary judgment against Svingos. Reversed.

In Zion v. Kurtz (50 N.Y.2d 92), the Court of Appeals interpreted analogous provisions of the Delaware General Corporation Law and held enforceable, as between the parties to it, a provision of a shareholders' agreement between all the shareholders, proscribing corporate action without the consent of a minority shareholder, even though the disputed provision was not incorporated in the corporate charter as required by Delaware's statute. Speaking for the majority, Judge Meyer stated ... "Since there are no intervening rights of third persons, the agreement requires nothing that is not permitted by statute, and all of the stockholders of the corporation assented to it, the certificate of incorporation may be ordered reformed, by requiring Kurtz [whose position was analogous to that of plaintiffs Adler and Shaw] to file the appropriate amendments, or more directly he may be held estopped to rely upon the absence of those amendments from the corporate charter".

The principles set forth in *Zion* are controlling here. We conclude that it was error to grant partial summary judgment to plaintiffs and to dismiss defendant's first counterclaim. Indeed, the record warrants granting the defendant's motion for partial summary judgment reforming the certificate to reflect the unanimity of the stockholders' agreement.

SECTION 4.   SUPERMAJORITY VOTING AND QUORUM REQUIREMENTS AT THE SHAREHOLDER AND BOARD LEVELS

Sutton v. Sutton

Court of Appeals of New York, 1994.
84 N.Y.2d 37, 637 N.E.2d 260, 614 N.Y.S.2d 369.

■ SIMONS, JUDGE.

In this CPLR article 78 proceeding, petitioners seek (1) a declaration that an amendment to the certificate of incorporation of Bag Bazaar, Ltd. is valid and (2) to compel respondent David S. Sutton, as a director of the corporation, to sign and deliver a certificate of amendment to petitioners for filing. Respondent has refused to execute the certificate, contending it is not valid because the amendment had the support of only 70% of the shareholders when the certificate of incorporation required unanimous approval. The appeal requires an interpretation of section 616(b) of the Business Corporation Law which states that supermajority provisions in a certificate of incorporation may be amended by a two-thirds vote unless the certificate "specifically" provides otherwise.

Petitioners contend that notwithstanding the general unanimity provision contained in Bag Bazaar's certificate, a two-thirds vote to amend is sufficient under this statute unless the certificate explicitly provides unanimous consent is required to amend the supermajority provision. As they see it, prior to a 1962 statutory amendment, which added the word "specifically", a general requirement of a unanimous vote for any amendment of the certificate—i.e., a provision like the one here—would be read to apply to the supermajority provision. Thus, they reason that the Legislature, by adding the word "specifically" in the 1962 amendment, intended to require an amendment provision explicitly directed at the procedure for changing a supermajority provision. The Appellate Division disagreed and held that the provision in Bag Bazaar's certificate of incorporation was sufficiently specific and that the amendment was not valid because it lacked unanimous shareholder approval (196 A.D.2d 411, 601 N.Y.S.2d 106). We now affirm.

In 1963, the certificate of incorporation of Bag Bazaar, Ltd. was amended to provide that "[t]he unanimous vote or consent of the holders of all the issued and outstanding shares of Common Stock of the corporation shall be necessary for the transaction of any business * * * of the corporation, including amendment to the certificate of incorporation''. At that time the business was run by Abraham Sutton and none of the parties to this litigation was a shareholder. In 1971 Abraham's brother, respondent David S. Sutton, purchased 30 shares. Two years later Abraham's son, petitioner Solomon A. Sutton, joined the business and subsequently acquired 30 shares. On Abraham's death, in 1987, his widow, petitioner Yvette Sutton, inherited Abraham's remaining 40 shares. Thus, petitioners now own 70% of the outstanding shares of the corporation and respondent and his wife own 30 shares. Petitioner Solomon A. Sutton serves as one of the two directors of the company and respondent David S. Sutton as the other.

The corporation was run without incident for nearly 30 years under Abraham's leadership. After he relinquished control of the company, however, disputes arose between Solomon and David Sutton concerning the management of the corporation. These disputes culminated in an April 1992 shareholders' meeting, where petitioners voted their 70% of the shares in favor of a resolution to strike the unanimity provision, while respondent's 30% of the shares voted against the resolution.

Respondent, as a director of the corporation, refused to sign a certificate of amendment reflecting the deletion of the unanimity provision, thereby preventing the amendment from taking effect. Accordingly, petitioners commenced this proceeding and moved for judgment declaring the resolution valid and enforceable and compelling respondent to sign the certificate of amendment. Respondent cross-moved to dismiss the petition, for reformation of the certificate of incorporation and to compel arbitration of the dispute. Supreme Court granted the petition and denied the cross motion. The Appellate Division reversed and denied the petition.

To support their position on this appeal, petitioners contend that the Legislature added the word ''specifically'' to section 616(b) because it recognized that a unanimity provision gives minority shareholders the ability to deadlock any and all corporate action. The amendment was intended to minimize deadlocks by permitting a two-thirds majority of the shareholders to alter or delete the unanimity requirement unless the certificate of incorporation explicitly stated otherwise. Respondent maintains that ''specifically'' was added to the statute to clarify that if more than a two-thirds vote was required to amend a unanimity provision, the certificate should state exactly what greater percentage is needed. They maintain that this certificate satisfied that requirement by declaring that a unanimous vote was required for any amendment.

The history of Business Corporation Law § 616(b) begins with Benintendi v. Kenton Hotel, 294 N.Y. 112, 60 N.E.2d 829, where this Court invalidated a unanimity provision adopted by unanimous shareholder vote. We reasoned that such a provision was antithetical to the basic concept of corporate governance by majority rule and contrary to public policy (id., at 118–119, 60 N.E.2d 829). In 1948, the Legislature abrogated *Benintendi* by enacting section 9 of the Stock Corporation Law, which authorized unanimity provisions when approved by a unanimous vote (see, L.1948, ch. 862). The effect of section 9 was to require unanimous shareholder consent to either add or amend a unanimity provision (see, 3 White, New York Corporations § 616.02, at 6–378 [13th ed.]). In 1951, this section was amended to allow adoption or change of a supermajority provision by a two-thirds or greater vote. A unanimous vote was still required, however, where the certificate called for a unanimous vote; where the unanimity provision itself required such a vote; or where the unanimity provision was adopted prior to the effective date of the 1951 amendment (see, L. 1951, ch. 717).

In 1961, the Business Corporation Law was adopted to replace the Stock Corporation Law, and section 9 was substantially reenacted as Business Corporation Law § 616(b) and § 709(b). However, in 1962, prior to the 1963 effective date of the Business Corporation Law, a series of changes were made, including the addition of the word "specifically" in section 616(b). As finally enacted, section 616(b) provides that "[a]n amendment of the certificate of incorporation which changes or strikes out a [supermajority] provision * * * shall be authorized at a meeting of shareholders by vote of the holders of two-thirds of all outstanding shares entitled to vote thereon, or of such greater proportion of shares * * * as may be provided specifically in the certificate of incorporation" (emphasis added). According to the Legislative Study Committee the word "specifically" was one of a number of "technical" amendments added to the chapter to clarify existing language and avoid minor inconsistencies. It was not intended to effect a substantive change in the law (Mem. of Joint Legis.Comm. To Study Revision of Corp. Laws, Bill Jacket, L.1962, ch. 834, at 86).

Thus, nothing in the legislative history or the statute itself suggests the necessity for a discrete paragraph addressed solely to the supermajority provision and explicitly declaring the vote required for its amendment. The history reveals that Stock Corporation Law § 9 stated that a provision in the certificate of incorporation requiring unanimous consent could only be amended by unanimous consent and this provision was substantially reenacted in the Business Corporation Law.* Inasmuch as the Legislature did not intend the "technical" revisions added before the effective date of the Business Corporation Law to change the existing law substantively, the present statute should be construed as section 9 of the Stock Corporation Law was. Unanimity was required under the prior law to amend a unanimity provision, such as this one, and the addition of the word "specifically" merely provides that a two-thirds majority may now amend a unanimity provision unless the certificate requires a greater percentage.

The provision in Bag Bazaar's certificate is unambiguous: it requires unanimous shareholder consent for the transaction of "any business * * * including amendment to the certificate of incorpo-

---

* While the 1951 amendments to that section allowed a unanimity provision to be amended by a two-thirds vote in certain instances, petitioners acknowledge that the provision at issue here would have required unanimous shareholder consent to amend, despite the 1951 amendment. (Footnote by the court.)

ration." To read section 616(b) as requiring more to address amendment of the super-majority provision would be unnecessarily restrictive in light of the legislative history. The certificate need only clearly state what vote, if greater than two thirds, is required to amend a unanimity provision. The certificate of Bag Bazaar, Ltd. does so....

Finally, petitioners note that unless section 616(b) is read as requiring an explicit certificate provision governing the amendment of unanimity provisions, majority shareholders will be unable to conduct the business of a corporation in the face of opposition from the minority. But as respondent notes, there is nothing inherently unfair or improper about a voluntary organization's consensual decision to assure protection for minority shareholders, and shareholders are not without remedies where deadlocks do arise (see generally, Business Corporation Law § 1104).

Accordingly, the order of the Appellate Division should be affirmed, with costs.

■ KAYE, C.J., and TITONE, BELLACOSA, SMITH, LEVINE and CIPARICK, JJ., concur.

Order affirmed, with costs.

———

N.Y. BUS. CORP. LAW §§ 616, 709

[See Statutory Supplement]

———

DEL. GEN. CORP. LAW §§ 102(b)(4), 141(b), 216

[See Statutory Supplement]

———

CAL. CORP. CODE §§ 204, 602

[See Statutory Supplement]

———

MODEL BUS. CORP. ACT §§ 7.27, 7.32, 8.24

[See Statutory Supplement]

———

SECTION 5. FIDUCIARY OBLIGATIONS OF SHAREHOLDERS IN CLOSE CORPORATIONS

———

Donahue v. Rodd Electrotype Co.

[See Section 1, supra.]

ROSENTHAL v. ROSENTHAL, 543 A.2d 348 (Me.1988). In this case, the trial court judge set out the following four specific fiduciary duties owed by the business associates in a close corporation to each other:

> (1) To act with that degree of diligence, care and skill which ordinarily prudent persons would exercise under similar circumstances in like positions;

> (2) To discharge the duties affecting their relationship in good faith with a view to furthering the interests of one another as to the matters within the scope of the relationship;

> (3) To disclose and not withhold from one another relevant information affecting the status and affairs of the relationship;

> (4) To not use their position, influence or knowledge respecting the affairs and organization that are subject to the relationship to gain any special privilege or advantage over the other person or persons involved in the relationship. . . .

On appeal, the Maine Supreme Court affirmed. "For the first time on appeal defendants object to the [trial judge's] definition of the scope of the [shareholders'] duties as including 'furthering the interests *of one another*,' rather than being restricted to furthering the interests of the business enterprise. We can find no clear error in that instruction, however, given the special nature of the [shareholders'] family business, which most closely resembles a single complex family partnership doing business through numerous entities of varied legal forms. . . . The duties owed in the circumstances here presented necessarily flowed to the other business associates, as well as to the [shareholders'] enterprise as a whole and the component entitles." (Emphasis by the court.)

Wilkes v. Springside Nursing Home, Inc.

Supreme Judicial Court of Massachusetts, 1976.
370 Mass. 842, 353 N.E.2d 657.

■ HENNESSEY, CHIEF JUSTICE.

[The plaintiff (Wilkes) filed a bill in equity for declaratory judgment, naming as defendants T. Edward Quinn,[3] Leon L. Riche, the executors of Lawrence R. Connor, and the Springside Nursing Home,

---

3. T. Edward Quinn died while this action was sub judice. The executrix of his estate has been substituted as a party-defendant. . . .

Inc. Wilkes sought, among other forms of relief, damages in the amount of the salary he would have received had he continued as a director and officer of Springside subsequent to March, 1967. The court referred the suit to a master. The master's report was confirmed, a judgment was entered dismissing Wilkes's action on the merits, and the Massachusetts Supreme Court granted direct appellate review.] On appeal, Wilkes argued in the alternative that (1) he should recover damages for breach of the alleged partnership agreement; and (2) he should recover damages because the defendants, as majority stockholders in Springside, breached their fiduciary duty to him as a minority stockholder by their action in February and March, 1967.

... [W]e reverse so much of the judgment as dismisses Wilkes's complaint and order the entry of a judgment substantially granting the relief sought by Wilkes under the second alternative set forth above.

A summary of the pertinent facts as found by the master is set out in the following pages....

In 1951 Wilkes acquired an option to purchase a building and lot located on the corner of Springside Avenue and North Street in Pittsfield, Massachusetts, the building having previously housed the Hillcrest Hospital. Though Wilkes was principally engaged in the roofing and siding business, he had gained a reputation locally for profitable dealings in real estate. Riche, an acquaintance of Wilkes, learned of the option, and interested Quinn (who was known to Wilkes through membership on the draft board in Pittsfield) and Pipkin (an acquaintance of both Wilkes and Riche) in joining Wilkes in his investment. The four men met and decided to participate jointly in the purchase of the building and lot as a real estate investment which, they believed, had good profit potential on resale or rental.

The parties later determined that the property would have its greatest potential for profit if it were operated by them as a nursing home. Wilkes consulted his attorney, who advised him that if the four men were to operate the contemplated nursing home as planned, they would be partners and would be liable for any debts incurred by the partnership and by each other. On the attorney's suggestion, and after consultation among themselves, ownership of the property was vested in Springside, a corporation organized under Massachusetts law.

Each of the four men invested $1,000 and subscribed to ten shares of $100 par value stock in Springside.[6] At the time of incorporation it was understood by all of the parties that each would be a director of Springside and each would participate actively in the management and decision making involved in operating the corporation.[7] It was, further, the understanding and intention of all the parties

---

6. On May 2, 1955, and again on December 23, 1958, each of the four original investors paid for and was issued additional shares of $100 par value stock, eventually bringing the total number of shares owned by each to 115.

7. Wilkes testified before the master that, when the corporate officers were elected, all four men "were ... guaranteed directorships." Riche's understanding of the parties' intentions was that they all wanted to play a part in the management of the corporation and wanted to have some "say"

that, corporate resources permitting, each would receive money from the corporation in equal amounts as long as each assumed an active and ongoing responsibility for carrying a portion of the burdens necessary to operate the business.

The work involved in establishing and operating a nursing home was roughly apportioned, and each of the four men undertook his respective tasks.[8] Initially, Riche was elected president of Springside, Wilkes was elected treasurer, and Quinn was elected clerk.[9] Each of the four was listed in the articles of organization as a director of the corporation.

At some time in 1952, it became apparent that the operational income and cash flow from the business were sufficient to permit the four stockholders to draw money from the corporation on a regular basis. Each of the four original parties initially received $35 a week from the corporation. As time went on the weekly return to each was increased until, in 1955, it totalled $100.

In 1959, after a long illness, Pipkin sold his shares in the corporation to Connor, who was known to Wilkes, Riche and Quinn through past transactions with Springside in his capacity as president of the First Agricultural National Bank of Berkshire County. Connor received a weekly stipend from the corporation equal to that received by Wilkes, Riche and Quinn. He was elected a director of the corporation but never held any other office. He was assigned no specific area of responsibility in the operation of the nursing home but did participate in business discussions and decisions as a director and served additionally as financial adviser to the corporation.

In 1965 the stockholders decided to sell a portion of the corporate property to Quinn who, in addition to being a stockholder in Springside, possessed an interest in another corporation which desired to operate a rest home on the property. Wilkes was successful in prevailing on the other stockholders of Springside to procure a higher sale price for the property than Quinn apparently anticipated paying or desired to pay. After the sale was consummated, the relationship between Quinn and Wilkes began to deteriorate.

The bad blood between Quinn and Wilkes affected the attitudes of both Riche and Connor. As a consequence of the strained relations among the parties, Wilkes, in January of 1967, gave notice of his intention to sell his shares for an amount based on an appraisal of

---

in the risks involved; that, to this end, they all would be directors; and that "unless you [were] a director and officer you could not participate in the decisions of [the] enterprise."

8. Wilkes took charge of the repair, upkeep and maintenance of the physical plant and grounds; Riche assumed supervision over the kitchen facilities and dietary and food aspects of the home; Pipkin was to make himself available if and when medical problems arose; and Quinn dealt with the personnel and administrative aspects of the nursing

home, serving informally as a managing director. Quinn further coordinated the activities of the other parties and served as a communication link among them when matters had to be discussed and decisions had to be made without a formal meeting.

9. Riche held the office of president from 1951 to 1963; Quinn served as president from 1963 on, as clerk from 1951 to 1967, and as treasurer from 1967 on; Wilkes was treasurer from 1951 to 1967.

their value. In February of 1967 a directors' meeting was held and the board exercised its right to establish the salaries of its officers and employees.[10] A schedule of payments was established whereby Quinn was to receive a substantial weekly increase and Riche and Connor were to continue receiving $100 a week. Wilkes, however, was left off the list of those to whom a salary was to be paid. The directors also set the annual meeting of the stockholders for March, 1967.

At the annual meeting in March,[11] Wilkes was not reelected as a director, nor was he reelected as an officer of the corporation. He was further informed that neither his services nor his presence at the nursing home was wanted by his associates.

The meetings of the directors and stockholders in early 1967, the master found, were used as a vehicle to force Wilkes out of active participation in the management and operation of the corporation and to cut off all corporate payments to him. Though the board of directors had the power to dismiss any officers or employees for misconduct or neglect of duties, there was no indication in the minutes of the board of directors' meeting in February, 1967, that the failure to establish a salary for Wilkes was based on either ground. The severance of Wilkes from the payroll resulted not from misconduct or neglect of duties, but because of the personal desire of Quinn, Riche and Connor to prevent him from continuing to receive money from the corporation. Despite a continuing deterioration in his personal relationship with his associates, Wilkes had consistently endeavored to carry on his responsibilities to the corporation in the same satisfactory manner and with the same degree of competence he had previously shown. Wilkes was at all times willing to carry on his responsibilities and participation if permitted so to do and provided that he receive his weekly stipend.

1. We turn to Wilkes's claim for damages based on a breach of the fiduciary duty owed to him by the other participants in this venture. In light of the theory underlying this claim, we do not consider it vital to our approach to this case whether the claim is governed by partnership law or the law applicable to business corporations. This is so because, as all the parties agree, Springside was at all times relevant to this action, a close corporation as we have recently defined such an entity in Donahue v. Rodd Electrotype Co. of New England, Inc.... [where] we held that "stockholders in the close corporation owe one another substantially the same fiduciary duty in the operation of the enterprise that partners owe to one another."

. . .

10. The by-laws of the corporation provided that the directors, subject to the approval of the stockholders, had the power to fix the salaries of all officers and employees. This power, however, up until February, 1967, had not been exercised formally; all payments made to the four participants in the venture had resulted from the informal but unanimous approval of all the parties concerned.

11. Wilkes was unable to attend the meeting of the board of directors in February or the annual meeting of the stockholders in March, 1967. He was represented, however, at the annual meeting by his attorney, who held his proxy.

In the *Donahue* case we recognized that one peculiar aspect of close corporations was the opportunity afforded to majority stockholders to oppress, disadvantage or "freeze out" minority stockholders....

... One ... device which has proved to be particularly effective in accomplishing the purpose of the majority is to deprive minority stockholders of corporate offices and of employment with the corporation ... This "freeze-out" technique has been successful because courts fairly consistently have been disinclined to interfere in those facets of internal corporate operations, such as the selection and retention or dismissal of officers, directors and employees, which essentially involve management decisions subject to the principle of majority control....

The denial of employment to the minority at the hands of the majority is especially pernicious in some instances. A guaranty of employment with the corporation may have been one of the "basic reason[s] why a minority owner has invested capital in the firm." ... The minority stockholder typically depends on his salary as the principal return on his investment, since the "earnings of a close corporation ... are distributed in major part in salaries, bonuses, and retirement benefits." 1 F.H. O'Neal, Close Corporations § 1.07 (1971).[13] Other noneconomic interests of the minority stockholder are likewise injuriously affected by barring him from corporate office. See F.H. O'Neal, "Squeeze–Outs" of Minority Shareholders 79 (1975). Such action severely restricts his participation in the management of the enterprise, and he is relegated to enjoying those benefits incident to his status as a stockholder. See Symposium—The Close Corporation, 52 Nw.U.L.Rev. 345, 386 (1957). In sum, by terminating a minority stockholder's employment or by severing him from a position as an officer or director, the majority effectively frustrate the minority stockholder's purposes in entering on the corporate venture and also deny him an equal return on his investment.

The *Donahue* decision acknowledged, as a "natural outgrowth" of the case law of this Commonwealth, a strict obligation on the part of majority stockholders in a close corporation to deal with the minority with the utmost good faith and loyalty. On its face, this strict standard is applicable in the instant case. The distinction between the majority action in *Donahue* and the majority action in this case is more one of form than of substance. Nevertheless, we are concerned that untempered application of the strict good faith standard enunciated in *Donahue* to cases such as the one before us will result in the imposition of limitations on legitimate action by the controlling group in a close corporation which will unduly hamper its effectiveness in managing the corporation in the best interests of all concerned. The majority, concededly, have certain rights to what has been termed "selfish ownership" in the corporation which should be balanced

---

13. We note here that the master found that Springside never declared or paid a dividend to its stockholders.

against the concept of their fiduciary obligation to the minority. See Hill, The Sale of Controlling Shares, 70 Harv.L.Rev. 986, 1013–1015 (1957); Note, 44 Iowa L.Rev. 734, 740–741 (1959); Symposium—The Close Corporation, 52 Nw.U.L.Rev. 345, 395–396 (1957).

Therefore, when minority stockholders in a close corporation bring suit against the majority alleging a breach of the strict good faith duty owed to them by the majority, we must carefully analyze the action taken by the controlling stockholders in the individual case. It must be asked whether the controlling group can demonstrate a legitimate business purpose for its action. See Bryan v. Brock & Blevins Co., 343 F.Supp. 1062, 1068 (N.D.Ga.1972), aff'd, 490 F.2d 563, 570–571 (5th Cir.1974); Schwartz v. Marien, 37 N.Y.2d 487, 492, 373 N.Y.S.2d 122, 335 N.E.2d 334 (1975).... In asking this question, we acknowledge the fact that the controlling group in a close corporation must have some room to maneuver in establishing the business policy of the corporation. It must have a large measure of discretion, for example, in declaring or withholding dividends, deciding whether to merge or consolidate, establishing the salaries of corporate officers, dismissing directors with or without cause, and hiring and firing corporate employees.

When an asserted business purpose for their action is advanced by the majority, however, we think it is open to minority stockholders to demonstrate that the same legitimate objective could have been achieved through an alternative course of action less harmful to the minority's interest. See Schwartz v. Marien, supra.... If called on to settle a dispute, our courts must weigh the legitimate business purpose, if any, against the practicability of a less harmful alternative.

Applying this approach to the instant case it is apparent that the majority stockholders in Springside have not shown a legitimate business purpose for severing Wilkes from the payroll of the corporation or for refusing to reelect him as a salaried officer and director....

It is an inescapable conclusion from all the evidence that the action of the majority stockholders here was a designed "freeze out" for which no legitimate business purpose has been suggested. Furthermore, we may infer that a design to pressure Wilkes into selling his shares to the corporation at a price below their value well may have been at the heart of the majority's plan.[14]

In the context of this case, several factors bear directly on the duty owed to Wilkes by his associates. At a minimum, the duty of utmost good faith and loyalty would demand that the majority consider that their action was in disregard of a long-standing policy of the stockholders that each would be a director of the corporation and that employment with the corporation would go hand in hand with stock ownership; that Wilkes was one of the four originators of the nursing

14. This inference arises from the fact that Connor, acting on behalf of the three controlling stockholders, offered to purchase Wilkes's shares for a price Connor admittedly would not have accepted for his own shares.

home venture; and that Wilkes, like the others, had invested his capital and time for more than fifteen years with the expectation that he would continue to participate in corporate decisions. Most important is the plain fact that the cutting off of Wilkes's salary, together with the fact that the corporation never declared a dividend (see note 13 supra), assured that Wilkes would receive no return at all from the corporation.

2.   The question of Wilkes's damages at the hands of the majority has not been thoroughly explored on the record before us. Wilkes, in his original complaint, sought damages in the amount of the $100 a week he believed he was entitled to from the time his salary was terminated up until the time this action was commenced. However, the record shows that, after Wilkes was severed from the corporate payroll, the schedule of salaries and payments made to the other stockholders varied from time to time. In addition, the duties assumed by the other stockholders after Wilkes was deprived of his share of the corporate earnings appear to have changed in significant respects.[15] Any resolution of this question must take into account whether the corporation was dissolved during the pendency of this litigation.

Therefore our order is as follows: So much of the judgment as dismisses Wilkes's complaint and awards costs to the defendants is reversed.[16] The case is remanded . . . for further proceedings concerning the issue of damages. Thereafter a judgment shall be entered declaring that Quinn, Riche and Connor breached their fiduciary duty to Wilkes as a minority stockholder in Springside, and awarding money damages therefor. Wilkes shall be allowed to recover from Riche, the estate of T. Edward Quinn and the estate of Lawrence R. Connor, ratably, according to the inequitable enrichment of each, the salary he would have received had he remained an officer and director of Springside. In considering the issue of damages the judge on remand shall take into account the extent to which any remaining corporate funds of Springside may be diverted to satisfy Wilkes's claim.

ZIMMERMAN v. BOGOFF, 402 Mass. 650, 524 N.E.2d 849 (1988). "[T]he *Donahue* remedy is not intended to place a strait jacket on legitimate corporate activity. Where the alleged wrongdoer can demonstrate a legitimate business purpose for his action, no liability will result unless the wronged shareholder succeeds in showing that the

---

15.   In fairness to Wilkes, who, as the master found, was at all times ready and willing to work for the corporation, it should be noted that neither the other stockholders nor their representatives may be heard to say that Wilkes's duties were performed by them and that Wilkes's damages should, for that reason, be diminished.

16.   We do not disturb the judgment in so far as it dismissed a counterclaim by Springside against Wilkes arising from the payment of money by Quinn to Wilkes after the sale in 1965 of certain property of Springside to a corporation owned at that time by Quinn and his wife. . . .

proffered legitimate objective could have been achieved through a less harmful, reasonably practicable, alternative mode of action. . . ."

———

Smith[1] v. Atlantic Properties, Inc.[2]

Appeals Court of Massachusetts, 1981.
12 Mass.App. 201, 422 N.E.2d 798.

■ CUTTER, JUSTICE. In December, 1951, Dr. Louis E. Wolfson agreed to purchase land in Norwood for $350,000, with an initial cash payment of $50,000 and a mortgage note of $300,000 payable in thirty-three months. Dr. Wolfson offered a quarter interest each in the land to Mr. Paul T. Smith, Mr. Abraham Zimble, and William H. Burke. Each paid to Dr. Wolfson $12,500, one quarter of the initial payment. Mr. Smith, an attorney, organized the defendant corporation (Atlantic) in 1951 to operate the real estate. Each of the four subscribers received twenty-five shares of stock. Mr. Smith included, both in the corporation's articles of organization and in its by-laws, a provision reading, "No election, appointment or resolution by the Stockholders and no election, appointment, resolution, purchase, sale, lease, contract, contribution, compensation, proceeding or act by the Board of Directors or by any officer or officers shall be valid or binding upon the corporation until effected, passed, approved or ratified by an affirmative vote of eighty (80%) per cent of the capital stock issued outstanding and entitled to vote." This provision (hereafter referred to as the 80% provision) was included at Dr. Wolfson's request and had the effect of giving to any one of the four original shareholders a veto in corporate decisions.

Atlantic purchased the Norwood land. Some of the land and other assets were sold for about $220,000. Atlantic retained twenty-eight acres on which stood about twenty old brick or wood mill-type structures, which required expensive and constant repairs. After the first year, Atlantic became profitable and showed a profit every year prior to 1969, ranging from a low of $7,683 in 1953 to a high of $44,358 in 1954. The mortgage was paid by 1958 and Atlantic has incurred no long-term debt thereafter. Salaries of about $25,000 were paid only in 1959 and 1960. Dividends in the total amount of $10,000 each were paid in 1964 and 1970. By 1961, Atlantic had about $172,000 in retained earnings, more than half in cash.

For various reasons, which need not be stated in detail, disagreements and ill will soon arose between Dr. Wolfson, on the one hand, and the other stockholders as a group.[3] Dr. Wolfson wished to see

1. Lillian Zimble, executrix of the will of Abraham Zimble, and Louis Zimble [are also plaintiffs]. William H. Burke was originally a plaintiff. Prior to his death, Atlantic Properties, Inc. purchased Burke's stock in the corporation and it is now held as treasury stock. Mr. Abraham Zimble, while living, sold twelve shares to Louis Zimble.

2. Dr. Louis E. Wolfson [is also a defendant].

3. At least one cause of ill will on Dr. Wolfson's part may have been the refusal of the other shareholders to consent to his transferring his shares in Atlantic to the Louis E. Wolfson Foundation, a charitable foundation created by Dr. Wolfson.

Atlantic's earnings devoted to repairs and possibly some improvements in its existing buildings and adjacent facilities. The other stockholders desired the declaration of dividends. Dr. Wolfson fairly steadily refused to vote for any dividends. Although it was pointed out to him that failure to declare dividends might result in the imposition by the Internal Revenue Service of a penalty under the Internal Revenue Code, I.R.C. § 531 et seq. (relating to unreasonable accumulation of corporate earnings and profits), Dr. Wolfson persisted in his refusal to declare dividends. The other shareholders did agree over the years to making at least the most urgent repairs to Atlantic's buildings, but did not agree to make all repairs and improvements which were recommended in a 1962 report by an engineering firm retained by Atlantic to make a complete estimate of all repairs and improvements which might be beneficial.

The fears of an Internal Revenue Service assessment of a penalty tax were soon realized. Penalty assessments were made in 1962, 1963, and 1964. These were settled by Dr. Wolfson for $11,767.71 in taxes and interest. Despite this settlement, Dr. Wolfson continued his opposition to declaring dividends. The record does not indicate that he developed any specific and definitive schedule or plan for a series of necessary or desirable repairs and improvements to Atlantic's properties. At least none was proposed which would have had a reasonable chance of satisfying the Internal Revenue Service that expenditures for such repairs and improvements constituted "reasonable needs of the business," I.R.C. § 534(c), a term which includes (see I.R.C. § 537) "the reasonably anticipated needs of the business." Predictably, despite further warnings by Dr. Wolfson's shareholder colleagues, the Internal Revenue Service assessed further penalty taxes for the years 1965, 1966, 1967, and 1968. These taxes were upheld by the United States Tax Court in Atlantic Properties, Inc. v. Commissioner of Int. Rev., 62 T.C. 644 (1974), and on appeal in 519 F.2d 1233 (1st Cir.1975). See the discussion of these opinions in Cathcart, Accumulated Earnings Tax: A Trap for the Wary, 62 A.B.A.J. 1197–1199 (1976). An examination of these decisions makes it apparent that Atlantic has incurred substantial penalty taxes and legal expense largely because of Dr. Wolfson's refusal to vote for the declaration of sufficient dividends to avoid the penalty, a refusal which was (in the Tax Court and upon appeal) attributed in some measure to a tax avoidance purpose on Dr. Wolfson's part.

On January 30, 1967, the shareholders, other than Dr. Wolfson, initiated this proceeding in the Superior Court, later supplemented to reflect developments after the original complaint. The plaintiffs sought a court determination of the dividends to be paid by Atlantic, the removal of Dr. Wolfson as a director, and an order that Atlantic be reimbursed by him for the penalty taxes assessed against it and related expenses. The case was tried before a justice of the Superior Court (jury waived) in September and October, 1979.

The trial judge made findings (but in more detail) of essentially the facts outlined above and concluded that Dr. "Wolfson's obstinate refusal to vote in favor of ... dividends was ... caused more by his dislike for other stockholders and his desire to avoid additional tax payments than ... by any genuine desire to undertake a program for improving ... [Atlantic] property." She also determined that Dr. Wolfson was liable to Atlantic for taxes and interest amounting to "$11,767.11 plus interest from the commencement of this action, plus $35,646.14 plus interest from August 11, 1975," the date of the First Circuit decision affirming the second penalty tax assessment. The latter amount includes an attorney's fee of $7,500 in the Federal tax cases. She also ordered the directors of Atlantic to declare "a reasonable dividend at the earliest practical date and reasonable dividends annually thereafter consistent with good business practice." In addition, the trial judge directed that jurisdiction of the case be retained in the Superior Court "for a period of five years to [e]nsure compliance." Judgment was entered pursuant to the trial judge's order. After the entry of judgment, Dr. Wolfson and Atlantic filed a motion for a new trial and to amend the judge's findings. This motion, after hearing, was denied, and Dr. Wolfson and Atlantic claimed an appeal from the judgment and the former from the denial of the motion. The plaintiffs (see note 1, supra) requested payment of their attorneys' fees in this proceeding and filed supporting affidavits. The motion was denied, and the plaintiffs appealed.

1.   The trial judge, in deciding that Dr. Wolfson had committed a breach of his fiduciary duty to other stockholders, relied greatly on broad language in Donahue v. Rodd Electrotype Co., 367 Mass. 578, 586–597, 328 N.E.2d 505 (1975).... Similar principles were stated in Wilkes v. Springside Nursing Home, Inc., 370 Mass. 842, 848–852, 353 N.E.2d 657 (1976), but with some modifications, mentioned in the margin,[5] of the sweeping language of the *Donahue* case. See Jessie v. Boynton, 372 Mass. 293, 304, 361 N.E.2d 1267 (1977); Hallahan v. Haltom Corp., 7 Mass.App. 68, 70–71, 385 N.E.2d 1033 (1979). See also Cain v. Cain, 3 Mass.App. 467, 473–479, 334 N.E.2d 650 (1975).

In the *Donahue* case, 367 Mass. at 593 n. 17, 328 N.E.2d 505, the court recognized that cases may arise in which, in a close corporation, majority stockholders may ask protection from a minority stockholder.

5. The court said (at 850–852, 353 N.E.2d 657) that it was "concerned that [the] untempered application of the strict good faith standard ... will result in the imposition of limitations on legitimate action by the *controlling group* in a close corporation which will unduly hamper its effectiveness.... The majority ... have certain rights to what has been termed 'selfish ownership' in the corporation which should be balanced against the concept of their fiduciary obligation to the minority.... [W]hen minority stockholders ... bring suit ... alleging a breach of the strict good faith duty ... we must carefully analyze the action taken by the *controlling stockholders* in the individual case. It must be asked whether the *controlling group* can demonstrate a legitimate business purpose for its action.... [T]he *controlling group* in a close corporation must have some room to maneuver in establishing the business policy of the corporation. It must have a large measure of discretion, for example, *in declaring or withholding dividends*" (emphasis supplied) and in certain other matters. "When an asserted business purpose ... is advanced by the majority, however, ... it is open to minority stockholders to demonstrate that the ... objective could have been achieved through an alternative course ... less harmful to the minority's interest."

Such an instance arises in the present case because Dr. Wolfson has been able to exercise a veto concerning corporate action on dividends by the 80% provision (in Atlantic's articles [of] organization and by-laws) already quoted. The 80% provision may have substantially the effect of reversing the usual roles of the majority and the minority shareholders. The minority, under that provision, becomes an ad hoc controlling interest.[6]

It does not appear to be argued that this 80% provision is not authorized by G.L. c. 156B (inserted by St.1964, c. 723, § 1). See especially § 8(a).* See also Seibert v. Milton Bradley Co., 380 Mass. 656, 405 N.E.2d 131 (1980). Chapter 156B was intended to provide desirable flexibility in corporate arrangements. The provision is only one of several methods which have been devised to protect minority shareholders in close corporations from being oppressed by their colleagues and, if the device is used reasonably, there may be no strong public policy considerations against its use. See 1 O'Neal, Close Corporations § 4.21 (2d ed. 1971 & Supp.1980). The textbook just cited contains in §§ 4.01–4.30 a comprehensive discussion of the business considerations (see especially §§ 4.02, 4.03, 4.06, & 4.24) which may recommend use of such a device. See also 2 O'Neal § 8.07 (& Supp.1980 which, at 84–90, discusses the Massachusetts decisions). In the present case, Dr. Wolfson testified that he requested the inclusion of the 80% provision "in case the people [the other share-holders] whom I knew, but not very well, ganged up on me." The possibilities of shareholder disagreement on policy made the provision seem a sensible precaution.[8] A question is presented, however, concerning the extent to which such a veto power possessed by a minority stockholder may be exercised as its holder may wish, without a violation of the "fiduciary duty" referred to in the *Donahue* case, 367 Mass. at 593, 328 N.E.2d 505, as modified in the *Wilkes* case. See note 5, supra.

---

6. The majority shareholders, in the event of a deadlock, at least may seek dissolution of the corporation if forty percent of the voting power can be mustered, whereas a single stockholder with only twenty-five percent of the stock may not do so. See G.L. c. 156B, § 99(b), as amended by St.1969, c. 392, § 23.

* M.G.L.A. c. 156B, § 8(a) provides that "Whenever, with respect to any action to be taken by the stockholders of a corporation, the articles of organization or by-laws require the vote or concurrence of the holders of all of the shares, or of any class or series thereof, or a greater proportion thereof than required by this chapter with respect to such action, the provisions of the articles of organization or by-laws shall control." (Footnote by ed.)

8. Dr. Wolfson himself had discovered the business opportunity which led to the formation of Atlantic, had made the initial $50,000 payment which made possible the Norwood land purchase, and had given the other shareholders an opportunity to share with him in what looked like a probably profitable enterprise. It was reasonably foreseeable that there might be differences of opinion between Dr. Wolfson, a man with substantial income likely to be in a high income tax bracket, and less affluent share-holders on such matters of policy as dividend declarations, salaries, and investment in improvements in the property. The other share-holders, two of whom were attorneys should have known that it was as open to Dr. Wolfson reasonably to exercise the veto provided to him by the 80% provision in favor of a policy of reinvestment of earnings in Atlantic's properties, which would probably avoid taxes and increase the value of the corporate assets, as it was for them (possessed of the same veto) to use reasonably their voting power in favor of a more generous dividend and salary policy.

The decided cases in Massachusetts do little to answer this question. The most pertinent guidance is probably found in the *Wilkes* case, 370 Mass. at 849–852, 353 N.E.2d 657, ... essentially to the effect that in any judicial intervention in such a situation there must be a weighing of the business interests advanced as reasons for their action (a) by the majority or controlling group and (b) by the rival persons or group.[9] It would obviously be appropriate, before a court-ordered solution is sought or imposed, for both sides to attempt to reach a sensible solution of any incipient impasse in the interest of all concerned after consideration of all relevant circumstances. See Helms v. Duckworth, 249 F.2d 482, 485–488 (D.C.Cir.1957).

2. With respect to the past damage to Atlantic caused by Dr. Wolfson's refusal to vote in favor of any dividends, the trial judge was justified in finding that his conduct went beyond what was reasonable. The other stockholders shared to some extent responsibility for what occurred by failing to accept Dr. Wolfson's proposals with much sympathy, but the inaction on dividends seems the principal cause of the tax penalties. Dr. Wolfson had been warned of the dangers of an assessment under the Internal Revenue Code, I.R.C. § 531 et seq. He had refused to vote dividends in any amount adequate to minimize that danger and had failed to bring forward, within the relevant taxable years, a convincing, definitive program of appropriate improvements which could withstand scrutiny by the Internal Revenue Service. Whatever may have been the reason for Dr. Wolfson's refusal to declare dividends (and even if in any particular year he may have gained slight, if any, tax advantage from withholding dividends) we think that he recklessly ran serious and unjustified risks of precisely the penalty taxes eventually assessed, risks which were inconsistent with any reasonable interpretation of a duty of "utmost good faith and loyalty." The trial judge (despite the fact that the other shareholders helped to create the voting deadlock and despite the novelty of the situation) was justified in charging Dr. Wolfson with the out-of-pocket expenditure incurred by Atlantic for the penalty taxes and related counsel fees of the tax cases.[10]

3. The trial judge's order to the directors of Atlantic, "to declare a reasonable dividend at the earliest practical date and reasonable dividends annually thereafter," presents difficulties. It may well not be a precise, clear, and unequivocal command which (without further explanation) would justify enforcement by civil contempt proceedings.... It also fails to order the directors to exercise similar business

---

9. The duties and quasi-fiduciary responsibilities of minority shareholders who find themselves in a position to control corporate action are discussed helpfully in Hetherington, The Minority's Duty of Loyalty in Close Corporations, 1972 Duke L.J. 921. The author recognizes (at 944) that, in disputes concerning the wisdom of a particular course of corporate action, the majority (or the ad hoc controlling minority) shareholder may be entitled to follow the course he or it thinks best.

10. We do not now suggest that the standard of "utmost good faith and loyalty" may require some relaxation when applied to a minority ad hoc controlling interest, created by some device, similar to the 80% provision, designed in part to protect the selfish interests of a minority shareholder. This seems to us a difficult area of the law best developed on a case by case basis. See note 4, supra.

judgment with respect to Dr. Wolfson's desire to make all appropriate repairs and improvements to Atlantic's factory properties. See the language of the Supreme Judicial Court in the *Wilkes* case, 370 Mass. at 850–852, 353 N.E.2d 657, see note 5, supra.

The somewhat ambiguous injunctive relief is made less significant by the trial judge's reservation of jurisdiction in the Superior Court, a provision which contemplates later judicial supervision. . . .

Although the reservation of jurisdiction is appropriate in this case . . . its purpose should be stated more affirmatively. Paragraph 2 of the judgment should be revised to provide: (a) a direction that Atlantic's directors prepare promptly financial statements and copies of State and Federal income and excise tax returns for the five most recent calendar or fiscal years, and a balance sheet as of as current a date as is possible; (b) an instruction that they confer with one another with a view to stipulating a general dividend and capital improvements policy for the next ensuing three fiscal years; (c) an order that, if such a stipulation is not filed with the clerk of the Superior Court within sixty days after the receipt of the rescript in the Superior Court, a further hearing shall be held promptly (either before the court or before a special master with substantial experience in business affairs), at which there shall be received in evidence at least the financial statements and tax returns above mentioned, as well as other relevant evidence. Thereafter, the court, after due consideration of the circumstances then existing, may direct the adoption (and carrying out), if it be then deemed appropriate, of a specific dividend and capital improvements policy adequate to minimize the risk of further penalty tax assessments for the then current fiscal year of Atlantic. The court also may reserve jurisdiction to take essentially the same action for each subsequent fiscal year until the parties are able to reach for themselves an agreed program. . . .

4.   The judgment is affirmed so far as it (par. 1) orders payments into Atlantic's treasury by Dr. Wolfson. Paragraph 2 of the judgment is to be modified in a manner consistent with part 3 of this opinion. . . .

So ordered.

———

SLETTELAND v. ROBERTS, 304 Mont. 21, 16 P.3d 1062 (2000). Sletteland was a shareholder in Billings Generation, Inc. (BGI), a closely held Montana corporation. The four other shareholders in BGI were Smith, Blendu, Orndorff and Roberts. BGI and Exxon Billings Cogeneration, Inc. were partners in Yellowstone Energy Limited Partnership (YELP). YELP owned and operated a cogeneration plant in Billings, Montana which generated steam and electric power. Sletteland had been removed as an officer of BGI by a vote of 60 percent of the shareholders, comprised of Orndorff, Roberts, and Smith. Thereafter, Sletteland brought a derivative action against Orndorff and Roberts, requesting a return of excessive legal fees that they had charged BGI, and removal of Orndorff and Roberts as directors. Orndorff and

Roberts counterclaimed, alleging that Sletteland brought the suit in bad faith, causing damage to the company and to the other shareholders.

At the time Sletteland's lawsuit was filed, YELP's project was in financial trouble due to high-interest debts and technical problems with the plant. YELP was attempting to refinance the high-interest debt with lower-interest financing. The window of opportunity for the financing was short, and the lawsuit became an issue hampering the refinancing. Ultimately, the refinancing fell through, and Sletteland's suit was a substantial factor in causing this result. Orndorff and Roberts claimed that the timing of the lawsuit by Sletteland was specifically intended to derail the financing. The District Court found that Sletteland was negligent and breached his fiduciary duties to BGI and his fellow shareholders by the timing of his filing of his action, and found Sletteland liable to Orndorff, Roberts, and Smith for $3,027,939. Affirmed:

> There was clearly animosity in the relationship between the business partners.... Ultimately, in June of 1996, Sletteland was removed as an officer of BGI. According to Roberts and Orndorff, Sletteland and Blendu wanted the other three shareholders to purchase their interests, and warned that "unpleasant things would happen" if their demands were not met.

> It appears that the suit was brought specifically to derail refinancing of the project. Sletteland admitted at trial that the timing of the suit was up to him and that he was not faced with any statute of limitations problem. The initial law suit was filed by Sletteland on October 2, 1996. This was immediately before the individuals involved in the refinancing were to meet to discuss the refinancing. He did no investigation to see what the effect of the lawsuit would be on the refinancing. The court concluded that "it only makes sense that he would be expected to know that the filing of his suit alleging director fraud would delay or derail the refinancing ... there was no particular reason to file this suit when he did." He was asked to withdraw the suit so that the refinancing could conclude, but he refused to do so.

Merola v. Exergen Corp.

Supreme Judicial Court of Massachusetts, 1996.
423 Mass. 461, 668 N.E.2d 351.

■ Before LIACOS, C.J., and WILKINS, LYNCH, O'CONNOR and GREANEY, JJ.

■ LYNCH, JUSTICE.

The plaintiff, a former vice president of Exergen Corporation (Exergen) and a former minority stockholder of that corporation, brought suit in the Superior Court against Exergen and the president and majority stockholder, Francesco Pompei, because of his termination as an officer and employee of Exergen.... [The complaint] alleged that the corporation was a "close corporation," and that Pompei, as the majority stockholder, violated his fiduciary obligations to the plaintiff as a minority stockholder by terminating his employment without cause.

The trial judge ruled that . . . she would make findings of fact and conclusions of law . . . following the verdict of the jury. The jury rendered a verdict . . . providing advisory answers. . . .

. . . [T]he judge found that the corporation was a "close corporation" and that Pompei had breached his fiduciary obligations to the plaintiff by failing to give him an opportunity to become a major stockholder and by terminating his employment. She adopted the jury's advisory conclusion that he had been damaged only by the termination of employment to the extent of $50,000.

The Appeals Court affirmed the judgment as to Pompei, but modified it as to the corporation, holding that there was no basis for liability by Exergen to the plaintiff. 38 Mass.App.Ct. 462, 471–472 (1995). We granted the defendants' application for further appellate review and now reverse the judgment of the Superior Court.

We summarize the facts found by the judge. Exergen was formed in May, 1980, as a corporation in the business of developing and selling infrared heat detection devices. From Exergen's inception to the date of trial, Pompei, the founder, was the majority shareholder in the corporation, as well as its president, owning over sixty per cent of the shares issued. At all relevant times, Pompei actively participated in and controlled the management of Exergen and, as the majority shareholder, had power to elect and change Exergen's board of directors.

The plaintiff began working for Exergen on a part-time basis in late 1980 while he was also employed full-time by Analogic Corporation. In the course of conversations with Pompei in late 1981, and early 1982, the plaintiff was offered full-time employment with Exergen, and he understood that, if he came to work there and invested in Exergen stock, he would have the opportunity to become a major shareholder of Exergen and for continuing employment with Exergen.

As of March 1, 1982, the plaintiff resigned from Analogic and began working full time for Exergen. He also then began purchasing shares in Exergen when the company made periodic offerings to its employees. From March, 1982, through June, 1982, the plaintiff purchased 4,100 shares at $2.25 per share, for a total of $9,225. Exergen announced at the Exergen shareholders meeting in September, 1982, another option program to purchase shares at $5 per share within one year. By late 1983, the plaintiff had exercised his option to purchase an additional 1,200 shares. The plaintiff was not offered additional stock options after late 1983. . . .

Principles of employment law permit the termination of employees at will, with or without cause excepting situations within a narrow public policy exception. *King v. Driscoll*, 418 Mass. 576, 581–582, 638 N.E.2d 488 (1994), and cases cited. However, the termination of a minority shareholder's employment may present a situation where the majority interest has breached its fiduciary duty to the minority interest. *Id.* at 586, 638 N.E.2d 488. *Wilkes v. Springside Nursing Home, Inc., supra* at 852–853, 353 N.E.2d 657. There the court concluded that the majority stockholders had attempted unfairly to "freeze out" a minority stockholder by terminating his employment, in part because their policy and practice was to divide the available resources of the corporation equally by way of salaries to the shareholders who all participated in the operation of the enterprise. *Id.* at 846, 353 N.E.2d 657. As the investment became more profitable, the salaries were increased. *Id.* The court recognized that "[t]he minority stockholder typically depends on his salary as the principal return on his investment, since the 'earnings of a close corporation . . . are distributed in major part in salaries, bonuses and retirement benefits.'" *Id.* at 850, 353 N.E.2d 657, quoting 1 F.H. O'Neal, Close Corporations § 1.07 (1971). Given those facts, this court concluded that the other shareholders did not show a legitimate business purpose for terminating the minority stockholder and that the other parties acted "in disregard of a longstanding policy of the stockholders that each would be a director of the corporation and that employment with the corporation would go hand in hand with stock ownership." *Id.* at 853, 353 N.E.2d 657.

Here, although the plaintiff invested in the stock of Exergen with the reasonable expectation of continued employment, there was no general policy regarding stock ownership and employment, and there was no evidence that any other stockholders had expectations of continuing employment because they purchased stock. The investment in the stock was an investment in the equity of the corporation which was not tied to employment in any formal way. The plaintiff acknowledged that he could have purchased 5,000 shares of stock while he was working part time before resigning from his position at Analogic Corporation and accepting full-time employment at Exergen. He testified that he was induced to work for Exergen with the promise that he could become a major stockholder. There was no testimony that he was ever required to buy stock as a condition of employment.

Unlike the *Wilkes* case, there was no evidence that the corporation distributed all profits to shareholders in the form of salaries. On the contrary, the perceived value of the stock increased during the time that the plaintiff was employed. The plaintiff first purchased his stock at $2.25 per share and, one year later, he purchased more for $5 per share. This indicated that there was some increase in value to the investment independent of the employment expectation. Neither was the plaintiff a founder of the business, his stock purchases were made after the business was established, and there was no suggestion that he had to purchase stock to keep his job.

The plaintiff testified that, when he sold his stock back to the corporation in 1991, he was paid $17 per share. This was a price that had been paid to other shareholders who sold their shares to the corporation at a previous date, and it is a price which, after consulting with his attorney, he concluded was a fair price. With this payment, the plaintiff realized a significant return on his capital investment independent of the salary he received as an employee.

We conclude that this is not a situation where the majority shareholder breached his fiduciary duty to a minority shareholder. "[T]he controlling group in a close corporation must have some room to maneuver in establishing the business policy of the corporation." *Wilkes v. Springside Nursing Home, Inc., supra* at 851, 353 N.E.2d 657. Although there was no legitimate business purpose for the termination of the plaintiff, neither was the termination for the financial gain of Pompei or contrary to established public policy. Not every discharge of an at-will employee of a close corporation who happens to own stock in the corporation gives rise to a successful breach of fiduciary duty claim. The plaintiff was terminated in accordance with his employment contract and fairly compensated for his stock. He failed to establish a sufficient basis for a breach of fiduciary duty claim under the principles of *Donahue v. Rodd Electrotype Co., supra....*

Judgment reversed.

SECTION 6. VALUATION

Many issues of corporate law are intimately related to problems of valuation. That is particularly true of the issues raised in sections 7, 8, and 10, infra, concerning restrictions on the transferability of shares, mandatory sales of shares, and dissolution. Now is therefore an appropriate time to provide an introduction to the general problem of valuing a business, and the special problem of valuing a business in corporate form.

This Section contains four selections. The first selection, Piemonte v. New Boston Garden, illustrates the Delaware Block Method of valuation. Under that method, the court normally values a corporation by first determining the market value of the corporation's stock, the value of the corporation's net assets, and the corporation's "earnings value." Next, the court assigns weights to each of the three values, depending on such factors as the comparative reliability of each factor in a particular case. Finally, the court sums the three elements of value, as adjusted by their relative weights. The Delaware Block Method is falling out of favor, but it is still used in some cases. More important for present purposes, even contemporary methods of valuation may involve individual elements of the Block Method.

The remaining three selections in this Section provide contemporary views on the valuation of business enterprises.

It may be useful, before studying the materials in this Section, to review the materials on the present-value rule in Chapter 3, Section 7.

Piemonte v. New Boston Garden Corp.[1]

Supreme Judicial Court of Massachusetts, 1979.
377 Mass. 719, 387 N.E.2d 1145.

■ WILKINS, JUSTICE.

The plaintiffs were stockholders in Boston Garden Arena Corporation (Garden Arena), a Massachusetts corporation whose stockholders voted on July 19, 1973, to merge with the defendant corporation in circumstances which entitled each plaintiff to "demand payment for his stock from the resulting or surviving corporation and an appraisal in accordance with the provisions of [G.L. c. 156B, §§ 86–98]." G.L. c. 156B, § 85, as amended by St.1969, c. 392, § 22. The plaintiffs commenced this action under G.L. c. 156B, § 90, seeking a judicial determination of the "fair value" of their shares "as of the day preceding the date of the vote approving the proposed corporate action."[2] G.L. c. 156B, § 92, inserted by St.1964, c. 723, § 1. Each party has appealed from a judgment determining the fair value of the plaintiffs' stock. We granted the defendant's application for direct appellate review.

On July 18, 1973, Garden Arena owned all the stock in a subsidiary corporation that owned both a franchise in the National Hockey League (NHL), known as the Boston Bruins, and a corporation that held a franchise in the American Hockey League (AHL), known as the Boston Braves. Garden Arena also owned and operated Boston Garden Sports Arena (Boston Garden), an indoor auditorium with facilities for the exhibition of sporting and other entertainment events, and a corporation that operated the food and beverage concession at the Boston Garden. A considerable volume of documentary material was introduced in evidence concerning the value of the stock of Garden Arena on July 18, 1973, the day before Garden Arena's stockholders approved the merger. Each side presented expert testimony. The judge gave consideration to the market value of the Garden Arena stock, to the value of its stock based on its earnings, and to the net asset value of Garden Arena's assets. Weighting these factors, the judge arrived at a total, per share value of $75.27.[3]

In this appeal, the parties raise objections to certain of the judge's conclusions. We will expand on the facts as necessary when we

---

1. The fifteen plaintiffs collectively owned 6,289 shares in Garden Arena Corporation, representing approximately 2.8% of its 224,892 shares of outstanding stock.

2. The plaintiffs took all the necessary, preliminary steps to preserve their rights. Each plaintiff objected in writing to the proposed merger; none of their shares was voted in favor of the proposed corporate action (see G.L. c. 156B, § 86); each plaintiff seasonably demanded in writing payment from the defendant for the fair value of his stock (see G.L. c. 156B, § 89); and no agreement as to that fair value was reached within thirty days of the demand (see G.L. c. 156B, § 90).

3. The judge determined the market value, earnings value, and net asset value of the stock and then weighted these values as follows:

	Value	Weight	Result
Market Value:	$ 26.50 ×	10%	= $ 2.65
Earnings Value:	$ 52.60 ×	40%	= $21.04
Net Asset Value:	$103.16 ×	50%	= $51.58
		Total Value Per Share:	$75.27

consider each issue. We conclude that the judge followed acceptable procedures in valuing the Garden Arena stock; that his determinations were generally within the range of discretion accorded a fact finder; but that, in three instances, the judge's treatment of the evidence was or may have been in error and, accordingly, the case should be remanded to him for further consideration of those three points.

General Principles of Law

The statutory provisions applicable to this case were enacted in 1964 as part of the Massachusetts Business Corporation Law. St.1964, c. 723, § 1....

[The judge in this case adopted the methodology known as the "Delaware block approach," which] calls for a determination of the market value, the earnings value, and the net asset value of the stock, followed by the assignment of a percentage weight to each of the elements of value. See generally, Note, Valuation of Dissenters' Stock under Appraisal Statutes, 79 Harv.L.Rev. 1453, 1456–1471 (1966)....

Market Value

The judge was acting within reasonable limits when he determined that the market value of Garden Arena stock on July 18, 1973, was $26.50 a share. Each party challenges this determination. The plaintiffs' contention is that market value should be disregarded because it was not ascertainable due to the limited trading in Garden Arena stock. The defendant argues that the judge was obliged to reconstruct market value based on comparable companies, and, in doing so, should have arrived at a market value of $22 a share.

Market value may be a significant factor, even the dominant factor, in determining the "fair value" of shares of a particular corporation under G.L. c. 156B, § 92. Shares regularly traded on a recognized stock exchange are particularly susceptible to valuation on the basis of their market price, although even in such cases the market value may well not be conclusive. See Martignette v. Sagamore Mfg. Co., 340 Mass. 136, 141–142, 163 N.E.2d 9 (1959). On the other hand, where there is no established market for a particular stock, actual market value cannot be used. In such cases, a judge might undertake to "reconstruct" market value, but he is not obliged to do so. Indeed, the process of the reconstruction of market value may actually be no more than a variation on the valuation of corporate assets and corporate earnings.

In this case, Garden Arena stock was traded on the Boston Stock Exchange, but rarely. Approximately ninety per cent of the company's stock was held by the controlling interests and not traded. Between January 1, 1968, and December 4, 1972, 16,741 shares were traded. During this period, an annual average of approximately 1.5% of the outstanding stock changed hands. In 1972, 4,372 shares were traded at prices ranging from $20.50 a share to $29 a share. The public announcement of the proposed merger was made on December 7, 1972. The last prior sale of 200 shares on December 4, 1972, was made at $26.50 a share. The judge accepted that sale price as the market price to be used in his determination of value.

The judge concluded that the volume of trading was sufficient to permit a determination of market value and expressed a preference for the actual sale price over any reconstruction of a market value, which he concluded would place "undue reliance on corporations, factors, and circumstances not applicable to Garden Arena stock." The decision to consider market value and the market value selected were within the judge's discretion.

Valuation Based on Earnings

The judge determined that the average per share earnings of Garden Arena for the five-fiscal-year period which ended June 30, 1973, was $5.26. To this amount he applied a factor, or multiplier, of 10 to arrive at $52.60 as the per share value based on earnings.

Each party objects to certain aspects of this process. We reject the plaintiffs' argument that the judge could not properly use any value based on earnings, and also reject the parties' various challenges to the judge's method of determining value based on earnings.

Delaware case law, which, as we have said, we regard as instructive but not binding, has established a method of computing value based on corporate earnings. The appraiser generally starts by computing the average earnings of the corporation for the past five years. Universal City Studios, Inc. v. Francis I. duPont & Co., 334 A.2d 216, 218 (Del.1975); Application of Del. Racing Ass'n, 213 A.2d 203, 212 (Del.1965). Extraordinary gains and losses are excluded from the average earnings calculation. Gibbons v. Schenley Indus., Inc., 339 A.2d 460, 468–470 (Del.Ch.1975); Felder v. Anderson, Clayton & Co., 39 Del.Ch. 76, 86–87, 159 A.2d 278 (1960). The appraiser then selects a multiplier (to be applied to the average earnings) which reflects the prospective financial condition of the corporation and the risk factor inherent in the corporation and the industry. Universal City Studios, Inc. v. Francis I. duPont & Co., supra. In selecting a multiplier, the appraiser generally looks to other comparable corporations. Universal City Studios, Inc. v. Francis I. duPont & Co., supra at 219–221 (averaging price-earnings ratios of nine other motion picture companies as of date of merger); Gibbons v. Schenley Indus., Inc., supra at 471 (using Standard & Poor's Distiller's Index as of date of merger); Felder v. Anderson, Clayton & Co., supra, 39 Del.Ch. at 87, 159 A.2d 278 (averaging price-earnings ratios of representative stocks over previous five-year period because of recent boom in industry). The appraiser's choice of a multiplier is largely discretionary and will be upheld if it is "within the range of reason." Universal City Studios, Inc. v. Francis I. duPont & Co., supra at 219 (approving multiplier of 16.1); Application of Del. Racing Ass'n, supra at 213 (approving multiplier of 10); Swanton v. State Guar. Corp., 42 Del.Ch. 477, 483, 215 A.2d 242 (1965) (approving multiplier of 14).[9]

9. Although Delaware courts have relied on, and continue to rely on, Professor Dewing's capitalization chart (see 1 A.S. Dewing, The Financial Policy of Corporations

The judge chose not to place "singular reliance on comparative data preferring to choose a multiplier based on the specific situation and prospects of the Garden Arena." He weighed the favorable financial prospects of the Bruins: the popularity and success of the team, the relatively low average age of its players, the popularity of Bobby Orr and Phil Esposito, the high attendance record at home games (each home team retained all gate receipts), and the advantageous radio and television contracts. On the other hand, he recognized certain risks, the negative prospects: the existence of the World Hockey Association with its potential, favorable impact on players' bargaining positions, and legal threats to the players' reserve clause. He concluded that a multiplier of 10 was appropriate. There was ample evidentiary support for his conclusion. He might have looked to and relied on price-earnings ratios of other corporations, but he was not obliged to.

The judge did not have to consider the dividend record of Garden Arena, as the defendant urges. Dividends tend to reflect the same factors as earnings and, therefore, need not be valued separately. See Felder v. Anderson, Clayton & Co., 39 Del.Ch. 76, 88–89, 159 A.2d 278 (1960). And since dividend policy is usually reflected in market value, the use of market value as a factor in the valuation process permitted the low and sporadic dividend rate to be given some weight in the process. Beyond that, the value of the plaintiffs' stock should not be depreciated because the controlling interests often chose to declare low dividends or none at all.

The judge did not abuse his discretion in including expansion income (payments from teams newly admitted to the NHL) received during two of the five recent fiscal years. His conclusion was well within the guidelines of decided cases. See Gibbons v. Schenley Indus., Inc., 339 A.2d 460, 470 (Del.Ch.1975) (gain from sale of real estate not extraordinary where corporation often sold such assets); Felder v. Anderson, Clayton & Co., 39 Del.Ch. 76, 86–87, 159 A.2d 278 (1960) (loss attributable to a drought not extraordinary). The Bruins first received expansion income ($2,000,000) during the fiscal year which ended on June 30, 1967, a year not included in the five-year average. The franchise received almost $1,000,000 more in 1970 and approximately $860,000 in 1972. This 1970 and 1972 income was reflected in the computation of earnings. Expansion income did not have to be treated as extraordinary income. The judge concluded that it did not distort "an accurate projection of the earnings value of Garden Arena" and noted, as of July 18, 1973, an NHL expansion plan for the admission of two more teams in 1974–1975 and for expansion thereafter.

390–391 [5th ed. 1953]), they have recognized that it is somewhat outdated and no longer the "be-all and end-all" on the subject of earnings value. See Universal City Studios, Inc. v. Francis I. duPont & Co., supra at 219; Swanton v. State Guar. Corp., 42 Del.Ch. 477, 483–484, 215 A.2d 242 (1965).

Valuation Based on Net Asset Value

The judge determined total net asset value by first valuing the net assets of Garden Arena apart from the Bruins franchise and the concession operations at Boston Garden. He selected $9,400,000 (the June 30, 1973, book value of Garden Arena) as representing that net asset value. Then, he added his valuations of the Bruins franchise ($9,600,000) and the concession operation ($4,200,000) to arrive at a total asset value of $23,200,000, or $103.16 a share.[10]

The parties raise various objections to these determinations. The defendant argues that the judge included certain items twice in his valuation of the net assets of Garden Arena and that he should have given no separate value to the concession operation. The plaintiff argues that the judge undervalued both the Boston Garden and the value of the Bruins franchise.

The defendant objects to the judge's refusal to deduct $1,116,000 from the $9,400,000 that represented the net asset value of Garden Arena (exclusive of the net asset value of the Bruins franchise and the concession operation). The defendant's expert testified that the $9,400,000 figure included $1,116,000 attributable to the goodwill of the Bruins, net player investment, and the value of the AHL franchise. The judge recognized that the items included in the $1,116,000 should not be valued twice and seemingly agreed that they would be more appropriately included in the value of the Bruins franchise than in the $9,400,000. He was not plainly wrong, however, in declining to deduct them from the $9,400,000, because, as is fully warranted from the testimony of the defendant's expert, the judge concluded that the defendant's expert did not include these items in his determination of the value of the Bruins franchise. The defendant's expert, whose determination the judge accepted, arrived at his value of the Bruins franchise by adding certain items to the cost of a new NHL franchise, but none of those items included goodwill, net player investment, or the value of an AHL franchise. Acceptance of the defendant's argument would have resulted in these items being entirely omitted from the net asset valuation of Garden Arena.

The plaintiffs object that the judge did not explicitly determine the value of the Boston Garden and implicitly undervalued it. Garden Arena had purchased the Boston Garden on May 25, 1973, for $4,000,000, and accounted for it on the June 30, 1973, balance sheet as a $4,000,000 asset with a corresponding mortgage liability of $3,437,065. Prior to the purchase, Garden Arena had held a long-term lease which was unfavorable to the owner of the Boston Garden.[13] The existence of the lease would tend to depress the purchase price.

The judge stated that the $9,400,000 book value *"includes* a reasonable value for Boston Garden" (emphasis supplied). He did not

---

10. $23,200,000 § 224,892 (the number of outstanding shares).

13. The lease, which ran until June 1, 1986, contained a fixed maximum rent and an obligation on the lessee to pay only two-thirds of any increase in local real estate taxes. In a period of inflation and rising local real estate taxes, the value of the lease to the lessor was decreasing annually.

indicate whether, if he had meant to value the Boston Garden at its purchase price (with an adjustment for the mortgage liabilities), he had considered the effect the lease would have had on that price. While we recognize that the fact-finding role of the judge permits him to reject the opinions of the various experts,[14] we conclude, in the absence of an explanation of his reasons, that it is possible that the judge did not give adequate consideration to the value of the Garden property. The judge should consider this subject further on remand.

A major area of dispute was the value of the Bruins franchise. The judge rejected the value advanced by the plaintiffs' expert ($18,000,-000), stating that "[a]lthough the defendant's figure of [$9,600,000] seems somewhat low in comparison with the cost of expansion team franchises, *the Court is constrained* to accept defendant's value as it is the more creditable and legally appropriate expert opinion in the record" (emphasis supplied). Although the choice of the word "constrained" may have been inadvertent, it connotes a sense of obligation. As the trier of fact, the judge was not bound to accept the valuation of either one expert or the other. He was entitled to reach his own conclusion as to value. . . .

Because the judge may have felt bound to accept the value placed on the Bruins franchise by the defendant's expert, we shall remand this case for him to arrive at his own determination of the value of the Bruins franchise. He would be warranted in arriving at the same valuation as that advanced on behalf of the defendant, but he is not obliged to do so.

The defendant argues that, in arriving at the value of the assets of Garden Arena, the judge improperly placed a separate value on the right to operate concessions at the Boston Garden. We agree with the judge. The fact that earnings from concessions were included in the computation of earnings value, one component in the formula, does not mean that the value of the concessions should have been excluded from the computation of net asset value, another such component.

The value of the concession operation was not reflected in the value of the real estate. Real estate may be valued on the basis of rental income, but it is not valued on the basis of the profitability of business operations within the premises. . . . Moreover, it is manifest that the value of the concession operation was not included in the value placed on the Boston Garden. The record indicates that Garden Arena already owned the concession rights when it purchased the Boston Garden. The conclusion that the value of the concession operation was not reflected in the value of the Boston Garden is particularly warranted because the determined value of the right to operate the concessions ($4,200,000) was higher than the May 25, 1973, purchase price ($4,000,000) of the *Boston Garden*.

14. The lowest value expressed by any expert for the plaintiffs was $8,250,000 (exclusive of mortgage liabilities), based on depreciated reproduction cost. The defendant offered no testimony concerning the value of the property on July 18, 1973.

We do conclude, however, that the judge may have felt unnecessarily bound to accept the plaintiffs' evidence of the value of the concession operation. He stated that "since the defendant did not submit evidence on this issue, the Court will accept plaintiffs' expert appraisal of the value of the concession operation." Although the judge did not express the view that he was "constrained" to accept the plaintiffs' valuation, as he did concerning the defendant's valuation of the Bruins franchise, he may have misconstrued his authority on this issue. The judge was not obliged to accept the plaintiffs' evidence at face value merely because no other evidence was offered. . . .

On remand, the judge should reconsider his determination of the value of the concession operation and exercise his own judgment concerning the bases for the conclusion arrived at by the plaintiffs' expert. However, the evidence did warrant the value selected by the judge, and no reduction in that value is required on this record.

Weighting of Valuations

The judge weighted the three valuations as follows:

Market Value	—	10%
Earnings Value	—	40%
Net Asset Value	—	50%

We accept these allocations as reasonable and within the range of the judge's discretion.

Any determination of the weight to be given the various elements involved in the valuation of a stock must be based on the circumstances. Heller v. Munsingwear, Inc., 33 Del.Ch. 593, 598, 98 A.2d 774 (1953). The decision to weight market value at only 10% was appropriate, considering the thin trading in the stock of Garden Arena. The decision to attribute 50% weight to net asset value was reasonably founded. The judge concluded that, because of tax reasons, the value of a sports franchise, unlike many corporate activities, depends more on its assets than on its earnings; that Garden Arena had been largely a family corporation in which earnings were of little significance; that Garden Arena had approximately $5,000,000 in excess liquid assets; and that the Garden property was a substantial real estate holding in an excellent location.

The judge might have reached different conclusions on this record. He was not obliged, however, to reconstruct market value and, as the defendant urges, attribute 50% weight to it. Nor was he obliged, as the plaintiffs argue, to consider only net asset value. See Martignette v. Sagamore Mfg. Co., 340 Mass. 136, 142, 163 N.E.2d 9 (1959). Market value and earnings value properly could be considered in these circumstances.

Although we would have found no fault with a determination to give even greater weight to the price per share based on the net asset value of Garden Arena, the judge was acting within an acceptable range of discretion in selecting the weights he gave to the various factors. . . .

Conclusion

We have concluded that the judge's method of valuing the Garden Arena stock was essentially correct. In this opinion, we have indicated, however, that the case should be remanded to him for clarification and further consideration on the record of three matters: his valuation of the Boston Garden, the Bruins franchise, and the concession operation.

So ordered.

———

L. Solomon, D. Schwartz, J. Bauman & E. Weiss, The Old Man and the Tree: A Parable of Valuation, in Corporations—Law and Policy 218–225

5th ed. 2003.

Once there was a wise old man who owned an apple tree. The tree was a fine tree, and with little care it produced a crop of apples each year which he sold for $100. The man was getting old, wanted to retire to a different climate and he decided to sell the tree. He enjoyed teaching a good lesson, and he placed an advertisement in the Business Opportunities section of the Wall Street Journal in which he said he wanted to sell the tree for "the best offer."

The first person to respond to the ad offered to pay the $50 which, the offeror said, was what he would be able to get for selling the apple tree for firewood after he had cut it down. "You are a very foolish person," said the old man. "You are offering to pay only the salvage value of this tree. That might be a good price for a pine tree or perhaps even this tree if it had stopped bearing fruit or if the price of apple wood had gotten so high that the tree was more valuable as a source of wood than as a source of fruit. But my tree is worth much more than $50."

The next person to come to see the old man offered to pay $100 for the tree. "For that," said she, "is what I would be able to get for selling this year's crop of fruit which is about to mature."

"You are not quite so foolish as the first one," responded the old man. "At least you see that this tree has more value as a producer of apples than it would as a source of firewood. But $100 is not the right price. You are not considering the value of next year's crop of apples, nor that of the years after. Please take your $100 and go elsewhere."

The next person to come along was a young man who had just started business school. "I am going to major in marketing," he said. "I figure that the tree should live for at least another fifteen years. If I sell the apples for $100 a year, that will total $1,500. I offer you $1,500 for your tree."

"You, too, are foolish," said the man. "Surely the $100 you would earn by selling the apples from the tree fifteen years from now cannot be worth $100 to you today. In fact, if you placed $41.73 today in a bank account paying 6% interest, compounded annually, that small sum would grow to $100 at the end of fifteen years. Therefore the present value of $100 worth of apples fifteen years from now, assuming an interest rate of 6%, is only $41.73, not $100. Pray," said the old man, "take your $1,500 and invest it safely in high-grade corporate bonds until you have graduated from business school and know more about finance."

Before long, there came a wealthy physician, who said, "I don't know much about apple trees, but I know what I like. I'll pay the market price for it. The last fellow was willing to pay you $1,500 for the tree, and so it must be worth that."

"Doctor," advised the old man, "you should get yourself a knowledgeable investment adviser. If there were truly a market in which apple trees were traded with some regularity, the prices at which they were sold would be a good indication of their value. But there is no such market. And the isolated offer I just received tells very little about how much my tree is really worth—as you would surely realize if you had heard the other foolish offers I have heard today. Please take your money and buy a vacation home."

The next prospective purchaser to come along was an accounting student. When the old man asked "What price are you willing to give me?" the student first demanded to see the old man's books. The old man had kept careful records and gladly brought them out. After examining them the accounting student said, "Your books show that you paid $75 for this tree ten years ago. Furthermore, you have made no deductions for depreciation. I do not know if that conforms with generally accepted accounting principles, but assuming that it does, the book value of your tree is $75. I will pay that."

"Ah, you students know so much and yet so little," chided the old man. "It is true that the book value of my tree is $75, but any fool can see that it is worth far more than that. You had best go back to school and see if you can find some books that will show you how to use your numbers to better effect."

The next prospective purchaser was a young stockbroker who had recently graduated from business school. Eager to test her new skills she, too, asked to examine the books. After several hours she came back to the old man and said she was now prepared to make an offer that valued the tree on the basis of the capitalization of its earnings.

For the first time the old man's interest was piqued and he asked her to go on.

The young woman explained that while the apples were sold for $100 last year, that figure did not represent profits realized from the tree. There were expenses attendant to the tree, such as the cost of fertilizer, the expense of pruning the tree, the cost of the tools, expenses in connection with picking the apples, carting them into town and selling them. Somebody had to do these things, and a portion of the salaries paid to those persons ought to be charged against the revenues from the tree. Moreover, the purchase price, or cost, of the tree was an expense. A portion of the cost is taken into account each year of the tree's useful life. Finally, there were taxes. She concluded that the profit from the tree was $50 last year.

"Wow!" exclaimed the old man. "I thought I made $100 off that tree."

"That's because you failed to match expenses with revenues, in accordance with generally accepted accounting principles," she explained. "You don't actually have to write a check to be charged with what accountants consider to be your expenses. For example, you bought a station wagon some time ago and you used it part of the time to cart apples to market. The wagon will last a while and each year some of the original cost has to be matched against revenues. A portion of the amount has to be spread out over the next several years even though you expended it all at one time. Accountants call that depreciation. I'll bet you never figured that in your calculation of profits."

"I'll bet you're right," he replied. "Tell me more."

"I also went back into the books for a few years and I saw that in some years the tree produced fewer apples than in other years, the prices varied and the costs were not exactly the same each year. Taking an average of only the last three years, I came up with a figure of $45 as a fair sample of the tree's earnings. But that is only half of what we have to do so as to figure the value."

"What's the other half?" he asked.

"The tricky part," she told him. "We now have to figure the value to me of owning a tree that will produce average annual earnings of $45 a year. If I believed that the tree was a one year wonder, I would say 100% of its value—as a going business—was represented by one year's earnings. But if I believe, as both you and I do, that the tree is more like a corporation, in that it will continue to produce earnings year after year, then the key is to figure out an appropriate rate of return. In other words, I will be investing my capital in the tree, and I need to compute the value to me of an investment that will produce $45 a year in income. We can call that amount the capitalized value of the tree."

"Do you have something in mind?" he asked.

"I'm getting there. If this tree produced steady and predictable earnings each year, it would be like a U.S. Treasury bond. But its earnings are not guaranteed. So we have to take into account risk and uncertainty. If the risk of its ruin is high, I will insist that a single year's earnings represent a higher percentage of the value of the tree. After all, apples could become a glut on the market one day and you would have to cut the price and increase the costs of selling them. Or some doctor could discover a link between eating an apple a day and heart disease. A drought could cut the yield of the tree. Or, heaven forbid, the tree could become diseased and die. These are all risks. And of course we do not know what will happen to costs that we know we have to bear."

"You are a gloomy one," reflected the old man. "There are treatments, you know, that could be applied to increase the yield of the tree. This tree could help spawn a whole orchard."

"I am aware of that," she assured him. "We will include that in the calculus. The fact is, we are talking about risk, and investment analysis is a cold business. We don't know with certainty what's going to happen. You want your money now and I'm supposed to live with the risk. That's fine with me, but then I have to look through a cloudy crystal ball, and not with 20/20 hindsight. And my resources are limited. I have to choose between your tree and the strawberry patch down the road. I cannot do both and the purchase of your tree will deprive me of alternative investments. That means I have to compare the opportunities and the risks."

"To determine a proper rate of return," she continued, "I looked at investment opportunities that are comparable to the apple tree, particularly in the agribusiness industry, where these factors have been taken into account. I have concluded that 20% would be an appropriate rate of return. In other words, average earnings over the last three years (which seems to be a representative period) are indicative of the return I will receive, I am prepared to pay a price for the tree that will give me a 20% return on my investment. I am not willing to accept any lower rate of return because I don't have to; I can always buy the strawberry patch instead. Now, to figure the price, we simply divide 45 by .20."

"Long division was never my long suit. Is there a simpler way of doing the figuring?" he asked hopefully.

"There is," she assured him. "We can use an approach we Wall Street types prefer, called a price-earnings (or P–E) ratio. To compute the ratio, we divide 100 by the rate of return we are seeking. If I was willing to settle for an 8% return, I would use a P–E ratio of 12.5 to 1. But since I want to earn 20% on my investment, I divided 100 by 20 and came up with a P–E ratio of 5:1. In other words, I am willing to pay five times the tree's estimated annual earnings. Multiplying $45 by 5, I get a value of $225. That's my offer."

The old man sat back and said he greatly appreciated the lesson. He would have to think about her offer, and he asked if she could come by the next day.

When the young woman returned she found the old man emerging from a sea of work sheets, small print columns of numbers and a calculator. "Glad to see you," he said. "I think we can do some business."

"It's easy to see how you Wall Street smarties make so much money, buying people's property for a fraction of the value. I think my tree is worth more than you figured, and I think I can get you to agree to that."

"I'm open minded," she assured him.

"The number you worked so hard over my books to come up with was something you called profits, or earnings that I earned in the past. I'm not so sure it tells you anything that important."

"Of course it does," she protested. "Profits measure efficiency and economic utility."

"Maybe," he mused, "but it sure doesn't tell you how much money you've got. I looked in my safe yesterday after you left and I saw I had some stocks that hadn't ever paid much of a dividend to me. And I kept getting reports each year telling me how great the earnings were, but I sure couldn't spend them. It's just the opposite with the tree. You figured the earnings were lower because of some amounts I'll never have to spend. It seems to me these earnings are an idea worked up by the accountants. Now I'll grant you that ideas, or concepts as you call them, are important and give you lots of useful information, but you can't fold them up, and put them in your pocket."

Surprised, she asked, "What is important, then?"

"Cash flow," he answered. "I'm talking about dollars you can spend, or save or give to your children. This tree will go on for years yielding revenues after costs. And it is the future, not the past, that we're trying to figure out."

"Don't forget the risks," she reminded him. "And the uncertainties."

"Quite right," he observed. "I think we can deal with that. Chances are that you and I could agree, after a lot of thought, on the possible range of future revenues and costs. I suspect we would estimate that for the next five years, there is a 25% chance that the cash flow will be $40, a 50% chance it will be $50 and a 25% chance it will be $60. That makes $50 our best guess, if you average it out. Then let us figure that for ten years after that the average will be $40. And that's it. The tree doctor tells me it can't produce any longer than that. Now all we have to do is figure out what you pay today to get $50 a year from now, two years from now, and so on for the first five years until we figure what you would pay to get $40 a year for each of the ten years after that. Then, throw in the [50] bucks we can get for firewood at that time, and that's that."

"Simple," she said. "You want to discount to the present value of future receipts including salvage value. Of course you need to determine the rate at which you discount."

"Precisely," he noted. "That's what all these charts and the calculator are doing." She nodded knowingly as he showed her discount tables that revealed what a dollar received at a later time is worth today, under different assumptions of the discount rate. It showed, for example, that at an 8% discount rate, a dollar delivered a year from now is worth $.93 today, simply because $.93 today, invested at 8%, will produce $1 a year from now.

"You could put your money in a savings bank or a savings and loan association and receive 3% interest, insured. But you could also put your money into obligations of the United States Government and earn 5% interest. That looks like the risk free rate of interest to me.* Anywhere else you put your money deprives you of the opportunity to earn 5% risk free. Discounting by 5% will only compensate you for the time value of the money you invest in the tree rather than in government securities. But the cash flow from the apple tree is not riskless, sad to say, so we need to use a higher discount rate to compensate you for the risk in your investment. Let us agree that we discount the receipt of $50 a year from now by 15%, and so on with the other deferred receipts. That is about the rate that is applied to investments with this magnitude of risk. You can check that out with my cousin who just sold his strawberry patch yesterday. According to my figures, the present value of the anticipated annual net revenues is $267.57, and today's value of the firewood is $6.14, making a grand total of $273.71. I'll take $270 even. You can see how much I'm allowing for risk because if I discounted the stream at 5%, it would come to $482.58."

* These numbers will vary with prevailing interest rates. The principle remains the same.

Year	Cash flow	Present value	
		5% discount rate	15% discount rate
1	$50	$ 47.62	$ 43.48
2	$50	$ 45.35	$ 37.81
3	$50	$ 43.19	$ 32.88
4	$50	$ 41.14	$ 28.59
5	$50	$ 39.18	$ 24.86
6	$40	$ 29.85	$ 17.29
7	$40	$ 28.43	$ 15.04
8	$40	$ 27.07	$ 13.08
9	$40	$ 25.78	$ 11.37
10	$40	$ 24.56	$ 9.89
11	$40	$ 23.39	$ 8.60
12	$40	$ 22.27	$ 7.48
13	$40	$ 21.21	$ 6.50
14	$40	$ 20.20	$ 5.65
15	$40	$ 19.24	$ 4.92
Salvage	$50	$ 24.05	$ 6.14
	TOTAL	$ 482.58	$ 273.71

After a few minutes reflection, the young woman said to the old man, "It was a bit foxy of you yesterday to let me appear to be teaching you something. Where did you learn so much about finance as an apple grower?"

"Don't be foolish, my young friend," he counseled her. "Wisdom comes from experience in many fields. Socrates taught us how to learn. I'll tell you a little secret; I spent a year in law school."

The young woman smiled at this last confession. "I have enjoyed this little exercise but let me tell you something that some of the financial whiz kids have told me. Whether we figure value on the basis of the discounted cash flow method or the capitalization of earnings, so long as we apply both methods perfectly we should come out at exactly the same point."

"Of course!" the old man exclaimed. "Some of the wunderkinds are catching on. But the clever ones are looking not at old earnings, but doing what managers are doing and projecting earnings into the future. The question is, however, which method is more likely to be misused. I prefer to calculate by my method because I don't have to monkey around with depreciation. You have to make these arbitrary assumptions about useful life and how fast you're going to depreciate. Obviously that's where you went wrong in your figuring."

"You are a crafty old devil," she rejoined. "There are plenty of places for your calculations to go off. It's easy to discount cash flows when they are nice and steady, but that doesn't help you when you've got some lumpy expenses that do not recur. For example, several years from now that tree will require some extensive pruning and spraying operations that simply do not show up in your flow. The labor and chemicals for that once-only occasion throw off the evenness of your calculations. But I'll tell you what, I'll offer you $250. My cold analysis tells me I'm overpaying, but I really like that tree. I think the psychic rewards of sitting in its shade must be worth something."

"It's a deal," said the old man. "I never said I was looking for the *perfect* offer, but only the *best* offer."

MORAL: There are several. Methods are useful as tools, but good judgment comes not from methods alone, but from experience. And experience comes from bad judgment.

Listen closely to the experts, and hear those things they don't tell you. Behind all the sweet sounds of their confident notes, there is a great deal of discordant uncertainty. One wrong assumption can carry you pretty far from the truth.

Finally, you are never too young to learn.

––––––

Warren Buffett, The Essays of Warren Buffett

19 Cardozo L.rev. 159 (1997).

. . . [W]hat may be called "owner earnings" . . . represent (a) reported earnings plus (b) depreciation, depletion, amortization, and certain other non-cash charges . . . less (c) the average annual amount of capitalized expenditures for plant and equipment, etc. that the business requires to fully maintain its long-term competitive position and its unit volume. . . .

Our owner-earnings equation does not yield the deceptively precise figures provided by GAAP, since (c) must be a guess—and one sometimes very difficult to make. Despite this problem, we consider the owner earnings figure, not the GAAP figure, to be the relevant item for valuation purposes—both for investors in buying stocks and for managers in buying entire businesses. We agree with Keynes's observation: "I would rather be vaguely right than precisely wrong." . . .

. . . [Calculations under our owner-earnings equation] usually do not provide . . . pleasant news. Most managers probably will acknowledge that they need to spend something more than (b) on their businesses over the longer term just to hold their ground in terms of both unit volume and competitive position. When this imperative exists—that is, when (c) exceeds (b)—GAAP earnings overstate owner earnings. Frequently this overstatement is substantial. The oil industry has in recent years provided a conspicuous example of this phenomenon. Had most major oil companies spent only (b) each year, they would have guaranteed their shrinkage in real terms.

All of this points up the absurdity of the "cash flow" numbers that are often set forth in Wall Street reports. These numbers routinely include (a) plus (b)—but do not subtract (c)....

"Cash Flow," true, may serve as a shorthand of some utility in descriptions of certain real estate businesses or other enterprises that make huge initial outlays and only tiny outlays thereafter. A company whose only holding is a bridge or an extremely long-lived gas field would be an example. But "cash flow" is meaningless in such businesses as manufacturing, retailing, extractive companies, and utilities because, for them, (c) is always significant. To be sure, businesses of this kind may in a given year be able to defer capital spending. But over a five-or ten-year period, they must make the investment—or the business decays.

Why, then, are "cash flow" numbers so popular today? In answer, we confess our cynicism: we believe these numbers are frequently used by marketers of businesses and securities in attempts to justify the unjustifiable (and thereby to sell what should be the unsalable). When (a)—that is, GAAP earnings—looks by itself inadequate to service debt of a junk bond or justify a foolish stock price, how convenient it becomes for salesmen to focus on (a) + (b). But you shouldn't add (b) without subtracting (c): though dentists correctly claim that if you ignore your teeth they'll go away, the same is not true for (c). The company or investor believing that the debt-servicing ability or the equity valuation or an enterprise can be measured by totaling (a) and (b) while ignoring (c) is headed for certain trouble....

[Intrinsic value is] an all-important concept that offers the only logical approach to evaluating the relative attractiveness of investments and businesses. Intrinsic value can be defined simply: It is the discounted value of the cash that can be taken out of a business during its remaining life.

The calculation of intrinsic value, though, is not so simple. As our definition suggests, intrinsic value is an estimate rather than a precise figure, and it is additionally an estimate that must be changed if interest rates move or forecasts of future cash flows are revised. Two people looking at the same set of facts, moreover ... will almost inevitably come up with at least slightly different intrinsic value figures....

Meanwhile, we [Berkshire Hathaway] regularly report our per-share book value, an easily calculable number, though one of limited use. The limitations do not arise from our holdings of marketable securities, which are carried on our books at their current prices. Rather the inadequacies of book value have to do with the companies we control, whose values as stated on our books may be far different from their intrinsic values.

The disparity can go in either direction. For example, in 1964 we could state with certitude that Berkshire's per-share book value was $19.46. However, that figure considerably overstated the company's intrinsic value, since all of the company's resources were tied up in a sub-profitable textile business. Our textile assets had neither going-concern nor liquidation values equal to their carrying values. Today, however, Berkshire's situation is reversed: Our March 31, 1996 book value of $15,180 far understates Berkshire's intrinsic value, a point true because many of the businesses we control are worth much more than their carrying value.

Inadequate though they are in telling the story, we give you Berkshire's book-value figures because they today serve as a rough, albeit significantly understated, tracking measure for Berkshire's intrinsic value. In other words, the percentage change in book value in any given year is likely to be reasonably close to that year's change in intrinsic value. . . .

———

LE BEAU v. M.G. BANCORPORATION, INC., 1998 WL 44993 (Del. Ch. 1998), aff'd in part, rev'd in part, 737 A.2d 513 (1999). This case concerned the valuation of a publicly held corporation, M.G. Bancorporation (MGB). MGB had two bank subsidiaries, Mount Greenwood Bank (Greenwood) and Worth Bancorp, Inc. (WBC). In the course of his opinion, Vice Chancellor Jacobs described the valuation techniques employed by David Clarke, an expert witness for the plaintiffs. Although Vice Chancellor Jacobs did not accept, in all respects, the manner in which Clarke applied the techniques to the case at hand, the techniques themselves nicely illustrate the contemporary theories of valuation developed in the two preceding selections. The description of the valuation methods employed by Clarke follows:

> The Petitioners commenced this appraisal proceeding on March 15, 1994. At trial the Petitioners' expert witness, David Clarke ("Clarke"), testified that as of the Merger date the fair value of MGB common stock was at least $85 per share. In arriving at that conclusion, Clarke used three distinct methodologies to value MGB's two operating bank subsidiaries: (i) the comparative publicly-traded company approach, (ii) the discounted cash flow ("DCF") method, and (iii) the comparative acquisition technique. Clarke then added a control premium to the values of the two subsidiaries to reflect the value of the holding company's (MGB's) controlling interest in those subsidiaries. Lastly, Clarke then added the value of MGB's remaining assets to the sum of his valuations of the two subsidiaries, to arrive at an overall fair value of $85 per share for MGB.
>
> What follows is a more detailed description of how Clarke performed his valuation(s) of MGB.

1.   Comparative Company Approach

Clarke's comparative publicly-traded company approach involved five steps: (1) identifying an appropriate set of comparable companies, (2) identifying the multiples of earnings and book value at which the comparable companies traded, (3) comparing certain of MGB's financial fundamentals (e.g., return on assets and return on equity) to those of the comparable companies, (4) making certain adjustments to those financial fundamentals, and (5) adding an appropriate control premium. After completing the first four steps, Clarke arrived at a value for WBC of $33.059 million ($48.02 per share), and for Greenwood of $20.952 million ($30.44 per share). Clarke next determined that during the period January 1989 to June 1993, acquirors of controlling interests in publicly-traded companies had paid an average premium of at least 35%. On that basis, Clarke concluded that a 35% premium was appropriate, and applied that premium to the values he had determined for Greenwood and WBC, to arrive at fair values of $43.3 million ($62.90 per share) for WBC and $27.1 million ($39.37 per share) for Greenwood, respectively. Clarke then valued MGB's 75.5% controlling interest in WBC at $32.691 million ($47.49 per share), and MGB's 100% interest in Greenwood at $27.1 million ($39.37 per share), under his comparative company approach.

2.   Discounted Cash Flow Approach

Clarke's DCF valuation analysis involved four steps: (1) projecting the future net cash flows available to MGB's shareholders for ten years after the Merger date, (2) discounting those future cash flows to present value as of the Merger date by using a discount rate based on the weighted average cost of capital ("WACC"), (3) adding a terminal value that represented the present value of all future cash flows generated after the ten year projection period, and (4) applying a control premium to the sum of (2) and (3).

. . . [Clarke] concluded that it would require ten years for MGB's cash flows to stabilize. Based on a 1996 Ibbotson Associates ("Ibbotson") study of the banking industry, Clarke concluded that the appropriate . . . discount rate (WACC), was 1%, and that the appropriate discount rate (WACC) for MGB was 12%. Applying that 12% discount rate, Clarke calculated the present value of WBC's future cash flows to be $17.251 million, and WBC's terminal value to be $14.824 million. Applying that same 12% discount rate, Clarke arrived at a present value of $10.937 million, and a terminal value of $9.138 million, for Greenwood.

Applying the same 35% control premium to those values of the two subsidiaries, Clarke calculated MGB's 75.5% interest in WBC at $33.824 million or $49.14 per share; and MGB's 100% interest in Greenwood at $28.3 million, or $41.11 per share.

3.   Comparative Acquisition Approach

Clarke's third valuation approach, the comparative acquisition method, focused upon multiples of MGB's last twelve months earnings and its tangible book value. Those multiples were determined by reference to the prices at which the stock of comparable companies had been sold in transactions involving the sale of control. Unlike the comparative company and DCF valuation approaches, this method did not require adding a control premium to the values of the subsidiaries because under that methodology, the parent holding company's controlling interest in the subsidiaries was already accounted for.

In valuing MGB under his third approach, Clarke identified three transactions involving community banks in the relevant geographic area that occurred within one year of the Merger. He also considered data published by The Chicago Corporation in its September 1993 issue of Midwest Bank & Thrift Survey.*** From these sources, Clarke determined that (i) control of WBC could be sold for a price between a multiple of 14 times WBC's last twelve months' earnings and 200% of WBC's tangible book value, and that (ii) control of Greenwood could be sold for a price between a multiple of 12 times Greenwood's last twelve months' earnings and 175% of its tangible book value. Giving equal weight to these two sets of values, Clarke valued MGB's 75.5% interest in WBC at $28.8 million (75.5% x $38.1 million) or $41.84 per share, and MGB's 100% interest in Greenwood, at $22.9 million, or $33.27 per share.

4.   MGB's Remaining Assets

Having valued MGB's two subsidiaries, Clarke then determined the fair value of MGB's remaining net assets, which included (i) a $6.83 million note payable by Southwest, (ii) certain intangibles that Clarke did not include in his valuation, (iii) $78,000 in cash, and (iv) other assets worth $2000. These assets totaled $6.91 million, from which Clarke subtracted liabilities of $96,000 to arrive at a net asset value of $6.814 million ($9.90 per share) for MGB's remaining assets.

5.   Fair Value Computation

Clarke then added the values he had determined under each of his valuation methodologies, for (i) MGB's 75.5% interest in WBC, (ii) MGB's 100% interest in Greenwood, and (iii) MGB's 100% interest in its remaining assets. Under his comparative publicly-traded method, Clarke concluded that MGB's value was $76.59 per share with no control premium, and $96.76 per share with a control premium. Under his DCF approach, Clarke determined that MGB's value was $74.75 per share with no control

*** That data reflected an analysis of 137 bank acquisitions announced from January 1, 1989 to June 1, 1993.

premium, and $100.15 per share with a control premium. And under his comparative acquisitions method, Clarke concluded that MGB's minimum fair value was $85 per share, which represented the median of the values described above.

The Chancery Court accepted the legitimacy of Clarke's valuation methods in principle, but concluded that there were various problems in the way that Clarke and the corporation's expert had actually applied most of the valuation methods they employed. However, the court accepted Clarke's valuation based on the comparative acquisition method, and concluded, largely on that basis, that the stock was worth $85/share. The Delaware Supreme Court affirmed on the valuation issue, but remanded on the issue whether compound or simple interest should be paid.

————

NOTE

The *control* premium to which the *LeBeau* opinion refers is based on the principle that the market value of stock includes a minority discount—that is, a discount for the fact that shares traded on the market are not controlling shares. However, a minority discount applicable to the valuation of noncontrolling stock is irrelevant when valuing the corporation. Therefore, if a given technique for valuing the *corporation* is based on the market price of *stock*, the minority discount applied to the stock must be reversed. The way to reverse the discount is to add back in a control premium, which should be the mirror image of, and identical to, the minority discount. See Rapid–American Corp. v. Harris, 603 A.2d 796 (Del.1992).

SECTION 7. RESTRICTIONS ON THE TRANSFERABILITY OF SHARES, AND MANDATORY-SALE PROVISIONS

————

INTRODUCTORY NOTE

This Section concerns the extent to which restrictions on transferability can be imposed on the stock of close corporations. Central to this issue is the problem of valuation. In theory, a shareholder might object to a restriction on transferability simply because as a matter of principle he wants to be free to sell to whoever he wants, on whatever conditions he wants. In practice, however, problems with a restriction on transferability usually arise where the restriction precludes the shareholder from realizing the full value of his shares on a transfer. If a restriction on transferability is coupled with some mechanism that provides a shareholder who wants to transfer his shares with the same economic value he could have realized in the absence of the restriction, he would be unlikely to complain.

———

F.B.I. Farms, Inc. v. Moore

Supreme Court of Indiana, 2003.
798 N.E.2d 440.

We hold that as a general proposition, restrictions on corporate share transfers may require approval of the transfer by the corporation's Board of Directors, at least in a family-owned corporation. Although generally valid against purchasers with notice of them, such restrictions may not prevent a creditor from foreclosing a lien on the shares, but a purchaser who buys at a foreclosure sale with notice of the restrictions acquires the shares subject to the restrictions. We also hold that if shares are subject to a right of first refusal, and the holder of the right has notice of the foreclosure, the holder cannot exercise the right against a purchaser at a foreclosure sale after the purchaser has taken title to the shares without objection from the holder of the rights.

Factual and Procedural Background

F.B.I. Farms, Inc., was formed in 1976 by Ivan and Thelma Burger, their children, Linda and Freddy, and the children's spouses. Each of the three couples transferred a farm and related machinery to the corporation in exchange for common stock in the corporation. At the time, Birchell Moore was married to Linda. Linda and Moore deeded a jointly-owned 180–acre farm to F.B.I., and 2,507 shares were issued to Moore and one to Linda. These 2,508 shares represented approximately fourteen percent of the capitalization of F.B.I.

In 1977, the Board of Directors of F.B.I. consisted of Moore, Ivan, Freddy and Linda. The minutes of a 1977 meeting of the Board recite that the following restrictions on the transfer of shares were "adopted":

1) No stock of said corporation shall be transferred, assigned and/or exchanged or divided, unless or until approved by the Directors thereof;

2) That if any stock be offered for sale, assigned and/or transferred, the corporation should have the first opportunity of purchasing the same at no more than the book value thereof;

3) Should said corporation be not interested, and could not economically offer to purchase said stock, any stockholder of record should be given the next opportunity to purchase said stock, at a price not to exceed the book value thereof;

4) That if the corporation was not interested in the stock, and any stockholders were not interested therein, then the same could be sold to any blood member of the family. Should they be

desirous of purchasing the same, then at not more than the book value thereof.

Linda's marriage to Moore was dissolved in 1982. As part of the dissolution proceedings, Linda was awarded all of the F.B.I. shares and Moore was awarded a monetary judgment in the amount of $155,889.80, secured by a lien on Linda's shares.

F.B.I. filed for bankruptcy protection in 1989 and emerged from Chapter 11 Bankruptcy in 1991. Moore's judgment against Linda remained unsatisfied, and in April 1998 he sought a writ of execution of his lien. The corporation, through its counsel, responded with a letter to Moore's counsel demanding payment of the $250,700 subscription price for the 2,507 shares that were initially issued to Moore but had since been transferred to Linda. Moore obtained the writ of execution in June 1999.... A sheriff's sale went forward and in February 2000 Moore purchased all 2,924 shares owned by Linda at the time for $290,450.67.

In December 2000 Moore instituted this suit against F.B.I., its shareholders, and Linda seeking a declaratory judgment that the attempted cancellation of the shares by the defendants was invalid, that Moore properly retained ownership of the shares, and that the shares were unencumbered by restrictions and were freely transferable. Moore also sought dissolution of the corporation, injunctive relief against alleged fraudulent practices by the defendants, and monetary damages. The trial court granted Moore's motion for partial summary judgment, finding (1) the shares were not "lawfully cancelled"; (2) Moore was the "lawful owner" of the disputed stock; (3) the restriction in paragraph one of the agreement requiring approval by F.B.I.'s directors for a share transfer was "manifestly unreasonable"; and, (4) the provision in paragraph four of the agreement giving "blood members" the option to purchase after the corporation and shareholders was "manifestly unreasonable" and unenforceable. The trial court's findings included those rendering the order appealable as a final judgment pursuant to Indiana Trial Rule 54(B).

On appeal, the Court of Appeals held that the transfer restrictions barred only voluntary transfers. *F.B.I. Farms, Inc. v. Moore,* 769 N.E.2d 688, 696 (Ind.Ct.App.2002). Because the sheriff's sale effectuated an involuntary transfer of Linda's shares, Moore, as the purchaser of the shares, acquired the shares. *Id.* at 692. Although the court found that future transfers of stock would be subject to the restrictions in Moore's hands, it also affirmed the trial court's finding that the two disputed restrictions were manifestly unreasonable. *Id.* at 695–96. The court reasoned that the several tumultuous years of dispute between the parties rendered the restriction requiring director approval before transfer unreasonable, and the reference to "blood members" of the family was sufficiently ambiguous that that restriction was unenforceable. *Id.* at 694–96. We granted transfer.

Standard of Review

To support an order granting a motion for summary judgment, the designated evidence must show that there is no genuine issue as to any material fact and that the moving party is entitled to a judgment as a matter of law. Ind. Trial Rule 56(C). On appeal, the standard of review of a grant or denial of a motion for summary judgment is the same as that used in the trial court. *Bemenderfer v. Williams,* 745 N.E.2d 212, 215 (Ind.2001).

I.   Transfer Restrictions

A.   *General Principles*

Most of the issues in this case are resolved by the Indiana statute governing share transfer restrictions. Indiana Code section 23–1–26–8 essentially mirrors Model Business Corporation Act § 6.27, which authorizes restrictions on the transfer of shares. The Indiana statute reads as follows:

(a) The articles of incorporation, bylaws, an agreement among shareholders, or an agreement between shareholders and the corporation may impose restrictions on the transfer or registration of transfer of shares of any class or series of shares of the corporation. A restriction does not affect shares issued before the restriction was adopted unless the holders of the shares are parties to the restriction agreement or voted in favor of the restriction.

(b) A restriction on the transfer or registration of transfer of shares is valid and enforceable against the holder or a transferee of the holder if the restriction is authorized by this section and its existence is noted conspicuously on the front or back of the certificate or is contained in the information statement required by section 7(b) [Ind.Code 23–1–26–7(b)] of this chapter. Unless so noted, a restriction is not enforceable against a person without knowledge of the restriction.

(c) A restriction on the transfer or registration of transfer of shares is authorized:

(1) to maintain the corporation's status when it is dependent on the number or identity of its shareholders;

(2) to preserve exemptions under federal or state securities law; or

(3) for any other reasonable purpose.

(d) A restriction on the transfer or registration of transfer of shares may, among other things:

(1) obligate the shareholder first to offer the corporation or other persons (separately, consecutively, or simultaneously) an opportunity to acquire the restricted shares;

(2) obligate the corporation or other persons (separately, consecutively, or simultaneously) to acquire the restricted shares;

(3) require the corporation, the holders of any class of its shares, or another person to approve the transfer of the

restricted shares, if the requirement is not manifestly unreasonable; or

(4) prohibit the transfer of the restricted shares to designated persons or classes of persons, if the prohibition is not manifestly unreasonable....

Corporate shares are personal property. At common law, any restriction on the power to alienate personal property was impermissible. *Doss v. Yingling,* 95 Ind.App. 494, 500, 172 N.E. 801, 803 (1930). Despite this doctrine, Indiana, like virtually all jurisdictions, allows corporations and their shareholders to impose restrictions on transfers of shares. The basic theory of these statutes is to permit owners of a corporation to control its ownership and management and prevent outsiders from inserting themselves into the operations of the corporation. *Id.* at 502–03, 172 N.E. 801; 12 William Meade Fletcher et al, *Fletcher Cyclopedia of the Law of Private Corporations,* § 5454 (1996). Chief Justice Holmes stated the matter succinctly a century ago: "Stock in a corporation is not merely property. It also creates a personal relation analogous otherwise than technically to a partnership.... [T]here seems to be no greater objection to retaining the right of choosing one's associates in a corporation than in a firm." *Barrett v. King,* 181 Mass. 476, 63 N.E. 934, 935 (1902). As applied to a family-owned corporation, this remains valid today.

Transfer restrictions are treated as contracts either between shareholders or between shareholders and the corporation.[35] *Doss,* 95 Ind.App. at 502, 172 N.E. at 803; *Butner v. United States,* 440 U.S. 48, 55, 99 S.Ct. 914, 59 L.Ed.2d 136 (1979) (the validity and enforcement of restrictions are governed by state law just like any other contract); *Boston Safe Deposit & Trust Co., et al. v. North Attleborough Chapter of the Am. Red Cross, et al.,* 330 Mass. 114, 111 N.E.2d 447, 449 (1953) (restrictions in the articles of organization are binding on a shareholder by reason of the contract made with the corporation when she accepted the certificates of stock containing the printed restrictions). Apart from any statutory requirements, restrictions on transfer are to be read, like any other contract, to further the manifest intention of the parties. Because they are restrictions on alienation and therefore disfavored, the terms in the restrictions are not to be expanded beyond their plain and ordinary meaning. 12 Fletcher § 5455 (1996).

---

35. The Indiana statute provides that restrictions are valid if included in the articles, the bylaws, an agreement among shareholders or an agreement between the corporation and shareholders. I.C. § 23–1–26–8(a) (1998). None of these was done here. However, no one challenges the restrictions as defective in their initial adoption. At least as to Moore, who approved them as a director and had actual knowledge of them, under these circumstances, the restrictions constitute a contract as to all of those shareholders who approved the adoption of the restrictions. *Shortridge v. Platis,* 458 N.E.2d 301, 304 (Ind.Ct.App.1984) (a buy-sell restriction is analyzed by the court as a contract); 18A Am.Jur.2d *Corporations* § 687 (1985) (courts sustain a restriction whether valid as a bylaw or not, on the ground that it constitutes a valid agreement between the stockholders and the corporation, particularly as applied to stockholders who assent to, or participate in, the adoption of the bylaw).

For a party to be bound by share transfer restrictions, that party must have notice of the restrictions. I.C. § 23–1–26–8(b) (1998). Here, the restrictions on transfer of F.B.I. shares were neither "noted conspicuously" on the certificates nor contained in the information statement referred to in Indiana Code 23–1–26–8(b), but there is no doubt that Moore, the buyer at the sheriff's sale, had notice of the restrictions. He was therefore bound by them. *State ex rel. Hudelson v. Clarks Hill Tel. Co.,* 139 Ind.App. 507, 510, 218 N.E.2d 154, 156 (1966).

Finally, a closely held corporation is a "corporation in which all of the outstanding stock is held by just a few individuals, or by a small group of persons belonging to a single family." J.R. Kemper, *Validity of "Consent Restraint" on Transfer of Shares of Close Corporation,* 69 A.L.R.3d 1327, 1328 (1976). In 1977, F.B.I. plainly fell within that description; it was owned by six individuals, all members of a single family. Closely held corporations have a viable interest in remaining the organization they envision at incorporation and transfer restrictions are an appropriate means of maintaining the status quo.

B. Rights of First Refusal

Paragraphs (2) and (3) of the restrictions created rights of first refusal in F.B.I. and its shareholders. A transfer in violation of restrictions is voidable at the insistence of the corporation. *Groves v. Prickett,* 420 F.2d 1119, 1122 (9th Cir.1970). F.B.I. and its shareholders argue that Moore should have been obliged to offer the shares to the corporation or a shareholder pursuant to those provisions. Moore responds, and the Court of Appeals agreed, that he was not a shareholder until he purchased the shares at the sheriff's sale. He contends he therefore had no power to offer the shares. This misses the point that before Linda could transfer her shares, she was obliged to offer them to F.B.I. and the other shareholders. Moore was on notice of that requirement. Moore, as the buyer, had the right to demand that Linda initiate the process to exercise or waive the right to first refusal.

Thus, if the corporation had insisted on its right of first refusal, Linda would have been obliged to sell to F.B.I. (or its shareholders). And Moore, as a buyer on notice of the restrictions, had the right to insist that that process go forward. But the corporation and its shareholders were aware of the sheriff's sale and did nothing to assert the right of first refusal. They cannot sit back and let the sale go forward, await future events, then claim a right to purchase on the same terms as Moore. *McCroden v. Case,* 602 N.W.2d 736, 743–44 (S.D.1999) (transfer restriction is waived by stockholder's failure to exercise "first option" preemptive rights); *Calton v. Calton,* 118 N.C.App. 439, 456 S.E.2d 520, 523 (1995) (no justiciable controversy existed where no shareholder exercised the right to purchase stock, intended to exercise the right, or was even financially able to do so at the time the action was filed; shareholders waived any right to object to the transfers where they had knowledge of both the testator's death and the restrictions contained on the stock certificates, no shareholder asked to purchase any of the stock, and shareholders waited eighteen months to file an action); *Puro v. Puro,* 40 A.D.2d 784, 337 N.Y.S.2d 586, 587 (N.Y.App.Div.1972) (transfer restrictions are not self-executing). In sum, F.B.I. and its shareholders had rights of first refusal, but failed to exercise them. As a result, the sale to Moore proceeded as if the shares had been offered and the corporation refused the opportunity. To hold otherwise would be to give F.B.I. and its shareholders a perpetual option to purchase but no obligation to do so. Having failed to demand their right to buy at the time of the sale, the rights of first refusal gave them no ability to upset the sale conducted by the sheriff.

C.   *Restrictions on Transfer with Board Approval*

The restrictions "adopted" in paragraphs (1) and (4) are more problematic. Indiana's statute, reflecting the common law, requires that restrictions on share transfers be reasonable. I.C. § 23–1–26–8(c)(3), (d)(3), and (d)(4). The general common law doctrine surrounding evaluation of the reasonableness of restrictions is well established. A restriction is reasonable if it is designed to serve a legitimate purpose of the party imposing the restraint and the restraint is not an absolute restriction on the recipient's right of alienability. Bernard F. Cataldo, *Stock Transfer Restrictions and the Closed Corporation,* 37 Va. L.Rev. 229, 232–33 (1951). The Indiana statute is somewhat more generous in allowing restrictions on classes of buyers unless "manifestly unreasonable." I.C. 23–1–26–8(d)(4). Several factors are relevant in determining the reasonableness of any transfer restriction, including the size of the corporation, the degree of restraint upon alienation; the time the restriction was to continue in effect, the method to be used in determining the transfer price of shares, the likelihood of the restriction's contributing to the attainment of corporate objectives, the possibility that a hostile stockholder might injure the corporation, and the probability of the restriction's promoting the best interests of the corporation. 18A Am.Jur.2d *Corporations* § 683 (1985). At one extreme, a restriction that merely prescribes procedures that must be observed before stock may be transferred is not unreasonable. *State ex rel. Howland v. Olympia Veneer Co.,* 138 Wash. 144, 244 P. 261 (1926). At the other end of the spectrum, restrictions that are fraudulent, oppressive, unconscionable, *Tourtelott v. Chestnuts Salon,* No. 00–5496 2001 R.I.Super. LEXIS 19 at * 6 (R.I. Sup.Ct. Jan. 17, 2001), 2001 WL 91393, or the result of a breach of the fiduciary duty that shareholders in a close corporation owe to one another, will not be upheld. *Cressy v. Shannon Cont'l Corp.,* 177 Ind.App. 224, 378 N.E.2d 941, 945 (1978); 12 Fletcher § 5455 (1996). The restrictions on F.B.I.'s shares, like most, are somewhere in the middle. They impose substantive limitations on transfer, but are not alleged to be the result of fraud or breach of fiduciary duty.

The trial court, in its order granting partial summary judgment, concluded that the restriction precluding transfer without Board approval was reasonable at the time that it was adopted, but the lengthy and difficult history between the parties had rendered the restriction unreasonable. Under basic contract law principles, the reasonableness of a term of a contract is evaluated at the time of its adoption. *First Fed. Sav. Bank v. Key Mkts.*, 559 N.E.2d 600, 603 (Ind.1990). The same is true of share transfer restrictions. As a result, evaluating the reasonableness of the restrictions in light of subsequent developments is inappropriate. For that reason, we do not agree that the restriction requiring director approval became unreasonable based upon events and disputes within the family that occurred after the restrictions had been adopted. To be sure, the parties find themselves in a difficult dispute as is sometimes the case in a family business following a dissolution. But when F.B.I. was formed and the family farms were effectively pooled, the shareholders agreed that the Board would be permitted to restrict access to the shares. To the extent that restriction devalues the shares in the hands of any individual shareholder by reason of lack of transferability, it is the result of the bargain they struck. The policy behind enforcement of these restrictions is to encourage entering into formal partnerships by permitting all parties to have confidence they will not involuntarily end up with an undesired co-venturer. Presumably for that reason, the statute permits a restriction that requires a transferee to be approved by the Board of Directors, and to that extent may severely limit transferability.

A "consent restriction" such as this has been considered unreasonable by some courts. 2 Cox, Hazen, O'Neal *Corporations* § 14.10 (2002); Harry G. Henn & John R. Alexander, *Laws of Corporations*, § 281 (1983). However, the General Assembly has allowed precisely this type of restriction in Indiana Code section 23–1–26–8(d)(3). That section provides that transfer restrictions may require the approval of "the corporation, the holders of any class of its shares, or another person" before the shares may be transferred. Board approval is one permissible way of implementing approval by "the Corporation" under this section. *See also Wright v. Iredell Telephone Co.*, 182 N.C. 308, 108 S.E. 744, 747 (1921) (upholding a restriction requiring the approval of the corporation's directors).

D. Restrictions on Transfer Except to "Blood Members of the Family"

We also find the "blood-member" restriction to be enforceable as protecting a viable interest. *Mathews v. United States*, 226 F.Supp. 1003, 1009 (E.D.N.Y.1964) (recognized "intact family ownership" as an interest worth protecting by a restriction). These are family farmers in corporate form. It is apparent from the nature of the corporation that the Burger family had an interest in maintaining ownership and operation of F.B.I. in the hands of family members. Although one may quibble with the terminology, and there may be some individuals where status as blood members is debatable, we think it plain enough that all parties to this dispute either are or are not blood members of the Burger family. All are either direct descendants of Ivan or spouses of Ivan or of one of his children....

III.   Restrictions as Applied to Involuntary Transfers

The Court of Appeals held that the restrictions on Linda's shares did not apply by their terms to the sheriff's sale and, as a result, did not bar the sheriff's sale to Moore. We agree that Moore acquired the shares at the sheriff's sale, but not because the restrictions were inapplicable by their terms.

The Court of Appeals relied on cases stating that involuntary transfers fall within the terms of a restriction only if the language of the restrictions specifically identifies them. *F.B.I. Farms,* 769 N.E.2d at 692. This doctrine has been developed largely in cases involving intestate transfers by a decedent, *Stern v. Stern,* 146 F.2d 870, 870 (D.C.Cir.1945), and in marriage dissolution proceedings where a transfer is made to a spouse. *Castonguay v. Castonguay,* 306 N.W.2d 143, 146 (Minn.1981).

The sheriff's sale where Moore purchased Linda's shares was an involuntary transfer. Transfers ordered incident to marriage dissolutions and transfers under intestate law may also be deemed involuntary. We think the governing principle is not the same for all forms of "involuntary" transfers. The language of the restrictions in this case does not specifically refer to involuntary transfers of any kind. Rather, it seems to contemplate restricting all transfers, voluntary and involuntary, by providing that no stock of the corporation should be "transferred, assigned, exchanged, divided, or sold" without complying with the restrictions. The intent of the parties is thus rather plain: to restrict ownership to the designated group, and to preclude transfer by any means. The question is whether that intent should be permitted to prevail in the face of countervailing policies.

Transfer by intestacy is in some sense involuntary, but it may also be viewed as a voluntary act of the decedent who had the option to leave a will. If a transfer could not be made by gift during lifetime, for example, to an offspring regarded by other shareholders as an undesirable partner, we see no reason to permit it at death by the decedent's choice to die intestate. There are, however, forms of involuntary transfers that a private agreement may not prevent because the agreement would unreasonably interfere with the rights of third parties. In a dissolution, the interests of the spouse require permitting transfer over the stated intent of the parties. Similarly, creditors of the shareholder cannot be stymied by a private agreement that renders foreclosure of a lien impossible. For that reason, we agree with the trial court that the sheriff's sale transferred the shares to Moore despite the restrictions. Transfer restrictions cannot preclude transfer in a foreclosure sale and thereby leave creditors without recourse. This does not turn on a doctrine of construction. Rather we hold that requiring an explicit bar specifically naming transfer by intestacy or by testamentary disposition should not be necessary. If the language purports to bar all transfers, and by its terms would apply to intestacy, devise or any other means of transfer, it should be given effect unless the restriction violates some policy.

Although we agree with Moore that he could purchase the shares at the sale, it is also the case that he purchased the shares with knowledge of the restrictions. We conclude that he could not acquire more property rights than were possessed by Linda as his seller. U.C.C. § 8–302 (1994) (the purchaser of an investment security acquires the rights in the security his transferor had or had actual authority to convey). The shares in Linda's hands were valued with restrictions in place, and therefore it is not unfair to her creditors that a purchaser at a foreclosure sale acquire the disputed shares subject to the same restrictions, and with whatever lessened value that produces. To be sure, the effect of such a restriction may be to make the shares unmarketable to any buyer. But the creditor retains the option to bid at the sale and, if successful, succeed to the shareholders' interest. The creditor then gets the assets the debtor used to secure the underlying obligation. If the creditor wants collateral free of restrictions, the creditor must negotiate for that at the outset of the arrangement.

Conclusion

We ... uphold the trial court's finding that the transfer restrictions did not prevent the sheriff's sale, and that the transfer restrictions remain applicable to the shares in Moore's hands. We reverse the trial court's ruling that the two disputed transfer restrictions are unreasonable and therefore unenforceable, and find that the director-approval and blood-member restrictions are reasonable and enforceable. The case is remanded for further proceedings consistent with this opinion.

■ SHEPARD, C.J., and DICKSON and SULLIVAN, JJ., concur.

■ RUCKER, J., concurs in result without opinion.

————

EVANGELISTA v. HOLLAND, 27 Mass.App.Ct. 244, 537 N.E.2d 589 (1989). A shareholders' agreement allowed the corporation to buy out, for $75,000, the estate of any deceased shareholder. The corporation brought suit against the estate of a deceased shareholder to enforce the agreement. There was strong evidence that the decedent's stock was worth at least $191,000. Held, for the corporation:

The executors suggest that to require them to part with their interest in the business for so much less than the [value of the stock] violates the duty of good faith and loyalty owed one another by stockholders in a closely held corporation.... Questions of good faith and loyalty do not arise when all the stockholders in advance enter into an agreement for the purchase of stock of a withdrawing or deceased stockholder.... That the price established by a stockholders' agreement may be less than the appraised or market value is unremarkable. Such agreements may have as their purpose: the payment of a price for a decedent's stock which will benefit the corporation or surviving stockholders by not unduly burdening them; the payment of a price tied to life insurance; or fixing a price which assures the beneficiaries of the deceased stockholder of a predetermined price for stock which might have little market value.... When the agreement was entered into in 1984, the order and time of death of stockholders was an unknown. There was a "mutuality of risk."

DEL. GEN. CORP. LAW §§ 202, 342, 347, 349

[See Statutory Supplement]

CAL. CORP. CODE §§ 204(a)(3), (b), 418

[See Statutory Supplement]

MODEL BUS. CORP. ACT § 6.27

[See Statutory Supplement]

NOTE ON RESTRICTIONS ON TRANSFERABILITY AND MANDATORY SALES OF STOCK

1. *Restrictions on Transferability.* Although some of the earlier cases held that any restriction on the transferability of shares constituted an illegal restraint on alienation, the modern cases hold that "reasonable" restrictions are valid and enforceable. Three basic types of restrictions are commonly used in the context of the close corporation: (1) First refusals, which prohibit a sale of stock unless the shares have been first offered to the corporation, the other shareholders, or both, on the terms offered by the third party. (2) First options, which prohibit a transfer of stock unless the shares have been first offered to the corporation, the other shareholders, or both, at a price fixed under the terms of the option. (3) Consent restraints, which prohibit a transfer of stock without the permission of the corporation's board or shareholders.

Of these three basic types, the *first refusal* is obviously least restrictive in its impact on a shareholder who wants to sell his stock, and such provisions are widely upheld. See, e.g., Groves v. Prickett, 420 F.2d 1119 (9th Cir.1970).

The restrictiveness of a *first option* depends largely on the relationship between the option price and a fair price at the time the option is triggered. The courts have been giving increasing latitude to this type of provision. See, e.g., In re Mather's Estate, 410 Pa. 361, 189 A.2d 586 (1963) where an agreement setting a price of $1 per share was enforced although the actual value was $1,060 per share.

A *consent restraint* is normally the most restrictive of the three basic types, and at one time such a restraint was almost certain to be deemed invalid. However, some recent statutes specifically contemplate the validity of such restraints (see, e.g., Del. § 202), and as *F.B.I.* suggests, the courts have also begun to be more tolerant.

In spite of the increasingly tolerant climate, however, the validity of consent restraints remains uncertain in the absence of statute or authoritative precedent. In Rafe v. Hindin, 29 A.D.2d 481, 288 N.Y.S.2d 662 (1968), P and D each owned 50% of the stock of Bil Cy Realty, which they had organized in 1963. A legend on each stock certificate made the stock nontransferable except to the other shareholder, and written permission from the other shareholder was required to record a transfer of the stock on Bil Cy's books. P brought an action for a declaratory judgment that the legend on the certificate was void, and that the stock was transferable without D's consent. The court so held:

> In New York certificates of stock are regarded as personal property and are subject to the rule that there be no unreasonable restraint on alienation....
>
> The legend on the stock certificate at bar contains no provision that the individual defendant's consent may not be unreasonably withheld. Since the individual defendant is thus given the arbitrary power to forbid a transfer of the shares of stock by the plaintiff, the restriction amounts to annihilation of property. The restriction is not only not reasonable, but it is against public policy and, therefore, illegal. It is an unwarrantable and unlawful restraint on the sale of personal property, the sale and interchange of which the law favors, and in restraint of trade.

2. *Mandatory Sales.* The three basic types of restraints discussed above limit the shareholders' power of transfer. Other types of arrangements go further, and give the corporation or the remaining shareholders an option to purchase a shareholder's stock upon the occurrence of one or more designated contingencies, even if the shareholder wants to retain the stock. A common example is an arrangement under which the corporation is given an option, in the event an employee is terminated, to repurchase stock that it has issued to the employee. The courts have tended to enforce such an arrangement even when the option price is quite low in relation to the value of the stock at the time the buyback right is triggered. See, e.g., St. Louis Union Trust Co. v. Merrill Lynch, Pierce, Fenner & Smith Inc., 562 F.2d 1040 (8th Cir.1977), cert. denied 435 U.S. 925, 98 S.Ct. 1490, 55 L.Ed.2d 519 (1978). Another common example is a buy-sell or survivor-purchase agreement, which provides that on the death of a shareholder in a close corporation, his estate has an obligation to sell its shares to the corporation or the remaining shareholders at a price fixed under the agreement, and the corporation or the remaining shareholders have an obligation (rather than an option) to purchase the shares. A major purpose of such agreements is to provide liquidity to the decedent's estate. If a corporation is closely held, the market for

its shares is usually negligible. In the absence of the agreement, therefore, the estate might be in a bad position if liquid assets are needed to meet tax liabilities or other needs. A buy-sell agreement provides the estate with funds to meet such needs. It also enables the corporation to control the identity of its shareholders. The corporation's obligation is often funded in whole or in part by insurance on the shareholders' lives.

3. *Problems of Interpretation.* Restrictions on transfer give rise to recurring problems of interpretation—in particular, whether a given type of disposition is within the scope of the restriction. The courts often give restrictions on transfer a strict interpretation. For example, some courts have held that unless explicitly otherwise provided, restrictions on transfer are inapplicable to testamentary transfers, see, e.g., Avrett and Ledbetter Roofing and Heating Co. v. Phillips, 85 N.C.App. 248, 354 S.E.2d 321 (1987) and to transfers by operation of law, such as divorce decrees. See, e.g., Castonguay v. Castonguay, 306 N.W.2d 143 (Minn.1981). Restrictions on transfer are also often interpreted as inapplicable to transfers between existing shareholders. See, e.g., Remillong v. Schneider, 185 N.W.2d 493 (N.D.1971). This rule of interpretation may result in an uncontemplated shift of control where a transfer between shareholders involves swing shares, that is, shares that when added to an existing holding will swing the balance of power to a shareholder who previously did not have that power. Cf. Lank v. Steiner, 43 Del.Ch. 262, 224 A.2d 242 (1966).

4. *Pricing Provisions.* Another kind of problem concerns the pricing clause in first-option, or buy-sell arrangements. Where shares are closely held, the price of the shares cannot realistically be set on the basis of market value. Some alternative pricing mechanism is therefore required.

a. *Book value.* One common approach is to use a pricing formula based on book value. Book value, however, may be an unreliable guide to a corporation's real worth: it reflects the historical cost of assets, rather than their present value, and usually ignores goodwill or going-concern value. The courts have tended to hold that a large disparity between book value and real value is not in itself sufficient to avoid the operation of a book-value pricing provision. Thus in Palmer v. Chamberlin, 191 F.2d 532 (5th Cir.1951), the court, quoting New England Trust Co. v. Abbott, 162 Mass. 148, 38 N.E. 432 (1894), stated, " '. . . specific performance of an agreement to convey will not be refused merely because the price is inadequate or excessive. The difference must be so great as to lead to a reasonable conclusion of fraud, mistake, or concealment in the nature of fraud, and to render it plainly inequitable and against conscience that the contract should be enforced.' " See also, e.g., In re Estate of Brown, 130 Ill.App.2d 514, 264 N.E.2d 287 (1970). Accordingly, a book-value formula may be disastrous for the selling shareholder or his estate where goodwill represents the most valuable component of the business—as is typical in non-capital-intensive enterprises, see, e.g., Jones v. Harris, 63 Wash.2d 559, 388 P.2d 539 (1964)—or where there is a significant disparity between historical costs and present values of tangible assets. See, e.g., S.C. Pohlman Co. v. Easterling, 211 Cal. App.2d 466, 27 Cal.Rptr. 450 (1962).

b. *Capitalized earnings.* A second common approach is to fix the price on the basis of a multiple of earnings. This approach is less likely than a book-value formula to produce an unfair price, but involves a number of drafting or interpretation problems, such as defining earnings and considering the impact of the selling shareholder's withdrawal on the value of the business.

c. *Periodic revisions.* A third common approach is to agree on a price when the provision is adopted, subject to periodic revision at agreed-upon intervals. This approach may lead to trouble when the parties fail to make periodic revisions through carelessness or inability to agree. In Helms v. Duckworth, 249 F.2d 482 (D.C.Cir.1957), Easterday, age 70, and Duckworth, age 37, formed a corporation and agreed that when one of them died his stock would be sold to the other at $10 a share, which was then a fair price, "provided, however, that such sale and purchase price may, from time to time, be re-determined . . . [annually] by an instrument in writing signed by the parties. . . ." When Easterday died six years later, the price had never been adjusted, although the actual value of the stock had risen to $80 a share. Easterday's administratrix brought suit to declare the agreement void, and Duckworth submitted an affidavit in which he stated that it was never his intention to consent to any change in the price provision. The district court granted summary judgment to Duckworth, but the Court of Appeals reversed:

> . . . Plainly [the agreement] implied a periodic bargaining or negotiating process in which each party must participate in good faith. . . .

> . . . We believe that the holders of closely held stock in a corporation such as shown here bear a fiduciary duty to deal fairly, honestly, and openly with their fellow stockholders and to make disclosure of all essential information.

> . . . [T]he very nature of Duckworth's secret intent was such that it had to be kept secret and undisclosed or it would fail of its purpose. . . . [Duckworth's] failure to disclose to his corporate business "partner" his fixed intent never to alter the original price constitutes a flagrant breach of a fiduciary duty. Standing alone this warrants cancellation of the agreement by a court of equity.

d. *Appraisal.* A fourth approach is to provide for appraisal by a third party at the time the option is triggered. See, e.g., Ginsberg v. Coating Products, Inc., 152 Conn. 592, 210 A.2d 667 (1965). This approach has the advantage of flexibility, but it may be coupled with an agreed-upon standard of valuation that can turn out to have unforeseen and undesired results.

5. *The UCC.* Uniform Commercial Code Article 8 deals with investment securities. Section 8–204 provides that "A restriction on transfer of a security imposed by the issuer, even if otherwise lawful, is

ineffective against a person without knowledge of the restriction unless: (1) the security is certificated and the restriction is noted conspicuously on the security certificate; or (2) the security is uncertif- icated and the registered owner has been notified of the restriction."

———

Gallagher v. Lambert

New York Court of Appeals, 1989.
74 N.Y.2d 562, 549 N.Y.S.2d 945, 549 N.E.2d 136.

OPINION OF THE COURT

■ BELLACOSA, JUDGE.

Plaintiff Gallagher purchased stock in the defendant close corpo- ration with which he was employed. The purchase of his 8.5% interest was subject to a mandatory buy-back provision: if the employment ended for any reason before January 31, 1985, the stock would return to the corporation for book value. The corporation fired plaintiff prior to the fulcrum date, after which the buy-back price would have been higher.

We must decide whether plaintiff's dismissed causes of action, seeking the higher repurchase price based on an alleged breach of a fiduciary duty, should be reinstated. We think not and affirm, conclud- ing that the Appellate Division did not err in dismissing these causes of action by summary judgment because there was no cognizable breach of any fiduciary duty owed to plaintiff under the plain terms of the parties' repurchase agreement.

Gallagher was employed by defendant Eastdil Realty as a mortgage broker from 1968 to 1973. Three years later, in 1976, he returned to the company as a broker, officer and director, serving additionally as president and chief executive officer of defendant's wholly owned subsidiary, Eastdil Advisors, Inc. Gallagher was at all times an employ- ee at will. Still later, in 1981, Eastdil offered all its executive employees an opportunity to purchase stock subject to a mandatory buy-back provision, which provided that upon "voluntary resignation or other termination" prior to January 31, 1985, an employee would be re- quired to return the stock for book value. After that date, the formula for the buy-back price was keyed to the company's earnings. Plaintiff accepted the offer and its terms.

On January 10, 1985, Gallagher was fired by Eastdil Realty. He did not and does not now contest the firing. But he demanded payment for his shares calculated on the post-January 31, 1985 buy-back formula. Eastdil refused and Gallagher sued, asserting eight causes of action. Only three claims, based on an alleged breach of fiduciary duty of good faith and fair dealing, are before us. The trial court denied defendants' motion for summary judgment on these claims, stating that factual issues were raised relating to defendants' motive in firing plaintiff. The Appellate Division, by divided vote, reversed, dismissed those claims and ordered payment for the shares at book value. 143

A.D.2d 313, 532 N.Y.S.2d 255. That court then granted leave and certified the following question to us: "Was the order of this Court, which modified the order of the Supreme Court, properly made?"

The parties negotiated a written contract containing a common and plain buy-back provision. Plaintiff got what he bargained for—book value for his minority shares if his employment in the corporation ended before January 31, 1985. There being no basis presented for the courts to interfere with the operation and consequences of this agreement between the parties, the order of the Appellate Division granting summary judgment to defendants, dismissing the first three causes of action, should be affirmed and the certified question answered in the affirmative. . . .

Accordingly, the order of the Appellate Division should be affirmed, with costs, and the certified question answered in the affirmative.

[The concurring opinion of Judge Hancock is omitted.]

■ KAYE, JUDGE (dissenting).

In summer 1984, Gallagher received 8.5% of Eastdil's stock, becoming the third largest shareholder, and he executed an amended stockholders' agreement. The agreement [provided] for mandatory repurchase at book value upon "voluntary resignation or other termination" of employment. But it also stipulated that after January 31, 1985, the buy-out price would be calculated by an escalating formula based on the company's earnings and the length of the shareholder's employment. According to Gallagher, the new buy-out price represented "golden handcuffs" designed to induce employees to remain on, at least until January 31, 1985.

On January 10, 1985—just 21 days before the new valuation formula became effective—Gallagher was fired and Eastdil invoked its right to repurchase his stock at book value. According to Gallagher, book value for the shares was $89,000; the price under the new valuation formula would have been around $3,000,000. . . .

Gallagher alleges that defendants had no bona fide, business-related reason to terminate his employment when they did—assertions we must accept as true on this summary judgment motion. He charges that defendants fired him for the sole purpose of recapturing his shares at an unfairly low price and redistributing them among themselves. . . .

If plaintiff were a minority shareholder, but not an employee, defendants would be barred from acting selfishly and opportunistically, for no corporate purpose, as he alleges they did. The controlling stockholders in a close corporation stand, in relation to minority owners, in the same fiduciary position as corporate directors generally, and are held "to the extreme measure of candor, unselfishness and good faith." (*Kavanaugh v. Kavanaugh Knitting Co.*, 226 N.Y. 185, 193, 123 N.E. 148.) Although, without more, the courts will not interfere when parties have set the repurchase price at book value (*Allen v. Biltmore Tissue Corp.*, 2 N.Y.2d 534, 542–543, 161 N.Y.S.2d

418, 141 N.E.2d 812), here plaintiff asserts there was more. The corporation agreed, commencing January 31, 1985, to pay a higher price, said to be more reflective of the true value of defendant's shares. Defendants' invocation of the pre-January 31 repurchase price was adverse to plaintiff's interests as a minority stockholder, and therefore subject to a standard of good faith under the foregoing principles. . . .

Defendants' broad interpretation of the "other termination" language of the repurchase clause amounts to an assertion that plaintiff agreed to waive substantial rights he might otherwise have possessed as a minority shareholder. However, in the absence of evidence that plaintiff knowingly assented to such a waiver, I cannot agree that the general language of the clause unambiguously expresses an understanding that the option could be exploited for the sole personal gain of the controlling shareholders in derogation of their fiduciary obligations to minority shareholders. Notably, the repurchase clause contains no reference to plaintiff's at-will employment status and no reservation of defendant's right to discharge plaintiff for any reason at all.

Moreover, defendants' interpretation denies that defendants themselves had any duty of good faith in connection with the shareholders' agreement. We have said that "there is an implied covenant that neither party shall do anything which will have the effect of destroying or injuring the right of the other party to receive the fruits of the contract, which means that in every contract there exists an implied covenant of good faith and fair dealing." (*Kirke La Shelle Co. v. Paul Armstrong Co.*, 263 N.Y. 79, 87, 188 N.E. 163.) This general rule does not apply to at-will employment relationships, as "it would be incongruous to say that an inference may be drawn that the employer impliedly agreed to a provision which would be destructive of his right of termination." (*Murphy v. American Home Prods. Corp.*, 58 N.Y.2d 293, 304–305, 461 N.Y.S.2d 232, 448 N.E.2d 86.) It does not follow, however, that there can be no covenant of good faith implicit in the shareholders' agreement that gives rise to obligations surviving termination of the employment relationship.

Assuming plaintiff's claims about the purpose of the amendments to be true, the expectations and relationship of the parties, as structured by the shareholders' agreement, dictate an implied contractual obligation of good faith, notwithstanding that there is none in their employment relationship (*see, Wakefield v. Northern Telecom*, 769 F.2d 109 [2d Cir.]). A covenant of good faith is anomalous in the context of at-will employment because performance and entitlement to benefits are simultaneous. Termination even without cause does not operate to deprive the employee of the benefits promised in return for performance.

But the alleged "golden handcuffs" agreement is different. An implied covenant of good faith *is* necessary to enable the employee to receive the benefits promised for performance. As one court noted, "an unfettered right to avoid payment * * * creates incentives counterproductive to the purpose of the contract itself in that the better the performance by the employee, the greater the temptation to terminate." (*Wakefield v. Northern Telecom, supra*, at 112–113; Note, *Exercising Options to Repurchase Employee–Held Stock: A Question of Good Faith*, 68 Yale L.J. 773, 779 [1959].) . . .

IV.

Denial of summary judgment would deprive defendants of no legitimate expectation or right, contractual or otherwise. Under the law, they remain free to terminate plaintiff's employment as agreed; they remain free to buy back his stock at book value as agreed—so long as there is a corporate purpose for their conduct. What controlling shareholders cannot do to a minority shareholder is take action against him solely for the self-aggrandizing, opportunistic purpose of themselves acquiring his shares at the low price, and they cannot do this because in the law it means something to be a shareholder, particularly a minority shareholder. . . .

■ SIMONS, ALEXANDER and TITONE, JJ., concur with BELLACOSA, J.

■ HANCOCK, J., concurs in a separate opinion.

■ KAYE, J., dissents and votes to reverse in another opinion in which WACHTLER, C.J., concurs.

Order affirmed, etc.

———

JENSEN v. CHRISTENSEN & LEE INSURANCE, INC., 157 Wis.2d 758, 460 N.W.2d 441 (App.1990). In this case, the court held that a shareholder who was discharged from his corporate position did not have an action for wrongful discharge, as such, because in Wisconsin actions for wrongful discharge are limited to discharges that violate public policy. However, the court added, the shareholder's allegations that his discharge triggered a stock buyout at a low purchase price that redounded to the financial benefit of the remaining shareholder-directors stated a claim that those directors had breached their fiduciary duties by failing to deal fairly in a matter in which they had a material conflict of interest.

———

JORDAN v. DUFF AND PHELPS, INC., 815 F.2d 429 (7th Cir. 1987). Duff & Phelps, Inc. was in the business of evaluating the risk and worth of firms and their securities. It sold credit ratings, investment research, and financial consulting services to both the firms under scrutiny and potential investors in those firms. Jordan started work at Duff & Phelps's Chicago office in May 1977, and was viewed as a successful securities analyst. In 1981, Duff & Phelps offered Jordan the opportunity to buy some of its stock. By November 1983, Jordan had purchased 188 of the 20,100 shares outstanding, and he was making installment payments on another 62 shares. Forty persons other than Jordan held stock in Duff & Phelps.

Jordan had purchased his stock at its book value. Before selling him any stock, Duff & Phelps required Jordan to sign a Stock Restriction and Purchase Agreement. This Agreement provided in part:

> Upon the termination of any employment with the Corporation ... for any reason, including resignation, discharge, death, disability or retirement, the individual whose employment is terminated or his estate shall sell to the Corporation, and the Corporation shall buy, all Shares of the Corporation then owned by such individual or his estate. The price to be paid for such Shares shall be equal to the adjusted book value (as hereinafter defined) of the Shares on the December 31 which coincides with, or immediately precedes, the date of termination of such individual's employment.

In late 1983, Jordan wanted to leave Duff & Phelps because tensions between his wife and his mother made it necessary for him to leave Chicago. Another firm, Underwood, offered Jordan a job at a salary substantially greater than his salary at Duff & Phelps. Jordan orally accepted, but Underwood would have allowed Jordan to withdraw his oral acceptance. On November 16, 1983, Jordan told Hansen, the chairman of Duff & Phelps's board, that he was going to resign and accept employment with Underwood. Jordan then delivered a letter of resignation, which Duff & Phelps accepted the same day. By mutual agreement, Jordan worked for Duff & Phelps the rest of the year, so that he could receive the book value of the stock as of December 31, 1983. (Under the Stock Restriction and Purchase Agreement, a departure before that date would have meant a valuation as of December 31, 1982.) Jordan delivered his stock certificates on December 30, 1983, and Duff & Phelps then mailed him a check for $23,225, the book value of the 188 shares of stock at $123.54 per share. Jordan surrendered, as worthless under the circumstances, the right to buy the remaining 62 shares on which he had been making installment payments.

On January 10, 1984, a merger was announced between Duff & Phelps and a subsidiary of Security Pacific. Under the terms of the merger Duff & Phelps was valued at $50 million. Hansen, the chairman of Duff & Phelps's board, had known on November 16 that negotiations for the merger were in process, but hadn't disclosed that fact to Jordan. If Jordan had been a Duff & Phelps employee on January 10, had still held his 188 shares, and had quickly paid for the additional 62 shares, and if the merger had closed that day, Jordan would have received $452,000 in cash and the opportunity to obtain as much as $194,000 more in an "earn out" (a percentage of Duff & Phelps's future profits to be paid to the former investors under the merger agreement), instead of the $23,225 he actually received. When Jordan learned these facts he demanded his stock back, but Duff & Phelps declined to return it. Jordan then sued Duff & Phelps, asking for damages measured by the value his stock would have had under the terms of the merger. The trial court granted summary judgement for Duff & Phelps. The Seventh Circuit reversed. Judge Easterbrook stated his reasons for reversal as follows:

A jury could find that the information withheld on November 16 is "material". A jury also could find that December 30, rather than November 16, is the date of the "sale" of the stock. If December 30 is the date of sale, the information withheld then was "material" ... as a matter of law. By then the negotiating teams for Duff & Phelps and Security Pacific had negotiated the price and structure of the deal. So there are two linked materiality questions for the jury: whether the information withheld on November 16 was material, and whether the sale took place on November 16 or December 30.

Duff & Phelps insists that nothing after November 16 matters.... Duff & Phelps treats the letter of resignation on November 16 as an irrevocable sale with deferred delivery. Yet if the "sale" occurred on November 16, then under the Agreement the stock would have been valued as of December 31, 1982. That Duff & Phelps valued the stock as of December 31, 1983, may persuade a jury that it treated the "sale" as made on that date. Moreover, Jordan insists that other employees were allowed to withdraw their resignations, and that he could have done so as late as December 31—if, say, his wife and his mother had reconciled.... The terms on which resignations may be withdrawn may be implicit parts of the relations between Duff & Phelps and its employees, and Jordan is entitled to an opportunity to demonstrate that he could have remained at the firm. If he can prove this, then December 30 rather than November 16 is the date on which the materiality of the firm's omissions must be assessed.

All of this supposes that Duff & Phelps had a duty to disclose anything to Jordan. Most people are free to buy and sell stock on the basis of valuable private knowledge without informing their trading partners. Strangers transact in markets all the time using private information that might be called "material" and, unless one has a duty to disclose, both may keep their counsel.

This argument is unavailing on the facts as we know them. The "duty" in question is the fiduciary duty of corporate law. Close corporations buying their own stock, like knowledgeable insiders of closely held firms buying from outsiders, have a fiduciary duty to disclose material facts....

... Jordan ... exercised choice about the date on which the formula would be triggered. He could have remained at Duff & Phelps; his decision to depart was affected by his wife's distress, his salary, his working conditions, the enjoyment he received from the job, and the value of his stock. The departure of such an employee is an investment decision as much as it is an employment decision. It is not fanciful to suppose that Mrs. Jordan would have found her mother in law a whole lot more tolerable if she had known that Jordan's stock might shortly be worth 20 times book value.

... That [Jordan] took the value of stock into account is evident from the timing of his departure. A few thousand dollars' increase in book value led the Jordans to stay in Chicago an extra six weeks. How long would they have stayed for the prospect of another $620,000?

Our dissenting colleague concludes that all of this is beside the point because Hansen could have said, on receiving Jordan's letter on November 16: "In a few weeks we will pull off a merger that would have made your stock 20 times more valuable. It's a shame you so foolishly resigned. But even if you hadn't resigned, we would have fired you, the better to engross the profits of the merger for ourselves. So long, sucker." This would have been permissible, under our colleague's interpretation, because Jordan was an employee at will and therefore could have been fired at any time, even the day before the merger, for any reason—including the desire to deprive Jordan of a share of the profits. The ability to fire Jordan enabled the firm to "call" his shares, at book value, on whim. On this view, it is foolish to say that Duff & Phelps had a duty to disclose, because disclosure would have been no use to Jordan. (Perhaps this is really an argument about "causation" rather than "duty," but the terminology is unimportant.) But Duff & Phelps itself does not press this argument, and in civil litigation an appellate court ought not put words in a party's mouth and use them as the grounds on which to decide.... Perhaps Duff & Phelps does not want to establish a reputation for shoddy dealing; as our dissenting brother observes, a firm's desire to preserve its reputation is a powerful inducement to treat its contractual partners well. To attribute to a litigant an argument that it will take every possible advantage is to assume that the party wishes to dissipate its reputation, and the assumption is unwarranted.

More than that, a person's status as an employee "at will" does not imply that the employer may discharge him for every reason. Illinois, where Jordan was employed, has placed some limits on the discharge of at-will employees.... We do not disparage the utility of at-will contracts; this very panel recently recognized the value of informal (meaning not legally binding) employment relations.... But employment "at will" is still a contractual relation, one in which a particular duration (at will) is implied in the absence of a contrary expression. E. Allan Farnsworth, Contracts 532 n. 29 (1982). The silence of the parties may make it necessary to imply other terms—those we are confident the parties would have bargained for if they had signed a written agreement. One term implied in every written contract and therefore, we suppose, every unwritten one, is that neither party will try to take opportunistic advantage of the other. "[T]he fundamental function of contract law (and recognized as such at least since Hobbes's day) is to deter people from behaving opportunistically toward their contracting parties, in order to encourage the optimal timing of economic activity and to make costly self-protective measures unnecessary." . . .

Employment creates occasions for opportunism. A firm may fire an employee the day before his pension vests, or a salesman the day before a large commission becomes payable. Cases of this sort may present difficult questions about the reasons for the decision (was it opportunism, or was it a decline in the employee's performance?). The difficulties of separating opportunistic conduct from honest differences of opinion about an employee's performance on the job may lead firms and their employees to transact on terms that keep such disputes out of court—which employment at will usually does. But no one . . . doubts that an *avowedly* opportunistic discharge is a breach of contract, although the employment is at-will. . . . The element of good faith dealing implied in a contract "is not an enforceable legal duty to be nice or to behave decently in a general way." . . . It is not a version of the Golden Rule, to regard the interests of one's contracting partner the same way you regard your own. An employer may be thoughtless, nasty, and mistaken. Avowedly opportunistic conduct has been treated differently, however.

The stock component in Jordan's package induced him to stick around and work well. Such an inducement is effective only if the employee reaps the rewards of success as well as the penalties of failure. We do not suppose for a second that if Jordan had not resigned on November 16, the firm could have fired him on January 9 with a little note saying: "Dear Mr. Jordan: There will be a lucrative merger tomorrow. You have been a wonderful employee, but in order to keep the proceeds of the merger for ourselves, we are letting you go, effective this instant. Here is the $23,000 for your shares." Had the firm fired Jordan for this stated reason, it would have broken an implied pledge to avoid opportunistic conduct. It may well be that Duff & Phelps could have fired Jordan without the slightest judicial inquiry; it does not follow that an opportunistic discharge would have allowed Duff & Phelps to cash out the stock on the eve of its appreciation. . . . Jordan's employment at will, the essential ingredient of our colleague's argument that Jordan waived the duty to disclose, does not establish that the firm had no duties concerning the stock.*

■ Judge Cudahy concurred; Judge Posner dissented.

SECTION 8.   DISSOLUTION FOR DEADLOCK

---

* Accord: Castellano v. Young & Rubicam, Inc., 257 F.3d 171 (2d Cir. 2001) (footnote by ed.).

DEL. GEN. CORP. LAW §§ 273, 355

[See Statutory Supplement]

MODEL BUS. CORP. ACT §§ 14.30, 14.34

[See Statutory Supplement]

N.Y. BUS. CORP. LAW §§ 1002, 1104, 1111

[See Statutory Supplement]

Wollman v. Littman

New York Supreme Court, Appellate Div., First Dept., 1970.
35 A.D.2d 935, 316 N.Y.S.2d 526.

■ PER CURIAM . . .

The stock of the corporation is held, fifty percent each, by two distinct groups, one of which, the Nierenberg sisters, are plaintiffs, and the other, the Littmans, defendants, each group having equal representation on the board of directors. The corporation's business is the selling of artificial fur fabrics to garment manufacturers. Defendants, the Littmans, allegedly had the idea for the business and developed a market for the fabrics among its manufacturing customers. Plaintiffs are the daughters of Louis Nierenberg, the main stockholder of Louis Nierenberg, Inc., who procures the fabrics and sells them to the corporation. The Littmans, in a separate action in which they are plaintiffs, charge the plaintiffs here (the Nierenberg sisters) and Louis Nierenberg Corporation with seeking to lure away the corporation's customers for Louis Nierenberg Corporation and with doing various acts to affect the corporation's business adversely. The Nierenberg faction countered with this suit, claiming that the bringing of the other action indicates that the corporate management is at such odds among themselves that effective management is impossible. Special Term agreed, but we do not. Irreconcilable differences even among an evenly divided board of directors do not in all cases mandate dissolution. . . . Here, two factors would require further exploration. The first is that the functions of the two disputing interests are distinct, one selling and the other procuring, and each can pursue its own without need for collaboration. The second is that a dissolution which will render nugatory the relief sought in the representative action would actually accomplish the wrongful purpose that defendants (Nierenberg) are charged with in that action. It would not only squeeze the Littmans out of the business but would require the receiver to dispose of the inventory with the Nierenbergs the only interested purchaser financially strong enough to take advantage of the situation. Such a result, if supported by the facts, would be intolerable to a court of equity. A trial of the issues is necessitated. On that trial it has been agreed by both counsel it would be advantageous to have the representative action and the action for dissolution tried together, though not consolidated (for a discussion of the distinction, see the comprehensive opinion in Padilla v. Greyhound Lines, 29 A.D.2d 495, 288 N.Y.S.2d 641), and it is so directed.

We affirm the appointment of a receiver. His function, however, should be limited to the necessities indicated, namely, to the orderly functioning of the regular course of business of the corporation until the further order of the court.

NOTE ON DISSOLUTION FOR DEADLOCK

1. A number of statutes provide for involuntary dissolution on a showing of deadlock. A few of the statutes define deadlock in terms of an "equally divided" board or body of shareholders, but most are phrased broadly enough to include deadlock brought about by super-majority or veto arrangements.

2. The deadlock statutes are generally interpreted to make dissolution discretionary even when deadlock is shown to exist, and the courts have often been reluctant to order the dissolution of a profitable corporation on deadlock grounds. However, profitability is not a *bar* to dissolution for deadlock. In Weiss v. Gordon, 32 A.D.2d 279, 301 N.Y.S.2d 839 (1969), the court stated, "The earlier thinking stressed the distinction between the corporation as an entity and the shareholders, and as long as the former could continue to function profitably the relationship between the shareholders was of no moment (cf. Matter of Radom & Neidorff, Inc., 307 N.Y. 1, 119 N.E.2d 563 (1954)). It is being increasingly realized that the relationship between the stockholders in a close corporation vis-a-vis each other in practice closely approximates the relationship between partners (see Mtr. of Surchin v. Approved Bus. Mach., 55 Misc.2d 888, 890, 286 N.Y.S.2d 580, 583 (1967)). As a consequence, when a point is reached where the shareholders who are actively conducting the business of the corporation cannot agree, it becomes in the best interests of those shareholders to order a dissolution. . . ."

SECTION 9.   PROVISIONAL DIRECTORS, AND CUSTODIANS

DEL. GEN. CORP. LAW §§ 226, 352, 353

[See Statutory Supplement]

CAL. CORP. CODE §§ 308, 1802

[See Statutory Supplement]

———

GIURICICH v. EMTROL CORP., 449 A.2d 232 (Del.1982). Plaintiffs owned 50% of the stock of Emtrol Corporation. Continental Boilerworks, Inc. controlled the other 50%. Plaintiffs petitioned the Delaware Court of Chancery for the appointment of a custodian pursuant to Del.Gen.Corp.Law § 226(a)(1), based on a shareholder deadlock between the plaintiffs and Continental. Appointment of a custodian was refused by the trial court, despite the existence of a shareholder deadlock preventing the election of successor directors, on the ground that there had been no injury to any vital interests of plaintiffs as stockholders or to Emtrol. Reversed.

... By § 226(a)(1), the Legislature has created a viable remedy for the injustices arising from a shareholder-deadlock which permits control of a corporation to remain indefinitely in the hands of a self-perpetuating board of directors, any gross unfairness to other major stockholders notwithstanding....

A custodian will be appointed by the Court of Chancery under § 226(a)(1) who is strictly impartial and has a proven business and executive background. The custodian will be empowered to act only in situations in which the board of directors of Emtrol have failed to reach a unanimous decision on any issue properly before them. In the event that the board is unable to reach unanimous accord on any such pending issue, the custodian will resolve the issue in such manner as he shall deem appropriate. His decision and action in such case shall be binding upon the officers and directors of Emtrol, and shall be deemed the official action of the corporation. The custodian may call a directors' meeting, or a stockholders' meeting, *sua sponte* or at the request of any director. The custodian shall serve for such time as the Court of Chancery shall deem necessary, or until there is a unanimous request to the Court for his discharge by all shareholders of Emtrol. The compensation of the custodian will be approved by the Court of Chancery and paid by Emtrol....

———

THOMPSON, THE SHAREHOLDER'S CAUSE OF ACTION FOR OPPRESSION, 48 Bus.Law. 699, 723 (1993). "[More than half of the states have added to the remedies available in shareholder disputes by providing for the appointment of a custodian. About twenty states authorize a court to appoint a provisional director to help resolve shareholder disputes.] ... Despite their widespread inclusion in statutes, these remedies are not used often. [The remedy is more important in states like Delaware, where it is the only effective remedy for shareholder dissension.] There is a cost to an additional layer of management, which would unduly burden a small enterprise, and the appointment of an outside party may not address the underlying differences among the participants."*

NOTE ON PROVISIONAL DIRECTORS AND CUSTODIANS

1. The appointment of a provisional director may enable one faction to make changes in the control structure of the corporation whose effects will persist even after the provisional director has left the scene. For example, in In re Jamison Steel Corp., 158 Cal.App.2d 27, 322 P.2d 246 (1958), one faction controlled 240 shares of stock, and the other controlled the remaining 160 shares. Under the corporation's articles, the board consisted of four directors, and under cumulative voting each faction could elect two of the four. Board meetings in December 1955 and December 1956 resulted in tie votes on several issues, including elections to certain offices and the size of the dividend. After the 1955 meeting, the majority faction petitioned the court for the appointment of a provisional director on the ground of deadlock. The lower court appointed a provisional director with authority to vote for an amendment to the articles of incorporation. The California Supreme Court affirmed, although recognizing that the provisional director might vote with the majority's two directors to increase the board to five, and thereby permanently alter the balance of power.

2. The distinctive aspect of the remedy of appointing a custodian is that unlike the remedy of dissolution, the business continues, and unlike the remedy of appointing a provisional director, the custodian normally has complete authority over the business.

3. Hetherington & Dooley argue that the provisional-director remedy is unsound:

> No state or public interest appears to justify [appointing a provisional director and thereby] depriving the resisting party of the right to veto corporate decisions. The power to veto is an important property right, to which the resisting party is entitled by virtue of his shareholdings. It is the best protection against exploitation and oppression that a shareholder in a close corporation can have, short of the power to impose his will on the other party.... The faction that has the support of the provisional director has little or no incentive to seek to settle its differences with the minority faction.

Hetherington & Dooley, Illiquidity and Exploitation: A Proposed Statutory Solution to the Remaining Close. Corporation Problem, 63 Va. L.Rev. 1, 21–22 (1977).

* The material in brackets has been transposed from footnotes to text. (Footnote by ed.)

SECTION 10.   DISSOLUTION FOR OPPRESSION, AND MANDATORY BUY-OUT

MODEL BUS. CORP. ACT § 14.30, 14.34

[See Statutory Supplement]

CAL. CORP. CODE §§ 1800, 1804, 2000

[See Statutory Supplement]

N.Y. BUS. CORP. LAW §§ 1104–a, 1111, 1118

[See Statutory Supplement]

NOTE ON HETHERINGTON AND DOOLEY

At one time, courts were extremely reluctant to order the involuntary dissolution of a profitable business, on the ground that it was bad social policy to break up such a business. In 1977, John Hetherington and Michael Dooley published a celebrated article on this problem, Illiquidity and Exploitation: A Proposed Statutory Solution to the Remaining Close Corporation Problem, 63 Va.L.Rev. 1 (1977). In this article, the authors pointed out that a judicial order to dissolve a corporation was unlikely to lead to the breakup of a profitable business. The reason is that if it is advantageous to continue a business, then after dissolution is ordered, normally one or more of the shareholders, or a third party, would purchase and continue the business. Hetherington & Dooley backed up this point with empirical data, by analyzing the fifty-four reported involuntary dissolution cases decided between 1960 and 1976. In half of the fifty-four cases, the plaintiff had been successful; in half, unsuccessful. Of the twenty-seven cases in which the plaintiff had been successful, the corporation was actually liquidated in only six. In seventeen of these twenty-seven cases, one party bought out the other. In three of the cases, the business was sold to an outsider. In one case, there was no buyout or other change. (In fourteen of the twenty-seven cases in which plaintiff was unsuccessful, one party bought out the other. In six of the cases, there was no change in ownership. In two of the cases, the business was sold to a third party. In three of the cases, the business was liquidated. In two of the cases, the result was unknown.)

Furthermore, Hetherington & Dooley pointed out, dissolution, or something like it, was a central remedy for disaffected shareholders in close corporations because, given the limits of reasonable foreseeability, shareholders who organized such corporations could not possibly plan in advance to deal with all the interpersonal problems that might occur between them. Therefore, Hetherington & Dooley concluded, in the case of a close corporation a remedy comparable to but stronger than dissolution—specifically, free exit through a mandatory buyout of the minority's interest on the minoroty's demand—should be available.

The emphasis on contractual arrangements [in close corporations] reveals a fundamental misunderstanding of the nature of close corporations. Whether the parties adopt special contractual arrangements is much less important than their ability to sustain a close, harmonious relationship over time. The continuance of such a relationship is crucial because it reflects what is perhaps the fundamental assumption made by those who decide to invest in a close corporation: they expect that during the life of the firm the shareholders will be in substantial agreement as to its operation.

Time and human nature may cause a divergence of interests and a breakdown in consensus, however. . . .

Our thesis is that the problem of exploitation is uniquely related to liquidity and, for that reason, it is resistant to solution by ex ante contractual arrangements or by ex post judicial relief for breach of fiduciary duty. Accordingly, we [propose that the law should require] the majority to repurchase the minority's interest at the request of the latter and subject to appropriate safeguards.

The insights and empirical data in the Hetherington & Dooley article form a backdrop to the materials in this section.

Matter of Kemp & Beatley, Inc.

Court of Appeals of New York, 1984.
64 N.Y.2d 63, 484 N.Y.S.2d 799, 473 N.E.2d 1173.

■ COOKE, CHIEF JUDGE. . . .

I

The business concern of Kemp & Beatley, incorporated under the laws of New York, designs and manufactures table linens and sundry tabletop items. The company's stock consists of 1,500 outstanding shares held by eight shareholders. Petitioner Dissin had been employed by the company for 42 years when, in June 1979, he resigned. Prior to resignation, Dissin served as vice-president and a director of Kemp & Beatley. Over the course of his employment, Dissin had acquired stock in the company and currently owns 200 shares.

Petitioner Gardstein, like Dissin, had been a long-time employee of the company. Hired in 1944, Gardstein was for the next 35 years involved in various aspects of the business including material procurement, product design, and plant management. His employment was terminated by the company in December 1980. He currently owns 105 shares of Kemp & Beatley stock.

Apparent unhappiness surrounded petitioners' leaving the employ of the company. Of particular concern was that they no longer received any distribution of the company's earnings. Petitioners considered themselves to be "frozen out" of the company; whereas it had been their experience when with the company to receive a distribution of the company's earnings according to their stockholdings, in the form of either dividends or extra compensation, that distribution was no longer forthcoming.

Gardstein and Dissin, together holding 20.33% of the company's outstanding stock, commenced the instant proceeding in June 1981, seeking dissolution of Kemp & Beatley pursuant to section 1104–a of the Business Corporation Law. Their petition alleged "fraudulent and oppressive" conduct by the company's board of directors such as to render petitioners' stock "a virtually worthless asset." Supreme Court referred the matter for a hearing, which was held in March 1982.

Upon considering the testimony of petitioners and the principals of Kemp & Beatley, the referee concluded that "the corporate management has by its policies effectively rendered petitioners' shares worthless, and ... the only way petitioners can expect any return is by dissolution". Petitioners were found to have invested capital in the company expecting, among other things, to receive dividends or "bonuses" based upon their stock holdings. Also found was the company's "established buyout policy" by which it would purchase the stock of employee shareholders upon their leaving its employ.

The involuntary-dissolution statute (Business Corporation Law, § 1104–a) permits dissolution when a corporation's controlling faction is found guilty of "oppressive action" toward the complaining shareholders. The referee considered oppression to arise when "those in control" of the corporation "have acted in such a manner as to defeat those expectations of the minority stockholders which formed the basis of [their] participation in the venture." The expectations of petitioners that they would not be arbitrarily excluded from gaining a return on their investment and that their stock would be purchased by the corporation upon termination of employment, were deemed defeated by prevailing corporate policies. Dissolution was recommended in the referee's report, subject to giving respondent corporation an opportunity to purchase petitioners' stock.

Supreme Court confirmed the referee's report. It, too, concluded that due to the corporation's new dividend policy petitioners had been prevented from receiving any return on their investments. Liquidation of the corporate assets was found the only means by which petitioners would receive a fair return. The court considered judicial dissolution of a corporation to be "a serious and severe remedy."

Consequently, the order of dissolution was conditioned upon the corporation's being permitted to purchase petitioners' stock. The Appellate Division affirmed, without opinion. 99 A.D.2d 445, 471 N.Y.S.2d 245.

At issue in this appeal is the scope of section 1104–a of the Business Corporation Law. Specifically, this court must determine whether the provision for involuntary dissolution when the "directors or those in control of the corporation have been guilty of ... oppressive actions toward the complaining shareholders" was properly applied in the circumstances of this case. We hold that it was, and therefore affirm.

II

Judicially ordered dissolution of a corporation at the behest of minority interests is a remedy of relatively recent vintage in New York. Historically, this State's courts were considered divested of equity jurisdiction to order dissolution, as statutory prescriptions were deemed exclusive (see Hitch v. Hawley, 132 N.Y. 212, 217, 30 N.E. 401). . . .

... [T]he Legislature has shown a special solicitude toward the rights of minority shareholders of closely held corporations by enacting section 1104–a of the Business Corporation Law. That statute provides a mechanism for the holders of at least 20% of the outstanding shares of a corporation whose stock is not traded on a securities market to petition for its dissolution "under special circumstances" (see Business Corporation Law, § 1104–a, subd. [a]). The circumstances that give rise to dissolution fall into two general classifications: mistreatment of complaining shareholders (subd. [a], par. [1]), or misappropriation of corporate assets (subd. [a], par. [2]) by controlling shareholders, directors or officers.

Section 1104–a (subd. [a], par. [1]) describes three types of proscribed activity: "illegal", "fraudulent", and "oppressive" conduct. The first two terms are familiar words that are commonly understood at law. The last, however, does not enjoy the same certainty gained through long usage. As no definition is provided by the statute, it falls upon the courts to provide guidance (see Goncalves v. Regent Int. Hotels, 58 N.Y.2d 206, 218, 460 N.Y.S.2d 750, 447 N.E.2d 693).

The statutory concept of "oppressive actions" can, perhaps, best be understood by examining the characteristics of close corporations and the Legislature's general purpose in creating this involuntary-dissolution statute. It is widely understood that, in addition to supplying capital to a contemplated or ongoing enterprise and expecting a fair and equal return, parties comprising the ownership of a close corporation may expect to be actively involved in its management and operation. . . . The small ownership cluster seeks to "contribute their capital, skills, experience and labor" toward the corporate enterprise. . . .

As a leading commentator in the field has observed: "Unlike the typical shareholder in a publicly held corporation, who may be simply an investor or a speculator and cares nothing for the responsibilities of management, the shareholder in a close corporation is a co-owner of the business and wants the privileges and powers that go with ownership. His participation in that particular corporation is often his principal or sole source of income. As a matter of fact, providing employment for himself may have been the principal reason why he participated in organizing the corporation. He may or may not anticipate an ultimate profit from the sale of his interest, but he normally draws very little from the corporation as dividends. In his capacity as an officer or employee of the corporation, he looks to his salary for the principal return on his capital investment, because earnings of a close corporation, as is well known, are distributed in major part in salaries, bonuses and retirement benefits." (O'Neal, Close Corporations [2d ed.], § 1.07, at pp. 21–22 [n. omitted].)

Shareholders enjoy flexibility in memorializing these expectations through agreements setting forth each party's rights and obligations in corporate governance (see, generally, Kessler, Shareholder–Managed Close Corporation Under the New York Business Corporation Law, 43 Fordham L.Rev. 197; Davidian, op. cit., 56 St. John's L.Rev. 24, 29–30, and nn. 21–22). In the absence of such an agreement, however, ultimate decision-making power respecting corporate policy will be reposed in the holders of a majority interest in the corporation (see, e.g., Business Corporation Law, §§ 614, 708). A wielding of this power by any group controlling a corporation may serve to destroy a stockholder's vital interests and expectations.

As the stock of closely held corporations generally is not readily salable, a minority shareholder at odds with management policies may be without either a voice in protecting his or her interests or any reasonable means of withdrawing his or her investment. This predicament may fairly be considered the legislative concern underlying the provision at issue in this case; inclusion of the criteria that the corporation's stock not be traded on securities markets and that the complaining shareholder be subject to oppressive actions supports this conclusion.

Defining oppressive conduct as distinct from illegality in the present context has been considered in other forums. The question has been resolved by considering oppressive actions to refer to conduct that substantially defeats the "reasonable expectations" held by minority shareholders in committing their capital to the particular enterprise (see, e.g., Mardikos v. Arger, 116 Misc.2d 1028, 457 N.Y.S.2d 371; Matter of Barry One Hour Photo Process, 111 Misc.2d 559, 444 N.Y.S.2d 540. . . .) This concept is consistent with the apparent purpose underlying the provision under review. A shareholder who reasonably expected that ownership in the corporation would entitle him or her to a job, a share of corporate earnings, a place in corporate management, or some other form of security, would be oppressed in a very real sense when others in the corporation seek to defeat those expectations and there exists no effective means of salvaging the investment.

Given the nature of close corporations and the remedial purpose of the statute, this court holds that utilizing a complaining shareholder's "reasonable expectations" as a means of identifying and measuring conduct alleged to be oppressive is appropriate. A court considering a petition alleging oppressive conduct must investigate what the majority shareholders knew, or should have known, to be the petitioner's expectations in entering the particular enterprise. Majority conduct should not be deemed oppressive simply because the petitioner's subjective hopes and desires in joining the venture are not fulfilled. Disappointment alone should not necessarily be equated with oppression.

Rather, oppression should be deemed to arise only when the majority conduct substantially defeats expectations that, objectively viewed, were both reasonable under the circumstances and were central to the petitioner's decision to join the venture. It would be inappropriate, however, for us in this case to delineate the contours of the courts' consideration in determining whether directors have been guilty of oppressive conduct. As in other areas of the law, much will depend on the circumstances in the individual case.

The appropriateness of an order of dissolution is in every case vested in the sound discretion of the court considering the application (see Business Corporation Law, § 1111, subd. [a]). Under the terms of this statute, courts are instructed to consider both whether "liquidation of the corporation is the only feasible means" to protect the complaining shareholder's expectation of a fair return on his or her investment and whether dissolution "is reasonably necessary" to protect "the rights or interests of any substantial number of shareholders" not limited to those complaining (Business Corporation Law, § 1104-a, subd. [b], pars. [1], [2]). Implicit in this direction is that once oppressive conduct is found, consideration must be given to the totality of circumstances surrounding the current state of corporate affairs and relations to determine whether some remedy short of or other than dissolution, constitutes a feasible means of satisfying both the petitioner's expectations and the rights and interests of any other substantial group of shareholders (see, also, Business Corporation Law, § 1111, subd. [b], par. [1]).

By invoking the statute, a petitioner has manifested his or her belief that dissolution may be the only appropriate remedy. Assuming the petitioner has set forth a prima facie case of oppressive conduct, it should be incumbent upon the parties seeking to forestall dissolution to demonstrate to the court the existence of an adequate, alternative remedy (cf. Baker v. Commercial Body Bldrs., 264 Or. 614, 507 P.2d 387, supra; White v. Perkins, 213 Va. 129, 189 S.E.2d 315). A court has broad latitude in fashioning alternative relief, but when fulfillment of the oppressed petitioner's expectations by these means is doubtful, such as when there has been a complete deterioration of relations between the parties, a court should not hesitate to order dissolution.

Every order of dissolution, however, must be conditioned upon permitting any shareholder of the corporation to elect to purchase the complaining shareholder's stock at fair value (see Business Corporation Law, § 1118).

One further observation is in order. The purpose of this involuntary dissolution statute is to provide protection to the minority shareholder whose reasonable expectations in undertaking the venture have been frustrated and who has no adequate means of recovering his or her investment. It would be contrary to this remedial purpose to permit its use by minority shareholders as merely a coercive tool (see Davidian, op. cit., 56 St. John's L.Rev. 24, 59–60, and nn. 159–160). Therefore, the minority shareholder whose own acts, made in bad faith and undertaken with a view toward forcing an involuntary dissolution, give rise to the complained-of oppression should be given no quarter in the statutory protection (cf. Mardikos v. Arger, 116 Misc.2d 1028, 1032, 457 N.Y.S.2d 371, supra).

III

There was sufficient evidence presented at the hearing to support the conclusion that Kemp & Beatley had a long-standing policy of awarding *de facto* dividends based on stock ownership in the form of "extra compensation bonuses." Petitioners, both of whom had extensive experience in the management of the company, testified to this effect. Moreover, both related that receipt of this compensation, whether as true dividends or disguised as "extra compensation", was a known incident to ownership of the company's stock understood by all of the company's principals. Finally, there was uncontroverted proof that this policy was changed either shortly before or shortly after petitioners' employment ended. Extra compensation was still awarded by the company. The only difference was that stock ownership was no longer a basis for the payments; it was asserted that the basis became services rendered to the corporation. It was not unreasonable for the fact finder to have determined that this change in policy amounted to nothing less than an attempt to exclude petitioners from gaining any return on their investment through the mere recharacterization of distributions of corporate income. Under the circumstances of this case, there was no error in determining that this conduct constituted oppressive action within the meaning of section 1104–a of the Business Corporation Law.

Nor may it be said that Supreme Court abused its discretion in ordering Kemp & Beatley's dissolution, subject to an opportunity for a buy-out of petitioners' shares. After the referee had found that the controlling faction of the company was, in effect, attempting to "squeeze-out" petitioners by offering them no return on their investment and increasing other executive compensation, respondents, in opposing the report's confirmation, attempted only to controvert the factual basis of the report. They suggested no feasible, alternative remedy to the forced dissolution. In light of an apparent deterioration in relations between petitioners and the governing shareholders of

Kemp & Beatley, it was not unreasonable for the court to have determined that a forced buy-out of petitioners' shares or liquidation of the corporation's assets was the only means by which petitioners could be guaranteed a fair return on their investments.

Accordingly, the order of the Appellate Division should be modified, with costs to petitioners-respondents, by affirming the substantive determination of that court but extending the time for exercising the option to purchase petitioners-respondents' shares to 30 days following this court's determination.

■ JASEN, JONES, WACHTLER, MEYER and SIMONS, JJ., concur.

■ KAYE, J., taking no part.

Order modified, with costs to petitioners-respondents, in accordance with the opinion herein and, as so modified, affirmed.

———

MEISELMAN v. MEISELMAN, 309 N.C. 279, 307 S.E.2d 551 (1983). "Professor O'Neal, perhaps the foremost authority on close corporations, points out that many close corporations are companies based on personal relationships that give rise to certain 'reasonable expectations' on the part of those acquiring an interest in the close corporation. Those 'reasonable expectations' include, for example, the parties' expectation that they will participate in the management of the business or be employed by the company. O'Neal, *Close Corporations: Existing Legislation and Recommended Reform,* 33 Bus.Law 873, 885 (1978) . . . .

"Thus, when personal relations among the participants in a close corporation break down, the 'reasonable expectations' the participants had, for example, an expectation that their employment would be secure, or that they would enjoy meaningful participation in the management of the business—become difficult if not impossible to fulfill. In other words, when the personal relationships among the participants break down, the majority shareholder, because of his greater voting power, is in a position to terminate the minority shareholder's employment and to exclude him from participation in management decisions.

"Some may argue that the minority shareholder should have bargained for greater protection before agreeing to accept his minority shareholder position in a close corporation. However, the practical realities of this particular business situation oftentimes do not allow for such negotiations. . . .

"Apparently in response to these commentators' uniform calls for reform in this area of corporate law, many state legislatures have enacted statutes giving the tribunals in their states the power to grant relief to minority shareholders under more liberal circumstances. . . .

"In helping to establish this growing trend toward enactment of more liberal grounds under which dissolution will be granted to a complaining shareholder, the legislature in this State enacted in 1955

N.C.G.S. § 55–125(a)(4), the statute granting superior court judges the 'power to liquidate the assets and business of a corporation in an action by a shareholder when it is established' that '[l]iquidation is reasonably necessary for the protection of the rights or interests of the complaining shareholder.' . . .

"[B]efore it can be determined whether, in any given case, it has been 'established' that liquidation is 'reasonably necessary' to protect the complaining shareholder's 'rights or interest,' the particular 'rights or interests' of the complaining shareholder must be articulated. This is so because N.C.G.S. § 55–125(a)(4) refers to the 'rights or interests' of *the complaining shareholder';* the statute does not refer to the 'rights or interests' of shareholders generally. . . . [W]e hold that a complaining shareholder's 'rights or interests' in a close corporation include the 'reasonable expectations' the complaining shareholder has in the corporation. These 'reasonable expectations' are to be ascertained by examining the entire history of the participants' relationship. That history will include the 'reasonable expectations' created at the inception of the participants' relationship; those 'reasonable expectations' as altered over time; and the 'reasonable expectations' which develop as the participants engage in a course of dealing in conducting the affairs of the corporation. The interests and views of the other participants must be considered in determining 'reasonable expectations.' The key is *'reasonable.'* In order for plaintiff's expectations to be reasonable, they must be known to or assumed by the other shareholders and concurred in by them. Privately held expectations which are not made known to the other participants are not 'reasonable.' Only expectations embodied in understandings, express or implied, among the participants should be recognized by the court. . . .

"Defendants argue, however, that . . . [a shareholder] is only entitled to relief if his traditional shareholder rights have been infringed. They contend that those traditional shareholder rights include the right to notice of stockholders' meetings, the right to vote cumulatively, the right of access to the corporate offices and to corporate financial information, and the right to compel the payment of dividends. . . .

"While it may be true that a shareholder in, for example, a publicly held corporation may have 'rights or interests' defined as defendants argue, a shareholder's rights in a closely held corporation may not necessarily be so narrowly defined. . . ."

––––––

NOTE ON EVOLVING EXPECTATIONS

In *Meiselman*, the court stated that what constitutes a shareholder's reasonable expectations can change over time. An example is A.W. Chesterton Co. v. Chesterton, 128 F.3d 1 (1st Cir.1997). Chesterton Co. had been a closely held corporation since 1885. In 1985, all the shareholders, including Arthur Chesterton, agreed to change the corporation's tax status under the Internal Revenue Code from a C corporation to an S corporation. In the early 1990s, Arthur Chesterton proposed to transfer some of his stock to two shell corporations that he wholly owned. To qualify for S Corporation status, a corporation may not have any shareholders who are themselves corporations. Therefore, Arthur Chesterton's proposed transfer would have resulted in a loss of J.W. Chesterton's favorable tax treatment under IRC subchapter S. Chesterton Co. and its other shareholders sued Arthur Chesterton to enjoin him from making the proposed transfer. The First Circuit granted the injunction. "Under Massachusetts law, the expectations and understanding of the shareholders are relevant to a breach of fiduciary duty determination ... The existence of the [1985] agreement ... sheds light on the Company's and other shareholders' expectations...." See also, e.g., Spurgeon Foster v. Foster Farms, 112 N.C.App. 700, 436 S.E.2d 843 (1993).

THOMPSON, THE SHAREHOLDER'S CAUSE OF ACTION FOR OPPRESSION, 48 Bus.Law. 699, 709–12, 715–716 (1993). "Oppression as a ground for dissolution was included in the Illinois and Pennsylvania corporations acts in 1933, in the first Model Business Corporation Act in 1946, and in the English Companies Act of 1948. Thirty-seven American states now include oppression or a similar term in their corporations statutes...."

HAYNSWORTH, THE EFFECTIVENESS OF INVOLUNTARY DISSOLUTION SUITS AS A REMEDY FOR CLOSE CORPORATION DISSENSION, 35 Clev.St. L.Rev. 25 (1987). "In recent years courts have increasingly focused on developing the concept of oppression, and proof of oppressive conduct is rapidly becoming the most likely avenue for minority shareholder relief in close corporations. Three definitions of oppression have been used in the cases.

"The first, drawn from English case law is:

burdensome, harsh and wrongful conduct ... a lack of probity and fair dealing in the affairs of a company to the prejudice of some portion of its members; or a visual departure from the standards of fair dealing, and a violation of fair play on which every shareholder who entrusts his money to a company is entitled to rely.

Under this definition, oppression is basically a breach of the general fiduciary duty of good faith and fair dealing that majority shareholders in a corporation owe to the minority shareholders.

"The second definition, first enunciated in the now famous case of *Donahue v. Rodd Electrotype Company of New England, Inc.*, is conduct that constitutes a violation of the strict fiduciary duty of 'utmost good faith and loyalty' owed by partners *inter se*. This

standard, which is based on the analogy of close corporation shareholders who are active in management to general partners in a
partnership, is theoretically higher than the 'good faith and inherent
fairness' standard normally applicable in a corporation.

"The third definition of oppression, initially derived from English
case law, and long advocated by Dean F. Hodge O'Neal as well as
other leading close corporation experts, is conduct which frustrates
the reasonable expectations of the investors. The reasonable expectations doctrine has been gaining wide acceptance in the past few years.
Decisions in at least eight states have explicitly adopted this concept,
and decisions in at least nine additional states have implicitly recognized it. The approval of the reasonable expectations doctrine by the
New York Court of Appeals in the 1984 case of *In re Kemp & Beatley,
Inc.* is quite significant and will undoubtedly influence other courts."

NOTE ON THE DUTY OF CARE AND THE DUTY OF LOYALTY IN THE CLOSELY HELD CORPORATION

Two legal bulwarks for minority shareholders in publicly held
corporations are the duty of care and the duty of loyalty imposed by
law on corporate directors and officers. These duties are extremely
complex in their details, and are the subject of Chapters 8–10. To
oversimplify somewhat, the duty of care may render a director or
officer liable for certain types of managerial negligence, and the duty
of loyalty may render a director or officer liable for unfair self-
interested transactions with the corporation or other types of improper self-interested conduct. However, under the business judgment rule
a decision by an officer or director will not subject her to liability for
violation of the duty of care even if the decision was unreasonable, if it
was taken in good faith, there was no self-interest, the director or
officer properly informed herself before making the decision, and the
decision was not so unreasonable as to be irrational. Under the duty of
loyalty, a self-interested transaction will not subject a director or
officer to liability if she made full disclosure and the transaction was
objectively fair.

The duties of care and loyalty protect minority shareholders in
closely held as well as publicly held corporations, but in the closely
held context they are often an insufficient protection. For example, the
discharge of a minority shareholder from corporate office might qualify for protection under the business judgment rule, and a purchase of
stock from majority shareholders might not violate the duty of loyalty
if the price paid for the stock was fair. The real vice of such actions lies
in the fact that they treat shareholders unequally, defeat legitimate
expectations of a sort found in closely but not publicly held corporations, or both. Accordingly, the "reasonable expectations" analysis that
is made explicit in cases like Meiselman v. Meiselman, that is implicit
in cases like Donahue v. Rodd, and that in part underlies the concept
of dissolution for oppression, fills a major gap in corporate law for
closely held corporations. It would be a mistake, however, to believe

that analysis based on reasonable expectations can be separated from the concept of fairness. One way in which a court determines whether reasonable expectations of minority shareholders have been defeated by majority shareholders is by asking itself what similarly situated shareholders would have probably expected. Often the only way to answer that question is to ask what similarly situated shareholders would have regarded as fair.

MICH. COMP. LAWS § 450.1489

[See Statutory Supplement]

MINN. STAT. ANN. § 302A.751

[See Statutory Supplement]

McCallum v. Rosen's Diversified, Inc.

United States Court of Appeals, Eighth Circuit, 1998.
153 F.3d 701.

■ Before BEAM, ROSS, and MAGILL, CIRCUIT JUDGES.

■ BEAM, CIRCUIT JUDGE.

William B. McCallum, a minority shareholder in Rosen's Diversified, Inc. (RDI), appeals from two adverse grants of summary judgment. McCallum seeks to have his shares in RDI redeemed for fair value pursuant to a court ordered buy-out. The district court held that McCallum failed to present evidence showing that RDI acted unfairly prejudicial toward him. We reverse and remand for a determination of the fair value of McCallum's shares.

I. BACKGROUND

This case involves a contentious dispute between the minority and controlling shareholders of a closely held Minnesota corporation. Two brothers, Elmer and Ludwig Rosen, founded RDI as a livestock trading business in the late 1940's. Today, RDI has grown into a thriving company, primarily engaged in meat packing and other agricultural businesses. In 1992, RDI had more than $400 million in sales. Members of the Rosen family own a majority of RDI's outstanding capital stock.

In January 1984, RDI hired McCallum, who had previously provided legal services to the company, as Executive Vice President and Chief Executive Officer (CEO). He was named a director in 1986. RDI performed well under McCallum's command. Accordingly, RDI rewarded McCallum—and three other key employees—with a bonus of

$186,815 in cash and 12,000 shares of common stock in the company.[2] According to RDI, these payments were made because the key employees were almost entirely responsible for the financial success of the corporation, because the compensation package of the employees had been artificially low, and in order to maintain the unswerving loyalty of these employees. The parties did not enter into a shareholder's agreement or provide any mechanism for the transfer of those shares if circumstances changed.

By 1991, the amiable relationship between McCallum and RDI deteriorated, ultimately resulting in McCallum's termination and removal from the board. Subsequently, McCallum proposed that RDI redeem his shares for $5 million. RDI responded with an offer to redeem the shares for $600,000, which was at a small premium over the value determined by the annual valuation for RDI's Employee Stock Ownership Program (ESOP). The parties could not agree on a price and extensive litigation has followed.... The present case involves McCallum's 12,000 shares of RDI common stock which is not contained in the ESOP.

McCallum alleges that RDI's controlling shareholders have acted unfairly prejudicial toward him because they: (1) undermined his authority as CEO; (2) excluded him from important company decisions; (3) engaged in conduct directed at minimizing the value of the company; (4) terminated his employment; (5) offered to redeem his shares at an artificially low price; (6) denied him access to company books, records, and financial information; (7) engaged in self-dealing, usurped company opportunities, and commingled personal ventures with the affairs of the company.

The district court dismissed many of McCallum's allegations as improperly pleaded derivative claims. The district court dismissed McCallum's request for a buyout of his stock on a subsequent motion for summary judgment. McCallum appeals.

II.   DISCUSSION . . .

Concerned with the vulnerable position of minority shareholders in closely held corporations, the Minnesota legislature has provided the courts with broad equitable authority to protect the interests of minority shareholders. See Minn.Stat. § 302A.751 (amended 1994) (hereinafter "Section 751"). Section 751 provides for the buy-out of a minority shareholder's interest when "the directors or those in control of the corporation have acted in a manner unfairly prejudicial toward one or more shareholders in their capacities as shareholders or directors . . . or as officers or employees of a closely held corporation."

The phrase "unfairly prejudicial" is to be interpreted liberally. See *Pedro v. Pedro*, 463 N.W.2d 285, 288–89 (Minn.Ct.App.1990). One

---

2. During the course of his employment, McCallum also received approximately 3,300 shares of common stock in RDI through an Employee Stock Ownership Program (ESOP). McCallum's total ownership represented nearly 3% of the company's capital stock.

commentator, who helped draft certain revisions to the Minnesota Business Corporation Act and Section 751, stated that:

> The section is remedial in nature and should be liberally construed as an addition to the rights afforded non-controlling shareholders by law and the corporation's governing documents. The broad scope of Section 751 reflects the Legislature's trust in the ability of the judiciary to achieve equitable results on the facts appearing in individual cases.

See Joseph Edward Olson, Statutory Changes Improve Position of Minority Shareholders in Closely Held Corporations, *The Hennepin Lawyer*, Sept.-Oct.1983, at 11. In deciding whether to order a buy-out, the courts should consider "the reasonable expectations of the shareholders" with respect to each other and the corporation. See Minn. Stat. § 302A.751, subd. 3a (amended 1994). Oftentimes, a shareholder's reasonable expectations include a significant voice in management and an opportunity to work. See Olson at 23.

We find that the uncontested facts demonstrate that McCallum's reasonable expectations were defeated. RDI terminated McCallum's employment as CEO and subsequently offered to purchase his RDI shares at a small premium over the value determined by an annual valuation for RDI's ESOP. McCallum had received these shares as compensation for his outstanding service and as an inducement to remain at RDI, in order to foster its continued growth. Although the employment relationship later deteriorated, our focus is on McCallum's reasonable expectations at the inception of the relationship. See Minn.Stat. § 302A.751, subd. 3a.

On his termination, McCallum was divested of his primary expectations as a minority shareholder in RDI—an active role in the "management of the corporation and input as an employee." Pedro, 463 N.W.2d at 289. This expectation was particularly reasonable since McCallum was CEO of RDI. We need not extend our holding as far as the Minnesota Court of Appeals, which held that controlling shareholders that terminate the employment of a minority shareholder must make a good-faith effort to buy out the shareholder at a fair price. See *Sawyer v. Curt & Co.*, 1991 WL 65320, at *2 (Minn.Ct.App. Feb.12, 1991) (publication order vacated). We simply hold that terminating the CEO—as opposed to an employee that did not have a significant role in management—and then offering to redeem his stock, which was issued partially to lure him to remain at the company, constituted conduct toward McCallum as a shareholder sufficient to invoke the requirements of the Minnesota Act. Accordingly, we remand the matter for a determination of the fair value of his stock.

On remand, the district court shall determine the fair value of McCallum's shares in accordance with Minn.Stat. § 302A.751, subd. 2 (amended 1994) and put an end to this pugnacious litigation. We express no opinion on the fair value of McCallum's shares or whether the ESOP valuation represents fair value.

III. CONCLUSION

For the foregoing reasons, we reverse the judgment of the district court and remand for further proceedings consistent with this opinion.

———

MUELLENBERG v. BIKON CORP., 143 N.J. 168, 669 A.2d 1382 (1996). Bikon Corporation was owned by Muellenberg, Passerini, and Burg. Muellenberg and Passerini were the majority shareholders. Burg, the minority shareholder, was Bikon's general manager. Burg sued Muellenberg and Passerini on the ground of oppression. The court held that Burg had been oppressed, and gave him the right to buy out the majority shareholders:

> The statute . . . plainly allows the minority to seek a court order for the sale of the stock of "any other shareholder." In most situations, oppressed minority shareholders will lack the resources to buy out the interests of controlling shareholders. As a result, claims of oppression are typically remedied by arranging for the corporation or the majority shareholders to buy out the interests of the minority shareholder. In this case, the record contained the following evidence in support of Burg: Burg was willing and able to purchase the shares of Muellenberg and Passerini; Burg, who owns the land on which BNJ's offices are located, was most active in operating the company since its inception; Burg is the only shareholder who works full-time for BNJ and the company has been his only source of income for over ten years; Burg was primarily responsible for developing the company's contacts in the United States and Canada and is best situated to maintain the existing operation; and finally, it was Burg who sought to preserve the corporation at a time when Muellenberg and Passerini attempted to dissolve it. . . .

> Thus, while a minority buy-out of the majority is an uncommon remedy, it was the appropriate one here. . . . This remedy is authorized by N.J.S.A. 14A:12–7(8) and is consistent with decisions holding that courts are not limited to statutory remedies, but have a wide variety of equitable remedies also available to them. *Brenner,* . . . 134 N.J. at 516. . . .

———

KELLEY v. AXELSON, 296 N.J.Super. 426, 687 A.2d 268 (1997), "[M]aintaining an accounting system whose shortcomings have the effect of substantially preventing the outside, minority shareholders from ascertaining and verifying the corporation's income [can] constitute unfairness and oppression toward the minority shareholders, entitling them to relief under [the dissolution-for-oppression statute]."

Haynsworth, The Effectiveness of Involuntary Dissolution Suits as a Remedy for Close Corporation Dissension

35 Cleve.St.L.Rev. 25 (1987).

What results actually occur in close corporation involuntary dissolution suits? One way to answer this question is to examine existing published opinions. For the purposes of this article, the opinions published in 1984 and 1985 in which involuntary dissolution was one of the major causes of action were analyzed. . . .

. . . [A] total of forty-seven cases . . . qualified for the sample [but ten of the cases involved technical legal issues in which no decision on the type of relief, if any, had been made at the time the opinion was issued].

Of the remaining thirty-seven cases, a buy-out was the most frequent relief ordered by the court or elected by the defendants. This result occurred in twenty of the decisions (fifty-four percent). Dissolution was ordered in ten of the cases (twenty-seven percent). In four of the cases (eleven percent), no substantial relief was granted to the plaintiff on the merits. Finally, in the three other cases (eight percent) relief other than either dissolution or a buy-out was the exclusive remedy ordered. . . .

What is somewhat surprising is the number of cases in which a court-supervised buy-out is the result of the involuntary dissolution suit. In a previous study of the fifty-four involuntary dissolution opinions decided between 1960–1976 conducted by [Hetherington and Dooley], a court-ordered or court supervised buy-out was involved in only three of the cases, whereas dissolution was ordered in sixteen of the twenty-seven cases in which some affirmative relief was granted [in the present sample]. . . .

NOTE ON DISSOLUTION

The evolution of the legal treatment of dissolution can, with some oversimplification, be divided into four stages.

1. *First Stage: Dissolution Granted Only for Deadlock, and Even Then Granted Very Sparingly.* In the first, original stage, which lasted until about the early 1960s, the courts typically granted dissolution only on the ground of deadlock. Furthermore, the courts were often reluctant to grant dissolution of a profitable corporation even on

that ground, partly on the theory that there was a public interest in preserving economically viable businesses.

2.   *Second Stage: Dissolution on the Ground of the Majority's Fault.* In the second stage, courts became more willing to grant dissolution, even of profitable corporations, not only on the ground of deadlock but also on the ground of oppression.[1] This increased willingness resulted in part from a wave of dissolution-for-oppression statutes. It also resulted from the influence of scholarship like that of Hetherington & Dooley, and also of F. Hodge O'Neal, who wrote extensively to show that dissolution was often a highly desirable remedy to resolve the problems of minority shareholders.

3.   *Third Stage: Dissolution on the Ground of Defeat of the Minority's Reasonable Expectations.* In the third stage, the emphasis shifted from an inquiry into whether there was fault on the part of majority shareholders to an inquiry into whether the reasonable expectations of the minority shareholders were being defeated. Often, this shift involved a reconstruction of the meaning of "oppression," as in *Kemp & Beatley, supra.*

4.   *Fourth Stage: Dissolution Converted into Mandatory Buy-Out.* In the fourth, present stage, there has been a marked tendency to grant relief even more freely to minority shareholders who petition for dissolution, but to cast that relief not in the form of dissolution, but in the form of requiring a mandatory buy-out, at fair value, of the interest of a shareholder who petitions for dissolution. In many cases, the dissolution statutes give the majority a right to buy out the minority. In other cases, the courts order buy-out as an alternative to dissolution, as a matter of discretion.

At present, therefore, a petition by a minority shareholder for dissolution is commonly just a trigger for requiring a mandatory buy-out of the minority shareholder's stock. To put this differently, the courts hold, with increasing frequency, that grounds for dissolution exist, but then substitute mandatory buy-out for dissolution as the appropriate remedy. This development has several implications.

First, because liquidation is not required under a mandatory buy-out, the power to order a mandatory buy-out serves to alleviate the persistent view that liquidation of a profitable corporation is against the public interest. As a result, the courts may now be more ready to find in favor of a minority shareholder in a dissolution proceeding, just because they know that such a finding will not necessarily result in a liquidation.

Second, the power to order a mandatory buy-out in lieu of dissolution obviates a concern that freely granting dissolution may enable minority shareholders to opportunistically use a petition for dissolution (or the threat of such a petition) to put undue pressure on the majority shareholders by making them fear that they will lose

---

1.   As stated in the Introduction to this Note, the evolution described in this Note is somewhat oversimplified. Even some very recent cases, such as Brenner v. Berkowitz, 134 N.J. 488, 634 A.2d 1019 (1993), contain expressions of concern about the dissolution of profitable corporations.

control of the business, and thereby extort an unduly high settlement from the majority. This possibility is sometimes referred to as "oppression by the minority."

Third, the easier it is to convert a dissolution proceeding into a mandatory buy-out, the less likely are the courts to require minority shareholders to satisfy a very high level of proof. In general, the less drastic is a remedy, the readier the courts will be to impose the remedy. This has been the trend of the law in the area of dissolution: As the remedy has been diluted from dissolution to buy-out, the standard for granting relief has also been diluted and the frequency of relief to minority shareholders has increased.

Fourth, to the extent that petitions for dissolution have become triggering events for mandatory buy-outs, and the courts grant such petitions without a showing of fault by the majority, in effect the law is edging toward the position advocated by Hetherington and Dooley, that minority shareholders in close corporations should be allowed exit on demand. (This position also moves close corporation law toward partnership law, which already allows dissolution on very free terms.)

Fifth, properly conceived and administered, mandatory buy-out may have important advantages over dissolution. The minority shareholder can get just what he wants—the cash value of his stock and exit from a bad situation. At the same time, the majority shareholders are given the right to continue the business if they wish to do so.

NOTE ON VALUATION OF THE MINORITY'S SHARES

To the extent that mandatory buy-out is substituted for dissolution, great pressure is put on how the value of the minority's shares is determined, because the remedy of mandatory buy-out works properly only if the minority interest is properly valued. Indeed, from the perspective of valuation, dissolution has a major advantage over a mandatory buy-out. In a mandatory buy-out the *court* must value the minority's interest. In contrast, in a dissolution there is a public sale of the corporation's business, so that the *market,* rather than the court, values the corporation and therefore the petitioner's shares. From a valuation perspective, therefore, dissolution may be preferable to mandatory buy-out on the ground that a valuation by the market is more accurate than a valuation by the court.

Against this view, it can be argued that a mandatory sale of close corporation's business in the context of a dissolution proceeding may not in fact realize the fair value of the business. The problem with such a sale is that there may be no ready market for the corporation's business, especially if one or more of the shareholder-managers will not continue to participate or if the only person who can realistically acquire the business is one of the shareholders, who might therefore be able to purchase the business at a public sale at an unduly low price. Professor Bahls has explained this problem especially well:

> ... When corporations are liquidated, they usually sell their assets for cash. Frequently, when a receiver or court-appointed auctioneer sells a business, the sale does not yield the maximum value for any of the shareholders. Auction sales are fire sales. Rather than selling the entire business as a going concern, the business assets might be sold separately. If so, the sale does not yield the full value of a going concern. In addition, the business is not always operated between the appointment of the receiver or court-appointed auctioneer and the date of sale. During this interim, the customers of the business may develop relationships and preferences for other vendors, often dealing a fatal blow to the corporation's ability to operate profitably.
>
> Compounding the problem, auction sales or other court-supervised sales usually require payment of the purchase price immediately or within a short period of time. This requirement excludes potential purchasers from the market and may result in lower purchase prices offered by those not excluded. Finally, purchase prices are depressed because it is difficult to insure that the buyer will reap the benefit of the seller's goodwill. Business management, as well as nonmanagement employees, often develop important customer contracts and special expertise. To the extent that management expertise and customer relationships cannot be sold with the business, buyers do not receive the benefit of, nor are they willing to pay for, these important elements of goodwill. . . .

Bahls, Resolving Shareholder Dissension: Selection of the Appropriate Equitable Remedy, [1990] J.Corp.Law 285, 297 (1990).

On the other hand, mandatory buy-outs also raise severe problems of valuation. To begin with, the valuation of a business by a nonmarket mechanism, like a court, is always a very difficult and problematic enterprise. Furthermore, two special problems are raised in the context of a mandatory buy-out. In valuing shares for some purposes, such as an estate-tax valuation a two-step approach is adopted. In the first step, the corporation is valued as a whole, and the shares are then valued on a pro rata basis. In the second step, a discount is applied to the first-step valuation if the shares are minority shares, not easily marketable, or both. Discounts for these factors can run 25% or more. Some courts have applied minority or marketability discounts in the mandatory buy-out context as well. The propriety of such discounts in that context is the subject of the following case.

————

Charland v. Country View Golf Club, Inc.

Supreme Court of Rhode Island, 1991.
588 A.2d 609.

OPINION

■ KELLEHER, JUSTICE.

The plaintiff in this litigation, Gilbert Charland, is a minority shareholder in a Rhode Island closely held corporation that owned and operated an eighteen-hole, 147–acre golf course located in the town of Burrillville. The defendant, Country View Golf Club, Inc., is the corporation. Hereafter we shall refer to the plaintiff as Charland and to the defendant as Country View.

On September 4, 1984, Charland, a 15 percent shareholder of Country View's stock, that is, an owner of fifteen shares, filed a complaint in the Superior Court asking that Country View be dissolved. Charland relied on G.L.1956 (1985 Reenactment) § 7–1.1–90, which provides:

> "(a) The superior court shall have full power to liquidate the assets and business of a corporation:
>
> (1) In an action by a shareholder when it is established that, whether or not the corporate business has been or could be operated at a profit, dissolution would be beneficial to the shareholders because . . .
>
> (B) The acts of the directors or those in control of the corporation are illegal, oppressive, or fraudulent."

Specifically Charland alleged that one of the officers of the corporation was engaging in illegal activities.

After filing an answer, Country View, acting pursuant to § 7–1.1–90.1, elected to purchase Charland's fifteen shares. Section 7–1.1–90.1 provides, in part:

> "Whenever a petition for dissolution of a corporation is filed by one or more shareholders (hereinafter in this section referred to as the 'petitioner') pursuant to * * * § 7–1.1–90 * * * the corporation or one or more of its other shareholders may avoid such dissolution by filing with the court * * * an election to purchase the shares owed by the petitioner *at a price equal to their fair value.* * * * If the parties are unable to reach an agreement as to the fair value of such shares, the court shall * * * stay the proceeding and determine the value of such shares, in accordance with the procedure set forth in § 7–1.1–74, *as of the close of business on the day on which the petition for dissolution was filed.*" (Emphasis added.)

Thus § 7–1.1–90.1 contains three provisions. First, a corporation, rather than be forced to dissolve by a shareholder dissolution petition, can elect to buy out the shareholder's stock. Second, the corporation must pay fair value for such shares. Third, if the fair value cannot be agreed upon, the court shall determine the value of such shares as of the close of business on the day on which the petition for dissolution was filed.

Charland and Country View could not agree on the fair value of Charland's shares. Therefore the court, in accordance with § 7–1.1–74, appointed an appraiser. Section 7–1.1–74(e) provides that "The court may, if it so elects, appoint one or more persons as appraisers to receive evidence and recommend a decision on the question of fair value. The appraisers shall have such power and authority as shall be specified in the order of their appointment or an amendment thereof.''

[The trial court designated Joseph R. Smith (Smith) as an appraiser to determine the fair value of Charland's shares.]

Smith's report to the trial justice noted the inherent difficulties in evaluating the value of a golf course in Burrillville. The appraiser then discussed the applicability of a minority discount in evaluating the shares. Smith concluded that a "minority discount" would be appropriate in determining the fair value of Charland's shares.[4]

Smith submitted two figures in his report. The first, or lower, valuation included a minority discount and was the one suggested by Smith. The trial justice, however, accepted the second, or higher, calculation.

The second figure of $9,273.05 per share, or $139,095.73, was arrived at in the following manner: first, Smith noted that the golf course was sold for $2 million in 1988; second, Smith used the present value procedure to discount the $2 million figure and arrive at the value of the entire golf course as of September 30, 1984; and finally, without applying an additional minority discount, Smith took 15 percent of the 1984 value in order to arrive at the value for Charland's 15 shares (out of 100) in the corporation. The trial justice ultimately awarded Charland the sum of $139,095.73. . . .

Although Charland raised a number of issues on appeal, he failed to furnish us with a complete transcript of the Superior Court proceeding. As a result, we shall consider. . . . [only] whether Charland received fair value for his shares pursuant to § 7–1.1–90.1.

Three separate issues must be resolved in determining fair value. The first issue is whether this court should apply a minority discount to Charland's shares. The second issue is whether this court should apply a discount for lack of marketability. The third issue is whether any discount was, in fact, applied to Charland's shares with the result that Charland received less than the fair value prescribed by § 7–1.1–90.1. We shall now consider each of these three issues.

A minority discount has been described as a second-stage adjustment for valuing minority shares. *See* Note, *Rejecting the Minority Discount*, 1989 Duke L.J. 258, 260. That is, after a minority shareholder's stock is initially discounted for the minority percentage owned, the pro rata value is determined. Then an additional discount is applied to the pro rata value because the minority shareholder lacks corporate decisionmaking power. *Id.* This second calculation is called a minority discount.

---

4. In his report, Smith failed to distinguish between a minority discount and a lack of marketability discount. Smith combined elements of both discounts but ultimately labeled the discount a "minority discount." Because of the ambiguity created by Smith's report, we will address the applicability of both a minority discount and a lack of marketability discount to Charland's shares.

The issue of whether to apply a minority discount in a situation in which a corporation elects to buy out a shareholder who has filed for dissolution has never been resolved by this court. In fact, few jurisdictions have decided this question.[5]

Most courts that have considered this question have agreed that no minority discount should be applied when a corporation elects to buy out the shareholder who petitions for dissolution of the corporation. *See, e.g., Brown v. Allied Corrugated Box Co.*, 91 Cal.App.3d 477, 485–87, 154 Cal.Rptr. 170, 173–76 (1979); *Blake v. Blake Agency, Inc.*, 107 A.D.2d 139, 486 N.Y.S.2d 341, *appeal denied*, 65 N.Y.2d 609, 484 N.E.2d 671, 494 N.Y.S.2d 1028 (1985). *But see McCauley v. Tom McCauley & Son, Inc.*, 104 N.M. 523, 535, 724 P.2d 232, 244 (1986) (trial justice has discretion in determining whether a minority discount is applicable).

[In *Brown v. Allied Corrugated Box Co.*, supra, the] court conceded that if the shares were placed on the open market, their minority status would substantially decrease their value. The court, however, went on to note that this devaluation has little validity when the shares are to be purchased by the corporation. When a corporation elects to buy out the shares of a dissenting shareholder, the fact that the shares are noncontrolling is irrelevant.

In addition the court in *Brown* observed that had the plaintiffs proved their case and had the corporation been dissolved, each shareholder would have been entitled to the same amount per share. There would be no consideration given to whether the shares were controlling or noncontrolling. Furthermore an unscrupulous controlling shareholder could avoid a proportionate distribution under dissolution by buying out the shares, and the very misconduct and unfairness that incited the minority shareholders to seek dissolution could be used to oppress them further. *Brown*, 91 Cal.App.3d at 486–87, 154 Cal.Rptr. at 176; *see also* Note, 1989 Duke L.J. at 269 n. 63.

We agree with the rationale of *Brown* and hereby adopt the rule that in circumstances in which a corporation elects to buy out a shareholder's stock pursuant to § 7–1.1–90.1, we shall not discount the shares solely because of their minority status.

A second and more difficult issue to resolve is whether a lack of marketability discount should be applied to Charland's shares. This discount is separate from and bears no relation to a minority discount. The courts that have addressed this question are divided.

The California courts have rejected a lack of marketability discount for the same reasons that they have rejected a minority dis-

---

5. Many jurisdictions, including this one, have decided the question of determining the fair value of shares when a *dissenting* shareholder elects to request the fair value of his or her shares in case of a merger or consolidation. *See* § 7–1.1–74; *see also Jeffrey v. American Screw Co.*, 98 R.I. 286, 201 A.2d 146 (1964) (appraiser given wide discretion to consider all relevant factors in determining fair value of dissenting shareholder's stock). This is a separate issue from whether a minority discount should be applied when a corporation elects to buy out a shareholder who has petitioned for *dissolution* proceedings.

count. *See Brown*, 91 Cal.App.3d at 483, 154 Cal.Rptr. at 175. That is, no lack of marketability discount should be applied because the shares are not being sold on the open market; they are purchased by the corporation. The New York courts, however, have decided to apply a lack of marketability discount to shares in a closely held corporation when the corporation elects to buy out a minority shareholder in order to avoid dissolution. The reason for applying this discount is that shares of a closely held corporation cannot readily be sold on the public market. *Blake v. Blake Agency, Inc.*, 107 A.D.2d at 149, 486 N.Y.S.2d at 349.

The difference between the approach taken by the New York and the California courts regarding the question of whether a lack of marketability discount should be applied when a corporation elects to buy out the shareholder who has filed for dissolution is based upon the statutes of each state. The California statute determines fair value "on the basis of the liquidation value as of the valuation date but taking into account the possibility, if any, of sale of the entire business as a going concern in a liquidation." Cal.Corp.Code Ann. § 2000(a) (West 1990). As there is no lack of marketability discount if the corporation dissolves, no such discount is applied by the California courts....

Furthermore ... a lack of marketability discount is inapposite when a corporation elects to buy out a shareholder who has filed for dissolution of a corporation. As a recent law review article noted:

> "In dissolution cases, strong reasons support the use of pro rata value without a discount * * *. A minority shareholder seeking dissolution claims that majority shareholders have engaged in some unfair, possibly tortious, action. If the minority shareholder succeeds in having the company dissolved, all shareholders will receive their pro rata share of the assets, with no account given to the minority [or illiquidity] status of their shares. Minority shareholders should not receive less than this value if, instead of fighting the dissolution action, the majority decides to seek appraisal of minority shares in order to buy out the minority and reduce corporate discord." Note, 1989 Duke L.J. at 269 n. 63.

We therefore today adopt the rule of not applying a discount for lack of marketability in § 7–1.1–90.1 proceedings....

[Because the trial justice applied a discount, we] remand this case to the Superior Court to determine the fair value of Charland's shares as of September 4, 1984, without applying a discount for either minority status or lack of marketability of his shares in Country View in conformity with the rules set forth herein.

———

NOTE ON MINORITY AND MARKETABILITY DISCOUNTS

A distinction must be drawn between the value of minority stock on the market and the value of minority stock to the majority shareholder. On the market, minority stock may be subject to a marketability discount, a minority discount, or both, because a third party who purchases minority stock will be in the same disadvantageous position as the selling minority shareholder. However, the majority shareholder will not be subject to these problems. Accordingly, the value of minority stock to a majority shareholder may be free of minority and marketability discounts. As stated in Robblee v. Robblee, 68 Wash.App. 69, 78–81, 841 P.2d 1289, 1294–95 (1992):

> In Columbia Management Co. v. Wyss, 94 Or.App. 195, 765 P.2d 207 (1988). . . . [t]he court rejected the minority discount as inappropriate to an "internal transaction", because market recognition of a minority discount has little validity when the corporation or someone already in control of the corporation is the purchaser. . . .
>
> [In the present case,] had the value of [the shares of Neil, the minority shareholder] to a third party been at stake, it would have been appropriate for the trial court to apply a minority discount to approximate the fair market value. We do not doubt the experts' opinions that the market value of Neil's minority shares is less per share than that of Dave's majority shares. But, as in a dissenting shareholder situation, here no third party was involved, and thus there was no "market" in fact or in theory—Dave was the only party contemplated to buy the stock.
>
> The [trial] court recognized the extra value that Neil's stock would have for Dave: "Dave's ownership will go to almost 80% and he will be ridding himself of a minority shareholder who had become, and would continue to be, extremely difficult." This, though, is one of the very reasons a minority shareholder's stock should not be discounted to fair market value, because the value to Dave is different from what it would be in the market.

––––––––

NOTE ON MATTER OF PACE PHOTOGRAPHERS

In Matter of Pace Photographers, Ltd., 71 N.Y.2d 737, 530 N.Y.S.2d 67, 525 N.E.2d 713 (1988), Pace Photographers had five shareholders, including Rosen, all of whom had entered into a shareholders' agreement. Paragraph 5 of the agreement fixed a method for determining the value of Pace shares for the purpose of paying out a shareholder who retired or withdrew from the business (the "withdrawal price"). Paragraph 12 of the agreement prohibited a sale by any shareholder of Pace stock to a third party for five years after the agreement was executed, unless all the other shareholders consented. A shareholder was permitted to sell his stock to one of the other shareholders during that period without such consent, but only for 50% of the withdrawal price.

Three years after the agreement was executed, a rift developed between Rosen and the other four shareholders. Rosen petitioned for dissolution under N.Y.B.C.L. § 1104–a, alleging oppression and wrongdoing. The other four shareholders responded by causing Pace to file an election under N.Y.B.C.L. § 1118, which allows a corporation to elect a mandatory buy-out of a shareholder who has petitioned under § 1104–a. The trial court held that Pace had a right to buy Rosen's shares under § 1118, and that the fair value of Rosen's shares under that section was 50% of the withdrawal price, pursuant to the shareholders' agreement. The Appellate Division affirmed, but the Court of Appeals reversed:

> As an abstract matter, it may well be that shareholders can agree in advance that an 1104–a dissolution proceeding will be deemed a voluntary offer to sell, or fix "fair value" in the event of judicial dissolution, and that their agreement would be enforced. . . . Participants in business ventures are free to express their understandings in written agreements, and such consensual arrangements are generally favored and upheld by the courts. . . .

> But in the absence of explicit agreement a shareholders' agreement fixing the terms of a sale voluntarily sought and desired by a shareholder does not equally control when the sale is the result of claimed majority oppression or other wrongdoing—in effect, a forced buyout . . .

> . . . The provisions of the shareholders' agreement regarding buyout within the first five years, at a 50% discount, were expressly limited to the situation where "a stockholder desires to sell his shares of the stock to the other stockholders" (para 12[e]), contemplating a voluntary sale at the convenience of and for the benefit of the selling shareholder, without regard to the inconvenience or detriment inflicted on the corporation or other shareholders. . . . It is plain . . . that a sale occasioned by an 1104–a petition premised on abuse by the majority does not fall within the contemplation of this shareholders' agreement regarding a sale of stock by a shareholder to the corporation. . . .

Less than a month after the Court of Appeals decision, the corporation sent a notice to Rosen, purporting to revoke its offer to buy his shares under N.Y.B.C.L. § 1118. In In re Pace Photographers, Ltd., 163 A.D.2d 316, 557 N.Y.S.2d 443 (1990), the court held that the corporation could not revoke its election. "Business Corporation Law § 1118(a) states in pertinent part that '[a]n election pursuant to this section shall be irrevocable unless the court, in its discretion, for just and equitable considerations, determines that such election be revocable. . . . [We do not] find any 'just and equitable considerations' that would allow us to authorize revocation of Pace's election. . . .'"

———

FRIEDMAN v. BEWAY REALTY CORP., 87 N.Y.2d 161, 638 N.Y.S.2d 399, 661 N.E.2d 972 (1995). "[I]n fixing fair value, courts should determine the minority shareholder's proportionate interest in the going concern value of the corporation as a whole, that is, 'what a willing purchaser, in an arm's length transaction, would offer for the *corporation* as an operating business' " (*Matter of Pace Photographers [Rosen]*, 71 N.Y.2d, at 748, *supra*, quoting *Matter of Blake v. Blake Agency*, 107 A.D.2d, at 146, *supra* [emphasis supplied]).

"Consistent with that approach, we have approved a methodology for fixing the fair value of minority shares in a close corporation under which the investment value of the entire enterprise was ascertained through a capitalization of earnings (taking into account the unmarketability of the corporate stock) and then fair value was calculated on the basis of the petitioners' proportionate share of all outstanding corporate stock (*Matter of Seagroatt Floral Co.*, 78 N.Y.2d, at 442, 446, *supra*).

"Imposing a discount for the minority status of the dissenting shares here, as argued by the corporations, would in our view conflict with two central equitable principles of corporate governance we have developed for fair value adjudications of minority shareholder interests under Business Corporation Law §§ 623 and 1118. A minority discount would necessarily deprive minority shareholders of their proportionate interest in a going concern, as guaranteed by our decisions previously discussed. Likewise, imposing a minority discount on the compensation payable to dissenting stockholders for their shares in a proceeding under Business Corporation Law §§ 623 or 1118 would result in minority shares being valued below that of majority shares, thus violating our mandate of equal treatment of all shares of the same class in minority stockholder buyouts.

"A minority discount on the value of dissenters' shares would also significantly undermine one of the major policies behind the appraisal legislation embodied now in Business Corporation Law § 623, the remedial goal of the statute to 'protect[ ] minority shareholders' from being forced to sell at unfair values imposed by those dominating the corporation while allowing the majority to proceed with its desired [corporate action]" (*Matter of Cawley v. SCM Corp.*, 72 N.Y.2d, at 471, *supra*, quoting *Alpert v. 28 Williams St. Corp.*, 63 N.Y.2d 557, 567–568). This protective purpose of the statute prevents the shifting of proportionate economic value of the corporation as a going concern from minority to majority stockholders. As stated by the Delaware Supreme Court, 'to fail to accord to a minority shareholder the full proportionate value of his [or her] shares imposes a penalty for lack of control, and unfairly enriches the majority stockholders who may reap a windfall from the appraisal process by cashing out a dissenting shareholder' (*Cavalier Oil Corp. v. Harnett*, 564 A.2d 1137, 1145 [Del.]).

"Furthermore, a mandatory reduction in the fair value of minority shares to reflect their owners' lack of power in the administration of the corporation will inevitably encourage oppressive majority conduct, thereby further driving down the compensation necessary to pay for the value of minority shares. 'Thus, the greater the misconduct by the majority, the less they need to pay for the minority's shares' (Murdock, *The Evolution of Effective Remedies for Minority Shareholders and Its*

Impact Upon Evaluation of Minority Shares, 65 Notre Dame L.Rev. 425, 487).

"We also note that a minority discount has been rejected in a substantial majority of other jurisdictions. 'Thus, statistically, minority discounts are almost uniformly viewed with disfavor by State courts' (*id.,* at 481). The imposition of a minority discount in derogation of minority stockholder appraisal remedies has been rejected as well by the American Law Institute in its Principles of Corporate Governance (*see,* 2 ALI, Principles of Corporate Governance § 7.22, at 314–315; comment *e* to § 7.22, at 324 [1994]) . . . .

"We likewise find no basis to disturb the trial court's discretion in failing to assign any additional diminution in value of petitioners' shares here because they were subject to contractual restrictions on voluntary transfer. As we noted in *Matter of Pace Photographers (Rosen) (supra),* a statutory acquisition of minority shares by a corporation pursuant to the Business Corporation Law is not a voluntary sale of corporate shares as contemplated by a restrictive stockholder agreement and, therefore, 'the express covenant is literally inapplicable' (71 N.Y.2d, at 749). Nor is there any reason to disturb Supreme Court's award of prejudgment interest."

However, the court approved a discount for marketability.

SECTION 11. ARBITRATION

Ringling v. Ringling Bros. Barnum & Bailey Circus

Section 2, supra.

APPLICATION OF VOGEL, 268 N.Y.S.2d 237, 25 A.D.2d 212 (1966), aff'd 19 N.Y.2d 589, 278 N.Y.S.2d 236, 224 N.E.2d 738 (1967). Certified Moving & Storage Co. was engaged in the moving-and-storage business and also owned a warehouse in which the business was operated. Prior to 1962, Certified's stock was owned by Vogel, Thomsky, and Horowitz. In 1962, Vogel and Lewis purchased all of the Certified stock, so that each owned 50%. However, the warehouse in which Certified's business was operated continued to be owned by Vogel, Thomsky, and Horowitz, Certified's former owners. When Vogel and Lewis took over Certified, they obtained a lease on the warehouse for five years and an option under which Certified could purchase the warehouse for $175,000.

Vogel and Lewis had a shareholders' agreement. Paragraph Sixth of the agreement provided that "The parties hereto hereby expressly agree that in the event of a dispute, or difference, arising between them in the course of their transaction with each other, under the terms of this agreement, such dispute or difference shall be settled between them by arbitration...." Lewis sought to have Certified exercise its option to purchase the warehouse, so as to strengthen and assure the continuance of Certified's business. If the warehouse was not acquired by Certified, and Vogel, Thomsky, and Horowitz did not renew Certified's lease, Certified would have to go out of business at the end of the lease term. The business would then effectively revert to Vogel, Thomsky, and Horowitz, as owners of the warehouse in which the business was operated.

In October 1964 there was a meeting of the board of directors of Certified, consisting of Vogel and Lewis. At that meeting, Lewis voted in favor of exercising the option to purchase the warehouse, and Vogel voted against. Vogel revealed that he had some sort of agreement with his former partners and considered himself morally and legally bound to them, and therefore could not agree to exercise the option to purchase. Vogel also made it clear it was to his own advantage and personal interest to keep the ownership of the property "as is." When further discussion failed to resolve the question of exercising the option to buy the warehouse, Lewis demanded arbitration, pursuant to paragraph Sixth, on two issues: (1) Should Certified exercise its option to purchase pursuant to terms of the Lease? (2) Should Vogel be removed as officer and director of Certified on the ground that he had interests adverse to the best interests of Certified? Vogel asserted that Paragraph Sixth did not cover the kinds of questions Lewis sought to arbitrate, and that the arbitration sought would be in violation of N.Y.Bus.Corp.Law § 701, which provided that the business of a corporation shall be managed by its board. The court ordered arbitration to proceed:

> ... [T]he question to exercise or not to exercise the option, under the circumstances here present, is not one which deals with problems of everyday corporate management or whether a particular deal in the exercise of business judgment would redound to the corporate benefit. It is more fundamental involving, as it does, continued corporate existence....

> ... [I]f all involved here were discretion and the exercise of business judgment in the management of corporate affairs it is doubtful that arbitration could be used or applied as a substitute in light of the language of the statute (Business Corporation Law § 701)....

> Obviously the question whether or not to exercise the option to purchase does not require assumption of any burden of continuing management, but rather if Certified is to have a measure of business security and assurance of continued existence.

> It must have reasonably been within the contemplation of the parties, acting in good faith when the corporation was formed, should the business prove successful, as is the case here, that all necessary or proper steps to assure its continued existence would

be cooperatively undertaken. Recognizing that disputes could arise the parties provided for arbitration. To read a limitation of exclusion at the price of continued corporate existence of this close corporation is to disregard the plain language of paragraph Sixth, and to impose a restriction, possibly fatal, where the issue sought to be arbitrated is nowise offensive to our public policy. This we should not do.

LANE v. ABEL–BEY, 70 A.D.2d 838, 418 N.Y.S.2d 25 (1979), aff'd, 50 N.Y.2d 864 (1980). A shareholders' agreement provided that "[a]ll disputes arising in connection with this agreement shall be finally settled by arbitration." One of the shareholders claimed that the corporation had failed to enter into an employment contract with him, as the agreement required; had paid excessive compensation; and had made improper payments to other shareholders. Held, the claims were subject to arbitration. "We do not agree with petitioner's argument that, because the second and third claims are in the nature of derivative suits, public policy precludes arbitration of such claims. . . . We are not concerned here with claims relating to the business conduct of a publicly held corporation, but rather with such claims addressed to the business conduct of a close corporation. Arbitration of claims of a derivative nature are not against public policy in a close corporation. . . ."

SHELL, ARBITRATION AND CORPORATE GOVERNANCE, 67 N.C.L.Rev. 517 (1989). "[Section 2 of the Federal Arbitration Act] makes enforceable any 'written provision in any . . . contract evidencing a transaction involving commerce to settle by arbitration' any existing or future dispute. . . .

". . . [A]fter nearly seventy years of legal evolution, arbitration is now utilized in New York as a close corporation remedy for virtually every kind of corporate dispute. Indeed, detailed case administration statistics compiled by the American Arbitration Association reveal that between 1984 and August 1988 the AAA received over one thousand claims and counterclaims worth over $118,000,000 under its case administration category dealing with close corporation disputes. These claims include disputes regarding stock valuation and appraisal, allegations of breach of contract, mismanagement, misrepresentation, wrongful discharge, and breach of fiduciary duty.

". . . [T]he Supreme Court has . . . [interpreted Federal Arbitration Act] as preempting attempts by the states to preclude access to the arbitral forum. When parties can convince a court that their close corporation dispute involves interstate commerce, they may be able to bypass even express statutory restrictions on arbitration, such as [a] . . . requirement that an arbitration clause appear in the charter." Id. at 524, 533.

CHAPTER VII

ALTERNATIVE FORMS OF BUSINESS ORGANIZATION: LIMITED PARTNERSHIPS, LIMITED LIABILITY COMPANIES, AND LIMITED LIABILITY PARTNERSHIPS

Although the different forms of business organization vary in a number of respects, traditionally the predominant considerations in selecting a form of organization have been taxation and liability: Owners want minimum taxation and maximum protection against individual liability. For many years, the major choice of prospective owners of a newly formed business association was between corporations and partnerships. Corporations offered maximum protection against liability. Partnerships (for reasons to be explained in this Chapter) normally offered minimum taxation. In recent years, however, new, alternative forms of unincorporated business organization have emerged that offer both protection against liability and minimum taxation. Three of these forms will be considered in this Chapter, in the order in which they evolved: limited partnerships, limited liability companies, and limited liability partnerships.

SECTION 1. LIMITED PARTNERSHIPS

(a) THE UNIFORM LIMITED PARTNERSHIP ACTS

The limited partnership is an historical form of business organization. As of 2002, there were 377,000 limited partnerships in the United States, with an average of 18 partners in each partnership. Wheeler & Parsons, Partnership Returns, 2002, Statistics of Income Bulletin, Fall 2004, at 46, 57.

Over the course of time, the Commissioners on Uniform State Laws have promulgated several uniform limited partnership acts.

In 1916, the Commissioners promulgated the original Uniform Limited Partnership Act. It was adopted in every state except Louisiana. In 1976, the Commissioners promulgated a replacement for the Uniform Limited Partnership Act, called the Revised Uniform Partnership Act. The new Act modernized the prior Act, and reflected the influence of the corporate model. It has been widely but not universally adopted.

In 1985, the Commissioners amended the Revised Uniform Limited Partnership Act in a number of important respects. The states are still in the process of adopting these amendments.

In 2001, the Commission adopted the Uniform Limited Partnership Act (2001). As of the time this casebook is written, that Act has been adopted in only four states. In the balance of this Section, the Uniform Limited Partnership Act will sometimes be referred to as the ULPA; the Revised Uniform Partnership Act, as amended in 1985, will sometimes be referred to as RULPA; and the Uniform Limited Partnership Act (2001) will sometimes be referred to as the 2001 Act.

(b) FORMATION OF A LIMITED PARTNERSHIP

———

REVISED UNIFORM LIMITED PARTNERSHIP ACT §§ 101, 201

[See Statutory Supplement]

———

UNIFORM LIMITED PARTNERSHIP ACT (2001) §§ 102, 201

———

NOTE

Unlike general partnerships, limited partnerships are basically creatures of statute, although they have nonstatutory historical antecedents. RULPA § 101 defines a limited partnership as "a partnership formed by two or more persons under the laws of this State and having one or more general partners and one or more limited partners." RULPA § 201 provides that in order to form a limited partnership a certificate of limited partnership must be filed in the office of the Secretary of State. The certificate must state the name of the limited partnership, the name and business address of each general partner, the latest date upon which the limited partnership is to dissolve, and the name and address of the agent for service of process. Sections 102 and 201 of the 2001 Act are comparable.

(c) LIABILITY OF LIMITED PARTNERS

———

REVISED UNIFORM LIMITED PARTNERSHIP ACT § 303

[See Statutory Supplement]

———

UNIFORM LIMITED PARTNERSHIP ACT (2001) § [303]

Gateway Potato Sales v. G.B. Investment Co.

Court of Appeals of Arizona, 1991.
170 Ariz. 137, 822 P.2d 490.

■ TAYLOR, JUDGE.

Gateway Potato Sales (Gateway), a creditor of Sunworth Packing Limited Partnership (Sunworth Packing), brought suit to recover payment for goods it had supplied to the limited partnership. Gateway sought recovery from Sunworth Packing, from Sunworth Corporation as general partner, and from G.B. Investment Company (G.B. Investment) as a limited partner, pursuant to Arizona Revised Statutes Annotated (A.R.S.) § 29–319. Under § 29–319, a limited partner may become liable for the obligations of the limited partnership under certain circumstances in which the limited partner has taken part in the control of the business.

G.B. Investment moved for summary judgment, urging that there was no evidence that the circumstances described in A.R.S. § 29–319 had occurred in this case. It argued that, as a limited partner, it was not liable to the creditors of the limited partnership except to the extent of its investment. The trial court agreed, granting G.B. Investment's motion for summary judgment.

Gateway appeals from the judgment and the denial of its motion for reconsideration, arguing the existence of conflicting evidence of material facts relating to the participation of the limited partner in the control of the partnership business. We agree and reverse the grant of summary judgment.

FACTS

On review from the trial court's order granting summary judgment, the facts are viewed in the light most favorable to the party against whom judgment is entered. Dolezal v. Carbrey, 161 Ariz. 365, 366, 778 P.2d 1261, 1262 (1989). Sunworth Corporation and G.B. Investment formed Sunworth Packing in November 1985 for the purpose of engaging in potato farming in Arizona. The limited partnership certificate and agreement of Sunworth Packing, filed with the office of the Arizona Secretary of State, specified Sunworth Corporation as the general partner and G.B. Investment Company as the limited partner. The agreement recited that the limited partner would not participate in the control of the business. The agreement further stated that the limited partner would not become liable to the creditors of the partnership, except to the extent of its initial contribution and any liability it may incur with an Arizona bank as a signatory party or guarantor of a loan and/or line of credit.

In late 1985, Robert C. Ellsworth, the president of Sunworth Corporation, called Robert Pribula, the owner of Gateway, located in

Minnesota, to see if Gateway would supply Sunworth Packing with seed potatoes. Pribula hesitated to supply the seed potatoes without receiving assurance of payment because Pribula was aware that Ellsworth had previously undergone bankruptcy. Pribula, however, decided to sell the seed potatoes to Sunworth Packing after being assured by Ellsworth that he was in partnership with a large financial institution, G.B. Investment Company, and that G.B. Investment was providing the financing, was actively involved in the operation of the business, and had approved the purchase of the seed potatoes. Thereafter, from February 1986 through April 1986, Gateway sold substantial quantities of seed potatoes to Sunworth Packing.

While supplying the seed potatoes, Pribula believed that he was doing business with a general partnership (i.e., Sunworth Packing Company, formed by Sunworth Corporation and G.B. Investment Company). The sales documents used by the parties specified "Sunworth Packing Company" as the name of the partnership. Pribula was neither aware of the true name of the partnership nor that it was a limited partnership.

All of Gateway's dealings were with Ellsworth. Pribula neither contacted G.B. Investment prior to selling the seed potatoes to the limited partnership nor did he otherwise attempt to verify any of the statements Ellsworth had made about G.B. Investment's involvement. The only direct contact between G.B. Investment and Gateway occurred some time after the sale of the seed potatoes. It is, however, disputed whether G.B. Investment ever provided any assurance of payment to Gateway.

G.B. Investment's vice-president, Darl Anderson, testified in his affidavit that G.B. Investment had exerted no control over the daily management and operation of the limited partnership, Sunworth Packing. This testimony was contradicted, however, by the affidavit testimony of Ellsworth which was presented by Gateway in opposing G.B. Investment's motion for summary judgment. According to Ellsworth, G.B. Investment's employees, Darl Anderson and Thomas McHolm, controlled the day-to-day affairs of the limited partnership and made Ellsworth account to them for nearly everything he did. This day-to-day contact included but was not limited to approval of most of the significant operational decisions and expenditures and the use and management of partnership funds without Ellsworth's involvement.[1]

1. Ellsworth described with some specificity the ways in which G.B. Investment's control was exerted:

a. During the early months of the Partnership, Thomas McHolm and/or Darl Anderson were at the Partnership's offices on a daily basis directing the operation of the Partnership, and thereafter, they were at the Partnership's offices at least 2–3 times per week reviewing the operations of the business, directing changes in operations, and instructing

me to make certain changes in operating the Partnership's affairs;

b. G.B. Investment Company was solely responsible for obtaining a $150,000.00 line-of-credit loan for the Partnership with Valley National Bank of Arizona, and it also signed documents guaranteeing the repayment of the loan;

c. As the President of the general partner, I was not permitted to make any significant independent business decisions concerning the operations of the Partnership, but was directed to have all

Ellsworth testified further that he had described G.B. Investment's control of the business operation to Pribula. Pribula confirmed that Ellsworth had informed him that G.B. Investment's employees, McHolm and Anderson, were at the partnership's office on a frequent basis, that Ellsworth reported directly to them, that daily operations of the partnership were reviewed by representatives of G.B. Investment, and that Ellsworth had to get their approval before making certain business decisions.

business decisions approved with Darl Anderson and/or Thomas McHolm, or was directed to carry out decisions made by Darl Anderson and/or Thomas McHolm. For example, instead of using Partnership funds to pay certain creditors and suppliers, I was directed by Darl Anderson and/or Thomas McHolm to use the Partnership funds to purchase additional machinery and equipment;

d. Prior to constructing improvements to the packaging facilities of the Partnership, Thomas McHolm and/or Darl Anderson had to approve all construction bids, individually selected some of the suppliers and subcontractors, and individually selected the equipment to be installed;

e. Thomas McHolm and/or Darl Anderson dictated the accounting procedures to be followed by the Partnership, reviewed the Partnership's books and accounts almost continually, dictated that the Partnership use the same accounting firm as that of G.B. Investment Company to do the Partnership accounting tasks, undertook the responsibility of having prepared all Partnership tax forms and returns, and I only signed tax returns after they had been prepared by G.B. Investment Company's accountants and reviewed by Darl Anderson or some other employee/agent of G.B. Investment Company;

f. During a great portion of the duration of the Partnership, Thomas McHolm and/or Darl Anderson oversaw the daily operations of the Partnership because I had to have all expenditures approved by Thomas McHolm and/or Darl Anderson and Darl Anderson had to approve and sign checks issued by the Partnership, including without limitation payroll checks and invoices for telephone charges, utilities, publications, interest payments, bank card charges, supplies, etc. Copies of a sampling of the invoices and the corresponding checks are attached hereto as Exhibit 2;

g. After it was decided to add a hydrocooler to the processing and packaging facilities of the Partnership, Thomas McHolm individually selected the refrigeration equipment and chose the contractor to install the refrigeration equipment on the hydrocooler, and even saw to it that G.B. Investment Company (not the partnership) directly paid the contractor for all of his services;

h. Thomas McHolm insisted that the Partnership use a particular supplier, to-wit: Allied Packaging, to supply packaging materials to the Partnership, he further took an active role in reviewing and modifying the art work for use on the packaging items, and personally approved the bid submitted for the art work;

i. At least on two separate occasions, approximately in August, 1986 and again in November, 1986, Darl Anderson caused sums of monies (approximately $8,000 and $7,000 respectively) to be withdrawn from the Partnership account (No. 2270-8018) with Valley National Bank without the prior knowledge or consent of myself, as the President of the general partner of the Partnership. These monies were paid directly to G.B. Investment, and the withdrawals caused other checks of the Partnership to be dishonored due to insufficient funds and left the Partnership without sufficient funds to meet its payroll obligations;

j. Darl Anderson and/or Thomas McHolm caused certain expenses of the Partnership to be paid directly by G.B. Investment Company, to-wit: refrigeration equipment; and

k. After the Partnership defaulted on its loan payments to Valley National Bank, a loan which had been guaranteed by G.B. Investment Company, Darl Anderson, without my knowledge or consent, instructed the Valley National Bank to proceed with declaring the loan to be in default and to pursue its remedies under its Security Agreement with the Partnership, to-wit: to sell the equipment and machinery that it held as collateral at a foreclosure auction. At the foreclosure auction held on March 3, 1987, by Valley National Bank, Darl Anderson, on behalf of G.B. Investment Company, bought the equipment and machinery previously owned by Sunworth Corporation.

DISCUSSION

Gateway argues that sufficient questions of fact exist which preclude the granting of summary judgment in favor of G.B. Investment. We will affirm the trial court's grant of summary judgment if there is no genuine issue of material fact in dispute and the moving party is entitled to judgment as a matter of law. Orme School v. Reeves, 166 Ariz. 301, 305, 802 P.2d 1000, 1004 (1990).

Subsection (a) of A.R.S. § 29–319 sets forth the general rule that a limited partner who is not also a general partner is not liable for the obligations of the limited partnership.

> [A] limited partner is not liable for the obligations of a limited partnership unless he is also a general partner or, in addition to the exercise of his rights and powers as a limited partner, he takes part in the control of the business. However, if the limited partner's participation in the control of the business is not substantially the same as the exercise of the powers of a general partner, he is liable only to persons who transact business with the limited partnership with actual knowledge of his participation in control.

In responding to the motion for summary judgment, Gateway urged the trial court to find that Gateway had presented a fact question of G.B. Investment's liability to it under A.R.S. § 29–319(a). Gateway argued that the statute imposes liability on a limited partner whose participation in the control of the business is substantially the same as the exercised power of a general partner. Gateway further argued that even if the person transacting business with the limited partnership did not know of the limited partner's participation in control, there is liability. Alternatively, Gateway argued that the statute imposes liability when the powers exercised in controlling the business might fall short of being "substantially the same as the exercise of powers of a general partner," but the person transacting business with the limited partnership had actual knowledge of the participation in control. Gateway asserted that the evidence it was presenting in response to the motion for summary judgment raised issues of material fact as to whether either of these situations had occurred. If either had occurred, Gateway argued, it would be entitled to recover from the limited partner, G.B. Investment.

In granting G.B. Investment's motion for summary judgment, the trial court gave two reasons for concluding that G.B. Investment could not be found liable under A.R.S. § 29–319(a) as a matter of law. First, as we interpret the trial court's comments, it read the statute as having a threshold requirement—that is, under all circumstances, a creditor of the limited partnership must have contact with the limited partner in order to impose liability on the limited partner. The evidence before the trial court showed that Gateway merely relied upon the statements made by Ellsworth, president of the general partner, and that Gateway did not contact G.B. Investment prior to transacting business with the limited partnership. Based upon these facts, the trial court concluded that liability could not be imposed upon G.B. Investment. The trial court's minute entry states, in relevant part:

> [I]t is undisputed that the plaintiff contracted with and sold seed potatoes to the limited partnership, without any direct contact with the movant. In other words, at the time the sale with the limited partnership was consummated and completed—plaintiff can not by the posture of the evidence—be said to have been a person who, while transacting business with the limited partnership, did so with actual knowledge of defendant G.B. Investment Company's participation in control with the limited partnership or its general partner.

> Consequently, plaintiff fails to leap the first "hurdle"; and neither the court nor the trier-of-fact need review plaintiff's factual assertions regarding "safe harbor" excesses or violations, if any, under A.R.S. § 29–319(B). The only purported contact between plaintiff and defendant G.B. Investment Company occurred in the fall of 1986, well after the last of the seed potatoes were delivered by plaintiff to the limited partnership.

> Notwithstanding the representations made by Robert C. Ellsworth, as the president of the general partner, Sunworth Corporation, regarding the movant, plaintiff admits it never directly contacted the movant, to inquire into or verify Ellsworth's authority to bind the movant by such representations.

> The court finds, given the present record, that movant G.B. Investment has no liability to plaintiff arising from movant being a limited partner in Sunworth Packing Limited Partnership.

After reaching this conclusion, the trial court also found that no specific facts had been presented which would support the application of A.R.S. § 29–319 so as to impose liability on G.B. Investment. As the minute entry states:

> The court further finds that while the statutory protection extended to limited partners is not absolute, there are no specific facts included within the plaintiff's response, supporting statement of facts, and supporting affidavits, which would support the applicability of A.R.S. § 29–319(A) so as to impose liability in favor of plaintiff and against the movant G.B. Investment.

To the extent that the trial court's ruling may have been based on a belief that a limited partner could never be liable under the statute unless the creditor had contact with the limited partner and learned directly from him of his participation and control of the business, we believe that ruling to be in error.

In A.R.S. § 29–319(a), the legislature stopped short of expressly stating that if the limited partner's participation in the control of the business is substantially the same as the exercise of the powers of a general partner, he is liable to persons who transact business with a limited partnership even though they have no knowledge of his participation and control. It has made this statement by implication, though, by stating to the opposite effect that "if the limited partner's participation in the control of the business is not substantially the same as the exercise of the powers of a general partner, he is liable only to persons who transact business with the limited partnership with actual knowledge of his participation in control." A.R.S. § 29–319(a).

We believe this interpretation is strengthened by an examination of the legislative history of Arizona's limited partnership statute. It is further strengthened by the legislature's refusal to modify this statute to correspond to the Revised Uniform Limited Partnership Act, as amended in 1985. Prior to 1982, Arizona's limited partnership statute was patterned after the Uniform Limited Partnership Act (ULPA), which was drafted in 1916. Section 7 of the ULPA provided that "[a] limited partner shall not become liable as a general partner unless, in addition to the exercise of his rights and powers as a limited partner, he takes part in the control of the business." Uniform Limited Partnership Act § 7, 6 U.L.A. 559 (1969).[3]

The Revised Uniform Limited Partnership Act (RULPA) was drafted in 1976. Revised Uniform Limited Partnership Act, 6 U.L.A. 239, 240 (Supp.1991). In 1982, the Arizona legislature adopted the RULPA after repealing its enactment of the ULPA. See 1982 Ariz.Sess.Laws, ch. 192, § 1 (effective July 24, 1982). Presently, A.R.S. § 29–319(a), dealing with a limited partner's liability to third parties, is very similar to the 1976 version of section 303(a) of the RULPA which stated:

> Except as provided in subsection (d), a limited partner is not liable for the obligations of a limited partnership unless he is also a general partner or, and in addition to the exercise of his rights and powers as a limited partner, he takes part in the control of the business. However, if the limited partner's participation in the control of the business is not substantially the same as the exercise of the powers of a general partner, he is liable only to persons who transact business with the limited partnership with actual knowledge of his participation in control.

Revised Uniform Limited Partnership Act § 303(a), 6 U.L.A. 239, 325 (Supp.1991). The drafters' comment to section 303 explained that limited partners exercising all of the powers of a general partner would not escape liability by avoiding direct dealings with third parties. The comment stated:

> Section 303 makes several important changes in Section 7 of the prior uniform law. The first sentence of Section 303(a) carries over the basic test from former Section 7 whether the limited partner "takes part in the control of the business" in order to ensure that judicial decisions under the prior uniform law remain applicable to the extent not expressly changed. The second sentence of Section 303(a) reflects a wholly new concept. Because of the difficulty of determining when the "control" line has been

3. The language of Arizona's then § 29–307 was taken verbatim from section 7 of the ULPA. For the text of Arizona's Uniform Limited Partnership Act, since repealed, see Uniform Limited Partnership Act, 1943 Ariz.Sess.Laws 124, reprinted in A.R.S. §§ 29–301 to –366 app. (1989) (as amended).

overstepped, it was thought it unfair to impose general partner's liability on a limited partner except to the extent that a third party had knowledge of his participation in control of the business. On the other hand, in order to avoid permitting a limited partner to exercise all of the powers of a general partner while avoiding any direct dealings with third parties, the "is not substantially the same as" test was introduced....

Id. at 326 cmt.

In 1985, the drafters of the RULPA backtracked from the position taken in section 303(a) of the 1976 Act. The new amendments reflect a reluctance to hold a limited partner liable if the limited partner had no direct contact with the creditor. The 1985 revised RULPA section 303(a) was amended to provide as follows:

Except as provided in Subsection (d), a limited partner is not liable for the obligations of a limited partnership unless he is also a general partner or, in addition to the exercise of his rights and powers as a limited partner, he participates in the control of the business. However, if the limited partner participates in the control of the business, he is liable only to persons who transact business with the limited partnership reasonably believing, based upon the limited partner's conduct, that the limited partner is a general partner.

Id. at 325 (emphasis added). The comment to section 303 was also revised to explain the reason for the amendment. The revised comment states:

Section 303 makes several important changes in Section 7 of the 1916 Act. The first sentence of Section 303(a) differs from the text of Section 7 of the 1916 Act in that it speaks of participating (rather than taking part) in the control of the business; this was done for the sake of consistency with the second sentence of Section 303(a), not to change the meaning of the text. It is intended that judicial decisions interpreting the phrase "takes part in the control of the business" under the prior uniform law will remain applicable to the extent that a different result is not called for by other provisions of Section 303 and other provisions of the Act. The second sentence of Section 303(a) reflects a wholly new concept in the 1976 Act that has been further modified in the 1985 Act. It was adopted partly because of the difficulty of determining when the "control" line has been overstepped, but also (and more importantly) because of a determination that it is not sound public policy to hold a limited partner who is not also a general partner liable for the obligations of the partnership except to persons who have done business with the limited partnership reasonably believing, based on the limited partner's conduct, that he is a general partner....

Id. at 326 cmt. (emphasis added).

The Arizona legislature, however, has not revised A.R.S. § 29–319(a) to correspond to the section 303 amendments. The Arizona statute continues to impose liability on a limited partner whenever the "substantially the same as" test is met, even though the creditor has no knowledge of the limited partner's control. It follows then that no contact between the creditor and the limited partner is required to impose liability.

Moreover, whereas section 303 of the RULPA states that the creditor's reasonable belief must be "based upon the limited partner's conduct," under A.R.S. § 29–319 the only requirement is that the creditor has had "actual knowledge of [the limited partner's] participation in control." The statute does not state that this knowledge must be based upon the limited partner's conduct. The comments to the original version of section 303 of the RULPA, from which Arizona's statute is taken, make it clear that only when the "substantially the same as" test is met is direct contact not a requirement. Conversely, if the "substantially the same as" test is not met, direct contact is required. Under the facts presented in this case, Gateway had no direct contact with G.B. Investment until after the sales were concluded. We conclude, therefore, that G.B. Investment would be liable only if the "substantially the same as" test was met.

Whether a limited partner has exercised the degree of control that will make him liable to a creditor has always been a factual question. This is so regardless of whether the particular statute involved is patterned after section 7 of the ULPA or after section 303 of the RULPA. E.g., Alzado v. Blinder, Robinson & Co., 752 P.2d 544 (Colo. 1988); Gast v. Petsinger, 228 Pa.Super. 394, 323 A.2d 371 (1974); Holzman v. DeEscamilla, 86 Cal.App.2d 858, 195 P.2d 833 (1948). Our current Arizona statute lists activities that a limited partner may undertake without participating in controlling the business. It also states that other activities may be excluded from the definition of such control. Where activities do not fall within the "safe harbor" of A.R.S. § 29–319(b), it is necessary for a trier-of-fact to determine whether such activities amount to "control." In the absence of actual knowledge of the limited partner's participation in the control of the partnership business, there must be evidence from which a trier-of-fact might find not only control, but control that is "substantially the same as the exercise of powers of a general partner."

We conclude that the evidence Gateway presented in this case should have allowed it to withstand summary judgment. The affidavit testimony of Ellsworth raises the issue whether he was merely a puppet for the limited partner, G.B. Investment. While a few of the activities Ellsworth listed may have fallen within the protected areas listed in A.R.S. § 29–319(b), others did not. Ellsworth's detailed statement raises substantial issues of material facts.

Viewing the facts in the light most favorable to Gateway, we cannot say as a matter of law that G.B. Investment was entitled to summary judgment. We conclude that Gateway is entitled to a determination by trial of the extent of control exercised by G.B. Investment over Sunworth Packing.

For the foregoing reasons, we reverse the judgment of the trial court and remand for further proceedings.

■ Ehrlich, P.J., and Claborne, J., concur.

————

(d) Corporate General Partners

————

NOTE ON CORPORATE GENERAL PARTNERS

It seems likely that the plaintiff in *Gateway* sued the limited partner, rather than the general partner, because the sole general partner was a corporation with limited assets. Ordinarily, shareholders are not liable for their corporation's debts. Therefore, if both the limited partnership and the corporate general partner had insufficient assets to pay the debt to the plaintiff, the plaintiff would have been unable to collect on the limited partnership's debt unless the limited partner was liable.

Section 303(b)(1) of RULPA and Section 601(4)(C) of the 2001 Act explicitly recognize that a corporation can be a general partner in a limited partnership. Although a director or officer of a corporate general partner is not liable for the debts of a limited partnership merely because he participates in the control of the partnership's business in his capacity as director or officer of the general partner, he may become liable if the corporate directors and officers fail to maintain their corporate identity in conducting partnership affairs through the corporation, or if corporate assets are intermingled with partnership assets, or if the corporation is not sufficiently capitalized. See Mursor Buildings, Inc. v. Crown Mountain Apartment Associates, 467 F.Supp. 1316 (D.V.I. (1978); Western Camps, Inc. v. Riverway Ranch Enterprises, 70 Cal.App.3d 714, 138 Cal.Rptr. 918 (1977), or under the principle of the following case.

————

In re USACafes, L.P. Litigation

Court of Chancery of Delaware, 1991.
600 A.2d 43.

■ Allen, Chancellor.

These consolidated actions arise out of the October 1989 purchase by Metsa Acquisition Corp. of substantially all of the assets of USACafes, L.P., a Delaware limited partnership (the "Partnership") at a cash price of $72.6 million or $10.25 per unit. Plaintiffs are holders of limited partnership units. They bring these cases as class actions on behalf of all limited partnership unitholders except defendants. The relief sought includes, inter alia, the imposition of constructive trusts on certain funds received by defendants in connection with the Metsa sale and an award of damages to the class resulting from the sale.

The Partnership was formed in the 1986 reorganization of the business of USACafes, Inc., a Nevada corporation. Also formed as part of that reorganization was USACafes General Partner, Inc. (the "General Partner"), a Delaware corporation that acts as the general partner of the Partnership. Both the Partnership and the General Partner are named as defendants in this action. A second category of defendants is composed of Sam and Charles Wyly, brothers who together own all of the stock of the General Partner, sit on its board, and who also personally, directly or indirectly, own 47% of the limited partnership units of the Partnership. Sam Wyly chairs the Board of the General Partner.

The third category of defendants are four other individuals who sit on the board of directors of the General Partner. All of these persons are alleged to have received substantial cash payments, loan forgiveness, or other substantial personal benefits in connection with the 1989 Metsa purchase.

The last of the defendants is Metsa, the buyer of the Partnership's assets. Metsa is not alleged to be related in any way to the Wylys or any other defendant except as a buyer in the transaction under review.

The Theories of the Amended Complaint

The amended complaint arrays four theories of liability against these defendants. The first and most central theory involves an alleged breach of the duty of loyalty. In essence, it claims that the sale of the Partnership's assets was at a low price, favorable to Metsa, because the directors of the General Partner all received substantial side payments that induced them to authorize the sale of the Partnership assets for less than the price that a fair process would have yielded. Specifically, it is alleged that, in connection with the sale, (1) the Wylys received from Metsa more than $11 million in payments (or promises to pay in the future) which were disguised as consideration for personal covenants not to compete; (2) the General Partner (which the Wylys wholly own) received a $1.5 million payment right in consideration of the release of a claim that plaintiffs assert was non-existent; (3) defendant Rogers, a director of the General Partner and President of the Partnership was forgiven the payment of a $956,169 loan from the Partnership and was given an employment agreement with the Partnership that contemplated a one million dollar cash payment in the event, then imminent, of a "change in control"; (4) defendant Tuley, also a director of the General Partner, was forgiven repayment of a $229,701 loan; and (5) the other directors were given employment agreements providing for a $60,000 payment in the event of a change in control. In sum, it is alleged that between $15 and $17 million was or will be paid to the directors and officers of the General Partner by or with the approval of Metsa; those payments are alleged to constitute financial inducements to the directors of the General Partner to refrain from searching for a higher offer to the Partnerships. Plaintiffs add that, even assuming that Metsa was the buyer willing to pay the best price, some part at least of these "side payments" should have gone to the Partnership.

The second theory of liability reflected in the amended complaint asserts that the General Partner was (or the directors of the General Partner were) not sufficiently informed to make a valid business judgment on the sale. This theory focuses upon the absence of shopping of the Partnership's assets, or of any post-agreement market check procedure, and on the alleged weakness of the investment banker's opinion. Thus, this claim is that the defendants were uninformed when they authorized the sale to Metsa.

The third theory of liability is asserted on behalf of a class of limited partnership unitholders who held stock in the predecessor Nevada corporation—USACafes, Inc.—and who were issued partnership units pursuant to the reorganization of the USACafes business into the limited partnership form. It is alleged that those persons were misled by a December 5, 1986, prospectus (the "Prospectus"), disseminated in conjunction with the issuance of the partnership units,[1] into believing, reasonably, that, under the then proposed and later adopted structure, any sale of substantially all of the Partnership assets would require the affirmative vote of a majority of all unitholders. The relief apparently sought on this theory is the judicial recognition of an implied right to vote on the Metsa transaction (which has long since closed) or rescission of it in absence of such a vote.

The last theory in the amended complaint is the only one asserted against Metsa, the buyer. It charges that Metsa knowingly participated in the other defendants' alleged breaches of duty in connection with the sale by offering and making (or, in the case of the forgiveness of partnership debt, in agreeing to) personal payments to those controlling the General Partner designed to induce those persons to breach fiduciary duties they owed to the limited partners. Plaintiffs claim that this course of action makes Metsa jointly liable for wrongs done to the class or injuries suffered by class members out of this transaction.

* * *

The Pending Motions

... [T]he Wyly defendants and the other director defendants move under Rule 12(b)(6) to dismiss the breach of fiduciary duty claims in the amended complaint asserting that, while the General Partner admittedly did owe fiduciary duties to the limited partners, they as directors of the General Partner owe no such duties to those persons. The whole remedy of the limited partners for breach of the duties of loyalty and care, it is said, is against the General Partner only and not its directors....

[The gist of] the director defendants' motion to dismiss for failure to state a claim with respect to the sale of the Partnership's assets ...

---

1. The prospectus did not seek a shareholders' vote, but rather informed the shareholders that the reorganization would be approved by shareholder action by consent.

is the assertion that the directors of the General Partner owed the limited partners no duty of loyalty or care. In their view their only duty of loyalty was to the General Partner itself and to its shareholders (i.e., the Wyly brothers). Thus, in alleging that the director defendants breached duties of loyalty and care running to them, the directors say the limited partners have asserted a legal nullity.

In my opinion the assertion by the directors that the independent existence of the corporate General Partner is inconsistent with their owing fiduciary duties directly to limited partners is incorrect. Moreover, even were it correct, their position on this motion would have to be rejected in any event because the amended complaint expressly alleges that they personally participated in the alleged breach by the General Partner itself, which admittedly did owe loyalty to the limited partners.

The first basis of this holding is the more significant. While I find no corporation law precedents directly addressing the question whether directors of a corporate general partner owe fiduciary duties to the partnership and its limited partners, the answer to it seems to be clearly indicated by general principles and by analogy to trust law. I understand the principle of fiduciary duty, stated most generally, to be that one who controls property of another may not, without implied or express agreement, intentionally use that property in a way that benefits the holder of the control to the detriment of the property or its beneficial owner. There are, of course, other aspects—a fiduciary may not waste property even if no self interest is involved and must exercise care even when his heart is pure—but the central aspect of the relationship is, undoubtedly, fidelity in the control of property for the benefit of another.[2] See generally Robert Flannigan, The Fiduciary Obligation, 9 Oxford J. Legal St. 285 (1989).

The law of trusts represents the earliest and fullest expression of this principle in our law, but courts of equity have extended it appropriately to achieve substantial justice in a wide array of situations. Thus, corporate directors, even though not strictly trustees, were early on regarded as fiduciaries for corporate stockholders. E.g., Koehler v. Black River Falls Iron Co., 67 U.S. (2 Black) 715, 17 L.Ed. 339 (1862); Wardell v. Union Pac. R.R. Co., 103 U.S. 651, 26 L.Ed. 509 (1880). When control over corporate property was recognized to be in the hands of shareholders who controlled the enterprise, the fiduciary obligation was found to extend to such persons as well. Allied Chemical & Dye Corp. v. Steel & Tube Co., 14 Del.Ch. 1, 120 A. 486, 491 (1923).

While the parties cite no case treating the specific question whether directors of a corporate general partner are fiduciaries for the limited partnership, a large number of trust cases do stand for a principle that would extend a fiduciary duty to such persons in certain circumstances. The problem comes up in trust law because modernly

2. Thus, for example, a borrower of money is not considered a fiduciary for the lender simply because she is bound to return the principle sum plus interest. The "property" is held by the borrower for her own benefit.

corporations may serve as trustees of express trusts. Thus, the question has arisen whether directors of a corporate trustee may personally owe duties of loyalty to cestui que trusts of the corporation. A leading authority states the accepted answer:

> The directors and officers of [a corporate trustee] are certainly under a duty to the beneficiaries not to convert to their own use property of the trust administered by the corporation.... Furthermore, the directors and officers are under a duty to the beneficiaries of trusts administered by the corporation not to cause the corporation to misappropriate the property.... The breach of trust need not, however, be a misappropriation.... Any officer [director cases are cited in support here] who knowingly causes the corporation to commit a breach of trust causing loss ... is personally liable to the beneficiary of the trust....
>
> Moreover, a director or officer of a trust institution who improperly acquires an interest in the property of a trust administered by the institution is subject to personal liability. He is accountable for any profit.... Even where the trustee [itself] is not liable, however, because it had no knowledge that the director was making the purchase ..., the director ... is liable to the beneficiaries.... The directors and officers are in a fiduciary relation not merely to the [corporation] ... but to the beneficiaries of the trust administered by the [corporation].

4 A. Scott & W. Fratcher, The Law of Trusts § 326.3, at 304–306 (4th ed. 1989) (citing cases) ["Scott on Trusts"].

The theory underlying fiduciary duties is consistent with recognition that a director of a corporate general partner bears such a duty towards the limited partnership. That duty, of course, extends only to dealings with the partnership's property or affecting its business, but, so limited, its existence seems apparent in any number of circumstances. Consider, for example, a classic self-dealing transaction: assume that a majority of the board of the corporate general partner formed a new entity and then caused the general partner to sell partnership assets to the new entity at an unfairly small price, injuring the partnership and its limited partners. Can it be imagined that such persons have not breached a duty to the partnership itself? And does it not make perfect sense to say that the gist of the offense is a breach of the equitable duty of loyalty that is placed upon a fiduciary? It appears true that the same result might be rationalized as aider and abettor liability, but I am unsure what such indirection would add that is useful where a self-dealing transaction or other diversion of partnership property is alleged. Indeed in some instances, for example the use by a director of confidential information concerning the partnership's business not yet known by the board of the general partner, there may be no breach of loyalty or care by the general partner itself to abet, yet there may be director liability to the partnership by the director. Cf. cases cited at 4 Scott on Trusts § 326.3, at n. 7.

Two courts have, in fact, held a sole shareholder/director of a corporate general partner personally liable for breach of fiduciary duty to limited partners, although without much discussion of the issue here considered. See Tobias v. First City National Bank and Trust Co., 709 F.Supp. 1266, 1277–78 (S.D.N.Y.1989); Remenchik v. Whittington, Tex.Ct.App., 757 S.W.2d 836 (1988); see also In re Integrated Resources, Inc., Case No. 90–B–10411 (CB) (Bankr.S.D.N.Y. Oct. 22, 1990) (controlling shareholder held liable).

While these authorities extend the fiduciary duty of the general partner to a controlling shareholder, they support as well, the recognition of such duty in directors of the General Partner who, more directly than a controlling shareholder, are in control of the partnership's property. It is not necessary here to attempt to delineate the full scope of that duty. It may well not be so broad as the duty of the director of a corporate trustee.[3] But it surely entails the duty not to use control over the partnership's property to advantage the corporate director at the expense of the partnership. That is what is alleged here.

The amended complaint contains the following allegations:

16. The General Partner and its directors, the named individual defendants, are in a fiduciary relationship with the plaintiffs and the other Unitholders of USACafes. . . .

17. . . . Through their unit ownership and executive positions [the director defendants] have dominated and controlled the affairs of USACafes. Among other things, they have . . . failed to adequately solicit or consider alternative proposals for USACafes, have failed to negotiate in good faith to enhance Unitholders' values and, instead, have agreed to sell all of its assets to Metsa, which will result in the minority limited partners receiving the grossly inadequate price of $10.25 per Unit. As inducement to the individual defendants to agree to the Metsa proposal, Metsa offered to pay and the individual defendants agreed to accept, certain additional payments (approximately $17 million) that were not offered to the classes. . . .

19. The individual defendants and the General Partner participated in the wrongdoing complained of in order to divert the valuable assets of USACafes for their own benefit by entering into highly favorable compensation arrangements with Metsa as part of the liquidation of USACafes.

I therefore conclude that the amended complaint does allege facts which if true establish that the director defendants have breached fiduciary obligations imposed upon them as directors of a Delaware corporation or have participated in a breach of such duties by the General Partner. The amended complaint does, in my opinion, state a claim upon which relief can be granted. . . .

---

3. For example, I imply nothing on such questions as whether a director of a corporate general partner might be held liable directly to the partnership on a "corporate" opportunity theory or for waste of partnership assets (two possible consequences of characterizing such persons as fiduciaries for the partnership).

The motions of the individual defendants, the General Partner, and the Partnership to dismiss the claims arising out of the sale of the Partnership's assets is denied....

———

NOTE ON THE TAXATION OF UNINCORPORATED BUSINESS ORGANIZATIONS

Taxation is a major issue in the choice of business form. There are two basic patterns of business taxation under the Internal Revenue Code, which may be called firm taxation and flow-through taxation.

Under *firm taxation*, a business firm is taxable on its income. Accordingly, if the firm has income or expenses, or gains or losses, those items go into the firm's taxable income, not into the taxable income of the firm's owners. If the firm then makes distributions to its owners out of after-tax income, the owners ordinarily pay taxes on those distributions. This is sometimes referred to as "double taxation."

Under *flow-through* taxation, a firm is not subject to taxation. Instead, all of the firm's income and expenses, and gains and losses, are taxable directly to the firm's owners. Distributions are not taxed. There is no "double taxation" effect. If the firm has losses, the owners can utilize the losses to offset their income from other sources.

Whether firm taxation or flow-through taxation is preferable for the owners of an enterprise depends in any given case on corporate and individual tax rates, the owners' circumstances, and other variables. Generally speaking, under present tax rates the owners of a firm will ordinarily regard flow-through taxation as preferable to firm taxation.

Historically, a firm-taxation pattern applied more or less automatically to corporations, and a flow-through taxation pattern applied more or less automatically to partnerships. Until recently, however, it was often less clear which type of taxation would be applied to forms of business organization that are intermediate between general partnerships and corporations—forms such as the limited partnership. This issue has now been resolved by the IRS's "check-the-box" Regulations. Under these Regulations, any domestic unincorporated business that constitutes an "eligible entity" can elect either flow-through taxation or firm (corporate) taxation. If an eligible entity has only one owner, the entity will be disregarded for tax purposes—that is, all of the entity's income and expenses and gains and losses will be attributed to the owner.

Generally speaking, an eligible entity is any business entity other than (i) a corporation or (ii) a business entity that is specifically made taxable as corporation under the Internal Revenue Code. The most important entity in the second category is the *master limited partnership*. Essentially, a master limited partnership is a limited partnership whose limited-partnership interests are publicly traded—that is, traded on an established securities market, or readily tradeable on a secondary market. With certain exceptions, under the Internal Revenue Code publicly traded limited partnerships are taxed as corporations, and cannot elect flow-through (partnership) taxation.

There is another important respect in which the tax comparison of the traditional forms has been blurred. Just as publicly traded limited partnerships are now normally taxed like corporations, so the Internal Revenue Code provides a route through which partnership-tax treatment can be achieved by certain corporate enterprises. Subchapter S of the Code (I.R.C. §§ 1361–1379) permits the owners of qualifying corporations to elect a special tax status under which the corporation and its shareholders receive flow-though taxation that is comparable (although not identical) to partnership taxation. The taxable income of an S corporation is computed essentially as if the corporation were an individual. With some exceptions, items of income, loss, deduction, and credit, are passed through to the shareholders on a pro rata basis, and added to or subtracted from each shareholder's gross income.

Among the conditions for making and maintaining a Subchapter S election are the following: (1) The corporation may not have more than one hundred shareholders. (2) The corporation may not have more than one class of stock. (3) All the shareholders must be individuals or qualified estates or trusts. (4) No shareholder may be a nonresident alien. The amount of the corporation's assets and income is immaterial under Subchapter S.

As of 2002, there were 4,474,000 corporations in the United States. Almost half—2,153,000—were S corporations. United States Bureau of the Census, Statistical Abstract of the United States (2004).

(e) FIDUCIARY OBLIGATIONS

Gotham Partners, L.P. v. Hallwood Realty Partners, L.P.

Supreme Court of Delaware, 2002.
817 A.2d 160.

■ Before: VEASEY, CHIEF JUSTICE, WALSH, HOLLAND and BERGER, JUSTICES and HARTNETT, JUSTICE (Retired), constituting the Court en Banc.

■ VEASEY, CHIEF JUSTICE:

In this appeal, we hold that a limited partnership agreement may provide for contractually created fiduciary duties substantially mirroring traditional fiduciary duties that apply in the corporation law. The Court of Chancery held that the limited partnership agreement here provided for such fiduciary duties by requiring the general partner and its controlling entity to treat the limited partners in accordance with the entire fairness standard. We agree with this holding. . . .

With respect to remedies for that breach, the plaintiff limited partner had demanded rescission or an adequate damage award and sterilization of the voting rights attached to the partnership units involved in the challenged transaction. The Court of Chancery refused to order rescission and awarded damages. We affirm the holding of the Vice Chancellor that he was not necessarily required to order rescission by the limited partnership contract or the application of equitable principles. Such a decision is properly within the discretion of a court of equity, but here the Court of Chancery did not fashion a remedy that is an appropriate substitute for rescission under the circumstances.

As the Court of Chancery noted, one effect of the challenged transaction was that the general partner and its corporate parent gained control of the limited partnership as a result of wrongdoing. In our view, the value of the control thus achieved was not properly compensated for by the award of damages because the trial court did not account properly for a control premium in its remedy calculation.

Consequently, we reverse the damages award and remand for such proceedings as may be necessary and appropriate: (1) to quantify how the challenged transaction would have been consummated had the defendants adhered to the entire fairness standards and procedures of the limited partnership agreement; and (2) to consider and award one or more of the various equitable remedies available to the limited partnership, including rescission, rescissory damages, sterilization of voting rights, or other appropriate methods of accounting for the control premium.

Facts

Hallwood Realty Partners, L.P. ("the Partnership") is a Delaware limited partnership that owns commercial office buildings and industrial parks in several locations in the United States and lists its partnership units on the American Stock Exchange. Gotham Partners, L.P. ("Gotham") is a hedge fund, the investments of which include real estate. It is the largest independent limited partner in the Partnership with approximately 14.8 percent of the outstanding partnership units. Hallwood Realty Corporation ("the General Partner") is the sole general partner and is a wholly-owned subsidiary of Hallwood Group Incorporated ("HGI"), which owned 5.1 percent of the outstanding partnership units before the transactions challenged in this case. Anthony Gumbiner and William Guzzetti were members of the board of directors of the General Partner. They were also officers of HGI at the time of the challenged transaction.[6]

6. Gumbiner, a corporate lawyer, owned 30 percent of HGI's shares between 1994 and 1995 and was the chairman of the board of directors and chief executive officer of the General Partner at the time of the challenged transactions. Guzzetti, a former lawyer, is an executive vice-president of HGI and was the president of the Partnership and a member of the General Partner's board of

In 1994, the Partnership's units were trading at a low price because of the ongoing economic recession in real estate. On October 12, 1994, Guzzetti proposed to the Partnership's board of directors that it approve a reverse split,[7] a unit option plan,[8] and an odd lot tender offer[9] subject to HGI's willingness to finance the transactions by buying any fractional units generated by a reverse split and any units purchased by the Partnership in an odd lot tender offer. At the time, more than half of the Partnership's units were held in odd lots and could be resold to HGI. Guzzetti told the board that HGI was the only source of financing available and that the transactions would, among other things, raise the trading price of the Partnership's units, reduce the Partnership's administrative costs, and give odd lot holders the chance to sell at market price without incurring brokerage fees. The Partnership's board approved the transactions, citing Guzzetti's reasons.

At first, HGI declined to provide funding for the reverse split and odd lot offer. But, by March 1995, HGI was willing to fund the Reverse Split and Option Plan, which were approved by the non-HGI directors on the General Partner's board. HGI purchased 30,000 units, approximately 1.6 percent of the Partnership's equity, through the Reverse Split. The Option Plan resulted in officers and employees of the General Partner purchasing 86,000 units or 4.7 percent of the Partnership's equity. Through these two transactions, HGI increased its ownership of outstanding Partnership units from 5.1 percent to approximately 11.4 percent.

By May 1995, HGI was willing to fund an odd lot tender offer. Guzzetti called a special meeting of the General Partner's board of directors after circulating a memorandum indicating that 55 percent of the Partnership's units were held in odd lots and thus could be tendered in the odd lot offer. The non-HGI directors voted as a "special committee" to approve the Odd Lot Offer. The purchase price of an odd lot was putatively set at the five-day market average referenced in Section 9.01(b) of the Partnership Agreement.[10] No valuation information was shared with the board.

The Odd Lot Offer began on June 5, 1995. The accompanying press release indicated that the Partnership would resell any tendered odd lot units to HGI, affiliates of HGI, or other institutional investors.

---

directors at the time of the challenged transactions.

7. A reverse split reduces the number of outstanding units and consequently increases the per unit value of each unit. Reverse splits usually create odd lots.

8. In this case, the option plan would sell post-reverse split units to officers and employees of the General Partner, including Gumbiner and Guzzetti.

9. An odd lot offer is a tender offer by the issuer for blocks of fewer than one hundred outstanding units or shares. Such "odd lots" are considered small and thus create inefficient administrative costs for issuers and may be difficult to sell at an attractive price. Odd lot offers are designed to provide liquidity to small holders and to reduce issuer costs.

10. Section 9.01(b) of the Partnership Agreement states: "Except as set forth above, the number of Units issued to the General Partners or any such Affiliate in exchange for any Capital Contribution shall not exceed the Net Agreed Value of the contributed property or amount of cash, as the case may be, divided by the Unit Price of a Unit as of the day of such issuance."

The Odd Lot Offer and Resale was pitched to the public and the American Stock Exchange as a resale to HGI of existing, listed Partnership units, not as an issuance of new, unlisted units. Consequently, the Partnership never filed a listing application with the American Stock Exchange for the units sold to HGI, and the Partnership's accounting books did not treat the Odd Lot Resale to HGI as an issuance of units.

From June 9 to July 25, 1995, when the Odd Lot Offer closed, the Partnership purchased 293,539 units from odd lot holders and placed them in a holding account. The Partnership then resold the units to HGI at the same price the Partnership paid for them, approximately $4.1 million. The Odd Lot Resale resulted in HGI purchasing approximately 23.4 percent of the Partnership's outstanding units. Thus, HGI increased its stake in the outstanding Partnership units from 11.4 percent to 29.7 percent and solidified its control over the Partnership. The Partnership Agreement requires the written consent or affirmative vote by at least 66 and 1/3 percent of the limited partners to remove a general partner.

Gotham began purchasing Partnership units in 1994 and owned 14.8 percent of the outstanding units as of September 1996. Gotham was aware of the Odd Lot Offer and Resale but did not complain to the Partnership until January 1997 when it requested access to the Partnership's books and records. The Partnership denied the request.

Preliminary Proceedings in the Court of Chancery

Gotham filed a books and records action in the Court of Chancery in February 1997. On June 20, 1997, Gotham filed another action in the Court of Chancery alleging derivative claims in connection with the Odd Lot Offer and Resale, the Reverse Split, and the Option Plan. Gotham alleged that these transactions were unfair to the Partnership's unitholders because HGI paid an unfairly low price to acquire control over the Partnership. Gotham's claims included breaches by the General Partner of traditional fiduciary duties and contractually based fiduciary duties.…

On summary judgment, the Court of Chancery sustained the contractual fiduciary duty claims and dismissed the traditional fiduciary duty claims on the ground that the Partnership Agreement supplanted traditional fiduciary duties and provided for contractual fiduciary duties by which the defendants' conduct would be measured.[11] The Vice Chancellor found that Sections 7.05[12] and 7.10(a)[13] of the Partner-

11. *Gotham Partners, L.P. v. Hallwood Realty Partners, L.P.* (*"Gotham S.J. Op."*), Del. Ch., C.A. No. 15754, 2000 WL 1476663 (Sept. 27, 2000), at 23–29.

12. Section 7.05 of the Partnership Agreement states: "Transactions with General Partner or Affiliates. The Partnership is expressly permitted to enter into transactions with the General Partner or any Affiliate thereof provided that the terms of any such

transaction are substantially equivalent to terms obtainable by the Partnership from a comparable unaffiliated third party."

13. Section 7.10(a) of the Partnership Agreement states in relevant part: "Audit Committee; Resolution of Conflicts of Interest. (a) The General Partner shall form an Audit Committee (the 'Audit Committee') to be comprised of two members of the board of directors of the General Partner who are not ship Agreement operate together as a contractual statement of the entire fairness standard, with Section 7.05 substantively requiring fair price and Section 7.10(a) substantively requiring fair dealing. No appeal has been taken from this ruling. . . .

Decision After Trial

After trial, the Court of Chancery found the defendants liable for their conduct associated with the Odd Lot Resale to HGI, but upheld their conduct connected with the Reverse Split and the Option Plan. The Vice Chancellor found that the Odd Lot Resale, unlike the other two transactions, did not involve an issuance of units, but rather a resale of existing units to HGI. As a result, the Vice Chancellor found "inapplicable" the protections of Section 9.01 of the Partnership Agreement, which authorizes the General Partner to issue Partnership Units of any kind to any person without the consent or approval of the Limited Partners. Instead, the Vice Chancellor continued, the Odd Lot Resale was subject to Partnership Agreement Sections 7.05 and 7.10(a), which provide for the contractually created fiduciary duties of entire fairness.

The Vice Chancellor found that the General Partner breached the contractual fiduciary duties of entire fairness because (1) the General Partner never formed the Audit Committee as required by Section 7.10(a) to review and approve the Odd Lot Offer and Resale, and (2) the General Partner failed to perform a market check or obtain any reliable financial analysis indicating that the Odd Lot Resale would be conducted on the same terms obtainable from a third party. The Court of Chancery thus held the General Partner liable for breach of the contractually created fiduciary duties of entire fairness contained in the Partnership Agreement. . . . .

Gotham requested rescission, or money damages and sterilization of voting rights. The Court of Chancery awarded money damages plus compound interest instead of rescission, in part because it found that Gotham delayed challenging the transaction "for nearly two years, and then filed suit to rescind only after it was clear that the market price [of the Partnership units] was up substantially and on a sustainable basis." The Vice Chancellor then went on to find that the challenged transactions were not "conceived of as a conscious scheme to entrench the General Partner's control and enrich HGI" improperly. He stated that if he had been convinced otherwise, "I might be inclined to grant rescission despite Gotham's torpid pace."

Gotham then filed a direct appeal in this Court contesting the remedy. The General Partner, HGI, Gumbiner, and Guzzetti filed cross appeals asserting that the Court of Chancery erred by finding Section 9.01(a) of the Partnership Agreement inapplicable to the Odd Lot Offer and Resale ... and by awarding compound interest on a damages award.

---

affiliated with the General Partner or its Affiliates except by reason of such directorship. The functions of the Audit Committee shall be to review and approve ... (ii) transactions between the Partnership and the General Partner and any of its Affiliates."

Issues on Appeal

On appeal, Gotham argues that the Court of Chancery was required to award rescission as a matter of law and, even if an award of monetary damages were appropriate, the Court of Chancery erred in its calculation of the damages by failing to account for a control premium. Gotham seeks reversal in part of the judgment of the Court of Chancery and a remand to the court with instructions to order rescission of the Odd Lot Resale to HGI. Alternatively, Gotham seeks an award of rescissory damages or sterilization of HGI's voting rights connected to the Odd Lot Resale units, or both.

The General Partner, HGI, Gumbiner, and Guzzetti, contend in their cross appeal that the Court of Chancery erred ... by finding the Odd Lot Resale to HGI subject to Sections 7.05 and 7.10(a) of the Partnership Agreement, which provide for contractual fiduciary duties of entire fairness, instead of Section 9.01, which authorizes the General Partner to issue Partnership Units of any kind to any person without the consent or approval of the Limited Partners.... We will address the cross appeals first.

Whether the Court of Chancery Erred By Ruling That the Odd Lot Resale to HGI Was a Resale of Partnership Units

This Court reviews de novo the Court of Chancery's interpretation of written agreements and Delaware law.

As the Vice Chancellor noted at summary judgment, a general partner owes the traditional fiduciary duties of loyalty and care to the limited partnership and its partners, but DRULPA § 17–1101(d)(2) "expressly authorizes the ... modification, or enhancement of these fiduciary duties in the written agreement governing the limited partnership."[14] Indeed, we have recognized that, by statute, the parties to a Delaware limited partnership have the power and discretion to form and operate a limited partnership "in an environment of private ordering" according to the provisions in the limited partnership agreement.[15] We have noted that DRULPA embodies "the policy of freedom of contract"[16] and "maximum flexibility."[17] DRULPA's "basic approach is to permit partners to have the broadest possible discretion in drafting their partnership agreements and to furnish answers only in situations where the partners have not expressly made provisions in their partnership agreement"[18] or "where the agreement is inconsistent with mandatory statutory provisions."[19] In those situations, a court will "look for guidance from the statutory default rules, tradi-

14. *Gotham S.J. Op.*, at 24, 2000 WL 1476663 at *10. DRULPA § 17–1101(d)(2), codified at 6 Del. C. § 17–1101(d)(2), reads: "To the extent that, at law or equity, a partner or other person has duties (including fiduciary duties) and liabilities relating thereto to a limited partnership or to another partner or to another person that is a party to or is otherwise bound by a partnership agreement, ... (2) the partner's or other person's duties and liabilities may be expand-ed or restricted by provisions in the partnership agreement."

15. *Elf Atochem North America, Inc. v. Jaffari*, 727 A.2d 286, 287 (Del.1999).

16. Id at 290....

17. *Elf Atochem*, 727 A.2d at 291 n. 27.

18. Id. at 291.

19. Id. at 292.

tional notions of fiduciary duties, or other extrinsic evidence."[20] But, if the limited partnership agreement unambiguously provides for fiduciary duties, any claim of a breach of a fiduciary duty must be analyzed generally in terms of the partnership agreement.[21]

The Vice Chancellor found, and the parties do not contest, that Partnership Agreement Sections 7.05 and 7.10(a) set forth fiduciary duties of entire fairness owed by the General Partner to its partners generally in self-dealing transactions, such as the Odd Lot Resale. Section 7.05 expressly permits the Partnership to enter into self-dealing transactions with the General Partner or its affiliate "provided that the terms of any such transaction are substantially equivalent to terms obtainable by the Partnership from a comparable unaffiliated third party."[22] Section 7.10(a) requires the General Partner to form an independent Audit Committee that shall review and approve self-dealing transactions between the Partnership and the General Partner and any of its affiliates.[23] The Vice Chancellor found, and the parties do not contest, that Sections 7.05 and 7.10(a) "operate together as a contractual statement of the traditional entire fairness standard [of fair price and fair dealing], with § 7.05 reflecting the substantive aspect of that standard and § 7.10 reflecting the procedural aspect of that standard."

Because the Partnership Agreement provided for fiduciary duties, the Vice Chancellor properly held that the Partnership Agreement, as a contract, provides the standard for determining whether the General Partner breached its duty to the Partnership through its execution of the Odd Lot Resale. As the Vice Chancellor stated, the Partnership Agreement "leaves no room for the application of common law fiduciary duty principles to measure the General Partner's conduct" because the Partnership Agreement "supplanted fiduciary duty and became the sole source of protection for the public unitholders of the Partnership." Thus, "the General Partner was subject, by contract, to a fairness standard akin to the common law one applicable to self-dealing transactions by fiduciaries."

The General Partner, HGI, Gumbiner, and Guzzetti apparently concede: (1) the General Partner's conduct associated with the Odd

20. *Sonet*, 722 A.2d at 324.

21. See id. ("[U]nder Delaware limited partnership law a claim of breach of fiduciary duty must first be analyzed in terms of the operating governing instrument—the partnership agreement—and only where that document is silent or ambiguous, or where the principles of equity are implicated, will a Court begin to look for guidance from the statutory default rules, traditional notions of fiduciary duties, or other extrinsic evidence.")....

22. Section 7.05 of the Partnership Agreement states in its entirety: "The Partnership is expressly permitted to enter into transactions with the General Partner or any Affiliate thereof provided that the terms of any such transaction are substantially equiv-

alent to terms obtainable by the Partnership from a comparable unaffiliated third party."

23. Section 7.10(a) states in its entirety: "The General Partner shall form an Audit Committee ("the Audit Committee") to be comprised of two members of the board of directors of the General Partner who are not affiliated with the General Partner or its Affiliates except by reason of such directorship. The functions of the Audit Committee shall be to review and approve (i) the expense reimbursements and compensation paid by the Partnership to the General Partner or any of its Affiliates and (ii) transactions between the Partnership and the General Partner and any of its Affiliates."

Lot Resale did not comply with Sections 7.05 and 7.10(a) of the Partnership Agreement because, as the Vice Chancellor found; (2) the Audit Committee never reviewed or approved the Odd Lot Resale to HGI; and (3) the General Partner never obtained a reliable financial analysis indicating that the Odd Lot Resale would be conducted on the same terms obtainable from an independent third party. Nonetheless, they argue that they are not liable for failing to comply with Sections 7.05 and 7.10(a) because Section 9.01 alone governed the Odd Lot Resale. They assert that the Odd Lot Resale was an issuance rather than a resale of Partnership units to HGI. The defendants seek the protection of Section 9.01, which gives the General Partner absolute and independent authority to issue additional Partnership units to any person or entity, including affiliates such as HGI.

The Vice Chancellor properly found that the Odd Lot Resale was a resale of Partnership units to HGI and thus Section 9.01 is inapplicable. It is undisputed that the Partnership's accounting books did not treat the sale of odd lots to HGI as an issuance of units. Furthermore, the Partnership units from the Odd Lot Resale were listed on the American Stock Exchange, but the Resale was presented to the Exchange as a resale, not as an issuance. The Vice Chancellor properly found that the Odd Lot Resale was structured as a resale, in part to avoid American Stock Exchange Rule 713, which requires that holders approve additional issuances as a prerequisite to the shares or units' listing on the Exchange. Thus, the General Partner is liable for breaching the contractually created fiduciary duties of entire fairness provided by Sections 7.05 and 7.10(a) of the Partnership Agreement. . . .

Whether the Court of Chancery Had Discretion Not to Grant Recission in This Case . . .

. . . Because Gotham unjustifiably delayed challenging the Odd Lot Resale and the defendants did not intend to entrench the General Partner or improperly enrich HGI, we find that the Vice Chancellor was within his discretion in refusing to grant rescission in this case, even though the result of the challenged transaction was to secure control by the defendants. Given the result of control and the defendants' conduct, however, an adequate, rationally-articulated substitute remedy must be awarded.

Whether the Court of Chancery Abused Its Discretion by Failing to Account for a Control Premium

The Court of Chancery awarded money damages of approximately $3.4 million based on a per unit value of $25.84 for each Partnership unit resold to HGI. The court gave equal weight to four factors: book value, Gotham's comparables for minority stakes in other limited partnerships, the per unit price of an unrelated Spring 1996 repurchase of Partnership units, and the average price paid by the Partnership during the Odd Lot Offer. Gotham notes that none of the four factors "takes account of the lock on control that HGI obtained in the Resale." Gotham emphasizes that, at trial, Gumbiner valued control of the Partnership at $50 to $55 million and that only a mere $3.4 million was awarded as monetary damages. Gotham argues that this Court should reverse on this issue and remand to the Court of Chancery for a new remedy calculation that accounts for the value of control of the Partnership. This Court reviews the Court of Chancery's fashioning of remedies for abuse of discretion.

The Partnership Agreement provides for contractual fiduciary duties of entire fairness. Although the contract could have limited the damage remedy for breach of these duties to contract damages, it did not do so. The Court of Chancery is not precluded from awarding equitable relief as provided by the entire fairness standard where, as here, the general partner breached its contractually created fiduciary duty to meet the entire fairness standard and the partnership agreement is silent regarding damages. The Court of Chancery in this case may award equitable relief as provided by the entire fairness standard and is not limited to contract damages for two reasons: (1) this case involves a breach of the duty of loyalty and such a breach permits broad, discretionary, and equitable remedies; and (2) courts will not construe a contract as taking away other forms of appropriate relief, including equitable relief, unless the contract explicitly provides for an exclusive remedy.

In this case, as the Vice Chancellor properly found, the fiduciary duties provided for by the Partnership Agreement supplanted common law fiduciary duty principles, but "some of the agreement's provisions were 'in some sense . . . an explicit acceptance of the default duty of loyalty and fair dealing.'" The General Partner breached its duty of loyalty by failing to comply with the contractually created entire fairness standard during the Odd Lot Resale, which resulted in the General Partner and its corporate parent solidifying their control over the Partnership. Where there is "a breach of the duty of loyalty, as here, 'potentially harsher rules come into play' and 'the scope of recovery for a breach of the duty of loyalty is not to be determined narrowly [because t]he strict imposition of penalties under Delaware law are designed to discourage disloyalty.'"[27] Therefore, the Court of Chancery's "powers are complete to fashion any form of equitable and monetary relief as may be appropriate."[28] . . .

. . . Although the Vice Chancellor found that the defendants did not intend for the General Partner to become entrenched or HGI to be unjustly enriched, the Odd Lot Resale had that effect. The Court of Chancery was thus required to remedy that effect by compensating the limited partners for a control premium. As the Vice Chancellor recog-

---

27. *Cantor Fitzgerald, L.P. v. Cantor,* 2001 WL 536911 (Del.Ch.), at *3 (quoting *Int'l Telecharge,* 766 A.2d at 441 (quoting *Thorpe v. CERBCO, Inc.,* 676 A.2d 436, 445 (Del.1996))).

28. *Weinberger,* 457 A.2d at 714. See also *Int'l Telecharge,* 766 A.2d at 440 (stating that "the powers of the Court of Chancery are very broad in fashioning equitable and monetary relief under the entire fairness standard as may be appropriate"); *Cantor Fitzgerald, L.P. v. Cantor,* 2000 WL 307370 (Del.Ch.), at *29–*30 (stating that "equity must try to right the wrongs with adequate remedies" and awarding a declaratory judgement and money damages for a breach of a contractually created fiduciary duty).

nized, the Audit Committee—whose contractually-mandated functions were not implemented—conceivably would have "taken into account the fact that the Odd Lot resales were of particular advantage to HGI and demanded value for that advantage in exchange" because "the Odd Lot resales solidified HGI's control." Consequently, we find that the Vice Chancellor abused his discretion in fashioning the remedy in this case by failing (1) to address and decide the applicability of rescissory damages, and (2) to include in the damages calculation a premium for the control acquired by HGI through the Odd Lot Resale.

The Partnership is entitled to receive, at a minimum, what the Partnership units sold to HGI would have been worth at the time of the Odd Lot Resale if the General Partner had complied with the Partnership Agreement. We thus reverse the judgment of the Court of Chancery regarding the remedy in this case, and we remand for procedures, such as expansion of the record, as may be necessary and appropriate to accomplish two objectives. First, the Court of Chancery should seek to quantify how the challenged transaction would have been consummated had the defendants adhered to the Partnership Agreement's contractual entire fairness provisions. Specifically, the court should determine and consider what price the Audit Committee would have approved for the Odd Lot Offer resales to HGI if the Audit Committee had been aware that the transaction would result in HGI solidifying control over the Partnership. Second, the Court of Chancery should reconsider and award some form or combination of the various equitable remedies available to the limited partnership, including rescissory damages, sterilization of voting rights, and other appropriate methods of accounting for a control premium. We note that the Court of Chancery has the discretion to consider afresh in light of the above analysis whether or not to order rescission.

Conclusion

We affirm the judgment of the Court of Chancery that . . . the contractual fiduciary duties of entire fairness contained in the Partnership Agreement applied to the disputed transaction in this case . . . [and that] the Court of Chancery has the discretion not to grant rescission where the plaintiff unjustifiably delays seeking that remedy, provided that the court articulates and orders a reasonable alternative remedy. . . .

We reverse the judgment of the Court of Chancery regarding the calculation of damages. We remand, as discussed above, for the court to fashion a remedy according to its discretion that accounts for a control premium. . . .

———

NOTE ON GOTHAM PARTNERS v. HALLWOOD

In a passage in Gotham Partners v. Hallwood that is is omitted from the opinion as edited above, the Delaware Supreme Court said:

The Vice Chancellor's summary judgment opinion in this case ... creates a separate problem. We refer to one aspect of the Vice Chancellor's discussion of the Delaware Revised Uniform Limited Partnership Act ("DRULPA") in his summary judgment opinion in this case where he stated that [DRULPA] section 17–1101(d)(2) "expressly authorizes the elimination, modification or enhancement of ... fiduciary duties in the written agreement governing the limited partnership." It is at least the second time the Court of Chancery has stated in dicta that DRULPA ... § 17–1101(d)(2) permits a limited partnership agreement to eliminate fiduciary duties.

Because the Vice Chancellor's summary judgment order in this matter has not been appealed, his opinion on this point is not before us for review on this appeal. In our view, however, this dictum should not be ignored because it could be misinterpreted in future cases as a correct rule of law. Accordingly, in the interest of avoiding the perpetuation of a questionable statutory interpretation that could be relied upon adversely by courts, commentators and practitioners in the future, we are constrained to draw attention to the statutory language and the underlying general principle in our jurisprudence that scrupulous adherence to fiduciary duties is normally expected.

[DRULPA] § 17–1101(d)(2) states: "the partner's or other person's duties and liabilities may be expanded or restricted by provisions in the partnership agreement." There is no mention in § 17–1101(d)(2), or elsewhere in DRULPA ... that a limited partnership agreement may eliminate the fiduciary duties or liabilities of a general partner.

Finally, we note the historic cautionary approach of the courts of Delaware that efforts by a fiduciary to escape a fiduciary duty, whether by a corporate director or officer or other type of trustee, should be scrutinized searchingly. Accordingly, although it is not appropriate for us to express an advisory opinion on a matter not before us, we simply raise a note of concern and caution relating to this dubious dictum in the Vice Chancellor's summary judgment opinion.

In 2004, after the decision in *Gotham Partners*, the Delaware Legislature amended the Delaware Revised Uniform Partnership Act, the Delaware Limited Liability Company Act, and the Delaware Revised Uniform Limited Partnership Act to make explicit that in these three forms of organization the governing agreement—partnership agreement, limited partnership agreement, or limited liability company agreement—can eliminate, as well as expand or restrict, fiduciary or other duties. At the same time, the amendments made clear that the implied contractual covenant of good faith and fair dealing cannot be eliminated by agreement.

———

SECTION 2.   LIMITED LIABILITY COMPANIES

___

UNIFORM LIMITED LIABILITY COMPANY ACT §§ 101, 103, 112, 201–203, 206, 301–303, 404, 405, 408, 409

[See Statutory Supplement]

___

DELAWARE LIMITED LIABILITY COMPANY ACT §§ 18–101, 18–107, 18–201, 18–206, 18–301, 18–303, 18–401, 18–402, 18–504

[See Statutory Supplement]

___

NOTE ON LIMITED LIABILITY COMPANIES

Limited liability companies (LLCs) are noncorporate entities that are created under special statutes that combine elements of corporation and partnership law. As under corporation law, the owners ("members") of LLCs have limited liability. As under partnership law, an LLC has great freedom to structure its internal governance by agreement. Like a corporation, an LLC is an entity, so that it can, for example, hold property and sue and be sued in its own name. LLCs come in two flavors: member-managed LLCs, which are managed by their members, and manager-managed LLCs, which are managed by managers who may or may not be members.

The LLC is a relatively new form. As a result, the LLC statutes are still evolving and the case law is still sparse. Moreover, unlike the limited partnership statutes of the various states, which tend to follow RULPA, the LLC statutes are highly variable. Part (although not all) of the reason for this variability is explained by tax issues. At the time LLCs first evolved, alternative forms of business organization (alternative, that is, to general partnerships and corporations) were not automatically entitled to the benefits of partnership taxation. Instead, whether any given firm that was cast in an alternative unincorporated form, such as an LLC, qualified for partnership taxation, depended on whether or not the firm had a certain number of characteristics that were deemed by the Internal Revenue Service to be "critical corporate characteristics," such as continuity of life and transferability of ownership interests.

The original LLC statutes were partly shaped by this tax rule. Some of the statutes were highly flexible, and allowed each LLC to choose its own characteristics. Other statutes, however, made certain LLC characteristics mandatory, in an effort to ensure that LLCs created under the statute would be bulletproof against an attack based on the

IRS's characteristic-counting test. Under the new, check-the-box approach to the taxation of alternative forms of business organization, no special purpose is served by making a statute bulletproof, rather than flexible. It is therefore to be expected that bulletproof LLC statutes will converge with flexible LLC statutes.

This Note will describe the central characteristics of LLCs in terms of prevailing statutory patterns. Bear in mind that as to any given characteristic there will usually be some LLC statutes that fall outside the major patterns this Note describes.*

1. *Formation; Articles of Organization; Powers.* An LLC is formed by filing articles of organization in a designated state office—usually, the office of the Secretary of State. All statutes allow LLCs to be formed by a single person. The articles must include the name of the LLC, the address of its principal place of business or registered office in the State, and the name and address of its agent for service of process. Many statutes also require the articles to state: (1) The purpose of the LLC. (2) If the LLC is to be manager-managed, the names of the initial managers. If the LLC is to be member-managed, the names of its initial members. (3) The duration of the LLC or the latest date on which it is to dissolve. Many statutes also require the articles to include various kinds of additional information, the nature of which varies considerably.

Most statutes either provide that LLCs have all powers necessary to effectuate their purposes or contain an exhaustive laundry list of an LLC's powers.

2. *Operating Agreements.* An LLC's articles of organization are usually very sketchy. In most LLCs, the critical foundational instrument is the *operating agreement* (sometimes called by another name, such as "limited liability company agreement"), which is an agreement among the members concerning the LLC's affairs. The operating agreement typically provides for the governance of the LLC, its capitalization, the admission and withdrawal of members, and distributions. The statutes vary on whether an operating agreement must be in writing.

3. *Management.* Almost all of the LLC statutes provide as a default rule, which prevails unless agreed otherwise, that an LLC is to be managed by its members. A few statutes provide as a default rule that an LLC is to be managed by managers—who may but need not be members—unless otherwise agreed. The most common statutory provision is that the default rule concerning management can be varied only by a provision in the LLC's articles of organization, but many statutes provide that the default rule can be varied in the operating agreement. One way to vary the statutory default rule is to completely reverse it—either by providing for manager management in a state where the default rule is member management, or by providing for member management in a state where the default rule is manager

* The descriptions of statutory patterns in this Note are based on the comprehensive tables in Ribstein & Keating, Limited Liability Companies (2004).

management. Another way to vary the statutory default rule is to distribute management functions between members and managers.

4. *Voting by Members*. Just over half the statutes provide as a default rule that members vote per capita—that is, one vote per member—unless otherwise agreed. This is like the partnership default rule. The remaining statutes provide that members vote pro rata, that is, by financial interest, unless otherwise agreed. This is the usual rule in corporations. Normally, members act by a majority vote, per capita or pro rata as the case may be. However, some of the statutes require a unanimous vote for certain designated actions, such as amendment of the articles or the operating agreement.

5. *Agency Powers*.

a. *Member-managed LLCs*. In a member-managed LLC, the apparent authority of a member is comparable to the apparent authority of a partner—that is, each member has power to bind the LLC for any act that is for apparently carrying on the business of the LLC in the usual way or ordinary course. Even if an action is not in the usual or ordinary course, the remaining members may confer on a given member actual authority to bind the LLC to an action or a given type of action. Conversely, the members as a group may withdraw the actual authority of one or more members to take a certain kind of action that is in the ordinary or usual course. In that case, if a member takes such an action the LLC will be bound by virtue of the member's apparent authority, but the member may be obliged to indemnify the LLC for any loss that results from her contravention of the other members' decision.

b. *Manager-managed LLCs*. In manager-managed firms, the rules concerning authority are comparable to those in the corporations—that is, typically only the managers have apparent authority to bind the firm. Members of a manager-managed LLC have no apparent authority to bind the LLC, just as shareholders have no apparent authority to bind a corporation. Most of the statutes provide that a manager in a manager-managed LLC has the same authority as a member in a member-managed firm.

c. *The Delaware statute*. Section 18–402 of the Delaware Limited Liability Company Act provides "Unless otherwise provided in a limited liability company agreement, each member and manager has the authority to bind the limited liability company." This section is unusual in two respects. First, it gives members wide apparent authority even in manager-managed LLC's. Second, it allows the apparent authority of both managers and members to be limited by the operating agreement, which is not a public document.

6. *Inspection of Books and Records*. The statutes generally provide that members are entitled to access to the LLC's books and records or to specified books and records. Many of the statutes include an explicit provision that the inspection must be for a proper purpose. Such a limitation might or might not be read into other statutes.

7. *Fiduciary Duties*. The fiduciary duties of managers and members of LLCs are largely unspecified by the LLC statutes, just as the fiduciary duties of directors, officers, and shareholders are largely unspecified by the corporate statutes. Presumably, the courts in deciding LLC cases involving fiduciary duties will borrow very heavily from the corporate and partnership case-law.

Despite the lack of extensive specification, the LLC statutes, like the corporate and partnership statutes, do include important provisions concerning particular issues of fiduciary duty. For example, most although not all of the statutes specify the elements of the duty of care. Some statutes provide that a manager will be liable only for gross negligence, bad faith, recklessness, or equivalent conduct. Others require a manager to act as would a prudent person in similar circumstances.

About two-thirds of the LLC statutes provide a mechanism for the authorization of self-interested transactions by disinterested managers or members. Many of the LLC statutes permit the operating agreement to limit fiduciary duties, and some permit the operating agreement to waive fiduciary duties entirely. Statutes that permit all fiduciaries to be waived may limit the force of such a waiver by prohibiting a waiver of the duty of good faith.

8. *Derivative Actions*. Most of the statutes explicitly permit members of LLCs to bring derivative actions on the LLC's behalf, based on a breach of fiduciary duties. Even where the statute does not explicitly permit such actions, courts are highly likely to permit them, both on analogy to corporation and limited-partnership law and because a failure to do so might allow fiduciaries who were in control of an LLC to violate their fiduciary duties without any sanction.

9. *Distributions*. Most LLC statutes that address the issue of distributions provide that in the absence of an agreement to the contrary, distributions to members are to be made pro rata according to the members' contributions, on analogy to corporation law, rather than per capita (the default rule in partnership law). However, a number of statutes provide that in the absence of an agreement to the contrary, distributions are to be made on a per capita basis.

10. *Members' Interests*. A member of an LLC has financial rights, and may also have governance rights as a member—that is, apart from any governance rights that she may have as a manager in a manager-managed LLC. A member's *financial* rights include her right to receive distributions. A member's *governance* rights include her right, if any, to participate in management, to vote on certain issues, and to be supplied with information. Most statutes define a member's *interest* in an LLC to consist of the member's financial rights, but some define a member's interest to include her governance rights.

Generally speaking, a member of an LLC can freely transfer her financial rights by transferring her interest in the LLC. Governance rights are treated differently. A majority of the statutes provide that a member can transfer her governance rights only with the unanimous consent of all the other members. Some statutes provide that a member can transfer her governance rights with the approval of a majority of the other members, or a majority of other members' financial interests, depending on the statute. Most statutes permit consent requirements for transfers of management interests to be varied in the articles of incorporation or operating agreement.

It is clear that a member who assigns her interest (that is, her financial rights) normally cannot include an assignment of her governance rights, unless otherwise agreed or approved by the other members, but it is not always clear whether a member who assigns her financial rights *retains* her governance rights. A number of statutes provide that a member who assigns her membership interest loses her membership status. Some statutes don't speak to the issue. A few provide that a member who assigns her membership interest loses her membership status if and when the assignee becomes a member. A few statutes provide that if a member assigns her membership interest, the remaining members can remove her as a member.

If a member of an LLC assigns her interest in the LLC as a *pledge* to secure a debt, rather than in an outright sale, and if the creditor gets a judgment against the member based on the debt, the creditor can get a charging order against the member's interest. A charging order gives the creditor the right to the member's share of any distributions.

11. *Liability*. All of the LLC statutes provide that the members and managers of an LLC are not liable for the LLC's debts, obligations, and other liabilities. However, members may become liable if the conditions for piercing an LLC's veil are satisfied. See Kaycee Land and Livestock v. Flahive, infra.

12. *Dissociation*. The LLC statutes vary considerably in their treatment of dissociation, that is, the termination of a member's interest in an LLC other than by the member's voluntary transfer of her interest. Ribstein describes the dissolution provisions of the LLC statutes as follows:

> LLC Statutes vary on members' power to voluntarily withdraw and receive the value of their interests. Some provide for withdrawal at any time subject to a notice requirement. This is justified by the need ... to provide some liquidity for otherwise locked-in interests. Some statutes eliminate any default right to withdraw or permit voluntary termination of membership status, but deny a default right to be paid on resignation. These statutes are based in part on the disruption a buyout right may cause a firm, and in part on the need to reduce the tax valuation of the departing partner's interest in familiar firms. ...

> Most LLC statutes provide that a withdrawing member is entitled to some payment on withdrawal. The statutes use different formulations. Some are based on a return of contributions, while others provide for payment of fair market value in addition to, or instead other distributions to which the member is entitled

(apparently including regular payouts that the member was entitled to receive before withdrawal). The statutes also provide for adjustment of the payment to exclude goodwill in the event of wrongful withdrawal. . . .

Consistent with [the] potential costs of dissolution at will, LLC statutes increasingly provide that dissociation does not dissolve or trigger liquidation of the firm. . . .

LLC statutes generally allow dissolution by judicial decree. Some allow judicial dissolution when it is "not reasonably practicable to carry on the business in conformity with the parties' agreement." Where the statute provides only for dissolution, it is not clear whether the court can order other relief, including buyout.

L. Ribstein, Limited Liability Companies 11–3—11–19 (2004).

———

As of 2002, there were 946,000 LLCs in the United States, with an average of 4 members in each LLC. The number of LLCs is growing rapidly: There were 17,000 LLCs in 1993, 48,000 LLCs in 1994, and 119,000 LLCs in 1995, and 221,000 as late as 1996. During the period 1996–2002, the number of LLCs increased more than 400% while the number of general partnerships decreased by 25%. In 2002, for the first time, the number of LLCs exceeded the number of general partnerships and the number of limited partnerships. However, the total number of the two partnership forms, combined, still exceeded the total number of LLCs; the total net income of general partnerships exceeded the total net income of LLCs; and so did the even higher total net income of limited partnerships. Wheeler & Parsons, Partnership Returns Statistics of Income Bulletin Fall 2004, at 57; Alan Zempel, Partnership Returns, 1996, 18 Statistics of Income Bulletin No. 2, at 49–50 (1998).

———

Kaycee Land and Livestock v. Flahive

Supreme Court of Wyoming, 2002.
46 P.3d 323

■ KITE, JUSTICE.

This matter comes before this court as a question certified to us by the district court for resolution under W.R.A.P. [Wisconsin Rules of Appellate Procedure] 11. The certified question seeks resolution of whether, in the absence of fraud, the entity veil of a limited liability company (LLC) can be pierced in the same manner as that of a corporation. We answer the certified question in the affirmative.

CERTIFIED QUESTION

The question we have agreed to answer is phrased as follows:

In the absence of fraud, is a claim to pierce the Limited Liability entity veil or disregard the Limited Liability Company entity in the same manner as a court would pierce a corporate veil or disregard a corporate shield, an available remedy against a Wyoming Limited Liability Company under Wyoming's Limited Liability Company Act, Wyo. Stat. §[§] 17–15–101 through 17–15–144.

FACTS

In a W.R.A.P. 11 certification of a question of law, we rely entirely upon the factual determinations made in the trial court.... The district court submitted the following statement of facts in its order certifying the question of law:

1.   Flahive Oil & Gas is a Wyoming Limited Liability Company with no assets at this time.

2.   [Kaycee Land and Livestock] entered into a contract with Flahive Oil & Gas LLC allowing Flahive Oil & Gas to use the surface of its real property.

3.   Roger Flahive is and was the managing member of Flahive Oil & Gas at all relevant times.

4.   [Kaycee Land and Livestock] alleges that Flahive Oil & Gas caused environmental contamination to its real property located in Johnson County, Wyoming.

5.   [Kaycee Land and Livestock] seeks to pierce the LLC veil and disregard the L[L]C entity of Flahive Oil & Gas Limited Liability Company and hold Roger Flahive individually liable for the contamination.

6.   There is no allegation of fraud.

DISCUSSION

The question presented is limited to whether, in the absence of fraud, the remedy of piercing the veil is available against a company formed under the Wyoming Limited Liability Company Act (Wyo. Stat. Ann. § § 17–15–101 to–144). To answer this question, we must first examine the development of the doctrine within Wyoming's corporate context. As a general rule, a corporation is a separate entity distinct from the individuals comprising it. *Opal Mercantile v. Tamblyn*, 616 P.2d 776, 778 (Wyo.1980). Wyoming statutes governing corporations do not address the circumstances under which the veil can be pierced. However, since 1932, this court has espoused the concept that a corporation's legal entity will be disregarded whenever the recognition thereof in a particular case will lead to injustice. *See Caldwell v. Roach*, 44 Wyo. 319, 12 P.2d 376, 380 (1932). In *Miles v. CEC Homes, Inc.*, 753 P.2d 1021, 1023 (Wyo.1988) (quoting *Amfac Mechanical Supply Co. v. Federer*, 645 P.2d 73, 77 (Wyo.1982)), this court summarized the circumstances under which the corporate veil would be pierced pursuant to Wyoming law:

" 'Before a corporation's acts and obligations can be legally recognized as those of a particular person, and vice versa, it must be made to appear that the corporation is not only influenced and governed by that person, but that there is such a unity of interest and ownership that the individuality, or separateness, of such person and corporation has ceased, and that the facts are such that an adherence to the fiction of the separate existence of the corporation would, under the particular circumstances, sanction a fraud or promote injustice.' Quoting *Arnold v. Browne*, 27 Cal. App.3d 386, 103 Cal.Rptr. 775 (1972) (overruled on other grounds)."

We provided the following factors to be considered in determining whether a corporate entity may be disregarded:

" 'Among the possible factors pertinent to the trial court's determination are: commingling of funds and other assets, failure to segregate funds of the separate entities, and the unauthorized diversion of corporate funds or assets to other than corporate uses; the treatment by an individual of the assets of the corporation as his own; the failure to obtain authority to issue or subscribe to stock; the holding out by an individual that he is personally liable for the debts of the corporation; the failure to maintain minutes or adequate corporate records and the confusion of the records of the separate entities; the identical equitable ownership in the two entities; the identification of the equitable owners thereof with the domination and control of the two entities; identification of the directors and officers of the two entities in the responsible supervision and management; the failure to adequately capitalize a corporation; the absence of corporate assets, and undercapitalization; the use of a corporation as a mere shell, instrumentality or conduit for a single venture or the business of an individual or another corporation; the concealment and misrepresentation of the identity of the responsible ownership, management and financial interest or concealment of personal business activities; the disregard of legal formalities and the failure to maintain arm's length relationships among related entities; the use of the corporate entity to procure labor, services or merchandise for another person or entity; the diversion of assets from a corporation by or to a stockholder or other person or entity, to the detriment of creditors, or the manipulation of assets and liabilities between entities so as to concentrate the assets in one and the liabilities in another; the contracting with another with intent to avoid performance by use of a corporation as a subterfuge of illegal transactions; and the formation and use of a corporation to transfer to it the existing liability of another person or entity [citation].' " 645 P.2d at 77–78 (quoting *Arnold v. Browne, supra,* 103 Cal.Rptr. at 781–82).

Miles, 753 P.2d at 1023–24.

Wyoming courts, as well as courts across the country, have typically utilized a fact driven inquiry to determine whether circumstances justify a decision to pierce a corporate veil. *Opal Mercantile,* 616 P.2d at 778. This case comes to us as a certified question in the abstract with little factual context, and we are asked to broadly pronounce that there are no circumstances under which this court will look through a failed attempt to create a separate LLC entity and prevent injustice. We simply cannot reach that conclusion and believe it is improvident for this court to prohibit this remedy from applying to any unforeseen circumstance that may exist in the future.

We have long recognized that piercing the corporate veil is an equitable doctrine. *State ex rel. Christensen v. Nugget Coal Co.*, 60 Wyo. 51, 144 P.2d 944, 952 (1944). The concept of piercing the corporate veil is a judicially created remedy for situations where corporations have not been operated as separate entities as contemplated by statute and, therefore, are not entitled to be treated as such. The determination of whether the doctrine applies centers on whether there is an element of injustice, fundamental unfairness, or inequity. The concept developed through common law and is absent from the statutes governing corporate organization. *See* Wyo. Stat. Ann. § § 17–16–101 to–1803 (LexisNexis 2001)....

We note that Wyoming was the first state to enact LLC statutes.... Wyoming's statute is very short and establishes only minimal requirements for creating and operating LLCs. It seems highly unlikely that the Wyoming legislature gave any consideration to whether the common-law doctrine of piercing the veil should apply to the liability limitation granted by that fledgling statute. It is true that some other states have adopted specific legislation extending the doctrine to LLCs while Wyoming has not. However, that situation seems more attributable to the fact that Wyoming was a pioneer in the LLC arena and states which adopted LLC statutes much later had the benefit of years of practical experience during which this issue was likely raised.

... It stands to reason that, because it is an equitable doctrine, "[t]he paucity of statutory authority for LCC piercing should not be considered a barrier to its application." [Karin Schwindt, Limited Liability Companies: Issues in Member Liability, 44 UCLA L. Rev. 1541, 1552 (1997).] Lack of explicit statutory language should not be considered an indication of the legislature's desire to make LLC members impermeable. *Id.* at 1555, 144 P.2d 944; Robert B. Thompson, *The Limits of Liability in the New Limited Liability Entities*, 32 Wake Forest L.Rev. 1, 19 (1997). Moreover,

> " 'It is not to be presumed that the legislature intended to abrogate or modify a rule of the common law by the enactment of a statute upon the same subject; it is rather to be presumed that no change in the common law was intended unless the language employed clearly indicates such an intention.... The rules of common law are not to be changed by doubtful implication, nor overturned except by clear and unambiguous language.' " *McKinney v. McKinney*, [59 Wyo. 204,] 135 P.2d [940,] 942 [(1943)], quoting from 25 R.C.L. 1054, § 280.

Allstate Insurance Company v. Wyoming Insurance Department, 672 P.2d 810, 824 (Wyo.1983).

With the dearth of legislative consideration on this issue in Wyoming, we are left to determine whether applying the well established common law to LLCs somehow runs counter to what the legislature would have intended had it considered the issue. In that regard, it is instructive that: "Every state that has enacted LLC piercing legislation has chosen to follow corporate law standards and not develop a separate LLC standard." Philip P. Whynott, The Limited Liability Company § 11:140 at 11–5 (3d ed.1999). Statutes which create corporations and LLCs have the same basic purpose—to limit the liability of individual investors with a corresponding benefit to economic development. Eric Fox, *Piercing the Veil of Limited Liability Companies*, 62 Geo. Wash. L.Rev. 1143, 1145–46 (1994). Statutes created the legal fiction of the corporation being a completely separate entity which could act independently from individual persons. If the corporation were created and operated in conformance with the statutory requirements, the law would treat it as a separate entity and shelter the individual shareholders from any liability caused by corporate action, thereby encouraging investment. However, courts throughout the country have consistently recognized certain unjust circumstances can arise if immunity from liability shelters those who have failed to operate a corporation as a separate entity. Consequently, when corporations fail to follow the statutorily mandated formalities, co-mingle funds, or ignore the restrictions in their articles of incorporation regarding separate treatment of corporate property, the courts deem it appropriate to disregard the separate identity and do not permit shareholders to be sheltered from liability to third parties for damages caused by the corporations' acts.

We can discern no reason, in either law or policy, to treat LLCs differently than we treat corporations. If the members and officers of an LLC fail to treat it as a separate entity as contemplated by statute, they should not enjoy immunity from individual liability for the LLC's acts that cause damage to third parties. Most, if not all, of the expert LLC commentators have concluded the doctrine of piercing the veil should apply to LLCs. *See generally* Fox, *supra;* Gelb, *supra;* Robert G. Lang, Note, *Utah's Limited Liability Company Act: Viable Alternative or Trap for the Unwary?*, 1993 Utah L.Rev. 941, 966 (1993) (Part 2); Stephen B. Presser, Piercing the Corporate Veil § 4.01[2] (2002); Ann M. Seward & Laura Stubberud, *The Limits of Limited Liability–Part Two*, Limited Liability Company Reporter 94–109 (January/February 1994); Schwindt, *supra.* It also appears that most courts faced with a similar situation—LLC statutes which are silent and facts which suggest the LLC veil should be pierced—have had little trouble concluding the common law should be applied and the factors weighed accordingly. *See, e.g., Hollowell v. Orleans Regional Hospital*, No. Civ. A. 95–4029, 1998 WL 283298 (E.D.La. May 29, 1998); *Ditty v. CheckRite, Ltd., Inc.*, 973 F.Supp. 1320 (D.Utah 1997); *Tom Thumb Food Markets, Inc. v. TLH Properties, LLC*, No. C9–98–1277, 1999 WL 31168 (Minn.Ct.App. Jan.26, 1999).

Certainly, the various factors which would justify piercing an LLC veil would not be identical to the corporate situation for the obvious reason that many of the organizational formalities applicable to corporations do not apply to LLCs. The LLC's operation is intended to be much more flexible than a corporation's. Factors relevant to determining when to pierce the corporate veil have developed over time in a multitude of cases. It would be inadvisable in this case, which lacks a complete factual context, to attempt to articulate all the possible factors to be applied to LLCs in Wyoming in the future. For guidance, we direct attention to commentators who have opined on the appropriate factors to be applied in the LLC context. Fox, *supra;* Gelb, *supra;* Curtis J. Braukmann, Comment, *Limited Liability Companies,* 39 U. Kan. L.Rev. 967 (1991); Presser, *supra;* Seward & Stubberud, *supra;* Larry E. Ribstein & Robert R. Keatinge, *Members' Limited Liability,* Limited Liability Companies § 12.03 (1999); Robert R. Keating et al., *The Limited Liability Company: A Study of the Emerging Entity,* 47 The Business Lawyer 375 (1992).

The certified question presents an interesting internal inconsistency. It begins, "In the absence of fraud," thereby presenting the assumption that a court may pierce an LLC's veil in a case of fraud. Thus, the certified question assumes that, when fraud is found, the courts are able to disregard the LLC entity despite the statutory framework which supposedly precludes such a result. Either the courts continue to possess the equitable power to take such action or they do not. Certainly, nothing in the statutes suggests the legislature gave such careful consideration and delineated the specific circumstances under which the courts can act in this arena. If the assumption is correct, individual LLC members can be held personally liable for damages to innocent third parties when the LLC has committed fraud. Yet, when the LLC has caused damage and has inadequate capitalization, co-mingled funds, diverted assets, or used the LLC as a mere shell, individual members are immune from liability. Legislative silence cannot be stretched to condone such an illogical result.

In *Amfac Mechanical Supply Co.,* this court clarified that a showing of fraud or an intent to defraud is not necessary to disregard a corporate entity. 645 P.2d at 79. We clearly stated: "Fraud is, of course, a matter of concern in suits to disregard corporate fictions, but it is not a prerequisite to such a result." *Id.* Other courts have echoed this view: "Liability on the basis of fraud, however, does not encompass the entire spectrum of cases in which the veil was pierced in the interest of equity." Fox, *supra* at 1169. Thus, even absent fraud, courts have the power to impose liability on corporate shareholders. *Id.* at 1170. This same logic should naturally be extended to the LLC context. We have made clear that: "Each case involving the disregard of the separate entity doctrine must be governed by the special facts of that case." *Opal Mercantile,* 616 P.2d at 778. Determinations of fact are within the trier of fact's province. *Id.* The district court must complete a fact intensive inquiry and exercise its equitable powers to determine whether piercing the veil is appropriate under the circumstances presented in this case.

CONCLUSION

No reason exists in law or equity for treating an LLC differently than a corporation is treated when considering whether to disregard the legal entity. We conclude the equitable remedy of piercing the veil is an available remedy under the Wyoming Limited Liability Company Act.

———

Solar Cells, Inc. v. True North Partners, LLC

Court of Chancery of Delaware.
2002 WL 749163

■ CHANDLER, J.

This action concerns the proposed merger of defendant First Solar, LLC ("First Solar" or the "Company") with and into First Solar Operating, LLC ("FSO"), the wholly-owned operating subsidiary of First Solar Ventures, LLC ("FSV"). The plaintiff, Solar Cells, Inc. ("Solar Cells"), alleges that the individual defendant managers of First Solar,[29] acting at the direction of defendant True North Partners, LLC ("True North" and, collectively, "the defendants"), acted in bad faith in approving the proposed merger and that the defendants will be unable to prove the entire fairness of that merger.

On March 13, 2002, Solar Cells filed a motion for a temporary restraining order requesting that this Court enjoin the proposed merger, which was scheduled to close two days later. The defendants agreed to postpone consummation of the merger in order to permit the parties to conduct the limited discovery necessary to present their positions at a preliminary injunction hearing. Solar Cells' motion for a preliminary injunction was fully briefed and then argued on April 17, 2002. Because I find that Solar Cells has met its burden of establishing a reasonable likelihood that it will be successful on the merits of its claim of a breach of fiduciary duty and that it is threatened by irreparable harm if the merger is consummated, I will enter an Order preliminarily enjoining the merger.

I. BACKGROUND FACTS

Solar Cells, an Ohio corporation, was founded in 1987 by Harold A. McMaster ("McMaster") to develop, design, and manufacture products and processes for photovoltaic electricity generation-technology commonly referred to as "solar power." McMaster designed technologies and processes for manufacturing photovoltaic cells making use of heretofore-unknown techniques that were predicted to revolutionize the solar power industry. These inventions purportedly would permit cost-effective manufacture of photovoltaic cells that produce energy at rates competitive with, or even less than, the present cost of electrical

---

29. The individual defendants are First Solar Managers elected by True North: Michael J. Ahearn ("Ahearn"), Michael L. Pierce ("Pierce"), and Michael Gallagher ("Gallagher").

generation using fossil fuels. In order to exploit the potential of these inventions, True North, an Arizona limited liability company, was brought in to provide needed financing. Solar Cells and True North formed First Solar as a Delaware limited liability company in February 1999 to commercialize McMaster's solar technology.

First Solar is managed pursuant to the Operating Agreement of First Solar, LLC ("Operating Agreement"). The Operating Agreement required Solar Cells to contribute patented and proprietary technology—valued in the Operating Agreement at $35 million—to First Solar. True North was to contribute $35 million in capital to First Solar and, also pursuant to the Operating Agreement, was required to, and did, loan First Solar an additional $8 million. In return for their contributions, Solar Cells and [True North] each received 4,500 of First Solar's Class A membership units. Solar Cells also received 100% of First Solar's Class B membership units.[30] The business and affairs of First Solar is conducted by five Managers. The Operating Agreement permits True North to elect three of those Managers (the "True North Managers") and Solar Cells to elect the remaining two Managers (the "Solar Cells Managers"). It is undisputed that, since its inception, First Solar has been managed by True North.

First Solar's continuing development and manufacturing expenditures, as well as its inability to produce a marketable product, eventually depleted the Company's initial funding. By early 2001 it became apparent that continued operations would require additional funding. To this end, in March 2001, First Solar retained investment banker Adams, Harkness & Hill, Inc. ("AHH") to find a strategic investor for the Company. In order for the Company to continue operating while AHH searched for a strategic investor, True North agreed to make an additional $15 million loan to First Solar.

The Loan Agreement between First Solar and True North bundled True North's original $8 million loan and the new $15 million loan and represented a funding commitment by True North of up to a total of $23 million through December 31, 2001. Upon either the receipt of outside investment or at the end of its funding commitment, the Loan Agreement gave True North the option of converting some or all of the loan amount into Class A Units of First Solar[31] or to retain the investment as a loan with liquidation preferences. For reasons disputed by the parties (but not relevant to this motion), no outside investors were brought into First Solar.

From December 2001 through March 2002, the parties engaged in unsuccessful negotiations regarding different alternatives for financing and restructuring First Solar. On March 5, 2002, True North purported to convert $250,000 of its outstanding loans to First Solar into Class A Units at a conversion ratio based on a January 8, 2002 AHH valuation of First Solar at $32,000,000. On March 7, 2002, the True North

---

30. According to the Operating Agreement, Class A Units had voting rights, and Class B Units had no voting rights.

31. The loan was convertible either at the same value as AHH proposed to outside investors or at a "conversion ratio" specified in the Loan Agreement.

Managers executed a written consent approving the challenged merger of First Solar into FSO, a Delaware limited liability company wholly owned by True North. On March 11, 2002, Solar Cells received notice of the proposed merger, which was scheduled to close on March 15, 2002, and the terms of that merger. In connection with the merger, True North would convert its remaining outstanding loans into equity at the same ratio as the March 5, 2002 conversion. The merger would occur based on a total valuation of First Solar at $32 million with First Solar ownership units being exchanged for ownership units of the surviving company. The end result of the merger-related transactions would be that Solar Cells would go from owning 50% of the Class A Units of First Solar to owning 5% of the membership units of the surviving company. On March 13, 2002, Solar Cells filed a complaint and request for temporary restraining order enjoining consummation of the proposed merger. True North agreed not to cause its Managers to close the merger before this Court's decision on Solar Cells' motion for a preliminary injunction filed in response to that agreement. . . .

IV. ANALYSIS

A. *Likelihood of Success on the Merits*

The defendants argue that all of the actions taken in connection with the proposed merger were clearly authorized by the Operating Agreement. They further argue that the Operating Agreement limited any fiduciary duties owed by True North Managers. Section 4.18(a) of the Operating Agreement provides, in relevant part:

> Solar Cells and [First Solar] acknowledge that the True North Managers have fiduciary obligations to both [First Solar] and to True North, which fiduciary obligations may, because of the ability of the True North Managers to control [First Solar] and its business, create a conflict of interest or a potential conflict of interest for the true North Managers. Both [First Solar] and Solar Cells hereby waive any such conflict of interest or potential conflict of interest and agree that neither True North nor any True North Manager shall have any liability to [First Solar] or to Solar Cells with respect to any such conflict of interest or potential conflict of interest, provided that the True North managers have acted in a manner which they believe in good faith to be in the best interest of [First Solar].

I note that this clause purports to limit *liability* stemming from any conflict of interest. Solar Cells has not requested that this Court impose liability on the individual defendants. It is currently only seeking to *enjoin* the proposed merger. Therefore, exculpation for personal liability has no bearing on the likelihood that Solar Cells would be successful on the merits of its contention that the proposed merger is inequitable and should be enjoined. Even if waiver of liability for engaging in conflicting interest transactions is contracted for, that does not mean that there is a waiver of all fiduciary duties to Solar Cells. Indeed, § 4.18(a) expressly states that the True North Managers must act in "good faith." It is undisputed that First Solar was, and is, in financial distress. Months of unsuccessful negotiations have been ongoing in an attempt to come to an agreement as to how to remedy that situation. On March 6, 2002, the full Board of Managers met and the True North Managers made no mention of the planned merger. The *very next day,* March 7, 2002, the three True North Managers met and by written consent approved the proposed merger. No effort was made to inform the Solar Cells Managers that this action was contemplated, or imminent, when those facts were surely known at the time of the March 6 meeting.[32] At the earliest, Solar Cells was given notice of the fact, and terms, of the proposed merger (which were presented as a *fait accompli*) via facsimile on March 8, 2002—a week before consummation of a merger that will apparently reduce Solar Cells' interest from 50% to 5%. These actions do not appear to be those of fiduciaries acting in good faith. As the Supreme Court and this Court have made clear, it is not an unassailable defense to say that what was done was in technical compliance with the law.[33] The facts before me make it likely, in my opinion, that the defendants would be required to show the entire fairness of the proposed merger.

The party with the burden of establishing entire fairness must establish that the challenged transaction was the result of fair dealing and offered a fair price. Fair dealing pertains to the process by which the transaction was approved and looks at the terms, structure, and timing of the transaction. Fair price includes all relevant factors "relat[ing] to the economic and financial considerations of the proposed merger."[34]

The defendants argue that there is nothing inherently unfair about the structure of the merger—a holding company with a wholly-owned operating subsidiary. Solar Cells points out, however, that there was no independent bargaining mechanism set up to protect its interests. In fact, there was no negotiation at all. All of the decisions regarding the terms of the merger and its approval were made unilaterally by True North through its representative Managers. No advance notice of this merger was given to Solar Cells. The fact that the Operating Agreement permits action by written consent of a majority of the Managers and permits interested transactions free from personal liability does not give a fiduciary free reign to approve any transaction he sees fit regardless of the impact on those to whom he owes a fiduciary duty.

The defendants contend that the timing of the merger was dictated by the Company's financial emergency, an emergency they say had been exacerbated by Solar Cells' refusal to negotiate, in good faith, a suitable plan for restructuring the Company. Solar Cells counters that the timing was driven by True North's desire to increase its propor-

---

32. The plaintiff contends that documents produced during discovery reveal that the defendants had been planning the proposed merger since at least February 27, 2002.

33. *See Schnell v. Chris–Craft Indus.,* 285 A.2d 437 (Del.1971).

34. *See Weinberger v. UOP, Inc.,* 457 A.2d 701, 711 (Del.1983).

tionate ownership while simultaneously squeezing out Solar Cells at an unfair price. Solar Cells argues that the effect of the merger is essentially the same as the terms of a restructuring plan Solar Cells had refused to agree to in February 2002. They contend, in the face of Solar Cells' refusal to accept an unfair restructuring offer voluntarily, that the defendants immediately sought to impose similar terms by way of the proposed merger.

I am unconvinced by defendants' argument that the merger was fair to Solar Cells because Solar Cells retains voting rights in the surviving company. On matters where the unit-holders can vote, Solar Cells is diluted from an equal (50%) voice, to only 5%.... In my opinion, the facts before me establish a reasonable likelihood that defendants will not be able to establish that the proposed merger was the result of fair dealing.

Application of the entire fairness standard requires a demonstration of both fair dealing and fair price. Having considered the fair dealing component of the standard, I turn now to the fair price analysis.

Solar Cells contends that True North manipulated the valuation of First Solar in order to advantage itself. That is, according to Solar Cells, when True North decided it would become a buyer of First Solar it unilaterally caused AHH to create a fundamentally flawed valuation that is less than one-third of the value calculated by AHH only five months earlier. On the other hand, True North insists that AHH's January 2002 $32 million valuation of First Solar, a calculation that forms the basis of the proposed merger terms, is a more credible calculation of First Solar's value than earlier calculations by AHH. True North contends that the earlier calculations were overly optimistic and were based on outdated financial projections as well as changed market conditions.

For purposes of the present motion only, I am satisfied that there is a reasonable probability that the Court will not find the January 2002 valuation to be entirely fair. First, the author of AHH's January 2002 valuation materials described those materials as a "quick and dirty" analysis of First Solar's value on that date. This contrasts with the earlier valuations in August and November of 2001, valuations that were based on multiple methodologies to arrive at a value for First Solar that ranged from $103 million in August 2001 to $72 million in November 2001, or almost two to three times the January 2002 valuation. Second, AHH's January 2002 valuation employed only a discounted cash flow analysis. Although the lower valuation in January 2002 was the basis upon which True North would acquire a 95% interest in First Solar and Solar Cells would fall to a 5% interest, the significantly lower valuation failed to employ any other method of valuation as a "crosscheck" to the discounted cash flow analysis. Because earlier valuations relied on multiple valuation methodologies, it is a reasonable inference that AHH's "quick and dirty" analysis is less reliable and authoritative. Third, the January 2002 formula used a much lower exit multiple (a 6.9 x free cash flow terminal year multiple) than did earlier valuation formulas (which used an 11 x free cash flow terminal year multiple), with no apparent rationale for that lower multiple. Fourth, AHH's lower valuation resulted from the use of a much higher discount rate (35%) than the valuations it performed only five months earlier (30%), even though the outlook for the solar cell industry was improving in that period and even though interest rates were generally falling.[35]

... I conclude that it is reasonably likely this Court will find the January 2002 $32 million valuation of First Solar not to be a fair price because it is irreconcilable with the earlier valuations only a few months before True North decided to go forward with the proposed merger. Because Solar Cells has demonstrated a reasonable likelihood of success on the merits of its entire fairness claim, I turn next to the irreparable harm and balance of the equities component of the preliminary injunction standard.

B.   Irreparable Harm

In order to show irreparable harm, the injury must be one for which money damages will not be an adequate remedy. Additionally, the threatened harm must be "imminent, unspeculative, and genuine."

Solar Cells argues that it will be harmed irreparably by the dilution of its equity position and voting power as unit-holders. It also alleges that the loss of its bargained-for participation in company management is an irreparable harm....

The defendants do not deny that Solar Cells will not have the right to appoint managers of the managing board of the surviving corporation. They argue that since True North had the right to nominate a majority of First Solar's Managers, True North could control the business and affairs of the Company. That reality is unaltered with the surviving company. The defendants reason, therefore, that Solar Cells has suffered no harm by losing its right to appoint managers. That argument carries no weight whatsoever. To accept that assertion would be to believe that every time the ability to elect a manager or director of a corporation is negotiated, there is no benefit derived therefrom if there is not a right to elect a majority of the managers or directors. Such a notion would certainly come as a

35. Even True North's litigation expert, Mr. Brian DiLucente, arrived at a much higher value for First Solar ($51.9 million). DiLucente was able to reduce his $51.9 million valuation to $31.1 million, but to do so, he was forced to apply a 40% "marketability" discount. The courts of this State, however, have repeatedly rejected the applicability of such discounts.... Furthermore, after putting to one side DiLucente's apparent improper application of a marketability discount, his $51.9 million valuation for First Solar likely was improperly depressed by other aspects of his discounted cash flow analysis. For example, DiLucente applied a discount rate as high as 45%, based on his subjective view of First Solar's Company specific risk. But Dilucente admitted in his deposition testimony that he had no expertise in the solar cell industry and limited knowledge of the specific company, First Solar, that his analysis purported to value. This Court has been, understandably in my view, suspicious of expert valuations offered at trial that incorporate subjective measures of company specific risk premia, as subjective measures may easily be employed as a means to smuggle improper risk assumptions into the discount rate so as to affect dramatically the expert's ultimate opinion on value....

surprise to all those who have given valuable consideration in negotiating such valueless rights. The right to participate in a management group is a valuable right whether or not that participation includes control of the group. In this case, it is undisputed that Solar Cells will lose that right if the proposed merger closes, thereby suffering an irreparable harm. . . .

V.   CONCLUSION

For the reasons stated, I grant plaintiff's motion for preliminary injunction. . . .

SECTION 3.   LIMITED LIABILITY PARTNERSHIPS

REVISED UNIFORM PARTNERSHIP ACT §§ 101(5), 306(c), 1001

[See Statutory Supplement]

NOTE ON LIMITED LIABILITY PARTNERSHIPS

Another important new form of business organization is the limited liability partnership ("LLP"). Essentially, LLPs are general partnerships, with one core difference and one ancillary difference. The core difference is that, as the name indicates, the liability of general partners of a limited liability partnership is less extensive than the liability of a general partner as discussed in the excerpt from Bromberg & Ribstein that follows. The ancillary difference is that LLPs must be registered with the appropriate state office. Although every state has adopted LLP provisions (normally by amendments to the general-partnership statutes), several states, including California and New York, permit only professional firms to be LLPs.

A variant on the LLP is the limited liability limited partnership, LLLP, in which the liability of the general partners in a limited partnership is limited.

Bromberg & Ribstein, Limited Liability Partnerships, The Revised Uniform Partnership Act, and the Uniform Limited Partnership Act

§ 3.02–3.04 (2003 ed.).

§ 3.02   LIMITED "TORT" LIABILITY IN LLPs

. . . [One] common form of LLP statute . . . limits liability for particular categories of conduct—that is, for negligence or other misconduct by a co-partner or other agent or employee of the firm [as opposed to breach of contract]. The model for these provisions is a prior version of the Delaware statute, which provides that a partner "is not liable for debts and obligations of or chargeable to the partnership arising from negligence, wrongful acts, or misconduct, whether characterized as tort, contract or otherwise, committed while the partnership is a registered limited partnership and in the course of the partnership business by another partner or an employee, agent, or representative of the partnership." . . .

Statutes that limit partners' liability only for misconduct-based claims raise some questions about the types of vicarious liability that are limited. The language clearly applies to any form of negligence or misconduct. . . . Professional malpractice liability arising out of partners' negligence is certainly included in the exception to vicarious liability despite the fact that this liability probably could be characterized as rising out of the contractual relationship between the professional and the client. . . . Thus it is significant that the original partial-shield Delaware statute was amended in 1994 to provide that it limits vicarious liability for conduct "whether characterized as tort, contract or otherwise." . . .

§ 3.03 LIMITED LIABILITY FOR ALL TYPES OF CLAIMS

. . . [Most LLP] statutes provide that liability is limited for all partnership debts and obligations. For example, the Revised Uniform Partnership Act provides:

> An obligation of partnership incurred while the partnership is a limited liability partnership, whether arising in contract, tort, or otherwise, is solely the obligation of the partnership. A partner is not personally liable, directly or indirectly, including by way of contribution or otherwise, for such a partnership obligation solely by reason of being or so acting as a partner. . . .

LLP statutes that eliminate partners' *vicarious* liability for all types of claims nevertheless preserve partners' liability for their own misconduct, including faulty supervision of other partners, discussed below in Section 3.04. . . . Also, it is important to keep in mind that the *partnership* retains vicarious liability for its' partners' acts. Partners therefore remain liable at least up to their investment in the firm, and perhaps beyond this if they have agreed with their co-partners to contribute toward partnership losses.

§ 3.04 PARTNERS' DIRECT LIABILITY

Nothing in the LLP statutes or in statutes . . . relieves owners from liability for their own misconduct. "Limited liability" means only that owners are not, solely as owners, vicariously liable for the firm's debts. . . .

The statutes both preserve whatever liability partners may have had under the common law and, perhaps, provide for an additional statutory category of liability for misconduct. . . . An important model is the original version of the Delaware statute, which provides that the liability limitation "shall not affect the liability of a partner in a registered limited liability partnership for his own negligence, wrongful acts, or misconduct, or that of any person under his direct supervision and control." . . .

It is uncertain under the supervision-type of provision whether the partner must be negligent or at fault in order to be held liable. Stating that the LLP provisions "shall not affect" the partner's liability suggests that the statute only continues any liability partners may have had for their own misconduct or for negligently failing to monitor or supervise others. But it is not clear to what pre-existing supervisory liability the statute might be referring other than partners' vicarious liability under traditional partnership law, which is supposedly eliminated by LLP registration.

. . . [N]ot all LLP statutes include potentially confusing language on supervisory or other indirect liability. Some provide for liability only for the partner's own wrongs or omit any extra language on liability of individual members and provide in varying terms that a partner in an LLP is not individually liable because of her partnership status. This preserves partners' common law liability for their own misconduct without risking creating new categories of statutory liability.

NOTE ON INVOLVEMENT

An issue that can arise in a professional LLP, when more than one partner was involved in a decision in some way, is what level of involvement will subject a partner to liability for his own conduct if the decision is later attacked. In Megadyne Information Systems v. Rosner, Owens & Nunziato, L.L.P., 2002 WL 31112563 (Cal. App. 2002), an unreported opinion, the court stated "All three partners offered declarations averring Owens was 'the sole attorney' who handled the Megadyne matter and that neither of the other two had 'any involvement' in the case. To contradict that showing, Megadyne [the plaintiff] offered Owens's testimony that 'there might have been discussions' with his two partners that Megadyne had a viable legal malpractice claim against Irell & Manella. This is sufficient to create a triable issue of fact as to whether the partners were personally involved in the firm's breach of fiduciary duties. If the partners had *discussions* that Megadyne could sue Irell & Manella for malpractice, it is reasonable to infer that they knew Megadyne's claim against OCTA was time-barred and that they participated in the decision to not disclose this fact to Megadyne while the firm continued to represent it."

According to Jonathan D. Glater, Fearing Liability, Law Firms Change Partnership Status, The New York Times, January 10, 2003, "[L]awyers at several large firms said they worried that becoming an L.L.P. could hamper their business in intangible ways. Lawyers who in a general partnership might have helped colleagues serving other clients might not do so in an L.L.P. to avoid taking on potential liability for the work, said one lawyer who insisted on anonymity. At Weil, Gotshal & Manges, which converted to an L.L.P. several years ago, the partners decided to indemnify one another in such a situation, said Richard J. Davis, a partner at the firm. That way, he said, a partner who was not primarily involved in a transaction would still be willing to provide advice.''

———

CHAPTER VIII

THE DUTY OF CARE AND THE DUTY TO ACT IN GOOD FAITH

SECTION 1. THE DUTY OF CARE

(a) THE BASIC STANDARD OF CARE

Francis v. United Jersey Bank

Supreme Court of New Jersey, 1981.
87 N.J. 15, 432 A.2d 814.

■ POLLOCK, J. The primary issue on this appeal is whether a corporate director is personally liable in negligence for the failure to prevent the misappropriation of trust funds by other directors who were also officers and shareholders of the corporation.

Plaintiffs are trustees in bankruptcy of Pritchard & Baird Intermediaries Corp. (Pritchard & Baird), a reinsurance broker or intermediary. Defendant Lillian P. Overcash is the daughter of Lillian G. Pritchard and the executrix of her estate. At the time of her death, Mrs. Pritchard was a director and the largest single shareholder of Pritchard & Baird. Because Mrs. Pritchard died after the institution of suit but before trial, her executrix was substituted as a defendant. United Jersey Bank is joined as the administrator of the estate of Charles Pritchard, Sr., who had been president, director and majority shareholder of Pritchard & Baird.

This litigation focuses on payments made by Pritchard & Baird to Charles Pritchard, Jr. and William Pritchard, who were sons of Mr. and Mrs. Charles Pritchard, Sr., as well as officers, directors and shareholders of the corporation. Claims against Charles, Jr. and William are being pursued in bankruptcy proceedings against them.

The trial court, sitting without a jury, characterized the payments as fraudulent conveyances within N.J.S.A. 25:2–10 and entered judgment of $10,355,736.91 plus interest against the estate of Mrs. Pritchard. 162 N.J.Super. 355, 392 A.2d 1233 (Law Div.1978). The judgment includes damages from her negligence in permitting payments from the corporation of $4,391,133.21 to Charles, Jr. and $5,483,799.02 to William. The trial court also entered judgment for payments of other

515

sums plus interest: (1) against the estate of Lillian Pritchard for $33,000 accepted by her during her lifetime; (2) against the estate of Charles Pritchard, Sr. for $189,194.17 paid to him during his lifetime and $168,454 for payment of taxes on his estate; and (3) against Lillian Overcash individually for $123,156.51 for payments to her.

The Appellate Division affirmed, but found that the payments were a conversion of trust funds, rather than fraudulent conveyances of the assets of the corporation. 171 N.J.Super. 34, 407 A.2d 1253 (1979). We granted certification limited to the issue of the liability of Lillian Pritchard as a director. 82 N.J. 285, 412 A.2d 791 (1980).

Although we accept the characterization of the payments as a conversion of trust funds, the critical question is not whether the misconduct of Charles, Jr. and William should be characterized as fraudulent conveyances or acts of conversion. Rather, the initial question is whether Mrs. Pritchard was negligent in not noticing and trying to prevent the misappropriation of funds held by the corporation in an implied trust. A further question is whether her negligence was the proximate cause of the plaintiffs' losses. Both lower courts found that she was liable in negligence for the losses caused by the wrongdoing of Charles, Jr. and William. We affirm.

I

The matrix for our decision is the customs and practices of the reinsurance industry and the role of Pritchard & Baird as a reinsurance broker. Reinsurance involves a contract under which one insurer agrees to indemnify another for loss sustained under the latter's policy of insurance. Insurance companies that insure against losses arising out of fire or other casualty seek at times to minimize their exposure by sharing risks with other insurance companies. Thus, when the face amount of a policy is comparatively large, the company may enlist one or more insurers to participate in that risk. Similarly, an insurance company's loss potential and overall exposure may be reduced by reinsuring a part of an entire class of policies (e.g., 25% of all of its fire insurance policies). The selling insurance company is known as a ceding company. The entity that assumes the obligation is designated as the reinsurer.

The reinsurance broker arranges the contract between the ceding company and the reinsurer. In accordance with industry custom before the Pritchard & Baird bankruptcy, the reinsurance contract or treaty did not specify the rights and duties of the broker. Typically, the ceding company communicates to the broker the details concerning the risk. The broker negotiates the sale of portions of the risk to the reinsurers. In most instances, the ceding company and the reinsurer do not communicate with each other, but rely upon the reinsurance broker. The ceding company pays premiums due a reinsurer to the broker, who deducts his commission and transmits the balance to the appropriate reinsurer. When a loss occurs, a reinsurer pays money due a ceding company to the broker, who then transmits it to the ceding company.

The reinsurance business was described by an expert at trial as having "a magic aura around it of dignity and quality and integrity." A telephone call which might be confirmed by a handwritten memorandum is sufficient to create a reinsurance obligation. Though separate bank accounts are not maintained for each treaty, the industry practice is to segregate the insurance funds from the broker's general accounts. Thus, the insurance fund accounts would contain the identifiable amounts for transmittal to either the reinsurer or the ceder. The expert stated that in general three kinds of checks may be drawn on this account: checks payable to reinsurers as premiums, checks payable to ceders as loss payments and checks payable to the brokers as commissions.

Messrs. Pritchard and Baird initially operated as a partnership. Later they formed several corporate entities to carry on their brokerage activities. The proofs supporting the judgment relate only to one corporation, Pritchard & Baird Intermediaries Corp. (Pritchard & Baird), and we need consider only its activities. When incorporated under the laws of the State of New York in 1959, Pritchard & Baird had five directors: Charles Pritchard, Sr., his wife Lillian Pritchard, their son Charles Pritchard, Jr., George Baird and his wife Marjorie. William Pritchard, another son, became director in 1960. Upon its formation, Pritchard & Baird acquired all the assets and assumed all the liabilities of the Pritchard & Baird partnership. The corporation issued 200 shares of common stock. Charles Pritchard, Sr. acquired 120 shares, his sons Charles Pritchard, Jr., 15 and William 15; Mr. and Mrs. Baird owned the remaining 50. In June 1964, Baird and his wife resigned as directors and sold their stock to the corporation. From that time on the corporation operated as a close family corporation with Mr. and Mrs. Pritchard and their two sons as the only directors. After the death of Charles, Sr. in 1973, only the remaining three directors continued to operate as the board. Lillian Pritchard inherited 72 of her husband's 120 shares in Pritchard & Baird, thereby becoming the largest stockholder in the corporation with 48% of the stock.

The corporate minute books reflect only perfunctory activities by the directors, related almost exclusively to the election of officers and adoption of banking resolutions and a retirement plan. None of the minutes for any of the meetings contain a discussion of the loans to Charles, Jr. and William or of the financial condition of the corporation. Moreover, upon instructions of Charles, Jr. that financial statements were not to be circulated to anyone else, the company's statements for the fiscal years beginning February 1, 1970, were delivered only to him.

Charles Pritchard, Sr. was the chief executive and controlled the business in the years following Baird's withdrawal. Beginning in 1966, he gradually relinquished control over the operations of the corporation. In 1968, Charles, Jr. became president and William became executive vice president. Charles, Sr. apparently became ill in 1971 and during the last year and a half of his life was not involved in the affairs of the business. He continued, however, to serve as a director until his death on December 10, 1973. Notwithstanding the presence of Charles, Sr. on the board until his death in 1973, Charles, Jr. dominated the management of the corporation and the board from 1968 until the bankruptcy in 1975.

Contrary to the industry custom of segregating funds, Pritchard & Baird commingled the funds of reinsurers and ceding companies with its own funds. All monies (including commissions, premiums and loss monies) were deposited in a single account. Charles, Sr. began the practice of withdrawing funds from the commingled account in transactions identified on the corporate books as "loans." As long as Charles, Sr. controlled the corporation, the "loans" correlated with corporate profits and were repaid at the end of each year. Starting in 1970, however, Charles, Jr. and William begin to siphon ever-increasing sums from the corporation under the guise of loans. As of January 31, 1970, the "loans" to Charles, Jr. were $230,932 and to William were $207,329. At least by January 31, 1973, the annual increase in the loans exceeded annual corporate revenues. By October 1975, the year of bankruptcy, the "shareholders' loans" had metastasized to a total of $12,333,514.47.

The trial court rejected the characterization of the payments as "loans." 162 N.J.Super. at 365, 392 A.2d 1233. No corporate resolution authorized the "loans," and no note or other instrument evidenced the debt. Charles, Jr. and William paid no interest on the amounts received. The "loans" were not repaid or reduced from one year to the next; rather, they increased annually.

The designation of "shareholders' loans" on the balance sheet was an entry to account for the distribution of the premium and loss money to Charles, Sr., Charles, Jr. and William. As the trial court found, the entry was part of a "woefully inadequate and highly dangerous bookkeeping system." 162 N.J.Super. at 363, 392 A.2d 1233.

The "loans" to Charles, Jr. and William far exceeded their salaries and financial resources. If the payments to Charles, Jr. and William had been treated as dividends or compensation, then the balance sheets would have shown an excess of liabilities over assets. If the "loans" had been eliminated, the balance sheets would have depicted a corporation not only with a working capital deficit, but also with assets having a fair market value less than its liabilities. The balance sheets for 1970–1975, however, showed an excess of assets over liabilities. This result was achieved by designating the misappropriated funds as "shareholders' loans" and listing them as assets offsetting the deficits. Although the withdrawal of the funds resulted in an obligation of repayment to Pritchard & Baird, the more significant consideration is that the "loans" represented a massive misappropriation of money belonging to the clients of the corporation.

The "loans" were reflected on financial statements that were prepared annually as of January 31, the end of the corporate fiscal year. Although an outside certified public accountant prepared the 1970 financial statement, the corporation prepared only internal financial statements from 1971–1975. In all instances, the statements were simple documents, consisting of three or four 8½ § 11 inch sheets.

The statements of financial condition from 1970 forward demonstrated:

	Working Capital Deficit	Shareholders' Loans	Net Brokerage Income
1970	$ 389,022	$ 509,941	$ 807,229
1971	not available	not available	not available
1972	$ 1,684,289	$ 1,825,911	$1,546,263
1973	$ 3,506,460	$ 3,700,542	$1,736,349
1974	$ 6,939,007	$ 7,080,629	$ 876,182
1975	$10,176,419	$10,298,039	$ 551,598.

Those financial statements showed working capital deficits increasing annually in tandem with the amounts that Charles, Jr. and William withdrew as "shareholders' loans." In the last complete year of business (January 31, 1974, to January 31, 1975), "shareholders' loans" and the correlative working capital deficit increased by approximately $3,200,000.

The funding of the "loans" left the corporation with insufficient money to operate. Pritchard & Baird could defer payment on accounts payable because its clients allowed a grace period, generally 30 to 90 days, before the payment was due. During this period, Pritchard & Baird used the funds entrusted to it as a "float" to pay current accounts payable. By recourse to the funds of its clients, Pritchard & Baird not only paid its trade debts, but also funded the payments to Charles, Jr. and William. Thus, Pritchard & Baird was able to meet its obligations as they came due only through the use of clients' funds.

The pattern that emerges from these figures is the substantial increase in the monies appropriated by Charles Pritchard, Jr. and William Pritchard after their father's withdrawal from the business and the sharp decline in the profitability of the operation after his death. This led ultimately to the filing in December, 1975, of an involuntary petition in bankruptcy and the appointments of the plaintiffs as trustees in bankruptcy of Pritchard & Baird.

Mrs. Pritchard was not active in the business of Pritchard & Baird and knew virtually nothing of its corporate affairs. She briefly visited the corporate offices in Morristown on only one occasion, and she never read or obtained the annual financial statements. She was unfamiliar with the rudiments of reinsurance and made no effort to assure that the policies and practices of the corporation, particularly pertaining to the withdrawal of funds, complied with industry custom or relevant law. Although her husband had warned her that Charles, Jr. would "take the shirt off my back," Mrs. Pritchard did not pay any attention to her duties as a director or to the affairs of the corporation. 162 N.J.Super. at 370, 392 A.2d 1233.

After her husband died in December 1973, Mrs. Pritchard became incapacitated and was bedridden for a six-month period. She became listless at this time and started to drink rather heavily. Her physical condition deteriorated, and in 1978 she died. The trial court rejected testimony seeking to exonerate her because she "was old, was grief-stricken at the loss of her husband, sometimes consumed too much alcohol and was psychologically overborne by her sons." 162 N.J.Super. at 371, 392 A.2d 1233. That court found that she was competent to act and that the reason Mrs. Pritchard never knew what her sons "were doing was because she never made the slightest effort to discharge any of her responsibilities as a director of Pritchard & Baird." 162 N.J.Super. at 372, 392 A.2d 1233.

II

A preliminary matter is the determination of whether New Jersey law should apply to this case. Although Pritchard & Baird was incorporated in New York, the trial court found that New Jersey had more significant relationships to the parties and the transactions than New York. The shareholder, officers and directors were New Jersey residents. The estates of Mr. and Mrs. Pritchard are being administered in New Jersey, and the bankruptcy proceedings involving Charles, Jr., William and Pritchard & Baird are pending in New Jersey. Virtually all transactions took place in New Jersey. Although many of the creditors are located outside the state, all had contacts with Pritchard & Baird in New Jersey. Consequently, the trial court applied New Jersey law. 162 N.J.Super. at 369, 392 A.2d 1233. The parties agree that New Jersey law should apply. We are in accord.

III

Individual liability of a corporate director for acts of the corporation is a prickly problem. Generally directors are accorded broad immunity and are not insurers of corporate activities. The problem is particularly nettlesome when a third party asserts that a director, because of nonfeasance, is liable for losses caused by acts of insiders, who in this case were officers, directors and shareholders. Determination of the liability of Mrs. Pritchard requires findings that she had a duty to the clients of Pritchard & Baird, that she breached that duty and that her breach was a proximate cause of their losses.

The New Jersey Business Corporation Act, which took effect on January 1, 1969, was a comprehensive revision of the statutes relating to business corporations. One section, N.J.S.A. 14A:6–14, concerning a director's general obligation had no counterpart in the old Act. That section makes it incumbent upon directors to discharge their duties in good faith and with that degree of diligence, care and skill which ordinarily prudent men would exercise under similar circumstances in like positions. [N.J.S.A. 14A:6–14] . . . .

. . . [The principle underlying] N.J.S.A. 14A:6–14 is . . . that directors must discharge their duties in good faith and act as ordinarily prudent persons would under similar circumstances in like positions. Although specific duties in a given case can be determined only after consideration of all of the circumstances, the standard of ordinary care is the wellspring from which those more specific duties flow.

As a general rule, a director should acquire at least a rudimentary understanding of the business of the corporation. Accordingly, a director should become familiar with the fundamentals of the business in which the corporation is engaged. [Campbell v. Watson, 62 N.J.Eq. 396, 50 A. 120 (Ch.1901)]. Because directors are bound to exercise ordinary care, they cannot set up as a defense lack of the knowledge needed to exercise the requisite degree of care. If one "feels that he has not had sufficient business experience to qualify him to perform the duties of a director, he should either acquire the knowledge by inquiry, or refuse to act." Ibid.

Directors are under a continuing obligation to keep informed about the activities of the corporation. Otherwise, they may not be able to participate in the overall management of corporate affairs. Barnes v. Andrews, 298 F. 614 (S.D.N.Y.1924)…. Directors may not shut their eyes to corporate misconduct, and then claim that because they did not see the misconduct, they did not have a duty to look. The sentinel asleep at his post contributes nothing to the enterprise he is charged to protect. Wilkinson v. Dodd, 42 N.J.Eq. 234, 245, 7 A. 327 (Ch.1886), aff'd 42 N.J.Eq. 647, 9 A. 685 (E. & A.1887).

Directorial management does not require a detailed inspection of day-to-day activities, but rather a general monitoring of corporate affairs and policies. Williams v. McKay, [46 N.J.Eq. 25, 36, 18 A. 824 (Ch.1889)]. Accordingly, a director is well advised to attend board meetings regularly. Indeed, a director who is absent from a board meeting is presumed to concur in action taken on a corporate matter, unless he files a "dissent with the secretary of the corporation within a reasonable time after learning of such action." N.J.S.A. 14A:6–13 (Supp.1981–1982). Regular attendance does not mean that directors must attend every meeting, but that directors should attend meetings as a matter of practice. A director of a publicly held corporation might be expected to attend regular monthly meetings, but a director of a small, family corporation might be asked to attend only an annual meeting. The point is that one of the responsibilities of a director is to attend meetings of the board of which he or she is a member. That burden is lightened by N.J.S.A. 14A:6–7(2) (Supp.1981–1982), which permits board action without a meeting if all members of the board consent in writing.

While directors are not required to audit corporate books, they should maintain familiarity with the financial status of the corporation by a regular review of financial statements. *Campbell,* supra, 62 N.J.Eq. at 415, 50 A. 120; *Williams,* supra, 46 N.J.Eq. at 38–39, 18 A. 824; see Section of Corporation, Banking and Business Law, American Bar Association, "Corporate Director's Guidebook," 33 Bus.Law. 1595, 1608 (1978) (Guidebook)…. In some circumstances, directors may be charged with assuring that bookkeeping methods conform to industry custom and usage. Lippitt v. Ashley, 89 Conn. 451, 464, 94 A. 995, 1000 (Sup.Ct.1915). The extent of review, as well as the nature and frequency of financial statements, depends not only on the customs of the industry, but also on the nature of the corporation and the business in which it is engaged. Financial statements of some small corporations may be prepared internally and only on an annual basis; in a large publicly held corporation, the statements may be produced monthly or at some other regular interval. Adequate financial review normally would be more informal in a private corporation than in a publicly held corporation.

Of some relevance in this case is the circumstance that the financial records disclose the "shareholders' loans". Generally directors are immune from liability if, in good faith,

> they rely upon the opinion of counsel for the corporation or upon written reports setting forth financial data concerning the corporation and prepared by an independent public accountant or certified public accountant or firm of such accountants or upon financial statements, books of account or reports of the corporation represented to them to be correct by the president, the officer of the corporation having charge of its books of account, or the person presiding at a meeting of the board. [N.J.S.A. 14A:6–14]

The review of financial statements, however, may give rise to a duty to inquire further into matters revealed by those statements. Corsicana Nat'l Bank v. Johnson, 251 U.S. 68, 71, 40 S.Ct. 82, 84, 64 L.Ed. 141 (1919).... Upon discovery of an illegal course of action, a director has a duty to object and, if the corporation does not correct the conduct, to resign. See Dodd v. Wilkinson, 42 N.J.Eq. 647, 651, 9 A. 685 (E. & A.1887); Williams v. Riley, 34 N.J.Eq. 398, 401 (Ch.1881).

In certain circumstances, the fulfillment of the duty of a director may call for more than mere objection and resignation. Sometimes a director may be required to seek the advice of counsel. *Guidebook*, supra, at 1631. One New Jersey case recognized the duty of a bank director to seek counsel where doubt existed about the meaning of the bank charter. Williams v. McKay, supra, 46 N.J.Eq. at 60, 18 A. 824. The duty to seek the assistance of counsel can extend to areas other than the interpretation of corporation instruments. Modern corporate practice recognizes that on occasion a director should seek outside advice. A director may require legal advice concerning the propriety of his or her own conduct, the conduct of other officers and directors or the conduct of the corporation. In appropriate circumstances, a director would be "well advised to consult with regular corporate counsel (or his own legal adviser) at any time in which he is doubtful regarding proposed action...." *Guidebook*, supra, at 1618. Sometimes the duty of a director may require more than consulting with outside counsel. A director may have a duty to take reasonable means to prevent illegal conduct by co-directors; in an appropriate case, this may include threat of suit. See Selheimer v. Manganese Corp., 423 Pa. 563, 572, 584, 224 A.2d 634, 640, 646 (Sup.Ct.1966) (director exonerated when he objected, resigned, organized shareholder action group, and threatened suit).

A director is not an ornament, but an essential component of corporate governance. Consequently, a director cannot protect himself

behind a paper shield bearing the motto, "dummy director." ...
Thus, all directors are responsible for managing the business and
affairs of the corporation. N.J.S.A. 14A:6–1 (Supp.1981–1982); 1 G.
Hornstein, Corporation Law and Practice § 431 at 525 (1959).

The factors that impel expanded responsibility in the large, publicly held corporation may not be present in a small, close corporation. Nonetheless, a close corporation may, because of the nature of
its business, be affected with a public interest. For example, the stock
of a bank may be closely held, but because of the nature of banking
the directors would be subject to greater liability than those of another
close corporation. Even in a small corporation, a director is held to the
standard of that degree of care that an ordinarily prudent director
would use under the circumstances. M. Mace, The Board of Directors
of Small Corporations 83 (1948).

A director's duty of care does not exist in the abstract, but must
be considered in relation to specific obligees. In general, the relationship of a corporate director to the corporation and its stockholders is
that of a fiduciary. Whitfield v. Kern, 122 N.J.Eq. 332, 341, 192 A. 48
(E. & A.1937). Shareholders have a right to expect that directors will
exercise reasonable supervision and control over the policies and
practices of a corporation. The institutional integrity of a corporation
depends upon the proper discharge by directors of those duties.

While directors may owe a fiduciary duty to creditors also, that
obligation generally has not been recognized in the absence of insolvency. *Whitfield,* supra, 122 N.J.Eq. at 342, 345, 192 A. 48. With
certain corporations, however, directors are [deemed] to owe a duty
to creditors and other third parties even when the corporation is
solvent. Although depositors of a bank are considered in some respects to be creditors, courts have recognized that directors may owe
them a fiduciary duty. See *Campbell,* supra, 62 N.J.Eq. at 406–407, 50
A. 120. Directors of nonbanking corporations may owe a similar duty
when the corporation holds funds of others in trust. Cf. McGlynn v.
Schultz, 90 N.J.Super. 505, 218 A.2d 408 (Ch.Div.1966), aff'd 95
N.J.Super. 412, 231 A.2d 386 (App.Div.), certif. den. 50 N.J. 409, 235
A.2d 901 (1967) (directors who did not insist on segregating trust
funds held by corporation liable to the *cestuis que trust*).

Courts in other states have imposed liability on directors of
nonbanking corporations for the conversion of trust funds, even
though those directors did not participate in or know of the conversion.... The distinguishing circumstances in regard to banks and
other corporations holding trust funds is that the depositor or beneficiary can reasonably expect the director to act with ordinary prudence
concerning the funds held in a fiduciary capacity. Thus, recognition of
a duty of a director to those for whom a corporation holds funds in
trust may be viewed as another application of the general rule that a
director's duty is that of an ordinary prudent person under the
circumstances.

The most striking circumstances affecting Mrs. Pritchard's duty as
a director are the character of the reinsurance industry, the nature of

the misappropriated funds and the financial condition of Pritchard & Baird. The hallmark of the reinsurance industry has been the unqualified trust and confidence reposed by ceding companies and reinsurers in reinsurance brokers. Those companies entrust money to reinsurance intermediaries with the justifiable expectation that the funds will be transmitted to the appropriate parties. Consequently, the companies could have assumed rightfully that Mrs. Pritchard, as a director of a reinsurance brokerage corporation, would not sanction the commingling and the conversion of loss and premium funds for the personal use of the principals of Pritchard & Baird.

As a reinsurance broker, Pritchard & Baird received annually as a fiduciary millions of dollars of clients' money which it was under a duty to segregate.[6] To this extent, it resembled a bank rather than a small family business. Accordingly, Mrs. Pritchard's relationship to the clientele of Pritchard & Baird was akin to that of a director of a bank to its depositors. All parties agree that Pritchard & Baird held the misappropriated funds in an implied trust. That trust relationship gave rise to a fiduciary duty to guard the funds with fidelity and good faith. Ellsworth Dobbs, Inc. v. Johnson, 50 N.J. 528, 553, 236 A.2d 843 (1967); General Films, Inc. v. Sanco Gen. Mfg. Corp., supra, 153 N.J.Super. at 372–373, 379 A.2d 1042.

As a director of a substantial reinsurance brokerage corporation, she should have known that it received annually millions of dollars of loss and premium funds which it held in trust for ceding and reinsurance companies. Mrs. Pritchard should have obtained and read the annual statements of financial condition of Pritchard & Baird. Although she had a right to rely upon financial statements prepared in accordance with N.J.S.A. 14A:6–14, such reliance would not excuse her conduct. The reason is that those statements disclosed on their face the misappropriation of trust funds.

From those statements, she should have realized that, as of January 31, 1970, her sons were withdrawing substantial trust funds under the guise of "Shareholders' Loans." The financial statements for each fiscal year commencing with that of January 31, 1970, disclosed that the working capital deficits and the "loans" were escalating in tandem. Detecting a misappropriation of funds would not have required special expertise or extraordinary diligence; a cursory reading of the financial statements would have revealed the pillage. Thus, if Mrs. Pritchard had read the financial statements, she would have known that her sons were converting trust funds. When financial statements demonstrate that insiders are bleeding a corporation to death, a director should notice and try to stanch the flow of blood.

In summary, Mrs. Pritchard was charged with the obligation of basic knowledge and supervision of the business of Pritchard & Baird. Under the circumstances, this obligation included reading and under-

---

6. Following the Pritchard & Baird bankruptcy, New York, a reinsurance center, adopted legislation regulating reinsurance intermediaries. One statute codified the industry standard by prohibiting reinsurance intermediaries from commingling their funds with funds of their principals. N.Y.Ins.Law § 122–a(9) (McKinney Supp.1980–1981).

standing financial statements, and making reasonable attempts at detection and prevention of the illegal conduct of other officers and directors. She had a duty to protect the clients of Pritchard & Baird against policies and practices that would result in the misappropriation of money they had entrusted to the corporation. She breached that duty.

IV

Nonetheless, the negligence of Mrs. Pritchard does not result in liability unless it is a proximate cause of the loss. . . .

Cases involving nonfeasance present a much more difficult causation question than those in which the director has committed an affirmative act of negligence leading to the loss. Analysis in cases of negligent omissions calls for determination of the reasonable steps a director should have taken and whether that course of action would have averted the loss.

Usually a director can absolve himself from liability by informing the other directors of the impropriety and voting for a proper course of action. Dyson, "The Director's Liability for Negligence," 40 Ind.L.J. 341, 365 (1965). . . .

Even accepting the hypothesis that Mrs. Pritchard might not be liable if she had objected and resigned, there are two significant reasons for holding her liable. First, she did not resign until just before the bankruptcy. Consequently, there is no factual basis for the speculation that the losses would have occurred even if she had objected and resigned. Indeed, the trial court reached the opposite conclusion: "The actions of the sons were so blatantly wrongful that it is hard to see how they could have resisted any moderately firm objection to what they were doing." 162 N.J.Super. at 372, 392 A.2d 1233. Second, the nature of the reinsurance business distinguishes it from most other commercial activities in that reinsurance brokers are encumbered by fiduciary duties owed to third parties. In other corporations, a director's duty normally does not extend beyond the shareholders to third parties.

In this case, the scope of Mrs. Pritchard's duties was determined by the precarious financial condition of Pritchard & Baird, its fiduciary relationship to its clients and the implied trust in which it held their funds. Thus viewed, the scope of her duties encompassed all reasonable action to stop the continuing conversion. Her duties extended beyond mere objection and resignation to reasonable attempts to prevent the misappropriation of the trust funds. *Campbell,* supra, 62 N.J.Eq. at 427, 50 A. 120. . . .

In assessing whether Mrs. Pritchard's conduct was a legal or proximate cause of the conversion, "[l]egal responsibility must be limited to those causes which are so closely connected with the result and of such significance that the law is justified in imposing liability." Prosser, supra, § 41 at 237. Such a judicial determination involves not only considerations of causation-in-fact and matters of policy, but also common sense and logic. Caputzal v. The Lindsay Co., 48 N.J. 69, 77–78 (1966). The act or the failure to act must be a substantial factor in producing the harm. Prosser, supra, § 41 at 240; Restatement (Second) of Torts, §§ 431, 432 (1965).

Within Pritchard & Baird, several factors contributed to the loss of the funds: comingling of corporate and client monies, conversion of funds by Charles, Jr. and William and dereliction of her duties by Mrs. Pritchard. The wrongdoing of her sons, although the immediate cause of the loss, should not excuse Mrs. Pritchard from her negligence which also was a substantial factor contributing to the loss. Restatement (Second) of Torts, supra, § 442B, comment b. Her sons knew that she, the only other director, was not reviewing their conduct; they spawned their fraud in the backwater of her neglect. Her neglect of duty contributed to the climate of corruption; her failure to act contributed to the continuation of that corruption. Consequently, her conduct was a substantial factor contributing to the loss.

Analysis of proximate cause is especially difficult in a corporate context where the allegation is that nonfeasance of a director is a proximate cause of damage to a third party. Where a case involves nonfeasance, no one can say "with absolute certainty what would have occurred if the defendant had acted otherwise." Prosser, supra, § 41 at 242. Nonetheless, where it is reasonable to conclude that the failure to act would produce a particular result and that result has followed, causation may be inferred. Ibid. We conclude that even if Mrs. Pritchard's mere objection had not stopped the depredations of her sons, her consultation with an attorney and the threat of suit would have deterred them. That conclusion flows as a matter of common sense and logic from the record. Whether in other situations a director has a duty to do more than protest and resign is best left to case-by-case determinations. In this case, we are satisfied that there was a duty to do more than object and resign. Consequently, we find that Mrs. Pritchard's negligence was a proximate cause of the misappropriations.

To conclude, by virtue of her office, Mrs. Pritchard had the power to prevent the losses sustained by the clients of Pritchard & Baird. With power comes responsibility. She had a duty to deter the depredation of the other insiders, her sons. She breached that duty and caused plaintiffs to sustain damages.

The judgment of the Appellate Division is affirmed.

■ For affirmance JUSTICES SULLIVAN, PASHMAN, CLIFFORD, SCHREIBER, HANDLER and POLLOCK—6.

For reversal—none.*

---

* Some earlier cases involving the liability of inactive spouse-or figurehead-directors went a different way. In Berman v. LeBeauInter–America, Inc., 509 F.Supp. 156, 161 (S.D.N.Y.), aff'd mem. 697 F.2d 879 (2d Cir. 1981), a director was held not liable on the ground that he was a "virtual figurehead." In Allied Freightways, Inc. v. Cholfin, 325 Mass. 630, 633, 91 N.E.2d 765, 768 (1950), the court rested nonliability on causa-

MODEL BUS. CORP. ACT §§ 8.30, 8.31

[See Statutory Supplement]

———

CAL. CORP. CODE § 309

[See Statutory Supplement]

———

NEW YORK BUS. CORP. LAW § 717

[See Statutory Supplement]

———

ALI, PRINCIPLES OF CORPORATE GOVERNANCE §§ 4.01(a), (b), 4.02, 4.03

[See Statutory Supplement]

———

ARONSON v. LEWIS, 473 A.2d 805, 812 (Del.1984). "[D]irectors have a duty to inform themselves, prior to making a business decision, of all material information reasonably available to them. Having become so informed, they must then act with requisite care in the discharge of their duties. While the Delaware cases use a variety of terms to describe the applicable standard of care, our analysis satisfies us that under the business judgment rule director liability is predicated upon concepts of gross negligence."

———

QUILLEN, *TRANS UNION,* **BUSINESS JUDGMENT, AND NEUTRAL PRINCIPLES,** 10 Del.J.Corp.L. 465, 497–98 (1985). "Even if one assumes that negligence law is the proper pigeonhole for director liability—a most questionable assumption at least at the decisional level—the concept of 'gross negligence' has been expressly rejected by the better tort scholarship as practically meaningless. Therefore its recent adoption in corporate law would appear, in some respects, to be an analytical step backwards....

"Perhaps we should say straight out that, on the threshold duty of care issue, the standard should be 'reasonable care under the circum-

tion grounds, concluding that it was doubtful whether, if the spouse, Mrs. Cholfin, had taken steps to familiarize herself with the conduct of the business by her husband she could have changed the situation. "Upon a careful reading of the evidence, we do not think that it can quite be said that the neglect of her official duties as a director was a contributing cause of the loss sustained by the corporation by the wrongful withdrawals of its funds, save only the amounts used for her personal benefits."

stances' as some argued all along. If that flexible standard includes all factors, e.g., director expertise [and], time pressures, ... as well as depth of inquiry, then one suspects the results probably would not radically change, but the judicial focus would be to a keener negligence standard and emphasis more on the qualitative nature of the varying circumstances.''

IN RE EMERGING COMMUNICATIONS, INC. SHAREHOLDERS LITIGATION, 2004 WL 1305745 (2004) (Jacobs, Justice, sitting by designation). 'The court also concludes, albeit with reluctance, that Muoio is ... liable [for his conduct as director]....

"Muoio is culpable because he voted to approve the transaction even though he knew, or at very least had strong reasons to believe, that the $ 10.25 per share merger price was unfair. Muoio was in a unique position to know that. He was a principal and general partner of an investment advising firm, with significant experience in finance and the telecommunications sector. From 1995 to 1996, Muoio had been a securities analyst for, and a vice president of, Lazard Freres & Co. in the telecommunications and media sector. From 1985 to 1995, he was a securities analyst for Gabelli and Co., Inc., in the communications sector, and from 1993 to 1995, he was a portfolio manager for Gabelli Global Communications Fund, Inc.

"Hence, Muoio possessed a specialized financial expertise, and an ability to understand ECM's [the corporation's] intrinsic value, that was unique to the ECM board members.... Informed by his specialized expertise and knowledge, Muoio conceded that the $10.25 price was 'at the low end of any kind of fair value you would put' and expressed ... his view that the [corporation] might be able to get up to $ 20 per share.... In these circumstances, it was incumbent upon Muoio, as a fiduciary, to advocate that the board reject the $10.25 price.... As a fiduciary knowledgeable of ECM's intrinsic value, Muoio should also have gone on record as voting against the proposed transaction at the $10.25 per share merger price. Muoio did neither. Instead he joined the other directors in voting, without objection, to approve the transaction.

"[Most of] ECM's directors ... could plausibly argue that they voted for the transaction in reliance on [the opinion of Houlihan, the corporation's outside financial advisor on the proposed transaction] that the merger term price was fair. In Muoio's case, however, the argument would be implausible. Muoio's expertise in this industry was equivalent, if not superior, to that of Houlihan.... That expertise gave Muoio far less reason to defer to Houlihan's valuation....''

NOTE ON CAUSATION

Cases in the duty-of-care area sometimes raise difficult causation issues. Two of these issues often arise together: (1) If the violation of the duty of care consists of an omission by a director, would the loss have occurred even if the director had not violated his duty? (2) If the whole board, or a substantial majority of the directors, violates the duty of care, can an individual director be excused on the ground that the result would have been the same even if she had acted differently?

These issues were addressed in the well-known case of Barnes v. Andrews, 298 Fed. 614 (S.D.N.Y.1924), decided by Judge Learned Hand, sitting as a trial judge. Liberty Starters Corporation was organized in 1918 to manufacture starters for Ford motors and airplanes. Andrews became a director in October 1919, and served until he resigned in June 1920. During Andrews's incumbency there had been only two board meetings, one of which he could not attend. Andrews was the largest shareholder and a friend of Liberty's president, Maynard, who had induced him to become a director. Andrews's only attention to Liberty's affairs consisted of talks with Maynard as they met from time to time. In 1921, Liberty went into receivership as a result of mismanagement. Andrews was sued for violating the duty of care by not paying sufficient attention to the corporation's affairs.

Judge Hand began by holding that Andrews had violated his duty of care:

> . . . It is not enough to content oneself with general answers that the business looks promising and that all seems prosperous. Andrews was bound, certainly as the months wore on, to inform himself of what was going on with some particularity, and, if he had done so, he would have learned that there were delays in getting into production which were putting the enterprise in most serious peril. . . . Having accepted a post of confidence, he was charged with an active duty to learn whether the company was moving to production, and why it was not, and to consider, as best he might, what could be done to avoid the conflicts among the personnel, or their incompetence, which was slowly bleeding it to death.

Id. at 615–16.

Hand went on to hold, however, that the plaintiff also had to prove that Liberty's losses would not have occurred if Andrews had properly performed his duties, and that no such showing had been made.

> . . . This cause of action rests upon a tort, as much though it be a tort of omission as though it had rested upon a positive act. The plaintiff must accept the burden of showing that the performance of the defendant's duties would have avoided loss, and what loss it would have avoided. . . .
>
> When the corporate funds have been illegally lent, it is a fair inference that a protest would have stopped the loan, and that the director's neglect caused the loss. But when a business fails from general mismanagement, business incapacity, or bad judgment, how is it possible to say that a single director could have made the company successful, or how much in dollars he could have

saved? Before this cause can go to a master, the plaintiff must show that, had Andrews done his full duty, he could have made the company prosper, or at least could have broken its fall. He must show what sum he could have saved the company. Neither of these has he made any effort to do.

The defendant is not subject to the burden of proving that the loss would have happened, whether he had done his duty or not. If he were, it would come to this: That, if a director were once shown slack in his duties, he would stand charged prima facie with the difference between the corporate treasury as it was, and as it would be, judged by a hypothetical standard of success. How could such a standard be determined? How could any one guess how far a director's skill and judgment would have prevailed upon his fellows, and what would have been the ultimate fate of the business, if they had? How is it possible to set any measure of liability, or to tell what he would have contributed to the event? Men's fortunes may not be subjected to such uncertain and speculative conjectures. It is hard to see how there can be any remedy, except one can put one's finger on a definite loss and say with reasonable assurance that protest would have deterred, or counsel persuaded, the managers who caused it. No men of sense would take the office, if the law imposed upon them a guaranty of the general success of their companies as a penalty for any negligence.

Id. at 616–18.

Some passages in Barnes v. Andrews may be read to suggest that an inattentive director will not be liable for a loss that would have been prevented by an attentive board unless it is shown that if the director had been attentive, his colleagues would have followed his lead. Such a suggestion would be out of keeping with general legal rules on the responsibility of joint actors, and hard to accept as a matter of either fairness or policy. However, Barnes v. Andrews can also be read to stand for the more modest proposition that an inattentive director will not be liable for a corporate loss if full attentiveness by *all* the directors would not have saved the situation, because in that case the inattentiveness of the director will not have been a cause-in-fact of the loss. That is the position taken in § 7.18(b) of the ALI's Principles of Corporate Governance. Under this section, if the board as a whole has violated its duty of care, by either commission or omission, each director will be liable for any loss of which the board's failure is the cause-in-fact and the legal (or proximate) cause:

> (b) A violation of [a standard of conduct] is the legal cause of loss if the plaintiff proves that (i) satisfaction of the applicable standard would have been a substantial factor in averting the loss, and (ii) the likelihood of injury would have been foreseeable to an ordinarily prudent person in a like position to that of the defendant and under similar circumstances. It is not a defense to liability in such cases that damage to the corporation would not have resulted but for the acts or omissions of other individuals.

The Comment to § 7.18 elaborates this position as follows:

> When multiple corporate officials fail to perform a duty whose omission is a legal cause of the loss, a problem of concurrent causation arises. Potentially, each defendant might claim that his or her conduct was less causally significant than that of others. To prevent each member of the collective body from evading liability by pointing to the concurrent omissions of others, the last sentence of § 7.18(b) specifies that "[i]t is not a defense to liability in such cases that damage to the corporation would not have resulted but for the acts or omissions of other individuals." This statement is consistent with the general approach of the law of torts to problems of concurrent causation, but § 7.18 takes no position on whether liability in such a case should be joint and several or should be apportioned in terms of culpability among those responsible.

In the duty-of-care case, Cede & Co. v. Technicolor, Inc., 634 A.2d 345 (Del. 1993), modified 636 A.2d (Del. 1994) (followed by extensive remands and appeals), the trial court rendered judgment for defendants on the ground that the plaintiff had the burden of proving injury and had not done so. The Delaware Supreme Court reversed. The Court concluded that based on the record, the directors had breached the duty of care. Given that conclusion, it held, the Chancellor's determination that the plaintiff had the burden of proving injury was erroneous. Bearing in mind that Delaware treats the business judgment rule as a presumption, the court held that if a plaintiff establishes that there was a breach of the duty of care, that showing overcomes the presumption of the rule and establishes a prima facie case of liability, even without a showing of injury. The burden then shifts to the defendants to show that the transaction was entirely fair. In the course of its opinion, the court explicitly rejected the reasoning of Barnes v. Andrews.

(b) THE BUSINESS JUDGMENT RULE

Kamin v. American Express Co.

Supreme Court, Special Term, N.Y. County, Part 1, 1976.
86 Misc.2d 809, 383 N.Y.S.2d 807, aff'd on opinion below 54 A.D.2d 654, 387 N.Y.S.2d 993 (1st Dept.1976).

■ EDWARD J. GREENFIELD, JUSTICE:

In this stockholders' derivative action, the individual defendants, who are the directors of the American Express Company, move for an order dismissing the complaint for failure to state a cause of action pursuant to CPLR 3211(a)(7), and alternatively, for summary judgment pursuant to CPLR 3211(c).

The complaint is brought derivatively by two minority stockholders of the American Express Company, asking for a declaration that a certain dividend in kind is a waste of corporate assets, directing the defendants not to proceed with the distribution, or, in the alternative, for monetary damages. The motion to dismiss the complaint requires the Court to presuppose the truth of the allegations. It is the defendants' contention that, conceding everything in the complaint, no viable cause of action is made out.

After establishing the identity of the parties, the complaint alleges that in 1972 American Express acquired for investment 1,954,418 shares of common stock of Donaldson, Lufken and Jenrette, Inc. (hereafter DLJ), a publicly traded corporation, at a cost of $29.9 million. It is further alleged that the current market value of those shares is approximately $4.0 million. On July 28, 1975, it is alleged, the Board of Directors of American Express declared a special dividend to all stockholders of record pursuant to which the shares of DLJ would be distributed in kind. Plaintiffs contend further that if American Express were to sell the DLJ shares on the market, it would sustain a capital loss of $25 million, which could be offset against taxable capital gains on other investments. Such a sale, they allege, would result in tax savings to the company of approximately $8 million, which would not be available in the case of the distribution of DLJ shares to stockholders. It is alleged that on October 8, 1975 and October 16, 1975, plaintiffs demanded that the directors rescind the previously declared dividend in DLJ shares and take steps to preserve the capital loss which would result from selling the shares. This demand was rejected by the Board of Directors on October 17, 1975.

It is apparent that all the previously-mentioned allegations of the complaint go to the question of the exercise by the Board of Directors of business judgment in deciding how to deal with the DLJ shares. The crucial allegation which must be scrutinized to determine the legal sufficiency of the complaint is paragraph 19, which alleges:

"19. All of the defendant Directors engaged in or acquiesced in or negligently permitted the declaration and payment of the Dividend in violation of the fiduciary duty owed by them to Amex to care for and preserve Amex's assets in the same manner as a man of average prudence would care for his own property."

Plaintiffs never moved for temporary injunctive relief, and did nothing to bar the actual distribution of the DLJ shares. The dividend was in fact paid on October 31, 1975. Accordingly, that portion of the complaint seeking a direction not to distribute the shares is deemed to be moot, and the Court will deal only with the request for declaratory judgment or for damages.

Examination of the complaint reveals that there is no claim of fraud or self-dealing, and no contention that there was any bad faith or oppressive conduct. The law is quite clear as to what is necessary to ground a claim for actionable wrongdoing.

"In actions by stockholders, which assail the acts of their directors or trustees, courts will not interfere unless the powers have been illegally or unconscientiously executed; or unless it be made to appear that the acts were fraudulent or collusive, and destructive of the rights of the stockholders. Mere errors of judgment are not sufficient as grounds for equity interference, for the powers of those entrusted with corporate management are largely discretionary." Leslie v. Lorillard, 110 N.Y. 519, 532, 18 N.E. 363, 365. . . .

More specifically, the question of whether or not a dividend is to be declared or a distribution of some kind should be made is exclusively a matter of business judgment for the Board of Directors.

". . . Courts will not interfere with such discretion unless it be first made to appear that the directors have acted or are about to act in bad faith and for a dishonest purpose. It is for the directors to say, acting in good faith of course, when and to what extent dividends shall be declared . . . The statute confers upon the directors this power, and the minority stockholders are not in a position to question this right, so long as the directors are acting in good faith . . ."

Thus, a complaint must be dismissed if all that is presented is a decision to pay dividends rather than pursuing some other course of conduct. Weinberger v. Quinn, 264 App.Div. 405, 35 N.Y.S.2d 567, affd. 290 N.Y. 635, 49 N.E.2d 131. A complaint which alleges merely that some course of action other than that pursued by the Board of Directors would have been more advantageous gives rise to no cognizable cause of action. Courts have more than enough to do in adjudicating legal rights and devising remedies for wrongs. The directors' room rather than the courtroom is the appropriate forum for thrashing out purely business questions which will have an impact on profits, market prices, competitive situations, or tax advantages. As stated by Cardozo, J., when sitting at Special Term, the substitution of someone else's business judgment for that of the directors "is no business for any court to follow." Holmes v. St. Joseph Lead Co., 84 Misc. 278, 283, 147 N.Y.S. 104, 107, quoting from Gamble v. Queens County Water Co., 123 N.Y. 91, 99, 25 N.E. 201, 208.

It is not enough to allege, as plaintiffs do here, that the directors made an imprudent decision, which did not capitalize on the possibility of using a potential capital loss to offset capital gains. More than imprudence or mistaken judgment must be shown.

"Questions of policy of management, expediency of contracts or action, adequacy of consideration, lawful appropriation of corporate funds to advance corporate interests, are left solely to their honest and unselfish decision, for their powers therein are without limitation and free from restraint, and the exercise of them for the common and general interests of the corporation may not be questioned, although the results show that what they did was unwise or inexpedient." Pollitz v. Wabash Railroad Co., 207 N.Y. 113, 124, 100 N.E. 721, 724.

Section 720 of the Business Corporation Law permits an action against directors for "the neglect of, or failure to perform, or other violations of his duties in the management and disposition of corporate assets committed to his charge." This does not mean that a director is chargeable with ordinary negligence for having made an improper decision, or having acted imprudently. The "neglect" referred to in the statute is neglect of duties (i.e., malfeasance or nonfeasance) and not misjudgment. To allege that a director "negligently permitted the declaration and payment" of a dividend without alleging fraud, dishonesty or nonfeasance, is to state merely that a decision was taken with which one disagrees.

Nor does this appear to be a case in which a potentially valid cause of action is inartfully stated.... The affidavits of the defendants and the exhibits annexed thereto demonstrate that the objections raised by the plaintiffs to the proposed dividend action were carefully considered and unanimously rejected by the Board at a special meeting called precisely for that purpose at the plaintiffs' request. The minutes of the special meeting indicate that the defendants were fully aware that a sale rather than a distribution of the DLJ shares might result in the realization of a substantial income tax saving. Nevertheless, they concluded that there were countervailing considerations primarily with respect to the adverse effect such a sale, realizing a loss of $25 million, would have on the net income figures in the American Express financial statement. Such a reduction of net income would have a serious effect on the market value of the publicly traded American Express stock. This was not a situation in which the defendant directors totally overlooked facts called to their attention. They gave them consideration, and attempted to view the total picture in arriving at their decision. While plaintiffs contend that according to their accounting consultants the loss on the DLJ stock would still have to be charged against current earnings even if the stock were distributed, the defendants' accounting experts assert that the loss would be a charge against earnings only in the event of a sale, whereas in the event of distribution of the stock as a dividend, the proper accounting treatment would be to charge the loss only against surplus. While the chief accountant for the SEC raised some question as to the appropriate accounting treatment of this transaction, there was no basis for any action to be taken by the SEC with respect to the American Express financial statement.

The only hint of self-interest which is raised, not in the complaint but in the papers on the motion, is that four of the twenty directors were officers and employees of American Express and members of its Executive Incentive Compensation Plan. Hence, it is suggested, by virtue of the action taken earnings may have been overstated and their compensation affected thereby. Such a claim is highly speculative and standing alone can hardly be regarded as sufficient to support an inference of self-dealing. There is no claim or showing that the four company directors dominated and controlled the sixteen outside members of the Board. Certainly, every action taken by the Board has some impact on earnings and may therefore affect the compensation of those whose earnings are keyed to profits. That does not disqualify the inside directors, nor does it put every policy adopted by the Board in question. All directors have an obligation, using sound business judgment, to maximize income for the benefit of all persons having a stake in the welfare of the corporate entity. See, Amdur v. Meyer, 15 A.D.2d 425, 224 N.Y.S.2d 440, appeal dismissed 14 N.Y.2d 541, 248 N.Y.S.2d 639, 198 N.E.2d 30. What we have here as revealed both by the complaint and by the affidavits and exhibits, is that a disagreement exists between two minority stockholders and a unanimous Board of Directors as to the best way to handle a loss already incurred on an investment. The directors are entitled to exercise their honest business judgment on the information before them, and to act within their corporate powers. That they may be mistaken, that other courses of action might have differing consequences, or that their action might benefit some shareholders more than others presents no basis for the superimposition of judicial judgment, so long as it appears that the directors have been acting in good faith. The question of to what extent a dividend shall be declared and the manner in which it shall be paid is ordinarily subject only to the qualification that the dividend be paid out of surplus (Business Corporation Law Section 510, subd. b). The Court will not interfere unless a clear case is made out of fraud, oppression, arbitrary action, or breach of trust.

Courts should not shrink from the responsibility of dismissing complaints or granting summary judgment when no legal wrongdoing is set forth....

In this case it clearly appears that the plaintiffs have failed as a matter of law to make out an actionable claim. Accordingly, the motion by the defendants for summary judgment and dismissal of the complaint is granted.

———

ALI, PRINCIPLES OF CORPORATE GOVERNANCE § 4.01(c)

[See Statutory Supplement]

———

W. Klein & J. Coffee, Business Organization and Finance 239–242

9th ed. 2004.

A. EXPECTED RETURN

Expected return is a measure of return that uses rudimentary concepts of probability to take account of risk or uncertainty as to outcome. Technically, expected return is the weighted average (or, if you prefer, arithmetic mean) of all possible outcomes. (The symbol commonly used to denote expected return is X.)

To illustrate, suppose that you bet $1 on the flip of a coin. If you win, you will have $2, and if you lose, nothing. The expected monetary value of that "investment" is $1, computed as follows:

Probability	Return	Value
.5	$2	$1
.5	0	0
1.0		$1

Note that here the expected return ignores the amount of the initial investment and thus tells us nothing about profitability. When we are concerned with profit we can use the concept of *expected rate of return,* which is likely to be expressed on an annual basis. Sometimes the term "expected return" is used to refer to rate of return. The meaning should be evident from the context.

Suppose that you buy 100 shares of stock of a corporation that does not pay dividends currently; that you pay $10 per share or $1,000 total; and that you expect to sell at the end of one year. Assume further that your estimate of the prospective sale prices and their probabilities is revealed in the first two columns below, with the corresponding expected return revealed by the third column:

Probability	Sale Price (return)	Value
.20	$ 900	$ 180
.50	1,000	500
.30	1,500	450
1.00		$1,130

The expected return calculation shows that in a statistical or probabilistic sense your investment is expected to yield $1,130, which is the expected return. The expected rate of return is 13 percent ($130 expected end-of-year gain on an investment of $1,000).

Where do these figures come from and how solid are they? The answer to that depends on facts that have not been developed. It is sufficient for our purposes to observe that people do, consciously or unconsciously, make calculations of this sort. Their information may be faulty. They may think in terms of a continuum of probabilities and outcomes or in terms of only two outcomes. The process may to some considerable extent be irrational or nonrational. Still, we need a term to describe the outcome of the process of considering and weighing prospects of various investment possibilities. "Expected return" is such a term.

B. RISK AND UNCERTAINTY ...

... In much of the professional literature of financial analysis, "risk" refers to the degree of dispersion or variation of possible outcomes. To illustrate, assume that you are confronted with two possible investments whose outcomes, probabilities, and expected returns are as follows:

INVESTMENT A

Probability	Outcome (return)	Value
.1	$ 900	$ 90
.8	1,000	800
.1	1,100	110
1.0		$1,000

INVESTMENT B

Probability	Outcome (return)	Value
.3	$ 0	$ 0
.4	1,000	400
.3	2,000	600
1.0		$1,000

The expected return of the two investments is the same but the risk associated with Investment B is much greater than that associated with Investment A. The range or dispersion of possible outcomes for B is greater. It is a potentially more volatile investment. For each investment the expected return or mean (weighted average) (X) is $1,000. For A, however, the combined chance of a return other than $1,000 is only 20 percent, and the difference between the expected return and extreme outcomes is only $100. For B, on the other hand, the combined chance of a return other than $1,000 is 60 percent and the difference between the expected return and extreme outcomes is $1,000. It can be seen, then, that the concept of volatility, or dispersion, or risk refers to a combination of the probability of deviation from the expected return and the amount of deviation—that is, to the degree of likelihood of receiving more or less than $1,000, and how much more or less. (Note that in the illustrations used above, the distributions of outcomes around the expected return are symmetrical—that is, there is an equal probability of deviation to each side of the expected return and the amount of deviation is the same to each side. This symmetrical kind of distribution has been used only for the sake of simplicity. It is not a necessary feature of the real world or of the analytic model, though it is commonly assumed to be a characteristic of the risks associated with investments in publicly traded common stocks.)

There are several statistical terms that are used to describe relative degrees of volatility (terms such as variance, standard deviation, and coefficient of variation) but we need not be concerned with their definition; they are simply measures of the degree of potential variation of possible outcomes. One investment is said to be more risky than another if the dispersion of potential outcomes is greater. We will refer to this concept of risk as *volatility risk* (recoiling only slightly at the now obvious redundancy of that phrase), though the term more commonly used by financial experts is *variance.*

Some economists have drawn a distinction between risk and uncertainty. "Risk" is then used to refer to variation depending purely on chance (e.g., the outcome of the flip of a coin) or, more broadly, to measurements as to which there is a large body of data or experience so that the probable outcomes can be estimated in a purely mechanical way. "Uncertainty," by contrast, refers to estimates made in situations where there is so little experience that the process of estimation is highly intuitive. It should be apparent from a moment's reflection that the distinction between risk and uncertainty is a fuzzy one and that the two concepts refer to ends of a spectrum....

NOTE ON JOY v. NORTH

In Joy v. North, 692 F.2d 880 (2d Cir. 1982), cert. denied, Citytrust v. Joy, 460 U.S. 1051, 103 S.Ct. 1498, 75 L.Ed.2d 930 (1983), the court, in discussing the duty of care, said:

Consider the choice between two investments in an example adapted from Klein, Business Organization and Finance 147–49 (1980):

INVESTMENT A

Estimated Probability of Outcome	Outcome Profit or Loss	Value
.4	+15	6.0
.4	+ 1	.4
.2	−13	−2.6
1.0		3.8

INVESTMENT B

Estimated Probability of Outcome	Outcome Profit or Loss	Value
.4	+6	2.4
.4	+2	.8
.2	+1	.2
1.0		3.4

Although A is clearly "worth" more than B, it is riskier because it is more volatile. Diversification lessens the volatility by allowing investors to invest in 20 or 200 A's which will tend to guarantee a total result near the value. Shareholders are thus better off with the various firms selecting A over B, although after the fact they will complain in each case of the 2.6 loss. If the courts did not abide by the business judgment rule, they might well penalize the choice of A in each such case and thereby unknowingly injure shareholders generally by creating incentives for management always to choose B.

NOTE ON THE DIVERGENCE OF STANDARDS OF CONDUCT AND STANDARDS OF REVIEW IN CORPORATE LAW, AND ON THE BUSINESS JUDGMENT RULE

A *standard of conduct* states how an actor should conduct a given activity or play a given role. A *standard of review* states the test a court should apply when it reviews an actor's conduct to determine whether to impose liability or grant injunctive relief. In many or most areas of law, standards of conduct and standards of review are identical. For example, the standard of conduct that governs an automobile driver is that he should drive carefully. Correspondingly, the standard of review in a liability claim against a driver is whether he drove carefully. The standard of conduct that governs an agent who engages in a transaction with his principal that involves the subject matter of the agency is that the agent must deal fairly. Correspondingly, the standard of review in a liability claim by the principal against an agent based on such a transaction is whether the agent dealt fairly.

An identity between standards of conduct and standards of review is so common that it is easy to overlook the fact that the two kinds of standards may diverge in any given area—that is, the standard of conduct that states how an actor should conduct himself may differ from the standard of review by which courts determine whether to impose liability on the basis of the actor's conduct. A divergence of standards of conduct and standards of review is particularly common in corporation law.

The duty of care is a leading example of this divergence. The traditional *standard of conduct* applicable to directors and officers in the performance of their functions, in relation to matters in which they are not interested, varies somewhat in its formulation, but the basic standard is set forth in Section 4.01(a) of the ALI's *Principles of Corporate Governance.* "A director or officer has a duty to the corporation to perform the director's or officer's functions in good faith, in a manner that he or she reasonably believes to be in the best interests of the corporation, and with the care that an ordinarily prudent person would reasonably be expected to exercise in a like position and under similar circumstances." The application of this standard of conduct to the functions of directors results in several distinct duties—in particular, the duty to monitor, the duty of inquiry, the duty to make prudent or reasonable decisions on matters that the board is obliged or chooses to act upon, and the duty to employ a reasonable process to make decisions.

Officers have comparable duties, although for most officers decisionmaking is likely to be more important than monitoring.

On their face, the duties of directors are fairly demanding, insofar as they are measured by reasonability. In practice, however, the standards of review applied to the performance of these duties are less stringent than the standards of conduct on which the duties are based. This is especially true when the quality of a decision—that is, the reasonableness of the decision, as opposed to the reasonableness of the decisionmaking process—is called into question. In such cases a much less demanding standard of review may apply, under the business judgment rule.

The business judgment rule consists of four conditions and, if the four conditions are satisfied, a special standard of review applicable to claims that are based on the quality of a decision.

The four conditions are as follows:

First, the director must have made a decision. So, for example, a director's failure to make due inquiry, or any other simple failure to take action (as opposed to a deliberative decision not to act), does not qualify for protection under the business judgment rule.

Second, the director must have informed himself with respect to the business judgment to the extent he reasonably believes appropriate under the circumstances—that is, he must have employed a reasonable decisionmaking process.

Third, the decision must have been made in good faith—a condition that is not satisfied if, among other things, the director knows that the decision violates the law.

Fourth, the director may not have a financial interest in the subject matter of the decision. For example, the business judgment rule is inapplicable to a director's decision to approve the corporation's purchase of his own property.

If the conditions of the business judgment rule are not satisfied, then the standard by which the quality of a decision is reviewed is comparable to the standard of conduct for making the decision—that is, the standard of review is based on entire fairness or reasonability. This is nicely illustrated by the Delaware Supreme Court's decision in Cede & Co. v. Technicolor, Inc., in 1993. Cede & Co. v. Technicolor, Inc., 634 A.2d 345 (Del.1993) (followed by extensive remands and appeals).

In that case, Perelman, the CEO of MacAndrews & Forbes, Inc. ("MAF"), entered into negotiations with Kamerman, the CEO of Technicolor, with a view to an acquisition of Technicolor by MAF. Goldman Sachs, the investment banker, told Kamerman, on the basis of limited information, that a price of $20–22 per share was worth pursuing, that a $25 price might be feasible, and that Kamerman should consider other possible purchasers. Six days later, Kamerman and Perelman agreed on a price of $23. That evening, Kamerman called a special meeting of Technicolor's Board, to be held two days later. At the meeting, the board approved an agreement with Pantry Pride that reflected the $23 price, and recommended that Technicolor's shareholders accept that price.

At the trial, the Chancellor found that it was a matter of grave doubt whether Technicolor's board had exercised due care in making its decision for the following reasons, among others: (1) The agreement was not preceded by a prudent search of alternatives. (2) Given the terms of the merger and the circumstances, the directors had no reasonable basis to assume that a better offer from a third party could be expected once the agreement was signed. (3) Most of the directors had little or no knowledge of an impending sale of the company until they arrived at the meeting, and only a few of them had any knowledge of the terms of the sale.

On the basis of these conclusions, the Delaware Supreme Court held that Technicolor's board failed to reach an informed decision when it made its decision, so that the business judgment rule did not apply. As a result, the directors had the burden of showing that the transaction was entirely fair. If the $23 price was not entirely fair, the directors would be liable for damages. And, the court added, because the business judgment rule did not apply, the directors had the burden of proving that the price was entirely fair.

In contrast, if the four conditions of the business judgment rule *are* satisfied, then the quality of a director's decision will be reviewed, not to determine whether the decision was reasonable, but only under a much more limited standard. There is some difference of opinion as to how that limited standard should be formulated. A few courts have stated that the standard is whether the director acted in good faith. See, e.g., In re RJR Nabisco, Inc. Shareholders Litig., [1988–89 Transfer Binder] Fed. Sec. L. Rep. (CCH) ¶ 94194, at 91,710 n.l3 (Del. Ch. Jan. 31, 1989). However, the prevalent formulation of the standard of review under the business judgment rule, if the four conditions of the rule are satisfied, is that the decision must be rational, or must have a rational basis, or the like. See ALI, Principles of Corporate Governance § 4.01(c)(3). This standard of review may be referred to as the business-judgment standard.

An example of a decision that fails to satisfy the rationality standard is a decision that cannot be coherently explained. For example, in Selheimer v. Manganese Corp. of America, 224 A.2d 634 (Pa.1966), a corporation's managers poured almost all of the corporation's funds into the development of a single plant even though they knew that the plant could not be operated profitably for a number of reasons, including lack of a railroad siding and proper storage areas. The court imposed liability because the managers' conduct "defie[d] explanation; in fact, the defendants have failed to give any satisfactory explanation or advance any justification for [the] expenditures." (In contrast, a decision may be *unreasonable*, but not *irrational*, if there are good reasons for and against the decision, but under the circumstances a person of sound judgment, giving appropriate weight to the reasons for and against, would not have made the decision. Accordingly, a decision may be unreasonable even though it was supported by some affirmative reasons and was therefore explicable, although on balance objectively undesirable.)

Although, as *Selheimer* shows, the rationality test has a bite, this standard of review is very much easier to satisfy than a reasonability standard. To see how exceptional a rationality standard is, we need only think about the judgments we make in everyday life. It is common to characterize a person's conduct as imprudent or unreasonable, but it is very uncommon to characterize a person's conduct as irrational.

Why should such a relatively undemanding standard of review, which differs so radically from the standard of conduct applicable to directors (and from the standards of both conduct and review applicable to persons who play most other life-roles) apply to the quality of decisions made by corporate directors? The answer to this question involves considerations of both fairness and policy.

To begin with, the application of a reasonableness standard of review to the quality of disinterested decisions by directors could result in the unfair imposition of liability. In paradigm negligence cases involving relatively simple decisions, such as automobile accidents, there is often little difference between decisions that turn out badly and bad decisions. In such cases, typically only one reasonable decision could have been made under a given set of circumstances, and decisions that turn out badly therefore almost inevitably turn out to have been bad decisions.

In contrast, in the case of business decisions it may often be difficult for fact-finders to distinguish between bad decisions and proper decisions that turn out badly. Business judgments are necessarily made on the basis of incomplete information and in the face of obvious risks, so that typically a range of decisions is reasonable. A decisionmaker faced with uncertainty must make a judgment concerning the relevant probability distribution and must act on that judgment. If the decisionmaker makes a reasonable assessment of the probability distribution, and the outcome falls on the unlucky tail, the decisionmaker has not made a bad decision, because in any normal probability distribution some outcomes will inevitably fall on the unlucky tail.

For example, a board faced with a promising but expensive and untried new technology may have to choose between investing in the technology or forgoing such an investment. Each alternative involves certain negative risks. If the board chooses one alternative and the associated negative risk materializes, the decision is "wrong" in the very restricted sense that if the board had it to do all over again it would make a different decision, but the decision is not for that reason a bad decision.

As a result of a systematic defect in cognition known as the hindsight bias, however, under a reasonableness standard of review fact-finders might too often erroneously treat decisions that turned out badly as bad decisions, and unfairly hold directors liable for such decisions. Experimental psychology has shown that in hindsight people consistently exaggerate the ease with which outcomes could have been anticipated in foresight. People view what has happened as relatively inevitable.[1] Accordingly, people who know that a bad *out-*

---

1. See Robyn M. Dawes, Rational Choice in an Uncertain World 119–20 (1988); Baruch Fischhoff, For Those Condemned to Study the Past: Heuristics and Biases in Hindsight, in Judgment Under Uncertainty: Heuristics and Biases 335, 341–43 (Daniel *come* resulted from a decision overestimate the extent to which the outcome was *predictable* and, therefore, the extent to which the decisionmaker was at fault for making the decision that led to the outcome.[2] Essentially, people find it difficult or even impossible to disregard information they possess about an outcome.[3] That information, in turn, renders the circumstances that pointed to the outcome more salient in their minds, because those circumstances can be integrated into a cohesive story that ends with the actual outcome, while circumstances pointing in other directions cannot.

The hindsight bias is nicely illustrated by an experiment in which 112 anesthesiologists reviewed the anesthesiological care in 21 paired cases that were based on actual files. Each of the anesthesiologists was presented with only one case from each pair. The patient and the treatments in each of the two paired cases were identical, and the results in all cases were as adverse. However, the files were edited so that in one case in each pair the adverse outcome was described as temporary, while in the other case the outcome was described as permanent. The reviewers were instructed to determine, in each of the 21 cases they reviewed, whether the anesthesiological care was less than appropriate, appropriate, or impossible to judge. When the adverse outcome was described as permanent rather than temporary, the overall distributions of the reviewers' judgments concerning the appropriateness of the care was shifted negatively by 30 percent.[4] Comparable results have been obtained in other experiments, even when the subjects have been explicitly instructed to disregard outcomes in evaluating fault.[5] The hindsight bias is also well-supported by survey evidence concerning the attribution of responsibility, and by casual empiricism.[6] The business judgment rule protects directors from the unfair imposition of liability as a result of the hindsight bias, by providing them with a large zone of protection when their decisions are attacked.

Furthermore, as a matter of policy the shareholders' own best interests may be served by conducting only a very limited review of the

Kahneman et al. eds., 1982) [hereinafter Heuristics and Biases]. Baruch Fischhoff & Ruth Beyth, "I Knew It Would Happen"—Remembered Probabilities of Once–Future Things, 13 Organizational Behav. and Hum. Performance 1–16 (1975) [hereinafter Fischhoff & Beyth].

2. See Hal Arkes & Cindy Schipani, Medical Malpractice and the Business Judgment Rule, 73 Ore. L. Rev. 587 (1994) [hereinafter Arkes & Schipani, Medical Malpractice]; Jonathan D. Casper et al., Juror Decision Making, Attitudes, and the Hindsight Bias, 13 L. & Hum. Behav. 291 (1989) [hereinafter Casper, Juror Decision Making]; Raanan Lipshitz, "Either a Medal or a Corporal:" The Effects of Success and Failure on the Evaluation of Decision Making and Decision Makers, 44 Organizational Behav. & Hum. Decision Processes 380 (1989) [hereinafter Lipshitz, Success and Failure].

3. See Michael J. Saks & Robert F. Kidd, Human Information processing and Adjudication: Trial by Heuristics, 15 L. & Soc'y Rev. 123, 144 (1980).

4. Robert A. Caplan et al., Effect of Outcome on Physician Judgments of Appropriateness of Care, 265 J. Am. Med. Ass'n 1957 (1991). This experiment, as well as the hindsight bias, its application to the business judgment rule, and other hindsight experiments in the medical area, are discussed in a very illuminating way in Arkes & Schipani, Medical Malpractice, supra note 3.

5. See, e.g., Casper, Juror Decision Making, supra note 2.

6. See Lipshitz, Success and Failure, supra note 2, at 381–82.

quality of directors' decisions. It is often in the interests of shareholders that directors choose the riskier of two alternative decisions, because the expected value of the more risky decision may be greater than the expected value of the less risky decision. For example, suppose that Corporation C has $100 million in assets. C's board must choose between decision X and decision Y. Each decision requires an investment of $1 million. Decision X has a 75% likelihood of succeeding. If the decision succeeds, C will gain $2 million. If it fails, C will lose its $1 million investment. Decision Y has a 90% chance of succeeding. If the decision succeeds, C will gain $1 million. If it fails, C will recover its investment. It is in the interest of C's shareholders that the board make decision X, even though it is riskier, because the expected value of decision X is $1.25 million (75% times the $2 million potential gain, minus 25% times the $1 million loss), while the expected value of decision Y is only $900,000 (90% of the $1 million potential gain). If, however, the board was concerned about liability for making an unreasonable decision it might choose decision Y, because as a practical matter it is almost impossible for a plaintiff to win a duty of care action on the theory that a board should have taken greater risks than it did. A standard of review of the quality of decisions that impose liability on a director for unreasonable, as opposed to irrational, decisions might therefore have the perverse incentive effect of discouraging bold but desirable decisions. Putting this more generally, under such a standard of review directors might tend to be unduly risk-averse, because if a highly risky decision had a positive outcome the corporation but not the directors would gain, while if it had a negative outcome the directors might be required to make up the corporate loss. The business judgment rule helps to offset that tendency.

—————

Smith v. Van Gorkom

Supreme Court of Delaware, 1985.
488 A.2d 858.

■ Before HERMANN, C.J., and McNEILLY, HORSEY, MOORE and CHRISTIE, JJ., constituting the Court en banc.

■ HORSEY, JUSTICE (for the majority):

This appeal from the Court of Chancery involves a class action brought by shareholders of the defendant Trans Union Corporation ("Trans Union" or "the Company"), originally seeking rescission of a cash-out merger of Trans Union into the defendant New T Company ("New T"), a wholly-owned subsidiary of the defendant, Marmon Group, Inc. ("Marmon"). Alternate relief in the form of damages is sought against the defendant members of the Board of Directors of Trans Union, New T, and Jay A. Pritzker and Robert A. Pritzker, owners of Marmon.[1]

1. The plaintiff, Alden Smith, originally sought to enjoin the merger; but, following extensive discovery, the Trial Court denied the plaintiff's motion for preliminary injunc-

Following trial, the former Chancellor granted judgment for the defendant directors by unreported letter opinion dated July 6, 1982.[2] Judgment was based on two findings: (1) that the Board of Directors had acted in an informed manner so as to be entitled to protection of the business judgment rule in approving the cash-out merger; and (2) that the shareholder vote approving the merger should not be set aside because the stockholders had been "fairly informed" by the Board of Directors before voting thereon. The plaintiffs appeal.

Speaking for the majority of the Court, we conclude that both rulings of the Court of Chancery are clearly erroneous. Therefore, we reverse and direct that judgment be entered in favor of the plaintiffs and against the defendant directors for the fair value of the plaintiffs' stockholdings in Trans Union. . . .

I.

The nature of this case requires a detailed factual statement. The following facts are essentially uncontradicted. . . .

Trans Union was a publicly-traded, diversified holding company, the principal earnings of which were generated by its railcar leasing business. During the period here involved, the Company had a cash flow of hundreds of millions of dollars annually. However, the Company had difficulty in generating sufficient taxable income to offset increasingly large investment tax credits (ITCs). . . .

B.

[Jerome Van Gorkom, Trans Union's Chairman and Chief Executive Officer, met with senior management on August 27, 1980, to discuss Trans Union's difficulty in producing sufficient taxable income to offset its increasing investment-tax credits and accelerated-depreciation deductions.] Donald Romans, Chief Financial Officer of Trans Union, stated that his department had done a "very brief bit of work on the possibility of a leveraged buy-out." . . . The work consisted of a "preliminary study" of the cash which could be generated by the Company if it participated in a leveraged buy-out. As Romans stated, this analysis "was very first and rough cut at seeing whether a cash flow would support what might be considered a high price for this type of transaction."

tion by unreported letter opinion dated February 3, 1981. On February 10, 1981, the proposed merger was approved by Trans Union's stockholders at a special meeting and the merger became effective on that date. Thereafter, John W. Gosselin was permitted to intervene as an additional plaintiff; and Smith and Gosselin were certified as representing a class consisting of all persons, other than defendants, who held shares of Trans Union common stock on all relevant dates. At the time of the merger, Smith owned 54,000 shares of Trans Union stock, Gosselin owned 23,600 shares, and members of Gosselin's family owned 20,000 shares.

2. Following trial, and before decision by the Trial Court, the parties stipulated to the dismissal, with prejudice, of the Messrs. Pritzker as parties defendant. However, all references to defendants hereinafter are to the defendant directors of Trans Union, unless otherwise noted.

On September 5, at another Senior Management meeting which Van Gorkom attended, Romans again brought up the idea of a leveraged buy-out as a "possible strategic alternative" to the Company's acquisition program. Romans and Bruce S. Chelberg, President and Chief Operating Officer of Trans Union, had been working on the matter in preparation for the meeting. According to Romans: They did not "come up" with a price for the Company. They merely "ran the numbers" at $50 a share and at $60 a share with the "rough form" of their cash figures at the time. Their "figures indicated that $50 would be very easy to do but $60 would be very difficult to do under those figures." This work did not purport to establish a fair price for either the Company or 100% of the stock. It was intended to determine the cash flow needed to service the debt that would "probably" be incurred in a leveraged buy-out, based on "rough calculations" without "any benefit of experts to identify what the limits were to that, and so forth." These computations were not considered extensive and no conclusion was reached.

At this meeting, Van Gorkom stated that he would be willing to take $55 per share for his own 75,000 shares. He vetoed the suggestion of a leveraged buy-out by Management, however, as involving a potential conflict of interest for Management. Van Gorkom, a certified public accountant and lawyer, had been an officer of Trans Union for 24 years, its Chief Executive Officer for more than 17 years, and Chairman of its Board for 2 years. It is noteworthy in this connection that he was then approaching 65 years of age and mandatory retirement.

For several days following the September 5 meeting, Van Gorkom pondered the idea of a sale. . . .

Van Gorkom decided to meet with Jay A. Pritzker, a well-known corporate takeover specialist and a social acquaintance. However, rather than approaching Pritzker simply to determine his interest in acquiring Trans Union, Van Gorkom assembled a proposed per share price for sale of the Company and a financing structure by which to accomplish the sale. Van Gorkom did so without consulting either his Board or any members of Senior Management except one: Carl Peterson, Trans Union's Controller. Telling Peterson that he wanted no other person on his staff to know what he was doing, but without telling him why, Van Gorkom directed Peterson to calculate the feasibility of a leveraged buy-out at an assumed price per share of $55. Apart from the Company's historic stock market price,[5] and Van Gorkom's long association with Trans Union, the record is devoid of any competent evidence that $55 represented the per share intrinsic value of the Company. . . .

---

5. The common stock of Trans Union was traded on the New York Stock Exchange. Over the five year period from 1975 through 1979, Trans Union's stock had traded within a range of a high of $39½ and a low of $24¼. Its high and low range for 1980 through September 19 (the last trading day before announcement of the merger) was $38¼–$29½.

Van Gorkom arranged a meeting with Pritzker at the latter's home on Saturday, September 13, 1980. Van Gorkom prefaced his presentation by stating to Pritzker: "Now as far as you are concerned, I can, I think, show how you can pay a substantial premium over the present stock price and pay off most of the loan in the first five years.... If you could pay $55 for this Company, here is a way in which I think it can be financed."

Van Gorkom then reviewed with Pritzker his calculations based upon his proposed price of $55 per share. Although Pritzker mentioned $50 as a more attractive figure, no other price was mentioned. However, Van Gorkom stated that to be sure that $55 was the best price obtainable, Trans Union should be free to accept any better offer. Pritzker demurred, stating that his organization would serve as a "stalking horse" for an "auction contest" only if Trans Union would permit Pritzker to buy 1,750,000 shares of Trans Union stock at market price which Pritzker could then sell to any higher bidder. After further discussion on this point, Pritzker told Van Gorkom that he would give him a more definite reaction soon.

On Monday, September 15, Pritzker advised Van Gorkom that he was interested in the $55 cash-out merger proposal and requested more information on Trans Union....

On Thursday, September 18, Van Gorkom met again with Pritzker. At that time, Van Gorkom knew that Pritzker intended to make a cash-out merger offer at Van Gorkom's proposed $55 per share. Pritzker instructed his attorney, a merger and acquisition specialist, to begin drafting merger documents. There was no further discussion of the $55 price. However, the number of shares of Trans Union's treasury stock to be offered to Pritzker was negotiated down to one million shares; the price was set at $38–75 cents above the per share price at the close of the market on September 19. At this point, Pritzker insisted that the Trans Union Board act on his merger proposal within the next three days, stating to Van Gorkom: "We have to have a decision by no later than Sunday [evening, September 21] before the opening of the English stock exchange on Monday morning." Pritzker's lawyer was then instructed to draft the merger documents, to be reviewed by Van Gorkom's lawyer, "sometimes with discussion and sometimes not, in the haste to get it finished."

On Friday, September 19, Van Gorkom, Chelberg, and Pritzker consulted with Trans Union's lead bank regarding the financing of Pritzker's purchase of Trans Union. The bank indicated that it could form a syndicate of banks that would finance the transaction. On the same day, Van Gorkom retained James Brennan, Esquire, to advise Trans Union on the legal aspects of the merger. Van Gorkom did not consult with William Browder, a Vice–President and director of Trans Union and former head of its legal department, or with William Moore, then the head of Trans Union's legal staff.

On Friday, September 19, Van Gorkom called a special meeting of the Trans Union Board for noon the following day. He also called a meeting of the Company's Senior Management to convene at 11:00

a.m., prior to the meeting of the Board. No one, except Chelberg and Peterson, was told the purpose of the meetings. Van Gorkom did not invite Trans Union's investment banker, Salomon Brothers or its Chicago-based partner, to attend.

Of those present at the Senior Management meeting on September 20, only Chelberg and Peterson had prior knowledge of Pritzker's offer. Van Gorkom disclosed the offer and described its terms, but he furnished no copies of the proposed Merger Agreement. Romans announced that his department had done a second study which showed that, for a leveraged buy-out, the price range for Trans Union stock was between $55 and $65 per share. Van Gorkom neither saw the study nor asked Romans to make it available for the Board meeting.

Senior Management's reaction to the Pritzker proposal was completely negative. No member of Management, except Chelberg and Peterson, supported the proposal. Romans objected to the price as being too low[6]. . . .

Ten directors served on the Trans Union Board, five inside (defendants Bonser, O'Boyle, Browder, Chelberg, and Van Gorkom) and five outside (defendants Wallis, Johnson, Lanterman, Morgan and Reneker). All directors were present at the meeting, except O'Boyle who was ill. Of the outside directors, four were corporate chief executive officers and one was the former Dean of the University of Chicago Business School. None was an investment banker or trained financial analyst. All members of the Board were well informed about the Company and its operations as a going concern. They were familiar with the current financial condition of the Company, as well as operating and earnings projections reported in the recent Five Year Forecast. The Board generally received regular and detailed reports and was kept abreast of the accumulated investment tax credit and accelerated depreciation problem.

Van Gorkom began the Special Meeting of the Board with a twenty-minute oral presentation. Copies of the proposed Merger Agreement were delivered too late for study before or during the meeting.[7] He reviewed the Company's ITC and depreciation problems and the efforts theretofore made to solve them. He discussed his initial meeting with Pritzker and his motivation in arranging that meeting. Van Gorkom did not disclose to the Board, however, the methodology by which he alone had arrived at the $55 figure, or the fact that he first proposed the $55 price in his negotiations with Pritzker.

6. Van Gorkom asked Romans to express his opinion as to the $55 price. Romans stated that he "thought the price was too low in relation to what he could derive for the company in a cash sale, particularly one which enabled us to realize the values of certain subsidiaries and independent entities."

7. The record is not clear as to the terms of the Merger Agreement. The Agreement, as originally presented to the Board on September 20, was never produced by defendants despite demands by the plaintiffs. Nor is it clear that the directors were given an opportunity to study the Merger Agreement before voting on it. All that can be said is that Brennan had the Agreement before him during the meeting.

Van Gorkom outlined the terms of the Pritzker offer as follows: Pritzker would pay $55 in cash for all outstanding shares of Trans Union stock upon completion of which Trans Union would be merged into New T Company, a subsidiary wholly-owned by Pritzker and formed to implement the merger; for a period of 90 days, Trans Union could receive, but could not actively solicit, competing offers; the offer had to be acted on by the next evening, Sunday, September 21; Trans Union could only furnish to competing bidders published information, and not proprietary information; the offer was subject to Pritzker obtaining the necessary financing by October 10, 1980; if the financing contingency were met or waived by Pritzker, Trans Union was required to sell to Pritzker one million newly-issued shares of Trans Union at $38 per share.

Van Gorkom took the position that putting Trans Union "up for auction" through a 90–day market test would validate a decision by the Board that $55 was a fair price. He told the Board that the "free market will have an opportunity to judge whether $55 is a fair price." Van Gorkom framed the decision before the Board not as whether $55 per share was the highest price that could be obtained, but as whether the $55 price was a fair price that the stockholders should be given the opportunity to accept or reject.[8]

Attorney Brennan advised the members of the Board that they might be sued if they failed to accept the offer and that a fairness opinion was not required as a matter of law.

Romans attended the meeting as chief financial officer of the Company. He told the Board that he had not been involved in the negotiations with Pritzker and knew nothing about the merger proposal until the morning of the meeting; that his studies did not indicate either a fair price for the stock or a valuation of the Company; that he did not see his role as directly addressing the fairness issue; and that he and his people "were trying to search for ways to justify a price in connection with such a [leveraged buy-out] transaction, rather than to say what the shares are worth." Romans testified:

> I told the Board that the study ran the numbers at 50 and 60, and then the subsequent study at 55 and 65, and that was not the same thing as saying that I have a valuation of the company at X dollars. But it was a way—a first step towards reaching that conclusion.

Romans told the Board that, in his opinion, $55 was "in the range of a fair price," but "at the beginning of the range." . . .

The Board meeting of September 20 lasted about two hours. Based solely upon Van Gorkom's oral presentation, Chelberg's supporting representations, Romans' oral statement, Brennan's legal advice, and their knowledge of the market history of the Company's stock, the directors approved the proposed Merger Agreement. However, the Board later claimed to have attached two conditions to its

---

8. In Van Gorkom's words: The "real decision" is whether to "let the stockholders decide it" which is "all you are being asked to decide today."

acceptance: (1) that Trans Union reserved the right to accept any better offer that was made during the market test period; and (2) that Trans Union could share its proprietary information with any other potential bidders. While the Board now claims to have reserved the right to accept any better offer received after the announcement of the Pritzker agreement (even though the minutes of the meeting do not reflect this), it is undisputed that the Board did not reserve the right to actively solicit alternate offers.

The Merger Agreement was executed by Van Gorkom during the evening of September 20 at a formal social event that he hosted for the opening of the Chicago Lyric Opera. Neither he nor any other director read the agreement prior to its signing and delivery to Pritzker. . . .

On Monday, September 22, the Company issued a press release announcing that Trans Union had entered into a "definitive" Merger Agreement with an affiliate of the Marmon Group, Inc., a Pritzker holding company. Within 10 days of the public announcement, dissent among Senior Management over the merger had become widespread. Faced with threatened resignations of key officers, Van Gorkom met with Pritzker who agreed to several modifications of the Agreement. Pritzker was willing to do so provided that Van Gorkom could persuade the dissidents to remain on the Company payroll for at least six months after consummation of the merger.

Van Gorkom reconvened the Board on October 8 and secured the directors' approval of the proposed amendments—sight unseen. The Board also authorized the employment of Salomon Brothers, its investment banker, to solicit other offers for Trans Union during the proposed "market test" period.

The next day, October 9, Trans Union issued a press release announcing: (1) that Pritzker had obtained "the financing commitments necessary to consummate" the merger with Trans Union; (2) that Pritzker had acquired one million shares of Trans Union common stock at $38 per share; (3) that Trans Union was now permitted to actively seek other offers and had retained Salomon Brothers for that purpose; and (4) that if a more favorable offer were not received before February 1, 1981, Trans Union's shareholders would thereafter meet to vote on the Pritzker proposal.

It was not until the following day, October 10, that the actual amendments to the Merger Agreement were prepared by Pritzker and delivered to Van Gorkom for execution. As will be seen, the amendments were considerably at variance with Van Gorkom's representations of the amendments to the Board on October 8; and the amendments placed serious constraints on Trans Union's ability to negotiate a better deal and withdraw from the Pritzker agreement. Nevertheless, Van Gorkom proceeded to execute what became the October 10 amendments to the Merger Agreement without conferring further with the Board members and apparently without comprehending the actual implications of the amendments. . . .

Salomon Brothers' efforts over a three-month period from October 21 to January 21 produced only one serious suitor for Trans Union–General Electric Credit Corporation ("GE Credit"), a subsidiary of the General Electric Company. However, GE Credit was unwilling to make an offer for Trans Union unless Trans Union first rescinded its Merger Agreement with Pritzker. When Pritzker refused, GE Credit terminated further discussions with Trans Union in early January.

In the meantime, in early December, the investment firm Kohlberg, Kravis, Roberts & Co. ("KKR"), the only other concern to make a firm offer for Trans Union, withdrew its offer under circumstances hereinafter detailed.

. . . On January 21, Management's Proxy Statement for the February 10 shareholder meeting was mailed to Trans Union's stockholders. On January 26, Trans Union's Board met and, after a lengthy meeting, voted to proceed with the Pritzker merger. . . .

On February 10, the stockholders of Trans Union approved the Pritzker merger proposal. Of the outstanding shares, 69.9% were voted in favor of the merger; 7.25% were voted against the merger; and 22.85% were not voted.

II.

We turn to the issue of the application of the business judgment rule to the September 20 meeting of the Board.

The Court of Chancery concluded from the evidence that the Board of Directors' approval of the Pritzker merger proposal fell within the protection of the business judgment rule. The Court found that the Board had given sufficient time and attention to the transaction, since the directors had considered the Pritzker proposal on three different occasions, on September 20, and on October 8, 1980 and finally on January 26, 1981. On that basis, the Court reasoned that the Board had acquired, over the four-month period, sufficient information to reach an informed business judgment on the cash-out merger proposal. The Court ruled:

> . . . that given the market value of Trans Union's stock, the business acumen of the members of the board of Trans Union, the substantial premium over market offered by the Pritzkers and the ultimate effect on the merger price provided by the prospect of other bids for the stock in question, that the board of directors of Trans Union did not act recklessly or improvidently in determining on a course of action which they believed to be in the best interest of the stockholders of Trans Union.

The Court of Chancery made but one finding; i.e., that the Board's conduct over the entire period from September 20 through January 26, 1981 was not reckless or improvident, but informed. This ultimate conclusion was premised upon three subordinate findings, one explicit and two implied. The Court's explicit finding was that Trans Union's Board was "free to turn down the Pritzker proposal" not only on September 20 but also on October 8, 1980 and on January 26, 1981.

The Court's implied, subordinate findings were: (1) that no legally binding agreement was reached by the parties until January 26; and (2) that if a higher offer were to be forthcoming, the market test would have produced it, and Trans Union would have been contractually free to accept such higher offer. However, the Court offered no factual basis or legal support for any of these findings; and the record compels contrary conclusions. . . .

Under Delaware law, the business judgment rule is the offspring of the fundamental principle, codified in 8 Del.C. § 141(a), that the business and affairs of a Delaware corporation are managed by or under its board of directors. . . . The rule itself "is a presumption that in making a business decision, the directors of a corporation acted on an informed basis, in good faith and in the honest belief that the action taken was in the best interests of the company." . . . [Aronson v. Lewis, 473 A.2d 805, 812 (Del.1984)]. Thus, the party attacking a board decision as uninformed must rebut the presumption that its business judgment was an informed one. Id.

The determination of whether a business judgment is an informed one turns on whether the directors have informed themselves "prior to making a business decision, of all material information reasonably available to them." Id.

Under the business judgment rule there is no protection for directors who have made "an unintelligent or unadvised judgment." Mitchell v. Highland–Western Glass, Del.Ch., 167 A. 831, 833 (1933). . . .

The standard of care applicable to a director's duty of care has also been recently restated by this Court. In Aronson, supra, we stated:

> While the Delaware cases use a variety of terms to describe the applicable standard of care, our analysis satisfies us that under the business judgment rule director liability is predicated upon concepts of gross negligence. (footnote omitted)

473 A.2d at 812.

We again confirm that view. We think the concept of gross negligence is also the proper standard for determining whether a business judgment reached by a board of directors was an informed one. . . .

It is against those standards that the conduct of the directors of Trans Union must be tested, as a matter of law and as a matter of fact, regarding their exercise of an informed business judgment in voting to approve the Pritzker merger proposal.

III. . . .

. . . [T]he question of whether the directors reached an informed business judgment in agreeing to sell the Company, pursuant to the terms of the September 20 Agreement presents, in reality, two questions: (A) whether the directors reached an informed business judgment on September 20, 1980; and (B) if they did not, whether the directors' actions taken subsequent to September 20 were adequate to cure any infirmity in their action taken on September 20. We first consider the directors' September 20 action in terms of their reaching an informed business judgment.

—A—

On the record before us, we must conclude that the Board of Directors did not reach an informed business judgment on September 20, 1980 in voting to "sell" the Company for $55 per share pursuant to the Pritzker cash-out merger proposal. Our reasons, in summary, are as follows:

The directors (1) did not adequately inform themselves as to Van Gorkom's role in forcing the "sale" of the Company and in establishing the per share purchase price; (2) were uninformed as to the intrinsic value of the Company; and (3) given these circumstances, at a minimum, were grossly negligent in approving the "sale" of the Company upon two hours' consideration, without prior notice, and without the exigency of a crisis or emergency.

As has been noted, the Board based its September 20 decision to approve the cash-out merger primarily on Van Gorkom's representations. None of the directors, other than Van Gorkom and Chelberg, had any prior knowledge that the purpose of the meeting was to propose a cash-out merger of Trans Union. . . .

Without any documents before them concerning the proposed transaction, the members of the Board were required to rely entirely upon Van Gorkom's 20–minute oral presentation of the proposal. No written summary of the terms of the merger was presented; the directors were given no documentation to support the adequacy of $55 price per share for sale of the Company; and the Board had before it nothing more than Van Gorkom's statement of his understanding of the substance of an agreement which he admittedly had never read, nor which any member of the Board had ever seen.

Under 8 Del.C. § 141(e), "directors are fully protected in relying in good faith on reports made by officers." Michelson v. Duncan, Del.Ch., 386 A.2d 1144, 1156 (1978); aff'd in part and rev'd in part on other grounds, Del.Supr., 407 A.2d 211 (1979). See also Graham v. Allis–Chalmers Mfg. Co., Del.Supr., 188 A.2d 125, 130 (1963); Prince v. Bensinger, Del.Ch., 244 A.2d 89, 94 (1968). The term "report" has been liberally construed to include reports of informal personal investigations by corporate officers, Cheff v. Mathes, Del.Supr., 199 A.2d 548, 556 (1964). However, there is no evidence that any "report," as defined under § 141(e), concerning the Pritzker proposal, was presented to the Board on September 20. Van Gorkom's oral presentation of his understanding of the terms of the proposed Merger Agreement, which he had not seen, and Romans' brief oral statement of his preliminary study regarding the feasibility of a leveraged buy-out of Trans Union do not qualify as § 141(e) "reports" for these reasons: The former lacked substance because Van Gorkom was basically uninformed as to the essential provisions of the very document about which he was talking. Romans' statement was irrelevant to the issues before the Board since it did not purport to be a valuation study. At a minimum for a report to enjoy the status conferred by § 141(e), it must be pertinent to the subject matter upon which a board is called to act, and otherwise be entitled to good faith, not blind, reliance. Considering all of the surrounding circumstances—hastily calling the meeting without prior notice of its subject matter, the proposed sale of the Company without any prior consideration of the issue or necessity therefor, the urgent time constraints imposed by Pritzker, and the total absence of any documentation whatsoever—the directors were duty bound to make reasonable inquiry of Van Gorkom and Romans, and if they had done so, the inadequacy of that upon which they now claim to have relied would have been apparent.

The defendants rely on the following factors to sustain the Trial Court's finding that the Board's decision was an informed one: (1) the magnitude of the premium or spread between the $55 Pritzker offering price and Trans Union's current market price of $38 per share; (2) the amendment of the Agreement as submitted on September 20 to permit the Board to accept any better offer during the "market test" period; (3) the collective experience and expertise of the Board's "inside" and "outside" directors; and (4) their reliance on Brennan's legal advice that the directors might be sued if they rejected the Pritzker proposal. We discuss each of these grounds *seriatim*:

(1)

A substantial premium may provide one reason to recommend a merger, but in the absence of other sound valuation information, the fact of a premium alone does not provide an adequate basis upon which to assess the fairness of an offering price. Here, the judgment reached as to the adequacy of the premium was based on a comparison between the historically depressed Trans Union market price and the amount of the Pritzker offer. Using market price as a basis for concluding that the premium adequately reflected the true value of the Company was a clearly faulty, indeed fallacious, premise....

The record is clear that before September 20, Van Gorkom and other members of Trans Union's Board knew that the market had consistently undervalued the worth of Trans Union's stock....

The parties do not dispute that a publicly-traded stock price is solely a measure of the value of a minority position and, thus, market price represents only the value of a single share. Nevertheless, on September 20, the Board assessed the adequacy of the premium over market, offered by Pritzker, solely by comparing it with Trans Union's current and historical stock price....

Indeed, as of September 20, the Board had no other information on which to base a determination of the intrinsic value of Trans Union as a going concern. As of September 20, the Board had made no evaluation of the Company designed to value the entire enterprise, nor had the Board ever previously considered selling the Company or consenting to a buy-out merger. Thus, the adequacy of a premium is indeterminate unless it is assessed in terms of other competent and sound valuation information that reflects the value of the particular business.

Despite the foregoing facts and circumstances, there was no call by the Board, either on September 20 or thereafter, for any valuation study or documentation of the $55 price per share as a measure of the fair value of the Company in a cash-out context. It is undisputed that the major asset of Trans Union was its cash flow. Yet, at no time did the Board call for a valuation study taking into account that highly significant element of the Company's assets.

We do not imply that an outside valuation study is essential to support an informed business judgment; nor do we state that fairness opinions by independent investment bankers are required as a matter of law. Often insiders familiar with the business of a going concern are in a better position than are outsiders to gather relevant information; and under appropriate circumstances, such directors may be fully protected in relying in good faith upon the valuation reports of their management. See 8 Del.C. § 141(e)....

Here, the record establishes that the Board did not request its Chief Financial Officer, Romans, to make any valuation study or review of the proposal to determine the adequacy of $55 per share for sale of the Company. On the record before us: The Board rested on Romans' elicited response that the $55 figure was within a "fair price range" within the context of a leveraged buy-out. No director sought any further information from Romans. No director asked him why he put $55 at the bottom of his range. No director asked Romans for any details as to his study, the reason why it had been undertaken or its depth. No director asked to see the study; and no director asked Romans whether Trans Union's finance department could do a fairness study within the remaining 36–hour period available under the Pritzker offer....

Thus, the record compels the conclusion that on September 20 the Board lacked valuation information adequate to reach an informed business judgment as to the fairness of $55 per share for sale of the Company.

(2)

This brings us to the post-September 20 "market test" upon which the defendants ultimately rely to confirm the reasonableness of their September 20 decision to accept the Pritzker proposal. In this connection, the directors present a two-part argument: (a) that by making a "market test" of Pritzker's $55 per share offer a condition of their September 20 decision to accept his offer, they cannot be found to have acted impulsively or in an uninformed manner on September 20; and (b) that the adequacy of the $17 premium for sale of the Company was conclusively established over the following 90 to 120 days by the most reliable evidence available—the marketplace. Thus, the defendants impliedly contend that the "market test" eliminated the need for the Board to perform any other form of fairness test either on September 20, or thereafter.

Again, the facts of record do not support the defendants' argument. There is no evidence: (a) that the Merger Agreement was effectively amended to give the Board freedom to put Trans Union up for auction sale to the highest bidder; or (b) that a public auction was in fact permitted to occur. The minutes of the Board meeting make no reference to any of this. Indeed, the record compels the conclusion that the directors had no rational basis for expecting that a market test was attainable, given the terms of the Agreement as executed during the evening of September 20. We rely upon the following facts which are essentially uncontradicted:

The Merger Agreement, specifically identified as that originally presented to the Board on September 20, has never been produced by the defendants, notwithstanding the plaintiffs' several demands for production before as well as during trial. No acceptable explanation of this failure to produce documents has been given to either the Trial Court or this Court. . . .

Van Gorkom states that the Agreement as submitted incorporated the ingredients for a market test by authorizing Trans Union to receive competing offers over the next 90–day period. However, he concedes that the Agreement barred Trans Union from actively soliciting such offers and from furnishing to interested parties any information about the Company other than that already in the public domain. Whether the original Agreement of September 20 went so far as to authorize Trans Union to receive competitive proposals is arguable. The defendants' unexplained failure to produce and identify the original Merger Agreement permits the logical inference that the instrument would not support their assertions in this regard. . . .

The defendant directors assert that they "insisted" upon including two amendments to the Agreement, thereby permitting a market test: (1) to give Trans Union the right to accept a better offer; and (2) to reserve to Trans Union the right to distribute proprietary information on the Company to alternative bidders. Yet, the defendants concede that they did not seek to amend the Agreement to permit Trans Union to solicit competing offers.

Several of Trans Union's outside directors resolutely maintained that the Agreement as submitted was approved on the understanding that, "if we got a better deal, we had a right to take it." Director Johnson so testified; but he then added, "And if they didn't put that in the agreement, then the management did not carry out the conclusion of the Board. And I just don't know whether they did or not." The only clause in the Agreement as finally executed to which the defendants can point as "keeping the door open" is the following underlined statement found in subparagraph (a) of section 2.03 of the Merger Agreement as executed:

The Board of Directors shall recommend to the stockholders of Trans Union that they approve and adopt the Merger Agreement ("the stockholders' approval") and to use its best efforts to obtain the requisite votes therefor. *GL acknowledges that Trans Union directors may have a competing fiduciary obligation to the shareholders under certain circumstances.*

Clearly, this language on its face cannot be construed as incorporating either of the two "conditions" described above: either the right to accept a better offer or the right to distribute proprietary information to third parties.... No reference to either of the so-called "conditions" or of Trans Union's reserved right to test the market appears in any notes of the Board meeting or in the Board Resolution accepting the Pritzker offer or in the Minutes of the meeting itself....

Thus, notwithstanding what several of the outside directors later claimed to have "thought" occurred at the meeting, the record compels the conclusion that Trans Union's Board had no rational basis to conclude on September 20 or in the days immediately following, that the Board's acceptance of Pritzker's offer was conditioned on (1) a "market test" of the offer; and (2) the Board's right to withdraw from the Pritzker Agreement and accept any higher offer received before the shareholder meeting.

(3)

The directors' unfounded reliance on both the premium and the market test as the basis for accepting the Pritzker proposal undermines the defendants' remaining contention that the Board's collective experience and sophistication was a sufficient basis for finding that it reached its September 20 decision with informed, reasonable deliberation....

(4) ...

We conclude that Trans Union's Board was grossly negligent in that it failed to act with informed reasonable deliberation in agreeing to the Pritzker merger proposal on September 20....

—B—

We now examine the Board's post-September 20 conduct for the purpose of determining first, whether it was informed and not grossly negligent; and second, if informed, whether it was sufficient to legally rectify and cure the Board's derelictions of September 20.[23]

(1)

First, as to the Board meeting of October 8....

The public announcement of the Pritzker merger resulted in an "en masse" revolt of Trans Union's Senior Management. The head of Trans Union's tank car operations (its most profitable division) informed Van Gorkom that unless the merger were called off, fifteen key personnel would resign.

---

23. As will be seen, we do not reach the second question.

Instead of reconvening the Board, Van Gorkom again privately met with Pritzker, informed him of the developments, and sought his advice. Pritzker then made the following suggestions for overcoming Management's dissatisfaction: (1) that the Agreement be amended to permit Trans Union to solicit, as well as receive, higher offers; and (2) that the shareholder meeting be postponed from early January to February 10, 1981. In return, Pritzker asked Van Gorkom to obtain a commitment from Senior Management to remain at Trans Union for at least six months after the merger was consummated.

Van Gorkom then advised Senior Management that the Agreement would be amended to give Trans Union the right to solicit competing offers through January, 1981, if they would agree to remain with Trans Union. Senior Management was temporarily mollified; and Van Gorkom then called a special meeting of Trans Union's Board for October 8.

Thus, the primary purpose of the October 8 Board meeting was to amend the Merger Agreement, in a manner agreeable to Pritzker, to permit Trans Union to conduct a "market test." Van Gorkom understood that the proposed amendments were intended to give the Company an unfettered "right to openly solicit offers down through January 31." Van Gorkom presumably so represented the amendments to Trans Union's Board members on October 8. In a brief session, the directors approved Van Gorkom's oral presentation of the substance of the proposed amendments, the terms of which were not reduced to writing until October 10. But rather than waiting to review the amendments, the Board again approved them sight unseen and adjourned, giving Van Gorkom authority to execute the papers when he received them.[25] . . .

The next day, October 9, and before the Agreement was amended, Pritzker moved swiftly to off-set the proposed market test amendment. First, Pritzker informed Trans Union that he had completed arrangements for financing its acquisition and that the parties were thereby mutually bound to a firm purchase and sale arrangement. Second, Pritzker announced the exercise of his option to purchase one million shares of Trans Union's treasury stock at $38 per share—75 cents above the current market price. Trans Union's Management responded the same day by issuing a press release announcing: (1) that all financing arrangements for Pritzker's acquisition of Trans Union had been completed; and (2) Pritzker's purchase of one million shares of Trans Union's treasury stock at $38 per share.

The next day, October 10, Pritzker delivered to Trans Union the proposed amendments to the September 20 Merger Agreement. Van Gorkom promptly proceeded to countersign all the instruments on

---

25. We do not suggest that a board must read *in haec verba* every contract or legal document which it approves, but if it is to successfully absolve itself from charges of the type made here, there must be some credible contemporary evidence demonstrat- ing that the directors knew what they were doing, and ensured that their purported action was given effect. That is the consistent failure which cast this Board upon its unredeemable course.

behalf of Trans Union without reviewing the instruments to determine if they were consistent with the authority previously granted him by the Board. The amending documents were apparently not approved by Trans Union's Board until a much later date, December 2. The record does not affirmatively establish that Trans Union's directors ever read the October 10 amendments.[26]

The October 10 amendments to the Merger Agreement did authorize Trans Union to solicit competing offers, but the amendments had more far-reaching effects. The most significant change was in the definition of the third-party "offer" available to Trans Union as a possible basis for withdrawal from its Merger Agreement with Pritzker. Under the October 10 amendments, a better *offer* was no longer sufficient to permit Trans Union's withdrawal. Trans Union was now permitted to terminate the Pritzker Agreement and abandon the merger only if, prior to February 10, 1981, Trans Union had either consummated a merger (or sale of assets) with a third party or had entered into a "definitive" merger agreement more favorable than Pritzker's and for a greater consideration—subject only to stockholder approval. Further, the "extension" of the market test period to February 10, 1981 was circumscribed by other amendments which required Trans Union to file its preliminary proxy statement on the Pritzker merger proposal by December 5, 1980 and use its best efforts to mail the statement to its shareholders by January 5, 1981. Thus, the market test period was effectively reduced, not extended. . . .

In our view, the record compels the conclusion that the directors' conduct on October 8 exhibited the same deficiencies as did their conduct on September 20. The Board permitted its Merger Agreement with Pritzker to be amended in a manner it had neither authorized nor intended. . . .

We conclude that the Board acted in a grossly negligent manner on October 8; and that Van Gorkom's representations on which the Board based its actions do not constitute "reports" under § 141(e) on which the directors could reasonably have relied. Further, the amended Merger Agreement imposed on Trans Union's acceptance of a third party offer conditions more onerous than those imposed on Trans Union's acceptance of Pritzker's offer on September 20. After October 10, Trans Union could accept from a third party a better offer only if it were incorporated in a definitive agreement between the parties, and not conditioned on financing or on any other contingency.

The October 9 press release, coupled with the October 10 amendments, had the clear effect of locking Trans Union's Board into the Pritzker Agreement. Pritzker had thereby foreclosed Trans Union's Board from negotiating any better "definitive" agreement over the remaining eight weeks before Trans Union was required to clear the Proxy Statement submitting the Pritzker proposal to its shareholders.

---

26. There is no evidence of record that Trans Union's directors ever raised any objections, procedural or substantive, to the October 10 amendments or that any of them, including Van Gorkom, understood the opposite result of their intended effect—until it was too late.

(2)

[On December 2, KKR offered to buy Trans–Union for $60/share. Van Gorkom apparently was resistant to this offer, and KKR withdrew it for reasons that were cloudy. In mid-January, GE Credit Corporation made a proposal which] was not in the form of an offer. Had there been time to do so, GE Credit was prepared to offer between $2 and $5 per share above the $55 per share price which Pritzker offered. But GE Credit needed an additional 60 to 90 days; and it was unwilling to make a formal offer without a concession from Pritzker extending the February 10 "deadline" for Trans Union's stockholder meeting.... Pritzker refused to grant such extension....

Our review of the record compels a finding that confirmation of the appropriateness of the Pritzker offer by an unfettered or free market test was virtually meaningless in the face of the terms and time limitations of Trans Union's Merger Agreement with Pritzker as amended October 10, 1980.

... [W]e hold that the defendants' post-September conduct did not cure the deficiencies of their September 20 conduct; and that, accordingly, the Trial Court erred in according to the defendants the benefits of the business judgment rule....

V.

The defendants ultimately rely on the stockholder vote of February 10 for exoneration. The defendants contend that the stockholders' "overwhelming" vote approving the Pritzker Merger Agreement had the legal effect of curing any failure of the Board to reach an informed business judgment in its approval of the merger.

The parties tacitly agree that a discovered failure of the Board to reach an informed business judgment in approving the merger constitutes a voidable, rather than a void, act. Hence, the merger can be sustained, notwithstanding the infirmity of the Board's action, if its approval by majority vote of the shareholders is found to have been based on an informed electorate.... the disagreement between the parties arises over ... the sufficiency of the evidence as to whether the Board satisfied that burden.

[The court rejected the shareholder-approval defense on the ground that Trans Union's stockholders were not fully informed of all facts material to their vote on the Pritzker Merger, and that the Trial Court's ruling to the contrary was clearly erroneous.] ...

VI.

... We hold, therefore, that the Trial Court committed reversible error in applying the business judgment rule in favor of the director defendants in this case.

On remand, the Court of Chancery shall conduct an evidentiary hearing to determine the fair value of the shares represented by the plaintiffs' class, based on the intrinsic value of Trans Union on September 20, 1980. Such valuation shall be made in accordance with

Weinberger v. UOP, Inc., supra.... Thereafter, an award of damages may be entered to the extent that the fair value of Trans Union exceeds $55 per share.

Reversed and Remanded for proceedings consistent herewith.

■ McNEILLY, JUSTICE, dissenting ...

I have no quarrel with the majority's analysis of the business judgment rule. It is the application of that rule to these facts which is wrong. An overview of the entire record, rather than the limited view of bits and pieces which the majority has exploded like popcorn, convinces me that the directors made an informed business judgment which was buttressed by their test of the market....

At the time of the September 20 meeting the 10 members of Trans Union's Board of Directors were highly qualified and well informed about the affairs and prospects of Trans Union. These directors were acutely aware of the historical problems facing Trans Union which were caused by the tax laws. They had discussed these problems *ad nauseam.* In fact, within two months of the September 20 meeting the board had reviewed and discussed an outside study of the company done by The Boston Consulting Group and an internal five year forecast prepared by management. At the September 20 meeting Van Gorkom presented the Pritzker offer, and the board then heard from James Brennan, the company's counsel in this matter, who discussed the legal documents. Following this, the Board directed that certain changes be made in the merger documents. These changes made it clear that the Board was free to accept a better offer than Pritzker's if one was made. The above facts reveal that the Board did not act in a grossly negligent manner in informing themselves of the relevant and available facts before passing on the merger. To the contrary, this record reveals that the directors acted with the utmost care in informing themselves of the relevant and available facts before passing on the merger....

[The dissenting opinion of Justice Christie is omitted.]

It is reported that after the decision of the Delaware Supreme Court, an agreement was reached to settle *Van Gorkom* by the payment of $23.5 million to the plaintiff class. Of that amount, $10 million, the policy limit, was provided by Trans Union's directors' and officers' liability-insurance carrier. Nearly all of the $13.5 million balance was paid by the Pritzker group on behalf of the Trans Union defendant directors, although the Pritzker group was not a defendant. See Manning, Reflections and Practical Tips on Life in the Boardroom After *Van Gorkom,* 41 Bus.Law. 1 (1985).

NOTE ON SUBSTANCE AND PROCESS IN THE DUTY OF CARE

In many areas of law, a distinction is drawn between substance and process. The duty of care may be understood in that way too. In effect, the business judgment rule gives wide latitude to a substantive decision of a director or senior executive if the *process* elements of the duty of care are satisfied. Under this distinction, the process elements of the duty of care, which involve such matters as preparing to make a decision, general monitoring, and following up suspicious circumstances, are governed by a standard of reasonability. However, if the process by which a decision was made satisfies the reasonability standard, the substantive decision itself will be reviewed only under the much looser standard of rationality.

———

(c) THE DUTY TO ENSURE THAT THE CORPORATION HAS EFFECTIVE INTERNAL CONTROLS

———

In re Caremark International Inc. Derivative Litigation

Delaware Court of Chancery, 1996.
698 A.2d 959.

■ ALLEN, CHANCELLOR.

Pending is a motion pursuant to Chancery Rule 23.1 to approve as fair and reasonable a proposed settlement of a consolidated derivative action on behalf of Caremark International, Inc. ("Caremark"). The suit involves claims that the members of Caremark's board of directors (the "Board") breached their fiduciary duty of care to Caremark in connection with alleged violations by Caremark employees of federal and state laws and regulations applicable to health care providers. As a result of the alleged violations, Caremark was subject to an extensive four year investigation by the United States Department of Health and Human Services and the Department of Justice. In 1994 Caremark was charged in an indictment with multiple felonies. It thereafter entered into a number of agreements with the Department of Justice and others. Those agreements included a plea agreement in which Caremark pleaded guilty to a single felony of mail fraud and agreed to pay civil and criminal fines. Subsequently, Caremark agreed to make reimbursements to various private and public parties. In all, the payments that Caremark has been required to make total approximately $250 million.

This suit was filed in 1994, purporting to seek on behalf of the company recovery of these losses from the individual defendants who constitute the board of directors of Caremark.[1] The parties now

---

1. Thirteen of the Directors have been members of the Board since November 30, 1992. Nancy Brinker joined the Board in October 1993.

propose that it be settled and, after notice to Caremark shareholders, a hearing on the fairness of the proposal was held on August 16, 1996.

A motion of this type requires the court to assess the strengths and weaknesses of the claims asserted in light of the discovery record and to evaluate the fairness and adequacy of the consideration offered to the corporation in exchange for the release of all claims made or arising from the facts alleged. The ultimate issue then is whether the proposed settlement appears to be fair to the corporation and its absent shareholders. In this effort the court does not determine contested facts, but evaluates the claims and defenses on the discovery record to achieve a sense of the relative strengths of the parties' positions. Polk v. Good, Del.Supr., 507 A.2d 531, 536 (1986). In doing this, in most instances, the court is constrained by the absence of a truly adversarial process, since inevitably both sides support the settlement and legally assisted objectors are rare. . . .

Legally, evaluation of the central claim made entails consideration of the legal standard governing a board of directors' obligation to supervise or monitor corporate performance. For the reasons set forth below I conclude, in light of the discovery record, that there is a very low probability that it would be determined that the directors of Caremark breached any duty to appropriately monitor and supervise the enterprise. Indeed the record tends to show an active consideration by Caremark management and its Board of the Caremark structures and programs that ultimately led to the company's indictment and to the large financial losses incurred in the settlement of those claims. It does not tend to show knowing or intentional violation of law. Neither the fact that the Board, although advised by lawyers and accountants, did not accurately predict the severe consequences to the company that would ultimately follow from the deployment by the company of the strategies and practices that ultimately led to this liability, nor the scale of the liability, gives rise to an inference of breach of any duty imposed by corporation law upon the directors of Caremark.

I. BACKGROUND

For these purposes I regard the following facts, suggested by the discovery record, as material. Caremark, a Delaware corporation with its headquarters in Northbrook, Illinois, was created in November 1992 when it was spun-off from Baxter International, Inc. ("Baxter") and became a publicly held company listed on the New York Stock Exchange. The business practices that created the problem pre-dated the spin-off. During the relevant period Caremark was involved in two main health care business segments, providing patient care and managed care services. As part of its patient care business, which accounted for the majority of Caremark's revenues, Caremark provided alternative site health care services, including infusion therapy, growth hormone therapy, HIV/AIDS-related treatments and hemophilia therapy. Caremark's managed care services included prescription drug programs and the operation of multi-specialty group practices.

A.   Events Prior to the Government Investigation

A substantial part of the revenues generated by Caremark's businesses is derived from third party payments, insurers, and Medicare and Medicaid reimbursement programs. The latter source of payments are subject to the terms of the Anti–Referral Payments Law ("ARPL") which prohibits health care providers from paying any form of remuneration to induce the referral of Medicare or Medicaid patients. From its inception, Caremark entered into a variety of agreements with hospitals, physicians, and health care providers for advice and services, as well as distribution agreements with drug manufacturers, as had its predecessor prior to 1992. Specifically, Caremark did have a practice of entering into contracts for services (e.g., consultation agreements and research grants) with physicians at least some of whom prescribed or recommended services or products that Caremark provided to Medicare recipients and other patients. Such contracts were not prohibited by the ARPL but they obviously raised a possibility of unlawful "kickbacks."

As early as 1989, Caremark's predecessor issued an internal "Guide to Contractual Relationships" ("Guide") to govern its employees in entering into contracts with physicians and hospitals. The Guide tended to be reviewed annually by lawyers and updated. Each version of the Guide stated as Caremark's and its predecessor's policy that no payments would be made in exchange for or to induce patient referrals. But what one might deem a prohibited quid pro quo was not always clear. Due to a scarcity of court decisions interpreting the ARPL, however, Caremark repeatedly publicly stated that there was uncertainty concerning Caremark's interpretation of the law.

To clarify the scope of the ARPL, the United States Department of Health and Human Services ("HHS") issued "safe harbor" regulations in July 1991 stating conditions under which financial relationships between health care service providers and patient referral sources, such as physicians, would not violate the ARPL. Caremark contends that the narrowly drawn regulations gave limited guidance as to the legality of many of the agreements used by Caremark that did not fall within the safe-harbor. Caremark's predecessor, however, amended many of its standard forms of agreement with health care providers and revised the Guide in an apparent attempt to comply with the new regulations.

B.   Government Investigation and Related Litigation

In August 1991, the HHS Office of the Inspector General ("OIG") initiated an investigation of Caremark's predecessor. Caremark's predecessor was served with a subpoena requiring the production of documents, including contracts between Caremark's predecessor and physicians (Quality Service Agreements ("QSAs")). Under the QSAs, Caremark's predecessor appears to have paid physicians fees for monitoring patients under Caremark's predecessor's care, including Medicare and Medicaid recipients. Sometimes apparently those monitoring patients were referring physicians, which raised ARPL concerns.

In March 1992, the Department of Justice ("DOJ") joined the OIG investigation and separate investigations were commenced by several additional federal and state agencies.[2]

C.   Caremark's Response to the Investigation

During the relevant period, Caremark had approximately 7,000 employees and ninety branch operations. It had a decentralized management structure. By May 1991, however, Caremark asserts that it had begun making attempts to centralize its management structure in order to increase supervision over its branch operations.

The first action taken by management, as a result of the initiation of the OIG investigation, was an announcement that as of October 1, 1991, Caremark's predecessor would no longer pay management fees to physicians for services to Medicare and Medicaid patients. Despite this decision, Caremark asserts that its management, pursuant to advice, did not believe that such payments were illegal under the existing laws and regulations.

During this period, Caremark's Board took several additional steps consistent with an effort to assure compliance with company policies concerning the ARPL and the contractual forms in the Guide. In April 1992, Caremark published a fourth revised version of its Guide apparently designed to assure that its agreements either complied with the ARPL and regulations or excluded Medicare and Medicaid patients altogether. In addition, in September 1992, Caremark instituted a policy requiring its regional officers, Zone Presidents, to approve each contractual relationship entered into by Caremark with a physician.

Although there is evidence that inside and outside counsel had advised Caremark's directors that their contracts were in accord with the law, Caremark recognized that some uncertainty respecting the correct interpretation of the law existed. In its 1992 annual report, Caremark disclosed the ongoing government investigations, acknowledged that if penalties were imposed on the company they could have a material adverse effect on Caremark's business, and stated that no assurance could be given that its interpretation of the ARPL would prevail if challenged.

Throughout the period of the government investigations, Caremark had an internal audit plan designed to assure compliance with business and ethics policies. In addition, Caremark employed Price Waterhouse as its outside auditor. On February 8, 1993, the [Audit &] Ethics Committee of Caremark's Board received and reviewed an outside auditors report by Price Waterhouse which concluded that there were no material weaknesses in Caremark's control structure.[3]

2. In addition to investigating whether Caremark's financial relationships with health care providers were intended to induce patient referrals, inquiries were made concerning Caremark's billing practices, activities which might lead to excessive and medically unnecessary treatments for patients, potentially improper waivers of patient co-payment obligations, and the adequacy of records kept at Caremark pharmacies.

3. At that time, Price Waterhouse viewed the outcome of the OIG Investigation

Despite the positive findings of Price Waterhouse, however, on April 20, 1993, the Audit & Ethics Committee adopted a new internal audit charter requiring a comprehensive review of compliance policies and the compilation of an employee ethics handbook concerning such policies.[4]

The Board appears to have been informed about this project and other efforts to assure compliance with the law. For example, Caremark's management reported to the Board that Caremark's sales force was receiving an ongoing education regarding the ARPL and the proper use of Caremark's form contracts which had been approved by in-house counsel. On July 27, 1993, the new ethics manual, expressly prohibiting payments in exchange for referrals and requiring employees to report all illegal conduct to a toll free confidential ethics hotline, was approved and allegedly disseminated.[5] The record suggests that Caremark continued these policies in subsequent years, causing employees to be given revised versions of the ethics manual and requiring them to participate in training sessions concerning compliance with the law.

During 1993, Caremark took several additional steps which appear to have been aimed at increasing management supervision. These steps included new policies requiring local branch managers to secure home office approval for all disbursements under agreements with health care providers and to certify compliance with the ethics program. In addition, the chief financial officer was appointed to serve as Caremark's compliance officer. In 1994, a fifth revised Guide was published.

D. Federal Indictments Against Caremark and Officers

On August 4, 1994, a federal grand jury in Minnesota issued a 47 page indictment charging Caremark, two of its officers (not the firm's chief officer), an individual who had been a sales employee of Genentech, Inc., and David R. Brown, a physician practicing in Minneapolis, with violating the ARPL over a lengthy period. According to the indictment, over $1.1 million had been paid to Brown to induce him to distribute Protropin, a human growth hormone drug marketed by Caremark.[6] The substantial payments involved started, according to the allegations of the indictment, in 1986 and continued through 1993.

as uncertain. After further audits, however, on February 7, 1995, Price Waterhouse informed the Audit & Ethics Committee that it had not become aware of any irregularities or illegal acts in relation to the OIG investigation.

4. Price Waterhouse worked in conjunction with the Internal Audit Department.

5. Prior to the distribution of the new ethics manual, on March 12, 1993, Caremark's president had sent a letter to all senior, district, and branch managers restating Caremark's policies that no physician be paid for referrals, that the standard contract forms in the Guide were not to be modified, and that deviation from such policies would result in the immediate termination of employment.

6. In addition to prescribing Protropin, Dr. Brown had been receiving research grants from Caremark as well as payments for services under a consulting agreement for several years before and after the investigation. According to an undated document from an unknown source, Dr. Brown and six other researchers had been providing patient referrals to Caremark valued at $6.55 for each $1 of research money they received.

Some payments were "in the guise of research grants", Ind. § 20, and others were "consulting agreements", Ind. § 19. The indictment charged, for example, that Dr. Brown performed virtually none of the consulting functions described in his 1991 agreement with Caremark, but was nevertheless neither required to return the money he had received nor precluded from receiving future funding from Caremark. In addition the indictment charged that Brown received from Caremark payments of staff and office expenses, including telephone answering services and fax rental expenses....

Subsequently, five stockholder derivative actions were filed in this court and consolidated into this action. The original complaint, dated August 5, 1994, alleged, in relevant part, that Caremark's directors breached their duty of care by failing adequately to supervise the conduct of Caremark employees, or institute corrective measures, thereby exposing Caremark to fines and liability....

After each complaint was filed, defendants filed a motion to dismiss. According to defendants, if a settlement had not been reached in this action, the case would have been dismissed on two grounds. First, they contend that the complaints fail to allege particularized facts sufficient to excuse the demand requirement under Delaware Chancery Court Rule 23.1. Second, defendants assert that plaintiffs had failed to state a cause of action due to the fact that Caremark's charter eliminates directors' personal liability for money damages, to the extent permitted by law.

E.   Settlement Negotiations

In September, following the announcement of the Ohio indictment, Caremark publicly announced that as of January 1, 1995, it would terminate all remaining financial relationships with physicians in its home infusion, hemophilia, and growth hormone lines of business.[9] In addition, Caremark asserts that it extended its restrictive policies to all of its contractual relationships with physicians, rather than just those involving Medicare and Medicaid patients, and terminated its research grant program which had always involved some recipients who referred patients to Caremark.

Caremark began settlement negotiations with federal and state government entities in May 1995. In return for a guilty plea to a single count of mail fraud by the corporation, the payment of a criminal fine, the payment of substantial civil damages, and cooperation with further federal investigations on matters relating to the OIG investigation, the government entities agreed to negotiate a settlement that would permit Caremark to continue participating in Medicare and Medicaid programs. On June 15, 1995, the Board approved a settlement ("Government Settlement Agreement") with the DOJ, OIG, U.S. Veterans Administration, U.S. Federal Employee Health Benefits Program, federal Civilian Health and Medical Program of the Uniformed Services, and

9. On June 1, 1993, Caremark had stopped entering into new contractual agreements in those business segments.

related state agencies in all fifty states and the District of Columbia.[10] No senior officers or directors were charged with wrongdoing in the Government Settlement Agreement or in any of the prior indictments. In fact, as part of the sentencing in the Ohio action on June 19, 1995, the United States stipulated that no senior executive of Caremark participated in, condoned, or was willfully ignorant of wrongdoing in connection with the home infusion business practices.

The federal settlement included certain provisions in a "Corporate Integrity Agreement" designed to enhance future compliance with law. The parties have not discussed this agreement, except to say that the negotiated provisions of the settlement of this claim are not redundant of those in that agreement.

Settlement negotiations between the parties in this action commenced in May 1995 as well, based upon a letter proposal of the plaintiffs, dated May 16, 1995. These negotiations resulted in a memorandum of understanding ("MOU"), dated June 7, 1995, and the execution of the Stipulation and Agreement of Compromise and Settlement on June 28, 1995, which is the subject of this action.[13] The MOU, approved by the Board on June 15, 1995, required the Board to adopt several resolutions, discussed below, and to create a new compliance committee. The Compliance and Ethics Committee has been reporting to the Board in accord with its newly specified duties....

F. The Proposed Settlement of this Litigation

In relevant part the terms upon which these claims asserted are proposed to be settled are as follows:

1. That Caremark undertakes that it and its employees and agents not pay any form of compensation to a third party in exchange for the referral of a patient to a Caremark facility or service or the prescription of drugs marketed or distributed by Caremark for which reimbursement may be sought from Medicare, Medicaid, or a similar state reimbursement program;

2. That Caremark undertakes for itself and its employees, and agents not to pay to or split fees with physicians, joint ventures, any business combination in which Caremark maintains a direct financial interest, or other health care providers with whom Caremark has a financial relationship or interest, in exchange for the referral of a patient to a Caremark facility or service or the prescription of drugs marketed or distributed by Caremark

---

10. The agreement, covering allegations since 1986, required a Caremark subsidiary to enter a guilty plea to two counts of mail fraud, and required Caremark to pay $29 million in criminal fines, $129.9 million relating to civil claims concerning payment practices, $3.5 million for alleged violations of the Controlled Substances Act, and $2 million, in the form of a donation, to a grant program set up by the Ryan White Comprehensive AIDS Resources Emergency Act.

Caremark also agreed to enter into a compliance agreement with the HHS.

13. Plaintiffs' initial proposal had both a monetary component, requiring Caremark's director-officers to relinquish stock options, and a remedial component, requiring management to adopt and implement several compliance related measures. The monetary component was subsequently eliminated.

for which reimbursement may be sought from Medicare, Medicaid, or a similar state reimbursement program;

3.   That the full Board shall discuss all relevant material changes in government health care regulations and their effect on relationships with health care providers on a semi-annual basis;

4.   That Caremark's officers will remove all personnel from health care facilities or hospitals who have been placed in such facility for the purpose of providing remuneration in exchange for a patient referral for which reimbursement may be sought from Medicare, Medicaid, or a similar state reimbursement program;

5.   That every patient will receive written disclosure of any financial relationship between Caremark and the health care professional or provider who made the referral;

6.   That the Board will establish a Compliance and Ethics Committee of four directors, two of which will be non-management directors, to meet at least four times a year to effectuate these policies and monitor business segment compliance with the ARPL, and to report to the Board semi-annually concerning compliance by each business segment; and

7.   That corporate officers responsible for business segments shall serve as compliance officers who must report semi-annually to the Compliance and Ethics Committee and, with the assistance of outside counsel, review existing contracts and get advance approval of any new contract forms.

II.   LEGAL PRINCIPLES

A.   Principles Governing Settlements of Derivative Claims

As noted at the outset of this opinion, this Court is now required to exercise an informed judgment whether the proposed settlement is fair and reasonable in the light of all relevant factors. Polk v. Good, Del.Supr., 507 A.2d 531 (1986). On an application of this kind, this Court attempts to protect the best interests of the corporation and its absent shareholders all of whom will be barred from future litigation on these claims if the settlement is approved. The parties proposing the settlement bear the burden of persuading the court that it is in fact fair and reasonable. Fins v. Pearlman, Del.Supr., 424 A.2d 305 (1980).

B.   Directors' Duties To Monitor Corporate Operations

The complaint charges the director defendants with breach of their duty of attention or care in connection with the ongoing operation of the corporation's business. The claim is that the directors allowed a situation to develop and continue which exposed the corporation to enormous legal liability and that in so doing they violated a duty to be active monitors of corporate performance. The complaint thus does not charge either director self-dealing or the more difficult loyalty-type problems arising from cases of suspect director motivation, such as entrenchment or sale of control contexts.[14] The theory here advanced is possibly the most difficult theory in corporation law upon which a plaintiff might hope to win a judgment. . . .

1. *Potential liability for directoral decisions:* Director liability for a breach of the duty to exercise appropriate attention may, in theory, arise in two distinct contexts. First, such liability may be said to follow from a board decision that results in a loss because that decision was ill advised or "negligent". Second, liability to the corporation for a loss may be said to arise from an unconsidered failure of the board to act in circumstances in which due attention would, arguably, have prevented the loss. See generally Veasey & Seitz, The Business Judgment Rule in the Revised Model Act . . . 63 TEXAS L.REV. 1483 (1985). The first class of cases will typically be subject to review under the director-protective business judgment rule. . . . See Aronson v. Lewis, Del.Supr., 473 A.2d 805 (1984); Gagliardi v. TriFoods Int'l, Inc., Del.Ch. 683 A.2d 1049 (July 19, 1996). . . .

2. *Liability for failure to monitor:* The second class of cases in which director liability for inattention is theoretically possible entail circumstances in which a loss eventuates not from a decision but, from unconsidered inaction. Most of the decisions that a corporation, acting through its human agents, makes are, of course, not the subject of director attention. Legally, the board itself will be required only to authorize the most significant corporate acts or transactions: mergers, changes in capital structure, fundamental changes in business, appointment and compensation of the CEO, etc. As the facts of this case graphically demonstrate, ordinary business decisions that are made by officers and employees deeper in the interior of the organization can, however, vitally affect the welfare of the corporation and its ability to achieve its various strategic and financial goals. If this case did not prove the point itself, recent business history would. Recall for example the displacement of senior management and much of the board of Salomon, Inc.;[18] the replacement of senior management of Kidder, Peabody following the discovery of large trading losses resulting from phantom trades by a highly compensated trader;[19] or the extensive financial loss and reputational injury suffered by Prudential Insurance as a result [of] its junior officers' misrepresentations in connection with the distribution of limited partnership interests. Financial and organizational disasters such as these raise the question, what is the board's responsibility with respect to the organization and monitoring of the enterprise to assure that the corporation functions within the law to achieve its purposes?

---

14. See Weinberger v. UOP, Inc., Del. Supr., 457 A.2d 701, 711 (1983) (entire fairness test when financial conflict of interest involved); Unitrin, Inc. v. American General Corp., Del.Supr., 651 A.2d 1361, 1372 (1995) (intermediate standard of review when "defensive" acts taken); Paramount Communications, Inc. v. QVC Network, Del.Supr., 637 A.2d 34, 45 (1994) (intermediate test when corporate control transferred).

18. See, e.g., Rotten at the Core, the Economist, August 17, 1991, at 69–70; The Judgment of Salomon: An Anticlimax, Bus. Week, June 1, 1992, at 106.

19. See Terence P. Pare, Jack Welch's Nightmare on Wall Street, Fortune, Sept. 5, 1994, at 40–48.

Modernly this question has been given special importance by an increasing tendency, especially under federal law, to employ the criminal law to assure corporate compliance with external legal requirements, including environmental, financial, employee and product safety as well as assorted other health and safety regulations. In 1991, pursuant to the Sentencing Reform Act of 1984,[21] the United States Sentencing Commission adopted Organizational Sentencing Guidelines which impact importantly on the prospective effect these criminal sanctions might have on business corporations. The Guidelines set forth a uniform sentencing structure for organizations to be sentenced for violation of federal criminal statutes and provide for penalties that equal or often massively exceed those previously imposed on corporations.[22] The Guidelines offer powerful incentives for corporations today to have in place compliance programs to detect violations of law, promptly to report violations to appropriate public officials when discovered, and to take prompt, voluntary remedial efforts.

In 1963, the Delaware Supreme Court in Graham v. Allis–Chalmers Mfg. Co.,[23] addressed the question of potential liability of board members for losses experienced by the corporation as a result of the corporation having violated the anti-trust laws of the United States. There was no claim in that case that the directors knew about the behavior of subordinate employees of the corporation that had resulted in the liability. Rather, as in this case, the claim asserted was that the directors ought to have known of it and if they had known they would have been under a duty to bring the corporation into compliance with the law and thus save the corporation from the loss. The Delaware Supreme Court concluded that, under the facts as they appeared, there was no basis to find that the directors had breached a duty to be informed of the ongoing operations of the firm. In notably colorful terms, the court stated that "absent cause for suspicion there is no duty upon the directors to install and operate a corporate system of espionage to ferret out wrongdoing which they have no reason to suspect exists."[24] The Court found that there were no grounds for suspicion in that case and, thus, concluded that the directors were blamelessly unaware of the conduct leading to the corporate liability.[25]

How does one generalize this holding today? Can it be said today that, absent some ground giving rise to suspicion of violation of law, that corporate directors have no duty to assure that a corporate information gathering and reporting system exists which represents a good faith attempt to provide senior management and the Board with information respecting material acts, events or conditions within the corporation, including compliance with applicable statutes and regulations? I certainly do not believe so. I doubt that such a broad

21. See Sentencing Reform Act of 1984, Pub.L. 98–473, Title II, § 212(a)(2) (1984); 18 U.S.C.A. §§ 3331–4120.

22. See United States Sentencing Commission, Guidelines Manual, Chapter 8 (U.S. Government Printing Office November 1994).

23. Del.Supr., 188 A.2d 125 (1963).

24. Id. at 130.

25. Recently, the *Graham* standard was applied by the Delaware Chancery in a case involving Baxter. In re Baxter International, Inc. Shareholders Litig., Del.Ch., 654 A.2d 1268, 1270 (1995).

generalization of the Graham holding would have been accepted by the Supreme Court in 1963. The case can be more narrowly interpreted as standing for the proposition that, absent grounds to suspect deception, neither corporate boards nor senior officers can be charged with wrongdoing simply for assuming the integrity of employees and the honesty of their dealings on the company's behalf. See 188 A.2d at 130–31.

A broader interpretation of *Graham v. Allis–Chalmers*—that it means that a corporate board has no responsibility to assure that appropriate information and reporting systems are established by management—would not, in any event, be accepted by the Delaware Supreme Court in 1996, in my opinion. In stating the basis for this view, I start with the recognition that in recent years the Delaware Supreme Court has made it clear—especially in its jurisprudence concerning takeovers, from *Smith v. Van Gorkom* through *Paramount Communications v. QVC*[26]—the seriousness with which the corporation law views the role of the corporate board. Secondly, I note the elementary fact that relevant and timely information is an essential predicate for satisfaction of the board's supervisory and monitoring role under Section 141 of the Delaware General Corporation Law. Thirdly, I note the potential impact of the federal organizational sentencing guidelines on any business organization. Any rational person attempting in good faith to meet an organizational governance responsibility would be bound to take into account this development and the enhanced penalties and the opportunities for reduced sanctions that it offers.

In light of these developments, it would, in my opinion, be a mistake to conclude that our Supreme Court's statement in *Graham* concerning "espionage" means that corporate boards may satisfy their obligation to be reasonably informed concerning the corporation, without assuring themselves that information and reporting systems exist in the organization that are reasonably designed to provide to senior management and to the board itself timely, accurate information sufficient to allow management and the board, each within its scope, to reach informed judgments concerning both the corporation's compliance with law and its business performance.

Obviously the level of detail that is appropriate for such an information system is a question of business judgment. And obviously too, no rationally designed information and reporting system will remove the possibility that the corporation will violate laws or regulations, or that senior officers or directors may nevertheless sometimes be misled or otherwise fail reasonably to detect acts material to the corporation's compliance with the law. But it is important that the board exercise a good faith judgment that the corporation's information and reporting system is in concept and design adequate to assure the board that appropriate information will come to its attention in a

---

26. E.g., Smith v. Van Gorkom, Del. Supr., 488 A.2d 858 (1985); Paramount Communications v. QVC Network, Del.Supr., 637 A.2d 34 (1994).

timely manner as a matter of ordinary operations, so that it may satisfy its responsibility.

Thus, I am of the view that a director's obligation includes a duty to attempt in good faith to assure that a corporate information and reporting system, which the board concludes is adequate, exists, and that failure to do so under some circumstances may, in theory at least, render a director liable for losses caused by non-compliance with applicable legal standards.[27] I now turn to an analysis of the claims asserted with this concept of the directors' duty of care, as a duty satisfied in part by assurance of adequate information flows to the board, in mind.

III. ANALYSIS OF THIRD AMENDED COMPLAINT AND SETTLEMENT

A. The Claims

On balance, after reviewing an extensive record in this case, including numerous documents and three depositions, I conclude that this settlement is fair and reasonable. In light of the fact that the Caremark Board already has a functioning committee charged with overseeing corporate compliance, the changes in corporate practice that are presented as consideration for the settlement do not impress one as very significant. Nonetheless, that consideration appears fully adequate to support dismissal of the derivative claims of director fault asserted, because those claims find no substantial evidentiary support in the record and quite likely were susceptible to a motion to dismiss in all events.

In order to show that the Caremark directors breached their duty of careby failing adequately to control Caremark's employees, plaintiffs would have to show either (1) that the directors knew or (2) should have known that violations of law were occurring and, in either event, (3) that the directors took no steps in a good faith effort to prevent or remedy that situation, and (4) that such failure proximately resulted in the losses complained of, although under Cede & Co. v. Technicolor, Inc., Del.Supr., 636 A.2d 956 (1994) this last element may be thought to constitute an affirmative defense. . . .

. . . I turn to a consideration of the [claim based on] . . . director inattention or "negligence." Generally where a claim of directorial liability for corporate loss is predicated upon ignorance of liability creating activities within the corporation, as in *Graham* or in this case, in my opinion only a sustained or systematic failure of the board to exercise oversight—such as an utter failure to attempt to assure a reasonable information and reporting system exits—will establish the

27. Any action seeking recover for losses would logically entail a judicial determination of proximate cause, since, for reasons that I take to be obvious, it could never be assumed that an adequate information system would be a system that would prevent all losses. I need not touch upon the burden allocation with respect to a proximate cause issue in such a suit. See Cede & Co. v. Technicolor, Inc., Del.Supr., 636 A.2d 956 (1994); Cinerama, Inc. v. Technicolor, Inc., Del.Ch., 663 A.2d 1134 (1994), aff'd., Del.Supr., 663 A.2d 1156 (1995). Moreover, questions of waiver of liability under certificate provisions authorized by 8 Del.C. § 102(b)(7) may also be faced.

lack of good faith that is a necessary condition to liability. Such a test of liability—lack of good faith as evidenced by sustained or systematic failure of a director to exercise reasonable oversight—is quite high. But, a demanding test of liability in the oversight context is probably beneficial to corporate shareholders as a class, as it is in the board decision context, since it makes board service by qualified persons more likely, while continuing to act as a stimulus to good faith performance of duty by such directors.

Here the record supplies essentially no evidence that the director defendants were guilty of a sustained failure to exercise their oversight function. To the contrary, insofar as I am able to tell on this record, the corporation's information systems appear to have represented a good faith attempt to be informed of relevant facts. If the directors did not know the specifics of the activities that lead to the indictments, they cannot be faulted.

The liability that eventuated in this instance was huge. But the fact that it resulted from a violation of criminal law alone does not create a breach of fiduciary duty by directors. The record at this stage does not support the conclusion that the defendants either lacked good faith in the exercise of their monitoring responsibilities or conscientiously permitted a known violation of law by the corporation to occur. The claims asserted against them must be viewed at this stage as extremely weak.

B.   The Consideration For Release of Claim

The proposed settlement provides very modest benefits. Under the settlement agreement, plaintiffs have been given express assurances that Caremark will have a more centralized, active supervisory system in the future. Specifically, the settlement mandates duties to be performed by the newly named Compliance and Ethics Committee on an ongoing basis and increases the responsibility for monitoring compliance with the law at the lower levels of management. In adopting the resolutions required under the settlement, Caremark has further clarified its policies concerning the prohibition of providing remuneration for referrals. These appear to be positive consequences of the settlement of the claims brought by the plaintiffs, even if they are not highly significant. Nonetheless, given the weakness of the plaintiffs' claims the proposed settlement appears to be an adequate, reasonable, and beneficial outcome for all of the parties. Thus, the proposed settlement will be approved. . . .

I am today entering an order consistent with the foregoing.

———

NOTE ON CORPORATE CRIMINAL LIABILITY, THE
SENTENCING GUIDELINES, AND COMPLIANCE PROGRAMS

Under 18 U.S.C.A. § 3553, a corporation that is found guilty of a crime may be sentenced to a fine, probation, or both. If the corporation is fined, the fine must normally be fixed within the range required by the Federal Sentencing Guidelines, promulgated by the Federal Sentencing Commission.

Under the Sentencing Guidelines, in setting a fine the court must determine four elements: the offense level of the crime; the base fine; the culpability score; and the fine range.

The offense level is essentially determined by the seriousness of the offense. The base fine is related to the offense level. The culpability score is based on various aggravating and mitigating factors. A low culpability score reduces the base fine; a high culpability score increases the base fine.

Under the mechanics of culpability scores, a corporation begins with a score of five, which is then increased upward by aggravating factors and decreased downward by mitigating factors. If a corporation had an effective compliance program in place at the time the crime was committed, the culpability score is reduced by three points. If a corporation fully cooperates with the government investigation and accepts responsibility for its criminal conduct, the culpability score is decreased by another two points. If no aggravating factors are present, these combined reductions would reduce the corporation's culpability score to zero. As a result, the corporation would be required to pay only 5–20% of its base fine. In contrast, with a culpability score of five, the corporation would be required to pay 100%–200% of its base fine. With a culpability score of 10 or more, the corporation would be required to pay 200%–400% of its base fine. Accordingly, the Criminal Sentencing Guidelines serve to reinforce the board's duty to monitor by providing a strong incentive to install effective compliance programs.

To constitute an effective program within the meaning of the Guidelines, the program must be reasonably designed, implemented, and enforced. The hallmark of an effective program is whether the corporation exercised due diligence in seeking to prevent and detect criminal conduct by its employees and other agents. At a minimum, due diligence requires that the corporation must have taken the following seven steps: (1) Establish standards and procedures, reasonably capable of reducing the prospect of criminal conduct, to be followed by employees and other agents of the corporation. (2) Assign specific high-level individuals overall responsibility to oversee compliance with the standards and procedures. (3) Exercise due care to not delegate substantial discretionary authority to those individuals whom the corporation knew or should have known have a propensity to engage in illegal activities. (4) Effectively communicate corporate standards and procedures to all employees and other agents through training programs or dissemination of written information. (5) Attempt to achieve compliance through the use of monitoring and auditing systems to detect criminal conduct by employees and agents, and by having in place and publicizing a reporting system whereby employees and agents can report criminal conduct by others within the organization anonymously, or confidentially report criminal or potential criminal conduct. (6) Enforce standards to achieve compliance through appropriate disciplinary mechanisms. (7) Respond appropriately if an offense is detected and take steps to prevent additional similar offenses. Sentencing Guidelines § 8A1.2, commentary (n. 3(k)).

A corporation that installs a compliance program will characteristically promulgate (i) a code of ethical conduct for its employees; (ii) procedures to ensure that the employees read, understand, and keep current on the code; and (iii) procedures to satisfy the due diligence inquiry requirement.

The Guidelines were recently amended, effective November 11, 2004, to make more stringent the criteria for what constitutes an effective compliance program. Although the overall structure of the Guidelines remains the same, the responsibilities of directors were significantly increased. The revised Guidelines require that directors be knowledgeable about the content and operation of the corporation's compliance and ethics program, and exercise reasonable oversight with respect to the program's implementation and effectiveness. The revised Guidelines also require the board to assign a specific high-level individual overall responsibility to oversee compliance, who regularly reports to the board and has day-to-day responsibility for the compliance-and-ethics program. This person must have direct access to the board or a designated subgroup. The Application Notes to the Guidelines recommend that this person should update the board or its designated subgroup on the status of the program no less than annually. All employees, including officers and directors, must participate in compliance training programs.

In addition to due diligence to prevent and detect criminal conduct, an effective compliance program must promote an organizational culture that encourages both ethical conduct and a commitment to compliance within the law.

The Supreme Court recently held that the Federal Sentencing Act, which authorizes the Sentencing Guidelines, was unconstitutional insofar as it made the Guidelines mandatory, because the Sixth Amendment requires sentencing determinations to be made by a jury, not a judge. United States v. Booker, 125 S.Ct. 738 (2005). The Court remedied the constitutional problem by removing the language in the Act that made the Guidelines mandatory. Although organizations don't enjoy the protection of the Sixth Amendment, the *Booker* revision of the Act will affect organizational sentencing provisions as well.

Although the Guidelines are no longer mandatory, sentencing judges are still required to consult the Guidelines: The Court stated in *Booker* that as "modified, the Federal Sentencing Act . . . *requires* a sentencing court to consider Guidelines ranges" (emphasis added). It is therefore highly likely that judges will continue to calculate an organization's culpability score and make sentencing decisions largely on the basis of the Guidelines. Accordingly, corporations that disregard the Guidelines would do so at their peril. Additionally, a prosecutor's decision whether or not to charge a corporation with a crime may be influenced by the corporation's ability to demonstrate that it has a well-documented and effective compliance program that is properly monitored by the board.

See generally Webb, Molo & Hurst, supra; Pitt & Groskaufmanis, Mischief Afoot: The Need for Incentives to Control Criminal Conduct. 71 B.U.L.Rev. 447 (1991); Pitt & Groskaufmanis, Minimizing Corporate Civil and Criminal Liability; A Second Look at Corporate Codes of Conduct, 78 Geo.L.J. 1559, 1561 (1990).

———

ABA Section of Business Law, Committee on Corporate Laws, Corporate Director's Guidebook

Fourth ed., 2004.

. . . LEGAL AND CONTRACTUAL COMPLIANCE

In recent years, particular attention has been given to the board's responsibility to oversee compliance with legal requirements. Many public companies assign such oversight to the audit committee, which meets regularly with the company's internal general counsel or regular external corporate counsel to be briefed on legal compliance and claims. With the increased burdens placed on public company audit committees, some boards have elected to form a separate compliance or legal affairs committee. Irrespective of which board committee is charged with oversight of legal compliance, directors should ensure that a process is in place to encourage appropriate attention to legal compliance issues (including compliance with contractual obligations) and claims against the corporation, and the timely reporting of significant legal matters to the board or an appropriate board committee. For public companies, the Sarbanes-Oxley Act and the SEC's lawyer conduct rules may require, in some circumstances, the legal counsel to report evidence of material violations of the securities laws or fiduciary duty to a committee of independent directors or to the board. The board should consider the processes in place to satisfy these requirements and how it will address any such reports.

———

Eisenberg, The Board of Directors and Internal Control

19 Cardozo L. Rev. 237, 1997.

I. The Meaning of Internal Control

In 1992, the Committee of Sponsoring Organizations (COSO) issued a comprehensive four-volume Report on internal control. The COSO Report defines internal control as "a process, effected by an entity's board of directors, management and other personnel, designed to provide reasonable assurance regarding the achievement of objectives" in three categories: "effectiveness and efficiency of operations, reliability of financial reporting, and compliance with applicable laws and regulations." Internal control over each of these objectives consists of five interrelated components: the control environment, risk assessment, control activities, information and communication, and monitoring. A system of internal control is deemed to be effective only if all five components are functioning effectively....

... In 1994, the ABA's Committee on Law and Accounting [stated] that "[t]he COSO Report may well become the standard for defining internal control and its interrelated components, and for measuring the effectiveness of internal control. The Report has serious implications for all entities and their managements and for their outside financial, accounting, legal, and other advisors as well."[30] Similarly, in SAS No. 78 the AICPA's Auditing Standards Board expressed its view that "the COSO Report is rapidly becoming a widely accepted framework for sound internal control among United States organizations and its acceptance and use will continue to grow."[31] ...

III.   What Board Responsibility for Internal Control Entails ...

... [T]he board's role is to use due care to assure itself that an internal control structure is in existence, is appropriate, and is effective. The board's responsibility in these matters is not to ensure that specific controls never fail. Accordingly, a breakdown in a specific control does not in itself establish that the board has not discharged its responsibility. Furthermore, the board need not ensure that every conceivable control is in place. In determining whether any given control should be installed, and the extent and contours of a control, the risk of failure if the control is not in place must be balanced with the control's costs.

The board should, however, be responsible for using due care to assure itself that the five components of internal control—control environment, risk assessment, control activities, information and communication, and monitoring—are in place in such a way as to provide reasonable assurance regarding the effectiveness and efficiency of operations, the reliability of financial reporting, and compliance with corporate policies and legal rules....

NOTE ON CIVIL LIABILITY OF DIRECTORS AND OFFICERS TO THIRD PERSONS

Most of the materials in this Section have concerned the liability of directors and officers to the *corporation* for failure to exercise due care. A director or officer may also be civilly liable to *third persons* for acts he commits in a corporate capacity. Robert Thompson has summarized the principles that govern the civil liability of directors and officers to third parties as follows:

30. [Committee on Law and Accounting, ABA, "Management" Reports on Internal Control: A Legal Respective, 49 Bus. Law, 889, 899 (1994)].

31. [Auditing Standards Board, AICPA, Statement on Auditing Standards No. 78, at 1].

Officers are agents of the corporation who act for the entity in a variety of day-to-day matters. . . . [A]ny individual liability [of officers] for enterprise obligations derives primarily from the common law. These principles, as reflected in the Restatement (Second) of Agency, usually insulate the officer [in the case of contracts entered into by the officer on the corporation's behalf]. An individual who signs a contract on behalf of the corporation is cloaked in the mantle of the enterprise and is not personally liable for action taken in the corporate name. If the enterprise defaults on an obligation under the contract, the creditor normally cannot proceed against the individual.

However, the same individual who acts for the same corporation in the same capacity in taking action deemed tortious loses the corporate cloak and is held individually liable along with the enterprise. . . .

Thus, as to direct participation, the corporate shield really only works for contracts, a narrowness of protection that may surprise many entrepreneurs who intend to use corporations to avoid liability. Note, however, that the corporate form [normally] does insulate corporate participants in a tort (or contract) setting against vicarious [civil] liability. . . .

Thompson, Unpacking Limited Liability: Direct and Vicarious Liability of Corporate Participants for Torts of the Enterprise, 47 Vand.L.Rev. 1, 6–7, 9, 24 (1994).

———

(d) LIABILITY SHIELDS

In assessing the duties of directors and officers to act with care, account must be taken of three elements that may serve to reduce or eliminate civil liability for breach of those duties: direct limits of liability, insurance, and indemnification. The first two elements is addressed in this Section. Insurance is addressed in Section 3. Indemnification is addressed in Chapter 11.

———

VIRGINIA CORPORATIONS CODE § 13.1–690

[See Statutory Supplement]

———

DEL. GEN. CORP. LAW § 102(b)(7)

[See Statutory Supplement]

———

MODEL BUSINESS CORP. ACT § 2.02(b)(4)

[See Statutory Supplement]

———

EMERALD PARTNERS v. BERLIN, 726 A.2d 1215 (Del. 1999). "[T]he shield from liability provided by a certificate of incorporation provision adopted pursuant to 8 Del. C. § 102(b)(7) is in the nature of an affirmative defense.... Defendants seeking exculpation under such a provision will normally bear the burden of establishing each of its elements. Here, the Court of Chancery incorrectly ruled that Emerald Partners [the plaintiff] was required to establish at trial that the individual defendants acted in bad faith or in breach of their duty of loyalty. To the contrary, the burden of demonstrating good faith, however slight it might be in given circumstances, is upon the party seeking the protection of the statute. Nonetheless, where the factual basis for a claim solely implicates a violation of the duty of care, this Court has indicated that the protections of such a charter provision may properly be invoked and applied."

———

Malpiede v. Townson

Supreme Court of Delaware, 2001.
780 A.2d 1075.

■ VEASEY, CHIEF JUSTICE:

In this appeal, we affirm ... the granting of a motion to dismiss the plaintiffs' due care claim on the ground that the exculpatory provision in the charter of the target corporation authorized by 8 Del. C. § 102(b)(7), bars any claim for money damages against the director defendants based solely on the board's alleged breach of its duty of care. Accordingly, we affirm the judgment of the Court of Chancery dismissing the amended complaint....

Facts

Frederick's of Hollywood ("Frederick's") is a retailer of women's lingerie and apparel with its headquarters in Los Angeles, California. This case centers on the merger of Frederick's into Knightsbridge Capital Corporation ("Knightsbridge") under circumstances where it became a target in a bidding contest. Before the merger, Frederick's common stock was divided into Class A shares (each of which has one vote) and Class B shares (which have no vote). As of December 6, 1996, there were outstanding 2,995,309 Class A shares and 5,903,118 Class B shares. Two trusts created by the principal founders of Frederick's, Frederick and Harriet Mellinger (the "Trusts"), held a total of about 41% of the outstanding Class A voting shares and a total of about 51% of the outstanding Class B non-voting shares of Frederick's.

On June 14, 1996, the Frederick's board announced its decision to retain an investment bank, Janney Montgomery Scott, Inc. ("JMS"), to advise the board in its search for a suitable buyer for the company. In January 1997, JMS initiated talks with Knightsbridge. Four months later, in April 1997, Knightsbridge offered to purchase all of the outstanding shares of Frederick's for between $6.00 and $6.25 per share. At Knightsbridge's request, the Frederick's board granted Knightsbridge the exclusive right to conduct due diligence.

On June 13, 1997, the Frederick's board approved an offer from Knightsbridge to purchase all of Frederick's outstanding Class A and Class B shares for $6.14 per share in cash in a two-step merger transaction.[39] The terms of the merger agreement signed by the Frederick's board prohibited the board from soliciting additional bids from third parties, but the agreement permitted the board to negotiate with third party bidders when the board's fiduciary duties required it to do so.[40] The Frederick's board then sent to stockholders a Consent Solicitation Statement recommending that they approve the transaction, which was scheduled to close on August 27, 1997.

On August 21, 1997, Frederick's received a fully financed, unsolicited cash offer of $7.00 per share from a third-party bidder, Milton Partners ("Milton"). Four days after the board received the Milton offer, Knightsbridge entered into an agreement to purchase all of the Frederick's shares held by the Trusts for $6.90 per share. Under the stock purchase agreement, the Trusts granted Knightsbridge a proxy to vote the Trusts' shares, but the Trusts had the right to terminate the agreement if the Frederick's board rejected the Knightsbridge offer in favor of a higher bid.

On August 27, 1997, the Frederick's board received a fully financed, unsolicited $7.75 cash offer from Veritas Capital Fund ("Veritas"). In light of these developments, the board postponed the Knightsbridge merger in order to arrange a meeting with the two new bidders. On September 2, 1997, the board sent a memorandum to Milton and Veritas outlining the conditions for participation in the bidding process. The memorandum required that the bidders each deposit $2.5 million in an escrow account and submit, before September 4, 1997, a marked-up merger agreement with the same basic terms as the Knightsbridge merger agreement. Veritas submitted a merger agreement and the $2.5 million escrow payment in accordance with these conditions. Milton did not.[41]

On September 3, 1997, the Frederick's board met with representatives of Veritas to discuss the terms of the Veritas offer. According to the plaintiffs, the board asserts that, at this meeting, it orally informed

39. Shortly before the board approved the merger on June 13, 1997, two directors, Sylvan Lefcor and Morton Fields, resigned from the board. The remaining five directors approved the merger agreement unanimously.

40. In the event that the Frederick's board terminated the merger agreement in order to accept a superior proposal by a third party bidder, the agreement entitled Knightsbridge to liquidated damages of $1.8 million.

41. Milton apparently discontinued its efforts to acquire Frederick's after Veritas submitted its higher bid.

Veritas that it was required to produce its "final, best offer" by September 4, 1997. The plaintiffs further allege that that board did not, in fact, inform Veritas of this requirement.

The same day that the board met with Veritas, Knightsbridge and the Trusts amended their stock purchase agreement to eliminate the Trusts' termination rights and other conditions on the sale of the Trusts' shares. On September 4, 1997, Knightsbridge exercised its rights under the agreement and purchased the Trusts' shares. Knightsbridge immediately informed the board of its acquisition of the Trusts' shares and repeated its intention to vote the shares against any competing third party bids.

One day after Knightsbridge acquired the Trusts' shares, the Frederick's board participated in a conference call with Veritas to discuss further the terms of the proposed merger. During this conference call, Veritas representatives suggested that, if the board elected to accept the Veritas offer, the board could issue an option to Veritas to purchase authorized but unissued Frederick's shares as a means to circumvent the 41% block of voting shares that Knightsbridge had acquired from the Trusts. Frederick's representatives also expressed some concern that Knightsbridge would sue the board if it decided to terminate the June 15, 1997 merger agreement. In response, Veritas agreed to indemnify the directors in the event of such litigation.

On September 6, 1997, Knightsbridge increased its bid to match the $7.75 Veritas offer, but on the condition that the board accept a variety of terms designed to restrict its ability to pursue superior offers.[42] On the same day, the Frederick's board approved this agreement and effectively ended the bidding process. Two days later, Knightsbridge purchased additional Frederick's Class A shares on the open market, at an average price of $8.21 per share, thereby acquiring a majority of both classes of Frederick's shares.

On September 11, 1997, Veritas increased its cash offer to $9.00 per share. Relying on (1) the "no-talk" provision in the merger agreement, (2) Knightsbridge's stated intention to vote its shares against third party bids, and (3) Veritas' request for an option to dilute Knightsbridge's interest, the board rejected the revised Veritas bid. On September 18, 1997, the board amended its earlier Consent Solicitation Statement to include the events that had transpired since July 1997. The deadline for responses to the consent solicitation was September 29, 1997, the scheduled closing date for the merger.

Before the merger closed, the plaintiffs filed in the Court of Chancery the purported class action complaint that is the predecessor of the amended complaint before us. The plaintiffs also moved for a

---

42. The terms included: a provision prohibiting any Frederick's representative from speaking to third party bidders concerning the acquisition of the company (the "no-talk" provision); a termination fee of $4.5 million (about 7% of the value of the transaction); the appointment of a non-voting Knightsbridge observer at Frederick's board meetings; and an obligation to grant Knightsbridge any stock option that Frederick's granted to a competing bidder. The revised merger agreement did not expressly permit the Frederick's board to pursue negotiations with third parties where its fiduciary duties required it to do so.

temporary restraining order enjoining the merger. The Court of Chancery denied the requested injunctive relief.

The plaintiffs then amended their complaint to include a class action claim for damages caused by the termination of the auction in favor of Knightsbridge and the rejection of the higher Veritas offer. The amended complaint alleged that the Frederick's board had breached its fiduciary duties in connection with the sale of the company....

The Court of Chancery granted the directors' motion to dismiss the amended complaint under Chancery Rule 12(b)(6), concluding that: (1) the complaint did not support a claim of breach of the board's duty of loyalty, [and] (2) the exculpatory provision in the Fredrick's charter precluded money damages against the directors for any breach of the board's duty of care....

Standard of Review

We review de novo the dismissal by the Court of Chancery of a complaint under Rule 12(b)(6)....

The Duty of Loyalty Claim

The central claim in the amended complaint is that the sale of Frederick's to Knightsbridge "constituted a breach of [the Frederick's board's] fiduciary obligation to maximize shareholder value" because the board did not "conduct an auction with a 'level playing field'" as required by Revlon, Inc. v. MacAndrews & Forbes Holdings, Inc.[43] The plaintiffs contend that this sort of allegation cannot be neatly divided into duty of care claims and duty of loyalty claims.

In our view, *Revlon* neither creates a new type of fiduciary duty in the sale-of-control context nor alters the nature of the fiduciary duties that generally apply. Rather, *Revlon* emphasizes that the board must perform its fiduciary duties in the service of a specific objective: maximizing the sale price of the enterprise. Although the *Revlon* doctrine imposes enhanced judicial scrutiny of certain transactions involving a sale of control, it does not eliminate the requirement that plaintiffs plead sufficient facts to support the underlying claims for a breach of fiduciary duties in conducting the sale. Accordingly, we proceed to analyze the amended complaint to determine whether it alleges sufficient facts to support a claim that the board breached any of its fiduciary duties.

The Court of Chancery concluded, and the plaintiffs do not appear to contest on appeal, that the amended complaint adequately alleges a conflict of interest with respect to only one of the directors who approved the Knightsbridge merger.[44] The amended complaint

43. Del. Supr., 506 A.2d 173, 182–83 (1985).

44. See January 2000 Mem. Op., 2000 Del. Ch. LEXIS 19, *17. In particular, the complaint alleges that the Knightsbridge merger agreement provided for several cash payments to George Townson, who was the CEO, President, and Chairman of Frederick's during the relevant period. The personal benefits allegedly received by Townson as a result of the Knightsbridge merger included: (1) a payment of $.05 for each "under water" option held by Townson with an exercise price below the merger price, (2) a severance does not allege that the lone conflicted director dominated the three other directors who approved the merger on September 6, 1997. The Court of Chancery therefore correctly held that the Knightsbridge merger was approved by a majority of disinterested directors....

The Due Care Claim

The primary due care issue is whether the board was grossly negligent, and therefore breached its duty of due care, in failing to implement a routine defensive strategy that could enable the board to negotiate for a higher bid or otherwise create a tactical advantage to enhance stockholder value.

In this case, that routine strategy would have been for the directors to use a poison pill to ward off Knightsbridge's advances and thus to prevent Knightsbridge from stopping the auction process. Had they done so, plaintiffs seem to allege that the directors could have preserved the appropriate options for an auction process designed to achieve the best value for the stockholders.

Construing the amended complaint most favorably to the plaintiffs, it can be read to allege that the board was grossly negligent in immediately accepting the Knightsbridge offer and agreeing to various restrictions on further negotiations without first determining whether Veritas would issue a counteroffer. Although the board had conducted a search for a buyer over one year, plaintiffs seem to contend that the board was imprudently hasty in agreeing to a restrictive merger agreement on the day it was proposed—particularly where other bidders had recently expressed interest.[45] Although the board's haste, in itself, might not constitute a breach of the board's duty of care because the board had already conducted a lengthy sale process, the plaintiffs argue that the board's decision to accept allegedly extreme contractual restrictions impacted its ability to obtain a higher sale price. Recognizing that, at the end of the day, plaintiffs would have an uphill battle in overcoming the presumption of the business judgment rule, we must give plaintiffs the benefit of the doubt at this pleading stage to determine if they have stated a due care claim. Because of our ultimate decision, however, we need not finally decide this question in this case.

We assume, therefore, without deciding, that a claim for relief based on gross negligence during the board's auction process is stated by the inferences most favorable to plaintiffs that flow from these

payment of $750,000 upon consummation of the merger, and (3) a payment of $250,000 on the date of the merger and sixteen quarterly payments of $100,000 under a noncompete and consulting agreement. The complaint also alleges that William Barrett, who was a Frederick's director and a vice president of JMS, the firm's financial advisor, had an interest in the merger transaction. Specifically, the complaint alleges that Barrett's firm received a $2 million fee upon consummation of the Knightsbridge merger. But because Barrett's firm was entitled to receive a fee upon the consummation of any merger and because the fee was proportional to the sale price, the Court of Chancery correctly concluded that the complaint was insufficient to establish a disabling conflict with respect to Barrett. See January 2000 Mem. Op., 2000 Del. Ch. LEXIS 19, *24....

45. Relatedly, the plaintiffs also argue that the board breached its fiduciary duties by favoring Knightsbridge over Veritas in the bidding process.

allegations. The issue then becomes whether the amended complaint may be dismissed upon a Rule 12(b)(6) motion by reason of the existence and the legal effect of the exculpatory provision of Article TWELFTH of Frederick's certificate of incorporation, adopted pursuant to 8 Del. C. § 102(b)(7). That provision would exempt directors from personal liability in damages with certain exceptions (e.g., breach of the duty of loyalty) that are not applicable here. . . . [46]

B.   Application of *Emerald Partners*

1.   The Court of Chancery Properly Dismissed Claims Based Solely on the Duty of Care

Plaintiffs here, while not conceding that the Section 102(b)(7) charter provision may be considered on this Rule 12(b)(6) motion nevertheless, in effect, conceded in oral argument in the Court of Chancery and similarly in oral argument in this Court that if a complaint unambiguously and solely asserted only a due care claim, the complaint is dismissible once the corporation's Section 102(b)(7) provision is invoked. . . .

Plaintiffs contended vigorously, however, that the Section 102(b)(7) charter provision does not apply to bar their claims in this case because the amended complaint alleges breaches of the duty of loyalty and other claims that are not barred by the charter provision. As a result, plaintiffs maintain, this case cannot be boiled down solely to a due care case. They argue, in effect, that their complaint is sufficiently well-pleaded that—as a matter of law—the due care claims are so inextricably intertwined with loyalty and bad faith claims that Section 102(b)(7) is not a bar to recovery of damages against the directors.

We disagree. It is the plaintiffs who have a burden to set forth "a short and plain statement of the claim showing that the pleader is entitled to relief."[47] The plaintiffs are entitled to all reasonable inferences flowing from their pleadings, but if those inferences do not support a valid legal claim, the complaint should be dismissed without the need for the defendants to file an answer and without proceeding with discovery. Here we have assumed, without deciding, that the amended complaint on its face states a due care claim. Because we have determined that the complaint fails properly to invoke loyalty and bad faith claims, we are left with only a due care claim. Defendants had the obligation to raise the bar of Section 102(b)(7) as a defense, and they did. As plaintiffs conceded in oral argument before this Court, if there is only an unambiguous, residual due care claim

---

46. Article TWELFTH provides:

TWELFTH. A director of this Corporation shall not be personally liable to the Corporation or its shareholders for monetary damages for breach of fiduciary duty as a director, except for liability (i) for any breach of the director's duty of loyalty to the Corporation or its shareholders, (ii) for acts or omissions not in good faith or which involve intentional misconduct or a knowing violation of law (iii) under Section 174 of the Delaware General Corporation Law, or (iv) for any transaction for which the director derived an improper personal benefit.

47. Chancery Rule 8(a).

and nothing else—as a matter of law—then Section 102(b)(7) would bar the claim. Accordingly, the Court of Chancery did not err in dismissing the plaintiffs due care claim in this case.

2.   The Court of Chancery Correctly Applied the Parties' Respective Burdens of Proof

Plaintiffs also assert that the trial court in the case before us incorrectly placed on plaintiffs a pleading burden to negate the elements of the 102(b)(7) charter provision. Plaintiffs argue that this ruling is inconsistent with the statement in *Emerald Partners* that "The shield from liability provided by a certificate of incorporation provision adopted pursuant to 8 Del. C. § 102(b)(7) is in the nature of an affirmative defense.... Defendants seeking exculpation under such a provision will normally bear the burden of establishing each of its elements."

The procedural posture here is quite different from that in *Emerald Partners*. There the Court stated that it was incorrect for the trial court to grant summary judgment on the record in that case because the defendants had the burden at trial of demonstrating good faith if they were invoking the statutory exculpation provision. In this case, we focus not on trial burdens, but only on pleading issues. A plaintiff must allege well-pleaded facts stating a claim on which relief may be granted. Had plaintiff alleged such well-pleaded facts supporting a breach of loyalty or bad faith claim, the Section 102(b)(7) charter provision would have been unavailing as to such claims, and this case would have gone forward.

But we have held that the amended complaint here does not allege a loyalty violation or other violation falling within the exceptions to the Section 102(b)(7) exculpation provision. Likewise, we have held that, even if the plaintiffs had stated a claim for gross negligence, such a well-pleaded claim is unavailing because defendants have brought forth the Section 102(b)(7) charter provision that bars such claims. This is the end of the case.

And rightly so, as a matter of the public policy of this State. Section 102(b)(7) was adopted by the Delaware General Assembly in 1986 following a directors and officers insurance liability crisis and the 1985 Delaware Supreme Court decision in Smith v. Van Gorkom. The purpose of this statute was to permit stockholders to adopt a provision in the certificate of incorporation to free directors of personal liability in damages for due care violations, but not duty of loyalty violations, bad faith claims and certain other conduct. Such a charter provision, when adopted, would not affect injunctive proceedings based on gross negligence. Once the statute was adopted, stockholders usually approved charter amendments containing these provisions because it freed up directors to take business risks without worrying about negligence lawsuits.

Our jurisprudence since the adoption of the statute has consistently stood for the proposition that a Section 102(b)(7) charter provision bars a claim that is found to state only a due care violation.[48] Because we have assumed that the amended complaint here does state a due care claim, the exculpation afforded by the statute must affirmatively be raised by the defendant directors.[49] The directors have done so in this case, and the Court of Chancery properly applied the Frederick's charter provision to dismiss the plaintiffs' due care claim. . . .

Conclusion

We have concluded that: (1) the amended complaint does not adequately allege a breach of the Frederick's board's duty of loyalty or its disclosure duty; (2) the exculpatory provision in the Frederick's charter operates to bar claims for money damages against the directors caused by the alleged breach of the board's duty of care. . . . Accordingly, we affirm the judgment of the Court of Chancery dismissing the amended complaint against the Frederick's board. . . .

SECTION 2.   THE DUTY TO ACT IN GOOD FAITH

In re The Walt Disney Company Derivative Litigation

Delaware Court of Chancery, 2003.
825 A.2d 275.

■ BEFORE: CHANDLER, CHIEF JUSTICE.

■ CHANDLER, J.

In this derivative action filed on behalf of nominal defendant Walt Disney Company, plaintiffs allege that the defendant directors breached their fiduciary duties when they blindly approved an employment agreement with defendant Michael Ovitz and then, again without any review or deliberation, ignored defendant Michael Eisner's dealings with Ovitz regarding his non-fault termination. Plaintiffs seek rescission and/or money damages from defendants and Ovitz, or compensation for damages allegedly sustained by Disney and disgorgement of Ovitz's unjust enrichment.

48. See, e.g., *Emerald Partners*, 726 A.2d at 1224; *Arnold v. Society for Savings Bancorp.*, Del. Supr., 650 A.2d 1270, 1288 (1994); *Zirn v. VLI Corp.*, Del. Supr., 681 A.2d 1050, 1061 (1996).

49. Although an exculpatory charter provision is in the nature of an affirmative defense under *Emerald Partners*, the board is not required to disprove claims based on alleged breaches of the duty of loyalty to gain the protection of the provision with respect to due care claims. Rather, proving the existence of a valid exculpatory provision in the corporate charter entitles directors to dismissal of any claims for money damages against them that are based solely on alleged breaches of the board's duty of care.

... Defendants moved to dismiss plaintiffs' second amended derivative complaint (hereinafter the "new complaint") pursuant to Court of Chancery Rules 12(b)(6) and 23.1....

As will be explained in greater detail below, I conclude that plaintiffs' new complaint sufficiently pleads a breach of fiduciary duty by the Old and the New Disney Board of Directors[25] so as to withstand a motion to dismiss under Chancery Rules 23.1 and 12(b)(6). Stated briefly, plaintiffs' new allegations give rise to a cognizable question whether the defendant directors of the Walt Disney Company should be held personally liable to the corporation for a knowing or intentional lack of due care in the directors' decision-making process regarding Ovitz's employment and termination. It is rare when a court imposes liability on directors of a corporation for breach of the duty of care, and this Court is hesitant to second-guess the business judgment of a disinterested and independent board of directors. But the facts alleged in the new complaint do not implicate merely negligent or grossly negligent decision making by corporate directors. Quite the contrary; plaintiffs' new complaint suggests that the Disney directors failed to exercise *any* business judgment and failed to make *any* good faith attempt to fulfill their fiduciary duties to Disney and its stockholders. Allegations that Disney's directors abdicated all responsibility to consider appropriately an action of material importance to the corporation puts directly in question whether the board's decision-making processes were employed in a good faith effort to advance corporate interests. In short, the new complaint alleges facts implying that the Disney directors failed to "act in good faith and meet minimal proceduralist standards of attention."[26] Based on the facts asserted in the new complaint, therefore, I believe plaintiffs have stated cognizable claims for which demand is excused and on which a more complete factual record is necessary.

I.   PROCEDURAL ... BACKGROUND

As mentioned, this case involves an attack on decisions of the Walt Disney Company's board of directors, approving an executive compensation contract for Michael Ovitz, as well as impliedly approving a non-fault termination that resulted in an award to Ovitz (allegedly exceeding $140,000,000) after barely one year of employment. After the Supreme Court's remand regarding plaintiffs' first amended complaint,[27] plaintiffs used the "tools at hand," a request for books and records as authorized under 8 *Del. C.* § 220, to obtain information about the nature of the Disney Board's involvement in the decision to hire and, eventually, to terminate Ovitz. Using the information gained from that request, plaintiffs drafted and filed the new complaint,

---

25. The Disney Board of Directors changed from the time Ovitz was hired to the time of his non-fault termination. Therefore, the board at the time Ovitz was hired is referred to as the "Old Board," and the board at the time of the non-fault termination is the "New Board."

26. *Gagliardi v. TriFoods Int'l, Inc.,* 683 A.2d 1049, 1052 (Del.Ch.1996).

27. *Brehm v. Eisner,* 746 A.2d 244, 249 (Del.2000).

which is the subject of the pending motions. The facts, as alleged in the new complaint, portray a markedly different picture of the corporate processes that resulted in the Ovitz employment agreement than that portrayed in the first amended complaint.[28] For that reason, it is necessary to set forth the repleaded facts in some detail. The facts set forth hereafter are taken directly from the new complaint and, for purposes of the present motions, are accepted as true. Of course, I hold no opinion as to the actual truth of any of the allegations set forth in the new complaint; nor do I hold any view as to the likely ultimate outcome on the merits of claims based on these asserted facts. I determine here only that the facts, if true, arguably support all three of plaintiffs' claims for relief, as asserted in the new complaint, and are sufficient to excuse demand and to state claims that warrant development of a full record.

II.   STANDARD OF REVIEW . . .

When the plaintiff alleges a derivative claim, demand must be made on the board or excused based upon futility. To determine whether demand would be futile, the Court must determine whether the particular facts, as alleged, create a reason to doubt that: "(1) the directors are disinterested and independent" or "(2) the challenged transaction was otherwise the product of a valid exercise of business judgment." . . . [31]

III.   ANALYSIS . . .

Defendants contend that the new complaint cannot be read reasonably to allege any fiduciary duty violation other than, at most, a breach of the directors' duty of due care. They further assert that even if the complaint states a breach of the directors' duty of care, Disney's charter provision, based on 8 *Del. C.* § 102(b)(7), would apply and the individual directors would be protected from personal damages liability for any breach of their duty of care. A § 102(b)(7) provision in a corporation's charter does not "eliminate or limit the liability of a director: (i)[f]or any breach of the director's duty of loyalty to the corporation or its stockholders; (ii) for acts or omissions not in good faith or which involve intentional misconduct or a knowing violation of the law; (iii) under § 174 of this title; or (iv) for any transaction from which the director derived an improper personal benefit."[33] A fair reading of the new complaint, in my opinion, gives rise to a reason to doubt whether the board's actions were taken honestly and in good faith. . . . Since acts or omissions not undertaken honestly and in good

28. This case is yet another example where a books and records request in the first instance might have prevented expensive and time-consuming procedural machinations that too often occur in derivative litigation. The Supreme Court and this Court have repeatedly urged derivative plaintiffs to seek books and records before filing a complaint. *See, e.g., Guttman v. Nvidia Corp.*, Del. Ch., C.A. No. 19571–NC, at 1–2, Strine, V.C. (May 5, 2003). The amended pleading in this case is a perfect illustration of the benefit of such an approach.

31. *Aronson v. Lewis*, 473 A.2d 805, 814 (Del.1984).

33. 8 *Del. C.* § 102(b)(7). As to (iii), § 174 deals with a director's liability for unlawful payment of dividends or unlawful stock purchase or redemption.

faith, or which involve intentional misconduct, do not fall within the protective ambit of § 102(b)(7), I cannot dismiss the complaint based on the exculpatory Disney charter provision.[34]

Defendants also argue that Ovitz's employment agreement was a reasonable exercise of business judgment. They argue that Ovitz's previous position as head of CAA required a large compensation package to entice him to become Disney's president. As to the non-fault termination, defendants contend that that decision was reasonable in that the board wished to avoid protracted litigation with Ovitz. The Court is appropriately hesitant to second-guess the business judgment of a disinterested and independent board of directors. As alleged in the new complaint, however, the facts belie any assertion that the New or Old Boards exercised any business judgment or made any good faith attempt to fulfill the fiduciary duties they owed to Disney and its shareholders.

A.   The Old and New Boards

[Michael Eisner is the chief executive officer ("CEO") of the Walt Disney Company. In 1994, Eisner's second-in-command, Frank Wells, died in a helicopter crash. Two other key executives—Jeffrey Katzenberg and Richard Frank—left Disney shortly thereafter, allegedly because of Eisner's management style. Eisner began looking for a new president for Disney and chose Michael Ovitz. Ovitz was founder and head of CAA, a talent agency; he had never been an executive for a publicly owned entertainment company. He had, however, been Eisner's close friend for over twenty-five years.]*

According to the new complaint, Eisner unilaterally made the decision to hire Ovitz, even in the face of internal documents warning of potential adverse publicity and with three members of the board of directors initially objecting to the hiring when Eisner first broached the idea in August 1995. No draft employment agreements were presented to the compensation committee or to the Disney board for review before the September 26, 1995 meetings. The compensation committee met for less than an hour on September 26, 1995, and spent most of its time on two other topics, including the compensation of director Russell for helping secure Ovitz's employment. With respect to the employment agreement itself, the committee received only a summary of its terms and conditions. No questions were asked about the employment agreement. No time was taken to review the documents for approval. Instead, the committee approved the hiring of Ovitz and directed Eisner, Ovitz's close friend, to carry out the negotiations with regard to certain still unresolved and significant details.[35]

---

34. See *Malpiede v. Townson*, 780 A.2d 1075, 1094 (Del.2001) (holding that, as a matter of law, § 102(b)(7) bars a claim only if there is an unambiguous, residual due care claim and nothing else).

* Passages in brackets have been relocated from the court's statement of the factual background. (Footnote by ed.).

35. The allegation that Eisner and Ovitz had been close friends for over twenty-five years is not mentioned to show self-interest or domination. Instead, the allegation is mentioned because it casts doubt on the good faith and judgment behind the Old and New

The Old Board met immediately after the committee did. Less than one and one-half pages of the fifteen pages of Old Board minutes were devoted to discussions of Ovitz's hiring as Disney's new president. Actually, most of that time appears to have been spent discussing compensation for director Russell. No presentations were made to the Old Board regarding the terms of the draft agreement. No questions were raised, at least so far as the minutes reflect. At the end of the meeting, the Old Board authorized Ovitz's hiring as Disney's president. No further review or approval of the employment agreement occurred. Throughout both meetings, no expert consultant was present to advise the compensation committee or the Old Board. Notably, the Old Board approved Ovitz's hiring even though the employment agreement was still a "work in progress." The Old Board simply passed off the details to Ovitz and his good friend, Eisner.

Negotiation over the remaining terms took place solely between Eisner, Ovitz, and attorneys representing Disney and Ovitz. The compensation committee met briefly in October to review the negotiations, but failed again to actually consider a draft of the agreement or to establish any guidelines to be used in the negotiations. The committee was apparently not otherwise involved in the negotiations. Negotiations with Eisner continued until mid-December, but Ovitz had already started serving as Disney's president as of October 1, 1995.

Eisner and Ovitz reached a final agreement on December 12, 1995. They agreed to backdate the agreement, however, to October 1, 1995. The final employment agreement also differed substantially from the original draft, but evidently no further committee or board review of it ever occurred. The final version of Ovitz's employment agreement was signed (according to the new complaint) without any board input beyond the limited discussion on September 26, 1995.

[Ovitz began serving as president of Disney on October 1, 1995, and became a Disney director in January 1996. Ovitz's tenure as Disney's president proved unsuccessful. Ovitz was not a good second-in-command, and he and Eisner were both aware of that fact. Eisner told defendant Watson, via memorandum, that he (Eisner) "had made an error in judgment in who I brought into the company." Other company executives were reported in the December 14, 1996 edition of the New York Times as saying that Ovitz had an excessively lavish office, an imperious management style, and had started a feud with NBC during his tenure. Even Ovitz admitted, during a September 30, 1996 interview on "Larry King Live," that he knew "about 1% of what I need to know."

[Even though admitting that he did not know his job, Ovitz studiously avoided attempts to be educated. Eisner instructed Ovitz to meet weekly with Disney's chief financial officer, defendant Bollenbach. The meetings were scheduled to occur each Monday at 2 p.m., but every week Ovitz cancelled at the last minute. Bollenbach was

Boards' decisions to allow two close personal friends to control the payment of shareholders' money to Ovitz.

quoted in a December 1996 issue of Vanity Fair as saying that Ovitz failed to meet with him at all, "didn't understand the duties of an executive at a public company[,] and he didn't want to learn."

[Instead of working to learn his duties as Disney's president, Ovitz began seeking alternative employment. He consulted Eisner to ensure that no action would be taken against him by Disney if he sought employment elsewhere. Eisner agreed that the best thing for Disney, Eisner, and Ovitz was for Ovitz to gain employment elsewhere. Eisner wrote to the chairman of Sony Japan that Ovitz could negotiate with Sony without any repercussions from Disney. Ovitz and Sony began negotiations for Ovitz to become head of Sony's entertainment business, but the negotiations ultimately failed. With the possibility of having another company absorb the cost of Ovitz's departure now gone, Eisner and Ovitz began in earnest to discuss a non-fault termination.

[Ovitz wanted to leave Disney, but could only terminate his employment if one of three events occurred: (1) he was not elected or retained as president and a director of Disney; (2) he was assigned duties materially inconsistent with his role as president; or (3) Disney reduced his annual salary or failed to grant his stock options, pay him discretionary bonuses, or make any required compensation payment. None of these three events occurred. If Ovitz resigned outright, he might have been liable to Disney for damages and would not have received the benefits of the non-fault termination. He also desired to protect his reputation when exiting from his position with Disney. Eisner agreed to help Ovitz depart Disney without sacrificing any of his benefits. Eisner and Ovitz worked together as close personal friends to have Ovitz receive a non-fault termination. Eisner stated in a letter to Ovitz that: "I agree with you that we must work together to assure a smooth transition and deal with the public relations brilliantly. I am committed to make this a win-win situation, to keep our friendship intact, to be positive, to say and write only glowing things.... Nobody ever needs to know anything other than positive things from either of us. This can all work out!"

[Eisner, Litvack [a Disney director] and Ovitz met at Eisner's apartment on December 11, 1996, to finalize Ovitz's non-fault termination. The new complaint alleges that the New Board was aware that Eisner was negotiating with Ovitz the terms of his separation. Litvack sent a letter to Ovitz on December 12, 1996, stating that, by "mutual agreement," (1) Ovitz's term of employment would end on January 31, 1997; and (2) "this letter will for all purposes of the Employment Agreement be given the same effect as though there had been a 'Non–Fault Termination,' and the Company will pay you, on or before February 5, 1997, all amounts due you under the Employment Agreement, including those under Section 11(c) thereof. In addition, the stock options granted pursuant to Option A, will vest as of January 31, 1997 and will expire in accordance with their terms on September 30, 2002." On December 12, 1996, Ovitz's departure from Disney became public. Neither the New Board of Directors nor the compensation committee had been consulted or given their approval for a non-fault termination. In addition, no record exists of any action by the New Board once the non-fault termination became public on December 12, 1996.

On December 27, 1996, Litvack sent Ovitz a new letter superseding the December 12th letter. The December 27th letter stated that Ovitz's termination would "be treated as a 'Non–Fault Termination.'" This differed from the December 12th letter, which treated Ovitz's termination "as though there had been a 'Non–Fault Termination.'" It also made the termination of Ovitz's employment and his resignation as a Disney director effective as of the close of business on December 27th, instead of on January 31, 1997, as in the December 12th letter. Additionally, it listed the amount payable to Ovitz as $38,888,230.77, and stated that the "A" options to purchase three million shares of Disney vested on December 27th, instead of January 31, 1997, as in the December 12th letter. Both Eisner and Litvack signed the letter. Again, however, neither the New Board nor the compensation committee reviewed or approved the December 27th letter. No record exists of any New Board action after the December 27th letter became public, nor had any board member raised any questions or concerns since the original December 12th letter became public.

According to the new complaint, Disney's bylaws required board approval for Ovitz's non-fault termination. Eisner and Litvack allegedly did not have the authority to provide for a non-fault termination without board consent. No documents or board minutes currently exist showing an affirmative decision by the New Board or any of its committees to grant Ovitz a non-fault termination. The New Board was already aware that Eisner was granting the non-fault termination as of December 12, 1996, the day it became public. No record of any action by the New Board affirming or questioning that decision by Eisner either before or after that date has been produced. There are also no records showing that alternatives to a non-fault termination were ever evaluated by the New Board or by any of its committees.]

Disney had lost several key executives in the months before Ovitz was hired. Moreover, the position of president is obviously important in a publicly owned corporation. But the Old Board and the compensation committee (it is alleged) each spent less than an hour reviewing Ovitz's possible hiring. According to the new complaint, neither the Old Board nor the compensation committee reviewed the actual draft employment agreement. Nor did they evaluate the details of Ovitz's salary or his severance provisions. No expert presented the board with details of the agreement, outlined the pros and cons of either the salary or non-fault termination provisions, or analyzed comparable industry standards for such agreements.[36] Notwithstanding this alleged

---

36. In the earlier proceedings in this case, defendants represented that Graef Crystal served as the expert with regard to Ovitz's employment, arguably providing the board with the statutory safe harbor under 8 Del. C. § 141(e). The new complaint, however, alleges that Graef Crystal was hired as the expert with regard to Eisner's new employment agreement, not Ovitz's agreement. Accepting this change in facts as true for information vacuum, the Old Board and the compensation committee approved Ovitz's hiring, appointed Eisner to negotiate with Ovitz directly in drafting the unresolved terms of his employment, never asked to review the final terms, and were never voluntarily provided those terms.

During the negotiation over the unresolved terms, the compensation committee was involved only once, at the very early stages in October 1995. The final agreement varied significantly from the draft agreement in the areas of both stock options and the terms of the non-fault termination. Neither the compensation committee nor the Old Board sought to review, nor did they review, the final agreement. In addition, both the Old Board and the committee failed to meet in order to evaluate the final agreement before it became binding on Disney. To repeat, no expert was retained to advise the Old Board, the committee, or Eisner during the negotiation process.

The new complaint, fairly read, also charges the New Board with a similar ostrich-like approach regarding Ovitz's non-fault termination. Eisner and Litvack granted Ovitz a non-fault termination on December 12, 1996, and the news became public that day. Although formal board approval appeared necessary for a non-fault termination, the new complaint alleges that no New Board member even asked for a meeting to discuss Eisner's and Litvack's decision. On December 27, 1996, when Eisner and Litvack accelerated Ovitz's non-fault termination by over a month, with a payout of more than $38 million in cash, together with the three million ''A'' stock options, the board again failed to do anything. Instead, it appears from the new complaint that the New Board played no role in Eisner's agreement to award Ovitz more than $38 million in cash and the three million ''A'' stock options, all for leaving a job that Ovitz had allegedly proven incapable of performing.

The New Board apparently never sought to negotiate with Ovitz regarding his departure. Nor, apparently, did it consider whether to seek a termination based on fault. During the fifteen-day period between announcement of Ovitz's termination and its effective date, the New Board allegedly chose to remain invisible in the process. The new complaint alleges that the New Board: (1) failed to ask why it had not been informed; (2) failed to inquire about the conditions and terms of the agreement; and (3) failed even to attempt to stop or delay the termination until more information could be collected. If the board had taken the time or effort to review these or other options, perhaps with the assistance of expert legal advisors, the business judgment rule might well protect its decision. In this case, however, the new complaint asserts that the New Board directors refused to explore any alternatives, and refused to even attempt to evaluate the implications of the non-fault termination—blindly allowing Eisner to

purposes of this motion, Disney's board is not entitled to invoke § 141(e)'s protection based on a board's reliance upon a qualified expert selected with reasonable care.

hand over to his personal friend, Ovitz, more than $38 million in cash and the three million "A" stock options.[37]

These facts, if true, do more than portray directors who, in a negligent or grossly negligent manner, merely failed to inform themselves or to deliberate adequately about an issue of material importance to their corporation. Instead, the facts alleged in the new complaint suggest that the defendant directors consciously and intentionally disregarded their responsibilities, adopting a "we don't care about the risks" attitude concerning a material corporate decision. Knowing or deliberate indifference by a director to his or her duty to act faithfully and with appropriate care is conduct, in my opinion, that may not have been taken honestly and in good faith to advance the best interests of the company. Put differently, all of the alleged facts, if true, imply that the defendant directors knew that they were making material decisions without adequate information and without adequate deliberation, and that they simply did not care if the decisions caused the corporation and its stockholders to suffer injury or loss. Viewed in this light, plaintiffs' new complaint sufficiently alleges a breach of the directors' obligation to act honestly and in good faith in the corporation's best interests for a Court to conclude, if the facts are true, that the defendant directors' conduct fell outside the protection of the business judgment rule.[38] . . .

I . . . conclude that plaintiffs' pleading is sufficient to withstand a motion to dismiss under Rule 12(b)(6). Specifically, plaintiffs' claims are based on an alleged knowing and deliberate indifference to a potential risk of harm to the corporation. Where a director consciously ignores his or her duties to the corporation, thereby causing economic injury to its stockholders, the director's actions are either "not in good faith" or "involve intentional misconduct."[40] Thus, plaintiffs' allegations support claims that fall outside the liability waiver provided under Disney's certificate of incorporation. . . .

IV. CONCLUSION

It is of course true that after-the-fact litigation is a most imperfect device to evaluate corporate business decisions, as the limits of human competence necessarily impede judicial review. But our corporation law's theoretical justification for disregarding honest errors simply does not apply to intentional misconduct or to egregious process failures that implicate the foundational directoral obligation to act honestly and in good faith to advance corporate interests. Because the facts alleged here, if true, portray directors consciously indifferent to a material issue facing the corporation, the law must be strong enough to intervene against abuse of trust. Accordingly, all three of plaintiffs' claims for relief concerning fiduciary duty breaches and waste survive defendants' motions to dismiss.

---

37. Plaintiffs allege that the present value of the cash and the value of the stock options totaled over $140 million to Ovitz as severance. At this time I need not determine whether plaintiffs' allegations as to the value of the payout are correct or incorrect.

38. *Aronson*, 473 A.2d at 812.

40. 8 *Del. C.* § 102(b)(7)(ii).

The practical effect of this ruling is that defendants must answer the new complaint and plaintiffs may proceed to take appropriate discovery on the merits of their claims. To that end, a case scheduling order has been entered that will promptly bring this matter before the Court on a fully developed factual record.

IT IS SO ORDERED.

————

Miller v. American Telephone & Telegraph Co.

United States Court of Appeals, Third Circuit, 1974.
507 F.2d 759.

■ Before Seitz, Chief Judge, Gibbons and Garth, Circuit Judges.

■ Seitz, Chief Judge.

Plaintiffs, stockholders in American Telephone and Telegraph Company ("AT & T"), brought a stockholders' derivative action in the Eastern District of Pennsylvania against AT & T and all but one of its directors. The suit centered upon the failure of AT & T to collect an outstanding debt of some $1.5 million owed to the company by the Democratic National Committee ("DNC") for communications services provided by AT & T during the 1968 Democratic national convention. Federal diversity jurisdiction was invoked under 28 U.S.C. § 1332.

Plaintiffs' complaint alleged that "neither the officers or directors of AT & T have taken any action to recover the amount owed" from on or about August 20, 1968, when the debt was incurred, until May 31, 1972, the date plaintiffs' amended complaint was filed. The failure to collect was alleged to have involved a breach of the defendant directors' duty to exercise diligence in handling the affairs of the corporation, to have resulted in affording a preference to the DNC in collection procedures in violation of § 202(a) of the Communications Act of 1934, 47 U.S.C. § 202(a) (1970), and to have amounted to AT & T's making a "contribution" to the DNC in violation of a federal prohibition on corporate campaign spending, 18 U.S.C. § 610 (1970).

Plaintiffs sought permanent relief in the form of an injunction requiring AT & T to collect the debt, an injunction against providing further services to the DNC until the debt was paid in full, and a surcharge for the benefit of the corporation against the defendant directors in the amount of the debt plus interest from the due date. A request for a preliminary injunction against the provision of services to the 1972 Democratic convention was denied by the district court after an evidentiary hearing.

On motion of the defendants, the district court dismissed the complaint for failure to state a claim upon which relief could be granted. 364 F.Supp. 648 (E.D.Pa.1973). The court stated that collection procedures were properly within the discretion of the directors whose determination would not be overturned by the court in the absence of an allegation that the conduct of the directors was "plainly illegal, unreasonable, or in breach of a fiduciary duty...." *Id.* at 651. Plaintiffs appeal from dismissal of their complaint.

In viewing the motion to dismiss, we must consider all facts alleged in the complaint and every inference fairly deductible therefrom in the light most favorable to the plaintiffs. A complaint should not be dismissed unless it appears that the plaintiffs would not be entitled to relief under any facts which they might prove in support of their claim. Judging plaintiffs' complaint by these standards, we feel that it does state a claim upon which relief can be granted for breach of fiduciary duty arising from the alleged violation of 18 U.S.C. § 610.

I.

The pertinent law on the question of the defendant directors' fiduciary duties in this diversity action is that of New York, the state of AT & T's incorporation.... The sound business judgment rule, the basis of the district court's dismissal of plaintiffs' complaint, expresses the unanimous decision of American courts to eschew intervention in corporate decision-making if the judgment of directors and officers is uninfluenced by personal considerations and is exercised in good faith. Pollitz v. Wabash Railroad Co., 207 N.Y. 113, 100 N.E. 721 (1912); Bayer v. Beran, 49 N.Y.S.2d 2, 4–7 (Sup.Ct.1944); 3 Fletcher, Private Corporations § 1039 (perm. ed. rev. vol. 1965). Underlying the rule is the assumption that reasonable diligence has been used in reaching the decision which the rule is invoked to justify....

Had plaintiffs' complaint alleged only failure to pursue a corporate claim, application of the sound business judgment rule would support the district court's ruling that a shareholder could not attack the directors' decision. *See* United Copper Securities Co. v. Amalgamated Copper Co., 244 U.S. 261, 37 S.Ct. 509, 61 L.Ed. 1119 (1917); Clifford v. Metropolitan Life Insurance Co., 264 App.Div. 168, 34 N.Y.S.2d 693 (2d Dept.1942); 13 Fletcher, Private Corporations § 5822 (perm. ed. rev. vol. 1970). Where, however, the decision not to collect a debt owed the corporation is itself alleged to have been an illegal act, different rules apply. When New York law regarding such acts by directors is considered in conjunction with the underlying purposes of the particular statute involved here, we are convinced that the business judgment rule cannot insulate the defendant directors from liability if they did in fact breach 18 U.S.C. § 610, as plaintiffs have charged.

Roth v. Robertson, 64 Misc. 343, 118 N.Y.S. 351 (Sup.Ct.1909), illustrates the proposition that even though committed to benefit the corporation, illegal acts may amount to a breach of fiduciary duty in New York. In *Roth,* the managing director of an amusement park company had allegedly used corporate funds to purchase the silence of persons who threatened to complain about unlawful Sunday operation of the park. Recovery from the defendant director was sustained on the ground that the money was an illegal payment:

> For reasons of public policy, we are clearly of the opinion that payments of corporate funds for such purposes as those disclosed in this case must be condemned, and officers of a corporation making them held to a strict accountability, and be compelled to

> refund the amounts so wasted for the benefit of stockholders....
> To hold any other rule would be establishing a dangerous prece-
> dent, tacitly countenancing the wasting of corporate funds for
> purposes of corrupting public morals. *Id.* at 346, 118 N.Y.S. at
> 353.

The plaintiffs' complaint in the instant case alleges a similar "waste" of
$1.5 million through an illegal campaign contribution.

Abrams v. Allen, 297 N.Y. 52, 74 N.E.2d 305 (1947), reflects an
affirmation by the New York Court of Appeals of the principle of *Roth*
that directors must be restrained from engaging in activities which are
against public policy. In *Abrams* the court held that a cause of action
was stated by an allegation in a derivative complaint that the directors
of Remington Rand, Inc., had relocated corporate plants and curtailed
production solely for the purpose of intimidating and punishing
employees for their involvement in a labor dispute. The Court of
Appeals acknowledged that, "depending on the circumstances," proof
of the allegations in the complaint might sustain recovery, *inter alia,*
under the rule that directors are liable for corporate loss caused by the
commission of an "unlawful or immoral act." *Id.* at 55, 74 N.E.2d at
306. In support of its holding, the court noted that the closing of
factories for the purpose alleged was opposed to the public policy of
the state and nation as embodied in the New York Labor Law and the
National Labor Relations Act. *Id.* at 56, 74 N.E.2d at 307.[3]

The alleged violation of the federal prohibition against corporate
political contributions not only involves the corporation in criminal
activity but similarly contravenes a policy of Congress clearly enunciated in 18 U.S.C. § 610.[4] That statute and its predecessor reflect
congressional efforts: (1) to destroy the influence of corporations over
elections through financial contributions and (2) to check the practice
of using corporate funds to benefit political parties without the
consent of the stockholders. United States v. CIO, 335 U.S. 106, 113,
68 S.Ct. 1349, 92 L.Ed. 1849 (1948).

The fact that shareholders are within the class for whose protection the statute was enacted gives force to the argument that the
alleged breach of that statute should give rise to a cause of action in
those shareholders to force the return to the corporation of illegally
contributed funds. Since political contributions by corporations can be
checked and shareholder control over the political use of general

---

3. That violation of a federal statute is
the basis of the breach of fiduciary duty and
that therefore the court is required to interpret the federal statute has not deterred New
York courts from entertaining such suits
against directors. *See* Knopfler v. Bohen, 15
A.D.2d 922, 225 N.Y.S.2d 609 (2d Dept.1962);
cf. Simon v. Socony–Vacuum Oil Co., 179
Misc. 202, 38 N.Y.S.2d 270 (Sup.Ct.1942).

4. We note that prior to June 1, 1974,
corporate political contributions made "directly or indirectly" violated New York law.
Law of July 20, 1965, ch. 1031, § 43, [1965]

N.Y.Laws 1783 (repealed 1974). Furthermore, apart from the statutory prohibition,
political donations by corporations were apparently ultra vires acts in New York. *See*
People ex rel. Perkins v. Moss, 187 N.Y. 410,
80 N.E. 383 (1907). Corporations or organizations financially supported by corporations
doing business in the state are now permitted
to make contributions up to $5,000 per year.
N.Y. Election Law § 480 (McKinney's Con-
sol.Laws, c. 17, Supp.1974).

corporate funds effectuated only if directors are restrained from causing the corporation to violate the statute, such a violation seems a particularly appropriate basis for finding breach of the defendant directors' fiduciary duty to the corporation. Under such circumstances, the directors cannot be insulated from liability on the ground that the contribution was made in the exercise of sound business judgment.

Since plaintiffs have alleged actual damage to the corporation from the transaction in the form of the loss of a $1.5 million increment to AT & T's treasury,[5] we conclude that the complaint does state a claim upon which relief can be granted sufficient to withstand a motion to dismiss.[6]

II.

We have accepted plaintiffs' allegation of a violation of 18 U.S.C. § 610 as a shorthand designation of the elements necessary to establish a breach of that statute. This is consonant with the federal practice of notice pleading. *See* Conley v. Gibson, 355 U.S. 41, 47–48, 78 S.Ct. 99, 2 L.Ed.2d 80 (1957); Fed.R.Civ.P. 8(f). That such a designation is sufficient for pleading purposes does not, however, relieve plaintiffs of their ultimate obligation to prove the elements of the statutory violation as part of their proof of breach of fiduciary duty. At the appropriate time, plaintiffs will be required to produce evidence sufficient to establish three distinct elements comprising a violation of 18 U.S.C. § 610: that AT & T (1) made a contribution of money or anything of value to the DNC (2) in connection with a federal election (3) for the purpose of influencing the outcome of that election. *See* United States v. Boyle, 157 U.S.App.D.C. 166, 482 F.2d 755, cert. denied, 414 U.S. 1076, 94 S.Ct. 593, 38 L.Ed.2d 483 (1973); United States v. Lewis Food Co., Inc., 366 F.2d 710 (9th Cir.1966)....[7]

The order of the district court will be reversed and the case remanded for further proceedings consistent with this opinion.

NOTE ON CRIMINAL LIABILITIES OF DIRECTORS AND OFFICERS

Miller concerns the liability of a director or officer to the corporation on the ground of illegal conduct. An officer (or, more rarely, a

---

5. Under New York law, allegation of breach even of a federal statute is apparently insufficient to state a cause of action unless the breach caused independent damage to the corporation. *See* Diamond v. Davis, 263 App. Div. 68, 31 N.Y.S.2d 582 (1st Dept.1941); Borden v. Cohen, 231 N.Y.S.2d 902 (Sup.Ct. 1962). *But see* Runcie v. Bankers Trust Co., 6 N.Y.S.2d 623 (Sup.Ct.1938).

6. We express no opinion today on the question of whether plaintiffs' complaint may also state a cause of action for breach of fiduciary duty arising from the alleged violation of 47 U.S.C. § 202(a).

7. As amended by the Federal Election Campaign Act of 1971 (effective April 7, 1972), the definition of "contribution" for purposes of 18 U.S.C. § 610 is a gift of money or anything of value "made for the purpose of influencing the nomination for election, or election" of any person to federal office or for influencing the outcome of a primary or national nominating convention. 18 U.S.C. § 591 (1970), as amended (Supp.II 1972).

director) may also be criminally liable for such conduct. Two kinds of statute are relevant to the potential criminal liability of officers and directors.

1. The first type of statute makes corporate managers criminally liable for unlawful corporate acts if the managers themselves performed or caused the performance of the act. An example is N.Y.Penal Law § 20.25: "A person is criminally liable for conduct constituting an offense which he performs or causes to be performed in the name of or in behalf of a corporation to the same extent as if such conduct were performed in his own name or behalf." A highly publicized case, People v. Film Recovery Systems, Inc., Nos. 83–11091, 84–5064 (Cook County Cir.Ct. of Ill., June 14, 1985), arose under an Illinois statute comparable to N.Y.Penal Law § 20.25. Film Recovery reclaimed silver from used photographic film, through a standard process called cyanide leaching, which involves a chemical that gives off poisonous cyanide gas. The ventilation and other conditions at Film Recovery's plant were unsafe, and most of the workers spoke little English and therefore could not read the sodium-cyanide warning label. In December 1982, Stefan Golab, a Polish immigrant, began working at Film Recovery, pumping and stirring the sodium cyanide solution in large vats. In February 1983, Golab complained of headaches and nausea, and asked the plant manager, through an interpreter, to transfer him from the vats. After four more days of working at the vats, Golab died of cyanide inhalation. Film Recovery's president, plant manager, and plant foreman were found guilty of murder, and sentenced to twenty-five years. See Note, Corporations Can Kill Too: After *Film Recovery*, Are Individuals Accountable for Corporate Crime?, 19 Loy.L.A.L.Rev. 1411 (1986). In 1990, *Film Recovery* was reversed on a technical ground and remanded for a new trial. People v. O'Neil, 194 Ill.App.3d 79, 141 Ill.Dec. 44, 550 N.E.2d 1090 (1990). On remand, the individual defendants pleaded guilty to lesser charges. Two were sentenced to two years, and the third received probation.

2. A second type of statute makes managers criminally liable for the unlawful acts of employees over whom they have the power of control, even if that power was not exercised. This type of statute gives rise to the "responsible-corporate-officer doctrine." The leading case is United States v. Park, 421 U.S. 658, 95 S.Ct. 1903, 44 L.Ed.2d 489 (1975). Acme Markets, Inc., was a national retail food chain with approximately 36,000 employees, 874 retail outlets, and 16 warehouses. Park was Acme's chief executive officer. In April 1970, the FDA advised Park by letter of unsanitary conditions, including rodent infestation, in Acme's Philadelphia warehouse. In late 1971, the FDA found that similar conditions existed in the Baltimore warehouse, and in January 1972 it sent a letter to that effect. In March 1972, a second inspection of the Baltimore warehouse showed improvement in the sanitary conditions but evidence of continued rodent activity and rodent-contaminated food. The Government then brought criminal proceedings against Acme and Park on the ground that food held for sale in Acme's Baltimore warehouse was exposed to contamination by rodents, in violation of 21 U.S.C.A. § 331(k). Park testified that al-

though all of Acme's employees were in a sense under his general direction, the company had an organizational structure according to which the responsibility for different phases of its operation were assigned to individuals who, in turn, had staff and departments under them. He identified those individuals responsible for sanitation, and stated that upon receipt of the FDA's January 1972 letter, he had conferred with Acme's vice-president for legal affairs, who informed him that the vice-president of Acme's Baltimore division "was investigating the situation immediately and would be taking corrective action and would be preparing a summary of the corrective action to reply to the letter." Id. at 664, 95 S.Ct. at 1907. Park conceded that providing sanitary conditions for food offered for sale to the public was something that he was "responsible for in the entire operation of the company," but said it was one of many phases of the company that he assigned to "dependable subordinates." Id.

Park was convicted, although he had not authorized the violations and the statute did not explicitly impose criminal liability on managers based on the acts of others. The Supreme Court upheld the conviction, relying in part on an earlier case, United States v. Dotterweich:

> In [United States v. Dotterweich, 320 U.S. 277, 64 S.Ct. 134, 88 L.Ed. 48 (1943)], a jury had disagreed as to the corporation, a jobber purchasing drugs from manufacturers and shipping them in interstate commerce under its own label, but had convicted Dotterweich, the corporation's president and general manager. . . .
>
> In reversing the judgment of the Court of Appeals and reinstating Dotterweich's conviction, this Court looked to the purposes of the Act and noted that they "touch phases of the lives and health of people which, in the circumstances of modern industrialism, are largely beyond self-protection." 320 U.S., at 280. It observed that the Act is of "a now familiar type" which "dispenses with the conventional requirement for criminal conduct—awareness of some wrongdoing. In the interest of the larger good it puts the burden of acting at hazard upon a person otherwise innocent but standing in responsible relation to a public danger." Id., at 280–281. . . .
>
> At the same time, however, the Court was aware of the concern which was the motivating factor in the Court of Appeals' decision, that literal enforcement "might operate too harshly by sweeping within its condemnation any person however remotely entangled in the proscribed shipment." Id., at 284. A limiting principle, in the form of "settled doctrines of criminal law" defining those who "are responsible for the commission of a misdemeanor," was available. In this context, the Court concluded, those doctrines dictated that the offense was committed "by all who . . . have . . . a responsible share in the furtherance of the transaction which the statute outlaws." Ibid. . . .
>
> . . . [T]he Act imposes not only a positive duty to seek out and remedy violations when they occur but also, and primarily, a

duty to implement measures that will insure that violations will not occur. The requirements of foresight and vigilance imposed on responsible corporate agents are beyond question demanding, and perhaps onerous, but they are no more stringent than the public has a right to expect of those who voluntarily assume positions of authority in business enterprises whose services and products affect the health and well-being of the public that supports them. . . .

Courts have extended criminal liability under the responsible-corporate-officer doctrine to directors and officers under a broad array of federal criminal statutes, including the Federal Hazardous Substances Act, the Sherman Act, the Economic Stabilization Act of 1970, the Occupational Safety & Health Act and the Federal Water Pollution Control Act. See Webb, Molo, and Hurst, Understanding and Avoiding Corporate and Executive Criminal Liability, 49 Bus.Law 617 (1994).

Meyer v. Holley, 537 U.S. 280 (2003), limited the sweep of the responsible-corporate-officer doctrine. *Meyer* arose under the Fair Housing Act. That Act forbids racial discrimination in respect to the sale or rental of a dwelling. Triad Inc. was a real estate corporation. David Meyer, Triad's president and sole shareholder, had listed for sale a house in Twenty–Nine Palms, California. Emma and David Holley, an interracial couple, tried to unsuccessfully to buy the house. The Holleys alleged that Grove Crank, a Triad salesman, prevented them from obtaining the house for racially discriminatory reasons, and sued Crank and Triad under the Fair Housing Act. They also sued Meyer, on the ground that he was vicariously liable, as Triad's president and sole shareholder, for Crank's unlawful actions. The Ninth Circuit held that the Fair Housing Act made corporate owners and officers liable for the unlawful acts of a corporate employee simply on the basis that the owner or officer controlled or had the right to control the employee's actions of that employee. The Supreme Court reversed. The Court pointed out that under traditional principles of agency law, one person, A, is not vicariously liable for the actions of another person, B, unless B was not only under or subject to A's control, but acted for and on B's behalf. Under these traditional principles, an owner or officer of a corporation is usually not vicariously liable in those capacities because a corporate employee acts on behalf of the corporation, not an owner or an officer:

> . . . Congress said nothing in the statute or on the legislative history about extending vicarious liability in this manner. And Congress' silence, while permitting an inference that Congress intended to apply ordinary background tort principles, cannot show that it intended to apply an unusual modification of those rules. . . .

> This Court has applied unusually strict rules only where Congress has specified that such was its intent. See, e.g., United States v. Dotterweich, 320 U.S. 277, 280–281 (1943) (Congress intended that a corporate officer or employee "standing in responsible relation" could be held liable in that capacity for a

corporation's violations of the Federal Food, Drug, and Cosmetic Act, congressional intent to impose a duty on "responsible corporate agents"); United States v. Wise, 370 U.S. 405, 411–414 (1962) (discussing 38 Stat. 736, currently 15 U.S.C. § 24, which provides: "Whenever a corporation shall violate any of the ... antitrust laws, such violation shall be deemed to be also that of the individual directors, officers, or agents of such corporation who shall have authorized, ordered, or done any of the acts constituting in whole or in part such violation") . . . .

. . . [W]hich "of two innocent people must suffer," *ibid.*, and just when, is a complex matter. We believe that courts ordinarily should determine that matter in accordance with traditional principles of vicarious liability—unless, of course, Congress, better able than courts to weigh the relevant policy considerations, has instructed the courts differently. Cf., *e.g.*, Sykes, the Economics of Vicarious Liability, 93 Yale L.J. 1231, 1236 (1984) (arguing that the expansion of vicarious liability or shifting of liability, due to insurance, may diminish an agent's incentives to police behavior). We have found no different instruction here.

SECTION 3.   DIRECTORS' AND OFFICERS' LIABILITY INSURANCE

FORM OF DIRECTORS' AND OFFICERS' LIABILITY INSURANCE

[See Statutory Supplement]

NOTE ON DIRECTORS' AND OFFICERS' LIABILITY INSURANCE

1. The liability and legal expenses of directors and officers who are the subject of claims based on a lack of due care, and for certain other wrongful acts, will often be covered by Directors' and Officers' ("D & O") Liability Insurance. Among approximately 2,049 U.S. participants in the Towers Perrin 2004 Directors and Officers Liability Survey, 99% reported purchasing D & O insurance. D & O insurance is commonly referred to as—and often captioned—"liability" insurance, because it insures against liability and legal expenses. Technically, however, D & O is indemnification insurance, because it does not require the insurer to defend (although it does require the insurer to indemnify for losses, including defense costs), and the insurer's obligations do not accrue until the claim is settled or adjudicated. See J. Bishop, The Law of Corporate Officers and Directors–Indemnification and Insurance § 8.05 (G. O'Gradney rev. 1994).

2. Typically, a D & O policy has two separate insurance agreements: (i) Corporate reimbursement, which insures the corporation against potential liability to officers and directors under the latters' right to indemnification from the corporation. (ii) Personal coverage, which insures the directors and officers themselves against losses based on claims against them for wrongful conduct when they are not indemnified for the loss by the corporation. There are various reasons why a director or officer may not be indemnified for such a loss by the corporation. For example, the law may prohibit such indemnification, as where the director's or officer's loss consists of a judgment against him in a duty-of-care action. Or the corporation may be insolvent, or it may refuse to make indemnification in a case where indemnification is discretionary rather than mandatory.

The precise scope of the personal coverage varies according to the policy form, but all policies would normally cover most liabilities arising in connection with claims based on a violation of the duty of care owed to the corporation, and many or most policies would normally cover liabilities for duties of care owed to the general public, barring either a specific exclusion in the insurance policy or a prohibition of public policy.

3. D & O insurance does not render directors and officers completely risk-free with regard to claims based on the duty of care. To begin with, a variety of claims are excluded from coverage, and some kinds of duty-of-care claims may fall within an exclusion, particularly claims owed to the public. Next, the policy limits in D & O insurance typically apply to the combined amount of liability and legal expenses, and in any given case the combination of the two may exceed the policy limit. See Helfand v. National Union Fire Ins. Co., 10 Cal.App.4th 869, 13 Cal.Rptr.2d 295 (1992). Furthermore, many D & O policies contain an "insured v. insured" exclusion, under which the insurer is not liable in connection with claims made against a director or officer by the corporation, except a claim made in a shareholder's derivative action (that is, a claim made by a shareholder on the corporation's behalf).

Another characteristic of D & O insurance that may be relevant to the protection afforded by such insurance is that such insurance is written on a "claims made" basis—that is, the insurance applies to, but only to, claims made while the policy is in force. To illustrate, suppose C Corporation procured a D & O policy from X Insurance Company for 2004. A *claim* made in 2004 that is based on events that occurred in 2003 may be covered by the 2004 policy even though X was not C's insurer in 2003. Conversely, however, a claim in 2005 based on *events* that occurred in 2004 may not be covered by the policy if the claim is not made before the 2004 policy expires or is canceled, unless a new 2005 policy is in effect or some exception applies.

The claims-made nature of D & O insurance is often modified by several features. First, a policy may contain a "retroactive date" provision, under which events occurring before a designated date will not be covered by the policy even if a claim based on the events is first made during the policy period. Second, a policy may include a right of "discovery," which allows an insured to extend the coverage for a claim made during a limited period after the policy has terminated, provided the claim is based on wrongful acts that occurred prior to termination of the policy. In addition, many policies permit an insured to present a notice of occurrence of a possible claim during the policy period, which has the same effect as an actual claim made against the insured. Subject to these exceptions, an effect of the claims-made nature of D & O insurance is that a director or officer cannot be positive that he will be covered for his present conduct if a claim concerning that conduct arises in the future, after the policy has expired or has been canceled.

Another factor that affects the risk of a director or officer for duty-of-care liability is that D & O insurers often seem to be exceptionally ready to litigate claims brought against them by their insureds. Some of the litigation concerns the interpretation of the policy language, which is often less than crystal clear. In addition, partly because D & O insurance is on a claims-made basis, the corporation and the directors and officers who are to be covered under a D & O policy must fill out extensive application questionnaires, which include questions on such issues as whether the applicant has knowledge or information of any act, error, or omission that might give rise to a claim under the policy. It is often easy for an insurer to argue that the policy is unenforceable on the ground that the questionnaire was not answered accurately. Furthermore, unless the policy has a provision to the contrary, the failure of only one director or officer to answer accurately may invalidate the coverage of all officers and directors. See, e.g., Bird v. Penn Central Co., 334 F.Supp. 255 (E.D.Pa.1971), 341 F.Supp. 291 (1972); Shapiro v. American Home Assurance Co., 584 F.Supp. 1245 (D.Mass.1984).

4.   In another recent development, the settlements in two high-profile cases, involving Enron and WorldCom, required directors to pay money out of their own pockets and not to seek reimbursement from the corporation's D&O insurance. In WorldCom, the directors were required to pay a total of $18 million out of their own pockets; each director was required to pay 20% of the director's net worth (with certain exclusions, such as primary residences). See WorldCom Ex-Directors Pony Up, Wall St. J. January 6, 2005, at p. A3. In Enron, the directors agreed to pay $13 million out of their own pockets. See Ex-Directors at Enron Chip In On Settlement, N.Y. Times, January 8, 2005, Section 2, p. 1.

CHAPTER IX

THE DUTY OF LOYALTY

SECTION 1. SELF-INTERESTED TRANSACTIONS

Marsh, Are Directors Trustees?—Conflicts of Interest and Corporate Morality

22 Bus.Law. 35, 36–43 (1966).

a. *Prohibition.*

In 1880 it could have been stated with confidence that in the United States the general rule was that any contract between a director and his corporation was voidable at the instance of the corporation or its shareholders, without regard to the fairness or unfairness of the transaction. This rule was stated in powerful terms by a number of highly regarded courts and judges in cases which arose generally out of the railroad frauds of the 1860's and 1870's....

Under this rule it mattered not the slightest that there was a majority of so-called disinterested directors who approved the contract. The courts stated that the corporation was entitled to the unprejudiced judgment and advice of all of its directors and therefore it did no good to say that the interested director did not participate in the making of the contract on behalf of the corporation. "... the very words in which he asserts his right declare his wrong; he ought to have participated...."[1] Furthermore, the courts said that it was impossible to measure the influence which one director might have over his associates, even though ostensibly abstaining from participation in the discussion or vote. "... a corporation, in order to defeat a contract entered into by directors, in which one or more of them had a private interest, is not bound to show that the influence of the director or directors having the private interest determined the action of the board. The law cannot accurately measure the influence of a trustee with his associates, nor will it enter into the inquiry...."[2]

Perhaps the strongest reason for this inflexibility of the law was given by the Maryland Supreme Court which stated that, when a contract is made with even one of the directors, "the remaining directors are placed in the embarrassing and invidious position of having to pass upon, scrutinize and check the transactions and accounts of one of their *own body, with* whom they are associated on

---

1. Stewart v. Lehigh Valley R.R. Co., 38 N.J.Law 505, at 523 (Ct.Err. & App.1875).

2. Munson v. Syracuse, G. & C. Ry. Co., 103 N.Y. 58, at 74, 8 N.E. 355, at 358 (1886).

terms of equality in the general management of all the affairs of the corporation."[3] Or, as Justice Davies of the New York Supreme Court expressed the same thought: "The moment the directors permit one or more of their number to deal with the property of the stockholders, they surrender their own independence and self control."[4]

This rule applied not only to individual contracts with directors, but also to the situation of interlocking directorates where even a minority of the boards were common to the two contracting corporations. Not only that, it was also applied to the situation where one corporation owned a majority of the stock of another and appointed its directors, even though they might not be the same men as sat on the board of the parent corporation. . . .

This principle, absolutely inhibiting contracts between a corporation and its directors or any of them, appeared to be impregnable in 1880. It was stated in ringing terms by virtually every decided case, with arguments which seemed irrefutable, and it was sanctioned by age. As Justice Davies stated:

> To hold otherwise, would be to overturn principles of equity which have been regarded as well settled since the days of Lord Keeper Bridgman, in the 22nd of Charles Second, to the present time—principles enunciated and enforced by Hardwicke, Thurlow, Loughborough, Eldon, Cranworth, Story and Kent, and which the highest courts in our country have declared to be founded on immutable truth and justice, and to stand upon our great moral obligation to refrain from placing ourselves in relations which excite a conflict between self interest and integrity.

Thirty years later this principle was dead.

b. *Approval by a disinterested majority of the board.*

It could have been stated with reasonable confidence in 1910 that the general rule was that a contract between a director and his corporation was valid if it was approved by a disinterested majority of his fellow directors and was not found to be unfair or fraudulent by the court if challenged; but that a contract in which a majority of the board was interested was voidable at the instance of the corporation or its shareholders without regard to any question of fairness.

One searches in vain in the decided cases for a reasoned defense of this change in legal philosophy, or for the slightest attempt to refute the powerful arguments which had been made in support of the previous rule. Did the courts discover in the last quarter of the Nineteenth Century that greed was no longer a factor in human conduct? If so, they did not share the basis of this discovery with the public; nor did they humbly admit their error when confronted with the next wave of corporate frauds arising out of the era of the formation of the "trusts" during the 1890's and early 1900's. . . .

---

3. Cumberland Coal and Iron Co. v. Parish, 42 Md. 598, at 606 (1875).

4. Cumberland Coal and Iron Co. v. Sherman, 30 Barb. 553, at 573 (N.Y.Sup.Ct. 1859).

The only explanation which seems to have been given for this change in position was the technical one that a trustee, while forbidden to deal with himself in connection with the trust property, could deal directly with the cestui que trust if he made full disclosure and took no unfair advantage; and that the case of a director who abstained from representing the corporation but dealt in his personal capacity with a majority of disinterested directors was properly analogized to a trustee dealing with the cestui que trust. As the Texas court said:[5]

> . . . we think it is not true that one who holds the position of director is incapable, under all circumstances, of divesting himself of his representative character in a particular transaction, and dealing with the corporation through others competent to represent it, as other trustees may deal directly with the beneficiaries. . . . [T]he company is represented by those who alone can act for it, and, if they are disinterested, he can, we think, deal with them as any other trustee can deal with the cestui que trust, if he makes a full disclosure of all facts known to him about the subject, takes no advantage of his position, deals honestly and openly, and concludes a contract fair and beneficial to the company.

But in no case is there any discussion or attempted refutation of the reasons previously given by the courts as to why it is impossible, in such a situation, for any director to be disinterested. Some courts seem simply to admit that the practice has grown too widespread for them to cope with. In *South Side Trust Co. v. Washington Tin Plate Co.* the Supreme Court of Pennsylvania said:[6] "The interests of corporations are sometimes so interwoven that it is desirable to have joint representatives in their respective managements, and at any rate it is a not uncommon and [therefore?] not unlawful practice." . . .

Under the rule that a disinterested majority of the directors must approve a transaction with one of their number, the question arose whether this meant a disinterested quorum (i.e., normally a majority of the whole board) or merely a disinterested majority of a quorum, so that the interested director or directors could be counted to make up the quorum. Virtually all of the cases held that the interested director could not be counted for quorum purposes. As the California court said, the interested director for this purpose was "as much a stranger to the board as if he had never been elected a director. . . . "[7]

c. *Judicial review of the fairness of the transaction.*

By 1960 it could be said with some assurance that the general rule was that no transaction of a corporation with any or all of its directors was automatically voidable at the suit of a shareholder, whether there was a disinterested majority of the board or not; but that the courts

---

5. Tenison v. Patton, 95 Tex. 284, at 292–93, 67 S.W. 92, at 95 (1902).

6. 252 Pa. 237 at 241, 97 A. 450 at 451 (1916).

7. Curtis v. Salmon River Hydraulic Gold–Mining & Dutch Co., . . . 10 Cal. at 349, 62 P. at 554.

would review such a contract and subject it to rigid and careful scrutiny, and would invalidate the contract if it was found to be unfair to the corporation. . . .

———

Lewis v. S.L. & E., Inc.

United States Court of Appeals, Second Circuit, 1980.
629 F.2d 764.

■ Before TIMBERS and KEARSE, CIRCUIT JUDGES, and LASKER, DISTRICT JUDGE.

■ KEARSE, CIRCUIT JUDGE:

This case arises out of an intra-family dispute over the management of two closely-held affiliated corporations. Plaintiff Donald E. Lewis ("Donald"), a shareholder of S.L. & E., Inc. ("SLE"), appeals from judgments entered against him in the United States District Court for the Western District of New York, Harold P. Burke, Judge, after a bench trial of his derivative claim against directors of SLE, and of a claim asserted against him by the other corporation, Lewis General Tires, Inc. ("LGT"), which intervened in the suit. The defendants Alan E. Lewis ("Alan"), Leon E. Lewis, Jr. ("Leon, Jr."), and Richard E. Lewis ("Richard"), are the brothers of Donald; they were, at pertinent times herein, directors of SLE and officers, directors and shareholders of LGT. Donald charged that his brothers had wasted the assets of SLE by causing SLE to lease business premises to LGT from 1966 to 1972 at an unreasonably low rental. LGT was permitted to intervene in the action, and filed a complaint seeking specific performance of an agreement by Donald to sell his SLE stock to LGT in 1972. The district court held that Donald had failed to prove waste by the defendant directors, and entered judgment in their favor. The court also awarded attorneys' fees to the defendant directors and to SLE, and granted LGT specific performance of Donald's agreement to sell his SLE stock.

On appeal, Donald argues that the district court improperly allocated to him the burden of proving his claims of waste, and that since defendants failed to prove that the transactions in question were fair and reasonable, he was entitled to judgment. Donald also argues that the awards of attorneys' fees were improper. We agree with each of these contentions, and therefore reverse and remand.

I

For many years Leon Lewis, Sr., the father of Donald and the defendant directors, was the principal shareholder of SLE and LGT. LGT, formed in 1933, operated a tire dealership in Rochester, New York. SLE, formed in 1943, owned the land and complex of buildings at 260 East Avenue in Rochester. This property was SLE's only significant asset. Prior to 1956 LGT occupied SLE's premises without benefit of a lease; the rent paid was initially $200 per month, and had increased over the years to $800 per month by 1956, when additional parcels were added. On February 28, 1956, SLE granted LGT a 10–year lease on the newly expanded property ("the Property"), for a rent of $1200 per month, or $14,400 per year. Under the terms of the lease, SLE was responsible for payment of real estate taxes on the Property, while all other current expenses were to be borne by the tenant, LGT.[1]

In 1962, Leon Lewis, Sr., transferred his SLE stock, 90 shares in all, to his six children (defendants Richard, Alan and Leon, Jr., plaintiff Donald, and two daughters, Margaret and Carol), giving 15 shares to each.[2] At that time Richard, Alan and Leon, Jr., were already shareholders, officers and directors of LGT. Contemporaneously with their receipt of SLE stock, all six of the children entered into a "shareholders' agreement" with LGT, under which each child who was not a shareholder of LGT on June 1, 1972 would be required to sell his or her SLE shares to LGT, within 30 days of that date, at a price equal to the book value of the SLE stock as of June 1, 1972.[3]

LGT's lease on the SLE property expired on February 28, 1966. At that time the directors of SLE were Richard, Alan, Leon, Jr., Leon, Sr., and Henry Etsberger; these five were also the directors of LGT. In 1966 Alan owned 44% of LGT, Richard owned 30%, Leon, Jr., owned 19%, and Leon, Sr., owned 7%. From 1967 to 1972 Richard owned 61% of LGT and Leon, Jr., owned the remaining 39%. When the lease expired in 1966, no new lease was entered into. LGT nonetheless continued to occupy the property and to pay SLE at the old rate, $14,400 per year. According to the defendants' testimony at trial, there was never any thought or discussion among the SLE directors of entering into a new lease or of increasing the rent. Richard testified: "We never gave consideration to a new lease." From all that appears, the defendant directors viewed SLE as existing purely for the benefit of LGT. Richard testified, for example, that although real estate taxes rose sharply during the period 1966–1971, from approximately $7,800 to more than $11,000, to be paid by SLE out of its constant $14,400 rental income, raising the rent was never mentioned. He testified that SLE was "only a shell to protect the operating company [LGT]." When this suit was commenced there had not been a formal meeting of either the shareholders or the directors of SLE since 1962. Richard, Alan and Leon, Jr., had largely ignored SLE's separate corporate existence[4] and disregarded the fact that SLE had shareholders who

---

1. It appears that SLE was also responsible for payments due on a mortgage on the Property. In addition, LGT charged SLE for the costs of certain capital improvements, such as the major structural repairs to the principal building's facade, carried out in 1969.

2. SLE had 150 shares outstanding, and each child thus received a ten percent interest. At the same time LGT purchased the remaining 60 outstanding shares from the elder Lewis's business partner, Henry Etsberger.

3. The agreement specified procedures by which the book value, and hence the price of the shares, would be determined.

4. For example, Richard's testimony includes the following statements:

Q Mr. Lewis, you have always looked at these two corporations as being one and the same, haven't you, Lewis General Tires and S.L. & E.?

A Yes.

* * *

I never really got into S.L. & E. at all. (Tr. 6/21/78, at 972–73.)

* * *

I don't think I ever looked at an operating statement of S.L. & E. seriously. (*Id.* at 991.)

were not shareholders of LGT and who therefore could not profit from actions that used SLE solely for the benefit of LGT.

Neither Donald nor his sisters ever owned LGT stock. As the June 1972 date approached for the required sale of their SLE stock to LGT, Donald apparently came to believe that SLE's book value was lower than it should have been. He sought SLE financial information from Richard, who had been president of SLE since 1967.[5] Richard refused to provide information. Donald therefore refused to sell his SLE shares in 1972,[6] and commenced this shareholders' derivative action in the district court in August 1973, basing jurisdiction on diversity of citizenship. The sole claim raised in the complaint was that the defendant directors had wasted the assets of SLE by "grossly undercharging" LGT for the latter's occupancy and use of the Property. Although the complaint charged such mismanagement for the period 1962 to 1973, plaintiff subsequently limited this claim to the period between February 28, 1966, the date on which the lease expired,[7] and June 1, 1972, the date contractually set for valuation of the SLE shares which plaintiff had agreed to sell to LGT. LGT intervened and demanded specific performance of Donald's agreement to sell his SLE stock. Donald did not contest his ultimate obligation to sell, but took the position that since the book value of the shares would be increased if he prevailed on his derivative claim, specific performance should be granted only after adjudication of that claim.

There ensured an eight-day bench trial, at which plaintiff sought to prove, by the testimony of several expert witnesses, that the fair rental value of the Property was greater than the $14,400 per year that SLE had been paid by LGT. Defendants sought to show that the rental paid was reasonable, by offering evidence concerning the financial straits of LGT, the cost to LGT of operating the Property, the general economic decline of the East Avenue neighborhood, and rentals paid on two other properties in that neighborhood. LGT presented expert testimony that the value of plaintiff's stock as of June 1972, assuming a successful defense of the derivative claims, was $15,650.

The district court subsequently filed lengthy and detailed findings of fact and conclusions of law. Many of the court's findings went to the validity and probative value of the testimony given by plaintiff's expert witnesses, and the court ultimately declined to credit that testimony. On this basis, the court held that Donald had failed to establish the rental value of the Property during the period at issue, and that

* * *

I had very little to do with S.L. & E. (Tr. 7/28/78, at 80.)

Alan testified that at no time after 1964 did he participate in any discussions of any increase in rent for SLE. (*Id.* at 160, 164.)

And Leon, Jr., testified, "I didn't have anything to do with running S.L. & E...." (*Id.* at 230.)

5. It does not appear that SLE paid salaries to any of its officers or directors.

6. Donald's sisters Carol and Margaret sold their SLE shares to LGT in 1972 and 1973 respectively. Alan, who had sold his LGT stock in 1967, sold his SLE stock to LGT in 1972.

7. Donald was not a shareholder of SLE in 1956 when the lease was entered into and hence had no standing to challenge its terms. BCL § 626(b); *Bernstein v. Polo Fashions, Inc.*, 55 A.D.2d 530, 389 N.Y.S.2d 368 (1st Dep't 1976).

defendants were therefore entitled to judgment on the derivative claims. Implicit in the district court's ruling, granting judgment for defendants upon plaintiff's failure to prove waste, was a determination that plaintiff bore the burden of proof on that issue. The court also ruled that LGT was entitled to specific performance of Donald's agreement to sell his SLE stock, and that Donald was not entitled to recover attorneys' fees from SLE, but that SLE and the individual defendants were entitled to attorneys' fees from Donald. This appeal followed.

II

Turning first to the question of burden of proof, we conclude that the district court erred in placing upon plaintiff the burden of proving waste. Because the directors of SLE were also officers, directors and/or shareholders of LGT, the burden was on the defendant directors to demonstrate that the transactions between SLE and LGT were fair and reasonable. New York Business Corporation Law ("BCL") § 713(b) (McKinney Supp.1979) (eff. September 1, 1971); BCL § 713(a)(3) (McKinney 1963) (repealed as of September 1, 1971); *see Cohen v. Ayers,* 596 F.2d 733, 739–40 (7th Cir.1979) (construing current BCL § 713); *Remillard Brick Co. v. Remillard–Dandini Co.,* 109 Cal. App.2d 405, 241 P.2d 66, 75 (1952) (construing California Corporations Code § 820, upon which the prior BCL § 713 was patterned).

Under normal circumstances the directors of a corporation may determine, in the exercise of their business judgment, what contracts the corporation will enter into and what consideration is adequate, without review of the merits of their decisions by the courts. The business judgment rule places a heavy burden on shareholders who would attack corporate transactions. *Galef v. Alexander,* 615 F.2d 51, 57–58 (2d Cir.1980); *Auerbach v. Bennett,* 47 N.Y.2d 619, 629, 419 N.Y.S.2d 920, 926, 393 N.E.2d 994, 1000 (1979); 3A Fletcher, *Cyclopedia of the Law of Private Corporations* § 1039 (perm. ed. 1975). But the business judgment rule presupposes that the directors have no conflict of interest. When a shareholder attacks a transaction in which the directors have an interest other than as directors of the corporation, the directors may not escape review of the merits of the transaction. At common law such a transaction was voidable unless shown by its proponent to be fair, and reasonable to the corporation.[11] BCL § 713, in both its current and its prior versions, carries forward this common law principle, and provides special rules for scrutiny of a transaction between the corporation and an entity in which its directors are directors or officers or have a substantial financial interest. . . .

The current version of § 713,* which became effective on September 1, 1971, and governs at least so much of the dealing between SLE

---

11. *E.g., Geddes v. Anaconda Copper Co.,* 254 U.S. 590, 599, 41 S.Ct. 209, 65 L.Ed. 425 (1921). . . .

* See New York Bus.Corp.Law § 713 in the Statutory Supplement. (Footnote by ed.)

and LGT as occurred after that date, expressly provides that a contract between a corporation and an entity in which its directors are interested may be set aside unless the proponent of the contract "shall establish affirmatively that the contract or transaction was fair and reasonable as to the corporation at the time it was approved by the board...." § 713(b). Thus when the transaction is challenged in a derivative action against the interested directors, they have the burden of proving that the transaction was fair and reasonable to the corporation. *Cohen v. Ayers, supra.*

The same was true under the predecessor to § 713(b), former § 713(a)(3), which was in effect prior to September 1, 1971....

During the entire period 1966–1972, Richard, Alan and Leon, Jr., were directors of both SLE and LGT;[14] there were no SLE directors who were not also directors of LGT. Richard, Alan and Leon, Jr., were all shareholders of LGT in 1966, and from 1967 to 1972 Richard and Leon, Jr., were the sole shareholders of LGT. Under BCL § 713, therefore, Richard, Alan and Leon, Jr., had the burden of proving that $14,400 was a fair and reasonable annual rent for the SLE property for the period February 28, 1966 through June 1, 1972.

Our review of the record convinces us that defendants failed to carry their burden. At trial, there was no direct testimony as to what would have been a fair rental during the relevant period, *i.e.*, 1966 to 1972, and the evidence that was introduced fell far short of establishing that $14,400 was a fair annual rental value for those years.

Quite clearly Richard, Alan and Leon, Jr., had made no effort to determine contemporaneously what rental would be fair during the years 1966–1972. Their view was that the rent should simply cover expenses and that SLE existed for the benefit of LGT.[15] During this period no appraisals were made; no attempts were made to sell or rent the Property; no thought whatever was given to whether $14,400 was a fair and reasonable rent even when real estate taxes had risen to consume nearly all of that amount.

Defendants offered instead evidence of rents paid on other properties. Among their best evidence was the expert testimony of Harvey Rosenbloom, a real estate appraiser. Rosenbloom testified that two other East Avenue buildings, which the district court found to be comparable to the 260 East Avenue premises, were leased at lower per-square-foot rentals than was paid by LGT to SLE. However, as to one of these properties, Rosenbloom testified only to rent paid in 1973 and 1974, and did not consider the 1966–1972 period. As to the other property, Rosenbloom described a fifteen year lease that was entered into in 1961. This testimony, while perhaps not wholly irrelevant to the issues in this suit, fell far short of demonstrating what rental the Property could have fetched in 1966, or in any other of the relevant years. Indeed, Rosenbloom himself testified that rental value

---

14. Alan ceased to be a director in November 1972; Leon, Jr., ceased to be a director in 1977. Richard remains a director.

15. *See* footnote 4 *supra*, and accompanying text.

could well be different for each year of the period. Thus, rentals that Rosenbloom testified were agreed to in 1961 or 1973 might well have been unfair in 1966 or 1967. This evidence thus could not support a finding that defendants acted fairly in maintaining an annual rental of $14,400 during the years from 1966 to 1972.[16]

Defendants also produced considerable evidence that over the relevant period, the East End neighborhood had been on an economic decline; that businesses had been leaving the area; that urban renewal projects and increased crime had depressed property values there; and that the area had, in general, become a less desirable place to do business. There was also evidence of specific developments that had an adverse effect on the Property: for example, the street running along one side of the Property was made a one-way street, thus limiting customers' access to LGT's premises. The district court credited all of this testimony, and it is fair to say that defendants proved that there was a general downward trend in the value of the Property. However, as noted above, defendants did not establish what was a fair rental value for the Property in 1966. Absent such a point of reference, a general downward trend in value is of no assistance in determining whether the rental actually paid was fair and reasonable during the ensuing years.

Moreover, working in reverse, some of defendants' own evidence as to the value of the Property at the end of the relevant period suggested that $14,400 was less than a fair rental in 1966, and that the figure of $38,099, estimated by plaintiff's expert, was perhaps not far off the mark.[17] First, there was a variety of evidence suggesting that in 1972 the Property was worth more than $200,000. An appraisal by defense witness Harold Grunert in 1972 set the fair market value of the Property as of June 30, 1972, at $220,000. In 1972 Leon, Jr., had offered personally to buy the Property for $200,000, an offer which Richard had rejected.[18] And in 1971, Richard had informed Donald that evaluations by another appraiser, Harold Galloway, had set the value of the Property at $200,000 and $236,000. Second, defendants' expert witness Rosenbloom, asked what he would consider a fair rent for the property, given Grunert's 1972 valuation of $220,000, stated that ten percent of the value would be inadequate and that fifteen to seventeen percent would be closer to adequate. Fifteen percent of $220,000 would have yielded a rent of $33,000 on the basis of the 1972 valuation. Grunert's own expert testimony was entirely consistent with this. While he had made no estimate as to the fair rental value of the property for 1966–1972, he opined that a fair rental as of June 30, 1972, would be $20–21,000 with the tenant paying all expenses

16. Defendant Richard E. Lewis testified that defendants tried, without success, to sell the Property in 1975, listing it with a realtor for $200,000. In addition he testified that an effort was made to rent the Property in 1973, and that only one offer, for $700 per month, was forthcoming. Since these efforts were made in 1973 and 1975, this evidence, like the evidence as to rentals of other property, was too remote in time to establish a fair rental value, especially as to the earlier years of the 1966–1972 period.

17. Plaintiff's expert made his evaluation as of February 1973. He did not make any evaluation for the period 1966–1972.

18. Leon, Jr., had just been fired from LGT by Richard.

including real estate taxes. According to Richard, SLE's real estate taxes in 1972 were about $12,000. Thus Grunert's testimony, too, suggests about $33,000 as the fair rental value in 1972. Finally, consistent with their view of the general downward economic trend, Richard and Alan conceded that, whatever the Property was worth in 1972, it was worth more in 1966.[19] Thus the evidence presented by defendants, far from carrying their burden of showing that $14,400 was a fair and reasonable annual rental in 1966–1972, suggested that the fair rental value of the Property throughout that period exceeded $33,000 per year.

The defendants argued, however, that LGT could not have afforded to pay SLE rent higher than $14,400. They produced evidence designed to show that LGT had made little profit; that this low profitability was due to the expenses of maintenance and upkeep of the 260 East Avenue property; and that LGT therefore would not have been able to pay a higher rent to SLE. The district court credited this evidence, finding that LGT had "experienced a number of years of very severe losses," that during the period from 1962–1973, LGT's overall profit was only $53,876, and that payment of rent at the rate of $39,099 per year during this period could have led to the "demise" of LGT. These findings have only a distorted relationship to this lawsuit.

The period in issue here is 1966–1972. The only "severe" losses shown, totaling nearly $83,000, occurred in 1963 and 1973. Their inclusion in the computation of what LGT could afford to pay in 1966–1972 was patently unfair. In fact LGT's only unprofitable year during the period in issue was 1969 when its loss was small: $1,168. LGT's after-tax profits in 1966–1972 in fact totaled $102,963, or an average of $14,709 per year. Thus, even on paper, LGT could have "afforded" to double its rent payments to SLE during the period in question.

Moreover, the proposition that LGT could not afford to pay as rent more than what its own books showed as profits ignores the fact that LGT was owned and managed by members of the Lewis family, some of whom were also employees of that corporation. It is entirely possible that these family members granted to themselves unusually high salaries or other perquisites, thus reducing LGT's paper profits. For example, in 1966 Richard's salary was approximately $21,000; Leon, Jr.'s compensation was $3,000 salary plus commissions. In 1967, LGT acquired all of Alan's LGT stock; and Richard and Leon, Jr., acquired all of the LGT stock of their father, agreeing to pay the purchase price over a ten-year period. Richard and Leon, Jr., thus became LGT's only shareholders, and their LGT salaries were immediately increased by a total of $23,000 per year (Richard's salary went from $21,000 to $36,000; Leon, Jr.'s went from $3,000 to $11,000), to cover the cost of the LGT stock they had just acquired.[20] Defendants bore the burden of proof on the question of a fair and reasonable

---

19. Leon, Jr., did not know whether the value had decreased from 1966 to 1972, but did not believe it had risen.

20. Richard had no doubt he could have paid for his newly acquired shares without the increase in his LGT salary. Leon, Jr., apparently lacked other resources from which to pay for the LGT stock (at least after he was fired from LGT in 1972).

rental; if they would rely on the proposition that LGT was unable to pay more, it was incumbent on them to demonstrate the fairness of the management and the reasonableness of the conduct of LGT's affairs. It does not appear that they made any effort to do so.

Finally, even if we were to assume that LGT's financial records provided a fair basis for evaluating the SLE–LGT transactions, defendants would not have carried their burden of proof. Defendants did not demonstrate that SLE could not have found some other tenant, stronger financially than LGT, which would have been willing and able to pay a higher rental. Even given the general downward trend of the East Avenue neighborhood, it is entirely possible that at least during the early years of the 1966–1972 period, such a tenant might have been secured. No effort was made during that period to rent to anyone other than LGT.

We conclude, therefore, that defendants failed to prove that the rental paid by LGT to SLE for the years 1966–1972 was fair and reasonable. Thus, Donald is not required to sell his SLE shares to LGT without such upward adjustment in the June 1, 1972, book value of SLE as may be necessary to reflect the amount by which the fair rental value of the Property exceeded $14,400 in any of the years 1966–1972. . . .

We remand to the district court (a) for the entry of judgment in favor of SLE against Richard, Alan and Leon, Jr., jointly and severally, in such amount as the district court shall determine to be equal to the amounts by which the annual fair rental value of the Property exceeded $14,400 in the period February 28, 1966–June 1, 1972, (b) for an accounting as to the value of Donald's SLE shares as of June 1, 1972, in light of such judgment, (c) for an order, following such accounting, of specific performance of the shareholders' agreement, and (d) for such other proceedings as are not inconsistent with this opinion.

NOTE ON REMEDIES FOR VIOLATION OF THE DUTY OF LOYALTY

The traditional remedies for violation of the duty of loyalty are restitutionary in nature. For example, if a director has engaged in improper self-dealing with the corporation, normally the remedy is rescission—or, if rescission is not feasible, an accounting for the difference between the contract price and a fair price. Similarly, if an officer has improperly appropriated a corporate opportunity (see Section 4, infra), normally the remedy is to impose a constructive trust in the corporation's favor, conditioned on reimbursement by the corporation of the officer's outlay in acquiring the opportunity.

The result of this restitutionary theory of remedies is that as a practical matter the legal sanctions for violation of the duty of loyalty are usually, although not invariably, much less severe than the legal sanctions for violation of the duty of care. If D, a director or officer, violates his duty of care, he must pay damages although he made no gain from his wrongful action. This leaves D much worse off than he was before the wrong. In contrast, if D violates his duty of fair dealing, under a restitutionary remedy he need only return a gain to which he was not entitled in the first place. This simply places D where he was before committing the wrong.

Indeed, putting aside important nonlegal remedies, such as discharge and damage to reputation, if a director or officer, D, is totally immoral, he would conclude that under a strictly restitutionary regime it normally paid him to engage in a course of wrongful self-interested transactions. Some of the transactions may remain undiscovered. Where D's wrongdoing is not discovered, he will retain his wrongful gains. Where D's wrongdoing is discovered, he will only be required to surrender his wrongful gains. If D engages in enough transactions, he will come out ahead.

In some cases, however, the remedies for violation of the duty of loyalty may make the director or officer worse off than he was before the wrong. For example:

(i) Where the director or officer sells property to the corporation at an unfairly high price, and the value of the property later drops below its fair value at the time of the transaction, rescission may leave him worse off than if he had sold the property to a third party. For instance, suppose that in 2005, D sells property to his corporation at $110,000 when it had a fair value of $100,000. In 2006, the corporation discovers the wrong and rescinds. Meanwhile, the market has fallen and the property is only worth $70,000. If D had sold the property for $100,000 to a third party, the third party would not be able to rescind. Thus D is $30,000 worse off than if he had not engaged in wrongful self-dealing. A comparable result may obtain where D buys property from the corporation, the market rises, and the corporation rescinds.

(ii) A director or officer who violates the duty of fair dealing may be required to repay the corporation any salary he earned during the relevant period in addition to making restitution of his wrongful gain. This remedy was granted, for example, in American Timber & Trading Co. v. Niedermeyer, 276 Or. 1135, 558 P.2d 1211 (1976), a case in which the fiduciary had depleted the corporation's assets by a series of unfair deals. The court there said:

> The remedy of restoration of compensation is an equitable principle and its applicability is dependent upon the individual facts of each case.... The general rule, however, is that a corporate officer who engages in activities which constitute either a breach of his duty of loyalty or a willful breach of his contract of employment is not entitled to any compensation for services rendered during that period of time even though part of those services may have been properly performed....

(iii) Courts have sometimes awarded punitive damages against directors or officers who have breached their duty of loyalty. See, e.g.,

Holden v. Construction Machinery Co., 202 N.W.2d 348 (Iowa 1972); Rowen v. Le Mars Mutual Insurance Co. of Iowa, 282 N.W.2d 639, 662 (Iowa 1979). In Goben v. Barry, 234 Kan. 721, 728, 676 P.2d 90, 97–98 (1984), the court said, "Punitive damages may be awarded in the trial court's discretion whenever there is proof of fraud. . . . Fraud itself is difficult to define, but it has been held [that] fraud 'in its general sense, is deemed to comprise anything calculated to deceive, including all acts, omissions, and concealments involving a breach of legal or equitable duty, trust, or confidence justly reposed, resulting in damage to another. . . .' Barry [the defendant] concealed his withdrawals [from the company], denied Goben [the plaintiff] had any interest in the company and ousted him, all to Goben's damage. That is sufficient evidence of fraud. The trial court did not err in awarding punitive damages."

(iv) ALI, Principles of Corporate Governance § 7.18(d) provides that a director or officer who violates the duty of fair dealing should normally be required to pay the counsel fees and other expenses incurred by the corporation in establishing the violation.

Talbot v. James

Supreme Court of South Carolina, 1972.
259 S.C. 73, 190 S.E.2d 759.

■ Moss, CHIEF JUSTICE:

This equitable action was brought by C.N. Talbot and Lula E. Talbot, appellants herein, against W.A. James, individually, and as President of Chicora Apartments, Inc., and Chicora Apartments, Inc., respondents herein, for an accounting. In the complaint it is alleged that W.A. James, as an officer and director of the Corporation, violated his fiduciary relationship to the Corporation and the appellants as stockholders thereof, by diverting specific funds to himself.

The respondents, by answer, denied the allegations of the complaint and alleged that W.A. James had received no funds from the Corporation except for the sums paid for the erection of Chicora Apartments, pursuant to a contract between Chicora Apartments, Inc., and the said W.A. James.

The case was referred to the Master in Equity for Horry County, who after taking the testimony, filed a report in which he found that W.A. James was not entitled to general overhead expense and profits arising out of the construction contract with Chicora Apartments, Inc., and recommended judgment in favor of Chicora Apartments, Inc., against him in the amount of $25,025.31.

The respondents timely appealed from the recommendations contained in the Report of the Master. The appeal was heard by the Honorable Dan F. Laney, Jr., presiding judge, and he issued his order reversing the findings of the Master and ordered judgment in favor of the respondents. This appeal followed.

This being an equity case and the Master and the Circuit Judge having disagreed and made contrary findings on the material issues in the case, this Court has jurisdiction to consider the evidence and make findings in accordance with our view of the preponderance or greater weight of the evidence. . . .

Lula E. Talbot owned a tract of land fronting on U.S. Highway 17, in Myrtle Beach, South Carolina. The title thereto was conveyed to her by her husband, C.N. Talbot. The appellants were approached by W.A. James with a proposal that the tract of land be used for the erection thereon of an apartment complex. After preliminary talks and negotiations, the parties on January 12, 1963, entered into a written agreement thereabout. Basically, the parties agreed to form a Corporation to construct and operate an apartment complex. Lula E. Talbot was to convey to said Corporation the tract of land owned by her and W.A. James agreed, as set forth in paragraph 5, of said contract,

"To promote the project aforementioned and shall be responsible for the planning, architectural work, construction, landscaping, legal fees, and loan processing of the entire project, same to contain at least fifty (50) one, two and three room air conditioned apartments for customer as approved by FHA appraisers."

It was further agreed that upon the formation of the Corporation that the appellants were to receive 50% of the stock of the Corporation in consideration for their transfer of the land to it. This was to be the absolute limit of the contribution of the appellants. W.A. James was to receive 50% of the stock of the Corporation in consideration of his efforts on its behalf.

It appears, that after the aforementioned contract was entered into, that W.A. James obtained the services of an architectural firm on a contingency basis and preliminary plans and sketches of the proposed apartment complex were made by such firm. James was also successful in obtaining commitments from the Federal Housing Administration and from an acceptable mortgagee with regard to financing. These commitments having been obtained, a corporation was formed to be known as Chicora Apartments, Inc., and a charter was duly issued by the Secretary of State on November 5, 1963.

Pursuant to the terms of the agreement dated January 12, 1963, 20 shares of no par value capital stock were issued, with W.A. James receiving 10 shares, C.N. Talbot one share and Lula E. Talbot 9 shares. At an organizational meeting of the corporation W.A. James was elected president, his wife, B.N. James, was elected secretary, C.N. Talbot was elected vice president, and Lula E. Talbot was elected treasurer. W.A. James and C.N. Talbot were elected as directors of the Corporation.

At a meeting of the Board of Directors held on November 5, 1963, a resolution was adopted accepting the offer of Lula E. Talbot to transfer the tract of land in question to Chicora Apartments, Inc., in exchange for 10 shares of the no par value capital stock thereof. In the said resolution, it was declared that the said property, to be so transferred, was of a value of $44,000.00. At the same meeting, a resolution was adopted accepting the offer of W.A. James to transfer to Chicora Apartments, Inc., in exchange for 10 shares of the no par value stock thereof, at a valuation of $44,000.00 the following:

"1. FHA Commitment issued pursuant to Title 2, Section 207 of the National Housing Act, whereby the FHA agrees to insure a mortgage loan in the amount of $850,700.00, on a parcel of land in Myrtle Beach, South Carolina, more particularly described in Schedule 'A' hereto attached, provided 66 apartment units are constructed thereon in accordance with plans and specifications as prepared by Lyles, Bissett, Carlisle & Wolff, Architects–Engineers, of Columbia, South Carolina.

"2. Commitment from United Mortgagee Servicing Corp. agreeing to make a mortgage loan on said property in the amount of $850,700.00 and also commitment from said mortgagee to make an interim construction loan in an identical amount.

"3. Certain contracts and agreements which W.A. James over the past two years have worked out and developed in connection with the architectural and construction services required for said project.

"4. The use of the finances and credit of W.A. James during the past two years (and including the construction period) in order to make it possible to proceed with the project."

The day following the election of the officers and the issuance of the capital stock, the Board of Directors of Chicora Apartments, Inc., met in Columbia, South Carolina, and passed a resolution authorizing the Corporation to borrow from United Mortgagee Servicing Corporation of Norfolk, Virginia, the sum of $850,700.00, upon the terms stated, said loan to be insured with the Federal Housing Administration. It was further resolved:

"That the President of the corporation, W.A. James, be authorized, empowered and directed to make, execute and deliver such documents and instruments as are required by the F.H.A. and the lender, in order to close the loan transaction; said documents including but not limited to, note, mortgage, Building Loan Agreement, Construction Contract, Architect's Agreement, Mortgagor's Certificate, Regulatory Agreement, Mortgagor's Oath and Agreement and Certificate."

The record shows that on November 6, 1963, James Construction Company entered into a construction contract with Chicora Apartments, Inc. This contract was executed by W.A. James, as president, and attested by B.N. James, secretary, on behalf of Chicora Apartments, Inc., and by W.A. James, sole proprietor, for James Construction Company. The contract sum was to be the actual cost of construction plus a fee equal to $20,000.00 but in no event was the contract price, including the fee, to exceed $736,000.00. Attached to the contract was a "Trade Payment Breakdown" which made an allowance for overhead expenses in the amount of $31,589.00, but, this said sum was to be paid by means other than cash. The aforementioned loan was obtained and the apartment complex was constructed. All funds from the mortgage loan were received and disbursed by W.A. James and the renting of the apartments was begun, such being conducted by a resident manager, who was an employee of the Corporation.

It appears . . . that in 1968, an accountant, who was employed by the corporation, advised James and C.N. Talbot that it was in financial straits. It was at this time that the appellants questioned the disbursement of the mortgage funds by W.A. James. Their demands to examine the corporate records were refused by James. Thereafter, an order was obtained from the Honorable James B. Morrison, Resident Judge of the Fifteenth Judicial Circuit, making available the corporate records to the appellants. This action was thereafter instituted.

The record in this case clearly shows that W.A. James personally received or there was paid for his benefit the sum of $25,025.31 from the proceeds of the mortgage loan. He received this directly or by payments of his own personal debts by the corporation. He contends that he was entitled to these funds and more under the construction contract which he had with Chicora Apartments, Inc. This raises the question of whether James, who was a stockholder, officer, and director of Chicora Apartments, Inc., could enter into a contract with himself as an individual and [make] a profit therefrom for himself.

The Master found that Chicora Apartments, Inc., through W.A. James as president thereof, entered into a contract with himself, as sole proprietor of James Construction Company, without disclosing his identity of interest to the other officers or stockholders of the corporation, and that such contract has not been acquiesced in or ratified by the other director, officers or stockholders. He further found that the initial agreement between the parties required W.A. James to perform the same duties that he later contracted with the corporation to perform and for which he now seeks to justify the payment to him from the mortgage funds of the corporation. It was also found that according to the initial agreement these services were to be performed and, in consideration of such performance, James was to receive one-half of the shares of the capital stock of Chicora Apartments, Inc. The trial judge, upon exceptions to the Master's Report, made contrary findings of fact and reversed the Master and entered judgment in favor of the respondents.

The first question for determination is whether the fiduciary relationship existing between W.A. James as a stockholder, officer and director of Chicora Apartments, Inc., prevented him from contracting with the said corporation for his profit without first having disclosed the terms of the contract to the disinterested officers and directors of the corporation.

The officers and directors of the corporation stand in a fiduciary relationship to the individual stockholders and in every instance must make a full disclosure of all relevant facts when entering into a contract with said corporation. *Jacobson v. Yaschik*, 249 S.C. 577, 155 S.E.(2d) 601. The object of this rule is to prevent directors from secretly using their fiduciary positions to their own advantage and to the detriment of the corporation and of the stockholders. . . .

... The testimony of C.N. Talbot is that he discussed with James as to who was going to construct the Chicora Apartments and was told that Dargan Construction Company was going to take the contract. He further testified that during the period of construction he saw Dargan Construction Company signs on the premises and also trucks bearing its name. This witness further testified that James never discussed with him or his wife the matter of his constructing the apartments. Talbot denied that he knew that James was to be the contractor.

James testified that he explained to C.N. Talbot that the only possible way that the apartments could be built without putting in money was that he be the building contractor. James further testified that the only way the project could survive and the only way that "we" could get the builder's equity was that he should be the builder. He says that everybody understood that because his attorney had explained it at a meeting of the directors.

Assuming that James revealed to Talbot that he was to be the building contractor for the Chicora Apartments complex, his testimony does not show that he disclosed his entitlement to a fee of $20,000.00 and an allowance for overhead expenses in the amount of $31,589.00. It is thus apparent that he did not make a full disclosure of the profits or monetary benefits that he was to receive under the terms of the contract. It was his duty to make such full disclosure and the burden of proof was upon him to show that such had been done.

We have carefully examined the minutes of the several meetings of the stockholders and directors of the corporation. We find from such examination that they reflect each and every detail and transaction looking toward the construction of the apartment complex but nowhere in said minutes is there any mention that James was to be the building contractor. The minutes reflect that there was a meeting of the directors of the corporation on November 6, 1963, and a resolution adopted at such meeting authorizing the borrowing of the sum of $850,700.00 from the United Mortgagee Servicing Corporation, and authorizing James, as president, to make, execute and deliver such documents and instruments as were required by the FHA and the lender. If James was to be the building contractor and such was discussed at this meeting, as he contends, the minutes should have reflected such, particularly in view of the fact that the building contract was being awarded to him when he was a director and president of the corporation. There is no explanation of why such a resolution or authorization was not considered or passed at this meeting of the Board of Directors.

The record shows that the appellants were stockholders and officers of the corporation. As such, they were entitled to inspect the books of the corporation at any and all times. Section 12–263 of the Code. When they demanded their right to exercise this privilege, such was refused by James and they only obtained the right to inspect the records and books of the corporation by an order of the court. James' only explanation was that the Talbots were not entitled to see the books. It is inferable from this action on the part of James that he did not want the appellants to discover how the funds of the corporation had been disbursed and see that he had received benefit in such disbursement.

It appears that at the meeting of the directors of the corporation held on November 6, 1963, W.A. James, as president, was authorized to execute and deliver several documents including a "construction contract." The respondents argue that this gave W.A. James the authority to make the construction contract here involved. It is true that he was authorized to sign a "construction contract" on behalf of the corporation but such resolution did not authorize him to sign one on behalf of the corporation in favor of himself individually.

The respondents contend and place great emphasis on the fact that the construction contract was approved by the Federal Housing Administration and the fees provided therein were allowed by it. This has no relevancy to the issue here.

Considering the entire record in this case, it is our conclusion that W.A. James, as president of Chicora Apartments, Inc., entered into a contract with himself as sole proprietor of James Construction Company without making full disclosure of his identity of interest to the other officers and stockholders of the corporation. In this conclusion, we agree with the findings of the Master. It follows that the Chicora Apartments, Inc., is entitled to judgment against the said W.A. James in the amount of $25,025.31, this being the amount of the corporate funds received by or paid in behalf of W.A. James.

The Master found that under the language in paragraph 5 of the pre-incorporation agreement, hereinbefore quoted, that W.A. James was to be responsible for overseeing, supervising and generally managing all aspects of the construction of the apartment complex. He found that W.A. James, as sole proprietor of James Construction Company, performed the contract obligations and for such he received one-half of the shares of the capital stock of Chicora Apartments, Inc. The trial judge reversed this finding of the Master. The appellants allege error.

James testified that he was the general contractor for the construction of the apartment complex. He testified further that the apartment complex was constructed by some eighteen to twenty subcontractors with whom he negotiated contracts. The record reveals that the only service that James rendered in connection with the construction of the apartment complex was supervisory. These duties were those contemplated by the pre-incorporation agreement of the parties. He was compensated for these services when he received one-half of the capital stock in the corporation. He was not entitled to any other compensation for the services rendered. We think the trial judge was in error in not so holding.

The order of the trial judge is reversed and this case remanded to the Court of Common Pleas for Horry County for an appropriate order to effectuate the views herein expressed.

Reversed and remanded.

■ LEWIS and LITTLEJOHN, JJ., concur.

■ BUSSEY and BRAILSFORD, JJ., dissent.

■ BUSSEY, JUSTICE (dissenting):

While admittedly there is some evidence tending to support the findings of fact by the master, adopted in the majority opinion, I have concluded after considerable study of the record and exhibits that the clear weight of the evidence preponderates in favor of the findings of fact by the circuit judge rather than those of the master. Being of this view, I am compelled to dissent.

The apartment complex was completed in July 1964, whereupon the plaintiff, C.N. Talbot, with the help of a resident manager, selected by him but approved by James, took charge of the management and operation of the apartment complex, all receipts being deposited by Talbot and all checks being written by Talbot. In 1968, after Talbot and his manager had been in charge of the apartment complex for nearly four years, the corporation was virtually insolvent and the recommendation of Talbot's auditor was that the project be surrendered to FHA as a failure. To this James did not agree; instead he took charge of the operation of the apartment complex himself for the corporation, and a little more than a year later the corporation had seventeen to eighteen thousand dollars in the bank with all current bills paid.

Talbot was obviously chagrined at this course of events and it was not until after he was ousted from management that he actively asserted any claim on behalf of the corporation against James. While he denied knowing that James Construction Company was the general contractor on the project, by his own testimony about January or February 1965 he knew that a check for more than fifteen thousand dollars had been drawn on the construction account for the benefit of James. There is no suggestion that he then made any issue thereabout; instead, he waited until nearly four years later and until after he had been ousted from the active management of the operation. . . .

The resolution of the Board of Directors at the meeting on November 5, 1963, unanimously confirmed by the meeting of the stockholders on the same date, as evidenced by their written signatures, clearly shows that all parties agreed that James' efforts over a two year period and the contracts and commitments thereby produced plus the continued use of the finances and credit of James during the actual construction period represented a value of $44,000, which was accepted in full payment for James' ten shares of stock. According to the literal terms of this resolution, nothing remained to be done by James to fully earn his ten shares except allow the use of his credit throughout the construction period. As president of the corporation, he would have been expected to at least reasonably supervise the construction of the project in the interest of the corporation, whether or not required to do so by either the resolution of November 5 or the pre-incorporation agreement between the parties. The general supervisory duties of a corporation president or a pre-incorporation promoter are a far cry from the arduous, time consuming and expensive duties of a general contractor.

Supervising a general contractor is one thing; while acting as a general contractor, engaging, supervising, and following up eighteen or twenty subcontractors is an entirely different thing. There is uncontradicted evidence of voluminous paper work, record keeping, reports, etc., on the part of James and his personnel in the performance of the general construction contract. The record leaves no doubt whatever, to my mind, that James Construction Company performed services to the corporation subsequent to November 5, 1963 far over and above the service contemplated by either the aforesaid resolution or the pre-incorporation agreement.

As mentioned in the majority opinion, the "Trade Payment Breakdown" attached to the approved FHA construction contract made an allowance for overhead expenses in the amount of $31,589, payable by means other than cash. Apparently from the evidence, this amount, otherwise drawable, as overhead by James, was to form a part of the equity of the corporation required for the FHA loan and, of course, not actually received by James. Aside, however, from this item, the record reflects that where, as here, there was an identity of interest between the contractor and the sponsor, FHA, within certain limitations, permitted the contractor to include in his certification of the actual cost of a project a reasonable allocation of his general overhead expense, *i.e.*, the proportion of his actual general overhead expense attributable to the particular contract job.

In his cost certification to FHA James showed the entire overhead of James Construction Company during the period that the apartment project was under construction, and represented that 88.98% thereof, or $22,817.34, was attributable to the construction of Chicora Apartments. Of this amount, FHA allowed only $21,231.90 (3% of other costs) as a portion of the actual cost of Chicora Apartments. James' figures as to his overhead and the portion thereof attributable to the construction of Chicora Apartments may or may not have been accurate, but he was not even cross-examined thereabout. Assuming the accuracy of his figures it follows that his net profit from this general construction contract was the sum of $25,025.31 less $22,817.34 overhead, or $2,207.97. Even Talbot had to frankly admit that he did not know of any loss suffered by the Talbots or the corporation as a result of the general contract being let to James. He tacitly, if not expressly, conceded that Dargan, or any other reputable contractor, would have cost the corporation some twenty-five or thirty thousand dollars more. . . .

For the foregoing reasons, I would affirm the judgment of the lower court, but at the very least, if the corporation is to recover at all from James, its recovery should be limited to any profit actually received, as opposed to his overhead expense. If the judgment below be not affirmed, the cause should be remanded for the purpose of determining the amount of actual overhead which James should equitably be allowed to retain.

■ BRAILSFORD, J., concurs.

NOTE ON THE DUTY OF LOYALTY

In the corporate context, fairness requires not only that the terms of a self-interested transaction be fair, but that entering into the transaction, even on fair terms, is in the corporation's interest. For example, in Fill Buildings, Inc. v. Alexander Hamilton Life Ins. Co. of America, 396 Mich. 453, 241 N.W.2d 466 (1976), Fill Buildings, Inc., which had leased premises to Wayne National Life Insurance Co., brought suit under the lease for past-due rent. The lease was a self-interested transaction: Leon Fill was the principal shareholder and a director of Wayne National and the sole shareholder and president of Fill Buildings. Wayne's corporate successor sought to avoid liability under the lease on the ground that the lease was unfair. The trial court held that Fill Buildings had not borne its burden of establishing that the lease was in the interests of Wayne National:

> Given an instance of alleged director enrichment at corporate expense such as in this case, the burden to establish fairness resting on the director requires not only a showing of "fair price" but also a showing of the fairness of the bargain to the interests of the corporation. Only when a convincing showing is made in both respects can "fairness" under the statute be said to have been established.

> We are inclined to agree with Fill Buildings' position that that corporation was entitled to make a profit on its lease and that a "fair price" for the leasehold agreement was established. The costs of extensive renovations and the thrust of expert testimony adduced at trial support this conclusion. The proofs respecting the showing that entry into the lease served the interests of Wayne National are, however, unconvincing. Evidence adduced at trial indicated that Wayne National was a corporation in trouble. The corporation had been warned against over-expansion. Yet here we have entry into a long-term lease (*i.e.,* expansion) at a time when the corporate future was in question....

NOTE ON ASSOCIATES OF DIRECTORS AND SENIOR EXECUTIVES

In the simplest type of self-interested transaction, a corporation deals with a director or senior executive. What if a corporation deals not with a director or senior executive, but with an enterprise or individual with whom a director or senior executive has a significant relationship? Such an enterprise or individual may be referred to as an "associate" of the director or senior executive. See ALI, Principles of Corporate Governance § 1.03.

Suppose, for example, that D, a director or senior executive, negotiates with the corporation on behalf of A, an associate of D, or otherwise knowingly advances A's interest. It seems pretty clear that the same rules of conduct should apply to D as if he had acted on his own behalf. The major problem would be remedy. Assume that D acted for A in a way that would have breached D's duty if he had acted for himself, and that D's breach resulted in a gain for A at the corporation's expense. If D will directly or indirectly derive all the gain—if, for example, A is a corporation wholly owned by D, or is D's minor child—damages equal to the gain are clearly appropriate. Suppose, however, that D will derive only part of the gain, as where A is a corporation that D controls but does not wholly own? On balance, the same result seems to be called for, because D has, by hypothesis, violated his duty, and the proximate result of that violation is that A will enjoy an unfair gain at the corporation's expense. That result should follow even if D will derive only a portion of the gain, as where A is D's spouse and the two spouses keep their finances on a separate basis.

Suppose now that the question is not the liability of D, but the liability of the associate, A, whose interest was knowingly advanced by D? If A knew or should have known that he was participating in a breach of fiduciary duty, he would be liable as an aider and abetter under the well-established rule against knowing participation in a breach of fiduciary duty. If A is a business organization controlled by D, D's knowledge should be imputed to A in considering A's responsibility. Even if A neither knew nor should have known that he was participating in a breach of fiduciary duty, he may be liable under established principles of restitution, if liability is required to prevent unjust enrichment. For example, Restatement, Second, Agency § 314 provides that a person who receives a principal's property from an agent, and is not a bona fide purchaser, is subject to liability to the extent he has been unjustly enriched even if he receives the property non-tortiously and is not on notice that the property belongs to the principal. See also Restatement of Restitution §§ 123, 201(1), 201(2).

Suppose, finally, that A deals with the corporation on his own behalf, without the intervention of D? Arguably, an associate, unlike the director or senior executive, owes no duty of loyalty to the corporation (at least, assuming the associate is not simply a vest pocket of the director or senior executive, like a wholly owned corporation). However, since an associate may receive favored treatment as a result of his association with the director or senior executive, it seems appropriate to subject such transactions to closer review than would be imposed in the case of transactions with strangers.

ALI, PRINCIPLES OF CORPORATE GOVERNANCE
§§ 1.14, 1.25, 5.02, 5.07, 5.08

[See Statutory Supplement]

SECTION 2.   STATUTORY APPROACHES

CAL. CORP. CODE § 310

[See Statutory Supplement]

DEL. GEN. CORP. LAW § 144

[See Statutory Supplement]

REV. MODEL BUS. CORP. ACT §§ 8.60–8.63

[See Statutory Supplement]

N.Y. BUS. CORP. LAW § 713

[See Statutory Supplement]

Cookies Food Products v. Lakes Warehouse

Supreme Court of Iowa, 1988.
430 N.W.2d 447.

■ NEUMAN, JUSTICE.

This is a shareholders' derivative suit brought by the minority shareholders of a closely held Iowa corporation specializing in barbeque sauce, Cookies Food Products, Inc. (Cookies). The target of the lawsuit is the majority shareholder, Duane "Speed" Herrig and two of his family-owned corporations, Lakes Warehouse Distributing, Inc. (Lakes) and Speed's Automotive Co., Inc. (Speed's). Plaintiffs alleged that Herrig, by acquiring control of Cookies and executing self-dealing contracts, breached his fiduciary duty to the company and fraudulently misappropriated and converted corporate funds. Plaintiffs sought actual and punitive damages. Trial to the court resulted in a verdict for the defendants, the district court finding that Herrig's actions benefited, rather than harmed, Cookies. We affirm.

I.   *Background.*

We review decisions in shareholders' derivative suits de novo, deferring especially to district court findings where the credibility of witnesses is a factor in the outcome. *Midwest Management Corp. v.*

Stephens, 353 N.W.2d 76, 78 (Iowa 1984). To better understand this dispute, and the issues this appeal presents, we shall begin by recounting in detail the facts surrounding the creation and growth of this corporation.

L.D. Cook of Storm Lake, Iowa, founded Cookies in 1975 to produce and distribute his original barbeque sauce. Searching for a plant site in a community that would provide financial backing, Cook met with business leaders in seventeen Iowa communities, outlining his plans to build a growth-oriented company. He selected Wall Lake, Iowa, persuading thirty-five members of that community, including Herrig and the plaintiffs, to purchase Cookies stock. All of the investors hoped Cookies would improve the local job market and tax base. The record reveals that it has done just that.

Early sales of the product, however, were dismal. After the first year's operation, Cookies was in dire financial straits. At that time, Herrig was one of thirty-five shareholders and held only two hundred shares. He was also the owner of an auto parts business, Speed's Automotive, and Lakes Warehouse Distributing, Inc., a company that distributed auto parts from Speed's. Cookies' board of directors approached Herrig with the idea of distributing the company's products. It authorized Herrig to purchase Cookies' sauce for twenty percent under wholesale price, which he could then resell at full wholesale price. Under this arrangement, Herrig began to market and distribute the sauce to his auto parts customers and to grocery outlets from Lakes' trucks as they traversed the regular delivery routes for Speed's Automotive.

In May 1977, Cookies formalized this arrangement by executing an exclusive distribution agreement with Lakes. Pursuant to this agreement, Cookies was responsible only for preparing the product; Lakes, for its part, assumed all costs of warehousing, marketing, sales, delivery, promotion, and advertising. Cookies retained the right to fix the sales price of its products and agreed to pay Lakes thirty percent of its gross sales for these services.

Cookies' sales have soared under the exclusive distributorship contract with Lakes. Gross sales in 1976, the year prior to the agreement, totaled only $20,000, less than half of Cookies' expenses that year. In 1977, however, sales jumped five-fold, then doubled in 1978, and have continued to show phenomenal growth every year thereafter. By 1985, when this suit was commenced, annual sales reached $2,400,000.

As sales increased, Cookies' board of directors amended and extended the original distributorship agreement. In 1979, the board amended the original agreement to give Lakes an additional two percent of gross sales to cover freight costs for the ever-expanding market for Cookies' sauce. In 1980, the board extended the amended agreement through 1984 to allow Herrig to make long-term advertising commitments. Recognizing the role that Herrig's personal strengths played in the success of their joint endeavor, the board also amended the agreement that year to allow Cookies to cancel the agreement with Lakes if Herrig died or disposed of the corporation's stock.

In 1981, L.D. Cook, the majority shareholder up to this time, decided to sell his interest in Cookies. He first offered the directors an opportunity to buy his stock, but the board declined to purchase any of his 8100 shares. Herrig then offered Cook and all other shareholders $10 per share for their stock, which was twice the original price. Because of the overwhelming response to these offers, Herrig had purchased enough Cookies stock by January 1982 to become the majority shareholder. His investment of $140,000 represented fifty-three percent of the 28,700 outstanding shares. Other shareholders had invested a total of $67,500 for the remaining forty-seven percent.

Shortly after Herrig acquired majority control he replaced four of the five members of the Cookies' board with members he selected. This restructuring of authority, following on the heels of an unsuccessful attempt by certain stockholders to prevent Herrig from acquiring majority status, solidified a division of opinion within the shareholder ranks. Subsequent changes made in the corporation under Herrig's leadership formed the basis for this lawsuit.

First, under Herrig's leadership, Cookies' board has extended the term of the exclusive distributorship agreement with Lakes and expanded the scope of services for which it compensates Herrig and his companies. In April 1982, when a sales increase of twenty-five percent over the previous year required Cookies to seek additional short-term storage for the peak summer season, the board accepted Herrig's proposal to compensate Lakes at the "going rate" for use of its nearby storage facilities. The board decided to use Lakes' storage facilities because building and staffing its own facilities would have been more expensive. Later, in July 1982, the new board approved an extension of the exclusive distributorship agreement. Notably, this agreement was identical to the 1980 extension that the former board had approved while four of the plaintiffs in this action were directors.

Second, Herrig moved from his role as director and distributor to take on an additional role in product development. This created a dispute over a royalty Herrig began to receive. Herrig's role in product development began in 1982 when Cookies diversified its product line to include taco sauce. Herrig developed the recipe because he recognized that taco sauce, while requiring many of the same ingredients needed in barbeque sauce, is less expensive to produce. Further, since consumer demand for taco sauce is more consistent throughout the year than the demand for barbeque sauce, this new product line proved to be a profitable method for increasing year-round utilization of production facilities and staff. In August 1982, Cookies' board approved a royalty fee to be paid to Herrig for this taco sauce recipe. This royalty plan was similar to royalties the board paid to L.D. Cook for the barbeque sauce recipe. That plan gives Cook three percent of the gross sales of barbeque sauce; Herrig receives a flat rate per case. Although Herrig's rate is equivalent to a sales percentage slightly higher than what Cook receives, it yields greater profit to Cookies because this new product line is cheaper to produce.

Third, since 1982 Cookies' board has twice approved additional compensation for Herrig. In January 1983, the board authorized payment of a $1000 per month "consultant fee" in lieu of salary, because accelerated sales required Herrig to spend extra time managing the company. Averaging eighty-hour work weeks, Herrig devoted approximately fifteen percent of his time to Cookies and eighty percent to Lakes business. In August, 1983, the board authorized another increase in Herrig's compensation. Further, at the suggestion of a Cookies director who also served as an accountant for Cookies, Lakes, and Speed's, the Cookies board amended the exclusive distributorship agreement to allow Lakes an additional two percent of gross sales as a promotion allowance to expand the market for Cookies products outside of Iowa. As a direct result of this action, by 1986 Cookies regularly shipped products to several states throughout the country.

As we have previously noted, however, Cookies' growth and success has not pleased all its shareholders. The discontent is motivated by two factors that have effectively precluded shareholders from sharing in Cookies' financial success: the fact that Cookies is a closely held corporation, and the fact that it has not paid dividends. Because Cookies' stock is not publicly traded, shareholders have no ready access to buyers for their stock at current values that reflect the company's success. Without dividends, the shareholders have no ready method of realizing a return on their investment in the company. This is not to say that Cookies has improperly refused to pay dividends. The evidence reveals that Cookies would have violated the terms of its loan with the Small Business Administration had it declared dividends before repaying that debt. That SBA loan was not repaid until the month before the plaintiffs filed this action.

Unsatisfied with the status quo, a group of minority shareholders commenced this equitable action in 1985. Based on the facts we have detailed, the plaintiffs claimed that the sums paid Herrig and his companies have grossly exceeded the value of the services rendered, thereby substantially reducing corporate profits and shareholder equity. Through the exclusive distributorship agreements, taco sauce royalty, warehousing fees, and consultant fee, plaintiffs claimed that Herrig breached his fiduciary duties to the corporation and its shareholders because he allegedly negotiated for these arrangements without fully disclosing the benefit he would gain. The plaintiffs sought recovery for lost profits, an accounting to determine the full extent of the damage, attorneys fees, punitive damages, appointment of a receiver to manage the company properly, removal of Herrig from control, and sale of the company in order to generate an appropriate return on their investment.

Having heard the evidence presented on these claims at trial, the district court filed a lengthy ruling that reflected careful attention to the testimony of the twenty-two witnesses and myriad of exhibits admitted. The court concluded that Herrig had breached no duties owed to Cookies or to its minority shareholders, and found that Herrig's compensation was fair and reasonable for each of the four challenged categories of service. In summary, the court found that: (1) the exclusive distributorship arrangement has been the "key to corporate growth and expansion" and the fees under the agreement were appropriate for the diverse services Lakes provided; (2) the warehousing agreement was fair because it allowed Cookies to store its goods at the "going rate" and the board had considered and rejected the idea of constructing its own warehouse as storage at the Lakes facility would be less expensive; (3) the taco sauce royalty agreement appropriately compensated Herrig for the value of his recipe; and (4) the consultant fee "is actually a management fee for services rendered seven days a week" and is "well within reason, considering the success of the business." Additionally, the district court found that Herrig had withheld no information from directors or other shareholders that he was obligated to provide. The court concluded its findings with the following observation:

> The Court believes that the plaintiffs' complaint is not that they have been damaged but that they have not been paid a profit for their investment yet. There is a vast difference. Plaintiffs have made a profit. That profit is in the form of increased value of their stocks rather than in the form of dividends because of the capital considerations of operating the company.

On appeal from this ruling, the plaintiffs challenge: (1) the district court's allocation of the burden of proof with regard to the four claims of self-dealing; (2) the standard employed by the court to determine whether Herrig's self-dealing was fair and reasonable to Cookies; (3) the finding that any self-dealing by Herrig was done in good faith, and with honesty and fairness; (4) the finding that Herrig breached no duty to disclose crucial facts to Cookies' board before it completed deliberations on Herrig's self-dealing transactions; and (5) the district court's denial of restitution and other equitable remedies as compensation for Herrig's alleged breach of his duty of loyalty. After a brief review of the nature and source of Herrig's fiduciary duties, we will address the appellants' challenges in turn.

II.   *Fiduciary Duties.*

Herrig, as an officer and director of Cookies, owes a fiduciary duty to the company and its shareholders. *See* Iowa Code § 496A.34 (1985) (director must serve in manner believed in good faith to be in best interest of corporation); *see also Schildberg Rock Prods. Co. v. Brooks,* 258 Iowa 759, 766–67, 140 N.W.2d 132, 136 (1966) (officers and directors occupy fiduciary relation to corporation and its stockholders). Herrig concedes that Iowa law imposed the same fiduciary responsibilities based on his status as majority stockholder. *See Des Moines Bank & Trust Co. v. George M. Bechtel & Co.,* 243 Iowa 1007, 1082–83, 51 N.W.2d 174, 217 (1952) (hereinafter *Bechtel*); *see also* 12B W. Fletcher, *Cyclopedia on the Law of Private Corporations*

§ 5810, at 149 (1986). Conversely, before acquiring majority control in February 1982, Herrig owed no fiduciary duty to Cookies or plaintiffs. *See* Fletcher § 5713, at 13 (stockholders not active in management of corporation owe duties radically different from director, and vote at shareholder's meetings merely for own benefit). Therefore, Herrig's conduct is subject to scrutiny only from the time he began to exercise control of Cookies. . . .

Appellants . . . claim that Herrig violated his duty of loyalty to Cookies. That duty derives from "the prohibition against self-dealing that inheres in the fiduciary relationship." *Norlin,* 744 F.2d at 264. As a fiduciary, one may not secure for oneself a business opportunity that "in fairness belongs to the corporation." *Rowen v. LeMars Mut. Ins. Co. of Iowa,* 282 N.W.2d 639, 660 (Iowa 1979). As we noted in *Bechtel:*

> Corporate directors and officers may under proper circumstances transact business with the corporation including the purchase or sale of property, but it must be done in the strictest good faith and with full disclosure of the facts to, and the consent of, all concerned. And the burden is upon them to establish their good faith, honesty and fairness. Such transactions are scanned by the courts with skepticism and the closest scrutiny, and may be nullified on slight grounds. It is the policy of the courts to put such fiduciaries beyond the reach of temptation and the enticement of illicit profit.

243 Iowa 1007, 1081, 51 N.W.2d 174, 216 (1952). We have repeatedly applied this standard, including the burden of proof and level of scrutiny, when a corporate director engages in self-dealing with another corporation for which he or she also serves as a director. *See Holden v. Construction Mach. Co.,* 202 N.W.2d 348, 356–57 (Iowa 1972).

Against this common law backdrop, the legislature enacted section 496A.34, quoted here in pertinent part, that establishes three sets of circumstances under which a director may engage in self-dealing without clearly violating the duty of loyalty:

> No contract or other transaction between a corporation and one or more of its directors or any other corporation, firm, association or entity in which one or more of its directors are directors or officers or are financially interested, shall be either void or voidable because of such relationship or interest . . . if any of the following occur:
>
> 1. The fact of such relationship or interest is disclosed or known to the board of directors or committee which authorizes, approves, or ratifies the contract or transaction . . . without counting the votes . . . of such interested director.
>
> 2. The fact of such relationship or interest is disclosed or known to the shareholders entitled to vote [on the transaction] and they authorize . . . such contract or transaction by vote or written consent.

3.   The contract or transaction is fair and reasonable to the corporation.

Some commentators have supported the view that satisfaction of any *one* of the foregoing statutory alternatives, in and of itself, would prove that a director has fully met the duty of loyalty. *See* Hansell, Austin, & Wilcox, *Director Liability Under Iowa Law-Duties and Protections,* 13 J.Corp.L. 369, 382. We are obliged, however, to interpret statutes in conformity with the common law wherever statutory language does not directly negate it. *See Hardwick v. Bublitz,* 253 Iowa 49, 59, 111 N.W.2d 309, 314 (1961); Iowa Code § 4.2 (1987). Because the common law and section 496A.34 require directors to show "good faith, honesty, and fairness" in self-dealing, we are persuaded that satisfaction of any one of these three alternatives under the statute would merely preclude us from rendering the transaction void or voidable *outright* solely on the basis "of such [director's] relationship or interest." Iowa Code § 496A.34; *see Bechtel,* 243 Iowa at 1081–82, 51 N.W.2d at 216. To the contrary, we are convinced that the legislature did not intend by this statute to enable a court, in a shareholder's derivative suit, to rubber stamp *any* transaction to which a board of directors or the shareholders of a corporation have consented. Such an interpretation would invite those who stand to gain from such transactions to engage in improprieties to obtain consent. We thus require directors who engage in self-dealing to establish the additional element that they have acted in good faith, honesty, and fairness. *Holi–Rest, Inc. v. Treloar,* 217 N.W.2d 517, 525 (Iowa 1974).

III.   *Burden of Proof.*

[The court held that the district court had appropriately placed the burden of proof on Herrig.]

IV.   *Standard of Law.*

Next, appellants claim the district court applied an inappropriate standard of law to determine whether Herrig's conduct was fair and reasonable to Cookies. Appellants correctly assert that self-dealing transactions must have the earmarks of arms-length transactions before a court can find them to be fair or reasonable. *See Bechtel,* 243 Iowa at 1023, 51 N.W.2d at 184. The crux of appellants' claim is that the court should have focused on the fair market value of Herrig's services to Cookies rather than on the success Cookies achieved as a result of Herrig's actions.

We agree with appellants' contention that corporate profitability should not be the sole criteria by which to test the fairness and reasonableness of Herrig's fees. In this connection, appellants cite authority from the Michigan Supreme Court that we find persuasive:

Given an instance of alleged director enrichment at corporate expense ... the burden to establish fairness resting on the director requires not only a showing of "fair price" but also a showing of the fairness of the bargain to the interests of the corporation.

Fill Bldgs., Inc. v. Alexander Hamilton Life Ins. Co., 396 Mich. 453, 241 N.W.2d 466, 469 (1976). Applying such reasoning to the record before us, however, we cannot agree with appellants' assertion that Herrig's services were either unfairly priced or inconsistent with Cookies corporate interest.

There can be no serious dispute that the four agreements in issue—for exclusive distributorship, taco sauce royalty, warehousing, and consulting fees—have all benefited Cookies, as demonstrated by its financial success. Even if we assume Cookies could have procured similar services from other vendors at lower costs, we are not convinced that Herrig's fees were therefore unreasonable or exorbitant. Like the district court, we are not persuaded by appellants' expert testimony that Cookies' sales and profits would have been the same under agreements with other vendors. As Cookies' board noted prior to Herrig's takeover, he was the driving force in the corporation's success. Even plaintiffs' expert acknowledged that Herrig has done the work of at least five people—production supervisor, advertising specialist, warehouseman, broker, and salesman. While eschewing the lack of internal control, for accounting purposes, that such centralized authority may produce, the expert conceded that Herrig may in fact be underpaid for all he has accomplished. We believe the board properly considered this source of Cookies' success when it entered these transactions, as did the district court when it reviewed them. . . .

V. *Denial of Equitable Relief.*

. . . [T]he record before us aptly demonstrates that all members of Cookies' board were well aware of Herrig's dual ownership in Lakes and Speed's. We are unaware of any authority supporting plaintiffs' contention that Herrig was obligated to disclose to Cookies' board or shareholders the extent of his profits resulting from these distribution and warehousing agreements; nevertheless, the exclusive distribution agreement with Lakes authorized the board to ascertain that information had it so desired. Appellants cannot reasonably claim that Herrig owed Cookies a duty to render such services at no profit to himself or his companies. Having found that the compensation he received from these agreements was fair and reasonable, we are convinced that Herrig furnished sufficient pertinent information to Cookies' board to enable it to make prudent decisions concerning the contracts. . . .

We concur in the trial court's assessment of the evidence presented and affirm its dismissal of plaintiffs' claims.

AFFIRMED.

All Justices concur except SCHULTZ, J., who dissents.

■ SCHULTZ, JUSTICE (dissenting) . . . .

Much of Herrig's evidence concerned the tremendous success of the company. I believe that the trial court and the majority opinion have been so enthralled by the success of the company that they have failed to examine whether these matters of self-dealing were fair to the stockholders. While much credit is due to Herrig for the success of the company, this does not mean that these transactions were fair to the company.

I believe that Herrig failed on his burden of proof by what he did not show. He did not produce evidence of the local going rate for distribution contracts or storage fees outside of a very limited amount of self-serving testimony. He simply did not show the fair market value of his services or expense for freight, advertising and storage cost. He did not show that his taco sauce royalty was fair. This was his burden. He cannot succeed on it by merely showing the success of the company.

The shareholders, on the other hand, produced testimony of what the fair market value of Herrig's services were. The majority discounts this testimony and chooses instead to focus on the success Cookies achieved as a result of Herrig's actions. They focus on the success of the company rather than whether his self-dealing actions were arms-length transactions that were fair and reasonable to the stockholders. The appellants have put forth convincing testimony that Herrig has been grossly over compensated for his services based on their fair market value. Appellant's expert witness, a CPA, performed an analysis to show what the company would have earned if it had hired a $65,000 a year executive officer, paid a marketing supervisor and an advertising agency a commission of five percent of the sales each, built a new warehouse and hired a warehouseman. It was compared with what the company actually did make under Herrig's management. The analysis basically shows what the operating cost of this company should be on the open market when hiring out the work to experts. In 1985 alone, the company's income would have doubled what it actually made were these changes made. The evidence clearly shows that the fair market value of those services is considerably less than what Herrig actually has been paid.

Similarly, appellant's food broker expert witness testified that for $110,865, what the CPA analysis stated was the fair market value for brokerage services, his company would have provided all of the services that Herrig had performed. The company actually paid $730,637 for the services, a difference of $620,000 in one year.

In summary, I believe the majority was dazzled by the tales of Herrig's efforts and Cookies' success in these difficult economic times. In the process, however, it is forgotten that Herrig owes a fiduciary duty to the corporation to deal fairly and reasonably with it in his self-dealing transactions. Herrig is not entitled to skim off the majority of the profits through self-dealing transactions unless they are fair to the minority stockholders. At trial, he failed to prove how his charges were in line with what the company could have gotten on the open market. Because I cannot ignore this inequity to the company and its shareholders, I must respectfully dissent.

———

NOTE ON THE EFFECT OF APPROVAL BY DISINTERESTED DIRECTORS OF SELF–INTERESTED TRANSACTIONS

Suppose that an interested transaction has been authorized by disinterested directors. There are several reasons why the transaction should nevertheless be subject to some review for substantive fairness, although a more limited review than would be applied in the absence of such an authorization. First, by virtue of their personal relationships, directors are unlikely to treat each other with the degree of wariness they would apply to third parties.

Second, a review of the *substantive* fairness of a self-interested transaction may be thought of as a surrogate for a review of the fairness of the *process* by which the transaction was approved. In a world of perfect information, a court could always determine, by direct means, whether directors who approved a self-interested transaction involving one or more of their colleagues were objective and impartial, and whether they approached the transaction with that degree of wariness with which they would approach transactions with third parties. In the real world, the courts may need to make these determinations by indirect means. If a self-interested transaction that has been approved by directors who are technically disinterested is substantively unfair, it can normally be inferred that either the approving directors were not objective and impartial in fact, or that they were not as wary as they should have been because they were dealing with a colleague.

Most states have adopted statutes, like those of California, Delaware, New York, and the Model Act, that address the effect of approval of self-interested transactions by disinterested directors. An important question under these statutes is whether they preclude a judicial inquiry into the fairness of self-interested transactions that have been approved by disinterested directors. Many of the statutes are susceptible to the interpretation that approval by disinterested directors precludes a judicial inquiry into fairness, but all or almost all the statutes can be interpreted not to preclude such an inquiry.

(i) Some of the statutes, such as the California statute, expressly require some form of fairness test even if transactions have been approved by disinterested directors.

(ii) Many of the statutes, such as the Delaware statute, explicitly require that approval by disinterested directors be in good faith, and such a requirement can be implied even where it is not explicit. It is often obscure whether a good-faith test is strictly subjective or has an objective content as well. For example, UCC § 2–103 provides that in the case of a merchant, good faith is defined to include "the observance of reasonable commercial standards of fair dealing in the trade." Similarly, in Sam Wong & Son, Inc. v. New York Mercantile Exchange, 735 F.2d 653, 671, 678 & n. 32 (2d Cir.1984), Judge Friendly held that the rationality of a decision was relevant in determining whether the decision had been made in good faith. "By this," he added, "we mean only a minimal requirement of some basis in reason. [A]bsent some basis in reason, action could hardly be in good faith even apart from ulterior motive." Even courts that seem to use the term "good faith" in a relatively subjective way characteristically go on to review decisions for quality under the guise of a rule that if a decision is irrational, egregious, or the like, this shows bad faith. Because of the uncertain meaning of good faith, a good-faith requirement opens the door to judicial scrutiny of the fairness of self-interested transactions that have been approved by disinterested directors.

(iii) Many of the remaining statutes can be interpreted to merely change the common law rule that self-interested transactions are voidable without regard to fairness, rather than to preclude review for fairness. Thus, some courts have held that such statutes only render a self-interested transaction not automatically voidable (that is, not voidable even if fair) or shifts the burden of proof. In addition to *Cookies Food Products,* see, e.g., Holi–Rest, Inc. v. Treloar, 217 N.W.2d 517, 525 (Iowa 1974); Cohen v. Ayers, 596 F.2d 733, 740–41 (7th Cir.1979); Remillard Brick Co. v. Remillard–Dandini Co., 109 Cal.App.2d 405, 241 P.2d 66 (1952); Gaillard v. Natomas Co., 208 Cal.App.3d 1250, 256 Cal.Rptr. 702 (1989).[24]

In contrast, in Marciano v. Nakash, 535 A.2d 400 (Del.1987), the Delaware Supreme Court stated that "approval by fully-informed disinterested directors under section 144(a)(1), or disinterested stockholders under section 144(a)(2), permits invocation of the business judgment rule and limits judicial review to issues of gift or waste with the burden of proof upon the party attacking the transaction." Similarly, in Oberly v. Kirby, 592 A.2d 445 (Del.1991) the Delaware Supreme Court said, again in dictum "The key to upholding an interested transaction is the approval of some neutral decision-making body. Under 8 *Del.C.* § 144, a transaction will be sheltered from shareholder challenge if approved by ... a committee of independent directors [or] the shareholders...."

[F]or me to conclude that the disinterested directors' approval of the transaction shifted the burden of demonstrating the unfairness of the transaction to the plaintiffs, the defendants must demonstrate that they are entitled to rely on section 144(a)(1). That is, they carry the burden of demonstrating that the directors approving the load were "truly independent, fully informed, and had the freedom to negotiate at arm's length." Evidence that the "action taken was as though each of the contending parties had in

---

24. In Scott v. Multi–Amp Corp., 386 F.Supp. 44 (D.N.J.1974), the court took just this approach to the then-New Jersey statute, N.J.S.A. 14A.6–8. However, the statute was subsequently amended "to make it clear that a transaction is not voidable solely because of a director conflict if any one of the following conditions are met: (i) the transaction was fair at the time it was authorized; (ii) disclosure was made to the directors of the conflict and disinterested directors approved; or (iii) disclosure was made to the shareholders and the shareholders approved." Id., Commissioner's Note. The Commissioner's Note continued, "Scott v. Multi–Amp Corp., 386 F.Supp. 44, 66–69 (D.N.J.1974), construed the word 'or' in the prior statutory provision in the conjunctive, rather than the disjunctive, thus requiring the statutory criterion of 'fairness' in every case. [The] revision to Section 14A:6–8 reflects what the Commission viewed to be a better reading of the section." See also Tennessee Dressed Beef Co. v. Hall, 519 S.W.2d 805 (Tenn.App.1974).

fact exerted its bargaining power against the other at arm's length is strong evidence that the transaction meets the test of fairness.''

It is widely believed that regardless of the form of the statute, at least outside of Delaware approval by disinterested directors will not prevent a court from reviewing self-interested transactions for obvious unfairness. Section 5.02(a)(2)(B) of the ALI's Principles of Corporate Governance makes this implicit rule explicit, by adopting a test intermediate between the business-judgment rule and a full-fairness test in cases where a self-interested transaction has been approved by disinterested directors. Under that Section, where there has been authorization by disinterested directors, the complainant must show that disinterested directors "could not [have] reasonably ... believed" the transaction to be fair to the corporation. This test is intended to be easier for the director or senior executive to satisfy than a full-fairness test, although harder to satisfy than the business-judgment standard. Even in Delaware, it may be necessary to show that the directors who approved the transaction were not only disinterested, but independent, and directors who passively approve a manifestly unfair transaction may be deemed to exhibit a lack of independence by virtue of their conduct.

NEW YORK STOCK EXCHANGE LISTED COMPANY MANUAL § 312.03(b)

[See Statutory Supplement]

NOTE ON WASTE AND SHAREHOLDER RATIFICATION

An outside limit on the power of even disinterested directors or shareholders is the principle of waste. This principle was defined and explained as follows by Chancellor Allen in Lewis v. Vogelstein, 699 A.2d 327 (1997):

> The judicial standard for determination of corporate waste is well developed. Roughly, a waste entails an exchange of corporate assets for consideration so disproportionately small as to lie beyond the range at which any reasonable person might be willing to trade. Most often the claim is associated with a transfer of corporate assets that serves no corporate purpose; or for which no consideration at all is received. Such a transfer is in effect a gift. If, however, there is any substantial consideration received by the corporation, and if there is a *good faith judgment* that in the circumstances the transaction is worthwhile, there should be no finding of waste, even if the fact finder would conclude ex post that the transaction was unreasonably risky. Any other rule would deter corporate boards from the optimal rational acceptance of risk, for reasons explained elsewhere. Courts are ill-fitted to attempt to weigh the "adequacy" of consideration under the

waste standard or, ex post, to judge appropriate degrees of business risk.

Chancellor Allen's definition was later quoted with approval by the Delaware Supreme Court in Brehm v. Eisner, 746 A.2d 244, n. 62 (2000). A similar definition is found in the ALI's Principles of Corporate Governance:

> A transaction constitutes a "waste of corporate assets" if it involves an expenditure of corporate funds or a disposition of corporate assets for which no consideration is received in exchange and for which there is no rational business purpose, or if consideration is received in exchange, the consideration the corporation receives is so inadequate in value that no person of ordinary sound business judgment would deem it worth that which the corporation has paid.

Id. § 1.42. Although the concept of waste is applicable to action by the board, it has greater bite as a limit on action by shareholders, because a board that commits waste would normally also violate the business judgment rule in any event. The issue of waste therefore overlaps with the issue, what is the effect of shareholder ratification of a conflict-of-interest transaction. In *Vogelstein*, Chancellor Allen stated:

> What is the effect under Delaware corporation law of shareholder ratification of an interested transaction? The answer to this apparently simple question appears less clear than one would hope or indeed expect. Four possible effects of shareholder ratification appear logically available: First, one might conclude that an effective shareholder ratification acts as a complete defense to any charge of breach of duty. Second, one might conclude that the effect of such ratification is to shift the substantive test on judicial review of the act from one of fairness that would otherwise be obtained (because the transaction is an interested one) to one of waste. Third, one might conclude that the ratification shifts the burden of proof of unfairness to plaintiff, but leaves that shareholder protective test in place. Fourth, one might conclude (perhaps because of great respect for the collective action disabilities that attend shareholder action in public corporations) that shareholder ratification offers no assurance of assent of a character that deserves judicial recognition. Thus, under this approach, ratification on full information would be afforded no effect. Excepting the fourth of these effects, there are cases in this jurisdiction that reflect each of these approaches to the effect of shareholder voting to approve a transaction. . . .
>
> 1. *Ratification generally:* I start with principles broader than those of corporation law. Ratification is a concept deriving from the law of agency which contemplates the ex post conferring upon or confirming of the legal authority of an agent in circumstances in which the agent had no authority or arguably had no authority. Restatement (Second) of Agency § 82 (1958). To be effective, of course, the agent must fully disclose all relevant circumstances with respect to the transaction to the principal

prior to the ratification. See, e.g., Breen Air Freight, Ltd. v. Air Cargo, Inc., et al., 470 F.2d 767, 773 (2d Cir.1972); Restatement (Second) of Agency § 91 (1958). Beyond that, since the relationship between a principal and agent is fiduciary in character, the agent in seeking ratification must act not only with candor, but with loyalty. Thus an attempt to coerce the principal's consent improperly will invalidate the effectiveness of the ratification. Restatement (Second) of Agency § 100 (1958). . . .

Assuming that a ratification by an agent is validly obtained, what is its effect? One way of conceptualizing that effect is that it provides, after the fact, the grant of authority that may have been wanting at the time of the agent's act. Another might be to view the ratification as consent or as an estoppel by the principal to deny a lack of authority. See Restatement (Second) of Agency § 103 (1958). In either event the effect of informed ratification is to validate or affirm the act of the agent as the act of the principal. Id. § 82. . . .

2. *Shareholder ratification:* [The] differences between shareholder ratification of director action and classic ratification by a single principal, . . . lead to a difference in the effect of a valid ratification in the shareholder context. The principal novelty added to ratification law generally by the shareholder context, is the idea—no doubt analogously present in other contexts in which common interests are held—that, in addition to a claim that ratification was defective because of incomplete information or coercion, shareholder ratification is subject to a claim by a member of the class that the ratification is ineffectual (1) because a majority of those affirming the transaction had a conflicting interest with respect to it or (2) because the transaction that is ratified constituted a corporate waste. As to the second of these, it has long been held that shareholders may not ratify a waste except by a unanimous vote. Saxe v. Brady, 40 Del.Ch. 474, 184 A.2d 602, 605 (1962). The idea behind this rule is apparently that a transaction that satisfies the high standard of waste constitutes a gift of corporate property and no one should be forced against their will to make a gift of their property. In all events, informed, uncoerced, disinterested shareholder ratification of a transaction in which corporate directors have a material conflict of interest has the effect of protecting the transaction from judicial review except on the basis of waste. . . .

SECTION 3. COMPENSATION

———

DEL. GEN. CORP. LAW §§ 141(h), 157

[See Statutory Supplement]

———

MODEL BUS. CORP. ACT §§ 6.24, 8.11

[See Statutory Supplement]

———

ALI, PRINCIPLES OF CORPORATE GOVERNANCE § 5.03

———

**IN RE THE WALT DISNEY COMPANY
DERIVATIVE LITIGATION**

[Chapter 8, Section 2, supra]

———

**NEW YORK STOCK EXCHANGE LISTED
COMPANY MANUAL § 312.03(a)**

[See Statutory Supplement]

———

NOTE ON COMPENSATION LITIGATION IN CLOSE CORPORATIONS

At least in the past, it has been difficult to successfully challenge executive compensation in a publicly held corporation when the compensation has been approved by disinterested directors or disinterested shareholders. In such corporations, executive compensation has at least the appearance, and perhaps the reality, of having been approved through a disinterested bureaucratic process. Furthermore, except in the most extreme cases, executive compensation in publicly held corporations constitutes only a very small fraction of the corporation's total earnings.

In contrast, the courts often hold executive compensation to be unreasonable in close corporations. The close-corporation case differs from the publicly held corporation case in two critical ways. First, in close corporations executive compensation usually is not approved by either disinterested directors or disinterested shareholders. Second, in close corporations executive compensation is likely to involve a very significant fraction of the corporation's earnings—often, half or more.

Close-corporation compensation cases arise in several basic contexts.

One of these contexts is taxation. A basic income-tax rule is that except in S corporations, compensation paid to a corporate executive or other employee is a deductible expense, which reduces taxable income, while a dividend paid to a shareholder is not deductible. (In S corporations, income and expense items flow through directly to the shareholders.) Accordingly, the payment of compensation reduces the corporation's taxable income, and therefore its taxes, while the payment of dividends does not. In the close corporation, the same persons are typically both shareholders and managers. If dividends and compensation were treated the same way for tax purposes, the shareholders would often be indifferent whether they took cash out of the corporation in the form of compensation or dividends. Given the tax laws, however, shareholders in close corporations other than S corporations will normally prefer to take out cash in the form of compensation, so as to reduce the corporation's taxes. The Internal Revenue Service regularly challenges compensation in close corporations as unreasonable, and the courts often agree with the IRS's position. See, e.g., RTS Investment Corp. v. Commissioner, 877 F.2d 647 (8th Cir.1989). In such cases, the excess of actual compensation over reasonable compensation is treated as a dividend, and is not deductible from the corporation's taxable income.

Another context in which the courts often hold compensation in close corporations to be unreasonable is derivative actions by shareholders in such corporations to recover the excess compensation. See, e.g., Crowley v. Communications For Hospitals, Inc., 30 Mass.App.Ct. 751, 573 N.E.2d 996 (1991), review denied, 410 Mass. 1104, 577 N.E.2d 309 (1991); Wilderman v. Wilderman, p. 699, supra; Hall v. Staha, 303 Ark. 673, 800 S.W.2d 396 (1990).

Compensation is also sometimes attacked indirectly in the context of a close corporation when compensation payments to the shareholders are not pro rata. For example, a shareholder may claim that payments that were cast in the form of compensation were unreasonable, and really constituted a dividend that should have been distributed pro rata to all shareholders. See, e.g., Alaska Plastics, Inc. v. Coppock, 621 P.2d 270 (Alaska 1980), on appeal following remand 705 P.2d 443 (1985). Or, a claim of unreasonable compensation to some shareholders may be advanced as a reason why dissolution for oppression should be granted. In these contexts, the courts are often ready to find compensation to be excessive where only one faction in a close corporation receives compensation and dividends are low or nonexistent.

———

WILDERMAN v. WILDERMAN, 315 A.2d 610, 615 (Del.Ch.1974). This was a case involving a claim of excessive compensation in a close corporation, in which the compensation had not been approved by disinterested directors or shareholders. The court said: "As to the facts to be considered in reaching a determination of the question as to whether or not defendant has met the burden he must carry there is little authority in Delaware. In Hall v. Isaacs, [37 Del.Ch. 530, 146 A.2d 602, aff'd in part 39 Del.Ch. 244, 163 A.2d 288 (1960),] the Court was of the view that evidence of what other executives similarly situated received was relevant, and in Meiselman v. Eberstadt, [39 Del.Ch. 563, 170 A.2d 720 (1961)], the ability of the executive was considered. Other factors which have been judicially recognized elsewhere are whether or not the Internal Revenue Service has allowed the corporation to deduct the amount of salary alleged to be unreasonable. Other relevant factors are whether the salary bears a reasonable relation to the success of the corporation, the amount previously received as salary, whether increases in salary are geared to increases in the value of services rendered, and the amount of the challenged salary compared to other salaries paid by the employer.''

Subcommittee on Executive Compensation of the ABA Section on Corporation, Banking and Business Law, Executive Compensation: A 1987 Road Map for the Corporate Advisor

43 Bus.Law. 185 (1987).

CHAPTER 3: STOCK–RELATED LONG– TERM INCENTIVE PROGRAMS

I. NON–QUALIFIED (NONSTATUTORY) STOCK OPTIONS ...

As used in the context of an executive compensation program, the term ''non-qualified stock option'' means a right granted to one or more employees or executives by a corporation (or by a parent or subsidiary corporation) to acquire shares of the corporation's stock (or stock of a parent or subsidiary). Non-qualified stock options derive their name from the fact that neither the options nor the shares issued upon exercise of the options satisfy the criteria of, or ''qualify'' for, the special, and heretofore generally favorable, income tax treatment provided under the Code for incentive stock options (formerly ''statutory'' or ''qualified'' options). Since non-qualified stock options are neither afforded special tax treatment under nor defined in the Code, by way of contrast to the old statutory stock options, such options are also sometimes referred to as ''nonstatutory options.''

Stock options often constitute an important part of the compensation and incentive program of a corporation. They may be offered pursuant to a plan applicable to one or more executives, or they may represent part of the premium offered to attract new executives or retain the services of valued existing executives. By obtaining the right to acquire an equity interest in the corporation, whether at a discount or at market value, the executive acquires a stake in the long-term growth of the corporation, benefits from the capital appreciation of the corporation's stock, and therefore presumably will work diligently for the success of the venture. However, there is little empirical evidence to prove that corporate performance can be improved by granting stock options. . . .

Neither grant nor vesting of a non-qualified stock option would ordinarily result in recognition of taxable income. First, the grant of an option does not constitute a transfer of the underlying stock. Second, the option itself is not treated as ''property'' for federal income tax purposes unless the option has a readily ascertainable fair market value. According to the regulations, an option has a readily ascertainable fair market value where either: (i) the option itself is actively traded on an established market, or (ii) if not so traded, the option is transferable, immediately exercisable in full, and subject to no restrictions which would affect the fair market value of the option, and the option privilege has a readily ascertainable fair market value....

At the time of exercise of a non-qualified stock option, if the stock received on exercise is not restricted, the executive will recognize income immediately [equal to the difference between the option price and the market value of the stock when the option is exercised]....

In connection with exercise of a non-qualified stock option, the employer is entitled to a business expense deduction in an amount equal to the ordinary income realized by the executive. The deduction is allowed at the same time the executive recognizes income....

II. INCENTIVE STOCK OPTIONS

One of the most significant developments in the area of executive compensation prior to the passage of the 1986 Tax Act was the reinstatement by the Economic Recovery Tax Act of 1981 ("ERTA") of a special class of statutory stock options known as "incentive stock options." Incentive stock options provided several advantages for executives over nonstatutory stock options and were generally well received by major employers....

[To qualify for incentive-stock-option (ISO) treatment, a number of conditions must be satisfied, including the following: (1) The option must be issued pursuant to a written plan which specifies the total number of employees, or the class of employees, who are eligible to receive the options. (2) The written plan must restrict the maximum aggregate fair market value of the stock, with respect to which any employee may exercise options, to no more than $100,000 during any calendar year. (3) The plan must be approved by the shareholders, within twelve months before or after it is adopted by the board. (4) The option must be granted within ten years after the plan has been adopted by the board or approved by the shareholders, whichever is earlier. (5) The option must be exercisable only during the executive's employment, or within three months after termination of employment, and may not be exercisable for more than ten years from the date of grant. (6) The option price must equal or exceed the fair market value of the stock on the date that the option is granted.]

If the requirements for incentive stock option treatment are satisfied, the executive is not subject to federal income tax either at the time of grant of the option or at the time of its exercise.... Upon disposition of stock acquired pursuant to an incentive stock option, the executive will be taxed at long-term capital gains rates, provided certain holding period requirements are satisfied....

[Stock acquired pursuant to an ISO cannot be disposed of until at least two years has elapsed since the option was granted, and one year has elapsed since the stock was acquired by the employee pursuant to exercise of the option.]

. . . [N]o deduction is allowed [to an employer] with respect to an incentive stock option. . . .

III.   STOCK APPRECIATION RIGHTS

A stock appreciation right is the right to be paid an amount equal to the increase in value or spread between the value (or a fraction of the value) of a share of employer stock on the date the SAR is granted and the value (or a fraction of the value) of the share on the date the SAR is exercised. SARs are distinguishable from "phantom stock" . . . units (discussed in the next section) because SARs are usually granted in tandem or in conjunction with another right, usually a stock option, and SARs generally do not include (as phantom stock often does) a right to receive the value of dividends payable on the underlying stock while the SAR is outstanding.

SARs can be granted in conjunction with stock options in order to allow the executive to realize the increase in market value of the underlying stock without having to expend cash or otherwise raise capital to pay the option exercise price. In that case, the executive usually may choose to exercise either the option or the SAR, and the exercise of one extinguishes the right to exercise the other. If the executive chooses to exercise the SAR in lieu of the stock option, he may also sometimes choose whether the value of the SAR will be paid to him in cash or in stock. If the executive chooses to receive stock, he will have the opportunity to enjoy future appreciation in the value of the stock, although he will have fewer shares than if he had exercised the option. If the executive chooses cash, future growth in value will obviously depend on how the cash is invested.

Alternatively, SARs may be granted in connection with stock options in order to provide a source of cash with which to pay taxes upon exercise of the associated option. In that case the SAR is usually exercisable (or automatically exercised) in addition to, rather than in lieu of, the associated option, and the SAR is usually payable in cash. However, the executive may be given the right to elect to have some or all of the SAR paid in stock. . . .

SARs also may be granted independently of the grant of any option. When granted in this manner, so-called "naked SARs" take the form of stock-related performance units, entitling the holder to a form of deferred compensation that may be made conditional on continued services, noncompetition, or other conduct not adverse to the employer during or after the executive's termination of employment. . . .

Upon the exercise of an SAR, the executive will normally have to include in gross income (and thus subject to federal income tax) compensation in an amount equal to the cash and/or the fair market value of the shares of stock received pursuant to such exercise. . . .

The principal advantage of SARs to the executive is that they permit the executive to realize the appreciation in the value of employer stock without making an investment, or provide cash with which to pay taxes on exercise of non-qualified stock options....

The employer is entitled to a tax deduction at the time of and equal to the amount the executive receives pursuant to the exercise of SARs....

IV. PHANTOM STOCK ...

The term "phantom stock" can be used to describe any form of long-term executive incentive arrangement using units that are equivalent to, but are not, actual shares of employer stock. Thus, a phantom stock plan might provide outright grants of phantom "shares" or options based on phantom stock.

Under a phantom stock arrangement, the value of a unit of phantom stock typically equals the appreciation in the market value of the underlying stock between the date the unit is acquired by the executive and its settlement date. In that case, a phantom stock unit is substantially similar to a "naked SAR" discussed in the preceding section of this report....

Phantom stock units can be settled in cash, stock, or some combination of the two forms. Furthermore, dividend equivalents are sometimes paid or accrued on phantom stock.

Phantom stock plans are among the least common forms of long-term incentive compensation plans, particularly among large publicly-held companies. For example, in 1986, only three Fortune 100 companies reported offering such plans. By contrast, ninety-five percent of these companies reported the use of stock option plans that year....

Executives generally are taxed on phantom stock awards at the time the awards are settled in stock, cash or both. Stock settlements are [normally] taxed at the stock's fair market value on the settlement date.... In general, the executive must pay tax on the award at the ordinary income tax rates....

Employers are generally entitled to tax deductions for phantom stock payments in the year in which the payments are made. The employer's federal income tax deduction will generally occur in the fiscal year in which the executive is subject to federal income tax....

V. RESTRICTED STOCK ...

"Restricted stock" is a term that defies brief definition. It is capital stock, generally the common stock of an employer, issued pursuant to a plan or agreement to an executive in connection with the performance of services to the employer. The shares may be issued without cost or for a nominal price. The ownership of the stock is subject to certain conditions or "restrictions." The executive's right to ownership in some or all of the shares of the stock, "vesting," is generally made contingent upon the executive's continued employment by the employer for a certain period. Furthermore, the stock may vest ratably over a period of time, or nonratably, according to a prearranged schedule. The plan or agreement typically requires forfeiture of unvested shares upon the participant's termination of employment during the restriction period. Occasionally vested shares may also be subject to repurchase. The repurchase price for the nonvested stock is likely to be the price, if any, paid by the executive, while the repurchase price for the vested stock may be its fair market value as determined by the board of directors, its book value, or the price offered by a third party. . . .

. . . [Under Section 83 of the Code, and the regulations thereunder, if stock that does not have a readily ascertainable fair market value] is transferred to an executive in connection with the performance of services, the executive must include in gross taxable income the excess of the then fair market value of the [stock] over the amount, if any, paid for it in the first taxable year in which his beneficial interest in the stock is either transferable or is not subject to a substantial risk of forfeiture, [but can defer taxation on the stock until that time. Accordingly, the executive will normally recognize ordinary income when the restrictions on transferability expire, but not until then.

[The employer is entitled to a deduction for the amount of ordinary income that the employee recognizes. The employer's deduction is taken in the same year that the employee recognizes the ordinary income.]

SEC REGULATION S–K, ITEM 402

[See Statutory Supplement]

NOTE ON CEO COMPENSATION

The issue of executive compensation today has a high place on the corporate and even the national agenda. Most of the concerns have centered on the compensation of the chief executive officers (CEOs) of publicly held corporations. These complaints have fallen into several categories.

One concern is that CEO compensation is too large as an absolute matter. The *mean annual* compensation of CEOs in the corporations in the S&P 500 index, expressed in constant dollars, grew from $3.7 million in 1993 to $10.3 million in 2002. (The S&P 500 is a group of stocks that is considered representative of the stock market in general.) Bebchuck & Grinstein, The Growth of Executive Pay, Table 5 (2005). This growth is not explained by inflation, because the figures are inflation-adjusted. Nor is it explained by changes in market capitalization or industry mix. Id. at 13. *Equity-based* compensation of CEOs in the S&P 500 rose from 41% of total compensation in 1993 to 67% in 2002. Id. at Table 5. Finally, *the ratio* between (i) the total of the compensation of the top five executives, and (ii) corporate net income, for all corporations in the S&P 500, the "Mid-Cap" 400, and "Small-Cap" 600, rose from 5.7% in 1993–1997 to 9.9% in 1998–2002. Id. at Table 10. (The Mid-Cap 400 is a group of corporations that generally have market capitalizations of $2 billion to $10 billion. The Small-Cap 600 is a group of corporations that generally have market capitalizations of $300 million to $2 billion. Market capitalization is the total stock market value of a corporation's stock.) Of course, this is only the median, and many compensation packages were much higher. For example, according to the *Wall Street Journal*, in 1999 Michael Eisner of Disney made $576 million; Sandy Weill of Citigroup made $167 million; and Douglas Ivester of Coca–Cola made $57 million. In those years, the total shareholder return for Disney, as calculated by the Journal, was minus 5%; the total shareholder return for Citigroup was minus 6.8%; and the total shareholder return for Coca–Cola was 1.3%. Skipping forward, the *Journal* reported that in 2004, Reuben Mark of Colgate–Palmolive Co. made $141 million; Steve Jobs of Apple made $75 million; and George David of United Technologies made $70 million.

A related concern is that there is too much disparity between CEO compensation and average salaries. "In 1992, the average large-company CEO received approximately 140 times the pay of an average worker; in 2003, the separation was about 500:1." Id. In contrast, the average Japanese CEO apparently makes only 16 times the pay of an average Japanese industrial worker, and the average German apparently makes about 21 times the pay of the average German factory worker. G. Crystal, In Search of Excess 27, 206–09 (1991).

Complaints about both the absolute and relative levels of CEO compensation leave many unpersuaded, especially in an era in which so many athletes and entertainment stars earn as much or more as the median CEO in the *Journal* survey. It has also been suggested that CEO compensation should be understood as the prize in a tournament, for which the corporation's vice-presidents joust. "On the day that a given individual is promoted from vice-president to president, his salary may triple. It is difficult to argue that his skills have tripled in that 1–day period. . . . It is not a puzzle, however, when interpreted in the context of a prize. . . . [A CEO's] wage is settled on not necessarily because it reflects his current productivity as president, but rather because it induces that individual and all other individuals to perform appropriately when they are in more junior positions." Edward Lazear, and Sherwin Rosen, Rank–Order Tournaments as Optimum Labor Contracts, 89 Journal of Political Economy 841 (1981). (This theory has not been empirically verified. See O'Reilly et al., CEO Compensation Tournament and Social Comparison: A Tale of Two Theories, 33 Admin.Sci.Q. 257, 266 (1988).)

Perhaps the more significant complaints, which have attracted a relatively widespread following, concern the process for setting CEO compensation and the relation, or lack of it, between CEO compensation and corporate performance. A major concern here is that CEOs often effectively set their own compensation, because they dominate their boards. In theory, a chief executive's compensation is determined by the board on the recommendation of an independent compensation committee, which in turn acts on the recommendation of an independent personnel department and an independent outside consulting firm, all without the chief executive's participation. In practice, however, "the chief executive often has his hand in the pay-setting process almost from the first step." Williams, Why Chief Executives' Pay Keeps Rising, Fortune, April 1, 1985, at 66, 67. The CEO "generally approves, or at least knows about, the recommendation of his personnel executive *before* it goes to the compensation committee, and may take a similar pregame pass at the consultant's recommendations too." Id. "[T]he reality at most companies is that top management itself usually devises the executive compensation plan—hiring the consultants whose scheme is then ratified by the board of directors and shareholders. . . ." Personnel executives who don't recommend what the chief executive officer wants may find that their jobs are at risk; consultants who don't recommend what the chief executive wants are unlikely to be invited back. See Louis, Business is Bungling Long–Term Compensation, Fortune, July 23, 1984, at 64, 65.

One response to this problem has been an increased emphasis on disclosure and on the makeup and role of the compensation committee. The SEC has periodically revised the Proxy Rules to enormously increase the amount of disclosure required in connection with executive compensation, and to give a critical role to the compensation committee. See Proxy Rules Schedule 14A, Items 8, 10, and Reg. S–K, Item 402, in the Statutory Supplement. Up to now, at least, these changes seem to have had little or no effect.

INTERNAL REVENUE CODE § 161(m) AND REGULATIONS THEREUNDER

[See Statutory Supplement]

NOTE ON THE EFFECT OF FEDERAL INCOME TAX RULES AND ACCOUNTING PRINCIPLES ON THE FORMS OF EXECUTIVE COMPENSATION

The federal income tax helps shape a variety of corporate decisions. Under existing tax law, compensation in the form of incentive stock options and non-qualified stock options is given highly favorable treatment. A non-qualified stock option is not taxable when issued, but only when the option is exercised. An incentive stock option is not taxable when issued or when exercised, but only when the stock is sold. Even then, tax is levied at only the capital-gains rate. From the executive's perspective, the tax law therefore provides a push toward using one or more of those forms of compensation.

In the past, accounting rules have also given a strong push in this direction. Until recently, those principles provided that most forms of executive compensation had to be *expensed*—that is, deducted—from the corporation's net income, but this rule did not apply to the value of executive stock options. Instead, corporations that granted stock options to employees could account for the cost of these options based on their "intrinsic value" at the moment they were granted. An option's "intrinsic value" is the difference between its exercise price and the current price of its underlying security. Accordingly, if a company granted options with an exercise price equal to the price of the company's stock at the time of the grant, the company could avoid deducting the value of the options from its income. The result was that corporations could give a CEO millions or even billions worth of stock options without counting the value of those options against its reported income or in the CEO's reported compensation.

In December 2004, the Financial Accounting Standards Board (FASB), which is the chief private rulemaking body for setting accounting principles, issued Statement of Financial Accounting Standards No. 123, which changes the generally accepted accounting principles (GAAP) that apply to stock-option compensation plans. FASB Statement No. 123 requires companies to measure the value of options by computing their "fair value" on the date they were granted. A standard way to compute the value of an option is by using the Black–Scholes option pricing model. The application of this model depends on five variables: (1) The risk-free rate of interest. (2) The market price of the underlying stock. (3) The volatility of the price of the underlying stock. (Volatility is the size of fluctuations of a stock's price.) (4) The exercise price of the option. (5) The length of the option's term. The value of an option will increase with increases in (i) the risk-free rate of interest; (ii) the excess (if any) of the market price of the stock over the exercise price of the option; (iii) the volatility of the underlying stock; and (iv) the length of the term of option. All of these variables except volatility can be easily determined. Volatility is estimated in significant part on the basis of the stock's historical performance. (Certain factors that are not incorporated into the Black–Scholes option-pricing model may also affect the value of an option. For example, the model is designed to value a "European call option," which is exercisable only at the end of the option's term. If an option is an "American option," which permits the option holder to exercise the option at any time during the option's term, then the option's value will be higher. Variations of the Black–Scholes model take such factors into account.) FASB Statement No. 123 is to take effect for public companies, except for small businesses, on June 15, 2005; it is to take effect for publicly held small businesses and privately held companies on December 15, 2005.

Even before FASB Statement No. 123, companies were permitted to measure the cost of options by their fair value instead of by their intrinsic value. FASB Statement No. 123 reports that before the new ruling, 750 public companies had voluntarily adopted—or announced their intention to voluntarily adopt—fair value measurement. Still, the

FASB ruling has led some companies that oppose fair-value measurement to lobby Congress and the SEC to override the the FASB ruling. See Carrie Johnson, FASB Orders Options Counted as Expenses; Lobbyists Look to Head Off Plan, Wash. Post., Dec. 17, 2004, at E01.

The Internal Revenue Code also has special provisions that can affect the form and even the size of compensation by limits on corporate deductibility. This is true, for example, of the special rules on the taxation of stock options. Another relevant provision is Internal Revenue Code § 161(m). Under that provision, a publicly held corporation normally cannot deduct any compensation of a CEO, or any of its other four most highly paid executives, in excess of $1 million, unless the excess is based on performance goals formulated by independent directors and approved by the shareholders. As a practical matter, this provision has a very limited bite, because it is easy to set up watered-down or easily attainable performance goals.

NOTE ON THE COMPENSATION OF NONEXECUTIVE DIRECTORS

The compensation of nonexecutive directors has drawn increasing attention within the last few years. The modern theory of the role of the board in publicly held corporations is that the board should monitor the executives' conduct of the business. This monitoring model assumes that directors will be independent of the executives they are to monitor, and will have the proper incentives to play a monitoring role. Directorial independence and incentives, in turn, are affected by the amount and form of directorial compensation.

1. *Amount of Compensation.* To understand the significance of the amount of a director's compensation, it must be borne in mind that although nominally the executives are selected by the board, in practice the chief executive officer plays a significant and often decisive role in selecting the board. The CEO's role in the selection of directors may be diminishing somewhat but it is still very important. Correspondingly, directors who displease a CEO will often find it difficult to retain their board seats. Accordingly, in most publicly held corporations a director who has material financial incentives to retain his directorship will not be independent of the CEO.

The greater a director's compensation, the greater the director's financial incentives to retain his seat. Thus all other things—such as personal integrity and individual wealth—being equal, the greater the director's compensation, the less the director's independence. To take a simple case, a director who earns, say, $200,000/year, and whose continuation in office is wholly or partly under the control of the CEO, normally could not be deemed independent of the CEO, unless he was extremely wealthy. The trick, therefore, is to compensate directors in an amount that is sufficient to give responsible persons an incentive to serve as directors, and rewards that service in an appropriate way, but is not so large as to compromise directorial independence.

In the 1980s, directors' fees averaged about $30,000/year. Since the early 1990s, however, directors' compensation has been growing much faster than inflation, partly because director compensation now often includes stock or stock options. In 1994, the average compensation of directors in Fortune 500 corporations (that is, in the country's 500 largest nonfinancial corporations) was $50,000. In 2002, director compensation averaged $152,000 in the largest 200 companies and $116,000 in the largest 1,000 companies. Moreover, many directors also provide side services to the corporation in nondirectorial capacities such as consultants, professionals, or the like, which further increases their compensation, and therefore further compromises their independence.

2. *Form of Compensation.* Directorial independence and incentives may be affected by the *form,* as well as the amount, of a director's compensation.

a. *Compensation for consulting and other nondirectorial services.* The effect of the form of a director's compensation is particularly dramatic in the case of side compensation for services that a director renders to the corporation in a nondirectorial capacity. The selection of consultants, professionals, and the like is normally within the sole control of the executives. Therefore, even if a director could retain his board seat against the wishes of the CEO, he would stand to lose his side compensation if he falls into the CEO's disfavor.

Side compensation for nondirectorial services can be very large, and may be further augmented by fringe benefits. For example, in 1995 American Express paid Henry Kissinger, a non-executive director, the following compensation: annual consulting fees of $350,000; an annual director's retainer of $64,000; a prospective annual director's pension of $30,000; free director's life insurance; and the right to have American Express make a $500,000 gift to a charity of his choice at the time of his death. Knecht & Lublin, American Express Bars Using Directors as Paid Consultants, Wall St. J. April 12, 1995, at A.3. American Express eventually adopted a policy that prohibits outside directors from serving as consultants, but Dr. Kissinger was exempted from the policy. Similarly, until 1995 W.R. Grace paid annual consulting fees totaling $1.5 million to five directors who were longtime friends of Grace's chairman. In that year, the chairman was ousted and Grace adopted a policy that no one with a consulting contract could serve as a director.

b. *Pensions.* Pensions for directors are a relatively new idea, but lately have become widespread. Like side compensation, directorial pensions present problems of independence and incentives. "The most common director retirement program involves an annual cash retirement fee equal to the board retainer at the time the director retires. The period of time for which a director receives a retirement fee typically is either (1) for the number of years for which the director has served, with some imposing a maximum of 10 years, or (2) for life if the director has served a minimum of 10 years. In some cases, the director's surviving spouse received part of the director's retirement fee upon the director's death—either until a designated number of years have elapsed, or for the spouse's life." Report on the National Association of Corporate Directors Blue Ribbon Commission on Director Compensation 29 (1995) ("NACD Report").

Some pensions are even more generous. At one time, Warner–Lambert Company paid a lifetime pension of $35,000/year to any director who had served five years and reached age 70. Lublin, More Big Companies Reconsider Lavish Pensions for Directors, Wall St. J., Sept. 7, 1995, at B1, Col. 3. The threat of losing a pension payoff may be even greater than the threat of losing annual directors' fees, especially as a director approaches retirement age. Moreover, pensions are associated with employment status, and therefore set a poor psychological tone for directorial independence. It is no coincidence that basic directorial compensation has been traditionally called a "fee," or sometimes a "retainer"—not "salary" which, like pensions, connotes employment status.

The NACD Report recommended that directors should be paid only cash and stock, and that pensions and other benefits should not be granted to directors.

c. *Payment in stock.* Paying directors in the form of stock, rather than cash, may also matter. Over the years, a director who is paid in stock may find that stock in the corporation represents a significant portion of her wealth, at least if the sale of her stock is restricted by its terms. This should tend to align the director's interest more closely with the shareholders, and thereby provide an incentive for monitoring. See Elson, The Duty of Care, Compensation, and Stock Ownership, 63 U.Cinn.L.Rev. 649 (1995).

SECTION 4.   USE OF CORPORATE ASSETS; COMPETITION WITH THE CORPORATION; THE CORPORATE OPPORTUNITY DOCTRINE

Hawaiian International Finances, Inc. v. Pablo

Supreme Court of Hawaii, 1971.
53 Haw. 149, 488 P.2d 1172.

■ Before RICHARDSON, C.J., ABE, LEVINSON and KOBAYASHI, JJ., and MENOR, CIRCUIT JUDGE, in place of MARUMOTO, J., disqualified.

■ KOBAYASHI, JUSTICE.

This is an appeal by Hawaiian International Finances, Inc., a Hawaii corporation (herein appellant), from a judgment of the circuit court providing that Pastor Pablo (herein Pablo), Rufina Pablo (herein Mrs. Pablo) and Pastor Pablo Realty, Inc., a Hawaii corporation (herein Pablo Realty) (all collectively herein appellees), are not liable to appellant for certain commissions received by appellees for their participation in the procurement of certain investment properties for appellant.

Although appellant appeals from both the conclusions of law and findings of fact of the trial court, the requisite facts necessary for a proper disposition of this case are not in dispute. As such, the factual rendition is concise and includes only those facts considered essential by this court. They are in part as follows:

FACTS

Pablo was president of appellant during the time the events pertinent to this case took place. In addition he and his wife, Rufina Pablo, were directors of Pablo Realty.

Pablo and Mrs. Pablo had been traveling to California in and prior to 1964, at their own expense, in connection with their private real estate business. Upon their return to Hawaii in early 1964, both Pablo and Mrs. Pablo advised appellant of attractive real estate investment opportunities in California. Appellant's board of directors appointed a subcommittee of four persons, including Pablo and three others who are non-litigants herein, to represent the corporation and go to California to investigate such investments. While in California, agreements were entered into by Pablo on behalf of appellant to purchase two parcels of land. The sellers were represented by separate California real estate brokers who eventually split their commissions from the sellers with Pablo. The trial court found that appellees had had no formal agreements with either of the California selling brokers for any commission splitting prior to the execution of the contracts to purchase the two properties. Pablo did testify, however, in response to questioning by the trial court, that he did expect, as a real estate broker, a commission for his participation in the transactions, and that he was told by one of the selling brokers that he would be paid after the transactions were closed.

After the closing of the escrows, the selling brokers in California paid, as commissions $4,800.00 to Pablo in May, 1964 and $17,594.20 to Pablo Realty in April, 1964. At this time appellant did not know of the receipt of these commissions and did not learn of them until the matter was brought up at a corporate meeting in September, 1964. The actual amounts were not disclosed by Pablo until March, 1965.

The trial court concluded as follows:

"That, although the general rule is that a person who is the president and a director of a corporation is a fiduciary of the corporation and cannot profit from any breach of the fiduciary obligation, nevertheless, under the particular facts of this case, PASTOR A. PABLO, acting for himself and as an officer of PASTOR PABLO REALTY, INC., committed no wrong in accepting the two partial real estate commissions from the California real estate brokers and the court cannot in good conscience compel him to turn those moneys over to the corporation."

ISSUE

The question on appeal centers around the trial court's construction of the law as applied to the facts in this case. Essentially the issue is whether a corporate officer and director, acting for the corporation in the purchase of investment real estate, can retain a commission received from the real estate brokers representing the sellers, absent disclosure and an agreement with the corporation.

CORPORATE FIDUCIARY—UNDISCLOSED PROFITS

It is widely held that a director while engaged in a transaction for his corporation cannot retain an undisclosed profit. . . .

The Restatement of Restitution, § 197, comment *c* at 809–810, speaks directly to the facts of the instant case and explains the rationale of the law in this area:

> *c. Where no harm to beneficiary.* The rule stated in this Section is applicable although the profit received by the fiduciary is not at the expense of the beneficiary. Thus, where an agent to purchase property for his principal acts properly in making the purchase but subsequently receives a bonus from the seller, he holds the money received upon a constructive trust for his principal. The rule * * * is not based on harm done to the beneficiary in the particular case, but rests upon a broad principle of preventing a conflict of opposing interests in the minds of fiduciaries, whose duty it is to act solely for the benefit of their beneficiaries. . . .

APPELLANT'S INTEREST IN THE UNDISCLOSED COMMISSION

In a case involving a trustee who received a bonus from a third party for placing trust business, we held that "when the opportunity to make a profit arises from the position occupied by a fiduciary the profit realized belongs to the principal, at least when the fiduciary has excluded his principal from any chance to enjoy the opportunity coming to the fiduciary in this manner." In re Dean's Trust, 47 Haw. 629, 640, 394 P.2d 432, 438 (1964). . . .

Appellees attempt to circumvent the rationale of cases [like *Dean's Trust*] by arguing that appellant could not lawfully have shared in the selling real estate brokers' commissions because appellant was not a licensed real estate broker. They therefore conclude that appellant was not excluded from enjoying the benefit received by appellees. We need not reach this question. In in re Dean's Trust it was pointed out that a line of cases have held "that the contention of *ultra vires* does not lie in the mouth of a corporate officer claiming the profits of a transaction for himself." In re Dean's Trust, *supra,* 47 Haw. at 638, 394 P.2d at 437. Even if it were decided that appellant itself could not have lawfully received the commissions that would not be determinative. In a case similar to the one at hand, involving a corporate fiduciary who made a secret profit from a seller of land to the corporation, the court said that "[i]t appears only reasonable that [the corporation] would have been more anxious to acquire the property at a price less the commission paid [the fiduciary] than they would have been to purchase the property paying the price including the commission." Pryor v. Oak Ridge Development Corp., 97 Fla. 1085, 1092, 119 So. 326, 329 (1928). The same holds true in this case. Had appellant known that one of its directors, Pablo, would be receiving a commission from its purchase, it is reasonable to assume that it would have been more anxious to acquire the property at a price less that commission.

Appellees' contention that Pablo's actions were in good faith and resulted in no loss to appellant is of no consequence. Had Pablo disclosed the fact that he anticipated receiving commissions, this case would be different. Then appellant would have had an opportunity to either attempt to obtain the property at a price less the commissions or it could have agreed with Pablo to acquiesce in letting him retain the commissions he received. This was not done. Appellant did not even learn of the commissions until months after their receipt when Pablo was directly questioned about them during a corporate meeting.

CONCLUSION

In accordance with the principles relating to corporate fiduciaries espoused herein, appellees Pablo and Pablo Realty are liable to appellant for the commissions they received and the trial court's judgment is reversed. As to appellee Mrs. Pablo, we affirm the judgment of the trial court, the trial court having specifically found, in its findings of fact, that Mrs. Pablo had no connection with the receipt of the commissions.

Remanded for entry of judgment consistent with this opinion.

———

FORKIN v. COLE, 192 Ill.App.3d 409, 139 Ill.Dec. 410, 548 N.E.2d 795 (1989). Cole, who controlled HPDI Corporation, mortgaged HPDI property to First National Bank to secure a personal loan made to Cole by the Bank. In affirming a judgment in favor of HPDI, the court said "Defendants ... contend the mortgage of the HPDI property to the First National Bank as security for a loan to Cole Sr. should not have resulted in judgment against Cole Sr., in that no material loss occurred to HPDI.... [However,] by encumbering the HPDI asset, Cole Sr. used a corporate asset for his own personal benefit. It also arguably could have prevented HPDI from taking advantage of a corporate opportunity had one arisen. The misappropriation of a corporate asset provided an advantage to Cole Sr."

———

AMERICAN LAW INSTITUTE, PRINCIPLES OF CORPORATE GOVERNANCE § 5.04

[See Statutory Supplement]

———

RESTATEMENT (SECOND) OF AGENCY § 388

[See Statutory Supplement]

Northeast Harbor Golf Club, Inc. v. Harris

Supreme Judicial Court of Maine, 1995.
661 A.2d 1146.

■ Before WATHEN, C.J., and ROBERTS, GLASSMAN, DANA, and LIPEZ, JJ.

■ ROBERTS, JUSTICE.

Northeast Harbor Golf Club, Inc., appeals from a judgment entered in the Superior Court (Hancock County, *Atwood, J.*) following a nonjury trial. The Club maintains that the trial court erred in finding that Nancy Harris did not breach her fiduciary duty as president of the Club by purchasing and developing property abutting the golf course. Because we today adopt principles different from those applied by the trial court in determining that Harris's activities did not constitute a breach of the corporate opportunity doctrine, we vacate the judgment.

I.

The Facts

Nancy Harris was the president of the Northeast Harbor Golf Club, a Maine corporation, from 1971 until she was asked to resign in 1990. The Club also had a board of directors that was responsible for making or approving significant policy decisions. The Club's only major asset was a golf course in Mount Desert. During Harris's tenure as president, the board occasionally discussed the possibility of developing some of the Club's real estate in order to raise money. Although Harris was generally in favor of tasteful development, the board always "shied away" from that type of activity.

In 1979, Robert Suminsby informed Harris that he was the listing broker for the Gilpin property, which comprised three noncontiguous parcels located among the fairways of the golf course. The property included an unused right-of-way on which the Club's parking lot and clubhouse were located. It was also encumbered by an easement in favor of the Club allowing foot traffic from the green of one hole to the next tee. Suminsby testified that he contacted Harris because she was the president of the Club and he believed that the Club would be interested in buying the property in order to prevent development.

Harris immediately agreed to purchase the Gilpin property in her own name for the asking price of $45,000. She did not disclose her plans to purchase the property to the Club's board prior to the purchase. She informed the board at its annual August meeting that she had purchased the property, that she intended to hold it in her own name, and that the Club would be "protected." The board took no action in response to the Harris purchase. She testified that at the time of the purchase she had no plans to develop the property and that no such plans took shape until 1988.

In 1984, while playing golf with the postmaster of Northeast Harbor, Harris learned that a parcel of land owned by the heirs of the Smallidge family might be available for purchase. The Smallidge parcel was surrounded on three sides by the golf course and on the fourth side by a house lot. It had no access to the road. With the ultimate goal of acquiring the property, Harris instructed her lawyer to locate the Smallidge heirs. Harris testified that she told a number of individual board members about her attempt to acquire the Smallidge parcel. At a board meeting in August 1985, Harris formally disclosed to the board that she had purchased the Smallidge property.[1] The minutes of that meeting show that she told the board she had no present plans to develop the Smallidge parcel. Harris testified that at the time of the purchase of the Smallidge property she nonetheless thought it might be nice to have some houses there. Again, the board took no formal action as a result of Harris's purchase. Harris acquired the Smallidge property from ten heirs, paying a total of $60,000. In 1990, Harris paid $275,000 for the lot and building separating the Smallidge parcel from the road in order to gain access to the otherwise landlocked parcel.

The trial court expressly found that the Club would have been unable to purchase either the Gilpin or Smallidge properties for itself, relying on testimony that the Club continually experienced financial difficulties, operated annually at a deficit, and depended on contributions from the directors to pay its bills. On the other hand, there was evidence that the Club had occasionally engaged in successful fundraising, including a two-year period shortly after the Gilpin purchase during which the Club raised $115,000. The Club had $90,000 in a capital investment fund at the time of the Smallidge purchase.

In 1987 or 1988, Harris divided the real estate into 41 small lots, 14 on the Smallidge property and 27 on the Gilpin property. Apparently as part of her estate plan, Harris conveyed noncontiguous lots among the 41 to her children and retained others for herself. In 1991, Harris and her children exchanged deeds to reassemble the small lots into larger parcels. At the time the Club filed this suit, the property was divided into 11 lots, some owned by Harris and others by her children who are also defendants in this case. Harris estimated the value of all the real estate at the time of the trial to be $1,550,000.

In 1988, Harris, who was still president of the Club, and her children began the process of obtaining approval for a five-lot subdivision known as Bushwood on the lower Gilpin property. Even when the board learned of the proposed subdivision, a majority failed to take any action. A group of directors formed a separate organization in order to oppose the subdivision on the basis that it violated the local zoning ordinance. After Harris's resignation as president, the Club also sought unsuccessfully to challenge the subdivision. *See Northeast*

---

1. In fact, it appears that Harris did not take title to the property until October 26, 1985. She had only signed a purchase and sale agreement at the time of the August board meeting.

Harbor Golf Club, Inc. v. Town of Mount Desert, 618 A.2d 225 (Me.1992). Plans of Harris and her family for development of the other parcels are unclear, but the local zoning ordinance would permit construction of up to 11 houses on the land as currently divided.

After Harris's plans to develop Bushwood became apparent, the board grew increasingly divided concerning the propriety of development near the golf course. At least two directors, Henri Agnese and Nick Ludington, testified that they trusted Harris to act in the best interests of the Club and that they had no problem with the development plans for Bushwood. Other directors disagreed.

In particular, John Schafer, a Washington, D.C., lawyer and long-time member of the board, took issue with Harris's conduct. He testified that he had relied on Harris's representations at the time she acquired the properties that she would not develop them. According to Schafer, matters came to a head in August 1990 when a number of directors concluded that Harris's development plans irreconcilably conflicted with the Club's interests. As a result, Schafer and two other directors asked Harris to resign as president. In April 1991, after a substantial change in the board's membership, the board authorized the instant lawsuit against Harris for the breach of her fiduciary duty to act in the best interests of the corporation. The board simultaneously resolved that the proposed housing development was contrary to the best interests of the corporation.

The Club filed a complaint against Harris, her sons John and Shepard, and her daughter-in-law Melissa Harris. As amended, the complaint alleged that during her term as president Harris breached her fiduciary duty by purchasing the lots without providing notice and an opportunity for the Club to purchase the property and by subdividing the lots for future development. The Club sought an injunction to prevent development and also sought to impose a constructive trust on the property in question for the benefit of the Club.

The trial court found that Harris had not usurped a corporate opportunity because the acquisition of real estate was not in the Club's line of business. Moreover, it found that the corporation lacked the financial ability to purchase the real estate at issue. Finally, the court placed great emphasis on Harris's good faith. It noted her long and dedicated history of service to the Club, her personal oversight of the Club's growth, and her frequent financial contributions to the Club. The court found that her development activities were "generally ... compatible with the corporation's business." This appeal followed.

II.

The Corporate Opportunity Doctrine

Corporate officers and directors bear a duty of loyalty to the corporations they serve. As Justice Cardozo explained the fiduciary duty in *Meinhard v. Salmon,* 249 N.Y. 458, 164 N.E. 545, 546 (1928):

A trustee is held to something stricter than the morals of the marketplace. Not honesty alone, but the punctilio of an honor the most sensitive, is then the standard of behavior. As to this there has developed a tradition that is unbending and inveterate.

Maine has embraced this "unbending and inveterate" tradition. Corporate fiduciaries in Maine must discharge their duties in good faith with a view toward furthering the interests of the corporation. They must disclose and not withhold relevant information concerning any potential conflict of interest with the corporation, and they must refrain from using their position, influence, or knowledge of the affairs of the corporation to gain personal advantage. *See Rosenthal v. Rosenthal*, 543 A.2d 348, 352 (Me.1988); 13–A M.R.S.A. § 716 (Supp. 1994).

Despite the general acceptance of the proposition that corporate fiduciaries owe a duty of loyalty to their corporations, there has been much confusion about the specific extent of that duty when, as here, it is contended that a fiduciary takes for herself a corporate opportunity. *See, e.g.,* Victor Brudney & Robert C. Clark, *A New Look at Corporate Opportunities,* 94 HARV.L.REV. 998, 998 (1981) ("Not only are the common formulations vague, but the courts have articulated no theory that would serve as a blueprint for constructing meaningful rules."). This case requires us for the first time to define the scope of the corporate opportunity doctrine in Maine.

Various courts have embraced different versions of the corporate opportunity doctrine. The test applied by the trial court and embraced by Harris is generally known as the "line of business" test. The seminal case applying the line of business test is *Guth v. Loft, Inc.,* 5 A.2d 503 (Del.1939). In *Guth,* the Delaware Supreme Court adopted an intensely factual test stated in general terms as follows:

> [I]f there is presented to a corporate officer or director a business opportunity which the corporation is financially able to undertake, is, from its nature, in the line of the corporation's business and is of practical advantage to it, is one in which the corporation has an interest or a reasonable expectancy, and, by embracing the opportunity, the self-interest of the officer or director will be brought into conflict with that of his corporation, the law will not permit him to seize the opportunity for himself.

Id. at 511. The "real issue" under this test is whether the opportunity "was so closely associated with the existing business activities . . . as to bring the transaction within that class of cases where the acquisition of the property would throw the corporate officer purchasing it into competition with his company." *Id.* at 513. The Delaware court described that inquiry as "a factual question to be decided by reasonable inferences from objective facts." *Id.*

The line of business test suffers from some significant weaknesses. First, the question whether a particular activity is within a corporation's line of business is conceptually difficult to answer. The facts of the instant case demonstrate that difficulty. The Club is in the business of running a golf course. It is not in the business of developing real estate. In the traditional sense, therefore, the trial court correctly observed that the opportunity in this case was not a corporate opportunity within the meaning of the *Guth* test. Nevertheless, the record would support a finding that the Club had made the policy judgment that development of surrounding real estate was detrimental to the best interests of the Club. The acquisition of land adjacent to the golf course for the purpose of preventing future development would have enhanced the ability of the Club to implement that policy. The record also shows that the Club had occasionally considered reversing that policy and expanding its operations to include the development of surrounding real estate. Harris's activities effectively foreclosed the Club from pursuing that option with respect to prime locations adjacent to the golf course.

Second, the *Guth* test includes as an element the financial ability of the corporation to take advantage of the opportunity. The court in this case relied on the Club's supposed financial incapacity as a basis for excusing Harris's conduct. Often, the injection of financial ability into the equation will unduly favor the inside director or executive who has command of the facts relating to the finances of the corporation. Reliance on financial ability will also act as a disincentive to corporate executives to solve corporate financing and other problems. In addition, the Club could have prevented development without spending $275,000 to acquire the property Harris needed to obtain access to the road.

The Massachusetts Supreme Judicial Court adopted a different test in *Durfee v. Durfee & Canning, Inc.*, 323 Mass. 187, 80 N.E.2d 522 (1948). The *Durfee* test has since come to be known as the "fairness test." According to *Durfee,* the

> true basis of governing doctrine rests on the unfairness in the particular circumstances of a director, whose relation to the corporation is fiduciary, taking advantage of an opportunity [for her personal profit] when the interest of the corporation justly call[s] for protection. This calls for application of ethical standards of what is fair and equitable . . . in particular sets of facts.

Id. at 529 (quoting *Ballantine on Corporations* 204–05 (rev. ed. 1946)). As with the *Guth* test, the *Durfee* test calls for a broad-ranging, intensely factual inquiry. The *Durfee* test suffers even more than the *Guth* test from a lack of principled content. It provides little or no practical guidance to the corporate officer or director seeking to measure her obligations.

The Minnesota Supreme Court elected "to combine the 'line of business' test with the 'fairness' test." *Miller v. Miller*, 301 Minn. 207, 222 N.W.2d 71, 81 (1974). It engaged in a two-step analysis, first determining whether a particular opportunity was within the corporation's line of business, then scrutinizing "the equitable considerations existing prior to, at the time of, and following the officer's acquisition." *Id.* The *Miller* court hoped by adopting this approach "to ameliorate the often-expressed criticism that the [corporate opportunity] doctrine is vague and subjects today's corporate management to the danger of unpredictable liability." *Id.* In fact, the test adopted in *Miller* merely piles the uncertainty and vagueness of the fairness test on top of the weaknesses in the line of business test.

Despite the weaknesses of each of these approaches to the corporate opportunity doctrine, they nonetheless rest on a single fundamental policy. At bottom, the corporate opportunity doctrine recognizes that a corporate fiduciary should not serve both corporate and personal interests at the same time. As we observed in *Camden Land Co. v. Lewis,* 101 Me. 78, 97, 63 A. 523, 531 (1905), corporate fiduciaries "owe their whole duty to the corporation, and they are not to be permitted to act when duty conflicts with interest. They cannot serve themselves and the corporation at the same time." The various formulations of the test are merely attempts to moderate the potentially harsh consequences of strict adherence to that policy. It is important to preserve some ability for corporate fiduciaries to pursue personal business interests that present no real threat to their duty of loyalty.

III.

The American Law Institute Approach

In an attempt to protect the duty of loyalty while at the same time providing long-needed clarity and guidance for corporate decision-makers, the American Law Institute has offered the most recently developed version of the corporate opportunity doctrine. PRINCIPLES OF CORPORATE GOVERNANCE § 5.05 (May 13, 1992), provides as follows:

§ **5.05 Taking of Corporate Opportunities by Directors or Senior Executives**

(a) *General Rule.* A director [§ 1.13] or senior executive [§ 1.33] may not take advantage of a corporate opportunity unless:

(1) The director or senior executive first offers the corporate opportunity to the corporation and makes disclosure concerning the conflict of interest [§ 1.14(a)] and the corporate opportunity [§ 1.14(b)];

(2) The corporate opportunity is rejected by the corporation; and

(3) Either:

(A) The rejection of the opportunity is fair to the corporation;

(B) The opportunity is rejected in advance, following such disclosure, by disinterested directors [§ 1.15], or, in the case of a senior executive who is not a director, by a disinterested superior, in a manner that satisfies the standards of the business judgment rule [§ 4.01(c)]; or

(C) The rejection is authorized in advance or ratified, following such disclosure, by disinterested shareholders [§ 1.16], and the rejection is not equivalent to a waste of corporate assets [§ 1.42].

(b) *Definition of a Corporate Opportunity.* For purposes of this Section, a corporate opportunity means:

(1) Any opportunity to engage in a business activity of which a director or senior executive becomes aware, either:

(A) In connection with the performance of functions as a director or senior executive, or under circumstances that should reasonably lead the director or senior executive to believe that the person offering the opportunity expects it to be offered to the corporation; or

(B) Through the use of corporate information or property, if the resulting opportunity is one that the director or senior executive should reasonably be expected to believe would be of interest to the corporation; or

(2) Any opportunity to engage in a business activity of which a senior executive becomes aware and knows is closely related to a business in which the corporation is engaged or expects to engage.

(c) *Burden of Proof.* A party who challenges the taking of a corporate opportunity has the burden of proof, except that if such party establishes that the requirements of Subsection (a)(3)(B) or (C) are not met, the director or the senior executive has the burden of proving that the rejection and the taking of the opportunity were fair to the corporation.

(d) *Ratification of Defective Disclosure.* A good faith but defective disclosure of the facts concerning the corporate opportunity may be cured if at any time (but no later than a reasonable time after suit is filed challenging the taking of the corporate opportunity) the original rejection of the corporate opportunity is ratified, following the required disclosure, by the board, the shareholders, or the corporate decisionmaker who initially approved the rejection of the corporate opportunity, or such decisionmaker's successor.

(e) *Special Rule Concerning Delayed Offering of Corporate Opportunities.* Relief based solely on failure to first offer an opportunity to the corporation under Subsection (a)(1) is not available if: (1) such failure resulted from a good faith belief that the business activity did not constitute a corporate opportunity, and (2) not later than a reasonable time after suit is filed challenging the taking of the corporate opportunity, the corporate opportunity is to the extent possible offered to the corporation and rejected in a manner that satisfies the standards of Subsection (a).

The central feature of the ALI test is the strict requirement of full disclosure prior to taking advantage of any corporate opportunity. *Id.,* § 5.05(a)(1). "If the opportunity is not offered to the corporation, the director or senior executive will not have satisfied § 5.05(a)." *Id.,* cmt.

to § 5.05(a). The corporation must then formally reject the opportunity. *Id.,* § 505(a)(2). The ALI test is discussed at length and ultimately applied by the Oregon Supreme Court in *Klinicki v. Lundgren,* 298 Or. 662, 695 P.2d 906 (1985). As *Klinicki* describes the test, "full disclosure to the appropriate corporate body is ... an absolute condition precedent to the validity of any forthcoming rejection as well as to the availability to the director or principal senior executive of the defense of fairness." *Id.* at 920. A "good faith but defective disclosure" by the corporate officer may be ratified after the fact only by an affirmative vote of the disinterested directors or shareholders. PRINCIPLES OF CORPORATE GOVERNANCE § 5.05(d).

The ALI test defines "corporate opportunity" broadly. It includes opportunities "closely related to a business in which the corporation is engaged." *Id.,* § 5.05(b). It also encompasses any opportunities that accrue to the fiduciary as a result of her position within the corporation. *Id.* This concept is most clearly illustrated by the testimony of Suminsby, the listing broker for the Gilpin property, which, if believed by the factfinder, would support a finding that the Gilpin property was offered to Harris specifically in her capacity as president of the Club. If the factfinder reached that conclusion, then at least the opportunity to acquire the Gilpin property would be a corporate opportunity. The state of the record concerning the Smallidge purchase precludes us from intimating any opinion whether that too would be a corporate opportunity.

Under the ALI standard, once the Club shows that the opportunity is a corporate opportunity, it must show either that Harris did not offer the opportunity to the Club or that the Club did not reject it properly. If the Club shows that the board did not reject the opportunity by a vote of the disinterested directors after full disclosure, then Harris may defend her actions on the basis that the taking of the opportunity was fair to the corporation. *Id.,* § 5.05(c). If Harris failed to offer the opportunity at all, however, then she may not defend on the basis that the failure to offer the opportunity was fair. *Id.,* cmt. to § 5.05(c).

The *Klinicki* court viewed the ALI test as an opportunity to bring some clarity to a murky area of the law. *Klinicki,* 695 P.2d at 915. We agree, and today we follow the ALI test. The disclosure-oriented approach provides a clear procedure whereby a corporate officer may insulate herself through prompt and complete disclosure from the possibility of a legal challenge. The requirement of disclosure recognizes the paramount importance of the corporate fiduciary's duty of loyalty. At the same time it protects the fiduciary's ability pursuant to the proper procedure to pursue her own business ventures free from the possibility of a lawsuit.

The importance of disclosure is familiar to the law of corporations in Maine. Pursuant to 13-A M.R.S.A. § 717 (1981), a corporate officer or director may enter into a transaction with the corporation in which she has a personal or adverse interest only if she discloses her interest in the transaction and secures ratification by a majority of the disinterested directors or shareholders. Section 717 is part of the Model Business Corporations Act, adopted in Maine in 1971. P.L.1971, ch. 439, § 1. Like the ALI rule, section 717 was designed to "eliminate the inequities and uncertainties caused by the existing rules." Model Business Corp. Act § 41, § 2, at 844 (1971).

IV.

Conclusion

The question remains how our adoption of the rule affects the result in the instant case. The trial court made a number of factual findings based on an extensive record.[3] The court made those findings, however, in the light of legal principles that are different from the principles that we today announce. Similarly, the parties did not have the opportunity to develop the record in this case with knowledge of the applicable legal standard. In these circumstances, fairness requires that we remand the case for further proceedings. Those further proceedings may include, at the trial court's discretion, the taking of further evidence.

The entry is:

Judgment vacated.

Remanded for further proceedings consistent with the opinion herein.

All concurring.

———

NOTE ON FURTHER PROCEEDINGS IN NORTHEAST HARBOR GOLF CLUB, INC. v. HARRIS

Following remand, the Superior Court entered judgment for the Club. On appeal, the Maine Supreme Court held that the Gilpin and Smallidge properties were both corporate opportunities, and that Harris breached her fiduciary obligations by not offering those opportunities to the Club's board:

> The subject of this lawsuit is land surrounding the Club that Harris purchased in her own name, some in 1979, and more in 1985. In 1979, in her capacity as Club president, Harris learned of an opportunity to purchase property owned by Lucy Gilpin. The Gilpin property adjoins Club property, including the driveway which provided access to the golf course, the clubhouse, and a portion of the Club's parking lot. Moreover, the Gilpin property is encumbered by an easement that allows golfers to travel from the green of one hole to the tee area of the next hole.

---

3. Harris raised the defense of laches and the statute of limitations but the court made no findings on those issues. We do not intimate what result the application of either doctrine would produce in this case....

Harris purchased the Gilpin property in her own name for $45,000. She did not disclose her plans to the board prior to acquiring the property. . . .

In 1984, Harris, independent of her position with the Club,[2] learned of the availability of property owned by the Smallidge family. The property was surrounded on three sides by the Club and on the fourth side by a house. Harris contracted to purchase eight of the ten interests of the Smallidge heirs in February of 1985, another in March, and the last in June of 1985, for a total of $60,000.[3] Harris disclosed the purchase to the board of directors at the Club's annual meeting on August 28, 1985. . . .

Harris concedes that, because she learned of the opportunity to purchase the Gilpin property in her capacity as president of the Club, her purchase of that property in 1979 constituted the taking of a corporate opportunity. See Principles of Corporate Governance § 5.05(b)(1)(A) (American Law Institute, May 13, 1992). . . .

Even if the opportunity to engage in a business activity, in which the officer or director becomes involved, is not learned of through her connection to the business of the corporation, nevertheless, such an opportunity may be considered a corporate opportunity if the officer or director knows it "is closely related to a business in which the corporation is engaged or expects to engage." Principles of Corporate Governance § 5.50(b)(2).

"The central feature of the ALI test is the strict requirement of full disclosure prior to taking advantage of any corporate opportunity." Northeast Harbor Golf Club, 661 A.2d at 1151. This feature was designed to prevent individual directors and officers from substituting their own judgment for that of the corporation when determining whether it would be in the corporate interest, or whether the corporation is financially or otherwise able to take advantage of an opportunity. . . . Doubt about the financial capacity of a corporation to pursue an opportunity may affect the incentive of a director or officer to solve corporate financing problems, and evidence regarding the corporation's financial status is often controlled by the usurping corporate director or officer. See Victor Brudney & Robert Charles Clark, A New Look at Corporate Opportunities, 94 HARV. L. REV. 998, 1020–22 (1981). The ALI approach recognizes the danger in allowing an individual director or officer to determine whether a corporation has the ability to take an opportunity, and accordingly disclosure to the corporation is required.

Full disclosure is likewise important to prevent individual directors and officers from using their own unfettered judgment to determine whether the business opportunity is related to the

---

2. While playing golf with the postmaster of Northeast Harbor, Harris learned that property owned by the heirs of the Smallidge family might be available for purchase.

3. In 1990, because the Smallidge property was landlocked, Harris purchased a house and property separating the Smallidge property from the road for $275,000.

corporation's business, such that it would be in the corporate interest to take advantage of that opportunity. "The appropriate method to determine whether or not a corporate opportunity exists is to let the corporation decide at the time the opportunity is presented." 3 FLETCHER CYC. CORP. § 861.10, p. 285 (1994). This rule protects individual directors and officers because after disclosing the potential opportunity to the corporation, they can pursue their own business ventures free from the possibility of a lawsuit. If there is doubt as to whether a business opportunity is closely related to the business of the corporation, that doubt must be resolved in favor of the corporation so that the officer or director will have a strong incentive to disclose any business opportunity even remotely related to the business of the corporation.

In this case, the Club's normal business is maintaining and operating a golf course. That business is dependent on having sufficient land for the course itself and ensuring that the activity of golf is not hindered or affected by development of adjacent and surrounding property. The Club had frequently discussed developing some of its own land and on one occasion talked about the possibility of purchasing and developing adjacent land. The purchase of the Smallidge land, surrounded as it is on three sides by the Club's land and adjacent to three of its golf holes, land that could be developed, is, in the circumstances of this case, sufficiently related to the Club's business to constitute a corporate opportunity. . . .

However, the court also concluded that the Club's action was barred by the statute of limitations.

———

BROZ v. CELLULAR INFORMATION SYSTEMS, INC., 673 A.2d 148 (Del.1996). Robert F. Broz was the President and sole stockholder of RFB Cellular, Inc. (RFBC), a Delaware corporation engaged in the business of providing cellular telephone service in the Midwest. RFBC held an FCC license known as the Michigan–4 Rural Service Area Cellular License (Michigan–4). The license entitled RFBC to provide cellular telephone service to its service area, a portion of rural Michigan. Broz was also an outside director of Cellular Information Systems, Inc. (CIS), a publicly held Delaware corporation and a competitor of RFBC. CIS was at all times fully aware of Broz's relationship with RFBC.

In April 1994, Mackinac Cellular Corp. wanted to sell an FCC cellular-phone-license area known as Michigan–2, which was immediately adjacent to Michigan–4. Mackinac's broker, Daniels, contacted Broz and broached the subject of RFBC's possible acquisition of Michigan–2. Daniels did not offer Michigan–2 to CIS. Apparently, Daniels did not consider CIS to be a viable purchaser for Michigan–2 because CIS had recently emerged from Chapter 11 bankruptcy proceedings, and had entered into a loan agreement that substantially impaired its ability to undertake new acquisitions or to incur new debt.

On June 1994, Broz spoke with CIS's Chief Executive Officer, Richard Treibick, concerning Broz's interest in acquiring Michigan–2. Treibick told Broz that CIS was not interested in Michigan–2. In August 1994, Broz contacted two other CIS directors, who expressed their belief that CIS had neither the resources nor the inclination to purchase Michigan–2. Ultimately, all the CIS directors testified at trial that if Broz had inquired at that time, they each would have expressed the opinion that CIS was not interested in Michigan–2.

In November 1994, Broz agreed to pay Mackinac $7.2 million for the Michigan–2 license. Thereafter, an asset-purchase agreement was executed by Mackinac and RFBC.

Meanwhile, between April 1994, when Broz had become aware of the opportunity to purchase the Michigan–2 license, and November 1994, when he purchased the license, a third party, PriCellular, Inc. had been in negotiations to purchase CIS's stock by negotiated transactions and a tender offer. The tender offer closed nine days after Broz purchased the license, and PriCellular became the owner of CIS. PriCellular then caused CIS to sue Broz, claiming that the purchase of the Michigan–2 license usurped a corporate opportunity of CIS. CIS admitted that at the time the opportunity was offered to Broz, the board of CIS would not have been interested in Michigan–2, but claimed that Broz was required to look not just to the interests of CIS at that time, but also to the articulated business plans of PriCellular, to determine whether PriCellular would be interested in acquiring Michigan–2. CIS contended that since Broz failed to do this, and instead acquired Michigan–2 without first considering the interests of PriCellular in its capacity as a potential acquiror of CIS, Broz must be held to account for breach of fiduciary duty. The Chancery court entered judgment for CIS. The Delaware Supreme Court reversed:

> The corporate opportunity doctrine, as delineated by [Guth v. Loft, Inc., 5 A.2d 503 (Del. 1939)] and its progeny, holds that a corporate officer or director may not take a business opportunity for his own if: (1) the corporation is financially able to exploit the opportunity; (2) the opportunity is within the corporation's line of business; (3) the corporation has an interest or expectancy in the opportunity; and (4) by taking the opportunity for his own, the corporate fiduciary will thereby be placed in a position inimicable to his duties to the corporation. The Court in *Guth* also derived a corollary which states that a director or officer may take a corporate opportunity if: (1) the opportunity is presented to the director or officer in his individual and not his corporate capacity; (2) the opportunity is not essential to the corporation; (3) the corporation holds no interest or expectancy in the opportunity; and (4) the director or officer has not wrongfully employed the resources of the corporation in pursuing or exploiting the opportunity. *Guth*, 5 A.2d at 509.

Thus, the contours of this doctrine are well established. It is important to note, however, that the tests enunciated in *Guth* and subsequent cases provide guidelines to be considered by a reviewing court in balancing the equities of an individual case. No one factor is dispositive and all factors must be taken into account insofar as they are applicable. Cases involving a claim of usurpation of a corporate opportunity range over a multitude of factual settings. Hard and fast rules are not easily crafted to deal with such an array of complex situations. As this Court noted in Johnston v. Greene, Del.Supr., 121 A.2d 919 (1956), the determination of "[w]hether or not a director has appropriated for himself something that in fairness should belong to the corporation is 'a factual question to be decided by reasonable inference from objective facts.' " Id. at 923 (quoting Guth, 5 A.2d at 513). In the instant case, we find that the facts do not support the conclusion that Broz misappropriated a corporate opportunity. . . .

First, we find that CIS was not financially capable of exploiting the Michigan–2 opportunity. . . .

Second, while it may be said with some certainty that the Michigan–2 opportunity was within CIS' line of business, it is not equally clear that CIS had a cognizable interest or expectancy in the license. Under the third factor laid down by this Court in *Guth*, for an opportunity to be deemed to belong to the fiduciary's corporation, the corporation must have an interest or expectancy in that opportunity. As this Court stated in Johnston, 121 A.2d at 924, "[f]or the corporation to have an actual or expectant interest in any specific property, there must be some tie between that property and the nature of the corporate business." Despite the fact that the nature of the Michigan–2 opportunity was historically close to the core operations of CIS, changes were in process. At the time the opportunity was presented, CIS was actively engaged in the process of divesting its cellular license holdings. CIS' articulated business plan did not involve any new acquisitions. Further, as indicated by the testimony of the entire CIS board, the Michigan–2 license would not have been of interest to CIS even absent CIS' financial difficulties and CIS' then current desire to liquidate its cellular license holdings. Thus, CIS had no interest or expectancy in the Michigan–2 opportunity. . . .

Finally, the corporate opportunity doctrine is implicated only in cases where the fiduciary's seizure of an opportunity results in a conflict between the fiduciary's duties to the corporation and the self-interest of the director as actualized by the exploitation of the opportunity. In the instant case, Broz' interest in acquiring and profiting from Michigan–2 created no duties that were inimicable to his obligations to CIS. Broz, at all times relevant to the instant appeal, was the sole party in interest in RFBC, a competitor of CIS. CIS was fully aware of Broz' potentially conflicting duties. Broz, however, comported himself in a manner that was wholly in accord with his obligations to CIS. Broz took care not to usurp any opportunity which CIS was willing and able to pursue. Broz sought only to compete with an outside entity, PriCellular, for acquisition of an opportunity which both sought to possess. Broz was not obligated to refrain from competition with PriCellular. Therefore, the totality of the circumstances indicates that Broz did not usurp an opportunity that properly belonged to CIS....

In concluding that Broz had usurped a corporate opportunity, the Court of Chancery placed great emphasis on the fact that Broz had not formally presented the matter to the CIS board. The court held that "in such circumstances as existed at the latest after October 14, 1994 (date of PriCellular's option contract on Michigan 2 RSA) it was the obligation of Mr. Broz as a director of CIS to take the transaction to the CIS board for its formal action...." 663 A.2d at 1185. In so holding, the trial court erroneously grafted a new requirement onto the law of corporate opportunity, viz., the requirement of formal presentation under circumstances where the corporation does not have an interest, expectancy or financial ability.

The teaching of *Guth* and its progeny is that the director or officer must analyze the situation ex ante to determine whether the opportunity is one rightfully belonging to the corporation. If the director or officer believes, based on one of the factors articulated above, that the corporation is not entitled to the opportunity, then he may take it for himself. Of course, presenting the opportunity to the board creates a kind of "safe harbor" for the director, which removes the specter of a post hoc judicial determination that the director or officer has improperly usurped a corporate opportunity. Thus, presentation avoids the possibility that an error in the fiduciary's assessment of the situation will create future liability for breach of fiduciary duty. It is not the law of Delaware that presentation to the board is a necessary prerequisite to a finding that a corporate opportunity has not been usurped....

In concluding that Broz usurped an opportunity properly belonging to CIS, the Court of Chancery held that "[f]or practical business reasons CIs' interests with respect to the Mackinac transaction came to merge with those of PriCellular, even before the closing of its tender offer for CIS stock." Based on this fact, the trial court concluded that Broz was required to consider PriCellular's prospective, post-acquisition plans for CIS in determining whether to forego the opportunity or seize it for himself. Had Broz done this, the Court of Chancery determined that he would have concluded that CIS was entitled to the opportunity by virtue of the alignment of its interests with those of PriCellular.

We disagree. Broz was under no duty to consider the interests of PriCellular when he chose to purchase Michigan–2. As stated in Guth, a director's right to "appropriate [an] ... opportunity depends on the circumstances existing at the time it presented itself to him without regard to subsequent events." Guth, 5 A.2d at 513. At the time Broz purchased Michigan–2, PriCellular had not yet acquired CIS. Any plans to do so would still have been wholly speculative. Accordingly, Broz was not required to consider the contingent and uncertain plans of PriCellular in reaching his determination of how to proceed.

Whether or not the CIS board would, at some time, have chosen to acquire Michigan–2 in order to make CIS a more attractive acquisition target for PriCellular or to enhance the synergy of any combined enterprise, is speculative. The trial court found this to be a plausible scenario and therefore found that, pursuant to the factors laid down in *Guth*, CIS had a valid interest or expectancy in the license. This speculative finding cuts against the statements made by CIS' Chief Executive and the entire CIS board of directors and ignores the fact that CIS still lacked the wherewithal to acquire Michigan–2, even if one takes into account the possible availability of PriCellular's financing. Thus, the fact of PriCellular's plans to acquire CIS is immaterial and does not change the analysis.

In reaching our conclusion on this point, we note that certainty and predictability are values to be promoted in our corporation law. See Williams v. Geier, Del.Supr., 671 A.2d 1368, 1385 n. 36 (1996). Broz, as an active participant in the cellular telephone industry, was entitled to proceed in his own economic interest in the absence of any countervailing duty. The right of a director or officer to engage in business affairs outside of his or her fiduciary capacity would be illusory if these individuals were required to consider every potential, future occurrence in determining whether a particular business strategy would implicate fiduciary duty concerns. In order for a director to engage meaningfully in business unrelated to his or her corporate role, the director must be allowed to make decisions based on the situation as it exists at the time a given opportunity is presented. Absent such a rule, the corporate fiduciary would be constrained to refrain from exploiting any opportunity for fear of liability based on the occurrence of subsequent events. This state of affairs would unduly restrict officers and directors and would be antithetical to certainty in corporation law.

———

Accord: Ostrowski v. Avery, 243 Conn. 355, 703 A.2d 117 (1997).

———

MODEL BUSINESS CORPORATION ACT § 8.70

[See Statutory Supplement]

———

ALI, PRINCIPLES OF CORPORATE GOVERNANCE §§ 5.05, 5.06

[See Statutory Supplement]

NOTE ON THE CORPORATE OPPORTUNITY DOCTRINE

1. *Tests*. A variety of tests have been formulated to determine whether a director or officer has wrongfully appropriated a corporate opportunity. Among these are three tests discussed in *Northeast Harbor*: (i) The line-of-business test, associated with Guth v. Loft, Inc., 23 Del.Ch. 255, 5 A.2d 503 (1939). (ii) The fairness test, associated with Durfee v. Durfee & Canning, Inc., 323 Mass. 187, 80 N.E.2d 522 (1948). (iii) The two-step test, associated with Miller v. Miller, 301 Minn. 207, 222 N.W.2d 71 (1974). Under another test, associated with Lagarde v. Anniston Lime & Stone Co., 126 Ala. 496, 502, 28 So. 199, 201 (1900), the corporate opportunity doctrine applies only when the director or officer has acquired property in which "the corporation has an interest already existing or in which it has an expectancy growing out of an existing right," or when his "interference will in some degree balk the corporation in effecting the purposes of its creation."

The application of the first branch of the *Lagarde* test (interest or expectancy) is uncertain, because the terms "interest" and "expectancy" have no fixed meaning in this context. See, e.g., Abbott Redmont Thinlite Corp. v. Redmont, 475 F.2d 85, 88–89 (2d Cir.1973). In *Lagarde* itself, the court held that real estate in which the corporation was a tenant constituted a corporate expectancy, but real estate in which the corporation owned an undivided one-third interest did not.

The application of the second branch of the *Lagarde* test (interference with the corporate purpose) is also uncertain. Presumably, it would cover cases in which the corporation's need for the property is very substantial. See, e.g., Harmony Way Bridge Co. v. Leathers, 353 Ill. 378, 187 N.E. 432 (1933) (a director purchased a right of way that was needed as an approach to the corporation's bridge); News–Journal Corp. v. Gore, 147 Fla. 217, 2 So.2d 741 (1941) (a director purchased a tract of land that the corporation leased for its building, and immediately increased the rent).

Insofar as the meaning of the *Lagarde* test can be determined, it is unduly narrow. Even the Alabama Supreme Court may now be seeking more leeway, by broadening the second branch of the test:

> The last restriction in *Lagarde,* that which prohibits "balking the corporate purpose," is really quite broad in its formulation, although the case has often been described as restrictive. . . . We think that *Lagarde* when properly read enforces responsibilities for the corporate officer or director comparable to those outlined in *Guth v. Loft, Inc.,* 23 Del.Ch. 255, 5 A.2d 503 (1939), where the Delaware Supreme Court employed the doctrine of corporate opportunity and observed that it

"... demands of a corporate officer or director, peremptorily and inexorably, the most scrupulous observance of his duty, not only affirmatively to protect the interests of the corporation committed to his charge, but also to refrain from doing anything that would work injury to the corporation, or to deprive it of profit or advantage which his skill and ability might properly bring to it, or to enable it to make in the reasonable and lawful exercise of its powers...."

Morad v. Coupounas, 361 So.2d 6, 8–9 (Ala.1978).

2. *Data.* A comprehensive analysis of corporate-opportunity cases reported between April 1977 and April 1988 found that disputes concerning corporate opportunities usually occur in close corporations, and that the opportunity is often directly competitive with the business of the corporation. Chew, Competing Interests in the Corporate Opportunity Doctrine, 67 N. C. L. Rev. 436 (1989).

3. *Different Types of Corporate Opportunities.* Traditionally, the body of law governing corporate opportunities has lacked clarity in two important respects. To begin with, the corporate-opportunity cases have often tended to lump all kinds of corporate opportunities together. In fact, however, there are two very different kinds of reasons why a *business* opportunity may be *a corporate* opportunity. Call an individual who is a director, officer, employee, or agent of a corporation, A, and call the Corporation C. One reason that a business opportunity may be a corporate opportunity is that A became aware of the opportunity through the use of corporate property, corporate information, or A's corporate position—that is, through the use of corporate assets. In such cases, the opportunity is Corporation C's property. If A took such an opportunity for herself without offering it to Corporation C, she has stolen it, just as much as if she had taken or used any other kind of corporate property for her own personal benefit.

A second, very different kind of reason why a business opportunity can constitute a corporate opportunity is that it is closely related to the corporation's business. If that is the *only* reason why an opportunity constitutes a corporate opportunity, then by hypothesis A will have found the opportunity on her own, rather than through the use of corporate property, information, or position. If an opportunity that A finds on her own constitutes a corporate opportunity, that is not because the discovery of the opportunity is a product of the use of corporate assets—it isn't—but because for some other reason A owes Corporation C a duty to turn over the opportunity to it.

If A is an officer of Corporation C, the reason why she might owe C the duty to turn over an opportunity that she found on her own is based on her duties (i) not to interfere with, and (ii) to advance, C's interests. Whether a given individual owes such duties may depend in part on the individual's position. The higher up in the corporate hierarchy the individual is, the more plausible it is that she owes such duties, and the more demanding the duties will normally be. Although a high-ranking executive can fairly be expected to turn over to the corporation any opportunity that is closely related to the corporation's business solely because it is so related, the same expectation may not apply to a blue-collar or clerical employee.

In short, a business opportunity that is discovered through the use of corporate property, information, or position should be a corporate opportunity regardless of *A*'s corporate position. In contrast, whether a business opportunity that *A* discovers on her own is a corporate opportunity solely because it is closely related to the corporation's business may partly depend on *A*'s corporate position.

4. *Ability of the Corporation to take the Opportunity*. Another area in which the traditional law of corporate opportunities has lacked clarity concerns the issue whether and to what extent *A* can raise, as a defense to a suit based on the taking of a business opportunity, that Corporation *C* was unable to take the opportunity. This issue usually, although not always, arises in the context of whether the corporation had the financial ability to take the relevant opportunity. The courts are all over the lot on this issue. At one extreme, some cases, such as Irving Trust Co. v. Deutsch, 73 F.2d 121 (2d Cir.1934), hold that the corporation's financial ability should be irrelevant, because it is too easy for executives who take a business opportunity to create a financial-inability excuse through manipulation of the corporation's financial picture. At the other extreme, some cases hold that not only is the corporation's financial ability relevant, but that a plaintiff who claims that a corporate opportunity has been taken has the burden of pleading and proving that the corporation had the financial ability to take the opportunity. See, e.g., Miller v. Miller, supra. Still other courts take some intermediate position between these two extremes. See, e.g., Klinicki v. Lundgren, 298 Or. 662, 695 P.2d 906 (1985) which allows financial inability to serve as a justification for the corporation's rejection of a corporate opportunity. Furthermore, there are a number of shadings on the issue how the corporation's financial ability should be measured in this context. See, e.g., Yiannatsis v. Stephanis, 653 A.2d 275 (Del.1995).

The problem in this area is that the courts have failed to disentangle two very different scenarios in which a corporate-inability defense may play a role. In one scenario, *A* first offers a business opportunity to the board of Corporation *C*; *C*'s board decides to reject the opportunity; and *A* then takes it for herself. A shareholder then brings a derivative action against *A*, and *A* raises as a defense that she did not take the opportunity until *C*'s board had rejected it. If, in such a case, the plaintiff puts into issue the fairness or reasonability of the board's rejection of the opportunity, *C*'s inability to take the opportunity is relevant, because it may justify the board's rejection.

In the second scenario, *A* takes an opportunity *without* having first offered it to the board of Corporation *C*. When *A* is sued for taking the opportunity, she raises as a defense that *C* did not have the ability to take the opportunity. In this scenario, *C*'s inability to take the opportunity should not be a defense, because if a business opportunity would be a corporate opportunity if the issue of the corporation's ability to take the opportunity is put aside, a fiduciary should always be obliged to offer the opportunity to the corporation in the first instance and let the *corporation* decide whether it is or can make itself able to take the opportunity. Business enterprises can be very adaptable when faced with a profitable business opportunity. For example, a corporation that doesn't have the cash to acquire a business opportunity may find that if the opportunity is profitable, a bank will lend the corporation money to acquire it. If *A* does not even offer the opportunity to the corporation, however, there is no way to tell whether the corporation would have been able to raise the money to acquire it, by bank financing or otherwise. That being so, it should be presumed against *A* that if she had offered the opportunity, the corporation would have adapted as necessary to take advantage of it. This is essentially the position taken in ALI, Principles of Corporate Governance § 5.05.

5. *The Relationship Between Corporate Opportunities; the Use of Corporate Information, Property, or Position; and Competition with the Corporation*. Three important principles of fiduciary duty overlap in a significant way. These are: (i) The corporate-opportunity principle, which prohibits a corporate fiduciary from taking a corporate opportunity. (ii) The use-of-corporate-assets principle, which prohibits a corporate fiduciary from using corporate property, information, or position for personal gain. (iii) The competition principle, which prohibits a corporate fiduciary from competing with the corporation.

Often, a given course of conduct violates all three principles. This would be the case, for example, if an executive appropriated a corporate opportunity that she learned of through the use of corporate information, and then exploited that opportunity in a way that competed with the corporation's business. Because of this potential for overlap, it is easy to think that the three principles express different facets of the same basic idea. In fact, however, the three principles express three different ideas, and despite the overlap, one of the principles may apply to a given case although the other principles do not.

For example, suppose that Officer O of Corporation X takes for herself an opportunity to buy Business B. O learned of the opportunity on her own, but Business B is closely related to A's business. In that case, O may violate the corporate-opportunity doctrine, but not the use-of-corporate-assets principle. Whether O violates the competition principle may depend on whether O remains in the corporation's employ after taking the opportunity. If O remains in the corporation's employ she may violate the competition principle, because by hypothesis Business B is closely related to the corporation's business. However, if O resigns immediately after acquiring Business B she may not violate the competition principle.

Suppose now that Business B is not closely related to Corporation X's business, but constituted a corporate opportunity because it came to O's attention through the use of corporate information, property, or position. In that case, if O buys Business B she may violate both the corporate-opportunity principle and the use-of corporate assets principle. However, she may not violate the competition principle, even if she remains in the corporation's employ after buying Business B, because Business B might not compete with Corporation X.

Finally, suppose that O inherits a business that is competitive with that of Corporation X. Here O has not taken a corporate opportunity. However, if O runs the business without resigning from Corporation X, she may be improperly competing with X. Similarly, suppose that O started a business that originally was not competitive with that of Corporation X, but that later becomes competitive because X itself expands its geographical or product-line reach, so that it begins going head-to-head with O's business. Here too O has not taken a corporate opportunity, but may be improperly competing with X.

IN RE eBAY, INC. SHAREHOLDERS LITIGATION, 2004 WL 253521 (Del. Ch. 2004). "In 1995, defendants Pierre M. Omidyar and Jeffrey Skoll founded nominal defendant eBay, a Delaware corporation, as a sole proprietorship. eBay is a pioneer in online trading platforms, providing a virtual auction community for buyers and sellers to list items for sale and to bid on items of interest. In 1998, eBay retained Goldman Sachs and other investment banks to underwrite an initial public offering of common stock. Goldman Sachs was the lead underwriter. The stock was priced at $18 per share. Goldman Sachs purchased about 1.2 million shares. Shares of eBay stock became immensely valuable during 1998 and 1999, rising to $175 per share in early April 1999. Around that time, eBay made a secondary offering, issuing 6.5 million shares of common stock at $170 per share for a total of $1.1 billion. Goldman Sachs again served as lead underwriter. Goldman Sachs was asked in 2001 to serve as eBay's financial advisor in connection with an acquisition by eBay of PayPal, Inc. For these services, eBay has paid Goldman Sachs over $8 million.

"During this same time period, Goldman Sachs 'rewarded' the individual defendants by allocating to them thousands of IPO shares, managed by Goldman Sachs, at the initial offering price. Because the IPO market during this particular period of time was extremely active, prices of initial stock offerings often doubled or tripled in a single day. Investors who were well connected, either to Goldman Sachs or to similarly situated investment banks serving as IPO underwriters, were able to flip these investments into instant profit by selling the equities in a few days or even in a few hours after they were initially purchased.

"The essential allegation of the complaint is that Goldman Sachs provided these IPO share allocations to the individual defendants to show appreciation for eBay's business and to enhance Goldman Sachs' chances of obtaining future eBay business. In addition to co-founding eBay, defendant Omidyar has been eBay's CEO, CFO and President. He is eBay's largest stockholder, owning more than 23% of the company's equity. Goldman Sachs allocated Omidyar shares in at least forty IPOs at the initial offering price. Omidyar resold these securities in the public market for millions of dollars in profit. Defendant Whitman owns 3.3% of eBay stock and has been President, CEO and a director since early 1998. Whitman also has been a director of Goldman Sachs since 2001. Goldman Sachs allocated Whitman shares in over 100 IPOs at the initial offering price. Whitman sold these equities in the open market and reaped millions of dollars in profit. Defendant Skoll, in addition to co-founding eBay, has served in various positions at the company, including Vice–President of Strategic Planning and Analysis and President. He served as an eBay director from December 1996 to March 1998. Skoll is eBay's second largest stockholder, owning about 13% of the company. Goldman Sachs has allocated Skoll shares in at least 75 IPOs at the initial offering price, which Skoll promptly resold on the open market, allowing him to realize millions of dollars in profit. Finally, defendant Robert C. Kagle has served as an eBay director since June 1997. Goldman Sachs allocated Kagle shares in at least 25 IPOs at the initial offering price. Kagle promptly resold these equities, and recorded millions of dollars in profit. . . .

"... [E]ven if one assumes that IPO allocations like those in question here do not constitute a corporate opportunity, a cognizable claim is nevertheless stated on the common law ground that an agent is under a duty to account for profits obtained personally in connection with transactions related to his or her company. The complaint gives rise to a reasonable inference that the insider directors accepted a commission or gratuity that rightfully belonged to eBay but that was improperly diverted to them. Even if this conduct does not run afoul of the corporate opportunity doctrine, it may still constitute a breach of the fiduciary duty of loyalty. Thus, even if one does not consider Goldman Sachs' IPO allocations to these corporate insiders—allocations that generated millions of dollars in profit—to be a corporate opportunity, the defendant directors were nevertheless not free to accept this consideration from a company, Goldman Sachs, that was doing significant business with eBay and that arguably intended the consideration as an inducement to maintaining the business relationship in the future."

SECTION 5.   DUTIES OF CONTROLLING SHAREHOLDERS

ALI, PRINCIPLES OF CORPORATE GOVERNANCE §§ 5.10–5.12

Zahn v. Transamerica Corporation

United States Circuit Court of Appeals, Third Circuit, 1947.
162 F.2d 36.

■ BIGGS, CIRCUIT JUDGE. Zahn, a holder of Class A common stock of Axton–Fisher Tobacco Company, a corporation of Kentucky, sued

Transamerica Corporation, a Delaware company, on his own behalf and on behalf of all stockholders similarly situated, in the District Court of the United States for the District of Delaware. His complaint as amended asserts that Transamerica caused Axton–Fisher to redeem its Class A stock at $80.80 per share on July 1, 1943, instead of permitting the Class A stockholders to participate in the assets on the liquidation of their company in June 1944. He alleges in brief that if the Class A stockholders had been allowed to participate in the assets on liquidation of Axton–Fisher and had received their respective shares of the assets, he and the other Class A stockholders would have received $240 per share instead of $80.80. Zahn takes the position that he has two separate causes of action, one based on the Class A shares which were not turned back to the company for redemption; another based on the shares which were redeemed.[1] He prayed the court below to direct Transamerica to pay over to the shareholders who had not surrendered their stock the liquidation value and to pay over to those shareholders who had surrendered their stock the liquidation value less $80.80. Transamerica filed a motion to dismiss. The court below granted the motion holding that Zahn had failed to state a cause of action. See 63 F.Supp. 243. He appealed.

The facts follow as appear from the pleadings, which recite provisions of Axton–Fisher's charter. Prior to April 30, 1943, Axton–Fisher had authorized and outstanding three classes of stock, designated respectively as preferred stock, Class A stock and Class B stock. Each share of preferred stock had a par value of $100 and was entitled to cumulative dividends at the rate of $6 per annum and possessed a liquidation value of $105 plus accrued dividends. The Class A stock, specifically described in the charter as a "common" stock, was entitled to an annual cumulative dividend of $3.20 per share. The Class B stock was next entitled to receive an annual dividend of $1.60 per share. If further funds were made available by action of the board of directors by way of dividends, the Class A stock and the Class B stock were entitled to share equally therein. Upon liquidation of the company and the payment of the sums required by the preferred stock, the Class A stock was entitled to share with the Class B stock in the distribution of the remaining assets, but the Class A stock was entitled to receive twice as much per share as the Class B stock.[2]

1. The plaintiff was originally the holder of 235 shares of Class A stock purchased on four occasions between July 23 and August 10, 1943, inclusive. Between August 2 and August 20, 1943, the plaintiff surrendered for redemption 215 shares and retained 20 shares.

2. The charter provides as follows:

"In the event of the dissolution, liquidation, merger or consolidation of the corporation, or sale of substantially all its assets, whether voluntary or involuntary, there shall be paid to the holders of the preferred stock then outstanding $105 per share, together with all unpaid accrued dividends thereon, before any sum shall be paid to or any assets distributed among the holders of the Class A common stock and/or the holders of the Class B common stock. After such payment to the holders of the preferred stock, and all unpaid accrued dividends on the Class A common stock shall have been paid, then all remaining assets and funds of the corporation shall be divided among and paid to the holders of the Class A common stock and to the holders of the Class B common stock in the ratio of 2 to 1; that is to say, there shall be paid upon each share of Class A common

Each share of Class A stock was convertible at the option of the shareholder into one share of Class B stock. All or any of the shares of Class A stock were callable by the corporation at any quarterly dividend date upon sixty days' notice to the shareholders, at $60 per share with accrued dividends.[3] The voting rights were vested in the Class B stock but if there were four successive defaults in the payment of quarterly dividends, the class or classes of stock as to which such defaults occurred gained voting rights equal share for share with the Class B stock. By reason of this provision the Class A stock had possessed equal voting rights with the Class B stock since on or about January 1, 1937.

On or about May 16, 1941, Transamerica purchased 80,160 shares of Axton–Fisher's Class B common stock. This was about 71.5% of the outstanding Class B stock and about 46.7% of the total voting stocks of Axton–Fisher. By August 15, 1942, Transamerica owned 5,332 shares of Class A stock and 82,610 shares of Class B stock. By March 31, 1943, the amount of Class A stock of Axton–Fisher owned by Transamerica had grown to 30,168 shares or about $66\frac{2}{3}\%$ of the total amount of this stock outstanding, and the amount of Class B stock owned by Transamerica had increased to 90,768 shares or about 80% of the total outstanding. Additional shares of Class B stock were acquired by Transamerica after April 30, 1943, and Transamerica converted the Class A stock owned by it into Class B stock so that on or about the end of May, 1944 Transamerica owned virtually all of the outstanding Class B stock of Axton–Fisher. Since May 16, 1941, Transamerica had control of and had dominated the management, directorate, financial policies, business and affairs of Axton–Fisher. Since the date last stated Transamerica had elected a majority of the board of directors of Axton–Fisher. These individuals are in large part officers or agents of Transamerica.

In the fall of 1942 and in the spring of 1943 Axton–Fisher possessed as its principal asset leaf tobacco which had cost it about $6,361,981. This asset was carried on Axton–Fisher's books in that amount. The value of leaf tobacco had risen sharply and to quote the words of the complaint, "unbeknown to the public holders of . . . Class A common stock of Axton–Fisher, but known to Transamerica, the market value of . . . [the] tobacco had, in March and April of 1943, attained the huge sum of about $20,000,000."

stock twice the amount paid upon each share of Class B common stock, in any such event."

3.   The charter provides as follows:

"The whole or any part of the Class A common stock of the corporation, at the option of the Board of Directors, may be redeemed on any quarterly dividend payment date by paying therefor in cash Sixty dollars ($60.00) per share and all unpaid and accrued dividends thereon at the date fixed for such redemption, upon sending by mail to the registered holders of the Class A common stock at least sixty (60) days' notice of the exercise of such option. If at any time the Board of Directors shall determine to redeem less than the whole amount of Class A common stock then outstanding, the particular stock to be so redeemed shall be determined in such manner as the Board of Directors shall prescribe; provided, however, that no holder of Class A common stock shall be preferred over any other holder of such stock."

The complaint then alleges the gist of the plaintiff's grievance, viz., that Transamerica, knowing of the great value of the tobacco which Axton–Fisher possessed, conceived a plan to appropriate the value of the tobacco to itself by redeeming the Class A stock at the price of $60 a share plus accrued dividends, the redemption being made to appear as if "incident to the continuance of the business of Axton–Fisher as a going concern," and thereafter, the redemption of the Class A stock being completed, to liquidate Axton–Fisher; that this would result, after the disbursal of the sum required to be paid to the preferred stock, in Transamerica gaining for itself most of the value of the warehouse tobacco. The complaint further alleges that in pursuit of this plan Transamerica, by a resolution of the Board of Directors of Axton–Fisher on April 30, 1943, called the Class A stock at $60 and, selling a large part of the tobacco to Phillip–Morris Company, Ltd., Inc., together with substantially all of the other assets of Axton–Fisher, thereafter liquidated Axton–Fisher, paid off the preferred stock and pocketed the balance of the proceeds of the sale. Warehouse receipts representing the remainder of the tobacco were distributed to the Class B stockholders.

Assuming as we must that the allegations of the complaint are true, it will be observed that agents or representatives of Transamerica constituted Axton–Fisher's board of directors at the times of the happening of the events complained of, and that Transamerica was Axton–Fisher's principal and controlling stockholder at such times. It will be observed also that jurisdiction in the suit at bar is based upon diversity of citizenship and jurisdictional amount. In such a suit the conflict-of-laws rule of Delaware requires the District Court of Delaware to refer to the law of the State of incorporation to determine the extent and nature of relationships between corporation and stockholder, corporate officer or director and stockholder and between stockholders *inter sese*. See Skillman v. Conner, 8 W.W.Harr. 402, 193 A. 563, and Black & Yates v. Mahogany Ass'n, 3 Cir., 129 F.2d 227, 233, 148 A.L.R. 841. As was well stated by the court below in Geller v. Transamerica Corporation, D.C., 53 F.Supp. 625, 629, 630, ". . . under the Delaware conflict of laws rule, the law of the place of the wrong determines the quantum of the breach of duty. . . . It would seem that the place of wrong is where the final act occurred which establishes liability." This court approved that reasoning by affirming per curiam the decision. See, 3 Cir., 151 F.2d 534.

The *loci* of the events complained of in the instant case are not set forth in the complaint. In Black & Yates v. Mahogany Ass'n, 129 F.2d at page 233, we stated, "We think that in the absence of allegations as to the place or places where the acts complained of occurred, the court below would have been entitled to assume that these operative facts took place within the State of Delaware," viz., the state of the forum. It is necessary therefore to assume that the events complained of took place within the State of Delaware. The law of Kentucky determines the existence of fiduciary duty, or the lack of it, between Transamerica (as the board of directors of Axton–Fisher, as its officership or as its controlling stockholder) and Axton–Fisher's minority Class A stockholders, and the law of Delaware determines the extent of the breach of fiduciary duty, if any. [At this point the court stated the case of Taylor v. Axton–Fisher Tobacco Co., 295 Ky. 226, 173 S.W.2d 377, 148 A.L.R. 834 (Ct.App.1943) which held that the action of the directors of Axton–Fisher in making the call gave the Class B shareholders the right to have the Class A shares redeemed and that a subsequent directors' resolution of June 16, 1943, purporting to give Class A shareholders the option not to have their shares redeemed, was an invalid resolution.]

The circumstances of the case at bar are *sui generis* and we can find no Kentucky decision squarely in point. In our opinion, however, the law of Kentucky imposes upon the directors of a corporation or upon those who are in charge of its affairs by virtue of majority stock ownership or otherwise the same fiduciary relationship in respect to the corporation and to its stockholders as is imposed generally by the laws of Kentucky's sister States or which was imposed by federal law prior to Erie R. Co. v. Tompkins, 304 U.S. 64, 58 S.Ct. 817, 82 L.Ed. 1188, 114 A.L.R. 1487.

The tenor of the federal decisions in respect to the general fiduciary duty of those in control of a corporation is unmistakable. The Supreme Court in Southern Pacific Co. v. Bogert, 250 U.S. 483, 487, 488, 39 S.Ct. 533, 535, 63 L.Ed. 1099, said: "The rule of corporation law and of equity invoked is well settled and has been often applied. The majority has the right to control; but when it does so, it occupies a fiduciary relation toward the minority, as much so as the corporation itself or its officers and directors." In Pepper v. Litton, 308 U.S. 295, 306, 60 S.Ct. 238, 245, 84 L.Ed. 281, the Supreme Court stated: "A director is a fiduciary.... So is a dominant or controlling stockholder or group of stockholders.... Their powers are powers in trust.... Their dealings with the corporation are subjected to rigorous scrutiny and where any of their contracts or engagements with the corporation is challenged the burden is on the director or stockholder not only to prove the good faith of the transaction but also to show its inherent fairness from the viewpoint of the corporation and those interested therein." ...

It is appropriate to emphasize at this point that the right to call the Class A stock for redemption was confided by the charter of Axton–Fisher to the directors and not to the stockholders of that corporation. We must also reemphasize the statement of the court in Haldeman v. Haldeman, supra, and its reiteration in Kirwan v. Parkway Distillery, supra, that there is a radical difference when a stockholder is voting strictly as a stockholder and when voting as a director; that when voting as a stockholder he may have the legal right to vote with a view of his own benefits and to represent himself only; but that when he votes as a director he represents all the stockholders in the capacity of a trustee for them and cannot use his office as a director for his personal benefit at the expense of the stockholders.

Two theories are presented on one of which the case at bar must be decided: One, vigorously asserted by Transamerica and based on its interpretation of the decision in the Taylor case, is that the board of directors of Axton–Fisher, whether or not dominated by Transamerica, the principal Class B stockholder, at any time and for any purpose, might call the Class A stock for redemption; the other, asserted with equal vigor by Zahn, is that the board of directors of Axton–Fisher as fiduciaries were not entitled to favor Transamerica, the Class B stockholder, by employing the redemption provisions of the charter for its benefit.

We must of course treat the decision of the Court of Appeals of Kentucky in the Taylor case as evidence of what is the law of Kentucky. The Court took the position on that record that the directors at any time might call the Class A stock for redemption and that the redemption provision of the charter was written as much for the benefit of the Class B stock as for the Class A stock. It is argued by Transamerica very persuasively that what the Court of Appeals of Kentucky held was that when the Class A stock received its allocation of $60 a share plus accrued dividends it received its full due and that the directors had the right at any time to eliminate Class A stock from the corporate setup for the benefit of the Class B stock.[4] It does not appear from the opinion of the Court of Appeals of Kentucky whether or not the subsequent liquidation of Axton–Fisher was brought to the attention of the Court. But it is clear from the pleading that the subsequent liquidation was not an issue in the case and from the language of the Court there is some indication that it believed that Axton–Fisher was to continue in existence because Commissioner Stanley spoke of the elimination of the Class A stock, which possessed voting rights, from the management and control of Axton–Fisher. Such surmises are hazardous, however, and are not really apposite since it is our duty to determine the law of Kentucky and not to delve into subjective mental processes. It should be noted that Commissioner Stanley stated the justiciable controversy before the Court of Appeals of Kentucky as follows: "The case presents a novel question of power of the board of directors of a corporation to rescind or modify its action in calling certain stock for redemption or retirement." This, and only this, was the question before the Court. It is notable that Commissioner Stanley said also that the acts of boards of directors "exercised in good faith and not in fraud of the rights of the stockholders" should not be interfered with by the courts and that he spoke as well of the "fair discretion" of directors to be exercised in the same manner as would be the case in the declaration of dividends.... We think that it is the settled law of Kentucky that directors may not declare or withhold the declaration of dividends for the purpose of personal profit or, by analogy, take any corporate action for such a purpose.

The difficulty in accepting Transamerica's contentions in the case at bar is that the directors of Axton–Fisher, if the allegations of the complaint be accepted as true, were the instruments of Transamerica,

4. The court said: "Manifestly, it was very much to the interest of the holders of Class B stock to have all these priorities, obligations and restrictions on and conditional joint control of the management eliminated. A substantial advantage was given to and acquired by the Class B stockholders...."

were directors voting in favor of their special interest, that of Transamerica, could not and did not exercise an independent judgment in calling the Class A stock, but made the call for the purpose of profiting their true principal, Transamerica. In short a puppet-puppeteer relationship existed between the directors of Axton–Fisher and Transamerica.

The act of the board of directors in calling the Class A stock, an act which could have been legally consummated by a disinterested board of directors, was here effected at the direction of the principal Class B stockholder in order to profit it. Such a call is voidable in equity at the instance of a stockholder injured thereby. It must be pointed out that under the allegations of the complaint there was no reason for the redemption of the Class A stock to be followed by the liquidation of Axton–Fisher except to enable the Class B stock to profit at the expense of the Class A stock. As has been hereinbefore stated the function of the call was confided to the board of directors by the charter and was not vested by the charter in the stockholders of any class. It was the intention of the framers of Axton–Fisher's charter to require the board of directors to act disinterestedly if that body called the Class A stock, and to make the call with a due regard for its fiduciary obligations. If the allegations of the complaint be proved, it follows that the directors of Axton–Fisher, the instruments of Transamerica, have been derelict in that duty. Liability which flows from the dereliction must be imposed upon Transamerica which, under the allegations of the complaint, constituted the board of Axton–Fisher and controlled it.

The *quantum* or extent of the breach of the fiduciary duty on the present record must be determined according to the law of Delaware for the reasons hereinbefore stated. The reaction of the law of Delaware to such a course as that pursued here by Transamerica is suggested by such decisions of the Supreme Court of Delaware as Bovay v. H.M. Byllesby & Co., Del.Sup., 38 A.2d 808, and Keenan v. Eshleman, 23 Del.Ch. 234, 2 A.2d 904, 120 A.L.R. 227. But whether the law of Delaware be applicable to determine the extent of the breach of fiduciary duty, or that of Kentucky or of New York, there will be found to be no substantial difference. The remedies to be afforded by the District Court of the United States for the District of Delaware, of course, must be those which may be available under the law of Delaware. See Guaranty Trust Co. v. York, 326 U.S. 99, 65 S.Ct. 1464, 89 L.Ed. 2079, 160 A.L.R. 1231, and Overfield v. Pennroad Corporation, 3 Cir., 146 F.2d 889.

As has been stated the plaintiff has endeavored to set up a "First Cause of Action" and a "Second Cause of Action" in his complaint. The first cause of action is based upon his ownership of shares of Class A stock not surrendered by him to Axton–Fisher for redemption and is asserted not only on his own behalf but also on behalf of other Class A stockholders retaining their stock. The second cause of action is asserted by him on his own behalf and on behalf of other Class A stockholders in respect to the value of the stock which was surrendered for redemption. The two alleged separate causes of action, however, are in reality one. In our opinion, if the allegations of the complaint be proved, Zahn may maintain his cause of action to recover from Transamerica the value of the stock retained by him as that shall be represented by its aliquot share of the proceeds of Axton–Fisher on dissolution. It is also our opinion that he may maintain a cause of action to recover the difference between the amount received by him for the shares already surrendered and the amount which he would have received on liquidation of Axton–Fisher if he had not surrendered his stock. . . .

––––––––

NOTE ON FURTHER PROCEEDINGS IN ZAHN v. TRANSAMERICA CORP.

The Third Circuit's original decision in *Zahn* used some language suggesting that the call of the Class A was wrongful in itself. However, in subsequent proceedings the Third Circuit held that the call was rightful, even though it benefited the Class B and Transamerica and hurt the Class A:

The first and principal question is the one raised by the holders of Class A stock as to the amount of damages to be awarded to them. The Class A stockholders contend that they are entitled to receive their aliquot shares in the liquidation distribution in the two-to-one ratio provided for in the charter for Class A stockholders participating in a liquidation. The district court held, however, that they are entitled only to recover as though they were Class B stockholders for the reason that a disinterested board of directors having knowledge of all the facts could and would have called the Class A stock for redemption in which event all of the Class A stockholders would have exercised their option to convert their shares into Class B stock on a one-for-one basis. We think that the district court was right in so holding.

The Court of Appeals of Kentucky has held that the Axton–Fisher Class A stock, although designated as a common stock was in the nature of a junior preferred stock, and that the provision of the charter for the redemption of the Class A stock was a continuing option allowed to the holders of the Class B common stock which the board of directors could exercise in their favor. This construction of the Axton–Fisher charter by the highest court of the state of its incorporation was, of course, binding on the district court. We agree with the district court that the provisions of the Axton–Fisher charter with respect to liquidation must be read realistically with the provisions for redemption of the Class A stock and its conversion into Class B stock. When so read it becomes apparent that a disinterested board of directors discharging its responsibility to the Class B stockholders in case of liquidation would call the Class A stock for redemption at $60 per share if it appeared that the distribution in liquidation to that stock would exceed that figure on a two-to-one basis. Since the board would have the right to do this and the Class B stockholders would be entitled to such action, the failure to do so would be an arbitrary act which would confer a windfall to which they were not entitled under the charter upon the Class A stockholders at the direct expense of the holders of the Class B stock. The district court was therefore quite right in determining that the damages to be awarded to the Class A stockholders should be measured by what they would have received if they had converted their shares into Class B stock prior to the liquidation.

Speed v. Transamerica Corp., 235 F.2d 369 (3d Cir.1956).

NOTE ON THE DUTY OF DISCLOSURE BY CONTROLLING SHAREHOLDERS UNDER DELAWARE LAW

The Delaware Court has been very rigorous in requiring full disclosure by controlling shareholders when they deal with the minority. In Lynch v. Vickers Energy Corp., 383 A.2d 278 (Del.1977),[1] Vickers, the majority shareholder of TransOcean stock, made a tender offer by for the 46% of TransOcean stock held by the public. The trial court held that in preparing the offering circular through which the tender offer was made, Vickers owed a fiduciary duty that required "complete candor" in disclosing fully "all of the facts and circumstances surrounding" the tender offer. The Delaware Supreme Court agreed with that rule, but reversed because the trial court had not applied the rule with sufficient vigor:

> ... [A]t the time of the offer, defendants were in possession of [an] estimate, prepared by Forrest Harrell, a petroleum engineer and a vice-president of TransOcean, fixing the net asset value [of TransOcean] at $250.8 million, which computes to approximately $20 per share, and from which one could conclude that the value could be as high as $300 million. Both of these estimates were ... substantially higher than the minimum amount stated in the tender offer.

> The Trial Court closely examined the Harrell report and concluded that nondisclosure thereof was not fatal; the Court reasoned that the [language used in the offering circular] "... furnished the TransOcean stockholders with adequate facts on which to make an educated choice...." ...

> This approach to the controversy was, in our view, mistaken in two respects: First, to reach such a conclusion it was necessary for the Court to weigh the merits of the Harrell report and, in the context of this case, that was error. The Court's function was not to go through Harrell's estimates of oil reserves and recoveries, for example, and make its own judgment about whether these

----

1. On subsequent appeal, 429 A.2d 497 (Del.Supr.1981), overruled on another issue, Weinberger v. UOP, Inc., 457 A.2d 701 (Del. Supr.1983).

should be "substantially discounted," nor should it have substituted its judgment for Harrell's about the rate which the Federal Power Commission would approve for a sale of natural gas. The stockholders and not the Court should have been permitted to make such qualitative judgments.

The Court's duty was to examine what information defendants had and to measure it against what they gave to the minority stockholders, in a context in which "complete candor" is required. In other words, the limited function of the Court was to determine whether defendants had disclosed all information in their possession germane to the transaction in issue. And by "germane" we mean, for present purposes, information such as a reasonable shareholder would consider important in deciding whether to sell or retain stock. . . .

A second reason why we think that the Court of Chancery was mistaken in applying the law was that it incorrectly substituted a "disclosure of adequate facts" standard . . . for the correct standard, which requires disclosure of *all* germane facts. Completeness, not adequacy, is both the norm and the mandate under present circumstances.

In Rosenblatt v. Getty Oil Co., 493 A.2d 929 (Del.1985), the Delaware Court substituted the term "material facts" for the term "germane facts," and explicitly adopted the test of materiality set out in TSC Industries, Inc. v. Northway, Inc., supra, Chapter 5. Subsequently, the Court dropped the "duty of candor" terminology in favor of terminology based on materiality, but made clear that the change in terminology did not signify a change in the underlying concept. Shell Petroleum, Inc. v. Smith, 606 A.2d 112, 113 n. 3 (Del.1992).

In Shell Petroleum, Inc. v. Smith, 606 A.2d 112 (Del. 1992), Royal Dutch Petroleum Co. owned 94.6% of Shell Oil Co. Royal Dutch decided to initiate a merger between Shell and SPNV Holdings ("Holdings"). Under the terms of the merger, each Shell minority shareholder would receive $58/share, or $60/share if he waived his right to appraisal before a fixed date. In conjunction with the merger, Holdings distributed several documents to the minority. Due to a computer-programming error, the documents understated Shell's discounted future net cash flows—an important element in the computation of the value of a business—by $3.00 to $3.45 per share. Former minority shareholders of Shell brought a class action. The Court of Chancery awarded damages to the shareholders for material misstatements. Affirmed.

Holdings' duty with respect to disclosure is clear. As the majority shareholder, Holdings bears the burden of showing complete disclosure of all material facts relevant to a minority shareholders' decision whether to accept the short-form merger consideration or seek an appraisal. . . . A fact is considered material if there is a "substantial likelihood that the disclosure of the omitted fact would have been viewed by the reasonable investor as having significantly altered the 'total mix' of information made available." ... "While it need not be shown that an omission or distortion would have made an investor change his overall view of a proposed transaction, it must be shown that the fact in question would have been relevant to him." ...

Holdings ... argues that a $3 per share error was not significant enough to make a reasonable stockholder change his decision and seek an appraisal. However, the question is not whether the information would have changed the stockholder's decision to accept the merger consideration, but whether "the fact in question would have been relevant to him." ...

See also Zirn v. VLI Corp., 621 A.2d 773, 777 (Del.1993); Arnold v. Society for Savings Bancorp, Inc., 650 A.2d 1270 (Del.1994).

NOTE ON THE TARGET OF SUITS BY MINORITY SHAREHOLDERS

Call a controlling shareholder S, and call the corporation that S controls C. Suppose that S and C have engaged in a transaction between themselves. Assume further that the transaction has been approved by C's board—as will often be the case. A minority shareholder of C who challenges the transaction could, in theory, sue both S and C's directors. As a practical matter, however, although C's directors may be joined as defendants, in many or most cases the real target of such a suit is the controlling shareholder, and typically (although not invariably) the court focuses on S's liability rather than on the liability of C's directors.

This phenomenon may be explained on two grounds. First, S, the controlling shareholder, usually has deep pockets; the directors of C may not. Therefore, it may not be worth adding the directors to a suit against the controlling shareholder. Second, C's directors are not self-interested, in the traditional sense, in transactions between C and S, because the directors will not directly profit from the transaction itself. Instead, the directors have a *positional* conflict; that is, it is in the directors' interests, if they want to maintain or augment their positions with C, to go along with S's proposals. Because the law concerning traditional conflicts of interest is better understood than the law concerning positional conflicts, it is easier for the plaintiff and the courts to focus on the liability of the controlling shareholder, who does have a traditional conflict, than on the directors of C, who have only positional conflicts.

Sinclair Oil Corporation v. Levien

Supreme Court of Delaware, 1971.
280 A.2d 717.

■ WOLCOTT, CHIEF JUSTICE. This is an appeal by the defendant, Sinclair Oil Corporation (hereafter Sinclair), from an order of the Court of Chancery, 261 A.2d 911, in a derivative action requiring Sinclair to account for damages sustained by its subsidiary, Sinclair Venezuelan Oil Company (hereinafter Sinven), organized by Sinclair for the purpose of operating in Venezuela, as a result of dividends paid by Sinven, the denial to Sinven of industrial development, and a breach of contract between Sinclair's wholly-owned subsidiary, Sinclair International Oil Company, and Sinven.

Sinclair, operating primarily as a holding company, is in the business of exploring for oil and of producing and marketing crude oil and oil products. At all times relevant to this litigation, it owned about 97% of Sinven's stock. The plaintiff owns about 3000 of 120,000 publicly held shares of Sinven. Sinven, incorporated in 1922, has been engaged in petroleum operations primarily in Venezuela and since 1959 has operated exclusively in Venezuela.

Sinclair nominates all members of Sinven's board of directors. The Chancellor found as a fact that the directors were not independent of Sinclair. Almost without exception, they were officers, directors, or employees of corporations in the Sinclair complex. By reason of Sinclair's domination, it is clear that Sinclair owed Sinven a fiduciary duty. Getty Oil Company v. Skelly Oil Co., 267 A.2d 883 (Del. Supr.1970); Cottrell v. Pawcatuck Co., 35 Del.Ch. 309, 116 A.2d 787 (1955). Sinclair concedes this.

The Chancellor held that because of Sinclair's fiduciary duty and its control over Sinven, its relationship with Sinven must meet the test of intrinsic fairness. The standard of intrinsic fairness involves both a high degree of fairness and a shift in the burden of proof. Under this standard the burden is on Sinclair to prove, subject to careful judicial scrutiny, that its transactions with Sinven were objectively fair. Guth v. Loft, Inc., 23 Del.Ch. 255, 5 A.2d 503 (1939); Sterling v. Mayflower Hotel Corp., 33 Del.Ch. 293, 93 A.2d 107, 38 A.L.R.2d 425 (Del. Supr.1952); Getty Oil Co. v. Skelly Oil Co., supra.

Sinclair argues that the transactions between it and Sinven should be tested, not by the test of intrinsic fairness with the accompanying shift of the burden of proof, but by the business judgment rule under which a court will not interfere with the judgment of a board of directors unless there is a showing of gross and palpable overreaching. Meyerson v. El Paso Natural Gas Co., 246 A.2d 789 (Del.Ch.1967). A board of directors enjoys a presumption of sound business judgment, and its decisions will not be disturbed if they can be attributed to any rational business purpose. A court under such circumstances will not substitute its own notions of what is or is not sound business judgment.

We think, however, that Sinclair's argument in this respect is misconceived. When the situation involves a parent and a subsidiary, with the parent controlling the transaction and fixing the terms, the test of intrinsic fairness, with its resulting shifting of the burden of proof, is applied. Sterling v. Mayflower Hotel Corp., supra; David J. Greene & Co. v. Dunhill International, Inc., 249 A.2d 427 (Del.Ch. 1968); Bastian v. Bourns, Inc., 256 A.2d 680 (Del.Ch.1969) aff'd. Per

Curiam (unreported) (Del.Supr.1970). The basic situation for the application of the rule is the one in which the parent has received a benefit to the exclusion and at the expense of the subsidiary.

Recently, this court dealt with the question of fairness in parent-subsidiary dealings in Getty Oil Co. v. Skelly Oil Co., supra. In that case, both parent and subsidiary were in the business of refining and marketing crude oil and crude oil products. The Oil Import Board ruled that the subsidiary, because it was controlled by the parent, was no longer entitled to a separate allocation of imported crude oil. The subsidiary then contended that it had a right to share the quota of crude oil allotted to the parent. We ruled that the business judgment standard should be applied to determine this contention. Although the subsidiary suffered a loss through the administration of the oil import quotas, the parent gained nothing. The parent's quota was derived solely from its own past use. The past use of the subsidiary did not cause an increase in the parent's quota. Nor did the parent usurp a quota of the subsidiary. Since the parent received nothing from the subsidiary to the exclusion of the minority stockholders of the subsidiary, there was no self-dealing. Therefore, the business judgment standard was properly applied.

A parent does indeed owe a fiduciary duty to its subsidiary when there are parent-subsidiary dealings. However, this alone will not evoke the intrinsic fairness standard. This standard will be applied only when the fiduciary duty is accompanied by self-dealing—the situation when a parent is on both sides of a transaction with its subsidiary. Self-dealing occurs when the parent, by virtue of its domination of the subsidiary causes the subsidiary to act in such a way that the parent receives something from the subsidiary to the exclusion of, and detriment to, the minority stockholders of the subsidiary.

We turn now to the facts. The plaintiff argues that, from 1960 through 1966, Sinclair caused Sinven to pay out such excessive dividends that the industrial development of Sinven was effectively prevented, and it became in reality a corporation in dissolution.

From 1960 through 1966, Sinven paid out $108,000,000 in dividends ($38,000,000 in excess of Sinven's earnings during the same period). The Chancellor held that Sinclair caused these dividends to be paid during a period when it had a need for large amounts of cash. Although the dividends paid exceeded earnings, the plaintiff concedes that the payments were made in compliance with 8 Del.C. § 170, authorizing payment of dividends out of surplus or net profits. However, the plaintiff attacks these dividends on the ground that they resulted from an improper motive—Sinclair's need for cash. The Chancellor, applying the intrinsic fairness standard, held that Sinclair did not sustain its burden of proving that these dividends were intrinsically fair to the minority stockholders of Sinven.

Since it is admitted that the dividends were paid in strict compliance with 8 Del.C. § 170, the alleged excessiveness of the payments alone would not state a cause of action. Nevertheless, compliance with the applicable statute may not, under all circumstances, justify all dividend payments. If a plaintiff can meet his burden of proving that a dividend cannot be grounded on any reasonable business objective, then the courts can and will interfere with the board's decision to pay the dividend.

Sinclair contends that it is improper to apply the intrinsic fairness standard to dividend payments even when the board which voted for the dividends is completely dominated. In support of this contention, Sinclair relies heavily on American District Telegraph Co. [ADT] v. Grinnell Corp., (N.Y.Sup.Ct.1969) aff'd. 33 A.D.2d 769, 306 N.Y.S.2d 209 (1969). Plaintiffs were minority stockholders of ADT, a subsidiary of Grinnell. The plaintiffs alleged that Grinnell, realizing that it would soon have to sell its ADT stock because of a pending anti-trust action, caused ADT to pay excessive dividends. Because the dividend payments conformed with applicable statutory law, and the plaintiffs could not prove an abuse of discretion, the court ruled that the complaint did not state a cause of action. Other decisions seem to support Sinclair's contention. In Metropolitan Casualty Ins. Co. v. First State Bank of Temple, 54 S.W.2d 358 (Tex.Civ.App.1932), rev'd. on other grounds, 79 S.W.2d 835 (Sup.Ct.1935), the court held that a majority of interested directors does not void a declaration of dividends because all directors, by necessity, are interested in and benefited by a dividend declaration. See, also, Schwartz v. Kahn, 183 Misc. 252, 50 N.Y.S.2d 931 (1944); Weinberger v. Quinn, 264 A.D. 405, 35 N.Y.S.2d 567 (1942).

We do not accept the argument that the intrinsic fairness test can never be applied to a dividend declaration by a dominated board, although a dividend declaration by a dominated board will not inevitably demand the application of the intrinsic fairness standard. Moskowitz v. Bantrell, 41 Del.Ch. 177, 190 A.2d 749 (Del.Supr.1963). If such a dividend is in essence self-dealing by the parent, then the intrinsic fairness standard is the proper standard. For example, suppose a parent dominates a subsidiary and its board of directors. The subsidiary has outstanding two classes of stock, X and Y. Class X is owned by the parent and Class Y is owned by minority stockholders of the subsidiary. If the subsidiary, at the direction of the parent, declares a dividend on its Class X stock only, this might well be self-dealing by the parent. It would be receiving something from the subsidiary to the exclusion of and detrimental to its minority stockholders. This self-dealing, coupled with the parent's fiduciary duty, would make intrinsic fairness the proper standard by which to evaluate the dividend payments.

Consequently it must be determined whether the dividend payments by Sinven were, in essence, self-dealing by Sinclair. The dividends resulted in great sums of money being transferred from Sinven to Sinclair. However, a proportionate share of this money was received by the minority shareholders of Sinven. Sinclair received nothing from Sinven to the exclusion of its minority stockholders. As such, these dividends were not self-dealing. We hold therefore that the Chancellor erred in applying the intrinsic fairness test as to these dividend payments. The business judgment standard should have been applied.

We conclude that the facts demonstrate that the dividend payments complied with the business judgment standard and with 8 Del.C. § 170. The motives for causing the declaration of dividends are immaterial unless the plaintiff can show that the dividend payments resulted from improper motives and amounted to waste. The plaintiff contends only that the dividend payments drained Sinven of cash to such an extent that it was prevented from expanding.

The plaintiff proved no business opportunities which came to Sinven independently and which Sinclair either took to itself or denied to Sinven. As a matter of fact, with two minor exceptions which resulted in losses, all of Sinven's operations have been conducted in Venezuela, and Sinclair had a policy of exploiting its oil properties located in different countries by subsidiaries located in the particular countries.

From 1960 to 1966 Sinclair purchased or developed oil fields in Alaska, Canada, Paraguay, and other places around the world. The plaintiff contends that these were all opportunities which could have been taken by Sinven. The Chancellor concluded that Sinclair had not proved that its denial of expansion opportunities to Sinven was intrinsically fair. He based this conclusion on the following findings of fact. Sinclair made no real effort to expand Sinven. The excessive dividends paid by Sinven resulted in so great a cash drain as to effectively deny to Sinven any ability to expand. During this same period Sinclair actively pursued a company-wide policy of developing through its subsidiaries new sources of revenue, but Sinven was not permitted to participate and was confined in its activities to Venezuela.

However, the plaintiff could point to no opportunities which came to Sinven. Therefore, Sinclair usurped no business opportunity belonging to Sinven. Since Sinclair received nothing from Sinven to the exclusion of and detriment to Sinven's minority stockholders, there was no self-dealing. Therefore, business judgment is the proper standard by which to evaluate Sinclair's expansion policies.

Since there is no proof of self-dealing on the part of Sinclair, it follows that the expansion policy of Sinclair and the methods used to achieve the desired result must, as far as Sinclair's treatment of Sinven is concerned, be tested by the standards of the business judgment rule. Accordingly, Sinclair's decision absent fraud or gross overreaching, to achieve expansion through the medium of its subsidiaries, other than Sinven, must be upheld.

Even if Sinclair was wrong in developing these opportunities as it did, the question arises, with which subsidiaries should these opportunities have been shared? No evidence indicates a unique need or ability of Sinven to develop these opportunities. The decision of which subsidiaries would be used to implement Sinclair's expansion policy was one of business judgment with which a court will not interfere absent a showing of gross and palpable overreaching. Meyerson v. El

Paso Natural Gas Co., 246 A.2d 789 (Del.Ch.1967). No such showing has been made here.

Next, Sinclair argues that the Chancellor committed error when he held it liable to Sinven for breach of contract.

In 1961 Sinclair created Sinclair International Oil Company (hereafter International), a wholly owned subsidiary used for the purpose of coordinating all of Sinclair's foreign operations. All crude purchases by Sinclair were made thereafter through International.

On September 28, 1961, Sinclair caused Sinven to contract with International whereby Sinven agreed to sell all of its crude oil and refined products to International at specified prices. The contract provided for minimum and maximum quantities and prices. The plaintiff contends that Sinclair caused this contract to be breached in two respects. Although the contract called for payment on receipt, International's payments lagged as much as 30 days after receipt. Also, the contract required International to purchase at least a fixed minimum amount of crude and refined products from Sinven. International did not comply with this requirement.

Clearly, Sinclair's act of contracting with its dominated subsidiary was self-dealing. Under the contract Sinclair received the products produced by Sinven, and of course the minority shareholders of Sinven were not able to share in the receipt of these products. If the contract was breached, then Sinclair received these products to the detriment of Sinven's minority shareholders. We agree with the Chancellor's finding that the contract was breached by Sinclair, both as to the time of payments and the amounts purchased.

Although a parent need not bind itself by a contract with its dominated subsidiary, Sinclair chose to operate in this manner. As Sinclair has received the benefits of this contract, so must it comply with the contractual duties.

Under the intrinsic fairness standard, Sinclair must prove that its causing Sinven not to enforce the contract was intrinsically fair to the minority shareholders of Sinven. Sinclair has failed to meet this burden. Late payments were clearly breaches for which Sinven should have sought and received adequate damages. As to the quantities purchased, Sinclair argues that it purchased all the products produced by Sinven. This, however, does not satisfy the standard of intrinsic fairness. Sinclair has failed to prove that Sinven could not possibly have produced or some way have obtained the contract minimums. As such, Sinclair must account on this claim.

Finally, Sinclair argues that the Chancellor committed error in refusing to allow it a credit or setoff of all benefits provided by it to Sinven with respect to all the alleged damages. The Chancellor held that setoff should be allowed on specific transactions, e.g., benefits to Sinven under the contract with International, but denied an overall setoff against all damages claimed. We agree with the Chancellor, although the point may well be moot in view of our holding that

Sinclair is not required to account for the alleged excessiveness of the dividend payments.

We will therefore reverse that part of the Chancellor's order that requires Sinclair to account to Sinven for damages sustained as a result of dividends paid between 1960 and 1966, and by reason of the denial to Sinven of expansion during that period. We will affirm the remaining portion of that order and remand the cause for further proceedings.

———

Accord: Ripley v. International Railways of Central America, 8 N.Y.2d 430, 209 N.Y.S.2d 289, 171 N.E.2d 443 (1960) (controlling shareholder of railroad was liable for the difference between (i) the transportation rates it paid for shipping commodities over the railroad and (ii) the fair and reasonable value of the transportation services).

———

DAVID J. GREENE AND CO. v. DUNHILL INTERNATIONAL, INC., 249 A.2d 427 (Del.Ch.1968). Dunhill was a diversified operating company. It manufactured and sold automotive equipment, infant-feeding equipment, and other products. Dunhill owned 80.3% of the stock of Spalding, which was a leading producer of athletic equipment and also had a toy division, which made and sold "Tinkertoys," and which accounted for about 4% of Spalding's sales. Dunhill did not make or sell toys of any kind. In 1968, Dunhill acquired Child Guidance Toys, which manufactured and distributed educational toys and visual-aid teaching devices. Minority shareholders in Spalding brought suit against Dunhill on the ground that Dunhill had appropriated a corporate opportunity that belonged to Spalding. Held, for plaintiffs:

> [T]he affidavit filed by Morris Shilensky, whose firm is counsel to Dunhill, shows that shortly after a prior merger by that company "there was widely circulated a description of a program for acquisition of businesses for Dunhill as well as for Spalding." He states that the Child Guidance opportunity came to Dunhill and not Spalding. That is perfectly understandable. The program Dunhill publicized *included* Spalding but asked that proposals be submitted to *Dunhill*. A reasonable inference from all of this is that Dunhill had taken over any acquisition program Spalding had.... And the Tinkertoy operation of Spalding is identified as the division interested in educational toys and equipment....
>
> In sum, the record makes out a sufficient showing of a business opportunity in the line of Spalding's business, which would have been of practical advantage to it and which it was financially able to undertake; that opportunity was acquired by Spalding's controlling stockholder.

———

Kahn v. Lynch Communication Systems, Inc.

Supreme Court of Delaware, 1994.
638 A.2d 1110.

■ Before MOORE, WALSH, and HOLLAND, JJ.

■ HOLLAND, JUSTICE:

This is an appeal by the plaintiff-appellant, Alan R. Kahn ("Kahn"), from a final judgment of the Court of Chancery which was entered after a trial. The action, instituted by Kahn in 1986, originally sought to enjoin the acquisition of the defendant-appellee, Lynch Communication Systems, Inc. ("Lynch"), by the defendant-appellee, Alcatel U.S.A. Corporation ("Alcatel"), pursuant to a tender offer and cash-out merger. Kahn amended his complaint to seek monetary damages after the Court of Chancery denied his request for a preliminary injunction. The Court of Chancery subsequently certified Kahn's action as a class action on behalf of all Lynch shareholders, other than the named defendants, who tendered their stock in the merger, or whose stock was acquired through the merger.

A three-day trial was held April 13–15, 1993. Kahn alleged that Alcatel was a controlling shareholder of Lynch and breached its fiduciary duties to Lynch and its shareholders. According to Kahn, Alcatel dictated the terms of the merger; made false, misleading, and inadequate disclosures; and paid an unfair price.

The Court of Chancery concluded that Alcatel was, in fact, a controlling shareholder that owed fiduciary duties to Lynch and its shareholders. It also concluded that Alcatel had not breached those fiduciary duties. Accordingly, the Court of Chancery entered judgment in favor of the defendants.

Kahn has raised three contentions in this appeal. Kahn's first contention is that the Court of Chancery erred by finding that "the tender offer and merger were negotiated by an independent committee," and then placing the burden of persuasion on the plaintiff, Kahn. Kahn asserts the uncontradicted testimony in the record demonstrated that the committee could not and did not bargain at arm's length with Alcatel. Kahn's second contention is that Alcatel's Offer to Purchase was false and misleading because it failed to disclose threats made by Alcatel to the effect that if Lynch did not accept its proposed price, Alcatel would institute a hostile tender offer at a lower price. Third, Kahn contends that the merger price was unfair. Alcatel contends that the Court of Chancery was correct in its findings, with the exception of concluding that Alcatel was a controlling shareholder.

This Court has concluded that the record supports the Court of Chancery's finding that Alcatel was a controlling shareholder. However, the record does not support the conclusion that the burden of persuasion shifted to Kahn. Therefore, the burden of proving the *entire* fairness of the merger transaction remained on Alcatel, the controlling shareholder. Accordingly, the judgment of the Court of Chancery is reversed. The matter is remanded for further proceedings in accordance with this opinion.

Facts

Lynch, a Delaware corporation, designed and manufactured electronic telecommunications equipment, primarily for sale to telephone operating companies. Alcatel, a holding company, is a subsidiary of Alcatel (S.A.), a French company involved in public telecommunications, business communications, electronics, and optronics. Alcatel (S.A.), in turn, is a subsidiary of Compagnie Generale d'Electricite ("CGE"), a French corporation with operations in energy, transportation, telecommunications and business systems.

In 1981, Alcatel acquired 30.6 percent of Lynch's common stock pursuant to a stock purchase agreement. As part of that agreement, Lynch amended its certificate of incorporation to require an 80 percent affirmative vote of its shareholders for approval of any business combination. In addition, Alcatel obtained proportional representation on the Lynch board of directors and the right to purchase 40 percent of any equity securities offered by Lynch to third parties. The agreement also precluded Alcatel from holding more than 45 percent of Lynch's stock prior to October 1, 1986. By the time of the merger which is contested in this action, Alcatel owned 43.3 percent of Lynch's outstanding stock; designated five of the eleven members of Lynch's board of directors; two of three members of the executive committee; and two of four members of the compensation committee.

In the spring of 1986, Lynch determined that in order to remain competitive in the rapidly changing telecommunications field, it would need to obtain fiber optics technology to complement its existing digital electronic capabilities. Lynch's management identified a target company, Telco Systems, Inc. ("Telco"), which possessed both fiber optics and other valuable technological assets. The record reflects that Telco expressed interest in being acquired by Lynch. Because of the supermajority voting provision, which Alcatel had negotiated when it first purchased its shares, in order to proceed with the Telco combination Lynch needed Alcatel's consent. In June 1986, Ellsworth F. Dertinger ("Dertinger"), Lynch's CEO and chairman of its board of directors, contacted Pierre Suard ("Suard"), the chairman of Alcatel's parent company, CGE, regarding the acquisition of Telco by Lynch. Suard expressed Alcatel's opposition to Lynch's acquisition of Telco. Instead, Alcatel proposed a combination of Lynch and Celwave Systems, Inc. ("Celwave"), an indirect subsidiary of CGE engaged in the manufacture and sale of telephone wire, cable and other related products.

Alcatel's proposed combination with Celwave was presented to the Lynch board at a regular meeting held on August 1, 1986. Although several directors expressed interest in the original combination which had been proposed with Telco, the Alcatel representatives on Lynch's board made it clear that such a combination would not be considered before a Lynch/Celwave combination. According to the minutes of the August 1 meeting, Dertinger expressed his opinion that Celwave would not be of interest to Lynch if Celwave was not owned by Alcatel.

At the conclusion of the meeting, the Lynch board unanimously adopted a resolution establishing an Independent Committee, consisting of Hubert L. Kertz ("Kertz"), Paul B. Wineman ("Wineman"), and Stuart M. Beringer ("Beringer"), to negotiate with Celwave and to make recommendations concerning the appropriate terms and conditions of a combination with Celwave. On October 24, 1986, Alcatel's investment banking firm, Dillon, Read & Co., Inc. ("Dillon Read") made a presentation to the Independent Committee. Dillon Read expressed its views concerning the benefits of a Celwave/Lynch combination and submitted a written proposal of an exchange ratio of 0.95 shares of Celwave per Lynch share in a stock-for-stock merger.

However, the Independent Committee's investment advisors, Thomson McKinnon Securities Inc. ("Thomson McKinnon") and Kidder, Peabody & Co. Inc. ("Kidder Peabody"), reviewed the Dillon Read proposal and concluded that the 0.95 ratio was predicated on Dillon Read's overvaluation of Celwave. Based upon this advice, the Independent Committee determined that the exchange ratio proposed by Dillon Read was unattractive to Lynch. The Independent Committee expressed its unanimous opposition to the Celwave/Lynch merger on October 31, 1986.

Alcatel responded to the Independent Committee's action on November 4, 1986, by withdrawing the Celwave proposal. Alcatel made a simultaneous offer to acquire the entire equity interest in Lynch, constituting the approximately 57 percent of Lynch shares not owned by Alcatel. The offering price was $14 cash per share.

On November 7, 1986, the Lynch board of directors revised the mandate of the Independent Committee. It authorized Kertz, Wineman, and Beringer to negotiate the cash merger offer with Alcatel. At a meeting held that same day, the Independent Committee determined that the $14 per share offer was inadequate. The Independent's Committee's own legal counsel, Skadden, Arps, Slate, Meagher & Flom ("Skadden Arps"), suggested that the Independent Committee should review alternatives to a cash-out merger with Alcatel, including a "white knight" third party acquiror, a repurchase of Alcatel's shares, or the adoption of a shareholder rights plan.

On November 12, 1986, Beringer, as chairman of the Independent Committee, contacted Michiel C. McCarty ("McCarty") of Dillon Read, Alcatel's representative in the negotiations, with a counteroffer at a price of $17 per share. McCarty responded on behalf of Alcatel with an offer of $15 per share. When Beringer informed McCarty of the Independent Committee's view that $15 was also insufficient, Alcatel raised its offer to $15.25 per share. The Independent Committee also rejected this offer. Alcatel then made its final offer of $15.50 per share.

At the November 24, 1986 meeting of the Independent Committee, Beringer advised its other two members that Alcatel was "ready to proceed with an unfriendly tender at a lower price" if the $15.50 per share price was not recommended by the Independent Committee and approved by the Lynch board of directors. Beringer also told the other members of the Independent Committee that the alternatives to a cash-out merger had been investigated but were impracticable.[52] After meeting with its financial and legal advisors, the Independent Committee voted unanimously to recommend that the Lynch board of directors approve Alcatel's $15.50 cash per share price for a merger with Alcatel. The Lynch board met later that day. With Alcatel's nominees abstaining, it approved the merger.

Alcatel Dominated Lynch

Controlling Shareholder Status

This Court has held that "a shareholder owes a fiduciary duty only if it owns a majority interest in or *exercises control* over the business affairs of the corporation." *Ivanhoe Partners v. Newmont Mining Corp.*, Del.Supr., 535 A.2d 1334, 1344 (1987) (emphasis added). With regard to the exercise of control, this Court has stated:

> [A] shareholder who owns less than 50% of a corporation's outstanding stocks does not, without more, become a controlling shareholder of that corporation, with a concomitant fiduciary status. For a dominating relationship to exist in the absence of controlling stock ownership, a plaintiff must allege domination by a minority shareholder through actual control of corporation conduct.

Citron v. Fairchild Camera & Instrument Corp., Del.Supr., 569 A.2d 53, 70 (1989) (quotations and citation omitted).

Alcatel held a 43.3 percent minority share of stock in Lynch. Therefore, the threshold question to be answered by the Court of Chancery was whether, despite its minority ownership, Alcatel exercised control over Lynch's business affairs. Based upon the testimony and the minutes of the August 1, 1986 Lynch board meeting, the Court of Chancery concluded that Alcatel did exercise control over Lynch's business decisions.

The standard of appellate review with regard to the Court of Chancery's factual findings is deferential. *Cede & Co. v. Technicolor, Inc.*, Del.Supr., 634 A.2d 345, 360 (1993). Those findings will not be set aside by this Court unless they are clearly erroneous or not the product of a logical and orderly deductive reasoning process. *Id.* The record supports the Court of Chancery's factual finding that Alcatel dominated Lynch.

At the August 1 meeting, Alcatel opposed the renewal of compensation contracts for Lynch's top five managers. According to Dertinger, Christian Fayard ("Fayard"), an Alcatel director, told the board members, "[y]ou must listen to us. We are 43 percent owner. You have to do what we tell you." The minutes confirm Dertinger's testimony. They recite that Fayard declared, "you are pushing us very much to

---

52. The minutes reflect that Beringer told the Committee the "white knight" alternative "appeared impractical with the 80% approval requirement"; the repurchase of Alcatel's shares would produce a "highly lever-aged company with a lower book value" and was an alternative "not in the least encouraged by Alcatel"; and a shareholder rights plan was not viable because of the increased debt it would entail.

take control of the company. Our opinion is not taken into consideration."

Although Beringer and Kertz, two of the independent directors, favored renewal of the contracts, according to the minutes, the third independent director, Wineman, admonished the board as follows:

> Mr. Wineman pointed out that the vote on the contracts is a "watershed vote" and the motion, due to Alcatel's "strong feelings," might not carry if taken now. Mr. Wineman clarified that "you [management] might win the battle and lose the war." With Alcatel's opinion so clear, Mr. Wineman questioned "if management wants the contracts renewed under these circumstances." He recommended that management "think twice." Mr. Wineman declared: "I want to keep the management. I can't think of a better management." Mr. Kertz agreed, again advising consideration of the "critical" period the company is entering.

The minutes reflect that the management directors left the room after this statement. The remaining board members then voted not to renew the contracts.

At the same meeting, Alcatel vetoed Lynch's acquisition of the target company, which, according to the minutes, Beringer considered "an immediate fit" for Lynch. Dertinger agreed with Beringer, stating that the "target company is extremely important as they have the products that Lynch needs now." Nonetheless, Alcatel prevailed. The minutes reflect that Fayard advised the board: "Alcatel, with its 44% equity position, would not approve such an acquisition as . . . it does not wish to be diluted from being the main shareholder in Lynch." From the foregoing evidence, the Vice Chancellor concluded:

> . . . Alcatel did control the Lynch board, at least with respect to the matters under consideration at its August 1, 1986 board meeting. The interplay between the directors was more than vigorous discussion, as suggested by defendants. The management and independent directors disagreed with Alcatel on several important issues. However, when Alcatel made its position clear, and reminded the other directors of its significant stockholdings, Alcatel prevailed. Dertinger testified that Fayard "scared [the non-Alcatel directors] to death." While this statement undoubtedly is an exaggeration, it does represent a first-hand view of how the board operated. I conclude that the non-Alcatel directors deferred to Alcatel because of its position as a significant stockholder and not because they decided in the exercise of their own business judgment that Alcatel's position was correct [citation omitted].

The record supports the Court of Chancery's underlying factual finding that "the non-Alcatel [independent] directors deferred to Alcatel because of its position as a significant stockholder and not because they decided in the exercise of their own business judgment that Alcatel's position was correct." The record also supports the subsequent factual finding that, notwithstanding its 43.3 percent minority shareholder interest, Alcatel did exercise actual control over

Lynch by dominating its corporate affairs. The Court of Chancery's legal conclusion that Alcatel owed the fiduciary duties of a controlling shareholder to the other Lynch shareholders followed syllogistically as the logical result of its cogent analysis of the record.

Entire Fairness Requirement

Dominating Interested Shareholder

A controlling or dominating shareholder standing on both sides of a transaction, as in a parent-subsidiary context, bears the burden of proving its entire fairness. *Weinberger v. UOP, Inc.,* Del.Supr., 457 A.2d 701, 710 (1983). *See Rosenblatt v. Getty Oil Co.,* Del.Supr., 493 A.2d 929, 937 (1985). The demonstration of fairness that is required was set forth by this Court in *Weinberger:*

> The concept of fairness has two basic aspects: fair dealing and fair price. The former embraces questions of when the transaction was timed, how it was initiated, structured, negotiated, disclosed to the directors, and how the approvals of the directors and the stockholders were obtained. The latter aspect of fairness relates to the economic and financial considerations of the proposed merger, including all relevant factors: assets, market value, earnings, future prospects, and any other elements that affect the intrinsic or inherent value of a company's stock. However, the test for fairness is not a bifurcated one as between fair dealing and price. All aspects of the issue must be examined as a whole since the question is one of entire fairness.

Weinberger v. UOP, Inc., 457 A.2d at 711 (citations omitted).

The logical question raised by this Court's holding in *Weinberger* was what type of evidence would be reliable to demonstrate entire fairness. That question was not only anticipated but also initially addressed in the *Weinberger* opinion. *Id.* at 709–10 n. 7. This Court suggested that the result "could have been entirely different if UOP had appointed an independent negotiating committee of its outside directors to deal with Signal at arm's length," because "fairness in this context can be equated to conduct by a theoretical, wholly independent, board of directors." *Id.* Accordingly, this Court stated, "a showing that the action taken was as though each of the contending parties had in fact exerted its bargaining power against the other at arm's length is strong *evidence* that the transaction meets the test of fairness." *Id.* (emphasis added).

In this case, the Vice Chancellor noted that the Court of Chancery has expressed "differing views" regarding the effect that an approval of a cash-out merger by a special committee of disinterested directors has upon the controlling or dominating shareholder's burden of demonstrating entire fairness. One view is that such approval shifts to the plaintiff the burden of proving that the transaction was unfair. *Citron v. E.I. Du Pont de Nemours & Co.,* Del.Ch., 584 A.2d 490, 500–02 (1990); *Rabkin v. Olin Corp,* Del.Ch., C.A. No. 7547 (Consolidated), Chandler, V.C., 1990 WL 47648, slip op. at 14–15 (Apr. 17, 1990), *reprinted in* 16 Del.J.Corp.L. 851, 861–62 (1991), *aff'd,* Del.Supr., 586 A.2d 1202 (1990). The other view is that such an approval renders the business judgment rule the applicable standard of judicial review. *In re Trans World Airlines, Inc. Shareholders Litig.,* Del.Ch., C.A. 9844 (Consolidated), Allen, C., 1988 WL 111271, slip op. at 15–16 (Oct. 21, 1988), *reprinted in* 14 Del.J.Corp.L. 870, 883 (1989). *See Cinerama, Inc. v. Technicolor, Inc.,* Del.Ch., C.A. No. 8358, Allen, C., 1991 WL 111134, slip op. at 47–48 (June 24, 1991), *reprinted in* 17 Del. J.Corp.L. 551, 570–72 (1992), *aff'd in part and rev'd in part on other grounds sub nom. Cede & Co. v. Technicolor, Inc.,* Del.Supr., 634 A.2d 345 (1993).

"It is often of critical importance whether a particular decision is one to which the business judgment rule applies or the entire fairness rule applies." *Nixon v. Blackwell,* Del.Supr., 626 A.2d 1366, 1376 (1993). The definitive answer with regard to the Court of Chancery's "differing views" is found in this Court's opinions in *Weinberger* and *Rosenblatt.* In *Weinberger,* this Court held that because

> of the fairness test which has long been applicable to parent-subsidiary mergers, the expanded appraisal remedy now available to shareholders, and the broad discretion of the [Court of Chancery] to fashion such relief as the facts of a given case may dictate, we do not believe that any additional meaningful protection is afforded minority shareholders by the business purpose requirement of the trilogy of *Singer* [*v. Magnavox Co.,* Del.Supr., 380 A.2d 969 (1977)], *Tanzer* [*v. International Gen. Indus., Inc.,* Del.Supr., 379 A.2d 1121 (1977)], [*Roland Int'l Corp. v.*] *Najjar* [Del.Supr., 407 A.2d 1032 (1979)], and their progeny. Accordingly, such requirement shall no longer be of any force or effect.

Weinberger v. UOP, Inc., 457 A.2d at 715 (citation and footnotes omitted). Thereafter, this Court recognized that it would be inconsistent with its holding in *Weinberger* to apply the business judgment rule in the context of an interested merger transaction which, by its very nature, did not require a business purpose. *See Rosenblatt v. Getty Oil Co.,* 493 A.2d at 937. Consequently, in *Rosenblatt,* in the context of a subsequent proceeding involving a parent-subsidiary merger, this Court held that the "approval of a merger, as here, by an informed vote of a majority of the minority stockholders, while not a legal prerequisite, shifts the burden of proving the unfairness of the merger entirely to the plaintiffs." *Id.*

Entire fairness remains the proper focus of judicial analysis in examining an interested merger, irrespective of whether the burden of proof remains upon or is shifted away from the controlling or dominating shareholder, because the unchanging nature of the underlying "interested" transaction requires careful scrutiny. *See Weinberger v. UOP, Inc.,* 457 A.2d at 710 (citing *Sterling v. Mayflower Hotel Corp.,* Del.Supr., 93 A.2d 107, 110 (1952)). The policy rationale for the exclusive application of the entire fairness standard to interested merger transactions has been stated as follows:

Parent subsidiary mergers, unlike stock options, are proposed by a party that controls, and will continue to control, the corporation, whether or not the minority stockholders vote to approve or reject the transaction. The controlling stockholder relationship has the potential to influence, however subtly, the vote of [ratifying] minority stockholders in a manner that is not likely to occur in a transaction with a noncontrolling party.

Even where no coercion is intended, shareholders voting on a parent subsidiary merger might perceive that their disapproval could risk retaliation of some kind by the controlling stockholder. For example, the controlling stockholder might decide to stop dividend payments or to effect a subsequent cash out merger at a less favorable price, for which the remedy would be time consuming and costly litigation. At the very least, the potential for that perception, and its possible impact upon a shareholder vote, could never be fully eliminated. Consequently, in a merger between the corporation and its controlling stockholder—even one negotiated by disinterested, independent directors—no court could be certain whether the transaction terms fully approximate what truly independent parties would have achieved in an arm's length negotiation. Given that uncertainty, a court might well conclude that even minority shareholders who have ratified a . . . merger need procedural protections beyond those afforded by full disclosure of all material facts. One way to provide such protections would be to adhere to the more stringent entire fairness standard of judicial review.

Citron v. E.I. Du Pont de Nemours & Co., 584 A.2d at 502.

Once again, this Court holds that the exclusive standard of judicial review in examining the propriety of an interested cash-out merger transaction by a controlling or dominating shareholder is entire fairness. *Weinberger v. UOP, Inc.,* 457 A.2d at 710–11. The initial burden of establishing entire fairness rests upon the party who stands on both sides of the transaction. *Id.* However, an approval of the transaction by an independent committee of directors or an informed majority of minority shareholders shifts the burden of proof on the issue of fairness from the controlling or dominating shareholder to the challenging shareholder-plaintiff. *See Rosenblatt v. Getty Oil Co.,* 493 A.2d at 937–38. Nevertheless, even when an interested cash-out merger transaction receives the informed approval of a majority of minority stockholders or an independent committee of disinterested directors, an entire fairness analysis is the only proper standard of judicial review. *See id.*

Independent Committees
Interested Merger Transactions

It is a now well-established principle of Delaware corporate law that in an interested merger, the controlling or dominating shareholder proponent of the transaction bears the burden of proving its entire fairness. *Weinberger v. UOP, Inc.,* Del.Supr., 457 A.2d 701, 710–11

(1983). It is equally well-established in such contexts that any shifting of the burden of proof on the issue of entire fairness must be predicated upon this Court's decisions in *Rosenblatt v. Getty Oil Co.*, Del.Supr., 493 A.2d 929 (1985) and *Weinberger v. UOP, Inc.*, Del. Supr., 457 A.2d 701 (1983). In *Weinberger*, this Court noted that "[p]articularly in a parent-subsidiary context, a showing that the action taken was as though each of the contending parties had *in fact* exerted its bargaining power against the other at arm's length is strong evidence that the transaction meets the test of fairness." 457 A.2d at 709–10 n. 7 (emphasis added). *Accord Rosenblatt v. Getty Oil Co.*, 493 A.2d at 937–38 & n. 7. In *Rosenblatt*, this Court pointed out that "[an] independent bargaining structure, while not conclusive, is strong evidence of the fairness" of a merger transaction. *Rosenblatt v. Getty Oil Co.*, 493 A.2d at 938 n. 7.

The same policy rationale which requires judicial review of interested cash-out mergers exclusively for entire fairness also mandates careful judicial scrutiny of a special committee's real bargaining power before shifting the burden of proof on the issue of entire fairness. A recent decision from the Court of Chancery articulated a two-part test for determining whether burden shifting is appropriate in an interested merger transaction. *Rabkin v. Olin Corp.*, Del.Ch., C.A. No. 7547 (Consolidated), Chandler, V.C., 1990 WL 47648, slip op. at 14–15 (Apr. 17, 1990), *reprinted in* 16 Del.J.Corp.L. 851, 861–62 (1991), *aff'd*, Del.Supr., 586 A.2d 1202 (1990). In *Olin*, the Court of Chancery stated:

> The mere existence of an independent special committee ... does not itself shift the burden. At least two factors are required. First, the majority shareholder must not dictate the terms of the merger. *Rosenblatt v. Getty Oil Co.*, Del.Ch., 493 A.2d 929, 937 (1985). Second, the special committee must have real bargaining power that it can exercise with the majority shareholder on an arms length basis.

Id., slip op. at 14–15, 16 Del.J.Corp.L. at 861–62.[53] This Court expressed its agreement with that statement by affirming the Court of Chancery decision in *Olin* on appeal.

Lynch's Independent Committee

In the case *sub judice*, the Court of Chancery observed that although "Alcatel did exercise control over Lynch with respect to the decisions made at the August 1, 1986 board meeting, it does not necessarily follow that Alcatel also controlled the terms of the merger

---

53. In *Olin*, the Court of Chancery concluded that because the special committee had been given "the narrow mandate of determining the monetary fairness of a non-negotiable offer," and because the majority shareholder "dictated the terms" and "there were no arm's-length negotiations," the burden of proof on the issue of entire fairness remained with the defendants. *Id.*, slip op. at 15, 16 Del.J.Corp.L. at 862. In making that determination, the Court of Chancery pointed out that the majority shareholder "could obviously have used its majority stake to effectuate the merger" regardless of the committee's or the board's disapproval, and that the record demonstrated that the directors of both corporations were "acutely aware of this fact." *Id.*, slip op. at 13, 16 Del.J.Corp.L. at 861.

and its approval." This observation is theoretically accurate, as this opinion has already stated. *Weinberger v. UOP, Inc.,* 457 A.2d at 709–10 n. 7. However, the performance of the Independent Committee merits careful judicial scrutiny to determine whether Alcatel's demonstrated pattern of domination was effectively neutralized so that "each of the contending parties had in fact exerted its bargaining power against the other at arm's length." *Id.* The fact that the same independent directors had submitted to Alcatel's demands on August 1, 1986 was part of the basis for the Court of Chancery's finding of Alcatel's domination of Lynch. Therefore, the Independent Committee's ability to bargain at arm's length with Alcatel was suspect from the outset.

The Independent Committee's original assignment was to examine the merger with Celwave which had been proposed by Alcatel. The record reflects that the Independent Committee effectively discharged that assignment and, in fact, recommended that the Lynch board reject the merger on Alcatel's terms. Alcatel's response to the Independent Committee's adverse recommendation was not the pursuit of further negotiations regarding its Celwave proposal, but rather its response was an offer to buy Lynch. That offer was consistent with Alcatel's August 1, 1986 expressions of an intention to dominate Lynch, since an acquisition would effectively eliminate once and for all Lynch's remaining vestiges of independence.

The Independent Committee's second assignment was to consider Alcatel's proposal to purchase Lynch. The Independent Committee proceeded on that task with full knowledge of Alcatel's demonstrated pattern of domination. The Independent Committee was also obviously aware of Alcatel's refusal to negotiate with it on the Celwave matter.

Burden of Proof Shifted

Court of Chancery's Finding

The Court of Chancery began its factual analysis by noting that Kahn had "attempted to shatter" the image of the Independent Committee's actions as having "appropriately simulated" an arm's length, third-party transaction. The Court of Chancery found that "to some extent, [Kahn's attempt] was successful." The Court of Chancery gave credence to the testimony of Kertz, one of the members of the Independent Committee, to the effect that he did not believe that $15.50 was a fair price but that he voted in favor of the merger because he felt there was no alternative.

The Court of Chancery also found that Kertz understood Alcatel's position to be that it was ready to proceed with an unfriendly tender offer at a lower price if Lynch did not accept the $15.50 offer, and that Kertz perceived this to be a threat by Alcatel. The Court of Chancery concluded that Kertz ultimately decided that, "although $15.50 was not fair, a tender offer and merger at that price would be better for Lynch's stockholders than an unfriendly tender offer at a significantly lower price." The Court of Chancery determined that "Kertz failed either to satisfy himself that the offered price was fair or oppose the merger."

In addition to Kertz, the other members of the Independent Committee were Beringer, its chairman, and Wineman. Wineman did not testify at trial.[54] Beringer was called by Alcatel to testify at trial. Beringer testified that at the time of the Committee's vote to recommend the $15.50 offer to the Lynch board, he thought "that *under the circumstances,* a price of $15.50 was fair and should be accepted" (emphasis added).

Wineman's failure to testify also permits both this Court and the Court of Chancery to draw the inference adverse to Alcatel, that Alcatel dictated the outcome of the November 24, 1986 meeting. As we have previously noted, the production of weak evidence when strong is, or should have been, available can lead only to the conclusion that the strong would have been adverse. *See Smith v. Van Gorkom,* Del.Supr., 488 A.2d 858, 878 (1985).

Kahn contends that these "circumstances" included those referenced in the minutes for the November 24, 1986 Independent Committee meeting: "Mr. Beringer added that Alcatel is 'ready to proceed with an unfriendly tender at a lower price' if the $15.50 per share price is not recommended to, and approved by, the Company's Board of Directors." In his testimony at trial, Beringer verified, albeit reluctantly, the accuracy of the foregoing statement in the minutes: "[Alcatel] *let us know* that they were giving serious consideration to making an unfriendly tender" (emphasis added).

The record reflects that Alcatel was "ready to proceed" with a hostile bid. This was a conclusion reached by Beringer, the Independent Committee's chairman and spokesman, based upon communications to him from Alcatel. Beringer testified that although there was no reference to a particular price for a hostile bid during his discussions with Alcatel, or even specific mention of a "lower" price, "the implication was clear to [him] that it probably would be at a lower price."[55]

According to the Court of Chancery, the Independent Committee rejected three lower offers for Lynch from Alcatel and then accepted the $15.50 offer "after being advised that [it] was fair and after considering the absence of alternatives." The Vice Chancellor expressly acknowledged the impracticability of Lynch's Independent Committee's alternatives to a merger with Alcatel:

> Lynch was not in a position to shop for other acquirors, since Alcatel could block any alternative transaction. Alcatel also made it clear that it was not interested in having its shares repurchased by Lynch. The Independent Committee decided that a stockholder rights plan was not viable because of the increased debt it would entail.

54. Based upon inferences from Kertz's testimony, the Court of Chancery noted that "Wineman apparently agreed" that $15.50 was a fair price. However, the record also reflects that it was Wineman who urged the other independent directors to yield to Alcatel's demands at the August 1, 1986 meeting.

55. On the other hand, Dertinger, an officer and director of Lynch, testified that he was informed by Alcatel that the price of an unfriendly tender offer would indeed be lower and would in fact be $12 per share.

Nevertheless, based upon the record before it, the Court of Chancery found that the Independent Committee had "appropriately simulated a third-party transaction, where negotiations are conducted at arms-length and there is no compulsion to reach an agreement." The Court of Chancery concluded that the Independent Committee's actions "as a whole" were "sufficiently well informed ... and aggressive to simulate an arms-length transaction," so that the burden of proof as to entire fairness shifted from Alcatel to the contending Lynch shareholder, Kahn. The Court of Chancery's reservations about that finding are apparent in its written decision.

The Power to Say No,

The Parties' Contentions,

Arm's Length Bargaining

The Court of Chancery properly noted that limitations on the alternatives to Alcatel's offer did not mean that the Independent Committee should have agreed to a price that was unfair:

> The power to say no is a significant power. It is the duty of directors serving on [an independent] committee to approve only a transaction that is in the best interests of the public shareholders, to say no to any transaction that is not fair to those shareholders and is not the best transaction available. It is not sufficient for such directors to achieve the best price that a fiduciary will pay if that price is not a fair price.

(Quoting *In re First Boston, Inc. Shareholders Litig.,* Del.Ch., C.A. 10338 (Consolidated), Allen, C., 1990 WL 78836, slip op. at 15–16 (June 7, 1990)).

The Alcatel defendants argue that the Independent Committee exercised its "power to say no" in rejecting the three initial offers from Alcatel, and that it therefore cannot be said that Alcatel dictated the terms of the merger or precluded the Independent Committee from exercising real bargaining power. *Compare Rabkin v. Olin Corp.,* Del.Ch., C.A. 7547 (Consolidated), Chandler, V.C., 1990 WL 47648, slip op. at 14–15 (Apr. 17, 1990), *reprinted in* 16 Del.J.Corp.L. 851, 861–62 (1991), *aff'd,* Del.Supr., 586 A.2d 1202 (1990).[56] The Alcatel defendants contend, alternatively, that "even assuming that such a threat [of a hostile takeover] could have had a coercive effect on the [Independent] Committee," the willingness of the Independent Committee to reject Alcatel's initial three offers suggests that "the alleged threat was either nonexistent or ineffective." *Braunschweiger v. American Home Shield Corp.,* Del.Ch., C.A. No. 10755, Allen, C., 1991 WL 3920, slip op. at 13 (Jan. 7, 1991), *reprinted in* 17 Del.J.Corp.L. 206, 219 (1992).

---

56. Alcatel also points to the fairness opinions of two investment banking firms employed by the Committee, Kidder Peabody and Thomson McKinnon, and the involvement of independent legal counsel, Skadden Arps, in considering and rejecting alternatives to the Alcatel cash offers.

Kahn contends the record reflects that the conduct of Alcatel deprived the Independent Committee of an effective "power to say no." Kahn argues that Alcatel not only threatened the Committee with a hostile tender offer in the event its $15.50 offer was not recommended and approved, but also directed the affairs of Lynch for Alcatel's benefit in such a way as to make it impossible for Lynch to continue as a public company under Alcatel's control without injury to itself and its minority shareholders. In support of this argument, Kahn relies upon another proceeding wherein the Court of Chancery has been previously presented with factual circumstances comparable to those of the case *sub judice,* albeit in a different procedural posture. *See American Gen. Corp. v. Texas Air Corp.,* Del.Ch., C.A. Nos. 8390, 8406, 8650 & 8805, Hartnett, V.C., 1987 WL 6337 (Feb. 5, 1987), *reprinted in* 13 Del.J.Corp.L. 173 (1988).

In *American General,* in the context of an application for injunctive relief, the Court of Chancery found that the members of the Special Committee were "truly independent and ... performed their tasks in a proper manner," but it also found that "at the end of their negotiations with [the majority shareholder] the Committee members were issued an ultimatum and told that they must accept the $16.50 per share price or [the majority shareholder] would proceed with the transaction without their input." *Id.,* slip op. at 11–12, 13 Del. J.Corp.L. at 181. The Court of Chancery concluded based upon this evidence that the Special Committee had thereby lost "its ability to negotiate in an arms-length manner" and that there was a reasonable probability that the burden of proving entire fairness would remain on the defendants if the litigation proceeded to trial. *Id.,* slip op. at 12, 13 Del.J.Corp.L. at 181.

Alcatel's efforts to distinguish *American General* are unpersuasive. Alcatel's reliance on *Braunschweiger* is also misplaced. In *Braunschweiger,* the Court of Chancery pointed out that "[p]laintiffs do not allege that [the management-affiliated merger partner] ever used the threat of a hostile takeover to influence the special committee." *Braunschweiger v. American Home Shield Corp.,* slip op. at 13, 17 Del.J.Corp.L. at 219. Unlike *Braunschweiger,* in this case the coercion was extant and directed to a specific price offer which was, in effect, presented in the form of a "take it or leave it" ultimatum by a controlling shareholder with the capability of following through on its threat of a hostile takeover.

Alcatel's Entire Fairness Burden Did Not Shift to Kahn

A condition precedent to finding that the burden of proving entire fairness has shifted in an interested merger transaction is a careful judicial analysis of the factual circumstances of each case. Particular consideration must be given to evidence of whether the special committee was truly independent, fully informed, and had the freedom to negotiate at arm's length. *Weinberger v. UOP, Inc.,* Del.Supr., 457 A.2d 701, 709–10 n. 7 (1983). *See also American Gen. Corp. v. Texas Air Corp.,* Del.Ch., C.A. Nos. 8390, 8406, 8650 & 8805, Hartnett,

V.C., 1987 WL 6337, slip op. at 11 (Feb. 5, 1987), *reprinted in* 13 Del.J.Corp.L. 173, 181 (1988). "Although perfection is not possible," unless the controlling or dominating shareholder can demonstrate that it has not only formed an independent committee but also replicated a process "as though each of the contending parties had in fact exerted its bargaining power at arm's length," the burden of proving entire fairness will not shift. *Weinberger v. UOP, Inc.*, 457 A.2d at 709–10 n. 7. *See also Rosenblatt v. Getty Oil Co.*, Del.Supr., 493 A.2d 929, 937–38 (1985).

Subsequent to *Rosenblatt*, this Court pointed out that "the use of an independent negotiating committee of outside directors may have significant advantages to the majority stockholder in defending suits of this type," but it does not *ipso facto* establish the procedural fairness of an interested merger transaction. *Rabkin v. Philip A. Hunt Chem. Corp.*, Del.Supr., 498 A.2d 1099, 1106 & n. 7 (1985). In reversing the granting of the defendants' motion to dismiss in *Rabkin*, this Court implied that the burden on entire fairness would not be shifted by the use of an independent committee which concluded its processes with "what could be considered a quick surrender" to the dictated terms of the controlling shareholder.[57] *Id.* at 1106. This Court concluded in *Rabkin* that the majority stockholder's "attitude toward the minority," coupled with the "apparent absence of any meaningful negotiations as to price," did not manifest the exercise of arm's length bargaining by the independent committee. *Id.*

The Court of Chancery's determination that the Independent Committee "appropriately simulated a third-party transaction, where negotiations are conducted at arm's-length and there is no compulsion to reach an agreement," is not supported by the record. Under the circumstances present in the case *sub judice*, the Court of Chancery erred in shifting the burden of proof with regard to entire fairness to the contesting Lynch shareholder-plaintiff, Kahn. The record reflects that the ability of the Committee effectively to negotiate at arm's length was compromised by Alcatel's threats to proceed with a hostile tender offer if the $15.50 price was not approved by the Committee and the Lynch board. The fact that the Independent Committee rejected three initial offers, which were well below the Independent

---

57. A "surrender" need not occur at the outset of the negotiation process in order to deny a controlling shareholder the burden-shifting function which might otherwise follow from establishing an independent committee bargaining structure. *See Freedman v. Restaurant Assocs. Indus., Inc.*, Del. Ch., C.A. No. 9212, Allen, C., 1990 WL 135923 (Sept. 19, 1990), *reprinted in* 16 Del.J.Corp.L. 1462 (1991). *See also* Block, Barton & Radin, *The Business Judgment Rule: Fiduciary Duties of Corporate Directors* 170–72 (4th ed. 1993). In *Freedman*, finding that there was no "fully functional" independent committee, the Court of Chancery stated:

[F]acts are alleged that would establish that [the] special committee was not given

the opportunity to select from among the range of alternatives that an independent, disinterested board would have had available to it; it was, in effect, 'hemmed in' by the management group's actions. Under these circumstances, where, according to the allegations contained in the amended complaint, the management group could (and did) veto any action of the special committee that was not agreeable to the conflicted interests of the management directors it would be for-malistically perverse to afford the special committee's action the effect of burden shifting of which that device is capable.

Freedman v. Restaurant Assocs. Indus., Inc., slip op. at 17–18, 16 Del.J.Corp.L. at 1475.

Committee's estimated valuation for Lynch and were not combined with an explicit threat that Alcatel was "ready to proceed" with a hostile bid, cannot alter the conclusion that any semblance of arm's length bargaining ended when the Independent Committee surrendered to the ultimatum that accompanied Alcatel's final offer. *See Rabkin v. Philip A. Hunt Chem. Corp.*, Del.Supr., 498 A.2d 1099, 1106 (1985).

Conclusion

Accordingly, the judgment of the Court of Chancery is reversed. This matter is remanded for further proceedings consistent herewith, including a redetermination of the entire fairness of the cash-out merger to Kahn and the other Lynch minority shareholders with the burden of proof remaining on Alcatel, the dominant and interested shareholder.

———

(Note: On remand, the Court of Chancery, applying the principles set out in Kahn v. Lynch, determined that the merger was entirely fair to the minority shareholders. The Delaware Supreme Court affirmed. Kahn v. Lynch Communication Systems, Inc., 669 A.2d 79 (Del. 1995).)

———

LEVCO ALTERNATIVE FUND v. THE READER'S DIGEST ASS'N, INC., 803 A.2d 428 (Del. 2002). Reader's Digest Association (RDA) had two classes of common stock: Class A, which was non-voting, and Class B, which had the right to vote. RDA proposed a recapitalization under which it would, among other things, (i) create a new class of voting common stock; (ii) purchase all the shares of its Class B voting stock at a premium of 1.24 to 1 to the new voting stock; and (iii) recapitalize each share of the Class A non-voting stock into one share of the new voting common stock. The key to the recapitalization proposal was an agreement by RDA to purchase 3,636,363 shares of Class B Voting Stock owned by two Funds at $27.50 per share, for an aggregate purchase price of approximately $100 million. Prior to recapitalization, the Funds controlled 50 percent of the Class B voting stock. Following the recapitalization, the funds would hold 14 percent of the new voting common stock.

Plaintiffs, Class A shareholders, sought a preliminary injunction against the recapitalization in Delaware Chancery Court. Plaintiffs alleged that the recapitalization would result in financial detriment to the Class A shareholders. Plaintiffs also argued that a Special Committee, composed of three outside directors and established to evaluate the fairness of the transaction, breached its fiduciary duty to consider the separate interests of the Class A shareholders. RDA and its directors did not dispute that the directors owed a fiduciary duty to the Class A shareholders, but contended that they had discharged that duty through intensive negotiations between the Funds and the Special Committee. Plaintiffs asserted that the directors, including the Special Committee, were subject to the Funds' control and therefore were required to demonstrate the entire fairness of the transaction. Plaintiffs further asserted that the directors breached their duty of care. The Court of Chancery ruled that regardless of where the burden of proof lay, the evidence did not support the view that plaintiffs would ultimately succeed in demonstrating that the activities of the Special Committee did not result in a "fair and genuinely negotiated price." Reversed.

Although the Court of Chancery did not elaborate on the burden of proof, we think it significant here that the initial burden of establishing entire fairness rests upon the party who stands on both sides of the transaction. *Kahn v. Lynch Comm. Sys., Inc.*, 638 A.2d 1110, 1117 (Del.1994). That burden may shift, of course, if an independent committee of directors has approved the transaction. *Emerald Partners v. Berlin*, 726 A.2d 1215, 1221 (Del.1999). While we agree with the Court of Chancery that the independent committee who negotiated the recapitalization believed it was operating in the interests of the corporation as an entity, we conclude that the committee's functioning, to the extent it was required to balance the conflicting interests of two distinct classes of shareholders, was flawed both from the standpoint of process and price.

With respect to the unfair dealing claim, the Special Committee never sought, nor did its financial advisor, Goldman Sachs, ever tender, an opinion as to whether the transaction was fair to the Class A shareholders. Goldman Sachs directed its fairness opinion to the interests of RDA as a corporate entity. Given the obvious conflicting interests of the shareholder classes, the conceded absence of an evaluation of the fairness of the recapitalization on the Class A shareholders is significant. While the Class A shareholders received voting rights, their equity interests decreased by at least $100 million without either their consent or an objective evaluation of the exchange. In short, while the Special Committee believed, perhaps in good faith, that the transaction was in the best interests of the corporation, arguably, it never focused on the specific impact upon the Class A shareholders of RDA's payment of $100 million to the Class B shareholders.

With respect to the premium paid to the Class B shareholders, given RDA's tenuous financial condition, having recently committed to a large acquisition, incurring additional debt in order to pay $100 million to the Class B shareholders is a matter of concern. The net result of the transaction was to significantly reduce the post-capitalization equity of the corporation. To the extent that the directors did not secure sufficient information concerning the effect of the recapitalization premium on the Class A shareholders, a serious question is raised concerning the discharge of their duty of care. *Kahn v. Tremont Corp.*, 694 A.2d 422, 430 (Del.1997)....

We are not required, nor was the Court of Chancery, to determine the final merits of appellants' claims but, in our view, they stand a reasonable probability of success. It is unquestioned that the appellants will be irreparably harmed. While future monetary relief may be available, the issuance of the shares contemplated by the recapitalization may place a practical remedy beyond judicial reach.

———

Jones v. H.F. Ahmanson & Co.

Supreme Court of California, 1969.
1 Cal.3d 93, 81 Cal.Rptr. 592, 460 P.2d 464.

■ TRAYNOR, C.J.—June K. Jones, the owner of 25 shares of the capital stock of United Savings and Loan Association of California brings this action on behalf of herself individually and of all similarly situated minority stockholders of the Association. The defendants are United Financial Corporation of California, fifteen individuals, and four corporations, all of whom are present or former stockholders or officers of the Association. Plaintiff seeks damages and other relief for losses allegedly suffered by the minority stockholders of the Association because of claimed breaches of fiduciary responsibility by defendants in the creation and operation of United Financial, a Delaware holding company that owns 87 percent of the outstanding Association stock.

Plaintiff appeals from the judgment entered for defendants after an order sustaining defendants' general and special demurrers to her third amended complaint without leave to amend. Defendants have filed a protective cross-appeal. We have concluded that the allegations of the complaint and certain stipulated facts sufficiently state a cause of action and that the judgment must therefore be reversed.

The following facts appear from the allegations of the complaint and stipulation.

United Savings and Loan Association of California is a California chartered savings and loan association that first issued stock on April 5, 1956. Theretofore it had been owned by its depositors, who, with borrowing members, elected the board of directors. No one depositor had sufficient voting power to control the Association.

The Association issued 6,568 shares of stock on April 5, 1956. No additional stock has been issued. Of these shares, 987 (14.8 percent) were purchased by depositors pursuant to warrants issued in proportion to the amount of their deposits. Plaintiff was among these purchasers. The shares allocated to unexercised warrants were sold to the then chairman of the board of directors who later resold them to defendants and others. The stockholders have the right to elect a majority of the directors of the Association.

The Association has retained the major part of its earnings in tax-free reserves with the result that the book value of the outstanding shares has increased substantially.[2] The shares were not actively traded. This inactivity is attributed to the high book value, the closely held nature of the Association,[3] and the failure of the management to provide investment information and assistance to shareholders, brokers, or the public. Transactions in the stock that did occur were primarily among existing stockholders. Fourteen of the nineteen defendants comprised 95 percent of the market for Association shares prior to 1959.

In 1958 investor interest in shares of savings and loan associations and holding companies increased. Savings and loan stocks that were publicly marketed enjoyed a steady increase in market price thereafter until June 1962, but the stock of United Savings and Loan Association was not among them. Defendants determined to create a mechanism by which they could participate in the profit taking by attracting investor interest in the Association. They did not, however, undertake to render the Association shares more readily marketable. Instead, the United Financial Corporation of California was incorporated in Delaware by all of the other defendants except defendant Thatcher on May 8, 1959. On May 14, 1959, pursuant to a prior agreement, certain Association stockholders who among them owned a majority of the Association stock exchanged their shares for those of United Financial, receiving a "derived block" of 250 United Financial shares for each Association share.[4]

After the exchange, United Financial held 85 percent of the outstanding Association stock. More than 85 percent of United Financial's consolidated earnings[5] and book value of its shares reflected its ownership of this Association stock. The former majority stockholders of the Association had become the majority shareholders of United Financial and continued to control the Association through the holding company. They did not offer the minority stockholders of the Association an opportunity to exchange their shares.

The first public offering of United Financial stock was made in June 1960. To attract investor interest, 60,000 units were offered, each of which comprised two shares of United Financial stock and one $100, 5 percent interest-bearing, subordinated, convertible debenture bond. The offering provided that of the $7,200,000 return from the sale of these units, $6,200,000 would be distributed immediately as a return of capital to the original shareholders of United Financial, *i.e.*, the former majority stockholders of the Association.[6] To obtain a permit from the California Corporations Commissioner for the sale, United Financial represented that the financial reserve requirement for

---

2. Between 1959 and 1966 the book value of each share increased from $1,131 to $4,143.70.

3. H.F. Ahmanson & Co. acquired a majority of the shares in May 1958. On May 14, 1959, the company owned 4,171 of the outstanding shares.

4. The number of shares in these derived blocks of United Financial stock was later modified by pro-rata surrenders and stock dividends in a series of transactions not pertinent here.

5. The balance reflected United Financial's ownership of three insurance agencies and stock in a fourth.

6. This distribution was equivalent to a $927.50 return of capital on each derived block of shares.

debenture repayment established by Commissioner's Rules 480 subdivision (a) and 486 would be met by causing the Association to liquidate or encumber its income producing assets for cash that the Association would then distribute to United Financial to service and retire the bonds.

In the Securities and Exchange Commission prospectus accompanying this first public offering, United Financial acknowledged that its prior earnings were not sufficient to service the debentures and noted that United Financial's direct earnings would have to be augmented by dividends from the Association.

A public offering of 50,000 additional shares by United Financial with a secondary offering of 600,000 shares of the derived stock by the original investors was made in February 1961 for a total price of $15,275,000. The defendants sold 568,190 shares of derived stock in this secondary offering. An underwriting syndicate of 70 brokerage firms participated. The resulting nationwide publicity stimulated trading in the stock until, in mid–1961, an average of 708.5 derived blocks were traded each month. Sales of Association shares decreased during this period from a rate of 170 shares per year before the formation of United Financial to half that number. United Financial acquired 90 percent of the Association shares that were sold.

Shortly after the first public offering of United Financial shares, defendants caused United Financial to offer to purchase up to 350 shares of Association stock for $1,100 per share. The book value of each of these shares was $1,411.57, and earnings were $301.15 per share. The derived blocks of United Financial shares then commanded an aggregate price of $3,700 per block exclusive of the $927.50 return of capital. United Financial acquired an additional 130 shares of Association stock as a result of this offer.

In 1959 and 1960 extra dividends of $75 and $57 per share had been paid by the Association, but in December 1960, after the foregoing offer had been made, defendants caused the Association's president to notify each minority stockholder by letter that no dividends other than the regular $4 per share annual dividend would be paid in the near future. The Association president, defendant M.D. Jameson, was then a director of both the Association and United Financial.

Defendants then proposed an exchange of United Financial shares for Association stock. Under this proposal each minority stockholder would have received approximately 51 United Financial shares of a total value of $2,400 for each Association share. When the application for a permit was filed with the California Corporations Commissioner on August 28, 1961, the value of the derived blocks of United Financial shares received by defendants in the initial exchange had risen to approximately $8,800.[9] The book value of the Association stock was in excess of $1,700 per share, and the shares were earning at an annual

9. The derived block sold for as much as $13,127.41 during 1960–1961. On January 30, 1962, the date upon which plaintiff commenced this action, the mean value was $9,116.08.

rate of $615 per share. Each block of 51 United Financial shares had a book value of only $210 and earnings of $134 per year, 85 percent of which reflected Association earnings. At the hearings held on the application by the Commissioner, representatives of United Financial justified the higher valuation of United Financial shares on the ground that they were highly marketable, whereas Association stock was unmarketable and poor collateral for loans. Plaintiff and other minority stockholders objected to the proposed exchange, contending that the plan was not fair, just, and equitable. Defendants then asked the Commissioner to abandon the application without ruling on it.

Plaintiff contends that in following this course of conduct defendants breached the fiduciary duty owed by majority or controlling shareholders to minority shareholders. She alleges that they used their control of the Association for their own advantage to the detriment of the minority when they created United Financial, made a public market for its shares that rendered Association stock unmarketable except to United Financial, and then refused either to purchase plaintiff's Association stock at a fair price or exchange the stock on the same basis afforded to the majority. She further alleges that they also created a conflict of interest that might have been avoided had they offered all Association stockholders the opportunity to participate in the initial exchange of shares. Finally, plaintiff contends that the defendants' acts constituted a restraint of trade in violation of common law and statutory antitrust laws. . . .

II

Majority Shareholders' Fiduciary Responsibility

Defendants take the position that as shareholders they owe no fiduciary obligation to other shareholders, absent reliance on inside information, use of corporate assets, or fraud. This view has long been repudiated in California. The Courts of Appeal have often recognized that majority shareholders, either singly or acting in concert to accomplish a joint purpose, have a fiduciary responsibility to the minority and to the corporation to use their ability to control the corporation in a fair, just, and equitable manner. Majority shareholders may not use their power to control corporate activities to benefit themselves alone or in a manner detrimental to the minority. Any use to which they put the corporation or their power to control the corporation must benefit all shareholders proportionately and must not conflict with the proper conduct of the corporation's business. (*Brown v. Halbert*, 271 Cal. App.2d 252 [76 Cal.Rptr. 781]; *Burt v. Irvine Co.*, 237 Cal.App.2d 828 [47 Cal.Rptr. 392]; *Efron v. Kalmanovitz*, 226 Cal.App.2d 546 [38 Cal.Rptr. 148]; *Remillard Brick Co. v. Remillard–Dandini Co.*, 109 Cal.App.2d 405 [241 P.2d 66].)

The extensive reach of the duty of controlling shareholders and directors to the corporation and its other shareholders was described by the Court of Appeal in *Remillard Brick Co. v. Remillard–Dandini Co., supra,* 109 Cal.App.2d 405, where, quoting from the opinion of the United States Supreme Court in *Pepper v. Litton,* 308 U.S. 295 [84

L.Ed. 281, 60 S.Ct. 238], the court held: " 'A director is a fiduciary . . . So is a dominant or controlling stockholder or group of stockholders . . . Their powers are powers of trust . . . Their dealings with the corporation are subjected to rigorous scrutiny and where any of their contracts or engagements with the corporation is challenged the burden is on the director or stockholder not only to prove the good faith of the transaction but also to show its inherent fairness from the viewpoint of the corporation and those interested therein . . .' " . . .

. . . The rule that has developed in California is a comprehensive rule of "inherent fairness from the viewpoint of the corporation and those interested therein." (*Remillard Brick Co. v. Remillard–Dandini Co., supra,* 109 Cal.App.2d 405, 420. See also, *In re Security Finance Co., supra,* 49 Cal.2d 370; *Brown v. Halbert, supra,* 271 Cal.App.2d 252; *Burt v. Irvine Co., supra,* 237 Cal.App.2d 828; *Efron v. Kalmanovitz, supra,* 226 Cal.App.2d 546.) The rule applies alike to officers, directors, and controlling shareholders in the exercise of powers that are theirs by virtue of their position and to transactions wherein controlling shareholders seek to gain an advantage in the sale or transfer or use of their controlling block of shares. . . .

The increasingly complex transactions of the business and financial communities demonstrate the inadequacy of the traditional theories of fiduciary obligation as tests of majority shareholder responsibility to the minority. These theories have failed to afford adequate protection to minority shareholders and particularly to those in closely held corporations whose disadvantageous and often precarious position renders them particularly vulnerable to the vagaries of the majority. Although courts have recognized the potential for abuse or unfair advantage when a controlling shareholder sells his shares at a premium over investment value (*Perlman v. Feldmann,* 219 F.2d 173 [50 A.L.R.2d 1134] [premium paid for control over allocation of production in time of shortage]; *Gerdes v. Reynolds,* 28 N.Y.S.2d 622 [sale of control to looters or incompetents]; *Porter v. Healy,* 244 Pa. 427 [91 A. 428]; *Brown v. Halbert, supra,* 271 Cal.App.2d 252 [sale of only controlling shareholder's shares to purchaser offering to buy assets of corporation or all shares]) or in a controlling shareholder's use of control to avoid equitable distribution of corporate assets (*Zahn v. Transamerica Corp.* (3rd Cir.1947) 162 F.2d 36 [172 A.L.R. 495] [use of control to cause subsidiary to redeem stock prior to liquidation and distribution of assets]), no comprehensive rule has emerged in other jurisdictions. Nor have most commentators approached the problem from a perspective other than that of the advantage gained in the sale of control. Some have suggested that the price paid for control shares over their investment value be treated as an asset belonging to the corporation itself (Berle and Means, The Modern Corporation and Private Property (1932) p. 243), or as an asset that should be shared proportionately with all shareholders through a general offer (Jennings, *Trading in Corporate Control* (1956) 44 Cal.L.Rev. 1, 39), and another contends that the sale of control at a premium is always evil (Bayne, *The Sale-of-Control Premium: the Intrinsic Illegitimacy* (1969) 47 Texas L.Rev. 215).

The additional potential for injury to minority shareholders from majority dealings in its control power apart from sale has not gone unrecognized, however. The ramifications of defendants' actions here are not unlike those described by Professor Gower as occurring when control of one corporation is acquired by another through purchase of less than all of the shares of the latter: "The [acquired] company's existence is not affected, nor need its constitution be altered; all that occurs is that its shareholders change. From the legal viewpoint this methodological distinction is formidable, but commercially the two things may be almost identical. If . . . a controlling interest is acquired, the [acquired] company . . . will become a subsidiary of the acquiring company . . . and cease, in fact though not in law, to be an independent entity.

"This may produce the situation in which a small number of dissentient members are left as a minority in a company intended to be operated as a member of a group. As such, their position is likely to be unhappy, for the parent company will wish to operate the subsidiary for the benefit of the group as a whole and not necessarily for the benefit of that particular subsidiary." (Gower, The Principles of Modern Company Law (2d ed. 1957) p. 561.) Professor Eisenberg notes that as the purchasing corporation's proportionate interest in the acquired corporation approaches 100 percent, the market for the latter's stock disappears, a problem that is aggravated if the acquiring corporation for its own business purposes reduces or eliminates dividends. (Eisenberg, *The Legal Role of Shareholders and Management in Modern Corporate Decision–Making* (1969) 57 Cal.L.Rev. 1, 132. See also, O'Neal and Derwin, Expulsion or Oppression of Business Associates (1961) *passim;* Leech, *Transactions in Corporate Control* (1956) 104 U.Pa.L.Rev. 725, 728; Comment, *The Fiduciary Relation of the Dominant Shareholder to the Minority Shareholders* (1958) 9 Hastings L.J. 306, 314.) The case before us, in which no sale or transfer of actual control is directly involved, demonstrates that the injury anticipated by these authors can be inflicted with impunity under the traditional rules and supports our conclusion that the comprehensive rule of good faith and inherent fairness to the minority in any transaction where control of the corporation is material properly governs controlling shareholders in this state.

We turn now to defendants' conduct to ascertain whether this test is met.

III

Formation of United Financial and Marketing its Shares

Defendants created United Financial during a period of unusual investor interest in the stock of savings and loan associations. They then owned a majority of the outstanding stock of the Association. This stock was not readily marketable owing to a high book value, lack of investor information and facilities, and the closely held nature of the Association. The management of the Association had made no effort to create a market for the stock or to split the shares and reduce their market price to a more attractive level. Two courses were available to defendants in their effort to exploit the bull market in savings and loan stock. Both were made possible by defendants' status as controlling stockholders. The first was either to cause the Association to effect a stock split (Corp.Code, § 1507) and create a market for the Association stock or to create a holding company for Association shares and permit all stockholders to exchange their shares before offering holding company shares to the public. All stockholders would have benefited alike had this been done, but in realizing their gain on the sale of their stock the majority stockholders would of necessity have had to relinquish some of their control shares. Because a public market would have been created, however, the minority stockholders would have been able to extricate themselves without sacrificing their investment had they elected not to remain with the new management.

The second course was that taken by defendants. A new corporation was formed whose major asset was to be the control block of Association stock owned by defendants, but from which minority shareholders were to be excluded. The unmarketable Association stock held by the majority was transferred to the newly formed corporation at an exchange rate equivalent to a 250 for 1 stock split. The new corporation thereupon set out to create a market for its own shares. Association stock constituted 85 percent of the holding company's assets and produced an equivalent proportion of its income. The same individuals controlled both corporations. It appears therefrom that the market created by defendants for United Financial shares was a market that would have been available for Association stock had defendants taken the first course of action.[13]

13. The situation of minority stockholders and the difficulties they faced in attempting to market their savings and loan stock were described in The Savings and Loan Industry in California, a report prepared by the Stanford Research Institute for the California Savings and Loan Commissioner, and published by the Commissioner in 1960. The attractiveness of the holding company as a device to enhance liquidity was recognized: "The majority and minority stockholders in the original associations often found that they had difficulties in selling their shares at a price approximating their book value. Their main difficulties arose from the fact that book values and prices of shares often ran into many thousands of dollars, a price not generally suitable for wide public sale. These shares were usually owned by a relatively small number of stockholders. When one of them, or his heirs, wished to sell his shares, he had to negotiate with a buyer in this small group or attempt to find an outside purchaser. Minority stockholders had a special problem, because they could not sell control with their stock.

"The holding company was regarded by many stockholders as an attractive device to solve the problem of the marketability of their shares. Through this method, the control of one, two, or several associations could be consolidated and offered to the investing public in a single large stock issue at relatively low prices, either over the counter or through a stock exchange. The wide public ownership of holding company shares would thus provide a more active market and more protection against large capital losses in the event the original owners or their heirs wished to sell their holding company stock.

" * * *

"Large capital gains on the sale of holding company stock to the public have been an important incentive and consequence of this form of organization. The issuance of holding company stock to the general public usually found an enthusiastic demand which made it possible to sell the stock for as much as two to three times book value. In many but not all cases the majority stockholders in the original associations have offered less than 50 percent of the holding company's stock to the public, thus retaining control of the association and the holding companies." (The Savings and Loan Industry in California (1960) pp. VI–6–VI–7.) Although defendants suggest that their transfer of the insurance busi-

After United Financial shares became available to the public it became a virtual certainty that no equivalent market could or would be created for Association stock. United Financial had become the controlling stockholder and neither it nor the other defendants would benefit from public trading in Association stock in competition with United Financial shares. Investors afforded an opportunity to acquire United Financial shares would not be likely to choose the less marketable and expensive Association stock in preference. Thus defendants chose a course of action in which they used their control of the Association to obtain an advantage not made available to all stockholders. They did so without regard to the resulting detriment to the minority stockholders and in the absence of any compelling business purpose. Such conduct is not consistent with their duty of good faith and inherent fairness to the minority stockholders. Had defendants afforded the minority an opportunity to exchange their stock on the same basis or offered to purchase them at a price arrived at by independent appraisal, their burden of establishing good faith and inherent fairness would have been much less. At the trial they may present evidence tending to show such good faith or compelling business purpose that would render their action fair under the circumstances. On appeal from the judgment of dismissal after the defendants' demurrer was sustained we decide only that the complaint states a cause of action entitling plaintiff to relief.

Defendants gained an additional advantage for themselves through their use of control of the Association when they pledged that control over the Association's assets and earnings to secure the holding company's debt, a debt that had been incurred for their own benefit. In so doing the defendants breached their fiduciary obligation to the minority once again and caused United Financial and its controlling shareholders to become inextricably wedded to a conflict of interest between the minority stockholders of each corporation. Alternatives were available to them that would have benefited all stockholders proportionately. . . .

In so holding we do not suggest that the duties of corporate fiduciaries include in all cases an obligation to make a market for and to facilitate public trading in the stock of the corporation. But when, as here, no market exists, the controlling shareholders may not use their power to control the corporation for the purpose of promoting a marketing scheme that benefits themselves alone to the detriment of the minority. Nor do we suggest that a control block of shares may not be sold or transferred to a holding company. We decide only that the circumstances of any transfer of controlling shares will be subject to judicial scrutiny when it appears that the controlling shareholders may

nesses and the later acquisition of another savings and loan association by United Financial were necessary to the creation of a market for United Financial shares and that no market could be created for the shares of a single savings and loan association, the study does not support their claim. Whether defendants could have created a market for a holding company that controlled a single association or reasonably believed that they could not, goes to their good faith and to the existence of a proper business purpose for electing the course that they chose to follow. At the trial of the cause defendants can introduce evidence relevant to the necessity for inclusion of other businesses.

have breached their fiduciary obligation to the corporation or the remaining shareholders.

IV

Damages ...

If, after the trial of the cause, plaintiff has established facts in conformity with the allegations of the complaint and stipulation, then upon tender of her Association stock to defendants she will be entitled to receive at her election either the appraised value of her shares on the date of the exchange, May 14, 1959, with interest at 7 percent a year from the date of this action, or a sum equivalent to the fair market value of a "derived block" of United Financial stock on the date of this action with interest thereon from that date, and the sum of $927.50 (the return of capital paid to the original United Financial shareholders) with interest thereon from the date United Financial first made such payments to its original shareholders, for each share tendered. The appraised or fair market value shall be reduced, however, by the amount by which dividends paid on Association shares during the period from May 14, 1959, to the present exceeds the dividends paid on a corresponding block of United Financial shares during the same period....

The judgment appealed from by plaintiff is reversed. The trial court is directed to overrule the demurrer in conformity with this opinion. Defendants' appeal is dismissed.

■ PETERS, J., TOBRINER, J., BURKE, J., SULLIVAN, J., and COUGHLIN, J. pro tem., concurred.

■ ... McCOMB, J., was of the opinion that the petition should be granted.

SECTION 6. SALE OF CONTROL

Zetlin v. Hanson Holdings, Inc.

New York Court of Appeals, 1979.
48 N.Y.2d 684, 421 N.Y.S.2d 877, 397 N.E.2d 387.

MEMORANDUM.

The order of the Appellate Division should be affirmed, with costs.

Plaintiff Zetlin owned approximately 2% of the outstanding shares of Gable Industries, Inc., with defendants Hanson Holdings, Inc., and Sylvestri, together with members of the Sylvestri family, owning 44.4% of Gable's shares. The defendants sold their interests to Flintkote Co. for a premium price of $15 per share, at a time when Gable stock was selling on the open market for $7.38 per share. It is undisputed that the 44.4% acquired by Flintkote represented effective control of Gable.

Recognizing that those who invest the capital necessary to acquire a dominant position in the ownership of a corporation have the right of controlling that corporation, it has long been settled law that, absent looting of corporate assets, conversion of a corporate opportunity, fraud or other acts of bad faith, a controlling stockholder is free to sell, and a purchaser is free to buy, that controlling interest at a premium price (see *Barnes v. Brown,* 80 N.Y. 527; *Levy v. American Beverage Corp.,* 265 App.Div. 208; *Essex Universal Corp. v. Yates,* 305 F.2d 572).

Certainly, minority shareholders are entitled to protection against such abuse by controlling shareholders. They are not entitled, however, to inhibit the legitimate interests of the other stockholders. It is for this reason that control shares usually command a premium price. The premium is the added amount an investor is willing to pay for the privilege of directly influencing the corporation's affairs.

In this action plaintiff Zetlin contends that minority stockholders are entitled to an opportunity to share equally in any premium paid for a controlling interest in the corporation. This rule would profoundly affect the manner in which controlling stock interests are now transferred. It would require, essentially, that a controlling interest be transferred only by means of an offer to all stockholders, i.e., a tender offer. This would be contrary to existing law and if so radical a change is to be effected it would best be done by the Legislature.

■ CHIEF JUDGE COOKE and JUDGES JASEN, GABRIELLI, JONES, WACHTLER, FUCHSBERG and MEYER concur in memorandum.

Order affirmed.

———

Andrews, The Stockholder's Right to Equal Opportunity in the Sale of Shares

78 Harv.L.Rev. 505, 515–22 (1965).

The rule to be considered can be stated thus: whenever a controlling stockholder sells his shares, every other holder of shares (of the same class) is entitled to have an equal opportunity to sell his shares, or a prorata part of them, on substantially the same terms. Or in terms of the correlative duty: before a controlling stockholder may sell his shares to an outsider he must assure his fellow stockholders an equal opportunity to sell their shares, or as high a proportion of theirs as he ultimately sells of his own. There are qualifications in the application of the rule, to which I will return; but for purposes of argument we can begin with this broad statement of it. . . .

[*Practical reasons for the proposed rule*] (*a*).—There is a substantial danger that following a transfer of controlling shares corporate affairs may be conducted in a manner detrimental to the interests of the stockholders who have not had an opportunity to sell their shares. The corporation may be looted; it may just be badly run. Or the sale of controlling shares may operate to destroy a favorable opportunity for corporate action. . . .

The equal opportunity rule does not deal directly with the problem of mismanagement, which may occur even after a transfer of control complying with the rule; but enforcement of the rule will remove much of the incentive a purchaser can offer a controlling stockholder to sell on profitable terms. Indeed, in the case of a purchasing looter there is nothing in it for the purchaser unless he can buy less than all the shares; there is no profit in stealing from a solvent corporation if the thief owns all the stock. But the controlling stockholder will be loath to sell only part of his shares (except at a price that compensates him for all of his shares) if he expects the purchaser to destroy the value of what he keeps. The rule forces the controlling stockholder to share equally with his fellow stockholders both the benefits of the price he receives for the shares he sells and the business risks incident to the shares he retains. This will tend strongly to discourage a sale of controlling shares when the risk of looting, or other harm to the corporation, is apparent; and it will provide the seller with a direct incentive to investigate and evaluate with care when the risks are not apparent, since his own financial interest continues to be at stake. . . .

Of course a transfer of control may have advantageous effects for a corporation and its stockholders—and these may be just as subtle as any adverse effects. Many sales of controlling shares come about because the selling stockholders are not doing as well with a business as a purchaser believes he can do; and the belief is often right. Often the sellers are members of a family that has simply run out of managerial talent or interest.

If the rule of equal opportunity would prevent sales in this sort of situation, that would be a high price to pay for the prevention of harm in other cases. . . . For my own part I do not believe the rule of equal opportunity would have much tendency to discourage beneficial transactions. After all, if the purchaser is optimistic—and can convince his bankers to share his optimism—he should be willing to buy out everyone. If the seller is optimistic about the consequences of the transfer, he should be willing to retain some of his shares. If minority stockholders are optimistic, they should be willing to hold their shares. If the financial community is optimistic (in the case of a publicly held corporation), the market itself should offer the minority stockholders a chance to sell at a price that satisfies the rule. Thus, on the face of it the rule would only operate to prevent a sale when all four of these—the seller, the purchaser, the minority stockholders, and the financial community—take a pessimistic view of the transfer. . . .

(b). . . . [A] purchaser attains control of the corporation's business and assets equally whether he purchases all the shares or a smaller controlling block. When a purchaser buys less than all the shares, he is acquiring a business worth more than what he pays in cash, and is financing the difference by leaving the minority shares outstanding. We think of mortgage debts that way; if a person buys property subject to a mortgage and leaves the mortgage outstanding, we recognize that the mortgage provides financing for the purchaser because it has the same effect, substantially, as a new loan with the proceeds of which the purchaser might have paid full value for the property. But stock provides financing just as much as a mortgage does. A purchaser who buys only part of the stock of an enterprise might have accomplished much the same net result by purchasing all the assets in the name of a newly organized corporation in which he takes only a part of the stock. The other stockholders in the new corporation would then be viewed as providing equity financing for the acquisition. The chief difference then between a sale of assets, or of all the stock, and a sale of a controlling block of shares only, is that in the latter case the purchaser has had his acquisition partially financed, perhaps unwillingly, by the stockholders from whom he does not buy. That is no reason to give the minority stockholders less protection than if the purchaser gave them an opportunity to sell, even at a lower price. . . .

(c).—A somewhat broader way of putting the argument is even simpler: each stockholder is entitled to share proportionately in the profits of the enterprise; from the stockholder's point of view a sale of stock is one very important way of realizing a profit on his investment; profits from stock sales ought to be regarded as profits of the enterprise subject to equal sharing among stockholders just as much as profits realized through corporate action.

A minority stockholder must invest largely on the strength of the expectation that decisions will tend to be made for his benefit because of the general identity of interest between him and those in control. This identity of interest is qualified when controlling stockholders have an opportunity to profit by entering into dealings with their corporation; this is permitted because such transactions may be mutually profitable, and there is no way to enforce equality of interest beyond allowing judicial scrutiny of such transactions for fairness. It would be impossible to insist, for example, that a publicly held corporation offer all its stockholders a proportionate opportunity to serve in an executive capacity. But when an opportunity arises for profit by selling shares, there is no such simple practical reason why it cannot be made equally available to all stockholders. . . .

———

Javaras, Equal Opportunity in the Sale of Controlling Shares: A Reply to Professor Andrews

32 U.Chi.L.Rev. 420, 425–27 (1965).

I believe that the gravest defect in Professor Andrews' theory is a grievous underassessment of the costs of a preventive rule in restraining beneficial transactions. Such restraint would operate on the purchaser by imposing higher required investment—the price of all the shares of the corporation rather than only those owned by the controlling shareholder. Professor Andrews minimizes the effects of this factor on two grounds. First, the controlling shareholder under the rule of equal opportunity, when confronted with a purchaser who wants the controlling shares and no more, may be induced to retain some of his shares and share the sale ratably with the non-controlling shareholders. Admittedly, this requires faith in the management of the purchaser. Second, a beneficial purchaser should be willing to buy all the shares because, after all, the non-controlling shares have the same investment value as the controlling shares. All the purchaser would have to do, therefore, if he did not have the capital is to borrow it. If he could not, that would be a reflection either of superior knowledge in the financial community or dislocations in the capital market.

It is doubtful whether sufficient controlling sellers can be induced to retain their shares so as to eliminate the higher capital requirement. First, . . . sales of securities are not dictated merely by an appraisal of investment value. Many sellers simply want immediate cash. Second, a controlling seller may not wish to hold, say twenty-five per cent as compared to his prior fifty per cent, because of the possibility of his views differing from those of the controlling purchaser in the future. This reticence would partly stem from . . . the controlling sellers assessment of the change in risks when he is deprived of control. The loss of control would subject him to the risk of poor management, which might dictate a lesser investment in this corporation on the principle of risk diversification.

Likewise the purchaser himself might be unwilling that the seller retain some of his shares, particularly where working control (less than fifty per cent) is the subject of the offer. He might well be reluctant to have a large block of stock outstanding whose owners, under conditions of dissension, could mobilize the other shareholders and displace his control of the board of directors.

In effect then, the rule of equal treatment would impose higher capital requirements on beneficial purchasers in a substantial number of transactions. Professor Andrews inappropriately assumes, however, that the purchasers should be willing to meet these higher costs because the investment value of the additional shares is the same. He errs in that his reasoning is incomplete. It is true that the investment value is the same. But even if the capital market did function perfectly and the purchaser could arrange the financing, a rational businessman might not want to buy all the shares at a premium price justified by the investment potential. It might be sensible to decline to buy more than the bare amount necessary for control on the principles of diversification of risk and of opportunity. This might render the equal treatment rule ineffectual as a means of automatically distinguishing "good" and "bad" purchasers. I would think that the number of prospective beneficial purchasers prevented because of a desire to diversify will be much larger than those simply unable to raise the capital. Until empirical evidence is adduced to the contrary, I am predisposed to consider this cost of restraining beneficial transactions substantial when compared with the cases of detriment with which the present law is incompetent to deal. . . .

———

Gerdes v. Reynolds

Supreme Court, Special Term, New York County, 1941.
28 N.Y.S.2d 622.

■ WALTER, JUSTICE. . . .

Defendants Clarence K. Reynolds and William F. Woodward, together with Richard S. Reynolds and Richard S. Reynolds, Jr., who are named as defendants but have not been served, were the officers and directors of Reynolds Investing Company, Inc., a Delaware corporation of the kind commonly known as an investment trust. They were also stockholders, and, with members of their families, owned a majority of its common stock, which was the only stock having voting power and was junior to debentures and preferred stock outstanding in the hands of the public. Ownership of such majority of the common stock was sold, and the persons just named resigned their offices and directorships and elected as their successors four persons designated by the purchaser. Assets of the company were then wasted and improperly applied, and the plaintiffs . . ., trustees of the company appointed in a proceeding under the Federal Bankruptcy Act, 11 U.S.C.A. § 1 et seq., here seek to hold accountable therefor both those who sold and those who bought and those who aided the transaction.

The negotiations which resulted in the transaction here complained of began in New York City about December 15, 1937, when defendant Mayer told defendant Woodward that he had a buyer [Sartell Prentice, of the firm of Prentice & Brady] "for the Reynolds Investing Company," and asked if the Reynolds family owned a majority of its stock and would sell it. Mayer knew, at least in large part, what assets Reynolds Investing Company had, such information being obtainable from regularly published statistics, and on that and the succeeding day he and Woodward discussed those assets at some length, and Mayer said his principal would pay $1.25 per share. . . .

[On December 31, 1937, Reynolds Investing Company had outstanding $3,446,900 face amount of 5 per cent debentures, $991,500 stated value of preferred stock, upon which there were $327,195 of accrued and unpaid dividends, a bank loan of $484,623, and accrued interest and taxes of $62,629. The total of those items was $5,312,847. It had cash and receivables of $149,218, a diversified portfolio of marketable securities, with a market value of $2,814,222, and 400 shares of Reynolds Research Corporation, worth $4,000. The total of those items was $2,967,440. Its other assets consisted of substantial blocks of stocks of a few companies, referred to as "special situations," including United States Foil Company and Reynolds Metals Company. Even with a liberal valuation of the "special situations," its holdings were worth just over $5 million, so that (after taking into account prior claims) the net asset value of Reynolds' common stock was only 6¢ per share.]

Woodward then telephoned an officer of the bank with which his company did business (one of the largest in New York City) for information as to Prentice. His request was transmitted to the bank's credit manager as a request for a report on Prentice & Brady, the firm of which Prentice was a member, and after communicating with other banks with which that firm did business that credit manager reported back to Woodward, a couple of hours after the request was made, that Prentice & Brady was a small Stock Exchange firm of good reputation and standing, with a capital of around half a million dollars, which sometimes was "spread out thin," (meaning that it did a large business for the amount of its capital) but because of a reputed relationship with the Rockefeller family it was assumed that it had access to large and substantial sums of money. There is no evidence that the reputed relationship to the Rockefeller family ever in fact existed....

[After negotiation, the parties agreed on a price of $2 per common share for a sale of not less than 1,035,000 shares and not more than 1,055,000 shares. Between December 31, 1937 and January 12, 1938, 1,055,000 shares were delivered in exchange for $2,110,000. On December 31, the incumbent directors resigned, and elected Mayer, Davis, McLanahan, and Prentice in their place.]

No notice of an intention to resign was given to other stockholders or to the debenture holders, and no substantial investigation of the character or ability of the persons so elected had been made by any of the resigning directors. Such persons were elected solely because the purchaser nominated them. Neither had the resigning directors made any investigation of the financial resources of Prentice other than the bank inquiry above mentioned. Further investigation would have disclosed that he bore an unblemished reputation among many social acquaintances but that such capital as he had in the firm of Prentice & Brady was borrowed and that he had practically no property other than that capital and no sources of income other than his share of the earnings of that firm and the income of a small trust.

The securities owned by Reynolds Investing Company, constituting substantially all its assets, were ... for the most part readily saleable and in practically negotiable form and of a value of over $5,000,000....

[Immediately after January 3, 1935, Prentice & Brady began converting Reynolds Investing Company's securities to its own use.]

Liability is asserted against ... [those who sold their stock and resigned as officers and directors] upon the grounds (a) that the sale of the stock, accompanied by their resignations and the election of successors nominated by the purchaser, was itself an illegal transaction because in violation of fiduciary duties owed to the corporation and the holders of its debentures and preferred stock and its minority common stockholders; and (b) that even if the transaction were not illegal in itself, it is made so because the selling defendants negligently or in bad faith failed to make proper investigation of the purchaser or to give advance notice to the other stockholders of an impending change of management, especially so inasmuch as what is claimed to be the excessive price paid was itself sufficient to put those defendants upon notice that some wrongful act was intended. Those contentions present interesting and important and difficult questions of law....

Officers and directors always and necessarily stand in a fiduciary relation to the corporation and to its stockholders and creditors. They undoubtedly may free themselves of that fiduciary relationship by ceasing to be officers and directors, but their right to resign, although sometimes stated with seeming absoluteness (Bruce v. Platt, 80 N.Y. 379, 383), is qualified by their fiduciary obligations to others. "Rights are never absolute and independent of those of others." O'Neill v. City of Port Jervis, 253 N.Y. 423, 430, 171 N.E. 694, 696. Officers and directors thus "cannot terminate their agency or accept the resignation of others if the immediate consequence would be to leave the interests of the company without proper care and protection." ...

Neither can they accept pay in any form or guise, direct or devious, for their own resignation or for the election of others in their place....

It is obvious, of course that it would be illegal for officers and directors to resign and elect as their successors persons who they knew intended to loot the corporation's treasury. Even stockholders, despite their right to sell their stock to whom they please, could not legally do that. Liability for such an act would not have to be predicated upon breach of a fiduciary relation, for the act would amount to a willful and malicious injury to property, tortious in its very nature.... I here find as a fact that none of the sellers of the stock of Reynolds Investing Company had any knowledge that the purchasers thereof, or any one acting for them, had any intention to loot the corporation or to pay any part of the purchase price out of the corporation's own assets. Whether or not the resigning officers and directors nevertheless are chargeable with notice of such an intention—whether or not it was, under all the circumstances, a risk reasonably to be perceived—is, of course, another question.

The questions determinative of the liability of corporate officers and directors in such a situation as is here disclosed thus appear to me to be these: (1) Are the circumstances such that, despite actual ignorance of unlawful plans and designs on the part of the purchasers, they are chargeable with notice of such plans and designs, or, perhaps more accurately, with notice that unlawful plans and designs are a risk reasonably to be perceived? "The risk reasonably to be perceived defines the duty to be obeyed." Palsgraf v. Long Island R.R. Co., 248 N.Y. 339, 344, 162 N.E. 99, 100, 59 A.L.R. 1253. (2) Is the price paid in reality a price paid for the stock, or is it, in part at least, a price paid for the resignations of the existing officers and directors and the election of the buyer's nominees? And the principal factors which must supply the answers to these questions are the nature of the assets which are to pass into the possession and control of the purchasers by reason of the transaction, the method by which the transaction is to be consummated, and the relation of the price paid to the value of the stock.

The immediate consequence of the resignation of the entire body of officers and directors of a corporation obviously is at least potentially different where the corporation's assets are land and buildings and where they are securities which to all intents and purposes are practically negotiable, and such potential difference must be taken into account, both by the officers and directors and by a court judging their conduct, in considering whether their en masse resignations would leave the assets without proper care and protection, because the risk of dissipation or speedy misapplication obviously is greater. Such difference in the nature of the assets must be considered, also, in gauging the significance of the purchaser's conceded requirement that custody and possession of the assets be accorded before payment of a substantial part of the purchase price. An assumption that the officers and directors of Reynolds Investing Company fully performed the fiduciary duty resting upon them thus requires an assumption that they realized that by doing what they did they were placing in the hands of those whom they elected as their successors the custody and possession of practically negotiable securities of a value of more than double the amount of the agreed purchase price, and were so placing such custody and possession at a time when a large part of the purchase price (over $600,000) still remained unpaid. For fiduciaries confronted with such a realization, I gravely doubt whether it is sufficient that they truthfully can say that they actually knew nothing against the character of the purchasers or of their nominees, or even that they had affirmative evidence that the purchasers were of good reputation. A man dealing with his own affairs may be as confiding and trusting as he pleases, and may be grossly negligent without being guilty of bad faith; but a fiduciary charged with the care of the property of others must be reasonably vigilant, and will not be heard to say that he did not know what the circumstances plainly indicated or that his faith in people was such that obvious opportunities for wrongdoing gave him no inkling that wrongdoing might be done, and schemes to acquire the stock of corporations by using assets of the corporation to pay the purchase price did not originate in the year 1937.

Precisely what would be the situation of directors who, by resignation and election, turned practically negotiable securities over to strangers who had not completed payment, need not be here determined, however, because here there is the added element that in connection with the same transaction a price was paid which is claimed to be grossly in excess of the value of the stock, and the situation of these directors must be considered in connection with that additional element.

Gross inadequacy of price long and frequently has been regarded as important evidence upon the question of good faith, and sometimes is sufficient in itself to charge a buyer with notice of fraudulent intent on the part of a seller. . . . For the same reasons, gross excessiveness of price may be equally significant in determining for what it really was paid, and may be sufficient to charge a seller with notice of a fraudulent intent on the part of a buyer. . . .

[The court then reviewed certain possible elements of value in the Reynolds Investing Company's common stock over and above its 6¢ per share asset value.]

One [expert] having much practical experience in the actual management of investment trusts expresses the view that in December, 1937, no prudent investor would have considered the purchase of this common stock—a view which he later qualified by adding "except at a nominal figure"—and after considering all speculative elements he concluded that the fair value was 25 cents per share, or $263,750 for 1,055,000 shares, to which he then added $32,000 for "control features," which he valued by taking one year's salaries and brokerage commissions which he figured the owner of the majority might obtain for himself, thus making a total of $295,750 for 1,055,000 shares. A security analyst testifying for plaintiffs fixed the value at 30 cents per share, allowed 10 cents per share additional if the block bought were large enough to secure control, and admitted the possibility of a value as high as 50 cents per share.

A feature which I regard as of great importance in considering the particular problems here involved is the almost complete lack of any distinctiveness in the assets of the company. It owned no land of special adaptability—in fact, no land at all. It owned no plant or structures or machinery which would take a long time to assemble. It had no clientele or customers, the mere existence of which sometimes gives great value to the stock of a company. It had no specially trained personnel or organization of any kind. Such position as it had in the canning industry of the country by reason of its holdings of the Stokely stocks could be duplicated by the purchase of the stocks of other canning companies. Therefore, with the exception of its holdings in United States Foil and Reynolds Metals Company, its entire assets could have been substantially duplicated by anyone in a very few days, by the simple device of giving some buying orders to a broker. Not even the sagacity and acumen displayed in selecting and assembling its portfolio was an element of value, because its portfolio was publicly disclosed in published statistics, and any admirer of the genius for security selection displayed by the company's managers could appropriate that genius for himself by examining printed volumes of security manuals which any broker expecting an order would have been only too glad to make available free of charge. Furthermore, there is no showing that the company's portfolio exhibited any exceptionally high character as an assemblage of securities. On the contrary, there is considerable evidence that in times of rising security prices it had advanced less than certain averages looked upon as fair standards of comparison, and in times of declining security prices it had receded greater than such averages.

Assuming, therefore, that in December, 1937, there was an investor with $2,110,000 in cash which he desired to invest in such a portfolio as was then owned by Reynolds Investing Company, and assuming that such investor shared to the fullest extent the optimistic viewpoint as to the future which defendants' expert says was justified, it is to my mind most improbable, if not inconceivable, that he would have put his $2,110,000 in a block of common stock which had ahead of it senior securities and obligations of $5,312,847. Even if he were so confident and optimistic of the future that he desired to corral bargains to an extent greater than he could do by buying $2,110,000 worth of securities for cash, the ordinary margin account with a broker would have presented as little risk of being wiped out by an unexpected decline in security prices as was entailed in buying common stock of Reynolds Investing Company, because the $3,446,900 of debentures of that company were issued under an indenture which contained a so-called "touch-off clause" which provided that if the value of the company's net assets fell below 110 per cent. of the amount of the debentures outstanding the debentures should be paid off at the next interest day....

Some trouble and expense undoubtedly would be saved by acquiring an existing investment trust instead of creating a new one, and I am willing to make the somewhat difficult assumption that an existing trust may have something in the nature of good-will or name which is valuable to the owner of the common stock, even though it be what is called a "closed-end" trust, i.e., one not engaged in selling additional stock or other securities. Such items, however, necessarily are small.

Viewing all the elements which the fiduciary obligations of the officers and directors of Reynolds Investing Company required them to view I am convinced that $2,110,000 was so grossly in excess of the value of the stock that it carried upon its face a plain indication that it was not for the stock alone but partly for immediate en masse resignations and immediate election of the purchasers' nominees as successors. The transaction was not one in which there was merely a sale of stock, with the right to elect directors passing to the purchasers as a legal incident of the sale, and I think it proper to add that these officers and directors did not submit to the lawyers whom they retained in the matter the question of the price paid or its significance. They had their eyes and minds so centered upon the personal interests of themselves and their families and associates as stockholders and upon a desire to get what they could for what they regarded as theirs, that they failed to consider their position as officers and directors, and the consequent duty they owed as such to the corporation itself and its creditors and other stockholders.

It thus becomes necessary to determine what part of the $2,110,000 was paid for the 1,055,000 shares of stock, and what part was paid for resignations and election of successors. Something more than the six cents per share which I have found to be the maximum asset value of the shares on December 31, 1937, obviously must be allowed to the shares because of permissible hopes and expectations and other considerations already mentioned, and what that additional something shall be is obviously a matter of judgment. It nevertheless is a matter of fact which the trier of facts must find, and with due allowance for all elements I think that 75 cents per share is as liberal a finding as the evidence warrants. That gives $791,250 as the price paid for 1,055,000 shares of stock, and $1,318,750 as the price paid for the resignations of the officers and directors and their election of the buyer's nominees as their successors, or, in other words, for what is termed the turning over of control.

The conclusion ordinarily to be drawn from the foregoing is that, having violated their fiduciary duty, these officers and directors must account to the corporation or to its duly appointed trustees for the sum of $1,318,750, and for all damages naturally resulting from their official misconduct. Bosworth v. Allen, 168 N.Y. 157, 165, 166, 61 N.E. 163, 55 L.R.A. 751, 85 Am.St.Rep. 667; McClure v. Law, 161 N.Y. 78, 55 N.E. 388, 76 Am.St.Rep. 262....

————

Accord: Insuranshares Corp. of Delaware v. Northern Fiscal Corp., 35 F.Supp. 22 (E.D.Pa.1940); DeBaun v. First Western Bank & Trust Co., 46 Cal.App.3d 686, 120 Cal.Rptr. 354 (1975).

————

NOTE ON FURTHER PROCEEDINGS IN GERDES v. REYNOLDS

Under the interlocutory judgment issued in *Gerdes v. Reynolds*, Reynolds and Woodward were directed to account "for all money and property of said Reynolds Investing Company, Inc., which were wrongfully diverted" to them by the payment of the premium, "and for all damages to Reynolds Investing Company," resulting from the transfer of control. 30 N.Y.S.2d 755, 770 (1941). In further proceedings, the damages to Reynolds Investing was determined to be over $900,000, consisting principally of the net proceeds realized by the buyers on their sale of securities belonging to Reynolds Investing, and the amount Reynolds Investing had to pay to obtain the release of converted securities that the buyers had pledged to two banks. Id. at 764, 770–73, 776.

Since the buyers paid over $2.1 million for control of Reynolds Investing, it seems likely that they originally planned to loot more than $900,000. Apparently, Mayer, who had represented the buyers and was elected an officer of Reynolds Investing, had a falling-out with some of the defendants shortly after the purchase. As a result, the affairs of Reynolds Investing were placed in the hands of a law firm, which conducted an investigation that unearthed and stopped the wrongdoing. See id. at 760.

————

Perlman v. Feldmann

United States Court of Appeals, Second Circuit, 1955.
219 F.2d 173, cert. denied 349 U.S. 952, 75 S.Ct. 880, 99 L.Ed. 1277 (1955).

■ CLARK, CHIEF JUDGE. This is a derivative action brought by minority stockholders of Newport Steel Corporation to compel accounting for, and restitution of, allegedly illegal gains which accrued to defendants as a result of the sale in August, 1950, of their controlling interest in the corporation. The principal defendant, C. Russell Feldmann, who represented and acted for the others, members of his family,[1] was at that time not only the dominant stockholder, but also the chairman of the board of directors and the president of the corporation. Newport, an Indiana corporation, operated mills for the production of steel sheets for sale to manufacturers of steel products, first at Newport, Kentucky, and later also at other places in Kentucky and Ohio. The buyers, a syndicate organized as Wilport Company, a Delaware corporation, consisted of end-users of steel who were interested in securing a source of supply in a market becoming ever tighter in the Korean War. Plaintiffs contend that the consideration paid for the stock included compensation for the sale of a corporate asset, a power held in trust for the corporation by Feldmann as its fiduciary. This power was the ability to control the allocation of the corporate product in a time of short supply, through control of the board of directors; and it was effectively transferred in this sale by having Feldmann procure the resignation of his own board and the election of Wilport's nominees immediately upon consummation of the sale.

The present action represents the consolidation of three pending stockholders' actions in which yet another stockholder has been permitted to intervene. Jurisdiction below was based upon the diverse citizenship of the parties. Plaintiffs argue here, as they did in the court below, that in the situation here disclosed the vendors must account to the nonparticipating minority stockholders for that share of their profit which is attributable to the sale of the corporate power. Judge Hincks denied the validity of the premise, holding that the rights involved in the sale were only those normally incident to the possession of a controlling block of shares, with which a dominant stockholder, in the absence of fraud or foreseeable looting, was entitled to deal according to his own best interests. Furthermore, he held that plaintiffs had failed to satisfy their burden of proving that the sales price was not a fair price for the stock per se. Plaintiffs appeal from these rulings of law which resulted in the dismissal of their complaint.

The essential facts found by the trial judge are not in dispute. Newport was a relative newcomer in the steel industry with predominantly old installations which were in the process of being supplemented by more modern facilities. Except in times of extreme shortage

---

1. The stock was not held personally by Feldmann in his own name, but was held by the members of his family and by personal corporations. The aggregate of stock thus [held] amounted to 33% of the outstanding Newport stock and gave working control to the holder. The actual sale included 55,552 additional shares held by friends and associates of Feldmann, so that a total of 37% of the Newport stock was transferred.

Newport was not in a position to compete profitably with other steel mills for customers not in its immediate geographical area. Wilport, the purchasing syndicate, consisted of geographically remote end-users of steel who were interested in buying more steel from Newport than they had been able to obtain during recent periods of tight supply. The price of $20 per share was found by Judge Hincks to be a fair one for a control block of stock, although the over-the-counter market price had not exceeded $12 and the book value per share was $17.03. But this finding was limited by Judge Hincks' statement that "[w]hat value the block would have had if shorn of its appurtenant power to control distribution of the corporate product, the evidence does not show." It was also conditioned by his earlier ruling that the burden was on plaintiffs to prove a lesser value for the stock.

Both as director and as dominant stockholder, Feldmann stood in a fiduciary relationship to the corporation and to the minority stockholders as beneficiaries thereof. Pepper v. Litton, 308 U.S. 295, 60 S.Ct. 238, 84 L.Ed. 281; Southern Pac. Co. v. Bogert, 250 U.S. 483, 39 S.Ct. 533, 63 L.Ed. 1099. His fiduciary obligation must in the first instance be measured by the law of Indiana, the state of incorporation of Newport. Rogers v. Guaranty Trust Co. of New York, 288 U.S. 123, 136, 53 S.Ct. 295, 77 L.Ed. 652; Mayflower Hotel Stockholders Protective Committee v. Mayflower Hotel Corp., 89 U.S.App.D.C. 171, 193 F.2d 666, 668. Although there is no Indiana case directly in point, the most closely analogous one emphasizes the close scrutiny to which Indiana subjects the conduct of fiduciaries when personal benefit may stand in the way of fulfillment of trust obligations. In Schemmel v. Hill, 91 Ind.App. 373, 169 N.E. 678, 682, 683, McMahan, J., said: "Directors of a business corporation act in a strictly fiduciary capacity. Their office is a trust. Stratis v. Andreson, 1926, 254 Mass. 536, 150 N.E. 832, 44 A.L.R. 567; Hill v. Nisbet, 1885, 100 Ind. 341, 353. When a director deals with his corporation, his acts will be closely scrutinized. Bossert v. Geis, 1914, 57 Ind.App. 384, 107 N.E. 95. Directors of a corporation are its agents, and they are governed by the rules of law applicable to other agents, and, as between themselves and their principal, the rules relating to honesty and fair dealing in the management of the affairs of their principal are applicable. They must not, in any degree, allow their official conduct to be swayed by their private interest, which must yield to official duty. Leader Publishing Co. v. Grant Trust Co., 1915, 182 Ind. 651, 108 N.E. 121. In a transaction between a director and his corporation, where he acts for himself and his principal at the same time in a matter connected with the relation between them, it is presumed, where he is thus potentially on both sides of the contract, that self-interest will overcome his fidelity to his principal, to his own benefit and to his principal's hurt." And the judge added: "Absolute and most scrupulous good faith is the very essence of a director's obligation to his corporation. The first principal duty arising from his official relation is to act in all things of trust wholly for the benefit of his corporation."

In Indiana, then, as elsewhere, the responsibility of the fiduciary is not limited to a proper regard for the tangible balance sheet assets of the corporation, but includes the dedication of his uncorrupted business judgment for the sole benefit of the corporation, in any dealings which may adversely affect it.... Although the Indiana case is particularly relevant to Feldmann as a director, the same rule should apply to his fiduciary duties as majority stockholder, for in that capacity he chooses and controls the directors, and thus is held to have assumed their liability. Pepper v. Litton, supra, 308 U.S. 295, 60 S.Ct. 238. This, therefore, is the standard to which Feldmann was by law required to conform in his activities here under scrutiny.

It is true, as defendants have been at pains to point out, that this is not the ordinary case of breach of fiduciary duty. We have here no fraud, no misuse of confidential information, no outright looting of a helpless corporation. But on the other hand, we do not find compliance with that high standard which we have just stated and which we and other courts have come to expect and demand of corporate fiduciaries. In the often-quoted words of Judge Cardozo: "Many forms of conduct permissible in a workaday world for those acting at arm's length, are forbidden to those bound by fiduciary ties. A trustee is held to something stricter than the morals of the market place. Not honesty alone, but the punctilio of an honor the most sensitive, is then the standard of behavior. As to this there has developed a tradition that is unbending and inveterate. Uncompromising rigidity has been the attitude of courts of equity when petitioned to undermine the rule of undivided loyalty by the 'disintegrating erosion' of particular exceptions." Meinhard v. Salmon, supra, 249 N.Y. 458, 464, 164 N.E. 545, 546, 62 A.L.R. 1. The actions of defendants in siphoning off for personal gain corporate advantages to be derived from a favorable market situation do not betoken the necessary undivided loyalty owed by the fiduciary to his principal.

The corporate opportunities of whose misappropriation the minority stockholders complain need not have been an absolute certainty in order to support this action against Feldmann. If there was possibility of corporate gain, they are entitled to recover....

... In the past Newport had used and profited by its market leverage by operation of what the industry had come to call the "Feldmann Plan." This consisted of securing interest-free advances from prospective purchasers of steel in return for firm commitments to them from future production. The funds thus acquired were used to finance improvements in existing plants and to acquire new installations. In the summer of 1950 Newport had been negotiating for cold-rolling facilities which it needed for a more fully integrated operation and a more marketable product, and Feldmann plan funds might well have been used toward this end.

Further, as plaintiffs alternatively suggest, Newport might have used the period of short supply to build up patronage in the geographical area in which it could compete profitably even when steel was more abundant. Either of these opportunities was Newport's, to be used to its advantage only. Only if defendants had been able to negate completely any possibility of gain by Newport could they have prevailed. It is true that a trial court finding states: "Whether or not, in August, 1950, Newport's position was such that it could have entered into 'Feldmann Plan' type transactions to procure funds and financing for the further expansion and integration of its steel facilities and whether such expansion would have been desirable for Newport, the evidence does not show." This, however, cannot avail the defendants, who—contrary to the ruling below—had the burden of proof on this issue, since fiduciaries always have the burden of proof in establishing the fairness of their dealings with trust property....

Defendants seek to categorize the corporate opportunities which might have accrued to Newport as too unethical to warrant further consideration. It is true that reputable steel producers were not participating in the gray market brought about by the Korean War and were refraining from advancing their prices, although to do so would not have been illegal. But Feldmann plan transactions were not considered within this self-imposed interdiction; the trial court found that around the time of the Feldmann sale Jones & Laughlin Steel Corporation, Republic Steel Company, and Pittsburgh Steel Corporation were all participating in such arrangements. In any event, it ill becomes the defendants to disparage as unethical the market advantages from which they themselves reaped rich benefits.

We do not mean to suggest that a majority stockholder cannot dispose of his controlling block of stock to outsiders without having to account to his corporation for profits or even never do this with impunity when the buyer is an interested customer, actual or potential, for the corporation's product. But when the sale necessarily results in a sacrifice of this element of corporate good will and consequent unusual profit to the fiduciary who has caused the sacrifice, he should account for his gains. So in a time of market shortage, where a call on a corporation's product commands an unusually large premium, in one form or another, we think it sound law that a fiduciary may not appropriate to himself the value of this premium. Such personal gain at the expense of his coventurers seems particularly reprehensible when made by the trusted president and director of his company. In this case the violation of duty seems to be all the clearer because of this triple role in which Feldmann appears, though we are unwilling to say, and are not to be understood as saying, that we should accept a lesser obligation for any one of his roles alone.

Hence to the extent that the price received by Feldmann and his codefendants included such a bonus, he is accountable to the minority stockholders who sue here. Restatement, Restitution §§ 190, 197 (1937); Seagrave Corp. v. Mount, supra, 6 Cir., 212 F.2d 389. And plaintiffs, as they contend, are entitled to a recovery in their own right, instead of in right of the corporation (as in the usual derivative actions), since neither Wilport nor their successors in interest should share in any judgment which may be rendered. See Southern Pacific Co. v. Bogert, 250 U.S. 483, 39 S.Ct. 533, 63 L.Ed. 1099. Defendants cannot well object to this form of recovery, since the only alternative, recovery for the corporation as a whole, would subject them to a greater total liability.

The case will therefore be remanded to the district court for a determination of the question expressly left open below, namely, the value of defendants' stock without the appurtenant control over the corporation's output of steel. We reiterate that on this issue, as on all others relating to a breach of fiduciary duty, the burden of proof must rest on the defendants. Bigelow v. RKO Radio Pictures, 327 U.S. 251, 265–266, 66 S.Ct. 574, 90 L.Ed. 652; Package Closure Corp. v. Sealright Co., 2 Cir., 141 F.2d 972, 979. Judgment should go to these plaintiffs and those whom they represent for any premium value so shown to the extent of their respective stock interests.

The judgment is therefore reversed and the action remanded for further proceedings pursuant to this opinion.

[The dissenting opinion of Judge Swan is omitted.]

NOTE ON PERLMAN v. FELDMANN

On remand, the district court determined the enterprise value of the corporation, based upon its book value and earnings potential, to be $15,825,777, or $14.67 per share. This made the premium $5.33 a share, or $2,126,280. The complaining stockholders, owning sixty-three percent of the stock, were therefore entitled to judgment of $1,339,769, with interest of 6 percent from the sale date, plus costs. Perlman v. Feldmann, 154 F.Supp. 436 (D.Conn.1957).

NOTE ON THE THEORY OF CORPORATE ACTION

Suppose a prospective purchaser, P, wants to acquire complete control of the assets and business of a corporation, C, and that C has a controlling shareholder, S. P then has a choice of several means to acquire C: (1) He can try to acquire all of C's shares. His first step would naturally be to approach S, without whom P's efforts will fail. (2) He can try to induce a sufficient number of C shareholders to vote for a sale of C's assets to D. (3) He can try to induce a sufficient number of C shareholders to vote for a merger with D, a corporation that P controls.

If P takes the first course, he deals with C's shareholders individually. Each C shareholder is free to make his own terms of sale, and S's shares may bring a better price than the remaining shares. If P takes the second course of action, involving a sale of C's assets, he is looking towards corporate action by C. If C sells its assets to D, the consideration will pass into C's treasury. Usually C will then be liquidated, and the net proceeds will be distributed pro rata to all C shareholders, so that each old C shareholder will receive the same amount per share. If P takes the third course of action, involving a merger of C and D, the plan of conversion of C shares into D shares will normally provide for equal treatment of all shareholders of the same class. Accordingly, the second and third courses of action provide equal treatment to shareholders, while the first course of action, involving the purchase of C shares, allows S to sell its shares at higher prices than the non-controlling shareholders. It may therefore be to the advantage of shareholders like S, who hold a control block of shares of a corporation, to have a purchaser like P take the first course of action.

If P originally proposes to take the second or third courses, but is persuaded by S to take the first course, and S realizes more per share for its holdings than the remaining shareholders, the latter may assert that the difference between the three courses of action is immaterial, that the first course of action should be treated as "corporate action," and that S acted improperly in switching P from one course of action to another. This theory has been successfully employed in several cases where the buyer began on the second or third course of action and the controlling shareholders switched him to the first. See Commonwealth Title Ins. & Trust Co. v. Seltzer, 227 Pa. 410, 76 A. 77 (1910); Dunnett v. Arn, 71 F.2d 912 (10th Cir.1934); Roby v. Dunnett, 88 F.2d 68 (10th Cir.1937), cert. denied 301 U.S. 706, 57 S.Ct. 940, 81 L.Ed. 1360; American Trust Co. v. California Western States Life Ins. Co., 15 Cal.2d 42, 98 P.2d 497 (1940).

The problem with the theory of corporate action is that a controlling shareholder cannot be compelled to sell his shares at a price he does not accept. A knowledgeable controlling shareholder therefore can avoid the application of the theory by simply voting down an offer to the corporation, and waiting for an offer to buy his shares. Accordingly, the theory of corporate action, although appealing, will affect only controlling shareholders who are not well-counseled.

Brecher v. Gregg

New York Supreme Court, 1975.
89 Misc.2d 457, 392 N.Y.S.2d 776.

OPINION OF THE COURT

■ NORMAN L. HARVEY, J.

This is a shareholder's derivative action brought on behalf of Lin Broadcasting Corporation (LIN) by Louis J. Brecher who, at the time this action was commenced, owned 200 shares of LIN common stock. No party challenges his right to bring the action.

LIN was incorporated in Delaware in 1961. By December, 1968 it had become a publicly-held corporation with assets of approximately $55,000,000. Currently it holds licenses issued by the Federal Communications Commission (FCC) to operate 10 radio and 2 television stations. Defendant Frederic Gregg was the principal founder of LIN and served as LIN's president from the time of incorporation until his resignation on January 10, 1969. In addition, Gregg was a member of the board of directors from October, 1961 to March, 1969 and chairman from February, 1967 to March, 1969. As of January 10, 1969 Gregg owned approximately 82,000 shares of LIN common stock—the largest block beneficially owned by any single person or entity.

The defendants Clyde W. Clifford, Peter J. Solomon, David Steine, Joel M. Thrope, Thomas I. Unterberg and Lind Carl Voth were directors of LIN at all times relevant herein. Defendant Alan J. Patricof was a director of LIN from February 19, 1967 until January 10, 1969 at which time an earlier tendered resignation was accepted by the LIN directors. He did not participate in any of the activities complained of by the plaintiff.

The controversy centers upon a transaction between the defendant Gregg and the Saturday Evening Post Company (SEPCO) in which the latter bought Gregg's 82,000 shares of LIN stock. The purchase price of the stock was $3,500,000, said amount being approximately $1,260,000 more than the market price on the date of sale. Plaintiff contends that SEPCO paid Gregg a premium for Gregg's promise to resign immediately as president of LIN; bring about the election of SEPCO's nominee as his successor to the presidency; bring about the immediate election of three SEPCO nominees as directors; and ultimately bring about an absolute numerical majority of SEPCO nominees to the board. Plaintiff contends that the acceptance of this premium amounted to a sale of corporate office, and therefore, was illegal.

Two specific contentions of the plaintiff are:

(1) That the corporation is entitled to receive $1,260,000 of the sale price paid to the defendant Gregg as a premium; and

(2) That because the remaining directors acquiesced in Gregg's promise and actually did vote to elect nominees of SEPCO as president and as three of its directors they are liable, jointly with Gregg and severally, for the premium resulting from the sale. . . .

Trial of the action was accomplished by the submission of certain exhibits which were agreed upon by all parties, the depositions of numerous witnesses, and answers to interrogatories. The court did not personally see or hear any of the witnesses when they gave their testimony.

Certain of the facts are undisputed. Sometime during the latter part of 1968 the defendant Frederic Gregg, Jr. and Martin Ackerman, then president of SEPCO, entered into negotiations for the purchase of the LIN stock owned by Gregg. Ultimately, an agreement was reached for the purchase of the stock by SEPCO for the total consideration of $3,500,000. In addition to that, Gregg agreed to relinquish certain rights that he had under an employment contract with LIN which included, among other things, stock options. The price of $3,500,000 was approximately $1,260,000 more than the then current price on the over-the-counter securities exchange in New York City.

Shortly after the agreement, defendant Gregg called a meeting of the LIN board of directors at which: defendant Alan Patricof's previously submitted resignation was accepted, thus creating a vacancy; the board voted to expand its size from 8 to 10 seats; the SEPCO nominees, Martin Ackerman, Alfred Driscoll and Milton Gould, were elected to fill the three vacancies; Gregg's resignation as president was tendered and accepted; and Ackerman was elected as his successor.

Within a few weeks thereafter, LIN's board of directors terminated Ackerman's tenure as president and all SEPCO directors resigned. SEPCO then sued Gregg, LIN and others for a refund of the premium alleging that, as conditions of its purchase, it was promised that SEPCO's nominee would be hired as president of LIN and be given a fair opportunity to supervise the management of its affairs; that SEPCO be given immediate minority representation on the board of directors and that best efforts be made to cause SEPCO to have majority representation on the board at an early date by seeking required approval from FCC. The complaint further alleged that the defendants breached the agreement by not permitting SEPCO's nominee to the presidency an ample opportunity to manage the corporation. The complaint was dismissed at Special Term because of the illegality of the agreement. Mr. Justice Saypol's opinion will be referred to later herein.

No evidence was introduced to establish that any of the director defendants, other than Gregg, was involved in the negotiations for the sale of Gregg's stock nor that they received any benefit therefrom.

The bulk of the evidence introduced concerned the negotiations between Martin S. Ackerman, president of SEPCO, and the defendant Gregg for the purchase of Gregg's stock. That evidence was conflicting as to the issue of the inducement for the payment of a premium. But, from all the evidence before it, the court concludes that the defendant Gregg and SEPCO agreed upon the purchase price of $3,500,000 for Gregg's stock (which also would result in his forfeiture of substantial stock option rights) and that the inducement for payment of a price more than $1,200,000 above the price quoted in the over-the-counter market was Gregg's promise to deliver effective control of LIN to SEPCO. Control was to be delivered by Gregg's resignation of the presidency and the election of SEPCO's nominees to the presidency and three directorships.

The court concludes as a matter of law that the agreement insofar as it provided for a premium in exchange for a promise of control, with only 4% of the outstanding shares actually being transferred, was contrary to public policy and illegal. The law as it pertains to these facts was succinctly stated by Mr. Justice Saypol in his determination of the motion previously referred to. (Brecher v. Gregg, NYLJ, June 15, 1970, p. 16, col. 1.)

> "The subject agreement to purchase an office is against public policy and unenforceable in this State. The employment contract cannot be saved by severance since it is an integral portion of the agreement having an illegal purpose.

"It is not alleged that by virtue of the stock purchase plaintiff acquired control with which it could then install officers and directors of its own selection. It appears on the face of the complaint that the transaction had no semblance of actual or practical control; rather, the designation of president and minority board representation remained in the actual control of the defendants but was bargained away to plaintiff.

"As stated in Matter of Lionel Corp. (NYLJ, Feb. 4, 1964, Schweitzer, J, Sup Ct NY County): 'As early as McClure v. Law (161 NY 78), and as late as Essex Universal Corp. v. Yates (305 F.2d 572), it is the law of this State that it is illegal to sell corporate office or management control by itself (that is, accompanied by no stock or insufficient stock to carry voting control).' (Affd sub nom Matter of Caplan v. Lionel Corp., 20 A.D.2d 301, affd 14 N.Y.2d 679.) Indeed, the illegal profit belongs to the corporation (Gabriel Ind. v. Defiance Ind., NYLJ, June 17, 1964, p 13, col 8; Sarafite, J., affd 23 A.D.2d 630)."

Clearly, the defendant Gregg must forfeit to the corporation any illegal profit derived from his sale of stock. . . .

Since there has been no showing that the actions of any directors other than Gregg either led to any pecuniary loss to the corporation or to the realization of any personal profit or gain to themselves, it follows that they cannot be held liable jointly, or severally, with Gregg for the payment of the premium over to the corporation.

In view of the fact that the court is charged with the duty to determine both the law and the facts, it must render a factual decision. There was no malfeasance or misfeasance demonstrated in the directors having voted to elect Messrs. Ackerman, Driscoll and Gould. That decision was as consistent with the future well-being and success of the corporation as the later vote to remove Ackerman. On the mere basis of hindsight, the court cannot inculpate these directors for what may or may not have been an unfortunate decision. . . .

It is the decision of the court that. . . . [Gregg] account to the corporation for any profits made in his sale to SEPCO over and above that which he would have realized, had the sale been consummated in an arm's length, over-the-counter transaction.

———

Essex Universal Corp. v. Yates

United States Court of Appeals, Second Circuit, 1962.
305 F.2d 572.

■ Before LUMBARD, CHIEF JUDGE, and CLARK and FRIENDLY, CIRCUIT JUDGES.

■ LUMBARD, CHIEF JUDGE.

This appeal from the district court's summary judgment in favor of the defendant raises the question whether a contract for the sale of 28.3 per cent of the stock of a corporation is, under New York law, invalid as against public policy solely because it includes a clause giving the purchaser an option to require a majority of the existing directors to replace themselves, by a process of seriatim resignation, with a majority designated by the purchaser. Despite the disagreement evidenced by the diversity of our opinions, my brethren and I agree that such a provision does not on its face render the contract illegal and unenforceable, and thus that it was improper to grant summary judgment. Judge Friendly would reject the defense of illegality without further inquiry concerning the provision itself (as distinguished from any contention that control could not be safely transferred to the particular purchaser). Judge Clark and I are agreed that on remand, which must be had in any event to consider other defenses raised by the pleadings, further factual issues may be raised by the parties upon which the legality of the clause in question will depend; we disagree, however, on the nature of those factual issues, as our separate opinions reveal. Accordingly, the grant of summary judgment is reversed and the case is remanded for trial of the question of the legality of the contested provision and such further proceedings as may be proper on the other issues raised by the pleadings.

Since we are in agreement on certain preliminary questions, this opinion constitutes the opinion of the court up to the point where it is indicated that it thenceforth states only my individual views.

The defendant Herbert J. Yates, a resident of California, was president and chairman of the board of directors of Republic Pictures Corporation, a New York corporation which at the time relevant to this suit had 2,004,190 shares of common stock outstanding. Republic's stock was listed and traded on the New York Stock Exchange. In August 1957, Essex Universal Corporation, a Delaware corporation owning stock in various diversified businesses, learned of the possibility of purchasing from Yates an interest in Republic. Negotiations proceeded rapidly, and on August 28 Yates and Joseph Harris, the president of Essex, signed a contract in which Essex agreed to buy, and Yates agreed "to sell or cause to be sold" at least 500,000 and not more than 600,000 shares of Republic stock. The price was set at eight dollars a share, roughly two dollars above the then market price on the Exchange. Three dollars per share was to be paid at the closing on September 18, 1957 and the remainder in twenty-four equal monthly payments beginning January 31, 1958. The shares were to be transferred on the closing date, but Yates was to retain the certificates, endorsed in blank by Essex, as security for full payment. In addition to other provisions not relevant to the present motion, the contract contained the following paragraph:

"6. Resignations.

Upon and as a condition to the closing of this transaction if requested by Buyer at least ten (10) days prior to the date of the closing:

(a) Seller will deliver to Buyer the resignations of the majority of the directors of Republic.

(b) Seller will cause a special meeting of the board of directors of Republic to be held, legally convened pursuant to law and the by-laws of Republic, and simultaneously with the acceptance of the directors' resignations set forth in paragraph 6(a) immediately preceding will cause nominees of Buyer to be elected directors of Republic in place of the resigned directors."

Before the date of the closing, as provided in the contract, Yates notified Essex that he would deliver 566,223 shares, or 28.3 per cent of the Republic stock then outstanding, and Essex formally requested Yates to arrange for the replacement of a majority of Republic's directors with Essex nominees pursuant to paragraph 6 of the contract. This was to be accomplished by having eight of the fourteen directors resign seriatim, each in turn being replaced by an Essex nominee elected by the others; such a procedure was *in form* permissible under the charter and by-laws of Republic, which empowered the board to choose the successor of any of its members who might resign.

On September 18, the parties met as arranged for the closing at Republic's office in New York City. Essex tendered bank drafts and cashier's checks totalling $1,698,690, which was the 37½ per cent of the total price of $4,529,784 due at this time. The drafts and checks were payable to one Benjamin C. Cohen, who was Essex' banker and had arranged for the borrowing of the necessary funds. Although Cohen was prepared to endorse these to Yates, Yates upon advice of his lawyer rejected the tender as "unsatisfactory" and said, according to his deposition testimony, "Well, there can be no deal. We can't close it."

Essex began this action in the New York Supreme Court, and it was removed to the district court on account of diversity of citizenship. Essex seeks damages of $2,700,000, claiming that at the time of the aborted closing the stock was in actuality worth more than $12.75 a share.[1] Yates' answer raised a number of defenses, but the motion for summary judgment now before us was made and decided only on the theory that the provision in the contract for immediate transfer of control of the board of directors was illegal *per se* and tainted the entire contract. We have no doubt, and the parties agree, that New York law governs.

Appellant's contention that the provision for transfer of director control is separable from the rest of the contract can quickly be rejected....

... [W]e hold the provision regarding directors inseparable from the sale of shares, and proceed to a consideration of its legality.

Up to this point my brethren and I are in agreement. The following analysis is my own, except insofar as the separate opinions of Judges Clark and Friendly may indicate agreement.

It is established beyond question under New York law that it is illegal to sell corporate office or management control by itself (that is,

---

1.   In 1959, while this action was pending, the stock was sold to another party for ten dollars a share.

accompanied by no stock or insufficient stock to carry voting control).... The rationale of the rule is undisputable: persons enjoying management control hold it on behalf of the corporation's stockholders, and therefore may not regard it as their own personal property to dispose of as they wish.[3] Any other rule would violate the most fundamental principle of corporate democracy, that management must represent and be chosen by, or at least with the consent of, those who own the corporation.

Essex was, however, contracting with Yates for the purchase of a very substantial percentage of Republic stock. If, by virtue of the voting power carried by this stock, it could have elected a majority of the board of directors, then the contract was not a simple agreement for the sale of office to one having no ownership interest in the corporation, and the question of its legality would require further analysis. Such stock voting control would incontestably belong to the owner of a majority of the voting stock, and it is commonly known that equivalent power usually accrues to the owner of 28.3% of the stock. For the purpose of this analysis, I shall assume that Essex was contracting to acquire a majority of the Republic stock, deferring consideration of the situation where, as here, only 28.3% is to be acquired.

Republic's board of directors at the time of the aborted closing had fourteen members divided into three classes, each class being "as nearly as may be" of the same size. Directors were elected for terms of three years, one class being elected at each annual shareholder meeting on the first Tuesday in April. Thus, absent the immediate replacement of directors provided for in this contract, Essex as the hypothetical new majority shareholder of the corporation could not have obtained managing control in the form of a majority of the board in the normal course of events until April 1959, some eighteen months after the sale of the stock. The first question before us then is whether an agreement to accelerate the transfer of management control, in a manner legal in form under the corporation's charter and by-laws, violates the public policy of New York.

There is no question of the right of a controlling shareholder under New York law normally to derive a premium from the sale of a controlling block of stock. In other words, there was no impropriety *per se* in the fact that Yates was to receive more per share than the generally prevailing market price for Republic stock. Levy v. American Beverage Corp., 265 App.Div. 208, 218, 38 N.Y.S.2d 517, 526 (1st Dept.1942); Stanton v. Schenck, 140 Misc. 621, 251 N.Y.S. 221 (N.Y.County Sup.Ct.1931); see Hill, supra, 70 Harv.L.Rev. at 991–92.

The next question is whether it is legal to give and receive payment for the immediate transfer of management control to one who has achieved majority share control but would not otherwise be able to convert that share control into operating control for some time. I think that it is.

---

3. The cases have made no distinction between contracts by directors or officers to resign and contracts by persons who in actu- ality control the actions of officers or directors to procure their resignations, and of course none should exist.

Of course under some circumstances controlling shareholders transferring immediate control may be compelled to account to the corporation for that part of the consideration received by them which exceeds the fair value of the block of stock sold, as well as for the injury which they may cause to the corporation.... Gerdes v. Reynolds, 28 N.Y.S.2d 622 (N.Y.County Sup.Ct.1941)....

A fair generalization from [Perlman v. Feldmann and other] cases may be that a holder of corporate control will not, as a fiduciary, be permitted to profit from facilitating actions on the part of the purchasers of control which are detrimental to the interests of the corporation or the remaining shareholders. There is, however, no suggestion that the transfer of control over Republic to Essex carried any such threat to the interests of the corporation or its other shareholders.

Our examination of the New York cases ... gives us no reason to regard as impaired the holding of the early case of Barnes v. Brown, 80 N.Y. 527 (1880), that a bargain for the sale of a majority stock interest is not made illegal by a plan for immediate transfer of management control by a program like that provided for in the Essex–Yates contract. Judge Earl wrote:

> "[The seller] had the right to sell out all his stock and interest in the corporation, ... and when he ceased to have any interest in the corporation, it was certainly legitimate and right that he should cease to control it ... It was simply the mode of transferring the control of the corporation to those who by the policy of the law ought to have it, and I am unable to see how any policy of the law was violated, or in what way, upon the evidence, any wrong was thereby done to anyone." 80 N.Y. at 537.

To be sure, in Barnes v. Brown no term of the contract of sale *required* the seller to effectuate the immediate replacement of directors, as did paragraph 6 of the Essex–Yates contract, but Judge Earl stated that "I shall assume that it was the understanding and a part of the scheme that he should do so." 80 N.Y. at 536....

The easy and immediate transfer of corporate control to new interests is ordinarily beneficial to the economy and it seems inevitable that such transactions would be discouraged if the purchaser of a majority stock interest were required to wait some period before his purchase of control could become effective. Conversely it would greatly hamper the efforts of any existing majority group to dispose of its interest if it could not assure the purchaser of immediate control over corporation operations. I can see no reason why a purchaser of majority control should not ordinarily be permitted to make his control effective from the moment of the transfer of stock.

Thus if Essex had been contracting to purchase a majority of the stock of Republic, it would have been entirely proper for the contract to contain the provision for immediate replacement of directors. Although in the case at bar only 28.3 per cent of the stock was involved, it is commonly known that a person or group owning so large a percentage of the voting stock of a corporation which, like Republic, has at least the 1,500 shareholders normally requisite to listing on the New York Stock Exchange, is almost certain to have share control as a practical matter. If Essex was contracting to acquire what in reality would be equivalent to ownership of a majority of stock, i.e., if it would as a practical certainty have been guaranteed of the stock voting power to choose a majority of the directors of Republic in due course, there is no reason why the contract should not similarly be legal.[6] Whether Essex was thus to acquire the equivalent of majority stock control would, if the issue is properly raised by the defendants, be a factual issue to be determined by the district court on remand.

Because 28.3 per cent of the voting stock of a publicly owned corporation is usually tantamount to majority control, I would place the burden of proof on this issue on Yates as the party attacking the legality of the transaction. Thus, unless on remand Yates chooses to raise the question whether the block of stock in question carried the equivalent of majority control, it is my view that the trial court should regard the contract as legal and proceed to consider the other issues raised by the pleadings. If Yates chooses to raise the issue, it will, on my view, be necessary for him to prove the existence of circumstances which would have prevented Essex from electing a majority of the Republic board of directors in due course. It will not be enough for Yates to raise merely hypothetical possibilities of opposition by the other Republic shareholders to Essex' assumption of management control. Rather, it will be necessary for him to show that, assuming neutrality on the part of the retiring management, there was at the time some concretely foreseeable reason why Essex' wishes would not have prevailed in shareholder voting held in due course. In other words, I would require him to show that there was at the time of the contract some other organized block of stock of sufficient size to outvote the block Essex was buying, or else some circumstance making it likely that enough of the holders of the remaining Republic stock would band together to keep Essex from control.

Reversed and remanded for further proceedings not inconsistent with the judgment of this court.

■ FRIENDLY, CIRCUIT JUDGE (concurring).

Chief Judge Lumbard's thoughtful opinion illustrates a difficulty, inherent in our dual judicial system, which has led at least one state to authorize its courts to answer questions about its law that a Federal court may ask. Here we are forced to decide a question of New York law, of enormous importance to all New York corporations and their stockholders, on which there is hardly enough New York authority for a really informed prediction what the New York Court of Appeals would decide on the facts here presented, see Cooper v. American Airlines, Inc., 149 F.2d 355, 359, 162 A.L.R. 318 (2 Cir., 1945); Pomerantz v. Clark, 101 F.Supp. 341 (D.Mass.1951); Corbin, The Laws of the Several States, 50 Yale L.J. 762, 775–776 (1941), yet too much

---

6. The fact that under the Essex–Yates contract only 37½% of the price of the stock was to be paid at the closing and the balance was not to be fully paid for twenty-eight months is irrelevant to this case. There is no indication that Essex did not have sound financial backing sufficient to discharge properly the obligation which had been incurred.

for us to have the freedom used to good effect in Perlman v. Feldmann, 219 F.2d 173 (2 Cir.), cert. denied, 349 U.S. 952, 75 S.Ct. 880, 99 L.Ed. 1277 (1955).

I have no doubt that many contracts, drawn by competent and responsible counsel, for the purchase of blocks of stock from interests thought to "control" a corporation although owning less than a majority, have contained provisions like paragraph 6 of the contract *sub judice*. However, developments over the past decades seem to me to show that such a clause violates basic principles of corporate democracy. To be sure, stockholders who have allowed a set of directors to be placed in office, whether by their vote or their failure to vote, must recognize that death, incapacity or other hazard may prevent a director from serving a full term, and that they will have no voice as to his immediate successor. But the stockholders are entitled to expect that, in that event, the remaining directors will fill the vacancy in the exercise of their fiduciary responsibility. A mass seriatim resignation directed by a selling stockholder, and the filling of vacancies by his henchmen at the dictation of a purchaser and without any consideration of the character of the latter's nominees, are beyond what the stockholders contemplated or should have been expected to contemplate. This seems to me a wrong to the corporation and the other stockholders which the law ought not countenance, whether the selling stockholder has received a premium or not. Right in this Court we have seen many cases where sudden shifts of corporate control have caused serious injury; Pettit v. Doeskin Products, Inc., 270 F.2d 95 (2 Cir., 1959), cert. denied, 362 U.S. 910, 80 S.Ct. 660, 4 L.Ed.2d 618 (1960); United States v. Crosby, 294 F.2d 928 (2 Cir., 1961), cert. denied Mittelman v. United States, 368 U.S. 984, 82 S.Ct. 599, 7 L.Ed.2d 523 (1962); and Kirtley v. Abrams, 299 F.2d 341 (2 Cir., 1962), are a few recent examples. To hold the seller for delinquencies of the new directors only if he knew the purchaser was an intending looter is not a sufficient sanction. The difficulties of proof are formidable even if receipt of too high a premium creates a presumption of such knowledge, and, all too often, the doors are locked only after the horses have been stolen. Stronger medicines are needed—refusal to enforce a contract with such a clause, even though this confers an unwarranted benefit on a defaulter, and continuing responsibility of the former directors for negligence of the new ones until an election has been held. Such prophylactics are not contraindicated, as Judge Lumbard suggests, by the conceded desirability of preventing the dead hand of a former "controlling" group from continuing to dominate the board after a sale, or of protecting a would-be purchaser from finding himself without a majority of the board after he has spent his money. A special meeting of stockholders to replace a board may always be called, and there could be no objection to making the closing of a purchase contingent on the results of such an election. I perceive some of the difficulties of mechanics such a procedure presents, but I have enough confidence in the ingenuity of the corporate bar to believe these would be surmounted.

Hence, I am inclined to think that if I were sitting on the New York Court of Appeals, I would hold a provision like [paragraph] 6 violative of public policy save when it was entirely plain that a new election would be a mere formality—i.e., when the seller owned more than 50% of the stock. I put it thus tentatively because, before making such a decision, I would want the help of briefs, including those of *amici curiae*, dealing with the serious problems of corporate policy and practice more fully than did those here, which were primarily devoted to argument as to what the New York law has been rather than what it ought to be. Moreover, in view of the perhaps unexpected character of such a holding, I doubt that I would give it retrospective effect.

As a judge of this Court, my task is the more modest one of predicting how the judges of the New York Court of Appeals would rule, and I must make this prediction on the basis of legal materials rather than of personal acquaintance or hunch. Also, for obvious reasons, the prospective technique is unavailable when a Federal court is deciding an issue of state law. Although Barnes v. Brown, 80 N.Y. 527 (1880), dealt with the sale of a majority interest, I am unable to find any real indication that the doctrine there announced has been thus limited. True, there are New York cases saying that the sale of corporate offices is forbidden; but the New York decisions do not tell us what this means and I can find nothing, save perhaps one unexplained sentence in the opinion of a trial court in Ballantine v. Ferretti, 28 N.Y.S.2d 668, 682 (Sup.Ct.N.Y.Co.1941), to indicate that New York would not apply Barnes v. Brown to a case where a stockholder with much less than a majority conditioned a sale on his causing the resignation of a majority of the directors and the election of the purchaser's nominees.

Chief Judge Lumbard's proposal goes part of the way toward meeting the policy problem I have suggested. Doubtless proceeding from what, as it seems to me, is the only justification in principle for permitting even a majority stockholder to condition a sale on delivery of control of the board—namely that in such a case a vote of the stockholders would be a useless formality, he sets the allowable bounds at the line where there is "a practical certainty" that the buyer would be able to elect his nominees and, in this case, puts the burden of disproving that on the person claiming illegality.

Attractive as the proposal is in some respects, I find difficulties with it. One is that I discern no sufficient intimation of the distinction in the New York cases, or even in the writers, who either would go further in voiding such a clause, see Berle, "Control" in Corporate Law, 58 Colum.L.Rev. 1212, 1224 (1958); Leech, Transactions in Corporate Control, 104 U.Pa.L.Rev. 725, 809 (1956) [proposing legislation], or believe the courts have not yet gone that far, see Baker & Cary, Corporations: Cases and Materials (3d ed. unabr. 1959) 590. To strike down such a condition only in cases falling short of the suggested line accomplishes little to prevent what I consider the evil; in most instances a seller will not enter into a contract conditioned on his "delivering" a majority of the directors unless he has good reason to think he can do that. When an issue does arise, the "practical certainty" test is difficult to apply. The existence of such certainty will depend not merely on the proportion of the stock held by the seller but on many other factors—whether the other stock is widely or closely held, how much of it is in "street names," what success the corporation has experienced, how far its dividend policies have satisfied its stockholders, the identity of the purchasers, the presence or absence of cumulative voting, and many others. Often, unless the seller has nearly 50% of the stock, whether he has "working control" can be determined only by an election; groups who thought they had such control have experienced unpleasant surprises in recent years. Judge Lumbard correctly recognizes that, from a policy standpoint, the pertinent question must be the buyer's prospects of election, not the seller's—yet this inevitably requires the court to canvass the likely reaction of stockholders to a group of whom they know nothing and seems rather hard to reconcile with a position that it is "right" to insert such a condition if a seller has a larger proportion of the stock and "wrong" if he has a smaller. At the very least the problems and uncertainties arising from the proposed line of demarcation are great enough, and its advantages small enough, that in my view a Federal court would do better simply to overrule the defense here, thereby accomplishing what is obviously the "just" result in this particular case, and leave the development of doctrine in this area to the State, which has primary concern for it.

I would reverse the grant of summary judgment and remand for consideration of defenses other than a claim that the inclusion of paragraph 6 *ex mero motu* renders the contract void.

[The concurring opinion of Judge Clark is omitted.]

———

NOTE ON ESSEX UNIVERSAL CORP. v. YATES

It is not at all clear that 28.3% will necessarily carry control of a publicly held corporation in and of itself, that is, unless coupled with control of the board. Consider Brannigan, Florida Businessman Seeks to Steer Bank Toward Sale, Wall Street Journal, Sept. 2, 1987, at 27, col. 1: "[Hugh F. Culverhouse] has launched a tender offer for 10% of Florida Commercial Banks Inc's shares, . . . He already holds . . . 39.9% of the bank's shares. Since 1984, Mr. Culverhouse has struggled unsuccessfully to win a seat on the company's board or to acquire control of the concern. As of earlier this year, 28.4% of the company's shares were controlled by a well-entrenched group of officers and directors that has opposed him. . . ."

———

SECURITIES EXCHANGE ACT RULE 14f–1

[See Statutory Supplement]

———

ALI, PRINCIPLES OF CORPORATE GOVERNANCE § 5.16

[See Statutory Supplement]

CHAPTER X

INSIDER TRADING

SECTION 1. THE COMMON LAW BACKGROUND

NOTE ON THE DUTIES OF DIRECTORS AND OFFICERS UNDER THE COMMON LAW WHEN TRADING IN THEIR CORPORATION'S STOCK

1. *Majority Rule*. At common law, the majority rule was that a director or officer of a corporation could trade in its stock without disclosing material nonpublic information concerning the corporation that he had acquired through his position—a type of information now referred to as *inside information*. A leading case was Goodwin v. Agassiz, 283 Mass. 358, 186 N.E. 659 (1933). Aggasiz was president of Cliff Mining Company and MacNaughton was Cliff's general manager. Both were also directors. In May 1926, Aggasiz and MacNaughton purchased a number of Cliff shares on the Boston Stock Exchange. Several hundred of these shares were owned by Goodwin. Because the trading was on an Exchange, neither the buyers nor the seller knew each other's identity. The background to the trading was set forth in the opinion as follows:

> [Agassiz and MacNaughton] had certain knowledge, material as to the value of the stock, which the plaintiff did not have. . . . That knowledge was that an experienced geologist had formulated in writing in March, 1926, a theory as to the possible existence of copper deposits under conditions prevailing in the region where the property of the company was located. That region was known as the mineral belt in northern Michigan, where are located mines of several copper mining companies. Another such company, of which the defendants were officers, had made extensive geological surveys of its lands. In consequence of recommendations resulting from that survey, exploration was started on property of the Cliff Mining Company in 1925. That exploration was ended in May, 1926, because completed unsuccessfully, and the equipment was removed. The defendants discussed the geologist's theory shortly after it was formulated. Both felt that the theory had value and should be tested, but they agreed that, before starting to test it, options should be obtained by another copper company of which they were officers on land adjacent to or nearby in the copper belt, that if the geologist's theory were known to the owners of such other land there might be difficulty in securing options, and that that theory should not be communicated to any

one unless it became absolutely necessary. Thereafter, options were secured which, if taken up, would involve a large expenditure by the other company. The defendants both thought, also, that, if there was any merit in the geologist's theory, the price of Cliff Mining Company stock in the market would go up. Its stock was quoted and bought and sold on the Boston stock exchange. Pursuant to agreement, they bought many shares of that stock through agents on joint account. The plaintiff first learned of the closing of exploratory operations on property of the Cliff Mining Company from an article in a paper on May 15, 1926, and immediately sold his shares of stock through brokers.... The plaintiff did not know that his stock was being bought for them.

Goodwin sued Agassiz and MacNaughton on the ground that they had a fiduciary duty to disclose the relevant information before purchasing Goodwin's shares. The Massachusetts Supreme Judicial Court held that directors and officers did not have such a duty, at least in an impersonal market.

Although the transactions in *Goodwin v. Agassiz* occurred in an impersonal market, there are cases in which the rule of that case was applied to face-to-face transactions. See, e.g., Lank v. Steiner, 43 Del.Ch. 262, 224 A.2d 242 (1966); Gladstone v. Murray Co., 314 Mass. 584, 50 N.E.2d 958 (1943). However, there was a minority rule, sometimes known as the Kansas rule, which required full disclosure by a director or officer, at least in face-to-face transactions. For example, in Hotchkiss v. Fischer, 136 Kan. 530, 16 P.2d 531 (1932), appeal after remand 139 Kan. 333, 31 P.2d 37 (1934), Hotchkiss, a widow in need of money, was a shareholder in Elmhurst Corporation. Hotchkiss came to Elmhurst's offices in advance of the corporation's annual meeting to ascertain whether a dividend would be declared. She had two interviews with Fischer, Elmhurst's president, who said he could not inform her whether a dividend would be declared until he conferred with directors coming from New York. Fischer showed Hotchkiss the year-end financial statements and explained the items on the statements, but painted a somewhat dark picture, saying finally, "[w]hat you regard your stock to be worth ... is a matter you have to determine yourself." 136 Kan. at 533, 16 P.2d at 532. In fact, the condition of the corporation was much better than the financial statements suggested. Hotchkiss sold her stock to Fischer for $1.25 per share. Three days later, the directors declared a dividend of $1.00 per share. In a suit for damages, the court held for Hotchkiss. The court likened a director's duty to that of a trustee, and said that a director is under a duty to deal fairly with the shareholder and "communicate ... all material facts in connection with the transaction which the [director] knows or should know." 136 Kan. at 537, 16 P.2d at 534. See also, e.g., Jacobson v. Yaschik, 249 S.C. 577, 155 S.E.2d 601 (1967).

2. *Fraud and Half–Truths.* The majority rule itself was subject to several very important exceptions. First, the rule did not apply when a director engaged in fraud. Under the common law, fraud occurs not

only when a speaker knowingly makes a false statement, but also when he knowingly tells a half-truth. "A representation stating the truth so far as it goes but which the maker knows or believes to be materially misleading because of his failure to state additional or qualifying matter is a fraudulent misrepresentation.... Thus, a statement that contains only favorable matters and omits all references to unfavorable matters is as much a false representation as if all the facts stated were untrue." Restatement (Second) of Torts § 529 and Comment a (1976).

3. *Fraudulent Concealment*. It is also fraudulent at common law to take affirmative steps to prevent the truth from being discovered. "One party to a transaction who by concealment or other action intentionally prevents the other from acquiring material information is subject to the same liability to the other, for pecuniary loss as though he had stated the nonexistence of the matter that the other was thus prevented from discovering.... Even a false denial of knowledge or information by one party to a transaction, who is in possession of the facts, may subject him to liability as fully as if he had expressly misstated the facts, if its effect upon the plaintiff is to lead him to believe that the facts do not exist or cannot be discovered." Id. § 550 and Comment b.

4. *"Special Facts."* Perhaps the most important exception to the majority rule was the "special facts" exception, adopted in Strong v. Repide, 213 U.S. 419, 29 S.Ct. 521, 53 L.Ed. 853 (1909) and later in many other cases. Repide was a director, the administrator general, and owner of nearly three-fourths of the shares, of Philippine Sugar. Strong, who owned shares in Philippine Sugar, had given Jones a power of attorney to sell her shares. Philippine Sugar owned certain lands in the Philippines that the United States government wished to buy. The corporation was without funds, and the value of its shares was wholly dependent on making an advantageous sale of its properties to the government. Repide was in charge of the negotiations with the government, which dragged on for months, primarily because Repide was holding out for a higher price. While negotiations with the government were pending, Repide, knowing that a sale to the government was probable, used an intermediary to employ a broker to purchase Strong's shares from Jones. Jones was given no information as to the state of the negotiations with the government, and neither Strong nor Jones knew that Repide was the purchaser. The price paid to Strong was about one-tenth what the shares became worth less than three months later, when the sale of the corporation's property to the government was consummated.

The Supreme Court affirmed an award of damages to Strong, on the ground that even if a director has no general duty to disclose facts known to him before he purchases shares, "there are cases where, by reason of the special facts, such duty exists." Id. at 431, 29 S.Ct. at 525. Jones sold Strong's shares because the corporation was paying no dividends and the negotiations with the government had gone on for so long that he thought that there was no prospect that a sale of the corporation's property would be made in the near term. Repide was not only a director but, by reason of his ownership of three-fourths of the shares, his position as administrator general, and the acquiescence of the other shareholders, was in full charge of the negotiations and was able to come to an agreement with the government if and when he chose to do so. He concealed his identity as a purchaser and dealt in a roundabout fashion with Jones. In view of all these facts, "the law would indeed be impotent if the sale could not be set aside or [Repide] cast in damages for his fraud." Id. at 433, 29 S.Ct. at 526.

Since there was no meaningful way to differentiate those cases that involved "special facts" from those that didn't, the special-facts exception either ate up the majority rule or made the rule impossible to administer in a consistent fashion. At bottom, the exception was inconsistent with the majority rule, and was employed by the courts as a mechanism to escape from that rule while purporting to follow it.

5. *Atrophy.* The common law rule concerning disclosure in the sale of securities atrophied after the 1940's, due to the development of Rule 10b–5 under the Securities Exchange Act, which came to occupy most of the field. It is conceivable that if Rule 10b–5 had not been adopted, and the common law concerning the obligations of directors and officers in the purchase and sale of stock had continued to develop, the majority rule would have withered, because in the last fifty years the common law has evolved in the direction of requiring greater disclosure. For example, Restatement (Second) of Contracts § 161 (1979) provides that a "person's nondisclosure of a fact known to him is equivalent to an assertion that the fact does not exist ... where the other person is entitled to know the fact because of a relation of trust and confidence between them." In Bailey v. Vaughan, 178 W.Va. 371, 359 S.E.2d 599 (1987), the court concluded that "there is presently no majority rule that enables a director to utilize insider information which points to substantial undervaluation of the corporate shares and then to purchase shares from an uninformed shareholder without any liability." In Lawton v. Nyman, 327 F.3d 30 (1st Cir. 2003), the court said "We hold, therefore, that it is a violation of a fiduciary duty for an officer or director of a closed corporation to purchase the stock of minority shareholders without disclosing material facts affecting the value of the stock, known to the purchasing officer or director by virtue of his position but not known to the selling shareholder."

SECTION 2.   SECURITIES EXCHANGE ACT § 10(b) AND RULE § 10(b)–5

_____

SECURITIES EXCHANGE ACT § 10(b)

[See Statutory Supplement]

_____

SECURITIES EXCHANGE ACT RULE 10b–5

[See Statutory Supplement]

———

The Wharf (Holdings) Limited v. United International Holdings, Inc.

Supreme Court of the United States, 2001.
532 U.S. 588.

■ JUSTICE BREYER delivered the opinion of the Court.

This securities fraud action focuses upon a company that sold an option to buy stock while secretly intending never to honor the option. The question before us is whether this conduct violates § 10(b) of the Securities Exchange Act of 1934, which prohibits using "any manipulative or deceptive device or contrivance" "in connection with the purchase or sale of any security." 48 Stat. 891, *15 U.S.C. § 78j(b)*; see also *17 C.F.R. § 240.10b–5 (2000)*. We conclude that it does.

I

Respondent United International Holdings, Inc., a Colorado-based company, sued petitioner The Wharf (Holdings) Limited, a Hong Kong firm, in Colorado's Federal District Court. United said that in October 1992 Wharf had sold it an option to buy 10% of the stock of a new Hong Kong cable system. But, United alleged, at the time of the sale Wharf secretly intended not to permit United to exercise the option. United claimed that Wharf's conduct amounted to a fraud "in connection with the . . . sale of [a] security," prohibited by § 10(b), and violated numerous state laws as well. A jury found in United's favor. The Court of Appeals for the Tenth Circuit upheld that verdict. *210 F.3d 1207 (2000)*. And we granted certiorari to consider whether the dispute fell within the scope of § 10(b).

The relevant facts, viewed in the light most favorable to the verdict winner, United, are as follows. In 1991, the Hong Kong government announced that it would accept bids for the award of an exclusive license to operate a cable television system in Hong Kong. Wharf decided to prepare a bid. Wharf's chairman, Peter Woo, instructed one of its managing directors, Stephen Ng, to find a business partner with cable system experience. Ng found United. And United sent several employees to Hong Kong to help prepare Wharf's application, negotiate contracts, design the system, and arrange financing.

United asked to be paid for its services with a right to invest in the cable system if Wharf should obtain the license. During August and September 1992, while United's employees were at work helping Wharf, Wharf and United negotiated about the details of that payment. Wharf prepared a draft letter of intent that contemplated giving United the right to become a co-investor, owning 10% of the system. But the parties did not sign the letter of intent. And in September, when Wharf submitted its bid, it told the Hong Kong authorities that Wharf would be the system's initial sole owner, although Wharf would also "consider" allowing United to become an investor.*

In early October 1992, Ng met with a United representative, who told Ng that United would continue to help only if Wharf gave United an enforceable right to invest. Ng then orally granted United an option with the following terms: (1) United had the right to buy 10% of the future system's stock; (2) the price of exercising the option would be 10% of the system's capital requirements minus the value of United's previous services (including expenses); (3) United could exercise the option only if it showed that it could fund its 10% share of the capital required for at least the first 18 months; and (4) the option would expire if not exercised within six months of the date that Wharf received the license. The parties continued to negotiate about how to write documents that would embody these terms, but they never reduced the agreement to writing.

In May 1993, Hong Kong awarded the cable franchise to Wharf. United raised $66 million designed to help finance its 10% share. In July or August 1993, United told Wharf that it was ready to exercise its option. But Wharf refused to permit United to buy any of the system's stock. Contemporaneous internal Wharf documents suggested that Wharf had never intended to carry out its promise. For example, a few weeks before the key October 1992 meeting, Ng had prepared a memorandum stating that United wanted a right to invest that it could exercise if it was able to raise the necessary capital. A handwritten note by Wharf's Chairman Woo replied, "No, no, no, we don't accept that." In September 1993, after meeting with the Wharf board to discuss United's investment in the cable system, Ng wrote to another Wharf executive, "How do we get out?" In December 1993, after United had filed documents with the Securities Exchange Commission representing that United was negotiating the acquisition of a 10% interest in the cable system, an internal Wharf memo stated that "[o]ur next move should be to claim that our directors got quite *upset* over these representations.... Publicly, we *do not* acknowledge [United's] opportunity" to acquire the 10% interest. In the margin of a December 1993 letter from United discussing its expectation of investing in the cable system, Ng wrote, "[B]e careful, must deflect this! [H]ow?" Other Wharf documents referred to the need to "back ped[al]," and "stall."

These documents, along with other evidence, convinced the jury that Wharf, through Ng, had orally sold United an option to purchase a 10% interest in the future cable system while secretly intending not to permit United to exercise the option, in violation of § 10(b) of the Securities Exchange Act and various state laws. The jury awarded United compensatory damages of $67 million and, in light of "circumstances of fraud, malice, or willful and wanton conduct," punitive damages of $58.5 million on the state-law claims. As we have said, the Court of Appeals upheld the jury's award. *210 F.3d 1207 (C.A.10*

---

* References to transcripts and briefs are omitted. (Footnote by ed.)

2000). And we granted certiorari to determine whether Wharf's oral sale of an option it intended not to honor is prohibited by § 10(b).

II

Section 10(b) of the Securities Exchange Act makes it "unlawful for any person ... [t]o use or employ, in connection with the purchase or sale of any security ..., any manipulative or deceptive device or contrivance in contravention of such rules and regulations as the [SEC] may prescribe." *15 U.S.C. § 78j.*

Pursuant to this provision, the SEC has promulgated Rule 10b–5. That Rule forbids the use, "in connection with the purchase or sale of any security," of (1) "any device, scheme, or artifice to defraud"; (2) "any untrue statement of a material fact"; (3) the omission of "a material fact necessary in order to make the statements made ... not misleading"; or (4) any other "act, practice, or course of business" that "operates ... as a fraud or deceit." *17 C.F.R. § 240.10b–5 (2000).*

To succeed in a Rule 10b–5 suit, a private plaintiff must show that the defendant used, in connection with the purchase or sale of a security, one of the four kinds of manipulative or deceptive devices to which the Rule refers, and must also satisfy certain other requirements not at issue here. See, *e.g., 15 U.S.C. § 78j* (requiring the "use of any means or instrumentality of interstate commerce or of the mails, or of any facility of any national securities exchange"); *Ernst & Ernst v. Hochfelder*, 425 U.S. 185, 193, 96 S.Ct. 1375, 47 L.Ed.2d 668 (1976) (requiring scienter, meaning "intent to deceive, manipulate, or defraud"); *Basic Inc. v. Levinson*, 485 U.S. 224, 231–232, 108 S.Ct. 978, 99 L.Ed.2d 194 (1988) (requiring that any misrepresentation be material); *id.,* at 243, 108 S.Ct. 978 (requiring that the plaintiff sustain damages through reliance on the misrepresentation).

In deciding whether the Rule covers the circumstances present here, we must assume that the "security" at issue is not the cable system stock, but the option to purchase that stock. That is because the Court of Appeals found that Wharf conceded this point. *210 F.3d, at 1221* ("Wharf does not contest on appeal the classification of the option as a security"). That concession is consistent with the language of the Securities Exchange Act, which defines "security" to include both "any ... option ... on any security" and "any ... right to ... purchase" stock. *15 U.S.C. § 78c(a)(10) (1994 ed., Supp. V)*; see also *Blue Chip Stamps v. Manor Drug Stores*, 421 U.S. 723, 751, 95 S.Ct. 1917, 44 L.Ed.2d 539 (1975) ("holders of ... options, and other contractual rights or duties to purchase ... securities" are " 'purchasers' ... of securities for purposes of Rule 10b–5"). And Wharf's current effort to deny the concession, by pointing to an ambiguous statement in its Court of Appeals reply brief, comes too late and is unconvincing. ... Consequently, we must decide whether Wharf's secret intent not to honor the option it sold United amounted to a misrepresentation (or other conduct forbidden by the Rule) in connection with the sale of the option.

Wharf argues that its conduct falls outside the Rule's scope for two basic reasons. First, Wharf points out that its agreement to grant United an option to purchase shares in the cable system was an oral agreement. And it says that § 10(b) does not cover oral contracts of sale. . . .

[There is no] convincing reason to interpret the Act to exclude oral contracts as a class. The Act itself says that it applies to "any contract" for the purchase or sale of a security. *15 U.S.C. §§ 78c(a)(13), (14).* Oral contracts for the sale of securities are sufficiently common that the Uniform Commercial Code and statutes of frauds in every State now consider them enforceable. See U.C.C. § 8–113 (Supp.2000) ("A contract . . . for the sale or purchase of a security is enforceable whether or not there is a writing signed or record authenticated by a party against whom enforcement is sought"). . . . Any exception for oral sales of securities would significantly limit the Act's coverage, thereby undermining its basic purposes. . . .

Second, Wharf argues that a secret reservation not to permit the exercise of an option falls outside § 10(b) because it does not "relat[e] to the value of a security purchase or the consideration paid"; hence it does "not implicate [§ 10(b)'s] policy of full disclosure." Brief for Petitioners 25, 26 (emphasis deleted). But even were it the case that the Act covers only misrepresentations likely to affect the value of securities, Wharf's secret reservation was such a misrepresentation. To sell an option while secretly intending not to permit the option's exercise is misleading, because a buyer normally presumes good faith. Cf., *e.g., Restatement (Second) of Torts § 530*, Comment *c* (1976) ("Since a promise necessarily carries with it the implied assertion of an intention to perform[,] it follows that a promise made without such an intention is fraudulent"). For similar reasons, the secret reservation misled United about the option's value. Since Wharf did not intend to honor the option, the option was, unbeknownst to United, valueless.

Finally, Wharf supports its claim for an exemption from the statute by characterizing this case as a "disput[e] over the ownership of securities." Brief for Petitioners 24. Wharf expresses concern that interpreting the Act to allow recovery in a case like this one will permit numerous plaintiffs to bring federal securities claims that are in reality no more than ordinary state breach-of-contract claims—actions that lie outside the Act's basic objectives. United's claim, however, is not simply that Wharf failed to carry out a promise to sell it securities. It is a claim that Wharf sold it a security (the option) while secretly intending from the very beginning not to honor the option. And United proved that secret intent with documentary evidence that went well beyond evidence of a simple failure to perform. . . .

For these reasons, the judgment of the Court of Appeals is

Affirmed.

NOTE ON PRIVATE ACTIONS UNDER RULE 10b–5

The Wharf (Holdings) Limited v. United International Holdings, Inc. was a private action; that is, it was an action brought by a private party for private relief—damages—rather rather than an action brought by the government. Neither section 10(b) of the Securities Exchange Act nor Rule 10b–5 explicitly provide for private actions. However, there is a long tradition in American law of allowing private parties to bring actions based on violations of statutes or administrative rules in appropriate cases. What kinds of cases are appropriate, for this purpose, is the subject of principles whose content has changed somewhat over time. The most salient principles, for present purposes, are summarized in the descriptions of J.I. Case Co v. Borak, Wyandotte v. United States, and Cort v. Ash, set out at the beginning of Chapter 5, Section 4, supra.

Under these principles, the courts have held that some provisions of the Securities Acts and the rules thereunder give rise to private actions, and others do not. It has become firmly established that section 10(b) and Rule 10b–5 give rise to private actions. The seminal case is a 1964 District Court decision, Kardon v. National Gypsum, 69 F.Supp. 512 (E.D. Pa. 1946).

NOTE ON BLUE CHIP STAMPS v. MANOR DRUG STORES

In Blue Chip Stamps v. Manor Drug Stores, 421 U.S. 723, 95 S.Ct. 1917, 44 L.Ed.2d 539 (1975), the Supreme Court held that under the "in connection with" clause of § 10(b), only a person who had purchased or sold stock had standing to bring a private action under Rule 10b–5. The Second Circuit had so held in 1952, in Birnbaum v. Newport Steel Corp., 193 F.2d 461 (1952), cert. denied 343 U.S. 956, 72 S.Ct. 1051, 96 L.Ed. 1356. The Supreme Court's opinion, by Justice Rehnquist, admitted that the language of section 10(b) itself was not conclusive on the issue, but supported its result on the basis of policy considerations:

> There has been widespread recognition that litigation under Rule 10b–5 presents a danger of vexatiousness different in degree and in kind from that which accompanies litigation in general. . . .

> We believe that the concern expressed for the danger of vexatious litigation which could result from a widely expanded class of plaintiffs under Rule 10b–5 is founded in something more substantial than the common complaint of the many defendants who would prefer avoiding lawsuits entirely to either settling them or trying them. These concerns have two largely separate grounds.

> The first of these concerns is that in the field of federal securities laws governing disclosure of information even a complaint which by objective standards may have very little chance of

success at trial has a settlement value to the plaintiff out of any proportion to its prospect of success at trial so long as he may prevent the suit from being resolved against him by dismissal or summary judgment. The very pendency of the lawsuit may frustrate or delay normal business activity of the defendant which is totally unrelated to the lawsuit. . . .

The potential for possible abuse of the liberal discovery provisions of the Federal Rules of Civil Procedure may likewise exist in this type of case to a greater extent than they do in other litigation. The prospect of extensive deposition of the defendant's officers and associates and the concomitant opportunity for extensive discovery of business documents, is a common occurrence in this and similar types of litigation. To the extent that this process eventually produces relevant evidence which is useful in determining the merits of the claims asserted by the parties, it bears the imprimatur of those Rules and of the many cases liberally interpreting them. But to the extent that it permits a plaintiff with a largely groundless claim to simply take up the time of a number of other people, with the right to do so representing an *in terrorem* increment of the settlement value, rather than a reasonably founded hope that the process will reveal relevant evidence, it is a social cost rather than a benefit. Yet to broadly expand the class of plaintiffs who may sue under Rule 10b-5 would appear to encourage the least appealing aspect of the use of the discovery rules.

Without the *Birnbaum* rule, an action under Rule 10b-5 will turn largely on which oral version of a series of occurrences the jury may decide to credit, and therefore no matter how improbable the allegations of the plaintiff, the case will be virtually impossible to dispose of prior to trial other than by settlement. . . .

The second ground for fear of vexatious litigation is based on the concern that, given the generalized contours of liability, the abolition of the *Birnbaum* rule would throw open to the trier of fact many rather hazy issues of historical fact the proof of which depended almost entirely on oral testimony. We in no way disparage the worth and frequent high value of oral testimony when we say that dangers of its abuse appear to exist in this type of action to a peculiarly high degree. . . .

The most significant bite of the *Blue Chip* doctrine is to bar private actions by persons who claim they *would have sold* stock that they owned had they not been induced to retain the stock by misrepresentations, or omissions, that violated Rule 10b-5. The bite of the doctrine in this regard, however, is not quite as wide as it might seem:

1. *Definition of "Sale."* The definitions of the term "sale" under the Securities Acts are very expansive, and therefore pick up many transactions that do not constitute a sale in the narrowest meaning of that term. For example, in Rubin v. United States, 449 U.S. 424, 101 S.Ct. 698, 66 L.Ed.2d 633 (1981), the Supreme Court held that a

pledge of securities was an "offer" or "sale" within § 17(a) of the Securities Act of 1933 (from whose language Rule 10b–5 was drawn). In Chemical Bank v. Arthur Andersen & Co., 726 F.2d 930, 939–40 (2d Cir.1984) (Friendly, J.), the court concluded that the *Rubin* reasoning applied under Rule 10b–5 as well.

2. *SEC Proceedings*. The *Blue Chip* doctrine does not affect the standing of the SEC to bring proceedings under Rule 10b–5, even though the SEC was neither a purchaser or a seller (as it never would be).

3. *Required Nexus*. Although some nexus between a violation of Rule 10b–5 and a purchase or sale is required, "[t]he courts have interpreted [the term 'in connection with'] broadly. Any statement that is reasonably calculated to affect the investment decision of a reasonable investor will satisfy the 'in connection with' requirement." 2 T. Hazen, Securities Regulation 108 (2d ed. 1990). Accordingly, it is well established that although the *plaintiff* in a private action under Rule 10b–5 must be a buyer or a seller, the *defendants* need not be. An action can be brought on the basis of a statement that influences trading but is made by a person who did not himself trade or tip.

4. *Injunctive Relief*. Several cases have held that a plaintiff in a private action for injunctive relief need not be a purchaser or a seller. See Kahan v. Rosenstiel, 424 F.2d 161, 173 (3d Cir.1970), cert. denied sub nom. Glen Alden Corp. v. Kahan, 398 U.S. 950, 90 S.Ct. 1870, 26 L.Ed.2d 290 (1970); Mutual Shares Corp. v. Genesco, Inc., 384 F.2d 540, 546–47 (2d Cir.1967). In Advanced Resources International v. Tri–Star Petroleum Co., 4 F.3d 327 (4th Cir.1993), the Fourth Circuit took a narrower view and held that a plaintiff in a private action for injunctive relief must be a purchaser or seller unless she falls within an appropriate exception.

NOTE ON THE SCIENTER REQUIREMENT

1. *Ernst & Ernst*. In Ernst & Ernst v. Hochfelder, 425 U.S. 185, 96 S.Ct. 1375, 47 L.Ed.2d 668 (1976), the Supreme Court held that a private action for damages under Rule 10b–5 will not lie "in the absence of any allegation of 'scienter,'" which the Court defined as an "intent to deceive, manipulate, or defraud" on the defendant's part. Loss and Seligman comment on this ruling as follows: "It is necessary [given the language of Section 10(b)] that some sort of watered-down scienter requirement be read into Clause (2) [of Rule 10b–5]. But why—in construing a fraud provision that was designed to *raise* the standards of securities trading, and that the courts have repeatedly interpreted as not limited to circumstances that would amount to common law deceit—did the majority opinion reach back in history to the strictest common law definition: not merely knowing falsity, but 'intent to deceive, manipulate, or defraud'?" 8 L. Loss & J. Seligman, Securities Regulation 3664 (3d ed. 1991).

2. *The Meaning of Scienter.* The opinion in *Ernst & Ernst* borrows the term "scienter" from tort law, but doesn't say much about what scienter means. The Prosser book has this to say about the scienter requirement in tort law:

> The intent which underlies an intentional misrepresentation is a more complex matter than the relatively simple intention in the case of assault and battery. It involves the intent that a representation shall be made, that it shall be directed to a particular person or class of persons, that it shall convey a certain meaning, that it shall be believed, and that it shall be acted upon in a certain way. In the usual case, all of this is present beyond dispute. . . .

W. Keeton, D. Dobbs, R. Keeton & D. Owen, Prosser & Keeton on The Law of Torts 741–42 (5th ed. 1984).

3. *Recklessness.* In footnote 12 of *Ernst & Ernst*, the Court stated:

> In this opinion the term "scienter" refers to a mental state embracing intent to deceive, manipulate, or defraud. In certain areas of the law recklessness is considered to be a form of intentional conduct for purposes of imposing liability for some act. We need not address here the question whether, in some circumstances, reckless behavior is sufficient for civil liability under § 10(b) and Rule 10b–5.

Decisions since *Ernst & Ernst* have unanimously held that recklessness satisfies the scienter requirement. What constitutes recklessness for purposes of Rule 10b–5 is less clear. Various courts have adopted, or cited with approval, observations in Sundstrand Corp. v. Sun Chemical Corp., 553 F.2d 1033 (7th Cir.1977), cert. denied 434 U.S. 875, 98 S.Ct. 224, 54 L.Ed.2d 155, and Sanders v. John Nuveen & Co., Inc., 554 F.2d 790 (7th Cir.1977). In *Sundstrand,* the court said:

> [R]eckless conduct may be defined as [highly unreasonable conduct], involving not merely simple, or even inexcusable negligence, but an extreme departure from the standards of ordinary care, and which presents a danger of misleading buyers or sellers that is either known to the defendant or is so obvious that the actor must have been aware of it.

553 F.2d at 1045. According to a gloss put on this test in Mansbach v. Prescott, Ball & Turben, 598 F.2d 1017, 1025 (6th Cir.1979), "[w]hile the danger need not be known, it must at least be so obvious that any reasonable man would have known of it." In *Sanders,* the court, after referring to the *Sundstrand* test, said:

> In view of the Supreme Court's analysis in *Hochfelder* of the statutory scheme of implied private remedies and express remedies, the definition of "reckless behavior" should not be a liberal one lest any discernible distinction between "scienter" and "negligence" be obliterated for these purposes. We believe "reckless" in these circumstances comes closer to being a lesser form of

intent than merely a greater degree of ordinary negligence. We perceive it to be not just a difference in degree, but also in kind. 554 F.2d at 793.

3. *Injunctive Relief.* In Aaron v. SEC, 446 U.S. 680, 100 S.Ct. 1945, 64 L.Ed.2d 611 (1980), the Supreme Court held that a showing of scienter was a requirement in an injunctive action under Rule 10b–5.

———

IN THE MATTER OF CADY, ROBERTS & CO., 40 S.E.C. 907, 911–12 (1961). "[Rule 10b–5 applies] to securities transactions by 'any person.' Misrepresentations will lie within [its] ambit, no matter who the speaker may be. An affirmative duty to disclose material information has been traditionally imposed on corporate 'insiders,' particularly officers, directors, or controlling stockholders. We, and the courts have consistently held that insiders must disclose material facts which are known to them by virtue of their position but which are not known to persons with whom they deal and which, if known, would affect their investment judgment. Failure to make disclosure in these circumstances constitutes a violation of the anti-fraud provisions. If, on the other hand, disclosure prior to effecting a purchase or sale would be improper or unrealistic under the circumstances, we believe the alternative is to forego the transaction. . . .

"We have already noted that the anti-fraud provisions are phrased in terms of 'any person' and that a special obligation has been traditionally required of corporate insiders, e.g., officers, directors and controlling stockholders. These three groups, however, do not exhaust the classes of persons upon whom there is such an obligation. Analytically, the obligation rests on two principal elements; first, the existence of a relationship giving access, directly or indirectly, to information intended to be available only for a corporate purpose and not for the personal benefit of anyone, and second, the inherent unfairness involved where a party takes advantage of such information knowing it is unavailable to those with whom he is dealing. In considering these elements under the broad language of the anti-fraud provisions we are not to be circumscribed by fine distinctions and rigid classifications. Thus our task here is to identify those persons who are in a special relationship with a company and privy to its internal affairs, and thereby suffer correlative duties in trading in its securities. Intimacy demands restraint lest the uninformed be exploited."

———

Securities and Exchange Commission v. Texas Gulf Sulphur Co.

United States Court of Appeals, Second Circuit, 1968.
401 F.2d 833 (in banc), cert. denied 394 U.S. 976, 89 S.Ct. 1454, 22 L.Ed.2d 756 (1969).

■ WATERMAN, CIRCUIT JUDGE:

[This was an action brought by the S.E.C. against Texas Gulf Sulphur (TGS) based on the issuance of a misleading press release, and against certain officers and employees of TGS based on their trading and tipping. The case grew out of an important mineral discovery by TGS. Four of the individual defendants were members of the geological exploration group that made the discovery: Mollison, a vice-president and mining engineer who headed the exploration group; Holyk, TGS' chief geologist; Clayton, an electrical engineer and geophysicist, and Darke, a geologist. The other individual defendants included Stephens, who was TGS's President; Fogarty, its Executive Vice–President; Kline, its Vice–President and General Counsel; and Coates, a director.

[Those portions of the opinion dealing with the liability of TGS for the misleading press release and the liability of individual defendants for tipping have been omitted, because the discussion of those issues has been largely superseded by later Supreme Court cases, set out below.]

This action derives from the exploratory activities of TGS begun in 1957 on the Canadian Shield in eastern Canada. In March of 1959, aerial geophysical surveys were conducted over more than 15,000 square miles of this area by a group led by defendant Mollison, a mining engineer and a Vice President of TGS. The group included defendant Holyk, TGS's chief geologist, defendant Clayton, an electrical engineer and geophysicist, and defendant Darke, a geologist. These operations resulted in the detection of numerous anomalies, i.e., extraordinary variations in the conductivity of rocks, one of which was on the Kidd 55 segment of land located near Timmins, Ontario.

On October 29 and 30, 1963, Clayton conducted a ground geophysical survey on the northeast portion of the Kidd 55 segment which confirmed the presence of an anomaly and indicated the necessity of diamond core drilling for further evaluation. Drilling of the initial hole, K–55–1, at the strongest part of the anomaly was commenced on November 8 and terminated on November 12 at a depth of 655 feet. Visual estimates by Holyk of the core of K–55–1 indicated an average copper content of 1.15% and an average zinc content of 8.64% over a length of 599 feet. This visual estimate convinced TGS that it was desirable to acquire the remainder of the Kidd 55 segment, and in order to facilitate this acquisition TGS President Stephens instructed the exploration group to keep the results of K–55–1 confidential and undisclosed even as to other officers, directors, and employees of TGS. The hole was concealed and a barren core was intentionally drilled off the anomaly. Meanwhile, the core of K–55–1 had been shipped to Utah for chemical assay which, when received in early December, revealed an average mineral content of 1.18% copper, 8.26% zinc, and 3.94% ounces of silver per ton over a length of 602 feet. These results were so remarkable that neither Clayton, an experienced geophysicist, nor four other TGS expert witnesses, had ever seen or heard of a comparable initial exploratory drill hole in a base metal deposit. So, the trial court concluded, "There is no doubt that the drill core of K–55–1 was unusually good and that it excited the interest and speculation of those who knew about it." Id. at 282. By March 27, 1964, TGS decided that the land acquisition program had advanced to such a point that the company might well resume drilling, and drilling was resumed on March 31.

During this period, from November 12, 1963 when K–55–1 was completed, to March 31, 1964 when drilling was resumed certain of the individual defendants . . . and persons . . . said to have received "tips" from them, purchased TGS stock or calls thereon. Prior to these transactions these persons had owned 1135 shares of TGS stock and possessed no calls; thereafter they owned a total of 8235 shares and possessed 12,300 calls.

On February 20, 1964, also during this period, TGS issued stock options to 26 of its officers and employees whose salaries exceeded a specified amount, five of whom were the individual defendants Stephens, Fogarty, Mollison, Holyk, and Kline. Of these, only Kline was unaware of the detailed results of K–55–1, but he, too, knew that a hole containing favorable bodies of copper and zinc ore had been drilled in Timmins. At this time, neither the TGS Stock Option Committee nor its Board of Directors had been informed of the results of K–55–1, presumably because of the pending land acquisition program which required confidentiality. All of the foregoing defendants accepted the options granted them.

When drilling was resumed on March 31, hole K–55–3 was commenced 510 feet west of K–55–1 and was drilled easterly at a 45– angle so as to cross K–55–1 in a vertical plane. Daily progress reports of the drilling of this hole K–55–3 and of all subsequently drilled holes were sent to defendants Stephens and Fogarty (President and Executive Vice President of TGS) by Holyk and Mollison. Visual estimates of K–55–3 revealed an average mineral content of 1.12% copper and 7.93% zinc over 641 of the hole's 876–foot length. On April 7, drilling of a third hole, K–55–4, 200 feet south of and parallel to K–55–1 and westerly at a 45_ angle, was commenced and mineralization was encountered over 366 of its 579–foot length. Visual estimates indicated an average content of 1.14% copper and 8.24% zinc. Like K–55–1, both K–55–3 and K–55–4 established substantial copper mineralization on the eastern edge of the anomaly. On the basis of these findings relative to the foregoing drilling results, the trial court concluded that the vertical plane created by the intersection of K–55–1 and K–55–3, which measured at least 350 feet wide by 500 feet deep extended southward 200 feet to its intersection with K–55–4, and that "There was real evidence that a body of commercially mineable ore might exist." Id. at 281–82.

On April 8 TGS began with a second drill rig to drill another hole, K–55–6, 300 feet easterly of K–55–1. This hole was drilled westerly at an angle of 60– and was intended to explore mineralization beneath K–55–1. While no visual estimates of its core were immediately available, it was readily apparent by the evening of April 10 that substantial copper mineralization had been encountered over the last 127 feet of the hole's 569–foot length. On April 10, a third drill rig commenced drilling yet another hole, K–55–5, 200 feet north of K–55–1, parallel to the prior holes, and slanted westerly at a 45_ angle. By the evening of April 10 in this hole, too, substantial copper mineralization had been encountered over the last 42 feet of its 97–foot length.

Meanwhile, rumors that a major ore strike was in the making had been circulating throughout Canada. On the morning of Saturday, April 11, Stephens at his home in Greenwich, Conn. read in the New York Herald Tribune and in the New York Times unauthorized reports of the TGS drilling which seemed to infer a rich strike from the fact that the drill cores had been flown to the United States for chemical assay. Stephens immediately contacted Fogarty at his home in Rye, N.Y., who in turn telephoned and later that day visited Mollison at Mollison's home in Greenwich to obtain a current report and evaluation of the drilling progress.[7] The following morning, Sunday, Fogarty again telephoned Mollison, inquiring whether Mollison had any further information and told him to return to Timmins with Holyk, the TGS Chief Geologist, as soon as possible "to move things along." With the aid of one Carroll, a public relations consultant, Fogarty drafted a press release designed to quell the rumors, which release, after having been channeled through Stephens and Huntington, a TGS attorney, was issued at 3:00 P.M. on Sunday, April 12, and which appeared in the morning newspapers of general circulation on Monday, April 13. It read in pertinent part as follows:

New York, April 12—The following statement was made today by Dr. Charles F. Fogarty, executive vice president of Texas Gulf Sulphur Company, in regard to the company's drilling operations near Timmins, Ontario, Canada. Dr. Fogarty said:

"During the past few days, the exploration activities of Texas Gulf Sulphur in the area of Timmins, Ontario, have been widely reported in the press, coupled with rumors of a substantial copper discovery there. These reports exaggerate the scale of operations, and mention plans and statistics of size and grade of ore that are without factual basis and have evidently originated by speculation of people not connected with TGS.

"The facts are as follows. TGS has been exploring in the Timmins area for six years as part of its overall search in Canada and elsewhere for various minerals—lead, copper, zinc, etc. During the course of this work, in Timmins as well as in Eastern Canada, TGS has conducted exploration entirely on its own, without the participation by others. Numerous prospects have been investigated by geophysical means and a large number of selected ones have been core-drilled. These cores are sent to the United States for assay and detailed examination as a

---

7. Mollison had returned to the United States for the weekend. Friday morning April 10, he had been on the Kidd tract "and had been advised by defendant Holyk as to the drilling results to 7:00 p.m. on April 10. At that time drill holes K–55–1, K–55–3 and K–55–4 had been completed; drilling of K–55–5 had started on Section 2200 S and had been drilled to 97 feet, encountering mineralization on the last 42 feet; and drilling of K–55–6 had been started on Section 2400 S and had been drilled to 569 feet, encountering mineralization over the last 127 feet." Id. at 294.

matter of routine and on advice of expert Canadian legal counsel. No inferences as to grade can be drawn from this procedure.

"Most of the areas drilled in Eastern Canada have revealed either barren pyrite or graphite without value; a few have resulted in discoveries of small or marginal sulphide ore bodies.

"Recent drilling on one property near Timmins has led to preliminary indications that more drilling would be required for proper evaluation of this prospect. The drilling done to date has not been conclusive, but the statements made by many outside quarters are unreliable and include information and figures that are not available to TGS.

"The work done to date has not been sufficient to reach definite conclusions and any statement as to size and grade of ore would be premature and possibly misleading. When we have progressed to the point where reasonable and logical conclusions can be made, TGS will issue a definite statement to its stockholders and to the public in order to clarify the Timmins project."

* * *

The release purported to give the Timmins drilling results as of the release date, April 12. From Mollison Fogarty had been told of the developments through 7:00 P.M. on April 10, and of the remarkable discoveries made up to that time, detailed supra, which discoveries, according to the calculations of the experts who testified for the SEC at the hearing, demonstrated that TGS had already discovered 6.2 to 8.3 million tons of proven ore having gross assay values from $26 to $29 per ton. TGS experts, on the other hand, denied at the hearing that proven or probable ore could have been calculated on April 11 or 12 because there was then no assurance of continuity in the mineralized zone.

The evidence as to the effect of this release on the investing public was equivocal and less than abundant. On April 13 the New York Herald Tribune in an article head-noted "Copper Rumor Deflated" quoted from the TGS release of April 12 and backtracked from its original April 11 report of a major strike but nevertheless inferred from the TGS release that "recent mineral exploratory activity near Timmins, Ontario, has provided preliminary favorable results, sufficient at least to require a step-up in drilling operations." Some witnesses who testified at the hearing stated that they found the release encouraging. On the other hand, a Canadian mining security specialist, Roche, stated that "earlier in the week [before April 16] we had a Dow Jones saying that they [TGS] didn't have anything basically" and a TGS stock specialist for the Midwest Stock Exchange became concerned about his long position in the stock after reading the release. The trial court stated only that "While, in retrospect, the press release may appear gloomy or incomplete, this does not make it misleading or deceptive on the basis of the facts then known." Id. at 296.

Meanwhile, drilling operations continued....

While drilling activity ensued to completion, TGS officials were taking steps toward ultimate disclosure of the discovery. On April 13, a previously-invited reporter for The Northern Miner, a Canadian mining industry journal, visited the drillsite, interviewed Mollison, Holyk and Darke, and prepared an article which confirmed a 10 million ton ore strike. This report, after having been submitted to Mollison and returned to the reporter unamended on April 15, was published in the April 16 issue. A statement relative to the extent of the discovery, in substantial part drafted by Mollison, was given to the Ontario Minister of Mines for release to the Canadian media. Mollison and Holyk expected it to be released over the airways at 11 P.M. on April 15th, but, for undisclosed reasons, it was not released until 9:40 A.M. on the 16th. An official detailed statement, announcing a strike of at least 25 million tons of ore, based on the drilling data set forth above, was read to representatives of American financial media from 10:00 A.M. to 10:10 or 10:15 A.M. on April 16, and appeared over Merrill Lynch's private wire at 10:29 A.M. and, somewhat later than expected, over the Dow Jones ticker tape at 10:54 A.M.

Between the time the first press release was issued on April 12 and the dissemination of the TGS official announcement on the morning of April 16, the only defendants before us on appeal who engaged in market activity were Clayton and Crawford and TGS director Coates. Clayton ordered 200 shares of TGS stock through his Canadian broker on April 15 and another 300 shares at 8:30 A.M. the next day, and these orders were executed over the Midwest Exchange in Chicago at its opening on April 16. Coates left the TGS press conference and called his broker son-in-law Haemisegger shortly before 10:20 A.M. on the 16th and ordered 2,000 shares of TGS for family trust accounts of which Coates was a trustee but not a beneficiary; Haemisegger executed this order over the New York and Midwest Exchanges, and he and his customers purchased 1500 additional shares.

During the period of drilling in Timmins, the market price of TGS stock fluctuated but steadily gained overall. On Friday, November 8, when the drilling began, the stock closed at $17\frac{3}{8}$; on Friday, November 15, after K–55–1 had been completed, it closed at 18. After a slight decline to $16\frac{3}{8}$ by Friday, November 22, the price rose to $20\frac{7}{8}$ by December 13, when the chemical assay results of K–55–1 were received, and closed at a high of $24\frac{1}{8}$ on February 21, the day after the stock options had been issued. It had reached a price of 26 by March 31, after the land acquisition program had been completed and drilling had been resumed, and continued to ascend to $30\frac{1}{8}$ by the close of trading on April 10, at which time the drilling progress up to then was evaluated for the April 12th press release. On April 13, the day on which the April 12 release was disseminated, TGS opened at $30\frac{1}{8}$, rose immediately to a high of 32 and gradually tapered off to close at $30\frac{7}{8}$. It closed at $30\frac{1}{4}$ the next day, and at $29\frac{3}{8}$ on April 15. On April 16, the day of the official announcement of the Timmins discovery, the price climbed to a high of 37 and closed at 36⅜. By May 15, TGS stock was selling at 58¼ . . . .*

I. The Individual Defendants

A. *Introductory*

. . . Whether predicated on traditional fiduciary concepts, see, e.g., Hotchkiss v. Fisher, 136 Kan. 530, 16 P.2d 531 (Kan.1932), or on

---

* The purchases by the parties during this period were:

Purchase Date		Purchaser	Shares Number	Price	Calls Number	Price

Purchase Date		Purchaser	Shares Number	Price	Calls Number	Price
Hole K–55–1 Completed November 12, 1963						
1963						
Nov.	12	Fogarty	300	17¾–18		
	15	Clayton	200	17¾		
	15	Fogarty	700	17⅝–17⅞		
	15	Mollison	100	17⅞		
	19	Fogarty	500	18⅛		
	26	Fogarty	200	17¾		
	29	Holyk (Mrs.)	50	18		
Chemical Assays of Drill Core of K–55–1 Received December 9–13, 1963						
Dec.	10	Holyk (Mrs.)	100	20⅜		
	12	Holyk (or wife)			200	21
	13	Mollison	100	21⅛		
	30	Fogarty	200	22		
	31	Fogarty	100	23¼		
1964						
Jan.	6	Holyk (or wife)			100	23⅝
	8	Murray			400	23¼
	24	Holyk (or wife)			200	22¼–22⅜
Feb.	10	Fogarty	300	22⅛–22¼		
	20	Darke	300	24⅛		
	24	Clayton	400	23⅞		
	24	Holyk (or wife)			200	24⅛
	26	Holyk (or wife)			200	23⅜
	26	Huntington	50	23¼		
	27	Darke (Moran as nominee)			1000	22⅝–22¾
Mar.	2	Holyk (Mrs.)	200	22⅜		
	3	Clayton	100	22¼		
	16	Huntington			100	22⅜
	16	Holyk (or wife)			300	23¼
	17	Holyk (Mrs.)	100	23⅞		
	23	Darke			1000	24¾
	26	Clayton	200	25		
Land Acquisition Completed March 27, 1964						
Mar.	30	Darke			100	25½
	30	Holyk (Mrs.)	100	25⅞		
Core Drilling of Kidd Segment Resumed March 31, 1964						
April	1	Clayton	60	26½		
	1	Fogarty	400	26½		
	2	Clayton	100	26⅞		
	6	Fogarty	400	28⅛–28⅞		
	8	Mollison (Mrs.)	100	28⅛		
First Press Release Issued April 12, 1964						
April	15	Clayton	200	29⅜		
	16	Crawford (and wife)	600	30⅛–30¼		
Second Press Release Issued 10:00–10:10 or 10:15 A.M., April 16, 1964 . . .						
1963						
April	16	(app. 10:20 A.M.)				
		Coates (for family trusts)	2000	31–31⅝		

[Footnote by the court; relocated by the editor.]

the "special facts" doctrine, see, e.g., Strong v. Repide, 213 U.S. 419, 29 S.Ct. 521, 53 L.Ed. 853 (1909), . . . Rule [10b–5] is based in policy on the justifiable expectation of the securities marketplace that all investors trading on impersonal exchanges have relatively equal access to material information, see Cary, Insider Trading in Stocks, 21 Bus. Law. 1009, 1010 (1966), Fleischer, Securities Trading and Corporation Information Practices: The Implications of the Texas Gulf Sulphur Proceeding, 51 Va.L.Rev. 1271, 1278–80 (1965). The essence of the Rule is that anyone who, trading for his own account in the securities of a corporation has "access, directly or indirectly, to information intended to be available only for a corporate purpose and not for the personal benefit of anyone" may not take "advantage of such information knowing it is unavailable to those with whom he is dealing," i.e., the investing public. Matter of Cady, Roberts & Co., 40 SEC 907, 912 (1961). Insiders, as directors or management officers are, of course, by this Rule, precluded from so unfairly dealing, but the Rule is also applicable to one possessing the information who may not be strictly termed an "insider" within the meaning of Sec. 16(b) of the Act. Cady, Roberts, supra. Thus, anyone in possession of material inside information must either disclose it to the investing public, or, if he is disabled from disclosing it in order to protect a corporate confidence, or he chooses not to do so, must abstain from trading in or recommending the securities concerned while such inside information remains undisclosed. So, it is here no justification for insider activity that disclosure was forbidden by the legitimate corporate objective of acquiring options to purchase the land surrounding the exploration site; if the information was, as the SEC contends, material, its possessors should have kept out of the market until disclosure was accomplished. Cady, Roberts, supra at 911.

B.   *Material Inside Information*

An insider is not, of course, always foreclosed from investing in his own company merely because he may be more familiar with company operations than are outside investors. An insider's duty to disclose information or his duty to abstain from dealing in his company's securities arises only in "those situations which are essentially extraordinary in nature and which are reasonably certain to have a substantial effect on the market price of the security if [the extraordinary situation is] disclosed." Fleischer, Securities Trading and Corporate Information Practices: The Implications of the Texas Gulf Sulphur Proceeding, 51 Va.L.Rev. 1271, 1289.

Nor is an insider obligated to confer upon outside investors the benefit of his superior financial or other expert analysis by disclosing his educated guesses or predictions. 3 Loss, op. cit. supra at 1463. The only regulatory objective is that access to material information be enjoyed equally, but this objective requires nothing more than the disclosure of basic facts so that outsiders may draw upon their own evaluative expertise in reaching their own investment decisions with knowledge equal to that of the insiders.

This is not to suggest, however, as did the trial court, that "the test of materiality must necessarily be a conservative one, particularly since many actions under Section 10(b) are brought on the basis of hindsight," 258 F.Supp. 262 at 280, in the sense that the materiality of facts is to be assessed solely by measuring the effect the knowledge of the facts would have upon prudent or conservative investors. As we stated in List v. Fashion Park, Inc., 340 F.2d 457, 462, "The basic test of materiality . . . is whether a *reasonable* man would attach importance . . . in determining his choice of action in the transaction in question. Restatement, Torts § 538(2)(a); accord Prosser, Torts 554–55; I Harper & James, Torts 565–66." (Emphasis supplied.) . . . [M]aterial facts include not only information disclosing the earnings and distributions of a company but also those facts which affect the probable future of the company and those which may affect the desire of investors to buy, sell, or hold the company's securities.

In each case, then, whether facts are material within Rule 10b–5 when the facts relate to a particular event and are undisclosed by those persons who are knowledgeable thereof will depend at any given time upon a balancing of both the indicated probability that the event will occur and the anticipated magnitude of the event in light of the totality of the company activity. Here, notwithstanding the trial court's conclusion that the results of the first drill core, K–55–1, were "too 'remote' . . . to have had any significant impact on the market, i.e., to be deemed material," 258 F.Supp. at 283, knowledge of the possibility, which surely was more than marginal, of the existence of a mine of the vast magnitude indicated by the remarkably rich drill core located rather close to the surface (suggesting mineability by the less expensive open pit method) within the confines of a large anomaly (suggesting an extensive region of mineralization) might well have affected the price of TGS stock and would certainly have been an important fact to a reasonable, if speculative, investor in deciding whether he should buy, sell, or hold. After all, this first drill core was "unusually good and . . . excited the interest and speculation of those who knew about it." 258 F.Supp. at 282.

. . . Our survey of the facts found below conclusively establishes that knowledge of the results of the discovery hole, K–55–1, would have been important to a reasonable investor and might have affected the price of the stock.[2] On April 16, The Northern Miner, a trade publication in wide circulation among mining stock specialists, called K–55–1, the discovery hole, "one of the most impressive drill holes completed in modern times." Roche, a Canadian broker whose firm

2. We do not suggest that material facts must be disclosed immediately; the timing of disclosure is a matter for the business judgment of the corporate officers entrusted with the management of the corporation within the affirmative disclosure requirements promulgated by the exchanges and by the SEC. Here, a valuable corporate purpose was served by delaying the publication of the K–55–1 discovery. We do intend to convey, however, that where a corporate purpose is thus served by withholding the news of a material fact, those persons who are thus quite properly true to their corporate trust must not during the period of non-disclosure deal personally in the corporation's securities or give to outsiders confidential information not generally available to all the corporations' stockholders and to the public at large.

specialized in mining securities, characterized the importance to investors of the results of K–55–1. He stated that the completion of "the first drill hole" with "a 600 foot drill core is very very significant ... anything over 200 feet is considered very significant and 600 feet is just beyond your wildest imagination." He added, however, that it "is a natural thing to buy more stock once they give you the first drill hole." Additional testimony revealed that the prices of stocks of other companies, albeit less diversified, smaller firms, had increased substantially solely on the basis of the discovery of good anomalies or even because of the proximity of their lands to the situs of a potentially major strike.

Finally, a major factor in determining whether the K–55–1 discovery was a material fact is the importance attached to the drilling results by those who knew about it. In view of other unrelated recent developments favorably affecting TGS, participation by an informed person in a regular stock-purchase program, or even sporadic trading by an informed person, might lend only nominal support to the inference of the materiality of the K–55–1 discovery; nevertheless, the timing by those who knew of it of their stock purchases and their purchases of *short-term* calls—purchases in some cases by individuals who had never before purchased calls or even TGS stock—virtually compels the inference that the insiders were influenced by the drilling results. This insider trading activity, which surely constitutes highly pertinent evidence and the only truly objective evidence of the materiality of the K–55–1 discovery, was apparently disregarded by the court below in favor of the testimony of defendants' expert witnesses, all of whom "agreed that one drill core does not establish an ore body, much less a mine," 258 F.Supp. at 282–283. Significantly, however, the court below, while relying upon what these defense experts said the defendant insiders *ought* to have thought about the worth to TGS of the K–55–1 discovery, and finding that from November 12, 1963 to April 6, 1964 Fogarty, Murray, Holyk and Darke spent more than $100,000 in purchasing TGS stock and calls on that stock, made no finding that the insiders were motivated by any factor other than the extraordinary K–55–1 discovery when they bought their stock and their calls. No reason appears why outside investors, perhaps better acquainted with speculative modes of investment and with, in many cases, perhaps more capital at their disposal for intelligent speculation, would have been less influenced, and would not have been similarly motivated to invest if they had known what the insider investors knew about the K–55–1 discovery.

Our decision to expand the limited protection afforded outside investors by the trial court's narrow definition of materiality is not at all shaken by fears that the elimination of insider trading benefits will deplete the ranks of capable corporate managers by taking away an incentive to accept such employment. Such benefits, in essence, are forms of secret corporate compensation, see Cary, Corporate Standards and Legal Rules, 50 Calif.L.Rev. 408, 409–10 (1962), derived at the expense of the uninformed investing public and not at the expense of the corporation which receives the sole benefit from insider incentives. Moreover, adequate incentives for corporate officers may be provided by properly administered stock options and employee purchase plans of which there are many in existence. In any event, the normal motivation induced by stock ownership, i.e., the identification of an individual with corporate progress, is ill-promoted by condoning the sort of speculative insider activity which occurred here; for example, some of the corporation's stock was sold at market in order to purchase short-term calls upon that stock, calls which would never be exercised to increase a stockholder equity in TGS unless the market price of that stock rose sharply.

The core of Rule 10b–5 is the implementation of the Congressional purpose that all investors should have equal access to the rewards of participation in securities transactions. It was the intent of Congress that all members of the investing public should be subject to identical market risks,—which market risks include, of course the risk that one's evaluative capacity or one's capital available to put at risk may exceed another's capacity or capital. The insiders here were not trading on an equal footing with the outside investors. They alone were in a position to evaluate the probability and magnitude of what seemed from the outset to be a major ore strike; they alone could invest safely, secure in the expectation that the price of TGS stock would rise substantially in the event such a major strike should materialize, but would decline little, if at all, in the event of failure, for the public, ignorant at the outset of the favorable probabilities would likewise be unaware of the unproductive exploration, and the additional exploration costs would not significantly affect TGS market prices. Such inequities based upon unequal access to knowledge should not be shrugged off as inevitable in our way of life, or, in view of the congressional concern in the area, remain uncorrected.

We hold, therefore, that all transactions in TGS stock or calls by individuals apprised of the drilling results[14] of K–55–1 were made in violation of Rule 10b–5.[15] Inasmuch as the visual evaluation of that drill core (a generally reliable estimate though less accurate than a chemical assay) constituted material information, those advised of the results of the visual evaluation as well as those informed of the chemical assay traded in violation of law. The geologist Darke possessed undisclosed material information and traded in TGS securities. Therefore we reverse the dismissal of the action as to him and his personal transactions. . . .

With reference to Huntington, the trial court found that he "had no detailed knowledge as to the work" on the Kidd–55 segment, 258 F.Supp. 281. Nevertheless, the evidence shows that he knew about and

14. The trial court found that defendant Murray "had no detailed knowledge as to the work" on the Kidd–55 segment. There is no evidence in the record suggesting that Murray purchased his stock on January 8, 1964, on the basis of material undisclosed information, and the disposition below is undisturbed as to him.

15. Even if insiders were in fact ignorant of the broad scope of the Rule and acted pursuant to a mistaken belief as to the applicable law such an ignorance does not insulate them from the consequences of their acts. Tager v. SEC, 344 F.2d 5, 8 (2 Cir.1965).

participated in TGS's land acquisition program which followed the receipt of the K–55–1 drilling results, and that on February 26, 1964 he purchased 50 shares of TGS stock. Later, on March 16, he helped prepare a letter for Dr. Holyk's signature in which TGS made a substantial offer for lands near K–55–1, and on the same day he, who had never before purchased calls on any stock, purchased a call on 100 shares of TGS stock. We are satisfied that these purchases in February and March, coupled with his readily inferable and probably reliable, understanding of the highly favorable nature of preliminary operations on the Kidd segment, demonstrate that Huntington possessed material inside information such as to make his purchase violative of the Rule and the Act.

C. *When May Insiders Act?*

Appellant Crawford, who ordered[17] the purchase of TGS stock shortly before the TGS April 16 official announcement, and defendant Coates, who placed orders with and communicated the news to his broker immediately after the official announcement was read at the TGS-called press conference, concede that they were in possession of material information. They contend, however, that their purchases were not proscribed purchases for the news had already been effectively disclosed. We disagree.

Crawford telephoned his orders to his Chicago broker about midnight on April 15 and again at 8:30 in the morning of the 16th, with instructions to buy at the opening of the Midwest Stock Exchange that morning. The trial court's finding that "he sought to, and did, 'beat the news,'" 258 F.Supp. at 287, is well documented by the record. The rumors of a major ore strike which had been circulated in Canada and, to a lesser extent, in New York, had been disclaimed by the TGS press release of April 12, which significantly promised the public an official detailed announcement when possibilities had ripened into actualities. The abbreviated announcement to the Canadian press at 9:40 A.M. on the 16th by the Ontario Minister of Mines and the report carried by The Northern Miner, parts of which had sporadically reached New York on the morning of the 16th through reports from Canadian affiliates to a few New York investment firms, are assuredly not the equivalent of the official 10–15 minute announcement which was not released to the American financial press until after 10:00 A.M. Crawford's orders had been placed before that. Before insiders may act upon material information, such information must have been effectively disclosed in a manner sufficient to insure its

---

17. The effective protection of the public from insider exploitation of advance notice of material information requires that the time that an insider places an order, rather than the time of its ultimate execution, be determinative for Rule 10b–5 purposes. Otherwise, insiders would be able to "beat the news," cf. Fleischer, supra, 51 Va.L.Rev. at 1291, by requesting in advance that their orders be executed immediately after the dis- semination of a major news release but before outsiders could act on the release. Thus it is immaterial whether Crawford's orders were executed before or after the announcement was made in Canada (9:40 A.M., April 16) or in the United States (10:00 A.M.) or whether Coates's order was executed before or after the news appeared over the Merrill Lynch (10:29 A.M.) or Dow Jones (10:54 A.M.) wires.

availability to the investing public. Particularly here, where a formal announcement to the entire financial news media had been promised in a prior official release known to the media, all insider activity must await dissemination of the promised official announcement.

Coates was absolved by the court below because his telephone order was placed shortly before 10:20 A.M. on April 16, which was after the announcement had been made even though the news could not be considered already a matter of public information. 258 F.Supp. at 288. This result seems to have been predicated upon a misinterpretation of dicta in *Cady, Roberts,* where the SEC instructed insiders to "keep out of the market until the established procedures for public release of the information are *carried out* instead of hastening to execute transactions in advance of, and in frustration of, the objectives of the release," 40 SEC at 915 (emphasis supplied). The reading of a news release, which prompted Coates into action, is merely the first step in the process of dissemination required for compliance with the regulatory objective of providing all investors with an equal opportunity to make informed investment judgments. Assuming that the contents of the official release could instantaneously be acted upon,[18] at the minimum Coates should have waited until the news could reasonably have been expected to appear over the media of widest circulation, the Dow Jones broad tape, rather than hastening to insure an advantage to himself and his broker son-in-law.[19] . . .

E.   *May Insiders Accept Stock Options Without Disclosing Material Information to the Issuer?*

On February 20, 1964, defendants Stephens, Fogarty, Mollison, Holyk and Kline accepted stock options issued to them and a number of other top officers of TGS, although not one of them had informed the Stock Option Committee of the Board of Directors or the Board of the results of K–55–1, which information we have held was then material. The SEC sought rescission of these options. The trial court, in addition to finding the knowledge of the results of the K–55 discovery to be immaterial, held that Kline had no detailed knowledge of the drilling progress and that Holyk and Mollison could reasonably assume that their superiors, Stephens and Fogarty, who were directors

18. Although the only insider who acted after the news appeared over the Dow Jones broad tape is not an appellant and therefore we need not discuss the necessity of considering the advisability of a "reasonable waiting period" during which outsiders may absorb and evaluate disclosures, we note in passing that, where the news is of a sort which is not readily translatable into investment action, insiders may not take advantage of their advance opportunity to evaluate the information by acting immediately upon dissemination. In any event, the permissible timing of insider transactions after disclosures of various sorts is one of the many areas of expertise for appropriate exercise of the SEC's rule-making power, which we hope will be utilized in the future to provide some predictability of certainty for the business community.

19. The record reveals that news usually appears on the Dow Jones broad tape 2–3 minutes after the reporter completes dictation. Here, assuming that the Dow Jones reporter left the press conference as early as possible, 10:10 A.M., the 10–15 minute release (which took at least that long to dictate) could not have appeared on the wire before 10:22, and for other reasons unknown to us did not appear until 10:54. Indeed, even the abbreviated version of the release reported by Merrill Lynch over its private wire did not appear until 10:29. Coates, however, placed his call no later than 10:20.

of the corporation, would report the results if that was advisable; indeed all employees had been instructed not to divulge this information pending completion of the land acquisition program, 258 F.Supp. at 291. Therefore, the court below concluded that only directors Stephens and Fogarty, of the top management, would have violated the Rule by accepting stock options without disclosure, but it also found that they had not acted improperly as the information in their possession was not material. 258 F.Supp. at 292. In view of our conclusion as to materiality we hold that Stephens and Fogarty violated the Rule by accepting them. However, as they have surrendered the options and the corporation has canceled them, supra at 292, n. 17, we find it unnecessary to order that the injunctions prayed for be actually issued. We point out, nevertheless, that the surrender of these options after the SEC commenced the case is not a satisfaction of the SEC claim, and a determination as to whether the issuance of injunctions against Stephens and Fogarty is advisable in order to prevent or deter future violations of regulatory provisions is remanded for the exercise of discretion by the trial court.

Contrary to the belief of the trial court that Kline had no duty to disclose his knowledge of the Kidd project before accepting the stock option offered him, we believe that he, a vice president, who had become the general counsel of TGS in January 1964, but who had been secretary of the corporation since January 1961, and was present in that capacity when the options were granted, and who was in charge of the mechanics of issuance and acceptance of the options, was a member of top management and under a duty before accepting his option to disclose any material information he may have possessed, and, as he did not disclose such information to the Option Committee we direct rescission of the option he received.[24] As to Holyk and Mollison, the SEC has not appealed the holding below that they, not being then members of top management (although Mollison was a vice president) had no duty to disclose their knowledge of the drilling before accepting their options. Therefore, the issue of whether, by

---

24. The options granted on February 20, 1964 to Mollison, Holyk, and Kline were ratified by the Texas Gulf directors on July 15, 1965 after there had been, of course, a full disclosure and after this action had been commenced. However, the ratification is irrelevant here, for we would hold with the district court that a member of top management, as was Kline, is required, before accepting a stock option, to disclose material inside information which, if disclosed, might affect the price of the stock during the period when the accepted option could be exercised. Kline had known since November 1962 that K–55–1 had been drilled, that the drilling had intersected a sulphide body containing copper and zinc, and that TGS desired to acquire adjacent property.

Of course, if any of the five knowledgeable defendants had rejected his option there might well have been speculation as to the reason for the rejection. Therefore, in a case where disclosure to the grantors of an option would seriously jeopardize corporate security, it could well be desirable, in order to protect a corporation from selling securities to insiders who are in a position to appreciate their true worth at a price which may not accurately reflect the true value of the securities and at the same time to preserve when necessary the secrecy of corporate activity, not to require that an insider possessed of undisclosed material information reject the offer of a stock option, but only to require that he abstain from exercising it until such time as there shall have been a full disclosure and, after the full disclosure, a ratification such as was voted here. However, as this suggestion was not presented to us, we do not consider it or make any determination with reference to it.

accepting, they violated the Act, is not before us, and the holding below is undisturbed....

■ FRIENDLY, CIRCUIT JUDGE (concurring):

Agreeing with the result reached by the majority and with most of Judge Waterman's searching opinion, I take a rather different approach to two facets of the case.

I.

The first is a situation that will not often arise, involving as it does the acceptance of stock options during a period when inside information likely to produce a rapid and substantial increase in the price of the stock was known to some of the grantees but unknown to those in charge of the granting. I suppose it would be clear, under Ruckle v. Roto American Corp., 339 F.2d 24 (2 Cir.1964), that if a corporate officer having such knowledge persuaded an unknowing board of directors to grant him an option at a price approximating the current market, the option would be rescindable in an action under Rule 10b–5. It would seem, by the same token, that if, to make the pill easier to swallow, he urged the directors to include others lacking the knowledge he possessed, he would be liable for all the resulting damage. The novel problem in the instant case is to define the responsibility of officers when a directors' committee administering a stock option plan proposes of its own initiative to make options available to them and others at a time when they know that the option price, geared to the market value of the stock, did not reflect a substantial increment likely to be realized in short order and was therefore unfair to the corporation.

A rule requiring a minor officer to reject an option so tendered would not comport with the realities either of human nature or of corporate life. If the SEC had appealed the ruling dismissing this portion of the complaint as to Holyk and Mollison, I would have upheld the dismissal quite apart from the special circumstance that a refusal on their part could well have broken the wall of secrecy it was important for TGS to preserve. Whatever they knew or didn't know about Timmins, they were entitled to believe their superiors had reported the facts to the Option Committee unless they had information to the contrary. Stephens, Fogarty and Kline stand on an altogether different basis; as senior officers they had an obligation to inform the Committee that this was not the right time to grant options at 95% of the current price. Silence, when there is a duty to speak, can itself be a fraud. I am unimpressed with the argument that Stephens, Fogarty and Kline could not perform this duty on the peculiar facts of this case, because of the corporate need for secrecy during the land acquisition program. Non-management directors would not normally challenge a recommendation for postponement of an option plan from the President, the Executive Vice President, and the Vice President and General Counsel. Moreover, it should be possible for officers to communicate with directors, of all people, without fearing a breach of confidence. Hence, as one of the foregoing hypotheticals suggests, I am not at all sure that a company in the position of TGS might not have a claim against top officers who breached their duty of disclosure for the entire damage suffered as a result of the untimely issuance of options, rather than merely one for rescission of the options issued to them.[2] Since that issue is not before us, I merely make the reservation of my position clear. . . .

[The opinions of Judges Kaufman and Anderson (concurring), Judge Hays (concurring in part and dissenting in part), and Judges Moore and Lumbard (dissenting) are omitted.]

————

SEC v. TEXAS GULF SULPHUR CO., 446 F.2d 1301, 1307–08 (2d Cir.1971). "[On remand, the] district court required Holyk, Huntington, Clayton, and Darke to pay to TGS the profits they had derived (and, in Darke's case, also the profits which his tippees had derived) from their TGS stock between their respective purchase dates and April 17, 1964, when the ore strike was fully known to the public. The payments are to be held in escrow in an interest-bearing account for a period of five years, subject to disposition in such manner as the court might direct upon application by the SEC or other interested person, or on the court's own motion. At the end of five years any money remaining undisposed of would become the property of TGS. To protect the appellants against double liability, any private judgments against these appellants arising out of the events of this case are to be paid from this fund. . . .

"Appellants, of course, contend that the required restitution is . . . a penalty assessment. . . . [However, restitution] of the profits on these transactions merely deprives the appellants of the gains of their wrongful conduct. . . .

"Finally, appellants contend that the order is punitive because it contains no element of compensation to those who have been damaged. However, as the New York Court of Appeals in Diamond v. Oreamuno, 24 N.Y.2d 494, 499, 301 N.Y.S.2d 78, 81–82, 248 N.E.2d 910, 912–913 (1969), recognized, a corporate enterprise may well suffer harm 'when officers and directors abuse their position to obtain personal profits' since 'the effect may be to cast a cloud on the corporation's name, injure stockholder relations and undermine public regard for the corporation's securities.' Although the sellers of TGS stock who sold before April 17, 1964, may have a higher equity than

2. Though the Board of Directors of TGS ratified the issuance of the options after the Timmins discovery had been fully publicized, it obviously was of the belief that Kline had committed no serious wrong in remaining silent. Throughout this litigation TGS has supported the legality of the actions of all the defendants—the company's counsel having represented, among others, Stephens, Fogarty and Kline. Consequently, I agree with the majority in giving the Board's action no weight here. If a fraud of this kind may ever be cured by ratification, compare Continental Securities Co. v. Belmont, 206 N.Y. 7, 99 N.E. 138, 51 L.R.A., N.S., 112 (1912), with Claman v. Robertson, 164 Ohio St. 61, 128 N.E.2d 429 (1955); cf. Wilko v. Swan, 346 U.S. 427, 74 S.Ct. 182, 98 L.Ed. 168 (1953), that cannot be done without an appreciation of the illegality of the conduct proposed to be excused, cf. United Hotels Co. v. Mealey, 147 F.2d 816, 819 (2 Cir.1945).

TGS to recover from appellants the wrongful profits appellants obtained, this fact does not preclude conditional compensation to TGS."

American Bar Association, Committee on Federal Regulation of Securities, Report of the Task Force on Regulation of Insider Trading, Part I: Regulation under the Antifraud Provisions of the Securities Exchange Act of 1934

41 Bus.Law. 223 (1985).

THE POLICY BASIS FOR INSIDER TRADING REGULATION

The task force first considered whether, in today's market and legal environment, a sound policy basis remains for prohibiting the use of nonpublic information by one trader to gain advantage over others. . . .

In today's securities markets, where vast amounts of information are quickly available about corporate issuers (at least widely followed ones) and electronic communication is instantaneous, some respected scholars have argued that the markets themselves provide an adequate corrective for temporary informational advantage by promptly reporting the trading that occurs. They argue that the economic incentive of allowing a trader to use nonpublic information is of social value because it encourages and rewards analytic research and initiative. But other scholars see valid policy bases for continued regulation of unfair informational advantage even in today's impersonal, high-speed securities markets. The task force has considered these policy arguments and is persuaded that there are still valid and persuasive reasons for continuing insider trading regulation.

In our society, we traditionally abhor those who refuse to play by the rules, that is, the cheaters and the sneaks. A spitball pitcher, or a card shark with an ace up his sleeve, may win the game but not our respect. And if we know such a person is in the game, chances are we won't play. These commonsense observations suggest that two of the traditional bases for prohibitions against insider trading are still sound: the "fair play" and "integrity of the markets" arguments. The first relies on the basic policy that cheating is wrong and on the traditional sympathy for the victim of the cheat. The second rests on the oft-repeated argument that people will not entrust their resources to a marketplace they don't believe is fair, any more than a card player will put his chips on the table in a poker game that may be fixed. Although the task force knows of no empirical research that directly demonstrates that concerns about integrity affect market activity, both authoritative commentators[8] and common sense tell us that if investors

---

8. *See, e.g.,* comments of Arthur Levitt, Jr., Chairman of the American Stock Exchange, *quoted in* Business Week, April 29, 1985, at 79 ("If the investor thinks he's not getting a fair share, he's not going to invest and that is going to hurt capital formation in the long run").

do not anticipate fair treatment, they will avoid investing in securities. As a result, capital formation through securities offerings will become less attractive and more difficult. . . .

Several other forceful policy arguments favor insider trading prohibitions. When the nonpublic information originates within the corporation—as in the case of a new product discovery or an unannounced earnings increase or decrease—the information itself is corporate property until publicly released. Those who "take" it for their own advantage rather than the corporate good may be sued for their "misappropriation" of it.

If there were no penalty for personal use of such nonpublic information to gain a market profit, then officers, employees, and even directors of a corporation might keep such information to themselves for a time and trade upon it, rather than act in the corporate interest by promptly communicating the information through appropriate corporate channels. The flow of information from its corporate source to officers, directors, and other decision makers and to the investing public could thus be impeded by the incentive to delay long enough to speculate on a stock market profit. Some have argued that such profits are an appropriate reward for corporate entrepreneurs. The task force disagrees. Unbridled insider trading would distort the intended impact of corporate compensation programs approved by directors and shareholders and based on business performance. Both the beneficiaries and the amount of benefit would be unpredictable and not subject to corporate control; the random rewards would be unrelated to overall corporate performance or to specific compensation objectives.

These corporate structure arguments certainly provide support for prohibiting trading on nonpublic, *inside* information, that is, information originating from within the corporation. But these arguments provide less support for prohibiting trading on *market* information, that is, information that comes from outside the issuer but may affect the value of its securities, such as advance news of an impending tender offer, a favorable newspaper article, or an announcement of a major governmental decision.

We continue to believe, however, that a "disclose or abstain" rule should be applied even when only *market* information is involved. The traditional fairness and market integrity bases for regulating insider trading are still important to uphold when market information is involved. Moreover, one can posit that, if those having material, nonpublic market information could trade on it without fear of liability, the incentive to promptly move such information into the marketplace would be greatly reduced. Rather, those "in the know" would keep secret, and accumulate or liquidate a position on the basis of, the information for as long as possible to maximize their gain or minimize their loss. The task force believes the result of such behavior would be a less informed (not to mention less attractive) marketplace.

The task force believes that fairness, information efficiency, and market integrity are served by laws that discourage retaining material market information for personal advantage.

Although it has been argued that insider trading activity affects the market quickly, so that the economic value of the undisclosed information is reflected in market prices even before the information is announced, at a minimum this involves some fundamental, and potentially costly, unfairness to the uninformed traders on the other side of the initial trades by the insiders and their tippees.

In the judgment of the task force, these policy bases provide persuasive support for prohibitions against trading on the basis of material, nonpublic "inside information." They also support extending the prohibitions beyond corporate insiders to others who may, through improper means, obtain or abuse selective access to either material "inside information" or material "market information."

In a federal system like ours, another question should be considered: to what extent are the above policies the concern of federal as opposed to state law? If insider trading prohibitions are to be imposed because of a concern for market integrity and market information efficiency, the interests would clearly be federal since the securities markets are an integral part of interstate commerce. Although the corporate structure and the misappropriation of business property are not traditional areas of federal interest, because the securities markets are national—even international—in scope, the task force believes that exclusive reliance on state regulation would be both impractical and unwise. Federal standards are required.

———

UNITED STATES v. CHESTMAN, 947 F.2d 551 (2d Cir.1991), cert. denied 503 U.S. 1004, 112 S.Ct. 1759, 118 L.Ed.2d 422 (1992). (Winter, J., dissenting). "One commentator has attempted to explain the Supreme Court [insider-trading] decisions in terms of [a] business-property rationale.... See Easterbrook, [Insider Trading, Secret Agents, Evidentiary Privileges, and the Production of Information, 1981 Sup.Ct.Rev. 309,] at 309–39. That rationale may be summarized as follows. Information is perhaps the most precious commodity in commercial markets. It is expensive to produce, and, because it involves facts and ideas that can be easily photocopied or carried in one's head, there is a ubiquitous risk that those who pay to produce information will see others reap the profit from it. Where the profit from an activity is likely to be diverted, investment in that activity will decline. If the law fails to protect property rights in commercial information, therefore, less will be invested in generating such information. Id. at 313.

"For example, mining companies whose investments in geological surveys have revealed valuable deposits do not want word of the strike to get out until they have secured rights to the land.[3] If word does get out, the price of the land not only will go up, but other mining companies may also secure the rights. In either case, the mining company that invested in geological surveys (including the inevitably sizeable number of unsuccessful drillings) will see profits from that investment enjoyed by others. If mining companies are unable to keep the results of such surveys confidential, less will be invested in them.

"Similarly, firms that invest money in generating information about other companies with a view to some form of combination will maintain secrecy about their efforts, and if secrecy cannot be maintained, less will be invested in acquiring such information. Hostile acquirers will want to keep such information secret lest the target mount defensive actions or speculators purchase the target's stock. Even when friendly negotiations with the other company are undertaken, the acquirer will often require the target corporation to maintain secrecy about negotiations, lest the very fact of negotiation tip off others on the important fact that the two firms think a combination might be valuable.... In the instant matter, A & P made secrecy a condition of its acquisition of Waldbaum's.

"Insider trading may reduce the return on information in two ways. First, it creates incentives for insiders to generate or disclose information that may disregard the welfare of the corporation. Easterbrook, supra, at 332–33. That risk is not implicated by the facts in the present case, and no further discussion is presently required.

"Second, insider trading creates a risk that information will be prematurely disclosed by such trading, and the corporation will lose part or all of its property in that information. Id. at 331. Although trades by an insider may rarely affect market price, others who know of the insider's trading may notice that a trader is unusually successful, or simply perceive unusual activity in a stock and guess the information and/or make piggyback trades. Id. at 336. A broker who executes a trade for a geologist or for a financial printer may well draw relevant conclusions. Or, as in the instant matter, the trader ... may tell his or her broker about the inside information, who may then trade on his or her account, on clients' accounts, or may tell friends and relatives. One inside trader has publicly attributed his exposure in part to the fact that the bank through which he made trades piggybacked on the trades, as did the broker who made the trades for the bank. See Levine, The Inside Story of An Inside Trader, Fortune, May 21, 1990, at 80. Once activity in a stock reaches an unusual stage, others may guess the reason for the trading—the corporate secret. Insider trading thus increases the risk that confidential information acquired at a cost may be disclosed. If so, the owner of the information may lose its investment."

---

3. Although [*Texas Gulf Sulphur*] stressed the unfairness of insider trading to those who deal with the trader, the reason for the nondisclosure that allowed insider trading in TGS stock was the company's insider trading in real estate.

SEMERENKO v. CENDANT CORP., 223 F.3d 165 (3d Cir. 2000). " ... [W]e are persuaded by recent decisions in the Second Circuit and the Ninth Circuit that have addressed the scope of the 'in connection with' requirement when the alleged fraud involves the public dissemination of false and misleading information.... Those courts have generally adopted the standard articulated in Securities & Exch. Comm'n v. Texas Gulf Sulphur Co., 401 F.2d 833, 862 (2d Cir.1968) (in banc), and ... have held that, where the fraud alleged involves the public dissemination of information in a medium upon which an investor would presumably rely, the 'in connection with' element may be established by proof of the materiality of the misrepresentation and the means of its dissemination. Under that standard, it is irrelevant that the misrepresentations were not made for the purpose or the object of influencing the investment decisions of market participants. See In re Ames Dep't Stores Inc. Stock Litig., 991 F.2d at 965 (holding that an investor's reliance need not be envisioned to give rise to liability under § 10(b) and Rule 10b–5)."

SEC v. Zandford

Supreme Court of the United States, 2002.
535 U.S. 813.

■ JUSTICE STEVENS delivered the opinion of the Court.

The Securities and Exchange Commission (SEC) filed a civil complaint alleging that a stockbroker violated both § 10(b) of the Securities Exchange Act of 1934, 48 Stat. 891, as amended, 15 U.S.C. § 78j(b), and the SEC's Rule 10b–5, by selling his customer's securities and using the proceeds for his own benefit without the customer's knowledge or consent. The question presented is whether the alleged fraudulent conduct was "in connection with the purchase or sale of any security" within the meaning of the statute and the rule.

I

Between 1987 and 1991, respondent was employed as a securities broker in the Maryland branch of a New York brokerage firm. In 1987, he persuaded William Wood, an elderly man in poor health, to open a joint investment account for himself and his mentally retarded daughter. According to the SEC's complaint, the "stated investment objectives for the account were 'safety of principal and income.' " App. to Pet. for Cert. 27a. The Woods granted respondent discretion to manage their account and a general power of attorney to engage in securities transactions for their benefit without prior approval. Relying on respondent's promise to "conservatively invest" their money, the Woods entrusted him with $419,255. Before Mr. Wood's death in 1991, all of that money was gone.

In 1991, the National Association of Securities Dealers (NASD) conducted a routine examination of respondent's firm and discovered that on over 25 separate occasions, money had been transferred from the Woods' account to accounts controlled by respondent. In due course, respondent was indicted in the United States District Court for the District of Maryland on 13 counts of wire fraud in violation of 18 U.S.C. § 1343. App. to Pet. for Cert. 40a. The first count alleged that respondent sold securities in the Woods' account and then made personal use of the proceeds. Id., at 42a. Each of the other counts alleged that he made wire transfers between Maryland and New York that enabled him to withdraw specified sums from the Woods' accounts. Id., at 42a–50a. Some of those transfers involved respondent writing checks to himself from a mutual fund account held by the Woods, which required liquidating securities in order to redeem the checks. Respondent was convicted on all counts, sentenced to prison for 52 months, and ordered to pay $10,800 in restitution.

After respondent was indicted, the SEC filed a civil complaint in the same District Court alleging that respondent violated § 10(b) and Rule 10b–5 by engaging in a scheme to defraud the Woods and by misappropriating approximately $343,000 of the Woods' securities without their knowledge or consent. Id., at 27a. The SEC moved for partial summary judgment after respondent's criminal conviction, arguing that the judgment in the criminal case estopped respondent from contesting facts that established a violation of § 10(b).[13] Respondent filed a motion seeking discovery on the question whether his fraud had the requisite "connection with" the purchase or sale of a security. The District Court refused to allow discovery and entered summary judgment against respondent. It enjoined him from engaging in future violations of the securities laws and ordered him to disgorge $343,000 in ill-gotten gains.

The Court of Appeals for the Fourth Circuit reversed the summary judgment and remanded with directions for the District Court to dismiss the complaint. 238 F.3d 559 (2001).... The court ... held that the civil complaint did not sufficiently allege the necessary connection because the sales of the Woods' securities were merely incidental to a fraud that "lay in absconding with the proceeds" of sales that were conducted in "a routine and customary fashion," 238 F.3d 559 at 564. Respondent's "scheme was simply to steal the Woods' assets" rather than to engage "in manipulation of a particular security." 238 F.3d 559 at 565. Ultimately, the court refused "to stretch the language of the securities fraud provisions to encompass every conversion or theft that happens to involve securities." 238 F.3d 559 at 566. Adopting what amounts to a "fraud on the market" theory of the statute's coverage, the court held that without some "relationship to market integrity or investor understanding," there is no violation of § 10(b). 238 F.3d 559 at 563.

We granted the SEC's petition for a writ of certiorari, 534 U.S. 1015, 151 L. Ed. 2d 418, 122 S. Ct. 510 (2001), to review the Court of

---

13. The scope of Rule 10b–5 is coextensive with the coverage of § 10(b), see United States v. O'Hagan, 521 U.S. 642, 651 (1997); Ernst & Ernst v. Hochfelder, 425 U.S. 185, 214, 47 L. Ed. 2d 668, 96 S. Ct. 1375 (1976); therefore, we use § 10(b) to refer to both the statutory provision and the Rule....

Appeals' construction of the phrase "in connection with the purchase or sale of any security." Because the Court of Appeals ordered the complaint dismissed rather than remanding for reconsideration, we assume the allegations contained therein are true and affirm that disposition only if no set of facts would entitle petitioner to relief. See Hartford Fire Ins. Co. v. California, 509 U.S. 764, 811, 125 L. Ed. 2d 612, 113 S. Ct. 2891 (1993). We do not reach the question whether the record supports the District Court's grant of summary judgment in the SEC's favor—a question that requires all potential factual disputes to be resolved in respondent's favor. We merely hold that the allegations of the complaint, if true, entitle the SEC to relief; therefore, the Court of Appeals should not have directed that the complaint be dismissed.

II

Section 10(b) of the Securities Exchange Act makes it "unlawful for any person . . . to use or employ, in connection with the purchase or sale of any security . . . , any manipulative or deceptive device or contrivance in contravention of such rules and regulations as the [SEC] may prescribe." 15 U.S.C. § 78j. Rule 10b–5, which implements this provision, forbids the use, "in connection with the purchase or sale of any security," of "any device, scheme, or artifice to defraud" or any other "act, practice, or course of business" that "operates . . . as a fraud or deceit." 17 CFR § 240.10b–5 (2000). Among Congress' objectives in passing the Act was "to insure honest securities markets and thereby promote investor confidence" after the market crash of 1929. United States v. O'Hagan, 521 U.S. 642, 658 (1997); see also United States v. Naftalin, 441 U.S. 768, 775, 60 L. Ed. 2d 624, 99 S. Ct. 2077 (1979). More generally, Congress sought " 'to substitute a philosophy of full disclosure for the philosophy of caveat emptor and thus to achieve a high standard of business ethics in the securities industry.' " Affiliated Ute Citizens of Utah v. United States, 406 U.S. 128, 151 (1972) (quoting SEC v. Capital Gains Research Bureau, Inc., 375 U.S. 180, 186, 11 L. Ed. 2d 237, 84 S. Ct. 275 (1963)).

Consequently, we have explained that the statute should be "construed 'not technically and restrictively, but flexibly to effectuate its remedial purposes.' " 406 U.S. 128 at 151 (quoting Capital Gains Research Bureau, Inc., 375 U.S., at 195). In its role enforcing the Act, the SEC has consistently adopted a broad reading of the phrase "in connection with the purchase or sale of any security." It has maintained that a broker who accepts payment for securities that he never intends to deliver, or who sells customer securities with intent to misappropriate the proceeds, violates § 10(b) and Rule 10b–5. See, e.g., In re Bauer, 26 S. E. C. 770 (1947); In re Southeastern Securities Corp., 29 S. E. C. 609 (1949). This interpretation of the ambiguous text of § 10(b), in the context of formal adjudication, is entitled to deference if it is reasonable, see United States v. Mead Corp., 533 U.S. 218, 229–230, and n. 12 (2001). For the reasons set forth below, we think it is. While the statute must not be construed so broadly as to convert every common-law fraud that happens to involve securities into a violation of § 10(b), Marine Bank v. Weaver, 455 U.S. 551, 556, 71 L. Ed. 2d 409, 102 S. Ct. 1220 (1982) ("Congress, in enacting the securities laws, did not intend to provide a broad federal remedy for all fraud"), neither the SEC nor this Court has ever held that there must be a misrepresentation about the value of a particular security in order to run afoul of the Act.

The SEC claims respondent engaged in a fraudulent scheme in which he made sales of his customer's securities for his own benefit. Respondent submits that the sales themselves were perfectly lawful and that the subsequent misappropriation of the proceeds, though fraudulent, is not properly viewed as having the requisite connection with the sales; in his view, the alleged scheme is not materially different from a simple theft of cash or securities in an investment account. We disagree.

According to the complaint, respondent "engaged in a scheme to defraud" the Woods beginning in 1988, shortly after they opened their account, and that scheme continued throughout the 2–year period during which respondent made a series of transactions that enabled him to convert the proceeds of the sales of the Woods' securities to his own use. App. to Pet. for Cert. 27a–29a. The securities sales and respondent's fraudulent practices were not independent events. This is not a case in which, after a lawful transaction had been consummated, a broker decided to steal the proceeds and did so. Nor is it a case in which a thief simply invested the proceeds of a routine conversion in the stock market. Rather, respondent's fraud coincided with the sales themselves.

Taking the allegations in the complaint as true, each sale was made to further respondent's fraudulent scheme; each was deceptive because it was neither authorized by, nor disclosed to, the Woods. With regard to the sales of shares in the Woods' mutual fund, respondent initiated these transactions by writing a check to himself from that account, knowing that redeeming the check would require the sale of securities. Indeed, each time respondent "exercised his power of disposition for his own benefit," that conduct, "without more," was a fraud. United States v. Dunn, 268 U.S. 121, 131, 69 L. Ed. 876, 45 S. Ct. 451 (1925). In the aggregate, the sales are properly viewed as a "course of business" that operated as a fraud or deceit on a stockbroker's customer. . . .

. . . [T]he Woods were injured as investors through respondent's deceptions, which deprived them of any compensation for the sale of their valuable securities. They were duped into believing respondent would "conservatively invest" their assets in the stock market and that any transactions made on their behalf would be for their benefit for the " 'safety of principal and income.' " App. to Pet. for Cert. 27a. The fact that respondent misappropriated the proceeds of the sales provides persuasive evidence that he had violated § 10(b) when he made the sales, but misappropriation is not an essential element of the offense. . . . It is enough that the scheme to defraud and the sale of securities coincide.

. . . Respondent was only able to carry out his fraudulent scheme without making an affirmative misrepresentation because the Woods had trusted him to make transactions in their best interest without prior approval. . . . Not only does such a fraud prevent investors from trusting that their brokers are executing transactions for their benefit, but it undermines the value of a discretionary account like that held by the Woods. The benefit of a discretionary account is that it enables individuals, like the Woods, who lack the time, capacity, or know-how to supervise investment decisions, to delegate authority to a broker who will make decisions in their best interests without prior approval. If such individuals cannot rely on a broker to exercise that discretion for their benefit, then the account loses its added value. Moreover, any distinction between omissions and misrepresentations is illusory in the context of a broker who has a fiduciary duty to her clients. . . .

. . . [T]he SEC complaint describes a fraudulent scheme in which the securities transactions and breaches of fiduciary duty coincide. Those breaches were therefore "in connection with" securities sales within the meaning of § 10(b).[14] Accordingly, the judgment of the Court of Appeals is reversed, and the case is remanded for further proceedings consistent with this opinion.

It is so ordered.

SEC v. TEXAS GULF SULPHUR CO., 401 F.2d 833 (2d Cir.1968), cert. denied 394 U.S. 976, 89 S.Ct. 1454, 22 L.Ed.2d 756 (1969). "[I]t seems clear . . . that Congress when it used the phrase 'in connection with the purchase or sale of any security' intended only that the device employed, whatever it might be, be of a sort that would cause reasonable investors to rely thereon, and, in connection therewith, so relying, cause them to purchase or sell a corporation's securities. There is no indication that Congress intended that the corporations or persons responsible for the issuance of a misleading statement would not violate the section unless they engaged in related securities transactions or otherwise acted with wrongful motives; indeed, the obvious purposes of the Act to protect the investing public and to secure fair dealing in the securities markets would be seriously undermined by applying such a gloss onto the legislative language. . . . The mere fact that an insider did not engage in securities transactions does not negate the possibility of wrongful purpose; perhaps the market did not react to the misleading statement as much as was anticipated

14. Contrary to the Court of Appeals' prediction, 238 F.3d 559, 566 (C.A.4 2001), our analysis does not transform every breach of fiduciary duty into a federal securities violation. If, for example, a broker embezzles cash from a client's account or takes advantage of the fiduciary relationship to induce his client into a fraudulent real estate transaction, then the fraud would not include the requisite connection to a purchase or sale of securities. Tr. of Oral Arg. 16. Likewise if the broker told his client he was stealing the client's assets, that breach of fiduciary duty might be in connection with a sale of securities, but it would not involve a deceptive device or fraud. Cf. Santa Fe Industries, Inc. v. Green, 430 U.S. 462, 474–476, 51 L. Ed. 2d 480, 97 S. Ct. 1292 (1977).

or perhaps the wrongful purpose was something other than the desire to buy at a low price or sell at a high price.''

———

Basic Inc. v. Levinson

Supreme Court of the United States, 1988.
485 U.S. 224, 108 S.Ct. 978, 99 L.Ed.2d 194.

■ JUSTICE BLACKMUN delivered the opinion of the Court.

This case requires us to apply the materiality requirement of § 10(b) of the Securities Exchange Act of 1934, 48 Stat. 881, as amended, 15 U.S.C. § 78a *et seq.* (1934 Act), and the Securities and Exchange Commission's Rule 10b–5, promulgated thereunder, see 17 CFR § 240.10b–5 (1987), in the context of preliminary corporate merger discussions. We must also determine whether a person who traded a corporation's shares on a securities exchange after the issuance of a materially misleading statement by the corporation may invoke a rebuttable presumption that, in trading, he relied on the integrity of the price set by the market.

I

Prior to December 20, 1978, Basic Incorporated was a publicly traded company primarily engaged in the business of manufacturing chemical refractories for the steel industry. As early as 1965 or 1966, Combustion Engineering, Inc., a company producing mostly alumina-based refractories, expressed some interest in acquiring Basic, but was deterred from pursuing this inclination seriously because of antitrust concerns it then entertained. See App. 81–83. In 1976, however, regulatory action opened the way to a renewal of Combustion's interest. The "Strategic Plan," dated October 25, 1976, for Combustion's Industrial Products Group included the objective: "Acquire Basic Inc. $30 million." App. 337.

Beginning in September 1976, Combustion representatives had meetings and telephone conversations with Basic officers and directors, including petitioners here,[2] concerning the possibility of a merger. During 1977 and 1978, Basic made three public statements denying that it was engaged in merger negotiations.[4] On December 18,

---

2. In addition to Basic itself, petitioners are individuals who had been members of its board of directors prior to 1979; Anthony M. Caito, Samuel Eells, Jr., John A. Gelbach, Harley C. Lee, Max Muller, H. Chapman Rose, Edmund Q. Sylvester, and John C. Wilson, Jr. Another former director, Mathew J. Ludwig, was a party to the proceedings below but died on July 17, 1986, and is not a petitioner here. See Brief for Petitioners ii.

4. On October 21, 1977, after heavy trading and a new high in Basic stock, the

following news item appeared in the Cleveland Plain Dealer:

"[Basic] President Max Muller said the company knew no reason for the stock's activity and that no negotiations were under way with any company for a merger. He said Flintkote recently denied Wall Street rumors that it would make a tender offer of $25 a share for control of the Cleveland-based maker of refractories for the steel industry." App. 363.

1978, Basic asked the New York Stock Exchange to suspend trading in its shares and issued a release stating that it had been "approached" by another company concerning a merger. *Id.,* at 413. On December 19, Basic's board endorsed Combustion's offer of $46 per share for its common stock, *id.,* at 335, 414–416, and on the following day publicly announced its approval of Combustion's tender offer for all outstanding shares.

Respondents are former Basic shareholders who sold their stock after Basic's first public statement of October 21, 1977, and before the suspension of trading in December 1978. Respondents brought a class action against Basic and its directors, asserting that the defendants issued three false or misleading public statements and thereby were in violation of § 10(b) of the 1934 Act and of Rule 10b–5. Respondents alleged that they were injured by selling Basic shares at artificially depressed prices in a market affected by petitioners' misleading statements and in reliance thereon.

The District Court adopted a presumption of reliance by members of the plaintiff class upon petitioners' public statements that enabled the court to conclude that common questions of fact or law predominated over particular questions pertaining to individual plaintiffs. See Fed.Rule Civ.Proc. 23(b)(3). The District Court therefore certified respondents' class. On the merits, however, the District Court granted summary judgment for the defendants. It held that, as a matter of law, any misstatements were immaterial: there were no negotiations ongoing at the time of the first statement, and although negotiations were taking place when the second and third statements were issued, those negotiations were not "destined, with reasonable certainty, to become a merger agreement in principle." App. to Pet. for Cert. 103a.

The United States Court of Appeals for the Sixth Circuit affirmed the class certification, but reversed the District Court's summary judgment, and remanded the case. 786 F.2d 741 (1986). The court reasoned that while petitioners were under no general duty to disclose their discussions with Combustion, any statement the company voluntarily released could not be " 'so incomplete as to mislead.' " *Id.,* at 746, quoting SEC v. Texas Gulf Sulphur Co., 401 F.2d 833, 862 (C.A.2 1968) (en banc), cert. denied *sub nom.* Coates v. SEC, 394 U.S. 976 (1969). In the Court of Appeals' view, Basic's statements that no negotiations were taking place, and that it knew of no corporate developments to account for the heavy trading activity, were misleading. With respect to materiality, the court rejected the argument that

---

On September 25, 1978, in reply to an inquiry from the New York Stock Exchange, Basic issued a release concerning increased activity in its stock and stated that

> "management is unaware of any present or pending company development that would result in the abnormally heavy trading activity and price fluctuation in company shares that have been experienced in the past few days." *Id.,* at 401.

On November 6, 1978, Basic issued to its shareholders a "Nine Months Report 1978." This Report stated:

> "With regard to the stock market activity in the Company's shares we remain unaware of any present or pending developments which would account for the high volume of trading and price fluctuations in recent months." *Id.,* at 403.

preliminary merger discussions are immaterial as a matter of law, and held that "once a statement is made denying the existence of any discussions, even discussions that might not have been material in absence of the denial are material because they make the statement made untrue." 786 F.2d, at 749.

The Court of Appeals joined a number of other circuits in accepting the "fraud-on-the-market theory" to create a rebuttable presumption that respondents relied on petitioners' material misrepresentations, noting that without the presumption it would be impractical to certify a class under Fed.Rule Civ.Proc. 23(b)(3). See 786 F.2d, at 750–751.

We granted certiorari, 479 U.S. 1083 (1987), to resolve the split, see Part III, *infra*, among the Courts of Appeals as to the standard of materiality applicable to preliminary merger discussions, and to determine whether the courts below properly applied a presumption of reliance in certifying the class, rather than requiring each class member to show direct reliance on Basic's statements.

II.   . . .

. . . The Court . . . [has] explicitly has defined a standard of materiality under the securities laws, see *TSC Industries, Inc. v. Northway, Inc.*, 426 U.S. 438 (1976), concluding in the proxy-solicitation context that "[a]n omitted fact is material if there is a substantial likelihood that a reasonable shareholder would consider it important in deciding how to vote." *Id.*, at 449.[7] Acknowledging that certain information concerning corporate developments could well be of "dubious significance," *id.*, at 448, the Court was careful not to set too low a standard of materiality; it was concerned that a minimal standard might bring an overabundance of information within its reach, and lead management "simply to bury the shareholders in an avalanche of trivial information—a result that is hardly conducive to informed decisionmaking." *Id.*, at 448–449. It further explained that to fulfill the materiality requirement "there must be a substantial likelihood that the disclosure of the omitted fact would have been viewed by the reasonable investor as having significantly altered the 'total mix' of information made available." *Id.*, at 449. We now expressly adopt the *TSC Industries* standard of materiality for the § 10(b) and Rule 10b–5 context.

III

The application of this materiality standard to preliminary merger discussions is not self-evident. Where the impact of the corporate development on the target's fortune is certain and clear, the *TSC Industries* materiality definition admits straightforward application. Where, on the other hand, the event is contingent or speculative in nature, it is difficult to ascertain whether the "reasonable investor" would have considered the omitted information significant at the time.

---

7. *TSC Industries* arose under § 14(a), as amended, of the 1934 Act, 15 U.S.C.   § 78n(a), and Rule 14a–9, 17 CFR § 240.14a–9 (1975).

Merger negotiations, because of the ever-present possibility that the contemplated transaction will not be effectuated, fall into the latter category. . . .

Petitioners urge upon us a Third Circuit test for resolving this difficulty. See Brief for Petitioners 20–22. Under this approach, preliminary merger discussions do not become material until "agreement-in-principle" as to the price and structure of the transaction has been reached between the would-be merger partners. See *Greenfield v. Heublein, Inc.,* 742 F.2d 751, 757 (C.A.3 1984), cert. denied, 469 U.S. 1215 (1985). By definition, then, information concerning any negotiations not yet at the agreement-in-principle stage could be withheld or even misrepresented without a violation of Rule 10b–5.

[The Court rejected the "agreement in principle" test, concluding that "We . . . find no valid justification for artificially excluding from the definition of materiality information concerning merger discussions, which would otherwise be considered significant to the trading decision of a reasonable investor, merely because agreement-in-principle as to price and structure has not yet been reached by the parties or their representatives.]" . . .

Even before this Court's decision in *TSC Industries,* the Second Circuit had explained the role of the materiality requirement of Rule 10b–5, with respect to contingent or speculative information or events, in a manner that gave that term meaning that is independent of the other provisions of the Rule. Under such circumstances, materiality "will depend at any given time upon a balancing of both the indicated probability that the event will occur and the anticipated magnitude of the event in light of the totality of the company activity." *SEC v. Texas Gulf Sulphur Co.,* 401 F.2d, at 849. Interestingly, neither the Third Circuit decision adopting the agreement-in-principle test nor petitioners here take issue with this general standard. Rather, they suggest that with respect to preliminary merger discussions, there are good reasons to draw a line at agreement on price and structure.

In a subsequent decision, the late Judge Friendly, writing for a Second Circuit panel, applied the *Texas Gulf Sulphur* probability/magnitude approach in the specific context of preliminary merger negotiations. After acknowledging that materiality is something to be determined on the basis of the particular facts of each case, he stated:

> "Since a merger in which it is bought out is the most important event that can occur in a small corporation's life, to wit, its death, we think that inside information, as regards a merger of this sort, can become material at an earlier stage than would be the case as regards lesser transactions—and this even though the mortality rate of mergers in such formative stages is doubtless high."

SEC v. Geon Industries, Inc., 531 F.2d 39, 47–48 (C.A.2 1976). We agree with that analysis.

Whether merger discussions in any particular case are material therefore depends on the facts. Generally, in order to assess the probability that the event will occur, a factfinder will need to look to indicia of interest in the transaction at the highest corporate levels. Without attempting to catalog all such possible factors, we note by way of example that board resolutions, instructions to investment bankers, and actual negotiations between principals or their intermediaries may serve as indicia of interest. To assess the magnitude of the transaction to the issuer of the securities allegedly manipulated, a factfinder will need to consider such facts as the size of the two corporate entities and of the potential premiums over market value. No particular event or factor short of closing the transaction need be either necessary or sufficient by itself to render merger discussions material.

As we clarify today, materiality depends on the significance the reasonable investor would place on the withheld or misrepresented information. The fact-specific inquiry we endorse here is consistent with the approach a number of courts have taken in assessing the materiality of merger negotiations. Because the standard of materiality we have adopted differs from that used by both courts below, we remand the case for reconsideration of the question whether a grant of summary judgment is appropriate on this record.

IV

A

We turn to the question of reliance and the fraud-on-the-market theory. Succinctly put:

> "The fraud on the market theory is based on the hypothesis that, in an open and developed securities market, the price of a company's stock is determined by the available material information regarding the company and its business. . . . Misleading statements will therefore defraud purchasers of stock even if the purchasers do not directly rely on the misstatements. . . . The causal connection between the defendants' fraud and the plaintiffs' purchase of stock in such a case is no less significant than in a case of direct reliance on misrepresentations." *Peil v. Speiser*, 806 F.2d 1154, 1160–61 (C.A.3 1986).

Our task, of course, is not to assess the general validity of the theory, but to consider whether it was proper for the courts below to apply a rebuttable presumption of reliance, supported in part by the fraud-on-the-market theory.

This case required resolution of several common questions of law and fact concerning the falsity or misleading nature of the three public statements made by Basic, the presence or absence of scienter, and the materiality of the misrepresentations, if any. In their amended complaint, the named plaintiffs alleged that in reliance on Basic's statements they sold their shares of Basic stock in the depressed market created by petitioners. See Amended Complaint in No. C79–1220 (ND Ohio) §§ 27, 29, 35, 40; see also *id.*, at § 33 (alleging effect on market price of Basic's statements). Requiring proof of individualized reliance from each member of the proposed plaintiff class effectively would have prevented respondents from proceeding with a class action, since individual issues then would have overwhelmed the common ones. The District Court found that the presumption of reliance created by the fraud-on-the-market theory provided "a practical resolution to the problem of balancing the substantive requirement of proof of reliance in securities cases against the procedural requisites of [Fed.Rule Civ.Proc.] 23." The District Court thus concluded that with reference to each public statement and its impact upon the open market for Basic shares, common questions predominated over individual questions, as required by Fed.Rule Civ.Proc. 23(a)(2) and (b)(3).

Petitioners and their *amici* complain that the fraud-on-the-market theory effectively eliminates the requirement that a plaintiff asserting a claim under Rule 10b–5 prove reliance. They note that reliance is and long has been an element of common-law fraud, see *e.g.*, Restatement (Second) of Torts § 525 (1977); Prosser and Keeton on The Law of Torts § 108 (5th ed. 1984), and argue that because the analogous express right of action includes a reliance requirement, see, *e.g.*, § 18(a) of the 1934 Act, as amended, 15 U.S.C. § 78r(a), so too must an action implied under § 10(b).

We agree that reliance is an element of a Rule 10b–5 cause of action. See *Ernst & Ernst v. Hochfelder*, 425 U.S., at 206 (quoting Senate Report). Reliance provides the requisite causal connection between a defendant's misrepresentation and a plaintiff's injury. See, *e.g.*, *Wilson v. Comtech Telecommunications Corp.*, 648 F.2d 88, 92 (C.A.2 1981); *List v. Fashion Park, Inc.*, 340 F.2d 457, 462 (CA2), cert. denied *sub nom. List v. Lerner*, 382 U.S. 811 (1965). There is, however, more than one way to demonstrate the causal connection. Indeed, we previously have dispensed with a requirement of positive proof of reliance, where a duty to disclose material information had been breached, concluding that the necessary nexus between the plaintiffs' injury and the defendant's wrongful conduct had been established. See *Affiliated Ute Citizens v. United States*, 406 U.S., at 153–154. Similarly, we did not require proof that material omissions or misstatements in a proxy statement decisively affected voting, because the proxy solicitation itself, rather than the defect in the solicitation materials, served as an essential link in the transaction. See *Mills v. Electric Auto–Lite Co.*, 396 U.S. 375, 384–385 (1970).

The modern securities markets, literally involving millions of shares changing hands daily, differ from the face-to-face transactions contemplated by early fraud cases, and our understanding of Rule 10b–5's reliance requirement must encompass these differences.

"In face-to-face transactions, the inquiry into an investor's reliance upon information is into the subjective pricing of that information by that investor. With the presence of a market, the market is interposed between seller and buyer and, ideally, transmits information to the investor in the processed form of a market price. Thus the market is performing a substantial part of the valuation process performed by the investor in a face-to-face transaction. The market is acting as the unpaid agent of the investor, informing him that given all the information available to it, the value of the stock is worth the market price." *In re LTV Securities Litigation,* 88 F.R.D. 134, 143 (N.D.Tex.1980).

Accord, *e.g., Peil v. Speiser,* 806 F.2d, at 1161 ("In an open and developed market, the dissemination of material misrepresentations or withholding of material information typically affects the price of the stock, and purchasers generally rely on the price of the stock as a reflection of its value"); *Blackie v. Barrack,* 524 F.2d 891, 908 (C.A.9 1975) ("the same causal nexus can be adequately established indirectly, by proof of materiality coupled with the common sense that a stock purchaser does not ordinarily seek to purchase a loss in the form of artificially inflated stock"), cert. denied, 429 U.S. 816 (1976).

B

Presumptions typically serve to assist courts in managing circumstances in which direct proof, for one reason or another, is rendered difficult. See, *e.g.,* D. Louisell & C. Mueller, Federal Evidence 541–542 (1977). The courts below accepted a presumption, created by the fraud-on-the-market theory and subject to rebuttal by petitioners, that persons who had traded Basic shares had done so in reliance on the integrity of the price set by the market, but because of petitioners' material misrepresentations that price had been fraudulently depressed. Requiring a plaintiff to show a speculative state of facts, *i.e.,* how he would have acted if omitted material information had been disclosed, see *Affiliated Ute Citizens v. United States,* 406 U.S., at 153–154, or if the misrepresentation had not been made, see *Sharp v. Coopers & Lybrand,* 649 F.2d 175, 188 (C.A.3 1981), cert. denied, 455 U.S. 938 (1982), would place an unnecessarily unrealistic evidentiary burden on the Rule 10b–5 plaintiff who has traded on an impersonal market. Cf. *Mills v. Electric Auto–Lite Co.,* 396 U.S., at 385.

Arising out of considerations of fairness, public policy, and probability, as well as judicial economy, presumptions are also useful devices for allocating the burdens of proof between parties. See E. Cleary, McCormick on Evidence 968–969 (3rd ed. 1984); see also Fed.Rule Evid. 301 and notes. The presumption of reliance employed in this case is consistent with, and, by facilitating Rule 10b–5 litigation, supports, the congressional policy embodied in the 1934 Act. In drafting that Act, Congress expressly relied on the premise that securities markets are affected by information, and enacted legislation to facilitate an investor's reliance on the integrity of those markets.…

The presumption is also supported by common sense and probability. Recent empirical studies have tended to confirm Congress' premise that the market price of shares traded on well-developed markets reflects all publicly available information, and, hence, any material misrepresentations. It has been noted that "it is hard to imagine that there ever is a buyer or seller who does not rely on market integrity. Who would knowingly roll the dice in a crooked crap game?" *Schlanger v. Four–Phase Systems, Inc.,* 555 F.Supp. 535, 538 (S.D.N.Y.1982). Indeed, nearly every court that has considered the proposition has concluded that where materially misleading statements have been disseminated into an impersonal, well-developed market for securities, the reliance of individual plaintiffs on the integrity of the market price may be presumed. Commentators generally have applauded the adoption of one variation or another of the fraud-on-the-market theory. An investor who buys or sells stock at the price set by the market does so in reliance on the integrity of that price. Because most publicly available information is reflected in market price, an investor's reliance on any public material misrepresentations, therefore, may be presumed for purposes of a Rule 10b–5 action.

C

The Court of Appeals found that petitioners "made public, material misrepresentations and [respondents] sold Basic stock in an impersonal, efficient market. Thus the class, as defined by the district court, has established the threshold facts for proving their loss." 786 F.2d, at 751. The court acknowledged that petitioners may rebut proof of the elements giving rise to the presumption, or show that the misrepresentation in fact did not lead to a distortion of price or that an individual plaintiff traded or would have traded despite his knowing the statement was false. *Id.,* at 750, n. 6.

Any showing that severs the link between the alleged misrepresentation and either the price received (or paid) by the plaintiff, or his decision to trade at a fair market price, will be sufficient to rebut the presumption of reliance. For example, if petitioners could show that the "market makers" were privy to the truth about the merger discussions here with Combustion, and thus that the market price would not have been affected by their misrepresentations, the causal connection could be broken: the basis for finding that the fraud had been transmitted through market price would be gone. Similarly, if, despite petitioners' allegedly fraudulent attempt to manipulate market price, news of the merger discussions credibly entered the market and dissipated the effects of the misstatements, those who traded Basic shares after the corrective statements would have no direct or indirect connection with the fraud. Petitioners also could rebut the presumption of reliance as to plaintiffs who would have divested themselves of their Basic shares without relying on the integrity of the market. For example, a plaintiff who believed that Basic's statements were false and that Basic was indeed engaged in merger discussions, and who consequently believed that Basic stock was artificially underpriced, but sold his shares nevertheless because of other unrelated concerns, *e.g.,* potential antitrust problems, or political pressures to divest from shares of certain businesses, could not be said to have relied on the integrity of a price he knew had been manipulated.

V

In summary:

1. We specifically adopt, for the § 10(b) and Rule 10b–5 context, the standard of materiality set forth in *TSC Industries, Inc. v. Northway, Inc.*, 426 U.S., at 449.

2. We reject "agreement-in-principle as to price and structure" as the bright-line rule for materiality. . . .

4. Materiality in the merger context depends on the probability that the transaction will be consummated, and its significance to the issuer of the securities. Materiality depends on the facts and thus is to be determined on a case-by-case basis.

5. It is not inappropriate to apply a presumption of reliance supported by the fraud-on-the-market theory.

6. That presumption, however, is rebuttable.

7. The District Court's certification of the class here was appropriate when made but is subject on remand to such adjustment, if any, as developing circumstances demand.

The judgment of the Court of Appeals is vacated and the case is remanded to that court for further proceedings consistent with this opinion.

It is so ordered.

■ THE CHIEF JUSTICE, JUSTICE SCALIA, and JUSTICE KENNEDY took no part in the consideration or decision of this case.

■ JUSTICE WHITE, with whom JUSTICE O'CONNOR joins, concurring in part and dissenting in part.

I join Parts I–III of the Court's opinion, as I agree that the standard of materiality we set forth in *TSC Industries, Inc. v. Northway, Inc.*, 426 U.S. 438, 449, 96 S.Ct. 2126, 48 L.Ed.2d 757 (1976), should be applied to actions under § 10(b) and Rule 10b–5. But I dissent from the remainder of the Court's holding because I do not agree that the "fraud-on-the-market" theory should be applied in this case. . . .

At the bottom of the Court's conclusion that the fraud-on-the-market theory sustains a presumption of reliance is the assumption that individuals rely "on the integrity of the market price" when buying or selling stock in "impersonal, well-developed market[s] for securities." *Ante,* at 21–22. Even if I was prepared to accept (as a matter of common sense or general understanding) the assumption that most persons buying or selling stock do so in response to the market price, the fraud-on-the-market theory goes further. For in adopting a "presumption of reliance," the Court *also* assumes that buyers and sellers rely—not just on the market price—but on the *"integrity"* of that price. It is this aspect of the fraud-on-the-market hypothesis which most mystifies me.

To define the term "integrity of the market price," the majority quotes approvingly from cases which suggest that investors are entitled to " 'rely on the price of a stock as a reflection of its value.' " But the meaning of this phrase eludes me, for it implicitly suggests that stocks have some "true value" that is measurable by a standard other than their market price. While the Scholastics of Medieval times professed a means to make such a valuation of a commodity's "worth," I doubt that the federal courts of our day are similarly equipped. . . .

————

SECURITIES ACT § 27A SECURITIES EXCHANGE ACT § 21E

[See Statutory Supplement]

————

SECURITIES ACT RULE 175

SECURITIES EXCHANGE ACT RULE 3b–6

[See Statutory Supplement]

————

IN RE VERIFONE SECURITIES LITIGATION, 784 F.Supp. 1471, 1479 (N.D.Cal.1992), aff'd sub nom. Halkin v. VeriFone, Inc., 11 F.3d 865 (9th Cir.1993). "[The] fraud-on-the-market theory recognizes that average investors in a developed securities market do not personally need access to the elaborate disclosure of documents and accounting data required by our securities laws. Market professionals obtain information from myriad sources, including the issuer, market analysts, and the financial and trade press. The professional traders analyze information about securities, and the trading activity of these knowledgeable investors pushes the price of the security toward a value which reflects all publicly available information. In this way, securities prices on the national exchanges reflect (albeit not perfectly) the expected future cash flows from the security. An investor making trades who has not relied on particular disclosures is presumed under the fraud-on-the-market theory to rely on the integrity of information reflected in the market price of the security. *Basic Inc.,* 485 U.S. at 247, 108 S.Ct. at 991. In this way, an investor who has never seen or heard of a fraudulent disclosure is no less a victim than one who pored over its details.

"The fraud-on-the-market theory thus shifts the inquiry from whether an individual investor was fooled to whether the market as a whole was fooled. Hence, the theory not so much eliminates the reliance requirement as subsumes it in the fraud-on-the-market analysis. In the same way, the theory also subsumes the inquiry into materiality, causation and damages. For if a misleading or fraudulent disclosure or omission could have had no effect on the security's market price, the information cannot have been material. Similarly, if a misstatement or omission had no effect on the market price (because, for example, the market already had the correct information from other sources) then there could be no causation and no damages."

––––––––

Richard A. Brealey & Stewart C. Myers, Principles of Corporate Finance

Seventh ed., 2003.

WHAT IS AN EFFICIENT MARKET?

A Startling Discovery: Price Changes Are Random

As is so often the case with important ideas, the concept of efficient capital markets stemmed from a chance discovery. In 1953 Maurice Kendall, a British statistician, presented a controversial paper to the Royal Statistical Society on the behavior of stock and commodity prices. Kendall had expected to find regular price cycles, but to his surprise they did not seem to exist. Each series appeared to be "a 'wandering' one, almost as if once a week the Demon of Chance drew a random number . . . and added it to the current price to determine the next week's price." In other words, the prices of stocks and commodities seemed to follow a random walk. . . .

When Maurice Kendall suggested that stock prices follow a random walk, he was implying that the price changes are independent of one another . . .

Three Forms of Market Efficiency

You should see . . . why prices in competitive markets must follow a random walk. If past price changes could be used to predict future price changes, investors could make easy profits. But in competitive markets easy profits don't last. As investors try to take advantage of the information in past prices, prices adjust immediately until the superior profits from studying past price movements disappear. As a result, all the information in past prices will be reflected in today's stock price, not tomorrow's. Patterns in prices will no longer exist and price changes in one period will be independent of changes in the next. In other words, the share price will follow a random walk.

In competitive markets today's stock price must already reflect the information in past prices. But why stop there? If markets are competitive, shouldn't today's stock price reflect all the information that is available to investors? If so, securities will be fairly priced and security returns will be unpredictable, whatever information you consider.

Economists often define three levels of market efficiency, which are distinguished by the degree of information reflected in security prices. In the first level, prices reflect the information contained in the record of past prices. This is called the weak form of efficiency. If markets are efficient in the weak sense, then it is impossible to make consistently superior profits by studying past returns. Prices will follow a random walk.

The second level of efficiency requires that prices reflect not just past prices but all other published information, such as you might get from reading the financial press. This is known as the semistrong form of market efficiency. If markets are efficient in this sense, then prices will adjust immediately to public information such as the announcement of the last quarter's earnings, a new issue of stock, a proposal to merge two companies, and so on.

Finally, we might envisage a strong form of efficiency, in which prices reflect all the information that can be acquired by painstaking analysis of the company and the economy. In such a market we would observe lucky and unlucky investors, but we wouldn't find any superior investment managers who can consistently beat the market.

PUZZLES AND ANOMALIES . . .

Almost without exception, early researchers concluded that the efficient market hypothesis was a remarkably good description of reality. So powerful was the evidence that any dissenting research was regarded with suspicion. But eventually the readers of finance journals grew weary of hearing the same message. The interesting articles became those that turned up some puzzle. Soon the journals were packed with evidence of anomalies that investors have apparently failed to exploit. . . .

Professional Investors, Irrational Exuberance, and the Dot.com Bubble

Investors in technology stocks in the 1990s saw an extraordinary run-up in the value of their holdings. The Nasdaq Composite Index, which has a heavy weighting in high-tech stocks, rose 580 percent from the start of 1995 to its high in March 2000. Then even more rapidly than it began, the boom ended. By November 2001 the Nasdaq index had fallen 64 percent.

Some of the largest price gains and losses were experienced by the new "dot.com stocks." For example, Yahoo! Shares, which began trading in April 1996, appreciated by 1,400 percent in just four years. At this point Yahoo! Stock was valued at $124 billion, more than that of GM, Heinz, and Boeing combined. It was not, however, to last; just over a year later Yahoo!'s market capitalization was little more than $6 billion.

What caused the boom in high-tech stocks? Alan Greenspan, chairman of the Federal Reserve, attributed the run-up in prices to "irrational exuberance," a view that was shared by Professor Robert Shiller from Yale. In his book *Irrational Exuberance*[18] Shiller argued that, as the bull market developed, it generated optimism about the future and stimulated demand for shares.[19] Moreover, as investors

18. See R.J. Shiller, *Irrational Exuberance*, Broadway Books, 2001. Shiller also discusses behavioral explanations for the boom in R.J. Shiller, "Bubbles, Human Judgment, and Expert Opinion," Cowles Foundation Discussion Paper No. 1303, Cowles Foundation for Research in Economics, Yale University, New Haven, CT, May 2001.

19. Some economists believe that the market price is prone to "bubbles"—situaracked up profits on their stocks, they became even more confident in their opinions.

But this brings us back to the $64,000 question. If Shiller was right and individual investors were carried away by irrational optimism, why didn't smart professional investors step in, sell high-tech stocks, and force their prices down to fair value? Were the pros also carried away on the same wave of euphoria? Or were they rationally reluctant to undertake more than a limited amount of selling if they could not be sure where and when the boom would end?

The Crash of 1987

On Monday, October 19, 1987, the Dow Jones Industrial Average (the Dow) fell 23 percent in one day. Immediately after the crash, everybody started to ask . . . "Do prices reflect fundamental values?" . . .

. . . [W]hy did prices fall so sharply? There was no obvious, new fundamental information to justify such a sharp and widespread decline in share values. For this reason, the idea that the market price is the best estimate of intrinsic value seems less compelling than before the crash. It appears that either prices were irrationally high before Black Monday or irrationally low afterward. Could the theory of efficient markets be another casualty of the crash?

The events of October 1987 remind us how exceptionally difficult it is to value common stocks from scratch. . . .

The extreme difficulty of valuing common stocks from scratch has two important consequences. First, investors almost always price a common stock relative to yesterday's price or relative to today's price of comparable securities. In other words, they generally take yesterday's price as correct, adjusting upward or downward on the basis of today's information. If information arrives smoothly, then as time passes, investors become more and more confident that today's market level is correct. However, when investors lose confidence in the benchmark of yesterday's price, there may be a period of confused trading and volatile prices before a new benchmark is established.

Second, the hypothesis that stock price always equals intrinsic value is nearly impossible to test, precisely because it's so difficult to calculate intrinsic value without referring to prices. Thus the crash didn't conclusively disprove the hypothesis, but many people now find it less plausible.

However, the crash does not undermine the evidence for market efficiency with respect to *relative* prices. Take, for example, Hershey stock, which sold for $66 in November 2001. Could we prove that true intrinsic value is $66? No, but we could be more confident that the price of Hershey should be roughly double that of Smucker ($33)

tions in which price grows faster than fundamental value, but investors don't sell because they expect prices to keep rising. Of course, all such bubbles pop eventually, but they can in theory be self-sustaining for a while. *The Journal of Economic Perspectives* 4 (Spring 1990) contains several nontechnical articles on bubbles.

since Hershey's earnings per share and dividend were about twice those of Smucker and the two shares had similar growth prospects. Moreover, if either company announced unexpectedly higher earnings, we could be quite confident that its share price would respond instantly and without bias. In other words, the subsequent price would be set correctly relative to the prior price. The most important lessons of market efficiency for the corporate financial manager are concerned with relative efficiency.

THE SIX LESSONS OF MARKET EFFICIENCY

Lesson 1: Markets Have No Memory

The weak form of the efficient-market hypothesis states that the sequence of past price changes contains no information about future changes. Economists express the same idea more concisely when they say that the market has no memory....

Lesson 2: Trust Market Prices

In an efficient market you can trust prices, for they impound all available information about the value of each security. This means that in an efficient market, there is no way for most investors to achieve consistently superior rates of return. To do so, you not only need to know more than anyone else, but you also need to know more than everyone else....

Lesson 3: Read the Entrails

If the market is efficient, prices impound all available information. Therefore, if we can only learn to read the entrails, security prices can tell us a lot about the future. For example, ... if the company's bonds are offering a much higher yield than the average, you can deduce that the firm is probably in trouble....

Lesson 4: There Are No Financial Illusions

In an efficient market there are no financial illusions. Investors are unromantically concerned with the firm's cash flows and the portion of those cash flows to which they are entitled....

Lesson 5: The Do–It–Yourself Alternative

In an efficient market investors will not pay others for what they can do equally well themselves.... [M]any of the controversies in corporate financing center on how well individuals can replicate corporate financial decisions. For example, companies often justify mergers on the grounds that they produce a more diversified and hence more stable firm. But if investors can hold the stocks of both companies why should they thank the companies for diversifying? It is much easier and cheaper for them to diversify than it is for the firm....

Lesson 6: Seen One Stock, Seen Them All

The elasticity of demand for any article measures the percentage change in the quantity demanded for each percentage addition to the price. If the article has close substitutes, the elasticity will be strongly negative; if not, it will be near zero. For example, coffee, which is a staple commodity, has a demand elasticity of about − .2. This means that a 5 percent increase in the price of coffee changes sales by − .2 − .05 = − .01; in other words, it reduces demand by only 1 percent. Consumers are likely to regard different brands of coffee as much closer substitutes for each other. Therefore, the demand elasticity for a particular brand could be in the region of, say, − 2.0. A 5 percent increase in the price of Maxwell House relative to that of Folgers would in this case reduce demand by 10 percent.

Investors don't buy a stock for its unique qualities; they buy it because it offers the prospect of a fair return for its risk. This means that stocks should be like very similar brands of coffee, almost perfect substitutes. Therefore, the demand for a company's stock should be highly elastic. If its prospective return is too low relative to its risk, nobody will want to hold that stock. If the reverse is true, everybody will scramble to buy.

Suppose that you want to sell a large block of stock. Since demand is elastic, you naturally conclude that you need only to cut the offering price very slightly to sell your stock. Unfortunately, that doesn't necessarily follow. When you come to sell your stock, other investors may suspect that you want to get rid of it because you know something they don't. Therefore, they will revise their assessment of the stock's value downward. Demand is still elastic, but the whole demand curve moves down. Elastic demand does not imply that stock prices never change when a large sale or purchase occurs; it does imply that you can sell large blocks of stock at close to the market price as long as you can convince other investors that you have no private information. . . .

———

DAINES & HANSON, THE CORPORATE LAW PARADOX: THE CASE FOR RESTRUCTURING CORPORATE LAW, 102 Yale L.J. 577, 614–15 (1992). "Beginning in the mid—1980's, doubts regarding the ECMH emerged first in the financial economics literature, and then began to trickle into the legal literature. But what began as a trickle has more recently become a deluge. Legal scholars familiar with current financial economics literature agree that there is now reason to doubt the efficiency of markets. Professors Macey, Miller, Mitchell and Netter summarize the current research as follows: '[W]e can at a minimum conclude that substantial disagreement exists among financial economists about what conclusions empirical tests of market efficiency support.' Indeed, 'substantial disagreement exists about to what degree markets are efficient, how to test for efficiency, and even the definition of efficiency.' Similarly, Professor Langevoort concludes from his review of the current financial economics literature that 'what is important for present purposes seems beyond debate: strong claims of efficiency are debatable.'

"To understand the source of the new doubts, it is helpful to recognize that the ECMH makes *two* general efficiency claims—namely, that the stock market is both informationally efficient and fundamentally efficient: The market is 'informationally efficient' if all public information is immediately incorporated into the stock price; it is 'fundamentally efficient' if stock prices accurately reflect only information relating to the net present value of the corporation's future profits. A growing body of work in financial economics now suggests, first, that informational efficiency—for which there *is* substantial empirical support—does not imply fundamental efficiency, and, second, that both the empirical and theoretical bases for the belief that markets are fundamentally efficient are suspect."

NOTE ON FRAUD ON THE MARKET

1. When is a market efficient for purposes on the fraud-on-the-market principle? In an influential decision, Cammer v. Bloom, 711 F.Supp. 1264, 1286–87 (D.N.J. 1989), the court set out a five-factor test: "Whether the stock trades at a high weekly volume; second, whether securities analysts follow and report on the stock; third, whether the stock has market makers and arbitrageurs; fourth, whether the company is eligible to file SEC registration form S–3, as opposed to form S–1 or S–2; and fifth, whether there are empirical facts showing a cause and effect relationship between unexpected corporate events or financial releases and an immediate response in the stock price."

2. A corollary of the fraud-on-the-market principle is the so-called "truth-on-the-market" principle. Under this corollary, a misrepresentation is immaterial if the information is already known to the market, because the misrepresentation cannot then defraud the market. See Ganino v. Citizens Utilities, 228 F.3d 154 (2d Cir. 2000).

NOTE ON CAUSATION AND RELIANCE

In principle, it is well-established that causation and reliance are required elements of a private action under Rule 10b–5. In practice, however, those requirements have sometimes proved to be elusive or even illusory.

1. *Causation.* In the area of causation, the case-law under Rule 10b–5 has distinguished between "transaction causation" and "loss causation."

Transaction causation means that there must be a causal connection between the defendant's violation of Rule 10b–5 and the plaintiff's purchase or sale of a security. To satisfy this requirement, a violation of rule 10b–5 must have caused the plaintiff to engage in the transaction in question. Schlick v. Penn–Dixie Cement Corp., 507 F.2d 374 (2d Cir. 1974). Accordingly, the plaintiff must allege and show that but for the fraudulent statement or omission, she would not have entered into the transaction. Transaction causation has been analogized to reliance. See Currie v. Cayman Resources Corp., 835 F.2d 780, 785 (11th Cir.1988).

The meaning of *loss causation* is harder to pin down. The best interpretation of this concept is that the defendant's wrongful act not only must have caused the plaintiff to buy or sell a security (transaction causation); it must also have been the cause of the plaintiff's *loss* on the security. In contrast to transaction causation, loss causation requires a showing that the violation of rule 10b–5 caused the economic harm of which the plaintiff complains. While transaction causation is generally understood as reliance, loss causation has often been described as proximate cause, meaning in part that the damages suffered by plaintiff must be a foreseeable consequence of any misrepresentation or material omission. An alternative formulation of loss causation is that it requires that "the misrepresentation touches upon the reasons for the investment's decline in value." Binder v. Gillespie, 184 F.3d 1059 (9th Cir. 1999). As stated in Suez Equity v. Toronto–Dominion Bank, 250 F.3d 87 (2d Cir. 2001), "[t]he loss causation inquiry typically examines how directly the subject of the [violation] caused the loss, and whether the resulting loss was a foreseeable outcome of the [violation]," while also taking into account issues such as the presence of intervening causes and the lapse of time between the behavior complained of and the loss.

Essentially, "loss causation" is a fancy name for the concept that even if an investment is induced by a violation of Rule 10b–5, the investor's loss may have been the result of an investment risk that was independent of the violation. "[W]hen an investor makes any investment he or she assumes certain investment risks. It may be too harsh a rule under rule 10b–5 that would place the wrongdoer in the position of insurer against those market risks. Otherwise, for example, a seller who fraudulently induced a purchase of securities in early October, 1987 would be an insurer against the precipitous price decline caused in large part by the market crash on October 19." 2 T. Hazen, *Securities Regulation 104* (2d ed. 1990). In Caremark, Inc. v. Coram Healthcare Corp., 113 F.3d 645 (7th Cir. 1997), the court said "To plead transaction causation, the plaintiff must allege that it would not have invested in the instrument if the defendant had stated truthfully the material facts at the time of the sale. To plead loss causation, the plaintiff must allege that [it] was the very facts about which the plaintiff lied which caused its injuries."

The meaning of the loss-causation concept, and the difficulty that can arise in applying the concept, are exemplified by a pair of cases, Huddleston v. Herman & MacLean, 640 F.2d 534, 549 n. 25 (5th Cir.1981), *aff'd in part, rev'd in part on other grounds* 459 U.S. 375,

103 S.Ct. 683, 74 L.Ed.2d 548 (1983), and *In re* Washington Public Power Supply System, 650 F.Supp. 1346, 1354 (W.D.Wash.1986). In *Huddleston*, the Fifth Circuit court used the following example to explain loss causation:

> [Assume that a vessel is described in a prospectus as having] a certain capacity when in fact it had less capacity than was represented in the prospectus. However, the prospectus does disclose truthfully that the vessel will not be insured. One week after the investment the vessel sinks as a result of a casualty and the stock becomes worthless. In such circumstances, a fact-finder might conclude that the misrepresentation was material and relied upon by the investor but that it did not cause the loss.

In *Washington Public Power*, the court criticized this example:

> By misrepresenting the capacity of the ship, the investor was induced to pay a certain price for stock in the venture. As a result of the misrepresentation, the investor paid more for the stock than it was worth. When the ship sank, the entire investment was lost. The investor, however, was injured by more than the true value of the investment because he paid an inflated price for the stock. His damages thus consist of two components: the value lost due to the casualty and the amount lost because he overpaid for the stock. This latter component of damages is related directly to the initial misrepresentation. Hence, this amount should be recoverable in an action for securities fraud.

2. *Reliance.* At one time, it seemed that the rule that reliance is an element of a private action would require the plaintiff to prove that he actually and specifically relied on the defendant's wrongful statement or omission. Later, however, the requirement of reliance became radically transformed. The reasons for the transformation differed somewhat as to (i) omissions or nondisclosure and (ii) affirmative misstatements.

(i) *Omissions or nondisclosure.* Reliance on an omission or nondisclosure is a questionable concept. We can say that *A* acted—bought or sold at a given price—in reliance on what *B* told him, but we can seldom say that *A* acted in reliance on *B*'s silence. What we *can* say in the latter case is that a reasonable investor who knew the omitted fact probably would or would not have bought or sold at the given price. In TSC Industries v. Northway, Inc., a major foundation for *Basic*, the Supreme Court held that the standard of *materiality* in a nondisclosure case is satisfied by "a showing of a substantial likelihood that, under all the circumstances, the omitted fact would have assumed actual significance in the deliberations of the reasonable shareholder." 426 U.S. 438, 449, 96 S.Ct. 2126, 2132, 48 L.Ed.2d 757 (1976). This standard is so close to what must be shown to prove causation in a nondisclosure case that for all intents and purposes, causation in such a case collapses into materiality. Thus in Affiliated Ute Citizens of Utah v. United States, 406 U.S. 128, 92 S.Ct. 1456, 31 L.Ed.2d 741 (1972), a bank purchased stock from a group of unsophisticated investors, without disclosing that the stock was selling at a higher price on a secondary market made by the bank. The Tenth Circuit denied recovery because the record failed to show that the plaintiffs relied on any misstatements made by the bank. The Supreme Court reversed:

> Under the circumstances of this case, involving primarily a failure to disclose, positive proof of reliance is not a prerequisite to recovery. All that is necessary is that the facts withheld be material in the sense that a reasonable investor might have considered them important in the making of this decision.

406 U.S. at 153–54, 92 S.Ct. at 1472.

On its face, *Ute* seemed to eliminate any requirement of reliance in a case of nondisclosure. In general, however, the cases have held that *Ute* "merely established a presumption that made it possible for the plaintiffs to meet their burden." Shores v. Sklar, 647 F.2d 462, 468 (5th Cir.1981) (en banc), cert. denied 459 U.S. 1102, 103 S.Ct. 722, 74 L.Ed.2d 949 (1983). The defendant can rebut this presumption "by showing that the . . . plaintiff would have followed the same course of conduct even with full and honest disclosure, [so that] the defendant's action (or lack thereof) cannot be said to have caused plaintiff's loss." Id. The defendant might carry this burden by showing, for example, that the plaintiff learned the omitted fact from an independent source before making his investment decision, so that the decision could not have been caused by the defendant's nondisclosure. Although the cases continue to use the language of "reliance" in the nondisclosure context, the real question is causation. When the question is properly framed in causation terms, once the plaintiff has shown that defendant omitted to disclose a material fact he was obliged to disclose, the burden is on the defendant to prove that the plaintiff would have made the same investment decision even if disclosure had been made.

(ii) *Misrepresentation*. Just as *Ute* diluted the requirement of reliance in the case of nondisclosure, *Basic* diluted the requirement in the case of misrepresentation, by adopting the fraud on-the-market theory. However, that theory is subject to various exceptions—for example, where there is no well-developed market for a security. The requirement of reliance remains meaningful in those cases and in the case of a face-to-face misrepresentation. For example, in a face-to-face case the defendant might be able to show that the plaintiff did not rely on a misrepresentation because he knew from other sources that the misrepresentation was false. However, although a lack of reliance in face-to-face misrepresentation cases is possible, it is extremely unlikely. People who trade soon after material misrepresentations have been made to them will have almost always have relied on the misrepresentations. Accordingly, once the plaintiff shows that a material misrepresentation was made to him, and that he traded soon thereafter, as a practical matter reliance will normally be presumed, and the burden will shift to the defendant to show that the plaintiff did not rely on the misrepresentation. In the end, therefore, the misrepresentation case is similar to the nondisclosure case—that is, as a practical matter, once the plaintiff makes a showing of materiality the burden shifts to the defendant to show that the plaintiff did not rely on the misrepresentation.

(iii) *Actions by SEC*. The reliance requirement applies only to determine when private parties can bring actions under rule 10b–5; it does not apply to actions by the SEC. Accordingly, the SEC can bring an action for injunctive or other appropriate relief based on a misrepresentation that violates rule 10b–5 even if no investors have relied upon the statement—because, for example, trading in the relevant stock was suspended immediately after the statement was made. SEC v. Rana Research, Inc., 8 F.3d 1358 (1993).

————

NOTE ON FORWARD–LOOKING STATEMENTS AND THE BESPEAKS–CAUTION DOCTRINE

1. *Forward-Looking Statements*. The securities acts, and the rules thereunder, provide special protection for most "forward-looking statements"—that is, statements about the future (for example, predictions of earnings). Section 21E(i) of the Securities Exchange Act defines a forward-looking statement to mean:

(A) a statement containing a projection of revenues, income (including income loss), earnings (including earnings loss) per share, capital expenditures, dividends, capital structure, or other financial items;

(B) a statement of the plans and objectives of management for future operations, including plans or objectives relating to the products or services of the issuer;

(C) a statement of future economic performance, including any such statement contained in a discussion and analysis of financial condition by the management or in the results of operations included pursuant to the rules and regulations of the Commission;

(D) any statement of the assumptions underlying or relating to any statement described in subparagraph (A), (B), or (C);

(E) any report issued by an outside reviewer retained by an issuer, to the extent that the report assesses a forward-looking statement made by the issuer; or

(F) a statement containing a projection or estimate of such other items as may be specified by rule or regulation of the Commission.

Section 21E(c)(1) provides two safe harbors against civil liability for written forward-looking statements, as defined, that are made (1) by a corporation that either has a security registered under section 12 of the Act or has filed a registration statement as described in section 15(d), or (2) by certain persons acting on behalf of such a corporation. Under the first safe harbor, there is no liability if the statement is identified as a forward-looking statement and is accompanied by meaningful cautionary statements identifying important factors that could cause actual results to differ materially from those in the statement. Under the second safe harbor, there is no liability if the plaintiff fails to prove that the statement was made with actual knowledge—not simply with recklessness—that the statement was false or misleading. Accordingly, Section 21E eliminates recklessness as sufficient scienter under Rule 10b–5 for forward-looking statements, although it does not affect omissions or statements that purport to concern historical or existing facts. Section 21E(c)(2) provides a special additional safe harbor applicable only to oral statements. (Comparable provisions are found in the Securities Act.)

2. *"Bespeaks Caution."* Under a doctrine known as "bespeaks caution," a forward-looking statement does not give rise to liability, even though it is misleading taken in isolation, if the document in which the statement is contained includes sufficient cautionary language. The applicability of the bespeaks-caution doctrine is highly fact-specific. To some extent, it is also court-specific; different Circuits have been either more or less ready to conclude that cautionary language was sufficient to protect against liability. It is fairly clear, however, that a generic, boiler-plate warning will not suffice. To have the desired effect, the cautionary language must be "tailored the specific future projections, estimates or opinions . . . which the plaintiffs challenge." Trump Casino Securities Litigation, 7 F.3d 357 (3d Cir. 1993), cert. denied sub. nom. Gollomp v. Trump, 510 U.S. 1178 (1994). By its terms, the bespeaks-caution doctrine, like the safe-harbor provisions in the Section 21E, is directed only to forward-looking statements, not to statements or present or historical facts. See EP MedSystems, Inc. v. EchoCath, Inc., 235 F.3d 865 (3d Cir. 2000). The doctrine is of special relevance when a forward-looking statement is made by a corporation or other person who is not within the safe harbor provided by Securities Exchange Act section 21E—for example, a corporation that does not have a class of stock registered under section 12 and has not filed a registration statement under section 15(d).

The bespeaks-caution doctrine was developed before the adoption of the statutory safe-harbors for certain forward-looking statements contained in Section 21E, but the doctrine is incorporated into the first of those safe harbors.

——————

NOTE ON THE PSLRA

As discussed in the Note on the Scienter Requirement, supra, liability under Rule 10b–5 usually requires a showing that the defendant had scienter. Normally for this purpose, scienter requires one of two forms of conscious misbehavior: either the defendant had a specific intent to mislead, or he acted recklessly. However, under the Private Securities Litigation Reform Act ("PSLRA") a plaintiff whose claim is based on an allegedly fraudulent forward-looking statement must establish that the misstatement was made with "actual knowledge." Accordingly, the PSLRA eliminated recklessness as sufficient scienter under Rule 10b–5 for forward-looking statements, within the limits discussed above. The PSLRA did not, on its face, eliminate recklessness in the case of statements of historical or existing (rather than forward-looking) facts. However, the PSLRA does bear on scienter even in those kinds of cases.

1. *Pleading.* Prior to the PSLRA, the pleading requirements in a securities-fraud case were governed only by Federal Rule of Civil Procedure 9(b), which requires that all types of fraud be pleaded with "particularity." The most stringent pleading *standard* in securities-act fraud cases under the requirement of Rule 9(b) was a standard established by the Second Circuit. This standard required the plaintiff to state with particularity facts that gave rise to a "strong inference" of the requisite intent, that is, of scienter. Under the Second Circuit *test* for applying that standard, the plaintiff could establish the required strong inference by detailed factual allegations that showed either direct evidence of scienter (conscious misbehavior or recklessness), circumstantial evidence of scienter, or that the defendant had the *motive and opportunity* to commit fraud.

To satisfy the motive element of the second branch of this test, it was not enough for a plaintiff to merely allege that the defendant had a motive of a kind possessed by virtually all corporate insiders, such as the desire to sustain the appearance of corporate profitability. Rather, the plaintiff had to allege that the defendant benefited in some concrete and personal way from his purported fraud. This requirement was normally satisfied when a corporate insider was alleged to have publicly misrepresented material facts about the corporation's performance or prospects to keep the stock price artificially high while he sold his own shares at a profit.

The PSLRA adopted the Second Circuit standard, but not necessarily the motive-and-opportunity test under that standard. Securities Exchange Act § 21D(b)(2) provides that a plaintiff who alleges securities fraud must "state with particularity *facts giving rise to a strong inference* that the defendant acted with the required state of mind"— that is, scienter. There are two issues concerning the meaning of this requirement. The first issue is what this standard entails—and in particular, whether a plaintiff can satisfy this standard solely by detailed factual allegations that the defendant had the motive and opportunity to commit fraud, as previously held by the Second Circuit, whose pleading standard the PSLRA had adopted. The second issue is whether the PSLRA was intended to change the rule that recklessness suffices to establish scienter.

A number of circuits have addressed the pleading issue. Three different views have been adopted.

Under one view, the PSLRA effectively adopted the Second Circuit's pleading standard and test wholesale. Accordingly, plaintiffs can state a claim by pleading either direct or strong circumstantial evidence of recklessness or conscious misbehavior, or motive and opportunity. Press v. Chemical Investment Services Corp., 166 F.3d 529 (2d

Cir. 1999); In re Advanta Corp. Securities Litigation, 180 F.3d 525 (3d Cir. 1999).

Under a second view, motive and opportunity may be relevant when combined with other facts, but as a matter of law they are never alone sufficient. Janas v. McCracken (In re Silicon Graphics Inc. Sec. Litig.), 183 F.3d 970, 977–79 (9th Cir. 1999); Bryant v. Avado Brands, Inc., 187 F.3d 1271, 1285–86 (11th Cir. 1999).

Finally, some Circuits explicitly refuse to decide whether motive and opportunity are or can be alone sufficient as a matter of law. Depending on the facts of the case, such pleadings might or might not be sufficient. For example, *Ottmann v. Hanger Orthopedic Group, Inc.*, 353 F.3d 338 (4th Cir. 2003), adopted a "flexible, case-specific analysis" because "Congress ultimately chose not to specify particular types of facts that would or would not show a strong inference of scienter." The flexible view, under which motive and opportunity are not alone either sufficient or insufficient in all cases, has been taken by most Circuits. Even the Second Circuit now takes the view that "Congress's failure to include language about motive and opportunity suggests that we need not be wedded to these concepts in articulating the prevailing standard." Novak v. Kasaks, 216 F.3d 300 (2d Cir. 2000). The position of the cases taking the flexible view has been summarized as follows in *Ottman v. Hanger Orthopedic Group, Inc.*:

> [Many courts have adopted] a case-specific approach that examines the particular allegations in their entirety to determine whether they provide the requisite strong inference, "without regard to whether those allegations fall into defined, formalistic categories such as 'motive and opportunity.'" . . . Still, these circuits generally agree that specific facts showing a motive and opportunity to commit fraud (or the absence of such facts) may be relevant in determining whether a plaintiff's complaint demonstrates a strong inference of scienter. . . .

> . . . [A] flexible, case-specific analysis is appropriate in examining scienter pleadings. . . . We therefore conclude that courts should not restrict their scienter inquiry by focusing on specific categories of facts, such as those relating to motive and opportunity, but instead should examine all of the allegations in each case to determine whether they collectively establish a strong inference of scienter. And, while particular facts demonstrating a motive and opportunity to commit fraud (or lack of such facts) may be relevant to the scienter inquiry, the weight accorded to those facts should depend on the circumstances of each case.

2. *Scienter.* A number of Circuits have concluded that the PSLRA did not alter the substantive definition of scienter. These courts opted to retain their pre–PSLRA definitions of recklessness. However, the Ninth Circuit has concluded that the PSLRA increased the substantive requirements of scienter, and strengthened its definition of scienter

from "recklessness" to "deliberate recklessness," *In re Silicon Graphics Inc. Securities Litigation*, 183 F.3d 970 (9th Cir. 1999).

NOTE ON THE USE TEST UNDER RULE 10b–5

In 1998, the Ninth and Eleventh Circuits held that Rule 10b–5 is not violated unless the defendant not only *possessed* material inside information when she traded, but actually *used* the information in deciding to buy or sell. These decisions were rested on the theory that having inside information in one's possession when trading does not wrongfully cause harm; only using such information wrongfully causes harm. SEC v. Adler, 137 F.3d 1325 (11th Cir.1998); United States v. Smith, 155 F.3d 1051 (9th Cir.1998).

This esoteric distinction between possession and use of inside information had been rejected by the Second Circuit in 1993, in United States v. Teicher, 987 F.2d 112. There the court said:

> . . . [A] "knowing possession" standard has the attribute of simplicity. It recognizes that one who trades while knowingly possessing material inside information has an informational advantage over other traders. Because the advantage is in the form of information, it exists in the mind of the trader. Unlike a loaded weapon which may stand ready but unused, material information can not lay idle in the human brain. The individual with such information may decide to trade upon that information, to alter a previously decided-upon transaction, to continue with a previously planned transaction even though publicly available information would now suggest otherwise, or simply to do nothing. In our increasingly sophisticated securities markets, where subtle shifts in strategy can produce dramatic results, it would be a mistake to think of such decisions as merely binary choices—to buy or to sell.

In 2000, the SEC promulgated Rule 10b5–1, which addresses the issue of whether liability under Rule 10b–5 is based on trading while in the knowing possession of material nonpublic information, or on using such information to trade. The general rule under Rule 10b5–1 is that the purchase or sale of a security violates Rule 10b–5 if the purchaser or seller was aware of material nonpublic information about the security or issuer at the time of the purchase or sale. However, the general rule is subject to an affirmative defense where the trade is made pursuant to certain kinds of definite contracts, instructions, or plans that were entered into before becoming aware of the information.

SECURITIES EXCHANGE ACT RULE 10b5–1

[See Statutory Supplement]

**SECURITIES AND EXCHANGE COMMISSION
RELEASE NO. 33–7881, Part III(A) (2000)**

**(TRADING "ON THE BASIS OF" MATERIAL
NONPUBLIC INFORMATION)**

[See Statutory Supplement]

————

NOTE ON AIDING AND ABETTING LIABILITY UNDER RULE 10b–5

In Central Bank of Denver v. First Interstate Bank of Denver, 511 U.S. 164, 114 S.Ct. 1439, 128 L.Ed.2d 119 (1994), the Supreme Court held that liability cannot be imposed on a person under Rule 10b–5 solely because that person aided and abetted a violation of the Rule. Prior to *Central Bank,* issues concerning aiding-and-abetting liability under Rule 10b–5 usually arose in the context of a suit against a primary violator, in which the plaintiff joined as defendants such secondary actors as lawyers, accountants, or banks who had somehow furthered the primary violator's course of conduct.

In re Enron Corp. Securities, Derivatives & ERISA Litigation, 235 F.Supp.2d 549 (S.D. Tex. 2002), a suit against several commercial and investment banks, an auditor, and two law firms, puts the following gloss on *Central Bank*:

> . . . [In *Central Bank*;] the Supreme Court did not conclude that secondary actors such as lawyers, accountants, banks, and underwriters were . . . always shielded from § 10(b) and Rule 10b–5 liability:
>
>> Because the text of § 10(b) does not prohibit aiding and abetting, we hold that a private plaintiff may not maintain an aiding and abetting suit under § 10(b). The absence of § 10(b) aiding and abetting liability does not mean that secondary actors in securities markets are always free from liability under the securities Act. Any person or entity, including a lawyer, accountant, or bank, who employs a manipulative device or makes a material misstatement (or omission) on which a purchaser or seller of securities relies may be liable as a primary violator under 10b–5, assuming *all* of the requirements for primary liability under Rule 10b–5 are met. . . . In any complex securities fraud, moreover, there are likely to be multiple violators. . . .

114 S.Ct. 1439. . . .

In sum, the Supreme Court left it to the lower courts to determine when the conduct of a secondary actor makes it a primary violator under the statute. In the aftermath of *Central Bank,* two divergent standards, the "bright line" test and the "substantial participation" test, have emerged.

Under the "bright line" test, in order for the conduct of a secondary actor to rise to the level of a primary violation, the secondary actor must not only make a material misstatement or omission, but "the misrepresentation must be attributed to the specific actor at the time of public dissemination," i.e., in advance of the investment decision, so as not to undermine the element of reliance required for § 10(b) liability. . . .

The less stringent "substantial participation" test provides for primary liability where there is "substantial participation or intricate involvement" of the secondary party in the preparation of fraudulent statements "even though that participation might not lead to the actor's actual making of the statements." *Howard v. Everex Systems, Inc.,* 228 F.3d 1057, 1061 n. 5 (9th Cir.2000). . . .

The SEC, [in the role of *amicus curiae,*] proposes . . . the following rule for primary liability of a secondary party under § 10(b): "when a person, acting alone or with others, creates a misrepresentation [on which the investor-plaintiffs relied], the person can be liable as a primary violator . . . if . . . he acts with the requisite scienter." . . . "Moreover it would not be necessary for a person to be the initiator of a misrepresentation in order to be a primary violator. Provided that a plaintiff can plead and prove scienter, a person can be a primary violator if he or she writes misrepresentations for inclusion in a document to be given to investors, even if the idea for those misrepresentations came from someone else." *Id.* Furthermore, "a person who prepares a truthful and complete portion of a document would not be liable as a primary violator for misrepresentations in other portions of the document. Even assuming such a person knew of misrepresentations elsewhere in the document and thus had the requisite scienter, he or she would not have created those misrepresentations." *Id.* at p. 19. Finally, of course, the plaintiff must plead and prove the elements of scienter and reliance. . . .

This Court finds that the SEC's approach to liability under § 10(b) and Rule 10b–5(b) is well reasoned and reasonable, balanced in its concern for protection for victimized investors as well as for meritlessly harassed defendants (including businesses, law firms, accountants and underwriters), in addition to the policies underlying the statutory private right of action for defrauded investors and the PSLRA. Moreover, it is consistent with the language of § 10b(b), Rule 10b–5, and *Central Bank.* Therefore since the SEC's proposed test is a reasonable interpretation of the text of the statute and serves its underlying policies, the Court adopts and applies it in this litigation to claims under § 10(b) and Rule 10b–5(b).

Applying this test, the court granted motions to dismiss made by one of the banks and one of the law firms, but denied the other defendants' motions.

———

NOTE ON REMEDIES IN PRIVATE ACTIONS UNDER RULE 10b–5

The determination of the appropriate remedy in a private action under Rule 10b–5 is a complex problem whose solution depends on a number of variables, including whether the corporation is closely or publicly held, whether the plaintiff is a buyer or a seller, whether the wrong is a misrepresentation or a wrongful nondisclosure, and whether the plaintiff dealt directly with the defendant. The common law rules governing remedies for fraud provide a good place to begin the analysis, because Rule 10b–5 cases often explicitly rely upon fraud concepts in the area of remedies.

1.   *Remedies for Fraud.* The basic remedies used by the courts in cases of common law fraud are damages and restitution.

a.   *Damages.* Two different damage measures are used by the courts in fraud cases: out-of-pocket damages and benefit-of-the-bargain damages. As explained by Dobbs:

The "Out-of-Pocket" Measure

. . . The out of pocket measure allows the plaintiff to recover the price paid for property he was induced to buy as a result of the misrepresentation, less the market value of the property. . . . The out of pocket measure is the limit of general damages recovery in a small group of states, even in cases of intentional fraud. . . . Anomalously, where this limit applies, the plaintiff will be better off to recover for contract or warranty breach than for deliberate fraud. . . .

Example of out-of-pocket measure. The defendant, by falsely representing authorship, induces the plaintiff to purchase a painting. The plaintiff pays $100,000 for the painting in reliance on the representation. In fact, because the painting was not authored by the artist named by the defendant, it is worth only $50,000. The out of pocket measure allows the plaintiff to recover $50,000 as the difference between the value and the price paid. The effect of this measure of damages is to leave the plaintiff with assets equal to those he had before the fraudulent transaction took place. . . .

The "Loss of Bargain" Measure

. . . [T]he benefit of the bargain or loss of bargain measure. The other measure of general damages is the loss of bargain measure, which is exactly like the expectancy measure of contract damages. The loss of bargain measure attempts to put the plaintiff in the economic position he would have been in had the representations been true. This rule not only guarantees that the plaintiff will have no loss; it also guarantees that the plaintiff will achieve any economic gains he would have had if the representations had been correct. The loss of bargain measure in some form has been used in most states, at least when the fraud is intentional, but it may be rejected in favor of the more conservative out of pocket rule when the misrepresentation is merely negligent.

... The traditional loss of bargain measure allows the plaintiff to recover the difference between (a) the value the thing would have had if the false representations had been true and (b) the price paid....

... For example, the defendant seller represents that spring water on Blackacre is pure, has been sold commercially and is of unlimited quantity. The plaintiff is induced to purchase Blackacre for $100,000, intending to bottle its water. Had the representations been true Blackacre would have been worth $150,000. In fact Blackacre's market value is only the price paid. The plaintiff is entitled to recover $50,000 under the loss of bargain rule....

2. D. Dobbs, Law of Remedies 548–553 (2d ed. 1993).

b. *Restitutionary relief.* A defrauded seller may seek restitutionary relief, rather than conventional damages. For example, he may sue for rescission, in which case he would return the purchase price and get back the property he sold. A defrauded buyer may also sue for rescission, in which case he would return the property he purchased and get back his purchase price.

Alternatively, a defrauded buyer or seller may be able to sue for the money equivalent of restitution, sometimes called "restitutionary," "rescissionary," or "rescissory" damages.

A major difference between conventional damages and restitutionary relief is that the latter tends to look to the defendant's wrongful gain, rather than to the plaintiff's loss:

Since the purpose is not to compensate the plaintiff's loss, but to restore what the defendant has received, the courts look to the inequity of allowing him to retain it, rather than to the damage which the plaintiff has sustained.

W. Keeton, D. Dobbs, R. Keeton, D. Owen, Prosser & Keeton on Torts 765–66 (5th ed. 1984).

2. *Rule 10b–5: Closely Held Corporations.*

Let us turn now to damages under Rule 10b–5 itself, beginning with closely held corporations.

Case 1. Plaintiff sells closely held stock to defendant based on defendant's misrepresentation. Suppose that S owns stock in C, a closely held corporation. B makes a material representation to S which, if true, would have a negative impact on the value of C stock. In reliance on the representation, S sells his C stock to B. Later, S learns that he was deceived. If S sues for conventional damages under Rule 10b–5, his recovery will normally be based on the out-of-pocket measure, so that he will be awarded the difference between the price he received for his stock and its higher actual value.

Alternatively, S may sue B for rescission. If he is successful, he will then return the purchase price to B, and recover the stock. This may be particularly desirable to S if C stock has substantially increased its value since he sold it. For example, suppose that S sold the stock to B for $12 at a time when the true value of the stock was $15. The value of the stock at the time of suit is $20. If S sues for conventional damages he will recover $3 in cash (the actual value of the stock, $15, minus the selling price, $12). If S sues for rescission, however, he will end up with a gain of $8 (stock worth $20 minus a $12 refund of the purchase price).

Suppose that B has meanwhile resold the stock? In Janigan v. Taylor, 344 F.2d 781 (1st Cir.1965), cert. denied 382 U.S. 879, 86 S.Ct. 163, 15 L.Ed.2d 120, the First Circuit held that S should be able to recover B's profit—that is, the difference between the price at which S sold the stock to B and the price at which B resold the stock—on the theory that B holds the profit in constructive trust for S. In effect, the money B received for the stock replaced the stock itself, and S should get the equivalent of rescission by recovering the difference between the price at which he sold to B and the proceeds of the sale by B. *Janigan* is based on equity and the principle that it is "more appropriate to give the defrauded party the benefit even of windfalls than to let the fraudulent party keep them." This is a form of rescissory damages. In Lawton v. Nyman, 327 F.3d 30 (1st Cir. 2003), the First Circuit limited the scope of *Janigan*, as follows:

> . . . *Janigan* does not embody a rule that plaintiffs are automatically entitled to all of defendants' profits from defendants' subsequent resale of stock regardless of circumstance. *Janigan* . . . does not state a per se rule that all subsequent profits accrue to plaintiffs; it is subject to significant restrictions. . . .

> *Janigan* . . . recognized at least two limits. First, it referred only to the profit which was "the proximate consequence of the fraud," itself a limiting factor. This court, sitting en banc, limited the application of the *Janigan* rule in the context of publicly traded companies. . . .

> Second, *Janigan* said that extraordinary gains in a company's affairs attributable to extra efforts by defendants are not part of the windfall profits. . . .

> As the *Janigan* doctrine has been refined, recovery of the defendants' later profits is usually applied when the subsequent resale follows fairly closely the original purchase from the plaintiffs. . . .

Case 2. Plaintiff sells closely held stock to defendant based on defendant's wrongful nondisclosure. Suppose now that instead of selling closely held stock in C on the basis of B's *misrepresentation*, S sells as a result of B's wrongful *nondisclosure* of a fact that, if known, would have a positive impact on the value of C stock. The analysis is essentially the same. Conventional damages would be based on the out-of-pocket rule. Rescission or rescissory damages should also be available. See Affiliated Ute Citizens of Utah v. United States, 406 U.S. 128, 154–55, 92 S.Ct. 1456, 1472–73, 31 L.Ed.2d 741 (1972).

Case 3. Plaintiff buys closely held stock from defendant based on defendant's wrongful nondisclosure. Suppose B *buys* closely held stock in C from S as a result of S's wrongful nondisclosure of a fact that, if known, would have a negative impact on the value of C stock. Conventional damages would normally be based on the out-of-pocket measure, but variations may be appropriate. In Chasins v. Smith, Barney & Co., 438 F.2d 1167 (2d Cir.1970), aff'g, 306 F.Supp. 177 (S.D.N.Y.1969), the Second Circuit allowed a purchaser in a nondisclosure case to recover the difference between the price he paid and the much lower price he received when he resold the stock prior to discovery of the wrongful omission. "Such a measurement is justified where, as here, the evil is not the price at which [the plaintiff] bought but the fact of being induced to buy and invest for some future growth in these stocks without disclosure . . .; the damages granted were proper under the circumstances." Id. at 1173.

Case 4. Plaintiff buys closely held stock from defendant based on defendant's misrepresentation. Suppose B buys closely held stock in C from S based on S's misrepresentation of a fact that, if true, would have a positive impact on the value of C stock. The courts generally employ the out-of-pocket measure in this kind of case. See Harris v. American Investment Co., 523 F.2d 220, 224–27 (8th Cir.1975), cert. denied 423 U.S. 1054, 96 S.Ct. 784, 46 L.Ed.2d 643 (1976). And, as in *Cases 1–3*, rescissory relief should also normally be available.

3.   *Rule 10b–5: Publicly Held Corporations—Misrepresentation.* Where a Rule 10b–5 case involves stock in a publicly held corporation, the situation may be much different. Begin with the case where the defendant has made a misrepresentation.

Case 5. Plaintiff sells publicly held stock based on defendant's misrepresentation. Suppose that S owns stock in P, a publicly held corporation. B makes a material misrepresentation concerning P. If the representation were true, it would have a negative impact on the value of P stock. In fact, it is false. In reliance on the misrepresentation, S sells his stock into the market. If a defendant has made a public misrepresentation that had the foreseeable effect of causing members of the public to sell (or buy) stock, the defendant is liable for the resulting damages. See, e.g., Blackie v. Barrack, 524 F.2d 891 (9th Cir.1975), cert. denied 429 U.S. 816, 97 S.Ct. 57, 50 L.Ed.2d 75 (1976).

a.   *Conventional damages.* Assume first that S sues for conventional damages. Under the out-of-pocket measure, S would recover the difference between the price at which he sold stock in P and the actual value of the stock. Actual value when? There are two strong reasons for measuring S's damages not by the value of the stock at the time of the wrong, but by its market value at the time of disclosure of the correct information.

(i) *The valuation idea and the modified out-of-pocket measure.* The first reason for using market value at the time of disclosure, in the case of a publicly held corporation, is that it provides the best indicator of actual value at the time of the wrong. Many think that the best indicator of the value of publicly held stock is the price of the stock on a fully informed market. The market price of P stock at the time of B's misrepresentation is *not* a good indicator of the stock's value, because the market will have been affected by the misrepresentation. The market price of P stock after the misrepresentation is corrected *is* a good indicator of the stock's value, because that price will reflect the market's valuation of P stock in light of the new, correct information. See Harris v. American Investment Co., 523 F.2d 220, 226–27 (8th Cir.1975), cert. denied 423 U.S. 1054, 96 S.Ct. 784, 46 L.Ed.2d 643 (1976). The use of market price at the time of disclosure to determine the actual value of the stock is sometimes referred to as a modified out-of-pocket measure.

Of course, the difference between the market price at the time of the wrong and the market price at the time of disclosure may be partly due to factors other than disclosure, such as changes in the economy. To the extent that the use of market price at the time of disclosure is based on the valuation idea—that the price at that time is the best indicator of the value of P's stock—the defendant should have the right to show that part of the price change was caused by other factors. This allocation of proof reflects the traditional rule that where damages are uncertain because of the defendant's wrong, the defendant should bear the burden of the uncertainty. See Bigelow v. RKO Radio Pictures, Inc., 327 U.S. 251, 264–65, 66 S.Ct. 574, 579–80, 90 L.Ed. 652 (1946).

(ii) *The cover idea.* There is a second reason why, in the case of stock in a publicly held corporation that is sold as a result of a violation of Rule 10b–5, damages should normally be based on the market value at, or a reasonable period after, the time of disclosure. Once disclosure has been made, so that the stock is correctly priced, the selling stockholder should have the opportunity to reinvest in the stock, or "cover," by purchasing the stock at the newly established price during a reasonable time after disclosure. "[A]fter the reasonable stockholder had opportunity to apprise himself [of the correct information,] a reasonable time lapse may be allowed to expire to permit the investor to decide whether or not he would reinvest.... The damages should then be based on the highest value of the [stock in question between the date of disclosure] and a reasonable time thereafter. In selecting the highest daily price the advantage works, to a greater degree, against the [wrongdoer]. But where ... the injury is suffered by an act makes difficult the exact computation of damages, the wrongdoer is not heard to complain." Mitchell v. Texas Gulf Sulphur Co., 446 F.2d 90, 105 (10th Cir.1971), cert. denied 404 U.S. 1004, 92 S.Ct. 564, 30 L.Ed.2d 558.

To recapitulate, measuring the market price at the time of disclosure, in the case of publicly held stock, reflects two basic ideas. The first is the valuation idea: such a measure allows the market to determine the value of the relevant information. The second is the cover idea: such a measure allows a selling plaintiff to restore himself to the position he would have been in if he had not been wrongfully induced to trade.

There are, however, certain tensions between these two ideas. The objective of allowing the market to determine the value of the relevant information might seem to require selecting a date promptly after disclosure has been made as the time for measuring damages. The objective of allowing a selling plaintiff to restore himself by making a purchase on the market might seem to require selecting a somewhat later date to give the plaintiff time to make the repurchase. In practice, the conflict is not likely to be severe. On the one hand, after an announcement is made the market needs a reasonable period of time, however short, to digest the new information. On the other, a reasonable time for a selling plaintiff to restore himself need not be very long. Thus the dates suggested by each concept may very well coincide in most cases.

A second tension is not so easily reconciled. If the law measures damages by the market price of the stock at the time of disclosure because that price is an indicator of the actual value of the stock at the time of the wrong, the defendant should be able to reduce damages if he can show that the difference between the market price at the time of the wrong and at the time of disclosure is partly attributable to factors other than the disclosure. If, however, the law uses the market price of the stock at the time of disclosure because a selling plaintiff should have an opportunity, after full disclosure, to replace himself on the market, the defendant should not be able to reduce damages by making such a showing.

b. *Rescissory damages.* In the case of stock in publicly held corporations *rescission* is usually not available as a practical matter, because a plaintiff seller usually sells into the market rather than to the defendant. Suppose, however, that instead of suing for rescission, a plaintiff seller sues for *rescissory damages*, based on the difference between the price he was paid for the stock and the price of the stock at the time of the trial. The emerging rule is that rescissory damages are unavailable in the case of publicly held stock, because they are unnecessary to protect the seller, S, or prevent unjust enrichment of the buyer, B. Where publicly held stock is involved, once the misrepresentation is corrected, S can replace himself by purchasing the stock on the market. Assume, for example, that on January 2, S sold stock in P, on the basis of B's misrepresentation, for $20. On January 8, B's misrepresentation was publicly corrected, and P stock went up to $25, where it hovered until January 22. At the time of trial, P stock is at $50. On these facts, after January 8, S and B are on an equal informational footing. S's failure to realize a gain from the run-up after January 22 does not derive from B's misrepresentation, but from S's fully-informed decision not to buy P stock at $25. Similarly, even if B bought S's stock, B's gain from January 8 forward reflects not his misrepresentation, but his investment decision to retain the stock, which he could have purchased at $25 on January 8 even without having made the earlier misrepresentation. See SEC v. MacDonald, 699 F.2d 47 (1st Cir.1983) (en banc).

This result is not inconsistent with allowing a selling plaintiff to recover the stock, or the defendant's profit, in the case of close corporations. Where a close corporation is involved, disclosure normally does not put the plaintiff and defendant on an equal footing, because a selling plaintiff cannot replace himself on the market after disclosure is made.

The principles applicable to cases in which the plaintiff sells publicly held stock on the basis of defendant's misrepresentation are also generally applicable to cases in which the plaintiff buys publicly held stock on the basis of a misrepresentation.[1]

4. *Rule 10b–5: Publicly Held Corporations—Nondisclosure.* Suppose, finally, that the plaintiff has purchased or sold publicly held stock at a time when the defendant wrongfully failed to disclose a material fact? Section 20A(a) of the Securities Exchange Act provides that any person who violates the Act or the Rules thereunder by purchasing or selling a security while in possession of material, nonpublic information shall be liable to any person who, contemporaneously with the purchase has sold, or contemporaneously with the sale has purchased, securities of the same class. Section 20A(b) then qualifies section 20A(a) by providing that the amount of damages imposed under that section shall not exceed the profit gained or loss avoided in the transaction that is the subject of the violation.

It should be noted that § 20A(b) does not limit the liability of defendants in Rule 10b–5 actions that do not fall within § 20A, because § 20A is expressly made nonexclusive by § 20A(d).

5. *Sanctions Other than Damages.* A person who violates Rule 10b–5 is subject to a variety of sanctions in addition to damages in a private action. The most salient sanctions are jail time, fines, and civil penalties, of up to three time the amount of the defendant's profit. (This penalty is in addition to a judgment or settlement in which the defendant is required to disgorge his profit.) Section 32(a) of the Securities Exchange Act provides for criminal penalties. Section 21A(a) provides for civil penalties. Because the penalty under § 21A is civil rather than criminal, the relevant standard of proof is whether the defendant's wrong has been established by a preponderance of the evidence, rather than whether it has been established beyond a reasonable doubt.

———

Chiarella v. United States

United States Supreme Court, 1980.
445 U.S. 222, 100 S.Ct. 1108, 63 L.Ed.2d 348.

■ MR. JUSTICE POWELL, delivered the opinion of the Court.

The question in this case is whether a person who learns from the confidential documents of one corporation that it is planning an

---

1. There may be special problems when a plaintiff buyer resells, or a plaintiff seller repurchases, before the information becomes publicly available. The plaintiff's damages in such cases should normally be limited to the difference between his purchase price and his resale price, or his sale price and his repurchase price. See Green v. Occidental Petroleum Corp., 541 F.2d 1335, 1341–46 (9th Cir.1976) (Sneed, J., concurring in part).

attempt to secure control of a second corporation violates § 10(b) of the Securities Exchange Act of 1934 if he fails to disclose the impending takeover before trading in the target company's securities.

I

Petitioner is a printer by trade. In 1975 and 1976, he worked as a "markup man" in the New York composing room of Pandick Press, a financial printer. Among documents that petitioner handled were five announcements of corporate takeover bids. When these documents were delivered to the printer, the identities of the acquiring and target corporations were concealed by blank spaces or false names. The true names were sent to the printer on the night of the final printing.

The petitioner, however, was able to deduce the names of the target companies before the final printing from other information contained in the documents. Without disclosing his knowledge, petitioner purchased stock in the target companies and sold the shares immediately after the takeover attempts were made public. By this method, petitioner realized a gain of slightly more than $30,000 in the course of 14 months. Subsequently, the Securities and Exchange Commission (Commission or SEC) began an investigation of his trading activities. In May 1977, petitioner entered into a consent decree with the Commission in which he agreed to return his profits to the sellers of the shares. On the same day, he was discharged by Pandick Press.

In January 1978, petitioner was indicted on 17 counts of violating § 10(b) of the Securities Exchange Act of 1934 (1934 Act) and SEC Rule 10b–5. After petitioner unsuccessfully moved to dismiss the indictment, he was brought to trial and convicted on all counts.

The Court of Appeals for the Second Circuit affirmed petitioner's conviction. 588 F.2d 1358 (2d Cir.1978). We granted certiorari, 441 U.S. 942, 99 S.Ct. 2158, 60 L.Ed.2d 1043 (1979), and we now reverse.

II . . .

This case concerns the legal effect of the petitioner's silence. The District Court's charge permitted the jury to convict the petitioner if it found that he willfully failed to inform sellers of target company securities that he knew of a forthcoming takeover bid that would make their shares more valuable. In order to decide whether silence in such circumstances violates § 10(b), it is necessary to review the language and legislative history of that statute as well as its interpretation by the Commission and the federal courts.

Although the starting point of our inquiry is the language of the statute, *Ernst & Ernst v. Hochfelder,* 425 U.S. 185, 197, 96 S.Ct. 1375, 47 L.Ed.2d 668 (1976), § 10(b) does not state whether silence may constitute a manipulative or deceptive device. Section 10(b) was designed as a catchall clause to prevent fraudulent practices. 425 U.S., at 202, 206. But neither the legislative history nor the statute itself affords specific guidance for the resolution of this case. When Rule

10b–5 was promulgated in 1942, the SEC did not discuss the possibility that failure to provide information might run afoul of § 10(b).

The SEC took an important step in the development of § 10(b) when it held that a broker-dealer and his firm violated that section by selling securities on the basis of undisclosed information obtained from a director of the issuer corporation who was also a registered representative of the brokerage firm. In *Cady, Roberts & Co.*, 40 S.E.C. 907 (1961), the Commission decided that a corporate insider must abstain from trading in the shares of his corporation unless he has first disclosed all material inside information known to him. The obligation to disclose or abstain derives from

> "[a]n affirmative duty to disclose material information[, which] has been traditionally imposed on corporate 'insiders,' particularly officers, directors, or controlling stockholders. We, and the courts have consistently held that insiders must disclose material facts which are known to them by virtue of their position but which are not known to persons with whom they deal and which, if known, would affect their investment judgment." *Id.*, at 911.

The Commission emphasized that the duty arose from (i) the existence of a relationship affording access to inside information intended to be available only for a corporate purpose, and (ii) the unfairness of allowing a corporate insider to take advantage of that information by trading without disclosure. *Id.*, at 912, and n. 15.[8]

That the relationship between a corporate insider and the stockholders of his corporation gives rise to a disclosure obligation is not a novel twist of the law. At common law, misrepresentation made for the purpose of inducing reliance upon the false statement is fraudulent. But one who fails to disclose material information prior to the consummation of a transaction commits fraud only when he is under a duty to do so. And the duty to disclose arises when one party has information "that the other [party] is entitled to know because of a fiduciary or other similar relation of trust and confidence between them."[9] In its *Cady, Roberts* decision, the Commission recognized a relationship of trust and confidence between the shareholders of a corporation and those insiders who have obtained confidential information by reason of their position with that corporation. This relationship gives rise to a duty to disclose because of the "necessity of preventing a corporate insider from . . . tak[ing] unfair advantage of

8. . . . The transaction in *Cady, Roberts* involved sale of stock to persons who previously may not have been shareholders in the corporation. 40 S.E.C., at 913, and n. 21. The Commission embraced the reasoning of Judge Learned Hand that "the director or officer assumed a fiduciary relation to the buyer by the very sale; for it would be a sorry distinction to allow him to use the advantage of his position to induce the buyer into the position of a beneficiary although he was forbidden to do so once the buyer had become one." *Id.*, at 914, n. 23, quoting *Gratz v. Claughton*, 187 F.2d 46, 49 (CA2), cert. denied, 341 U.S. 920, 71 S.Ct. 741, 95 L.Ed. 1353 (1951).

9. Restatement (Second) of Torts § 551(2)(a) (1976). See James & Gray, Misrepresentation—Part II, 37 Md.L.Rev. 488, 523–527 (1978). As regards securities transactions, the American Law Institute recognizes that "silence when there is a duty to . . . speak may be a fraudulent act." ALI, Federal Securities Code § 262(b) (Prop.Off. Draft 1978).

the uninformed minority stockholders." *Speed v. Transamerica Corp.,* 99 F.Supp. 808, 829 (Del.1951).

The federal courts have found violations of § 10(b) where corporate insiders used undisclosed information for their own benefit. *E.g., SEC v. Texas Gulf Sulphur Co.,* 401 F.2d 833 (C.A.2 1968), cert. denied, 404 U.S. 1005 (1971). The cases also have emphasized, in accordance with the common-law rule, that "[t]he party charged with failing to disclose market information must be under a duty to disclose it." *Frigitemp Corp. v. Financial Dynamics Fund, Inc.,* 524 F.2d 275, 282 (C.A.2 1975). Accordingly, a purchaser of stock who has no duty to a prospective seller because he is neither an insider nor a fiduciary has been held to have no obligation to reveal material facts. See *General Time Corp. v. Talley Industries, Inc.,* 403 F.2d 159, 164 (C.A.2 1968), cert. denied, 393 U.S. 1026, 89 S.Ct. 631, 21 L.Ed.2d 570 (1969) . . . .

Thus, administrative and judicial interpretations have established that silence in connection with the purchase or sale of securities may operate as a fraud actionable under § 10(b) despite the absence of statutory language or legislative history specifically addressing the legality of nondisclosure. But such liability is premised upon a duty to disclose arising from a relationship of trust and confidence between parties to a transaction. Application of a duty to disclose prior to trading guarantees that corporate insiders, who have an obligation to place the shareholder's welfare before their own, will not benefit personally through fraudulent use of material, nonpublic information.[12]

III

In this case, the petitioner was convicted of violating § 10(b) although he was not a corporate insider and he received no confidential information from the target company. Moreover, the "market information" upon which he relied did not concern the earning power or operations of the target company, but only the plans of the acquiring company. Petitioner's use of that information was not a fraud under § 10(b) unless he was subject to an affirmative duty to disclose it before trading. In this case, the jury instructions failed to specify any such duty. In effect, the trial court instructed the jury that petitioner owed a duty to everyone; to all sellers, indeed, to the market as a whole. The jury simply was told to decide whether petitioner used material, nonpublic information at a time when "he knew other people trading in the securities market did not have access to the same information." Record 677.

The Court of Appeals affirmed the conviction by holding that "[a]nyone—corporate insider or not—who regularly receives material

---

12. "Tippees" of corporate insiders have been held liable under § 10(b) because they have a duty not to profit from the use of inside information that they know is confidential and know or should know came from a corporate insider, *Shapiro v. Merrill Lynch,* *Pierce, Fenner & Smith, Inc.,* 495 F.2d 228, 237–238 (C.A.2 1974). The tippee's obligation has been viewed as arising from his role as a participant after the fact in the insider's breach of a fiduciary duty . . . .

nonpublic information may not use that information to trade in securities without incurring an affirmative duty to disclose." 588 F.2d, at 1365 (emphasis in original). Although the court said that its test would include only persons who regularly receive material, nonpublic information, *id.,* at 1366, its rationale for that limitation is unrelated to the existence of a duty to disclose.[14] The Court of Appeals, like the trial court, failed to identify a relationship between petitioner and the sellers that could give rise to a duty. Its decision thus rested solely upon its belief that the federal securities laws have "created a system providing equal access to information necessary for reasoned and intelligent investment decisions." *Id.,* at 1362. The use by anyone of material information not generally available is fraudulent, this theory suggests, because such information gives certain buyers or sellers an unfair advantage over less informed buyers and sellers.

This reasoning suffers from two defects. First, not every instance of financial unfairness constitutes fraudulent activity under § 10(b). See *Santa Fe Industries, Inc. v. Green,* 430 U.S. 462, 474–477, 97 S.Ct. 1292, 51 L.Ed.2d 480 (1977). Second, the element required to make silence fraudulent—a duty to disclose—is absent in this case. No duty could arise from petitioner's relationship with the sellers of the target company's securities, for petitioner had no prior dealings with them. He was not their agent, he was not a fiduciary, he was not a person in whom the sellers had placed their trust and confidence. He was, in fact, a complete stranger who dealt with the sellers only through impersonal market transactions.

We cannot affirm petitioner's conviction without recognizing a general duty between all participants in market transactions to forgo actions based on material, nonpublic information. Formulation of such a broad duty, which departs radically from the established doctrine that duty arises from a specific relationship between two parties, see n. 9, *supra,* should not be undertaken absent some explicit evidence of congressional intent.

As we have seen, no such evidence emerges from the language or legislative history of § 10(b). Moreover, neither the Congress nor the Commission ever has adopted a parity-of-information rule. Instead the problems caused by misuse of market information have been addressed by detailed and sophisticated regulation that recognizes when use of market information may not harm operation of the securities markets. For example, the Williams Act[15] limits but does not completely prohibit a tender offeror's purchases of target corporation stock before public announcement of the offer. Congress' careful action in

---

14. The Court of Appeals said that its "regular access to market information" test would create a workable rule embracing "those who occupy ... strategic places in the market mechanism." 588 F.2d, at 1365. These considerations are insufficient to support a duty to disclose. A duty arises from the relationship between parties, see nn. 9 and 10, *supra,* and accompanying text, and not merely from one's ability to acquire information because of his position in the market....

15. Title 15 U.S.C. § 78m(d)(1) (1976 ed., Supp. II) permits a tender offeror to purchase 5% of the target company's stock prior to disclosure of its plan for acquisition.

this and other areas contrasts, and is in some tension, with the broad rule of liability we are asked to adopt in this case. . . .

. . . As we have emphasized before, the 1934 Act cannot be read " 'more broadly than its language and the statutory scheme reasonably permit.' " *Touche Ross & Co. v. Redington,* 442 U.S. 560, 578, 99 S.Ct. 2479, 61 L.Ed.2d 82 (1979), quoting *SEC v. Sloan,* 436 U.S. 103, 116, 98 S.Ct. 1702, 56 L.Ed.2d 148 (1978). Section 10(b) is aptly described as a catchall provision, but what it catches must be fraud. When an allegation of fraud is based upon nondisclosure, there can be no fraud absent a duty to speak. We hold that a duty to disclose under § 10(b) does not arise from the mere possession of nonpublic market information. The contrary result is without support in the legislative history of § 10(b) and would be inconsistent with the careful plan that Congress has enacted for regulation of the securities markets. Cf. *Santa Fe Industries, Inc. v. Green,* 430 U.S., at 479.[20]

IV

In its brief to this Court, the United States offers an alternative theory to support petitioner's conviction. It argues that petitioner breached a duty to the acquiring corporation when he acted upon information that he obtained by virtue of his position as an employee of a printer employed by the corporation. The breach of this duty is said to support a conviction under § 10(b) for fraud perpetrated upon both the acquiring corporation and the sellers.

We need not decide whether this theory has merit for it was not submitted to the jury. . . .

The jury instructions demonstrate that petitioner was convicted merely because of his failure to disclose material, nonpublic information to sellers from whom he bought the stock of target corporations. The jury was not instructed on the nature or elements of a duty owed by petitioner to anyone other than the sellers. Because we cannot affirm a criminal conviction on the basis of a theory not presented to the jury, *Rewis v. United States,* 401 U.S. 808, 814, 91 S.Ct. 1056, 28 L.Ed.2d 493 (1971), see *Dunn v. United States,* 442 U.S. 100, 106, 99 S.Ct. 2190, 60 L.Ed.2d 743 (1979), we will not speculate upon whether such a duty exists, whether it has been breached, or whether such a breach constitutes a violation of § 10(b).

The judgment of the Court of Appeals is

Reversed.

[The concurring opinions of Justices Stevens and Brennan are omitted.]

■ Mr. Chief Justice Burger, dissenting.

20. . . . It is worth noting that this is apparently the first case in which criminal liability has been imposed upon a purchaser for § 10(b) nondisclosure. Petitioner was sentenced to a year in prison, suspended except for one month, and a 5–year term of probation. 588 F.2d, at 1373, 1378 (Meskill, J., dissenting).

I believe that the jury instructions in this case properly charged a violation of § 10(b) and Rule 10b–5, and I would affirm the conviction.

I

As a general rule, neither party to an arm's-length business transaction has an obligation to disclose information to the other unless the parties stand in some confidential or fiduciary relation. See W. Prosser, Law of Torts § 106 (2d ed. 1955). This rule permits a businessman to capitalize on his experience and skill in securing and evaluating relevant information; it provides incentive for hard work, careful analysis, and astute forecasting. But the policies that underlie the rule also should limit its scope. In particular, the rule should give way when an informational advantage is obtained, not by superior experience, foresight, or industry, but by some unlawful means. One commentator has written:

> "[T]he way in which the buyer acquires the information which he conceals from the vendor should be a material circumstance. The information might have been acquired as the result of his bringing to bear a superior knowledge, intelligence, skill or technical judgment; it might have been acquired by mere chance; or it might have been acquired by means of some tortious action on his part. . . . *Any time information is acquired by an illegal act it would seem that there should be a duty to disclose that information.*" Keeton, Fraud—Concealment and Non–Disclosure, 15 Texas L.Rev. 1, 25–26 (1936) (emphasis added).

I would read § 10(b) and Rule 10b–5 to encompass and build on this principle: to mean that a person who has misappropriated nonpublic information has an absolute duty to disclose that information or to refrain from trading.

The language of § 10(b) and of Rule 10b–5 plainly supports such a reading. By their terms, these provisions reach *any* person engaged in *any* fraudulent scheme. This broad language negates the suggestion that congressional concern was limited to trading by "corporate insiders" or to deceptive practices related to "corporate information."[1] Just as surely Congress cannot have intended one standard of fair dealing for "white collar" insiders and another for the "blue collar" level. The very language of § 10(b) and Rule 10b–5 "by repeated use of the word 'any' [was] obviously meant to be inclusive." *Affiliated Ute Citizens v. United States,* 406 U.S. 128, 151, 92 S.Ct. 1456, 31 L.Ed.2d 741 (1972).

---

1. Academic writing in recent years has distinguished between "corporate information"—information which comes from within the corporation and reflects on expected earnings or assets—and "market information." See, *e.g.,* Fleischer, Mundheim, & Murphy, An Initial Inquiry into the Responsibility to Disclose Market Information, 121 U.Pa. L.Rev. 798, 799 (1973). It is clear that § 10(b) and Rule 10b–5 by their terms and by their history make no such distinction. See Brudney, Insiders, Outsiders, and Informational Advantages Under the Federal Securities Laws, 93 Harv.L.Rev. 322, 329–333 (1979).

The history of the statute and of the Rule also supports this reading. The antifraud provisions were designed in large measure "to assure that dealing in securities is fair and without undue preferences or advantages among investors." H.R.Conf.Rep. No. 94–229, p. 91 (1975). These provisions prohibit "those manipulative and deceptive practices which have been demonstrated to fulfill no useful function." S.Rep. No. 792, 73d Cong., 2d Sess., 6 (1934). An investor who purchases securities on the basis of misappropriated nonpublic information possesses just such an "undue" trading advantage; his conduct quite clearly serves no useful function except his own enrichment at the expense of others.

This interpretation of § 10(b) and Rule 10b–5 is in no sense novel. It follows naturally from legal principles enunciated by the Securities and Exchange Commission in its seminal *Cady, Roberts* decision. 40 S.E.C. 907 (1961). There, the Commission relied upon two factors to impose a duty to disclose on corporate insiders: (1) " ... access ... to information intended to be available only for a corporate purpose *and not for the personal benefit of anyone*"(emphasis added); and (2) the unfairness inherent in trading on such information when it is inaccessible to those with whom one is dealing. Both of these factors are present whenever a party gains an informational advantage by unlawful means. Indeed, in *In re Blyth & Co.*, 43 S.E.C. 1037 (1969), the Commission applied its *Cady, Roberts* decision in just such a context. In that case a broker-dealer had traded in Government securities on the basis of confidential Treasury Department information which it received from a Federal Reserve Bank employee. The Commission ruled that the trading was "improper use of inside information" in violation of § 10(b) and Rule 10b–5. 43 S.E.C., at 1040. It did not hesitate to extend *Cady, Roberts* to reach a "tippee" of a Government insider.

Finally, it bears emphasis that this reading of § 10b and Rule 10b–5 would not threaten legitimate business practices. So read, the antifraud provisions would not impose a duty on a tender offeror to disclose its acquisition plans during the period in which it "tests the water" prior to purchasing a full 5% of the target company's stock. Nor would it proscribe "warehousing." See generally SEC, Institutional Investor Study Report, H.R.Doc. No. 92–64, pt. 4, p. 2273 (1971). Likewise, market specialists would not be subject to a disclose-or-refrain requirement in the performance of their everyday market functions. In each of these instances, trading is accomplished on the basis of material, nonpublic information, but the information has not been unlawfully converted for personal gain.

II

The Court's opinion, as I read it, leaves open the question whether § 10(b) and Rule 10b–5 prohibit trading on misappropriated nonpublic information.[4] Instead, the Court apparently concludes that

---

4. There is some language in the Court's opinion to suggest that only "a relationship between petitioner and the sellers ... could give rise to a duty [to disclose]."

this theory of the case was not submitted to the jury. In the Court's view, the instructions given the jury were premised on the erroneous notion that the mere failure to disclose nonpublic information, however acquired, is a deceptive practice. . . .

The Court's reading of the District Court's charge is unduly restrictive. Fairly read as a whole and in the context of the trial, the instructions required the jury to find that Chiarella obtained his trading advantage by misappropriating the property of his employer's customers. . . .

In sum, the evidence shows beyond all doubt that Chiarella, working literally in the shadows of the warning signs in the printshop, misappropriated—stole to put it bluntly—valuable nonpublic information entrusted to him in the utmost confidence. He then exploited his ill-gotten informational advantage by purchasing securities in the market. In my view, such conduct plainly violates § 10(b) and Rule 10b–5. Accordingly, I would affirm the judgment of the Court of Appeals.

■ [The dissenting opinions of Justices Blackman and Marshall are omitted.]

———

AFTER THE FALL, Wall St.J., November 18, 1987, at 1, col. 6. " . . . Vincent Chiarella will always rate at least a footnote in the history of Wall Street: In 1978, he became the first person in modern times convicted of criminal insider trading.

"A financial printer, Mr. Chiarella had made about $29,000 trading on information gleaned from tender-offer documents that he had seen in the course of his job. His conviction was reversed in a landmark Supreme Court decision in 1980; nevertheless, he 'went through hell' for seven years, he says, explaining that he was shunned by friends and blackballed by the printing industry. His conclusion: 'I was a martyr for insider trading.' . . .

" . . . [A]fter 20 years as a printer, he was forced to drift from job to job, two months there, two days there, always living near the poverty line. Extra cash went to pay legal bills. One year he listed 18 separate printing jobs on his W–2 form; every mention of his past in the press presaged the end of each job.

" 'All my life I was a printer, a good worker, no trouble,' says Mr. Chiarella. 'All of a sudden, you're nothing anymore. What do you do?'

"Insider trading seemed a lofty term for the guessing game he and other printers played at Pandick Press in New York in the 1970s. They

... The Court's holding, however, is much more limited, namely, that mere possession of material, nonpublic information is insufficient to create a duty to disclose or to refrain from trading. . . . Accordingly, it is my understanding that the Court has not rejected the view, advanced above, that an absolute duty to disclose or refrain arises from the very act of misappropriating nonpublic information.

spent hours trying to decode identities of buyers and sellers in tender-offer documents they prepared; only Mr. Chiarella, however, played the market with his hunches. To this day, he doesn't know how he was caught. . . .

"Today, Mr. Chiarella is back at his old job at Pandick after winning an arbitration suit suggested by his union a couple of years ago. He walks to work each day at 4 p.m., a bitter man. 'I was the guinea pig,' he says. 'I disgorged $29,000 to the SEC. Ivan Boesky could buy cigarettes with that.'

"He wants little except to be left alone. 'I'm at the twilight of my career as a printer,' he says. 'I hope to just fade away.' "

SECURITIES EXCHANGE ACT § 14(e) AND RULE 14(e)(3)

[See Statutory Supplement]

Dirks v. Securities and Exchange Commission

Supreme Court of the United States, 1983.
463 U.S. 646, 103 S.Ct. 3255, 77 L.Ed.2d 911.

■ JUSTICE POWELL delivered the opinion of the Court.

Petitioner Raymond Dirks received material nonpublic information from "insiders" of a corporation with which he had no connection. He disclosed this information to investors who relied on it in trading in the shares of the corporation. The question is whether Dirks violated the antifraud provisions of the federal securities laws by this disclosure.

I

In 1973, Dirks was an officer of a New York broker-dealer firm who specialized in providing investment analysis of insurance company securities to institutional investors. On March 6, Dirks received information from Ronald Secrist, a former officer of Equity Funding of America. Secrist alleged that the assets of Equity Funding, a diversified corporation primarily engaged in selling life insurance and mutual funds, were vastly overstated as the result of fraudulent corporate practices. Secrist also stated that various regulatory agencies had failed to act on similar charges made by Equity Funding employees. He urged Dirks to verify the fraud and disclose it publicly.

Dirks decided to investigate the allegations. He visited Equity Funding's headquarters in Los Angeles and interviewed several officers and employees of the corporation. The senior management denied any wrongdoing, but certain corporation employees corroborated the charges of fraud. Neither Dirks nor his firm owned or traded any Equity Funding stock, but throughout his investigation he openly discussed the information he had obtained with a number of clients and investors. Some of these persons sold their holdings of Equity Funding securities, including five investment advisers who liquidated holdings of more than $16 million.[2]

While Dirks was in Los Angeles, he was in touch regularly with William Blundell, the Wall Street Journal's Los Angeles bureau chief. Dirks urged Blundell to write a story on the fraud allegations. Blundell did not believe, however, that such a massive fraud could go undetected and declined to write the story. He feared that publishing such damaging hearsay might be libelous.

During the two-week period in which Dirks pursued his investigation and spread word of Secrist's charges, the price of Equity Funding stock fell from $26 per share to less than $15 per share. This led the New York Stock Exchange to halt trading on March 27. Shortly thereafter California insurance authorities impounded Equity Funding's records and uncovered evidence of the fraud. Only then did the Securities and Exchange Commission (SEC) file a complaint against Equity Funding[3] and only then, on April 2, did the Wall Street Journal publish a front-page story based largely on information assembled by Dirks. Equity Funding immediately went into receivership.[4]

The SEC began an investigation into Dirks' role in the exposure of the fraud. After a hearing by an administrative law judge, the SEC found that Dirks had aided and abetted violations of § 17(a) of the Securities Act of 1933, 15 U.S.C. § 77q(a), § 10(b) of the Securities Exchange Act of 1934, 15 U.S.C. § 78j(b), and SEC Rule 10b–5, 17 CFR § 240.10b–5 (1982), by repeating the allegations of fraud to members of the investment community who later sold their Equity Funding stock. The SEC concluded: "Where 'tippees'—regardless of their motivation or occupation—come into possession of material 'information that they know is confidential and know or should know came from a corporate insider,' they must either publicly disclose that information or refrain from trading." 21 S.E.C. Docket 1401, 1407 (1981) (footnote omitted) (quoting Chiarella v. United States, 445 U.S. 222, 230 n. 12, 100 S.Ct. 1108, 1115 n. 12, 63 L.Ed.2d 348 (1980)). Recognizing, however, that Dirks "played an important role in bringing [Equity

2. Dirks received from his firm a salary plus a commission for securities transactions above a certain amount that his clients directed through his firm. See 21 S.E.C. Docket, at 1402, n. 3. But "[i]t is not clear how many of those with whom Dirks spoke promised to direct some brokerage business through [Dirks' firm] to compensate Dirks, or how many actually did so." 220 U.S.App. D.C., at 316, 681 F.2d, at 831. The Boston Company Institutional Investors, Inc., promised Dirks about $25,000 in commissions, but it is unclear whether Boston actually generated any brokerage business for his firm. See App. 199, 204–205; 21 S.E.C. Docket, at 1404, n. 10; 220 U.S.App.D.C., at 316, n. 5, 681 F.2d, at 831, n. 5.

3. As early as 1971, the SEC had received allegations of fraudulent accounting practices at Equity Funding. Moreover, on March 9, 1973, an official of the California Insurance Department informed the SEC's regional office in Los Angeles of Secrist's charges of fraud. Dirks himself voluntarily presented his information at the SEC's regional office beginning on March 27.

4. A federal grand jury in Los Angeles subsequently returned a 105–count indictment against 22 persons, including many of Equity Funding's officers and directors. All defendants were found guilty of one or more counts, either by a plea of guilty or a conviction after trial. See Brief for Petitioner 15; App. 149–153.

Funding's] massive fraud to light," 21 S.E.C. Docket, at 1412, the SEC only censured him.

Dirks sought review in the Court of Appeals for the District of Columbia Circuit. The court entered judgment against Dirks....

In view of the importance to the SEC and to the securities industry of the question presented by this case, we granted a writ of certiorari. 459 U.S. 1014, 103 S.Ct. 371, 74 L.Ed.2d 506 (1982). We now reverse.

II

In the seminal case of In re Cady, Roberts & Co., 40 S.E.C. 907 (1961), the SEC recognized that the common law in some jurisdictions imposes on "corporate 'insiders,' particularly officers, directors, or controlling stockholders" an "affirmative duty of disclosure ... when dealing in securities." Id., at 911, and n. 13.[10] The SEC found that not only did breach of this common-law duty also establish the elements of a Rule 10b–5 violation, but that individuals other than corporate insiders could be obligated either to disclose material non-public information before trading or to abstain from trading altogether. Id., at 912. In *Chiarella,* we accepted the two elements set out in *Cady, Roberts* for establishing a Rule 10b–5 violation: "(i) the existence of a relationship affording access to inside information intended to be available only for a corporate purpose, and (ii) the unfairness of allowing a corporate insider to take advantage of that information by trading without disclosure." 445 U.S., at 227, 100 S.Ct. at 1114. In examining whether Chiarella had an obligation to disclose or abstain, the Court found that there is no general duty to disclose before trading on material nonpublic information, and held that "a duty to disclose under § 10(b) does not arise from the mere possession of nonpublic market information." Id., at 235, 100 S.Ct., at 1118. Such a duty arises rather from the existence of a fiduciary relationship. See id., at 227–235, 100 S.Ct., at 1114–1118.

Not "all breaches of fiduciary duty in connection with a securities transaction," however, come within the ambit of Rule 10b–5. Santa Fe Industries, Inc. v. Green, 430 U.S. 462, 472, 97 S.Ct. 1292, 1300, 51 L.Ed.2d 480 (1977). There must also be "manipulation or deception." Id., at 473, 97 S.Ct., at 1300. In an inside-trading case this fraud derives from the "inherent unfairness involved where one takes advantage" of "information intended to be available only for a corporate purpose and not for the personal benefit of anyone." In re Merrill Lynch, Pierce, Fenner & Smith, Inc., 43 S.E.C. 933, 936 (1968). Thus,

---

10. The duty that insiders owe to the corporation's shareholders not to trade on inside information differs from the common-law duty that officers and directors also have to the corporation itself not to mismanage corporate assets, of which confidential information is one. See 3 Fletcher Cyclopedia of the Laws of Private Corporations §§ 848, 900 (1975 ed. and Supp.1982); 3A Fletcher §§ 1168.1, 1168.2. In holding that breaches of this duty to shareholders violated the Securities Exchange Act, the *Cady, Roberts* Commission recognized, and we agree, that "[a] significant purpose of the Exchange Act was to eliminate the idea that use of inside information for personal advantage was a normal emolument of corporate office." See 40 S.E.C., at 912, n. 15.

an insider will be liable under Rule 10b–5 for inside trading only where he fails to disclose material nonpublic information before trading on it and thus makes "secret profits." *Cady, Roberts,* 40 S.E.C., at 916, n. 31.

III

We were explicit in *Chiarella* in saying that there can be no duty to disclose where the person who has traded on inside information "was not [the corporation's] agent, . . . was not a fiduciary, [or] was not a person in whom the sellers [of the securities] had placed their trust and confidence." 445 U.S., at 232, 100 S.Ct., at 1116. Not to require such a fiduciary relationship, we recognized, would "depar[t] radically from the established doctrine that duty arises from a specific relationship between two parties" and would amount to "recognizing a general duty between all participants in market transactions to forgo actions based on material, nonpublic information." Id., at 232, 233, 100 S.Ct., at 1116, 1117. This requirement of a specific relationship between the shareholders and the individual trading on inside information has created analytical difficulties for the SEC and courts in policing tippees who trade on inside information. Unlike insiders who have independent fiduciary duties to both the corporation and its shareholders, the typical tippee has no such relationships.[14] In view of this absence, it has been unclear how a tippee acquires the *Cady, Roberts* duty to refrain from trading on inside information. . . .

A

The SEC's position, as stated in its opinion in this case, is that a tippee "inherits" the *Cady, Roberts* obligation to shareholders whenever he receives inside information from an insider . . .

. . . This [position] conflicts with the principle set forth in *Chiarella* that only some persons, under some circumstances, will be barred from trading while in possession of material nonpublic information. . . . See *Chiarella,* 445 U.S., at 235, n. 20, 100 S.Ct., at 1118, n. 20. We reaffirm today that "[a] duty [to disclose] arises from the relationship between parties . . . and not merely from one's ability to acquire information because of his position in the market." [Chiarella,] 445 U.S., at 232–233, n. 14, 100 S.Ct., at 1116–1117, n. 14.

---

14. Under certain circumstances, such as where corporate information is revealed legitimately to an underwriter, accountant, lawyer, or consultant working for the corporation, these outsiders may become fiduciaries of the shareholders. The basis for recognizing this fiduciary duty is not simply that such persons acquired nonpublic corporate information, but rather that they have entered into a special confidential relationship in the conduct of the business of the enterprise and are given access to information solely for corporate purposes. See SEC v. Monarch Fund, 608 F.2d 938, 942 (C.A.2 1979); In re Investors Management Co., 44 S.E.C. 633, 645 (1971); In re Van Alystne, Noel & Co., 43 S.E.C. 1080, 1084–1085 (1969); In re Merrill Lynch, Pierce, Fenner & Smith, Inc., 43 S.E.C. 933, 937 (1968); *Cady, Roberts,* 40 S.E.C., at 912. When such a person breaches his fiduciary relationship, he may be treated more properly as a tipper than a tippee. See Shapiro v. Merrill Lynch, Pierce, Fenner & Smith, Inc., 495 F.2d 228, 237 (C.A.2 1974) (investment banker had access to material information when working on a proposed public offering for the corporation). For such a duty to be imposed, however, the corporation must expect the outsider to keep the disclosed nonpublic information confidential, and the relationship at least must imply such a duty.

Imposing a duty to disclose or abstain solely because a person knowingly receives material nonpublic information from an insider and trades on it could have an inhibiting influence on the role of market analysts, which the SEC itself recognizes is necessary to the preservation of a healthy market. It is commonplace for analysts to "ferret out and analyze information," 21 S.E.C., at 1406,[18] and this often is done by meeting with and questioning corporate officers and others who are insiders. And information that the analysts obtain normally may be the basis for judgments as to the market worth of a corporation's securities. The analyst's judgment in this respect is made available in market letters or otherwise to clients of the firm. It is the nature of this type of information, and indeed of the markets themselves, that such information cannot be made simultaneously available to all of the corporation's stockholders or the public generally.

B

The conclusion that recipients of inside information do not invariably acquire a duty to disclose or abstain does not mean that such tippees always are free to trade on the information. The need for a ban on some tippee trading is clear. Not only are insiders forbidden by their fiduciary relationship from personally using undisclosed corporate information to their advantage, but they may not give such information to an outsider for the same improper purpose of exploiting the information for their personal gain. See 15 U.S.C. § 78t(b) (making it unlawful to do indirectly "by means of any other person" any act made unlawful by the federal securities laws). Similarly, the transactions of those who knowingly participate with the fiduciary in such a breach are "as forbidden" as transactions "on behalf of the trustee himself." Mosser v. Darrow, 341 U.S. 267, 272, 71 S.Ct. 680, 683, 95 L.Ed. 927 (1951). See Jackson v. Smith, 254 U.S. 586, 589, 41 S.Ct. 200, 202, 65 L.Ed. 418 (1921); Jackson v. Ludeling, 21 Wall. 616, 88 U.S. 616, 631–632, 22 L.Ed. 492 (1874). As the Court explained in *Mosser,* a contrary rule "would open up opportunities for devious dealings in the name of the others that the trustee could not conduct in his own." 341 U.S., at 271, 71 S.Ct., at 682. See SEC v. Texas Gulf Sulphur Co., 446 F.2d 1301, 1308 (CA2), cert. denied, 404 U.S. 1005, 92 S.Ct. 561, 30 L.Ed.2d 558 (1971). Thus, the tippee's duty to disclose or abstain is derivative from that of the insider's duty. See Tr. of Oral Arg. 38. Cf. *Chiarella,* 445 U.S., at 246, n. 1, 100 S.Ct., at 1122,

---

18. On its facts, this case is the unusual one. Dirks is an analyst in a broker-dealer firm, and he did interview management in the course of his investigation. He uncovered, however, startling information that required no analysis or exercise of judgment as to its market relevance. Nonetheless, the principle at issue here extends beyond these facts. The SEC's rule—applicable without regard to any breach by an insider—could have serious ramifications on reporting by analysts of investment views.

Despite the unusualness of Dirks' "find," the central role that he played in uncovering the fraud at Equity Funding, and that analysts in general can play in revealing information that corporations may have reason to withhold from the public, is an important one. Dirks' careful investigation brought to light a massive fraud at the corporation. And until the Equity Funding fraud was exposed, the information in the trading market was grossly inaccurate. But for Dirks' efforts, the fraud might well have gone undetected longer. See n. 8, supra.

n. 1 (Blackmun, J., dissenting). As we noted in *Chiarella,* "[t]he tippee's obligation has been viewed as arising from his role as a participant after the fact in the insider's breach of a fiduciary duty." 445 U.S., at 230, n. 12, 100 S.Ct., at 1115, n. 12.

Thus, some tippees must assume an insider's duty to the shareholders not because they receive inside information, but rather because it has been made available to them *improperly*. And for Rule 10b–5 purposes, the insider's disclosure is improper only where it would violate his *Cady, Roberts* duty. Thus, a tippee assumes a fiduciary duty to the shareholders of a corporation not to trade on material nonpublic information only when the insider has breached his fiduciary duty to the shareholders by disclosing the information to the tippee and the tippee knows or should know that there has been a breach. As Commissioner Smith perceptively observed in *Investors Management Co.:* "[T]ippee responsibility must be related back to insider responsibility by a necessary finding that the tippee knew the information was given to him in breach of a duty by a person having a special relationship to the issuer not to disclose the information...." 44 S.E.C., at 651 (concurring in the result). Tipping thus properly is viewed only as a means of indirectly violating the *Cady, Roberts* disclose-or-abstain rule.

C

In determining whether a tippee is under an obligation to disclose or abstain, it thus is necessary to determine whether the insider's "tip" constituted a breach of the insider's fiduciary duty. All disclosures of confidential corporate information are not inconsistent with the duty insiders owe to shareholders. In contrast to the extraordinary facts of this case, the more typical situation in which there will be a question whether disclosure violates the insider's *Cady, Roberts* duty is when insiders disclose information to analysts. See n. 16, supra. In some situations, the insider will act consistently with his fiduciary duty to shareholders, and yet release of the information may affect the market. For example, it may not be clear—either to the corporate insider or to the recipient analyst—whether the information will be viewed as material nonpublic information. Corporate officials may mistakenly think the information already has been disclosed or that it is not material enough to affect the market. Whether disclosure is a breach of duty therefore depends in large part on the purpose of the disclosure. This standard was identified by the SEC itself in *Cady, Roberts:* a purpose of the securities laws was to eliminate "use of inside information for personal advantage." 40 S.E.C., at 912, n. 15. See n. 10, supra. Thus, the test is whether the insider personally will benefit, directly or indirectly, from his disclosure. Absent some personal gain, there has been no breach of duty to stockholders. And absent a breach by the insider, there is no derivative breach. As Commissioner Smith stated in *Investors Management Co.* "It is important in this type of case to focus on policing insiders and what they do ... rather than on policing information *per se* and its possession...." 44 S.E.C., at 648 (concurring in the result).

The SEC argues that, if inside-trading liability does not exist when the information is transmitted for a proper purpose but is used for trading, it would be a rare situation when the parties could not fabricate some ostensibly legitimate business justification for transmitting the information. We think the SEC is unduly concerned. In determining whether the insider's purpose in making a particular disclosure is fraudulent, the SEC and the courts are not required to read the parties' minds. Scienter in some cases is relevant in determining whether the tipper has violated his *Cady, Roberts* duty. But to determine whether the disclosure itself "deceive[s], manipulate[s], or defraud[s]" shareholders, Aaron v. SEC, 446 U.S. 680, 686, 100 S.Ct. 1945, 1950, 64 L.Ed.2d 611 (1980), the initial inquiry is whether there has been a breach of duty by the insider. This requires courts to focus on objective criteria, i.e., whether the insider receives a direct or indirect personal benefit from the disclosure, such as a pecuniary gain or a reputational benefit that will translate into future earnings. Cf. 40 S.E.C., at 912, n. 15; Brudney, Insiders, Outsiders, and Informational Advantages Under the Federal Securities Laws, 93 Harv.L.Rev. 324, 348 (1979) ("The theory . . . is that the insider, by giving the information out selectively, is in effect selling the information to its recipient for cash, reciprocal information, or other things of value for himself . . ."). There are objective facts and circumstances that often justify such an inference. For example, there may be a relationship between the insider and the recipient that suggests a *quid pro quo* from the latter, or an intention to benefit the particular recipient. The elements of fiduciary duty and exploitation of nonpublic information also exist when an insider makes a gift of confidential information to a trading relative or friend. The tip and trade resemble trading by the insider himself followed by a gift of the profits to the recipient.

Determining whether an insider personally benefits from a particular disclosure, a question of fact, will not always be easy for courts. But it is essential, we think, to have a guiding principle for those whose daily activities must be limited and instructed by the SEC's inside-trading rules, and we believe that there must be a breach of the insider's fiduciary duty before the tippee inherits the duty to disclose or abstain. In contrast, the rule adopted by the SEC in this case would have no limiting principle.

IV

Under the inside-trading and tipping rules set forth above, we find that there was no actionable violation by Dirks. It is undisputed that Dirks himself was a stranger to Equity Funding, with no pre-existing fiduciary duty to its shareholders. He took no action, directly or indirectly, that induced the shareholders or officers of Equity Funding to repose trust or confidence in him. There was no expectation by Dirks' sources that he would keep their information in confidence. Nor did Dirks misappropriate or illegally obtain the information about Equity Funding. Unless the insiders breached their *Cady, Roberts* duty to shareholders in disclosing the nonpublic information to Dirks, he breached no duty when he passed it on to investors as well as to the Wall Street Journal.

It is clear that neither Secrist nor the other Equity Funding employees violated their *Cady, Roberts* duty to the corporation's shareholders by providing information to Dirks. The tippers received no monetary or personal benefit for revealing Equity Funding's secrets, nor was their purpose to make a gift of valuable information to Dirks. As the facts of this case clearly indicate, the tippers were motivated by a desire to expose the fraud.... In the absence of a breach of duty to shareholders by the insiders, there was no derivative breach by Dirks. See n. 20, supra. Dirks therefore could not have been "a participant after the fact in [an] insider's breach of a fiduciary duty." *Chiarella*, 445 U.S., at 230, n. 12, 100 S.Ct., at 1115, n. 12.

V

We conclude that Dirks, in the circumstances of this case, had no duty to abstain from use of the inside information that he obtained. The judgment of the Court of Appeals therefore is reversed.

■ JUSTICE BLACKMUN, with whom JUSTICE BRENNAN and JUSTICE MARSHALL join, dissenting.

The Court today takes still another step to limit the protections provided investors by § 10(b) of the Securities Exchange Act of 1934.... The device employed in this case engrafts a special motivational requirement on the fiduciary duty doctrine. This innovation excuses a knowing and intentional violation of an insider's duty to shareholders if the insider does not act from a motive of personal gain. Even on the extraordinary facts of this case, such an innovation is not justified.

I

As the Court recognizes, ... the facts here are unusual. After a meeting with Ronald Secrist, a former Equity Funding employee, on March 7, 1973, App. 226, petitioner Raymond Dirks found himself in possession of material nonpublic information of massive fraud within the company.[2] In the Court's words, "[h]e uncovered ... startling information that required no analysis or exercise of judgment as to its market relevance." ... In disclosing that information to Dirks, Secrist intended that Dirks would disseminate the information to his clients, those clients would unload their Equity Funding securities on the market, and the price would fall precipitously, thereby triggering a reaction from the authorities. App. 16, 25, 27.

---

2. Unknown to Dirks, Secrist also told his story to New York insurance regulators the same day. App. 23. They immediately assured themselves that Equity Funding's New York subsidiary had sufficient assets to cover its outstanding policies and then passed on the information to California regulators who in turn informed Illinois regulators. Illinois investigators, later joined by California officials, conducted a surprise audit of Equity Funding's Illinois subsidiary, id., at 87–88, to find $22 million of the subsidiary's assets missing. On March 30, these authorities seized control of the Illinois subsidiary. Id., at 271.

Dirks complied with his informant's wishes. Instead of reporting that information to the Securities and Exchange Commission (SEC or Commission) or to other regulatory agencies, Dirks began to disseminate the information to his clients and undertook his own investigation. One of his first steps was to direct his associates at Delafield Childs to draw up a list of Delafield clients holding Equity Funding securities. On March 12, eight days before Dirks flew to Los Angeles to investigate Secrist's story, he reported the full allegations to Boston Company Institutional Investors, Inc., which on March 15 and 16 sold approximately $1.2 million of Equity securities.[4] See id., at 199. As he gathered more information, he selectively disclosed it to his clients. To those holding Equity Funding securities he gave the "hard" story—all the allegations; others received the "soft" story—a recitation of vague factors that might reflect adversely on Equity Funding's management. See id., at 211, n. 24.

Dirks' attempts to disseminate the information to nonclients were feeble, at best. On March 12, he left a message for Herbert Lawson, the San Francisco bureau chief of The Wall Street Journal. Not until March 19 and 20 did he call Lawson again, and outline the situation. William Blundell, a Journal investigative reporter based in Los Angeles, got in touch with Dirks about his March 20 telephone call. On March 21, Dirks met with Blundell in Los Angeles. Blundell began his own investigation, relying in part on Dirks' contacts, and on March 23 telephoned Stanley Sporkin, the SEC's Deputy Director of Enforcement. On March 26, the next business day, Sporkin and his staff interviewed Blundell and asked to see Dirks the following morning. Trading was halted by the New York Stock Exchange at about the same time Dirks was talking to Los Angeles SEC personnel. The next day, March 28, the SEC suspended trading in Equity Funding securities. By that time, Dirks' clients had unloaded close to $15 million of Equity Funding stock and the price had plummeted from $26 to $15. The effect of Dirks' selective dissemination of Secrist's information was that Dirks' clients were able to shift the losses that were inevitable due to the Equity Funding fraud from themselves to uninformed market participants.

II

A

No one questions that Secrist himself could not trade on his inside information to the disadvantage of uninformed shareholders and purchasers of Equity Funding securities. See Brief for United

---

4. The Court's implicit suggestion that Dirks did not gain by this selective dissemination of advice, ante, at . . . n. 2, is inaccurate. The [Administrative Law Judge] found that because of Dirks' information, Boston Company Institutional Investors, Inc., directed business to Delafield Childs that generated approximately $25,000 in commissions. App. 199, 204–205. While it is true that the exact economic benefit gained by Delafield Childs due to Dirks' activities is unknowable because of the structure of compensation in the securities market, there can be no doubt that Delafield and Dirks gained both monetary rewards and enhanced reputations for "looking after" their clients.

States as *Amicus Curiae* 19, n. 12. Unlike the printer in *Chiarella,* Secrist stood in a fiduciary relationship with these shareholders....

The Court also acknowledges that Secrist could not do by proxy what he was prohibited from doing personally.... Mosser v. Darrow, 341 U.S. 267, 272, 71 S.Ct. 680, 685, 95 L.Ed. 927 (1951). But this is precisely what Secrist did. Secrist used Dirks to disseminate information to Dirks' clients, who in turn dumped stock on unknowing purchasers. Secrist thus intended Dirks to injure the purchasers of Equity Funding securities to whom Secrist had a duty to disclose. Accepting the Court's view of tippee liability,[5] it appears that Dirks' knowledge of this breach makes him liable as a participant in the breach after the fact....; *Chiarella,* 445 U.S., at 230, n. 12, 100 S.Ct., at 1115, n. 12.

B

The Court holds, however, that Dirks is not liable because Secrist did not violate his duty; according to the Court, this is so because Secrist did not have the improper purpose of personal gain.... In so doing, the Court imposes a new, subjective limitation on the scope of the duty owed by insiders to shareholders. The novelty of this limitation is reflected in the Court's lack of support for it....

C

The fact that the insider himself does not benefit from the breach does not eradicate the shareholder's injury. Cf. Restatement (Second) of Trusts § 205, Comments c and d (1959) (trustee liable for acts causing diminution of value of trust); 3 A. Scott on Trusts § 205, p. 1665 (1967) (trustee liable for any losses to trust caused by his breach). It makes no difference to the shareholder whether the corporate insider gained or intended to gain personally from the transaction; the shareholder still has lost because of the insider's misuse of nonpublic information. The duty is addressed not to the insider's motives, but to his actions and their consequences on the shareholder. Personal gain is not an element of the breach of this duty.[11] ...

Although Secrist's general motive to expose the Equity Funding fraud was laudable, the means he chose were not. Moreover, even assuming that Dirks played a substantial role in exposing the fraud,[15]

5. I interpret the Court's opinion to impose liability on tippees like Dirks when the tippee knows or has reason to know that the information is material and nonpublic and was obtained through a breach of duty by selective revelation or otherwise. See In re Investors Management Co., 44 S.E.C. 633, 641 (1971).

11. The Court seems concerned that this case bears on insiders' contacts with analysts for valid corporate reasons.... When the disclosure is to an investment banker or some other adviser, however, there is normally no breach because the insider does not have scienter: he does not intend that the inside information be used for trading purposes to the disadvantage of shareholders....

The situation here, of course, is radically different.... Secrist divulged the information for the precise purpose of causing Dirks' clients to trade on it. I fail to understand how imposing liability on Dirks will affect legitimate insider-analyst contacts.

15. The Court uncritically accepts Dirks' own view of his role in uncovering the he and his clients should not profit from the information they obtained from Secrist. . . .

IV

In my view, Secrist violated his duty to Equity Funding shareholders by transmitting material nonpublic information to Dirks with the intention that Dirks would cause his clients to trade on that information. Dirks, therefore, was under a duty to make the information publicly available or to refrain from actions that he knew would lead to trading. Because Dirks caused his clients to trade, he violated § 10(b) and Rule 10b–5. Any other result is a disservice to this country's attempt to provide fair and efficient capital markets. I dissent.

AFTER THE FALL, Wall St. J., November 18, 1987, at 1, col. 6. "As a securities analyst in 1973, [Raymond L. Dirks] uncovered the Equity Funding stock-fraud case and alerted the SEC to it. The agency told Mr. Dirks it was too busy to probe the matter, but it eventually looked into Equity Funding—and slapped Mr. Dirks with an insider-trading action for notifying his clients before the matter became public. He fought that all the way to the Supreme Court and won in 1983.

"His luck ran out, however, when John Muir & Co., a highflying brokerage firm, collapsed in 1980 amid SEC charges of misplaced funds. Mr. Dirks, who was in charge of underwritings at Muir, denies any wrongdoing. He was suspended from acting as a principal in a securities firm for six months, a period that ended this year after appeals petered out.

"After Muir's collapse, Mr. Dirks scraped for work as a self-employed analyst. He resurfaced in 1985 at the firm of Steinberg & Lyman, helping bring fledgling insurance companies public. Last November, he moved to the New York brokerage firm of Baird, Patrick & Co., where he now heads an 18–person insurance-analyst unit. 'I'm excited about insurance stocks again,' says Mr. Dirks, who is now 53. 'They're tremendously undervalued.' . . .

"Fourteen years of legal battles have left Ray Dirks older, wiser—and better connected. 'Some of the biggest money managers in the country return my phone calls now because they've heard my name,' he says. 'People want to know what I'm like. I can generally get in to see anybody I want.'

"He plays down the rigors of his long fight. 'I am a rebel by nature. I thrived on it,' Mr. Dirks says. 'But reality sets in when you have to pay lawyers. It was depressing.'

Equity Funding fraud. . . . It ignores the fact that Secrist gave the same information at the same time to state insurance regulators, who proceeded to expose massive fraud in a major Equity Funding subsidiary. The fraud surfaced before Dirks ever spoke to the SEC.

"He adds: 'I still get calls from guys wanting me to uncover some scams. I tell 'em I'm too busy. Besides, there's no money in it.' "

––––––

SEC v. YUN, 327 F.3d 1263 (11th Cir. 2003). "[In cases involving tippee liability,] the SEC must establish that [the tippers intended] to benefit from their disclosure of confidential information. . . .

"The showing needed to prove an intent to benefit is not extensive. The Supreme Court in *Dirks*, after establishing the tipper benefit requirement, proceeded to define 'benefit' in very expansive terms. The Court declared that not only does an actual pecuniary gain, such as a kickback or an expectation of a reciprocal tip in the future, suffice to create a 'benefit,' but also cases where the tipper sought to enhance his reputation (which would translate into future earnings) or to make a gift to a trading relative or friend." . . .

"In this case, the SEC presented evidence that the two [tipper and tippee] were 'friendly,' worked together for several years, and split commissions on various real estate transactions over the years. This evidence is sufficient for a jury reasonably to conclude that Donna [the tipper] expected to benefit from her tip to Burch [the tippee] by maintaining a good relationship between a friend and frequent partner in real estate deals. See SEC v. Sargent, 229 F.3d at 68 (finding evidence of personal benefit when the tipper passed on information 'to effect a reconciliation with his friend and to maintain a useful networking contact')."

See also United States v. Falcone, 257 F.3d 226 (2d Cir. 2001).

––––––

United States v. O'Hagan

United States Supreme Court, 1997.
521 U.S. 642, 117 S.Ct. 2199, 138 L.Ed.2d 724.

■ JUSTICE GINSBURG delivered the opinion of the Court.

This case concerns the interpretation and enforcement of § 10(b) and § 14(e) of the Securities Exchange Act of 1934, and rules made by the Securities and Exchange Commission pursuant to these provisions, Rule 10b–5 and Rule 14e–3(a). Two prime questions are presented. The first relates to the misappropriation of material, nonpublic information for securities trading; the second concerns fraudulent practices in the tender offer setting. In particular, we address and resolve these issues: (1) Is a person who trades in securities for personal profit, using confidential information misappropriated in breach of a fiduciary duty to the source of the information, guilty of violating § 10(b) and Rule 10b–5? (2) Did the Commission exceed its rulemaking authority by adopting Rule 14e–3(a), which proscribes trading on undisclosed information in the tender offer setting, even in the absence of a duty to disclose? Our answer to the first question is yes, and to the second question, viewed in the context of this case, no.

I

Respondent James Herman O'Hagan was a partner in the law firm of Dorsey & Whitney in Minneapolis, Minnesota. In July 1988, Grand Metropolitan PLC (Grand Met), a company based in London, England, retained Dorsey & Whitney as local counsel to represent Grand Met regarding a potential tender offer for the common stock of the Pillsbury Company, headquartered in Minneapolis. Both Grand Met and Dorsey & Whitney took precautions to protect the confidentiality of Grand Met's tender offer plans. O'Hagan did no work on the Grand Met representation. Dorsey & Whitney withdrew from representing Grand Met on September 9, 1988. Less than a month later, on October 4, 1988, Grand Met publicly announced its tender offer for Pillsbury stock.

On August 18, 1988, while Dorsey & Whitney was still representing Grand Met, O'Hagan began purchasing call options for Pillsbury stock. Each option gave him the right to purchase 100 shares of Pillsbury stock by a specified date in September 1988. Later in August and in September, O'Hagan made additional purchases of Pillsbury call options. By the end of September, he owned 2,500 unexpired Pillsbury options, apparently more than any other individual investor. See App. 85, 148. O'Hagan also purchased, in September 1988, some 5,000 shares of Pillsbury common stock, at a price just under $39 per share. When Grand Met announced its tender offer in October, the price of Pillsbury stock rose to nearly $60 per share. O'Hagan then sold his Pillsbury call options and common stock, making a profit of more than $4.3 million.

The Securities and Exchange Commission (SEC or Commission) initiated an investigation into O'Hagan's transactions, culminating in a 57–count indictment. The indictment alleged that O'Hagan defrauded his law firm and its client, Grand Met, by using for his own trading purposes material, nonpublic information regarding Grand Met's planned tender offer. Id., at 8. According to the indictment, O'Hagan used the profits he gained through this trading to conceal his previous embezzlement and conversion of unrelated client trust funds. Id., at 10.[2] O'Hagan was charged with 20 counts of mail fraud, in violation of 18 U.S.C. § 1341; 17 counts of securities fraud, in violation of § 10(b) of the Securities Exchange Act of 1934 (Exchange Act), 48 Stat. 891, 15 U.S.C. § 78j(b), and SEC Rule 10b–5, 17 CFR § 240.10b–5 (1996); 17 counts of fraudulent trading in connection with a tender offer, in violation of § 14(e) of the Exchange Act, 15 U.S.C. § 78n(e), and SEC Rule 14e–3(a), 17 CFR § 240.14e–3(a) (1996); and 3 counts of violating federal money laundering statutes, 18 U.S.C. §§ 1956(a)(1)(B)(i),

---

2. O'Hagan was convicted of theft in state court, sentenced to 30 months' imprisonment, and fined. See State v. O'Hagan, 474 N.W.2d 613, 615, 623 (Minn.App.1991). The Supreme Court of Minnesota disbarred O'Hagan from the practice of law. See In re O'Hagan, 450 N.W.2d 571 (Minn.1990).

1957. See App. 13–24. A jury convicted O'Hagan on all 57 counts, and he was sentenced to a 41–month term of imprisonment.

A divided panel of the Court of Appeals for the Eighth Circuit reversed all of O'Hagan's convictions. 92 F.3d 612 (1996). Liability under § 10(b) and Rule 10b–5, the Eighth Circuit held, may not be grounded on the "misappropriation theory" of securities fraud on which the prosecution relied. Id., at 622. The Court of Appeals also held that Rule 14e–3(a)—which prohibits trading while in possession of material, nonpublic information relating to a tender offer—exceeds the SEC's § 14(e) rulemaking authority because the rule contains no breach of fiduciary duty requirement. Id., at 627. The Eighth Circuit further concluded that O'Hagan's mail fraud and money laundering convictions rested on violations of the securities laws, and therefore could not stand once the securities fraud convictions were reversed. Id., at 627–628. Judge Fagg, dissenting, stated that he would recognize and enforce the misappropriation theory, and would hold that the SEC did not exceed its rulemaking authority when it adopted Rule 14e–3(a) without requiring proof of a breach of fiduciary duty. Id., at 628.

Decisions of the Courts of Appeals are in conflict on the propriety of the misappropriation theory under § 10(b) and Rule 10b–5, see infra this page and n. 3, and on the legitimacy of Rule 14e–3(a) under § 14(e), see infra, at 25. We granted certiorari, 519 U.S. 1037 (1997), and now reverse the Eighth Circuit's judgment.

II

We address first the Court of Appeals' reversal of O'Hagan's convictions under § 10(b) and Rule 10b–5. Following the Fourth Circuit's lead, see United States v. Bryan, 58 F.3d 933, 943–959 (1995), the Eighth Circuit rejected the misappropriation theory as a basis for § 10(b) liability. We hold, in accord with several other Courts of Appeals, that criminal liability under § 10(b) may be predicated on the misappropriation theory.[4]

A . . .

[Section] 10(b) of the Exchange Act proscribes (1) using any deceptive device (2) in connection with the purchase or sale of securities, in contravention of rules prescribed by the Commission. The provision, as written, does not confine its coverage to deception of a purchaser or seller of securities, see United States v. Newman, 664

---

4. Twice before we have been presented with the question whether criminal liability for violation of § 10(b) may be based on a misappropriation theory. In Chiarella v. United States, 445 U.S. 222, 235–237 (1980), the jury had received no misappropriation theory instructions, so we declined to address the question.... In Carpenter v. United States, 484 U.S. 19, 24 (1987), the Court divided evenly on whether, under the circumstances of that case, convictions resting on the misappropriation theory should be affirmed. See Aldave, The Misappropriation Theory: Carpenter and Its Aftermath, 49 Ohio St. L.J. 373, 375 (1988) (observing that "Carpenter was, by any reckoning, an unusual case," for the information there misappropriated belonged not to a company preparing to engage in securities transactions, e.g., a bidder in a corporate acquisition, but to the Wall Street Journal).

F.2d 12, 17 (C.A.2 1981); rather, the statute reaches any deceptive device used "in connection with the purchase or sale of any security."

Pursuant to its § 10(b) rulemaking authority, the Commission has adopted Rule 10b–5. . . .

Under the "traditional" or "classical theory" of insider trading liability, § 10(b) and Rule 10b–5 are violated when a corporate insider trades in the securities of his corporation on the basis of material, nonpublic information. Trading on such information qualifies as a "deceptive device" under § 10(b), we have affirmed, because "a relationship of trust and confidence [exists] between the shareholders of a corporation and those insiders who have obtained confidential information by reason of their position with that corporation." Chiarella v. United States, 445 U.S. 222, 228 (1980). That relationship, we recognized, "gives rise to a duty to disclose [or to abstain from trading] because of the 'necessity of preventing a corporate insider from . . . taking unfair advantage of . . . uninformed . . . stockholders.' " Id., at 228–229 (citation omitted). The classical theory applies not only to officers, directors, and other permanent insiders of a corporation, but also to attorneys, accountants, consultants, and others who temporarily become fiduciaries of a corporation. See Dirks v. SEC, 463 U.S. 646, 655, n. 14 (1983).

The "misappropriation theory" holds that a person commits fraud "in connection with" a securities transaction, and thereby violates § 10(b) and Rule 10b–5, when he misappropriates confidential information for securities trading purposes, in breach of a duty owed to the source of the information. See Brief for United States 14. Under this theory, a fiduciary's undisclosed, self-serving use of a principal's information to purchase or sell securities, in breach of a duty of loyalty and confidentiality, defrauds the principal of the exclusive use of that information. In lieu of premising liability on a fiduciary relationship between company insider and purchaser or seller of the company's stock, the misappropriation theory premises liability on a fiduciary-turned-trader's deception of those who entrusted him with access to confidential information.

The two theories are complementary, each addressing efforts to capitalize on nonpublic information through the purchase or sale of securities. The classical theory targets a corporate insider's breach of duty to shareholders with whom the insider transacts; the misappropriation theory outlaws trading on the basis of nonpublic information by a corporate "outsider" in breach of a duty owed not to a trading party, but to the source of the information. The misappropriation theory is thus designed to "protect the integrity of the securities markets against abuses by 'outsiders' to a corporation who have access to confidential information that will affect the corporation's security price when revealed, but who owe no fiduciary or other duty to that corporation's shareholders." Ibid.

In this case, the indictment alleged that O'Hagan, in breach of a duty of trust and confidence he owed to his law firm, Dorsey & Whitney, and to its client, Grand Met, traded on the basis of nonpublic information regarding Grand Met's planned tender offer for Pillsbury common stock. App. 16. This conduct, the Government charged, constituted a fraudulent device in connection with the purchase and sale of securities.[5]

B

We agree with the Government that misappropriation, as just defined, satisfies § 10(b)'s requirement that chargeable conduct involve a "deceptive device or contrivance" used "in connection with" the purchase or sale of securities. We observe, first, that misappropriators, as the Government describes them, deal in deception. A fiduciary who "[pretends] loyalty to the principal while secretly converting the principal's information for personal gain," Brief for United States 17, "dupes" or defrauds the principal. See Aldave, Misappropriation: A General Theory of Liability for Trading on Nonpublic Information, 13 Hofstra L.Rev. 101, 119 (1984).

We addressed fraud of the same species in Carpenter v. United States, 484 U.S. 19 (1987), which involved the mail fraud statute's proscription of "any scheme or artifice to defraud," 18 U.S.C. § 1341. Affirming convictions under that statute, we said in Carpenter that an employee's undertaking not to reveal his employer's confidential information "became a sham" when the employee provided the information to his co-conspirators in a scheme to obtain trading profits. 484 U.S. at 27. A company's confidential information, we recognized in Carpenter, qualifies as property to which the company has a right of exclusive use. Id., at 25–27. The undisclosed misappropriation of such information, in violation of a fiduciary duty, the Court said in Carpenter, constitutes fraud akin to embezzlement—" 'the fraudulent appropriation to one's own use of the money or goods entrusted to one's care by another.' " Id., at 27 (quoting Grin v. Shine, 187 U.S. 181, 189 (1902)); see Aldave, 13 Hofstra L.Rev., at 119. Carpenter's discussion of the fraudulent misuse of confidential information, the Government notes, "is a particularly apt source of guidance here, because [the mail fraud statute] (like Section 10(b)) has long been held to require deception, not merely the breach of a fiduciary duty." Brief for United States 18, n. 9 (citation omitted).

Deception through nondisclosure is central to the theory of liability for which the Government seeks recognition. As counsel for the Government stated in explanation of the theory at oral argument: "To satisfy the common law rule that a trustee may not use the property that [has] been entrusted [to] him, there would have to be consent. To satisfy the requirement of the Securities Act that there be

---

5. The Government could not have prosecuted O'Hagan under the classical theory, for O'Hagan was not an "insider" of Pillsbury, the corporation in whose stock he traded. Although an "outsider" with respect to Pillsbury, O'Hagan had an intimate association with, and was found to have traded on confidential information from Dorsey & Whitney, counsel to tender offeror Grand Met. Under the misappropriation theory, O'Hagan's securities trading does not escape Exchange Act sanction, as it would under the dissent's reasoning, simply because he was associated with, and gained nonpublic information from, the bidder, rather than the target.

no deception, there would only have to be disclosure." Tr. of Oral Arg. 12; see generally Restatement (Second) of Agency §§ 390, 395 (1958) (agent's disclosure obligation regarding use of confidential information).[6]

. . . [F]ull disclosure forecloses liability under the misappropriation theory: Because the deception essential to the misappropriation theory involves feigning fidelity to the source of information, if the fiduciary discloses to the source that he plans to trade on the nonpublic information, there is no "deceptive device" and thus no § 10(b) violation—although the fiduciary-turned-trader may remain liable under state law for breach of a duty of loyalty.[7]

We turn next to the § 10(b) requirement that the misappropriator's deceptive use of information be "in connection with the purchase or sale of [a] security." This element is satisfied because the fiduciary's fraud is consummated, not when the fiduciary gains the confidential information, but when, without disclosure to his principal, he uses the information to purchase or sell securities. The securities transaction and the breach of duty thus coincide. This is so even though the person or entity defrauded is not the other party to the trade, but is, instead, the source of the nonpublic information. See Aldave, 13 Hofstra L.Rev., at 120 ("a fraud or deceit can be practiced on one person, with resultant harm to another person or group of persons"). A misappropriator who trades on the basis of material, nonpublic information, in short, gains his advantageous market position through deception; he deceives the source of the information and simultaneously harms members of the investing public. See id., at 120–121, and n. 107.

The misappropriation theory targets information of a sort that misappropriators ordinarily capitalize upon to gain no-risk profits through the purchase or sale of securities. Should a misappropriator put such information to other use, the statute's prohibition would not be implicated. The theory does not catch all conceivable forms of fraud involving confidential information; rather, it catches fraudulent means of capitalizing on such information through securities transactions.

The Government notes another limitation on the forms of fraud § 10(b) reaches: "The misappropriation theory would not . . . apply to a case in which a person defrauded a bank into giving him a loan or embezzled cash from another, and then used the proceeds of the

6. Under the misappropriation theory urged in this case, the disclosure obligation runs to the source of the information, here, Dorsey & Whitney and Grand Met. Chief Justice Burger, dissenting in Chiarella, advanced a broader reading of § 10(b) and Rule 10b–5; the disclosure obligation, as he envisioned it, ran to those with whom the misappropriator trades. 445 U.S., at 240 ("a person who has misappropriated nonpublic information has an absolute duty to disclose that information or to refrain from trading"); see also id., at 243, n. 4. The Government does not propose that we adopt a misappropriation theory of that breadth.

7. Where, however, a person trading on the basis of material, nonpublic information owes a duty of loyalty and confidentiality to two entities or persons—for example, a law firm and its client—but makes disclosure to only one, the trader may still be liable under the misappropriation theory.

misdeed to purchase securities." Brief for United States 24, n. 13. In such a case, the Government states, "the proceeds would have value to the malefactor apart from their use in a securities transaction, and the fraud would be complete as soon as the money was obtained." Ibid. In other words, money can buy, if not anything, then at least many things; its misappropriation may thus be viewed as sufficiently detached from a subsequent securities transaction that § 10(b)'s "in connection with" requirement would not be met. Ibid. . . .

The misappropriation theory comports with § 10(b)'s language, which requires deception "in connection with the purchase or sale of any security," not deception of an identifiable purchaser or seller. The theory is also well-tuned to an animating purpose of the Exchange Act: to insure honest securities markets and thereby promote investor confidence. See 45 Fed.Reg. 60412 (1980) (trading on misappropriated information "undermines the integrity of, and investor confidence in, the securities markets"). Although informational disparity is inevitable in the securities markets, investors likely would hesitate to venture their capital in a market where trading based on misappropriated nonpublic information is unchecked by law. An investor's informational disadvantage vis-a-vis a misappropriator with material, nonpublic information stems from contrivance, not luck; it is a disadvantage that cannot be overcome with research or skill. See Brudney, Insiders, Outsiders, and Informational Advantages Under the Federal Securities Laws, 93 Harv.L.Rev. 322, 356 (1979) ("If the market is thought to be systematically populated with . . . transactors [trading on the basis of misappropriated information] some investors will refrain from dealing altogether, and others will incur costs to avoid dealing with such transactors or corruptly to overcome their unerodable informational advantages."); Aldave, 13 Hofstra L.Rev., at 122–123.

In sum, considering the inhibiting impact on market participation of trading on misappropriated information, and the congressional purposes underlying § 10(b), it makes scant sense to hold a lawyer like O'Hagan a § 10(b) violator if he works for a law firm representing the target of a tender offer, but not if he works for a law firm representing the bidder. The text of the statute requires no such result.[9] The misappropriation at issue here was properly made the subject of a § 10(b) charge because it meets the statutory requirement that there be "deceptive" conduct "in connection with" securities transactions.

9. As noted earlier, however, see supra, at 9–10, the textual requirement of deception precludes § 10(b) liability when a person trading on the basis of nonpublic information has disclosed his trading plans to, or obtained authorization from, the principal—even though such conduct may affect the securities markets in the same manner as the conduct reached by the misappropriation theory. . . . [T]he fact that § 10(b) is only a partial antidote to the problems it was designed to allevi-

ate does not call into question its prohibition of conduct that falls within its textual proscription. Moreover, once a disloyal agent discloses his imminent breach of duty, his principal may seek appropriate equitable relief under state law. Furthermore, in the context of a tender offer, the principal who authorizes an agent's trading on confidential information may, in the Commission's view, incur liability for an Exchange Act violation under Rule 14e–3(a).

C

... [T]he misappropriation theory, as we have examined and explained it in this opinion, is both consistent with the statute and with our precedent.[11] ...

The Eighth Circuit erred in holding that the misappropriation theory is inconsistent with § 10(b). The Court of Appeals may address on remand O'Hagan's other challenges to his convictions under § 10(b) and Rule 10b–5.

III

We consider next the ground on which the Court of Appeals reversed O'Hagan's convictions for fraudulent trading in connection with a tender offer, in violation of § 14(e) of the Exchange Act and SEC Rule 14e–3(a). A sole question is before us as to these convictions: Did the Commission, as the Court of Appeals held, exceed its rulemaking authority under § 14(e) when it adopted Rule 14e–3(a) without requiring a showing that the trading at issue entailed a breach of fiduciary duty? We hold that the Commission, in this regard and to the extent relevant to this case, did not exceed its authority.

The governing statutory provision, § 14(e) of the Exchange Act, reads in relevant part:

"It shall be unlawful for any person ... to engage in any fraudulent, deceptive, or manipulative acts or practices, in connection with any tender offer.... The [SEC] shall, for the purposes of this subsection, by rules and regulations define, and prescribe means reasonably designed to prevent, such acts and practices as are fraudulent, deceptive, or manipulative." 15 U.S.C. § 78n(e).

Section 14(e)'s first sentence prohibits fraudulent acts in connection with a tender offer. This self-operating proscription was one of several provisions added to the Exchange Act in 1968 by the Williams Act, 82 Stat. 454. The section's second sentence delegates definitional and prophylactic rulemaking authority to the Commission. Congress added this rulemaking delegation to § 14(e) in 1970 amendments to the Williams Act. See § 5, 84 Stat. 1497.

Through § 14(e) and other provisions on disclosure in the Williams Act, Congress sought to ensure that shareholders "confronted

---

11. The United States additionally argues that Congress confirmed the validity of the misappropriation theory in the Insider Trading and Securities Fraud Enforcement Act of 1988 (ITSFEA), § 2(1), 102 Stat. 4677, note following 15 U.S.C. § 78u–1. See Brief for United States 32–35. ITSFEA declares that "the rules and regulations of the Securities and Exchange Commission under the Securities Exchange Act of 1934 ... governing trading while in possession of material, nonpublic information are, as required by such Act, necessary and appropriate in the public interest and for the protection of investors." Note following 15 U.S.C. § 78u–1.

ITSFEA also includes a new § 20A(a) of the Exchange Act expressly providing a private cause of action against persons who violate the Exchange Act "by purchasing or selling a security while in possession of material, nonpublic information", such an action may be brought by "any person who, contemporaneously with the purchase or sale of securities that is the subject of such violation, has purchased ... or sold ... securities of the same class." 15 U.S.C. § 78u–1(a). Because we uphold the misappropriation theory on the basis of § 10(b) itself, we do not address ITSFEA's significance for cases of this genre.

by a cash tender offer for their stock [would] not be required to respond without adequate information." Rondeau v. Mosinee Paper Corp., 422 U.S. 49, 58 (1975); see Lewis v. McGraw, 619 F.2d 192, 195 (C.A.2 1980) (per curiam) ("very purpose" of Williams Act was "informed decisionmaking by shareholders"). As we recognized in Schreiber v. Burlington Northern, Inc., 472 U.S. 1 (1985), Congress designed the Williams Act to make "disclosure, rather than court-imposed principles of 'fairness' or 'artificiality,' ... the preferred method of market regulation." Id., at 9, n. 8. Section 14(e), we explained, "supplements the more precise disclosure provisions found elsewhere in the Williams Act, while requiring disclosure more explicitly addressed to the tender offer context than that required by § 10(b)." Id., at 10–11.

Relying on § 14(e)'s rulemaking authorization, the Commission, in 1980, promulgated Rule 14e–3(a). That measure provides:

> "(a) If any person has taken a substantial step or steps to commence, or has commenced, a tender offer (the 'offering person'), it shall constitute a fraudulent, deceptive or manipulative act or practice within the meaning of section 14(e) of the [Exchange] Act for any other person who is in possession of material information relating to such tender offer which information he knows or has reason to know is nonpublic and which he knows or has reason to know has been acquired directly or indirectly from:
>
>> "(1) The offering person,
>>
>> "(2) The issuer of the securities sought or to be sought by such tender offer, or
>>
>> "(3) Any officer, director, partner or employee or any other person acting on behalf of the offering person or such issuer,
>
> to purchase or sell or cause to be purchased or sold any of such securities or any securities convertible into or exchangeable for any such securities or any option or right to obtain or to dispose of any of the foregoing securities, unless within a reasonable time prior to any purchase or sale such information and its source are publicly disclosed by press release or otherwise." 17 CFR § 240.14e–3(a) (1996).

As characterized by the Commission, Rule 14e–3(a) is a "disclose or abstain from trading" requirement. 45 Fed.Reg. 60410 (1980).[15] The Second Circuit concisely described the rule's thrust:

> "One violates Rule 14e–3(a) if he trades on the basis of material nonpublic information concerning a pending tender offer that he knows or has reason to know has been acquired 'directly or indirectly' from an insider of the offeror or issuer, or someone

---

15. The rule thus adopts for the tender offer context a requirement resembling the one Chief Justice Burger would have adopted in Chiarella for misappropriators under § 10(b). See supra, at 10, n. 6.

working on their behalf. Rule 14e–3(a) is a disclosure provision. It creates a duty in those traders who fall within its ambit to abstain or disclose, without regard to whether the trader owes a pre-existing fiduciary duty to respect the confidentiality of the information." United States v. Chestman, 947 F.2d 551, 557 (1991) (en banc) (emphasis added), cert. denied, 503 U.S. 1004 (1992). See also SEC v. Maio, 51 F.3d 623, 635 (C.A.7 1995) ("Rule 14e–3 creates a duty to disclose material nonpublic information, or abstain from trading in stocks implicated by an impending tender offer, regardless of whether such information was obtained through a breach of fiduciary duty.") (emphasis added); SEC v. Peters, 978 F.2d 1162, 1165 (C.A.10 1992) (as written, Rule 14e–3(a) has no fiduciary duty requirement).

In the Eighth Circuit's view, because Rule 14e–3(a) applies whether or not the trading in question breaches a fiduciary duty, the regulation exceeds the SEC's § 14(e) rulemaking authority....

The Eighth Circuit homed in on the essence of § 14(e)'s rulemaking authorization: "The statute empowers the SEC to 'define' and 'prescribe means reasonably designed to prevent' 'acts and practices' which are 'fraudulent.' " Id., at 624. All that means, the Eighth Circuit found plain, is that the SEC may "identify and regulate," in the tender offer context, "acts and practices" the law already defines as "fraudulent"; but, the Eighth Circuit maintained, the SEC may not "create its own definition of fraud." Ibid. (internal quotation marks omitted)....

We need not resolve in this case whether the Commission's authority under § 14(e) to "define ... such acts and practices as are fraudulent" is broader than the Commission's fraud-defining authority under § 10(b), for we agree with the United States that Rule 14e–3(a), as applied to cases of this genre, qualifies under § 14(e) as a "means reasonably designed to prevent" fraudulent trading on material, non-public information in the tender offer context. A prophylactic measure, because its mission is to prevent, typically encompasses more than the core activity prohibited.... [Section] 14(e)'s rulemaking authorization gives the Commission "latitude," even in the context of a term of art like "manipulative," "to regulate nondeceptive activities as a 'reasonably designed' means of preventing manipulative acts, without suggesting any change in the meaning of the term 'manipulative' itself." 472 U.S., at 11, n. 11. We hold, accordingly, that under § 14(e), the Commission may prohibit acts, not themselves fraudulent under the common law or § 10(b), if the prohibition is "reasonably designed to prevent ... acts and practices [that] are fraudulent." 15 U.S.C. § 78n(c)....

[I]t is a fair assumption that trading on the basis of material, nonpublic information [in connection with a tender offer] will often involve a breach of a duty of confidentiality to the bidder or target company or their representatives. The SEC, cognizant of the proof problem that could enable sophisticated traders to escape responsibility, placed in Rule 14e–3(a) a "disclose or abstain from trading" command that does not require specific proof of a breach of fiduciary duty. That prescription, we are satisfied, applied to this case, is a "means reasonably designed to prevent" fraudulent trading on material, nonpublic information in the tender offer context. See Chestman, 947 F.2d, at 560 ("While dispensing with the subtle problems of proof associated with demonstrating fiduciary breach in the problematic area of tender offer insider trading, [Rule 14e–3(a)] retains a close nexus between the prohibited conduct and the statutory aims."); accord, Maio, 51 F.3d, at 635, and n. 14; Peters, 978 F.2d, at 1167. Therefore, insofar as it serves to prevent the type of misappropriation charged against O'Hagan, Rule 14e–3(a) is a proper exercise of the Commission's prophylactic power under § 14(e).

As an alternate ground for affirming the Eighth Circuit's judgment, O'Hagan urges that Rule 14e–3(a) is invalid because it prohibits trading in advance of a tender offer—when "a substantial step . . . to commence" such an offer has been taken—while § 14(e) prohibits fraudulent acts "in connection with any tender offer." See Brief for Respondent 41–42. O'Hagan further contends that, by covering pre-offer conduct, Rule 14e–3(a) "fails to comport with due process on two levels": The rule does not "give fair notice as to when, in advance of a tender offer, a violation of § 14(e) occurs," id., at 42; and it "disposes of any scienter requirement," id., at 43. The Court of Appeals did not address these arguments, and O'Hagan did not raise the due process points in his briefs before that court. We decline to consider these contentions in the first instance.[23] The Court of Appeals may address on remand any arguments O'Hagan has preserved.

IV

Based on its dispositions of the securities fraud convictions, the Court of Appeals also reversed O'Hagan's convictions, under 18 U.S.C. § 1341, for mail fraud. See 92 F.3d, at 627–628. Reversal of the securities convictions, the Court of Appeals recognized, "did not as a matter of law require that the mail fraud convictions likewise be reversed." Id., at 627 (citing Carpenter, 484 U.S., at 24, in which this Court unanimously affirmed mail and wire fraud convictions based on the same conduct that evenly divided the Court on the defendants' securities fraud convictions). But in this case, the Court of Appeals said, the indictment was so structured that the mail fraud charges could not be disassociated from the securities fraud charges, and absent any securities fraud, "there was no fraud upon which to base the mail fraud charges." 92 F.3d, at 627–628.[24]

. . . We need not linger over this matter, for our rulings on the securities fraud issues require that we reverse the Court of Appeals

---

23. As to O'Hagan's scienter argument, ... 15 U.S.C. § 78ff(a) requires the Government to prove "willful violation" of the securities laws, and that lack of knowledge of the relevant rule is an affirmative defense to a sentence of imprisonment. . . .

24. The Court of Appeals reversed respondent's money laundering convictions on similar reasoning. See 92 F.3d, at 628. Because the United States did not seek review of that ruling, we leave undisturbed that portion of the Court of Appeals' judgment.

judgment on the mail fraud counts as well.[25] . . .

The judgment of the Court of Appeals for the Eighth Circuit is reversed, and the case is remanded for further proceedings consistent with this opinion.

It is so ordered.

■ DISSENT: JUSTICE SCALIA, concurring in part and dissenting in part.

I join Parts I, III, and IV of the Court's opinion. I do not agree, however, with Part II of the Court's opinion, containing its analysis of respondent's convictions under § 10(b) and Rule 10b–5. . . .

While the Court's explanation of the scope of § 10(b) and Rule 10b–5 would be entirely reasonable in some other context, it does not seem to accord with the principle of lenity we apply to criminal statutes. . . .

In light of that principle, it seems to me that the unelaborated statutory language: "to use or employ in connection with the purchase or sale of any security . . . any manipulative or deceptive device or contrivance," § 10(b), must be construed to require the manipulation or deception of a party to a securities transaction.

[The opinion of Justice Thomas, concurring with the majority on the Mail Fraud Act issue, but dissenting on the Rule 10b–5 and Rule 14e–3(a) issues, is omitted. Chief Justice Rehnquist concurred in Justice Thomas's opinion.]

———

SEC RULE 10b5–2

[See Statutory Supplement]

———

SECURITIES AND EXCHANGE COMMISSION RELEASE NO. 33–7881, Part III(B) (2000)

(RULE 10b5–2: DUTIES OF TRUST OR CONFIDENCE IN MISAPPROPRIATION INSIDER TRADING CASES)

[See Statutory Supplement]

———

25. The dissent finds O'Hagan's convictions on the mail fraud counts, but not on the securities fraud counts, sustainable. . . . Under the dissent's view, securities traders like O'Hagan would escape SEC civil actions and federal prosecutions under legislation targeting securities fraud, only to be caught for their trading activities in the broad mail fraud net. If misappropriation theory cases could proceed only under the federal mail and wire fraud statutes, practical consequences for individual defendants might not be large, see Aldave, 49 Ohio St. L.J., at 381, and n. 60; however, "proportionally more persons accused of insider trading [might] be pursued by a U.S. Attorney, and proportionally fewer by the SEC," id., at 382. Our decision, of course, does not rest on such enforcement policy considerations.

Santa Fe Industries, Inc. v. Green

Supreme Court of the United States, 1977.
430 U.S. 462, 97 S.Ct. 1292, 51 L.Ed.2d 480.

■ MR. JUSTICE WHITE delivered the opinion of the Court.

The issue in this case involves the reach and coverage of § 10(b) of the Securities Exchange Act of 1934 and Rule 10b–5 thereunder in the context of a Delaware short-form merger transaction used by the majority stockholder of a corporation to eliminate the minority interest.

I

In 1936, petitioner Santa Fe Industries, Inc. (Santa Fe), acquired control of 60% of the stock of Kirby Lumber Corp. (Kirby), a Delaware corporation. Through a series of purchases over the succeeding years, Santa Fe increased its control of Kirby's stock to 95%; the purchase prices during the period 1968–1973 ranged from $65 to $92.50 per share. In 1974, wishing to acquire 100% ownership of Kirby, Santa Fe availed itself of § 253 of the Delaware Corporation Law, known as the "short-form merger" statute. Section 253 permits a parent corporation owning at least 90% of the stock of a subsidiary to merge with that subsidiary, upon approval by the parent's board of directors, and to make payment in cash for the shares of the minority stockholders. The statute does not require the consent of, or advance notice to, the minority stockholders. However, notice of the merger must be given within 10 days after its effective date, and any stockholder who is dissatisfied with the terms of the merger may petition the Delaware Court of Chancery for a decree ordering the surviving corporation to pay him the fair value of his shares, as determined by a court-appointed appraiser subject to review by the court. Del.Code Ann., Tit. 8, §§ 253, 262 (1975 ed. and Supp.1976).

Santa Fe obtained independent appraisals of the physical assets of Kirby—land, timber, buildings, and machinery—and of Kirby's oil, gas, and mineral interests. These appraisals, together with other financial information, were submitted to Morgan Stanley & Co. (Morgan Stanley), an investment banking firm retained to appraise the fair market value of Kirby stock. Kirby's physical assets were appraised at $320 million (amounting to $640 for each of the 500,000 shares); Kirby's stock was valued by Morgan Stanley at $125 per share. Under the terms of the merger, minority stockholders were offered $150 per share.

The provisions of the short-form merger statute were fully complied with. The minority stockholders of Kirby were notified the day after the merger became effective and were advised of their right to obtain an appraisal in Delaware court if dissatisfied with the offer of $150 per share. They also received an information statement containing, in addition to the relevant financial data about Kirby, the appraisals of the value of Kirby's assets and the Morgan Stanley appraisal concluding that the fair market value of the stock was $125 per share.

Respondents, minority stockholders of Kirby, objected to the terms of the merger, but did not pursue their appraisal remedy in the Delaware Court of Chancery.[4] Instead, they brought this action in federal court on behalf of the corporation and other minority stockholders, seeking to set aside the merger or to recover what they claimed to be the fair value of their shares. The amended complaint asserted that, based on the fair market value of Kirby's physical assets as revealed by the appraisal included in the information statement sent to minority shareholders, Kirby's stock was worth at least $772 per share.[5] The complaint alleged further that the merger took place without prior notice to minority stockholders; that the purpose of the merger was to appropriate the difference between the "conceded pro rata value of the physical assets," App. 103a, and the offer of $150 per share—to "freez[e] out the minority stockholders at a wholly inadequate price," *id.*, at 100a; and that Santa Fe, knowing the appraised value of the physical assets, obtained a "fraudulent appraisal" of the stock from Morgan Stanley and offered $25 above that appraisal "in order to lull the minority stockholders into erroneously believing that [Santa Fe was] generous." *Id.*, at 103a. This course of conduct was alleged to be "a violation of Rule 10b–5 because defendants employed a 'device, scheme, or artifice to defraud' and engaged in an 'act, practice or course of business which operates or would operate as a fraud or deceit upon any person, in connection with the purchase or sale of any security.' " *Ibid.* Morgan Stanley assertedly participated in the fraud as an accessory by submitting its appraisal of $125 per share although knowing the appraised value of the physical assets. . . .

The District Court dismissed the complaint for failure to state a claim upon which relief could be granted. 391 F.Supp. 849 (S.D.N.Y. 1975). . . .

As for the claim that actionable fraud inhered in the allegedly gross undervaluation of the minority shares, the District Court observed that respondents valued their shares at a minimum of $772 per share, "basing this figure on the *pro rata* value of Kirby's physical assets." *Id.*, at 853. Accepting this valuation for purposes of the motion to dismiss, the District Court further noted that, as revealed by the complaint, the physical asset appraisal, along with other information relevant to Morgan Stanley's valuation of the shares, had been included with the information statement sent to respondents within the time required by state law. It thought that if "full and fair disclosure is made, transactions eliminating minority interests are beyond the purview of Rule 10b–5," and concluded that the "com-

---

4. On August 21, 1974, respondents petitioned for an appraisal of their Kirby stock, but they withdrew that petition on September 9 and the next day commenced this lawsuit.

5. The figure of $772 per share was calculated as follows:

"The difference of $311,000,000 ($622 per share) between the fair market value of Kirby's land and timber, alone, as per defendants' own appraisal thereof at $320,000,000 and the $9,000,000 book value of said land and timber, added to the $150 per share, yields a pro rata share of the value of the physical assets of Kirby of at least $772 per share. The value of the stock was at least the pro rata value of the physical assets." App. 102a.

plaint fail[ed] to allege an omission, misstatement or fraudulent course of conduct that would have impeded a shareholder's judgment of the value of the offer." *Id.*, at 854. The complaint therefore failed to state a claim and was dismissed.

A divided Court of Appeals for the Second Circuit reversed. 533 F.2d 1283 (1976).... The court [held] that the complaint, taken as a whole, stated a cause of action under the Rule:

> "We hold that a complaint alleges a claim under Rule 10b–5 when it charges, in connection with a Delaware short-form merger, that the majority has committed a breach of its fiduciary duty to deal fairly with minority shareholders by effecting the merger without any justifiable business purpose. The minority shareholders are given no prior notice of the merger, thus having no opportunity to apply for injunctive relief, and the proposed price to be paid is substantially lower than the appraised value reflected in the Information Statement." *Id.*, at 1291....

We granted the petition for certiorari challenging this holding because of the importance of the issue involved to the administration of the federal securities laws. 429 U.S. 814 (1976). We reverse.

II

Section 10(b) of the 1934 Act makes it "unlawful for any person ... to use or employ ... any manipulative or deceptive device or contrivance in contravention of [Securities and Exchange Commission rules]"; Rule 10b–5, promulgated by the SEC under § 10(b), prohibits, in addition to nondisclosure and misrepresentation, any "artifice to defraud" or any act "which operates or would operate as a fraud or deceit." ... The Court of Appeals' approach to the interpretation of Rule 10b–5 is inconsistent with that taken by the Court last Term in Ernst & Ernst v. Hochfelder, 425 U.S. 185, 96 S.Ct. 1375, 47 L.Ed.2d 668 (1976)....

The language of § 10(b) gives no indication that Congress meant to prohibit any conduct not involving manipulation or deception. Nor have we been cited to any evidence in the legislative history that would support a departure from the language of the statute. "When a statute speaks so specifically in terms of manipulation and deception, ... and when its history reflects no more expansive intent, we are quite unwilling to extend the scope of the statute...." *Id.*, at 214. Thus the claim of fraud and fiduciary breach in this complaint states a cause of action under any part of Rule 10b–5 only if the conduct alleged can be fairly viewed as "manipulative or deceptive" within the meaning of the statute.

III

It is our judgment that the transaction, if carried out as alleged in the complaint, was neither deceptive nor manipulative and therefore did not violate either § 10(b) of the Act or Rule 10b–5.

As we have indicated, the case comes to us on the premise that the complaint failed to allege a material misrepresentation or material failure to disclose. The finding of the District Court, undisturbed by the Court of Appeals, was that there was no "omission" or "misstatement" in the information statement accompanying the notice of merger. On the basis of the information provided, minority shareholders could either accept the price offered or reject it and seek an appraisal in the Delaware Court of Chancery. Their choice was fairly presented, and they were furnished with all relevant information on which to base their decision.

We therefore find inapposite the cases relied upon by respondents and the court below, in which the breaches of fiduciary duty held violative of Rule 10b–5 included some element of deception. Those cases forcefully reflect the principle that "[§] 10(b) must be read flexibly, not technically and restrictively" and that the statute provides a cause of action for any plaintiff who "suffer[s] an injury as a result of deceptive practices touching its sale [or purchase] of securities...." *Superintendent of Insurance v. Bankers Life & Cas. Co.*, 404 U.S. 6, 12–13, 92 S.Ct. 165, 30 L.Ed.2d 128 (1971). But the cases do not support the proposition, adopted by the Court of Appeals below and urged by respondents here, that a breach of fiduciary duty by majority stockholders, without any deception, misrepresentation, or nondisclosure, violates the statute and the Rule.

It is also readily apparent that the conduct alleged in the complaint was not "manipulative" within the meaning of the statute. "Manipulation" is "virtually a term of art when used in connection with securities markets." *Ernst & Ernst*, 425 U.S., at 199. The term refers generally to practices, such as wash sales, matched orders, or rigged prices, that are intended to mislead investors by artificially affecting market activity.... Section 10(b)'s general prohibition of practices deemed by the SEC to be "manipulative"—in this technical sense of artificially affecting market activity in order to mislead investors—is fully consistent with the fundamental purpose of the 1934 Act " 'to substitute a philosophy of full disclosure for the philosophy of *caveat emptor*....' " *Affiliated Ute Citizens v. United States*, 406 U.S. 128, 151, 92 S.Ct. 1456, 31 L.Ed.2d 741 (1972), quoting *SEC v. Capital Gains Research Bureau*, 375 U.S. 180, 186, 84 S.Ct. 275, 11 L.Ed.2d 237 (1963). Indeed, nondisclosure is usually essential to the success of a manipulative scheme. 3 Loss, *supra*, at 1565. No doubt Congress meant to prohibit the full range of ingenious devices that might be used to manipulate securities prices. But we do not think it would have chosen this "term of art" if it had meant to bring within the scope of § 10(b) instances of corporate mismanagement such as this, in which the essence of the complaint is that shareholders were treated unfairly by a fiduciary.

IV

The language of the statute is, we think, "sufficiently clear in its context" to be dispositive here, *Ernst & Ernst, supra*, at 201; but even if it were not, there are additional considerations that weigh heavily against permitting a cause of action under Rule 10b–5 for the breach of corporate fiduciary duty alleged in this complaint. Congress did not expressly provide a private cause of action for violations of § 10(b). Although we have recognized an implied cause of action under that section in some circumstances, *Superintendent of Insurance v. Bankers Life & Cas. Co., supra,* at 13 n. 9, we have also recognized that a private cause of action under the antifraud provisions of the Securities Exchange Act should not be implied where it is "unnecessary to ensure the fulfillment of Congress' purposes" in adopting the Act. *Piper v. Chris–Craft Industries, ante,* at 41. Cf. *J.I. Case Co. v. Borak,* 377 U.S. 426, 431–433, 84 S.Ct. 1555, 12 L.Ed.2d 423 (1964). As we noted earlier, ... the Court repeatedly has described the "fundamental purpose" of the Act as implementing a "philosophy of full disclosure"; once full and fair disclosure has occurred, the fairness of the terms of the transaction is at most a tangential concern of the statute. Cf. *Mills v. Electric Auto–Lite Co.,* 396 U.S. 375, 381–385, 90 S.Ct. 616, 24 L.Ed.2d 593 (1970). As in *Cort v. Ash,* 422 U.S. 66, 80, 95 S.Ct. 2080, 45 L.Ed.2d 26 (1975), we are reluctant to recognize a cause of action here to serve what is "at best a subsidiary purpose" of the federal legislation.

A second factor in determining whether Congress intended to create a federal cause of action in these circumstances is "whether 'the cause of action [is] one traditionally relegated to state law....' " *Piper v. Chris–Craft Industries, Inc., ante,* at 40, quoting *Cort v. Ash, supra,* at 78. The Delaware Legislature has supplied minority shareholders with a cause of action in the Delaware Court of Chancery to recover the fair value of shares allegedly undervalued in a short-form merger.... Of course, the existence of a particular state-law remedy is not dispositive of the question whether Congress meant to provide a similar federal remedy, but as in *Cort* and *Piper,* we conclude that "it is entirely appropriate in this instance to relegate respondent and others in his situation to whatever remedy is created by state law." 422 U.S., at 84; *ante,* at 41.

The reasoning behind a holding that the complaint in this case alleged fraud under Rule 10b–5 could not be easily contained. It is difficult to imagine how a court could distinguish, for purposes of Rule 10b–5 fraud, between a majority stockholder's use of a short-form merger to eliminate the minority at an unfair price and the use of some other device, such as a long-form merger, tender offer, or liquidation, to achieve the same result; or indeed how a court could distinguish the alleged abuses in these going private transactions from other types of fiduciary self-dealing involving transactions in securities. The result would be to bring within the Rule a wide variety of corporate conduct traditionally left to state regulation. In addition to posing a "danger of vexatious litigation which could result from a widely expanded class of plaintiffs under Rule 10b–5," *Blue Chip Stamps v. Manor Drug Stores,* 421 U.S., at 740, this extension of the federal securities laws would overlap and quite possibly interfere with state corporate law. Federal courts applying a "federal fiduciary principle" under Rule 10b–5 could be expected to depart from state fiduciary standards at least to the extent necessary to ensure uniformity within the federal system.[16] Absent a clear indication of congressional intent, we are reluctant to federalize the substantial portion of the law of corporations that deals with transactions in securities, particularly where established state policies of corporate regulation would be overridden. As the Court stated in *Cort v. Ash, supra:* "Corporations are creatures of state law, and investors commit their funds to corporate directors on the understanding that, except where federal law *expressly* requires certain responsibilities of directors with respect to stockholders, state law will govern the internal affairs of the corporation." 422 U.S., at 84 (emphasis added).

We thus adhere to the position that "Congress by § 10(b) did not seek to regulate transactions which constitute no more than internal corporate mismanagement." *Superintendent of Insurance v. Bankers Life & Cas. Co.,* 404 U.S., at 12. There may well be a need for uniform federal fiduciary standards to govern mergers such as that challenged in this complaint. But those standards should not be supplied by judicial extension of § 10(b) and Rule 10b–5 to "cover the corporate universe."

The judgment of the Court of Appeals is reversed, and the case is remanded for further proceedings consistent with this opinion.

So ordered.

[The dissenting opinion of Justice Brennan is omitted.]

■ Mr. Justice Blackmun, concurring in part.

Like Mr. Justice Stevens, I refrain from joining Part IV of the Court's opinion. I, too, regard that part as unnecessary for the decision in the instant case.... I, however, join the remainder of the Court's opinion and its judgment.

■ Mr. Justice Stevens, concurring in part.

... [T]he entire discussion in Part IV is unnecessary to the decision of this case. Accordingly, I join only Parts I, II, and III of the Court's opinion. I would also add further emphasis to the fact that the controlling stockholders in this case did not breach any duty owed to the minority shareholders because (a) there was complete disclosure of the relevant facts, and (b) the minority are entitled to receive the

---

16. For example, some States apparently require a "valid corporate purpose" for the elimination of the minority interest through a short-form merger, whereas other States do not. Compare *Bryan v. Brock & Blevins Co.,* 490 F.2d 563 (CA5), cert. denied, 419 U.S. 844, 95 S.Ct. 77, 42 L.Ed.2d 72 (1974) (merger arranged by controlling stockholder for no business purpose except to eliminate 15% minority stockholder violated Georgia short-form merger statute) with *Stauffer v. Standard Brands, Inc.,* 41 Del.Ch. 7, 187 A.2d 78 (1962) (Delaware short-form merger statute allows majority stockholder to eliminate minority interest without any corporate purpose and subject only to an appraisal remedy). Thus to the extent that Rule 10b–5 is interpreted to require a valid corporate purpose for elimination of minority shareholders as well as a fair price for their shares, it would impose a stricter standard of fiduciary duty than that required by the law of some States.

fair value of their shares.[2] The facts alleged in the complaint do not constitute "fraud" within the meaning of Rule 10b–5.

———

NOTE ON GOLDBERG v. MERIDOR

Although the language of the majority opinion in *Santa Fe* indicates a reluctance to extend Rule 10b–5 into the province of state law regarding corporate mismanagement, *Santa Fe* does not carry quite that far. For example, if D, a director of Corporation C, persuades C's board, by fraud, to sell him stock, C can sue D under Rule 10b–5 even though C can also sue D for breach of fiduciary duty. Similarly, if C's board doesn't sue D, a shareholder could sue D under Rule 10b–5 in a derivative action.

Suppose that a controlling shareholder causes a corporation to issue stock to him at an unfair price, with the approval of a majority of the directors, when material facts are not disclosed to the minority shareholders. In Schoenbaum v. Firstbrook, 405 F.2d 215 (2d Cir. 1968) (en banc), cert. denied 395 U.S. 906, 89 S.Ct. 1747, 23 L.Ed.2d 219 (1969), decided before *Santa Fe,* Aquitaine was a majority shareholder of Banff Oil Ltd. and had appointed three of its eight directors. It was alleged that Aquitaine used its controlling influence to cause Banff to sell Banff shares to Aquitaine for wholly inadequate consideration. The Second Circuit held that a Banff minority shareholder could bring a derivative action on Banff's behalf under Rule 10b–5:

> ... [I]t is alleged that Aquitaine exercised a controlling influence over the issuance to it of treasury stock of Banff for a wholly inadequate consideration. If it is established that the transaction took place as alleged, it constituted a violation of Rule 10b–5, subdivision (3), because Aquitaine engaged in an "act, practice or course of business which operates or would operate as a fraud or deceit upon any person, in connection with the purchase or sale of any security." Moreover, Aquitaine and the directors of Banff were guilty of deceiving the stockholders of Banff (other than Aquitaine).

In Goldberg v. Meridor, 567 F.2d 209 (2d Cir.1977), cert. denied 434 U.S. 1069, 98 S.Ct. 1249, 55 L.Ed.2d 771 (1978), decided shortly after *Santa Fe,* UGO Corporation was controlled by Maritimecor, which in turn was controlled by Maritime Fruit. An UGO shareholder alleged that Maritimecor, Maritime Fruit, and directors of the various companies had caused UGO to acquire Maritimecor's assets in exchange for UGO stock, and that the agreement "was fraudulent and unfair in that the assets of Maritimecor were overpriced." Id. at 211. Press releases that described the agreement failed to disclose certain material facts concerning the value of Maritimecor's assets. The Se-

---

2. The motivation for the merger is a matter of indifference to the minority stockholders because they retain no interest in the corporation after the merger is consummated.

cond Circuit, in an opinion by Judge Friendly, held that *Schoenbaum* had survived *Santa Fe.* A derivative action could be brought under Rule 10b–5 on the basis of an unfair transaction between a corporation and a controlling shareholder if (1) the transaction involved stock and (2) material facts concerning the transaction had not been disclosed to all shareholders:

> *Schoenbaum* . . . can rest solidly on the now widely recognized ground that there is deception of the corporation (in effect, of its minority shareholders) when the corporation is influenced by its controlling shareholder to engage in a transaction adverse to the corporation's interests (in effect, the minority shareholders' interests) and there is nondisclosure or misleading disclosures as to the material facts of the transaction. . . .
>
> Here the complaint alleged "deceit . . . upon UGO's minority shareholders". . . . The nub of the matter is that the conduct attacked in *[Santa Fe]* did not violate the " 'fundamental purpose' of the Act as implementing a 'philosophy of full disclosure' ", . . . [T]he conduct here attacked does. . . .

Id. at 217–18.

Goldberg v. Meridor has been widely followed. See, e.g., Kas v. Financial General Bankshares, Inc., 796 F.2d 508, 512 (D.C.Cir.1986). The courts are in agreement that to succeed under the principle of Goldberg v. Meridor, the plaintiff must show a misrepresentation or nondisclosure that caused a loss to the shareholders. If the controlling shareholder did not need approval by the minority shareholders to effectuate the relevant transaction, then to show causation the plaintiff normally must establish that as a result of the lack of full disclosure, a state remedy was forgone. Most commonly, the plaintiff attempts to satisfy this requirement by arguing that if full disclosure had been made, the shareholders could have sought injunctive relief against the proposed transaction under state law.

The courts are in disagreement about the nature of the showing that the plaintiff must make concerning the likelihood that the forgone remedy would have been successful.

In Kidwell ex rel. Penfold v. Meikle, 597 F.2d 1273, 1294 (1979), the Ninth Circuit held that the plaintiff must show the shareholders would actually have succeeded if they had brought the forgone suit.

In Healey v. Catalyst Recovery, 616 F.2d 641, 647–48 (1980) the Third Circuit rejected the *Kidwell* test, and instead held that the plaintiff must show "there was a reasonable probability of ultimate success." The court explained:

> [W]e frame the test in terms of a reasonable probability for two reasons. First, we believe absolute certainty to be both an impossible goal as well as an impracticable standard for a jury to implement. Second, in most cases the state remedy will be a preliminary injunction, which looks to the likelihood of ultimate success.

In Alabama Farm Bureau Mutual Casualty Co. v. American Fidelity Life Insurance Co., 606 F.2d 602, 614 (1979), cert. denied 449 U.S. 820, 101 S.Ct. 77, 66 L.Ed.2d 22 (1980), the Fifth Circuit also rejected the *Kidwell* test, adopting instead a requirement "that state law remedies were available and that the facts shown make out a prima facie case for relief".

In Madison Consultants v. FDIC, 710 F.2d 57, 64–65 (1983), the Second Circuit adopted the *Kidwell* test, but put a gloss on the test that reduces its bite:

> We believe that the correct view is that the plaintiff must show that he would have succeeded in preventing the loss he in fact suffered. See *Kidwell*.... This standard does not obligate a plaintiff to prove beyond a reasonable doubt or to an absolute certainty that he would have won the state court suit or otherwise prevented the injury that he in fact suffered. He needs to prove only by a fair preponderance of the evidence that he would have succeeded.... [If] the plaintiff's burden in the state court action were lower, such as when preliminary injunction relief would have been tantamount to success, that factor would be taken into account in the federal suit under the standard we require.

The Seventh Circuit has rejected *Goldberg*. See, e.g., Isquith v. Caremark International, 136 F.3d 531 (7th Cir. 1998):

> *Goldberg* would allow every complaint about the mismanagement of a corporation that issues securities subject to federal law to be shoe-horned into federal court on the theory that management had defrauded the shareholders by concealing the mismanagement. This would carry the securities law far outside their intended domain. And it would violate the principle that the only loss of which complaint is possible under the antifraud provisions of those laws is a loss that candor would have averted.

NOTE ON THE OBLIGATIONS OF A NONTRADING CORPORATION UNDER RULE 10b–5

Most private actions under Rule 10b–5 are brought against persons who have traded or tipped, but as *Basic* shows, a corporation that makes *misstatements* may be liable under Rule 10b–5 even if it does not trade. The imposition of Rule 10b–5 liability on a nontrading corporation for *nondisclosure* is much less usual. In the area of disclosure, a distinction is drawn between periodic, continuous, and transactional disclosure. *Periodic disclosure* is the disclosure of events that have occurred within a given past period, such as a fiscal year, a fiscal quarter, or a month. *Continuous disclosure* is the disclosure of material information as soon as the material information arises. *Transactional disclosure* is disclosure of information that concerns a given transaction.

Traditionally, the Securities Exchange Act and the rules thereunder required three basic kinds of periodic disclosure: annual disclosure in Form 10–K and the Proxy Statement; quarterly disclosure in Form 10–Q; and monthly disclosure of a limited number of events in Form 8–K. The Act and the Rules thereunder also required transactional disclosure when shareholder approval was required for a transaction. In addition, the rules of the Stock Exchanges require certain kinds of continuous disclosure, although typically the only sanction for noncompliance with those rules would be delisting, and that sanction has seldom or never been imposed for mere nondisclosure. In contrast, traditionally the Securities Exchange Act and the Rules thereunder did not require continuous disclosure. That situation has changed to a significant extent, because under recent revisions of the Rules under the Securities Exchange Act, a Form 8–K must be filed promptly after the occurrence of many kinds of material events. Nevertheless, although the revision of Form 8–K has led to a system that makes an approach to a regime of continuous disclosure, Form 8–K still covers only specified events, so that there is still no legal obligation on a corporation to make general continuous disclosure.

In *Texas Gulf Sulphur Co.,* the court stated that "the timing of the disclosure [of material facts] is a matter for the business judgment of the corporate officers entrusted with the management of the corporation within the affirmative disclosure requirements promulgated by the exchanges and by the SEC." Id. at 850 n. 12. This is still the rule. See, e.g., Staffin v. Greenberg, 672 F.2d 1196, 1204 (3d Cir.1982). There are, however, several exceptions to this rule.

1. If the corporation makes a statement that is misleading—inaccurate—when made, even though not intentionally or recklessly so, and the corporation later learns that the statement was misleading, it is under a duty to *correct* the statement if the statement is still "alive," rather than "stale"—that is, if the statement would still be likely to be material to investors. See, e.g., Backman v. Polaroid Corp., 910 F.2d 10 (1st Cir.1990) (en banc).

2. A corporation may so involve itself in the preparation of statements about the corporation by outsiders—such as analysts' reports or earnings projections—that it assumes a duty to correct material errors in those statements. Such a duty "may occur when officials of the company have, by their activity, made an implied representation that the information they have reviewed is true or at least in accordance with the company's views." Elkind v. Liggett & Myers, Inc., 635 F.2d 156, 163 (2d Cir.1980).

3. A corporation may be under a duty to correct erroneous rumors resulting from leaks by the corporation or its agents. See, e.g., State Teachers Retirement Board v. Fluor Corp., 654 F.2d 843, 850 (2d Cir.1981) (dictum).

4. A more difficult question is whether a corporation has a duty to *update* a forward-looking statement that was correct—or more accurately, reasonable—when made but later comes to be materially misleading. In Gallagher v. Abbott Laboratories, 269 F.3d 806 (7th Cir.

2001), the court said "a statement may be 'corrected' only if it was *in*correct when made. . . . In order to maintain the difference between periodic-disclosure and continuous-disclosure systems, it is essential to draw a sharp line between duties to correct and duties to update. If, for example, [Abbot's] 10–K report had said that Abbott's net income for 1998 was $500 million, and the actual income was $400 million, Abbott would have had to fix the error. But if the 10–K report had projected a net income of $125 million for the first quarter of 1999, and accountants determined in May that the actual profit was only $100 million, there would have been nothing to correct; a projection is not rendered false when the world turns out otherwise." However, several courts have held that if a corporation makes a public statement that is correct when made, but that becomes materially misleading in light of subsequent events, the corporation may have a duty to update the statement.

In Greenfield v. Heublein, Inc., 742 F.2d 751, 758 (3d Cir.1984), cert. denied 469 U.S. 1215, 105 S.Ct. 1189, 84 L.Ed.2d 336 (1985), the court said, "[a]lthough a corporation may be under no duty to disclose . . ., if a corporation voluntarily makes a public statement that is correct when issued, [the corporation] has a duty to update the statement if it becomes materially misleading in light of subsequent events." See also In re Time Warner Inc. Securities Litigation, 9 F.3d 259, 167 (2d Cir.1993), cert. denied 511 U.S. 1017, 114 S.Ct. 1397, 128 L.Ed.2d 70 (1994) ("a duty to update opinions and projections may arise if the original opinions or projections have become misleading as the result of intervening events.") See also Backman v. Polaroid Corp., supra:

> [T]he duty to correct can also apply to a certain narrow set of forward-looking statements. We will attempt to illustrate the kinds of circumstances we have in mind with an example.

> Imagine the following situation. A public company in Manhattan makes a forecast that appears to it to be reasonable at the time made. Subsequently, the company discovers that it misread a vital piece of data that went into its forecast. Perhaps a fax sent by the company's factory manager in some remote location was blurry and was reasonably misread by management in Manhattan as representing sales for the past quarter as 100,000 units as opposed to 10,000 units. Manhattan management then makes an erroneous forecast based on the information it has at the time. A few weeks later, management receives the correct sales figures by mail. So long as the correction in the sales figures was material to the forecast that was discussed earlier, we think there would likely be a duty on the part of the company to disclose either the corrected figures or a corrected forecast. In other words, there is an implicit representation in any forecast (or statement of historical fact) that errors of the type we have identified will be corrected. This duty derives from the implicit factual representation that a public company makes whenever it makes a forecast, i.e., that the forecast was reasonable at the time made. What is crucial to

recognize is that the error, albeit an honest one, was one that had to do with information available at the time the forecast was made and that the error in the information was subsequently discovered. . . .

The scope of a duty to update has been brought into question by the safe-harbor provisions by Section 21E(d) of the Securities Exchange Act, added by the Private Securities Litigation Reform Act of 1995. This section provides that "nothing in this section shall impose a duty to update a forward-looking statement," as defined in Section 21E. See the Note on Forward–Looking Statements and the Bespeaks–Caution Doctrine, supra.

5.   Finally, if a corporation makes a voluntary disclosure, under Regulation FD it may not make the disclosure on a selective basis.

REGULATION FD

[See Statutory Supplement]

**SECURITIES AND EXCHANGE COMMISSION
RELEASE NO. 33–7881, PART II (2000)**

(SELECTIVE DISCLOSURE: REGULATION FD)

[See Statutory Supplement]

SECTION 3.   LIABILITY FOR SHORT-SWING TRADING UNDER § 16(b) OF THE SECURITIES EXCHANGE ACT

SECURITIES EXCHANGE ACT § 16

[See Statutory Supplement]

SECURITIES EXCHANGE ACT RULES 3a–11–1, 3b–2, 16a–1, 16a–2, 16a–3, 16a–10, 16b–3, 16b–5, 16b–6, 16b–7, 16b–9; FORM 3; FORM 4; FORM 5

[See Statutory Supplement]

FELDMAN & TEBERG, BENEFICIAL OWNERSHIP UNDER SECTION 16 OF THE SECURITIES EXCHANGE ACT OF 1934, 17 Western Res.L.Rev. 1054, 1063–65 (1966). "The juxtaposition of section 16(a) and 16(b), plus the fact that both operate with respect to the same persons, has led many to erroneously conclude that section 16(a) was enacted only to reveal transactions within the scope of section 16(b). That section 16(a) is not confined to transactions within the scope of section 16(b) is clear not only from the fact that section 16(a) pre-existed section 16(b) [as a matter of legislative history], but also from the different language of the two subsections. For while section 16(b) speaks of purchases and sales within six months of each other, section 16(a) speaks of changes in beneficial ownership, a much broader concept. . . .

"Since the terms of section 16(a) require insiders to disclose any changes in their beneficial ownership of securities, it provides a means for bringing to light possible violations of . . . Rule 10b–5, as well as a 'purchase and sale' within the scope of section 16(b). However, two other functions of the section 16(a) reports are equally important to the efficacious operations of the Exchange Act's scheme to banish investors' ignorance and upgrade the ethics of corporate managers. Its second function is to reveal information which may be used in evaluating the securities of the issuer. This is a pure disclosure device in which the conclusions to be drawn from the reports and the weight to be attached thereto are left to the judgment of the individual investor. The information contained in the reports may be used (1) as a guide to the insiders' current confidence or lack thereof in the company's fortunes or (2) to detect an evolving change in control in the company. Undoubtedly this investment information function of the section largely explains why the Commission's monthly summary of transactions reported under section 16(a) has become a perennial best seller. Finally, section 16(a) is itself a deterrent to the misuse of inside information through the publicity which attaches to the reports, apart from any other statutory prohibition or liability. This is a standard by-product or goal of any disclosure provision, since presumably people are likely to refrain from improper acts, or acts which may appear improper, if they know such acts will be exposed to public scrutiny."

———

NOTE ON GOLLUST v. MENDELL

In Gollust v. Mendell, 501 U.S. 115, 111 S.Ct. 2173, 115 L.Ed.2d 109 (1991), the Supreme Court made the following observations on the procedural aspects of § 16(b):

> To enforce this strict liability rule on insider trading, Congress chose to rely solely on the issuers of stock and their security holders. Unlike most of the federal securities laws, § 16(b) does not confer enforcement authority on the Securities and Exchange Commission. It is, rather, the security holders of an issuer who have the ultimate authority to sue for enforcement of § 16(b). If the issuer declines to bring a § 16(b) action within 60 days of a demand by a security holder, or fails to prosecute the action

"diligently" ... then the security holder may "institut[e]" an action to recover insider shortswing profits for the issuer....

Although plaintiffs seeking to sue under the statute must own a "security," § 16(b) places no significant restriction on the type of security adequate to confer standing. "[A]ny security" will suffice, ... the statutory definition being broad enough to include stock, notes, warrants, bonds, debentures, puts, calls, and a variety of other financial instruments; it expressly excludes only "currency or any note, draft, bill of exchange, or banker's acceptance which has a maturity at the time of issuance of not exceeding nine months...."

Report of the Task Force on Regulation of Insider Trading, Part II: Reform of Section 16

42 Bus.Law. 1087, 1091–92 (1987).

In recent years, a number of commentators have suggested that section 16(b) causes more harm than good and that it should be repealed. It has been argued that section 16(b) is ineffectual in preventing insider trading and does not even address all of the ways in which insider trades can be perpetrated, while it imposes punitive liability on the innocent, the naive, and the unaware corporate officers who unwittingly sell in violation of, for example, the labyrinthine restrictions of rule 16b–3. These commentators raise the question: Given the development of the insider trading doctrine under rule 10b–5, the substantial limitations of section 16(b) in preventing insider trading, and the hardships that it imposes, is the statute needed?

The task force believes that it is. Section 16(b) has a different legislative focus than the prohibition of trading on inside information. Indeed, it is the only provision of the 1934 Act that specifically regulates insider trading. It is aimed at three specific types of insider trading abuses, only one of which involves abuse of inside information.

First, section 16(b) was intended to remove the temptation for corporation executives to profit from short-term stock price fluctuations at the expense of the long-term financial health of their companies. It prevents insiders from being obsessed with trading in their companies' securities to the detriment of their managerial and fiduciary responsibilities. In this regard, based on the testimony of insider abuses presented at the hearings, it was Congress's judgment that short-swing trading by corporate executives is not good for their companies or the American capital markets.

Second, the section was intended to penalize the unfair use of inside information by insiders. This includes both trading on inside information in violation of rule 10b–5 and the use of "softer" information of the type that insiders often have but that members of the investing public do not: the ability to make better informed guesses as to the success of new products, the likely results of negotiations, and the real risks of contingencies and other uncertainties, the underlying facts of which have been publicly disclosed.

Third, section 16(b) was designed to eliminate the temptation for insiders to manipulate corporate events so as to maximize their own short-term trading profits. Before the enactment of section 16(b), insiders had been able to make quick profits from short-term price swings by such practices as the announcement of generous (but imprudent) dividend programs followed by postinsider trading dividend reductions. Thus, the section provides a minimum standard of fiduciary conduct for corporate insiders.

The task force thus concludes that section 16 remains a useful tool for preventing speculative abuses by insiders and for focusing their attention on their fiduciary duty and on long-term corporate health, rather than on short-term trading profits.

Gratz v. Claughton

United States Court of Appeals, Second Circuit, 1951.
187 F.2d 46, cert. denied 341 U.S. 920, 71 S.Ct. 741, 95 L.Ed. 1353 (1951).

■ Before L. HAND, CHIEF JUDGE, and SWAN and AUGUSTUS N. HAND, CIRCUIT JUDGES.

■ L. HAND, CHIEF JUDGE.

This is an appeal by the defendant, Claughton, from a judgment against him, entered upon the report of a master, in an action by a shareholder of the Missouri–Kansas–Texas Railroad Company under § 16(b) of the Securities Exchange Act of 1934.... The court first granted a summary judgment as to all the issues except the amount of the profits made by the defendant, which it referred to a master, on whose report it entered final judgment. The defendant does not dispute the propriety of a summary disposition of all the issues except that referred, but he does dispute the propriety of the judgment in law. First, he argues that the venue was wrong because he was domiciled in Florida, and the summons was served upon him in that state. Second, he disputes the rule adopted by the master in computing his profits. Third, he challenges the constitutionality of the statute which imposes the liability, and of the provisions for venue. We shall take up the first and third in sequence, reserving the second for the last.

[The court held that venue was proper.] ...

The challenge to the constitutionality of § 16(b) we have answered twice before. For many years a grave omission in our corporation law had been its indifference to dealings of directors or other corporate officers in the shares of their companies. When they bought shares, they came literally within the conventional prohibitions of the law of trusts; yet the decisions were strangely slack in so deciding. When they sold shares, it could indeed be argued that they were not dealing with a beneficiary, but with one whom his purchase made a beneficiary. That should not, however, have obscured the fact that the director or officer assumed a fiduciary relation to the buyer by the very sale; for it would be a sorry distinction to allow him to use the advantage of his position to induce the buyer into the position of a beneficiary, although he was forbidden to do so, once the buyer had become one. Certainly this is true, when the buyer knows he is buying of a director or officer, for he expects to become the seller's *cestui que* trust. If the buyer does not know, he is entitled to assume that if his seller in fact is already a director or officer, he will remain so after the sale. Nor was it necessary to confine this disability to directors or other officers of the corporation. The reason for the doctrine was that a director or officer may have information not accessible to a shareholder, actual or prospective, and that advantage is not confined to them. We take judicial notice that an effective control over the affairs of a corporation often does not require anything approaching a majority of the shares; and this is particularly true in the case of those corporations whose shares are dealt in upon national exchanges. Nor is it common for the control so obtained to be in the hands of one individual; more often a number share it, who are all in a position to gain a more intimate acquaintance with the enterprise and its prospects than the shareholders at large. It is of course true that the ownership of ten per cent of the shares does not always put the owner among those who do control; but neither Congress, nor any other legislature, is obliged to limit the means which it chooses so exactly to its ends that the correspondence is exact. If only those persons were liable, who could be proved to have a bargaining advantage, the execution of the statute would be so encumbered as to defeat its whole purpose. We do not mean that the interest, of which a statute deprives an individual, may never be so vital that he must not be given a trial of his personal guilt; but that is not so when all that is at stake is a director's, officer's or "beneficial owner's" privilege to add to, or subtract from, his holdings for a period of six months. In such situations it is well settled that a statute may provide any means which can reasonably be thought necessary to deal with the evil, even though they may cover instances where it is not present....

There remains the question of the computation of profits, which we dealt with in Smolowe v. Delendo Corporation....[8] Section 16(b) declares that "any profit realized ... from any purchase and sale, or any sale and purchase ... within any period of less than six months ... shall inure to and be recoverable by the issuer": the corporation. It is plain that this presupposes some matching of (1) purchases against sales, or of (2) sales against purchases, and that there must therefore be some principle upon which both the minuend—the sale price—and the subtrahend—the purchase price—can be determined. At first blush it might seem that the statute limited the recovery to profits derived from transactions in the same shares; as, for example, that a dealer's profit upon the sale of any given number of shares was

---

8. 2 Cir., 136 F.2d 231, 148 A.L.R. 300.

to be measured by subtracting what he paid for those shares from what he got upon a sale of the same certificate. However, as we observed in Smolowe v. Delendo Corporation, supra, that would allow an easy avoidance of the statute; in order to speculate freely an officer, director, or "beneficial owner" need only hold a substantial block of shares for more than six months. If, for example, on January 1st, he had 10,000 shares which he had bought before October 1st, he could buy 1,000 shares on February 1st and sell 1,000 shares at a profit on April 1st, making delivery out of certificates from the 10,000 shares purchased before October 1st. After the two transactions his position would be what it had been on January 1st save that in two months he had made a profitable turn in 1,000 shares—exactly the evil against which the statute is directed. Moreover, there is an added reason for this interpretation, if one be needed. In the case of a sale followed by a purchase it is impossible to identify any purchase with any previous sale; one would have to confine such transactions to the practically non-existent occasions when the proceeds of the sale were used to purchase. Thus it appears, regardless of anything said during the passage of the bill through Congress and of the different forms it took, that the Act does not demand—that the same shares should be sold which were bought. This accords with the fungible nature of shares of stock. Indeed, if we translate the transaction into sales and purchases, or purchases and sales, of gallons of oil in a single tank, or of bushels of wheat in a single bin, it at once appears that the ascertainment of the particular shares bought or sold must be wholly irrelevant.

Although for these reasons it appears that the transactions—sales and purchases, or purchases and sales—are not to be matched by identifying the shares dealt in, we are no nearer than before to finding an answer as to how transactions shall be matched; all that so far appeared, is that the matching is to be between contracts of sale and contracts of purchase, or vice versa. On the other hand it is manifest that the intent of the fiduciary cannot be the test; first, because he generally has no ascertainable intent; and second, because that would open the door even more widely to the evil in question. The statute does not allow the fiduciary to minimize his profits, any more than to set off his losses against them. We can therefore find no principle by which to select any two transactions which are to be matched; and, so far as we can see, we are forced to one of two alternatives: to match any given sale taken as minuend, against any given purchase, taken as subtrahend, in such a way as to reduce profits to their lowest possible amount, or in such a way as to increase them to the greatest possible amount. The master adopted the second course, following what he supposed to be the doctrine of Smolowe v. Delendo Corporation, supra. We think that he was right for the following reasons.

The question is in substance the same as when a trustee's account is to be surcharged, for, as we have said, the statute makes the fiduciary a constructive trustee for any profits he may make. It is true that on the beneficiary in an accounting rests the burden of proof of a surcharge,[9] although the fiduciary has the burden of establishing any credits.[10] Since the plaintiff was seeking to surcharge the defendant we will therefore assume that it rested upon her to show how the transactions are to be matched; and, that, if there were nothing more, since she cannot do so, she must be content to have them matched in the way that shows the least profit. Obviously that cannot be the right answer, for the reasons we have given; and perhaps the fact that it cannot be, is reason enough for adopting the alternative. But there is another ground for reaching the same result. As we have said, the statute makes all such dealings unlawful, and makes the fiduciary accountable to the corporation. Although it is impossible in the case at bar to compute the defendant's profits, except that they must fall between two limits—the minimum and the maximum—the cause of this uncertainty is the number of transactions within six months: that is, the number of defendant's derelictions. The situation falls within the doctrine which has been law since the days of the "Chimney Sweeper's Jewel Case,"[11] that when damages are at some unascertainable amount below an upper limit and when the uncertainty arises from the defendant's wrong, the upper limit will be taken as the proper amount.[12]

This results in looking for six months both before and after any sale, and not for three months only, as the defendant insists. If one is seeking an equation of purchase and sale, one may take any sale as the minuend and look back for six months for a purchase at less price to match against it. On the other hand, if one is looking for an equation of sale and purchase, one may take the same sale and look forward for six months for any purchase at a lower price. Although obviously no transaction can figure in more than one equation, with that exception we can see no escape from what we have just said. It is true that this means that no director, officer, or "beneficial owner" may safely buy and sell, or sell and buy, shares of stock in the company except at intervals of six months. Whether that is too drastic a means of meeting the evil, we have not to decide; it is enough that we can find no other way to administer the statute. Therefore, not only will we follow Smolowe v. Delendo Corporation, supra, as a precedent; but as *res integra* and after independent analysis we reassert its doctrine. The defendant concedes that, except for carrying the transactions backward and forward for six months, instead of for three, the master followed the rule laid down in that decision; and the plaintiff has not appealed, so that she is not entitled to any more than she has recovered. On this account we have not examined the master's computations in detail and are not to be understood to have passed upon them. The crushing liabilities which § 16(b) may impose are apparent from this action in

9. Ewen v. Peoria & Eastern Ry., D.C., 78 F.Supp. 312, 334.

10. Wootton Land and Fuel Co. v. Ownbey, 8 Cir., 265 F. 91.

11. Armory v. Delamirie, 1722, 1 Strange 505.

12. ... Story Parchment Co. v. Paterson Parchment Paper Co., 282 U.S. 555, 563–565, 51 S.Ct. 248, 75 L.Ed. 544; Bigelow v. R.K.O. Radio Pictures, Inc., 327 U.S. 251, 264, 265, 66 S.Ct. 574, 90 L.Ed. 652....

which the judgment was for over $300,000; it should certainly serve as a warning, and may prove a deterrent.[1]

Judgment affirmed.

––––––––––

NOTE ON THE COMPUTATION OF PROFITS UNDER § 16(b)

1. In Smolowe v. Delendo Corporation, 136 F.2d 231 (2d Cir. 1943), cert. denied 320 U.S. 751, 64 S.Ct. 56, 88 L.Ed. 446, which was cited and relied upon in Gratz v. Claughton, the court considered and rejected several formulas for computing profits under § 16(b) other than those analyzed in *Gratz:*

> Once the principle of [measuring damages based on the identification of the stock certificates involved] is rejected, its corollary, the first-in, first-out rule, is left at loose ends. . . . Its rationalization is the same as that for the identification rule, for which it operates as a presumptive principle; and it has no other support. If we reject one, we reject the other and for like reasons. Its application would render the large stockholder with a backlog of stock not immediately devoted to trading immune from the Act. Further, we should note that it does not fit the broad statutory language; a purchase followed immediately by a sale, albeit a transaction within the exact statutory language, would often be held immune from the statutory penalty because the purchase would be deemed by arbitrary rule to have been made at an earlier date; while a sale followed by purchase would never even be within the terms of the rule. . . .

> Another possibility might be the striking of an average purchase price and an average sale price during the period, and using these as bases of computation. What this rule would do in concrete effect is to allow as offsets all losses made by such trading. This in effect the district court first planned to do. . . . But it corrected this in its supplemental opinion, properly pointing out that the statute provided for the recovery of "any" profit realized and obviously precluded a setting off of losses. Even had the statutory language been more uncertain, this rule seems one not to be favored in the light of the statutory purpose. Compared to other possible rules, it tends to stimulate more active trading by reducing the chance of penalty. . . . Its application to a case where trading continued more than six months might be most uncertain, depending upon how the beginning of each six months' period was ascertained. It is not a clear-cut taking of "any profit" for the corporation, and we agree with the district court in rejecting it.

––––––––––

1. In Adler v. Klawans, 267 F.2d 840, 848 (2d Cir.1959), it is reported that "during the pertinent periods, [Gratz] suffered a net loss of $400,000 on trading in the stock for which he was charged under section 16(b)." (Footnote by ed.)

2.   The formula adopted in *Smolowe* and *Gratz* has been general-ly approved by the courts. It is often referred to the "lowest purchase price, highest sale price" method. See, e.g., Whittaker v. Whittaker Corp., 639 F.2d 516, 530 (9th Cir.1981). Here are three illustrations of this method. Assume in all three illustrations that D is a director of C Corporation, whose stock is traded on a national securities exchange.

(i) On January 2, D purchases 1,000 shares of C at $10. On April 1, D sells 1,000 shares of C at $15. This is a short-swing "purchase and sale," and D is liable under § 16(b) for his profit of $5,000.

(ii) On January 2, D purchases 1,000 shares of C at $10. On August 1, D sells 1,000 shares at $15. On November 1, D purchases 1,000 shares at $10. D has no § 16(b) liability on the basis of the January–August swing, because the two ends of the swing did not occur within six months. However, the August and November transac-tions constitute a short-swing "sale and purchase," and D would be liable under § 16(b) for a profit of $5,000 on these two transactions. Why has D made a $5,000 "profit"? Because after D's November 1 purchase, his position in C Corporation's stock is exactly as it was just before August 1 (that is, he owns 1,000 C shares) but he has also added $5,000 cash to his bank account. D may have accomplished this result by using inside information. The sale at $15 may have been made on the basis of undisclosed bad news. The purchase at $10 may have been made on the basis of undisclosed good news.

(iii) D engages in the following pattern of activity:

Date	Action	Amount	Price
2/1	Purchase	1,000	$30
3/1	Sale	1,000	$25
4/1	Purchase	1,000	$20
5/1	Sale	1,000	$15

Under the *Smolowe/Gratz* formula, D has a profit of $5,000, because the purchase at $20 on 4/1 can be matched with the sale at $25 on 3/1. At first glance, this looks counterintuitive: it seems that D has a $10,000 loss in his total trading, not a $5,000 profit. But it may be that except for inside information, D would not have sold on 3/1, and instead would have ridden the C stock all the way down from $30 to $15, for a loss of $15,000. Accordingly, there is a possibility (which is all that § 16(b) requires) that D has profited by $5,000 by holding his loss to $10,000 through the use of inside information.[1]

NOTE ON SECTION 16(b)

Section 16(b) is often criticized on the ground that it can result in liability in cases where there has been no insider trading, and in cases

---

1. For a hypothetical in which a finding of profits under the *Smolowe/Gratz* formula does seem counterintuitive, see Lowenfels, Section 16(b): A New Trend in Regulating Insider Trading, 54 Cornell L.Rev. 45, 46–47 n. 6 (1968).

where there has been no real profit. As the Report of the ABA Task Force makes clear, however, this criticism has failed to strike a responsive chord among most members of the corporate bar. The ABA Task Force Report addresses these kinds of criticisms by giving affirmative justifications for the operation of § 16(b). See also Fox, Insider Trading Deterrence versus Managerial Incentives: A Unified Theory of Section 16(b), 92 Mich.L.Rev. 2088.

Furthermore, it's hard to see that § 16(b) has any significant capacity for harm. It's often thought to be desirable to encourage directors and executives to become shareholders, so as to tie their fortunes more closely to those of the corporation's owners. However, it is seldom thought to be desirable to encourage directors and executives to engage in short-swing in-and-out trading. In the overwhelming majority of cases, all that § 16(b) does is to disincentive such trading. Moreover, if we put aside exotic scenarios that could occur in theory, but almost never occur in practice, the sanction of § 16(b) is exceptionally mild, because normally all § 16(b) does is put the director or executive back where she was before she engaged in the relevant transactions.

————

NOTE ON THE INTERPRETATION OF § 16(b)

The courts have tended to use two somewhat different approaches in cases in which the applicability of § 16(b) is contestable. Until the early 1960s, the predominant theory of interpreting § 16(b) was that the section should be construed to cover all transactions within its literal reach. "[T]he statute was intended to be thoroughgoing, to squeeze all possible profits out of stock transactions, and thus to establish a standard so high as to prevent any conflict between the selfish interest of [an insider] and the faithful performance of his duty." Smolowe v. Delendo Corp., 136 F.2d 231, 239 (2d Cir.1943), cert. denied 320 U.S. 751, 64 S.Ct. 56, 88 L.Ed. 446. This theory of interpreting § 16(b) was known as the "objective" approach, although it has been aptly suggested that "automatic" would be more descriptive. Blau v. Lamb, 363 F.2d 507, 520 (2d Cir.1966), cert. denied 385 U.S. 1002, 87 S.Ct. 707, 17 L.Ed.2d 542 (1967).

Beginning in the mid–1960s, § 16(b) came to be perceived by some as overly harsh, because it operates without regard to fault. A different theory of interpretation, known as the "subjective" or "pragmatic" approach, then set in. Under this approach, in *borderline* cases—particularly cases involving an "*unorthodox*" transaction, rather than a garden-variety purchase or sale—the statute would be interpreted to impose liability only if the insider actually had access to inside information, or the transaction was of a type that carries a potential for insider abuse. See Whittaker v. Whittaker Corp., 639 F.2d 516, 522 (9th Cir.1981), cert. denied, 454 U.S. 1031, 102 S.Ct. 566, 70 L.Ed.2d 473; Lowenfels, Section 16(b): A New Trend in Regulating Insider Trading, 54 Cornell L.Rev. 45 (1968).

The names given to these two approaches are misleading. The "subjective" approach does not turn, as its name suggests, on the defendant's subjective intent to use inside information. Conversely, the "objective" approach can be just as pragmatic as the "pragmatic" approach. If the names of the two approaches are put aside, the conflict is between an approach that treats § 16(b) as a prophylactic rule of thumb, whose purpose would be defeated if defendants could escape liability on the ground that in their particular case no abuse could have occurred, and an approach that treats § 16(b) as inviting an inquiry into the possibility of abuse, at least in borderline cases. To a certain extent, which approach is adopted in a given case may depend on whether the court perceives § 16(b) as a good idea or a bad idea.

It should be emphasized that although the tension between the approaches to the interpretation of § 16(b) is real and important, it is a tension only at the margins. In the great bulk of potential cases, the application of § 16(b) is relatively straightforward. As pointed out in *Whittaker*, supra:

> [T]he pragmatic approach has not ousted the objective view. Rather, the pragmatic approach is used to determine the boundaries of the statute's definitional scope in borderline situations, especially unorthodox transactions.... For a garden-variety transaction which cannot be regarded as unorthodox, the pragmatic approach is not applicable.... In such cases, if the situation is within the requirements established by Congress for § 16, then the mechanical, "objective," operation of the statute imposes liability.

––––––––

ARROW DISTRIBUTING CORP. v. BAUMGARTNER, 783 F.2d 1274 (1986). "Congress adopted § 16(b) of the Act, which Professor Louis Loss characterizes as a 'nice example of "native American radicalism," 'to prevent insiders of publicly-held corporations, who had advance knowledge of facts that, upon public disclosure, would produce either a rise or fall in the market price of the stock, from realizing a personal profit by buying or selling the corporation's shares before the good or bad news was made public. The exploitation by insiders of information not available to the public was considered unfair to the public investors who were not privy to the information. Moreover, the profit potential prompted some insiders to manipulate the market price of their corporation's shares by causing the corporation to inaugurate and follow financial policies calculated to produce sudden fluctuations in that price.

"Considering any case-by-case rule impracticable, Congress adopted 'a flat rule taking the profits out of a class of transactions in which the possibility of abuse was believed to be intolerably great.'[10]

---

10. Texas Int'l Airlines v. National Airlines, Inc., 714 F.2d 533, 538 (5th Cir.1983), cert. denied, 465 U.S. 1052, 104 S.Ct. 1326, 79 L.Ed.2d 721 (1984) (quoting Kern County

The general rule used to compute recoverable profits under § 16(b) is to match the shares bought at the lowest price against an equal number of shares sold at the highest price within six months of such purchase. It was described to Congress by the spokesman for the Roosevelt administration who advocated its adoption as a 'crude rule of thumb.' The rule is frequently and properly referred to as prophylactic because it is designed to preserve the health of the securities market and prevent the disease of insider trading. . . .

"The insiders contend, in a last-ditch defense, that § 16(b) should not be applied to them because in this case there was no possibility of speculative abuse. The existence of that possibility is irrelevant, for neither actual use of inside information nor intention to exploit such information is required to establish § 16(b) liability. In the 'garden variety' insider purchase and sale, or sale and purchase, of securities within a period of less than six months, proof of the possibility of speculative abuse is wholly immaterial.

"The officers contend that the contemporary view is to read § 16(b) liberally. They point out that § 16(b) was interpreted in the 1940s and 1950s to 'squeeze all possible profits out of stock transactions' by corporate insiders. But they say that in the § 16(b) cases the Supreme Court has decided in the last fifteen years, it has each time found § 16(b) inapplicable and has rejected a literal interpretation of the statute in favor of a pragmatic approach that reflects the economic realities of the transaction. Additionally, they note that commentators have criticized the arbitrary and often unfair operation of § 16(b).

"The officers misconstrue the jurisprudence. The courts developed this 'pragmatic approach' to cover cases involving the application of § 16(b) to transactions that were not classic purchases and sales for cash, but were more accurately characterized as 'unorthodox transactions.' Using this analysis, courts found § 16(b) liability whenever the challenged transactions were likely to involve the potential for speculative abuse that the statute was designed to prevent. A common thread in the § 16(b) cases in which no liability was assessed, however, was the involuntary participation of those alleged to have engaged in short-swing trading. Such a factor was not present in this case. The officers had complete control over the timing of the exercise of their respective stock options.

"Moreover, such a hortatory argument, as Judge Curtis Bok wrote, leads to no clear conclusion: 'They might as well have said, if you meet a monster in a dark street, construe it liberally and everything will be all right.' The argument suggests that we read into court decisions dealing with other, albeit related, issues, intimations of liberality that simply are not there. The defendants invite judicial repeal of a rule because it is arbitrary, although it is no more so than thousands of other statutory bright lines. Our response is that their invitation is

Land Co. v. Occidental Petroleum Corp., 411 U.S. 582, 592, 93 S.Ct. 1736, 1743, 36 L.Ed.2d 503, 513 (1973), quoting Reliance Elec. Co. v. Emerson Elec. Co., 404 U.S. 418, 422, 92 S.Ct. 596, 599, 30 L.Ed.2d 575, 579 (1972)).

misaddressed. Congress has not altered the language of § 16(b) for over half a century, and it is not the judiciary's task to revise the rule into what might be in some eyes a more equitable rule.

''The insiders' companion economic-reality argument points to no specific direction. '[T]he economists are not of one persuasion.' The strictly economic arguments, moreover, display 'apparent scorn for the moral or public opinion factor.' 'Why should the public enter the market,' Professor Loss writes, 'if the rules of the game make it perfectly legitimate for insiders (and their friends and business associates) to play with marked cards?' Section 16(b) is a strict-liability rule. It was enacted precisely because of the difficulty of establishing whether an insider did indeed benefit from the information available to him in his strategic position. It adopts a purely objective test: if a sale and a purchase or a purchase and a sale result in net gain, the gain is recoverable.''

Kern County Land Co. v. Occidental Petroleum Corp.

Supreme Court of the United States, 1973.
411 U.S. 582, 93 S.Ct. 1736, 36 L.Ed.2d 503.

■ MR. JUSTICE WHITE delivered the opinion of the Court.

Section 16(b) of the Securities Exchange Act of 1934, 48 Stat. 896, 15 U.S.C. § 78p(b), provides that officers, directors, and holders of more than 10% of the listed stock of any company shall be liable to the company for any profits realized from any purchase and sale or sale and purchase of such stock occurring within a period of six months. Unquestionably, one or more statutory purchases occur when one company, seeking to gain control of another, acquires more than 10% of the stock of the latter through a tender offer made to its shareholders. But is it a § 16(b) ''sale'' when the target of the tender offer defends itself by merging into a third company and the tender offeror then exchanges his stock for the stock of the surviving company and also grants an option to purchase the latter stock that is not exercisable within the statutory six-month period? This is the question before us in this case.

I

On May 8, 1967, after unsuccessfully seeking to merge with Kern County Land Co. (Old Kern),[2] Occidental Petroleum Corp. (Occidental)[3] announced an offer, to expire on June 8, 1967, to purchase on a

---

2. Old Kern was a California corporation having substantial real estate holdings, including oil-producing lands, oil-exploration activities, cattle ranching, cattle-feeding operations, and interests in the manufacture of automotive parts, electronic systems and devices, and farm machinery and construction equipment. After the reorganization described in the text, Old Kern became known as the 600 California Corporation until its eventual dissolution under California law on October 6, 1967.

3. Occidental is the respondent in this Court. A California corporation with its principal place of business in California, Occidental is engaged in the production and sale of oil, gas, coal, sulphur, and fertilizers.

first-come, first-served basis 500,000 shares of Old Kern common stock[4] at a price of $83.50 per share plus a brokerage commission of $1.50 per share.[5] By May 10, 1967, 500,000 shares, more than 10% of the outstanding shares of Old Kern,[6] had been tendered. On May 11, Occidental extended its offer to encompass an additional 500,000 shares. At the close of the tender offer, on June 8, 1967, Occidental owned 887,549 shares of Old Kern.[7]

Immediately upon the announcement of Occidental's tender offer, the Old Kern management undertook to frustrate Occidental's take-over attempt. A management letter to all stockholders cautioned against tender and indicated that Occidental's offer might not be the best available, since the management was engaged in merger discussions with several companies. When Occidental extended its tender offer, the president of Old Kern sent a telegram to all stockholders again advising against tender. In addition, Old Kern undertook merger discussions with Tenneco, Inc. (Tenneco),[8] and, on May 19, 1967, the Board of Directors of Old Kern announced that it had approved a merger proposal advanced by Tenneco.[9] Under the terms of the merger, Tenneco would acquire the assets, property, and goodwill of Old Kern, subject to its liabilities, through "Kern County Land Co." (New Kern),[10] a new corporation to be formed by Tenneco to receive the assets and carry on the business of Old Kern. The shareholders of Old Kern would receive a share of Tenneco cumulative convertible preference stock in exchange for each share of Old Kern common

4. The Old Kern stock was registered pursuant to § 12 of the Securities Exchange Act of 1934, as amended, 15 U.S.C. § 78l. The stock was a nonexempt, equity security for purposes of § 16(b).

5. The Old Kern stock closed at 63⅝ on Friday, May 8, 1967, the last trading day prior to the announcement of the tender offer. It had reached a high of 64⅞ and a low of 57⅞ in 1967, a high of 76¼ and a low of 51¾ in 1966, a high of 71⅝ and a low of 56 in 1965, and a high of 70⅜ and a low of 56⅝ in 1964. Thus, the $85–per–share tender-offer price represented a substantial profit for shareholders of Old Kern.

6. On May 10, Old Kern had 4,328,000 shares outstanding.

7. On May 18, 1967, Occidental filed a Form 3, Initial Statement of Beneficial Ownership of Securities, with the Securities and Exchange Commission indicating direct ownership of 507,055 shares of Old Kern stock; on June 9, 1967, Occidental filed a Form 4, Statement of Changes in Beneficial Ownership of Securities, for the month of May, indicating the purchase of an additional 376,326 shares of Old Kern stock, for a total ownership as of May 31, 1967, of 883,381 shares. An additional 4,168 shares were purchased by June 8, 1967, so that as of June 30, 1967, Occidental held 887,549 shares of Old Kern stock. This figure included 1,900 shares

which Occidental purchased on the open market in April 1967. Section 16(b) liability is not asserted with respect to these shares, because these purchases did not make Occidental a "beneficial owner" for purposes of § 16(b).

8. Tenneco, a Delaware corporation, is a diversified industrial company with operations in natural gas transmission, oil and gas, chemicals, packaging, manufacturing, and shipbuilding. Tenneco is not a party to this litigation.

9. Although technically a sale of assets, the corporate combination has been consistently referred to by the parties as a "merger" and will be similarly denominated in this opinion. The only significance of the characterization is the fact that a sale of assets required, under California law, approval of only a majority of the Old Kern shareholders and provided no appraisal rights for dissenters.

10. New Kern, a Delaware corporation with its principal place of business in California, is the petitioner in this Court and is a wholly owned subsidiary of Tenneco Corp. Tenneco Corp. is, in turn, a wholly owned subsidiary of Tenneco and owns all of the capital stock or controlling interests in most of Tenneco's nonpipeline operating subsidiaries. When first incorporated, New Kern was known as KCL Corp.

stock which they owned. On the same day, May 19, Occidental, in a quarterly report to stockholders, appraised the value of the new Tenneco stock at $105 per share.[11]

Occidental, seeing its tender offer and takeover attempt being blocked by the Old Kern–Tenneco "defensive" merger, countered on May 25 and 31 with two mandamus actions in the California courts seeking to obtain extensive inspection of Old Kern books and records.[12] Realizing that, if the Old Kern–Tenneco merger were approved and successfully closed, Occidental would have to exchange its Old Kern shares for Tenneco stock and would be locked into a minority position in Tenneco, Occidental took other steps to protect itself. Between May 30 and June 2, it negotiated an arrangement with Tenneco whereby Occidental granted Tenneco Corp., a subsidiary of Tenneco, an option to purchase at $105 per share all of the Tenneco preference stock to which Occidental would be entitled in exchange for its Old Kern stock when and if the Old Kern–Tenneco merger was closed.[13] The premium to secure the option, at $10 per share, totaled $8,866,230 and was to be paid immediately upon the signing of the option agreement.[14] If the option were exercised, the premium was to be applied to the purchase price. By the terms of the option agreement, the option could not be exercised prior to December 9, 1967, a date six months and one day after expiration of Occidental's tender offer. On June 2, 1967, within six months of the acquisition by Occidental of more than 10% ownership of Old Kern, Occidental and Tenneco Corp. executed the option.[15] Soon thereafter, Occidental announced that it would not oppose the Old Kern–Tenneco merger and dismissed its state court suits against Old Kern.[16]

The Old Kern–Tenneco merger plan was presented to and approved by Old Kern shareholders at their meeting on July 17, 1967. Occidental refrained from voting its Old Kern shares, but in a letter read at the meeting Occidental stated that it had determined prior to

---

11. The annual dividend of $5.50 per share on the new Tenneco stock would be more than double the current annual dividend of $2.60 per share on the Old Kern stock. Each share of the new Tenneco preference stock was convertible into 3.6 shares of Tenneco common stock. During 1967, Tenneco common stock had sold at a high of $32\frac{1}{2}$ and a low of $20\frac{7}{8}$. Moreover, in contrast to Occidental's cash offer, the Tenneco exchange was expected to be, and was ultimately approved by the Internal Revenue Service as, free of capital gains tax.

12. Prior to any court ruling on Occidental's mandamus petitions, Old Kern voluntarily permitted inspection of Old Kern's general ledger, consolidated financial statements, consolidated journal entries, details of cash receipts from oil operations, supporting trial balances, and other records over a six-day period. A list of stockholders, however, was withheld.

13. The agreement covered 886,623 shares. This figure is 926 shares less than the number of Old Kern shares ultimately owned by Occidental. This discrepancy apparently results from uncertainty as to the number of shares tendered.

14. An outside investment banking firm in New York had determined that between $9 and $12 per share was a fair premium on an option on the Old Kern stock.

15. On that date, and on the date of the exercise of the option, Old Kern common stock was selling at approximately $95 per share.

16. Seeking to prevent its acquisition of Tenneco shares pursuant to the merger from being matched with the sale of those shares upon exercise of the option for purposes of establishing § 16(b) liability, Occidental asked that the new Tenneco stock not be immediately registered pursuant to § 12 of the Securities Exchange Act of 1934, 15 U.S.C. § 78l. See 450 F.2d 157, 160 n. 6.

June 2 not to oppose the merger and that it did not consider the plan unfair or inequitable.[17] Indeed, Occidental indicated that, had it been voting, it would have voted in favor of the merger.

Meanwhile, the Securities and Exchange Commission had refused Occidental's request to exempt from possible § 16(b) liability Occidental's exchange of its Old Kern stock for the Tenneco preference shares that would take place when and if the merger transaction were closed. Various Old Kern stockholders, with Occidental's interests in mind, thereupon sought to delay consummation of the merger by instituting various lawsuits in the state and federal courts. These attempts were unsuccessful, however, and preparations for the merger neared completion with an Internal Revenue Service ruling that consummation of the plan would result in a tax-free exchange with no taxable gain or loss to Old Kern shareholders, and with the issuance of the necessary approval of the merger closing by the California Commissioner of Corporations.

The Old Kern–Tenneco merger transaction was closed on August 30. Old Kern shareholders thereupon became irrevocably entitled to receive Tenneco preference stock, share for share in exchange for their Old Kern stock. Old Kern was dissolved and all of its assets, including "all claims, demands, rights and choses in action accrued or to accrue under and by virtue of the Securities Exchange Act of 1934 . . .," were transferred to New Kern.

The option granted by Occidental on June 2, 1967, was exercised on December 11, 1967. Occidental, not having previously availed itself of its right, exchanged certificates representing 887,549 shares of Old Kern stock for a certificate representing a like number of shares of Tenneco preference stock. The certificate was then endorsed over to the optionee-purchaser, and in return $84,229,185 was credited to Occidental's accounts at various banks. Adding to this amount the $8,886,230 premium paid in June, Occidental received $93,905,415 for its Old Kern stock (including the 1,900 shares acquired prior to issuance of its tender offer). In addition, Occidental received dividends totaling $1,793,439.22. Occidental's total profit was $19,506,419.22 on the shares obtained through its tender offer.

On October 17, 1967, New Kern instituted a suit under § 16(b) against Occidental to recover the profits which Occidental had realized as a result of its dealings in Old Kern stock. The complaint alleged that the execution of the Occidental–Tenneco option on June 2, 1967, and the exchange of Old Kern shares for shares of Tenneco to which Occidental became entitled pursuant to the merger closed on August 30, 1967, were both "sales" within the coverage of § 16(b). Since both acts took place within six months of the date on which Occidental

---

17. The letter indicated that Occidental "did not consider it to be in its best interest, or the best interest of its shareholders, or the best interest of KCL Shareholders generally for it to [oppose] the transaction." However, Occidental stated that "[i]n view of the fact that we would rather have worked out our own transaction with KCL, we shall not vote our KCL shares at the KCL Shareholder's Meeting on July 17, 1967." Under applicable California law, the abstention from voting was tantamount to opposing the merger.

became the owner of more than 10% of the stock of Old Kern, New Kern asserted that § 16(b) required surrender of the profits realized by Occidental. New Kern eventually moved for summary judgment, and, on December 27, 1970, the District Court granted summary judgment in favor of New Kern. *Abrams v. Occidental Petroleum Corp.,* 323 F.Supp. 570 (S.D.N.Y.1970). The District Court held that the execution of the option on June 2, 1967, and the exchange of Old Kern shares for shares of Tenneco on August 30, 1967, were "sales" under § 16(b). The Court ordered Occidental to disgorge its profits plus interest. In a supplemental opinion, Occidental was also ordered to refund the dividends which it had received plus interest.

On appeal, the Court of Appeals reversed and ordered summary judgment entered in favor of Occidental. *Abrams v. Occidental Petroleum Corp.,* 450 F.2d 157 (C.A.2 1971). The Court held that neither the option nor the exchange constituted a "sale" within the purview of § 16(b).[20] We granted certiorari. 405 U.S. 1064, 92 S.Ct. 1498, 31 L.Ed.2d 793 (1972). We affirm.

II

Section 16(b) provides, *inter alia,* that a statutory insider must surrender to the issuing corporation "any profit realized by him from any purchase and sale, or any sale and purchase, of any equity security of such issuer ... within any period of less than six months." As specified in its introductory clause, § 16(b) was enacted "[f]or the purpose of preventing the unfair use of information which may have been obtained by [a statutory insider] ... by reason of his relationship to the issuer." Congress recognized that short-swing speculation by stockholders with advance, inside information would threaten the goal of the Securities Exchange Act to "insure the maintenance of fair and honest markets." 15 U.S.C. § 78b. Insiders could exploit information not generally available to others to secure quick profits. As we have noted, "the only method Congress deemed effective to curb the evils of insider trading was a flat rule taking the profits out of a class of transactions in which the possibility of abuse was believed to be intolerably great." *Reliance Electric Co. v. Emerson Electric Co.,* 404 U.S. 418, 422, 92 S.Ct. 596, 30 L.Ed.2d 575 (1972). As stated in the report of the Senate Committee, the bill aimed at protecting the public "by preventing directors, officers, and principal stockholders of a corporation ... from speculating in the stock on the basis of information not available to others." S.Rep. No. 792, 73d Cong., 2d Sess., 9 (1934).

Although traditional cash-for-stock transactions that result in a purchase and sale or a sale and purchase within the six-month, statutory period are clearly within the purview of § 16(b), the courts

---

20. In view of its disposition, the Court of Appeals did not reach Occidental's contentions that only the purchases in excess of 10% of Old Kern's stock, rather than all purchases made pursuant to the tender offer, should be included in calculating liability and that the awards of prejudgment interest and dividends were improper. Occidental also appealed from the dismissal of its counterclaims. The Court of Appeals dismissed Occidental's appeal as moot.

have wrestled with the question of inclusion or exclusion of certain "unorthodox" transactions.[24] The statutory definitions of "purchase" and "sale" are broad and, at least arguably, reach many transactions not ordinarily deemed a sale or purchase. In deciding whether border-line transactions are within the reach of the statute, the courts have come to inquire whether the transaction may serve as a vehicle for the evil which Congress sought to prevent—the realization of short-swing profits based upon access to inside information[25]—thereby endeavoring to implement congressional objectives without extending the reach of the statute beyond its intended limits. The statute requires the inside, short-swing trader to disgorge all profits realized on all "purchases" and "sales" within the specified time period, without proof of actual abuse of insider information, and without proof of intent to profit on the basis of such information. Under these strict terms, the prevailing view is to apply the statute only when its application would serve its goals. "[W]here alternative constructions of the terms of § 16(b) are possible, those terms are to be given the construction that best serves the congressional purpose of curbing short-swing specula-tion by corporate insiders." *Reliance Electric Co. v. Emerson Electric Co.,* 404 U.S., at 424. See *Blau v. Lamb,* 363 F.2d 507 (C.A.2 1966), cert. denied, 385 U.S. 1002, 87 S.Ct. 707, 17 L.Ed.2d 542 (1967). Thus, "[i]n interpreting the terms 'purchase' and 'sale,' courts have properly asked whether the particular type of transaction involved is one that gives rise to speculative abuse." *Reliance Electric Co. v. Emerson Electric Co., supra,* at 424 n. 4.

In the present case, it is undisputed that Occidental became a "beneficial owner" within the terms of § 16(b) when, pursuant to its tender offer, it "purchased" more than 10% of the outstanding shares of Old Kern. We must decide, however, whether a "sale" within the ambit of the statute took place either when Occidental became irrevocably bound to exchange its shares of Old Kern for shares of Tenneco pursuant to the terms of the merger agreement between Old Kern and Tenneco or when Occidental gave an option to Tenneco to purchase from Occidental the Tenneco shares so acquired.[28]

24. The term, see 2 L. Loss, Securities Regulation 1069 (2d ed. 1961), has been ap-plied to stock conversions, exchanges pursu-ant to mergers and other corporate reorgani-zations, stock reclassifications, and dealings in options, rights, and warrants.

25. Several decisions have been read as to apply a so-called "objective" test in inter-preting and applying § 16(b). See, *e.g., Smo-lowe v. Delendo Corp., supra; Park & Tilford v. Schulte,* 160 F.2d 984 (CA2), cert. denied, 332 U.S. 761, 68 S.Ct. 64, 92 L.Ed. 347 (1947); *Heli-Coil Corp. v. Webster,* 352 F.2d 156 (C.A.3 1965). Under some broad lan-guage in those decisions, § 16(b) is said to be applicable whether or not the transaction in question could possibly lend itself to the types of speculative abuse that the statute was designed to prevent. By far the greater weight of authority is to the effect that a "pragmatic" approach to § 16(b) will best serve the statutory goals. . . .

28. Both events occurred within six months of Occidental's first acquisition of Old Kern shares pursuant to its tender offer. Although Occidental did not exchange its Old Kern shares until December 11, 1967, it is not contended that that date, rather than the date on which Occidental became irrevocably bound to do so, should control. Similarly, although the option was not exercised until December 11, 1967, no liability is asserted with respect to that event, because it oc-curred more than six months after Occiden-tal's last acquisition of Old Kern stock.

III

On August 30, 1967, the Old Kern–Tenneco merger agreement was signed, and Occidental became irrevocably entitled to exchange its shares of Old Kern stock for shares of Tenneco preference stock. Concededly, the transaction must be viewed as though Occidental had made the exchange on that day. But, even so, did the exchange involve a "sale" of Old Kern shares within the meaning of § 16(b)? We agree with the Court of Appeals that it did not, for we think it totally unrealistic to assume or infer from the facts before us that Occidental either had or was likely to have access to inside information, by reason of its ownership of more than 10% of the outstanding shares of Old Kern, so as to afford it an opportunity to reap speculative, short-swing profits from its disposition within six months of its tender-offer purchases.

It cannot be contended that Occidental was an insider when, on May 8, 1967, it made an irrevocable offer to purchase 500,000 shares of Old Kern stock at a price substantially above market. At that time, it owned only 1,900 shares of Old Kern stock, far fewer than the 432,000 shares needed to constitute the 10% ownership required by the statute. There is no basis for finding that, at the time the tender offer was commenced, Occidental enjoyed an insider's opportunity to acquire information about Old Kern's affairs.

It is also wide of the mark to assert that Occidental, as a sophisticated corporation knowledgeable in matters of corporate affairs and finance, knew that its tender offer would either succeed or would be met with a "defensive merger." If its takeover efforts failed, it is argued, Occidental knew it could sell its stock to the target company's merger partner at a substantial profit. Calculations of this sort, however, whether speculative or not and whether fair or unfair to other stockholders or to Old Kern, do not represent the kind of speculative abuse at which the statute is aimed, for they could not have been based on inside information obtained from substantial stockholdings that did not yet exist. Accepting both that Occidental made this very prediction and that it would recurringly be an accurate forecast in tender-offer situations,[29] we nevertheless fail to perceive how the fruition of such anticipated events would require, or in any way depend upon, the receipt and use of inside information. If there are evils to be redressed by way of deterring those who would make tender offers, § 16(b) does not appear to us to have been designed for this task.

29. Although a "defensive merger" is one tactic available to incumbent management in its arsenal of antitender-offer weapons, it is by no means a foregone conclusion that it is the response that will be most often, much less invariably, employed. Incumbent management might, for instance, choose to exhort shareholders not to tender, employ various techniques to elevate the market price of the company's stock in order to make the tender offer less attractive, institute legal proceedings, or increase the company's outstanding stock. Any one of these devices might prove more attractive to incumbent management than a defensive merger which could prove to be highly detrimental to the enterprise. See Note, Defensive Tactics Employed by Incumbent Managements in Contesting Tender Offers, 21 Stan.L.Rev. 1104 (1969).

By May 10, 1967, Occidental had acquired more than 10% of the outstanding shares of Old Kern. It was thus a statutory insider when, on May 11, it extended its tender offer to include another 500,000 shares. We are quite unconvinced, however, that the situation had changed materially with respect to the possibilities of speculative abuse of inside information by Occidental. Perhaps Occidental anticipated that extending its offer would increase the likelihood of the ultimate success of its takeover attempt or the occurrence of a defensive merger. But, again, the expectation of such benefits was unrelated to the use of information unavailable to other stockholders or members of the public with sufficient funds and the intention to make the purchases Occidental had offered to make before June 8, 1967.

The possibility that Occidental had, or had the opportunity to have, any confidential information about Old Kern before or after May 11, 1967, seems extremely remote. Occidental was, after all, a tender offeror, threatening to seize control of Old Kern, displace its management, and use the company for its own ends. The Old Kern management vigorously and immediately opposed Occidental's efforts. Twice it communicated with its stockholders, advising against acceptance of Occidental's offer and indicating prior to May 11 and prior to Occidental's extension of its offer, that there was a possibility of an imminent merger and a more profitable exchange. Old Kern's management refused to discuss with Occidental officials the subject of an Old Kern–Occidental merger. Instead, it undertook negotiations with Tenneco and forthwith concluded an agreement, announcing the merger terms on May 19. Requests by Occidental for inspection of Old Kern records were sufficiently frustrated by Old Kern's management to force Occidental to litigate to secure the information it desired.

There is, therefore, nothing in connection with Occidental's acquisition of Old Kern stock pursuant to its tender offer to indicate either the possibility of inside information being available to Occidental by virtue of its stock ownership or the potential for speculative abuse of such inside information by Occidental. Much the same can be said of the events leading to the exchange of Occidental's Old Kern stock for Tenneco preferred, which is one of the transactions that is sought to be classified a "sale" under § 16(b). The critical fact is that the exchange took place and was required pursuant to a merger between Old Kern and Tenneco. That merger was not engineered by Occidental but was sought by Old Kern to frustrate the attempts of Occidental to gain control of Old Kern. Occidental obviously did not participate in or control the negotiations or the agreement between Old Kern and Tenneco. Cf. *Newmark v. RKO General,* 425 F.2d 348 (CA2), cert. denied, 400 U.S. 854, 91 S.Ct. 64, 27 L.Ed.2d 91 (1970); *Park & Tilford v. Schulte,* 160 F.2d 984 (CA2), cert. denied, 332 U.S. 761, 68 S.Ct. 64, 92 L.Ed. 347 (1947). Once agreement between those two companies crystallized, the course of subsequent events was out of Occidental's hands. Old Kern needed the consent of its stockholders, but as it turned out, Old Kern's management had the necessary votes without the affirmative vote of Occidental. The merger agreement was approved by a majority of the stockholders of Old Kern, excluding the votes to which Occidental was entitled by virtue of its ownership of Old Kern shares. See generally *Ferraiolo v. Newman,* 259 F.2d 342 (C.A.6 1958), cert. denied, 359 U.S. 927, 79 S.Ct. 606, 3 L.Ed.2d 629 (1959); *Roberts v. Eaton,* 212 F.2d 82 (C.A.2 1954). Occidental, although registering its opinion that the merger would be beneficial to Old Kern shareholders, did not in fact vote at the stockholders' meeting at which merger approval was obtained. Under California law, its abstention was tantamount to a vote against approval of the merger. Moreover, at the time of stockholder ratification of the merger, Occidental's previous dealing in Old Kern stock was, as it had always been, fully disclosed.

Once the merger and exchange were approved, Occidental was left with no real choice with respect to the future of its shares of Old Kern. Occidental was in no position to prevent the issuance of a ruling by the Internal Revenue Service that the exchange of Old Kern stock for Tenneco preferred would be tax free; and, although various lawsuits were begun in state and federal courts seeking to postpone the merger closing beyond the statutory six-month period, those efforts were futile. The California Corporation Commissioner issued the necessary permits for the closing that took place on August 30, 1967. The merger left no right in dissenters to secure appraisal of their stock. Occidental could, of course, have disposed of its shares of Old Kern for cash before the merger was closed. Such an act would have been a § 16(b) sale and would have left Occidental with a prima facie § 16(b) liability. It was not, therefore, a realistic alternative for Occidental as long as it felt that it could successfully defend a suit like the present one. See generally *Petteys v. Butler,* 367 F.2d 528 (C.A.8 1966), cert. denied, 385 U.S. 1006, 87 S.Ct. 712, 17 L.Ed.2d 545 (1967); *Ferraiolo v. Newman, supra; Lynam v. Livingston,* 276 F.Supp. 104 (Del.1967); *Blau v. Hodgkinson,* 100 F.Supp. 361 (S.D.N.Y.1951). We do not suggest that an exchange of stock pursuant to a merger may never result in § 16(b) liability. But the involuntary nature of Occidental's exchange, when coupled with the absence of the possibility of speculative abuse of inside information, convinces us that § 16(b) should not apply to transactions such as this one.

IV

Petitioner also claims that the Occidental–Tenneco option agreement should itself be considered a sale, either because it was the kind of transaction the statute was designed to prevent or because the agreement was an option in form but a sale in fact. But the mere execution of an option to sell is not generally regarded as a "sale." See *Booth v. Varian Associates,* 334 F.2d 1 (C.A.1 1964), cert. denied, 379 U.S. 961, 85 S.Ct. 651, 13 L.Ed.2d 556 (1965); *Allis–Chalmers Mfg. Co. v. Gulf & Western Industries,* 309 F.Supp. 75 (E.D.Wis.1970); *Marquette Cement Mfg. Co. v. Andreas,* 239 F.Supp. 962 (S.D.N.Y.1965). And we do not find in the execution of the Occidental–Tenneco option agreement a sufficient possibility for the speculative abuse of inside information with respect to Old Kern's affairs to warrant holding that the option agreement was itself a ''sale'' within the meaning of § 16(b). The mutual advantages of the arrangement appear quite clear. As the District Court found, Occidental wanted to avoid the position of a minority stockholder with a huge investment in a company over which it had no control and in which it had not chosen to invest. On the other hand, Tenneco did not want a potentially troublesome minority stockholder that had just been vanquished in a fight for the control of Old Kern. Motivations like these do not smack of insider trading; and it is not clear to us, as it was not to the Court of Appeals, how the negotiation and execution of the option agreement gave Occidental any possible opportunity to trade on inside information it might have obtained from its position as a major stockholder of Old Kern. Occidental wanted to get out, but only at a date more than six months thence. It was willing to get out at a price of $105 per share, a price at which it had publicly valued Tenneco preferred on May 19 when the Tenneco–Old Kern agreement was announced. In any event, Occidental was dealing with the putative new owners of Old Kern, who undoubtedly knew more about Old Kern and Tenneco's affairs than did Occidental. If Occidental had leverage in dealing with Tenneco, it is incredible that its source was inside information rather than the fact of its large stock ownership itself.

Neither does it appear that the option agreement, as drafted and executed by the parties, offered measurable possibilities for speculative abuse. What Occidental granted was a ''call'' option. Tenneco had the right to buy after six months, but Occidental could not force Tenneco to buy. The price was fixed at $105 for each share of Tenneco preferred. Occidental could not share in a rising market for the Tenneco stock. See *Silverman v. Landa*, 306 F.2d 422 (C.A.2 1962). If the stock fell more than $10 per share, the option might not be exercised, and Occidental might suffer a loss if the market further deteriorated to a point where Occidental was forced to sell. Thus, the option, by its very form, left Occidental with no choice but to sell if Tenneco exercised the option, which it was almost sure to do if the value of Tenneco stock remained relatively steady. On the other hand, it is difficult to perceive any speculative value to Occidental if the stock declined and Tenneco chose not to exercise its option. See generally Note, Put and Call Options Under Section 16 of the Securities Exchange Act, 69 Yale L.J. 868 (1960); H. Filer, Understanding Put and Call Options 96–111 (1959); G. Leffler, The Stock Market 363–378 (2d ed. 1957).

The option, therefore, does not appear to have been an instrument with potential for speculative abuse, whether or not Occidental possessed inside information about the affairs of Old Kern. In addition, the option covered Tenneco preference stock, a stock as yet unissued, unregistered, and untraded. It was the value of this stock that underlay the option and that determined whether the option would be exercised, whether Occidental would be able to profit from the exercise, and whether there was any real likelihood of the exploitation of inside information. If Occidental had inside information when it negotiated and signed the option agreement, it was inside information with respect to Old Kern. Whatever it may have known or expected as to the future value of Old Kern stock, Occidental had no ownership position in Tenneco giving it any actual or presumed insights into the future value of Tenneco stock. That was the critical item of intelligence if Occidental was to use the option for purposes of speculation. Also, the date for exercise of the option was over six months in the future, a period that, under the statute itself, is assumed to dissipate whatever trading advantage might be imputed to a major stockholder with inside information. See Comment, Stock Exchanges Pursuant to Corporate Consolidation: A Section 16(b) "Purchase or Sale?," 117 U.Pa.L.Rev. 1034, 1054 (1969); *Silverman v. Landa, supra.* By enshrining the statutory period into the option, Occidental also, at least if the statutory period is taken to accomplish its intended purpose, limited its speculative possibilities. Nor should it be forgotten that there was no absolute assurance that the merger, which was not controlled by Occidental, would be consummated. In the event the merger did not close, the option itself would become null and void.

Nor can we agree that we must reverse the Court of Appeals on the ground that the option agreement was in fact a sale because the premium paid was so large as to make the exercise of the option almost inevitable, particularly when coupled with Tenneco's desire to rid itself of a potentially troublesome stockholder. The argument has force, but resolution of the question is very much a matter of judgment, economic and otherwise, and the Court of Appeals rejected the argument. That court emphasized that the premium paid was what experts had said the option was worth, the possibility that the market might drop sufficiently in the six months following execution of the option to make exercise unlikely, and the fact that here, unlike the situation in *Bershad v. McDonough,* 428 F.2d 693 (C.A.7 1970), the optionor did not surrender practically all emoluments of ownership by executing the option. Nor did any other special circumstances indicate that the parties understood and intended that the option was in fact a sale.[30] We see no satisfactory basis or reason for disagreeing with the judgment of the Court of Appeals in this respect.

The judgment of the Court of Appeals is affirmed.

---

30. In *Bershad v. McDonough,* 428 F.2d 693 (C.A.7 1970), the defendants were directors and greater-than-ten-percent stockholders of Cudahy Co. The defendants, within six months of their acquisition of beneficial ownership of Cudahy, granted an option to Smelting Refining & Mining Co. to purchase their Cudahy stock. The Seventh Circuit held that the grant of the option was a § 16(b) "sale" of the Cudahy stock. The Court of Appeals in the present case distinguished *Bershad* as follows:

"That case came before the court of appeals on a finding by the district court that, under the circumstances there presented, the stock had in fact been sold within the six months period, although the option was not formally exercised until later. The district court had relied on a number of circumstances, the most significant being that the optionor gave the optionee an irrevocable proxy to vote the shares and that the optionor and one of his associate directors resigned as directors within a few days after the grant of the option and were replaced by officers of the optionee. In other words, the district court found in effect that the 'option' was accompanied by a wink of the eye, and the court of appeals sustained this. Here there is no such finding, and no basis for one." 450 F.2d, at 165.

So ordered.

■ MR. JUSTICE DOUGLAS, with whom MR. JUSTICE BRENNAN and MR. JUSTICE STEWART concur, dissenting.

The Court, in resorting to an *ad hoc* analysis of the "possibility for the speculative abuse of inside information," charts a course for the interpretation of § 16(b) of the Securities Exchange Act of 1934, 15 U.S.C. § 78p(b), that in my mind undermines the congressional purpose. I respectfully dissent.

<h1 style="text-align:center">I</h1>

"The statute is written broadly, and the liability it imposes is strict." *Reliance Electric Co. v. Emerson Electric Co.*, 404 U.S. 418, 431, 92 S.Ct. 596, 30 L.Ed.2d 575 (DOUGLAS, J., dissenting). Except for narrowly drawn exceptions, it is all-inclusive. The operative language provides:

> "[A]ny profit realized by [a beneficial owner, director, or officer] from *any purchase and sale,* or any sale and purchase, of any equity security of such issuer (other than an exempted security) *within any period of less than six months,* unless such security was acquired in good faith in connection with a debt previously contracted, shall inure to and be recoverable by the issuer, *irrespective of any intention* on the part of such beneficial owner, director, or officer in entering into such transaction of holding the security purchased or of not repurchasing the security sold for a period exceeding six months." (Emphasis added.)

By its own terms, the section subsumes *all* transactions that are technically purchases and sales and applies irrespective of any actual or potential use of inside information to gain a trading advantage. See *Feder v. Martin Marietta Corp.*, 406 F.2d 260, 262 (C.A.2 1969). The conclusion seems inescapable that Occidental Petroleum Corp. (Occidental) purchased and sold shares of Kern County Land Co. (Old Kern) within a six-month period and that this "round trip" in Old Kern stock is covered by the literal terms of § 16(b).

Occidental, pursuant to a cash tender offer, acquired in excess of 880,000 shares of Old Kern during May and June 1967. It is undisputed that these acquisitions were purchases within the meaning of the section.[2] On August 30, 1967, Old Kern sold its assets to a newly formed subsidiary of Tenneco Corp., Kern County Land Co. (New Kern), in exchange for cumulative convertible preference stock of Tenneco, Inc. (Tenneco), Tenneco Corp.'s parent. Old Kern was dissolved in October 1967 (within six months of the tender offer), and each shareholder became irrevocably entitled to receive, share for

---

2. ... The District Court held that "[t]he tender offer constituted a single act of Occidental, whereby the company became a beneficial owner of more than 10 percent of Old Kern's capital stock." 323 F.Supp. 570, 579. Thus, the District Court ruled that the profit made on all stock purchased in the tender offer, not only the profit on the purchases in excess of 10%, would have to be surrendered. The Court of Appeals did not reach this issue.

share, for his Old Kern stock the cumulative convertible preference stock of Tenneco.

The question presented to us is whether this exchange of shares constituted a "sale" of the Old Kern shares. The term "sale," as used in the Securities Exchange Act, includes "any contract to sell or otherwise dispose of." 15 U.S.C. § 78c(a)(14). Clearly, Occidental "disposed" of its Old Kern shares through the Old Kern–Tenneco consolidation. Its status as a shareholder of Old Kern terminated, and it became instead a shareholder of Tenneco, privy to all the rights conferred by the Tenneco shares.[3] See *Newmark v. RKO General,* 425 F.2d 348 (C.A.2 1970); *Park & Tilford v. Schulte,* 160 F.2d 984 (C.A.2 1947).[4] In my view, we need look no further. As my Brother Blackmun, then Circuit Judge, stated in dissent in *Petteys v. Butler,* 367 F.2d 528, 538 (C.A.8 1966):

> "My own reaction is that either the statute means what it literally says or that it does not; that if the Congress intended to provide additional exceptions, it would have done so in clear language; and that the recognized purpose and aim of the statute are more consistently and protectively to be served if the statute is construed literally and objectively rather than non-literally and subjectively on a case-by-case application. The latter inevitably is a weakening process."

The majority finesses the literal impact of § 16(b) by examining Occidental's willfulness and its access to inside information. It concludes: "But the involuntary nature of Occidental's exchange, when coupled with the absence of the possibility of speculative abuse of inside information, convinces us that § 16(b) should not apply to transactions such as this one." . . . This approach is plainly contrary to the legislative purpose.

The purpose of § 16(b) is stated in its preamble: "preventing the unfair use of information which may have been obtained by such beneficial owner, director, or officer by reason of his relationship to the issuer. . . ." The congressional investigations that led to the enactment of the Securities Exchange Act revealed widespread use of confidential information by corporate insiders to gain an unfair advantage in trading their corporations' securities. Unlike other remedial provisions of the Act, the most noteworthy being § 10(b), 15 U.S.C. § 78j(b), Congress drafted § 16(b) as an objective rule, designed to have a clearly "prophylactic" effect. *Blau v. Lehman,* 368 U.S. 403, 414, 82 S.Ct. 451, 7 L.Ed.2d 403. See *Heli–Coil Corp. v. Webster,* 352 F.2d 156, 165–166 (C.A.3 1965); *Smolowe v. Delendo Corp.,* 136 F.2d

3. This is not a case where the stock surrendered and the stock received in the exchange were economic equivalents. Cf., *e.g., Blau v. Lamb,* 363 F.2d 507, 523–525 (C.A.2 1966); *Blau v. Max Factor & Co.,* 342 F.2d 304, 308–309 (C.A.9 1965). . . .

4. Judge Clark, in *Park & Tilford v. Schulte,* adopted a straightforward approach to defining "acquisition": "Defendants did not own the common stock in question before they exercised their option to convert; they did afterward. Therefore they acquired the stock, within the meaning of the Act." 160 F.2d 984, 987. The same analysis holds for "disposition."

231, 235 (C.A.2 1943). As Thomas Corcoran, a principal draftsman of the Act, explained to Congress:

> "You hold the director, irrespective of any intention or expectation to sell the security within 6 months after, because it will be absolutely impossible to prove the existence of such intention or expectation, and you have to have this crude rule of thumb, because you cannot undertake the burden of having to prove that the director intended, at the time he bought, to get out on a short swing."[6]

In *Reliance Electric, supra,* the Court noted that "the only method Congress deemed effective to curb the evils of insider trading was a flat rule taking the profits out of a *class of transactions* in which the possibility of abuse was believed to be intolerably great." 404 U.S., at 422 (emphasis added). Certainly, mergers are such a class of transactions....

    ... It is true that in some cases an insider may be required to disgorge profits even though his transactions do not lend themselves to the abuses that underlay the enactment of § 16(b). The draftsmen carefully weighed this eventuality and opted for a bright-line rule. As Thomas Corcoran stated: "You have to have a general rule. In particular transactions it might work a hardship, but those transactions that are a hardship represent the sacrifice to the necessity of having a general rule."[9]

The very construction of § 16(b) reinforces the conclusion that the section is based in the first instance[10] on a totally objective appraisal of the relevant transactions. See *Smolowe v. Delendo Corp., supra,* at 236. Had the draftsmen intended that the operation of the section hinge on abuse of access to inside information it would have been anomalous to limit the section to purchases and sales occurring within six months.[12] Indeed, the purpose of the six-month limitation, coupled with the definition of an insider, was to create a *conclusive presumption* that an insider who turns a short-swing profit in the stock of his corporation had access to inside information *and* capitalized on that information by speculating in the stock. But, the majority departs from the benign effects of this presumption when it assumes that it is "totally unrealistic to assume or infer from the facts before us that Occidental either had or was likely to have access to inside information...." .... The majority abides by this assumption even for that period after which Occidental became a 10% shareholder and then extended its tender offer in order to purchase additional Old Kern shares.

---

6. Hearings on Stock Exchange Practices before the Senate Committee on Banking and Currency, 73d Cong., 2d Sess., pt. 15, p. 6557 (1934).

9. Hearings, *supra,* n. 6, at 6558.

10. The objective approach may have to yield to a more flexible interpretation of the terms "purchase" and "sale" to include transactions which present the evil Congress sought to eliminate or transactions which are designed to evade § 16(b)....

12. In addition, there would have been no reason to exempt transactions wherein the "security was acquired in good faith in connection with a debt previously contracted...."

The majority takes heart from those decisions of lower federal courts which endorse a "pragmatic" approach to § 16(b).... But, by sanctioning the approach of these cases, the majority brings to fruition Louis Loss' prophecy that they will "continue to rule us from their graves,"[16] for henceforth they certainly will be applied by analogy to the area of mergers and other consolidations.

Thus, the courts will be caught up in an *ad hoc* analysis of each transaction, determining both from the economics of the transaction and the *modus operandi* of the insider whether there exists the possibility of speculative abuse of inside information. Instead of a section that is easy to administer and by its clearcut terms discourages litigation, we have instead a section that fosters litigation because the Court's decision holds out the hope for the insider that he may avoid § 16(b) liability. In short, the majority destroys much of the section's prophylactic effect.... Certainly we cannot allow transactions which present the possibility of abuse but do not fall within the classic conception of a purchase or sale to escape the confines of § 16(b). It is one thing to interpret the terms "purchase" and "sale" liberally in order to include those transactions which evidence the evil Congress sought to eliminate; it is quite another to abandon the bright-line test of § 16(b) for those transactions which clearly fall within its literal bounds. Section 16(b), because of the six-month limitation, allows some to escape who have abused their inside information. It should not be surprising, given the objective nature of the rule, if some are caught unwillingly.

In *Reliance Electric, supra,* at 422, the Court quoted with approval the following language from *Bershad v. McDonough,* 428 F.2d 693, 696 (C.A.7 1970):

> "In order to achieve its goals, Congress chose a relatively arbitrary rule capable of easy administration. The objective standard of Section 16(b) imposes strict liability upon substantially all transactions occurring within the statutory time period, regardless of the intent of the insider or the existence of actual speculation. This approach maximized the ability of the rule to eradicate speculative abuses by reducing difficulties in proof. Such arbitrary and sweeping coverage was deemed necessary to insure the optimum prophylactic effect."

It is this "objective standard" that the Court hung to so tenaciously in *Reliance Electric,* but now apparently would abandon to a large extent. In my view, the Court improperly takes upon itself the task of refashioning the contours of § 16(b) and changing its essential thrust....

NOTE, SHORT–SWING PROFITS IN FAILED TAKEOVER BIDS— THE ROLE OF SECTION 16(b), 59 Wash.L.Rev. 895 (1984). "Al-

16. 5 L. Loss, Securities Regulation 3029 (Supp. to 2d ed. 1969).

though the *Kern* decision did not state the threshold requirement for application of the pragmatic approach, subsequent courts have generally held that an involuntary transaction is [a necessary condition to the application of that approach]. To prove that a particular transaction is involuntary, the insider must apparently show that it had no control over the timing of the transaction. If the insider fails to make this showing, liability attaches automatically. If the insider does make this showing, however, courts will regard the transaction as unorthodox and will then ask whether the defendant had access to inside information. This inquiry, though secondary, is critical. One with access to inside information can speculate profitably by relying on an imminent 'involuntary' transaction. A finding of involuntariness, therefore, does not guarantee exoneration...."

———

COLAN v. MESA PETROLEUM CO., 951 F.2d 1512 (9th Cir. 1991), cert. denied 504 U.S. 911, 112 S.Ct. 1943, 118 L.Ed.2d 548 (1992). In October 1984, Mesa Partners began accumulating Unocal stock. By February 22, 1985, Mesa owned 9.7 percent of Unocal's outstanding shares. On March 27, Mesa increased its ownership interest to 13.6 percent. To discourage a takeover by Mesa, on April 16 Unocal initiated a self-tender, under which it offered to exchange a package of its own debt securities for up to one-half of its own outstanding common stock. Unocal stated that one of the express purposes of the self-tender was to make it more difficult for Mesa to take over Unocal, and expressly excluded Mesa from participating in the Unocal offer. After negotiations, however, Mesa and Unocal made an agreement under which Mesa was allowed to, and did, participate in Unocal's self-tender. Plaintiff, a Unocal shareholder, then sued Mesa under § 16(b) to recover Mesa's short-swing profit on its exchange of Unocal stock for Unocal negotiable debt securities pursuant to Unocal's self-tender. Mesa argued that the exchange was not a sale because it fell within the "unorthodox transaction" exception. Held, the exception did not apply, the exchange was a sale, and Mesa was liable under § 16(b).

The exchange of Unocal stock for debt securities pursuant to Unocal's tender offer is factually distinguishable from the transaction in *Kern County*. [In that case, the] exchange of Occidental's stock for equity shares of the new corporation which was formed as the result of the merger in *Kern County* was involuntary and automatic. The ... exchange of stock for debt securities by the Mesa Defendants was not an involuntary or automatic transaction. Unocal did not merge into a new corporation so as to compel its shareholders to exchange their stock.

The Mesa Defendants not only were not compelled to exchange their stock for Unocal's debt securities, but Unocal expressly excluded them from its self-tender offer. The Mesa Defendants filed [an unsuccessful] suit in Delaware seeking an injunction to force Unocal to permit the Mesa Defendants to participate in Unocal's tender offer.

The Mesa Defendants had the choice of participating in the tender offer or holding onto their stock. The record shows that it was anticipated that Unocal's stock would sell at $30 a share as a result of the exchange set forth in the tender offer. One of the choices available to the Mesa Defendants was to buy up Unocal's stock at the reduced price of $30 a share and acquire control of the corporation. . . .

Courts following *Kern County* have recognized that involuntariness is an important factor in determining whether or not a transaction constitutes a "sale" or "purchase" within section 16(b).

The Mesa Defendants argue that "otherwise volitional transactions" are unorthodox under section 16(b) if a beneficial owner is coerced economically into exchanging his common stock or suffer a financial loss. In *Oliff v. Exchange Int'l Corp.*, 669 F.2d 1162 (7th Cir.1980), *cert. denied,* 450 U.S. 915, 101 S.Ct. 1358, 67 L.Ed.2d 340 (1981), the Seventh Circuit found that although a 205% tax payment was not a "reasonable alternative" to the repurchase of shares which gave rise to section 16(b) liability, the acquisition of the stock was not "so involuntary as to take it out of the definition of 'purchase' for 16(b) purposes." . . .

An economic coercion test would allow corporate insiders to avoid section 16(b) liability by presenting evidence of a variety of unfortunate circumstances that forced them to sell their common stock. The objective standards of section 16(b) were adopted to avoid the necessity for an inquiry into an insider's subjective "intent." . . . We reject the "economic coercion" test as contrary to the intent of Congress in enacting the bright-line, flat rule set forth in section 16(b) requiring disgorgement of profits.

We conclude that the facts in this matter do not come within the holding of *Kern County* that an involuntary transaction that results from a merger is "unorthodox."

The cases that have applied the *Kern County* "unorthodox" transaction defense to a short-swing sale by a beneficial owner have characterized it as a narrow exception to section 16(b). . . . The Supreme Court did not indicate that the courts should conduct an ad hoc, case-by-case analysis of all securities transactions involving a sale by a beneficial owner. The Court in *Kern County* simply held that an automatic exchange of stock in one company for stock in another company pursuant to a merger between the two companies, over which the shareholder had no control, is not a form of transaction covered by section 16(b). . . .

The majority of the transactions which have been considered "unorthodox" within the narrow exception announced in *Kern County* involve exchanges of stock pursuant to a merger. . . .

Those courts that have directly addressed the issue of section 16(b) liability in a tender offer or hostile takeover context have concluded that the disposition of shares pursuant to a tender offer, or in the face of defeat in a takeover contest, is not an unorthodox transaction under Kern County. . . .

. . . The Mesa Defendants rely primarily on the Supreme Court's comment in footnote 24 in *Kern County*. . . . In footnote 24, the Court observed that "[t]he term [unorthodox transaction] . . . has been applied to stock conversions, exchanges pursuant to mergers and other corporate reorganizations, stock reclassifications, and dealings in options, rights, and warrants." *Id.* The Mesa Defendants reason that since a recapitalization is a form of corporate reorganization, it must constitute an "unorthodox transaction."

The comment in footnote 24 in *Kern County* was not necessary to the opinion in *Kern County*. The Court, without expressing its approval, enumerated the types of business transactions that others have labeled as "unorthodox." The Court did not cite any authority to support its observation in footnote 24. Thus, we cannot determine whether the Court was referring to decisions construing section 16(b).

————

NOTE ON ATTRIBUTION OF OWNERSHIP UNDER SECTIONS 16(a) AND (b)

Sections 16(a) and (b) use the term or the concept of "beneficial ownership" for several different purposes.

Under § 16(a), a person who is either "a beneficial owner of more than 10 per centum of any class of equity security" (hereafter, a "more-than–10–percent owner"), or an officer or director, must report the amount of all equity securities of the issuer "of which he is the beneficial owner."

Under § 16(b), a director, officer, or more-than–10–percent owner is liable for short-swing profits "realized by him from any purchase and sale, or any sale and purchase, of any equity security" of the issuer. Given both the purpose of the statute and the context, § 16(b) seems generally intended to cover the purchase and sale of those equity securities of which a person is a beneficial owner for purposes of § 16(a).

If a person is the record owner of an equity security and also has a pecuniary interest in the security, he is undoubtedly a beneficial owner for all purposes under § 16. Problems of interpretation arise, however, if a person is a record owner of shares but has no pecuniary interest; or if a person has a pecuniary interest but is not the record owner; or if a person is neither the record owner nor has a pecuniary interest, but there is nevertheless an important relationship between the person and the security, such as the right to control the security.

For most although not all practical purposes, the problem can be stated as follows: when should an equity security that is not legally owned by a person, in the conventional sense, nevertheless be *attributed* to the person under § 16, so that either (i) the security counts toward determining whether the person's ownership crosses the 10-percent-beneficial-ownership line, (ii) the person's transactions in the security must be reported under § 16(a), or (iii) the person's transactions in the security may subject him to liability under § 16(b)?

These problems are addressed in detail by the Rules under § 16. Those Rules draw a distinction between (1) what constitutes beneficial ownership for purposes of determining whether a person is a more-than-10-percent owner, and (2) what constitutes beneficial ownership for purposes of determining whether a person who *is* a more-than-10-percent owner, or a director or officer, must report under § 16(a) and may be liable for short-swing profits under § 16(b).

As to the first problem (whether a person is a more-than-10-percent owner), Rule 16a–1(a)(1) provides that, with certain exceptions, "*solely for purposes of determining whether a person is a beneficial owner of more than ten percent of* any class of equity securities registered pursuant to § 12 of the Act, the term 'beneficial owner' shall mean any person who is deemed a beneficial owner pursuant to § 13(d) of the Act and the rules thereunder...." (emphasis added). Rule 13d–3, in turn, provides that a beneficial owner of a security includes "any person who, directly or indirectly, through any contract, arrangement, understanding, relationship, or otherwise has or shares: (1) *Voting power* which includes the power to vote, or to direct the voting of, such security; and/or, (2) *Investment power* which includes the power to dispose, or to direct the disposition of, such security." (Emphasis added.) In short, in determining *whether* a person is a more-than-10-percent owner of stock, the emphasis, under Rule 16a–1, is on the person's *control* over the stock.

As to the second problem (what constitutes beneficial ownership for *reporting* and *liability* purposes) Rule 16a–1(a)(2) provides that as a general principle, with certain exceptions and elaborations, (1) "*other than for purposes of determining whether a person is a beneficial owner of more than ten percent of any class of equity securities* registered under § 12 of the Act, the term 'beneficial owner' shall mean any person who, directly or indirectly, through any contract, arrangement, understanding, relationship or otherwise, has or shares a direct or indirect *pecuniary interest* in the equity securities...."; and (2) "[t]he term 'pecuniary interest' in any class of equity securities shall mean the opportunity, directly or indirectly, *to profit or share in any profit* derived from a transaction in the subject securities." (Emphasis added.) In short, unlike Rule 16a–1(a)(1), which emphasizes *control* for purposes of determining who is a more-than-10-percent owner, Rule 16a–1(a)(2) emphasizes *pecuniary interest* for purposes of determining what transactions in equity securities must be reported and may give rise to liability.

After stating the pecuniary-interest test as a general principle to govern the determination of beneficial ownership for reporting and liability purposes, Rule 16a–1(a)(2) then goes on to deal with certain recurring cases in which problems of attribution based on a pecuniary interest may arise. Some of these cases are as follows:

Family members. Rule 16a–1(a)(2)(ii)(A) provides that "[t]he term 'indirect pecuniary interest' [under Rule 16a–2] in any class of equity securities shall include, but not be limited to ... securities held by members of a person's immediate family sharing the same household; *provided, however,* that the presumption of such beneficial ownership may be rebutted...." Rule 16a–1(e) then provides that "[t]he term 'immediate family', shall mean any child, stepchild, grand-child, parent, stepparent, grandparent, spouse, sibling, mother-in-law, father-in-law, son-in-law, daughter-in-law, brother-in-law, or sister-in-law, and shall include adoptive relationships."

Partnerships. Rule 16a–1(a)(2)(ii)(B) provides that the term "indirect pecuniary interest" [under Rule 16a–1(a)(2)] includes "a general partner's proportionate interest in the portfolio securities held by a general or limited partnership."

Corporations. Rule 16a–1(a)(2)(iii) provides that "[a] shareholder shall not be deemed to have a pecuniary interest in the portfolio securities held by a corporation or similar entity in which the person owns securities if the shareholder is not a controlling shareholder of the entity and does not have or share investment control over the entity's portfolio...." Note that this Rule does not state specify a general principle for determining when a corporation's portfolio securities will be attributed to shareholders in the corporation, but only provides a safe harbor in the cases that the rule specifies.

The Rules under § 16 also contain elaborate provisions dealing with such matters as when a trustee is a beneficial owner for reporting and liability purposes, and when the ownership of a derivative security makes a person the beneficial owner of the derivative security.

———

NOTE ON INSIDER STATUS AT ONLY ONE END OF A SWING

The last sentence of § 16(b) sets out an exemptive provision under which "[T]his subsection shall not be construed to cover any transaction where [a more-than–10–percent] beneficial owner was not such both at the time of the purchase and sale, or the sale and purchase, of the security involved." Suppose a person, S, owns a more-than–10–percent block, but is not a director or officer. S makes a sale that reduces his block to less than 10 percent, but leaves him with the remainder. Are S's later sales of some or all of the remainder of his block, covered by § 16? The Supreme Court has held that the later sales are not covered, because the person is not a 10 percent owner at the time of those sales. Reliance Electric Co. v. Emerson Electric Co.,

404 U.S. 418, 92 S.Ct. 596, 30 L.Ed.2d 575 (1972). This result is codified in Rule 16a–2(c).

What about the very purchase that makes a person a more-than–10–percent beneficial owner? Can that purchase be matched with a subsequent sale within six months? In Foremost–McKesson, Inc. v. Provident Securities Co., 423 U.S. 232, 96 S.Ct. 508, 46 L.Ed.2d 464 (1976) the Supreme Court held, largely on the basis of the exemptive provision and legislative history, that in the case of a *purchase-sale sequence*, a more-than–10–percent beneficial owner is not liable unless he was such *before* he made the purchase in question. To put this differently, the purchase that first lifts a beneficial owner above 10 percent cannot be matched with a subsequent sale under § 16(b).

Suppose a person who is a more-than–10–percent owner sells enough stock to get below the 10 percent line, and then buys stock within six months after that sale? This kind of case is called a sale-repurchase sequence. The *Foremost* opinion did not cover this case, and left considerable room for arguing that this sequence should result in liability under § 16(b).

Suppose a person is a director or officer at only one end of a swing? Since the exemptive clause provides that "this subsection shall not be construed to cover any transaction where [*a more–than–10–percent*] *beneficial owner* was not such both at the time of the purchase and sale, or the sale and purchase" (emphasis added), the clear implication is that § 16(b) *does* apply to a short-swing transaction by a director or officer even where the director or officer "was not such both at the time of purchase and sale, or the sale and purchase." In Feder v. Martin Marietta Corp., 406 F.2d 260 (2d Cir.1969), cert. denied 396 U.S. 1036, 90 S.Ct. 678, 24 L.Ed.2d 681 (1970), the court held that a director or officer who purchases, resigns, and then sells within six months of the purchase, is liable under § 16(b). However, no liability will be imposed if both ends of a swing occur after the director or officer resigns. Lewis v. Mellon Bank, N.A., 513 F.2d 921 (3d Cir.1975); Lewis v. Varnes, 505 F.2d 785 (2d Cir.1974). Prior to 1991, it had been held that § 16(b) applies to a purchase or sale of shares by a person who becomes a director or officer after the transaction, and engages in a matching transaction within six months of the original transaction. In such a case, the director or officer will have had an opportunity to utilize inside information at the second end of the swing, but not at the first. This issue is now governed by Rule 16a–2(a), adopted by the SEC in 1991, which provides that purchases and sales by a director or officer before she became a director or officer are not subject to § 16.

NOTE ON WHO IS AN "OFFICER" UNDER § 16(b)

The battle between "objective" and "subjective" approaches to the interpretations of Section 16(b) has played a dramatic role in the question who is an "officer" for purposes of that Section. Under the objective view, an officer *title* would give rise to § 16(b) liability. Under the subjective view, liability would depend on whether the person had access to inside information by virtue of her position. An intermediate view is that liability should turn on a person's corporate role or function (rather than her title), but that the issue is whether the function is "officer-like," not whether the person's corporate function gives her access to inside information.

For many years, SEC Rule 3b–2 provided that the term officer "means a president, vice president, secretary, treasurer or principal financial officer, comptroller or principal accounting officer, and any person routinely performing corresponding functions with respect to any organization whether incorporated or unincorporated."

The first part of this rule (up to the phrase "and any person") was objective—it imposed liability based on a person's title. The second part of the rule (beginning with the phrase "and any person") reflected the intermediate view—it made liability turn on the functions a person actually performed. Neither part of the rule, however, was explicitly keyed into whether a person's officer role was likely to give her access to inside information. Presumably, the theory of Rule 3b–2 was either that (1) in using the term "officer" § 16(b) intended to pick up any person commonly regarded as an officer for non–16(b) purposes; (2) a person who held one of the titles designated in the rule, or performed the kinds of functions identified in the rule, should be conclusively presumed to have access to material inside information; or (3) both.

In the early case of *Colby v. Klune,* 178 F.2d 872 (2d Cir.1949), rev'g 83 F.Supp. 159 (S.D.N.Y.), the plaintiff sought to hold a corporation's "production manager" liable under § 16(b). The Second Circuit criticized Rule 3b–2 as too limited, and therefore not authorized by the statute. The court said: "[W]e construe 'officer,' as used in section 16(b) of the Securities Exchange Act, thus: It includes, *inter alia,* a corporate employee performing important executive duties of such character that he would be likely, in discharging these duties, to obtain confidential information about the company's affairs that would aid him if he engaged in personal market transactions."

In contrast, in Merrill Lynch, Pierce, Fenner & Smith, Inc. v. Livingston, 566 F.2d 1119 (9th Cir.1978), in which an account executive at a stockbroker had been given an honorary title as vice-president, with no change in his duties, as a reward for an outstanding sales record, the Ninth Circuit held that Rule 3b–2 was too expansive. The court said: "Liability under Section 16(b) is not based simply upon a person's title within his corporation; rather, liability follows from the existence of a relationship with the corporation that makes it more probable than not that the individual has access to insider information." Id. at 1121. Later, however, in National Medical Enterprises, Inc. v. Small, 680 F.2d 83 (9th Cir.1982), the Ninth Circuit drastically restricted *Merrill Lynch,* and endorsed the concept of liability based on a person's title, with only a very limited exception:

In designing section 16, "Congress chose a relatively arbitrary rule capable of easy administration." . . . It does not matter whether the insider actually received the information, or utilized it; his mere status makes him liable.

. . . The defendants mistakenly . . . argue that although they are officers of National Medical, they did not have access to material inside information and therefore should not be considered section 16(b) "officers." Whether an individual is an "officer" for purposes of section 16(b) is determined by the title that he holds, with a very limited exception applicable only where the title is essentially honorary or ceremonial. . . .

Eventually, the SEC itself adopted a new definition of "officer" which is essentially function-based, and much more limited in its coverage than was Rule 3b–2. The new rule, Rule 16a–1(f), provides that:

[T]he term "officer" shall mean an issuer's president, principal financial officer, or principal accounting officer (or, if there is no such accounting officer, the controller), any vice-president of the issuer in charge of a principal business unit, division or function (such as sales, administration or finance), any other officer who performs a policy-making function, or any other person who performs similar policy-making functions for the issuer.

In a note to Rule 16a–1(f), the SEC states that the term "policy-making function" is not intended to include policy-making functions that are not significant.

The Chairman of the SEC, in his opening remarks at the meeting at which the new rule was adopted, stated that:

The definition of officer has been revised to make clear that a person's functions and not simply title will determine the applicability of Section 16. The definition . . . is intended to make clear that individuals with executive functions do not avoid liability under Section 16 simply by foregoing title, and those with a title but no significant executive responsibilities are not subject to the automatic short-swing profit liability of Section 16(b). Thus, for example, a vice-president of a bank, who has no policy-making responsibility would not have to be concerned with possible liability under Section 16(b), if because of an unexpected family emergency, he needed to sell securities.

Barron, Control and Restricted Securities, 19 Sec.Reg.L.J. 292, 294–95 (1991).

___

NOTE ON DEPUTIZATION

Closely related to the theory of attribution under § 16(b) is the theory of deputization. In Blau v. Lehman, 368 U.S. 403, 82 S.Ct. 451, 7 L.Ed.2d 403 (1962), the Supreme Court held that one enterprise, A, could be a "director" of second enterprise, B, within the meaning of § 16(b), if one of B's directors had been deputized by A to act on its behalf. In *Blau*, Thomas, a partner in Lehman Brothers (Enterprise A) sat on the board of Tide Water (Enterprise B), and Lehman profited from short-swing trading in Tide Water stock. The Court approved the deputization theory:

> No doubt Lehman Brothers, though a partnership, could for purposes of § 16 be a "director" of Tide Water and function through a deputy, since § 3(a)(9) of the Act provides that " 'person' means ... partnership" and § 3(a)(7) that " 'director' means any director of a corporation or any person performing similar functions with respect to any organization, whether incorporated or unincorporated." Consequently, Lehman Brothers would be a "director" of Tide Water, if as petitioner's complaint charged Lehman actually functioned as a director through Thomas, who had been deputized by Lehman to perform a director's duties not for himself but for Lehman.

Id. at 409. However, the courts below had made findings that the Supreme Court believed precluded the conclusion that deputization had actually occurred, and Lehman Brothers was therefore not held liable. (Thomas himself was held liable below for his pro rata share of the short-swing profits made by Lehman, and this aspect of the case was not appealed.)

Deputization *was* found to be present in Feder v. Martin Marietta Corp., 406 F.2d 260 (2d Cir.1969), cert. denied 396 U.S. 1036, 90 S.Ct. 678, 24 L.Ed.2d 681 (1970). Bunker, the president of Martin Marietta (Enterprise A), had become a director of Sperry (Enterprise B), in which Martin Marietta held substantial stock. Bunker was ultimately responsible for the total operation of Martin Marietta, and personally approved all of the firm's financial investments—in particular, its purchase of the Sperry stock. Bunker's control over Martin Marietta, coupled with his membership on Sperry's Board, placed him in a position in which he could acquire inside information concerning Sperry and could utilize such information for Martin. Further, Bunker admitted discussing Sperry's affairs with two officials at Martin Marietta and participating in sessions when Martin Marietta's investment in Sperry was reviewed, and Bunker's ultimate letter of resignation to Martin Marietta's president stated that "When I became a member of the [Sperry] board ... it appeared to your associates that the Martin Marietta ownership of a substantial number of shares of Sperry Rand should have representation on your Board." On these facts, the Second Circuit concluded that "The control possessed by Bunker, his letter of resignation, the approval by the Martin Board of Bunker's directorship with Sperry and the functional similarity between Bunker's acts as a Sperry director and the acts of Martin's representatives on other boards ... are all definite and concrete indicatives that Bunker, in fact, was a Martin deputy." Martin Marietta was therefore held liable, as a director, for its short-swing profits in Sperry stock.

SECTION 4.   THE COMMON LAW REVISITED

Diamond v. Oreamuno

New York Court of Appeals, 1969.
24 N.Y.2d 494, 301 N.Y.S.2d 78, 248 N.E.2d 910.

■ CHIEF JUDGE FULD. Upon this appeal from an order denying a motion to dismiss the complaint as insufficient on its face, the question presented—one of first impression in this court—is whether officers and directors may be held accountable to their corporation for gains realized by them from transactions in the company's stock as a result of their use of material inside information.

The complaint was filed by a shareholder of Management Assistance, Inc. (MAI) asserting a derivative action against a number of its officers and directors to compel an accounting for profits allegedly acquired as a result of a breach of fiduciary duty. It charges that two of the defendants—Oreamuno, chairman of the board of directors, and Gonzalez, its president—had used inside information, acquired by them solely by virtue of their positions, in order to reap large personal profits from the sale of MAI shares and that these profits rightfully belong to the corporation. Other officers and directors were joined as defendants on the ground that they acquiesced in or ratified the assertedly wrongful transactions.

MAI is in the business of financing computer installations through sale and lease back arrangements with various commercial and industrial users. Under its lease provisions, MAI was required to maintain and repair the computers but, at the time of this suit, it lacked the capacity to perform this function itself and was forced to engage the manufacturer of the computers, International Business Machines (IBM), to service the machines. As a result of a sharp increase by IBM of its charges for such service, MAI's expenses for August of 1966 rose considerably and its net earnings declined from $262,253 in July to $66,233 in August, a decrease of about 75%. This information, although earlier known to the defendants, was not made public until October of 1966. Prior to the release of the information, however, Oreamuno and Gonzalez sold off a total of 56,500 shares of their MAI stock at the then current market price of $28 a share.

After the information concerning the drop in earnings was made available to the public, the value of a share of MAI stock immediately fell from the $28 realized by the defendants to $11. Thus, the plaintiff alleges, by taking advantage of their privileged position and their access to confidential information, Oreamuno and Gonzalez were able to realize $800,000 more for their securities than they would have had this inside information not been available to them. Stating that the defendants were "forbidden to use [such] information . . . for their own personal profit or gain", the plaintiff brought this derivative action seeking to have the defendants account to the corporation for this difference. A motion by the defendants to dismiss the complaint—pursuant to CPLR 3211 (subd. [a], par. 7)—for failure to state a cause of action was granted by the court at Special Term. The Appellate Division, with one dissent, modified Special Term's order by reinstating the complaint as to the defendants Oreamuno and Gonzalez. The appeal is before us on a certified question.

In reaching a decision in this case, we are, of course, passing only upon the sufficiency of the complaint and we necessarily accept the charges contained in that pleading as true.

It is well established, as a general proposition, that a person who acquires special knowledge or information by virtue of a confidential or fiduciary relationship with another is not free to exploit that knowledge or information for his own personal benefit but must account to his principal for any profits derived therefrom. (See, e.g., *Byrne v. Barrett,* 268 N.Y. 199.) This, in turn, is merely a corollary of the broader principle, inherent in the nature of the fiduciary relationship, that prohibits a trustee or agent from extracting secret profits from his position of trust.

In support of their claim that the complaint fails to state a cause of action, the defendants take the position that, although it is admittedly wrong for an officer or director to use his position to obtain trading profits for himself in the stock of his corporation, the action ascribed to them did not injure or damage MAI in any way. Accordingly, the defendants continue, the corporation should not be permitted to recover the proceeds. They acknowledge that, by virtue of the exclusive access which officers and directors have to inside information, they possess an unfair advantage over other shareholders and, particularly, the persons who had purchased the stock from them but, they contend, the corporation itself was unaffected and, for that reason, a derivative action is an inappropriate remedy.

It is true that the complaint before us does not contain any allegation of damages to the corporation but this has never been considered to be an essential requirement for a cause of action founded on a breach of fiduciary duty. (See, e.g., *Matter of People [Bond & Mtge. Guar. Co.],* 303 N.Y. 423, 431; *Wendt v. Fischer,* 243 N.Y. 439, 443; *Dutton v. Willner,* 52 N.Y. 312, 319.) This is because the function of such an action, unlike an ordinary tort or contract case, is not merely to *compensate* the plaintiff for wrongs committed by the defendant but, as this court declared many years ago (*Dutton v. Willner,* 52 N.Y. 312, 319, *supra*), "to *prevent* them, by removing from agents and trustees all inducement to attempt dealing for their own benefit in matters which they have undertaken for others, or to which their agency or trust relates." (Emphasis supplied.)

Just as a trustee has no right to retain for himself the profits yielded by property placed in his possession but must account to his beneficiaries, a corporate fiduciary, who is entrusted with potentially valuable information, may not appropriate that asset for his own use even though, in so doing, he causes no injury to the corporation. The primary concern, in a case such as this, is not to determine whether the corporation has been damaged but to decide, as between the corporation and the defendants, who has a higher claim to the proceeds derived from the exploitation of the information. In our opinion, there can be no justification for permitting officers and directors, such as the defendants, to retain for themselves profits which, it is alleged, they derived solely from exploiting information gained by virtue of their inside position as corporate officials.

In addition, it is pertinent to observe that, despite the lack of any specific allegation of damage, it may well be inferred that the defendants' actions might have caused some harm to the enterprise. Although the corporation may have little concern with the day-to-day transactions in its shares, it has a great interest in maintaining a reputation of integrity, an image of probity, for its management and in insuring the continued public acceptance and marketability of its stock. When officers and directors abuse their position in order to gain personal profits, the effect may be to cast a cloud on the corporation's name, injure stockholder relations and undermine public regard for the corporation's securities. As Presiding Justice BOTEIN aptly put it, in the course of his opinion for the Appellate Division, "[t]he prestige and good will of a corporation, so vital to its prosperity, may be undermined by the revelation that its chief officers had been making personal profits out of corporate events which they had not disclosed to the community of stockholders." (29 A.D.2d, at p. 287.)

The defendants maintain that extending the prohibition against personal exploitation of a fiduciary relationship to officers and directors of a corporation will discourage such officials from maintaining a stake in the success of the corporate venture through share ownership, which, they urge, is an important incentive to proper performance of their duties. There is, however, a considerable difference between corporate officers who assume the same risks and obtain the same benefits as other shareholders and those who use their privileged position to gain special advantages not available to others. The sale of shares by the defendants for the reasons charged was not merely a wise investment decision which any prudent investor might have made. Rather, they were assertedly able in this case to profit solely because they had information which was not available to any one else—including the other shareholders whose interests they, as corporate fiduciaries, were bound to protect.

Although no appellate court in this State has had occasion to pass upon the precise question before us, the concept underlying the present cause of action is hardly a new one. (See, e.g., Securities Exchange Act of 1934 [48 U.S.Stat. 881], § 16[b]; U.S.Code, tit. 15, § 78p, subd. [b]; *Brophy v. Cities Serv. Co.,* 31 Del.Ch. 241; Restatement, 2d, Agency, § 388, comment *c*; Israels, A New Look at Corporate Directorship, 24 Business Lawyer 727, 732 *et seq.;* Note, 54 Cornell L.Rev. 306, 309–312.) Under Federal law (Securities Exchange Act of 1934, § 16[b]), for example, it is conclusively presumed that, when a director, officer or 10% shareholder buys and sells securities of his corporation within a six-month period, he is trading on inside information. The remedy which the Federal statute provides in that situation is precisely the same as that sought in the present case under State law, namely, an action brought by the corporation or on its behalf to recover all profits derived from the transactions.

In providing this remedy, Congress accomplished a dual purpose. It not only provided for an efficient and effective method of accomplishing its primary goal—the protection of the investing public from unfair treatment at the hands of corporate insiders—but extended to the corporation the right to secure for itself benefits derived by those insiders from their exploitation of their privileged position. The United States Court of Appeals for the Second Circuit has stated the policy behind section 16(b) in the following terms (*Adler v. Klawans*, 267 F.2d 840, 844):

> "The undoubted congressional intent in the enactment of § 16(b) was to discourage what was reasonably thought to be a widespread abuse of a fiduciary relationship—specifically to discourage if not prevent three classes of persons from making private and gainful use of information acquired by them by virtue of their official relationship to a corporation."

Although the provisions of section 16(b) may not apply to all cases of trading on inside information, it demonstrates that a derivative action can be an effective method for dealing with such abuses which may be used to accomplish a similar purpose in cases not specifically covered by the statute. In *Brophy v. Cities Serv. Co.* (31 Del.Ch. 241, *supra*), for example, the Chancery Court of Delaware allowed a similar remedy in a situation not covered by the Federal legislation. One of the defendants in that case was an employee who had acquired inside information that the corporate plaintiff was about to enter the market and purchase its own shares. On the basis of this confidential information, the employee, who was not an officer and, hence, not liable under Federal law, bought a large block of shares and, after the corporation's purchases had caused the price to rise, resold them at a profit. The court sustained the complaint in a derivative action brought for an accounting, stating that "[p]ublic policy will not permit an employee occupying a position of trust and confidence toward his employer to abuse that relation to his own profit, regardless of whether his employer suffers a loss" (31 Del.Ch., at p. 246). And a similar view has been expressed in the Restatement, 2d, Agency (§ 388, comment *c*):

> "*c. Use of confidential information.* An agent who acquires confidential information in the course of his employment or in violation of his duties has a duty . . . to account for any profits made by the use of such information, although this does not harm the principal. . . . So, if [a corporate officer] has 'inside' information that the corporation is about to purchase or sell securities, or to declare or to pass a dividend, profits made by him in stock

transactions undertaken because of his knowledge are held in constructive trust for the principal."

In the present case, the defendants may be able to avoid liability to the corporation under section 16(b) of the Federal law since they had held the MAI shares for more than six months prior to the sales. Nevertheless, the alleged use of the inside information to dispose of their stock at a price considerably higher than its known value constituted the same sort of "abuse of a fiduciary relationship" as is condemned by the Federal law. Sitting as we are in this case as a court of equity, we should not hesitate to permit an action to prevent any unjust enrichment realized by the defendants from their allegedly wrongful act.

The defendants recognize that the conduct charged against them directly contravened the policy embodied in the Securities Exchange Act but, they maintain, the Federal legislation constitutes a comprehensive and carefully wrought plan for dealing with the abuse of inside information and that allowing a derivative action to be maintained under State law would interfere with the Federal scheme. Moreover, they urge, the existence of dual Federal and State remedies for the same act would create the possibility of double liability.

An examination of the Federal regulatory scheme refutes the contention that it was designed to establish any particular remedy as exclusive. In addition to the specific provisions of section 16(b), the Securities and Exchange Act contains a general anti-fraud provision in section 10(b), (U.S.Code, tit. 15, § 78j, subd. [b]) which, as implemented by rule 10b–5 (Code of Fed.Reg., tit. 17, § 240.10b–5) under that section, renders it unlawful to engage in a variety of acts considered to be fraudulent. In interpreting this rule, the Securities and Exchange Commission and the Federal courts have extended the common-law definition of fraud to include not only affirmative misrepresentations, relied upon by the purchaser or seller, but also a failure to disclose material information which might have affected the transaction. (See, e.g., *Securities & Exch. Comm. v. Texas Gulf Sulphur Co.*, 401 F.2d 833, 847–848; *Myzel v. Fields*, 386 F.2d 718, 733–735.)

Accepting the truth of the complaint's allegations, there is no question but that the defendants were guilty of withholding material information from the purchasers of the shares and, indeed, the defendants acknowledge that the facts asserted constitute a violation of rule 10b–5. The remedies which the Federal law provides for such violation, however, are rather limited. An action could be brought, in an exceptional case, by the SEC for injunctive relief. This, in fact, is what happened in the *Texas Gulf Sulphur* case (401 F.2d 833, *supra*). The purpose of such an action, however, would appear to be more to establish a principle than to provide a regular method of enforcement. A class action under the Federal rule might be a more effective remedy but the mechanics of such an action have, as far as we have been able to ascertain, not yet been worked out by the Federal courts and several questions relating thereto have never been resolved. These include the definition of the class entitled to bring such an action, the measure of damages, the administration of the fund which would be recovered and its distribution to the members of the class. (See Note, 54 Cornell L.Rev. 306, 309, *supra.*) Of course, any individual purchaser, who could prove his own injury as a result of a rule 10b–5 violation can bring an action for rescission but we have not been referred to a single case in which such an action has been successfully prosecuted where the public sale of securities is involved. The reason for this is that sales of securities, whether through a stock exchange or over-the-counter, are characteristically anonymous transactions, usually handled through brokers, and the matching of the ultimate buyer with the ultimate seller presents virtually insurmountable obstacles. Thus, unless a section 16(b) violation is also present, the Federal law does not yet provide a really effective remedy.

In view of the practical difficulties inherent in an action under the Federal law, the desirability of creating an effective common-law remedy is manifest. "Dishonest directors should not find absolution from retributive justice", Ballantine observed in his work on Corporations ([rev. ed., 1946], p. 216), "by concealing their identity from their victims under the mask of the stock exchange." There is ample room in a situation such as is here presented for a "private Attorney General" to come forward and enforce proper behavior on the part of corporate officials through the medium of the derivative action brought in the name of the corporation. (See, e.g., *Associated Ind. v. Ickes,* 134 F.2d 694, 704; *Cherner v. Transitron Electronic Corp.,* 201 F.Supp. 934, 936.) Only by sanctioning such a cause of action will there be any effective method to prevent the type of abuse of corporate office complained of in this case.

There is nothing in the Federal law which indicates that it was intended to limit the power of the States to fashion additional remedies to effectuate similar purposes. Although the impact of Federal securities regulation has on occasion been said to have created a "Federal corporation law," in fact, its effect on the duties and obligations of directors and officers and their relation to the corporation and its shareholders is only occasional and peripheral. The primary source of the law in this area ever remains that of the State which created the corporation. Indeed, Congress expressly provided against any implication that it intended to pre-empt the field by declaring, in section 28(a) of the Securities Exchange Act of 1934 (48 U.S.Code 903), that "[t]he rights and remedies provided by this title shall be in addition to any and all other rights and remedies that may exist at law or in equity".

Nor should we be deterred, in formulating a State remedy, by the defendants' claim of possible double liability. Certainly, as already indicated, if the sales in question were publicly made, the likelihood that a suit will be brought by purchasers of the shares is quite remote. But, even if it were not, the mere possibility of such a suit is not a defense nor does it render the complaint insufficient. It is not unusual for an action to be brought to recover a fund which may be subject to a superior claim by a third party. If that be the situation, a defendant should not be permitted to retain the fund for his own use on the chance that such a party may eventually appear. A defendant's course, if he wishes to protect himself against double liability, is to interplead any and all possible claimants and bind them to the judgment (CPLR 1006, subd. [b]).

In any event, though, no suggestion has been made either in brief or on oral argument that any purchaser has come forward with a claim against the defendants or even that anyone is in a position to advance such a claim.[1] As we have stated, the defendants' assertion that such a party may come forward at some future date is not a basis for permitting them to retain for their own benefit the fruits of their allegedly wrongful acts. For all that appears, the present derivative action is the only effective remedy now available against the abuse by these defendants of their privileged position.

As we have previously indicated, what we have written must be read in the light of the charges contained in the complaint, and it must be borne in mind that "it will be incumbent upon the plaintiff, if he is to succeed, to prove upon the trial the truth and correctness of his allegations." (*Walkovszky v. Carlton*, 23 N.Y.2d 714, 715.)

The order appealed from should be affirmed, with costs, and the question certified answered in the affirmative.

■ JUDGES BURKE, SCILEPPI, BERGAN, KEATING, BREITEL and JASEN concur.

Order affirmed, etc.

———

Accord: Brophy v. Cities Service Co., 31 Del.Ch. 241, 70 A.2d 5 (1949). See also Thomas v. Roblin Indus., Inc., 520 F.2d 1393, 1397 (3d Cir.1975); In re ORFA Securities Litigation, 654 F.Supp. 1449 (D.N.J.1987). Contra: Freeman v. Decio, 584 F.2d 186 (7th Cir.1978); Schein v. Chasen, 313 So.2d 739 (Fla.1975).

———

Malone v. Brincat

Supreme Court of Delaware, 1998.
722 A.2d 5.

■ Before VEASEY, CHIEF JUSTICE, WALSH, HOLLAND, HARTNETT and BERGER, JUSTICES (constituting the Court en Banc).

■ HOLLAND, JUSTICE:

Doran Malone, Joseph P. Danielle, and Adrienne M. Danielle, the plaintiffs-appellants, filed this individual and class action in the Court of Chancery. The complaint alleged that the directors of Mercury Finance Company ("Mercury"), a Delaware corporation, breached

---

1. In the absence of any such appearance by adverse claimants, we need not now decide whether the corporation's recovery would be affected by any amounts which might have to be refunded by the defendant to the injured purchasers.

their fiduciary duty of disclosure. The individual defendant-appellee directors are John N. Brincat, Dennis H. Chookaszian, William C. Croft, Clifford R. Johnson, Andrew McNally, IV, Bruce I. McPhee, Fred G. Steingraber, and Phillip J. Wicklander. The complaint also alleged that the defendant-appellee, KPMG Peat Marwick LLP ("KPMG") aided and abetted the Mercury directors' breaches of fiduciary duty. The Court of Chancery dismissed the complaint with prejudice pursuant to Chancery Rule 12(b)(6) for failure to state a claim upon which relief may be granted.

The complaint alleged that the director defendants intentionally overstated the financial condition of Mercury on repeated occasions throughout a four-year period in disclosures to Mercury's shareholders. Plaintiffs contend that the complaint states a claim upon which relief can be granted for a breach of the fiduciary duty of disclosure. Plaintiffs also contend that, because the director defendants breached their fiduciary duty of disclosure to the Mercury shareholders, the Court of Chancery erroneously dismissed the aiding and abetting claim against KPMG.

This Court has concluded that the Court of Chancery properly granted the defendants' motions to dismiss the complaint. That dismissal, however, should have been without prejudice. Plaintiffs are entitled to file an amended complaint. Therefore, the judgment of the Court of Chancery is affirmed in part, reversed in part, and remanded for further proceedings consistent with this opinion.

Facts

Mercury is a publicly-traded company engaged primarily in purchasing installment sales contracts from automobile dealers and providing short-term installment loans directly to consumers. This action was filed on behalf of the named plaintiffs and all persons (excluding defendants) who owned common stock of Mercury from 1993 through the present and their successors in interest, heirs and assigns (the "putative class"). The complaint alleged that the directors "knowingly and intentionally breached their fiduciary duty of disclosure because the SEC filings made by the directors and every communication from the company to the shareholders since 1994 was materially false" and that "as a direct result of the false disclosures ... the Company has lost all or virtually all of its value (about $2 billion)." The complaint also alleged that KPMG knowingly participated in the directors' breaches of their fiduciary duty of disclosure.

According to plaintiffs, since 1994, the director defendants caused Mercury to disseminate information containing overstatements of Mercury's earnings, financial performance and shareholders' equity. Mercury's earnings for 1996 were actually only $56.7 million, or $33 a share, rather than the $120.7 million, or $.70 a share, as reported by the director defendants. Mercury's earnings in 1995 were actually $76.9 million, or $.44 a share, rather than $98.9 million, or $.57 a share, as reported by the director defendants. Mercury's earnings for 1994 were $83 million, or $.47 a share, rather than $86.5 million, or

$.49 a share, as reported by the director defendants. Mercury's earnings for 1993 were $64.2 million, rather than $64.9 million, as reported by the director defendants. Shareholders' equity on December 31, 1996 was disclosed by the director defendants as $353 million, but was only $263 million or less. The complaint alleged that all of the foregoing inaccurate information was included or referenced in virtually every filing Mercury made with the SEC and every communication Mercury's directors made to the shareholders during this period of time.

Having alleged these violations of fiduciary duty, which (if true) are egregious, plaintiffs alleged that as "a direct result of [these] false disclosures ... the company has lost all or virtually all its value (about $2 billion)," and seeks class action status to pursue damages against the directors and KPMG for the individual plaintiffs and common stockholders. The individual director defendants filed a motion to dismiss, contending that they owed no fiduciary duty of disclosure under the circumstances alleged in the complaint. KPMG also filed a motion to dismiss the aiding and abetting claim asserted against it.

After briefing and oral argument, the Court of Chancery granted both of the motions to dismiss with prejudice. The Court of Chancery held that directors have no fiduciary duty of disclosure under Delaware law in the absence of a request for shareholder action. In so holding, the Court stated:

> The federal securities laws ensure the timely release of accurate information into the marketplace. The federal power to regulate should not be duplicated or impliedly usurped by Delaware. When a shareholder is damaged merely as a result of the release of inaccurate information into the marketplace, unconnected with any Delaware corporate governance issue, that shareholder must seek a remedy under federal law.

We disagree, and although we hold that the Complaint as drafted should have been dismissed, our rationale is different.

Standard of Review

A motion to dismiss a complaint presents the trial court with a question of law and is subject to de novo review by this Court on appeal. This Court and the trial court must accept all well-pleaded allegations of fact as true. A complaint should be dismissed for failure to state a claim only when it appears "with a reasonable certainty that a plaintiff would not be entitled to the relief sought under any set of facts which could be proven to support the action."

Issue On Appeal

This Court has held that. a board of directors is under a fiduciary duty to disclose material information when seeking shareholder action:

> It is well-established that the duty of disclosure "represents nothing more than the well-recognized proposition that directors

of Delaware corporations are under a fiduciary duty to disclose fully and fairly all material information within the board's control when it seeks shareholder action."[1]

The majority of opinions from the Court of Chancery have held that there may be a cause of action for disclosure violations only where directors seek shareholder action.[2] The present appeal requires this Court to decide whether a director's fiduciary duty arising out of misdisclosure is implicated in the absence of a request for shareholder action. We hold that directors who knowingly disseminate false information that results in corporate injury or damage to an individual stockholder violate their fiduciary duty, and may be held accountable in a manner appropriate to the circumstances.

Fiduciary Duty
Delaware Corporate Directors

An underlying premise for the imposition of fiduciary duties is a separation of legal control from beneficial ownership. Equitable principles act in those circumstances to protect the beneficiaries who are not in a position to protect themselves. One of the fundamental tenets of Delaware corporate law provides for a separation of control and ownership. The board of directors has the legal responsibility to manage the business of a corporation for the benefit of its shareholder owners. Accordingly, fiduciary duties are imposed on the directors of Delaware corporations to regulate their conduct when they discharge that function.

The directors of Delaware corporations stand in a fiduciary relationship not only to the stockholders but also to the corporations upon whose boards they serve.[3] The director's fiduciary duty to both the corporation and its shareholders has been characterized by this Court as a triad: due care, good faith, and loyalty.[4] That triparte fiduciary duty does not operate intermittently but is the constant compass by which all director actions for the corporation and interactions with its shareholders must be guided.

Although the fiduciary duty of a Delaware director is unremitting, the exact course of conduct that must be charted to properly discharge that responsibility will change in the specific context of the action the director is taking with regard to either the corporation or its shareholders. This Court has endeavored to provide the directors with clear signal beacons and brightly lined-channel markers as they navigate with due care, good faith, and loyalty on behalf of a Delaware corporation and its shareholders. This Court has also endeavored to mark the safe harbors clearly.

1. Zirn v. VLI Corp., Del.Supr., 681 A.2d 1050, 1056 (1996) quoting *Stroud v. Grace*, 606 A.2d at 84 (emphasis added). [Editor's Note: A number of the footnotes in this opinion have been deleted. The balance have been renumbered.]

2. *Kahn v. Roberts*, Del.Supr., 679 A.2d 460, 467 (1996) (collecting cases). *Cf. Ciro,*

Inc. v. Gold, D. Del. 816 F.Supp. 253, 267 (1993).

3. *Guth v. Loft*, Del.Supr., 5 A.2d 503, 510 (1939). *See David A. Drexler et al.*, Delaware Corporation Law § 15.02 (Matthew Bender 1998).

4. *Cede & Co. v. Technicolor, Inc.*, Del. Supr., 734 A.2d 345, 361 (1993).

Director Communications
Shareholder Reliance Justified

The shareholder constituents of a Delaware corporation are entitled to rely upon their elected directors to discharge their fiduciary duties at all times. Whenever directors communicate publicly or directly with shareholders about the corporation's affairs, with or without a request for shareholder action, directors have a fiduciary duty to shareholders to exercise due care, good faith and loyalty. It follows a fortiori that when directors communicate publicly or directly with shareholders about corporate matters the sine qua non of directors' fiduciary duty to shareholders is honesty.[5]

According to the appellants, the focus of the fiduciary duty of disclosure is to protect shareholders as the "beneficiaries" of all material information disseminated by the directors. The duty of disclosure is, and always has been, a specific application of the general fiduciary duty owed by directors. The duty of disclosure obligates directors to provide the stockholders with accurate and complete information material to a transaction or other corporate event that is being presented to them for action.

The issue in this case is not whether Mercury's directors breached their duty of disclosure. It is whether they breached their more general fiduciary duty of loyalty and good faith by knowingly disseminating to the stockholders false information about the financial condition of the company. The directors' fiduciary duties include the duty to deal with their stockholders honestly.

Shareholders are entitled to rely upon the truthfulness of all information disseminated to them by the directors they elect to manage the corporate enterprise. Delaware directors disseminate information in at least three contexts: public statements made to the market, including shareholders; statements informing shareholders about the affairs of the corporation without a request for shareholder action; and, statements to shareholders in conjunction with a request for shareholder action. Inaccurate information in these contexts may be the result of violation of the fiduciary duties of care, loyalty or good faith. We will examine the remedies that are available to shareholders for misrepresentations in each of these three contexts by the directors of a Delaware corporation.

State Fiduciary Disclosure Duty
Shareholder Remedy In Action Requested Context

In the absence of a request for stockholder action, the Delaware General Corporation Law does not require directors to provide shareholders with information concerning the finances or affairs of the corporation. Even when shareholder action is sought, the provisions in

---

5. *Marhart, Inc. v. Calmat Co.,* Del. Ch., CA No. 11820, Berger, V.C., 1992 WL 212587 (Apr. 22, 1992), slip op. At 6 (reported in 18 Del. J. Corp. L. 330 (1992)) ("Delaware directors are fiduciaries and are held to a high standard of conduct.... It is entirely consistent with this settled principle of law that fiduciaries who undertake the responsibility of informing shareholders about corporate affairs, be required to do so honestly.").

the General Corporation Law requiring notice to the shareholders of the proposed action do not require the directors to convey substantive information beyond a statutory minimum.[6] Consequently, in the context of a request for shareholder action, the protection afforded by Delaware law is a judicially recognized equitable cause of action by shareholders against directors.

The fiduciary duty of directors in connection with disclosure violations in Delaware jurisprudence was restated in Lynch v. Vickers Energy Corp., Del.Supr., 383 A.2d 278 (1977). In *Lynch*, this Court held that, in making a tender offer to acquire the stock of the minority stockholders, a majority stockholder "owed a fiduciary duty ... which required 'complete candor' in disclosing fully 'all the facts and circumstances surrounding the' tender offer."[7] In *Stroud v. Grace,* we noted that the language of our jurisprudence should be clarified to the extent that "candor" requires no more than the duty to disclose all material facts when seeking stockholder action.[8] An article by Professor Lawrence Hamermesh[9] includes an excellent historical summary of the content, context, and parameters of the law of disclosure, as it has been developed in a series of decisions during the last two decades.

The duty of directors to observe proper disclosure requirements derives from the combination of the fiduciary duties of care, loyalty and good faith.[10] The plaintiffs contend that, because directors fiduciary responsibilities are not "intermittent duties," there is no reason why the duty of disclosure should not be implicated in every public communication by a corporate board of directors. The directors of a Delaware corporation are required to disclose fully and fairly all material information within the board's control when it seeks shareholder action. When the directors disseminate information to stockholders when no stockholder action is sought, the fiduciary duties of care, loyalty and good faith apply. Dissemination of false information could violate one or more of those duties.

An action for a breach of fiduciary duty arising out of disclosure violations in connection with a request for stockholder action does not include the elements of reliance, causation and actual quantifiable monetary damages.[11] Instead, such actions require the challenged

---

6. *See Stroud v. Grace,* 606 A.2d at 85 (discussing 8 Del. C. § 222(a) and 242(b)(1)).

7. *Lynch v. Vickers Energy Corp.,* Del. Supr., 383 A.2d 278, 279 (1977) quoting *Lynch v. Vickers Energy Corp.,* Del. Ch., 351 A.2d 570, 573 (1976); *accord Shell Petroleum, Inc. v. Smith,* Del. Supr., 606 A.2d 112, 114–15 (1992) (majority stockholder bears burden of showing full disclosure of all facts within its knowledge that are material to stockholder action). The fiduciary duty of disclosure is also applicable to directors of a Delaware corporation, *In re Anderson, Clayton Shareholders Litig.,* Del. Ch., 519 A.2d 680, 688–90 (1986); *Smith v. Van Gorkom,* Del. Supr., 488 A.2d 858, 890 (1985) and to less-than-majority shareholders who control or affirmatively

attempt to mandate the destiny of the corporation. *In re Tri–Star Pictures, Inc. Litig.,* 634 A.2d at 328–29.

8. *Stroud v. Grace,* 606 A.2d at 84.

9. Lawrence A. Hamermesh, Calling Off the Lynch Mob: A Corporate Director's Fiduciary Disclosure Duty, 49 Vand. L. Rev. 1087, 1174 n.394 (1996).

10. *See Cinerama, Inc. v. Technicolor, Inc.,* Del.Supr., 663 A.2d 1156, 1160 (1995); *Zirn v. VLI Corp.,* 621 A.2d at 778.

11. *See Cinerama, Inc. v. Technicolor, Inc.,* Del.Supr., 663 A.2d 1163; *In re Tri–Star Pictures, Inc. Litig.,* 634 A.2d at 327 n.10 and 333. *Loudon v. Archer–Daniels–Midland Co.,* 700 A.2d at 142 ("where di-

disclosure to have a connection to the request for shareholder action. The essential inquiry in such an action is whether the alleged omission or misrepresentation is material. Materiality is determined with respect to the shareholder action being sought.

The directors' duty to disclose all available material information in connection with a request for shareholder action must be balanced against its concomitant duty to protect the corporate enterprise, in particular, by keeping certain financial information confidential. Directors are required to provide shareholders with all information that is material to the action being requested and to provide a balanced, truthful account of all matters disclosed in the communications with shareholders.[12] Accordingly, directors have definitive guidance in discharging their fiduciary duty by an analysis of the factual circumstances relating to the specific shareholder action being requested and an inquiry into the potential for deception or misinformation.[13]

Fraud On Market Regulated by Federal Law

When corporate directors impart information they must comport with the obligations imposed by both the Delaware law and the federal statutes and regulations of the United States Securities and Exchange Commission ("SEC"). Historically, federal law has regulated disclosures by corporate directors into the general interstate market. This Court has noted that "in observing its congressional mandate the SEC has adopted a 'basic philosophy of disclosure.' "[14] Accordingly, this Court has held that there is "no legitimate basis to create a new cause of action which would replicate, by state decisional law, the provisions of . . . the 1934 Act."[15] In deference to the panoply of federal protections that are available to investors in connection with the purchase or sale of securities of Delaware corporations, this Court has decided not to recognize a state common law cause of action against the directors of Delaware corporations for "fraud on the market."[16] Here, it is to be noted, the claim appears to be made by those who did not sell and, therefore, would not implicate federal securities laws which relate to the purchase or sale of securities.

rectors have breached their disclosure duties in a corporate transaction . . . there must at least be an award of nominal damages.").

12. *Zirn v. VLI Corp.*, 681 A.2d at 1056. In *Zirn II*, this Court held, "in addition to the traditional duty to disclose all facts material to the proffered transaction, directors are under a fiduciary obligation to avoid misleading partial disclosures. The law of partial disclosure is likewise clear: Once defendants travel down the road of partial disclosure they have an obligation to provide the stockholders with an accurate, full and fair characterization of those historic events." (Internal quotations omitted).

13. *See Zirn v. VLI Corp.*, 681 A.2d at 1062 ("a good faith erroneous judgment as to the proper scope or content of required disclosure implicates the duty of care rather

than the duty of loyalty."); *Arnold v. Society for Savings Bancorp*, 650 A.2d at 1287–88 & no. 36.

14. *Stroud v. Grace*, Del.Supr. 606 A.2d 75, 86 (1992). *See, e.g.,* Randall S. Thomas & Catherine T. Dixon, *Aranow & Einhorn on Proxy Contents for Corporation Control*, § 21.02 (3d ed. 1998).

15. *Arnold v. Society for Savings Bankcorp, Inc.*, Del. Supr., 678 A.2d 533, 539 (1996).

16. *Gaffin v. Teledyne, Inc.*, Del.Supr., 611 A.2d 467, 471 (1992). *See Basic Incorporated v. Levinson*, 485 U.S. 224, 241–42, 108 S.Ct. 978, 99 L.Ed.2d 194 (1988) (discussing the theory of fraud on the market.)

The historic roles played by state and federal law in regulating corporate disclosures have been not only compatible but complementary.[17] That symbiotic relationship has been perpetuated by the recently enacted federal Securities Litigation Uniform Standards Act of 1998.[18] Although that statute by its terms does not apply to this case, the new statute will require securities class actions involving the purchase or sale of nationally traded securities, based upon false or misleading statements, to be brought exclusively in federal court under federal law. The 1998 Act, however, contains two important exceptions:[19] the first provides that an "exclusively derivative action brought by one or more shareholders on behalf of a corporation" is not preempted; the second preserves the availability of state court class actions, where state law already provides that corporate directors have fiduciary disclosure obligations to shareholders.[20] These exceptions have become known as the "Delaware carve-outs."[21]

We need not decide at this time, however, whether this new Act will have any effect on this litigation if plaintiffs elect to replead. See Section (c) of the Act:

17. *See Santa Fe Industries, Inc. v. Green*, 430 U.S. 462, 474–80, 97 S.Ct. 1292, 51 L.Ed.2d 480 (1977) (discussing state corporation law and the purpose of disclosure in federal securities law). *Cf.* Roberta Romano, Empowering Investors: A Market Approach to Securities Regulation 107 Yale L.J. 2359 (1998) ("Advocating fundamental reform of the current strategy toward securities regulation by implementing a regulatory approach of competitive federalism.").

18. Securities Litigation Uniform Standards Act of 1998, Pub.L. No. 105–353, 112 Stat. 3227 (1998).

19. Section 16(d) of the Act provides:

(d) Preservation of Certain Actions.—

(1) Actions under state law of state of incorporation.—

(A) Actions preserved.—Notwithstanding subsection (b) or (c), a covered class action described in subparagraph (B) of this paragraph that is based upon the statutory or common law of the State in which the issuer is incorporated (in the case of a corporation) or organized (in the case of any other entity) may be maintained in a State or Federal court by a private party.

(B) Permissible actions.—A covered class action is described in this subparagraph if it involves—

(i) the purchase or sale of securities by the issuer or an affiliate of the issuer exclusively from or to holders of equity securities of the issuer; or

(ii) any recommendation, position, or other communication with respect to the sale of securities of the issuer securities by the issuer or an affiliate

that—

(I) is made by or on behalf of the issuer or an affiliate of the issuer to holders of equity securities of the issuer; and

(II) concerns decisions of those equity holders with respect to voting their securities, acting in response to a tender or exchange offer, or exercising dissenters' or appraisal rights.

20. *See, e.g., Zirn v. VLI Corp.*, 621 A.2d 773; *Zirn v. VLI Corp.*, 681 A.2d at 1060–61. *See also* Michael A. Perino, Fraud and Federalism: Preempting Private State Securities Fraud Causes of Action, 50 Stan. L.Rev. 273 (1998).

21. The Senate Committee Report on the Act is instructive. It states, in part:

The Committee is keenly aware of the importance of state corporate law, specifically those states that have laws that establish a fiduciary duty of disclosure. It is not the intent of the Committee in adopting this legislation to interfere with state law regarding the duties and performance of an issuer's directors or officers in connection with a purchase or sale of securities by the issuer or an affiliate from current shareholders or communicating with existing shareholders with respect to voting their shares, acting in response to a tender or exchange offer, or exercising dissenters' or appraisal rights.

S. Rep. No. 105–182, at 11–12 (May 4, 1998).

(c) Applicability.—The amendments made by this section shall not affect or apply to any action commenced before and pending on the date of enactment of this Act.

State Common Law Shareholder Remedy
In Nonaction Context

Delaware law also protects shareholders who receive false communications from directors even in the absence of a request for shareholder action. When the directors are not seeking shareholder action, but are deliberately misinforming shareholders about the business of the corporation, either directly or by a public statement, there is a violation of fiduciary duty. That violation may result in a derivative claim on behalf of the corporation or a cause of action for damages. There may also be a basis for equitable relief to remedy the violation.

Complaint Properly Dismissed
No Shareholder Action Requested

Here the complaint alleges (if true) an egregious violation of fiduciary duty by the directors in knowingly disseminating materially false information. Then it alleges that the corporation lost about $2 billion in value as a result. Then it merely claims that the action is brought on behalf of the named plaintiffs and the putative class. It is a non sequitur rather than a syllogism.

The allegation in paragraph 3 that the false disclosures resulted in the corporation losing virtually all its equity seems obliquely to claim an injury to the corporation. The plaintiffs, however, never expressly assert a derivative claim on behalf of the corporation or allege compliance with Court of Chancery Rule 23.1, which requires pre-suit demand or cognizable and particularized allegations that demand is excused.[22] If the plaintiffs intend to assert a derivative claim,[23] they should be permitted to replead to assert such a claim and any damage or equitable remedy sought on behalf of the corporation.[24] Likewise, the plaintiffs should have the opportunity to replead to assert any individual cause of action and articulate a remedy that is appropriate on behalf of the named plaintiffs individually, or a properly recognizable class consistent with Court of Chancery Rule 23, and our decision in Gaffin.[25]

---

22. It seems that plaintiffs have attempted to allege the basis for demand excusal by the very nature of the central claim that the directors knowingly misstated the company's financial condition, thus seemingly taking this case out of the business judgment rule because all the directors are alleged to be implicated in the wrongdoing.

23. This will require an articulation of the classic "direct v. derivative" theory. See Grimes v. Donald, Del.Supr., 673 A.2d 1207 (1996) (distinguishing individual and derivative actions).

24. We express no opinion whether equitable remedies such as injunctive relief, ju-dicial removal of directors or disqualification from directorship could be asserted here. No such equitable relief has been sought in the current complaint. See Randall S. Thomas & Catherine T. Dixon, Aranow & Einhorn on Proxy Contests for Corporate Control, § 19.01 (3d ed. 1998).

25. Gaffin v. Teledyne, Inc., 611 A.2d 467, 474 (1992) ("A class action may not be maintained in a purely common law or equitable fraud case since individual questions of law or fact, particularly as to the element of justifiable reliance, will inevitably predominate over common questions of law or fact.").…

The Court of Chancery properly dismissed the complaint before it against the individual director defendants, in the absence of well-pleaded allegations stating a derivative, class or individual cause of action and properly assertable remedy. Without a well-pleaded allegation in the complaint for a breach of fiduciary duty, there can be no claim for aiding and abetting such a breach. Accordingly, the plaintiffs' aiding and abetting claim against KPMG was also properly dismissed.

Nevertheless, we disagree with the Court of Chancery's holding that such a claim cannot be articulated on these facts. The plaintiffs should have been permitted to amend their complaint, if possible, to state a properly cognizable cause of action against the individual defendants and KPMG. Consequently, the Court of Chancery should have dismissed the complaint *without* prejudice.

Conclusion

The judgment of the Court of Chancery to dismiss the complaint is affirmed. The judgment to dismiss the complaint with prejudice is reversed. This matter is remanded for further proceedings in accordance with this opinion.

CHAPTER XI

SHAREHOLDER SUITS

SECTION 1. INTRODUCTION

BACKGROUND NOTE

If the fiduciary duties owed by directors, officers, and controlling shareholders could be enforced only in suits by the corporation, many wrongs would never be remedied. If a controlling shareholder breaches its duty, it will normally cause the corporation to not institute litigation to remedy the wrong. Similarly, directors will seldom bring suit against one of their colleagues or top executives for such a breach. To overcome these obstacles, and hold wrongdoing managers and controlling shareholders to account, the law permits shareholders to bring suit for breach of fiduciary duty on the corporation's behalf.

In Ross v. Bernhard, 396 U.S. 531, 534–35, 90 S.Ct. 733, 735–6, 24 L.Ed.2d 729 (1970), the Supreme Court sketched the background and nature of such suits in the following terms:

> The common law refused ... to permit stockholders to call corporate managers to account in actions at law. The possibilities for abuse, thus presented, were not ignored by corporate officers and directors. Early in the 19th century, equity provided relief both in this country and in England. Without detailing these developments, it suffices to say that the remedy in this country, first dealt with by this Court in Dodge v. Woolsey, 18 How. 331, 15 L.Ed. 401 (1855), provided redress ... against faithless officers and directors.... The remedy made available in equity was the derivative suit, viewed in this country as a suit to enforce a *corporate* cause of action against officers, directors, and third parties. As elaborated in the cases, one precondition for the suit was a valid claim on which the corporation could have sued; another was that the corporation itself had refused to proceed after suitable demand, unless excused by extraordinary conditions. Thus the dual nature of the stockholder's action: first, the plaintiff's right to sue on behalf of the corporation and, second, the merits of the corporation's claim itself.

This type of suit is commonly known as a *derivative action*, since the shareholder's right to bring the suit derives from the corporation.

Two features of the derivative action warrant highlighting at the outset. First is the extraordinary procedural complexity inherent in such actions—complexity involving, for example, proper parties and their alignment, jurisdiction, demand on the board, demand on the shareholders, right to sue, intervention, settlement, and dismissal. Second is the difficult problem of social policy raised by such actions, particularly in the publicly held corporation. Through the derivative action, a shareholder with a tiny investment can force an expenditure by the corporation of a large amount of funds and executive time. The question is whether the overall benefits of such actions justify their overall costs, which are, in effect, borne involuntarily by the noncomplaining shareholders.

Where the corporation is publicly held, the plaintiff-shareholder's gain is not only indirect, but usually very small and often infinitesimal. For example, the defendants' briefs in Hornstein v. Paramount Pictures, Inc., 37 N.Y.S.2d 404 (Sup.Ct. 1942), aff'd, 266 App.Div. 659, 41 N.Y.S.2d 210 (1943), aff'd 292 N.Y. 468, 55 N.E.2d 740 (1944), asserted that the five plaintiffs in that case stood to gain $3.57, $.41, $2.41, $.17 and $.65, respectively. In another well-known case, Winkelman v. General Motors Corp., 44 F.Supp. 960 (S.D.N.Y.1942), the three plaintiffs gained 8¢/share for the eighty shares held between them.

In contrast, the plaintiff's lawyer stands to be awarded a very substantial fee out of the proceeds of any judgment or settlement—a fee that often runs into many hundreds of thousands, or even millions, of dollars. Furthermore, defendants in derivative actions are sometimes able to make settlements involving the illicit use of corporate funds to discharge their own liabilities. As a result of these elements, a concern exists that unscrupulous lawyers will exploit either the nuisance value of a nonmeritorious claim, or management's desire to cover up its own wrongdoing, through the institution of suits essentially brought to extract an exorbitant attorneys' fee.

Many or most of the issues to be considered in this chapter, although couched in technical terms, reflect an underlying tension between a concern that managers be held accountable for their wrongdoing, on the one hand, and a concern with the abusive or *strike suit* potential of derivative actions, on the other. Emphasis on the former element leads to liberality in permitting derivative actions; emphasis on the latter leads to rules that restrict such actions. In weighing these opposed concerns, it should be borne in mind that the derivative action and the disclosure requirements of the securities acts constitute the two major legal bulwarks against managerial self-dealing. In considering the various rules taken up in this chapter, it is therefore critical to evaluate the extent to which each rule cuts into the effectiveness of the derivative action, and whether the benefits of the rule justify that cost.

It should also be kept in mind, when considering the problems raised in this chapter, that significant substantive consequences often turn on the success of a motion to dismiss a derivative action on procedural grounds. If the plaintiff can survive such a motion, the facts that he already knows, together with the material that he can develop through discovery, will often lead to a substantial settlement. If the defendant can get the case dismissed on procedural grounds, however, no other plaintiff may come forward—either because no other shareholder who would bring suit knows all the relevant facts, or because the statute of limitations has run. Accordingly, for practical purposes many derivative actions will be won or lost on the basis of procedural issues that do not go to the merits of the case.

———

FEDERAL RULES OF CIVIL PROCEDURE, RULE 11

[See Statutory Supplement]

———

Macey & Miller, The Plaintiffs' Attorneys' Role in Class Actions and Derivative Litigation: Economic Analysis and Recommendations for Reform

58 U.Chi.L.Rev. 1, 3, 8–11, 78 (1991).

Plaintiffs' attorneys in class action and derivative suits occupy an uneasy place in the American legal system. The traditional image of the lawyer is of an independent professional providing advice and advocacy on behalf of a client. The attorney, in this view, is an agent of the client and subject to the client's control in all important matters. Plaintiffs' class action and derivative attorneys do not fit this mold. They are subject to only minimal monitoring by their ostensible "clients," who are either dispersed and disorganized (in the case of class action litigation) or under the control of hostile forces (in the case of derivative litigation). Accordingly, plaintiffs' class and derivative attorneys function essentially as entrepreneurs who bear a substantial amount of the litigation risk and exercise nearly plenary control over all important decisions in the lawsuit. . . .

[The] regulatory structure [that governs derivative and class actions] is poorly designed in a number of respects, particularly when applied to "large-scale, small-claim" litigation in which the overall liability is large but the individual interests of the class members or corporate shareholders are small. . . . Many regulatory shortfalls can be traced ultimately to a single fundamental error: the inappropriate attempt to treat entrepreneurial litigation as if it were essentially the same as standard litigation, in which the client exercises substantial influence. . . .

The class action is a tool for overcoming the free-rider[5] and other collective action[6] problems that impair any attempt to organize a large number of discrete individuals in any common project. These kinds of problems are prevalent in situations when a large number of people

---

5. Freeriding, as the name implies, simply refers to a situation where a person can obtain a benefit (or avoid a cost) without paying for it. . . .

6. Collective action is used in the public choice literature to refer to any procedure for making decisions by groups of people. . . .

have been injured by another person's conduct, but when the injury to many of these individuals is small. In the absence of a class action device, such injuries would often go unremedied because most individual plaintiffs would not themselves have a sufficient economic stake in the litigation to incur the litigation costs. Of course, some particularly aggrieved individual might attempt to bring a large group together in a single lawsuit by using standard joinder and intervention devices. But bringing large numbers of additional parties in by this method would be very costly. Organizing the conduct of litigation with large numbers of additional parties would be a nightmare. The organizer, moreover, would have no effective way of obtaining reimbursement from other plaintiffs for these costs.

The class action procedure partially overcomes these difficulties by providing an effective and inexpensive procedure for joining large numbers of individual plaintiffs. . . .

The economic rationale for the [Rule 23] (b)(3) class action—as a method for overcoming free-rider and other collective action problems—stands in sharp contrast to the rationale for the shareholder's derivative suit. Shareholder's derivative actions are not premised on collective action problems in the *litigation*. On the contrary, they presuppose the existence of a corporate form that is already organized to overcome such collective action problems. The corporation has standing and is fully competent to bring legal actions to redress injuries to its rights. The problem, rather, is with collective action *within* the corporate form itself. As scholars since Berle and Means have observed, corporate managers typically have only a small ownership stake in the firms they manage. Thus, their interests deviate from those of shareholders: they may prefer to consume excessive perquisites or practice their golf whereas shareholders would want them to work diligently at maximizing profits.

The shareholder's derivative suit is one of many devices in corporate law for controlling these conflicts between managers and shareholders. Many cases arise in which a corporation has an enforceable legal claim against others for harm to the corporation. Like other matters affecting the corporation, pursuit of the claim is left initially to the managers. But if the suit would potentially harm the managers' personal interests, the managers may be unwilling to prosecute the claim, even when doing so would serve the best interests of the corporation. The classic case is the action for breach of fiduciary duty against corporate directors. Obviously the directors cannot be trusted to cause the corporation to sue themselves. The derivative action allows a representative shareholder in such circumstances to take over the litigation from recalcitrant managers and prosecute it on behalf of the corporation. Unlike the class action, in which the relief is given to the plaintiff class members, any relief recovered in a derivative action (net of expenses including attorneys' fees) is returned to the corporation. . . .

. . . Although a theoretical model exists in which suits are brought solely for their nuisance settlement value, the frequency of strike suits in derivative and class litigation remains an open question. Most observers agree that strike suit litigation is relatively uncommon. Defendants in class action and derivative litigation are typical repeat players, in that they are vulnerable to frequent lawsuits brought by entrepreneurial attorneys. It would not appear particularly desirable for such defendants (or their insurers, as the case may be) to settle cases for their nuisance value, because doing so would predictably establish a reputation as an easy mark and thus generate even more frivolous litigation. Conversely, a defendant that vigorously contests derivative or class action litigation, even when meritorious, is likely to gain a reputation as a party that derivative attorneys take on at their peril. Moreover, a plaintiffs' attorney who brings a strike suit incurs substantial risk; she must fund and staff the litigation subject to a high probability of non-success at the end. The true strike suit, where it occurs, is unlikely to be overly costly for defendants because the plaintiff would be likely to settle at a very low figure.

AMERICAN LAW INSTITUTE, PRINCIPLES OF CORPORATE GOVERNANCE §§ 7.04(a)(1), (b), (d)

[See Statutory Supplement]

NOTE ON WHO CAN BRING A DERIVATIVE ACTION

1. *Shareholder Status.* It is generally agreed that the plaintiff in a derivative action must be a shareholder at the time the action is begun, e.g., Vista Fund v. Garis, 277 N.W.2d 19 (Minn.1979), and must remain a shareholder during the pendency of the action, see, e.g., Schilling v. Belcher, 582 F.2d 995 (5th Cir.1978). An implication of this rule is that if S, a shareholder of C Corporation, brings a derivative action on C's behalf, and C then merges into T Corporation, which is the survivor of the merger, S loses standing to continue prosecuting the action, since she is no longer a shareholder in C. This rule was adopted in Delaware in the leading case of Lewis v. Anderson, 477 A.2d 1040 (Del. 1984), recently reaffirmed in Lewis v. Ward, 852 A.2d 896 (Del. 2004). However, both cases recognize two exceptions: (1) Where the merger is subject to the claim that it was perpetrated merely to deprive shareholders of the right to bring a derivative action; and (2) Where the merger is in reality a reorganization that does not affect the plaintiff's ownership of the business enterprise.

What constitutes shareholdership for derivative-action purposes? In a few states, a statute or rule speaks to the issue directly. For example, N.Y.Bus.Corp.Law § 626(a) provides that the plaintiff in a derivative suit must be "a holder of shares or of voting trust certificates ... or of a beneficial interest in such shares or certificates." Where the statute is silent, courts normally define shareholdership in a very expansive manner. First, record ownership is generally not required; an unregistered shareholder will qualify. See, e.g., Rosenthal v. Burry Biscuit Corp., 30 Del.Ch. 299, 60 A.2d 106 (Ch.1948). Second, legal ownership is not required—equitable ownership suffices. The latter category has been held to include, among others, an owner of stock held by a broker in a margin account in the broker's street name, a pledgee, the beneficiary of a trust, a legatee, a surviving spouse with a community interest in stock held in the deceased spouse's name, and a person who has contracted to purchase stock.

It is also established that in an appropriate case a shareholder in a parent corporation can bring a derivative action on behalf of a subsidiary, despite the fact that he is not a shareholder in the subsidiary. See Painter, Double Derivative Suits and Other Remedies With Regard to Damaged Subsidiaries, 36 Ind.L.J. 143, 147–49 (1961).

2. *Creditors.* An implication from the rule that the plaintiff in a derivative action must be a shareholder at the time he brings suit is that a creditor (including a bondholder) ordinarily has no right to bring a derivative action. See, e.g., Harff v. Kerkorian, 324 A.2d 215 (Del.Ch.1974), aff'd in pertinent part 347 A.2d 133 (Del.1975). Professor DeMott comments, "Convertible debentures present a more complicated problem. Some courts have held that the holder lacks standing to sue derivatively until the debenture has been converted, while others have held that the conversion feature provides the holder a sufficient equity interest to confer standing to sue derivatively—or have recognized that the question is disputed. More generally, in analyzing the status of holders of rights related to stocks, most courts focus on whether the holder has the right or an obligation to acquire shares of stock." Deborah DeMott, Shareholder Derivative Actions § 4:3 (2003).

However, if a corporation is insolvent, the directors owe fiduciary duties to the creditors, whether or not there has been a statutory filing under bankruptcy law. See Geyer v. Ingersoll Publications Co., 621 A.2d 784 (Del.Ch.1992). Presumably, therefore, in that situation creditors could bring an action against directors for violation of those duties. Moreover, in Credit Lyonnais Bank Nederland, N.V. v. Pathe Communications Corp., 1991 WL 277613 (Del.Ch.1991), Chancellor Allen stated that "At least where a corporation is operating *in the vicinity* of bankruptcy, a board of directors is not merely the agent of the [shareholders], but owes its duty to the corporate enterprise." (Emphasis added.) And in Francis v. United Jersey Bank, Chapter 8, supra, the court stated that in the case of certain kinds of corporations and creditors—such as banks and bank depositors—directors owe a duty to creditors even while the corporation is solvent.

3. *Directors.* Occasionally a statute gives an officer or director the right to bring a derivative action. See N.Y.Bus.Corp.Law § 720(b).

NOTE ON PERSONAL DEFENSES

It is generally held that a shareholder is barred from bringing a derivative action if either (1) she participated in the alleged wrong; (2)

she consented to the wrong or explicitly ratified it; (3) she is guilty of laches; or (4) (under a few opinions) she "acquiesced" in the wrong by failing to object. The theory of these rules is that in such cases the plaintiff is "estopped" to bring the action, or lacks "clean hands." See, e.g., Bloodworth v. Bloodworth, 225 Ga. 379, 169 S.E.2d 150 (1969). These defenses are therefore known as "personal" defenses, because they do not relate to the merits of the action, but only to whether a particular shareholder can bring it.

Recognition of personal defenses seems inconsistent with the nature of a derivative action. In Kullgren v. Navy Gas & Supply Co., 112 Colo. 331, 149 P.2d 653 (1944), the court said:

> The finding of the trial court on which it based its order of dismissal . . . is in part as follows: "If the defendants named in this case are wolves, as the plaintiff so vigorously contends, then the plaintiff was running with the pack. . . . If they are thieves, as plaintiff strongly urges, then they are all thieves together, and a court of equity will not undertake to adjust equities between thieves." . . . [W]e cannot think [this] is sound in a situation, where, as here, the only judgment sought is in behalf of the corporation. Based on the implication that the three moving defendants and plaintiff are "thieves together," . . . the result . . . is that all—the three defendants and plaintiff—are beholden to the corporation.

Despite this reasoning, most courts not only allow personal defenses, but go one step further and adopt the so-called "tainted share" rule. Under this rule, if a shareholder is barred from bringing an action by virtue of a personal defense, so also is any transferee of that shareholder. For discussions of the rule, see Note, 54 Boston U.L.Rev. 355, 362–66 (1974); Note, 46 Mich.L.Rev. 429, 430 (1948).

———

NOTE ON THE CORPORATION AS AN INDISPENSABLE PARTY

It is well established that the corporation is an indispensable party to a derivative action, and therefore must be joined in the suit:

> If the defendants account, it must be to the corporation and not to the shareholders. As to the defendants charged with defrauding it, the corporation is an indispensable party. . . . Furthermore, the decree must protect the defendants against any further suit by the corporation, and this will not be true unless it properly be made a party to the action. . . . The usual American practice is to name the beneficiary corporation as a party defendant, although in substance it is a party plaintiff; the flexibility of equity procedure permits an affirmative judgment to be entered in favor of one defendant against other defendants.

Dean v. Kellogg, 294 Mich. 200, 207–08, 292 N.W. 704, 707–08 (1940).

SECTION 2.   THE NATURE OF THE DERIVATIVE ACTION

———

Tooley v. Donaldson, Lufkin, & Jenrette, Inc.

Supreme Court of Delaware, 2004.
845 A.2d 1031.

■ Before VEASEY, CHIEF JUSTICE, HOLLAND, BERGER, STEELE and JACOBS, JUSTICES, constituting the Court en Banc.

■ VEASEY, CHIEF JUSTICE:

Plaintiff-stockholders brought a purported class action in the Court of Chancery, alleging that the members of the board of directors of their corporation breached their fiduciary duties by agreeing to a 22–day delay in closing a proposed merger. Plaintiffs contend that the delay harmed them due to the lost time-value of the cash paid for their shares. The Court of Chancery granted the defendants' motion to dismiss on the sole ground that the claims were, "at most," claims of the corporation being asserted derivatively. They were, thus, held not to be direct claims of the stockholders, individually. Thereupon, the Court held that the plaintiffs lost their standing to bring this action when they tendered their shares in connection with the merger.

Although the trial court's legal analysis of whether the complaint alleges a direct or derivative claim reflects some concepts in our prior jurisprudence, we believe those concepts are not helpful and should be regarded as erroneous. We set forth in this Opinion the law to be applied henceforth in determining whether a stockholder's claim is derivative or direct. That issue must turn *solely* on the following questions: (1) who suffered the alleged harm (the corporation or the suing stockholders, individually); and (2) who would receive the benefit of any recovery or other remedy (the corporation or the stockholders, individually)? . . .

Facts

Patrick Tooley and Kevin Lewis are former minority stockholders of Donaldson, Lufkin & Jenrette, Inc. (DLJ), a Delaware corporation engaged in investment banking. DLJ was acquired by Credit Suisse Group (Credit Suisse) in the Fall of 2000. Before that acquisition, AXA Financial, Inc.(AXA), which owned 71% of DLJ stock, controlled DLJ. Pursuant to a stockholder agreement between AXA and Credit Suisse, AXA agreed to exchange with Credit Suisse its DLJ stockholdings for a mix of stock and cash. The consideration received by AXA consisted primarily of stock. Cash made up one-third of the purchase price. Credit Suisse intended to acquire the remaining minority interests of publicly-held DLJ stock through a cash tender offer, followed by a merger of DLJ into a Credit Suisse subsidiary.

The tender offer price was set at $90 per share in cash. The tender offer was to expire 20 days after its commencement. The merger agreement, however, authorized two types of extensions. First, Credit Suisse could unilaterally extend the tender offer if certain conditions were not met, such as SEC regulatory approvals or certain payment obligations. Alternatively, DLJ and Credit Suisse could agree to postpone acceptance by Credit Suisse of DLJ stock tendered by the minority stockholders.

Credit Suisse availed itself of both types of extensions to postpone the closing of the tender offer. The tender offer was initially set to expire on October 5, 2000, but Credit Suisse invoked the five-day unilateral extension provided in the agreement. Later, by agreement between DLJ and Credit Suisse, it postponed the merger a second time so that it was then set to close on November 2, 2000.

Plaintiffs challenge the second extension that resulted in a 22–day delay. They contend that this delay was not properly authorized and harmed minority stockholders while improperly benefitting AXA. They claim damages representing the time-value of money lost through the delay.

The Decision of the Court of Chancery

The order of the Court of Chancery dismissing the complaint, and the Memorandum Opinion upon which it is based, state that the dismissal is based on the plaintiffs' lack of standing to bring the claims asserted therein. Thus, when plaintiffs tendered their shares, they lost standing under Court of Chancery Rule 23.1, the contemporaneous holding rule. The ruling before us on appeal is that the plaintiffs' claim is derivative, purportedly brought on behalf of DLJ. The Court of Chancery, relying upon our confusing jurisprudence on the direct/derivative dichotomy, based its dismissal on the following ground: "Because this delay affected all DLJ shareholders equally, plaintiffs' injury was not a special injury, and this action is, thus, a derivative action, at most."

Plaintiffs argue that they have suffered a "special injury" because they had an alleged contractual right to receive the merger consideration of $90 per share without suffering the 22–day delay arising out of the extensions under the merger agreement. But the trial court's opinion convincingly demonstrates that plaintiffs had no such contractual right that had ripened at the time the extensions were entered into:

> *Here, it is clear that plaintiffs have no separate contractual right to bring a direct claim, and they do not assert contractual rights under the merger agreement.* First, the merger agreement specifically disclaims any persons as being third party beneficiaries to the contract. Second, any contractual shareholder right to payment of the merger consideration did not ripen until the conditions of the agreement were met. The agreement stated that Credit Suisse Group was not required to accept any shares for tender, or could extend the offer, under certain conditions—one condition of

which included an extension or termination by agreement between Credit Suisse Group and DLJ. *Because Credit Suisse Group and DLJ did in fact agree to extend the tender offer period, any right to payment plaintiffs could have did not ripen until this newly negotiated period was over. The merger agreement only became binding and mutually enforceable at the time the tendered shares ultimately were accepted for payment by Credit Suisse Group.* It is at that moment in time, November 3, 2000, that the company became bound to purchase the tendered shares, making the contract mutually enforceable. *DLJ stockholders had no individual contractual right to payment until November 3, 2000, when their tendered shares were accepted for payment.* Thus, they have no contractual basis to challenge a delay in the closing of the tender offer up until November 3. *Because this is the date the tendered shares were accepted for payment, the contract was not breached and plaintiffs do not have a contractual basis to bring a direct suit.*

Moreover, no other individual right of these stockholder-plaintiffs was alleged to have been violated by the extensions.

That conclusion could have ended the case because it portended a definitive ruling that plaintiffs have no claim whatsoever on the facts alleged. But the defendants chose to argue, and the trial court chose to decide, the standing issue, which is predicated on an assertion that this claim is a derivative one asserted on behalf of the corporation, DLJ.

The Court of Chancery correctly noted that "[t]he Court will independently examine the nature of the wrong alleged and any potential relief to make its own determination of the suit's classification. . . . Plaintiffs' classification of the suit is not binding." The trial court's analysis was hindered, however, because it focused on the confusing concept of "special injury" as the test for determining whether a claim is derivative or direct. The trial court's premise was as follows:

> In order to bring a *direct* claim, a plaintiff must have experienced some "special injury." [citing *Lipton v. News Int'l*, 514 A.2d 1075, 1079 (Del.1986)]. A special injury is a wrong that "is separate and distinct from that suffered by other shareholders, . . . or a wrong involving a contractual right of a shareholder, such as the right to vote, or to assert majority control, which exists independently of any right of the corporation." [citing *Moran v. Household Int'l. Inc.*, 490 A.2d 1059, 1070 (Del.Ch.1985), *aff'd* 500 A.2d 1346 (Del.1986 [1985])].

In our view, the concept of "special injury" that appears in some Supreme Court and Court of Chancery cases is not helpful to a proper analytical distinction between direct and derivative actions. We now disapprove the use of the concept of "special injury" as a tool in that analysis.

The Proper Analysis to Distinguish Between
Direct and Derivative Actions

The analysis must be based solely on the following questions: Who suffered the alleged harm—the corporation or the suing stockholder individually—and who would receive the benefit of the recovery or other remedy? This simple analysis is well imbedded in our jurisprudence,[3] but some cases have complicated it by injection of the amorphous and confusing concept of "special injury."

The Chancellor, in the very recent *Agostino* case,[4] correctly points this out and strongly suggests that we should disavow the concept of "special injury." In a scholarly analysis of this area of the law, he also suggests that the inquiry should be whether the stockholder has demonstrated that he or she has suffered an injury that is not dependent on an injury to the corporation. In the context of a claim for breach of fiduciary duty, the Chancellor articulated the inquiry as follows: "Looking at the body of the complaint and considering the nature of the wrong alleged and the relief requested, has the plaintiff demonstrated that he or she can prevail without showing an injury to the corporation?"[5] We believe that this approach is helpful in analyzing the first prong of the analysis: what person or entity has suffered the alleged harm? The second prong of the analysis should logically follow.

A Brief History of Our Jurisprudence

The derivative suit has been generally described as "one of the most interesting and ingenious of accountability mechanisms for large formal organizations."[6] It enables a stockholder to bring suit on behalf of the corporation for harm done to the corporation. Because a derivative suit is being brought on behalf of the corporation, the recovery, if any, must go to the corporation. A stockholder who is directly injured, however, does retain the right to bring an individual action for injuries affecting his or her legal rights as a stockholder. Such a claim is distinct from an injury caused to the corporation alone. In such individual suits, the recovery or other relief flows directly to the stockholders, not to the corporation.

---

3. See, e.g., Kramer v. Western Pacific Industries, Inc., 546 A.2d 348 (Del.1988).

4. Agostino v. Hicks, No. Civ. A. 20020-NC, 2004 WL 443987 (Del.Ch. March 11, 2004).

5. Agostino, 2004 WL 443987, at * 7. The Chancellor further explains that the focus should be on the person or entity to whom the relevant duty is owed. Id. at *7 n. 54. As noted in Agostino, id., this test is similar to that articulated by the American Law Institute (ALI), a test that we cited with approval in Grimes v. Donald, 673 A.2d 1207 (Del.1996). The ALI test is as follows:

A direct action may be brought in the name and right of a holder to redress an injury sustained by, or enforce a duty owed to, the holder. An action in which the holder can prevail without showing an injury or breach of duty to the corporation should be treated as a direct action that may be maintained by the holder in an individual capacity.

2 American Law Institute, PRINCIPLES OF CORPORATE GOVERNANCE: ANALYSIS AND RECOMMENDATIONS § 7.01(b) at 17.

6. Kramer v. Western Pacific Industries, Inc., 546 A.2d at 351 (quoting R. Clark, Corporate Law 639–40 (1986)).

Determining whether an action is derivative or direct is sometimes difficult and has many legal consequences, some of which may have an expensive impact on the parties to the action. For example, if an action is derivative, the plaintiffs are then required to comply with the requirements of Court of Chancery Rule 23.1, that the stockholder: (a) retain ownership of the shares throughout the litigation; (b) make presuit demand on the board; and (c) obtain court approval of any settlement. Further, the recovery, if any, flows only to the corporation. The decision whether a suit is direct or derivative may be outcome-determinative. Therefore, it is necessary that a standard to distinguish such actions be clear, simple and consistently articulated and applied by our courts.

In *Elster v. American Airlines, Inc.*,[7] the stockholder sought to enjoin the grant and exercise of stock options because they would result in a dilution of her stock personally. In *Elster*, the alleged injury was found to be derivative, not direct, because it was essentially a claim of mismanagement of corporate assets. Then came the complication in the analysis: The Court held that where the alleged injury is to both the corporation *and* to the stockholder, the stockholder must allege a "special injury" to maintain a direct action. The Court did not define "special injury," however. By implication, decisions in later cases have interpreted *Elster* to mean that a "special injury" is alleged where the wrong is inflicted upon the stockholder alone or where the stockholder complains of a wrong affecting a particular right. Examples would be a preemptive right as a stockholder, rights involving control of the corporation or a wrong affecting the stockholder, qua individual holder, and not the corporation.

In *Bokat v. Getty Oil Co.*,[8] a stockholder of a subsidiary brought suit against the director of the parent corporation for causing the subsidiary to invest its resources wastefully, resulting in a loss to the subsidiary. The claim in *Bokat* was essentially for mismanagement of corporate assets. Therefore, the Court held that any recovery must be sought on behalf of the corporation, and the claim was, thus, found to be derivative.

In describing how a court may distinguish direct and derivative actions, the *Bokat* Court stated that a suit must be maintained derivatively if the injury falls equally upon all stockholders. Experience has shown this concept to be confusing and inaccurate. It is confusing because it appears to have been intended to address the fact that an injury to the corporation tends to diminish each share of stock equally because corporate assets or their value are diminished. In that sense, the *indirect* injury to the stockholders arising out of the harm to the corporation comes about solely by virtue of their stockholdings. It does not arise out of any independent or direct harm to the stockholders, individually. That concept is also inaccurate because a direct, individual claim of stockholders that does not depend on harm to the

---

7.   100 A.2d 219, 222 (Del.Ch.1953).   **8.**   262 A.2d 246 (Del.1970).

corporation can also fall on all stockholders equally, without the claim thereby becoming a derivative claim.

In *Lipton v. News International, Plc.,*[9] this Court applied the "special injury" test. There, a stockholder began acquiring shares in the defendant corporation presumably to gain control of the corporation. In response, the defendant corporation agreed to an exchange of its shares with a friendly buyer. Due to the exchange and a supermajority voting requirement on certain stockholder actions, the management of the defendant corporation acquired a veto power over any change in management.

The *Lipton* Court concluded that the critical analytical issue in distinguishing direct and derivative actions is whether a "special injury" has been alleged. There, the Court found a "special injury" because the board's manipulation worked an injury upon the plaintiff-stockholder unlike the injury suffered by other stockholders. That was because the plaintiff-stockholder was actively seeking to gain control of the defendant corporation. Therefore, the Court found that the claim was direct. Ironically, the Court could have reached the same correct result by simply concluding that the manipulation directly and individually harmed the stockholders, without injuring the corporation. . . .

In *Grimes v. Donald,*[10] we sought to distinguish between direct and derivative actions in the context of employment agreements granted to certain officers that allegedly caused the board to abdicate its authority. Relying on the [*Elster*] that the court must look to the nature of the wrong and to whom the relief will go, we concluded that the plaintiff was not seeking to recover any damages for injury to the corporation. Rather, the plaintiff was seeking a declaration of the invalidity of the agreements on the ground that the board had abdicated its responsibility to the stockholders. Thus, based on the relief requested, we affirmed the judgment of the Court of Chancery that the plaintiff was entitled to pursue a direct action.

Grimes was followed by *Parnes v. Bally Entertainment Corp.,* which held, among other things, that the injury to the stockholders must be "independent of any injury to the corporation."[11] As the Chancellor correctly noted in *Agostino,* neither *Grimes* nor *Parnes* applies the purported "special injury" test.

Thus, two confusing propositions have encumbered our caselaw governing the direct/derivative distinction. The "special injury" concept, applied in cases such as *Lipton,* can be confusing in identifying the nature of the action. The same is true of the proposition that stems from *Bokat*—that an action cannot be direct if all stockholders are equally affected or unless the stockholder's injury is separate and distinct from that suffered by other stockholders. The proper analysis has been and should remain that stated in *Grimes*. . . . That is, a court should look to the nature of the wrong and to whom the relief should go. The stockholder's claimed direct injury must be independent of

---

9. . . . . 514 A.2d at 1078 [Del. 1988].

10.   673 A.2d 1207, 1213 (Del.1996).

11.   722 A.2d 1243, 1245 (Del.1999).

any alleged injury to the corporation. The stockholder must demonstrate that the duty breached was owed to the stockholder and that he or she can prevail without showing an injury to the corporation.

Standard to Be Applied in This Case

In this case it cannot be concluded that the complaint alleges a derivative claim. There is no derivative claim asserting injury to the corporate entity. There is no relief that would go the corporation. Accordingly, there is no basis to hold that the complaint states a derivative claim.

But, it does not necessarily follow that the complaint states a direct, individual claim. While the complaint purports to set forth a direct claim, in reality, it states no claim at all. The trial court analyzed the complaint and correctly concluded that it does not claim that the plaintiffs have any rights that have been injured. Their rights have not yet ripened. The contractual claim is nonexistent until it is ripe, and that claim will not be ripe until the terms of the merger are fulfilled, including the extensions of the closing at issue here. Therefore, there is no direct claim stated in the complaint before us.

Accordingly, the complaint was properly dismissed. But, due to the reliance on the concept of "special injury" by the Court of Chancery, the ground set forth for the dismissal is erroneous, there being no derivative claim. That error is harmless, however, because, in our view, there is no direct claim either.

Conclusion

For purposes of distinguishing between derivative and direct claims, we expressly disapprove both the concept of "special injury" and the concept that a claim is necessarily derivative if it affects all stockholders equally. In our view, the tests going forward should rest on those set forth in this opinion.

We affirm the judgment of the Court of Chancery dismissing the complaint, although on a different ground from that decided by the Court of Chancery. We reverse the dismissal with prejudice and remand this matter to the Court of Chancery to amend the order of dismissal: (a) to state that the complaint is dismissed on the ground that it does not state a claim upon which relief can be granted; and (b) that the dismissal is without prejudice.

Because our determination that there is no valid claim whatsoever in the complaint before us was not argued by the defendants and was not the basis of the ruling of the Court of Chancery, the interests of justice will be best served if the dismissal is without prejudice, and plaintiffs have an opportunity to replead if they have a basis for doing so. . . .

———

Barth v. Barth

Supreme Court of Indiana, 1995.
659 N.E.2d 559.

■ JUDGES: SULLIVAN, JUSTICE, SHEPARD, C.J., and DEBRULER, DICKSON and SELBY, JJ., concur.

■ SULLIVAN, JUSTICE.

Background

This lawsuit was brought against defendants Barth Electric Co., Inc., and its president and majority shareholder Michael G. Barth, Jr., by plaintiff minority shareholder Robert Barth individually (rather than derivatively on behalf of the corporation).[3] Plaintiff Robert Barth alleged that defendant Michael Barth had taken certain actions which had the effect of "substantially reducing the value of Plaintiff's shares of common stock" in the corporation. Specifically, plaintiff contended that defendant Michael Barth had: (1) paid excessive salaries to himself and to members of his immediate family; (2) used corporate employees to perform services on his and his son's homes without compensating the corporation; (3) dramatically lowered dividend payments; and (4) appropriated corporate funds for personal investments. *Barth v. Barth* (Ind.App.1995), 651 N.E.2d 291. Michael Barth and the corporation moved to dismiss Robert Barth's complaint for the failure to state a claim upon which relief can be granted, Ind. Trial Rule 12(B)(6), arguing that a derivative action was required to redress claims of this nature. The trial court granted the motion to dismiss. The Court of Appeals acknowledged that the "well-established general rule" prohibits a shareholder from maintaining an action in the shareholder's own name but found that requiring a derivative action here would "exalt form over substance" since Robert Barth could have satisfied the requirements for bringing a derivative action and that none of the reasons underlying the general derivative action requirement were present. *Barth v. Barth*, 651 N.E.2d at 293. The Court of Appeals reversed the trial court; the corporation and Michael Barth seek transfer.

Discussion

As the Court of Appeals made clear, the well-established general rule is that shareholders of a corporation may not maintain actions at law in their own names to redress an injury to the corporation even if the value of their stock is impaired as a result of the injury. *Moll v. South Central Solar Systems, Inc.* (Ind.App.1981), 419 N.E.2d 154, 161. . . . In *Moll*, Judge Ratliff discussed the purpose of the rule in the following terms:

> The rationale supporting this rule is based on sound public policy considerations. It is recognized that authorization of shareholder actions in such cases would constitute authorization of multitudinous litigation and disregard for the corporate entity. . . . Sound

---

3. Michael Barth owns 51% of the shares of the corporation. Robert Barth owns 29.8%. A third individual owns the remaining shares.

policy considerations have been said to require that a single action be brought rather than to permit separate suits by each shareholder even when the corporation and the shareholder are the same. . . .

Moll, 419 N.E.2d at 161. In W & W Equipment Co., Inc. v. Mink (1991), Ind.App., 568 N.E.2d 564, Judge Baker set forth additional reasons for this rule: the protection of corporate creditors by putting the proceeds of the recovery back in the corporation; the protection of the interests of all the shareholders rather than allowing one shareholder to prejudice the interests of other shareholders; and the adequate compensation of the injured shareholder by increasing the value of the shares when recovery is put back into the corporation. *Id.,* 568 N.E.2d at 571 (citing *Caswell v. Jordan* (1987), 184 Ga.App. 755, 362 S.E.2d 769, cert. denied).

While we affirm the general rule requiring a shareholder to bring a derivative rather than direct action when seeking redress for injury to the corporation, we nevertheless observe two reasons why this rule will not always apply in the case of closely-held corporations.[5] First, shareholders in a close corporation stand in a fiduciary relationship to each other, and as such, must deal fairly, honestly, and openly with the corporation and with their fellow shareholders. *W & W Equipment Co.,* 568 N.E.2d at 570; *Krukemeier v. Krukemeier Machine and Tool Co., Inc.* (Ind.App.1990), 551 N.E.2d 885; *Garbe v. Excel Mold, Inc.* (Ind.App.1979), 397 N.E.2d 296.[6] Second, shareholder litigation in the closely-held corporation context will often not implicate the policies that mandate requiring derivative litigation when more widely-held corporations are involved. W & W Equipment Co., Inc. v. Mink is a leading case in this regard. There our Court of Appeals was faced with a lawsuit filed by one of two 50% shareholders of a corporation after the other shareholder joined with nonshareholder directors to fire the plaintiff shareholder and arrange for the payment of certain corporate assets to the other shareholder. The court concluded that no useful purpose would be served by forcing the plaintiff to proceed derivatively where the policies favoring derivative actions were not implicated—direct corporate recovery was not necessary to protect absent shareholders or creditors as none existed. *Id.,* 568 N.E.2d at 571.

Because shareholders of closely-held corporations have very direct obligations to one another and because shareholder litigation in the closely-held corporation context will often not implicate the principles which gave rise to the rule requiring derivative litigation, courts in many cases are permitting direct suits by shareholders of closely-held

5. A closely-held corporation is one which typically has relatively few shareholders and whose shares are not generally traded in the securities market. *W & W Equipment Co., Inc. v. Mink* (Ind.App.1991), 568 N.E.2d 564, 570 (citing F. Hodge O'Neal & Robert B. Thompson, O'Neal's Close Corporations § 1.02 (3d ed.)). Accord, American Law Institute, Principles of Corporate Governance: Analysis and Recommendations § 1.06 (1994).

6. This principle of Indiana corporate law mirrors that reached by the Supreme Judicial Court of Massachusetts in. . . . *Donahue v. Rodd Electrotype Co. of New England, Inc.,* 367 Mass. 578, 328 N.E.2d 505, 515 (Mass.1975). . . .

corporations where the complaint is one that in a public corporation would have to be brought as a derivative action. See F. Hodge O'Neal & Robert B. Thompson, O'Neal's Close Corporations § 8.16 n. 32 (3d ed. & 1995 Cum.Supp.) (collecting cases); American Law Institute, Principles of Corporate Governance: Analysis and Recommendations § 7.01, reporter's n. 4 (1994) (collecting cases). However, it is important to keep in mind that the principles which gave rise to the rule requiring derivative actions will sometimes be present even in litigation involving closely-held corporations. For example, because a corporate recovery in a derivative action will benefit creditors while a direct recovery by a shareholder will not, the protection of creditors principle could well be implicated in a shareholder suit against a closely-held corporation with debt. . . .

In its recently-completed corporate governance project, the American Law Institute proposed the following rule for determining when a shareholder of a closely-held corporation may proceed by direct or derivative action:

> In the case of a closely held corporation, the court in its discretion may treat an action raising derivative claims as a direct action, exempt it from those restrictions and defenses applicable only to derivative actions, and order an individual recovery, if it finds that to do so will not (i) unfairly expose the corporation or the defendants to a multiplicity of actions, (ii) materially prejudice the interests of creditors of the corporation, or (iii) interfere with a fair distribution of the recovery among all interested persons.

A.L.I., Principles of Corporate Governance § 7.01(d). We have studied this rule and find that it is consistent with the approach taken by our Court of Appeals and by most other jurisdictions in similar cases and that it represents a fair and workable approach for balancing the relative interests in closely-held corporation shareholder litigation.

In determining that a trial court has discretion to decide whether a plaintiff must proceed by direct or by derivative action, we make the following observations, drawn largely from the Comment to § 7.01(d). First, permitting such litigation to proceed as a direct action will exempt the plaintiff from the requirements of Ind.Code § 23–1–32–1 et seq., including the provisions that permit a special committee of the board of directors to recommend dismissal of the lawsuit. Ind.Code § 23–1–32–4. As such, the court in making its decision should consider whether the corporation has a disinterested board that should be permitted to consider the lawsuit's impact on the corporation. A.L.I., Corporate Governance Project § 7.01 comment e. Second, in some situations it may actually be to the benefit of the corporation to permit the plaintiff to proceed by direct action. This will permit the defendant to file a counterclaim against the plaintiff, whereas counterclaims are generally prohibited in derivative actions. Also, in a direct action each side will normally be responsible for its own legal expenses; the plaintiff, even if successful, cannot ordinarily look to the corporation for attorney's fees. Id.

Conclusion

We grant transfer, vacate the opinion of the Court of Appeals, and remand this cause to the trial court for reconsideration of its order of dismissal in light of the rule adopted in this opinion.

■ SHEPARD, C.J., and DEBRULER, DICKSON and SELBY, JJ., concur.

———

BAGDON v. BRIDGESTONE/FIRESTONE, INC., 916 F.2d 379 (7th Cir.1990), cert. denied 500 U.S. 952, 111 S.Ct. 2257, 114 L.Ed.2d 710 (1991). "Delaware follows the venerable rule that a claim is derivative if injury is mediated through the corporation. *Elster v. American Airlines, Inc.,* 34 Del.Ch. 94, 100 A.2d 219 (1953). It also follows the 'special injury' exception to this rule, *id.* 100 A.2d at 222, allowing a shareholder to litigate independently if the wrong to the corporation inflicts a distinct and disproportionate injury on the investor....

"Ohio, like a few other states, has expanded the 'special injury' doctrine into a general exception for closely held corporations, treating them as if they were partnerships. *Crosby [v. Beam]* follows *Donahue v. Rodd Electrotype Co.,* 367 Mass. 578, 328 N.E.2d 505 (1975), and *Jones v. H.F. Ahmanson & Co.,* 1 Cal.3d 93, 460 P.2d 464, 81 Cal.Rptr. 592 (1969). The American Law Institute recommends that other states do the same. *Principles of Corporate Governance* § 7.01(d) and pp. 22–25 (comment), 30–36 (reporter's note). The premise of this extension may be questioned. Corporations are *not* partnerships. Whether to incorporate entails a choice of many formalities. Commercial rules should be predictable; this objective is best served by treating corporations as what they are, allowing the investors and other participants to vary the rules by contract if they think deviations are warranted. So it is understandable that not all states have joined the parade.

"Delaware, for one, has not. When the controlling stockholder of a family corporation transferred its assets for inadequate consideration, Delaware required the minority investors to pursue derivative litigation, observing that the value of the minority shares went down only to the extent the corporation as an entity was worth less. *Taormina v. Taormina Corp.,* 32 Del.Ch. 18, 78 A.2d 473 (1951). When the owner of 95% of a closely held firm's stock proposed to liquidate the corporation at what the minority thought was an inadequate price, Delaware again required the minority to bring the objection derivatively. *Abelow v. Symonds,* 38 Del.Ch. 572, 156 A.2d 416 (1959). In neither case did the Chancellor think it important that the wrong alleged involved the controlling stockholder enriching itself at corporate expense, or that the corporation was closely held.... The Reporter of the ALI's corporate governance project disapproves, *Principles of Corporate Governance* at 36, but *Abelow* is the law of Delaware today...."

———

NOTE ON THE DISTINCTION BETWEEN DERIVATIVE AND DIRECT ACTIONS

1. *The Impact of a Determination that an Action is Derivative.* What's the difference whether a shareholder's action is properly characterized as derivative or direct? The answer is that, as shown in the balance of this Chapter, a number of special procedural rules apply to—and set hurdles to—derivative actions, but not to direct actions. A shareholder who is concerned whether she can leap these hurdles will therefore prefer that her action is characterized as direct.

2. *Reasons for Distinguishing Between Direct and Derivative Actions.* Two kinds of reasons are commonly advanced for distinguishing between a *derivative* action, which is brought on the corporation's behalf against either corporate fiduciaries or third persons, and a *direct* action, which is brought on a shareholder's own behalf against either corporate fiduciaries or the corporation itself. The first kind of reason is theoretical: Since a corporation is a legal person separate from its shareholders, an injury to the corporation is not an injury to its shareholders. This proposition is somewhat dubious, because every injury to a corporation must also have an impact, however slight, on the shareholders as well. The second kind of reason is pragmatic: "(1) To avoid a multiplicity of suits by each injured shareholder, (2) to protect the corporate creditors, and (3) to protect all the stockholders since a corporate recovery benefits all equally," while a direct action does not. Watson v. Button, 235 F.2d 235 (9th Cir.1956).

3. *Easy Cases.* Some principles concerning the distinction between derivative and direct actions are relatively well-established. At one end of the spectrum, a wrongful act that depletes corporate assets, and affects the shareholder only by reducing the value of his stock, gives rise only to an action on the corporation's behalf. At the other end of the spectrum, a wrongful act that does not deplete corporate assets, and interferes with rights that are traditionally viewed as either incident to the ownership of stock or inhering in the shares themselves (such as voting or pre-emptive rights), gives rise only to a direct action by the injured shareholders.

4. *Harder Cases.* Many kinds of cases fall between the two ends of the spectrum described in the preceding paragraph. In some of these cases, the rules are relatively clear; in others, rules are just beginning to emerge. For example, it is relatively clear that a direct action will lie based on the issuance of stock for the wrongful purpose of perpetuating or shifting control (e.g., Sheppard v. Wilcox, 210 Cal.App.2d 53, 26 Cal.Rptr. 412 (1962)), or to enjoin a threatened ultra vires act (e.g., Alexander v. Atlanta & West Point R.R., 113 Ga. 193, 38 S.E. 772 (1901)). A rule permitting a direct action seems to be emerging in suits based on wrongs by controlling against noncontrolling shareholders. Suits to enjoin improperly authorized corporate actions are also commonly treated as direct actions, either implicitly (that is, without discussion of the issue), or explicitly, but the authorities are in conflict on this type of case.

5. *Actions that can be Characterized as Either Direct or Derivative.* In many cases a wrongful act both depletes corporate assets *and* interferes with rights traditionally viewed as inhering in shares. The general principle governing such cases is that a direct action is not precluded simply because the same facts could also give rise to a derivative action. For example, in Bennett v. Breuil Petroleum Corp., 34 Del.Ch. 6, 99 A.2d 236 (1953), the plaintiff claimed that the controlling shareholders had caused the corporation to issue stock for an improper purpose—impairing his interest and forcing him out on management's terms—and at a grossly inadequate consideration. The court held that the first claim stated a direct and the second a derivative cause of action. See also, e.g., Buschmann v. Professional Men's Ass'n, 405 F.2d 659 (7th Cir.1969).

Another important kind of case in which suit may be either direct or derivative is one involving proxy-rule violations. Insofar as such a violation interferes with the individual shareholder's voting right, the suit can be regarded as direct; insofar as it involves a breach of management's fiduciary obligations, the suit can be regarded as derivative.

AMERICAN LAW INSTITUTE, PRINCIPLES OF CORPORATE GOVERNANCE § 7.01

[See Statutory Supplement]

SECTION 3. INDIVIDUAL (PRO RATA) RECOVERY IN DERIVATIVE ACTIONS

Glenn v. Hoteltron Systems, Inc.

Court of Appeals of New York, 1989.
74 N.Y.2d 386, 547 N.Y.S.2d 816, 547 N.E.2d 71.

■ WACHTLER, CHIEF JUDGE....

The dispute here is between Jacob Schachter and Herbert Kulik, the founders of Ketek Electric Corporation. Schachter and Kulik each own 50% of the corporation's shares and serve as the corporation's only officers.... [T]he Appellate Division, on [a] prior appeal, found Schachter liable for diverting Ketek assets and opportunities to Hoteltron Systems, Inc., a corporation wholly owned by Schachter.

Following the trial on damages, Supreme Court concluded that Hoteltron had earned profits of $362,242.84 from Schachter's usurpation of Ketek assets and opportunities....

On Schachter's appeal, the Appellate Division . . . concluded that the Hoteltron profits should be awarded to the injured corporation, Ketek, rather than the innocent shareholder Kulik. . . .

It is the general rule that, because a shareholders' derivative suit seeks to vindicate a wrong done to the corporation through enforcement of a corporate cause of action, any recovery obtained is for the benefit of the injured corporation. . . .

Kulik argues that this result is inequitable because Schachter, as a shareholder of Ketek, will ultimately share in the proceeds of the damage award. But that prospect exists in any successful derivative action in which the wrongdoer is a shareholder of the injured corporation. An exception based on that fact alone would effectively nullify the general rule that damages for a corporate injury should be awarded to the corporation.

It is true that this anomaly is magnified in cases involving closely held corporations, because the errant fiduciary is likely to own a large share of the corporation—as Schachter owns 50% of Ketek—and will share proportionately in the restitution to the corporation generated by a successful suit against him. Thus, it may be argued that in such circumstances an award of damages to the corporation does not provide a sufficient deterrent to the potential wrongdoer. We conclude, however, that this consideration does not require a different damage rule for close corporations.

While awarding damages directly to the innocent shareholder may seem equitable with respect to the parties before the court, other interests, particularly those of the corporation's creditors, should not be overlooked. The fruits of a diverted corporate opportunity are properly a corporate asset. Awarding that asset directly to a shareholder could impair the rights of creditors whose claims may be superior to that of the innocent shareholder. . . .

Thus, while we do not rule out the possibility that an award to innocent shareholders rather than to the corporation would be appropriate in some circumstances, we find no need to invoke such an exception here.

Accordingly, the order of the Appellate Division should be affirmed, without costs.

■ SIMONS, KAYE, ALEXANDER, TITONE, HANCOCK and BELLACOSA, JJ., concur.

Order affirmed, without costs.

———————

PERLMAN v. FELDMANN

[Chapter 9, supra.]

———————

NOTE ON INDIVIDUAL RECOVERY IN DERIVATIVE ACTIONS

1. *The Basic Principle.* Pro-rata recovery cases involve derivative actions that take a sudden turn at the remedy stage. Normally, in a derivative action the recovery goes to the corporation, in whose name the action is brought. When pro rata recovery is granted, however, the recovery goes directly to the shareholders—more accurately, to certain shareholders. Each shareholder who is entitled to participate in a pro rata recovery gets a share of the recovery equal to her percentage ownership of stock. For example, suppose A owns 20% of Azure Corporation's stock, B owns 20%, and C owns 60%. A brings a derivative action against C on Azure's behalf. The court awards damages of $1 million against C, in favor of Azure. In a normal derivative action, the $1 million would go to Azure. If pro rata recovery is granted to A and B, A will get $200,000 (20% of $1 million), B will get $200,000 (same), C will get nothing, and Azure will got nothing.

Pro rata recovery is a useful tool to achieve justice in a variety of cases that are properly characterized as derivative actions. Although pro rata recovery results in direct payments by the defendants to shareholders, rather than a payment solely to the corporation, pro rata recovery is consistent with characterizing an action as derivative rather than as direct, for two reasons. First, the plaintiff in such an action must satisfy all the relevant requirements for bringing a derivative action. Second, the amount of damages is measured by the injury to the corporation—although once that measurement is made, a portion of the amount is distributed directly to certain shareholders.

2. *Preventing Wrongdoers from Sharing in the Recovery.* It is frequently said that pro rata recovery may be decreed to prevent the wrongdoers from sharing in the recovery. See, e.g., Atkinson v. Marquart, 112 Ariz. 304, 541 P.2d 556 (1975). However, in most derivative actions the defendants own stock in the corporation, and this in itself seldom leads to pro rata recovery. Nor should it, in the typical case. For example, suppose D, the owner of forty percent of Blue Corporation, is found liable in a derivative suit in the amount of $1 million. If corporate recovery is decreed, D must pay Blue $1 million. Since D "shares" in the recovery, his net output is only $600,000 (assuming that he can recover the balance through a dividend or appreciation in the value of his stock). But if pro rata recovery is decreed, D's output will also be $600,000. Indeed, for reasons of liquidity D may very well prefer the pro rata alternative. The fact that D "shares" in a corporate recovery is therefore not sufficient in itself to justify pro rata relief.

3. *Wrongdoers are Still in Control.* Similarly, it is sometimes said that pro rata recovery is appropriate where the wrongdoers are still in control of the corporation, and therefore would control any corporate recovery. See Backus v. Finkelstein, 23 F.2d 357, 366 (D.C.Minn.1927); Note, 69 Harv.L.Rev. 1314, at 1314–16 (1956). However, derivative actions in situations where the wrongdoers still control the corporation are legion, and pro rata recovery will normally not be decreed on this ground alone.

4. *Most of the Shareholders are Subject to Personal Defenses.* The cases suggest that pro rata relief will be decreed where the great bulk of the corporation's shares are held by persons who could not themselves have brought suit because they are subject to a personal defense. For example, in Young v. Columbia Oil Co., 110 W.Va. 364, 158 S.E. 678 (1931), pro rata recovery was decreed where thirteen of sixteen shareholders were barred by laches or acquiescence, and the remaining three shareholders owned only 145 of the corporation's 5000 outstanding shares. In Joyce v. Congdon, 114 Wash. 239, 195 P. 29 (1921), pro rata recovery was decreed where 423 out of the corporation's 429 shares were owned by either the wrongdoers, persons alleged by the plaintiff to be in collusion with the wrongdoers, or persons who had acquired their stock from the wrongdoers. In Chounis v. Laing, 125 W.Va. 275, 23 S.E.2d 628 (1942), more than ninety-five percent of the shareholders had either ratified or participated in the defendant's wrongful actions. The court held that the ratification was not effective as against innocent minority shareholders, but decreed pro rata relief, excluding all those shareholders who had either participated or ratified. See also, e.g., May v. Midwest Refining Co., 121 F.2d 431 (1st Cir.1941), cert. denied 314 U.S. 668, 62 S.Ct. 129, 86 L.Ed. 534, noted, 30 Calif.L.Rev. 338 (1942).

5. *The Injured Corporation has been Merged.* Still another type of case in which pro rata recovery may be decreed is that in which Corporation A, against whom a wrong was committed, is merged into Corporation B, and some or all of B's shareholders are barred from bringing a derivative suit—for example, because they had all participated in the wrong. In Gabhart v. Gabhart, 267 Ind. 370, 370 N.E.2d 345 (1977) the court said that in such cases, "[s]ince no wrong should be without a remedy a Court of Equity may grant relief, pro-rata, to a former shareholder of a merged corporation, whose equity was adversely affected by the fraudulent act of an officer or director and whose means of redress otherwise would be cut off by the merger, if there is no shareholder of the surviving corporation eligible to maintain a derivative action for such wrong and said shareholder had no prior opportunity for redress by derivative action against either the merged or the surviving corporation."

6. *Residual Cases.* Over the long run, perhaps the most important category of pro rata cases is the residual category where such relief is the most effective technique for dealing with the parties' varying equities on a case-by-case basis. Perlman v. Feldmann, supra Chapter 4, Section 5, is one such case. Another is Rankin v. Frebank Co., 47 Cal.App.3d 75, 121 Cal.Rptr. 348 (1975). Frebank Corporation was engaged in the sale, engineering, research, development, and manufacturing of missile parts and components. It had 200 shares outstanding. In late 1953, McCoy became the owner of 100 shares. The other 100 were owned, thirty-three and one-third shares each, by Bankey, Myers, and Rankin, but for some reason these three shareholders determined to give McCoy the impression that their 100 shares were owned only by Bankey. In September 1954, McCoy and Bankey organized Bancoy Corporation for the purpose of carrying out

the manufacturing aspects of Frebank's business, and each took fifty percent of Bancoy's stock. Aside from taxes, McCoy gained no financial advantage from organizing Bancoy, because he had the same proportionate interest (50%) in both Frebank and Bancoy. Bankey, however, gained a substantial advantage, since instead of having a one-sixth interest in the manufacturing proceeds of Frebank's business, Bankey obtained a one-half interest in Bancoy, in which Rankin and Myers did not share. Subsequently, Rankin and Myers brought a derivative action against Bankey and McCoy for the profits they received from Bancoy. The court began by holding that although Bankey had violated his fiduciary obligations, McCoy had not, because he had acted in good faith and had received no more than what he would have received if Bancoy not been organized. The court then decreed pro rata relief, excluding McCoy:

> [I]t seems inequitable ... [for the funds] acquired by Bankey from Bancoy to be distributed to all of the shareholders of [Frebank]. If this were done, McCoy would receive one-half of these funds despite the fact that he has no right to receive them because he had retained his [50%] proportion of the dividends and retained earnings received from Bancoy. Instead, an equitable distribution of those funds would require that only Bankey, Rankin, and Myers each receive one-third of the dividends and retained earnings received by Bankey from Bancoy. Other courts have been willing to equitably distribute damages in stockholders' derivative actions. (Perlman v. Feldmann (2d Cir.1955) 219 F.2d 173, 178.) There is good reason to do so here....

> This case illustrates that shareholders' derivative suits cannot all be pressed into a single mold.... A rule which permits a court to equitably distribute damages in a derivative action safeguards the interests of creditors while simultaneously protecting the interests of shareholders. We adopt it as the most effective method of accommodating the relevant interests involved in this case.

Id. at 96, 121 Cal.Rptr. at 361–62.

7. *Who Should Participate in the Recovery?* Assuming that pro rata recovery is decreed in derivative action brought on behalf of a *publicly held corporation* (as in Perlman v. Feldmann), who should be allowed to participate in the recovery—those persons who were shareholders at the time of the wrong; those who were shareholders at the time of the complaint; or those who were shareholders at some later time, such as the time of the decision or the decree? In *Perlman* itself, the recovery was distributed to those persons who were shareholders at the time of the decree. See Perlman v. Feldmann, 160 F.Supp. 310 (D.Conn.1958).

SECTION 4.   THE CONTEMPORANEOUS-OWNERSHIP RULE

FEDERAL RULES OF CIVIL PROCEDURE, RULE 23.1

[See Statutory Supplement]

———

DELAWARE GEN. CORP. LAW § 327

[See Statutory Supplement]

———

MODEL BUS. CORP. ACT § 7.41

[See Statutory Supplement]

———

CAL. CORP. CODE § 800(b)(1)

[See Statutory Supplement]

———

ALI, PRINCIPLES OF CORPORATE GOVERNANCE § 7.02(a)

[See Statutory Supplement]

———

Bangor Punta Operations, Inc. v. Bangor & Aroostook R.R.

Supreme Court of the United States, 1974.
417 U.S. 703, 94 S.Ct. 2578, 41 L.Ed.2d 418.

■ MR. JUSTICE POWELL delivered the opinion of the Court....

I

[Prior to October 1964, Bangor & Aroostook Corporation ("B & A") held 98.3% of the stock of the Bangor & Aroostook Railroad Company ("BAR"), a Maine corporation. In October 1964, B & A sold its BAR stock to Bangor Punta, a Delaware corporation. Bangor Punta held the stock for five years, and then sold it in October 1969 to Amoskeag Co. for $5 million. Amoskeag later acquired additional shares which gave it ownership of more than 99% (but less than 100%) of BAR.]*

In 1971, BAR ... filed the present action against Bangor Punta ... in the United States District Court for the District of Maine. The complaint specified 13 counts of alleged mismanagement, misappro-

---

* In the interests of clarity, the statement of facts eliminates subsidiaries that do not figure in the opinion. (Footnote by ed.)

priation, and waste of BAR's corporate assets occurring during the period from 1960 through 1967 when B & A and then Bangor Punta controlled BAR.[1] Damages were sought in the amount of $7,000,000 for violations of both federal and state laws. The federal statutes and regulations alleged to have been violated included § 10 of the Clayton Act, 15 U.S.C.A. § 20; § 10(b) of the Securities Exchange Act of 1934, 15 U.S.C.A. § 78j(b); and Rule 10b–5.... The state claims were grounded on § 104 of the Maine Public Utilities Act, Maine Rev.Stat. Ann., Tit. 35, § 104 (1965), and the common law of Maine.

The complaint focused on four intercompany transactions which allegedly resulted in injury to BAR. Counts I and II averred that B & A, and later Bangor Punta, overcharged BAR for various legal, accounting, printing, and other services. Counts III, IV, V, and VI averred that B & A improperly acquired the stock of the St. Croix Paper Co. which BAR owned through its subsidiary. Counts VII, VIII, IX, and X charged that B & A and Bangor Punta improperly caused BAR to declare special dividends to its stockholders, including B & A and Bangor Punta, and also caused BAR's subsidiary to borrow in order to pay regular dividends. Counts XI, XII, and XIII charged that B & A improperly caused BAR to excuse payment by B & A and Bangor Punta of the interest due on a loan made by BAR to B & A. In sum, the complaint alleged that during the period of their control of BAR, Bangor Punta, and its predecessor in interest B & A, "exploited it solely for their own purposes" and "calculatedly drained the resources of BAR in violation of law for their own benefit."

The District Court granted petitioners' motion for summary judgment and dismissed the action. 353 F.Supp. 724 (1972). The court first observed that although the suit purported to be a primary action brought in the name of the corporation, the real party in interest and hence the actual beneficiary of any recovery, was Amoskeag, the present owner of more than 99% of the outstanding stock of BAR. The court then noted that Amoskeag had acquired all of its BAR stock long after the alleged wrongs occurred and that Amoskeag did not contend that it had not received full value for its purchase price, or that the purchase transaction was tainted by fraud or deceit. Thus, any recovery on Amoskeag's part would constitute a windfall because it had sustained no injury. With this in mind, the court then addressed the claims based on federal law and determined that Amoskeag would have been barred from maintaining a shareholder derivative action because of its failure to satisfy the "contemporaneous ownership" requirement of Fed.Rule Civ.Proc. 23.1(1).[3] Finding that equitable

---

1. Several of the alleged acts of corporate mismanagement occurred between 1960 and 1964 when B & A ... was in control of the railroad. Liability for these acts was nevertheless sought to be imposed on Bangor Punta, even though it had no interest in either BAR or B & A during this period. The apparent basis for liability was the 1964 purchase agreement between B & A and Bangor Punta. The complaint in the instant case alleged that under the agreement Bangor Punta, through its subsidiary, assumed "all ... debts, obligations, contracts and liabilities" of B & A.

3. Rule 23.1(1), which specifies the requirements applicable to shareholder derivative actions, states that the complaint shall aver that "the plaintiff was a shareholder or member at the time of the transaction of principles prevented the use of the corporate fiction to evade the proscription of Rule 23.1, the court concluded that Amoskeag's efforts to recover under the Securities Exchange Act and the Clayton Act must fail. Turning to the claims based on state law, the court recognized that the applicability of Rule 23.1(1) has been questioned where federal jurisdiction is based on diversity of citizenship.[4] The court found it unnecessary to resolve this issue, however, since its examination of state law indicated that Maine probably followed the "prevailing rule" requiring contemporaneous ownership in order to maintain a shareholder derivative action. Thus, whether the federal rule or state substantive law applied, the present action could not be maintained.

The United States Court of Appeals for the First Circuit reversed....

We granted petitioners' application for certiorari. 414 U.S. 1127 (1974). We now reverse.

II

A

We first turn to the question whether respondent corporations* may maintain the present action under § 10 of the Clayton Act, 15 U.S.C.A. § 20, and § 10(b) of the Securities Exchange Act of 1934, 15 U.S.C.A. § 78j(b), and Rule 10b–5, 17 CFR § 240.10b–5. The resolution of this issue depends upon the applicability of the settled principle of equity that a shareholder may not complain of acts of corporate mismanagement if he acquired his shares from those who participated or acquiesced in the allegedly wrongful transactions. See, e.g., Bloodworth v. Bloodworth, 225 Ga. 379, 387, 169 S.E.2d 150, 156–157 (1969)....[5] This principle has been invoked with special force where a shareholder purchases all or substantially all the shares of a corporation from a vendor at a fair price, and then seeks to have the corporation recover against that vendor for prior corporate mismanagement. See, e.g., Matthews v. Headley Chocolate Co., 130 Md. 523, 532–535, 100 A. 645, 650–651 (1917); Home Fire Insurance Co. v. Barber, 67 Neb. 644, 661–662, 93 N.W. 1024, 1030–1031 (1903). See also Amen v. Black, 234 F.2d 12, 23 (C.A.10 1956). The equitable considerations precluding recovery in such cases were explicated long ago by Dean (then Commissioner) Roscoe Pound in Home Fire

which he complains...." This provision is known as the "contemporaneous ownership" requirement. See 3B J. Moore, Federal Practice § 23.1 et seq. (2d ed. 1974).

4. The "contemporaneous ownership" requirement in shareholder derivative actions was first announced in Hawes v. Oakland, 104 U.S. 450, 26 L.Ed. 827 (1881), and soon thereafter adopted as Equity Rule 97. This provision was later incorporated in Equity Rule 27 and finally in the present Rule 23.1. After the decision in Erie R. Co. v. Tompkins, 304 U.S. 64, 58 S.Ct. 817, 82 L.Ed. 1188 (1938), the question arose whether the contemporaneous-ownership requirement was one of procedure or substantive law. If the

requirement were substantive, then under the regime of *Erie* it could not be validly applied in federal diversity cases where state law permitted a noncontemporaneous shareholder to maintain a derivative action. See 3B J. Moore, Federal Practice §§ 23.1.01–23.1.15[2] (2d ed. 1974). Although most cases treat the requirement as one of procedure, this Court has never resolved the issue. Ibid.

* The respondents were BAR and a wholly owned subsidiary. (Footnote by ed.)

5. This principle obtains in the great majority of jurisdictions. See, e.g., Russell v. Louis Melind Co., 331 Ill.App. 182, 72 N.E.2d 869 (1947).

Insurance Co. v. Barber, supra. Dean Pound, writing for the Supreme Court of Nebraska, observed that the shareholders of the plaintiff corporation in that case had sustained no injury since they had acquired their shares from the alleged wrongdoers after the disputed transactions occurred and had received full value for their purchase price. Thus, any recovery on their part would constitute a windfall, for it would enable them to obtain funds to which they had no just title or claim. Moreover, it would in effect allow the shareholders to recoup a large part of the price they agreed to pay for their shares, notwithstanding the fact that they received all they had bargained for. Finally, it would permit the shareholders to reap a profit from wrongs done to others, thus encouraging further such speculation. Dean Pound stated that these consequences rendered any recovery highly inequitable and mandated dismissal of the suit.

The considerations supporting the *Home Fire* principle are especially pertinent in the present case. As the District Court pointed out, Amoskeag, the present owner of more than 99% of the BAR shares, would be the principal beneficiary of any recovery obtained by BAR. Amoskeag, however, acquired 98.3% of the outstanding shares of BAR from petitioner Bangor Punta in 1969, well after the alleged wrongs were said to have occurred. Amoskeag does not contend that the purchase transaction was tainted by fraud or deceit, or that it received less than full value for its money. Indeed, it does not assert that it has sustained any injury at all. Nor does it appear that the alleged acts of prior mismanagement have had any continuing effect on the corporations involved or the value of their shares.[6] Nevertheless, by causing the present action to be brought in the name of respondent corporations, Amoskeag seeks to recover indirectly an amount equal to the $5,000,000 it paid for its stock, plus an additional $2,000,000. All this would be in the form of damages for wrongs petitioner Bangor Punta is said to have inflicted, not upon Amoskeag, but upon respondent corporations during the period in which Bangor Punta owned 98.3% of the BAR shares. In other words, Amoskeag seeks to recover for wrongs Bangor Punta did to *itself* as owner of the railroad.[7] At the same time it reaps this windfall, Amoskeag desires to retain all its BAR stock. Under *Home Fire,* it is evident that Amoskeag would have no standing in equity to maintain the present action.[8]

We are met with the argument, however, that since the present action is brought in the name of respondent corporations, we may not

6. In *Home Fire,* Dean Pound suggested that equitable principles might not prevent recovery where the effects of the wrongful acts continued and resulted in injury to present shareholders. 67 Neb. 644, 662, 93 N.W. 1024, 1031. In their complaint in the instant case, respondents alleged that "[t]he injury to BAR is a continuing one surviving the aforesaid sale [from petitioner BPO] to Amoskeag." The District Court noted that respondents alleged no facts to support this contention and therefore found any such exception inapplicable. 353 F.Supp. 724, 727 n. 1 (1972). Respondents apparently did not renew this contention on appeal.

7. Similarly, as to the period before October 1964, Amoskeag seeks to recover for wrongs B & A and its shareholders did to *themselves* as owners of the railroad.

8. Conceding the lack of equity in any recovery by Amoskeag, the dissent argues that the present action can nevertheless be maintained because there are 20 minority shareholders, holding less than 1% of the BAR stock, who owned their shares "during the period from 1960 through 1967 when the transactions underlying the railroad's complaint took place, and who still owned that stock in 1971 when the complaint was filed."

look behind the corporate entity to the true substance of the claims and the actual beneficiaries. The established law is to the contrary. Although a corporation and its shareholders are deemed separate entities for most purposes, the corporate form may be disregarded in the interests of justice where it is used to defeat an overriding public policy. New Colonial Ice Co. v. Helvering, 292 U.S. 435, 442, 54 S.Ct. 788, 78 L.Ed. 1348 (1934); Chicago, M. & St. P.R. Co. v. Minneapolis Civic Assn., 247 U.S. 490, 501, 38 S.Ct. 553, 62 L.Ed. 1229 (1918). In such cases, courts of equity, piercing all fictions and disguises, will deal with the substance of the action and not blindly adhere to the corporate form. Thus, where equity would preclude the shareholders from maintaining an action in their own right, the corporation would also be precluded. Amen v. Black, supra; Capitol Wine & Spirit Corp. v. Pokrass, 277 App.Div. 184, 98 N.Y.S.2d 291 (1950), aff'd, 302 N.Y. 734, 98 N.E.2d 704 (1951); Matthews v. Headley Chocolate Co., supra; Home Fire Insurance Co. v. Barber, supra. It follows that Amoskeag, the principal beneficiary of any recovery and itself estopped from complaining of petitioners' alleged wrongs, cannot avoid the command of equity through the guise of proceeding in the name of respondent corporations which it owns and controls.

B

Respondents fare no better in their efforts to maintain the present actions under state law, specifically § 104 of the Maine Public Utilities Act, Maine Rev.Stat.Ann., Tit. 35, § 104 (1965), and the common law of Maine. In Forbes v. Wells Beach Casino, Inc., 307 A.2d 210, 223 n. 10 (1973), the Maine Supreme Judicial Court recently declared that it had long accepted the equitable principle that a "stockholder has no standing if either he or his vendor participated or acquiesced in the wrong...." See Hyams v. Old Dominion Co., 113 Me. 294, 302, 93 A. 747, 750 (1915).[9] ...

III

In reaching the contrary conclusion, the Court of Appeals stated that it could not accept the proposition that Amoskeag would be the

---

... The dissent would conclude that the existence of these innocent minority shareholders entitled BAR, and hence Amoskeag, to recover the entire $7,000,000 amount of alleged damages.

Aside from the illogic of such an approach, the dissent's position is at war with the precedents, for the *Home Fire* principle has long been applied to preclude full recovery by a corporation even where there are innocent minority shareholders who acquired their shares prior to the alleged wrongs. See cases cited at n. 5, supra, and accompanying text. The dissent also mistakes the factual posture of this case, since the respondent corporations did not institute this action for the benefit of the minority shareholders. See discussion at n. 15, infra.

9. In addition, the new Maine Business Corporation Act adopts the contemporaneous-ownership requirement for shareholder derivative actions. See Maine Rev.Stat.Ann., Tit. 13–A, § 627.1.A (1974). This provision apparently became effective two days after the present action was filed. As the District Court noted, it is an open question whether Maine in fact had a contemporaneous-ownership requirement prior to that time. 353 F.Supp., at 727. See R. Field, V. McKusick & L. Wroth, Maine Civil Practice § 23.2, p. 393 (2d ed. 1970). In the absence of any indication that Maine would not have followed the "prevailing view," the District Court determined that the contemporaneous-ownership requirement of Fed.Rule Civ.Proc. 23.1 applied.

"sole beneficiary" of any recovery by BAR. 482 F.2d, at 868. The court noted that in view of the railroad's status as a "quasi-public" corporation and the essential nature of the services it provides, the public had an identifiable interest in BAR's financial health. Thus, any recovery by BAR would accrue to the benefit of the public through the improvement in BAR's economic position and the quality of its services. The court thought that this factor rendered any windfall to Amoskeag irrelevant.

At the outset, we note that the Court of Appeals' assumption that any recovery would necessarily benefit the public is unwarranted. As that court explicitly recognized, any recovery by BAR could be diverted to its shareholders, namely Amoskeag, rather than re-invested in the railroad for the benefit of the public. . . .

The Court of Appeals' position also appears to overlook the fact that Amoskeag, the actual beneficiary of any recovery through its ownership of more than 99% of the BAR shares, would be unjustly enriched since it has sustained no injury. . . .

The Court of Appeals further stated that it was important to insure that petitioners would not be immune from liability for their wrongful conduct and noted that BAR's recovery would provide a needed deterrent to mismanagement of railroads. Our difficulty with this argument is that it proves too much. If deterrence were the only objective, then in logic any plaintiff willing to file a complaint would suffice. No injury or violation of a legal duty to the particular plaintiff would have to be alleged. The only prerequisite would be that the plaintiff agree to accept the recovery, lest the supposed wrongdoer be allowed to escape a reckoning. Suffice it to say that we have been referred to no authority which would support so novel a result, and we decline to adopt it.

We therefore conclude that respondent corporations may not maintain the present action.[15] The judgment of the Court of Appeals is reversed.

■ MR. JUSTICE MARSHALL, with whom MR. JUSTICE DOUGLAS, MR. JUSTICE BRENNAN, and MR. JUSTICE WHITE join, dissenting. . . .

---

15. Our decision rests on the conclusion that equitable principles preclude recovery by Amoskeag, the present owner of more than 99% of the BAR shares. The record does not reveal whether the minority shareholders who hold the remaining fraction of 1% of the BAR shares stand in the same position as Amoskeag. Some courts have adopted the concept of a pro-rata recovery where there are innocent minority shareholders. Under this procedure, damages are distributed to the minority shareholders individually on a proportional basis, even though the action is brought in the name of the corporation to enforce primary rights. See, e.g., Matthews v. Headley Chocolate Co., 130 Md. 523, 536–540, 100 A. 645, 650–652 (1917). In the present case, respondents have expressly disavowed any intent to obtain a pro-rata recovery on behalf of the 1% minority shareholders of BAR. We therefore do not reach the question whether such recovery would be appropriate.

The dissent asserts that the alleged acts of corporate mismanagement have placed BAR "close to the brink of bankruptcy" and that the present action is maintained for the benefit of BAR's creditors. . . . With all respect, it appears that the dissent has sought to redraft respondents' complaint. As the District Court noted, respondents have not brought this action on behalf of any creditors. 353 F.Supp., at 726. Indeed, they have never so contended. Moreover, respondents have conceded that the financial health of the railroad is excellent. Tr. of Oral Arg. 18.

The majority places primary reliance on Dean Pound's decision in Home Fire Insurance Co. v. Barber, supra. In that case, *all* of the shares of the plaintiff corporation had been acquired from the alleged wrongdoers after the transactions giving rise to the causes of action stated in the complaint. Since none of the corporation's shareholders held stock at the time of the alleged wrongful transactions, none had been injured thereby. Dean Pound therefore held that equity barred the corporation from pursuing a claim where none of its shareholders could complain of injury.

Dean Pound thought it clear, however, that the opposite result would obtain if *any* of the present shareholders

> "are entitled to complain of the acts of the defendant and of his past management of the company; for if any of them are so entitled, there can be no doubt of the right and duty of the corporation to maintain this suit. It would be maintainable in such a case even though the wrongdoers continued to be stockholders and would share in the proceeds." 67 Neb., at 655, 93 N.W., at 1028.

Cf. Capitol Wine & Spirit Corp. v. Pokrass, 277 App.Div. 184, 186, 98 N.Y.S.2d 291, 293 (1950), aff'd, 302 N.Y. 734, 98 N.E.2d 704 (1951).

The rationale for the distinction drawn by Dean Pound is simple enough. The sole shareholder who defrauds or mismanages his own corporation hurts only himself. For the corporation to sue him for his wrongs is simply to take money out of his right pocket and put it in his left. It is therefore appropriate for equity to intervene to pierce the corporate veil. But where there are minority shareholders, misappropriation and conversion of corporate assets injure their interests as well as the interest of the majority shareholder. The law imposes upon the directors of a corporation a fiduciary obligation to all of the corporation's shareholders, and part of that obligation is to use due care to ensure that the corporation seek redress where a majority shareholder has drained the corporation's resources for his own benefit and to the detriment of minority shareholders.[1] . . .

———

Rifkin v. Steele Platt

Colorado Court of Appeals, 1991.
824 P.2d 32.

■ Opinion by JUDGE PLANK.

Defendants, Steele Platt and Fas–Wok, Inc. (sellers), appeal the judgment of the trial court in favor of the corporate plaintiff, The

---

1. Under a separate rule, the plaintiff must be a shareholder at the time the action is brought. See Note on Who Can Bring a Derivative Action, Section 1, supra. The two rules are bridged by a third rule requiring that the plaintiff's ownership between the time of the wrong and the time of the suit must be uninterrupted. Vista Fund v. Garis, 277 N.W.2d 19 (Minn.1979); Gresov v. Shattuck Denn Mining Corp., 40 Misc.2d 569, 243 N.Y.S.2d 760 (1963).

Boiler Room, Inc. (the corporation). Plaintiffs cross-appeal the award of damages. We affirm in part and remand for further proceedings consistent with this opinion.

This matter involves the sale of the controlling shares of the corporation, which owns a restaurant of the same name located in the Tivoli Shopping Center in Denver, Colorado. Plaintiffs include the corporation and its present principal shareholders, Robert C. Rifkin, Gerald N. Kernis, and Gary G. Kortz (buyers). Sellers are the former controlling shareholders.

Buyers and sellers executed a Stock Purchase Agreement to effectuate the sale of the corporation. After the closing, the buyers discovered inaccuracies in financial representations made in the agreement. Consequently, they filed suit against the sellers asserting claims of breach of contract, breach of good faith, breach of fiduciary duty, and unjust enrichment.

The complaint alleged, in part, that Platt, as officer and director of the corporation, had misappropriated funds from it and that certain assets on the balance sheet were actually owned by Platt or other entities that he controlled. Sellers counterclaimed seeking rescission of the agreement.

After a trial to the court, judgment was entered in favor of the buyers on the breach of contract claim and the corporation on the breach of fiduciary duty claim. The court also awarded attorney fees pursuant to the agreement. Sellers do not appeal that part of the judgment concerning the breach of contract claim. . . .

Sellers . . . contend that the trial court erred in awarding the corporation damages for breach of fiduciary duty for conduct which occurred prior to buyers' acquisition of stock. They cite *Bangor Punta Operations, Inc. v. Bangor & Aroostook R. Co.,* 417 U.S. 703, 94 S.Ct. 2578, 41 L.Ed.2d 418 (1974) in support of this argument. We agree that *Bangor Punta* raises issues which must be resolved in this matter.

In *Bangor Punta,* the new shareholders of the corporation, in the name of the corporation, sought damages from the former shareholders for violations of state and federal law which occurred before the sale. The United States Supreme Court held that the corporation could not maintain the action for wrongs that occurred before the new shareholders' acquisition of the shares. The court reasoned that the real parties that would gain from a successful lawsuit would be the new shareholders. It presumed that the purchase price that they paid reflected the prior wrongdoings. Thus, the shareholders would improperly receive a windfall if allowed to recover damages.

Here, it is undisputed that the acts which constituted Platt's breach of fiduciary duty occurred prior to the buyers' acquisition of stock in The Boiler Room. However, the parties dispute whether the purchase price reflected the prior wrongdoings. The trial court did not make a finding on this issue. Therefore, we remand it to the trial court for further findings. *See El Dorado Bancshares v. Martin,* 701 F.Supp. 1515 (D.Kan.1988).

If on review the court finds that the price, in fact, reflected Platt's wrongdoings, it must dismiss the breach of fiduciary duty claim. If, on the other hand, it finds that the purchase price of the shares did not reflect the wrongdoings, then the corporation's previous damage award may stand. . . .

■ HUME and NEY, JJ., concur.

———

NOTE ON THE CONTEMPORANEOUS–OWNERSHIP RULE

1.   *The Basic Rule and Three Standard Exceptions.* At early common law, the cases were divided on whether a shareholder was barred from bringing a derivative action if he was not a "contemporaneous shareholder"—that is, if he did not hold his shares when the wrong occurred. Today, however, most jurisdictions have adopted some version of the contemporaneous-ownership rule by case-law, statute, or court rule. The rule is subject to several important exceptions:

(a) Devolution by Operation of Law. A non-contemporaneous shareholder is normally allowed to bring a derivative action if his shares devolved upon him "by operation of law"—for example, by inheritance. (This exception is sometimes made applicable only where the shares have devolved from a person who was a shareholder at the time of the wrong.)

(b) Continuing–Wrong Theory. Under the continuing-wrong theory, a plaintiff can bring an action to challenge a wrong that began before he acquired his shares but continued thereafter. In principle this may not seem to be an exception at all, since the plaintiff is only complaining about what happened after he became a shareholder. In practice, however, it is often difficult to distinguish between a wrongful continuing course of conduct, on the one hand, and the continued effect of a completed wrongful transaction, on the other. Therefore, while the continuing-wrong exception is widely accepted in principle, in practice there is considerable divergence in the way it is applied, and different cases often seem to come out differently on virtually the same facts.

For example, in Forbes v. Wells Beach Casino, Inc., 307 A.2d 210 (Me.1973), the continuing-wrong theory was deemed applicable, and the plaintiff was allowed to bring suit, where the plaintiff had purchased his stock after a fiduciary had wrongfully taken possession of corporate property, but while the fiduciary continued to hold the property. In contrast, in Weinhaus v. Gale, 237 F.2d 197 (7th Cir. 1956), the continuing-wrong theory was deemed inapplicable, and the plaintiff was not allowed to bring suit, where the plaintiff had purchased his stock after a subsidiary had sold stock to its parent at a price alleged to be unfairly low, but before the parent had resold the stock. In Palmer v. Morris, 316 F.2d 649 (5th Cir.1963), the continuing-wrong theory was deemed applicable, and the plaintiff was allowed to bring suit, where the plaintiff had purchased his stock after an allegedly wrongful deal had been made, but while payments under the deal continued. In contrast, in Chaft v. Kass, 19 A.D.2d 610, 241 N.Y.S.2d 284 (1963), the continuing-wrong theory was deemed inapplicable, and the plaintiff was not allowed to bring suit, where the plaintiff purchased his stock after the corporation had entered into an allegedly invalid contract, but while payments under the contract were still being made.

Several statutes provide that the plaintiff must allege that he was a shareholder at the time of the transaction "or any part thereof." E.g., Cal. § 800(b)(1); Wis. § 180.405. Where there is a close question whether the continuing-wrong theory applies to a given case, such a statute might tip the scale in the plaintiff's favor.

(c) Section 16(b). Despite the fact that FRCP 23.1 contains a contemporaneous-ownership rule, it has been held that a non-contemporaneous shareholder can bring a derivative action to recover short-swing profits under § 16(b) of the 1934 Securities Exchange Act. See, e.g., Blau v. Mission Corp., 212 F.2d 77, 79 (2d Cir.1954), cert. denied 347 U.S. 1016, 74 S.Ct. 872, 98 L.Ed. 1138. The theory is that FRCP 23.1 "cannot, even if so perhaps intended, override the direct mandate of § 16(b) that suit may be brought 'by the owner of any security' without qualification." Blau v. Mission Corp., supra.

2. *Federalism.* In footnote 4 of *Bangor Punta,* the Court adverted to the question whether Erie v. Tompkins prohibits application of the contemporaneous-ownership requirement of FRCP 23.1 to a diversity action in cases where the forum state does not impose such a requirement. In Cohen v. Beneficial Industrial Loan Corp., 337 U.S. 541, 556, 69 S.Ct. 221, 1238, 93 L.Ed. 1528, 1541 (1949), the Supreme Court stated in dicta that the contemporaneous-ownership requirements under the Federal Rules was "procedural." The principles that determine whether a legal rule is procedural or substantive have changes since *Cohen* was decided. In Hanna v. Plumer, 380 U.S. 460, 472, 85 S.Ct. 1136, 14 L.Ed.2d 8 (1965), the Court held that when the applicability of a federal rule of civil procedure to a diversity action is involved, the question is not simply whether the rule is "substantive" or "procedural" within the meaning of *Erie,* but whether it is authorized by the Rules Enabling Act.[1] A rule could be authorized by that Act, the Court concluded, even though it might be considered substantive. "[T]he constitutional provision for a federal court system (augmented by the Necessary and Proper Clause) carries with it congressional power to make rules governing the practice and pleadings in those courts, which in turn includes a power to regulate matters which, though falling within the uncertain area between substance and procedure, are rationally capable of classification as either." In Kona Enterprises, Inc. v. Estate of Bishop, 179 F.3d 767, 769 (9th Cir. 1999), the

---

1. 28 U.S.C.A. § 2072. Under that Act, the Supreme Court is empowered "to prescribe, by general rules ... the practice and procedure of the district courts.... Such rules shall not abridge, enlarge or modify any substantive right...."

court held that the federal contemporaneous-ownership rule was applicable in diversity cases.

3. *Special Problems and Special Solutions.* Several cases prior to *Bangor Punta* had applied the principle of the contemporaneous-ownership rule to bar corporate recovery when *all* of the corporation's shareholders had purchased their stock after the wrong had been committed. See, e.g., Capitol Wine & Spirit Corp. v. Pokrass, 277 App.Div. 184, 98 N.Y.S.2d 291 (1950), aff'd per curiam 302 N.Y. 734, 98 N.E.2d 704 (1951). Suppose a large proportion of a corporation's stock is held by noncontemporaneous shareholders, but more than a minimal amount of stock is held by contemporaneous shareholders? It has been suggested that in such cases the court might impose liability but limit damages by granting pro rata relief to the contemporaneous shareholders.

For example, suppose A and B each own 50% of Blue Corporation. Among Blue's assets is a property, Appleacre, that is carried on the books at $1 million but is really worth $2 million. A, as Blue's active manager, knows Appleacre's real value; B, as a passive investor, does not. A causes Blue to sell Appleacre to him for $1 million. A then sells his Blue stock to C for a fair price based on Blue's assets at the time of sale. Subsequently, B and C learn the real value of Appleacre, and cause Blue Corporation to bring an action against A based on unfair self-dealing. Here a corporate recovery of $1 million by Blue Corporation seems inappropriate. C, the owner of Blue, has no injury, because he paid fair value for Blue stock, based on the value of Blue's assets at the time he purchased the stock. Therefore, a $1 million recovery for Blue would give C a windfall of $500,000. The real loser is B, whose Blue stock is worth $500,000 less than it was before A bought Appleacre. If A had given B $500,000 at the time he purchased Appleacre for $1 Million, B would have suffered no injury. Accordingly, one way to adjust the equities of the parties is to allow *suit* by (or in the right of) Blue, but limit *relief* to pro rata recovery by B in the amount of $500,000.

This technique, however, will not work in all cases. For example, suppose that after the Appleacre transaction, A and B *both* sell their stock to C for a fair price based on the value of Blue's assets at the time of the sale of stock. Here either a corporate recovery or a pro rata recovery by Blue's present shareholder, C, would give C a windfall gain of $1 million. Suit by Blue (or in its name) with pro rata recovery by B also will not work: C has no economic incentive to cause Blue to bring such a suit, and B cannot bring suit on Blue's behalf because he is no longer a Blue shareholder. (See Note on Who Can Bring a Derivative Action, Section 1, supra.) In Watson v. Button, 235 F.2d 235 (9th Cir.1956), the court held, on comparable facts, that B could sue A *directly.* "Suits against directors for violations of fiduciary duties are equitable in nature. It is unlikely that the Oregon courts would allow a director to misappropriate funds and leave those injured without a remedy."

SECTION 5. THE RIGHT TO TRIAL BY JURY IN DERIVATIVE ACTIONS

———

NOTE ON THE RIGHT TO TRIAL BY JURY IN DERIVATIVE ACTIONS

Since a derivative action has traditionally been conceived as an equitable remedy, until recently it did not carry the right to a trial by jury. In 1970, however, the Supreme Court held in Ross v. Bernhard, 396 U.S. 531, 90 S.Ct. 733, 24 L.Ed.2d 729 that under the Seventh Amendment to the federal Constitution, in a derivative action brought in federal court the parties have a right to a jury where the action would be triable to a jury if it had been brought by the corporation itself, rather than by a shareholder:

> We have noted that the derivative suit has dual aspects: first, the stockholder's right to sue on behalf of the corporation, historically an equitable matter; second, the claim of the corporation against directors or third parties on which, if the corporation had sued and the claim presented legal issues, the company could demand a jury trial.... [L]egal claims are not magically converted into equitable issues by their presentation to a court of equity in a derivative suit. The claim pressed by the stockholder against directors or third parties "is not his own but the corporation's." ... The heart of the action is the corporate claim. If it presents a legal issue, one entitling the corporation to a jury trial under the Seventh Amendment, the right to a jury is not forfeited merely because the stockholder's right to sue must first be adjudicated as an equitable issue triable to the court.[1]

The question remains, what kinds of derivative actions are legal, and what kinds are equitable, within the meaning of *Ross?* Two passages in that opinion are suggestive. First:

> [T]he "legal" nature of an issue is determined by considering, first, the pre-merger custom with reference to such questions; second, the remedy sought; and, third, the practical abilities and limitations of juries. Of these factors, the first, requiring extensive and possibly abstruse historical inquiry, is obviously the most difficult to apply....

Id. at 538 n. 10, 90 S.Ct. at 738 n. 10. And second:

> In the instant case we have no doubt that the corporation's claim is, at least in part, a legal one. The relief sought is money

---

1. Id. at 538–39, 90 S.Ct. at 738. It is reported that after Ross v. Bernhard was decided, several cases were settled in which the defendants would have gone to trial had the case been triable to the judge. Rosenfeld, Plaintiff's Strategy in Prosecuting and Defending Stockholders Suits 241, 250 (S. Wechsler ed. 1972).

damages. There are allegations in the complaint of a breach of fiduciary duty, but there are also allegations of ordinary breach of contract and gross negligence. The corporation, had it sued on its own behalf, would have been entitled to a jury's determination, at a minimum, of its damages against its broker under the brokerage contract and of its rights against its own directors because of their negligence. Under these circumstances it is unnecessary to decide whether the corporation's other claims are also properly triable to a jury. Dairy Queen, Inc. v. Wood, 369 U.S. 469, 82 S.Ct. 894, 8 L.Ed.2d 44 (1962)....

Id. at 542–43, 90 S.Ct. at 740. (The citation to *Dairy Queen* apparently refers to the holding in that decision that legal claims must be submitted to a jury even where a case also involves equitable claims.) For further treatment of this issue, see Dasho v. Susquehanna Corp., 461 F.2d 11 (7th Cir.1972), cert. denied 408 U.S. 925, 92 S.Ct. 2496, 33 L.Ed.2d 336.

The Seventh Amendment applies only to federal proceedings. State-court decisions vary. Professor DeMott comments, "Ten states have directly resolved this issue. Cases in four states—Alabama, Alaska, New Mexico, and New York—hold that parties to a derivative action have a right to trial by jury if the underlying corporate claim asserted by the plaintiff on the corporation's behalf would have entitled the corporation to a jury trial, that is, if the corporation had itself brought an action to enforce the claim. The dispositive Wyoming case examines the substantive issues raised by the complaint, along with the relief demanded, to determine whether the suit is primarily equitable in nature and thus not susceptible to a jury trial. In Arkansas, California, Florida, Iowa, and Massachusetts, the form of the action is dispositive: even when the substantive claim involves a legal rather than an equitable claim, the equitable nature of a derivative suit excludes any right to a jury trial.... The authority on this question is less direct in other states. In Delaware, language in one opinion could be understood to imply that a right to a jury trial is not available in derivative actions. In five other states, there are cases in which the circumstances arguably provide a basis for inferring that a right to jury trial does exist." Deborah DeMott, Shareholder Derivative Actions § 4:18 (2003).

SECTION 6.   DEMAND ON THE BOARD AND TERMINATION OF DERIVATIVE ACTIONS ON THE RECOMMENDATION OF THE BOARD OR A COMMITTEE

CAL. CORP. CODE § 800(b)(2)

[See Statutory Supplement]

FEDERAL RULES OF CIVIL PROCEDURE RULE 23.1

[See Statutory Supplement]

———

INTRODUCTORY NOTE

Until about the 1970s, it was well settled that before bringing a derivative action, a shareholder was required to make a demand on the board, unless demand was excused. However, two related issues were much less settled. The first issue was, when was demand on the board excused? The general rule was that demand was excused if it was futile. The most important application of this rule was that demand was excused as futile if a majority of the directors were interested. It was not clear, however, what constituted *interest* for these matters. For example, it was not clear whether a director was interested merely because he or she was named as a defendant, and if not, how much more had to be shown.

The second unsettled issue was the consequence of *not* making demand. In most of the reported cases, demand had not been made, and the corporation moved to dismiss the action on the ground that demand was required. The courts in such cases often simply held that demand was or was not required, without getting into what consequences would follow if a required demand was made and rejected—although some courts did say or hold that if demand was required and rejected, and the rejection was by disinterested directors who constituted a majority of the board, a derivative action could not proceed unless in rejecting demand the board violated the business judgment rule.

The picture was further complicated in the 1970s, when a series of cases held that even when a majority of directors were interested, so that demand was not required, the board could appoint a committee to consider whether the derivative action was in the best interests of the corporation. If the committee concluded that the action was not in the corporation's best interests, and the committee had engaged in an adequate investigation, the court could dismiss the action on the committee's motion, subject to a designated standard of review. If the board was disinterested, the board itself could conduct the investigation and make the motion.

In short, as of the 1970s a cluster of related issues were raised concerning the role and power of the board in derivative actions. When was demand on the board excused? What were the consequences if demand was required, made, and denied? What, if anything, could a board do if demand was excused?

It was against this background that the cases in this Section were decided.

———

Marx v. Akers

New York Court of Appeals, 1996.
88 N.Y.2d 189, 644 N.Y.S.2d 121, 666 N.E.2d 1034.

◼ JUDGES: Opinion by JUDGE SMITH. CHIEF JUDGE KAYE and JUDGES SIMONS, TITONE, LEVINE and CIPARICK concur. JUDGE BELLACOSA took no part.

◼ SMITH, J.:

Plaintiff commenced this shareholder derivative action against International Business Machines Corporation (IBM) and IBM's board of directors without first demanding that the board initiate a lawsuit. The amended complaint (complaint) alleges that the board wasted corporate assets by awarding excessive compensation to IBM's executives and outside directors. The issues raised on this appeal are whether the Appellate Division abused its discretion by dismissing plaintiff's complaint for failure to make a demand and whether plaintiff's complaint fails to state a cause of action. We affirm the order of the Appellate Division because we conclude that plaintiff was not excused from making a demand with respect to the executive compensation claim and that plaintiff has failed to state a cause of action for corporate waste in connection with the allegations concerning payments to IBM's outside directors.

Facts and Procedural History

The complaint alleges that during a period of declining profitability at IBM the director defendants engaged in self-dealing by awarding excessive compensation to the 15 outside directors on the 18–member board. Although the complaint identifies only one of the three inside directors as an IBM executive (defendant Akers is identified as a former chief executive officer of IBM), plaintiff also appears to allege that the director defendants violated their fiduciary duties to IBM by voting for unreasonably high compensation for IBM executives.[2]

Defendants moved to dismiss the complaint for (1) failure to state a cause of action, and (2) failure to serve a demand on IBM's board to initiate a lawsuit based on the complaint's allegations. The Supreme Court dismissed, holding that plaintiff failed to establish the futility of a demand. Supreme Court concluded that excusing a demand here would render Business Corporation Law § 626(c) "virtually meaningless in any shareholders' derivative action in which all members of a corporate board are named as defendants." Having decided the demand issue in favor of defendants, the court did not reach the issue of whether plaintiff's complaint stated a cause of action. The Appellate Division affirmed the dismissal, concluding that the complaint did not contain any details from which the futility of a demand could be inferred. The Appellate Division found that plaintiff's objections to the

---

2. Executives at IBM are compensated through a fixed salary and performance incentives. Payouts on the performance incentives are based on IBM's earnings per share, return on equity and cash flow. Plaintiff's complaint criticizes only the performance incentive component of executive compensation as excessive because of certain accounting practices which plaintiff alleges artificially inflate earnings, return on equity and cash flow.

level of compensation were not stated with sufficient particularity in light of statutory authority permitting directors to set their own compensation.

Background

A shareholder's derivative action is an action "brought in the right of a domestic or foreign corporation to procure a judgment in its favor, by a holder of shares or of voting trust certificates of the corporation or of a beneficial interest in such shares or certificates" (Business Corporation Law § 626[a]). "Derivative claims against corporate directors belong to the corporation itself" (Auerbach v. Bennett, 47 N.Y. 2d 619, 631).

> "The remedy sought is for wrong done to the corporation; the primary cause of action belongs to the corporation; recovery must enure to the benefit of the corporation. The stockholder brings the action, in behalf of others similarly situated, to vindicate the corporate rights and a judgment on the merits is a binding adjudication of these rights (citations omitted)" (Isaac v. Marcus, 258 N.Y. 257, 264).

... Business Corporation Law § 626(c) provides that in any shareholders' derivative action, "the complaint shall set forth with particularity the efforts of the plaintiff to secure the initiation of such action by the board or the reasons for not making such effort." Enacted in 1961 (L 1961, ch 855), section 626(c) codified a rule of equity developed in early shareholder derivative actions requiring plaintiffs to demand that the corporation initiate an action, unless such demand was futile, before commencing an action on the corporation's behalf (Barr v. Wackman, 36 N.Y. 2d 371, 377). The purposes of the demand requirement are to (1) relieve courts from deciding matters of internal corporate governance by providing corporate directors with opportunities to correct alleged abuses, (2) provide corporate boards with reasonable protection from harassment by litigation on matters clearly within the discretion of directors, and (3) discourage "strike suits" commenced by shareholders for personal gain rather than for the benefit of the corporation (Barr, 36 NY2d at 378). "The demand is generally designed to weed out unnecessary or illegitimate shareholder derivative suits" (id.).

By their very nature, shareholder derivative actions infringe upon the managerial discretion of corporate boards. "As with other questions of corporate policy and management, the decision whether and to what extent to explore and prosecute such [derivative] claims lies within the judgment and control of the corporation's board of directors" (Auerbach, supra, 47 NY2d at 631). Consequently, we have historically been reluctant to permit shareholder derivative suits, noting that the power of courts to direct the management of a corporation's affairs should be "exercised with restraint" (Gordon v. Elliman, 306 N.Y. 456, 462).

In permitting a shareholder derivative action to proceed because a demand on the corporation's directors would be futile, "the object is for the court to chart the course for the corporation which the directors should have selected, and which it is presumed that they would have chosen if they had not been actuated by fraud or bad faith. Due to their misconduct, the court substitutes its judgment ad hoc for that of the directors in the conduct of its business" (id. at 462).

Achieving a balance between preserving the discretion of directors to manage a corporation without undue interference, through the demand requirement, and permitting shareholders to bring claims on behalf of the corporation when it is evident that directors will wrongfully refuse to bring such claims, through the demand futility exception, has been accomplished by various jurisdictions in different ways. One widely cited approach to demand futility which attempts to balance these competing concerns has been developed by Delaware courts and applies a two-pronged test to each case to determine whether a failure to serve a demand is justified. At the other end of the spectrum is a universal demand requirement which would abandon particularized determinations in favor of requiring a demand in every case before a shareholder derivative suit may be filed.

The Delaware Approach

Delaware's demand requirement, codified in Delaware Chancery Court Rule 23.1, provides, in relevant part,

"In a derivative action brought by 1 or more shareholders or members to enforce a right of a corporation * * * [the complaint shall allege] with particularity the efforts, if any, made by the plaintiff to obtain the action the plaintiff desires from the directors or comparable authority and the reasons for the plaintiff's failure to obtain the action or for not making the effort."

Interpreting Rule 23.1, the Delaware Supreme Court in Aronson v. Lewis (473 A.2d 805) developed a two-prong test for determining the futility of a demand. Plaintiffs must allege particularized facts which create a reasonable doubt that,

"(1) the directors are disinterested and independent and (2) the challenged transaction was otherwise the product of a valid exercise of business judgment. Hence, the Court of Chancery must make two inquiries, one into the independence and disinterestedness of the directors and the other into the substantive nature of the challenged transaction and the board's approval thereof" (473 A2d at 814).

The two branches of the *Aronson* test are disjunctive (see, Levine v. Smith, 591 A.2d 194, 205). Once director interest has been established, the business judgment rule becomes inapplicable and the demand excused without further inquiry (*Aronson*, 473 A2d at 814). Similarly, a director whose independence is compromised by undue influence exerted by an interested party cannot properly exercise business judgment and the loss of independence also justifies the excusal of a demand without further inquiry (see, Levine, supra, 591

A2d at 205–206). Whether a board has validly exercised its business judgment must be evaluated by determining whether the directors exercised procedural (informed decision) and substantive (terms of the transaction) due care (Grobow v. Perot, 539 A.2d 180, 189).

The reasonable doubt threshold of Delaware's two-fold approach to demand futility has been criticized. The use of a standard of proof which is the heart of a jury's determination in a criminal case has raised questions concerning its applicability in the corporate context (see, Starrels v. First Natl. Bank, 870 F.2d 1168, 1175 (7th Cir.)) [Easterbrook, J, concurring]. The reasonable doubt standard has also been criticized as overly subjective, thereby permitting a wide variance in the application of Delaware law to similar facts (2 American Law Institute, Principles of Corporate Governance: Analysis and Recommendations § 7.03, Comment d at 57 [1992]).

Universal Demand

A universal demand requirement would dispense with the necessity of making case-specific determinations and impose an easily applied bright line rule. The Business Law Section of the American Bar Association has proposed requiring a demand in all cases, without exception, and permits the commencement of a derivative proceeding within 90 days of the demand unless the demand is rejected earlier (Model Business Corporation Act § 7.42[1] [1995 Supplement]). However, plaintiffs may file suit before the expiration of 90 days, even if their demand has not been rejected, if the corporation would suffer irreparable injury as a result (Model Business Corporation Act § 7.42[2]).

The American Law Institute (ALI) has also proposed a "universal" demand. Section 7.03 of ALI's Principles of Corporate Governance would require shareholder derivative action plaintiffs to serve a written demand on the corporation unless a demand is excused because "the plaintiff makes a specific showing that irreparable injury to the corporation would otherwise result" (2 American Law Institute, Principles of Corporate Governance: Analysis and Recommendations, § 7.03[b] at 53–54, [1992]). Once a demand has been made and rejected, however, the ALI would subject the board's decision to "an elaborate set of standards that calibrates the deference afforded the decision of the directors to the character of the claim being asserted" (Kamen v. Kemper Financial Services, Inc., 500 U.S. 90, 104).

At least 11 states have adopted, by statute, the universal demand requirement proposed in the Model Business Corporation Act. Georgia, Michigan, Wisconsin, Montana, Virginia, New Hampshire, Mississippi, Connecticut, Nebraska and North Carolina require shareholders to wait 90 days after serving a demand before filing a derivative suit unless the demand is rejected before the expiration of the 90 days, or irreparable injury to the corporation would result. . . . Arizona additionally permits shareholders to file suit before the expiration of 90 days if the statute of limitations would expire during the 90 day period. . . . Florida also appears to have adopted a universal demand requirement, although the statutory language does not track the Model Business Corporation Act. Florida's statute provides, "A complaint in a proceeding brought in the right of a corporation must be verified and allege with particularity the demand made to obtain action by the board of directors and that the demand was refused or ignored (emphasis added)". . . .

New York State has also considered and continues to consider implementing a universal demand requirement. However, even though bills to adopt a universal demand have been presented over three legislative sessions, the Legislature has yet to enact a universal demand requirement. . . .

New York's Approach to Demand Futility

Although instructive, neither the universal demand requirement nor the Delaware approach to demand futility is adopted here. Since New York's demand requirement is codified in Business Corporation Law § 626(c), a universal demand can only be adopted by the Legislature. Delaware's approach, which resembles New York law in some respects, incorporates a "reasonable doubt" standard which, as we have already pointed out, has provoked criticism as confusing and overly subjective. An analysis of the *Barr* decision compels the conclusion that in New York, a demand would be futile if a complaint alleges with particularity that (1) a majority of the directors are interested in the transaction, or (2) the directors failed to inform themselves to a degree reasonably necessary about the transaction, or (3) the directors failed to exercise their business judgment in approving the transaction.

In Barr v. Wackman (36 N.Y. 2d 371, supra), we considered whether the plaintiff was excused from making a demand where the board of Talcott National Corporation (Talcott), consisting of 13 outside directors, a director affiliated with a related company and four interested inside directors, rejected a merger proposal involving Gulf & Western Industries (Gulf & Western) in favor of another proposal on allegedly less favorable terms for Talcott and its shareholders. The merger proposal, memorialized in a board-approved "agreement in principle," proposed exchanging one share of Talcott common stock for approximately $24.00 consisting of $17.00 in cash and 0.6 of a warrant to purchase Gulf & Western stock, worth approximately $7.00. This proposal was abandoned in favor of a cash tender offer for Talcott shares by Associated First Capital Corporation (a Gulf & Western subsidiary) at $20.00 per share—four dollars less than proposed for the merger.

The plaintiff in *Barr* alleged that Talcott's board discarded the merger proposal after the four "controlling" inside directors received pecuniary and personal benefits from Gulf & Western in exchange for ceding control of Talcott on terms less favorable to Talcott's shareholders. As alleged in the complaint, these benefits included new and favorable employment contracts for nine Talcott officers, including five-year employment contracts for three of the controlling directors. In addition to his annual salary of $125,000 with Talcott, defendant

Silverman (a controlling director) would allegedly receive $60,000 a year under a five year employment contract with Associated First Capital, and an aggregate of $275,000 for the next five years in an arrangement with Associated First Capital to serve as a consultant. This additional compensation would be awarded to Silverman after control of Talcott passed to Associated First Capital and Gulf & Western. Plaintiff also alleged that Gulf & Western and Associated First Capital paid an excessive "finder's fee" of $340,000 to a company where Silverman's son was an executive vice president. In addition to alleging that the controlling defendants obtained personal benefits, the complaint also alleged that Talcott's board agreed to sell a Talcott subsidiary at a net loss of $6,100,000 solely to accommodate Gulf & Western.

In *Barr*, we held that insofar as the complaint attacked the controlling directors' acts in causing the corporation to enter into a transaction for their own financial benefit, demand was excused because of the self-dealing, or self-interest of those directors in the challenged transaction. Specifically, we pointed to the allegation that the controlling directors "breached their fiduciary obligations to Talcott in return for personal benefits" (id., at 376).

We also held in *Barr*, however, that as to the disinterested outside directors, demand could be excused even in the absence of their receiving any financial benefit from the transaction. That was because the complaint alleged that, by approving the terms of the less advantageous offer, those directors were guilty of a "breach of their duties of due care and diligence to the corporation" (id., at 380). Their performance of the duty of care would have "put them on notice of the claimed self-dealing of the affiliated directors" (id.). The complaint charged that the outside directors failed "to do more than passively rubber stamp the decisions of the active managers" (id., at 381) resulting in corporate detriment. These allegations, the *Barr* Court concluded, also excused demand as to the charges against the disinterested directors.

Barr also makes clear that "it is not sufficient * * * merely to name a majority of the directors as parties defendant with the conclusory allegation of wrongdoing or control by wrongdoers" (id., at 379) to justify failure to make a demand. Thus, *Barr* reflects the statutory requirement that the complaint "must set forth with particularity the * * * reasons for not making such effort" (Business Corporation Law § 626[c]).

Unfortunately, various courts have overlooked the explicit warning that conclusory allegations of wrongdoing against each member of the board are not sufficient to excuse demand and have misinterpreted *Barr* as excusing demand whenever a majority of the board members who approved the transaction are named as defendants (see, Miller v. Schreyer, 200 A.D. 2d 492; Curreri v. Verni, 156 A.D. 2d 420; MacKay v. Pierce, 86 A.D. 2d 655; Joseph v. Amrep Corp., 59 A.D. 2d 841; see also, Allison Publications Incorporated v. Mutual Benefit Life Insurance, 197 A.D. 2d 463). As stated most recently, "the rule is clear in this State that no demand is necessary 'if the complaint alleges acts for which a majority of the directors may be liable and plaintiff reasonably concluded that the board would not be responsive to a demand' " (Miller v. Schreyer, supra, at 494 [quoting from *Barr,* supra, 36 N.Y.2d at 371]; but see, Lewis v. Welch, 126 A.D. 2d 519, 521). The problem with such an approach is that it permits plaintiffs to frame their complaint in such a way as to automatically excuse demand, thereby allowing the exception to swallow the rule.

We thus deem it necessary to offer the following elaboration of *Barr's* demand/futility standard. (1) Demand is excused because of futility when a complaint alleges with particularity that a majority of the board of directors is interested in the challenged transaction. Director interest may either be self-interest in the transaction at issue (see, Barr v. Wackman, supra, at 376 [receipt of "personal benefits"]), or a loss of independence because a director with no direct interest in a transaction is "controlled" by a self-interested director. (2) Demand is excused because of futility when a complaint alleges with particularity that the board of directors did not fully inform themselves about the challenged transaction to the extent reasonably appropriate under the circumstances (see, *Barr,* supra, at 380, 368 N.Y.S.2d 497, 329 N.E.2d 180). The "long-standing rule" is that a director "does not exempt himself from liability by failing to do more than passively rubber-stamp the decisions of the active managers" (id., at 381). (3) Demand is excused because of futility when a complaint alleges with particularity that the challenged transaction was so egregious on its face that it could not have been the product of sound business judgment of the directors.

The Current Appeal

Plaintiff argues that the demand requirement was excused both because the outside directors awarded themselves generous compensation packages and because of the acquiescence of the disinterested directors in the executive compensation schemes. The complaint states:

> "Plaintiff has made no demand upon the directors of IBM to institute this lawsuit because such demand would be futile. As set forth above, each of the directors authorized, approved, participated and/or acquiesced in the acts and transactions complained of herein and are liable therefor. Further, each of the Non–Employee [outside] Directors has received and retained the benefit of his excessive compensation and each of the other directors has received and retained the benefit of the incentive compensation described above. The defendants cannot be expected to vote to prosecute an action against themselves. Demand upon the company to bring action (sic) to redress the wrongs herein is therefore unnecessary."

Defendants argue that neither the Supreme Court nor the Appellate Division abused its discretion in holding that plaintiff's complaint did not set forth the futility of a demand with particularity.

As in *Barr*, we look to the complaint here to determine whether the allegations are sufficient and establish with particularity that demand would have been futile. Here, the plaintiff alleges that the compensation awarded to IBM's outside directors and certain IBM executives was excessive.

Defendant's motion to dismiss for failure to make a demand as to the allegations concerning the compensation paid to IBM's executive officers was properly granted. A board is not interested "in voting compensation for one of its members as an executive or in some other nondirectorial capacity, such as a consultant to the corporation," although "so-called 'back-scratching' arrangements, pursuant to which all directors vote to approve each other's compensation as officers or employees, do not constitute disinterested directors' action" (1 ALI, supra, at 250). Since only three directors are alleged to have received the benefit of the executive compensation scheme, plaintiff has failed to allege that a majority of the board was interested in setting executive compensation. Nor do the allegations that the board used faulty accounting procedures to calculate executive compensation levels move beyond "conclusory allegations of wrongdoing" (Barr v. Wackman, supra, at 379) which are insufficient to excuse demand. The complaint does not allege particular facts in contending that the board failed to deliberate or exercise its business judgment in setting those levels. Consequently, the failure to make a demand regarding the fixing of executive compensation was fatal to [the] portion of the complaint challenging that transaction.

However, a review of the complaint indicates that plaintiff also alleged that a majority of the board was self-interested in setting the compensation of outside directors because the outside directors comprised a majority of the board.

Directors are self-interested in a challenged transaction where they will receive a direct financial benefit from the transaction which is different from the benefit to shareholders generally (see, Rales v. Blasband, 634 A.2d 927, 936 [Del Sup Ct]; Bergstein v. Texas Intern. Co., 453 A.2d 467, 472–473 [Del Ch]; ALI, Principles of Corporate Governance § 1.23, at 25; 13 Fletcher, Cyclopedia Corporations § 5965, at 138). A director who votes him or herself a raise in directors' compensation is always "interested" because that person will receive a personal financial benefit from the transaction not shared in by stockholders (see, 1 ALI Principles of Corporate Governance § 5.03, comment g, at 250 ["if the board votes directorial compensation for itself, the board is interested"]; see also, Steiner v. Meyerson, [1995 Transfer Binder], Fed. Sec. L. Rep. P 98857 [Del Ch], 1995 WL 441999, at 12 ["As the outside directors comprise a majority of the Telxon board and are personally interested in their compensation levels, demand upon them to challenge or decrease their own compensation is excused"]). Consequently, a demand was excused as to plaintiff's allegations that the compensation set for outside directors was excessive.

Corporate Waste

Our conclusion that demand should have been excused as to the part of the complaint challenging the fixing of directors' compensation does not end our inquiry, however. We must also determine whether plaintiff has stated a cause of action regarding that transaction, i.e., some wrong to the corporation. We conclude that plaintiff has not, and thus dismiss the complaint in its entirety.

Historically, directors did not receive any compensation for their work as directors (see, Fletcher, Cyclopedia Corporations, § 2109). Thus, a bare allegation that corporate directors voted themselves excessive compensation was sufficient to state a cause of action (e.g., Walsh v. Van Ameringen–Haebler, Inc., 257 N.Y. 478, 480; Jacobson v. Brooklyn Lumber Co., 184 N.Y. 152, 162). Many jurisdictions, including New York, have since changed the common law rule by statute providing that a corporation's board of directors has the authority to fix director compensation unless the corporation's charter or bylaws provides otherwise. Thus, the allegation that directors have voted themselves compensation is clearly no longer an allegation which gives rise to a cause of action, as the directors are statutorily entitled to set those levels. Nor does a conclusory allegation that the compensation directors have set for themselves is excessive give rise to a cause of action.

> The courts will not undertake to review the fairness of the official salaries, at the suit of a shareholder attacking them as excessive, unless wrongdoing and oppression or possible abuse of a fiduciary position are shown. However, the courts will take a hand in the matter at the instance of the corporation or of shareholders in extreme cases. A case of fraud is presented where directors increase their collective salaries so as to use up nearly the entire earnings of a company; where directors or officers appropriate the income so as to deprive shareholders of reasonable dividends, or perhaps so reduce to assets as to threaten the corporation with insolvency * * * (Fletcher, Cyclopedia Corporations, § 2122, at 46–47).

Thus, a complaint challenging the excessiveness of director compensation must—to survive a dismissal motion—allege compensation rates excessive on their face or other facts which call into question whether the compensation was fair to the corporation when approved, the good faith of the directors setting those rates, or that the decision to set the compensation could not have been a product of valid business judgment.[3]

---

3. There is general agreement that the allocation of the burden of proof differs depending on whether the compensation was approved by disinterested directors or shareholders, or by interested directors. Plaintiffs must prove wrongdoing or waste as to compensation arrangements regarding disinterested directors or shareholders, but directors who approve their own compensation bear the burden of proving that the transaction was fair to the corporation (see, Block, et al, The Business Judgment Rule, at 149 [4th ed.]; Fletcher, supra, § 514.1, 632; ALI, supra, § 5.03). However, at the pleading stage we are not concerned with burdens of proof.

Applying the foregoing principles to plaintiff's complaint, it is clear that it must be dismissed. The complaint alleges that the directors increased their compensation rates from a base of $20,000 plus $500 for each meeting attended to a retainer of $55,000 plus 100 shares of IBM stock over a five-year period. The complaint also alleges that "this compensation bears little relation to the part-time services rendered by the Non–Employee Directors or to the profitability of IBM. The board's responsibilities have not increased, its performance, measured by the company's earnings and stock price, has been poor yet its compensation has increased far in excess of the cost of living."

These conclusory allegations do not state a cause of action. There are no factually-based allegations of wrongdoing or waste which would, if true, sustain a verdict in plaintiff's favor. Plaintiff's bare allegations that the compensation set lacked a relationship to duties performed or to the cost of living are insufficient as a matter of law to state a cause of action.

Accordingly, the order of the Appellate Division should be affirmed, with costs.

———

Auerbach v. Bennett

Court of Appeals of New York, 1979.
47 N.Y.2d 619, 419 N.Y.S.2d 920, 393 N.E.2d 994.

■ JONES, JUDGE.

While the substantive aspects of a decision to terminate a shareholders' derivative action against defendant corporate directors made by a committee of disinterested directors appointed by the corporation's board of directors are beyond judicial inquiry under the business judgment doctrine, the court may inquire as to the disinterested independence of the members of that committee and as to the appropriateness and sufficiency of the investigative procedures chosen and pursued by the committee. In this instance, however, no basis is shown to warrant either inquiry by the court. Accordingly we hold that it was error to reverse the lower court's dismissal of the shareholders' derivative action.

In the summer of 1975 the management of General Telephone & Electronics Corporation, in response to reports that numerous other multinational companies had made questionable payments to public officials or political parties in foreign countries, directed that an internal preliminary investigation be made to ascertain whether that corporation had engaged in similar transactions. On the basis of the report of this survey, received in October, 1975, management brought the issue to the attention of the corporation's board of directors. At a meeting held on November 6 of that year the board referred the matter to the board's audit committee. The audit committee retained as its special counsel the Washington, D.C., law firm of Wilmer, Cutler & Pickering which had not previously acted as counsel to the corporation. With the assistance of such special counsel and Arthur Andersen & Co., the corporation's outside auditors, the audit committee engaged in an investigation into the corporation's worldwide operations, focusing on whether, in the period January 1, 1971 to December 31, 1975, corporate funds had been (1) paid directly or indirectly to any political party or person or to any officer, employee, shareholder or director of any governmental or private customer, or (2) used to reimburse any officer of the corporation or other person for such payments.

On March 4, 1976 the audit committee released its report which was filed with the Securities and Exchange Commission and disclosed to the corporation's shareholders in a proxy statement prior to the annual meeting of shareholders held in April, 1976. The audit committee reported that it had found evidence that in the period from 1971 to 1975 the corporation or its subsidiaries had made payments abroad and in the United States constituting bribes and kickbacks in amounts perhaps totaling more than 11 million dollars and that some of the individual defendant directors had been personally involved in certain of the transactions.

Almost immediately Auerbach, a shareholder in the corporation, instituted the present shareholders' derivative action on behalf of the corporation against the corporation's directors, Arthur Andersen & Co. and the corporation. The complaint alleged that in connection with the transactions reported by the audit committee defendants, present and former members of the corporation's board of directors and Arthur Andersen & Co., are liable to the corporation for breach of their duties to the corporation and should be made to account for payments made in those transactions.

On April 21, 1976 the board of directors of the corporation adopted a resolution creating a special litigation committee "for the purpose of establishing a point of contact between the Board of Directors and the Corporation's General Counsel concerning the position to be taken by the Corporation in certain litigation involving shareholder derivative claims on behalf of the Corporation against certain of its directors and officers" and authorizing that committee "to take such steps from time to time as it deems necessary to pursue its objectives including the retention of special outside counsel." The special committee comprised three disinterested directors who had joined the board after the challenged transactions had occurred. The board subsequently additionally vested in the committee "all of the authority of the Board of Directors to determine, on behalf of the Board, the position that the Corporation shall take with respect to the derivative claims alleged on its behalf" in the present and similar shareholder derivative actions.

The special litigation committee reported under date of November 22, 1976. It found that defendant Arthur Andersen & Co. had conducted its examination of the corporation's affairs in accordance with generally accepted auditing standards and in good faith and concluded that no proper interest of the corporation or its shareholders would be served by the continued assertion of a claim against it. The committee also concluded that none of the individual defendants had violated the New York State statutory standard of care, that none had profited personally or gained in any way, that the claims asserted in the present action are without merit, that if the action were allowed to proceed the time and talents of the corporation's senior management would be wasted on lengthy pretrial and trial proceedings, that litigation costs would be inordinately high in view of the unlikelihood of success, and that the continuing publicity could be damaging to the corporation's business. The committee determined that it would not be in the best interests of the corporation for the present derivative action to proceed, and, exercising the authority delegated to it, directed the corporation's general counsel to take that position in the present litigation as well as in pending comparable shareholders' derivative actions.

On December 17, 1976 the corporation and the four individual defendants who had been served moved for an order pursuant to CPLR 3211 (subd. [a], pars. [3], [7]) dismissing the complaint or in the alternative for an order pursuant to CPLR 3211 (subd. [c]) for summary judgment. On January 7, 1977 Arthur Andersen & Co. made a similar motion. On May 13, 1977 Supreme Court, Special Term, granted the motions of all defendants and dismissed the complaint on the merits. . . .

As all parties and both courts below recognize, the disposition of this case on the merits turns on the proper application of the business judgment doctrine, in particular to the decision of a specially appointed committee of disinterested directors acting on behalf of the board to terminate a shareholders' derivative action. That doctrine bars judicial inquiry into actions of corporate directors taken in good faith and in the exercise of honest judgment in the lawful and legitimate furtherance of corporate purposes. "Questions of policy of management, expediency of contracts or action, adequacy of consideration, lawful appropriation of corporate funds to advance corporate interests, are left solely to their honest and unselfish decision, for their powers therein are without limitation and free from restraint, and the exercise of them for the common and general interests of the corporation may not be questioned, although the results show that what they did was unwise or inexpedient." (Pollitz v. Wabash, R.R. Co., 207 N.Y. 113, 124, 100 N.E. 721, 724.)

In this instance our inquiry, to the limited extent to which it may be pursued, has a two-tiered aspect. The complaint initially asserted liability on the part of defendants based on the payments made to foreign governmental customers and privately owned customers, some unspecified portions of which were allegedly passed on to officials of the customers, i.e., the focus was on first-tier bribes and kickbacks. Then subsequent to the service of the complaint there came the report of a special litigation committee, particularly appointed by the corporation's board of directors to consider the merits of the present and similar shareholders' derivative actions, and its determination that it would not be in the best interests of the corporation to press claims against defendants based on their possible first-tier liability. The motions for summary judgment were predicated principally on the report and determination of the special litigation committee and on the contention that this second-tier corporate action insulated the first-tier transactions from judicial inquiry and was itself subject to the shelter of the business judgment doctrine. The disposition at Special Term was predicated on this analysis; its decision focused on the actions of the special litigation committee, and the motions for summary judgment were granted on the ground that the business judgment doctrine precluded the courts from going back of the decision of the special litigation committee on behalf of the corporation not to pursue the claims alleged in the complaint. Similarly the reversal at the Appellate Division was based on that court's perception of the proper application of the business judgment rule to the actions and determination of the special litigation committee. We proceed on the same analysis, concluding, however, on the record before us, at variance with the Appellate Division, that the determination of the special litigation committee forecloses further judicial inquiry in this case.

It appears to us that the business judgment doctrine, at least in part, is grounded in the prudent recognition that courts are ill equipped and infrequently called on to evaluate what are and must be essentially business judgments. The authority and responsibilities vested in corporate directors both by statute and decisional law proceed on the assumption that inescapably there can be no available objective standard by which the correctness of every corporate decision may be measured, by the courts or otherwise. Even if that were not the case, by definition the responsibility for business judgments must rest with the corporate directors; their individual capabilities and experience peculiarly qualify them for the discharge of that responsibility. Thus, absent evidence of bad faith or fraud (of which there is none here) the courts must and properly should respect their determinations.

Derivative claims against corporate directors belong to the corporation itself. As with other questions of corporate policy and management, the decision whether and to what extent to explore and prosecute such claims lies within the judgment and control of the corporation's board of directors. Necessarily such decision must be predicated on the weighing and balancing of a variety of disparate considerations to reach a considered conclusion as to what course of action or inaction is best calculated to protect and advance the interests of the corporation. This is the essence of the responsibility and role of the board of directors, and courts may not intrude to interfere.

In the present case we confront a special instance of the application of the business judgment rule and inquire whether it applies in its full vigor to shield from judicial scrutiny the decision of a three-person minority committee of the board acting on behalf of the full board not to prosecute a shareholder's derivative action. The record in this case reveals that the board is a 15-member board, and that the derivative suit was brought against four of the directors. Nothing suggests that any of the other directors participated in any of the challenged first-tier transactions. Indeed the report of the audit committee on which the complaint is based specifically found that no other directors had any prior knowledge of or were in any way involved in any of these transactions. Other directors had, however, been members of the board in the period during which the transactions occurred. Each of the three director members of the special litigation committee joined the board thereafter.

The business judgment rule does not foreclose inquiry by the courts into the disinterested independence of those members of the board chosen by it to make the corporate decision on its behalf—here the members of the special litigation committee. Indeed the rule shields the deliberations and conclusions of the chosen representatives of the board only if they possess a disinterested independence and do not stand in a dual relation which prevents an unprejudicial exercise of judgment. (Cf. Koral v. Savory, Inc., 276 N.Y. 215, 11 N.E.2d 883.)

We examine then the proof submitted by defendants. It is not disputed that the members of the special litigation committee were not members of the corporation's board of directors at the time of the first-tier transactions in question. Howard Blauvelt, chairman of the board of Continental Oil Company, had been elected to the corporation's board of directors on October 9, 1975. Dr. John T. Dunlop, Lamont University professor at the Graduate School of Business Administration of Harvard University had been elected to the board on April 21, 1976. James R. Barker, chairman of the board and chief executive officer of Moore McCormack Resources, Inc., was added as the third member of the committee when he was elected to the board on July 19, 1976. None of the three had had any prior affiliation with the corporation. Notwithstanding the vigorous and imaginative hypothesizing and innuendo of counsel there is nothing in this record to raise a triable issue of fact as to the independence and disinterested status of these three directors.

The contention of Wallenstein that any committee authorized by the board of which defendant directors were members must be held to be legally infirm and may not be delegated power to terminate a derivative action must be rejected. In the very nature of the corporate organization it was only the existing board of directors which had authority on behalf of the corporation to direct the investigation and to assure the cooperation of corporate employees, and it is only that same board by its own action—or as here pursuant to authority duly delegated by it—which had authority to decide whether to prosecute the claims against defendant directors. The board in this instance, with slight adaptation, followed prudent practice in observing the general policy that when individual members of a board of directors prove to have personal interests which may conflict with the interests of the corporation, such interested directors must be excluded while the remaining members of the board proceed to consideration and action.

(Cf. Business Corporation Law, § 713, which contemplates such situations and provides that the interested directors may nonetheless be included in the quorum count.) Courts have consistently held that the business judgment rule applies where some directors are charged with wrongdoing, so long as the remaining directors making the decision are disinterested and independent. (Swanson v. Traer, 249 F.2d 854, 858–859; Gall v. Exxon Corp., 418 F.Supp. 508, supplemented 75 Civ. 3582 [U.S.Dist.Ct., S.D.N.Y., Jan. 17, 1977]; Issner v. Aldrich, 254 F.Supp. 696, 701–702; Republic Nat. Life Ins. Co. v. Beasley, 73 F.R.D. 658, 668–669; Gilbert v. Curtiss–Wright Corp., 179 Misc. 641, 645, 38 N.Y.S.2d 548, 552.)

To accept the assertions of the intervenor and to disqualify the entire board would be to render the corporation powerless to make an effective business judgment with respect to prosecution of the derivative action. The possible risk of hesitancy on the part of the members of any committee, even if composed of outside, independent, disinterested directors, to investigate the activities of fellow members of the board where personal liability is at stake is an inherent, inescapable, given aspect of the corporation's predicament. To assign responsibility of the dimension here involved to individuals wholly separate and apart from the board of directors would, except in the most extraordinary circumstances, itself be an act of default and breach of the nondelegable fiduciary duty owed by the members of the board to the corporation and to its shareholders, employees and creditors. For the courts to preside over such determinations would similarly work an ouster of the board's fundamental responsibility and authority for corporate management.

We turn then to the action of the special litigation committee itself which comprised two components. First, there was the selection of procedures appropriate to the pursuit of its charge, and second, there was the ultimate substantive decision; predicated on the procedures chosen and the data produced thereby, not to pursue the claims advanced in the shareholders' derivative actions. The latter, substantive decision falls squarely within the embrace of the business judgment doctrine, involving as it did the weighing and balancing of legal, ethical, commercial, promotional, public relations, fiscal and other factors familiar to the resolution of many if not most corporate problems. To this extent the conclusion reached by the special litigation committee is outside the scope of our review. Thus, the courts cannot inquire as to which factors were considered by that committee or the relative weight accorded them in reaching that substantive decision—"the reasons for the payments, the advantages or disadvantages accruing to the corporation by reason of the transactions, the extent of the participation or profit by the respondent directors and the loss, if any, of public confidence in the corporation which might be incurred" (64 A.D.2d, at p. 107, 408 N.Y.S.2d at pp. 87–88). Inquiry into such matters would go to the very core of the business judgment made by the committee. To permit judicial probing of such issues would be to emasculate the business judgment doctrine as applied to the actions and determinations of the special litigation committee. Its substantive evaluation of the problems posed and its judgment in their resolution are beyond our reach.

As to the other component of the committee's activities, however, the situation is different, and here we agree with the Appellate Division. As to the methodologies and procedures best suited to the conduct of an investigation of facts and the determination of legal liability, the courts are well equipped by long and continuing experience and practice to make determinations. In fact they are better qualified in this regard than are corporate directors in general. Nor do the determinations to be made in the adoption of procedures partake of the nuances or special perceptions or comprehensions of business judgment or corporate activities or interests. The question is solely how appropriately to set about to gather the pertinent data.

While the court may properly inquire as to the adequacy and appropriateness of the committee's investigative procedures and methodologies, it may not under the guise of consideration of such factors trespass in the domain of business judgment. At the same time those responsible for the procedures by which the business judgment is reached may reasonably be required to show that they have pursued their chosen investigative methods in good faith. What evidentiary proof may be required to this end will, of course, depend on the nature of the particular investigation, and the proper reach of disclosure at the instance of the shareholders will in turn relate inversely to the showing made by the corporate representatives themselves. The latter may be expected to show that the areas and subjects to be examined are reasonably complete and that there has been a good-faith pursuit of inquiry into such areas and subjects. What has been uncovered and the relative weight accorded in evaluating and balancing the several factors and considerations are beyond the scope of judicial concern. Proof, however, that the investigation has been so restricted in scope, so shallow in execution, or otherwise so *pro forma* or halfhearted as to constitute a pretext or sham, consistent with the principles underlying the application of the business judgment doctrine, would raise questions of good faith or conceivably fraud which would never be shielded by that doctrine.

In addition to the issue of the disinterested independence of the special litigation committee, addressed above, the disposition of the present appeal turns, then, on whether on defendants' motions for summary judgment predicated on the investigation and determination of the special litigation committee, Wallenstein by tender of evidentiary proof in admissible form has shown facts sufficient to require a trial of any material issue of fact as to the adequacy or appropriateness of the *modus operandi* of that committee or has demonstrated acceptable excuse for failure to make such tender. (Friends of Animals v. Associated Fur Mfrs., 46 N.Y.2d 1065, 416 N.Y.S.2d 790, 390 N.E.2d 298; CPLR 3212, subd. [b].) We conclude that the requisite showing has not been made on this record. . . .

On the submissions made by defendants in support of their motions, we do not find either insufficiency or infirmity as to the procedures and methodologies chosen and pursued by the special litigation committee. That committee promptly engaged eminent special counsel to guide its deliberations and to advise it. The committee reviewed the prior work of the audit committee, testing its completeness, accuracy and thoroughness by interviewing representatives of Wilmer, Cutler & Pickering, reviewing transcripts of the testimony of 10 corporate officers and employees before the Securities and Exchange Commission, and studying documents collected by and work papers of the Washington law firm. Individual interviews were conducted with the directors found to have participated in any way in the questioned payments, and with representatives of Arthur Andersen & Co. Questionnaires were sent to and answered by each of the corporation's nonmanagement directors. At the conclusion of its investigation the special litigation committee sought and obtained pertinent legal advice from its special counsel. The selection of appropriate investigative methods must always turn on the nature and characteristics of the particular subject being investigated, but we find nothing in this record that requires a trial of any material issue of fact concerning the sufficiency or appropriateness of the procedures chosen by this special litigation committee. Nor is there anything in this record to raise a triable issue of fact as to the good-faith pursuit of its examination by that committee.

Finally, there should be a word as to the contention advanced by the intervenor that summary judgment should at least be withheld until there has been opportunity for disclosure. We note preliminarily as a matter of procedure that there was no application at Special Term for any such relief nor is there in the record any opposing affidavit from which it appears that essential facts may exist which could be obtained by disclosure (CPLR 3212, subd. [f]). It is also significant that neither in his brief nor on oral argument did Wallenstein identify any particulars as to which he desires discovery relating to the disinterestedness of the members of the special litigation committee or to the procedures followed by that committee. To speculate that something might be caught on a fishing expedition provides no basis to postpone decision on the summary judgment motions under the authority of CPLR 3212 (subd. [f]). The disclosure proposed and described by Wallenstein on oral argument would go only to particulars as to the results of the committee's investigation and work, the factors bearing on its substantive decision not to prosecute the derivative actions and the factual aspects of the underlying first-tier activities of defendants—all matters falling within the ambit of the business judgment doctrine and thus excluded from judicial scrutiny.

For the reasons stated the order of the Appellate Division should be modified, with costs to defendants, by reversing so much thereof as reversed the order of Supreme Court, and, as so modified, affirmed.

[The dissenting opinion of Chief Judge Cooke is omitted.]

■ JASEN, WACHTLER, FUCHSBERG and MEYER, JJ., concur with JONES, J.

■ COOKE, C.J., dissents and votes to affirm in a separate opinion.

◼ GABRIELLI, J., taking no part.

Order modified, with costs to defendants, in accordance with the opinion herein and, as so modified, affirmed. Question certified answered in the negative.

———

Zapata Corp. v. Maldonado

Supreme Court of Delaware, 1981.
430 A.2d 779.

◼ Before DUFFY, QUILLEN and HORSEY, JJ.

[The claims on which this case was apparently based are stated as follows in Maldonado v. Flynn, 597 F.2d 789 (2d Cir.1979): A stock-option plan had been adopted by the board of Zapata Corporation in 1970 and approved by Zapata's shareholders in 1971. The board was authorized to amend the plan freely. The options were exercisable in five equal installments; the last exercise date was July 14, 1970. Flynn, the chief executive officer and a director of Zapata, as well as other senior officers of Zapata, were granted options under the plan to purchase Zapata stock at $12.15 per share.

[In 1974, Flynn and the board had decided Zapata should make a cash tender offer for its own stock at $25–$30 per share. Since Zapata stock was then trading at only $19 per share, the announcement of the tender offer would trigger a sharp rise in the price of Zapata stock. The tender offer was to be publicly announced on July 2, 1974. Early that day, trading in Zapata stock on the New York Stock Exchange was suspended at the request of Zapata's management, pending the announcement. Before trading resumed, the board accelerated the final exercise date for the options held by Flynn and the other senior officers from July 14, 1974 to July 2, 1974. The board also modified the plan to authorize Zapata to make interest-free loans to Flynn and the other senior officers in the amount of (i) the purchase price of the options they exercised and (ii) the tax liability they would incur by exercising the options. The purpose and effect of these amendments were to permit Flynn and the other senior officers to benefit at Zapata's expense. Under applicable federal tax laws, on the exercise of the option Flynn and the other senior officers would realize ordinary income in the amount of the spread between the option price and the fair market price of the stock at the time the option was exercised. Correspondingly, Zapata could deduct the amount of that spread as a business expense. By accelerating the last exercise date, and allowing Flynn and the other senior officers to exercise their options before the market price of the stock rose as a result of the tender offer, the board permitted the optionees to save a considerable amount of taxes but prevented Zapata from enjoying a correspondingly higher tax deduction.]

◼ QUILLEN, JUSTICE. This is an interlocutory appeal from an order entered on April 9, 1980, by the Court of Chancery denying appellant-defendant Zapata Corporation's (Zapata) alternative motions to dismiss the complaint or for summary judgment. The issue to be addressed has reached this Court by way of a rather convoluted path.

In June, 1975, William Maldonado, a stockholder of Zapata, instituted a derivative action in the Court of Chancery on behalf of Zapata against ten officers and/or directors of Zapata, alleging, essentially, breaches of fiduciary duty. Maldonado did not first demand that the board bring this action, stating instead such demand's futility because all directors were named as defendants and allegedly participated in the acts specified.[1] In June, 1977, Maldonado commenced an action in the United States District Court for the Southern District of New York against the same defendants, save one, alleging federal security law violations as well as the same common law claims made previously in the Court of Chancery.

By June, 1979, four of the defendant-directors were no longer on the board, and the remaining directors appointed two new outside directors to the board. The board then created an "Independent Investigation Committee" (Committee), composed solely of the two new directors, to investigate Maldonado's actions . . . and to determine whether the corporation should continue any or all of the litigation. The Committee's determination was stated to be "final, . . . not . . . subject to review by the Board of Directors and . . . in all respects . . . binding upon the Corporation."

Following an investigation, the Committee concluded, in September, 1979, that each action should "be dismissed forthwith as their continued maintenance is inimical to the Company's best interests. . . ." Consequently, Zapata moved for dismissal or summary judgment. . . .

On March 18, 1980, the Court of Chancery, in a reported opinion, the basis for the order of April 9, 1980, denied Zapata's motions, holding that Delaware law does not sanction this means of dismissal. . . .

[T]he focus in this case is on the power to speak for the corporation as to whether the lawsuit should be continued or terminated. As we see it, this issue in the current appellate posture of this case . . . [concerns] the corporate power under Delaware law of an authorized board committee to cause dismissal of litigation instituted for the benefit of the corporation; and the role of the Court of Chancery in resolving conflicts between the stockholder and the committee. . . .

Consistent with the purpose of requiring a demand, a board decision to cause a derivative suit to be dismissed as detrimental to the company, after demand has been made and refused, will be respected

---

1. Court of Chancery Rule 23.1 states in part: "The complaint shall also allege with particularity the efforts, if any, made by the plaintiff to obtain the action he desires from the directors or comparable authority and the reasons for his failure to obtain the action or for not making the effort."

unless it was wrongful.[10] . . . A claim of a wrongful decision not to sue is thus the first exception and the first context of dispute. Absent a wrongful refusal, the stockholder in such a situation simply lacks legal managerial power. . . .

But it cannot be implied that, absent a wrongful board refusal, a stockholder can never have an individual right to initiate an action. For, as is stated in *[McKee]*, a "well settled" exception exists to the general rule.

> "[A] stockholder may sue in equity in his derivative right to assert a cause of action in behalf of the corporation, *without prior demand* upon the directors to sue, when it is apparent that a demand would be futile, that the officers are under an influence that sterilizes discretion and could not be proper persons to conduct the litigation."

156 A. at 193 (emphasis added). . . .[11]

These comments in *McKee* . . . make obvious sense. A demand, when required and refused (if not wrongful), terminates a stockholder's legal ability to initiate a derivative action. But where demand is properly excused, the stockholder does possess the ability to initiate the action on his corporation's behalf.

These conclusions, however, do not determine the question before us. Rather, they merely bring us to the question to be decided. . . .

The question to be decided becomes: When, if at all, should an authorized board committee be permitted to cause litigation, properly initiated by a derivative stockholder in his own right, to be dismissed? As noted above, a board has the power to choose not to pursue litigation when demand is made upon it, so long as the decision is not wrongful. If the board determines that a suit would be detrimental to the company, the board's determination prevails. Even when demand is excusable, circumstances may arise when continuation of the litigation would not be in the corporation's best interests. Our inquiry is whether, under such circumstances, there is a permissible procedure under § 141(a) by which a corporation can rid itself of detrimental litigation. If there is not, a single stockholder in an extreme case might control the destiny of the entire corporation. This concern was bluntly expressed by the Ninth Circuit in Lewis v. Anderson, 9th Cir., 615 F.2d 778, 783 (1979), cert. denied, 449 U.S. 869, 101 S.Ct. 206, 66 L.Ed.2d 89 (1980): "To allow one shareholder to incapacitate an entire board of directors merely by leveling charges against them gives too much leverage to dissident shareholders." But, when examining the means,

---

10. In other words, when stockholders, after making demand and having their suit rejected, attack the board's decision as improper, the board's decision falls under the "business judgment" rule and will be respected if the requirements of the rule are met. . . . That situation should be distinguished from the instant case, where demand was not made, and the *power* of the board to seek a dismissal, due to disqualification, presents a threshold issue. . . .

11. These statements are consistent with Rule 23.1's "reasons for . . . failure" to make demand. . . .

including the committee mechanism examined in this case, potentials for abuse must be recognized. This takes us to the second and third aspects of the issue on appeal. . . .

The corporate power inquiry then focuses on whether the board, tainted by the self-interest of a majority of its members, can legally delegate its authority to a committee of two disinterested directors. We find our statute clearly requires an affirmative answer to this question. As has been noted, under an express provision of the statute, § 141(c), a committee can exercise all of the authority of the board to the extent provided in the resolution of the board. Moreover, at least by analogy to our statutory section on interested directors, 8 Del.C. § 141, it seems clear that the Delaware statute is designed to permit disinterested directors to act for the board.[14] Compare Puma v. Marriott, Del.Ch., 283 A.2d 693, 695–96 (1971).

We do not think that the interest taint of the board majority is per se a legal bar to the delegation of the board's power to an independent committee composed of disinterested board members. The committee can properly act for the corporation to move to dismiss derivative litigation that is believed to be detrimental to the corporation's best interest.

Our focus now switches to the Court of Chancery which is faced with a stockholder assertion that a derivative suit, properly instituted, should continue for the benefit of the corporation and a corporate assertion, properly made by a board committee acting with board authority, that the same derivative suit should be dismissed as inimical to the best interests of the corporation.

At the risk of stating the obvious, the problem is relatively simple. If, on the one hand, corporations can consistently wrest bona fide derivative actions away from well-meaning derivative plaintiffs through the use of the committee mechanism, the derivative suit will lose much, if not all, of its generally-recognized effectiveness as an intra-corporate means of policing boards of directors. See Dent, [supra note 5,] 75 Nw.U.L.Rev. at 96 & n. 3, 144 & n. 241. If, on the other hand, corporations are unable to rid themselves of meritless or harmful litigation and strike suits, the derivative action, created to benefit the corporation, will produce the opposite, unintended result. . . . It thus appears desirable to us to find a balancing point where bona fide stockholder power to bring corporation causes of action cannot be unfairly trampled on by the board of directors, but the corporation can rid itself of detrimental litigation.

[T]he question has been treated by other courts as one of the "business judgment" of the board committee. If a "committee, composed of independent and disinterested directors, conducted a proper review of the matters before it, considered a variety of factors and reached, in good faith, a business judgment that [the] action was not in the best interest of [the corporation]", the action must be dismissed. See, e.g., Maldonado v. Flynn, . . . 485 F.Supp. at 282, 286.

---

14. [The court quoted Del. § 144.]

The issues become solely independence, good faith, and reasonable investigation. The ultimate conclusion of the committee, under that view, is not subject to judicial review.

We are not satisfied, however, that acceptance of the "business judgment" rationale at this stage of derivative litigation is a proper balancing point. While we admit an analogy with a normal case respecting board judgment, it seems to us that there is sufficient risk in the realities of a situation like the one presented in this case to justify caution beyond adherence to the theory of business judgment.

The context here is a suit against directors where demand on the board is excused. We think some tribute must be paid to the fact that the lawsuit was properly initiated. It is not a board refusal case. Moreover, this complaint was filed in June of 1975 and, while the parties undoubtedly would take differing views on the degree of litigation activity, we have to be concerned about the creation of an "Independent Investigation Committee" four years later, after the election of two new outside directors. Situations could develop where such motions could be filed after years of vigorous litigation for reasons unconnected with the merits of the lawsuit.

Moreover, notwithstanding our conviction that Delaware law entrusts the corporate power to a properly authorized committee, we must be mindful that directors are passing judgment on fellow directors in the same corporation and fellow directors, in this instance, who designated them to serve both as directors and committee members. The question naturally arises whether a "there but for the grace of God go I" empathy might not play a role. And the further question arises whether inquiry as to independence, good faith and reasonable investigation is sufficient safeguard against abuse, perhaps subconscious abuse.

There is another line of exploration besides the factual context of this litigation which we find helpful. The nature of this motion finds no ready pigeonhole, as perhaps illustrated by its being set forth in the alternative. It is perhaps best considered as a hybrid summary judgment motion for dismissal because the stockholder plaintiff's standing to maintain the suit has been lost. But it does not fit neatly into a category described in Rule 12(b) of the Court of Chancery Rules nor does it correspond directly with Rule 56 since the question of genuine issues of fact on the merits of the stockholder's claim are not reached.

It seems to us that there are two other procedural analogies that are helpful in addition to reference to Rules 12 and 56. There is some analogy to a settlement in that there is a request to terminate litigation without a judicial determination of the merits. See Perrine v. Pennroad Corp., Del.Super., 47 A.2d 479, 487 (1946). "In determining whether or not to approve a proposed settlement of a derivative stockholders' action [when directors are on both sides of the transaction], the Court of Chancery is called upon to exercise its own business judgment." Neponsit Investment Co. v. Abramson, Del.Super., 405 A.2d 97, 100 (1979) and cases therein cited. In this case, the litigating stockholder plaintiff facing dismissal of a lawsuit properly commenced ought, in our judgment, to have sufficient status for strict Court review.

Finally, if the committee is in effect given status to speak for the corporation as the plaintiff in interest, then it seems to us there is an analogy to Court of Chancery Rule 41(a)(2) where the plaintiff seeks a dismissal after an answer. Certainly, the position of record of the litigating stockholder is adverse to the position advocated by the corporation in the motion to dismiss. Accordingly, there is perhaps some wisdom to be gained by the direction in Rule 41(a)(2) that "an action shall not be dismissed at the plaintiff's instance save upon order of the Court and upon such terms and conditions as the Court deems proper."

Whether the Court of Chancery will be persuaded by the exercise of a committee power resulting in a summary motion for dismissal of a derivative action, where a demand has not been initially made, should rest, in our judgment, in the independent discretion of the Court of Chancery. We thus steer a middle course between those cases which yield to the independent business judgment of a board committee and this case as determined below which would yield to unbridled plaintiff stockholder control. In pursuit of the course, we recognize that "[t]he final substantive judgment whether a particular lawsuit should be maintained requires a balance of many factors—ethical, commercial, promotional, public relations, employee relations, fiscal as well as legal." Maldonado v. Flynn, [supra,] 485 F.Supp. at 285. But we are content that such factors are not "beyond the judicial reach" of the Court of Chancery which regularly and competently deals with fiduciary relationships, disposition of trust property, approval of settlements and scores of similar problems. We recognize the danger of judicial overreaching but the alternatives seem to us to be outweighed by the fresh view of a judicial outsider. Moreover, if we failed to balance all the interests involved, we would in the name of practicality and judicial economy foreclose a judicial decision on the merits. At this point, we are not convinced that is necessary or desirable.

After an objective and thorough investigation of a derivative suit, an independent committee may cause its corporation to file a pretrial motion to dismiss in the Court of Chancery. The basis of the motion is the best interests of the corporation, as determined by the committee. The motion should include a thorough written record of the investigation and its findings and recommendations. Under appropriate court supervision, akin to proceedings on summary judgment, each side should have an opportunity to make a record on the motion. As to the limited issues presented by the motion noted below, the moving party should be prepared to meet the normal burden under Rule 56 that there is no genuine issue as to any material fact and that the moving party is entitled to dismiss as a matter of law.[15] The Court should apply a two-step test to the motion.

---

15. We do not foreclose a discretionary trial of factual issues but that issue is not presented in this appeal. See Lewis v. Anderson, supra, 615 F.2d at 780. Nor do we

First, the Court should inquire into the independence and good faith of the committee and the bases supporting its conclusions. Limited discovery may be ordered to facilitate such inquiries. The corporation should have the burden of proving independence, good faith and a reasonable investigation, rather than presuming independence, good faith and reasonableness.[17] If the Court determines that the committee is not independent or has not shown reasonable bases for its conclusions, or, if the Court is not satisfied for other reasons relating to the process, including but not limited to the good faith of the committee, the Court shall deny the corporation's motion. If, however, the Court is satisfied under Rule 56 standards that the committee was independent and showed reasonable bases for good faith findings and recommendations, the Court may proceed, in its discretion, to the next step.

The second step provides, we believe, the essential key in striking the balance between legitimate corporate claims as expressed in a derivative stockholder suit and a corporation's best interests as expressed by an independent investigating committee. The Court should determine, applying its own independent business judgment, whether the motion should be granted.[18] This means, of course, that instances could arise where a committee can establish its independence and sound bases for its good faith decisions and still have the corporation's motion denied. The second step is intended to thwart instances where corporate actions meet the criteria of step one, but the result does not appear to satisfy its spirit, or where corporate actions would simply prematurely terminate a stockholder grievance deserving of further consideration in the corporation's interest. The Court of Chancery of course must carefully consider and weigh how compelling the corporate interest in dismissal is when faced with a nonfrivolous lawsuit. The Court of Chancery should, when appropriate, give special consideration to matters of law and public policy in addition to the corporation's best interests.

If the Court's independent business judgment is satisfied, the Court may proceed to grant the motion, subject, of course, to any equitable terms or conditions the Court finds necessary or desirable.

The interlocutory order of the Court of Chancery is reversed and the cause is remanded for further proceedings consistent with this opinion.

---

foreclose the possibility that other motions may proceed or be joined with such a pretrial summary judgment motion to dismiss, e.g., a partial motion for summary judgment on the merits.

17. Compare Auerbach v. Bennett, 47 N.Y.2d 619, 419 N.Y.S.2d 920, 928–29, 393 N.E.2d 994 (1979). Our approach here is analogous to and consistent with the Delaware approach to "interested director" transactions, where the directors, once the

transaction is attacked, have the burden of establishing its "intrinsic fairness" to a court's careful scrutiny. See, e.g., Sterling v. Mayflower Hotel Corp., Del.Supr., 93 A.2d 107 (1952).

18. This step shares some of the same spirit and philosophy of the statement by the Vice Chancellor: "Under our system of law, courts and not litigants should decide the merits of litigation." 413 A.2d at 1263.

ARONSON v. LEWIS, 473 A.2d 805 (Del.1984). "[T]he *Zapata* demand-excused/demand-refused bifurcation ... has left a crucial issue unanswered: when is demand futile and, therefore, excused?

"Delaware courts have addressed the issue of demand futility on several earlier occasions.... The rule emerging from these decisions is that where officers and directors are under an influence which sterilizes their discretion, they cannot be considered proper persons to conduct litigation on behalf of the corporation. Thus, demand would be futile. See e.g., McKee v. Rogers, Del.Ch., 156 A. 191, 192 (1931) (holding that where a defendant controlled the board of directors, '[i]t is manifest then that there can be no expectation that the corporation would sue him, and if it did, it can hardly be said that the prosecution of the suit would be entrusted to proper hands')....

"However, those cases cannot be taken to mean that any board approval of a challenged transaction automatically connotes 'hostile interest' and 'guilty participation' by directors, or some other form of sterilizing influence upon them. Were that so, the demand requirements of our law would be meaningless, leaving the clear mandate of Chancery Rule 23.1 devoid of its purpose and substance....

"Our view is that in determining demand futility the Court of Chancery in the proper exercise of its discretion must decide whether, under the particularized facts alleged, a reasonable doubt is created that: (1) the directors are disinterested and independent and (2) the challenged transaction was otherwise the product of a valid exercise of business judgment. Hence, the Court of Chancery must make two inquiries, one into the independence and disinterestedness of the directors and the other into the substantive nature of the challenged transaction and the board's approval thereof. As to the latter inquiry the court does not assume that the transaction is a wrong to the corporation requiring corrective steps by the board. Rather, the alleged wrong is substantively reviewed against the factual background alleged in the complaint. As to the former inquiry, directorial independence and disinterestedness, the court reviews the factual allegations to decide whether they raise a reasonable doubt, as a threshold matter, that the protections of the business judgment rule are available to the board. Certainly, if this is an 'interested' director transaction, such that the business judgment rule is inapplicable to the board majority approving the transaction, then the inquiry ceases. In that event futility of demand has been established by any objective or subjective standard.[8] See, e.g., Bergstein v. Texas International Co., Del.Ch., 453 A.2d 467, 471 (1982) (because five of nine directors approved stock appreciation rights plan likely to benefit them, board

---

8. We recognize that drawing the line at a majority of the board may be an arguably arbitrary dividing point. Critics will charge that we are ignoring the structural bias common to corporate boards throughout America, as well as the other unseen socialization processes cutting against independent discussion and decisionmaking in the board-room. The difficulty with structural bias in a demand futile case is simply one of establishing it in the complaint for purposes of Rule 23.1. We are satisfied that discretionary review by the Court of Chancery of complaints alleging specific facts pointing to bias on a particular board will be sufficient for determining demand futility.

was interested for demand purposes and demand held futile). This includes situations involving self-dealing directors....

"However, the mere threat of personal liability for approving a questioned transaction, standing alone, is insufficient to challenge either the independence or disinterestedness of directors, although in rare cases a transaction may be so egregious on its face that board approval cannot meet the test of business judgment, and a substantial likelihood of director liability therefore exists.... In sum the entire review is factual in nature. The Court of Chancery in the exercise of its sound discretion must be satisfied that a plaintiff has alleged facts with particularity which, taken as true, support a reasonable doubt that the challenged transaction was the product of a valid exercise of business judgment. Only in that context is demand excused."

NOTE: The Delaware Supreme Court later changed the formulation, although not the substance, of the *Aronson* test by changing the connective from "and" to "or." Accordingly, the test now reads: "whether under the particularized facts alleged, a reasonable doubt is created that: (1) the directors are disinterested and independent [or] (2) the challenged transaction was otherwise the product of a valid exercise of business judgment." See Rales v. Blasband, 634 A.2d 927 (Del. 1993); Brehm v. Eisner, 746 A.2d 244 (1998).

––––––

GROBOW v. PEROT, 539 A.2d 180 (Del.1988). "[G]iven the highly factual nature of the inquiry presented to the Trial Court by a Rule 23.1 defense, we conclude that it would be neither practicable nor wise to attempt to formulate a criterion of general application for determining reasonable doubt [under *Aronson v. Lewis*]. The facts necessary to support a finding of reasonable doubt either of director disinterest or independence, or whether proper business judgment was exercised in the transaction will vary with each case. Reasonable doubt must be decided by the trial court on a case-by-case basis employing an objective analysis. Were we to adopt a standard criterion for resolving a motion to dismiss based on Rule 23.1, the test for demand excusal would, in all likelihood, become rote and inelastic....

"We think it sufficient simply to say that the Court of Chancery must weigh the presumption of the business judgment rule that attaches to a board of directors' decision against the well-pleaded facts alleged in a plaintiff's demand-futility complaint."

See also Levine v. Smith, 591 A.2d 194 (Del.Supr.1991).

––––––

NOTE ON CUKER v. MIKALAUSKAS

In Cuker v. Mikalauskas, 547 Pa. 600, 692 A.2d 1042 (Pa. 1997), PECO Energy Co. filed a motion for summary judgment seeking termination of minority shareholder derivative actions. The motion was filed on behalf of the board, which had adopted the report of a special litigation committee that proceeding with the actions would not be in the corporation's best interests. The trial court rejected PECO's motion for summary judgment. The Pennsylvania Supreme Court reversed and remanded, with the following instructions:

> Decisions regarding litigation by or on behalf of a corporation, including shareholder derivative actions, are business decisions as much as any other financial decisions. As such, they are within the province of the board of directors [and within the scope of the business judgment rule]. . . .
>
> . . . [T]he practical effect of this holding needs elaboration. Assuming that an independent board of directors may terminate shareholder derivative actions, what is needed is a procedural mechanism for implementation and judicial review of the board's decision. Without considering the merits of the action, a court should determine the validity of the board's decision to terminate the litigation; if that decision was made in accordance with the appropriate standards, then the court should dismiss the derivative action prior to litigation on the merits.
>
> The business judgment rule should insulate officers and directors from judicial intervention in the absence of fraud or self-dealing, if challenged decisions were within the scope of the directors' authority, if they exercised reasonable diligence, and if they honestly and rationally believed their decisions were in the best interests of the company. It is obvious that a court must examine the circumstances surrounding the decisions in order to determine if the conditions warrant application of the business judgment rule. If they do, the court will never proceed to an examination of the merits of the challenged decisions, for that is precisely what the business judgment rule prohibits. In order to make the business judgment rule meaningful, the preliminary examination should be limited and precise so as to minimize judicial involvement when application of the business judgment rule is warranted.
>
> To achieve these goals, a court might stay the derivative action while it determines the propriety of the board's decision. The court might order limited discovery or an evidentiary hearing to resolve issues respecting the board's decision. Factors bearing on the board's decision will include whether the board or its special litigation committee was disinterested, whether it was assisted by counsel, whether it prepared a written report, whether it was independent, whether it conducted an adequate investigation, and whether it rationally believed its decision was in the best interests of the corporation (i.e., acted in good faith). If all of these criteria are satisfied, the business judgment rule applies and the court should dismiss the action.
>
> These considerations and procedures are all encompassed in Part VII, chapter 1 of the *ALI Principles* (relating to the derivative

action), which provides a comprehensive mechanism to address shareholder derivative actions. A number of its provisions are implicated in the action at bar. Sections 7.02 (standing), 7.03 (the demand rule), 7.04 (procedure in derivative action), 7.05 (board authority in derivative action), 7.06 (judicial stay of derivative action), 7.07, 7.08, and 7.09 (dismissal of derivative action), 7.10 (standard of judicial review), and 7.13 (judicial procedures) are specifically applicable to this case.[3] These sections set forth guidance which is consistent with Pennsylvania law and precedent, which furthers the policies inherent in the business judgment rule, and which provides an appropriate degree of specificity to guide the trial court in controlling the proceedings in this litigation.

We specifically adopt §§ 7.02–7.10, and § 7.13 of the *ALI Principles*.[5] In doing so we have weighed many considerations. First, the opinion of the trial court, the questions certified to the Superior Court, and the inability of PECO to obtain a definitive ruling from the lower courts all demonstrate the need for specific guidance from this court on how such litigation should be managed; the ALI principles provide such guidance in specific terms which will simplify this litigation. Second, we have often found ALI guidance helpful in the past, most frequently in adopting or citing sections of various Restatements; the scholarship reflected in work of the American Law Institute has been consistently reliable and useful. Third, the principles set forth by the ALI are generally consistent with Pennsylvania precedent. Fourth, although the *ALI Principles* incorporate much of the law of New York and Delaware, other states with extensive corporate jurisprudence, the ALI Principles better serve the needs of Pennsylvania. Although New York law parallels Pennsylvania law in many respects, it does not set forth any procedures to govern the review of corporate decisions relating to derivative litigation, and this omission would fail to satisfy the needs evident in this case. Delaware law permits a court in some cases ("demand excused" cases) to apply its own business judgment in the review process when deciding to honor the directors' decision to terminate derivative litigation. In our view, this is a defect which could

---

3. *ALI Principles* §§ 4.01, 4.02, and 4.03 (duties of directors and officers; the business judgment rule; reliance on committees and other persons) are similar but not identical to the statutory standards found in 15 Pa.C.S. §§ 512, 513, 515, 1712, 1713, and 1715. The statutory standards, of course, control the duties of directors and the application of the business judgment rule in Pennsylvania.

5. Our adoption of these sections is not a rejection of other sections not cited. We have identified and studied the sections which apply to this case and have adopted those which appear most relevant.

The entire publication, all seven parts, is a comprehensive, cohesive work more than a decade in preparation. Additional sections of the publication, particularly procedural ones due to their interlocking character, may be adopted in the future. Issues in future cases or, perhaps, further proceedings in this case might implicate additional sections of the *ALI Principles*. Courts of the Commonwealth are free to consider other parts of the work and utilize them if they are helpful and appear to be consistent with Pennsylvania law.

eviscerate the business judgment rule and contradict a long line of Pennsylvania precedents. Delaware law also fails to provide a procedural framework for judicial review of corporate decisions under the business judgment rule.

Accordingly, we adopt the specified sections of the *ALI Principles*, reverse the orders of the court of common pleas, and remand the matter for further proceedings consistent with this opinion.

In an Appendix to its opinion, the court set out Principles of Corporate Governance §§ 7.02–7.10 and 7.13 in full.

————

IN RE PSE&G SHAREHOLDER LITIGATION, 173 N.J. 258, 801 A.2d 295 (2002). Plaintiffs filed derivative actions. The board directed an investigation by a law firm, and, based on the law firm's report, moved for summary judgment. The New Jersey court adopted the following standard of review: "We believe that the trial court correctly declined to apply the traditional business judgment rule in this case. Instead, we shall apply a modified business judgment rule that imposes an initial burden on a corporation to demonstrate that in deciding to reject or terminate a shareholder's suit the members of the board (1) were independent and disinterested, (2) acted in good faith and with due care in their investigation of the shareholder's allegations, and that (3) the board's decision was reasonable.... All three elements must be satisfied. Moreover, shareholders in these circumstances must be permitted access to corporate documents and other discovery 'limited to the narrow issue of what steps the directors took to inform themselves of the shareholder demand and the reasonableness of its decision.' " ...

————

MODEL BUSINESS CORPORATION ACT §§ 7.42–7.44

[See Statutory Supplement]

————

AMERICAN LAW INSTITUTE, PRINCIPLES OF CORPORATE GOVERNANCE §§ 7.03, 7.04, 7.08–7.13

[See Statutory Supplement]

————

NOTE ON INDEPENDENCE

The concept of independence is in some ways new in corporate law. It figures in a variety of contexts, including, but not limited to, derivative actions.

1. *Board Composition.* Until around 1970, for purposes board composition a distinction was drawn between "outside" and "inside" directors. Inside directors were directors who were also officers. All other directors were outside directors. Gradually, a recognition emerged that a director could be an outside director and yet not an independent director—that is, not independent of management—because even though a director wasn't an employee, she might have important economic ties to the corporation that could affect her independence from the senior executives, whose performance she was supposed to monitor. Today, it is generally recognized that rather than having simply a majority of outside directors, the board of a publicly held corporation should have a majority of directors who are independent of the senior executives.

2. *Conflict-of-Interest Transactions.* Similarly, in considering the board's review of a director's conflict-of-interest transaction, the courts at one time focused almost exclusively on whether the reviewing directors were "disinterested," in the sense that they did not have a financial stake in the relevant transaction, rather than "independent," in the sense that they were independent of the director who engaged in the transaction. In contrast, today the courts are increasingly requiring both disinterestedness and independence in this context.

3. *Excuse of Demand.* In Beam v. Martha Stewart, 845 A.2d 1040 (Del. Supr. 2004), the issue of independence arose in the context of whether the plaintiff in a derivative action was excused from making a demand on the board on the ground that a majority of the directors were not disinterested and independent. Martha Stewart was an officer, director, and 94% owner of Martha Stewart Living Omnimedia, Inc. ("MSO"). Beam, the derivative-action plaintiff, was a minority shareholder. Beam's complaint alleged that Martha Stewart had breached her fiduciary duties of loyalty and care to MSO by illegally selling stock she owned in another company and mishandling the media attention that followed, thereby jeopardizing MSO's financial position. Beam did not make a demand on the board before bringing suit. The Chancellor dismissed one count of Beam's complaint on the ground that Beam had failed to plead particularized facts demonstrating demand futility.

MSO's board of directors consisted of six members: Stewart, Patrick, Martinez, Moore, Seligman, and Ubben. The Chancellor found that Stewart's potential civil and criminal liability for the acts underlying Beam's claim rendered her an interested party, and therefore unable to consider demand. The Chancellor also found that Patrick's position as an officer and inside director, together with the substantial compensation she received from MSO, raised a reasonable doubt as to her ability objectively to consider a demand. Beam claimed, among other things, that Martinez was also not independent in view of his longstanding personal friendship with both Patrick and Stewart, and that Moore was not independent in view of her longstanding personal relationship with Stewart. The Chancellor determined that the complaint failed to raise a reasonable doubt that Martinez and Patrick were independent, despite their personal ties to Stewart. The Delaware Supreme Court affirmed, but made clear that in an appropriate case, strong ties of personal friendship or other nonfinancial relationships could lead to a conclusion that a director lacked independence:

> A variety of motivations, including friendship, may influence the demand futility inquiry. But, to render a director unable to consider demand, a relationship must be of a bias-producing nature. Allegations of mere personal friendship or a mere outside business relationship, standing alone, are insufficient to raise a reasonable doubt about a director's independence. In this connection, we adopt as our own the Chancellor's analysis in this case:
>
> > [S]ome professional or personal friendships, which may border on or even exceed familial loyalty and closeness, may raise a reasonable doubt whether a director can appropriately consider demand. This is particularly true when the allegations raise serious questions of either civil or criminal liability of such a close friend. Not all friendships, or even most of them, rise to this level and the Court cannot make a *reasonable* inference that a particular friendship does so without specific factual allegations to support such a conclusion....
>
> Allegations that Stewart and the other directors moved in the same social circles, attended the same weddings, developed business relationships before joining the board, and described each other as "friends," even when coupled with Stewart's 94% voting power, are insufficient, without more, to rebut the presumption of independence.... [S]uch affinities—standing alone—will not render pre-suit demand futile.
>
> That is not to say that personal friendship is always irrelevant to the independence calculus. But, for presuit demand purposes, friendship must be accompanied by substantially more in the nature of serious allegations that would lead to a reasonable doubt as to a director's independence. That a much stronger relationship is necessary to overcome the presumption of independence at the demand futility stage becomes especially compelling when one considers the risks that directors would take by protecting their social acquaintances in the face of allegations that those friends engaged in misconduct. To create a reasonable doubt about an outside director's independence, a plaintiff must plead facts that would support the inference that because of the nature of a relationship or additional circumstances other than the interested director's stock ownership or voting power, the non-interested director would be more willing to risk his or her reputation than risk the relationship with the interested director.

4. *Special Litigation Committees.* In In re Oracle Corp. Derivative Litigation, 824 A.2d 917 (Del. Ch. 2003), a derivative action had been brought which alleged that several Oracle directors and officers had engaged in illegal insider trading. A two-person litigation special litigation committee ("SLC") moved to dismiss the action. The issue

arose whether the members of the committee were independent. Both committee members were professors at Stanford, and the defendants also had important ties to Stanford. Vice Chancellor Strine noted that the directors who were accused of insider trading included:

> (1) another Stanford professor, who taught one of the SLC members when the SLC member was a Ph.D. candidate and who serves as a senior fellow and a steering committee member alongside that SLC member at the Stanford Institute for Economic Policy Research or "SIEPR"; (2) a Stanford alumnus who has directed millions of dollars of contributions to Stanford during recent years, serves as Chair of SIEPR's Advisory Board and has a conference center named for him at SIEPR's facility, and has contributed nearly $600,000 to SIEPR and the Stanford Law School, both parts of Stanford with which one of the SLC members is closely affiliated; and (3) Oracle's CEO, who has made millions of dollars in donations to Stanford through a personal foundation and large donations indirectly through Oracle, and who was considering making donations of his $100 million house and $170 million for a scholarship program as late as August 2001, at around the same time period the SLC members were added to the Oracle board.

On these facts, Vice Chancellor Strine concluded that there was a reasonable doubt about the impartiality of the SLC:

> It is no easy task to decide whether to accuse a fellow director of insider trading. For Oracle to compound that difficulty by requiring SLC members to consider accusing a fellow professor and two large benefactors of their university of conduct that is rightly considered a violation of criminal law was unnecessary and inconsistent with the concept of independence recognized by our law. The possibility that these extraneous considerations biased the inquiry of the SLC is too substantial for this court to ignore. I therefore deny the SLC's motion to terminate.

In *Martha Stewart*, the Delaware Supreme Court commented on *Oracle* as follows:

> An SLC is a unique creature that was introduced into Delaware law by *Zapata v. Maldonado* in 1981. The SLC procedure is a method sometimes employed where presuit demand has already been excused and the SLC is vested with the full power of the board to conduct an extensive investigation into the merits of the corporate claim with a view toward determining whether—in the SLC's business judgment—the corporate claim should be pursued. Unlike the demand-excusal context, where the board is presumed to be independent, the SLC has the burden of establishing its own independence by a yardstick that must be "like Caesar's wife"—"above reproach." Moreover, unlike the presuit demand context, the SLC analysis contemplates not only a shift in the burden of persuasion but also the availability of discovery into various issues, including independence.

We need not decide whether the substantive standard of independence in an SLC case differs from that in a pre-suit demand case. As a practical matter, the procedural distinction relating to the diametrically-opposed burdens and the availability of discovery into independence may be outcome-determinative on the issue of independence. Moreover, because the members of an SLC are vested with enormous power to seek dismissal of a derivative suit brought against their director-colleagues in a setting where presuit demand is already excused, the Court of Chancery must exercise careful oversight of the bona fides of the SLC and its process. Aside from the procedural distinctions, the Stanford connections in *Oracle* are factually distinct from the relationships here.

5. *Special Negotiating Committees.* In a footnote in *Martha Stewart*, the court also commented on independence in the context of a special negotiating committee in a merger. The court here pointed out still another facet of independence: It is not always enough to be independent *on paper*; the director must sometimes also demonstrate independence on the ground, by *acting* independent:

> The analysis applied to determine the independence of a special committee in a merger case also has its own special procedural characteristics. In such cases, courts evaluate not only whether the relationships among members of the committee and interested parties placed them in a position objectively to consider a proposed transaction, but also whether the committee members *in fact* functioned independently. *See, e.g., Kahn v. Tremont Corp.*, 694 A.2d 422, 429–30 (Del.1997) ("[T]he Special Committee— did not function independently.... From its inception, the Special Committee failed to operate in a manner which would create the appearance of objectivity in Tremont's decision to purchase the NL stock. As this Court has previously stated in defining director independence: 'it is the care, attention and sense of individual responsibility to the performance of one's duties ... that generally touches on independence.' The record amply demonstrates that neither Stafford nor Boushka possessed the 'care, attention and sense of responsibility' necessary to afford them the status of independent directors." ...)

SECTION 7. DEMAND ON THE SHAREHOLDERS

NOTE ON DEMAND ON SHAREHOLDERS

The rules governing demand on the shareholders vary widely.

1. *Demand Not Required.* Under the law of many jurisdictions, demand on shareholders is not required. For example, the California

and New York statutory counterparts to FRCP 23.1 omit any reference to demand on the shareholders, and it is clear that this omission was deliberate. See Syracuse Television, Inc. v. Channel 9, Syracuse, Inc., 51 Misc.2d 188, 273 N.Y.S.2d 16 (1966).

2. *Demand Required; Exceptions*. A substantial minority of jurisdictions, including Massachusetts, continue to require that demand be made on other shareholders. "The rationale for demand on other shareholders is that such a requirement allows the majority of shareholders to determine whether legal action is in the corporation's best interest." Harhen v. Brown, 431 Mass. 838, 730 N.E.2d 859 (Mass. 2000). Even in these jurisdictions, demand may be excused, but there is considerable divergence concerning what constitutes an acceptable excuse.

a. *Wrongdoers hold a majority of the stock*. All courts agree that demand on shareholders is excused when the alleged wrongdoers hold a majority of the stock. See, e.g., Heilbrunn v. Hanover Equities Corp., 259 F.Supp. 936 (S.D.N.Y.1966). Most courts would probably come to the same result where the wrongdoers hold a controlling but less-than-majority interest. See Gottesman v. General Motors Corp., 268 F.2d 194 (2d Cir.1959). But see Levitan v. Stout, 97 F.Supp. 105 (W.D.Ky.1951).

b. *Demand otherwise futile*. All courts would probably agree that demand on shareholders is also excused when it is futile for other reasons, although there might be considerable divergence as to whether a given state of facts constitutes futility. See, e.g., Pioche Mines Consolidated, Inc. v. Dolman, 333 F.2d 257, 264–65 (9th Cir.1964), cert. denied 380 U.S. 956, 85 S.Ct. 1081, 13 L.Ed.2d 972 (1965) (demand excused where only one shareholders' meeting had been held for many years, and management had ignored earlier demands that such meetings be held).

c. *Large number of shareholders*. The cases are split on whether demand on shareholders is excused because the corporation has a large number of shareholders. In Harhen v. Brown, supra, the Massachusetts court said, "Although we have not previously recognized such an exception, we conclude today that an exception to the shareholder demand requirement, where a very large number of shareholders is involved, as in this case, is eminently reasonable, and we therefore adopt such an exception. To hold otherwise would place a tremendous financial and administrative burden on plaintiffs; in this case requiring the plaintiff to make demand on the seven million other policyholders."

d. *Nonratifiable wrong*. The cases are also split on whether demand on shareholders is excused where the alleged wrong could not be ratified. The majority rule, reflected in Mayer v. Adams, 37 Del.Ch. 298, 141 A.2d 458 (1958) is that nonratifiability excuses demand. However, there is a very strong minority view. For example, in Bell v. Arnold, supra, the court stated:

One reason set forth in the complaint for not making a demand on the shareholders is that they could not ratify the alleged wrongs because of the illegal nature of the wrongs. We hold this is not an acceptable reason or a valid excuse for not making a demand on the shareholders here. The purpose of making demand on the shareholders is to inform them of the alleged nonratifiable wrongs; to seek their participation in available courses of action, such as, the removal of the involved directors and the election of new directors who will seek the redress required in the circumstances; or to secure shareholder approval of an action for damages to the corporation caused by the alleged wrongdoing directors.

See also Claman v. Robertson, 164 Ohio St. 61, 128 N.E.2d 429 (1955).

3. *Two Distinctions.* A distinction must be drawn between the question whether a plaintiff must make a demand on shareholders and the question whether shareholder ratification has a substantive effect. A further distinction is drawn by some courts (most notably Massachusetts), which hold that the shareholders have power to preclude suit even where they do not have power to ratify. The leading case is S. Solomont & Sons Trust v. New England Theatres Operating Corp., 326 Mass. 99, 111–12, 93 N.E.2d 241, 247–48 (1950).

SECTION 8.   PLAINTIFF'S COUNSEL FEES

Sugarland Industries, Inc. v. Thomas

Supreme Court of Delaware, 1980.
420 A.2d 142.*

■ Before DUFFY, QUILLEN and HORSEY, JJ.

■ DUFFY, JUSTICE:

This is an appeal from an order of the Court of Chancery awarding $3.5 million in attorney fees. Counsel's efforts in the case are separable into two phases, and the appeal places both of them in issue, that is, a Phase I award of $3 million and a Phase II award of $500,000. Plaintiffs have cross-appealed as to the orders governing interest on the awards.

I

The relevant facts are as follows:

In January 1973, Sugarland Industries, Inc., a Delaware corporation (defendant) controlled by the Kempner family,[1] owned 7,500 acres of land in Texas south of Houston which it was attempting to

* On appeal after remand, 431 A.2d 1271 (Del.1981) (footnote by ed.)

1. All members of the Board of Directors of Sugarland are members of the Kempner family, with one exception.

sell. Lyda Ann Q. Thomas and her husband, J. Redmond Thomas (plaintiffs), who are members of the Kempner family and shareholders in Sugarland, were concerned about a proposed sale of the so-called South Tract (which is the major part of the property and includes some 5,900 acres) to White and Hill, a Texas partnership involved in real estate development, for $23,800,000. Plaintiffs considered the price to be inadequate and retained Brantly Harris, a Houston lawyer and a partner in the firm of Prappas, Caldwell & Moncure (now, Prappas, Moncure, Harris & Termini) to represent their interest in the proposed sale. Shortly thereafter, and at least partially as a result of Mr. Harris' efforts, a syndicate known as R–S–C was formed and it offered to buy the South Tract for $27,000,000, or $3.2 million more than White and Hill had offered.

Ignoring the higher bid by R–S–C, Sugarland's directors continued to favor White and Hill and gave notice that a special meeting of stockholders would be held on March 7, 1973, to consider and accept the $23.8 million proposal. After being informed of such a meeting, the Prappas firm, concerned that the Sugarland directors had excluded the possibility of selling the property to anyone other than White and Hill, consulted counsel in Delaware about litigation to block the sale. Prappas had suggested to R–S–C that it would be helpful if R–S–C, which would benefit if plaintiffs prevailed in such litigation, advanced $10,000 as a retainer for Delaware counsel; under this plan, plaintiffs would pay any fees in excess of the $10,000. Both R–S–C and plaintiffs agreed to that arrangement.

Shortly thereafter, on March 6, plaintiffs filed a stockholders' derivative action in the Court of Chancery to enjoin the proposed sale of the South Tract to White and Hill. On March 9, Mr. Prappas wrote a letter to the Thomases confirming their fee arrangement with his firm . . . .

[The court held that the fee agreement entered into by the plaintiffs' lawyers did not preclude their application to the court for attorneys' fees on a basis other than hourly rates.]

On March 22, the Chancellor filed an opinion in which he ruled that Sugarland would be enjoined from accepting the White and Hill proposal and ordered competitive bidding for the Sugarland properties. The opinion was implemented by order dated April 10. Because this created a conflict between the Thomases who, as Sugarland shareholders, wanted the sale to bring top dollar, and R–S–C, which wanted the property at the lowest possible price, the Prappas firm (by letter dated April 6, 1973) withdrew from its representation of R–S–C.

Thereafter, Sugarland conducted a sale by sealed bids, and on April 30, the Gerald D. Hines Interests submitted the highest bid, an offer of $37,229,069 for the South Tract. Hines later negotiated for Sugarland's North Tract and on July 3 entered into a contract for both the North and South Tracts. Hines' bid on the North Tract similarly exceeded the next highest bid on that tract by about $1,243,139. The total price for both properties was about $44,000,000. (The closing was held on December 14, 1973.)

On July 25, after Hines had contracted to buy both Tracts, the Prappas firm wrote to the Thomases "releasing" them from the fee agreement....

Meanwhile, on April 30, a second action on behalf of the same plaintiffs by the same attorneys against the same defendants had been filed in the Court of Chancery; on November 12, a supplemental complaint was filed, thereby beginning the "damage" or Phase II of this controversy. That action was essentially a claim for damages against the Sugarland directors. Unlike the first or injunctive phase which was swiftly concluded, the second phase remained unresolved over the next three years and consumed some 13,000 hours on the part of lawyers (and their respective staffs) representing plaintiffs.

On November 10, 1977, a settlement of the Phase II litigation was finally made and approved by the Court of Chancery. While the complaint addressed to the second phase had alleged wrongdoing involving Sugarland, the terms of settlement did not directly affect the corporation; they centered, rather, on a reorganization of the management of various other business entities owned by the Kempner family.

After the settlement had been approved, plaintiffs' attorneys filed an application in the Court of Chancery seeking a combined fee of approximately $6 million for their services as to Phases I and II of the litigation.

The United States National Bank of Galveston, Trustee (intervenor) owns some 47,500 shares (about 23%) of Sugarland stock. It entered the litigation as an objector to the fee application.

On January 26, 1979, the Chancellor awarded plaintiffs' counsel[2] a fee of $3,500,000 computed as follows: (a) as to Phase I, a fee equal to 20% of the benefit created by their efforts, with a cap of $3 million, and (b) as to Phase II, the sum of $500,000 for time expended in achieving the settlement. An order implementing the opinion was entered on May 11, 1979. It directed that $1,376,130 be paid within the month, and required that the remainder be paid "if, as, and when" Sugarland received additional monies in the future from Hines. It also provided that petitioners would be entitled to 6% interest on any late payments made by Sugarland.

Defendant and the intervenor have docketed this appeal....

II

We consider, first, the arguments made by the United States National Bank of Galveston, Trustee.... [The Bank contends that] Sugarland did not benefit from the Phase II efforts of counsel and, therefore, should not be obliged to pay for them....

The Phase II settlement did not result in the creation of a fund or transfer of a tangible benefit to Sugarland. The Bank concedes, tacitly

---

2. For convenience, we will hereafter refer to the attorneys whose compensation is in issue as "petitioners." They include, of course, both the Delaware and Texas firms.

All parties tacitly concede that whatever fee arrangements plaintiffs made with Prappas are equally applicable to Delaware counsel.

at least, that the case was settled in the interest of "family harmony" by effecting a reorganization of the personnel of the boards or management of the various Kempner entities.

In his opinion, the Chancellor described in some detail the changes in management effected by the settlement agreement, and it is unnecessary to repeat them here. It is enough to say that they were numerous and relatively complex; they involved some eight or nine separate entities and a seemingly endless series of personnel changes and power balancing. As we see it, the result was accurately summarized in the Chancellor's opinion, thus:

> ". . . As to the second phase application, I am satisfied that petitioners are entitled to be compensated on the non-pecuniary results of their effort to bring harmony to the Kempner family although such benefit does not inure directly to the benefit of Sugarland Industries and its stockholders. . . .
>
> Petitioners will be allowed the amount of $500,000 for the time expended and effort exerted by them during the second phase of this case, which resulted in a settlement which promises to terminate the feud which has split the Kempner family in recent years, thus indirectly benefiting Sugarland Industries and its stockholders. . . . "

It is undisputed that the settlement agreement was the culmination of long and intensive efforts by counsel over many years. Sugarland was not a direct beneficiary of the "family harmony" which, legally speaking at least, resulted from the settlement. But it was very much involved in both lawsuits and it was a party to the settlement of both of them. Indeed, the purpose of the settlement agreement was to "settle all claims" in both actions[5] and thus to put an end to the controversy and the issues in litigation. A hearing was held and the settlement was approved on the basis of Sugarland participation in it. Prior thereto, notice as to the agreement, the stipulation of settlement, the other pertinent documents and the date of hearing was sent to all Sugarland stockholders, including the Bank. The Bank elected not to appear nor to challenge the settlement. It arrived only after the *fait accompli* to challenge the right of the settling corporation to pay counsel fees.

In the stipulation of settlement, Sugarland reserved the right "to object to any application for allowance of fees and expenses of plaintiffs and their attorneys," but the stipulation also provides that

---

5. The agreement provides in part, as follows:

"I. 1. The purpose of this agreement is to settle all claims remaining in the above litigation, and the agreement and actions contemplated in Section II hereof are the direct result of the assertion and prosecution of such claims, derivatively by plaintiffs for the benefit of defendant Sugarland Industries, Inc. ('Sugarland').

2. Section II of this agreement and the actions that it contemplates provide a substantial, real benefit to the body of stockholders of Sugarland, constituting a proper basis and appropriate, commensurate consideration for the settlement of the remaining claims of Sugarland, which is itself in the course of liquidation.

3. The parties will each support the settlement and will each promptly seek the required judicial approval for it."

"Sugarland has determined that this settlement is beneficial to it and in the best interests of Sugarland and its stockholders." Given that representation by Sugarland to the Court before the settlement was approved, Sugarland's reservations as to fees might well be construed as going to the amount of any allowance, not to whether it had, in principle, any duty to pay an allowance.

In any event, we are satisfied that the Chancellor properly invoked his power to order Sugarland to pay fees to petitioners for Phase II services. In saying this, we note that most of the stockholders of Sugarland are also (in the same proportion) stockholders in or beneficial owners of other Kempner enterprises, and that Sugarland was in liquidation. Compare *Mills v. Electric Auto–Lite Co.,* 396 U.S. 375, 90 S.Ct. 616, 24 L.Ed.2d 593 (1970); *Richman v. DeVal Aerodynamics, Inc.,* Del.Ch., 185 A.2d 884 (1962).

III

We now consider Sugarland's argument that the fee awarded for Phase I is grossly excessive under any standard. The thrust of the argument is that petitioners had expended only $122,881 worth of time, at their regular hourly rates, and that the percentage approach adopted by the Chancellor was arbitrary under the circumstances.

The standard of review of an award of attorney fees in Chancery is well settled under Delaware case law: the test is abuse of discretion. *Chrysler Corporation v. Dann,* Del.Supr., 223 A.2d 384 (1966)....

As to the amount of the fee, Sugarland observes that there is no real dispute between the parties as to the "elements of the Delaware standard" governing fees. It argues that the "results achieved" by counsel plus the following factors stated by the Chancellor are pertinent:

> "... the amount of time and effort applied to a case by counsel for plaintiff, the relative complexities of the litigation, the skills applied to their resolution by counsel, as well as any contingency factor and the standing and ability of petitioning counsel are, of course, considered in the award of fees in an appropriate case...."

Sugarland invites our attention to *Lindy I* [Lindy Bros. Buildings, Inc. v. American Radiator & Standard Sanitary Corp., 487 F.2d 161 (1973)], an opinion authored by Chief Judge Seitz, who served as Chancellor of Delaware (and before then as Vice Chancellor) for some twenty years during which he ruled on many applications for counsel fees. Sugarland argues that Delaware should adopt the *Lindy I* guidelines as other jurisdictions have done.[8]

The evolution of *Lindy I* has not been limited to jurisdictions other than the Third Circuit. Indeed, the case has its own progeny in

---

8. See, for example, *City of Detroit v. Grinnell Corporation,* 2 Cir., 495 F.2d 448 (1974); *Grunin v. International House of Pancakes,* 8 Cir., 513 F.2d 114 (1975), *cert. de-* nied 423 U.S. 864, 96 S.Ct. 124, 46 L.Ed.2d 93 (1975); *National Treasury Employees Union v. Nixon,* D.C.Cir., 521 F.2d 317 (1975).

Lindy II, an *en banc* ruling by the Third Circuit [540 F.2d 102 (1976)]; see also *Baughman v. Wilson Freight Forwarding Co.,* 3 Cir., 583 F.2d 1208 (1978).

As we understand Sugarland's contention, *Lindy I's* principal significance for Phase I purposes is its emphasis on the "time factor" and because petitioners' entire fee was not "at risk."

Under *Lindy I,* the Court's analysis must begin with a calculation of the number of hours to be credited to the attorney seeking compensation. The total hours multiplied by the approved hourly rate is the "lodestar" in the Third Circuit's formulation. It has, indeed, been said that the time approach is virtually the sole consideration in making a fee ruling under *Lindy I.* Be that as it may, we conclude that our Chancery Judges should not be obliged to make the kind of elaborate analyses called for by the several opinions in *Lindy I* and *Lindy II.* To put it another way, while *Lindy's* careful craftsmanship has much to commend it, we are not persuaded that our case law governing fee applications is an inadequate criterion for a fair judgment in this case, nor that new guidelines are needed for the Court of Chancery.

It is undisputed that the White and Hill offer was $23,800,000, so, in one sense, petitioners are entitled to "some" credit for any amount received by Sugarland in excess of that sum.

The Chancellor determined that petitioners are entitled to a fair percentage of the benefit inuring to Sugarland and its stockholders from the sale of both Tracts to the Hines group; he computed the monetary benefit to Sugarland, as a result of petitioners' efforts, to be about $21,812,000. That figure gives petitioners full credit for all of the additional cash received or to be received, including principal and interest, from the sale of both tracts. The Chancellor held that petitioners are entitled to 20% of the fund thus created through their efforts, but subject to a $3,000,000 cap. Petitioners say that with that limitation, the award computes to about 14% of the benefit conferred.

We agree with substantially all of the Chancellor's findings and most of his conclusions, but we are unable to agree with him on one significant element in his formulations: in measuring benefit, he credited petitioners with all amounts received or to be received by Sugarland in excess of the White and Hill offer of $23,800,000. In our view of the case, petitioners' services and the nature of the benefits separate into two distinct parts and the R–S–C offer is at the dividing line between them.

It is crystal clear from the record that the services of petitioners benefited Sugarland to the extent of the difference between the White and Hill offer of $23,800,000 and the $27,000,000 which was submitted by R–S–C. But how one should view the amount received by Sugarland in excess of the $27,000,000 is not so clear. Petitioners had sought the best price obtainable and but for their initiative (and success) at the injunctive stage, Sugarland might not have received anything over the White and Hill offer. Thus, there is, as we have noted, "some" cause and effect between what petitioners did and the ultimate price received. But petitioners are attorneys seeking compensation for services rendered in litigation. They are not brokers or real estate agents seeking a commission or a percentage of sale price for having produced a buyer. And how much anyone would pay, at least in excess of the $27,000,000 offered by R–S–C, was a circumstance neither caused nor influenced by petitioners. The highest offer eventually made has in it something in the nature of [a] "windfall".... [P]etitioners here cannot take full credit for the price which Hines was willing to pay for both tracts.

There is also another factor which relates to the amount of compensation.... [The Prappas firm's contract] did assure *some* compensation for services, at least through the restraining order phrase, and thus petitioners were not providing services entirely on a contingent basis.

Sugarland has taken the position that if the Court reduces the fee award, we should, in the interest of justice and judicial economy, determine the appropriate fee. We conclude that it is appropriate for us to do so in this case.

In making the award, the Chancellor used a 20%–of–benefit factor and that seems reasonable to us when applied to the difference between the respective offers. But for the reasons we have discussed, it is unreasonable when applied to the amounts paid by the buyer in excess of the $27,000,000. We have held that petitioners are entitled to some credit for the benefit received in excess of that sum and, in view of the circumstances, any percentage is arguably fair or not, depending on one's point of view. In our judgment, based on the various factors we have noted, compensation at the rate of 5% of the benefit achieved is fair and should be applied to the additional benefits Sugarland received from the sale of both the North and South Tracts. Given the fee which that percentage generates (about $573,609 in all), we conclude that it is reasonable (and perhaps generous) compensation for the significant skills and expertise which petitioners demonstrated in identifying an inadequate price for the Tracts, in stimulating the competitive offer from R–S–C, in quickly initiating the litigation, in successfully carrying it to a conclusion against highly competent counsel and thus opening the door for entry by the Hines Interests with their offers.

The total amount to be allowed to petitioners as compensation for Phase I services (on an "if, as and when" received basis) is computed as follows:

South Tract	
R–S–C Offer	$27,000,000
White and Hill Offer	23,800,000
	$ 3,200,000
Hines Purchase Price	$37,229,069
R–S–C Offer	27,000,000
	$10,229,069

North Tract
  Additional Benefit (Cash) $ 1,243,139

Computation of the Fee
  20% × $ 3,200,000 $ 640,000
   5% ×   10,229,069   511,453
   5% ×   1,243,139   62,156
                     Total $ 1,213,609

It is difficult to test this allowance on an hourly rate basis because that was not determined by the Chancellor and, indeed, was not crucial to the awards he made. And the allocation of hours is a matter of dispute in this Court. For present purposes, we note only that Sugarland agreed that the total time given to both phases of the litigation by petitioners and their staffs totals 15,110.8 hours. Petitioners say that it amounts to more than that, including about 2,800[10] hours in 1973 for the Phase I representation. In our view of the appeal, we need not resolve the time controversy.

IV

Turning now to Phase II, Sugarland also argues that the $500,000 allowed by the Chancellor is grossly excessive, under any standard.

It is apparent that the Chancellor based the award for this phase largely on a "time and effort" basis. Specifically, he said:

"As to the second phase application, I am satisfied that petitioners are entitled to be compensated on the nonpecuniary results of their efforts to bring harmony to the Kempner family although such benefit does not inure directly to the benefit of Sugarland Industries and its stockholders.

* * *

Petitioners will be allowed the amount of $500,000 for the time expended and effort exerted by them during the second phase of this case.... "

Given the extraordinary difficulties involved in this phase and the central purpose accomplished (family peace by litigation settlement), we conclude that the Chancellor did not abuse his discretion in making the award. Tested on an hourly rate basis, the $500,000 computes to $50 per hour, if only 10,000 of the agreed 15,110.8 hours were assigned to this phase. And that is a modest rate....

Affirmed in part and reversed in part with directions to enter judgment in accordance herewith.

[A motion by the petitioners for reargument was denied. 420 A.2d 142, 146.]

---

10. All of Phase I was completed in 1973. Accepting petitioners' representations that they gave 2,800 hours to that Phase, then the allowance made herein computes to about $433 per hour.

TANDYCRAFTS, INC. v. INITIO PTNRS., 562 A.2d 1162 (Del. Supr.1989). Initio Partners, a limited partnership, was the largest independent shareholder of Tandycrafts, Inc., owning 9.9% of Tandycraft's stock. Tandycraft proposed to amend its charter, and issued a proxy statement in connection with the vote on the proposed amendment at the annual meeting. Initio sought a temporary injunction against holding Tandycraft's annual meeting, on the ground that the proxy statement was materially misleading.

Tandycraft then prepared a supplement to its proxy statement that made clarifications and new disclosures on the subjects Initio had complained of. The annual meeting was held, and the charter amendments were soundly defeated. Initio then moved for the award of counsel fees and expenses. Tandycraft opposed the motion, on the grounds that the changes in the proxy statement were not attributable to Initio's litigation and that counsel fees could not be awarded to a plaintiff that had sued on its own behalf (as had Initio), rather than derivatively or on behalf of a class. The Vice Chancellor awarded counsel fees to Initio. Affirmed. "In the realm of corporate litigation, the Court may order the payment of counsel fees and related expenses to a plaintiff whose efforts result in the creation of a common fund . . . or the conferring of a corporate benefit. . . . Typically, successful derivative or class action suits which result in the recovery of money or property wrongfully diverted from the corporation, or which result in the imposition of changes in internal operating procedures that are designed to produce such monetary savings in the future, are viewed as fund creating actions. . . .

"The definition of a corporate benefit, however, is much more elastic. While the benefit achieved may have an indirect economic effect on the corporation, in the sense that the interests of the plaintiff class reflect a value not theretofore apparent, the benefit need not be measurable in economic terms. Changes in corporate policy or, as here, a heightened level of corporate disclosure, if attributable to the filing of a meritorious suit, may justify an award of counsel fees. *See* Chrysler Corp. v. Dann, 223 A.2d at 386; Allied Artists Pictures Corp. v. Baron, 413 A.2d at 878.

"Once it is determined that action benefiting the corporation chronologically followed the filing of a meritorious suit, the burden is upon the corporation to demonstrate 'that the lawsuit did not in any way cause their action.' Allied Artists Pictures Corp. v. Baron, 413 A.2d at 880. . . .

"Although this Court has not adopted an expansive approach to fee shifting in corporate litigation, the critical inquiry is not the status of the plaintiff but the nature of the corporate or class benefit which is causally related to the filing of suit. It is to be expected that litigation to force compliance with fiduciary standards or statutory duties will be initiated by a shareholder who has standing to sue for the benefit of the corporation. For the most part, such claims are clearly derivative, or class based. But where the shareholder's individual interests are directly and equally implicated, as in proxy contests, the distinction between individual and representative claims may become blurred. Indeed, the same wrong may give rise to both an individual and derivative action. . . .

"Having concluded that, under these circumstances, Initio had standing to seek an award of counsel fees as an individual plaintiff, we summarily address Tandycrafts' claim that the Vice Chancellor abused his discretion in the fee allowance. The sequence of events is not in dispute and the correction or clarification of the proxy material chronologically followed the filing of the Initio suit attacking the accuracy of the material. It was thus incumbent upon Tandycrafts to demonstrate that there was no causal connection between the suit and the subsequent action. . . . Although Tandycrafts argues that the corrective action would have been taken in any event, we are not persuaded that the Vice Chancellor abused his discretion in ruling to the contrary."

ALI, PRINCIPLES OF CORPORATE GOVERNANCE § 7.17

[See Statutory Supplement]

G & N AIRCRAFT, INC. v. BOEHM, 743 N.E.2d 227 (Ind. 2001). "The trial court awarded Boehm 'attorney's fees in this action,' but did not specify for what or from whom. The Court of Appeals modified this award to allow for attorney's fees against G & N [the corporation] for the derivative action, but no fees against Goldsmith [an individual defendant] in the direct action. We agree with the Court of Appeals that Boehm is not entitled to attorney's fees from Goldsmith in his direct action. The 'United States Rule' is that parties bear their own fees in the absence of a statute or a basis in quantum meruit for reimbursing a party who has benefited others. The direct action by Boehm fits neither category."

Macey & Miller, The Plaintiffs' Attorneys' Role in Class Actions and Derivative Litigation: Economic Analysis and Recommendations for Reform

58 U.Chi.L.Rev. 1, 22–26 (1991).

. . . [Under the lodestar approach, in which the primary determinant of attorneys' fees is the attorney's time, attorneys] have an incentive to run up excessive hours, delay the litigation unnecessarily, or even to exaggerate the number of hours expended in order to obtain a larger fee. Plaintiffs' attorneys may also wish to settle for a relatively low sum on the eve of trial, knowing that in so doing they obtain most of the benefits they can expect from the litigation while eliminating their downside risk. . . .

Further, plaintiffs' attorneys may sometimes substantially reduce their risk by reaching an understanding with defense counsel early on about the contours of the eventual settlement. Then they can expend a mutually acceptable number of additional hours on the case, charging them against the settlement fund under the lodestar calculation. The social disutility of this procedure is obvious; it represents an essentially meaningless exercise that ties up the resources of plaintiffs' counsel, defense counsel, and others such as witnesses who must submit to depositions that all parties understand will never be used in court. The principal losers are members of the plaintiff class who must pay over part of their recovery to counsel for work that serves no purpose other than to justify an enhanced attorney's fee.

. . . There are obvious incentive problems with [the percentage-of-recovery method] as well. First, plaintiffs' attorneys will earn windfall profits, at the expense of the class members, in cases presenting large damages and low proof costs. More generally, it would appear that the percentage method effectively guarantees that plaintiffs' attorneys will be systematically compensated at a rate higher than the rate they would demand in an efficiently functioning competitive market. To illustrate this point, consider the thought process of a plaintiffs' attorney in deciding whether to bring a given cause of action. The attorney operating in a percentage-of-the-recovery system will never bring an action when the expected opportunity costs to the attorney of bringing the suit (as measured by the value the attorney places on his or her time) exceed the expected award of attorneys' fees (equal to the present value of the expected recovery for the class multiplied by the fee percentage used in the jurisdiction and further discounted by the attorney's estimate of the probability of success in the litigation). The plaintiffs' attorney faces a distribution of cases in which one tail—representing cases where the expected payoff to the attorney falls short of the attorney's expected costs—is cut off. On the other hand, the attorney can be expected to bring all cases where the expected payoff equals or exceeds the attorney's expected costs.

Among the cases that are brought will be a wide range of cases in which the expected payoff exceeds the attorney's expected costs. Because the applicable fee percentage is not adjusted downward in such cases—as it would be in an efficiently functioning market for contingency fee representation—these excess profits are not dissipated by competition. In theory, a court could reduce a percentage award downward in such cases, but such judicial reductions would not necessarily be reliable, and would add an additional level of complexity and cost to fee calculations. Thus, plaintiffs' attorneys can be expected to reap systematic excess profits, of which windfall cases are only the most noteworthy examples, under a percentage method. These excess profits are earned at the expense of the plaintiff class.

The second incentive problem in percentage-of-the-recovery cases is settlement. Attorneys compensated on a percentage method have an incentive to settle early for an amount lower than what might be obtained by further efforts. The attorney who puts in relatively few hours to obtain an early settlement is likely to earn a much greater compensation per hour of effort than an attorney who expends greater efforts and litigates a case to the point where the plaintiffs' recovery is maximized. Again the plaintiff class loses.

Consider now common benefit ... cases. Common benefit cases are typically shareholder's derivative suits in which the plaintiffs' attorney does not generate a fund, but rather causes the defendant to do something that confers a nonpecuniary benefit on the corporation. In common benefit ... cases the attorneys' fee comes from the defendant rather than from the class recovery. Unlike common fund cases, therefore, there is a counter-party in common benefit and fee-shifting cases with an incentive to bargain over the fee in order to keep it within reasonable limits.

This feature, however, does not effectively obviate the attorney-client conflict. Defendants in common benefit and fee-shifting cases typically wish to minimize the sum of three costs: the costs of the relief on the merits, the costs of their own attorney's fees, and the costs of the plaintiffs' attorney's fees. Defendants are typically indifferent about how the total cost of litigation is distributed among these elements. Plaintiffs' attorneys, on the other hand, have an interest in increasing their own fees, even at the expense of a reduction in the relief afforded to the putative client. Thus the conditions are present for a bargain under which the plaintiffs' attorneys agree to a lower overall settlement on the merits of the litigation in exchange for a higher fee....

———

BACKGROUND NOTE ON THE AWARD OF COUNSEL FEES TO SUCCESSFUL DERIVATIVE–ACTION PLAINTIFFS

1. *Rationale.* The derivative action constitutes a major legal bulwark against managerial self-dealing. As a practical matter this means that the rules governing plaintiffs' legal fees are critical to the operation of the corporate system: Because very few shareholders would pay, out of their own pockets, the attorney's fee for a suit that is brought on the corporation's behalf and will benefit all shareholders, with only a slight and indirect benefit for the plaintiff, very few derivative actions would be brought if the law did not allow the plaintiff's attorney to be compensated by a contingent fee payable out of the corporate recovery.

As a conceptual matter, the award of counsel fees to successful plaintiffs in derivative actions has been justified by several overlapping rationales, none of which is unique to derivative actions. The most important of these is the "common fund" theory, under which a plaintiff who has successfully established a fund under the control of the court, from which many besides himself will benefit, may recover his counsel fees out of that fund. As stated in the seminal case of Trustees v. Greenough, 105 U.S. (15 Otto) 527, 532, 26 L.Ed. 1157 (1881), to deny an allowance for fees in such circumstances "would not only be unjust to [plaintiff], but ... would give to the other parties entitled to participate in the benefits of the fund an unfair advantage." This theory was later elaborated, under the heading of the "substantial benefit" or "common benefit" theory, to cover cases where the plaintiff had not brought a fund into the court's control but had established a right to a fund from which others would benefit. See Sprague v. Ticonic Nat. Bank, 307 U.S. 161, 59 S.Ct. 777, 83 L.Ed. 1184 (1939). Eventually, the common-benefit theory was extended to cover cases involving the establishment of nonpecuniary benefits.

Another basic rationale for the award of attorneys' fees to successful plaintiffs in derivative actions is the "private attorney-general" doctrine—that plaintiff's counsel fees should be awarded in appropriate cases to encourage the initiation of private actions that vindicate important legal policies. See Newman v. Piggie Park Enterprises, Inc., 390 U.S. 400, 402, 88 S.Ct. 964, 966, 19 L.Ed.2d 1263 (1968).

In the corporate area, this doctrine is important chiefly as a reinforcement to the common-fund or common-benefit theory, particularly where the benefit is not pecuniary. For example, in Mills v. Electric Auto–Lite Co., 396 U.S. 375, 90 S.Ct. 616, 24 L.Ed.2d 593 (1970), plaintiffs, who were former Auto–Lite shareholders, alleged that defendants had violated the Proxy Rules in connection with a merger of Auto–Lite into Mergenthaler. The Court held that plaintiffs were entitled to summary judgment on the merits. It then went on to award interim counsel fees, although it recognized that if on remand the merger were found to be fair, there might be no feasible way to remedy the violation, and therefore no economically measurable benefit to either Auto–Lite or its shareholders. The opinion began by attempting to bring the case within the common-benefit rule: "In many suits under § 14(a) ... it may be impossible to assign monetary value to the benefit. Nevertheless, the stress placed by Congress on the importance of fair and informed corporate suffrage leads to the conclusion that, in vindicating the statutory policy, petitioners have rendered a substantial service to the corporation and its shareholders." However, the Court then seemed to shift rationales by stressing that the action conferred a benefit on a subsector of the public, that is, shareholders as a class.

In Alyeska Pipeline Service Co. v. Wilderness Society, 421 U.S. 240, 95 S.Ct. 1612, 44 L.Ed.2d 141 (1975), the Supreme Court held that in the absence of statutory authorization, attorney's fees may not be awarded on the private-attorney-general theory in suits brought under federal statutes. While the opinion left the common-fund theory (and its derivative, the common-benefit theory) undisturbed, and cited

Sprague and *Mills* with approval, it is open to question whether the Supreme Court would again go as far as it did in *Mills* in determining what constitutes a benefit for these purposes in a suit brought under federal law.

2. *Criteria*. For many years, the criteria to be considered in setting counsel fees were as set out in Angoff v. Goldfine, 270 F.2d 185, 189 (1st Cir.1959):

> [T]he amount recovered for the corporation; the time fairly required to be spent on the case; the skill required and employed on the case with reference to the intricacy, novelty and complexity of issues; the difficulty encountered in unearthing the facts and the skill and resourcefulness of opposing counsel; the prevailing rate of compensation for those with the skill, experience and standing of the attorneys, accountants or others involved; the contingent nature of the fees, with the accompanying risk of wasting hours of work, overhead and expenses (for it is clearly established that compensation is awarded only in the event of success); and the benefits accruing to the public from such suits as this.

Traditionally, the most important of these elements was the first—the amount recovered by the corporation—and as a practical matter the courts tended to calculate counsel fees in derivative actions as a percentage of that amount.[2] Although the percentage varied from case to case, awards calculated on this basis traditionally tended to run around 20–35% of the recovery when the recovery was less than $1 million, and 15–25% when it was more.

In contrast, the 1973 revision of the Federal Judicial Manual for Complex Litigation stated that "the reasonableness of the fee arrived at [in class actions] should not rest primarily on the selection of a percentage of the total recovery," and suggested instead emphasizing "the time and labor required and the effect of the allowance on the public interest and the reputation of the courts." Id. at § 1.47. This approach was adopted by the Third Circuit in the leading case of Lindy Bros. Builders, Inc. v. American Radiator & Standard Sanitary Corp., 487 F.2d 161 (3d Cir.1973), a class action under the antitrust laws. Under *Lindy*, the value of the lawyer's time is made the dominant factor:

> . . . [T]he first inquiry of the court should be into the hours spent by the attorneys. . . .

> After determining . . . the services performed by the attorneys, the district court must attempt to value those services. . . .

> The value of an attorney's time generally is reflected in his normal billing rate. A logical beginning in valuing an attorney's services is to fix a reasonable hourly rate for his time—taking

---

2. "[These cases] find their true analogue in salvage causes on a pure salvage basis of no cure no pay. . . . [B]enefits conferred in the light of the efforts required are the real basis of the salvage awards, as they should be in causes like these." Murphy v. North American Light & Power Co., 33 F.Supp. 567, 570–571 (S.D.N.Y.1940).

account of the attorney's legal reputation and status (partner, associate)....

While the amount thus found to constitute reasonable compensation should be the lodestar of the court's fee determination, there are at least two other factors that must be taken into account in computing the value of attorneys' services. The first of these is the contingent nature of success....

The second additional factor the district court must consider is the extent, if any, to which the quality of an attorney's work mandates increasing or decreasing the amount to which the court has found the attorney reasonably entitled.

Under this approach, which is known as the "lodestar" approach (because hourly time is used as a lodestar), the benefit produced is important chiefly insofar as it bears on the quality of the lawyer's work, as where "a particularly resourceful attorney ... secures a substantial benefit for his clients with a minimum of time invested...."

In 1974 the Second Circuit fell into line with *Lindy* in Detroit v. Grinnell Corp., 495 F.2d 448 (2d Cir.1974). Since a derivative action is in effect a special type of class action, the emphasis placed on lawyer's time by cases like *Lindy* and *Grinnell* came to figure prominently in derivative actions.

There is considerable variation in the percentages applied to basic hourly rates, under the lodestar approach, to adjust for contingency and quality factors. Increases of 50 or 100% are common. Higher and lower increases can also be found.

Even at the height of the lodestar approach, the data suggested that courts managed to apply the lodestar formula in such a way as to produce results comparable to those obtained under the percentage-of-the-benefit formula. See Mowrey, Attorney Fees in Securities Class Actions and Derivative Suits, 3 J.Corp.Law 267 (1978). In 1984, the Supreme Court explicitly stated—albeit in a footnote—that in a common-fund case, a reasonable fee "is based on the percentage of the fund bestowed on the class." Blum v. Stenson, 465 U.S. 886, 900 n. 16, 104 S.Ct. 1541, 1550 n. 16, 79 L.Ed.2d 891 (1984). The Court contrasted this approach to that under the Civil Rights Attorney's Fee Awards Act, where, the Court said, a reasonable fee was based on the attorney's time. The following year, the Third Circuit, which had begun the movement to the lodestar approach with its decision in *Lindy,* issued a Task Force Report that advocated a return to the percentage-of-recovery approach in common-fund cases.

————

GOODRICH v. E.F. HUTTON GROUP, 681 A.2d 1039 (Del. Supr.1996). The court here summarized current federal law as follows: "In the 1970s, courts began to use the 'lodestar' approach to calculate fee awards in common fund cases. *Lindy Bros. Builders, Inc. of Phila.*

v. American Radiator & Standard Sanitary Corp., 487 F.2d 161, 167–68 (3d Cir.1973). *See* Report of the Third Circuit Task Force, *Court Awarded Attorney Fees*, 108 F.R.D. 237, 242 (1985). That method requires a court to calculate the product of an attorney's reasonable hours expended on the litigation and reasonable hourly rate to arrive at the 'lodestar.' *Swedish Hosp. Corp. v. Shalala*, 1 F.3d at 1266. That lodestar calculation can then be adjusted, through application of a 'multiplier' or fee enhancer, to account for additional factors, *e.g.*, the contingent nature of the case and the quality of an attorney's work. *Lindy Bros. Builders, Inc. of Phila. v. American Radiator & Standard Sanitary Corp.*, 540 F.2d 102, 112 (3d Cir.1976); *Swedish Hosp. Corp. v. Shalala*, 1 F.3d at 1266. During the 1970s, the 'lodestar/multiplier' method of awarding fees was frequently invoked in common fund cases, instead of determining a reasonable percentage of recovery from the fund, based upon a multifactor analysis. *Johnson v. Georgia Highway Express, Inc.*, 488 F.2d 714, 716–19 (5th Cir.1974) ('*Johnson*' factors); *Lindy Bros. Builders, Inc. v. American Radiator & Standard Sanitary Corp.*, 487 F.2d at 164–69 ('*Lindy*' factors).

"In the 1980s, however, two events led to a reconsideration of the lodestar method of calculating common fund fee awards. First, in 1984, the Supreme Court distinguished the calculation of awards under fee-shifting statutes from the calculation of attorney's fees under the common fund doctrine. In doing so, the Supreme Court suggested that an award in a common fund case should be based upon a percentage of the fund:

> Unlike the calculation of attorney's fees under the 'common fund doctrine,' where a reasonable fee is based on a percentage of the fund bestowed on the class, a reasonable fee under [42 U.S.C.] § 1988 reflects the amount of attorney time reasonably expended on the litigation.

Blum v. Stenson, 465 U.S. 886, 900 n. 16, 104 S.Ct. 1541, 1550 n. 16, 79 L.Ed.2d 891 (1984). Footnote 16 in *Blum* has been cited for the proposition that the Supreme Court's approval of the lodestar method in the fee-shifting context was not intended to overrule decisions which had approved percentage of the fund awards of attorney's fees in common fund cases. *Swedish Hosp.*, 1 F.3d at 1268. *See, e.g., Sprague v. Ticonic National Bank*, 307 U.S. 161, 59 S.Ct. 777, 83 L.Ed. 1184 (1939); *Central Railroad & Banking Co. v. Pettus*, 113 U.S. 116, 5 S.Ct. 387, 28 L.Ed. 915 (1885). That interpretation of *Blum* did not change when the Supreme Court held that the lodestar should not be enhanced through the use of a multiplier in statutory fee-shifting cases. *City of Burlington v. Dague*, 505 U.S. 557, 565–67, 112 S.Ct. 2638, 2642–44, 120 L.Ed.2d 449 (1992).

"The second significant event in the 1980s was the report issued in 1985 by a Task Force the Third Circuit had appointed to evaluate the practical effectiveness of the lodestar method in making attorney fee awards. *See* Report of the Third Circuit Task Force, *Court Awarded Attorney Fees*, 108 F.R.D. 237 (1985). The Task Force recommended continued use of the lodestar technique in statutory fee-shifting cases.

Id. See also City of Burlington v. Dague, 505 U.S. at 562, 112 S.Ct. at 2641 (acknowledging, in the statutory fee-shifting context, 'a strong presumption that the lodestar represents the reasonable fee'). The Task Force concluded, however, that all attorney fee awards in common fund cases should be structured as a percentage of the fund. Report of the Third Circuit Task Force, *Court Awarded Attorney Fees,* 108 F.R.D. at 255.

"At the present time, the majority of federal courts use a reasonable percentage of the fund method when making attorney fee awards in common fund cases. *See Swedish Hosp. Corp. v. Shalala,* 1 F.3d at 1266 (chronicling history of the methodologies). *See also* FEDERAL JUDICIAL CENTER, AWARDING ATTORNEYS' FEES AND MANAGING FEE LITIGATION 63–64 (1994) (canvassing case law.) The Third Circuit has recently held that the percentage of the fund is generally the preferable method for awarding fees in common fund cases, but noted that a lodestar analysis might be used to cross check the propriety of the award (a 'hybrid' approach). *See In re General Motors Corp. Pick–Up Truck Fuel Tank Products Liability Litigation,* 55 F.3d at 821. Ultimately, however, the Third Circuit permits the trial court to exercise its discretion in choosing *either* the percentage method *or* the lodestar method, *or* some combination or hybrid, as the circumstances warrant, in making common fund fee awards. *Id."*

––––––

FURTHER NOTE ON PLAINTIFF'S COUNSEL FEES

1.   The Third Circuit Task Force Report was extremely influential. Since 1985, a number of Circuits have held that the percentage-of-recovery method is mandatory or permissible in common-fund cases. In a striking and widely remarked-upon opinion in In re Oracle Securities Litigation, 131 F.R.D. 688 (N.D.Cal.1990) (a class-action securities case), Judge Vaughan Walker said, "the lodestar approach . . . is now thoroughly discredited by experience. The lodestar approach is unworkable because, among other things, it abandons the adversary process upon which our judicial system is based. . . ."

2.   In a widely cited decision, In re Activision Securities Litigation, 723 F.Supp. 1373 (N.D.Cal.1989), the court determined, on the basis of a review of recent reported cases, that in nearly all common-fund cases the attorney's fee award ranges around 30% of the fund, even if the fee is purportedly calculated under the lodestar or related methods. The court observed that "[m]ost of these cases achieve this result after lengthy motion practice, volumes of discovery, and hence, the accumulation of extensive attorney time on behalf of all parties." Id. at 1377. Accordingly, the court concluded that the better practice in common-fund cases is to set a percentage fee, and that the percentage should be 30%, absent extraordinary circumstances. Other courts have mentioned other benchmark percentages. For example, in Paul, Johnson, Alston & Hunt v. Graulty, 886 F.2d 268 (9th Cir.1989), the court noted with approval a benchmark fee of 25%. In In re

Warner Communications Securities Litigation, 618 F.Supp. 735, 750 (S.D.N.Y.1985), aff'd 798 F.2d 35 (2d Cir.1986), the court concluded that fee awards had averaged 20%–30% in the Second Circuit.

3.   While *success* is a prerequisite to an award of counsel fees, a *judgment* is not. Counsel fees may be awarded even if a case is settled or the defendants or the corporation takes a unilateral act that renders the plaintiff's demand or complaint moot. See, e.g., Bird v. Lida, Inc., 681 A.2d 399 (Allen, Ch.1996). In the latter kind of case, the plaintiff must show that his course of action was a significant cause of the act. Normally, however, the plaintiff is allowed to prove causation indirectly, by showing that his claim or demand was meritorious and that corrective action followed. It has been said that "[a] claim is meritorious within the meaning of the rule if it can withstand a motion to dismiss on the pleadings [and] if, at the same time, the plaintiff possesses knowledge of provable facts which hold out some reasonable likelihood of ultimate success. It is not necessary that factually there be absolute assurance of ultimate success, but only that there be some reasonable hope." Chrysler Corp. v. Dann, 43 Del.Ch. 252, 256–57, 223 A.2d 384, 387 (1966). Although a few cases suggest that meritoriousness is the only relevant issue in such cases, the rule seems to be that the plaintiff has the burden of showing meritoriousness, and once that showing is made the burden shifts to defendants to show that their actions did not result from plaintiff's course of action. See, e.g., Baron v. Allied Artists Pictures Corp., 395 A.2d 375 (Del.Ch.1978).

4.   It is a well-established rule that attorneys' fees can be awarded to a plaintiff on the basis of a common but nonmonetary benefit, such as the corporation's agreement to change its governance structure, as opposed to the creation of a common fund. This rule has two important implications in derivative actions.

First, it is often very difficult to attribute any realistic value to nonmonetary benefits. As a result, in such cases attorney's fees usually are measured under the lodestar method, even by courts that employ the percentage-of-the-benefit test in common-fund cases.

Second, the rule that a plaintiff's attorney is entitled to a fee for producing a nonmonetary benefit opens the door to the possibility of collusive settlements in which the real defendants in a derivative action (the directors or officers) pay little or nothing; the corporation agrees to a change that is largely cosmetic; plaintiff's attorney and the corporation join hands to inflate the importance of the change; and plaintiff's attorney is then paid a fee that is supposed to be justified by that importance, but is really a bribe to drop the case. The real defendants are happy, because they get a release although they have paid little or nothing. Plaintiff's counsel is happy, because she gets a very nice fee. The shareholders aren't unhappy, because they don't realize what happened. If they did realize what happened, they would be very unhappy.

This doesn't mean that every settlement involving only a nonmonetary benefit is collusive. Nevertheless, the possibility that settlements involving only nonmonetary benefits may be collusive suggests that the courts should be especially cautious in reviewing such settlements.

SECTION 9. SECURITY FOR EXPENSES

N.Y. BUS. CORP. LAW § 627

[See Statutory Supplement]

CAL. CORP. CODE § 800(c)–(f)

[See Statutory Supplement]

SECURITIES ACT § 11(e), 27(c)

[See Statutory Supplement]

SECURITIES EXCHANGE ACT § 21D(c)

Alcott v. M.E.V. Corp.

California Court of Appeal, Sixth District, 1987.
193 Cal.App.3d 797, 238 Cal.Rptr. 520.

■ BRAUER, J.—This stockholder derivative action collapsed after all defendants had prevailed in pretrial skirmishes: one defendant obtained dismissal for failure to serve summons in time, and the others secured either summary judgment or judgment upon demurrer sustained without leave to amend. Thereafter defendants filed cost bills containing demands for attorneys' fees. This appeal is taken from an order awarding defendants their attorneys' fees.... Plaintiffs also challenge the amount of the fees awarded, an issue we do not reach in view of our conclusion that no attorneys' fees are recoverable here....

The action was commenced in 1980 under authority of Corporations Code section 800....

No security was ever sought or posted. The attorneys' fees clause in section 800, subdivision (d) is the only statutory basis for the trial court's ruling.

Section 800 is susceptible of two constructions: (1) Attorneys' fees are recoverable only out of the security, if posted; (2) Prevailing defendants are entitled to their attorneys' fees. . . .

In *Freeman v. Goldberg* (1961) 55 Cal.2d 622 [12 Cal.Rptr. 668, 361 P.2d 244], a derivative suit was dismissed after plaintiffs failed to post the security demanded. Thereafter the prevailing defendants filed a cost bill including attorneys' fees. [The Supreme Court unanimously held] that the statute "contains no provision for an award of attorney's fees where, as here, security is not furnished. . . ." (*Id.*, at p. 626.) The court was interpreting section 834, the predecessor to section 800, which was identical in all relevant respects to section 800 as it read in 1980. . . .

Judgment reversed. Costs on appeal to appellants.

■ AGLIANO, P.J., and CAPACCIOLI, J., concurred.

BACKGROUND NOTE ON SECURITY–FOR–EXPENSES STATUTES

Security-for-expenses statutes must be considered against the background of the general American rule that the losing party in a lawsuit does not have to pay the winner's expenses, except for "taxable costs," such as clerk's, witness, docket, and transcript fees. Accordingly, security-for-expenses statutes are normally not interpreted to impose *individual* liability on the plaintiff for expenses—that is, liability beyond the amount of his bond.

A shareholder who wants to bring a derivative action in a state that has a security-for-expenses statute is under heavy pressure to find some way to bring suit without posting security. Since the statutes are normally interpreted to be inapplicable to direct (as opposed to derivative) actions, one alternative is to frame the suit as a direct action. A second alternative is to bring the action under some provision of federal law, such as the Proxy Rules or Rule 10b–5. The security-for-expenses requirement may also be avoided in certain types of cases by petitioning for dissolution or the appointment of a receiver. See Leibert v. Clapp, 13 N.Y.2d 313, 247 N.Y.S.2d 102, 196 N.E.2d 540 (1963).

Even where these alternatives are infeasible, two judicial practices tend to soften the impact of the security-for-expenses statutes. The first practice is to stay the effectiveness of an order to post security, so that the plaintiff can find intervenors to help qualify under a statutory exemption based on the percentage or dollar value of complaining shares. See Baker v. MacFadden Publications, 300 N.Y. 325, 90 N.E.2d 876 (1950).

A second judicial practice, which builds on the first, is to order a corporation that moves for the posting of security to produce a shareholders' list, so that during the period of the stay the plaintiff can solicit other shareholders to join the action. A study based on interviews with knowledgeable plaintiffs' and defense attorneys in New York concluded that the courts have been extremely permissive in granting these motions. The study continued:

> [Thus if] the motion for security for expenses were to be made, it is likely that the plaintiff would request and obtain a 60–day stay and access to the corporate stocklist. By granting the plaintiff access to the list, defendants have hurt themselves in several ways. The motion involves additional expense in corporate time and effort in furnishing a stockholders' list to the plaintiff. Moreover, circularization by the plaintiff apprises stockholders and the press that a lawsuit involving management is pending. "Most if not all directors don't like to have their deeds or misdeeds advertised. They are sensitive to public opinion, particularly when a proxy fight is involved or imminent." Further, the plaintiffs' counsel now has a list of potential plaintiffs which may be used against the corporation in future litigation. Finally, there is a risk that a motion for security may cause the plaintiff to discontinue the original action and start another in a sister-state having no security-for-expenses statute....

As a result, it is not uncommon for defendants in New York cases to refrain from moving for security for expenses. Note, Security for Expenses in Shareholders' Derivative Suits: 23 Years' Experience, 4 Colum.J.L. & Soc.Prob. 50, 62–65 (1968).

In Cohen v. Beneficial Industrial Loan Corp., 337 U.S. 541, 69 S.Ct. 1221, 93 L.Ed. 1528 (1949), the Supreme Court held that security-for-expenses statutes are substantive for *Erie* purposes—that is, if such a statute would apply to an action brought in a court of the forum state, it will also apply to a diversity action brought in a federal court in that state. However, a state security-for-expenses statute is not applicable to derivative actions brought on *federal* grounds, e.g., under § 16(b) or Rule 10b–5. McClure v. Borne Chemical Co., 292 F.2d 824 (3d Cir.1961), cert. denied 368 U.S. 939, 82 S.Ct. 382, 7 L.Ed.2d 339. On the other hand, where an action arising under a federal statute is brought in federal court, and the plaintiff brings a related state-law action before the court under the doctrine of pendent jurisdiction, any relevant state security-for-expenses statute will apply to the pendent action.

SECTION 10. INDEMNIFICATION AND INSURANCE

(a) INDEMNIFICATION

DEL. GEN. CORP. LAW § 145

[See Statutory Supplement]

MODEL BUS. CORP. ACT §§ 8.50–8.59

[See Statutory Supplement]

N.Y. BUS. CORP. LAW §§ 721–726

[See Statutory Supplement]

CAL. CORP. CODE § 317

[See Statutory Supplement]

ALI, PRINCIPLES OF CORPORATE GOVERNANCE § 7.20

[See Statutory Supplement]

Waltuch v. Conticommodity Services, Inc.

United States Court of Appeals, Second Circuit, 1996.
88 F.3d 87.

■ Before: VAN GRAAFEILAND, JACOBS and PARKER, CIRCUIT JUDGES.

■ JACOBS, CIRCUIT JUDGE:

Famed silver trader Norton Waltuch spent $2.2 million in unreimbursed legal fees to defend himself against numerous civil lawsuits and an enforcement proceeding brought by the Commodity Futures Trading Commission (CFTC). In this action under Delaware law, Waltuch seeks indemnification of his legal expenses from his former employer. The district court denied any indemnity, and Waltuch appeals.

As vice-president and chief metals trader for Conticommodity Services, Inc., Waltuch traded silver for the firm's clients, as well as for his own account. In late 1979 and early 1980, the silver price spiked upward as the then-billionaire Hunt brothers and several of Waltuch's foreign clients bought huge quantities of silver futures contracts. Just as rapidly, the price fell until (on a day remembered in trading circles as "Silver Thursday") the silver market crashed. Between 1981 and 1985, angry silver speculators filed numerous lawsuits against Waltuch and Conticommodity, alleging fraud, market manipulation, and antitrust violations. All of the suits eventually settled and were dismissed with prejudice, pursuant to settlements in which Conticommodity paid over $35 million to the various suitors. Waltuch himself was dismissed from the suits with no settlement contribution. His unreimbursed legal expenses in these actions total approximately $1.2 million.

Waltuch was also the subject of an enforcement proceeding brought by the CFTC, charging him with fraud and market manipulation. The proceeding was settled, with Waltuch agreeing to a penalty that included a $100,000 fine and a six-month ban on buying or selling futures contracts from any exchange floor. Waltuch spent $1 million in unreimbursed legal fees in the CFTC proceeding.[1]

Waltuch brought suit in the United States District Court for the Southern District of New York (Lasker, J.) against Conticommodity and its parent company, Continental Grain Co. (together "Conti"), for indemnification of his unreimbursed expenses.[2] Only two of Waltuch's claims reach us on appeal.

Waltuch first claims that Article Ninth of Conticommodity's articles of incorporation requires Conti to indemnify him for his expenses in both the private and CFTC actions. Conti responds that this claim is barred by subsection (a) of § 145 of Delaware's General Corporation Law, which permits indemnification only if the corporate officer acted "in good faith," something that Waltuch has not established. Waltuch counters that subsection (f) of the same statute permits a corporation to grant indemnification rights outside the limits of subsection (a), and that Conticommodity did so with Article Ninth (which has no stated good-faith limitation). The district court held that, notwithstanding § 145(f), Waltuch could recover under Article Ninth only if Waltuch met the "good faith" requirement of § 145(a).[3] 833 F.Supp. 302, 308–09 (S.D.N.Y.1993). On the factual issue of whether Waltuch had acted "in good faith," the court denied Conti's summary judgment motion and cleared the way for trial. Id. at 313. The parties then stipulated that they would forgo trial on the issue of Waltuch's "good faith," agree to an entry of final judgment against Waltuch on his claim under Article Ninth and § 145(f), and allow Waltuch to take an immediate appeal of the judgment to this Court. Thus, as to Waltuch's first claim, the only question left is how to interpret §§ 145(a) and 145(f), assuming Waltuch acted with less than "good faith." As we explain in part I below, we affirm the district court's judgment as to this claim

---

1. The parties have stipulated that Waltuch's "reasonable attorney's fees and costs" for the private lawsuits totaled $1,228,586.67, and that the comparable expenses for the CFTC proceeding are an even $1 million.

2. Conticommodity and Continental Grain are incorporated in Delaware and have their principal places of business in New York; Waltuch is a New Jersey citizen. We therefore have diversity jurisdiction under 28 U.S.C. § 1332. All parties agree that Delaware law governs.

3. A Special Committee of Continental Grain Co.'s Board of Directors reached the same conclusion in November 1991. Waltuch filed his complaint two months later. In the district court, Conti argued that under the business judgment rule, the Special Committee's decision was immune from challenge, an argument the district court rejected. 833 F.Supp. at 305. Although the parties signed a stipulation preserving Conti's right to contest the district court's ruling on this issue, Conti has abandoned its business judgment rule argument on appeal.

and hold that § 145(f) does not permit a corporation to bypass the "good faith" requirement of § 145(a).

Waltuch's second claim is that subsection (c) of § 145 requires Conti to indemnify him because he was "successful on the merits or otherwise" in the private lawsuits.[4] The district court ruled for Conti on this claim as well. The court explained that, even though all the suits against Waltuch were dismissed without his making any payment, he was not "successful on the merits or otherwise," because Conti's settlement payments to the plaintiffs were partially on Waltuch's behalf. Id. at 311. For the reasons stated in part II below, we reverse this portion of the district court's ruling, and hold that Conti must indemnify Waltuch under § 145(c) for the $1.2 million in unreimbursed legal fees he spent in defending the private lawsuits.

I

Article Ninth, on which Waltuch bases his first claim, is categorical and contains no requirement of "good faith":

> The Corporation shall indemnify and hold harmless each of its incumbent or former directors, officers, employees and agents ... against expenses actually and necessarily incurred by him in connection with the defense of any action, suit or proceeding threatened, pending or completed, in which he is made a party, by reason of his serving in or having held such position or capacity, except in relation to matters as to which he shall be adjudged in such action, suit or proceeding to be liable for negligence or misconduct in the performance of duty.[5]

Conti argues that § 145(a) of Delaware's General Corporation Law, which does contain a "good faith" requirement, fixes the outer limits of a corporation's power to indemnify; Article Ninth is thus invalid under Delaware law, says Conti, to the extent that it requires indemnification of officers who have acted in bad faith. The affirmative grant of power in § 145(a) is as follows:

> *A corporation shall have power to indemnify* any person who was or is a party or is threatened to be made a party to any threatened, pending or completed action, suit or proceeding, whether civil, criminal, administrative or investigative (other than an action by or in the right of the corporation) by reason of the fact that he is or was a director, officer, employee or agent of the corporation, or is or was serving at the request of the corporation as a director, officer, employee or agent of another corporation, partnership, joint venture, trust or other enterprise, against expenses (including attorneys' fees), judgments, fines and amounts paid in settlement actually and reasonably incurred by him in

4. The district court held that Waltuch was not successful "on the merits or otherwise" in the CFTC proceeding. 833 F.Supp. at 311. Waltuch does not appeal this aspect of the court's ruling.

5. Because the private suits and the CFTC proceeding were settled, it is undisputed that Waltuch was not "adjudged ... to be liable for negligence or misconduct in the performance of duty."

connection with such action, suit or proceeding *if he acted in good faith and in a manner he reasonably believed to be in or not opposed to the best interests of the corporation,* and, with respect to any criminal action or proceeding, had no reasonable cause to believe his conduct was unlawful.

56 Del.Laws 50, § 1 at 170–71 (1967) (emphasis added) (rewriting Delaware's General Corporation Law, title 8, chapter 1 of the Delaware Code), *codified at* 8 Del.Code Ann. tit. 8, § 145(a) (Michie 1991). Key language in the Delaware Code Annotated's version of this subsection is in error, as explained in the margin.[6]

In order to escape the "good faith" clause of § 145(a), Waltuch argues that § 145(a) is not an *exclusive* grant of indemnification power, because § 145(f) expressly allows corporations to indemnify officers in a manner broader than that set out in § 145(a). The "nonexclusivity" language of § 145(f) provides:

> The indemnification and advancement of expenses provided by, or granted pursuant to, the other subsections of this section *shall not be deemed exclusive of any other rights* to which those seeking indemnification or advancement of expenses may be entitled under any bylaw, agreement, vote of stockholders or disinterested directors or otherwise, both as to action in his official capacity and as to action in another capacity while holding such office.

56 Del.Laws 50, § 1 at 172 (emphasis added), *as amended and codified* at 8 Del.Code Ann. tit. 8, § 145(f). Waltuch contends that the "nonexclusivity" language in § 145(f) is a separate grant of indemnification power, not limited by the good faith clause that governs the power granted in § 145(a). Conti on the other hand contends that

---

6. There is some confusion about whether this subsection begins, "A corporation *shall have power* to indemnify ..." or "A corporation *may* indemnify ...". As originally enacted, § 145(a) contained the phrase "shall have power". 56 Del.Laws 50, § 1 at 170 (1967). According to the annotations in the *Delaware Code Annotated* (and confirmed by a review of the legislative records since 1967), § 145(a) has never been amended. *See* 8 Del.Code Ann. tit. 8, § 145(a) (1991 & 1995 Supp.).

Nevertheless, the *Delaware Code Annotated,* a private compilation by the Michie Company of all Delaware legislative acts, at some point began using the phrase "may" in place of "shall have power". *See* 8 Del.Code Ann. tit. 8, § 145(a) (1974). We have not been able to explain this non-legislative change in statutory language. The *Delaware Corporation Law Annotated,* published by the Corporation Trust Company, continues to use the phrase "shall have power". Del.Corp. L.Ann. § 145(a) (20th ed. Corp.Trust Co.1991).

One treatise uses the phrase "shall have power", *see* Ernest L. Folk, III, et al., *Folk on the Delaware General Corporation Law* at 145:1 (3d ed. 1994), while another uses "may". *See* 5 R. Franklin Balotti & Jesse A. Finkelstein, *The Delaware Law of Corporations and Business Organizations* at 100 (1990 & 1993 Supp.) ("Balotti & Finkelstein"). The parties to this appeal perpetuate the confusion: their joint appendix contains a version of § 145(a) that says "shall have power", but one of the briefs quotes a version that says "may".

When there is a conflict between an original enactment of the Delaware Legislature and the codification of the law, the original enactment controls. *Elliott v. Blue Cross & Blue Shield,* 407 A.2d 524, 528 (Del.1979); *Kimmey v. Farmers Bank,* 373 A.2d 569, 570 (Del.1977). We therefore employ the Legislature's version of § 145(a), which says "shall have power".

We are indebted to Lesley Lawrence and the staff at the Third Circuit library in Wilmington for their assistance on this issue.

§ 145(f) must be limited by "public policies," one of which is that a corporation may indemnify its officers only if they act in "good faith."

In a thorough and scholarly opinion, Judge Lasker agreed with Conti's reading of § 145(f), writing that "it has been generally agreed that there are public policy limits on indemnification under Section 145(f)," although it was "difficult ... to define precisely what limitations on indemnification public policy imposes." 833 F.Supp. at 307, 308. After reviewing cases from Delaware and elsewhere and finding that they provided no authoritative guidance, Judge Lasker surveyed the numerous commentators on this issue and found that they generally agreed with Conti's position. *Id.* at 308–09. He also found that Waltuch's reading of § 145(f) failed to make sense of the statute as a whole:

> [T]here would be no point to the carefully crafted provisions of Section 145 spelling out the permissible scope of indemnification under Delaware law if subsection (f) allowed indemnification in additional circumstances without regard to these limits. The exception would swallow the rule.

Id. at 309. The fact that § 145(f) was limited by § 145(a) did not make § 145(f) meaningless, wrote Judge Lasker, because § 145(f) "still 'may authorize the adoption of various procedures and presumptions to make the process of indemnification more favorable to the indemnitee without violating the statute.' " *Id.* at 309 (quoting 1 Balotti & Finkelstein § 4.16 at 4–321). As will be evident from the discussion below, we adopt much of Judge Lasker's analysis.

A.   Delaware Cases

No Delaware court has decided the very issue presented here; but the applicable cases tend to support the proposition that a corporation's grant of indemnification rights cannot be *inconsistent* with the substantive statutory provisions of § 145, notwithstanding § 145(f). We draw this rule of "consistency" primarily from our reading of the Delaware Supreme Court's opinion in *Hibbert v. Hollywood Park, Inc.*, 457 A.2d 339 (Del.1983). In that case, Hibbert and certain other directors sued the corporation and the remaining directors, and then demanded indemnification for their expenses and fees related to the litigation. The company refused indemnification on the ground that directors were entitled to indemnification only as *defendants* in legal proceedings. The court reversed the trial court and held that Hibbert was entitled to indemnification under the plain terms of a company bylaw that did not draw an express distinction between plaintiff directors and defendant directors. *Id.* at 343. The court then proceeded to test the bylaw for consistency with § 145(a):

> Furthermore, *indemnification here is consistent with current Delaware law.* Under 8 Del.C. § 145(a) ..., "a corporation may indemnify any person who was or is a party or is threatened to be made a party to any threatened, pending or completed" derivative or third-party action. By this language, indemnity is *not limited to* only those who stand as a defendant in the main action. The

corporation can also grant indemnification rights beyond those provided by statute. 8 Del.C. § 145(f).

Id. at 344 (emphasis added and citations omitted). *See supra* note 6 (explaining the error in the *Delaware Code Annotated*'s use of the phrase "may indemnify" in § 145(a)). This passage contains two complementary propositions. Under § 145(f), a corporation may provide indemnification rights that go "beyond" the rights provided by § 145(a) and the other substantive subsections of § 145. At the same time, any such indemnification rights provided by a corporation must be "consistent with" the substantive provisions of § 145, including § 145(a). In *Hibbert,* the corporate bylaw was "consistent with" § 145(a), because this subsection was "not limited to" suits in which directors were defendants. *Hibbert*'s holding may support an inverse corollary that illuminates our case: if § 145(a) had been expressly limited to directors who were named as defendants, the bylaw could not have stood, regardless of § 145(f), because the bylaw would not have been "consistent with" the substantive statutory provision.[7] . . .

B. Statutory Reading

The "consistency" rule suggested by [the] Delaware cases is reinforced by our reading of § 145 as a whole. Subsections (a) (indemnification for third-party actions) and (b) (similar indemnification for derivative suits) expressly grant a corporation the power to indemnify directors, officers, and others, if they "acted in good faith and in a manner reasonably believed to be in or not opposed to the best interest of the corporation." These provisions thus limit the scope of the power that they confer. They are permissive in the sense that a corporation may exercise less than its full power to grant the indemnification rights set out in these provisions. *See Essential Enter. Corp. v. Dorsey Corp.,* 182 A.2d 647, 653 (Del.Ch.1962). By the same token, subsection (f) permits the corporation to grant additional rights: the rights provided in the rest of § 145 "shall not be deemed exclusive of any other rights to which those seeking indemnification may be entitled." But crucially, subsection (f) merely acknowledges that one seeking indemnification may be entitled to "other rights" (of indemnification or otherwise); it does not speak in terms of corporate power,

---

7. The *Hibbert* court cites to a 1978 article by Samuel Arsht, chairman of the committee of experts that drafted Delaware's General Corporation Law in 1967, *id.,* which supports our conclusion that indemnification rights permitted under § 145(f) must be consistent with the other substantive provisions of § 145. At the pages cited by the court, Arsht writes:

> The question most frequently asked by practicing lawyers is what subsection (f), the nonexclusive clause, means. . . . The question which subsection (f) invariably raises is whether a corporation can adopt a by-law or make a contract with its directors providing that they will be in-

demnified for whatever they may have to pay if they are sued and lose or settle. The answer to this question is "no." Subsection (f) . . . permits additional rights to be created, but *it is not a blanket authorization to indemnify directors against all expenses, fines, or settlements of whatever nature and regardless of the directors' conduct.* The statutory language is circumscribed by limits of public policy. . . .

S. Samuel Arsht, *Indemnification Under Section 145 of Delaware General Corporation Law,* 3 Del.J.Corp.L. 176, 176–77 (1978) (emphasis added).

and therefore cannot be read to free a corporation from the "good faith" limit explicitly imposed in subsections (a) and (b).

An alternative construction of these provisions would effectively force us to ignore certain explicit terms of the statute. Section 145(a) gives Conti the power to indemnify Waltuch "*if* he acted in good faith and in a manner reasonably believed to be in or not opposed to the best interest of the corporation." 56 Del.Laws 50, § 1 at 171 (emphasis added). This statutory limit must mean that there is *no power* to indemnify Waltuch if he did not act in good faith. Otherwise, as Judge Lasker pointed out, § 145(a)—and its good faith clause—would have no meaning: a corporation could indemnify whomever and however it wished regardless of the good faith clause or anything else the Delaware Legislature wrote into § 145(a).

When the Legislature intended a subsection of § 145 to augment the powers limited in subsection (a), it set out the additional powers expressly. Thus subsection (g) explicitly allows a corporation to circumvent the "good faith" clause of subsection (a) by purchasing a directors and officers liability insurance policy. Significantly, that subsection is framed as a grant of corporate power:

> A corporation shall have power to purchase and maintain insurance on behalf of any person who is or was a director, officer, employee or agent of the corporation ... against any liability asserted against him and incurred by him in any such capacity, or arising out of his status as such, *whether or not the corporation would have the power to indemnify him against such liability under this section.*

56 Del.Laws 50, § 1 at 172 (1967) (emphasis added), *codified at* 8 Del.Code Ann. tit. 8, § 145(g) (Michie 1991). The italicized passage reflects the principle that corporations have the power under § 145 to indemnify in some situations and not in others. Since § 145(f) is neither a grant of corporate power nor a limitation on such power, subsection (g) must be referring to the limitations set out in § 145(a) and the other provisions of § 145 that describe corporate power. If § 145 (through subsection (f) or another part of the statute) gave corporations unlimited power to indemnify directors and officers, then the final clause of subsection (g) would be unnecessary: that is, its grant of "power to purchase and maintain insurance" (exercisable regardless of whether the corporation itself would have the power to indemnify the loss directly) is meaningful only because, in some insurable situations, the corporation simply lacks the power to indemnify its directors and officers directly.

A contemporaneous account from the principal drafter of Delaware's General Corporation Law confirms what an integral reading of § 145 demonstrates: the statute's affirmative grants of power also impose limitations on the corporation's power to indemnify. Specifically, the good faith clause (unchanged since the Law's original enactment in 1967) was included in subsections (a) and (b) as a carefully calculated improvement on the prior indemnification provision and as an explicit limit on a corporation's power to indemnify:

During the three years of the Revision Committee's study, no subject was more discussed among members of the corporate bar than the subject of indemnification of officers and directors. As far as Delaware law was concerned, the existing statutory provision on the subject had been found inadequate. Numerous by-laws and charter provisions had been adopted clarifying and extending its terms, but *uncertainty existed in many instances as to whether such provisions transgressed the limits* which the courts had indicated they would establish based on public policy.

. . . .

It was ... apparent that revision was appropriate with respect to *the limitations which must necessarily be placed on the power to indemnify* in order to prevent the statute from undermining the substantive provisions of the criminal law and corporation law....

[There was a] need for a ... provision to protect the corporation law's requirement of loyalty to the corporation.... Ultimately, it was decided that *the power to indemnify should not be granted unless* it appeared that the person seeking indemnification had "acted in good faith and in a manner reasonably believed to be in or not opposed to the best interest of the corporation."

S. Samuel Arsht & Walter K. Stapleton, *Delaware's New General Corporation Law: Substantive Changes,* 23 Bus.Law. 75, 77–78 (1967).[8] This passage supports *Hibbert's* rule of "consistency" and makes clear that a corporation has no power to transgress the indemnification limits set out in the substantive provisions of § 145.

Waltuch argues at length that reading § 145(a) to bar the indemnification of officers who acted in bad faith would render § 145(f) meaningless. This argument misreads § 145(f). That subsection refers to "any other rights to which those seeking indemnification or advancement of expenses may be entitled." Delaware commentators have identified various indemnification rights that are "beyond those provided by statute," *Hibbert,* 457 A.2d at 344, and that are at the same time consistent with the statute:

[S]ubsection (f) provides general authorization for the adoption of various procedures and presumptions making the process of indemnification more favorable to the indemnitee. For example, indemnification agreements or by-laws could provide for: (i) mandatory indemnification unless prohibited by statute; (ii) mandatory advancement of expenses, which the indemnitee can, in many instances, obtain on demand; (iii) accelerated procedures for the "determination" required by section 145(d) to be made in the "specific case"; (iv) litigation "appeal" rights of the indemnitee in the event of an unfavorable determination; (v) procedures

---

8. Delaware commentators consider this article to be part of (if not all of) "[t]he legislative history of Section 145." A. Gilchrist Sparks, III, et al., *Indemnification, Directors and Officers Liability Insurance and* *Limitations of Director Liability Pursuant to Statutory Authorization: The Legal Framework Under Delaware Law,* 696 PLI/Corp. 941 (1990) (at page 10 out of 123 on WESTLAW)....

under which a favorable determination will be deemed to have been made under circumstances where the board fails or refuses to act; [and] (vi) reasonable funding mechanisms.

E. Norman Veasey, et al., *Delaware Supports Directors With a Three–Legged Stool of Limited Liability, Indemnification, and Insurance*, 42 Bus.Law. 399, 415 (1987).[9] Moreover, subsection (f) may reference nonindemnification rights, such as advancement rights or rights to other payments from the corporation that do not qualify as indemnification.

We need not decide in this case the precise scope of those "other rights" adverted to in § 145(f). We simply conclude that § 145(f) is not rendered meaningless or inoperative by the conclusion that a Delaware corporation lacks power to indemnify an officer or director "unless [he] 'acted in good faith and in a manner reasonably believed to be in or not opposed to the best interest of the corporation.' " *See* Arsht & Stapleton, 23 Bus.Law. at 78. As a result, we hold that Conti's Article Ninth, which would require indemnification of Waltuch even if he acted in bad faith, is inconsistent with § 145(a) and thus exceeds the scope of a Delaware corporation's power to indemnify. Since Waltuch has agreed to forgo his opportunity to prove at trial that he acted in good faith, he is not entitled to indemnification under Article Ninth for the $2.2 million he spent in connection with the private lawsuits and the CFTC proceeding. We therefore affirm the district court on this issue.

II

Unlike § 145(a), which grants a discretionary indemnification power, § 145(c) affirmatively *requires* corporations to indemnify its officers and directors for the "successful" defense of certain claims:

> To the extent that a director, officer, employee or agent of a corporation has been successful on the merits or otherwise in defense of any action, suit or proceeding referred to in subsections (a) and (b) of this section, or in defense of any claim, issue or matter therein, he shall be indemnified against expenses (including attorneys' fees) actually and reasonably incurred by him in connection therewith.

56 Del.Laws 50, § 1 at 171 (1967), *codified at* 8 Del.Code Ann. tit. 8, § 145(c) (Michie 1991). Waltuch argues that he was "successful on the merits or otherwise" in the private lawsuits, because they were dismissed with prejudice without any payment or assumption of liability by him. Conti argues that the claims against Waltuch were dismissed only because of Conti's $35 million settlement payments, and that this payment was contributed, in part, "on behalf of Waltuch."[10]

---

9. Veasey is now Chief Justice of the Delaware Supreme Court. *See also* 1 Balotti & Finkelstein § 4.16 at 4–321, which makes the same suggestions. Other suggestions are made in Joseph F. Johnston, Jr., *Corporate Indemnification and Liability Insurance for Directors and Officers*, 33 Bus.Law. 1993, 1996, 2009–10 (1978).

10. Although this is not essential to our holding, we note that Conti points to no evidence in support of its contention that the plaintiffs would have continued to pursue their suits as to Waltuch if Conti had paid some lesser amount.

The district court agreed with Conti that "the successful settlements cannot be credited to Waltuch but are attributable solely to Conti's settlement payments. It was not Waltuch who was successful, but Conti who was successful for him." 833 F.Supp. at 311. The district court held that § 145(c) mandates indemnification when the director or officer "is vindicated," but that there was no vindication here:

> Vindication is also ordinarily associated with a dismissal with prejudice without any payment. However, a director or officer is not vindicated when the reason he did not have to make a settlement payment is because someone else assumed that liability. Being bailed out is not the same thing as being vindicated.

Id. We believe that this understanding and application of the "vindication" concept is overly broad and is inconsistent with a proper interpretation of § 145(c).

No Delaware court has applied § 145(c) in the context of indemnification stemming from the settlement of civil litigation. One lower court, however, has applied that subsection to an analogous case in the criminal context, and has illuminated the link between "vindication" and the statutory phrase, "successful on the merits or otherwise." In *Merritt–Chapman & Scott Corp. v. Wolfson*, 321 A.2d 138 (Del.Super.Ct.1974), the corporation's agents were charged with several counts of criminal conduct. A jury found them guilty on some counts, but deadlocked on the others. The agents entered into a "settlement" with the prosecutor's office by pleading nolo contendere to one of the counts in exchange for the dropping of the rest. *Id.* at 140. The agents claimed entitlement to mandatory indemnification under § 145(c) as to the counts that were dismissed. In opposition, the corporation raised an argument similar to the argument raised by Conti:

> [The corporation] argues that the statute and sound public policy require indemnification only where there has been vindication by a finding or concession of innocence. *It contends that the charges against [the agents] were dropped for practical reasons,* not because of their innocence. . . .
>
> The statute requires indemnification to the extent that the claimant "has been successful on the merits or otherwise." *Success is vindication.* In a criminal action, any result other than conviction must be considered success. *Going behind the result,* as [the corporation] attempts, is neither authorized by subsection (c) nor consistent with the presumption of innocence.

Id. at 141 (emphasis added).

Although the underlying proceeding in *Merritt* was criminal, the court's analysis is instructive here. The agents in *Merritt* rendered consideration—their guilty plea on one count—to achieve the dismissal of the other counts. The court considered these dismissals both "success" and (therefore) "vindication," and refused to "go[ ] behind the result" or to appraise the reason for the success. In equating "success" with "vindication," the court thus rejected the more expansive view of vindication urged by the corporation. Under *Merritt*'s holding, then, vindication, when used as a synonym for "success" under § 145(c), does not mean moral exoneration. Escape from an adverse judgment or other detriment, for whatever reason, is determinative. According to *Merritt*, the only question a court may ask is what the result was, not why it was.[12]

Conti's contention that, because of its $35 million settlement payments, Waltuch's settlement without payment should not really count as settlement without payment, is inconsistent with the rule in *Merritt*. Here, Waltuch was sued, and the suit was dismissed without his having paid a settlement. Under the approach taken in *Merritt*, it is not our business to ask why this result was reached. Once Waltuch achieved his settlement gratis, he achieved success "on the merits or otherwise." And, as we know from *Merritt*, success is sufficient to constitute vindication (at least for the purposes of § 145(c)). Waltuch's settlement thus vindicated him.

The concept of "vindication" pressed by Conti is also inconsistent with the fact that a director or officer who is able to defeat an adversary's claim by asserting a technical defense is entitled to indemnification under § 145(c). *See* 1 Balotti & Finkelstein, § 4.13 at 4–302. In such cases, the indemnitee has been "successful" in the palpable sense that he has won, and the suit has been dismissed, whether or not the victory is deserved in merits terms. If a technical defense is deemed "vindication" under Delaware law, it cannot matter why Waltuch emerged unscathed, or whether Conti "bailed [him] out", or whether his success was deserved. Under § 145(c), mere success is vindication enough.

This conclusion comports with the reality that civil judgments and settlements are ordinarily expressed in terms of cash rather than moral victory. No doubt, it would make sense for Conti to buy the dismissal of the claims against Waltuch along with its own discharge from the case, perhaps to avoid further expense or participation as a non-party, potential cross-claims, or negative publicity. But Waltuch apparently did not accede to that arrangement, and Delaware law cannot allow an

---

12. Our adoption of *Merritt*'s interpretation of the statutory term "successful" does not necessarily signal our endorsement of the result in that case. The *Merritt* court sliced the case into individual counts, with indemnification pegged to each count independently of the others. We are not faced with a case in which the corporate officer claims to have been "successful" on some parts of the case but was clearly "unsuccessful" on others, and therefore take no position on this feature of the *Merritt* holding.

We also do not mean our discussion of *Merritt* to suggest that the line between success and failure in a criminal case may be drawn in the same way in the civil context. In a criminal case, conviction on a particular count is obvious failure, and dismissal of the charge is obvious success. In a civil suit for damages, however, there is a monetary continuum between complete success (dismissal of the suit without any payment) and complete failure (payment of the full amount of damages requested by the plaintiff). Because Waltuch made no payment in connection with the dismissal of the suits against him, we need not decide whether a defendant's settlement payment automatically renders that defendant "unsuccessful" under § 145(c).

indemnifying corporation to escape the mandatory indemnification of subsection (c) by paying a sum in settlement on behalf of an unwilling indemnitee.

... In *Wisener v. Air Express Int'l Corp.*, 583 F.2d 579 (2d Cir.1978), we construed an Illinois indemnification statute that was intentionally enacted as a copy of Delaware's § 145. *See id.* at 582 n. 3; 1 Balotti & Finkelstein, § 4.12 at 4–296 n. 1048 (§ 145 was the "prototype" for Illinois's indemnification statute). Our holding in that case is perfectly applicable here:

> It is contended that [the director] was not "successful" in the litigation, since the third-party claims against him never proceeded to trial. The statute, however, refers to success "on the merits or otherwise," which surely is broad enough to cover a termination of claims by agreement without any payment or assumption of liability.

583 F.2d at 583. It is undisputed that the private lawsuits against Conti and Waltuch were dismissed with prejudice, "without any payment of assumption of liability" by Waltuch. Applying the analysis of *Wisener,* Conti must indemnify Waltuch for his expenses in connection with the private lawsuits.

... [T]he extent of Waltuch's success] is not lessened by Conti's payments, even if it is true (as it stands to reason) that his success was achieved because Conti was willing to pay. Whatever the impetus for the plaintiffs' dismissal of their claims against Waltuch, he still walked away without liability and without making a payment. This constitutes a success that is untarnished by the process that achieved it.

For all of these reasons, we agree with Waltuch that he is entitled to indemnification under § 145(c) for his expenses pertaining to the private lawsuits.

III

The judgment of the district court is affirmed in part and reversed in part. This case is remanded to the district court so that judgment may be entered in favor of Waltuch on his claim for $1,228,586.67, representing the unreimbursed expenses from the private lawsuits. *See supra* note 1.

IN RE LANDMARK LAND CO., 76 F.3d 553. "An agent who has intentionally participated in illegal activity or wrongful conduct against third persons cannot be said to have acted in good faith, even if the conduct benefits the corporation. *Plate [v. Sun–Diamond Growers], 275 Cal.Rptr. at 672.*" For example, corporate executives who participate in a deliberate price-fixing conspiracy with competing firms could not be found to have acted in good faith, even though they may have reasonably believed that a deliberate flouting of the antitrust laws would increase the profits of the corporation. "1 Harold Marsh, Jr. and

R. Roy Finkle, Marsh's California Corporation Law (3d ed.) § 10.43, at 751; see *Plate, 275 Cal.Rptr. at 672* (citing same language from second edition).... [A] deliberate attempt to undermine the regulatory authority of a government agency cannot constitute good faith conduct, even if such actions benefit the corporation.''

PLATE v. SUN–DIAMOND GROWERS, 225 Cal.App.3d 1115, 275 Cal.Rptr. 667 (1990). "The first prerequisite to indemnification under section 317, subdivision (b) [of the California Corporation Code] is that the action against the person is brought 'by reason of the fact that the person is or was an agent of the corporation.' Marsh, in his treatise on California corporation law, explains: 'In other words, the conduct of the agent which gives rise to the claim against him must have been performed in connection with his corporate functions and not with respect to purely personal matters.' (1 Marsh, Cal.Corporation Law (2d ed.) § 9.36, p. 536.) Where personal motives, not the corporate good, are predominant in a transaction giving rise to an action, indemnification is not warranted. For example, '[i]t would ... appear unlikely that an officer could properly claim that he was entitled to indemnification as the result of litigation brought to recover short-swing profits or profits from trading in the stock of his corporation on the basis of inside information....' (Heyler, *Indemnification of Corporate Agents* (1976) 23 UCLA L.Rev. 1255, 1258, fn. 24.)

"Sister-state authorities illustrate this rule. In *Tomash v. Midwest Technical Development Corp.* (1968) 281 Minn. 21, 160 N.W.2d 273, 277–278, where the Minnesota indemnification statute contained the 'by reason of the fact' requirement, the court held that directors seeking indemnification for defending themselves in an SEC proceeding stemming from their personal investments in certain stock, did not meet the requirement because the statute 'speak[s] in terms of indemnification to one who defends himself as a director or officer of the corporation' whereas 'the officers and directors [seeking indemnification] were defending themselves from alleged violations of the Investment Company Act, from which they personally profited. The two are not the same.' (*Ibid.*)...."

STIFEL FINANCIAL CORP. v. COCHRAN, 809 A.2d 555 (Del. Supr. 2002). Cochran, an investment banker, had been discharged as an officer and director of Stifel Nicolaus corporation, a wholly owned subsidiary of Stifel Financial Corporation ("Stifel"). Cochran then refused to repay to Stifel Nicolaus excess compensation and the balance of a promissory note, as required by his employment agreement. To recover these amounts, Stifel Nicolaus instituted an arbitration proceeding against Cochran. The arbitrators ruled in favor of Stifel Nicolaus on the excess-compensation and promissory-note claims, and ordered Cochran to repay Stifel Nicolaus approximately

$1.2 million. The arbitration award was confirmed by the United States District Court for the Eastern District of Missouri.

Stifel's bylaws contained the following indemnification provision:

The Corporation [Stifel] shall indemnify to the full extent authorized by law any person made or threatened to be made a party to any action, suit, or proceeding, whether criminal, civil, administrative or investigative, by reason of the fact that he . . . is or was a director, officer or employee of the Corporation or any predecessor of the Corporation or serves or served any other enterprise as a director, officer or employee at the request of the Corporation or any predecessor of the Corporation.

Cochran filed an action seeking indemnification from Stifel pursuant to this bylaw. The Delaware Supreme Court held that Cochran was not entitled to indemnification for the amounts he was required to pay to Stifel on the basis of the compensation and promissory note claims because the liability did not result from actions by Stifel in his official capacity:

The arbitration action was brought against Cochran to enforce certain provisions of an employment contract and promissory note, which Cochran had entered into with Stifel Nicolaus. The Court of Chancery's explanation bears repeating:

When a corporate officer signs an employment contract committing to fill an office, he is acting in a personal capacity in an adversarial, arms-length transaction. To the extent that he binds himself to certain obligations under that contract, he owes a personal obligation to the corporation. When the corporation brings a claim and proves its entitlement to relief because the officer has breached his individual obligations, it is problematic to conclude that the suit has been rendered an "official capacity" suit subject to indemnification under § 145 and implementing bylaws. Such a conclusion would render the officer's duty to perform his side of the contract in many respects illusory.

We agree that the claims litigated in the arbitration action were properly characterized as personal, not directed at Cochran in his "official capacity" as an officer and director of Stifel Nicolaus. . . . Stifel Nicolaus based the Compensation Claim [and] the Promissory Note Claim . . . on the employment contract Cochran entered into with the company. Although Cochran's termination is the event that triggered the relevant provisions of the employment contract, Cochran's decision to breach the contract was entirely a personal one, pursued for his sole benefit. . . .

————

NOTE ON ADVANCES

In *Advanced Mining Systems, Inc. v. Fricke*, 623 A.2d 82 (Del.Ch. 1992), the Delaware court held that indemnification rights and advancement rights stand apart as two "distinct types of legal rights," so that a bylaw provision that required a corporation to "indemnify . . . to the extent permitted" under Delaware law did not wrest from a corporation the ability to refuse advances. See also Rev. Model Bus. Corp. Act § 8.58(a) and Official Comment.

———

BACKGROUND NOTE ON INDEMNIFICATION

1. The right of a director or officer to indemnification under the common law was not completely clear. New York Dock Co. v. McCollom, 173 Misc. 106, 16 N.Y.S.2d 844 (1939), decided prior to the enactment of the New York indemnification statute, held that directors who had successfully defended themselves in a derivative suit were not entitled to reimbursement of their counsel fees, absent a showing that the corporation had benefited. Later decisions in other jurisdictions, however, upheld the common law right of a vindicated director to recover the expenses of his defense without any showing of a specific benefit to the corporation. In re E.C. Warner Co., 232 Minn. 207, 45 N.W.2d 388 (1950); Solimine v. Hollander, 129 N.J.Eq. 264, 19 A.2d 344 (Ch.1941). The policy reasons why the corporation should indemnify a director, as set forth in *Solimine,* are (1) to encourage innocent directors to resist unjust charges and provide them an opportunity to hire competent counsel; (2) to induce "responsible business men to accept the post of directors": and (3) "to discourage in large measure stockholders' litigation of the strike variety." Id. at 272, 19 A.2d at 348. Today, virtually every state has an indemnification statute, but the statutes vary widely in detail.

2. In Globus v. Law Research Service, Inc., 418 F.2d 1276 (2d Cir.1969), cert. denied 397 U.S. 913, 90 S.Ct. 913, 25 L.Ed.2d 93 (1970) plaintiffs, who had purchased stock under an allegedly misleading offering circular, brought actions under § 17(a) of the 1933 Act and Rule 10b–5 against the issuer, the underwriter, and the issuer's president. The underwriter cross-claimed against the issuer pursuant to an agreement under which the issuer had promised to indemnify the underwriter for any loss arising out of defects in the offering circular, except for those attributable to the underwriter's "willful misfeasance, bad faith or gross negligence . . . or . . . reckless disregard of its obligations under the agreement." Id. at 1287. The court concluded that the underwriter had actual knowledge of material misstatements in the circular, and denied the cross-claim both because it fell within the exception to the agreement and on grounds of public policy:

> Given [the underwriter's actual knowledge of material misstatements], ... to tolerate indemnity under these circumstances would encourage flouting the policy of the common law and the Securities Act. . . .
>
> Civil liability under section 11 and similar provisions was designed not so much to compensate the defrauded purchaser as

to promote enforcement of the Act and to deter negligence by providing a penalty for those who fail in their duties. And Congress intended to impose a "high standard of trusteeship" on underwriters. Thus, what Professor Loss terms the "*in terrorem* effect" of civil liability might well be thwarted if underwriters were free to pass their liability on to the issuer. Underwriters who knew they could be indemnified simply by showing that the issuer was "more liable" than they (a process not too difficult when the issuer is inevitably closer to the facts) would have a tendency to be lax in their independent investigations. Cases upholding indemnity for negligence in other fields are not necessarily apposite. The goal in such cases is to compensate the injured party. But the Securities Act is more concerned with prevention than cure.

Globus involved "a sin graver than ordinary negligence," and left open the propriety of indemnification for negligence or other lesser sins. Some later cases have held that the policy of the Securities Acts bars indemnification for negligence; others have held indemnification for negligence permissible under the Securities Acts where the indemnitor's conduct was significantly more wrongful than that of the indemnitee. See Donaldson Lufkin & Jenrette Securities Corp. v. Star Technologies, 148 Misc.2d 880, 561 N.Y.S.2d 371 (1990), aff'd, Donaldson, Lufkin & Jenrette Sec. Corp. v. Star Technologies, Inc., 180 A.D.2d 495, 580 N.Y.S.2d 657 (1st Dep't 1992) (reviewing cases); ALI, Principles of Corporate Governance § 7.20, Reporter's Note 7. It has been held that indemnification for liability under section 16(b) would violate public policy, even though section 16(b) does not require proof of fraudulent intent. See First Golden Bancorporation v. Weiszmann, 942 F.2d 726 (10th Cir.1991).

Under SEC Regulation S–K, Item 512(h), if a registrant seeks acceleration of a prospectus (as all registrants do), and any provision or agreement exists under which the registrant may indemnify a director or officer against liabilities arising under the Securities Act, then unless the right to indemnification is waived, the registrant must include the following statement in the Prospectus:

> Insofar as indemnification for liabilities arising under the Securities Act of 1933 may be permitted to directors, officers and controlling persons of the registrant pursuant to the foregoing provisions, or otherwise, the registrant has been advised that in the opinion of the Securities and Exchange Commission such indemnification is against public policy as expressed in the Act and is, therefore, unenforceable. In the event that a claim for indemnification against such liabilities (other than the payment by the registrant of expenses incurred or paid by a director, officer or controlling person of the registrant in the successful defense of any action, suit or proceeding) is asserted by such director, officer or controlling person in connection with the securities being registered, the registrant will, unless in the opinion of its counsel the matter has been settled by controlling precedent, submit to a court of appropriate jurisdiction the question whether such in-

demnification by it is against public policy as expressed in the Act and will be governed by the final adjudication of such issue.

———

(b) INSURANCE

[See Chapter 8.]

———

SECTION 11. SETTLEMENT OF DERIVATIVE ACTIONS

———

Clarke v. Greenberg

Court of Appeals of New York, 1947.
296 N.Y. 146, 71 N.E.2d 443.

■ Dye, Judge. The challenge to the within complaint, for failure to state a cause of action, raises the question of whether a plaintiff in a stockholder's derivative action may be required to account to the corporation for moneys received in private settlement for discontinuance of the action.

The complaint alleges that the defendants commenced a stockholder's derivative action in behalf of the Associated Gas & Electric Company (called AGECO) entitled "Greenberg v. Mange et al." in which it was alleged that the defendants, as officers and directors, had so mismanaged its affairs that the company and its stockholders were damaged and prayed that an accounting be had, and that the court "impress a trust in favor of the Company (AGECO) upon all secret profits and gains obtained by any of the defendant directors," etc. No individual relief was asked except reimbursement for expenses. Later and before trial, a stipulation was made settling and discontinuing the action without notice to other stockholders and without approval of the court, by the terms of which Greenberg executed releases in his individual and representative capacity and transferred and delivered his stock, having a market value of $51.88, to the defendant directors and defendants herein received from them the sum of $9,000.

The complaint in this action alleges that the defendants received the money "to the use of, and in trust for AGECO"; that they had failed to account to it or its trustee, the plaintiff herein, and had accordingly unjustly enriched themselves in the sum of $8,948.12 which, in equity, should be paid over to the plaintiff, and prayed judgment accordingly.

The Appellate Division unanimously affirmed the dismissal of the complaint by the Special Term which relied upon Manufacturers Mutual Fire Ins. Co. of Rhode Island v. Hopson, 176 Misc. 220, 25

N.Y.S.2d 502, affirmed 262 App.Div. 731, 29 N.Y.S.2d 139, affirmed 288 N.Y. 668, 43 N.E.2d 71 in which we refused to set aside a stipulation settling a stockholder's derivative suit and revive the action. That case was limited to the right to discontinue and it did not consider whether the moneys received in settlement were impressed with a trust in favor of the corporation for which an accounting should be made.

The very nature of the derivative suit by a stockholder-plaintiff suing in the corporation's behalf suggests the application of the fiduciary principle to the proceeds realized from such litigation whether received by way of judgment, by settlement with approval of the court, which presupposes stockholders' approval, or by private settlement and discontinuance of the action at any stage of the proceeding. Such action, we have held, belongs primarily to the corporation, the real party in interest ... and a judgment so obtained, as well as the proceeds of a settlement with court approval belongs to it and not the individual stockholder plaintiffs.... While the stockholder-plaintiff, with such others as join with him, controls the course of the litigation at all stages of the proceeding before final judgment, he does not bind the nonparticipating stockholders by his action, or deprive them of their own right of action against the unfaithful directors, nor is he subject to their interference.... When, however, success crowns his effort, the amount received is in behalf and for the account of the corporation. This is so because the action belongs primarily to it. The manner and method by which such success is accomplished whether by way of judgment, settlement with court approval or by stipulation of the parties, makes no substantial difference in the interest of the corporation upon distribution of the proceeds. Requiring an accounting for moneys received in a private settlement introduces no new element. It simply amounts to a logical application of a fundamental principle inherent in the representative relation. When one assumes to act for another, regardless of the manner or method used in accomplishing a successful termination, he should willingly account for his stewardship. The plaintiff-stockholder, in good conscience, should not be allowed to retain the proceeds of a derivative suit discontinued by stipulation, to his individual use, in opposition to the corporation, any more than the proceeds of a judgment or a settlement with court approval.

The complaint, we believe, states a cause of action.

The judgments should be reversed and the motion to dismiss the complaint denied, with costs in all courts.

■ LOUGHRAN, C.J., and LEWIS, CONWAY, DESMOND, THACHER, and FULD, JJ., concur.

Judgments reversed, etc.*

---

* Cf. Young v. Higbee Co., 324 U.S. 204, 65 S.Ct. 594, 89 L.Ed. 890 (1945). In Certain–

Teed Products Corporation v. Topping, 171 F.2d 241 (2d Cir.1948) a shareholder-plaintiff

BACKGROUND NOTE ON THE PROBLEM OF ILLICIT SETTLEMENTS

In Manufacturers Mutual Fire Ins. Co. v. Hopson, cited in Clarke v. Greenberg, shareholders of Associated Gas & Electric had brought a derivative action against AG&E directors for mismanagement and waste. Thereafter the plaintiffs had agreed to discontinue the action in exchange for a payment made to them in their individual capacities. (The payment took the form of a purchase of the plaintiffs' AG&E stock for seven times its market value.) On petition by other shareholders and AG&E's trustee in bankruptcy, the court refused to set aside the discontinuance:

> If this were a case of first impression, my conclusion might be otherwise. But this court is bound by a line of cases in New York, to the effect that a minority stockholder may discontinue his action at any time before another stockholder has intervened or judgment has been entered. The exclusive control of the action belongs to him and he can settle his individual damages, leaving other shareholders to seek their remedy in a new action.

176 Misc. at 223, 25 N.Y.S.2d at 505. While not all courts took the position reflected in *Manufacturer's Mutual,* that position was the majority rule at common law:

> ... From the early days of the class suit, it had been widely accepted doctrine that a ... derivative plaintiff ... was the *dominus litis;* since he bore all the expenses of the action, he could dismiss or compromise it at pleasure and on any terms he saw fit. . . .

> The prevailing state of the law plainly invited abuse. Most stockholders' suits involve corporate or class claims of considerable magnitude. The temptation for the defendants to buy off the plaintiff by a relatively modest private settlement was therefore great. Many stockholders' actions of doubtful merit were brought simply to secure private settlements for the plaintiff and his lawyer. Private settlements also were employed to stifle meritorious suits brought initially in good faith. In derivative suits, the corporation, frequently controlled by the alleged wrong-doers or their allies, could not be expected to resist the sacrifice of claims which it had been unwilling to assert by direct action. Even without a private settlement, complaining stockholders often dropped their suits simply to avoid further expense and trouble. By the time the class suit was dismissed, the statute of limitations or laches often barred other stockholders from bringing actions of their own; advantages already gained in the litigation were lost. The termination of the action without notice to the class also served to conceal whatever wrongs had been done, so that

in a derivative suit consented to the entry of a summary judgment in favor of the individual defendant on payment of $5,000 to the plaintiff's attorney. Plaintiff was held liable to the corporation for the $5,000 less such amount as the district court might allow as a reasonable attorney's fee. (Footnote by ed.)

uninformed class members were unable to safeguard their rights. The stockholder's suit was in danger of becoming a tool for defeating the class rights it was intended to protect.

Haudek, The Settlement and Dismissal of Stockholders' Actions–Part I, 22 Sw.L.J. 767, 768–70 (1968).

The problems described by Haudek led to the adoption, in many though not all jurisdictions, of rules like Fed.R.Civ.P. 23.1, which provides that a derivative action "shall not be dismissed or compromised without the approval of the court, and notice of the proposed dismissal or compromise shall be given to shareholders or members in such manner as the court directs."[1]

FEDERAL RULES OF CIVIL PROCEDURE, RULE 23.1

[See Statutory Supplement]

MODEL BUSINESS CORPORATION ACT § 7.45

[See Statutory Supplement]

NEW YORK BUS. CORP. LAW § 626(d), (e)

[See Statutory Supplement]

IN RE CAREMARK, INTERNATIONAL, INC. DERIVATIVE LITIGATION

[Chapter 8, supra]

ALI, PRINCIPLES OF CORPORATE GOVERNANCE §§ 7.14–7.16

[See Statutory Supplement]

DESIMONE v. INDUSTRIAL BIO–TEST LABORATORIES, INC., 83 F.R.D. 615 (S.D.N.Y.1979). "The court will approve a proposed settlement of a class action if the proposal is fair, reasonable and

---

1. Settlements are often submitted for judicial approval even in jurisdictions that do not have such rules, either because the jurisdiction does not follow the theory of *Manu-* *facturer's Mutual* or because the defendants want to secure the res judicata effect that follows from judicial approval.

adequate. This determination requires three levels of analysis. First, the proponents have the burden of proving that (1) the settlement is not collusive but was reached after arm's length negotiation; (2) the proponents are counsel experienced in similar cases; (3) there has been sufficient discovery to enable counsel to act intelligently and (4) the number of objectants or their relative interest is small. If the proponents establish these propositions, the burden of attacking the settlement then shifts to the objectants, if any. Finally, the court must approve the settlement only after finding it to be reasonable in light of the plaintiffs' ultimate probability of success in the lawsuit....

"In determining reasonableness, the courts in this circuit have not applied any single, inflexible test. Instead, they have considered the amount of the settlement in light of all the circumstances, including such factors as: (1) the best possible recovery; (2) the likely recovery if the claims were fully litigated; (3) the complexity, expense and probable duration of continued litigation; (4) the risk of establishing liability; (5) the risk of establishing damages; (6) the risk of maintaining the class action throughout trial; (7) the reaction of the class to the settlement; (8) the stage of the proceedings and (9) the ability of the defendants to withstand a greater judgment." ...

BACKGROUND NOTE ON JUDICIAL APPROVAL OF SETTLEMENTS

Once notice of settlement has been given, a shareholder who objects to the proposed settlement can enter the case. If he succeeds in improving the settlement, he—or more accurately his lawyer—is entitled to counsel fees. White v. Auerbach, 500 F.2d 822 (2d Cir. 1974), noted, 1 J.Corp.Law 194 (1975). Not infrequently the efforts of objectors result in a significant improvement of the settlement. In a well-known episode involving the Alleghany Corporation, a settlement involving a cash payment of $700,000 was increased under objection to $1,000,000, and under continued objection was further increased to $3 million. See Alleghany Corp. v. Kirby, 333 F.2d 327 (2d Cir.1964), aff'd in banc by an equally divided court 340 F.2d 311 (2d Cir.1965), cert. dismissed 384 U.S. 28, 86 S.Ct. 1250, 16 L.Ed.2d 335 (1966).

As a practical matter, the engine that normally drives a derivative action involving a publicly held corporation is not the plaintiff, but the plaintiff's attorney. The plaintiff typically makes little or no investment in the action and stands to gain very little benefit. His attorney, on the other hand, makes a very substantial investment (in the form of his time and disbursements) and stands to reap a very substantial benefit (in the form of a fee). This raises the unwholesome possibility that the defendants may be able to make an improper settlement by giving their acquiescence to an inflated fee in exchange for acquiescence by plaintiff's counsel to an inadequate corporate recovery. In Alleghany Corp. v. Kirby, supra, Judge Friendly remarked on the manner in which the interests of a plaintiff's attorney may conflict with the interests of the shareholders in settling cases where very large amounts are at stake:

I cannot at all agree ... that standard procedures for the approval of settlements afford sufficient safeguards in the "big" case.... The plaintiff stockholders or, more realistically, their attorneys have every incentive to accept a settlement that runs into high six figures or more regardless of how strong the claims for much larger amounts may be. The percentage allowance in stockholders' actions is "reduced as the amount of recovery passes the million dollar mark," 2 Hornstein, Corporation Law and Practice 253 (1959) ... the income tax also plays a role; and a juicy bird in the hand is worth more than the vision of a much larger one in the bush, attainable only after years of effort not currently compensated and possibly a mirage. Once a settlement is agreed, the attorneys for the plaintiff stockholders link arms with their former adversaries to defend the joint handiwork—as is vividly shown here where the stockholders' general counsel sometimes opposed [the objector's] efforts to gain information, although the settlement so vigorously defended before the Referee would have produced less than a quarter as much cash for Alleghany, $700,000, as the $3,000,000 ultimately secured....

Given the problems to which Judge Friendly pointed, as a practical matter the amount of a settlement in any given case may depend in significant part on whether an intervener appears in court to attack the settlement by bringing up problems that the attorneys for the settling parties might gloss over.

Macey & Miller, The Plaintiffs' Attorneys' Role in Class Actions and Derivative Litigation: Economic Analysis and Recommendations for Reform

58 U.Chi.L.Rev. 1, 44–48 (1991).

Most class action and derivative litigation is settled prior to judgment. When such litigation is settled, the problem of agency costs appears in a particularly problematic form. As already discussed, the plaintiffs' attorney often faces a severe conflict of interest in settling class and derivative litigation. In common fund cases where the attorney earns a percentage of the judgment, the attorney has an incentive to settle early at a relatively low figure in order to maximize her profit. In common fund cases in which the attorney is compensated according to the lodestar formula, the attorney has an incentive to delay reaching a settlement in order to increase the hours upon which the compensation is calculated. The attorney may also agree to an inappropriately low settlement on the merits in exchange for the defendant's implicit or explicit promise to allow the attorney to expend additional risk-free hours in order to build up a fee. In common benefit and fee-shifting cases the attorney has an incentive both to delay settlement and to agree to inappropriately low settlements in exchange for generous negotiated attorney's fees....

The regulatory response to these conflicts is to require judicial scrutiny of proposed settlements. Unfortunately, judicial approval appears to be highly imperfect as a protection for the plaintiffs' interests, for several reasons. First, and most important, the judge herself has a powerful interest in approving the settlement. Judges' calendars are crowded with cases, and despite various reform efforts, the workload only seems to increase. If the judge approves the settlement, the result will be to remove a potentially complex and time-consuming case from the judge's calendar; if she rejects it she faces a substantial probability of further litigation. A judge faces virtually no prospect of reversal for approving a settlement, whereas a decision rejecting a settlement might well be appealed. Moreover, trial judges are heavily conditioned by the ethos of their jobs to view settlements as desirable; they routinely encourage settlement in other contexts. It would be unrealistic to expect trial judges to shift gears suddenly and view settlements with suspicion rather than approbation when they arise in the class action or derivative contexts.

Second, trial courts may simply lack information to make an informed evaluation of the fairness of the settlement. Typically, when a case is settled well in advance of trial, the only information available to the judge is found in papers filed in court—pleadings, briefs, and supporting materials filed on motions—and materials submitted to the judge in connection with the settlement hearing. Such evidence is likely to be highly incomplete and, in the case of materials submitted to support the proposed settlement, biased in favor of the settlement. The matters on which the judge must rule are also highly subjective and imprecise. Even if the judge had adequate information on which to decide, it would be difficult to make reliable estimates of the settlement value of a case.

Third, settlement hearings are typically pep rallies jointly orchestrated by plaintiffs' counsel and defense counsel. Because both parties desire that the settlement be approved, they have every incentive to present it as entirely fair. Objectors to the settlement, on the other hand, are uncommon; those who do object are often either disgruntled plaintiffs' attorneys who have fallen out with others in the plaintiffs' consortium, or naive class members who demonstrate their ignorance of the issues in dispute. The deck is heavily stacked toward approval of the settlement.

Trial courts happily play along with the camaraderie. In approving settlement, courts often engage in paeans of praise for counsel or lambaste anyone rash enough to object to the settlement. Not surprisingly, it is uncommon to find cases where trial courts reject settlements that are presented to them by defense counsel and plaintiffs' attorneys. Given that settlements are nearly always approved, one might well question the efficacy of judicial review of class action and derivative settlements.

ALI, PRINCIPLES OF CORPORATE GOVERNANCE § 7.15

[See Statutory Supplement]

NOTE ON SETTLEMENTS WITHOUT THE PLAINTIFF'S CONSENT

Wolf v. Barkes, 348 F.2d 994 (2d Cir.1965), cert. denied 382 U.S. 941, 86 S.Ct. 395, 15 L.Ed.2d 351, was a derivative action that had been brought in federal court by a shareholder-plaintiff against director and officer defendants. The defendants, over the plaintiff's objection, proposed to settle the claims underlying the action directly with the corporation. The corporation and the defendants did not propose to comply with the notice and judicial-approval requirements of then-Rule 23 for the settlement of a derivative action. Plaintiffs attempted to enjoin the settlement on that ground. The court held that the proposed settlement did not fall within Rule 23, because no one was attempting to settle the *suit*, as opposed to the *claim* on which the suit was brought. The court emphasized that if (as might be expected) the defendants moved to dismiss the suit on the basis of the release they obtained as part of the settlement of the claim, the validity of the release could be contested—for example, if it involved a self-interested transaction.

ALI, Principles of Corporate Governance § 7.15, Reporters Note, points out that "[a]lthough Wolf v. Barkes ... establishes that the Federal Rules of Civil Procedure do not require judicial approval of a settlement between the corporation and a defendant in a derivative action, other decisions have held that interested directors may not settle a derivative action, at least not without court approval.... In practice, it appears that on the few occasions when boards have settled with a defendant after the action's commencement, they have sought judicial approval.... Although these cases were arguably voluntary elections, it still appears that the use of the technique *Wolf* affords has been 'infrequent in practice,' and this infrequency appears largely attributable to the uncertainties surrounding such settlements."

SECTION 12. THE ROLE OF CORPORATE COUNSEL

NOTE ON PROBLEMS CONCERNING THE LAW GOVERNING LAWYERS IN DERIVATIVE ACTIONS

1. *Attorney Conflicts of Interest in Derivative Litigation; Garner v. Wolfinbarger.* Partly because of their complex four-party structure—involving nominal plaintiffs, entrepreneurial attorneys, the corporation, and defendants who in their director or officer capacities have or share control of the corporation—derivative actions present a number of severe problems that fall under the heading of the law governing lawyers.

On one side of the case, there may be a conflict between the interests of the shareholders as a class, who are the ultimate beneficiaries of a derivative action, and the interests of the entrepreneurial attorney who brings the action. On the other side, the interests of the corporation may diverge from the interests of defendants who control the corporation, and the corporation's lawyers may as a practical matter regard themselves as working for the latter.

Against this background, problems may also arise concerning the lawyer-client and work-product privileges. In doctrinal terms, the issue can be phrased in terms of whether the corporation's attorney can assert the privilege in a way that favors the defendants even though at least nominally the attorney's client was not the defendants, but rather the corporation in whose right the action is brought. In substantive terms, the issue can be phrased as whether which one of the following rules best serves the interests of the shareholder-owners: (1) A rule that gives inviolate protection to management communications with lawyers, on the ground that to do so will make managers more secure in seeking advice from corporate counsel. (2) A rule that permits exceptions when the very issue is whether a manager's conduct injured rather than served the corporation by whom the attorney was retained or employed.

In Garner v. Wolfinbarger, 430 F.2d 1093 (5th Cir.1970), cert. denied 401 U.S. 974, 91 S.Ct. 1191, 28 L.Ed.2d 323 (1971), the court attempted to balance the various interests involved by adopting the rule that in a derivative action, invocation of the attorney-client privilege was subject to the right of the plaintiff-shareholders to show good cause why the privilege should not be invoked:

> It is urged that disclosure is injurious to both the corporation and the attorney. Corporate management must manage. It has the duty to do so and requires the tools to do so. Part of the managerial task is to seek legal counsel when desirable, and, obviously, management prefers that it confer with counsel without the risk of having the communications revealed at the instance of one or more dissatisfied stockholders. The managerial preference is a rational one, because it is difficult to envision the management of any sizeable corporation pleasing all of its stockholders all of the time, and management desires protection from those who might second-guess or even harass in matters purely of judgment.
>
> But in assessing management assertions of injury to the corporation it must be borne in mind that management does not manage for itself and that the beneficiaries of its action are the stockholders. Conceptualistic phrases describing the corporation as an entity separate from its stockholders are not useful tools of analysis. They serve only to obscure the fact that management has duties which run to the benefit ultimately of the stockholders. For example, it is difficult to rationally defend the assertion of the privilege if all, or substantially all, stockholders desire to inquire into the attorney's communications with corporate representatives who have only nominal ownership interests, or even none at all. There may be reasonable differences over the manner of characterizing in legal terminology the duties of management, and over

the extent to which corporate management is less of a fiduciary than the common law trustee. There may be many situations in which the corporate entity or its management, or both, have interests adverse to those of some or all stockholders. But when all is said and done management is not managing for itself. . . .

In summary, we say this. The attorney-client privilege still has viability for the corporate client. The corporation is not barred from asserting it merely because those demanding information enjoy the status of stockholders. But where the corporation is in suit against its stockholders on charges of acting inimically to stockholder interests, protection of those interests as well as those of the corporation and of the public require that the availability of the privilege be subject to the right of the stockholders to show cause why it should not be invoked in the particular instance. . . .

There are many indicia that may contribute to a decision of presence or absence of good cause, among them the number of shareholders and the percentage of stock they represent; the bona fides of the shareholders; the nature of the shareholders' claim and whether it is obviously colorable; the apparent necessity or desirability of the shareholders having the information and the availability of it from other sources; whether, if the shareholders' claim is of wrongful action by the corporation, it is of action criminal, or illegal but not criminal, or of doubtful legality; whether the communication related to past or to prospective actions; whether the communication is of advice concerning the litigation itself; the extent to which the communication is identified versus the extent to which the shareholders are blindly fishing; the risk of revelation of trade secrets or other information in whose confidentiality the corporation has an interest for independent reasons. The court can freely use *in camera* inspection or oral examination and freely avail itself of protective orders, a familiar device to preserve confidentiality in trade secret and other cases where the impact of revelation may be as great as in revealing a communication with counsel.

On remand, the district court held that the lawyer-client privilege was inapplicable under the standards *Garner* set out. Garner v. Wolfinbarger, 56 F.R.D. 499 (S.D.Ala.1972).

There is a split among the Circuits concerning whether the *Garner* principle is applicable to shareholder class actions. Compare Weil v. Investment/Indicators, Research & Management, 647 F.2d 18 (9th Cir. 1981) (*Garner* is not applicable to class actions), with Ward v. Succession of Freeman, 854 F.2d 780 (5th Cir. 1988), cert. denied, 490 U.S. 1065, 109 S.Ct. 2064, 104 L.Ed.2d 629 (1989) (*Garner* is applicable to class actions) and Fausek v. White, 965 F.2d 126 (6th Cir.), cert. denied, 506 U.S. 1034, 113 S.Ct. 814 (1992) (same).

2. *Upjohn.* In Upjohn Co. v. United States, 449 U.S. 383, 101 S.Ct. 677, 66 L.Ed.2d 584 (1981), Upjohn's independent accountant discovered that an Upjohn subsidiary had made improper payments to secure foreign government business. After consultation among Up-

john's general counsel, outside counsel, and chairman of the board, it was decided that the company would conduct an internal investigation of "questionable payments." As part of this investigation the attorneys prepared a letter containing a questionnaire which was sent to "All Foreign General and Area Managers" over the chairman's signature. Subsequently, the Internal Revenue Service issued a summons demanding production of certain records, including the questionnaires. The Supreme Court held that the questionnaires were protected from disclosure by the attorney-client privilege. Unlike *Garner, Upjohn* involved an action by a third party against the corporation, rather than a derivative action on the corporation's behalf against some of its managers.

3. *Work–Product.* In In re International Systems & Controls Corp. Securities Litigation, 693 F.2d 1235 (5th Cir.1982), the court held that the good-cause standard of *Garner* is inapplicable to material covered by the work-product immunity, that is, material prepared in anticipation of litigation, as opposed to the communications between managers and counsel in the course of business decisionmaking. The court said the discoverability of work product in this context is governed by the general principle concerning the discoverability of work product under FRCP Rule 26(b)(3), which turns on a general principle concerning substantial need/undue hardship test. See also *Upjohn*, supra; Cox v. Administrator U.S. Steel & Carnegie, 17 F.3d 1386, 1423 (11th Cir.1994).

ABA MODEL RULES OF PROFESSIONAL CONDUCT, RULES 1.6, 1.7, 1.13

[See Statutory Supplement]

SECTION 13. CLASS ACTIONS

Particularly in the light of the growth of Rule 10b–5 litigation, the procedural aspects of class actions have become highly significant in corporate practice. Some of the problems raised by such actions are virtually identical to those raised by derivative suits—for example, how counsel fees are determined, how duplicate actions are handled, and when a settlement is binding upon the class. Some issues, however, are relatively unique, such as when individual rights can be bundled into a class action, and when members of a class must be given notice that a class action has been filed.

FEDERAL RULES OF CIVIL PROCEDURE, RULE 23

[See Statutory Supplement]

———

NOTE ON CLASS ACTIONS

As discussed in Section 2, supra, in certain cases shareholders can bring suit in their own right. An individual suit is often more attractive to a plaintiff and his attorney than a derivative suit, because it avoids such hurdles as security for expenses, demand on the board, and demand on the shareholders. An individual suit is not economical, however, unless either the plaintiff's shareholding is so large that the probable recovery will cover attorneys' fees, or it can be confidently predicted that attorneys' fees can be collected from other shareholders under the common-fund theory or a variant (see Section 8, supra). Since these conditions are not often satisfied, suits to vindicate shareholders' individual rights are commonly cast as class actions, because attorneys' fees can then be paid out of the benefits accruing to the entire class. Suits under the securities acts are a common example, but suits based on state corporation law are also frequently brought as class actions—for example, suits to require the declaration of a dividend, to enjoin an allegedly unauthorized transaction, to set aside an improper vote, or to enforce a preemptive or conversion right.

In Zahn v. International Paper Co., 414 U.S. 291, 94 S.Ct. 505, 38 L.Ed.2d 511 (1973), the Court held that in Rule 23(b)(3) actions brought in federal court on diversity grounds, the claim of each member of the class must involve the jurisdictional amount for diversity cases (now $75,000). However, most corporate class actions brought in federal courts are brought on federal grounds under the securities acts, and in such cases there is no jurisdictional minimum.

The status of *Zahn* is uncertain. The Judicial Improvement Act, 28 U.S.C. § 1367, adopted in 1990, provides that where a district court has original jurisdiction over a claim, the court will also have supplemental jurisdiction over claims that are so related that they form part of the same case or controversy. Read literally, this provision overrules *Zahn*, because if the claims of one or more members of the class involve $75,000 each, then section 1367 gives the court jurisdiction over the claims of all the other members of the class, even if those claims do not satisfy the amount-in-controversy requirement. However, the legislative history expressly states that section 1367 was not intended to overrule *Zahn*. The circuit courts have divided on the issue. Compare e.g., Rosmer v. Pfizer, Inc., 263 F.3d 110 (4th Cir. 2001) (holding that the text of section 1367 is unambiguous, and overrules Zahn) and Olden v. LaFarge Corp., 383 F.3d 495 (6th Cir. 2004) (same) with Meritcare Inc. v. St. Paul Mercury Ins. Co., 166 F.3d 214 (3d Cir. 1999) (holding that based on the legislative history, section 1367 does not overrule Zahn) and Trimble v. Asarco, Inc., 232 F.3d 946 (8th Cir. 2000) (same).

SECTION 14. A LOOK BACK

AMERICAN LAW INSTITUTE, PRINCIPLES OF CORPORATE GOVERNANCE, INTRODUCTION TO PART VII, REPORTER'S NOTE

[See Statutory Supplement]

NOTE ON SHAREHOLDER LITIGATION

Based on studies of certain data concerning settlement and success rates in derivative actions, Professor Roberta Romano has concluded that "shareholder litigation is a weak, if not ineffective, instrument of corporate governance," and that "the principal beneficiaries of the litigation ... appear to be the [plaintiffs'] attorneys." Romano, The Shareholder Suit: Litigation Without Foundation?, 7 J. of Law, Economics, & Organization 55, 84 (1991). Some others have drawn comparable conclusions.

These conclusions seem either questionable or incorrect. To begin with, the samples from which the relevant data have been drawn have all been seriously flawed. For example, Romano's own sample excluded all actions involving corporations whose stock was not publicly traded. However, litigation involving such corporations may have a different degree of merit than litigation involving publicly held corporations, because the incentive structures for bringing shareholder actions in the two types of corporations differ substantially.

Furthermore, even the data that has been used does not support the conclusions that are drawn. Several kinds of arguments are often made on the basis of the data. One is that the data shows that an extremely high proportion of derivative actions settle. That argument, however, is a non-starter. As Romano points out, "[t]his aspect of shareholder litigation is unremarkable; most civil suits settle." Id. at 60.

A second kind of argument is that the data shows that settlements don't, on average, confer a benefit on the corporation. In Romano's sample, about half the settlements during the relevant period resulted in monetary recovery, with an average recovery of $9 million and a median recovery of $2 million. A number of the remaining settlements involved changes in corporate governance but no monetary recovery. In most of the cases, the plaintiffs' attorney was awarded attorneys' fees. Because the monetary recoveries were very small in relation to firm assets, Romano states that "One interpretation [of this data] is that most fiduciary breaches involve only minor harm to shareholders. But the settlement pattern is consistent with another, more troubling explanation, that a significant proportion of shareholder suits are without merit." Id. at 61. Others have drawn similar conclusions.

There are several problems with this explanation. To begin with, as Romano states, the data on which she relies can be explained in a much different way. Next, there are methodological problems. Apart from the flaws in the sample, no baseline data is provided concerning suits other than shareholder suits. Some percentage of all cases that appear to have merit ex ante turn out to be without merit ex post. No baseline data is provided by Romano or others against which to measure whether the percentage of shareholder litigation that is without merit is higher or lower than the percentage of all litigation that is without merit. Similarly, some percentage of all settlements are low, and no baseline data is provided by critics of shareholder suits comparing settlements in shareholder actions with settlements in other kinds of actions.

Furthermore, most of the data on the settlement of derivative actions is simply not persuasive concerning the merits of shareholder litigation. In Romano's sample, the average monetary settlement was $9 million and the median was $2 million. Those are not insignificant amounts. A director who sells property to the corporation at $2 million more than its market value has committed a serious wrong that should be remedied, and a derivative action may be the only way to accomplish that end.

Similarly, the fact that a relatively high proportion of shareholder suits involve nonmonetary settlements is not in itself dispositive concerning the merits of these cases. Corporations are governance systems. Accordingly, in a number of shareholder suits a change in governance would be extremely valuable. Additionally, in the case of many or most civil suits, the only thing the defendant has that the plaintiff wants is money. Shareholder suits, in contrast, offer a greater opportunity for win/win outcomes, because the defendants can trade not only money, but also changes in governance rules and conduct. Therefore, a certain percentage of nonmonetary settlements of derivative actions are to be expected simply as a matter of the dynamics of the corporate context. Some nonmonetary settlements do indeed involve relief that is only cosmetic. Others, however, involve very substantial benefits, such as the termination of inside directors' employment contracts or a systematic change in the corporation's governance structure.

Moreover, although it is possible that a significant proportion of nonmonetary settlements do not involve substantial relief, even that may not show that the underlying cases lacked substantive merit. Weak settlements may be due not to a lack of substantive merit, but to the role of the special procedural obstacles to derivative actions. Professor John Coffee has made the following observations concerning arguments that derivative actions produce only limited financial benefits in relation to their costs:

What does this evidence really prove? First, the same critique could be made of the criminal law; the fines imposed by a criminal court may often fall below the state's cost of prosecution. Nonetheless, criminal prosecutions continue, either because society believes in general deterrence or because it enjoys retribution. Similarly, the value of the derivative action arguably lies in its deterrent capacity, which such studies do not measure. Although the deterrent threat of the derivative action may be undercut to some degree by liability insurance, most D & O policies do not cover repayment of an improper benefit. In addition, there are also non-monetary sanctions, such as loss of reputation and social stigma. These intangibles are even harder to estimate, but only a fool ignores them.

Second, the real problem with any study finding a negligible benefit is that it cannot measure the deterrent or compensatory capacity of the derivative action in the abstract but only under a specific set of legal rules. Recent studies, which have focused on publicly listed companies, are thus principally measuring the effectiveness of Delaware law, because Delaware is the corporate home for nearly half of such companies. That these studies find only negligible benefits and substantial costs is hardly reassuring about Delaware's legal rules for the derivative action. But, by the same token, such studies prove little about alternative legal regimes.

The bottom line then is that any claim that the empirical data proves the derivative action useless is circular. The outcome of derivative actions is determined largely by the incentives that the law holds out to private enforcers to bring them. If the operative legal rules tell the plaintiff's attorney that there is a high probability of dismissal, regardless of the action's merit, the predictable result of such rules will be small settlements. All this proves is the truism that the parties "bargained in the shadow of the law."

Another argument that is sometimes made against the efficacy of shareholder actions is that the data shows that plaintiffs have a very low rate of success in those cases that are disposed of through adjudication, rather than settlement. Certainly this data is troubling. However, this data too is difficult to evaluate. Because there are so many special, procedural defenses to derivative actions—such as contemporaneous ownership and demand on the board—a low rate of success in derivative actions is not surprising, and may only be evidence that the special procedural hurdles couldn't be jumped, not that the suits lacked substantive merit. As a practical matter, a typical strategy of defendants in derivative actions is to try to get rid of a case on the basis of a special procedural defense before discovery, and to settle if the plaintiff survives the procedural attacks and begins unearthing all the facts in discovery.

Finally, in evaluating shareholder litigation *all* benefits and losses must be taken into account. One benefit is general deterrence. General deterrence is, of course, important for any class of litigation, but it may be especially important in the case of shareholder litigation, because corporations, directors, and officers are more likely to get legal messages—to be law-sensitive—than most private actors.

Another benefit of shareholder litigation is the public knowledge that directors and officers who engage in misconduct are subject to such litigation. This knowledge increases public confidence in, and therefore the efficiency of, the capital markets.

A third benefit of derivative actions is that, as Romano states, "legal rules are public goods. All firms benefit from a judicial decision clarifying the scope of permissible conduct." Id. at 85. In assessing derivative actions, Romano, like others who have drawn negative conclusions concerning the benefits of such actions, left the calculation of the public-good aspect of derivative actions "for another study." But any argument that the costs of derivative actions exceed their benefits entirely depends on taking into account all costs and all benefits. That is not what the critics of derivative actions have done. Instead, most critics count all the costs of derivative actions but only a fraction of the benefits, and then—not surprisingly—conclude that the costs exceed the benefits.

It is possible that if all the costs and benefits of shareholder litigation were added up, we would conclude that the costs would exceed the benefits. Whether that conclusion is probable, however, is a much different question. Recall, in this connection, the conclusion of Macey & Miller, supra, that "Although a theoretical model exists in which [shareholder] suits are brought solely for their nuisance settlement value, the frequency of strike suits in derivative and class litigation remains an open question. Most observers agree that strike suit litigation is relatively uncommon."

The most recent scholarship in the area attests to the benefits of shareholder suits. Delaware is by far the most important corporate jurisdiction, and corporate litigation in Delaware begins in the Chancery Court. In a pair of articles, Robert Thompson and Randall Thomas studied all the complaints filed in Delaware Chancery court in the two-year period 1999–2000. Thompson & Thomas, The Public and Private Faces of Derivative Lawsuits, 57 Vanderbilt Law Rev. 1747 (2004); Thompson & Thomas, The New Look of Shareholder Litigation: Acquisition-Oriented Class Actions, 57 Vanderbilt Law. Rev. 133 (2004). The former article focuses on derivative actions, and the latter focuses on class actions brought for violations of state corporate law (as opposed to securities class actions).

Thompson & Thomas found that during 1999–2000, on a consolidated basis 348 shareholder fiduciary-duty suits were filed in the Delaware Chancery Court. Of these, 84 were derivative actions, 74 were direct actions, and 223 were class actions. Taken together, fiduciary-duty cases accounted for most of the shareholder suits in Delaware during the relevant period. (The remaining suits were based on statutory or contractual claims. These claims concerned such matters as inspection of books and records, petitions for dissolution or the appointment of a receiver or custodian, appraisal proceedings, suits for indemnification, and so forth.)

Of the derivative actions involving private corporations, about one-third resulted in affirmative relief. The relief included money payments to minority owners, changes in the allocation of ownership, and a purchase by the corporation of the complaining shareholders' shares. Of the derivative actions involving publicly held corporations, about 28% ended in affirmative relief. This relief included money damages and nonmonetary relief, such as rescission of a purchase agreement and rescission of substantial executive compensation. All together, nine cases ended in monetary relief. Almost all the monetary settlements were for $9 million or more. In one case, the settlement was for $140 million, and in one case it was for $165 million. In the latter two cases, the attorneys' fees were less than 10% of the settlement amount.

Overall, as to derivative actions, Thompson & Thomas conclude as follows:

> ... The impact of decisions in derivative cases like *Caremark*,[9] *Disney*,[10] and *Oracle*[11] goes well beyond the outcome of the cases themselves—these decisions changed the rules for future legal practice by allowing well motivated legal counselors to force their clients to accept better conduct and procedures. Moreover, derivative suits at private companies perform an important, if less heralded, role in policing conflict of interest transactions and duty of care violations.
>
> To support our claim, we present the data from a study of all corporate litigation in Delaware for a two year period. We find that there are a small number of derivative suits, about 30 per year, brought against public companies incorporated in Delaware. Contrary to earlier studies, we do not find evidence that these cases are "strike suits" yielding little benefit. Instead, roughly 30% of the derivative suits provide relief to the corporation or the shareholders, while the others are usually dismissed quickly with little apparent litigation activity. In cases producing a recovery to shareholders, the amount of recovery typically exceeds the amount of attorneys' fees awarded by a significant margin. The cases do demonstrate some indicia of litigation agency costs (for example suits being filed quickly, multiple suits per controversy, and repeat plaintiffs' law firms) but each of these costs is much less pronounced for derivative suits than for other forms of representative litigation. Overall, the claim that derivative suits are strike suits is much weaker than in earlier periods.

Public and Private Faces of Derivative Actions, supra, at 1749–50.

9. Caremark International Inc. Derivative Litigation, 698 A.2d 959 (Del. Ch. 1996) (finding in dicta that boards had a duty to consider whether to create internal monitoring systems).

10. In re The Walt Disney Company Derivative Litigation, 825 A.2d 275 (Del. Ch. 2003) (denying motion to dismiss complaint alleging that board had breached the duty of good faith in determining executive compensation package).

11. In re Oracle Corp. Derivative Litigation, 824 A.2d 917 (Del. Ch. 2003) (finding that tenured professors who were members of special litigation committee were not independent where financial ties between university and corporation were substantial).

Thompson's and Thomas's findings on state-law class actions is even more striking than their findings on derivative actions. One important finding was that while the derivative actions generally involved traditional duty-of-loyalty claims, most of the class actions involved director or controlling shareholder conduct in mergers and other acquisitions. Another important finding was that class actions account for a much higher percentage of corporate-law litigation in Delaware than derivative actions. Thompson and Thomas also found that "There is no pattern [in the class-action cases] of modest settlements for the shareholder group and most of that money going to the attorneys, as was sometimes found in earlier representative suits. Instead, we find that there were large monetary settlements paid to shareholders in many of these cases and that these settlements involved a substantially lower percentage level of attorneys' fees as compared to securities fraud class actions.... The pattern of affirmative relief was strongest in those cases in which there was a controlling shareholder who has proposed an acquisition that will effectively cash-out the minority shareholders...." In 20 of 65 of the controlling-shareholder acquisition cases, as a result of the class action additional consideration was paid to the minority shareholders. In the controlling-shareholder acquisition cases that did not result in a monetary settlement, the premium of the acquisition price over the market price was 25.5%. In the cases that did result in a monetary settlement, the premium was only 15%, but the settlement lifted the premium to more than 25.5%. Accordingly, the impact of the monetary class-action settlements was "to raise the premium paid in the lowest-priced control shareholder transactions above the average level for all of these transactions in our sample. In other words, acquisition-oriented class action litigation polices the worst control shareholder deals, and benefits target company shareholders by insuring that they get compensated as well as, or better than, shareholders in deals that are more fully priced."

Overall, as to acquisition-oriented class actions, Thompson and Thomas conclude as follows:

> [An] optimistic perspective would be that these acquisition-driven suits serve an important effect a priori: corporate planners know the relative strength of the different legal doctrines associated with different forms of acquisitions, and try to minimize the costs of shareholder litigation by invoking procedural protections like the use of special committees and by offering shareholders a sufficiently high price for their shares that they do not file suit. If they ignore this information, and do not offer shareholders a sufficient premium for their stock, shareholder litigation forces them to do so in many instances....

> Placing our findings in the historical context of the debate over the value of representative shareholder litigation, we believe that acquisition-oriented class actions substantially reduce management agency costs, while the litigation agency costs they create do not appear excessive. For these suits, we therefore disagree with earlier studies that have claimed that all representative

shareholder litigation has little, if any, effect in reducing management agency costs and should be evaluated solely in terms of its litigation agency costs. . . .

. . . [I]f we take only those control shareholder transactions that evidence a larger likelihood of conflict of interest, we find that affirmative relief occurs only in those cases in which the initial premium offered by the conflicted controlling shareholder was the lowest in relation to the prior market price. This finding suggests that the merits of litigation do make a difference, and that shareholder litigation deserves a seat at the table of corporate governance.

The New Look of Shareholder Litigation, supra, at 139–40, 208.

Thompson and Thomas analyzed only state-law class actions. Similar trends are emerging in securities-law class actions. In 2003, U.S. companies and foreign firms operating in the United States made settlement payments in securities actions that totaled over $5 billion. Twenty two of the settlements exceeded $20 million. Colter, Bull Market for Securities Lawsuits, Wall St. J., March 30, 2005, at C3, col. 1.

CHAPTER XII

STRUCTURAL CHANGES: CORPORATE COMBINATIONS AND TENDER OFFERS

SECTION 1. CORPORATE COMBINATIONS

———

(a) SALE OF SUBSTANTIALLY ALL ASSETS

———

DEL. GEN. CORP. LAW § 271

[See Statutory Supplement]

———

MODEL BUS. CORP. ACT §§ 12.01, 12.02, 13.02(3)

[See Statutory Supplement]

———

Hollinger, Inc. v. Hollinger International, Inc.

Court of Chancery of Delaware, 2004.
858 A.2d 342.

Opinion

■ STRINE, VICE CHANCELLOR. . . .

Hollinger Inc. (or "Inc.") seeks a preliminary injunction preventing Hollinger International, Inc. (or "International") from selling the *Telegraph* Group Ltd. (England) to Press Holdings International, an entity controlled by Frederick and David Barclay (hereinafter, the "Barclays"). The *Telegraph* Group is an indirect, wholly owned subsidiary of International and publishes the *Telegraph* newspaper and the *Spectator* magazine. The *Telegraph* newspaper is a leading one in the United Kingdom, both in terms of its circulation and its journalistic reputation.

The key question addressed in this decision is whether Inc. and the other International stockholders must be provided with the opportunity to vote on the sale of the *Telegraph* Group because that sale involves "substantially all" the assets of International within the meaning of 8 Del. C. §271. The sale of the *Telegraph* followed a lengthy auction process whereby International and all of Hollinger's operating assets were widely shopped to potential bidders. As a practical matter, Inc.'s vote would be the only one that matters because although it now owns only 18% of International's total equity, it, through high-vote Class B shares, controls 68% of the voting power....

... Does § 271 Apply to a Sale of Assets By an Indirect, Wholly Owned Subsidiary?

International [first] argues that the sale of the *Telegraph* Group simply does not implicate § 271 at all. The reason is that the operating assets that the Barclays are buying and that comprise the *Telegraph* Group are actually held by a 6th tier U.K. subsidiary and not by International.

It is undisputed that the chain of subsidiaries through which International controlled the *Telegraph* Group maintained the corporate formalities necessary for it to comply with U.K. and U.S. regulatory requirements. It is also undisputed that these subsidiaries are long-standing parts of the International structure and were formed because they had valuable tax, financial, and liability-insulating purposes. There is no indication that any third parties dealing with the subsidiaries in the ordinary course of business or any tort plaintiff allegedly injured by one of the subsidiaries would have been entitled to pierce their corporate veil and seek recourse directly against International.

On the other hand, the chain of subsidiaries is wholly owned by International. The Strategic Process that resulted in the proposal to sell the *Telegraph* Group was, as a matter of obvious reality, conducted entirely at the International level....

Notably, the contract for sale of the *Telegraph* Group does not run simply between the Barclays and the U.K. subsidiary that directly own the *Telegraph* Group. Instead, International is a direct signatory to that agreement and its lawyers negotiated its terms....

In essence, it is clear to me that the *Telegraph* sale was directed and controlled by International and that its wholly owned subsidiaries did what wholly owned subsidiaries do—the bidding of their sole owner. It is no disrespect to the employees who populated the subsidiary boards to recognize this obvious reality.

From this, to my view, clear factual picture, the parties draw starkly different legal conclusions. For its part, International contends that it is plain that § 271 does not contemplate ignoring the separate existence of subsidiary corporations unless the stringent test for veil piercing is met....

If International's argument is accepted, § 271's vote requirement will be rendered largely hortatory—reduced to an easily side-stepped gesture, but little more, towards the idea that transactions that dispose of substantially all of a corporation's economic value need stockholders' assent to become effective. An example tied to this case points out this implication. Assume that the [board, acting through its Corporate Review Committee] decided to sell all four of International's operating groups. Further assume that each is held by subsidiaries that would not be subject to veil piercing but that it is equally clear that International dictated the sale of the assets and was a signatory to and guarantor of the sales contracts. Under International's view, even that sale would not constitute a sale of substantially all of its assets. This would be the case even though the sales would, taken together, result in a de facto liquidation of the firm's operating assets into a pool of cash, a result akin to a sale of the entire company for cash or a liquidation. . . .

In drawing lines under § 271 itself, moreover, the facts of this case suggest a possible demarcation point. When an asset sale by the wholly owned subsidiary is to be consummated by a contract in which the parent entirely guarantees the performance of the selling subsidiary that is disposing of all of its assets and in which the parent is liable for any breach of warranty by the subsidiary, the direct act of the parent's board can, without any appreciable stretch, be viewed as selling assets of the parent itself. By its direct contractual action, the parent board is promising to dispose of all of the underlying assets of the subsidiaries by having the parent cause its wholly owned subsidiaries to sell, by promising to bear all the economic risks of the asset sale itself, and by therefore essentially eliminating the subsidiary's purpose and existence and monetizing for itself as parent the value of the assets held by that subsidiary. To find that § 271's vote requirement were implicated by such a contract if it involved the sale of assets that would, if owned directly by the parent, comprise substantially all of the parent's assets would not, despite International's well-stated arguments to the contrary, be an irrational implementation of the legislative intent expressed in that section of our corporation code.

I need not reach that conclusion, or a contrary one, in this case, however. This motion can be resolved without rendering any definitive pronouncement on this area of our law and, given the limited time for reflection on the question presented, prudential considerations counsel in favor of leaving the question to be answered in another case, or at later stage of this one, if that becomes necessary.

. . . As a Matter of Economic Substance, Does the Telegraph Group Comprise Substantially All of International's Assets?

I now discuss the major question presented by this motion: whether the *Telegraph* Group comprises "substantially all" of International's assets, such that its sale requires a vote under § 271.

1. The Legal Standards to Measure Whether the Telegraph Group Comprises Substantially All of International's Assets

Section 271 of the Delaware General Corporation Law authorizes a board of directors of a Delaware corporation to sell "all or substantially all of its property and assets, including goodwill and corporate franchises" only with the approval of a stockholder vote. . . .

Therefore, I begin my articulation of the applicable legal principles with the words of the statute itself. . . . A fair and succinct equivalent to the term "substantially all" would . . . be "essentially everything."

In our jurisprudence, however, words of this kind arguably long ago passed from the sight of our judicial rear view mirrors, to be replaced by an inquiry more focused on the judicial gloss put on the statute than on the words of the statute itself. The need for some gloss is understandable, of course. There are various metrics that can be used to determine how important particular assets are in the scheme of things. Should a court look to the percentage of the corporation's potential value as a sales target to measure the statute's application? Or measures of income-generating potential, such as contributions to revenues or operating income? To what extent should the flagship nature of certain assets be taken into account? For all these reasons,

> The Supreme Court has long held that a determination of whether there is a sale of substantially all assets so as to trigger section 271 depends upon the particular qualitative and quantitative characteristics of the transaction at issue. Thus, the transaction must be viewed in terms of its overall effect on the corporation, and there is no necessary qualifying percentage.[51]

In other words,

> Our jurisprudence eschewed a definitional approach to § 271 focusing on the interpretation of the words "substantially all," in favor of a contextual approach focusing upon whether a transaction involves the sale "of assets quantitatively vital to the operation of the corporation and is out of the ordinary and substantially affects the existence and purpose of the corporation." *Gimbel v. Signal Cos., Inc.*, Del.Ch., 316 A.2d 599, 606, *aff'd*, Del.Supr., 316 A.2d 619 (1974). . . .[52]

. . . *Gimbel* set forth a quantitative and qualitative test designed to help determine whether a particular sale of assets involved substantially all the corporation's assets. That test has been adopted by our Supreme Court as a good metric for determining whether an asset sale triggers the vote requirement of § 271. . . .[55]

The test that *Gimbel* articulated—requiring a stockholder vote if the assets to be sold "are quantitatively vital to the operation of the corporation' and 'substantially affect[ ] the existence and purpose of the corporation"—must . . . be read as an attempt to give practical life to the words "substantially all." It is for that reason that *Gimbel* emphasized that a vote would never be required for a transaction in

---

51. *Winston v. Mandor*, 710 A.2d 835, 843 (Del.Ch.1997) (footnotes omitted).

52. *In re General Motors Class H S'holders Litig.*, 734 A.2d 611, 623 (Del.Ch. 1999).

55. *Oberly v. Kirby*, 592 A.2d 445, 464 (Del.1991); *see also Thorpe v. CERBCO, Inc.*, 676 A.2d 436, 444 (Del.1996).

the ordinary course of business and that the mere fact that an asset sale was out of the ordinary had little bearing on whether a vote was required.

Indeed, *Gimbel* stressed that "the statute does not speak of a requirement of shareholder approval simply because an independent, important branch of a corporate business is being sold." In that case, the court expressly rejected the argument that Delaware law ought to follow the law of other states that subjected all such major sales to stockholder approval. . . .

To underscore the point that the test it was articulating was tied directly to the statute, *Gimbel* noted that its examination of the quantitative and qualitative importance of the transaction at issue was intended to determine whether the transaction implicated the statute because it struck "at the heart of the corporate existence and purpose," in the sense that it involved the " 'destruction of the means to accomplish the purposes or objects for which the corporation was incorporated and actually performs.' " It was in that sense, Gimbel said, that the "statute's applicability was to be determined."

And it is in that sense that I apply the *Gimbel* test in this case.

2.   *Is the Telegraph Group Quantitatively Vital to the Operations of International?*

The first question under the *Gimbel* test is whether the *Telegraph* Group is quantitatively vital to the operations of International. The short answer to that question is no, it is not quantitatively vital within the meaning of *Gimbel*.

Why?

Because it is clear that International will retain economic vitality even after a sale of the *Telegraph* because it is retaining other significant assets, one of which, the Chicago Group [which owned, among other things, the Chicago *Sun-Times* and Jerusalem *Post* newspapers], has a strong record of past profitability and expectations of healthy profit growth.

Now, it is of course clear that the *Telegraph* Group is a major quantitative part of International's economic value and an important contributor to its profits. I am even prepared to decide this motion on the assumption that the *Telegraph* Group is the single most valuable asset that International possesses, even more valuable than the Chicago Group.

If one were to use the actual high bids received for each of the *Telegraph* and Chicago Groups as a result of the Strategic [Auction] Process and assume that those were the only assets of International—which is not an accurate assumption—the *Telegraph* Group accounts for 56–57% of International's asset value, while the Chicago Group accounts for only 43–44% of the value. Recognizing that quantitative vitality must be defined in light of the statutory language "substantially all," this breakdown does little to support Inc.'s position. It is less than 60% and the remaining asset is itself a quantitatively vital economic asset....

Let's consider the relative contribution to International's revenues of the *Telegraph* Group and the Chicago Group....

Put simply, the *Telegraph* Group has accounted for less than half of International's revenues during the last three years and the Chicago Group's contribution has been in the same ballpark....

In book value terms, neither the *Telegraph* Group nor the Chicago Group approach 50% of International's asset value because the company's other operating groups and non-operating assets have value....

In terms of vitality, however, a more important measure is EBITDA [Earnings Before Interest, Taxes, Depreciation, and Amortization] contribution, as that factor focuses on the free cash flow that assets generate for the firm, a key component of economic value....

The [EBITDA] picture that emerges is one of rough equality between the two Groups—with any edge tilting in the Chicago Group's direction....

Importantly, the record evidence regarding the future of both Groups also suggests that their cash flow-generating potential and sale value are not greatly disparate....

The evidence therefore reveals that neither the *Telegraph* Group nor the Chicago Group is quantitatively vital in the sense used in the *Gimbel* test. Although both Groups are profitable, valuable economic assets and although the *Telegraph* Group is somewhat more valuable than the Chicago Group, International can continue as a profitable entity without either one of them....

[A] sale of either Group leaves International as a profitable entity, even if it chooses to distribute a good deal of the cash it receives from the *Telegraph* sale to its stockholders through a dividend or share repurchase.

3. Does the Telegraph Sale "Substantially Affect the Existence and Purpose of" International?

The relationship of the qualitative element of the *Gimbel* test to the quantitative element is more than a tad unclear. If the assets to be sold are not quantitatively vital to the corporation's life, it is not altogether apparent how they can "substantially affect the existence and purpose of" the corporation within the meaning of *Gimbel*, suggesting either that the two elements of the test are actually not distinct or that they are redundant. In other words, if quantitative vitality takes into account factors such as the cash-flow generating value of assets and not merely book value, then it necessarily captures qualitative considerations as well.... Rather than endeavor to explore the relationship between these factors, however, I will just dive into my analysis of the qualitative importance of the *Telegraph* Group to International.

Inc.'s demand for a vote places great weight on the qualitative element of *Gimbel*. In its papers, Inc. stresses the journalistic superiority of the *Telegraph* over the *Sun–Times* and the social cachet the *Telegraph* has....

The argument ... misconceives the qualitative element of *Gimbel*. That element is not satisfied if the court merely believes that the economic assets being sold are aesthetically superior to those being retained; rather, the qualitative element of *Gimbel* focuses on economic quality and, at most, on whether the transaction leaves the stockholders with an investment that in economic terms is qualitatively different than the one that they now possess. Even with that focus, it must be remembered that the qualitative element is a gloss on the statutory language "substantially all" and not an attempt to identify qualitatively important transactions but ones that "strike at the heart of the corporate existence."

The *Telegraph* sale does not strike at International's heart or soul, if that corporation can be thought to have either one....

... Whatever the social importance of the *Telegraph* in Great Britain, the economic value of that importance to International as an entity is what matters for the *Gimbel* test, not how cool it would be to be the *Telegraph's* publisher. The expected cash flows from the *Telegraph* Group take that into account, as do the bids that were received for the *Telegraph* Group....

After the *Telegraph* Sale, International's stockholders will remain investors in a publication company with profitable operating assets, a well-regarded tabloid newspaper of good reputation and large circulation, a prestigious newspaper in Israel, and other valuable assets. While important, the sale of the *Telegraph* does not strike a blow to International's heart.

4.   Summary of § 271 Analysis

When considered quantitatively and qualitatively, the *Telegraph* sale does not amount to a sale of substantially all of International's assets. This conclusion is consistent with the bulk of our case law under § 271. Although by no means wholly consistent, that case law has, by and large, refused to find that a disposition involved substantially all the assets of a corporation when the assets that would remain after the sale were, in themselves, substantial and profitable. As *Gimbel* noted, § 271 permits a board to sell "one business ... without shareholder approval when other substantial businesses are retained." In the cases when asset sales were deemed to involve substantially all of a corporation's assets, the record always revealed great doubt about the viability of the business that would remain, primarily because the remaining operating assets were not profitable.[77]

---

77. *E.g., Winston v. Mandor*, 710 A.2d 835, 843 (Del.Ch.1997) (assets comprising 60% of net asset value might be substantially all assets for pleading purposes in situation when they allegedly constituted the only "income-generating assets"); *Thorpe v. CERB-CO, Inc.*, 1995 WL 478954, at *9–*10 (Del.Ch. Aug.9, 1995) (assets that were held likely to

But, "if the portion of the business not sold constitutes a substantial, viable, ongoing component of the corporation, the sale is not subject to Section 271."[78]

To conclude that the sale of the *Telegraph* Group was a sale of substantially all of International's assets would involve a determination that International possesses two operating assets, the sale of either of which would trigger a stockholder vote under § 271. That is, because there is no significant distinction between the economic importance of the Chicago and *Telegraph* Groups to International, a conclusion that the *Telegraph* Group was substantially all of International's assets would (impliedly but undeniably) supplant the plain language and intended meaning of the General Assembly with an "approximately half" test.[79] I decline Inc.'s invitation for me to depart so markedly

constitute substantially all the assets comprised at least 68% of corporation's assets and were the corporation's "primary income-generating asset[s]"), *rev'd in part, aff'd in relevant part*, 676 A.2d 436 (Del.1996); *Katz v. Bregman*, 431 A.2d 1274, 1275 (Del.Ch. 1981) (only case finding assets worth less than 60% of a company's value to be "substantially all" the company's assets, and doing so when sale at issue came on heels of other substantial asset sales and where the assets to be sold had been the company's only income-producing facility during the previous four years).

78. 1 R. Franklin Balotti & Jesse A. Finkelstein, DELAWARE LAW OF CORPORATIONS & BUSINESS ORGANIZATIONS § 10.2, at 10–7 (3d ed. Supp. 2004).

79. As International points out, the MBCA now includes a safe harbor provision that is intended to provide a "greater measure of certainty than is provided by interpretations of the current case law." MODEL BUS. CORP. ACT § 12.02 cmt. 1 (2002). The safe harbor is an objective test involving two factors:

> If a corporation retains a business activity that represented at least 25 percent of total assets at the end of the most recently completed fiscal year, and 25 percent of either income from continuing operations before taxes or revenues from continuing operations for that fiscal year, in each case of the corporation and its subsidiaries on a consolidated basis, the corporation will conclusively be deemed to have retained a significant continuing business activity.

Id. § 12.02(a).

Moreover, both the MBCA and the ALI Principles of Corporate Governance usefully turn the 'substantially all' inquiry on its head by focusing, as *Gimbel* does in a more oblique way, on what remains after a sale. *See* MODEL BUS. CORP. ACT § 12.02 cmt. 1 (2002) (stockholder vote required if asset sale would "leave the corporation without a significant continuing business activity"); PRINCIPLES OF CORP. GOVERNANCE §§ 1.38(a)(2), 6.01(b) (text requiring stockholder approval when asset sale "would leave the corporation without a significant continuing business"); *id.* § 1.38 cmt. 3 (commentary indicating that if a company has two principal operating divisions and one will remain following the asset sale, "there should normally be no doubt concerning the significance of the remaining division, even if the division to be sold represented a majority of the corporation's operating assets"). The MBCA, in particular, recognizes that while the "significant continuing business activity" test differs verbally from the "substantially all" language employed in many state corporation statutes, adoption of the MBCA provision would not entail a substantive change from existing law, because "[i]n practice, ... courts interpreting these statutes [using the phrase 'substantially all'] have commonly employed a test comparable to that embodied in 12.02(a)." MODEL BUS. CORP. ACT § 12.02 cmt. 1 (2002). The commentary specifically cites several Delaware judicial decisions as examples of cases employing such a test. *Id.* These approaches support the conclusion I reach.

Although not binding on me, these interpretative approaches provide a valuable perspective on § 271 because they are rooted, as is *Gimbel*, in the intent behind the statute (and statutes like it in other jurisdictions). Indeed, taken together, a reading of § 271 that: 1) required a stockholder vote for any sales contract to which a parent was a party that involved a sale by a wholly owned subsidiary that, in economic substance, amounted to a disposition of substantially all the parent's assets; combined with 2) a strict adherence to the words "substantially all" (a la the MBCA), could be viewed as the most faithful way to give life to the General Assembly's intended use of § 271. That is, § 271 would have substantive force but only from our legislature's mandate. By any reasonable interpretation, the *Telegraph* sale does not involve substantially all of International's assets as substantial operating (and non-operating) assets will be retained, and International will remain a profitable publishing concern.

. . . Conclusion

Inc.'s motion for a preliminary injunction is DENIED. . . .

———

NOTE ON SALE OF SUBSTANTIALLY ALL ASSETS

At common law, a sale of substantially all assets required unanimous shareholder approval, on the theory that it breached an implied contract among the shareholders to further the corporate enterprise. See, e.g., Fontaine v. Brown County Motors Co., 251 Wis. 433, 437, 29 N.W.2d 744, 746–47 (1947). The statutory sale-of-substantially-all-assets provisions were enacted against this backdrop. It has been held that under those statutes a sale of substantially all assets in the ordinary course of business does not require shareholder approval. See Jeppi v. Brockman Holding Co., 34 Cal.2d 11, 206 P.2d 847 (1949). The theory is that because such a sale does not prevent furtherance of the corporate enterprise, it would not have required unanimous shareholder approval at common law, and the statutory sale-of-substantially-all-assets provisions were not intended to change that result.

———

(b) THE APPRAISAL REMEDY

———

DEL. GEN. CORP. LAW § 262

[See Statutory Supplement]

———

MODEL BUS. CORP. ACT §§ 13.01–13.03, 13.20–13.26, 13.30–13.31

[See Statutory Supplement]

———

ALI, PRINCIPLES OF CORPORATE GOVERNANCE §§ 7.21–7.23

[See Statutory Supplement]

———

with regard to transactions that genuinely involved substantially all of the corporation's assets. . . .

CAL. CORP. CODE §§ 1300, 1311

[See Statutory Supplement]

———

PIEMONTE v. NEW BOSTON GARDEN CORP.

[See Chapter 6, supra]

———

BACKGROUND NOTE ON APPRAISAL RIGHTS

The value and function of the appraisal right are intimately related to the way in which the value of dissenting shares is determined. The most common statutory formula instructs the courts to determine the "fair value" of such shares. This formula obviously leaves considerable room for elaboration. Unfortunately, there is often a very substantial difference between the elements of valuation under the "block method" used by some courts in appraisal proceedings, and exemplified in *Piemonte,* Chapter 6, *supra,* and the elements of valuation in the real world. This in turn diminishes the usefulness of the appraisal right and opens up the possibility of manipulation, by those in control, to freeze out the minority at unfairly low prices.

In Weinberger v. UOP, 457 A.2d 701 (1983), the Delaware Supreme Court overturned the traditional Delaware block method of valuation:

> Turning to the matter of price, plaintiff also challenges its fairness. His evidence was that on the date the merger was approved the stock was worth at least $26 per share. In support, he offered the testimony of a chartered investment analyst who used two basic approaches to valuation: a comparative analysis of the premium paid over market in ten other tender offer-merger combinations, and a discounted cash flow analysis.

> In this breach of fiduciary duty case, the Chancellor perceived that the approach to valuation was the same as that in an appraisal proceeding. Consistent with precedent, he rejected plaintiff's method of proof and accepted defendants' evidence of value as being in accord with practice under prior case law. This means that the so-called "Delaware block" or weighted average method was employed wherein the elements of value, i.e., assets, market price, earnings, etc., were assigned a particular weight and the resulting amounts added to determine the value per share. This procedure has been in use for decades.... However, to the extent it excludes other generally accepted techniques used in the financial community and the courts, it is now clearly outmoded. It is time we recognize this in appraisal and other stock valuation proceedings and bring our law current on the subject.

... Accordingly, the standard "Delaware block" or weighted average method of valuation, formerly employed in appraisal and other stock valuation cases, shall no longer exclusively control such proceedings. We believe that a more liberal approach must include proof of value by any techniques or methods which are generally considered acceptable in the financial community and otherwise admissible in court, subject only to our interpretation of 8 Del.C.§ 262(h), infra.... This will obviate the very structured and mechanistic procedure that has heretofore governed such matters....

It is significant that section 262 now mandates the determination of "fair" value based upon "all relevant factors". Only the speculative elements of value that may arise from the "accomplishment or expectation" of the merger are excluded. We take this to be a very narrow exception to the appraisal process, designed to eliminate use of *pro forma* data and projections of a speculative variety relating to the completion of a merger. But elements of future value, including the nature of the enterprise, which are known or susceptible of proof as of the date of the merger and not the product of speculation, may be considered. When the trial court deems it appropriate, fair value also includes any damages, resulting from the taking, which the stockholders sustain as a class. If that was not the case, then the obligation to consider "all relevant factors" in the valuation process would be eroded.

NEW YORK BUS. CORP. LAW § 623(h)(4)

[See Statutory Supplement]

LEADER v. HYCOR, INC., 395 Mass. 215, 479 N.E.2d 173 (1985). "Because the issue of the continuing validity of the 'Delaware block method' of stock valuation is likely to arise on remand, we express our opinion on this matter. We do not agree that the 'Delaware block method' for valuing closely held stock, as set forth in our decision in *Piemonte v. New Boston Garden Corp.*, 377 Mass. 719, 387 N.E.2d 1145 (1979), is outmoded. Citing *Weinberger v. UOP, Inc.*, 457 A.2d 701 (Del.1983), the plaintiffs contend that the Delaware Supreme Court has rejected this valuation method. The *Weinberger* court stated that this method is outmoded 'to the extent it excludes other generally accepted techniques used in the financial community and the courts' and that it would no longer '*exclusively* control such proceedings' (emphasis added). *Weinberger, supra* at 712–713. We need not accept judicial interpretations of Delaware law made subsequent to our Legislature's adoption of c. 156B. *Id.* at 723. In any event, we have never held that the Delaware block method is the only approach that a judge may employ in valuing stock. In *Piemonte,* we stated that a judge 'might appropriately follow' this general approach. *Id.* at 723–724."

———

CHARLAND v. COUNTRY VIEW GOLF CLUB, INC.

[See Chapter 6, supra]

———

NOTE ON IN RE VALUATION OF COMMON STOCK OF McCLOON OIL CO.

In *Charland,* the Rhode Island Court held that in valuing stock pursuant to a mandatory buy-out in a dissolution proceeding, minority and nonmarketability discounts should not be applied. The propriety of these discounts can also arise in the context of an appraisal proceeding. In In re Valuation of Common Stock of McLoon Oil Co., 565 A.2d 997 (Me.1989), shareholders of corporations that merged into Lido Co. had dissented from the merger and exercised their appraisal rights. The Maine Supreme Court addressed the discount issues as follows:

> . . . Should the dissenting shareholder's proportionate part of that whole firm value as so determined be discounted because of the minority status and lack of marketability of his stock? The Delaware Supreme Court . . . has recently said no: Delaware emphatically rejects the application of those discounts in determining the fair value of a dissenting shareholder's stock. See Cavalier Oil Corp. v. Harnett, 564 A.2d 1137, 1141 (Del.1989) ("application of a discount to a minority shareholder is contrary to the requirement that the company be viewed as a going concern"). See also . . . Haynsworth, *Valuation of Business Interests,* 33 Mercer L.Rev. 457, 489 (1982) [hereinafter "Haynsworth"] . . .

> The appraisal remedy has deep roots in equity. The traditional rule through much of the 19th century was that any corporate transaction that changed the rights of common shareholders required unanimous consent. The appraisal remedy for dissenting shareholders evolved as it became clear that unanimous consent was inconsistent with the growth and development of large business enterprises. By the bargain struck in enacting an appraisal statute, the shareholder who disapproves of a proposed merger or other major corporate change gives up his right of veto in exchange for the right to be bought out—not at market value, but at "fair value.". . . . Methods used in valuing stock for tax, probate, ERISA, and like purposes in which market value is of the essence are inapposite to the determination of the fair value owed to dissenting shareholders. See Haynsworth at 459 ("The purpose of applying these discount variables is to determine the invest-

ment value or fair market value of a minority interest in the context of a hypothetical sale between a willing seller and buyer, a situation that does not exist in the dissenting shareholder situation''). In the statutory appraisal proceeding, the involuntary change of ownership caused by a merger requires as a matter of fairness that a dissenting shareholder be compensated for the loss of his proportionate interest in the business as an entity. The valuation focus under the appraisal statute is not the stock as a commodity, but rather the stock only as it represents a proportionate part of the enterprise as a whole. The question for the court becomes simple and direct: What is the best price a single buyer could reasonably be expected to pay for the firm as an entirety? The court then prorates that value for the whole firm equally among all shares of its common stock. The result is that all of those shares have the same fair value.

Our view of the appraisal remedy is obviously inconsistent with the application of minority and nonmarketability discounts. Lido would have us discount the stock for minority status and lack of marketability in order to reflect what it calls the "real world" value of the stock to the Dissenters.... Especially in fixing the appraisal remedy in a close corporation, the relevant inquiry is what is the highest price a single buyer would reasonably pay for the whole enterprise, not what a willing buyer and a willing seller would bargain out as the sales price of a dissenting shareholder's shares in a hypothetical market transaction. Any rule of law that gave the shareholders less than their proportionate share of the whole firm's fair value would produce a transfer of wealth from the minority shareholders to the shareholders in control. Such a rule would inevitably encourage corporate squeeze-outs. See Haynsworth at 489. As the Delaware Supreme Court stated recently in Cavalier Oil Corp. v. Harnett,

> to fail to accord to a minority shareholder the full proportionate value of his shares imposes a penalty for lack of control, and unfairly enriches the majority shareholders who may reap a windfall from the appraisal process by cashing out a dissenting shareholder, a clearly undesirable result.

Cavalier Oil Corp. v. Harnett, 564 A.2d at 1141. We agree.

... As a matter of law, the Dissenters are entitled to their proportionate share of each Maine company at its full fair value....

———

MT PROPERTIES, INC. v. CMC REAL ESTATE CORP., 481 N.W.2d 383 (Minn.App.1992). "[The issue of minority discounts] involves highly conflicting policy considerations. Either resolution of the issue risks unduly enlarging the value of some shares, either those of the remaining shareholders or those of the dissenter. However, because the legislature has enacted the statute with the evident aim to protect the dissenting shareholder, we must prohibit application of minority discounts when determining 'fair value' in statutory dissenter's rights cases in Minnesota. This result is also in accord with the approach of the majority of states which have addressed this issue."

————

NOTE ON EXCLUSIVITY OF THE APPRAISAL REMEDY

The question frequently arises whether the appraisal right is intended by the legislature as an exclusive remedy, so that the availability of appraisal precludes shareholders from seeking equitable relief such as injunction or rescission. This question does not always admit of a hard-and-fast answer.

In some cases the issue is specifically addressed by language in the appraisal statute itself. In the absence of explicit statutory language, it is clear that the availability of appraisal rights normally does not preclude an attack based on any of the following grounds:

(a) That the transaction is illegal under corporation law in that it is not authorized by the statute. See, e.g., Eisenberg v. Central Zone Property Corp., 306 N.Y. 58, 115 N.E.2d 652 (1953).

(b) That the transaction is illegal under corporation law in that the procedural steps required to authorize the transaction were not properly taken. See, e.g., Johnson v. Spartanburg County Fair Ass'n, 210 S.C. 56, 41 S.E.2d 599 (1947) (required number of votes not validly cast).

(c) That shareholder approval of the transaction was improperly obtained, as through fraudulent misrepresentation or violation of the Proxy Rules. See, e.g., Victor Broadcasting Co. v. Mahurin, 236 Ark. 196, 365 S.W.2d 265 (1963).

At least in the past, it has also been clear that the availability of appraisal rights normally *does* preclude a shareholder from seeking to recover the money value of his shares under a nonstatutory remedy in connection with transactions for which appraisal rights are given. See, e.g., Adams v. United States Distributing Corp., 184 Va. 134, 34 S.E.2d 244 (1945).

Beyond this, the matter is less clear. A few cases have suggested or implied that even in the absence of explicit statutory language, the availability of appraisal rights precludes an attack based on any ground other than illegality or *fraudulent misrepresentation*. The general rule, however, is that the mere availability of appraisal rights does not preclude shareholders from seeking injunctive relief or rescission for *fraud*, using that term in the broad sense to include unfair self-dealing by fiduciaries. For example, in Cohen v. Mirage Resorts, 62 P.3d 720 (Nev. 2003), the court stated:

A dissenting shareholder who wishes to attack the validity of the merger or seek monetary damages based upon improper actions during the merger process must allege wrongful conduct that goes to the approval of the merger. Our conclusion is supported by case law from other jurisdictions. Shareholders are limited to appraisal-type actions unless they allege wrongful conduct or procedures in the approval process. In addition, the term "fraudulent," as used in the Model Act, has not been limited to the elements of common-law fraud; it encompasses a variety of acts involving breach of fiduciary duties imposed upon corporate officers, directors, or majority shareholders. We conclude that the term fraudulent as used in [the statute] has a similar scope....

See also, e.g., John R. Behrmann Revocable Trust v. Szaloczi, 2002 WL 31600856 (Colo. App. 2002); Pupecki v. James Madison Corp., 376 Mass. 212, 382 N.E.2d 1030 (1978).

The Delaware courts are especially reluctant to make appraisal rights exclusive in unfair self-dealing cases. In Andra v. Blount, 772 A.2d 183 (Del. Ch. 2000), the court stated:

... [I]t has become nearly impossible for a judge of this court to dismiss a well-pled unfair dealing claim on the basis that appraisal is available as a remedy and is fully adequate. Although the Supreme Court has never held that this court cannot limit a plaintiff to an appraisal remedy if that remedy is fully adequate, its prior holdings are reasonably read as indicating that so long as a plaintiff can state a claim for breach of fiduciary duty in connection with the merger, he can press an unfair dealing claim. The unavailability of a class action and fee shifting in appraisal actions makes an unfair dealing action more attractive from the perspective of plaintiffs, thus leading to the litigation of lawsuits that require a determination of the fairness of the process used and the price paid when appraisal lawsuits addressing solely the issue of fair price would otherwise be sufficient.

[Footnote 22] Vice Chancellor Jacobs has succinctly captured the essential differences between a statutory appraisal action and an equitable fiduciary action:

Appraisal is purely a creature of statute. Its underlying concept is that a stockholder dissenting from a merger or other triggering transaction is entitled, without having to prove wrongdoing or liability on anyone's part, to a determination of the fair value of his investment by an independent agency, usually a court. The only party held liable is the surviving corporation, and the measure of recovery is the fair or intrinsic value of the corporation's stock immediately before the merger. Post-merger synergies or values are not to be considered. In most states, including Delaware, the right to court-awarded attorneys fees in an appraisal is highly limited.

In contrast, a stockholders' class action for breach of fiduciary duty is a creature of equity. To obtain a monetary recovery, the plaintiff shareholder must prove wrongdoing and establish liability. The parties from whom the recovery is sought are normally the corporation's directors and executive officers. The measure of the recovery is not limited to the statutorily appraised value, and in some cases, may include post-merger values computed as rescissory damages. Because the proceeding is equitable in nature, a court-awarded fee, payable by the corporation or from any fund created by a successful plaintiff, is available....

. . . Because an entire fairness action permits this court the flexibility to shape a remedy fitting to the breach (e.g., rescissory damages when justified), a plaintiff who can state a claim for breach of fiduciary duty ordinarily should not be relegated to the (implicitly less adequate) remedy of appraisal, where the only remedy is the fair value of plaintiff's stock. Otherwise, there is a risk that victims of fiduciary breaches will be less than wholly compensated for the harm done them, thus creating less than an adequate incentive for fiduciaries to comply with their "unremitting" duties of loyalty and care....

. . . [Consider] the obvious situation where an appraisal would not be an adequate remedy. Posit a scenario where a 43% stockholder who is the company's chairman and chief executive officer consummates a tender offer followed by a back-end, squeeze-out merger. Suppose the stockholder offered $25 a share, which is by any measure "fair," and obtains tenders from enough minority stockholders to enable him to cash out the remaining minority stockholders in a short-form merger at the same price. Undisclosed by the 43% stockholder, however, is the fact that a well-funded third party was willing to make a tender offer for $28 a share but had been rebuffed by the 43% stockholder, who did not even disclose the offer to the rest of his hand-picked board. In such a scenario, an appraisal remedy would not be sufficient to remedy the monetary harm that might have been suffered by the stockholders as a result of any breach of fiduciary duty they might prove had been committed by the 43% stockholder. While $25 is a fair price, they had arguably been wrongfully denied the opportunity for $28....

The net result is that, in the absence of explicit statutory language, the availability of appraisal rights may preclude a shareholder from attacking an *arm's-length* transaction on the ground of unfairness, but will usually not insulate *self-interested* transactions from an attack on that ground—although in the latter case it may lead the court to impose a somewhat less rigorous standard of fairness than would otherwise prevail. See Vorenberg, Exclusiveness of the Dissenting Stockholder's Appraisal Right, 77 Harv.L.Rev. 1189, 1214–15 (1964).

CAL. CORP. CODE § 1312

[See Statutory Supplement]

MODEL BUS. CORP. ACT § 13.02(d)

[See Statutory Supplement]

————

ALI, PRINCIPLES OF CORPORATE GOVERNANCE §§ 7.24, 7.25

[See Statutory Supplement]

————

(c) STATUTORY MERGERS

————

(1) CLASSICAL MERGERS

————

DEL. GEN. CORP. LAW §§ 251(a)–(e), 259–261

[See Statutory Supplement]

————

MODEL BUS. CORP. ACT §§ 11.01, 11.02, 11.04, 11.06, 11.07

[See Statutory Supplement]

————

NOTE ON STATUTORY MERGERS

1. *Statutory Mergers.* Del.Gen.Corp.Law §§ 251(a)–(e), 259–61 and Model Bus.Corp.Act §§ 11.01, 11.03 authorize a type of transaction commonly referred to as a statutory merger. Although the term *merger* is often used by nonlawyers to describe any form of combination, to a lawyer a merger is a combination involving the fusion of two constituent corporations pursuant to a formal agreement executed with reference to specific statutory merger provisions under which one corporation (the survivor) succeeds to the assets and liabilities of the other corporation by operation of law.

While details vary from state to state, generally the first formal step in such a merger, after negotiations have been completed, is a preliminary agreement (often embodied in a "letter of intent") signed by representatives of the constituent corporations. If the merger is approved by the board and shareholders of each constituent corporation, then: (1) articles of merger are filed with the secretary of state; and (2) stock or other consideration issued by the surviving corporation is exchanged for the stock and other securities of the disappearing corporation, which is fused into the survivor and loses its identity.

In general, no deeds, bills of sale, or other instruments of conveyance, are necessary to pass title from the "disappearing" or nonsurviving corporation to the survivor: By operation of law, the survivor acquires all the rights, privileges, franchises, and assets of the disappearing corporation, and assumes all of its liabilities.

2. *Abandonment*. In most merger agreements, authority is given to the boards of both constituents to abandon the merger at any time up to the effective date of the merger, upon the occurrence of certain defined conditions—for example, if a constituent suffers substantial loss as a result of catastrophe, or suffers any material adverse change in its condition, or if any material litigation or governmental proceeding is instituted against a constituent, or if more than a defined percentage of shareholders exercise appraisal rights.

3. *Consolidations*. A statutory *consolidation* is identical to a statutory merger, except for the fact that in a merger one constituent fuses into another, while in a consolidation two (or more) constituents fuse to form a new corporation. Because the consolidation technique is seldom employed, and when employed is treated almost identically to a merger, no separate attention will be given in this Chapter to statutory consolidations.

4. *Short-Form and Small-Scale Mergers*. At one time, virtually all statutory mergers required approval by a majority or two-thirds vote of the outstanding shares of each constituent, and also triggered appraisal rights for the shareholders of each constituent. Many statutes now carve out exceptions to these requirements in the case of "short-form" and "small-scale" mergers. These types of merger will be considered in the next two sections.

——————

(2) SMALL-SCALE MERGERS

——————

DEL. GEN. CORP. LAW § 251(f)

[See Statutory Supplement]

——————

MODEL BUS. CORP. ACT § 11.04(g)

[See Statutory Supplement]

——————

R. Ward, E. Welch & A. Turezyn, Folk on the Delaware General Corporation Law § 251.2.2.1

(4th ed. 1999).

(1) [The requirement of Del. § 251(f) that the survivor's certificate of incorporation not be amended] is designed to assure that the

merger technique cannot be used to deprive stockholders of the voting rights that they would enjoy if the certificate were being amended under section 242....

(2) The theory underlying the ... 20 percent limitation on increasing the number of common shares—is that a merger that involves less than 20 percent of the survivor's shares is not such a major change as to require a stockholder vote, and is really no more than an enlargement of the business that could be achieved by other means without triggering voting rights. For instance, a corporation purchasing assets need not secure approval of its stockholders to issue already authorized shares to the seller. Nor would voting rights exist if a corporation offered its own authorized shares in exchange for the shares of another corporation and thereby gained control, or if the corporation were to sell its authorized shares for cash and then use the proceeds of the sale to purchase assets. When business needs demand that the acquisition take the form of a merger rather than a purchase of assets or shares, the premise of the statute is that the merger should not require a stockholder vote when other procedures with nearly identical economic consequences do not require a stockholder vote. Stated otherwise, [§ 251(f)] puts mergers more on a parity with acquisition of assets or shares so far as the legal requirements are concerned.

---

(3) SHORT-FORM MERGERS

DEL. GEN. CORP. LAW § 253

[See Statutory Supplement]

MODEL BUS. CORP. ACT § 11.05

[See Statutory Supplement]

NOTE ON SHORT–FORM MERGERS

Most or all of the corporate statutes now include provisions authorizing the so-called short-form merger, under which certain parent-subsidiary mergers can be effected simply by vote of the parent's board—that is, without a vote of the parent's or the subsidiary's shareholders, without appraisal rights in the parent's shareholders, and frequently without a vote of the subsidiary's board. Most of the early short-form statutes were applicable only to mergers involving a parent and its 100%-owned subsidiary, and were probably conceived as procedural in nature, designed to simplify the mechanics of mergers. Today, however, the reach of short-form merger provisions has been substantively extended in two important ways. First, many such provisions are now applicable to mergers between parents and less-than-100%-owned subsidiaries: typically, although not invariably, the floor is set at 90 percent. Second, it has been held that the purpose of these statutes is to provide the parent corporation with a means of eliminating the minority shareholder's interest in the enterprise by issuing cash rather than stock to the minority. See e.g., Beloff v. Consolidated Edison Co., 300 N.Y. 11, 87 N.E.2d 561 (1949). To the extent this view is followed, these statutory provisions operate as *cash-out* rather than *merger* statutes. Furthermore, they are cash-out statutes that run in one direction only: the parent can force the minority to sell at any time, but the minority cannot force the parent to buy.

(d) TAX ASPECTS OF CORPORATE COMBINATIONS

NOTE ON THE TAX TREATMENT OF CORPORATE COMBINATIONS

Much is made of taxation as a principal motive for corporate combinations, but this factor, while significant, can be exaggerated. Whatever its role as a motive, however, taxation is often very important in determining *how* a combination will be effected. The principal issue is whether the combination will be tax-free—which means, essentially, that taxes on the transferor's gain will be postponed, that the transferor's basis in the stock or property received will remain unchanged from the transferee's basis, and that past operating losses of both companies can generally be carried over to apply against future earnings. See IRC §§ 354(a)(1), 358, 361(a), 381, 382.

In general, the Code provides three basic routes by which a tax-free combination—or, in tax parlance, a "reorganization"—can be achieved. These routes are popularly known as Type A, B, and C reorganizations, and are the tax counterparts of statutory mergers, stock-for-stock combinations, and stock-for-assets combinations, respectively.

a. A "Type A" reorganization—covered by IRC § 368(a)(1)(A)—is defined as a statutory merger or consolidation.

b. A "Type B" reorganization—covered by § 368(a)(1)(B)—is defined as the acquisition by one corporation, in exchange solely for all or part of its voting stock (or the voting stock of a parent corporation) of stock of another corporation, if the acquiring corporation has control of the acquired corporation immediately after the acquisition. Control is defined by § 368(c) as the ownership of stock possessing at least 80 percent of total combined voting power, plus at least 80 percent of the total number of shares of all other classes of stock.

c. A "Type C" reorganization—covered by § 368(a)(1)(C)—is defined as the acquisition by one corporation, in exchange for all or part of its voting stock (or the voting stock of a parent corporation), of substantially all the properties of another corporation.

In a Type B reorganization, the consideration given by the acquiring corporation must consist solely of voting stock. In a Type C reorganization, the consideration must consist primarily of voting stock, but the use of money or other property is permitted if at least 80 percent of the fair market value of all the property of the acquired corporation is taken in exchange for voting stock.[1] Section 368(a)(1)(A), which covers Type A reorganizations, does not explicitly restrict the consideration issued by the survivor to voting stock, or indeed to stock. Thus the survivor in a statutory merger can use consideration other than voting stock ("boot")—including bonds, nonvoting stock, short-term notes, and cash. However, if property other than stock or securities is permissibly issued to the transferor or its shareholders under a Type A or Type C reorganization, gain will be recognized in an amount not exceeding the value of this property. IRC § 356. Furthermore, under the "continuity of interest" doctrine, in a statutory merger the transferor's shareholders must receive a significant equity interest in the survivor if the merger is to qualify as a tax-free Type A reorganization. See Treas.Reg. § 1.368–1(b), (c). In Helvering v. Minnesota Tea Co., 296 U.S. 378, 56 S.Ct. 269, 80 L.Ed. 284 (1935), the Supreme Court held that under this doctrine the equity issued to the transferor must represent a "substantial part of the value of the [transferred assets]," and that 56 percent was sufficient under this standard. See also May B. Kass, 60 T.C. 218, 1973 WL 2497 (1973) (16 percent insufficient); Yoc Heating Corp., 61 T.C. 168, 1973 WL 2680 (1973) (15 percent insufficient); Miller v. Commissioner, 84 F.2d 415 (6th Cir.1936) (25% sufficient). The illustrations to proposed new Treasury Regulations suggest that in the current view of the Internal Revenue Service, there will be continuity of interest if at least 40% of the consideration in a merger is in the form of equity, but not if 30% or less is in that form.

———

(e) THE STOCK MODES AND THE DE FACTO MERGER THEORY

Having considered the traditional form of combination, mergers, we now pass to a consideration of two newer modes of corporate combination: stock-for-assets combinations and stock-for-stock combinations. In a *stock-for-assets* combination, Corporation A issues shares of its own stock to Corporation B in exchange for substantially all of B's assets. Often, in such a combination, A agrees to assume B's

---

1. IRC § 368(a)(2)(B). The survivor's assumption of the transferor's liabilities is not treated as money paid for the transferor's property unless the survivor uses consideration other than voting stock. Id.

liabilities. In some cases, however, A may assume B's liabilities on only a selective basis. Indeed, one reason for using this mode in preference to a statutory merger may be A's desire to avoid assuming all of B's liabilities. Usually, B agrees that upon completion of the exchange it will dissolve and distribute its stock in A to its own shareholders. The major reason for this is that A does not want a large block of its stock concentrated in a single holder. Frequently, it is also agreed or understood that some or all of B's officers and directors will join A's management.

In a *stock-for-stock* combination, Corporation A issues shares of its own stock directly to the shareholders of Corporation B in exchange for an amount of B stock—normally at least a majority—sufficient to carry control. By virtue of such a combination the shareholder groups of the two corporations are combined to a substantial extent, and B becomes a subsidiary of A. Frequently B is then liquidated or merged into A, but whether or not this occurs, B's assets will be under A's control. Such a combination does not require approval by B's management, since corporate action by B is not required. Often, however, the terms of the exchange of stock are worked out beforehand by the managements of both corporations, and often too, it is agreed or understood that some or all of B's management will stay on with B in its new role as a subsidiary, or will join Corporation A itself.

There has been a sharp division of opinion on the issue, how to characterize such combinations. Take, for example, a stock-for-assets combination in which A acquires substantially all of the assets of B in exchange for A's common stock; A assumes all of B's liabilities; and B agrees to dissolve and to distribute to its shareholders the A common stock it receives.

One possible way to view such a combination is as a de facto merger. This is the position taken in Farris v. Glen Alden Corp. and Rath v. Rath Packing Co., infra. If the combination is viewed as a de facto merger, then in the normal case (that is, in the absence of some special exception) it requires a vote of both A's shareholders and B's shareholders, and triggers appraisal rights in both A's shareholders and B's shareholders.

Alternatively, the transaction could be characterized as a purchase by A and a sale of substantially all assets by B. That is the position taken in Hariton v. Arco Electronics Corp. and Heilbrunn v. Sun Packing Co., infra. Under traditional corporate statutes, a purchase does not require shareholder approval and does not trigger appraisal rights. Therefore, if the combination is treated as a purchase by A, it neither requires a vote of A's shareholders nor triggers appraisal rights for those shareholders—although it would have required a shareholder vote, and triggered appraisal rights, if it had been characterized as a merger.

Now turn to B's shareholders. Under the corporate statutes, a sale of substantially all assets, unlike a purchase, does require shareholder approval. Therefore, the combination will require the approval of B's shareholders. Furthermore, most statutes provide that if a corporation sells substantially all of its assets, the transaction triggers appraisal rights in the corporation's shareholders. Therefore, B's shareholders, unlike A's shareholders, will usually have appraisal rights. However, under some statutes, most notably the Delaware statute, a sale of substantially all assets does not trigger appraisal rights. Under such statutes, if a stock-for-assets combination is treated as a purchase by A and a sale by B, rather than as a merger of A and B, B's shareholders will not have appraisal rights, although they would have had appraisal rights if the transaction had been characterized as a merger.

Hariton v. Arco Electronics, Inc.

Supreme Court of Delaware, 1963.
41 Del.Ch. 74, 188 A.2d 123.

■ SOUTHERLAND, CHIEF JUSTICE: This case involves a sale of assets under § 271 of the corporation law, 8 Del.C. It presents for decision the question presented, but not decided, in Heilbrunn v. Sun Chemical Corporation, 38 Del.Ch. 321, 150 A.2d 755. It may be stated as follows:

A sale of assets is effected under § 271 in consideration of shares of stock of the purchasing corporation. The agreement of sale embodies also a plan to dissolve the selling corporation and distribute the shares so received to the stockholders of the seller, so as to accomplish the same result as would be accomplished by a merger of the seller into the purchaser. Is the sale legal?

The facts are these:

The defendant Arco and Loral Electronics Corporation, a New York corporation, are both engaged, in somewhat different forms, in the electronic equipment business. In the summer of 1961 they negotiated for an amalgamation of the companies. As of October 27, 1961, they entered into a "Reorganization Agreement and Plan." The provisions of this Plan pertinent here are in substance as follows:

1. Arco agrees to sell all its assets to Loral in consideration (*inter alia*) of the issuance to it of 283,000 shares of Loral.

2. Arco agrees to call a stockholders meeting for the purpose of approving the Plan and the voluntary dissolution.

3. Arco agrees to distribute to its stockholders all the Loral shares received by it as a part of the complete liquidation of Arco.*

At the Arco meeting all the stockholders voting (about 80%) approved the Plan. It was thereafter consummated.

---

* According to the Vice Chancellor's opinion below, 40 Del.Ch. 326, 182 A.2d 22 (1962), the agreement also provided that Loral would assume and pay all of Arco's debts and liabilities, and that after the closing date Arco would not engage in any business or activity except as might be required to complete the liquidation and dissolution of Arco. (Footnote by ed.)

Plaintiff, a stockholder who did not vote at the meeting, sued to enjoin the consummation of the Plan on the grounds (1) that it was illegal, and (2) that it was unfair. The second ground was abandoned. Affidavits and documentary evidence were filed, and defendant moved for summary judgment and dismissal of the complaint. The Vice Chancellor granted the motion and plaintiff appeals.

The question before us we have stated above. Plaintiff's argument that the sale is illegal runs as follows:

The several steps taken here accomplish the same result as a merger of Arco into Loral. In a "true" sale of assets, the stockholder of the seller retains the right to elect whether the selling company shall continue as a holding company. Moreover, the stockholder of the selling company is forced to accept an investment in a new enterprise without the right of appraisal granted under the merger statute. § 271 cannot therefore be legally combined with a dissolution proceeding under § 275 and a consequent distribution of the purchaser's stock. Such a proceeding is a misuse of the power granted under § 271, and a *de facto* merger results.

The foregoing is a brief summary of plaintiff's contention.

Plaintiff's contention that this sale has achieved the same result as a merger is plainly correct. The same contention was made to us in Heilbrunn v. Sun Chemical Corporation, 38 Del.Ch. 321, 150 A.2d 755. Accepting it as correct, we noted that this result is made possible by the overlapping scope of the merger statute and section 271, mentioned in Sterling v. Mayflower Hotel Corporation, 33 Del.Ch. 293, 93 A.2d 107, 38 A.L.R.2d 425. We also adverted to the increased use, in connection with corporate reorganization plans, of § 271 instead of the merger statute. Further, we observed that no Delaware case has held such procedure to be improper, and that two cases appear to assume its legality. Finch v. Warrior Cement Corporation, 16 Del.Ch. 44, 141 A. 54, and Argenbright v. Phoenix Finance Co., 21 Del.Ch. 288, 187 A. 124. But we were not required in the *Heilbrunn* case to decide the point.

We now hold that the reorganization here accomplished through § 271 and a mandatory plan of dissolution and distribution is legal. This is so because the sale-of-assets statute and the merger statute are independent of each other. They are, so to speak, of equal dignity, and the framers of a reorganization plan may resort to either type of corporate mechanics to achieve the desired end. This is not an anomalous result in our corporation law. As the Vice Chancellor pointed out, the elimination of accrued dividends, though forbidden under a charter amendment (Keller v. Wilson Co., 21 Del.Ch. 391, 190 A. 115) may be accomplished by a merger. Federal United Corporation v. Havender, 24 Del.Ch. 318, 11 A.2d 331.

In Langfelder v. Universal Laboratories, D.C., 68 F.Supp. 209, Judge Leahy commented upon "the general theory of the Delaware Corporation Law that action taken pursuant to the authority of the various sections of that law constitute acts of independent legal significance and their validity is not dependent on other sections of the Act." 68 F.Supp. 211, footnote.

In support of his contentions of a *de facto* merger plaintiff cites Finch v. Warrior Cement Corporation, 16 Del.Ch. 44, 141 A. 54, and Drug Inc. v. Hunt, 5 W.W.Harr. 339, 35 Del. 339, 168 A. 87. They are patently inapplicable. Each involved a disregard of the statutory provisions governing sales of assets. Here it is admitted that the provisions of the statute were fully complied with.

Plaintiff concedes, as we read his brief, that if the several steps taken in this case had been taken separately they would have been legal. That is, he concedes that a sale of assets, followed by a separate proceeding to dissolve and distribute, would be legal, even though the same result would follow. This concession exposes the weakness of his contention. To attempt to make any such distinction between sales under § 271 would be to create uncertainty in the law and invite litigation.

We are in accord with the Vice Chancellor's ruling, and the judgment below is affirmed.

———

NOTE ON HEILBRUNN v. SUN CHEMICAL CORPORATION

In *Hariton*, suit was brought by a shareholder of the transferor in a stock-for-assets combination. In the earlier case of Heilbrunn v. Sun Chemical Corporation, 38 Del.Ch. 321, 150 A.2d 755 (1959), referred to in the *Hariton* opinion, suit was brought by the shareholders of Sun, the survivor in a stock-for-assets combination between Sun and Ansbacher. Plaintiff claimed that the transaction was a merger, and therefore gave rise to appraisal rights. The court rejected this claim:

> The argument that the result of this transaction is substantially the same as the result that would have followed a merger may be readily accepted. As plaintiffs correctly say, the Ansbacher enterprise is continued in altered form as a part of Sun. This is ordinarily a typical characteristic of a merger.... Moreover the plan of reorganization *requires* the dissolution of Ansbacher and the distribution to its stockholders of the Sun stock received by it for the assets. As a part of the plan, the Ansbacher stockholders are compelled to receive Sun stock. From the viewpoint of Ansbacher, the result is the same as if Ansbacher had formally merged into Sun.

> This result is made possible, of course, by the overlapping scope of the merger statute and the statute authorizing the sale of all the corporate assets....

> Our Court of Chancery has said that the appraisal right is given to the stockholder in compensation for his former right at common law to prevent a merger.... By the use of the sale-of-assets method of reorganization, it is contended, he has been unjustly deprived of this right.

... [W]e do not reach this question, because we fail to see how any injury has been inflicted upon the Sun stockholders. Their corporation has simply acquired property and paid for it in shares of stock. The business of Sun will go on as before, with additional assets. The Sun stockholder is not forced to accept stock in another corporation. Nor has the reorganization changed the essential nature of the enterprise of the purchasing corporation. . . .

Farris v. Glen Alden Corp.

Supreme Court of Pennsylvania, 1958.
393 Pa. 427, 143 A.2d 25.

■ COHEN, JUSTICE. We are required to determine on this appeal whether, as a result of a Reorganization Agreement executed by the officers of Glen Alden Corporation and List Industries Corporation, and approved by the shareholders of the former company, the rights and remedies of a dissenting shareholder accrue to the plaintiff.

Glen Alden is a Pennsylvania corporation engaged principally in the mining of anthracite coal and lately in the manufacture of air conditioning units and fire-fighting equipment. In recent years the company's operating revenue has declined substantially, and in fact, its coal operations have resulted in tax loss carryovers of approximately $14,000,000. In October 1957, List, a Delaware holding company owning interests in motion picture theaters, textile companies and real estate, and to a lesser extent, in oil and gas operations, warehouses and aluminum piston manufacturing, purchased through a wholly owned subsidiary 38.5% of Glen Alden's outstanding stock.[1] This acquisition enabled List to place three of its directors on the Glen Alden board.

On March 20, 1958, the two corporations entered into a reorganization agreement, subject to stockholder approval, which contemplated the following actions:

1.   Glen Alden is to acquire all of the assets of List, excepting a small amount of cash reserved for the payment of List's expenses in connection with the transaction. These assets include over $8,000,000 in cash held chiefly in the treasuries of List's wholly owned subsidiaries.

2.   In consideration of the transfer, Glen Alden is to issue 3,621,-703 shares of stock to List. List in turn is to distribute the stock to its shareholders at a ratio of five shares of Glen Alden stock for each six shares of List stock. In order to accomplish the necessary distribution, Glen Alden is to increase the authorized number of its shares of capital stock from 2,500,000 shares to 7,500,000 shares without according preemptive rights to the present shareholders upon the issuance of any such shares.

---

1.   Of the purchase price of $8,719,109, $5,000,000 was borrowed.

3.   Further, Glen Alden is to assume all of List's liabilities including a $5,000,000 note incurred by List in order to purchase Glen Alden stock in 1957, outstanding stock options, incentive stock options plans, and pension obligations.

4.   Glen Alden is to change its corporate name from Glen Alden Corporation to List Alden Corporation.

5.   The present directors of both corporations are to become directors of List Alden.

6.   List is to be dissolved and List Alden is to then carry on the operations of both former corporations.

Two days after the agreement was executed notice of the annual meeting of Glen Alden to be held on April 11, 1958, was mailed to the shareholders together with a proxy statement analyzing the reorganization agreement and recommending its approval as well as approval of certain amendments to Glen Alden's articles of incorporation and bylaws necessary to implement the agreement. At this meeting the holders of a majority of the outstanding shares, (not including those owned by List), voted in favor of a resolution approving the reorganization agreement.

On the day of the shareholders' meeting, plaintiff, a shareholder of Glen Alden, filed a complaint in equity against the corporation and its officers seeking to enjoin them temporarily until final hearing, and perpetually thereafter, from executing and carrying out the agreement.

The gravamen of the complaint was that the notice of the annual shareholders' meeting did not conform to the requirements of the Business Corporation Law, 15 P.S. § 2852–1 et seq., in three respects: (1) It did not give notice to the shareholders that the true intent and purpose of the meeting was to effect a merger or consolidation of Glen Alden and List; (2) It failed to give notice to the shareholders of their right to dissent to the plan of merger or consolidation and claim fair value for their shares, and (3) It did not contain copies of the text of certain sections of the Business Corporation Law as required.[3]

By reason of these omissions, plaintiff contended that the approval of the reorganization agreement by the shareholders at the annual meeting was invalid and unless the carrying out of the plan were enjoined, he would suffer irreparable loss by being deprived of substantial property rights.

The defendants answered admitting the material allegations of fact in the complaint but denying that they gave rise to a cause of action because the transaction complained of was a purchase of corporate assets as to which shareholders had no rights of dissent or appraisal.

---

3. The proxy statement included the following declaration: Appraisal Rights.

"In the opinion of counsel, the shareholders of neither Glen Alden nor List Industries will have any rights of appraisal or similar rights of dissenters with respect to any matter to be acted upon at their respective meetings."

For these reasons the defendants then moved for judgment on the pleadings.[4]

The court below concluded that the reorganization agreement entered into between the two corporations was a plan for a *de facto* merger, and that therefore the failure of the notice of the annual meeting to conform to the pertinent requirements of the merger provisions of the Business Corporation Law rendered the notice defective and all proceedings in furtherance of the agreement void. Wherefore, the court entered a final decree denying defendants' motion for judgment on the pleadings, entering judgment upon plaintiff's complaint and granting the injunctive relief therein sought. This appeal followed.

When use of the corporate form of business organization first became widespread, it was relatively easy for courts to define a "merger" or a "sale of assets" and to label a particular transaction as one or the other. See, e.g., 15 Fletcher, Corporations §§ 7040–7045 (rev. vol. 1938); In re Buist's Estate, 1929, 297 Pa. 537, 541, 147 A. 606; Koehler v. St. Mary's Brewing Co., 1910, 228 Pa. 648, 653–654, 77 A. 1016. But prompted by the desire to avoid the impact of adverse, and to obtain the benefits of favorable, government regulations, particularly federal tax laws, new accounting and legal techniques were developed by lawyers and accountants which interwove the elements characteristic of each, thereby creating hybrid forms of corporate amalgamation. Thus, it is no longer helpful to consider an individual transaction in the abstract and solely by reference to the various elements therein determine whether it is a "merger" or a "sale". Instead, to determine properly the nature of a corporate transaction, we must refer not only to all the provisions of the agreement, but also to the consequences of the transaction and to the purposes of the provisions of the corporation law said to be applicable. We shall apply this principle to the instant case.

Section 908, subd. A of the Pennsylvania Business Corporation Law provides: "If any shareholder of a domestic corporation which becomes a party to a plan of merger or consolidation shall object to such plan of merger or consolidation . . . such shareholder shall be entitled to . . . [the fair value of his shares upon surrender of the share certificate or certificates representing his shares]." Act of May 5, 1933, P.L. 364, as amended, 15 P.S. §§ 2852–908, subd. A.[5]

---

4. Counsel for the defendants concedes that if the corporation is required to pay the dissenting shareholders the appraised fair value of their shares, the resultant drain of cash would prevent Glen Alden from carrying out the agreement. On the other hand, plaintiff contends that if the shareholders had been told of their rights as dissenters, rather than specifically advised that they had no such rights, the resolution approving the reorganization agreement would have been defeated.

5. Furthermore, section 902, subd. B provides that notice of the proposed merger and of the right to dissent thereto must be given the shareholders. "There shall be included in, or enclosed with . . . notice [of meeting of shareholders to vote on plan of merger] a copy or a summary of the plan of merger or plan of consolidation, as the case may be, and . . . a copy of subsection A of section 908 and of subsections B, C and D of section 515 of this act." Act of May 5, 1933, P.L. 364, § 902, subd. B, as amended, 15 §§ P.S. 2852–902, subd. B.

This provision had its origin in the early decision of this Court in Lauman v. Lebanon Valley R.R. Co., 1858, 30 Pa. 42. There a shareholder who objected to the consolidation of his company with another was held to have a right in the absence of statute to treat the consolidation as a dissolution of his company and to receive the value of his shares upon their surrender.

The rationale of the Lauman case, and of the present section of the Business Corporation Law based thereon, is that when a corporation combines with another so as to lose its essential nature and alter the original fundamental relationships of the shareholders among themselves and to the corporation, a shareholder who does not wish to continue his membership therein may treat his membership in the original corporation as terminated and have the value of his shares paid to him. See Lauman v. Lebanon Vally R.R. Co., supra, 30 Pa. at pages 46–47. See also Bloch v. Baldwin Locomotive Works, C.P., Del.1950, 75 Pa.Dist. Co.R. 24, 35–38.

Does the combination outlined in the present "reorganization" agreement so fundamentally change the corporate character of Glen Alden and the interest of the plaintiff as a shareholder therein, that to refuse him the rights and remedies of a dissenting shareholder would in reality force him to give up his stock in one corporation and against his will accept shares in another? If so, the combination is a merger within the meaning of section 908, subd. A of the corporation law. See Bloch v. Baldwin Locomotive Works, supra. Cf. Marks v. Autocar Co., D.C.E.D.Pa.1954, 153 F.Supp. 768. See also Troupiansky v. Henry Disston & Sons, D.C.E.D.Pa.1957, 151 F.Supp. 609.

If the reorganization agreement were consummated plaintiff would find that the "List Alden" resulting from the amalgamation would be quite a different corporation than the "Glen Alden" in which he is now a shareholder. Instead of continuing primarily as a coal mining company, Glen Alden would be transformed, after amendment of its articles of incorporation, into a diversified holding company whose interests would range from motion picture theaters to textile companies. Plaintiff would find himself a member of a company with assets of $169,000,000 and a long-term debt of $38,000,000 in lieu of a company one-half that size and with but one-seventh the long-term debt.

While the administration of the operations, and properties of Glen Alden as well as List would be in the hands of management common to both companies, since all executives of List would be retained in List Alden, the control of Glen Alden would pass to the directors of List; for List would hold eleven of the seventeen directorships on the new board of directors.

As an aftermath of the transaction plaintiff's proportionate interest in Glen Alden would have been reduced to only two-fifths of what it presently is because of the issuance of an additional 3,621,703 shares to List which would not be subject to pre-emptive rights. In fact, ownership of Glen Alden would pass to the stockholders of List who would hold 76.5% of the outstanding shares as compared with but 23.5% retained by the present Glen Alden shareholders.

Perhaps the most important consequence to the plaintiff, if he were denied the right to have his shares redeemed at their fair value, would be the serious financial loss suffered upon consummation of the agreement. While the present book value of his stock is $38 a share after combination it would be worth only $21 a share. In contrast, the shareholders of List who presently hold stock with a total book value of $33,000,000 or $7.50 a share, would receive stock with a book value of $76,000,000 or $21 a share.

Under these circumstances it may well be said that if the proposed combination is allowed to take place without right of dissent, plaintiff would have his stock in Glen Alden taken away from him and the stock of a new company thrust upon him in its place. He would be projected against his will into a new enterprise under terms not of his own choosing. It was to protect dissident shareholders against just such a result that this Court one hundred years ago in the Lauman case, and the legislature thereafter in section 908, subd. A, granted the right of dissent. And it is to accord that protection to the plaintiff that we conclude that the combination proposed in the case at hand is a merger within the intendment of section 908, subd. A.

Nevertheless, defendants contend that the 1957 amendments to sections 311 and 908 of the corporation law preclude us from reaching this result and require the entry of judgment in their favor. Subsection F of section 311 dealing with the voluntary transfer of corporate assets provides: "The shareholders of a business corporation which acquires by sale, lease or exchange all or substantially all of the property of another corporation by the issuance of stock, securities or otherwise shall not be entitled to the rights and remedies of dissenting shareholders...." Act of July 11, 1957, P.L. 711, § 1, 15 P.S. §§ 2852–311, subd. F.

And the amendment to section 908 reads as follows: "The right of dissenting shareholders ... shall not apply to the purchase by a corporation of assets whether or not the consideration therefor be money or property, real or personal, including shares of bonds or other evidences of indebtedness of such corporation. The shareholders of such corporation shall have no right to dissent from any such purchase." Act of July 11, 1957, P.L. 711, § 1, 15 P.S. §§ 2852–908, subd. C.

Defendants view these amendments as abridging the right of shareholders to dissent to a transaction between two corporations which involves a transfer of assets for a consideration even though the transfer has all the legal incidents of a merger. They claim that only if the merger is accomplished in accordance with the prescribed statutory procedure does the right of dissent accrue. In support of this position they cite to us the comment on the amendments by the Committee on Corporation Law of the Pennsylvania Bar Association, the committee which originally drafted these provisions. The comment states that the provisions were intended to overrule cases which granted shareholders the right to dissent to a sale of assets when accompanied by the legal incidents of a merger. See 61 Ann.Rep.Pa.Bar Ass'n. 277, 284 (1957). Whatever may have been the intent of the *committee,* there is no evidence to indicate that the *legislature* intended the 1957 amendments to have the effect contended for. But furthermore, the language of these two provisions does not support the opinion of the committee and is inept to achieve any such purpose. The amendments of 1957 do not provide that a transaction between two corporations which has the effect of a merger but which includes a transfer of assets for consideration is to be exempt from the protective provisions of sections 908, subd. A and 515. They provide only that the shareholders of a corporation which acquires the property or purchases the assets of another corporation, *without more,* are not entitled to the right to dissent from the transaction. So, as in the present case, when as part of a transaction between two corporations, one corporation dissolves, its liabilities are assumed by the survivor, its executives and directors take over the management and control of the survivor, and, as consideration for the transfer, its stockholders acquire a majority of the shares of stock of the survivor, then the transaction is no longer simply a purchase of assets or acquisition of property to which sections 311, subd. F and 908, subd. C apply, but a merger governed by section 908, subd. A of the corporation law. To divest shareholders of their right of dissent under such circumstances would require express language which is absent from the 1957 amendments.

Even were we to assume that the combination provided for in the reorganization agreement is a "sale of assets" to which section 908, subd. A does not apply, it would avail the defendants nothing; we will not blind our eyes to the realities of the transaction. Despite the designation of the parties and the form employed, Glen Alden does not in fact acquire List, rather, List acquires Glen Alden, cf. Metropolitan Edison Co. v. Commissioner, 3 Cir., 1938, 98 F.2d 807, affirmed sub nom., Helvering v. Metropolitan Edison Co., 1939, 306 U.S. 522, 59 S.Ct. 634, 83 L.Ed. 957, and under section 311, subd. D[8] the right of dissent would remain with the shareholders of Glen Alden.

We hold that the combination contemplated by the reorganization agreement, although consummated by contract rather than in accordance with the statutory procedure, is a merger within the protective purview of sections 908, subd. A and 515 of the corporation law. The shareholders of Glen Alden should have been notified accordingly and advised of their statutory rights of dissent and appraisal. The failure of the corporate officers to take these steps renders the stockholder approval of the agreement at the 1958 shareholders' meeting invalid.

---

8. "If any shareholder of a business corporation which sells, leases or exchanges all or substantially all of its property and assets otherwise than (1) in the usual and regular course of its business, (2) for the purpose of relocating its business, or (3) in connection with its dissolution and liqui- dation, shall object to such sale, lease or exchange and comply with the provisions of section 515 of this act, such shareholder shall be entitled to the rights and remedies of dissenting shareholders as therein provided." . . .

The lower court did not err in enjoining the officers and directors of Glen Alden from carrying out this agreement.

Decree affirmed at appellants' costs.

———

NOTE ON FARRIS

1. *Reasons for the Form in Which the Transaction was Cast.* It is clear that a major reason for structuring the transaction in *Farris* as a stock-for-assets combination, rather than as a statutory merger, was to avoid conferring appraisal rights on the Glen Alden shareholders. But given that reason for using the stock-for-assets mode, why did the parties also use an upside-down format, in which the smaller corporation nominally purchased the larger corporation's assets? Why didn't the parties arrange the transaction in a more natural way, by having the larger corporation, List, issue shares for assets of the smaller corporation, Glen Alden?

Again, one reason had to do with appraisal rights. List was a Delaware corporation. Under Delaware law, in a purchase and sale of assets, neither the purchaser's shareholders nor the seller's shareholders had appraisal rights. Under Pennsylvania law, however, a seller's shareholders did have appraisal rights, while a purchaser's did not—or so counsel thought. Therefore, by making List, a Delaware corporation, the nominal seller and Glen Alden, a Pennsylvania corporation, the nominal purchaser, the parties hoped to avoid giving appraisal rights to the shareholders of either corporation.

A second reason for the upside-down format may have been a desire to keep alive Glen Alden's tax loss carryover. While the rules governing the survival of such carryovers were complex, in general survival was more likely if the entity of the carryover corporation was left intact.

A third reason is given in the Supplemental Brief for Appellee: "In answer to the question of Mr. Justice Bell as to why List did not purchase the assets of Glen Alden, Mr. Littleton answered that the one percent Pennsylvania realty tax on the transfer of [the huge coalmining] holdings of Glen Alden would make such a sale prohibitive."

Following the decision in Farris v. Glen Alden, the two corporations were combined pursuant to a statutory merger. Probably for some of the reasons just given, Glen Alden was the surviving corporation. The List shareholders received one Glen Alden share for each List share, and the Glen Alden shareholders ended up with five Glen Alden shares for each four they had previously held. New York Times, March 7, 1959; Moody's Industrial Manual 954 (1972).

2. *Subsequent Legislation.* After the decision in *Farris*, Pa. §§ 311(F) and 908(B) were amended, and now read as follows:

§ [311]. Voluntary Transfer of Corporate Assets . . .

F. The shareholders of a business corporation which acquires by purchase, lease or exchange all or substantially all of the property of another corporation by the issuance of shares, evidences of indebtedness or otherwise, with or without assuming the liabilities of such other corporation, shall be entitled to the rights and remedies of dissenting shareholders provided in ... this act, if any, if, but only if, such acquisition shall have been accomplished by the issuance of voting shares of such corporation to be outstanding immediately after the acquisition sufficient to elect a majority of the directors of the corporation.

§ [908].   Rights of Dissenting Shareholders ...

B.   Where a corporation acquires assets by purchase, lease or exchange, by the issuance of shares, evidences of indebtedness or otherwise, with or without assuming liabilities other than by the procedure for merger or consolidation prescribed in this Article IX, the rights, if any, of dissenting shareholders shall be governed by section [311] and not by this section.

————

NOTE ON RATH v. RATH PACKING CO.

In Rath v. Rath Packing Co., 257 Iowa 1277, 136 N.W.2d 410 (1965), Rath Packing, an Iowa corporation, entered into a "Plan and Agreement of Reorganization" with Needham Packing. Under the Plan, Rath was to (1) amend its articles to double the number of shares of its common shares, create a new class of preferred shares, and change its name to Rath–Needham Corporation; (2) issue Rath common and preferred in exchange for substantially all of Needham's assets; (3) assume all of Needham's liabilities; and (4) elect two Needham officers and directors to its board. Needham would then distribute the new Rath–Needham shares to its shareholders and dissolve. If the new preferred was fully converted, the Needham shareholders would end up with about 54 per cent of Rath–Needham's common stock.

At a meeting of Rath shareholders, 60% of its outstanding shares were voted in favor of the certificate amendments. Under Iowa law a merger required two-thirds shareholder approval, and shareholders in Rath Packing sued to enjoin the transaction on the ground that it was a merger and accordingly had not been properly approved. Rath argued that the transaction constituted only an amendment of Rath's certificate and an issuance of its stock, and accordingly did not need to meet the requirements of Iowa's merger provisions, under the equal-dignity theory. The Iowa Supreme Court, reversing the decision below, concluded the transaction was a merger, and ordered the issuance of an injunction.

We can agree all provisions of our [corporation law] are of equal dignity. But we cannot agree any provisions of the act are legally independent of others if this means that in arriving at the correct interpretation thereof and the legislative intent expressed therein we are not to consider the entire act and, so far as possible, construe its various provisions in the light of their relation to the whole act....

The "Plan and Agreement of Reorganization" clearly provides for what amounts to a merger of Rath and Needham under any definition of merger we know.

... "A merger of corporations consists of a combination whereby one of the constituent companies remains in being—absorbing or merging in itself all the other constituent corporations." 19 Am.Jur.2d, Corporations, section 1492.... "It (merger) is the uniting of two or more corporations by the transfer of property to one of them, which continues in existence, the others being merged therein." Id., pages 9–10....

If, as we hold, this agreement provides for what amounts to a merger of Rath and Needham, calling it a Plan and Agreement of Reorganization does not change its essential character. A fundamental maxim of equity, frequently applied, is that equity regards substance rather than form....

In seeking the scope and effect of the two sets of sections relied upon at least one fundamental rule of statutory construction is applicable. As stated, the merger sections specifically provide for a particular thing—mergers. The sections authorizing amendment of articles and issuance of stock apply to all amendments and stock issues, whether or not amending the articles or issuing stock is part of a merger, as they may or may not be. As applied to mergers, the sections on which plaintiffs rely are specific provisions, those on which defendants rely are not....

A ... rule, many times applied by us, is that where a general statute, if standing alone, would include the same matter as a special statute and thus conflict with it, the latter will prevail and the former must give way....

It is apparent that if the sections pertaining to amending articles and issuing stock are construed to authorize a merger by a majority vote of shareholders they conflict with the sections specifically dealing with the one matter of mergers which require a two-thirds vote of shareholders. The two sets of sections may be harmonized by holding, as we do, that the merger sections govern the matter of merger and must be regarded as an exception to the sections dealing with amending articles and issuing stock, which may or may not be involved in a merger....

The merger sections make it clear the legislature intended to require a two-thirds vote of shareholders and accord so-called appraisal rights to dissenters in case of a merger. It is unreasonable to ascribe to the same legislature an intent to provide in the same act a method of evading the required two-thirds vote and the grant of such appraisal rights. The practical effect of the decision appealed from is to render the requirements of a two-thirds vote and appraisal rights meaningless in virtually all mergers. It is scarcely an exaggeration to say the decision amounts to judicial repeal of the merger sections in most instances of merger.

It is obvious, as defendants' counsel frankly stated in oral argument, that corporate management would naturally choose a method which requires only majority approval of shareholders and does not grant dissenters the right to be paid the fair value of their stock. The legislature could hardly have intended to vest in corporate management the option to comply with the requirements just referred to or to proceed without such compliance, a choice that would invariably be exercised in favor of the easier method....

NEW YORK STOCK EXCHANGE, LISTED COMPANY MANUAL § 312.00

[See Statutory Supplement]

CAL. CORP. CODE §§ 152, 160, 168, 181, 187, 194.5, 1001, 1101, 1200, 1201, 1300

[See Statutory Supplement]

MODEL BUS. CORP. ACT § 6.21(f)

[See Statutory Supplement]

NOTE ON THE SURVIVOR'S LIABILITY TO THE TRANSFEROR'S CREDITORS IN STOCK-FOR-ASSETS COMBINATIONS

Stock-for-assets transactions are often used in preference to a statutory merger or a stock-for-stock combination because of a desire to avoid assuming the acquired corporation's liabilities—particularly undisclosed or contingent liabilities. In a statutory merger, the surviving corporation becomes liable by operation of law for all of the transferor's obligations, including those that are contingent or undisclosed. In a stock-for-stock combination, the survivor does not become directly liable for the debts of the acquired corporation, although the acquired corporation is now a subsidiary of the survivor, and carries its obligations along.

In contrast, in a stock-for-assets combination, the survivor may remain free of those liabilities it does not expressly assume, on the theory that it merely engaged in a purchase. Frequently, however, this theory is not accepted by the courts. The following formulation, or one very much like it, is found in a great number of cases:

The general rule is that "a mere sale of corporate property by one company to another does not make the purchaser liable for the liabilities of the seller not assumed by it...." There are, however, certain exceptions to this rule. Liability for obligations of a selling corporation may be imposed on the purchasing corporation when (1) the purchaser expressly or impliedly agrees to assume such obligations; (2) the transaction amounts to a consolidation or merger of the selling corporation with or into the purchasing corporation; (3) the purchasing corporation is merely a continuation of the selling corporation; or (4) the transaction is entered into fraudulently to escape liability for such obligations.

Where the second or third exceptions apply, many (though not all) cases make the survivor in a typical stock-for-assets transaction liable to the transferor's shareholders under a de facto merger theory.

(f) TRIANGULAR MERGERS AND SHARE EXCHANGES

Terry v. Penn Central Corp.

United States Court of Appeals, Third Circuit, 1981.
668 F.2d 188.

■ Before ADAMS, MARIS and HIGGINBOTHAM, CIRCUIT JUDGES....

■ ADAMS, CIRCUIT JUDGE.

The Penn Central Corporation ("Penn Central"), an appellee in this case, has sought to acquire Colt Industries Inc. ("Colt"), also an appellee, by merging Colt with PCC Holdings, Inc. ("Holdings"), a wholly-owned subsidiary of Penn Central. Howard L. Terry and W.H. Hunt, the appellants, are shareholders of Penn Central who objected to the transaction. In a diversity action before the United States District Court for the Eastern District of Pennsylvania, appellants sought injunctive and declaratory relief to enforce voting and dissenters' rights to which appellants asserted they were entitled. Appellants further sought to enjoin Holdings from proceeding with the proposed merger, and in particular moved to enjoin a vote on the transaction, scheduled for October 29, 1981, by the shareholders of Penn Central. In an opinion issued on October 22, 1981, Judge Pollak denied appellants' requests. Appellants thereupon filed an appeal in this Court, and then petitioned for a temporary injunction against the proposed shareholder vote until the appeal on the merits of the district court order could be heard. On October 27, following oral argument, we entered an order denying the petition for temporary injunction, stating that appellants had failed to demonstrate a sufficient likelihood of prevailing on the merits. C.A. No. 81–3955. The shareholders of Penn Central voted, as scheduled, on October 29. Pursuant to an expedited hearing schedule, the appeal from the district court's denial of injunctive and declaratory relief was submitted to this Court following oral argument on November 5.

After argument on appeal, the shareholders disapproved of the merger, and the corporations thereafter publicly announced their abandonment of this particular merger. Penn Central, however, has not abandoned its proposed series of acquisitions, of which the Colt acquisition was merely one instance.

I.

Penn Central is the successor to the Penn Central Transportation Corporation, which underwent a reorganization under the bankruptcy laws that was completed in 1978. No longer involved in the railroading business, Penn Central, since 1978, has had the advantage, for tax purposes, of a large loss carry-forward. In order to put that loss carry-forward to its best use, Penn Central has embarked on a program of acquiring corporations whose profits could be sheltered. To this end Penn Central created Holdings, a wholly-owned subsidiary which was to acquire the businesses that Penn Central desired. The first acquisition under the plan was Marathon Manufacturing Company ("Marathon"), in 1979. In the Marathon acquisition, a class of preferred Penn Central stock was created, and 30 million shares of "First Series Preference Stock" was issued to the owners of Marathon stock. Appellants were shareholders of Marathon who thereby obtained shares of this First Series Preference Stock. Terry was promptly elected to the Penn Central board of directors.

In 1981, Penn Central decided upon another acquisition: Colt. The management and directors of Colt and Penn Central agreed upon a merger of Colt into Holdings, compensated for by issuance of a second series of Penn Central preference stock to Colt shareholders. Terry opposed the merger at the directors' meeting, and sought to preclude the consummation of the transaction.

... [A]ppellants argue that under Pennsylvania's corporate law, they are entitled to dissent and appraisal rights if the merger is adopted over their opposition.[2] ...

Because Colt and Penn Central have now announced their abandonment of the proposed merger, the request for injunctive relief considered by the district court is now conceded by all parties to be moot. However, the appellants' request for declaratory relief, which the appellants now contend is moot as well, involves legal questions that go to Penn Central's plan of acquisitions, rather than to the Colt transaction alone, and these questions appear likely to recur in future disputes between the parties here.... In a case such as this, a

---

2. In addition, appellants claim a right under Pennsylvania law to require approval of an absolute majority vote of the shares outstanding on the proposed merger, relying on § 902(B) of the Pennsylvania Business Corporation Law (PBCL), 15 P.S. § 1902(B) (Purdon Supp.1981–82). For the reasons discussed in Part III of this opinion, we conclude that Penn Central is not a "party" to the merger, within the technical meaning of the term under that section and the related Section 908 of the PBCL, 15 P.S. § 1908 (Purdon Supp.1981–82). Accordingly, section 902 does not apply to the Penn Central vote on the merger.

voluntary termination by the parties of the specific activity challenged in the lawsuit—here, the proposed treatment of the dissenting preferred shareholders in the Colt–Holdings plan—does not render the action moot because there is "a reasonable likelihood that the parties or those in privity with them will be involved in a suit on the same issues in the future." American Bible Society v. Blount, 446 F.2d 588, 595 (3d Cir.1971)....

III.

Terry and Hunt contend that under Pennsylvania law they are entitled to dissent and appraisal rights if a merger is approved by the Penn Central shareholders. As the district court concluded, this assertion is unsupported by Pennsylvania statute or caselaw. Sitting as a court in diversity, we are not at liberty to diverge from the outcome that the Pennsylvania legislature and the Pennsylvania courts prescribe. Briefly, appellants' argument is that the proposed merger between Holdings and Colt constitutes a *de facto* merger between Colt and Penn Central, and that the Penn Central shareholders are therefore entitled to the protections for dissenting shareholders that Pennsylvania corporate law provides for shareholders of parties to a merger. Although this reasoning, with its emphasis on the substance of the transaction rather than its formal trappings, may be attractive as a matter of policy, see, e.g., Note, Three–Party Mergers: The Fourth Form of Corporate Acquisition, 57 Va.L.Rev. 1242 (1971), it contravenes the language employed by the Pennsylvania legislature in setting out the rights of shareholders.

Section 908 of the Pennsylvania Business Corporation Law (PBCL), 15 P.S. § 1908, provides that shareholders of corporations that are parties to a plan of merger are entitled to dissent and appraisal rights, but adds that for an acquisition other than such a merger, the only rights are those provided for in Section 311 of the PBCL, 15 P.S. § 1311 (Purdon 1967 Supp.1981–82). Section 311, in turn, provides for dissent and appraisal rights only when an acquisition has been accomplished by "the issuance of voting shares of such corporation to be outstanding immediately after the acquisition sufficient to elect a majority of the directors of the corporation." In this case the shares of Penn Central stock to be issued in the Colt transaction do not exceed the number of shares already existing, and thus the transaction is not covered by Section 311. Any statutory dissent and appraisal rights for Penn Central shareholders are therefore contingent upon Penn Central's status as a party to the merger within the meaning of Section 908. And as the district court points out, the PBCL describes the parties to a merger as those entities that are *actually* combined into a single corporation. Section 907, 15 P.S. § 1907 (Purdon Supp.1981–82), states that:

> Upon the merger or consolidation becoming effective, the several corporations parties to the plan of merger or consolidation shall be a single corporation which, in the case of a merger,

shall be that corporation designated in the plan of merger as the surviving corporation. . . .

At the consummation of the proposed merger plan here, both Holdings and Penn Central would survive as separate entities, and it would therefore appear that Penn Central is not a party within the meaning of . . . Section 907. We can discern no reason to infer that the legislature intended the word "party" to have different meanings in Sections 907 and 908, and accordingly conclude that Penn Central is not a party to the merger.

Appellants argue that Penn Central is nevertheless brought into the amalgamation by the *de facto* merger doctrine as set out in Pennsylvania law in Farris v. Glen Alden Corp., 393 Pa. 427, 143 A.2d 25 (1958). *Farris* was the penultimate step in a *pas de deux* involving the Pennsylvania courts and the Pennsylvania legislature regarding the proper treatment for transactions that reached the same practical result as a merger but avoided the legal form of merger and the concomitant legal obligations. In the 1950s the Pennsylvania courts advanced the doctrine that a transaction having the effect of an amalgamation would be treated as a *de facto* merger. See, e.g., Bloch v. The Baldwin Locomotive Works, 75 Pa.D. & C. 24 (1951). The legislature responded with efforts to constrict the *de facto* merger doctrine. *Farris*, addressing those efforts, held that the doctrine still covered a reorganization agreement that had the effect of merging a large corporation into a smaller corporation. In a 1959 response to *Farris*, the legislature made explicit its objection to earlier cases that found certain transactions to be *de facto* mergers. The legislature enacted a law, modifying *inter alia* Sections 311 and 908, entitled in part:

> An Act . . . changing the law as to . . . the acquisition or transfer of corporate assets, the rights of dissenting shareholders, . . . abolishing the doctrine of de facto mergers or consolidation and reversing the rules laid down in *Bloch v. Baldwin Locomotive Works*, 75 Pa. D. & C. 24, and *Marks v. The Autocar Co.*, 153 F.Supp. 768, ...

Act of November 10, 1959 (P.L. 1406, No. 502).

Following this explicit statement, the *de facto* merger doctrine has rarely been invoked by the Pennsylvania courts. Only once has the Pennsylvania Supreme Court made reference to it, in In re Jones Laughlin Steel Corp., 488 Pa. 524, 412 A.2d 1099 (1980). Even there, the Court's reference was oblique. It merely cited *Farris* for the proposition that shareholders have the right to enjoin "proposed unfair or fraudulent corporate actions." 488 Pa. at 533, 412 A.2d at 1104. This Court, sitting in diversity in Knapp v. North American Rockwell Corp., 506 F.2d 361 (3d Cir.1974), cert. denied, 421 U.S. 965, 95 S.Ct. 1955, 44 L.Ed.2d 452 (1975), made reference to the *de facto* merger doctrine to hold that a transaction structured as a sale of assets could nevertheless be deemed a merger for purposes of requiring the merging corporation to assume the acquired corporation's liability for damages to a worker who was injured by a faulty piece of equipment manufactured by the acquired company....

None of [the] cases persuades us that a Pennsylvania court would apply the *de facto* merger doctrine to the situation before us. Although *Jones & Laughlin Steel* suggests that dissent and appraisal rights might be available if fraud or fundamental unfairness were shown, we are not faced with such a situation. No allegation of fraud has been advanced, and the only allegation of fundamental unfairness is that the appellants will, if the merger is consummated, be forced into what they consider a poor investment on the part of Penn Central without the opportunity to receive an appraised value for their stock. Even if appellants' evaluation of the merits of the proposed merger is accurate, poor business judgment on the part of management would not be enough to constitute unfairness cognizable by a court. And the denial of appraisal rights to dissenters cannot constitute fundamental unfairness, or the *de facto* merger doctrine would apply in every instance in which dissenters' rights were sought and the 1959 amendments by the legislature would be rendered nugatory.[7] ...

In the absence of any explicit guidance to the contrary by the Pennsylvania courts, we conclude that the language of the legislature in 1959 precludes a decision that the transaction in this case constitutes a *de facto* merger sufficient to entitle Penn Central shareholders to dissent and appraisal rights. We therefore hold that appellants do not possess such rights if a transaction such as the one involved here is consummated....

NOTE ON TRIANGULAR MERGERS AND SHARE EXCHANGES

1. *Triangular Mergers.* A statutory merger is often preferable to either a stock-for-assets or a stock-for-stock combination. To begin with, the Internal Revenue Code provides greater liberality as to the type of consideration that can be given in an A reorganization (a statutory merger) than in a B reorganization (a stock-for-stock combination) or a C reorganization (a stock-for-assets combination). See Section 1(e), supra. Furthermore, a stock-for-assets combination may involve sales taxes, while a statutory merger ordinarily will not. A stock-for-assets combination also ordinarily involves a great amount of paperwork, in the form of deeds and assignments of the transferor's property and (in some cases) notice to creditors in compliance with the applicable bulk sales law. In contrast, in a statutory merger the survivor succeeds to the transferor's assets by operation of law, so that neither individual documents of title nor compliance with the bulk sales law is ordinarily required.

7. A different result might be reached if here, as in *Farris,* the acquiring corporation were significantly smaller than the acquired corporation such that the acquisition greatly transformed the nature of the successor corporation. But in this situation we do not have such a case; after the merger Penn Central would remain a major, diversified corporation, and would continue on the course of acquiring other corporations.

On the other hand, in a statutory merger the surviving corporation assumes the disappearing corporation's liabilities by operation of law. Furthermore, a statutory merger normally triggers voting and appraisal rights in the shareholders of both constituents. In contrast, in a stock-for-stock or stock-for-assets combination, the acquiring corporation does not necessarily assume the transferor corporation's liabilities. Moreover, these forms of combination may require a vote only by the shareholders of one constituent, and may not trigger appraisal rights. Accordingly, the management of a corporation that proposes to engage in a corporate combination may prefer to use the statutory-merger form except for the voting and appraisal rights entailed by that form. The triangular merger is a technique designed to give management the best of both possible worlds: the form of a merger, but without necessarily assuming the liabilities of the disappearing corporation and without voting or appraisal rights in the survivor's shareholders.

A conventional (or "foreward") triangular merger works this way: Assume that Corporations S and T want to engage in a merger in which S will be the survivor and T's shareholders will end up with 100,000 shares of S. In a normal merger this would be accomplished by having S issue 100,000 shares of its own stock to T's shareholders. In a conventional triangular merger, however, S instead begins by creating a new subsidiary, S/Sub, and then transfers 100,000 shares of its own stock to S/Sub in exchange for all of S/Sub's stock. S/Sub and T then engage in a statutory merger, but instead of issuing its *own* stock to T's shareholders, S/Sub issues its 100,000 shares of S stock. The net result is that T's business is now owned by S's wholly owned subsidiary (rather than by S itself, as in a normal merger), and T's shareholders now own 100,000 shares of S stock. By use of this technique, S may therefore achieve the advantages of a statutory merger while insulating itself from direct responsibility for T's liabilities.[1]

Such a transaction would probably not have been permissible under the traditional statutory merger provisions, because those provisions usually contemplated that the surviving corporation would issue its *own* shares or securities. However, the merger statutes of most or all jurisdictions have now been amended to permit the survivor to issue shares or securities of *any* corporation. (See, e.g., Del. § 251(b)(4).) In tandem with this development, the Internal Revenue Code was amended by adding § 368(a)(2)(D), which permits a conventional triangular merger to qualify as a tax-free A reorganization, if (i) substantially all of T's properties are acquired by S/Sub; (ii) the merger would have qualified as an A reorganization if T had merged directly into S; and (iii) no stock of S/Sub is used in the transaction.

A *reverse* triangular merger proceeds like a conventional triangular merger, except that instead of merging T into S/Sub, S/Sub is merged into T. The merger agreement provides that all previously outstanding T shares are automatically converted into the 100,000

---

1. However, a court might impose these liabilities on S under the de facto merger doctrine, on the theory that in effect S itself is a constituent to the merger.

shares of S held by S/Sub, and that all shares in S/Sub (which are held by S) are automatically converted into shares in T. When all the shooting is over, therefore, S/Sub will have disappeared, T will be a wholly owned subsidiary of S, and T's shareholders will own 100,000 shares of S stock. By use of this technique S may therefore achieve the advantages of a statutory merger while preserving T's legal status, which could be important where T has valuable but non-assignable rights under contracts, leases, licenses, or franchises. Under IRC § 368(a)(2)(E), a reverse triangular merger will qualify as a tax-free A reorganization, if (i) T ends up with substantially all of the properties of both S/Sub and T, and (ii) S voting stock is exchanged for at least 80% of T's voting and nonvoting stock. (The balance of T's stock can be acquired for other types of consideration.)

An important problem raised by triangular mergers is that they may allow subversion of shareholder voting and appraisal rights. To avoid this result, it can be argued that despite the form of such transactions, voting and appraisal rights on the survivor's side are vested not in S, as the sole shareholder of S/Sub, but in S's shareholders. This argument was rejected in Terry v. Penn Central Corp., supra, but that case was at least partly controlled by the unusual Pennsylvania legislative history. Ideally, this problem should be dealt with by statute. For example, under Cal. §§ 1200(d), 1201, a merger reorganization must be approved by the shareholders of a corporation which is "in control of any constituent ... corporation ... and whose equity securities are issued or transferred in the reorganization." Even where a statute does not deal with the problem explicitly, it can be argued that a triangular merger triggers voting and appraisal rights in S's shareholders on the theory that S should be deemed a constituent to the merger, or alternatively that such a result is necessary to prevent subversion of the merger statutes.

2. *Share Exchanges.* Another new mode of combination is known as a share exchange. In a share exchange, the shareholders of the acquired corporation vote on whether to exchange their shares for designated consideration from the acquiring corporation. If the proposed transaction is approved by a majority of that corporation's outstanding shares, all of the shares must be surrendered—including those of nonconsenting shareholders (unless they exercise appraisal rights).

(g) FREEZEOUTS

NOTE ON FREEZEOUT TECHNIQUES

A freezeout is a corporate transaction whose principal purpose is to reconstitute the corporation's ownership by involuntarily eliminating the equity interest of minority shareholders. Until twenty-five or thirty years ago, freezeouts tended to take one of three forms, all of which met with only indifferent success at the hands of the courts.

1. *Dissolution Freezeouts.* Assume that S (who may be an individual, a group, or a corporation) owns 70% of C Corporation, and wishes to eliminate C's minority shareholders. In a dissolution freezeout, S causes C to dissolve under a plan of dissolution which provides that C's productive assets will be distributed to S (or to an entity S controls), while cash or notes will be distributed to C's minority shareholders. This technique has been held illegal in a number of cases, most of which stress that such a plan of dissolution violates a corporate norm of equal treatment among all shareholders of the same class. See e.g., In re San Joaquin Light & Power Corp., 52 Cal.App.2d 814, 127 P.2d 29 (1942).

2. *Sale-of-Assets Freezeouts.* In a sale-of-assets freezeout, C's controlling shareholder, S, organizes a new corporation, T, all of whose stock S owns. S then causes C to sell its assets to T for cash or notes. Result: S owns C's business through T, while the equity interest of C's minority shareholders in C's business is involuntarily terminated. (C is then normally dissolved, although a freezeout will be effected even without dissolution.) Such a procedure has been disapproved in several cases. See, e.g., Theis v. Spokane Falls Gaslight Co., 34 Wash. 23, 74 P. 1004 (1904).

3. *Debt or Redeemable–Preferred Mergers.* A debt or redeemable-preferred merger begins like a sale-of-assets freezeout, with the organization by S of a new corporation, T. However, instead of causing C to transfer its assets to T, S causes C to merge into T; and instead of issuing common stock in the merger, T issues either short-term debentures or redeemable preferred stock. Accordingly, the interest of C's minority shareholders in T either terminates automatically after a period of years (in the case of debentures) or is terminable at T's election (in the case of redeemable preferred).

4. *Cashout Mergers.* Modern freezeouts commonly employ still a fourth technique. Most states now allow the survivor in any type of merger to issue cash as well as, or instead of, stock or other securities. This opens the door to cash mergers, which resemble debt or redeemable-stock mergers, except that the survivor issues cash rather than stock or other securities. Under this technique, the freezeout possibilities of the short-form merger are extended to cases where the parent does not own the percentage of stock requisite for a short-form merger.

A recurrent issue in the freezeout area is whether such a transaction is permissible if it is effected with no business purpose other than to increase the controlling shareholders' portion of the pie. That issue is addressed in the materials that follow.

Weinberger v. UOP, Inc.

Supreme Court of Delaware, 1983.
457 A.2d 701.

■ Before HERMANN, C.J., McNEILLY, QUILLEN, HORSEY and MOORE, JJ., constituting the Court en Banc.

■ MOORE, JUSTICE:

This post-trial appeal was reheard en banc from a decision of the Court of Chancery. It was brought by the class action plaintiff below, a former shareholder of UOP, Inc., who challenged the elimination of UOP's minority shareholders by a cash-out merger between UOP and its majority owner, The Signal Companies, Inc. [T]he defendants in this action are Signal, UOP, [and] certain officers and directors of those companies.... The present Chancellor held that the terms of the merger were fair to the plaintiff and the other minority shareholders of UOP. Accordingly, he entered judgment in favor of the defendants.

Numerous points were raised by the parties, but we address only the following questions presented by the trial court's opinion:

(1) The plaintiff's duty to plead sufficient facts demonstrating the unfairness of the challenged merger;

(2) The burden of proof upon the parties where the merger has been approved by the purportedly informed vote of a majority of the minority shareholders;

(3) The fairness of the merger in terms of adequacy of the defendants' disclosures to the minority shareholders;

(4) The fairness of the merger in terms of adequacy of the price paid for the minority shares and the remedy appropriate to that issue; and

(5) The continued force and effect of Singer v. Magnavox Co., Del.Supr., 380 A.2d 969, 980 (1977), and its progeny.

In ruling for the defendants, the Chancellor re-stated his earlier conclusion that the plaintiff in a suit challenging a cash-out merger must allege specific acts of fraud, misrepresentation, or other items of misconduct to demonstrate the unfairness of the merger terms to the minority. We approve this rule and affirm it.

The Chancellor also held that even though the ultimate burden of proof is on the majority shareholder to show by a preponderance of the evidence that the transaction is fair, it is first the burden of the plaintiff attacking the merger to demonstrate some basis for invoking the fairness obligation. We agree with that principle. However, where corporate action has been approved by an informed vote of a majority of the minority shareholders, we conclude that the burden entirely shifts to the plaintiff to show that the transaction was unfair to the minority. See, e.g., Michelson v. Duncan, Del.Supr., 407 A.2d 211, 224 (1979). But in all this, the burden clearly remains on those relying on the vote to show that they completely disclosed all material facts relevant to the transaction.

Here, the record does not support a conclusion that the minority stockholder vote was an informed one. Material information, necessary to acquaint those shareholders with the bargaining positions of Signal and UOP, was withheld under circumstances amounting to a breach of fiduciary duty. We therefore conclude that this merger does not meet the test of fairness, at least as we address that concept, and no burden thus shifted to the plaintiff by reason of the minority shareholder vote. Accordingly, we reverse and remand for further proceedings consistent herewith.

In considering the nature of the remedy available under our law to minority shareholders in a cash-out merger, we believe that it is, and hereafter should be, an appraisal under 8 Del.C. § 262 as hereinafter construed. We therefore overrule Lynch v. Vickers Energy Corp., Del.Supr., 429 A.2d 497 (1981) (*Lynch II*) to the extent that it purports to limit a stockholder's monetary relief to a specific damage formula. See *Lynch II*. 429 A.2d at 507–08 (McNeilly Quillen, JJ., dissenting). But to give full effect to section 262 within the framework of the General Corporation Law we adopt a more liberal, less rigid and stylized, approach to the valuation process than has heretofore been permitted by our courts. While the present state of these proceedings does not admit the plaintiff to the appraisal remedy per se, the practical effect of the remedy we do grant him will be co-extensive with the liberalized valuation and appraisal methods we herein approve for cases coming after this decision.

Our treatment of these matters has necessarily led us to a reconsideration of the business purpose rule announced in the trilogy of Singer v. Magnavox Co., supra; Tanzer v. International General Industries, Inc., Del.Supr., 379 A.2d 1121 (1977); and Roland International Corp. v. Najjar, Del.Supr., 407 A.2d 1032 (1979). For the reasons hereafter set forth we consider that the business purpose requirement of these cases is no longer the law of Delaware.

I.

The facts found by the trial court, pertinent to the issues before us, are supported by the record, and we draw from them as set out in the Chancellor's opinion.

Signal is a diversified, technically based company operating through various subsidiaries. Its stock is publicly traded on the New York, Philadelphia and Pacific Stock Exchanges. UOP, formerly known as Universal Oil Products Company, was a diversified industrial company engaged in various lines of business, including petroleum and petro-chemical services and related products, construction, fabricated metal products, transportation equipment products, chemicals and plastics, and other products and services including land development, lumber products and waste disposal. Its stock was publicly held and listed on the New York Stock Exchange.

In 1974 Signal sold one of its wholly-owned subsidiaries for $420,000,000 in cash. See Gimbel v. Signal Companies, Inc., Del.Ch., 316 A.2d 599, aff'd, Del.Supr., 316 A.2d 619 (1974). While looking to invest this cash surplus, Signal became interested in UOP as a possible acquisition. Friendly negotiations ensued, and Signal proposed to acquire a controlling interest in UOP at a price of $19 per share. UOP's representatives sought $25 per share. In the arm's length bargaining that followed, an understanding was reached whereby Signal agreed to purchase from UOP 1,500,000 shares of UOP's authorized but unissued stock at $21 per share.

This purchase was contingent upon Signal making a successful cash tender offer for 4,300,000 publicly held shares of UOP, also at a price of $21 per share. This combined method of acquisition permitted Signal to acquire 5,800,000 shares of stock, representing 50.5% of UOP's outstanding shares. The UOP board of directors advised the company's shareholders that it had no objection to Signal's tender offer at that price. Immediately before the announcement of the tender offer, UOP's common stock had been trading on the New York Stock Exchange at a fraction under $14 per share.

The negotiations between Signal and UOP occurred during April 1975, and the resulting tender offer was greatly oversubscribed. However, Signal limited its total purchase of the tendered shares so that, when coupled with the stock bought from UOP, it had achieved its goal of becoming a 50.5% shareholder of UOP.

Although UOP's board consisted of thirteen directors, Signal nominated and elected only six. Of these, five were either directors or employees of Signal. The sixth, a partner in the banking firm of Lazard Freres & Co., had been one of Signal's representatives in the negotiations and bargaining with UOP concerning the tender offer and purchase price of the UOP shares.

However, the president and chief executive officer of UOP retired during 1975, and Signal caused him to be replaced by James V. Crawford, a long-time employee and senior executive vice president of one of Signal's wholly-owned subsidiaries. Crawford succeeded his predecessor on UOP's board of directors and also was made a director of Signal.

By the end of 1977 Signal basically was unsuccessful in finding other suitable investment candidates for its excess cash, and by February 1978 considered that it had no other realistic acquisitions available to it on a friendly basis. Once again its attention turned to UOP.

The trial court found that at the instigation of certain Signal management personnel, including William W. Walkup, its board chairman, and Forrest N. Shumway, its president, a feasibility study was made concerning the possible acquisition of the balance of UOP's outstanding shares. This study was performed by two Signal officers, Charles S. Arledge, vice president (director of planning), and Andrew J. Chitiea, senior vice president (chief financial officer). Messrs. Walkup, Shumway, Arledge and Chitiea were all directors of UOP in addition to their membership on the Signal board.

Arledge and Chitiea concluded that it would be a good investment for Signal to acquire the remaining 49.5% of UOP shares at any price up to $24 each. Their report was discussed between Walkup and Shumway who, along with Arledge, Chitiea and Brewster L. Arms, internal counsel for Signal, constituted Signal's senior management. In particular, they talked about the proper price to be paid if the acquisition was pursued, purportedly keeping in mind that as UOP's majority shareholder, Signal owed a fiduciary responsibility to both its own stockholders as well as to UOP's minority. It was ultimately agreed that a meeting of Signal's Executive Committee would be called to propose that Signal acquire the remaining outstanding stock of UOP through a cash-out merger in the range of $20 to $21 per share.

The Executive Committee meeting was set for February 28, 1978. As a courtesy, UOP's President, Crawford, was invited to attend, although he was not a member of Signal's executive committee. On his arrival, and prior to the meeting, Crawford was asked to meet privately with Walkup and Shumway. He was then told of Signal's plan to acquire full ownership of UOP and was asked for his reaction to the proposed price range of $20 to $21 per share. Crawford said he thought such a price would be "generous", and that it was certainly one which should be submitted to UOP's minority shareholders for their ultimate consideration. He stated, however, that Signal's 100% ownership could cause internal problems at UOP. He believed that employees would have to be given some assurance of their future place in a fully-owned Signal subsidiary. Otherwise, he feared the departure of essential personnel. Also, many of UOP's key employees had stock option incentive programs which would be wiped out by a merger. Crawford therefore urged that some adjustment would have to be made, such as providing a comparable incentive in Signals' shares, if after the merger he was to maintain his quality of personnel and efficiency at UOP.

Thus, Crawford voiced no objection to the $20 to $21 price range, nor did he suggest that Signal should consider paying more than $21 per share for the minority interests. Later, at the Executive Committee meeting the same factors were discussed, with Crawford repeating the position he earlier took with Walkup and Shumway. Also considered was the 1975 tender offer and the fact that it had been greatly oversubscribed at $21 per share. For many reasons, Signal's management concluded that the acquisition of UOP's minority shares provided the solution to a number of its business problems.

Thus, it was the consensus that a price of $20 to $21 per share would be fair to both Signal and the minority shareholders of UOP. Signal's executive committee authorized its management "to negotiate" with UOP "for a cash acquisition of the minority ownership in UOP, Inc., with the intention of presenting a proposal to [Signal's] board of directors ... on March 6, 1978. Immediately after this February 28, 1978" meeting, Signal issued a press release stating:

The Signal Companies, Inc. and UOP, Inc. are conducting negotiations for the acquisition for cash by Signal of the 49.5 per cent of UOP which it does not presently own, announced Forrest N. Shumway, president and chief executive officer of Signal, and James V. Crawford, UOP president.

Price and other terms of the proposed transaction have not yet been finalized and would be subject to approval of the boards of directors of Signal and UOP, scheduled to meet early next week, the stockholders of UOP and certain federal agencies.

The announcement also referred to the fact that the closing price of UOP's common stock on that day was $14.50 per share.

Two days later, on March 2, 1978, Signal issued a second press release stating that its management would recommend a price in the range of $20 to $21 per share for UOP's 49.5% minority interest. This announcement referred to Signal's earlier statement that "negotiations" were being conducted for the acquisition of the minority shares.

Between Tuesday, February 28, 1978 and Monday, March 6, 1978, a total of four business days, Crawford spoke by telephone with all of UOP's non-Signal, i.e., outside, directors. Also during that period, Crawford retained Lehman Brothers to render a fairness opinion as to the price offered the minority for its stock. He gave two reasons for this choice. First, the time schedule between the announcement and the board meetings was short (by then only three business days) and since Lehman Brothers had been acting as UOP's investment banker for many years, Crawford felt that it would be in the best position to respond on such brief notice. Second, James W. Glanville, a long-time director of UOP and a partner in Lehman Brothers, had acted as a financial advisor to UOP for many years. Crawford believed that Glanville's familiarity with UOP, as a member of its board, would also be of assistance in enabling Lehman Brothers to render a fairness opinion within the existing time constraints.

Crawford telephoned Glanville, who gave his assurance that Lehman Brothers had no conflicts that would prevent it from accepting the task. Glanville's immediate personal reaction was that a price of $20 to $21 would certainly be fair, since it represented almost a 50% premium over UOP's market price. Glanville sought a $250,000 fee for Lehman Brothers' services, but Crawford thought this too much. After further discussions Glanville finally agreed that Lehman Brothers would render its fairness opinion for $150,000.

During this period Crawford also had several telephone contacts with Signal officials. In only one of them, however, was the price of the shares discussed. In a conversation with Walkup, Crawford advised that as a result of his communications with UOP's non-Signal directors, it was his feeling that the price would have to be the top of the proposed range, or $21 per share, if the approval of UOP's outside directors was to be obtained. But again, he did not seek any price higher than $21.

Glanville assembled a three-man Lehman Brothers team to do the work on the fairness opinion. These persons examined relevant documents and information concerning UOP, including its annual reports and its Securities and Exchange Commission filings from 1973 through 1976, as well as its audited financial statements for 1977, its interim reports to shareholders, and its recent and historical market prices and trading volumes. In addition, on Friday, March 3, 1978, two members of the Lehman Brothers team flew to UOP's headquarters in Des Plaines, Illinois, to perform a "due diligence" visit, during the course of which they interviewed Crawford as well as UOP's general counsel, its chief financial officer, and other key executives and personnel.

As a result, the Lehman Brothers team concluded that "the price of either $20 or $21 would be a fair price for the remaining shares of UOP". They telephoned this impression to Glanville, who was spending the weekend in Vermont.

On Monday morning, March 6, 1978, Glanville and the senior member of the Lehman Brothers team flew to Des Plaines to attend the scheduled UOP directors meeting. Glanville looked over the assembled information during the flight. The two had with them the draft of a "fairness opinion letter" in which the price had been left blank. Either during or immediately prior to the directors' meeting, the two-page "fairness opinion letter" was typed in final form and the price of $21 per share was inserted.

On March 6, 1978, both the Signal and UOP boards were convened to consider the proposed merger. Telephone communications were maintained between the two meetings. Walkup, Signal's board chairman, and also a UOP director, attended UOP's meeting with Crawford in order to present Signal's position and answer any questions that UOP's non-Signal directors might have. Arledge and Chitiea, along with Signal's other designees on UOP's board, participated by conference telephone. All of UOP's outside directors attended the meeting either in person or by conference telephone.

First, Signal's board unanimously adopted a resolution authorizing Signal to proposed to UOP a cash merger of $21 per share as outlined in a certain merger agreement and other supporting documents. This proposal required that the merger be approved by a majority of UOP's outstanding minority shares voting at the stockholders meeting at which the merger would be considered, and that the minority shares voting in favor of the merger, when coupled with Signal's 50.5% interest would have to comprise at least two-thirds of all UOP shares. Otherwise the proposed merger would be deemed disapproved.

UOP's board then considered the proposal. Copies of the agreement were delivered to the directors in attendance, and other copies had been forwarded earlier to the directors participating by telephone. They also had before them UOP financial data for 1974–1977, UOP's most recent financial statements, market price information, and budget projections for 1978. In addition they had Lehman Brothers' hurriedly prepared fairness opinion letter finding the price of $21 to be fair. Glanville, the Lehman Brothers partner, and UOP director, commented on the information that had gone into preparation of the letter.

Signal also suggests that the Arledge–Chitiea feasibility study, indicating that a price of up to $24 per share would be a "good investment" for Signal, was discussed at the UOP directors' meeting. The Chancellor made no such finding, and our independent review of the record, detailed infra, satisfies us by a preponderance of the evidence that there was no discussion of this document at UOP's board meeting. Furthermore, it is clear beyond peradventure that nothing in that report was ever disclosed to UOP's minority shareholders prior to their approval of the merger.

After consideration of Signal's proposal, Walkup and Crawford left the meeting to permit a free and uninhibited exchange between UOP's non-Signal directors. Upon their return a resolution to accept Signal's offer was then proposed and adopted. While Signal's men on UOP's board participated in various aspects of the meeting they abstained from voting. However, the minutes show that each of them "if voting would have voted yes".

On March 7, 1978, UOP sent a letter to its shareholders advising them of the action taken by UOP's board with respect to Signal's offer. This document pointed out, among other things, that on February 28, 1978 "both companies had announced negotiations were being conducted."

Despite the swift board action of the two companies, the merger was not submitted to UOP's shareholders until their annual meeting on May 26, 1978. In the notice of that meeting and proxy statement sent to shareholders in May, UOP's management and board urged that the merger be approved. The proxy statement also advised:

> The price was determined after *discussions* between James V. Crawford, a director of Signal and Chief Executive Officer of UOP, and officers of Signal which took place during meetings on February 28, 1978, and in the course of several subsequent telephone conversations. (Emphasis added.)

In the original draft of the proxy statement the word "negotiations" had been used rather than "discussions". However, when the Securities and Exchange Commission sought details of the "negotiations" as part of its review of these materials, the term was deleted and the word "discussions" was substituted. The proxy statement indicated that the vote of UOP's board in approving the merger had been unanimous. It also advised the shareholders that Lehman Brothers had given its opinion that the merger price of $21 per share was fair to UOP's minority. However, it did not disclose the hurried method by which this conclusion was reached.

As of the record date for UOP's annual meeting, there were 11,488,302 shares of UOP common stock outstanding, 5,688,302 of which were owned by the minority. At the meeting only 56%, or 3,208,652, of the minority shares were voted. Of these, 2,953,812, or

51.9% of the total minority, voted for the merger, and 254,840 voted against it. When Signal's stock was added to the minority shares voting in favor, a total of 76.2% of UOP's outstanding shares approved the merger while only 2.2% opposed it.

By its terms the merger became effective on May 26, 1978, and each share of UOP's stock held by the minority was automatically converted into a right to receive $21 cash.

II.

A.

A primary issue mandating reversal is the preparation by two UOP directors, Arledge and Chitiea, of their feasibility study for the exclusive use and benefit of Signal. This document was of obvious significance to both Signal and UOP. Using UOP data, it described the advantages to Signal of ousting the minority at a price range of $21–$24 per share. Mr. Arledge, one of the authors, outlined the benefits to Signal:*

Purpose of the Merger

(1) Provides an outstanding investment opportunity for Signal—(Better than any recent acquisition we have seen.)

(2) Increases Signal's earnings.

(3) Facilitates the flow of resources between Signal and its subsidiaries—(Big factor—works both ways.)

(4) Provides cost savings potential for Signal and UOP.

(5) Improves the percentage of Signal's "operating earnings" as opposed to "holding company earnings".

(6) Simplifies the understanding of Signal.

(7) Facilitates technological exchange among Signal's subsidiaries.

(8) Eliminates potential conflicts of interest.

Having written those words, solely for the use of Signal, it is clear from the record that neither Arledge nor Chitiea shared this report with their fellow directors of UOP. We are satisfied that no one else did either. This conduct hardly meets the fiduciary standards applicable to such a transaction. While Mr. Walkup, Signal's chairman of the board and a UOP director, attended the March 6, 1978 UOP board meeting and testified at trial that he had discussed the Arledge–Chitiea report with the UOP directors at this meeting, the record does not support this assertion. Perhaps it is the result of some confusion on Mr. Walkup's part. In any event Mr. Shumway, Signal's president, testified that he made sure the Signal outside directors had this report prior to the March 6, 1978 Signal board meeting, but he did not testify that the Arledge–Chitiea report was also sent to UOP's outside directors.

---

* The parentheses indicate certain hand-written comments of Mr. Arledge.

Mr. Crawford, UOP's president, could not recall that any documents, other than a draft of the merger agreement, were sent to UOP's directors before the March 6, 1978 UOP meeting. Mr. Chitiea, an author of the report, testified that it was made available to Signal's directors, but to his knowledge it was not circulated to the outside directors of UOP. He specifically testified that he "didn't share" that information with the outside directors of UOP with whom he served.

None of UOP's outside directors who testified stated that they had seen this document. The minutes of the UOP board meeting do not identify the Arledge–Chitiea report as having been delivered to UOP's outside directors. This is particularly significant since the minutes describe in considerable detail the materials that actually were distributed. While these minutes recite Mr. Walkup's presentation of the Signal offer, they do not mention the Arledge–Chitiea report or any disclosure that Signal considered a price of up to $24 to be a good investment. If Mr. Walkup had in fact provided such important information to UOP's outside directors, it is logical to assume that these carefully drafted minutes would disclose it. The post-trial briefs of Signal and UOP contain a thorough description of the documents purportedly available to their boards at the March 6, 1978, meetings. Although the Arledge–Chitiea report is specifically identified as being available to the Signal directors, there is no mention of it being among the documents submitted to the UOP board. Even when queried at a prior oral argument before this Court, counsel for Signal did not claim that the Arledge–Chitiea report had been disclosed to UOP's outside directors. Instead, he chose to belittle its contents. This was the same approach taken before us at the last oral argument.

Actually, it appears that a three-page summary of figures was given to all UOP directors. Its first page is identical to one page of the Arledge–Chitiea report, but this dealt with nothing more than a justification of the $21 price. Significantly, the contents of this three-page summary are what the minutes reflect Mr. Walkup told the UOP board. However, nothing contained in either the minutes or this three-page summary reflects Signal's study regarding the $24 price.

The Arledge–Chitiea report speaks for itself in supporting the Chancellor's finding that a price of up to $24 was a "good investment" for Signal. It shows that a return on the investment at $21 would be 15.7% versus 15.5% at $24 per share. This was a difference of only two-tenths of one percent, while it meant over $17,000,000 to the minority. Under such circumstances, paying UOP's minority shareholders $24 would have had relatively little long-term effect on Signal, and the Chancellor's findings concerning the benefit to Signal, even at a price of $24, were obviously correct. Levitt v. Bouvier, Del.Supr., 287 A.2d 671, 673 (1972).

Certainly, this was a matter of material significance to UOP and its shareholders. Since the study was prepared by two UOP directors, using UOP information for the exclusive benefit of Signal, and nothing whatever was done to disclose it to the outside UOP directors or the minority shareholders, a question of breach of fiduciary duty arises.

This problem occurs because there were common Signal–UOP directors participating, at least to some extent, in the UOP board's decision-making processes without full disclosure of the conflicts they faced.[7]

B.

In assessing this situation, the Court of Chancery was required to:

examine what information defendants had and to measure it against what they gave to the minority stockholders, in a context in which "complete candor" is required. In other words, the limited function of the Court was to determine whether defendants had disclosed all information in their possession germane to the transaction in issue. And by "germane" we mean, for present purposes, information such as a reasonable shareholder would consider important in deciding whether to sell or retain stock.

* * *

... Completeness, not adequacy, is both the norm and the mandate under present circumstances.

Lynch v. Vickers Energy Corp., Del.Supr., 383 A.2d 278, 281 (1977) (*Lynch I*). This is merely stating in another way the long-existing principle of Delaware law that these Signal designated directors on UOP's board still owed UOP and its shareholders an uncompromising duty of loyalty. The classic language of Guth v. Loft, Inc., Del.Supr., 5 A.2d 503, 510 (1939), requires no embellishment:

A public policy, existing through the years, and derived from a profound knowledge of human characteristics and motives, has established a rule that demands of a corporate officer or director, peremptorily and inexorably, the most scrupulous observance of his duty, not only affirmatively to protect the interests of the corporation committed to his charge, but also to refrain from doing anything that would work injury to the corporation, or to deprive it of profit or advantage which his skill and ability might properly bring to it, or to enable it to make in the reasonable and lawful exercise of its powers. The rule that requires an undivided and unselfish loyalty to the corporation demands that there shall be no conflict between duty and self-interest.

Given the absence of any attempt to structure this transaction on an arm's length basis, Signal cannot escape the effects of the conflicts

---

7. Although perfection is not possible, or expected, the result here could have been entirely different if UOP had appointed an independent negotiating committee of its outside directors to deal with Signal at arm's length. See, e.g., Harriman v. E.I. du Pont De Nemours & Co., 411 F.Supp. 133 (D.Del. 1975). Since fairness in this context can be equated to conduct by a theoretical, wholly independent, board of directors acting upon the matter before them, it is unfortunate that this course apparently was neither considered nor pursued. Johnston v. Greene, Del.Supr., 121 A.2d 919, 925 (1956). Particularly in a parent-subsidiary context, a showing that the action taken was as though each of the contending parties had in fact exerted its bargaining power against the other at arm's length is strong evidence that the transaction meets the test of fairness. Getty Oil Co. v. Skelly Oil Co., Del.Supr., 267 A.2d 883, 886 (1970); Puma v. Marriott, Del.Ch., 283 A.2d 693, 696 (1971).

it faced, particularly when its designees on UOP's board did not totally abstain from participation in the matter. There is no "safe harbor" for such divided loyalties in Delaware. When directors of a Delaware corporation are on both sides of a transaction, they are required to demonstrate their utmost good faith and the most scrupulous inherent fairness of the bargain. Gottlieb v. Heyden Chemical Corp., Del.Supr., 91 A.2d 57, 57–58 (1952). The requirement of fairness is unflinching in its demand that where one stands on both sides of a transaction, he has the burden of establishing its entire fairness, sufficient to pass the test of careful scrutiny by the courts. Sterling v. Mayflower Hotel Corp., Del.Supr., 93 A.2d 107, 110 (1952); Bastian v. Bourns, Inc., Del.Ch., 256 A.2d 680, 681 (1969), aff'd, Del.Supr., 278 A.2d 467 (1970); David J. Greene & Co. v. Dunhill International Inc., Del.Ch., 249 A.2d 427, 431 (1968).

There is no dilution of this obligation where one holds dual or multiple directorships, as in a parent-subsidiary context. Levien v. Sinclair Oil Corp., Del.Ch., 261 A.2d 911, 915 (1969). Thus, individuals who act in a dual capacity as directors of two corporations, one of whom is parent and the other subsidiary, owe the same duty of good management to both corporations, and in the absence of an independent negotiating structure (see note 7, supra), or the directors' total abstention from any participation in the matter, this duty is to be exercised in light of what is best for both companies. Warshaw v. Calhoun, Del.Supr., 221 A.2d 487, 492 (1966). The record demonstrates that Signal has not met this obligation.

C.

The concept of fairness has two basic aspects: fair dealing and fair price. The former embraces questions of when the transaction was timed, how it was initiated, structured, negotiated, disclosed to the directors, and how the approvals of the directors and the stockholders were obtained. The latter aspect of fairness relates to the economic and financial considerations of the proposed merger, including all relevant factors: assets, market value, earnings, future prospects, and any other elements that affect the intrinsic or inherent value of a company's stock. Moore, The "Interested" Director or Officer Transaction, 4 Del.J.Corp.L. 674, 676 (1979); Nathan Shapiro, Legal Standard of Fairness of Merger Terms Under Delaware Law, 2 Del.J.Corp.L. 44, 46–47 (1977). See Tri-Continental Corp. v. Battye, Del.Supr., 74 A.2d 71, 72 (1950); 8 Del.C. § 262(h). However, the test for fairness is not a bifurcated one as between fair dealing and price. All aspects of the issue must be examined as a whole since the question is one of entire fairness. However, in a non-fraudulent transaction we recognize that price may be the preponderant consideration outweighing other features of the merger. Here, we address the two basic aspects of fairness separately because we find reversible error as to both.

D.

Part of fair dealing is the obvious duty of candor required by *Lynch I*, supra. Moreover, one possessing superior knowledge may not mislead any stockholder by use of corporate information to which the latter is not privy. Lank v. Steiner, Del.Supr., 224 A.2d 242, 244 (1966). Delaware has long imposed this duty even upon persons who are not corporate officers or directors, but who nonetheless are privy to matters of interest or significance to their company. Brophy v. Cities Service Co., Del.Ch., 70 A.2d 5, 7 (1949). With the well-established Delaware law on the subject, and the Court of Chancery's findings of fact here, it is inevitable that the obvious conflicts posed by Arledge and Chitiea's preparation of their "feasibility study", derived from UOP information, for the sole use and benefit of Signal, cannot pass muster.

The Arledge–Chitiea report is but one aspect of the element of fair dealing. How did this merger evolve? It is clear that it was entirely initiated by Signal. The serious time constraints under which the principals acted were all set by Signal. It had not found a suitable outlet for its excess cash and considered UOP a desirable investment, particularly since it was now in a position to acquire the whole company for itself. For whatever reasons, and they were only Signal's, the entire transaction was presented to and approved by UOP's board within four business days. Standing alone, this is not necessarily indicative of any lack of fairness by a majority shareholder. It was what occurred, or more properly, what did not occur, during this brief period that makes the time constraints imposed by Signal relevant to the issue of fairness.

The structure of the transaction, again, was Signal's doing. So far as negotiations were concerned, it is clear that they were modest at best. Crawford, Signal's man at UOP, never really talked price with Signal, except to accede to its management's statements on the subject, and to convey to Signal the UOP outside directors' view that as between the $20–$21 range under consideration, it would have to be $21. The latter is not a surprising outcome, but hardly arm's length negotiations. Only the protection of benefits for UOP's key employees and the issue of Lehman Brothers' fee approached any concept of bargaining.

As we have noted, the matter of disclosure to the UOP directors was wholly flawed by the conflicts of interest raised by the Arledge–Chitiea report. All of those conflicts were resolved by Signal in its own favor without divulging any aspect of them to UOP.

This cannot but undermine a conclusion that this merger meets any reasonable test of fairness. The outside UOP directors lacked one material piece of information generated by two of their colleagues, but shared only with Signal. True, the UOP board had the Lehman Brothers' fairness opinion, but that firm has been blamed by the plaintiff for the hurried task it performed, when more properly the responsibility for this lies with Signal. There was no disclosure of the circumstances surrounding the rather cursory preparation of the Lehman Brothers' fairness opinion. Instead, the impression was given UOP's minority that a careful study had been made, when in fact speed was the hallmark, and Mr. Glanville, Lehman's partner in charge of the matter, and also a UOP director, having spent the weekend in Vermont, brought a draft of the "fairness opinion letter" to the UOP directors' meeting on March 6, 1978 with the price left blank. We can only conclude from the record that the rush imposed on Lehman Brothers by Signal's timetable contributed to the difficulties under which this investment banking firm attempted to perform its responsibilities. Yet, none of this was disclosed to UOP's minority.

Finally, the minority stockholders were denied the critical information that Signal considered a price of $24 to be a good investment. Since this would have meant over $17,000,000 more to the minority, we cannot conclude that the shareholder vote was an informed one. Under the circumstances, an approval by a majority of the minority was meaningless. *Lynch I,* 383 A.2d at 279, 281; Cahall v. Lofland, Del.Ch., 114 A. 224 (1921).

Given these particulars and the Delaware law on the subject, the record does not establish that this transaction satisfies any reasonable concept of fair dealing, and the Chancellor's findings in that regard must be reversed.

E.

Turning to the matter of price, plaintiff also challenges its fairness. His evidence was that on the date the merger was approved the stock was worth at least $26 per share. In support, he offered the testimony of a chartered investment analyst who used two basic approaches to valuation: a comparative analysis of the premium paid over market in ten other tender offer-merger combinations, and a discounted cash flow analysis.

In this breach of fiduciary duty case, the Chancellor perceived that the approach to valuation was the same as that in an appraisal proceeding. Consistent with precedent, he rejected plaintiff's method of proof and accepted defendants' evidence of value as being in accord with practice under prior case law. This means that the so-called "Delaware block" or weighted average method was employed wherein the elements of value, i.e., assets, market price, earnings, etc., were assigned a particular weight and the resulting amounts added to determine the value per share.

[The court held that the use of this valuation technique was in error. See Chapter 6, supra.]

Although the Chancellor received the plaintiff's evidence, his opinion indicates that the use of it was precluded because of past Delaware practice. While we do not suggest a monetary result one way or the other, we do think the plaintiff's evidence should be part of the factual mix and weighed as such. Until the $21 price is measured on remand by the valuation standards mandated by Delaware law, there can be no finding at the present stage of these proceedings that the price is fair. Given the lack of any candid disclosure of the material facts surrounding establishment of the $21 price, the majority of the minority vote, approving the merger, is meaningless.

The plaintiff has not sought an appraisal, but rescissory damages of the type contemplated by Lynch v. Vickers Energy Corp., Del.Supr., 429 A.2d 497, 505–06 (1981) (*Lynch II*). In view of the approach to valuation that we announce today, we see no basis in our law for *Lynch II*'s exclusive monetary formula for relief. On remand the plaintiff will be permitted to test the fairness of the $21 price by the standards we herein establish, in conformity with the principle applicable to an appraisal—that fair value be determined by taking into account all relevant factors [see 8 Del.C. § 262(h), supra]. In our view this includes the elements of rescissory damages if the Chancellor considers them susceptible of proof and a remedy appropriate to all the issues of fairness before him. To the extent that *Lynch II*, 429 A.2d at 505–06, purports to limit the Chancellor's discretion to a single remedial formula for monetary damages in a cash-out merger, it is overruled.

While a plaintiff's monetary remedy ordinarily should be confined to the more liberalized appraisal proceeding herein established, we do not intend any limitation on the historic powers of the Chancellor to grant such other relief as the facts of a particular case may dictate. The appraisal remedy we approve may not be adequate in certain cases, particularly where fraud, misrepresentation, self-dealing, deliberate waste of corporate assets, or gross and palpable overreaching are involved. Cole v. National Cash Credit Association, Del.Ch., 156 A. 183, 187 (1931). Under such circumstances, the Chancellor's powers are complete to fashion any form of equitable and monetary relief as may be appropriate, including rescissory damages. Since it is apparent that this long completed transaction is too involved to undo, and in view of the Chancellor's discretion, the award, if any, should be in the form of monetary damages based upon entire fairness standards, i.e., fair dealing and fair price.

Obviously, there are other litigants, like the plaintiff, who abjured an appraisal and whose rights to challenge the element of fair value must be preserved.[8] Accordingly, the quasi-appraisal remedy we grant the plaintiff here will apply only to: (1) this case; (2) any case now pending on appeal to this Court; (3) any case now pending in the Court of Chancery which has not yet been appealed but which may be eligible for direct appeal to this Court; (4) any case challenging a cash-out merger, the effective date of which is on or before February 1, 1983; and (5) any proposed merger to be presented at a shareholders' meeting, the notification of which is mailed to the stockholders on or before February 23, 1983. Thereafter, the provisions of 8 Del.C. § 262, as herein construed, respecting the scope of an appraisal and the means for perfecting the same, shall govern the financial remedy available to minority shareholders in a cash-out merger. Thus, we return to the well established principles of Stauffer v. Standard Brands, Inc., Del.Supr., 187 A.2d 78 (1962) and David J. Greene & Co. v.

---

8. Under 8 Del.C. § 262(a), (d) & (e), a stockholder is required to act within certain time periods to perfect the right to an appraisal.

Schenley Industries, Inc., Del.Ch., 281 A.2d 30 (1971), mandating a stockholder's recourse to the basic remedy of an appraisal.

III.

Finally, we address the matter of business purpose. The defendants contend that the purpose of this merger was not a proper subject of inquiry by the trial court. The plaintiff says that no valid purpose existed—the entire transaction was a mere subterfuge designed to eliminate the minority. The Chancellor ruled otherwise, but in so doing he clearly circumscribed the thrust and effect of *Singer*. Weinberger v. UOP, 426 A.2d at 1342–43, 1348–50. This has led to the thoroughly sound observation that the business purpose test "may be . . . virtually interpreted out of existence, as it was in *Weinberger*".[9]

The requirement of a business purpose is new to our law of mergers and was a departure from prior case law. See Stauffer v. Standard Brands, Inc., supra; David J. Greene & Co. v. Schenley Industries, Inc., supra.

In view of the fairness test which has long been applicable to parent-subsidiary mergers, Sterling v. Mayflower Hotel Corp., Del. Supr., 93 A.2d 107, 109–10 (1952), the expanded appraisal remedy now available to shareholders, and the broad discretion of the Chancellor to fashion such relief as the facts of a given case may dictate we do not believe that any additional meaningful protection is afforded minority shareholders by the business purpose requirement of the trilogy of *Singer, Tanzer,*[10] *Najjar,*[11] and their progeny. Accordingly, such requirement shall no longer be of any force or effect.

The judgment of the Court of Chancery, finding both the circumstances of the merger and the price paid the minority shareholders to be fair, is reversed. The matter is remanded for further proceedings consistent herewith. Upon remand the plaintiff's post-trial motion to enlarge the class should be granted.

* * *

Reversed and Remanded.

KAHN v. LYNCH COMMUNICATION SYSTEMS

Chapter 9, supra

---

9. Weiss, The Law of Take Out Mergers: A Historical Perspective, 56 N.Y.U.L.Rev. 624, 671, n. 300 (1981).

10. Tanzer v. International General Industries, Inc., Del.Supr., 379 A.2d 1121, 1124–25 (1977).

11. Roland International Corp. v. Najjar, Del.Supr., 407 A.2d 1032, 1036 (1979).

Glassman v. Unocal Exploration Corp.

Supreme Court of Delaware, 2001.
777 A.2d 242.

■ Before VEASEY, CHIEF JUSTICE, WALSH, HOLLAND, BERGER and STEELE, JUSTICES, constituting the Court en Banc.

■ BERGER, JUSTICE.

In this appeal, we consider the fiduciary duties owed by a parent corporation to the subsidiary's minority stockholders in the context of a "short-form" merger. Specifically, we take this opportunity to reconcile a fiduciary's seemingly absolute duty to establish the entire fairness of any self-dealing transaction with the less demanding requirements of the short-form merger statute. The statute authorizes the elimination of minority stockholders by a summary process that does not involve the "fair dealing" component of entire fairness. Indeed, the statute does not contemplate any "dealing" at all. Thus, a parent corporation cannot satisfy the entire fairness standard if it follows the terms of the short-form merger statute without more.

Unocal Corporation addressed this dilemma by establishing a special negotiating committee and engaging in a process that it believed would pass muster under traditional entire fairness review. We find that such steps were unnecessary. By enacting a statute that authorizes the elimination of the minority without notice, vote, or other traditional indicia of procedural fairness, the General Assembly effectively circumscribed the parent corporation's obligations to the minority in a short-form merger. The parent corporation does not have to establish entire fairness, and, absent fraud or illegality, the only recourse for a minority stockholder who is dissatisfied with the merger consideration is appraisal.

I. Factual and Procedural Background

Unocal Corporation is an earth resources company primarily engaged in the exploration for and production of crude oil and natural gas. At the time of the merger at issue, Unocal owned approximately 96% of the stock of Unocal Exploration Corporation ("UXC"), an oil and gas company operating in and around the Gulf of Mexico. In 1991, low natural gas prices caused a drop in both companies' revenues and earnings. Unocal investigated areas of possible cost savings and decided that, by eliminating the UXC minority, it would reduce taxes and overhead expenses.

In December 1991 the boards of Unocal and UXC appointed special committees to consider a possible merger. The UXC committee consisted of three directors who, although also directors of Unocal, were not officers or employees of the parent company. The UXC committee retained financial and legal advisors and met four times before agreeing to a merger exchange ratio of .54 shares of Unocal stock for each share of UXC. Unocal and UXC announced the merger on February 24, 1992, and it was effected, pursuant to *8 Del. C. § 253*, on May 2, 1992. The Notice of Merger and Prospectus stated the terms of the merger and advised the former UXC stockholders of their appraisal rights.

Plaintiffs filed this class action, on behalf of UXC's minority stockholders, on the day the merger was announced. They asserted, among other claims, that Unocal and its directors breached their fiduciary duties of entire fairness and full disclosure. The Court of Chancery conducted a two day trial and held that: (i) the Prospectus did not contain any material misstatements or omissions; (ii) the entire fairness standard does not control in a short-form merger; and (iii) plaintiffs' exclusive remedy in this case was appraisal. The decision of the Court of Chancery is affirmed.

II. Discussion

The short-form merger statute, as enacted in 1937, authorized a parent corporation to merge with its wholly-owned subsidiary by filing and recording a certificate evidencing the parent's ownership and its merger resolution. In 1957, the statute was expanded to include parent/subsidiary mergers where the parent company owns at least 90% of the stock of the subsidiary. The 1957 amendment also made it possible, for the first time and only in a short-form merger, to pay the minority cash for their shares, thereby eliminating their ownership interest in the company. In its current form, which has not changed significantly since 1957, *8 Del. C. § 253* provides in relevant part:

> (a) In any case in which at least 90 percent of the outstanding shares of each class of the stock of a corporation ... is owned by another corporation ..., the corporation having such stock ownership may ... merge the other corporation ... into itself ... by executing, acknowledging and filing, in accordance with § 103 of this title, a certificate of such ownership and merger setting forth a copy of the resolution of its board of directors to so merge and the date of the adoption; provided, however, that in case the parent corporation shall not own all the outstanding stock of ... the subsidiary corporation[ ], ... the resolution ... shall state the terms and conditions of the merger, including the securities, cash, property or rights to be issued, paid delivered or granted by the surviving corporation upon surrender of each share of the subsidiary corporation....

> * * *

> (d) In the event that all of the stock of a subsidiary Delaware corporation ... is not owned by the parent corporation immediately prior to the merger, the stockholders of the subsidiary Delaware corporation party to the merger shall have appraisal rights as set forth in Section 262 of this Title....

The ... question [was then] presented to this Court ... whether any equitable relief is available to minority stockholders who object to a short-form merger. In *Stauffer v. Standard Brands Incorporated*,[15]

---

15. Del.Supr., 187 A.2d 78 (1962).

minority stockholders sued to set aside the contested merger or, in the alternative, for damages. They alleged that the merger consideration was so grossly inadequate as to constitute constructive fraud and that Standard Brands breached its fiduciary duty to the minority by failing to set a fair price for their stock. The Court of Chancery held that appraisal was the stockholders' exclusive remedy, and dismissed the complaint. This Court affirmed, but explained that appraisal would not be the exclusive remedy in a short-form merger tainted by fraud or illegality:

> [T]he exception [to appraisal's exclusivity] ... refers generally to all mergers, and is nothing but a reaffirmation of the ever-present power of equity to deal with illegality or fraud. But it has no bearing here. No illegality or overreaching is shown. The dispute reduces to nothing but a difference of opinion as to value. Indeed it is difficult to imagine a case under the short merger statute in which there could be such actual fraud as would entitle a minority to set aside the merger. This is so because the very purpose of the statute is to provide the parent corporation with a means of eliminating the minority shareholder's interest in the enterprise. Thereafter the former stockholder has only a monetary claim.[16]

The *Stauffer* doctrine's viability rose and fell over the next four decades ...

In 1977, this Court [held in] ... *Singer v. Magnavox Co.*[17] ... that a controlling stockholder breaches its fiduciary duty if it effects a cash-out merger under § 251 for the sole purpose of eliminating the minority stockholders....

Singer's business purpose test was extended to short-form mergers two years later in *Roland International Corporation v. Najjar*....[18]

After *Roland*, there was not much of *Stauffer* that safely could be considered good law.... But that changed in 1983, in *Weinberger v. UOP, Inc.*,[19] when the Court dropped the business purpose test, made appraisal a more adequate remedy, and said that it was "return[ing] to the well established principles of *Stauffer* ... mandating a stockholder's recourse to the basic remedy of an appraisal." *Weinberger* focused on two subjects—the "unflinching" duty of entire fairness owed by self-dealing fiduciaries, and the "more liberalized appraisal" it established.

With respect to entire fairness, the Court explained that the concept includes fair dealing (how the transaction was timed, initiated, structured, negotiated, disclosed and approved) and fair price (all elements of value); and that the test for fairness is not bifurcated. On the subject of appraisal, the Court made several important statements: (i) courts may consider "proof of value by any techniques or methods which are generally considered acceptable in the financial community

---

16. 187 A.2d at 80.

17. Del. Supr., 380 A.2d 969 (1977).

18. Del. Supr., 407 A.2d 1032 (1979).

19. Del.Supr., 457 A.2d 701 (1983).

and otherwise admissible in court....;" (ii) fair value must be based on "all relevant factors," which include not only "elements of future value ... which are known or susceptible of proof as of the date of the merger" but also, when the court finds it appropriate, "damages, resulting from the taking, which the stockholders sustain as a class;" and (iii) "a plaintiff's monetary remedy ordinarily should be confined to the more liberalized appraisal proceeding herein established...."

By referencing ... *Stauffer* ..., one might have thought that the *Weinberger* court intended appraisal to be the exclusive remedy "ordinarily" in non-fraudulent mergers where "price ... [is] the preponderant consideration outweighing other features of the merger." In *Rabkin v. Philip A. Hunt Chemical Corp.*,[20] however, the Court dispelled that view. The *Rabkin* plaintiffs claimed that the majority stockholder breached its fiduciary duty of fair dealing by waiting until a one year commitment to pay $25 per share had expired before effecting a cash-out merger at $20 per share. The Court of Chancery dismissed the complaint, reasoning that, under *Weinberger*, plaintiffs could obtain full relief for the alleged unfair dealing in an appraisal proceeding. This Court reversed, holding that the trial court read *Weinberger* too narrowly and that appraisal is the exclusive remedy only if stockholders' complaints are limited to "judgmental factors of valuation."

Rabkin, through its interpretation of *Weinberger*, effectively eliminated appraisal as the exclusive remedy for any claim alleging breach of the duty of entire fairness. But *Rabkin* involved a long-form merger, and the Court did not discuss, in that case or any others, how its refinement of *Weinberger* impacted short-form mergers....

Mindful of this history, we must decide whether a minority stockholder may challenge a short-form merger by seeking equitable relief through an entire fairness claim. Under settled principles, a parent corporation and its directors undertaking a short-form merger are self-dealing fiduciaries who should be required to establish entire fairness, including fair dealing and fair price. The problem is that § 253 authorizes a summary procedure that is inconsistent with any reasonable notion of fair dealing. In a short-form merger, there is no agreement of merger negotiated by two companies; there is only a unilateral act—a decision by the parent company that its 90% owned subsidiary shall no longer exist as a separate entity. The minority stockholders receive no advance notice of the merger; their directors do not consider or approve it; and there is no vote. Those who object are given the right to obtain fair value for their shares through appraisal.

The equitable claim plainly conflicts with the statute. If a corporate fiduciary follows the truncated process authorized by § 253, it will not be able to establish the fair dealing prong of entire fairness. If, instead, the corporate fiduciary sets up negotiating committees, hires independent financial and legal experts, etc., then it will have lost the

---

20. *Del.Supr.*, 498 A.2d 1099 (1985).

very benefit provided by the statute—a simple, fast and inexpensive process for accomplishing a merger. We resolve this conflict by giving effect the intent of the General Assembly.[21] In order to serve its purpose, *§ 253* must be construed to obviate the requirement to establish entire fairness.

Thus, we again return to *Stauffer*, and hold that, absent fraud or illegality, appraisal is the exclusive remedy available to a minority stockholder who objects to a short-form merger. In doing so, we also reaffirm *Weinberger's* statements about the scope of appraisal. The determination of fair value must be based on *all* relevant factors, including damages and elements of future value, where appropriate. So, for example, if the merger was timed to take advantage of a depressed market, or a low point in the company's cyclical earnings, or to precede an anticipated positive development, the appraised value may be adjusted to account for those factors. We recognize that these are the types of issues frequently raised in entire fairness claims, and we have held that claims for unfair dealing cannot be litigated in an appraisal.[22] But our prior holdings simply explained that equitable claims may not be engrafted onto a statutory appraisal proceeding; stockholders may not receive rescissionary relief in an appraisal. Those decisions should not be read to restrict the elements of value that properly may be considered in an appraisal.

Although fiduciaries are not required to establish entire fairness in a short-form merger, the duty of full disclosure remains, in the context of this request for stockholder action. Where the only choice for the minority stockholders is whether to accept the merger consideration or seek appraisal, they must be given all the factual information that is material to that decision. The Court of Chancery carefully considered plaintiffs' disclosure claims and applied settled law in rejecting them. We affirm this aspect of the appeal on the basis of the trial court's decision.

III.   Conclusion

Based on the foregoing, we affirm the Court of Chancery and hold that plaintiffs' only remedy in connection with the short-form merger of UXC into Unocal was appraisal.

———

Solomon v. Pathe

Supreme Court of Delaware, 1996.
672 A.2d 35.

■ Before HOLLAND, HARTNETT, and BERGER, JJ.

■ HARTNETT, JUSTICE.

21. *Klotz v. Warner Communications, Inc.*, Del.Supr., 674 A.2d 878, 879 (1995).

22. *Alabama By-Products Corporation v. Neal*, Del.Supr., 588 A.2d 255, 257 (1991).

In this appeal, we affirm the dismissal of this action by the Court of Chancery which held that the complaint fails to state a claim upon which relief can be granted. . . .

The suit dismissed is a putative shareholder class action that challenges the fairness of a tender offer made by Credit Lyonnais Banque Nederland N.V. ("CLBN") to purchase 5.9 million shares of the publicly-traded common stock of Pathe Communications Corporation ("Pathe"). . . . The Plaintiff-Appellant, Robert Solomon ("Solomon"), is a shareholder who purportedly represents a class holding ten percent of Pathe's common stock.

CLBN is a Netherlands corporation. Giancarlo Parretti ("Parretti") was the Chief Executive Officer of Pathe when it purchased MGM/UA Communications Corporation ("MGM"). The purchase price was funded principally by loans from CLBN totalling approximately one billion dollars. As part of this loan transaction, CLBN took a perfected security interest in eighty-nine percent of Pathe's stock and ninety-eight percent of MGM's stock. Additionally, in exchange for the granting of credit, CLBN acquired the right, under two voting trust agreements, to vote 89.5 percent of Pathe's shares and substantially all of MGM's shares. . . .

. . . [Prior to May 1992,] CLBN offered to make a tender offer for an unspecified number of Pathe's publicly held shares of common stock. In response, Pathe appointed a special committee to review the proposal with the assistance of its own legal and financial advisers.

On May 1, 1992 . . . CLBN agreed to make a public tender offer of $1.50 per share for up to 5.8 million of Pathe's publicly held shares. . . . On May 7th, CLBN . . . made the promised tender offer for the Pathe shares.

. . . The amended complaint asserted that the tender offer was unfair to all shareholders (except the Defendants) who tendered their shares in response to the tender offer. Additionally, it asserted that the tender offer price was "coercive" and amounted to a breach of loyalty by CLBN as controlling shareholder of Pathe and MGM. Solomon also asserted in his amended complaint that the Pathe Board was under the control of CLBN; that the Defendants exhibited impropriety by failing to retain independent advisers; and that the Defendants failed "to assure that no conflict of interest existed."

CLBN moved, pursuant to Chancery Rule 12(b), to dismiss the suit, arguing that . . . the complaint failed to state a claim upon which relief could be granted. . . . [The Court of Chancery dismissed the complaint with prejudice.]

After a careful review of the amended complaint, we agree with the Chancellor that it fails to state a claim upon which relief can be granted. . . .

. . . [The complaint] attempts to assert a breach of the duty of fair dealing by the directors because they did not oppose the tender offer. The asserted unfairness of the tender offer is based on its allegedly inadequate price. The Chancellor's holding that none of the facts cited by Solomon "can be said to arouse as much as a fleeting doubt of the fairness of the [disclosure] or the $1.50 tender offer" price is correct as a matter of law.

In the case of totally voluntary tender offers, as here, courts do not impose any right of the shareholders to receive a particular price.... Delaware law recognizes that, as to allegedly voluntary tender offers (in contrast to cash-out mergers), the determinative factor as to voluntariness is whether coercion is present, or whether there is "materially false or misleading disclosures made to shareholders in connection with the offer." *Eisenberg v. Chicago Milwaukee Corp.*, Del.Ch., 537 A.2d 1051, 1056 (1987) (citations omitted). A transaction may be considered involuntary, despite being voluntary in appearance and form, if one of these factors is present. *Id.* There is no well-plead allegation of any coercion or false or misleading disclosures in the present case, however.

Moreover, in the absence of coercion or disclosure violations, the adequacy of the price in a voluntary tender offer cannot be an issue. *Weinberger*, 457 A.2d at 703.... Solomon has plead no facts from which there could be drawn a reasonable inference that there was coercion or lack of complete disclosure. The amended complaint focuses mainly on a conclusory allegation that coercion was present. The complaint, therefore, falls well short of the minimum notice requirements. "Conclusions ... will not be accepted as true without specific allegations of fact to support them." ...

For the foregoing reasons, the Court of Chancery's dismissal of Solomon's claim under Rule 12(b)(6) for failure to state a claim upon which relief can be granted is AFFIRMED.

NOTE ON PURE RESOURCES, INC. SHAREHOLDERS LITIGATION

In In re Pure Resources, Inc. Shareholders Litigation, 808 A.2d 421 (Del. Ch. 2002), Unocal, which owned 65% of Pure Resources, made a tender offer for the remaining 35%. The tender offer included a non-waivable condition under which the offer would be effective only if a majority of the shares not owned by Unocal were tendered. Shareholders in Pure Resources sought to enjoin the tender offer on the ground that the entire fairness standard of Kahn v. Lynch, supra, was applicable to the transaction, and the transaction did not satisfy that standard because the tender-offer price was inadequate. Unocal replied that Kahn v. Lynch was inapplicable, because that case applied only to negotiated transactions between a controlling shareholder and a controlled corporation, and Unocal had made a tender offer, rather than entering into a negotiated transaction. Accordingly, Unocal argued, under Solomon v. Pathe Communications, supra, Unocal was free to make the offer at whatever price it chose, so long Unocal did not (i) "structurally coerce" the Pure Resources minority by suggesting explicitly or implicitly that injurious events would occur to those shareholders who failed to tender; or (ii) mislead the Pure Resources minority into tendering by concealing or misstating material facts.

Vice Chancellor Strine held that the entire-fairness standard of Kahn v. Lynch was not applicable to a tender offer by a controlling shareholder, but that such a tender offer should be deemed non-coercive only when it is subject to the condition that a majority of the minority accept the tender; the controlling shareholder promises to consummate a prompt short-form merger at the same price if as a result of the tender it acquires ends up owning more that 90% of the controlled corporation's shares; and the controlling shareholder has made no threats that if the tender offer fails there will be retribution:

> This case ... involves an aspect of Delaware law fraught with doctrinal tension: what equitable standard of fiduciary conduct applies when a controlling shareholder seeks to acquire the rest of the company's shares? ...

> In building the common law, judges ... cannot escape making normative choices, based on imperfect information about the world. This reality clearly pervades the area of corporate law implicated by this case. When a transaction to buy out the minority is proposed, is it more important to the development of strong capital markets to hold controlling stockholders and target boards to very strict (and litigation-intensive) standards of fiduciary conduct? Or is more stockholder wealth generated if less rigorous protections are adopted, which permit acquisitions to proceed so long as the majority has not misled or strong-armed the minority? Is such flexibility in fact beneficial to minority stockholders because it encourages liquidity-generating tender offers to them and provides incentives for acquirers to pay hefty premiums to buy control, knowing that control will be accompanied by legal rules that permit a later "going private" transaction to occur in a relatively non-litigious manner?

> At present, the Delaware case law has two strands of authority that answer these questions differently. In one strand, which deals with situations in which controlling stockholders negotiate a merger agreement with the target board to buy out the minority, our decisional law emphasizes the protection of minority stockholders against unfairness. In the other strand, which deals with situations when a controlling stockholder seeks to acquire the rest of the company's shares through a tender offer followed by a short-form merger under 8 Del.C. § 253, Delaware case precedent facilitates the free flow of capital between willing buyers and willing sellers of shares, so long as the consent of the sellers is not procured by inadequate or misleading information or by wrongful compulsion.

> These strands appear to treat economically similar transactions as categorically different simply because the method by which the controlling stockholder proceeds varies. This disparity in treatment persists even though the two basic methods (negotiated merger versus tender offer/short-form merger) pose similar

threats to minority stockholders. Indeed, it can be argued that the distinction in approach subjects the transaction that is more protective of minority stockholders when implemented with appropriate protective devices—a merger negotiated by an independent committee with the power to say no and conditioned on a majority of the minority vote—to more stringent review than the more dangerous form of a going private deal—an unnegotiated tender offer made by a majority stockholder. The latter transaction is arguably less protective than a merger of the kind described, because the majority stockholder-offeror has access to inside information, and the offer requires disaggregated stockholders to decide whether to tender quickly, pressured by the risk of being squeezed out in a short-form merger at a different price later or being left as part of a much smaller public minority. This disparity creates a possible incoherence in our law. . . .

To illustrate this possible incoherence in our law, it is useful to sketch out these two strands. I begin with negotiated mergers. In *Kahn v. Lynch Communication Systems, Inc.*, the Delaware Supreme Court addressed the standard of review that applies when a controlling stockholder attempts to acquire the rest of the corporation's shares in a negotiated merger pursuant to 8 Del.C. § 251. The Court held that the stringent entire fairness form of review governed regardless of whether: i) the target board was comprised of a majority of independent directors; ii) a special committee of the target's independent directors was empowered to negotiate and veto the merger; and iii) the merger was made subject to approval by a majority of the disinterested target stockholders. . . .

The second strand of cases involves tender offers made by controlling stockholders—i.e., the kind of transaction Unocal has proposed. The prototypical transaction addressed by this strand involves a tender offer by the controlling stockholder addressed to the minority stockholders. In that offer, the controlling stockholder promises to buy as many shares as the minority will sell but may subject its offer to certain conditions. For example, the controlling stockholder might condition the offer on receiving enough tenders for it to obtain 90% of the subsidiary's shares, thereby enabling the controlling stockholder to consummate a short-form merger under 8 Del.C. § 253 at either the same or a different price. . . .

Before *Glassman*, transactional planners had wondered whether the back-end of the tender offer/short-form merger transaction would subject the controlling stockholder to entire fairness review. *Glassman* seemed to answer that question favorably from the standpoint of controlling stockholders, and to therefore encourage the tender offer/short-form merger form of acquisition as presenting a materially less troublesome method of proceeding than a negotiated merger.

Why? Because the legal rules that governed the front end of the tender offer/short-form merger method of acquisition had already provided a more flexible, less litigious path to acquisition for controlling stockholders than the negotiated merger route. Tender offers are not addressed by the Delaware General Corporation Law ("DGCL"), a factor that has been of great importance in shaping the line of decisional law addressing tender offers by controlling stockholders—but not, as I will discuss, tender offers made by third parties.

Because no consent or involvement of the target board is statutorily mandated for tender offers, our courts have recognized that "[i]n the case of totally voluntary tender offers ... courts do not impose any right of the shareholders to receive a particular price. Delaware law recognizes that, as to allegedly voluntary tender offers (in contrast to cash-out mergers), the determinative factors as to voluntariness are whether coercion is present, or whether there are materially false or misleading disclosures made to stockholders in connection with the offer.[28]" ...

The differences between this approach, which I will identify with the *Solomon* line of cases, and that of *Lynch* are stark. To begin with, the controlling stockholder is said to have no duty to pay a fair price, irrespective of its power over the subsidiary. Even more striking is the different manner in which the coercion concept is deployed. In the tender offer context addressed by *Solomon* and its progeny, coercion is defined in the more traditional sense as a wrongful threat that has the effect of forcing stockholders to tender at the wrong price to avoid an even worse fate later on, a type of coercion I will call structural coercion. The inherent coercion that *Lynch* found to exist when controlling stockholders seek to acquire the minority's stake is not even a cognizable concern for the common law of corporations if the tender offer method is employed.

This latter point is illustrated by those cases that squarely hold that a tender is not actionably coercive if the majority stockholder decides to: (i) condition the closing of the tender offer on support of a majority of the minority and (ii) promise that it would consummate a short-form merger on the same terms as the tender offer. In those circumstances, at least, these cases can be read to bar a claim against the majority stockholder even if the price offered is below what would be considered fair in an entire fairness hearing ("fair price") or an appraisal action ("fair value"). That is, in the tender offer context, our courts consider it sufficient protection against coercion to give effective veto power over the offer to a majority of the minority. Yet that very same protection is considered insufficient to displace fairness review in the negotiated merger context....

28. *Solomon v. Pathe Communications Corp.*, 672 A.2d 35, 39 (Del.1996) (citations and quotations omitted).

The problem is that nothing about the tender offer method of corporate acquisition makes the 800 pound gorilla's retributive capabilities less daunting to minority stockholders. Indeed, many commentators would argue that the tender offer form is more coercive than a merger vote. In a merger vote, stockholders can vote no and still receive the transactional consideration if the merger prevails. In a tender offer, however, a non-tendering shareholder individually faces an uncertain fate. That stockholder could be one of the few who holds out, leaving herself in an even more thinly traded stock with little hope of liquidity and subject to a § 253 merger at a lower price or at the same price but at a later (and, given the time value of money, a less valuable) time. The 14D–9 warned Pure's minority stockholders of just this possibility. For these reasons, some view tender offers as creating a prisoner's dilemma—distorting choice and creating incentives for stockholders to tender into offers that they believe are inadequate in order to avoid a worse fate. But whether or not one views tender offers as more coercive of shareholder choice than negotiated mergers with controlling stockholders, it is difficult to argue that tender offers are materially freer and more reliable measures of stockholder sentiment. . . .

. . . [T]he preferable policy choice is to continue to adhere to the more flexible and less constraining *Solomon* approach, while giving some greater recognition to the inherent coercion and structural bias concerns that motivate the *Lynch* line of cases. Adherence to the *Solomon* rubric as a general matter, moreover, is advisable in view of the increased activism of institutional investors and the greater information flows available to them. Investors have demonstrated themselves capable of resisting tender offers made by controlling stockholders on occasion, and even the lead plaintiff here expresses no fear of retribution. This does not mean that controlling stockholder tender offers do not pose risks to minority stockholders; it is only to acknowledge that the corporate law should not be designed on the assumption that diversified investors are infirm but instead should give great deference to transactions approved by them voluntarily and knowledgeably. . . .

The potential for coercion and unfairness posed by controlling stockholders who seek to acquire the balance of the company's shares by acquisition requires some equitable reinforcement, in order to give proper effect to the concerns undergirding *Lynch*. In order to address the prisoner's dilemma problem, our law should consider an acquisition tender offer by a controlling stockholder non-coercive only when: 1) it is subject to a non-waivable majority of the minority tender condition; 2) the controlling stockholder promises to consummate a prompt § 253 merger at the same price if it obtains more than 90% of the shares; and 3) the controlling stockholder has made no retributive threats. Those protections . . . minimize the distorting influence of the tendering process on voluntary choice. They also recognize the adverse conditions that confront stockholders who find themselves owning what have become very thinly traded shares. These conditions also provide a partial cure to the disaggregation problem, by providing a realistic non-tendering goal the minority can achieve to prevent the offer from proceeding altogether.

The informational and timing advantages possessed by controlling stockholders also require some countervailing protection if the minority is to truly be afforded the opportunity to make an informed, voluntary tender decision. In this regard, the majority stockholder owes a duty to permit the independent directors on the target board both free rein and adequate time to react to the tender offer, by (at the very least) hiring their own advisors, providing the minority with a recommendation as to the advisability of the offer, and disclosing adequate information for the minority to make an informed judgment. For their part, the independent directors have a duty to undertake these tasks in good faith and diligently, and to pursue the best interests of the minority. . . .

Turning specifically to Unocal's Offer, I conclude that the application of these principles yields the following result. The Offer, in its present form, is coercive because it includes within the definition of the "minority" those stockholders who are affiliated with Unocal as directors and officers. It also includes the management of Pure, whose incentives are skewed by their employment, their severance agreements [which gave the managers the right to severance payments, up to three times their annual salaries and bonuses, upon successful completion of the tender offer], and their Put Agreements [which give the managers the right to sell their Pure shares to Unocal upon the occurrence of certain events, arguably including the successful completion of Unocal's tender offer, at an amount that could exceed the tender-offer price]. This is, of course, a problem that can be cured if Unocal amends the Offer to condition it on approval of a majority of Pure's unaffiliated stockholders. Requiring the minority to be defined exclusive of stockholders whose independence from the controlling stockholder is compromised is the better legal rule (and result). Too often, it will be the case that officers and directors of controlled subsidiaries have voting incentives that are not perfectly aligned with their economic interest in their stock and who are more than acceptably susceptible to influence from controlling stockholders. Aside, however, from this glitch in the majority of the minority condition, I conclude that Unocal's Offer satisfies the other requirements of "non-coerciveness." Its promise to consummate a prompt § 253 merger is sufficiently specific, and Unocal has made no retributive threats. . . .

For all these reasons, therefore, I find that the plaintiffs do not have a probability of success on the merits of their attack on the Offer, with the exception that the majority of the minority condition is flawed. . . .

NOTE ON MERGER FREEZEOUTS

In a freezeout of minority shareholders in a publicly held corporation by a majority shareholder that is itself publicly held, it is at least arguable that (i) the expectations of the transferor corporation's shareholders are purely centered on a passive investment, which has ready financial substitutes; (ii) efficiency gains are likely to result from the combination, and (iii) the frozen-out minority shareholders "are free, if they wish, to restore their participation by purchasing [the survivor's] shares in the market. That a 'transaction' is required is simply a cost (possibly one that ought to be reimbursed) of using cash or debt instead of stock [to effect the merger], but the exchange is nevertheless 'fair' if the amount received is sufficient to enable a recipient to obtain the same stock interest that he would have had if the parent had issued its shares in a ratio reflecting the premerger values of the companies." Brudney Chirelstein, A Restatement of Corporate Freezeouts, 87 Yale L.J. 1354, 1374–75 (1978). This reasoning would not apply where the survivor is closely held, and several cases have struck down cash mergers into closely held corporations organized by the transferor's controlling shareholders for the sole purpose of effecting the freezeout.

———

COGGINS v. NEW ENGLAND PATRIOTS FOOTBALL CLUB, INC., 397 Mass. 525, 492 N.E.2d 1112 (1986). "Unlike the Delaware court . . . we believe that the 'business-purpose' test is an additional useful means under our statutes and case law for examining a transaction in which a controlling stockholder eliminates the minority interest in a corporation. . . . This concept of fair dealing is not limited to close corporations but applies to judicial review of cash freeze-out mergers. . . .

"The defendants argue that judicial review of a merger cannot be invoked by disgruntled stockholders, absent illegal or fraudulent conduct. They rely on G.L. c. 156B, § 98 (1984 ed.).[12] In the defendants' view, 'the Superior Court's finding of liability was premised solely on the claimed inadequacy of the offering price.' Any dispute over offering price, they urge, must be resolved solely through the statutory remedy of appraisal. . . .

"We have held in regard to so called 'close corporations' that the statute does not divest the courts of their equitable jurisdiction to assure that the conduct of controlling stockholders does not violate the fiduciary principles governing the relationship between majority and minority stockholders. *Pupecki v. James Madison Corp.*, 376 Mass. 212, 216–217, 382 N.E.2d 1030 (1978) (when controlling stockholder

---

12. The enforcement by a stockholder of his right to receive payment for his shares in the manner provided in this chapter shall be an exclusive remedy except that this chapter shall not exclude the right of such stock-holder to bring or maintain an appropriate proceeding to obtain relief on the ground that such corporate action will be or is illegal or fraudulent as to him. G.L. c. 156B, § 98.

fails to assure that corporation receives adequate consideration for its assets, transaction is illegal or fraudulent, and G.L. c. 156B, § 98, does not foreclose review). 'Where the director's duty of loyalty to the corporation is in conflict with his self-interest the court will vigorously scrutinize the situation.' *American Discount Corp. v. Kaitz,* 348 Mass. 706, 711, 206 N.E.2d 156 (1965). The court is justified in exercising its equitable power when a violation of fiduciary duty is claimed.

"The dangers of self-dealing and abuse of fiduciary duty are greatest in freeze-out situations like the Patriots merger, where a controlling stockholder and corporate director chooses to eliminate public ownership. It is in these cases that a judge should examine with closest scrutiny the motives and the behavior of the controlling stockholder. A showing of compliance with statutory procedures is an insufficient substitute for the inquiry of the courts when a minority stockholder claims that the corporate action 'will be or is illegal or fraudulent as to him.' G.L. c. 156B, § 98. *Leader v. Hycor, Inc.,* 395 Mass. 215, 221, 479 N.E.2d 173 (1985) (judicial review may be had of claims of breach of fiduciary duty and unfairness).

"Judicial scrutiny should begin with recognition of the basic principle that the duty of a corporate director must be to further the legitimate goals of the corporation. The result of a freeze-out merger is the elimination of public ownership in the corporation. The controlling faction increases its equity from a majority to 100%, using corporate processes and corporate assets. The corporate directors who benefit from this transfer of ownership must demonstrate how the legitimate goals of the corporation are furthered. A director of a corporation violates his fiduciary duty when he uses the corporation for his or his family's personal benefit in a manner detrimental to the corporation. *Widett Widett v. Snyder,* 392 Mass. 778, 785–786, 467 N.E.2d 1312 (1984). See *Buckman v. Elm Hill Realty Co. of Peabody,* 312 Mass. 10, 15, 42 N.E.2d 814 (1942). Because the danger of abuse of fiduciary duty is especially great in a freeze-out merger, the court must be satisfied that the freeze-out was for the advancement of a legitimate corporate purpose. If satisfied that elimination of public ownership is in furtherance of a business purpose, the court should then proceed to determine if the transaction was fair by examining the totality of the circumstances. . . .' "

ALPERT v. 28 WILLIAMS ST. CORP., 63 N.Y.2d 557, 483 N.Y.S.2d 667, 473 N.E.2d 19 (1984). "In the context of a freeze-out merger, variant treatment of the minority shareholders—i.e., causing their removal will be justified when related to the advancement of a general corporate interest. The benefit need not be great, but it must be for the corporation. For example, if the sole purpose of the merger is reduction of the number of profit sharers—in contrast to increasing the corporation's capital or profits, or improving its management structure—there will exist no 'independent corporate interest' (see Schwartz v. Marien, 37 N.Y.2d 487, 492, 373 N.Y.S.2d 122, 335 N.E.2d

334, supra). All of these purposes ultimately seek to increase the individual wealth of the remaining shareholders. What distinguishes a proper corporate purpose from an improper one is that, with the former, removal of the minority shareholders furthers the objective of conferring some general gain upon the corporation. Only then will the fiduciary duty of good and prudent management of the corporation serve to override the concurrent duty to treat all shareholders fairly (see Klurfeld v. Equity Enterprises, 79 A.D.2d 124, 136, 436 N.Y.S.2d 303, supra). We further note that a finding that there was an independent corporate purpose for the action taken by the majority will not be defeated merely by the fact that the corporate objective could have been accomplished in another way, or by the fact that the action chosen was not the best way to achieve the bona fide business objective.''

NOTE ON FREEZEOUTS BY REVERSE STOCK SPLITS

Most states allow a corporation to amend its certificate to either split or consolidate its outstanding shares, so that the number of shares held by each shareholder is increased (in the case of a split) or reduced (in the case of a consolidation). A consolidation of outstanding stock—commonly referred to as a ''reverse split''—often results in some shareholders becoming entitled to fractional shares, as where the stock is consolidated in the ratio of 3:1 and some holdings are not divisible by 3. Because fractional shares can raise administrative difficulties, most statutes allow a corporation to compel shareholders to accept cash in lieu of such shares. Some corporations have used these statutory provisions to effect a freezeout. This is done by (1) adopting a reverse split that employs a ratio whose numerator is higher than the largest minority shareholding, so that all minority holdings are reduced to fractional shares, and then (2) compelling the minority shareholders to accept cash in lieu of their fractional shares. For example, in Teschner v. Chicago Title & Trust Co., 59 Ill.2d 452, 322 N.E.2d 54 (1974), Lincoln National Corp. had acquired 2,233,321 shares of the stock of Chicago Title—constituting 99.9% of Chicago Title's outstanding common stock—through a tender offer and private purchases. However, 1,890 shares, including 63 held by plaintiff, remained outstanding. To eliminate these shares Lincoln caused Chicago Title to adopt a plan involving a 600:1 reverse split and a compulsory surrender of fractional shares for cash. Since no single minority shareholder owned 600 shares, under the plan all of the minority's stock would be converted into fractional shares and thereby eliminated. The court upheld the transaction, on analogy to the short-form merger statutes:

> . . . It can be said in general that unless there is fraud which would entitle dissenting shareholders to other relief, interests of minority shareholders can be terminated. . . . For a specific example, a majority of jurisdictions, among them Illinois . . . provide

for short-mergers.... The statutes in effect allow the termination of the minority shareholders' interests by the payment of cash for the minority's shares....

We do not say that under all circumstances minority shareholders will be denied relief when the majority has proceeded under the provisions of the Act, but we do not consider that the plaintiff here has shown grounds for the relief she seeks.

... The plaintiff's complaint made no claim of fraud or deceptive conduct by the defendants. It did not charge that the exchange offer was unfair or that the price later offered for the shares was inadequate. The defendants stated in the circuit court that the corporate action of reclassifying stock and eliminating fractional shares was basically to reduce corporate expenses and simplify and facilitate procedures. The plaintiff did not allege or show any improper purpose on the part of the defendants. Considering the circumstances the judgment in favor of the defendants was proper.

See also Leader v. Hycor, Inc., 395 Mass. 215, 479 N.E.2d 173 (1985).

However, in Clark v. Pattern Analysis & Recognition Corp., 87 Misc.2d 385, 384 N.Y.S.2d 660 (1976), the court issued a temporary injunction against a similar plan. Plaintiffs had purchased Pattern stock during their employment by the corporation. After they left Pattern's employ, Pattern adopted a plan involving a 4000:1 reverse stock split and a compulsory exchange of fractional shares for cash, which would have eliminated plaintiffs' interests. Pattern justified the plan on the ground that if plaintiffs were eliminated, all remaining shareholders would be Pattern employees, and the confidentiality of Pattern's financial statements could be better maintained. Plaintiffs showed, however, that other non-employees, who were close relatives of the controlling shareholders, would remain as shareholders, and that Pattern had never issued a financial statement. The court stated, "Where there is an allegation of fraud, illegality or bad faith, coupled with a tenuous showing of legitimate corporate business purpose, fairness requires that a minority shareholder be afforded an opportunity to fully contest the actions of the majority before he is deprived of his property. Where a strong and compelling corporate business purpose is shown, however, the courts should not interfere at the mere whim of a dissident shareholder."

CAL. CORP. CODE § 407

[See Statutory Supplement]

ALI, PRINCIPLES OF CORPORATE GOVERNANCE §§ 5.15, 7.25

[See Statutory Supplement]

(h) GOING PRIVATE

"Going private" involves the conversion of a corporation that is publicly held into one that is privately held—or, more particularly, the conversion of a corporation whose stock is registered under the 1934 Act, and listed on a Stock Exchange or actively traded over the counter, into one whose stock is unregistered, unlisted, and traded thinly, if at all. While going private is often accomplished through a freezeout, the two categories are not entirely coextensive: going private, unlike freezeouts, does not necessarily involve *legal* compulsion, since it may be accomplished through purchases of minority shares. As the following material shows, however, such purchases, while apparently involving voluntary action on the minority's part, may in fact involve very little meaningful choice, and are often accomplished in part by the implicit or explicit threat that those who do not sell voluntarily will be made to sell involuntarily, through use of a cashout merger or other freezeout device.

Address by A.A. Sommer, Jr., Commissioner, Securities and Exchange Commission, CCH, Fed'l Sec.L.Rep.

[1974–75 transfer binder] ¶ 80,010.

During the sixties and early seventies innumerable companies "went public," that is, publicly offered their securities.... All of these companies invited the public to share in their fortunes....

What is happening now is this: as market prices of stock have plummeted, often to levels below book value, many companies have commenced the process of going private....

The simplest way is an offer to pay the shareholders who accept a stipulated price, usually something in excess of the market price. This seems simple enough: the shareholder can take the offer or leave it, he is under no compulsion, and in fact, the offer may be a significant favor to him, since it may be the highest price he will see for some time. But even this simple approach has within it, in my estimation, troublesome elements. Usually, because of the necessities of full disclosure in our corporate life—largely policed and demanded by the SEC—the document which communicates the tender offer tells the awful truth. First, if significant numbers of shareholders respond to the tender, the shareholder who considers staying aboard faces significant losses. If the number of shareholders drops under 300 he will lose the network of federal protections built over a period of forty years for his benefit: no assurance of comprehensive disclosure, only limited protections against insider chicanery and so on. If he chooses to stay aboard he may find the liquidity of his investment—the ability to sell readily at a price reasonably proximate to the last sale—reduced, perhaps completely destroyed. Further, if management buys or otherwise acquires or has the power to bring it about, it may "merge out" the remaining minority and compel them in effect to sell their investments. Under the laws of the states in which most public corporations are incorporated, so-called cash mergers are allowed, that is, the shareholders of a company being acquired by another, instead of receiving stock of the acquiring company (the pattern of the typical merger) can be compelled to take cash in the amount determined by the merger agreement. . . .

Faced with the prospect of a force-out merger, or a market reduced to glacial activity and the liquidity of the Mojave Desert, and deprived of most of the benefits of the federal securities laws, how real is the choice of the shareholder confronting the offer of management to acquire his shares, usually not with their own resources, but with the corporation's resources that really belong to him and his fellow shareholders? In short, he usually decides he damn well better take the money and run. . . .

Is all this ethical? I would say to you there is at the minimum deep doubt of that. The spectacle of entrepreneurs inviting the public in when they can command high prices for their stock, and then squeezing them out with little or no practical choice in the matter at substantially reduced prices is hardly one to warm the soul of Thomas Aquinas or Aristotle. The corporation, and often the controlling interests, have been enriched with the proceeds of the public offerings of the past; with those proceeds the corporation grew and prospered, then, with the power deriving from their managerial positions and shareholdings, the insiders take over the whole corporation for themselves.

In one recent instance public offerings netted $696,000 for the corporation, over $12,500,000 for the offering shareholders. The corporation has now proposed to acquire all the stock held by minority shareholders for $11.00 per share. If all of the minority shareholders tender, they would receive $3.00 in cash and $8.00 in ten year subordinated debentures (which the company believes will sell at a substantial discount) for shares which were originally offered at $17.50 a share and three years ago at $21.75 a share; the dominant shareholder would go from a 7% interest to 43%, with over 3.7 million dollars (less taxes) provided by the public now safely locked up for her benefit. On a pro forma basis, had all public shares been repurchased on the basis proposed at the beginning of 1973, the corporate profits attributable to her interest would have risen from $236,000 to $1,107,000 in 1973—over 400%—and from $167,000 to $688,000 for the first ten months of 1974—again over 400%—and without a single dime of additional investment by her!

I would suggest there is something wrong with that. . . .[1]

---

1. See also Kahn v. United States Sugar Corp., 1985 WL 4449 (Del.Ch.1985). (Footnote by ed.)

SECURITIES EXCHANGE ACT RULE 13e–3 AND SCHEDULE 13E–3

[See Statutory Supplement]

———

SECTION 2.   TENDER OFFERS

———

SECURITIES EXCHANGE ACT §§ 13(d), (e), 14(d), (e)

[See Statutory Supplement]

———

SECURITIES EXCHANGE ACT RULES 13d–1, 13d–3, 13d–5, 13e–1, 13e–4, 14d1 to 14d–4, 14d–6 TO 14d–10, 14e–1 TO 14e–3, 14e–5

———

SCHEDULE TO

[See Statutory Supplement]

———

SCHEDULE [I4D–9]

[See Statutory Supplement]

———

HART-SCOTT-RODINO ACT

[See Statutory Supplement]

———

NOTE ON TERMINOLOGY

The legal profession has developed a rich terminology in connection with tender offers. The terms are too numerous and change too quickly to permit a comprehensive glossary, and some of the terms are fairly well defined in the cases that follow. This Note defines a few of the more important terms that are not defined in those cases.

Raider. The term *raider* refers to a person (normally, although not necessarily, a corporation) that makes a tender offer. The term is invidious; a more accurate term is *bidder.*

Target. The corporation whose shares the raider or bidder seeks to acquire is referred to as the *target.*

White knight. Often the management of a target realizes that it will be taken over, but prefers a takeover by someone (sometimes, anyone) other than the original bidder. The management therefore solicits competing tender offers from other corporations. These more friendly corporations are known as *white knights.*

Lock-up. A *lock-up* is a device that is designed to protect one bidder (normally, a friendly bidder or white knight) against competition by other bidders (deemed less friendly). The favored bidder is given an option to acquire selected assets, or a given amount of shares, of the target at a favorable price under designated conditions. These conditions usually involve either defeat of the favored bidder's attempt to acquire the corporation, or the occurrence of events that would make that defeat likely.

Crown jewels. To defeat or discourage a takeover bid by a disfavored bidder, the target's management may sell or (more usually) give to a white knight a lock-up option that covers the target's most desirable business or, at least, the business most coveted by the disfavored bidder—its *crown jewels.*

Fair-price provisions. A *fair-price provision* requires that a super-majority (usually eighty percent) of the voting power of a corporation must approve any merger or similar combination with an acquiror who owns a specified interest in the corporation (usually twenty percent of the voting power). The supermajority vote is not required under certain conditions—most notably, if the transaction is approved by a majority of those directors who are not affiliated with the acquiror and who were directors at the time the acquiror reached the specified level of ownership of the company, or if certain minimum-price criteria and procedural requirements are satisfied. A fair-price provision discourages purchasers whose objective is to seek control of a corporation at a relatively cheap price, and discourages accumulations of large blocks, because it reduces the options that an acquiror has once it reaches the specified level of shares.

Management buyout. A *management buyout (MBO)* is an acquisition for cash or non-convertible senior securities of the business of a public corporation, by a newly organized corporation in which members of the former management of the public corporation will have a significant equity interest, pursuant to a merger or other form of combination. See Lowenstein, Management Buyouts, 85 Colum.L.Rev. 730, 732 (1985).

Leverage. *Leverage* involves the use of debt to increase the return on equity. The extent of leverage is measured by the ratio of debt to equity. The higher the ratio, the greater the leverage (or, to put it differently, the more highly leveraged the corporation is).

Leveraged buyout. A *leveraged buyout (LBO)* is an MBO that is highly leveraged—that is, in which the newly organized acquiring corporation has a very high amount of debt in relation to its equity.

Characteristically, an LBO is arranged by a firm that specializes in such transactions; can find investors (or will itself invest) along with senior management in the new firm's securities; and can arrange for (or help arrange for) placement of the massive amount of debt that the new corporation must issue to finance the acquisition of the old corporation's business.

Junk bonds. A *junk bond* is a bond that has an unusually high risk of default (and is therefore below investment grade), but correspondingly carries an unusually high yield. (The theory is that by diversification—that is, by holding a portfolio of junk bonds—investors in junk bonds can insulate themselves from catastrophic loss if any one bond issue goes under.) Because an LBO is so highly leveraged, much or most of the debt issued to finance an LBO usually consists of junk bonds.

No-shop clauses. A board of a corporation that enters into an agreement for a merger or other corporate combination (whether with a white knight or otherwise) may agree that it will recommend the combination to its shareholders, that it will not shop around for a more attractive deal, or both.

Poison pills. In essence, a *poison pill* (also known as a *Rights Plan* or a *Shareholder Rights Plan*) is a plan under which the board of directors of a corporation creates Rights that are distributed or distributable to shareholders. Under the Rights, upon the occurrence of certain events shareholders *other than a tender-offer bidder or prospective bidder* have the right to purchase stock in the corporation, or under certain circumstances in an acquiror, at a deep discount—normally, half-price. Because the potential exercise of the Rights would dramatically dilute the value of the target stock that the bidder proposes to acquire, the mere potential that the Rights will be exercised may serve as a deterrent to making a bid in the first place (although for reasons that will be explored in the materials that follow, a pill is usually not a complete show-stopper).

The actual mechanics of pills are highly complex, and have evolved over time. Here is a description of a fairly standard modern version of the pill, taken from Carmody v. Toll Brothers, Inc., 723 A.2d 1180 (Del.Ch. 1998). The corporation whose pill is described was named Toll Brothers:

> The Rights Plan would operate as follows: there would be a dividend distribution of one preferred stock purchase right (a "Right") for each outstanding share of common stock as of July 11, 1997. Initially the Rights would attach to the company's outstanding common shares, and each Right would initially entitle the holder to purchase one thousandth of a share of a newly registered series Junior A Preferred Stock for $100. The Rights would become exercisable, and would trade separately from the common shares, after the "Distribution Date," which is defined as the earlier of (a) ten business days following a public announcement that an acquiror has acquired, or obtained the right to acquire, beneficial ownership of 15% or more of the company's

outstanding common shares (the "Stock Acquisition Date"), or (b) ten business days after the commencement of a tender offer or exchange offer that would result in a person or group beneficially owning 15% or more of the company's outstanding common shares. Once exercisable, the Rights remain exercisable until their Final Expiration Date (June 12, 2007, ten years after the adoption of the Plan), unless the Rights are earlier redeemed by the company.

The dilutive mechanism of the Rights is "triggered" by certain defined events. One such event is the acquisition of 15% or more of Toll Brothers' stock by any person or group of affiliated or associated persons. Should that occur, each Rights holder (except the acquiror and its affiliates and associates) becomes entitled to buy two shares of Toll Brothers common stock or other securities at half price. That is, the value of the stock received when the Right is exercised is equal to two times the exercise price of the Right. In that manner, this so-called "flip in" feature of the Rights Plan would massively dilute the value of the holdings of the unwanted acquiror. . . .

The "flip-in" feature of a rights plan is triggered when the acquiror crosses the specified ownership threshold, regardless of the acquiror's intentions with respect to the use of the shares. At that point, rights vest in all shareholders other than the acquiror, and as a result, those holders become entitled to acquire additional shares of voting stock at a substantially discounted price, usually 50% of the market price. Commonly, rights plans also contain a "flip-over" feature entitling target company shareholders (again, other than the acquiror) to purchase shares of the acquiring company at a reduced price. That feature is activated when, after a "flip-in" triggering event, the acquiror initiates a triggering event, such as a merger, self-dealing transaction, or sale of assets. . . .

The Rights [in the case at bar] have a standard "flip over" feature, which is triggered if after the Stock Acquisition Date, the company is made a party to a merger in which Toll Brothers is not the surviving corporation, or in which it is the surviving corporation and its common stock is changed or exchanged. In either event, each Rights holder becomes entitled to purchase common stock of the acquiring company, again at half-price, thereby impairing the acquiror's capital structure and drastically diluting the interest of the acquiror's other stockholders.

Id. at 1183–84 n.5.

A flip-over pill is normally triggered only by a corporate combination between the bidder and the target following the initial tender offer. The effect of a flip-over pill may therefore be moderated where the bidder's business plan allows it to forgo such a merger. A flip-in pill is much more wide-ranging in its applicability, but usually the Rights issued under such a pill can be redeemed by the target's board for a nominal consideration at any time before a triggering event and, often, for a brief period thereafter.

Standstill. A target may seek an accommodation with a shareholder who has acquired a significant amount of stock, under which the shareholder agrees to limit his stock purchases—hence, *standstill.* In the typical standstill agreement, the shareholder makes one or more commitments: (i) it will not increase its shareholdings above designated limits for a specified period of time; (ii) it will not sell its shares without giving the corporation a right of first refusal; (iii) it will not engage in a proxy contest; and (iv) it will vote its stock in a designated manner in the election of directors, and perhaps on other issues. In return, the corporation may agree to give the shareholder board representation, to register the shareholder's stock under the Securities Act on demand, and to not oppose the shareholder's acquisition of more stock up to the specified limit.

NOTE ON THE WILLIAMS ACT

Tender offers, and the initial or *toehold* share acquisitions by the bidder that often precede them, are regulated in a great number of respects by the Williams Act, which added sections 13(d) and (e), and 14(d), (e), and (f), to the Securities Exchange Act. Section 14(d), and Rule 14d thereunder, apply to tender offers for more than 5% of any class of equity security that is registered under Section 12 of the Act. Section 14(e), and Rule 14e thereunder, apply to any tender offer for any class of security. Accordingly, in theory section 14(e) and Rule 14e cover more tender offers than section 14(d) and Rule 14d. In practice, however, most tender offers will be covered by both sections and both rules. For ease of exposition, in the balance of this Note all references to tender offers will mean tender offers that are covered by the relevant sections and rules, unless otherwise stated.

1. *Toehold Acquisitions.* Under section 13(d) of the Securities Exchange Act, a person who has acquired beneficial ownership of more than 5% of any class of equity securities registered under section 12 of the Act must file a Schedule 13D within 10 days of the acquisition. The Schedule 13D must include the purchaser's identity and background; the amount and sources of the funds for the purchase; the purpose of the purchase; any plans with respect to extraordinary corporate transactions involving the corporation whose stock has been acquired; and any contracts, arrangements, or understandings with other persons regarding the corporation's securities. Under Rule 13d–2, any material changes in the information disclosed in a Schedule 13D must be promptly updated, and any further acquisitions of an additional 1% or more of the corporation's stock will be deemed a material change. Even further acquisitions of less than 1% of the corporation's stock may be deemed material, depending on the circumstances.

Furthermore, under section 13(d)(3) of the Securities Exchange Act, as implemented by Rule 13d–5(b), when two or more persons agree to act together for the purpose of acquiring, holding, voting, or disposing of an issuer's equity securities, the group formed by the agreement is deemed to have acquired ownership of all securities of that issuer owned by any member of the group, for purposes of section 13(d). Even acting in concert may create a group for these purposes.

Wholly aside from the Williams Act, the Hart-Scott-Rodino Antitrust Improvements Act requires notification of acquisitions of stock in medium-size and large publicly held companies, if the acquisition will result in the acquiror's owning voting stock in the corporation in excess of $75 million. For many corporations that are likely to be made subject to a tender offer, $75 million of the corporation's stock will be substantially less than 5% of its stock. Thus Hart-Scott-Rodino effectively lowers the reporting threshold for many toehold acquisitions.

2. *What Constitutes a Tender Offer.* What constitutes a "tender offer" within the meaning of the Williams Act is not completely settled. At one extreme, a public offer, made by a bidder to all shareholders, to purchase, at a fixed stated price, shares that are tendered into the offer during a stated period of time, will almost certainly be deemed a tender offer within the meaning of the Williams Act. At the other extreme, purchases that a buyer makes anonymously in the stock market will almost certainly not be deemed a tender offer within the meaning of the Act. Kennecott Copper Corp. v. Curtiss–Wright Corp., 584 F.2d 1195 (2d Cir.1978); Calumet Industries, Inc. v. MacClure, 464 F.Supp. 19 (N.D.Ill.1978). The problem concerns transactions that fall between these two extremes, such as a series of private offers made to a limited number of potential sellers. Some courts have adopted an eight-factor test to determine whether offers like this are tender offers under the Act. These factors are: (i) Whether the purchasers engage in active and widespread solicitation of public shareholders. (ii) Whether the solicitation is made for a substantial percentage of the corporation's stock. (iii) Whether the offer to purchase is made at a premium over the prevailing market price. (iv) Whether the terms of the offer are firm rather than negotiable. (v) Whether the offer is contingent on the tender of a fixed number of shares. (vi) Whether the offer is open only for a limited person of time. (vii) Whether the offerees are under pressure to sell their stock. (viii) Whether public announcements of a purchasing program preceded or accompanied a rapid accumulation of large amounts of the corporation's stock. Wellman v. Dickinson, 475 F.Supp. 783 (S.D.N.Y.1979), aff'd on other grounds 682 F.2d 355 (2d Cir.1982), cert. denied 460 U.S. 1069, 103 S.Ct. 1522, 75 L.Ed.2d 946 (1983); SEC v. Carter Hawley Hale Stores, Inc., 760 F.2d 945 (9th Cir.1985).

In Hanson Trust PLC v. SCM Corp., 774 F.2d 47 (2d Cir.1985), the Second Circuit rejected the eight-factor test, and held instead that whether an offer to buy stock constitutes a tender offer under the Williams Act turns on whether there appears to be a likelihood that unless the Act's rules are followed, there will be a substantial risk that solicited shareholders will lack information needed to make a carefully considered appraisal of the offer. Applying that standard, the Second Circuit held in *Hanson* that the offer before it was not a tender offer. The target had 22,800 shareholders and offers were made to only six. At least five of the sellers were highly sophisticated professionals, knowledgeable in the market place and well aware of the essential facts needed to exercise their professional skills and to appraise the offer. The sellers were not pressured to sell their shares by any conduct that the Williams Act was designed to alleviate, but only by the forces of the marketplace. There was no active or widespread advance publicity or public solicitation. The price received by the six sellers was not at a premium over the then-market price. The purchases were not made contingent upon acquiring a fixed minimum number or percentage of the target's outstanding shares. There was no time limit within which the buyer would purchase the target's stock.

3. *Schedule TO.* Section 14(d) of the Securities Exchange Act requires a schedule TO to be filed by any person who makes a tender offer for a class of registered equity securities that would result in that person owning more than 5% of the class. The Schedule TO must contain extensive disclosure of such matters as the offer; the identity of the bidder; past dealings between the bidder and the target corporation; the bidder's source of funds; the bidder's purposes and plans concerning the target; the bidder's contracts and understandings or relationships with respect to securities of the target; financial statements of the bidder, if they are material and the bidder is not an individual; and arrangements between the bidder and persons holding important positions with the target.

4. *Regulation of the Terms of Tender Offers.* Section 14(d) of the Securities Exchange Act, and Rules 14d and 14e, regulate the terms of tender offers. These provisions impose the following requirements, among others:

(i) *Minimum duration.* Under Rule 14e–1, a tender offer must be held open for at least twenty business days.

(ii) *All-holders rule.* Rule 14d–10 provides that a bidder may not make a tender offer for a class of securities unless the offer is open, at the same price and on the same terms, to all holders of the class. This rule is called the "all holders rule." Under the Supremacy Clause, the all-holders rule displaces the outcome of the *Unocal* case, infra, which held that under Delaware law a corporation can make an exclusionary self-tender—that is, a tender offer that excludes certain shares of the class for which the offer is made.

(iii) *Best-price rule.* Rule 14d–10 also provides that the price paid to any security holder pursuant to a tender offer must equal the highest price that the bidder pays to any other security holder during the tender offer. See Epstein v. MCA, Inc., 54 F.3d 1422 (9th Cir. 1995), rev'd on other grounds sub nom. Matsushita Electrical Industrial Corp. v. Epstein, 516 U.S. 367, 116 S.Ct. 873, 134 L.Ed.2d 6 (1996), reaffirmed on remand, 126 F.3d 1235 (9th Cir. 1997). Under this rule, if, as frequently occurs, the bidder increases the bid price during a tender offer, the new, higher price must be made retroactively available to all holders who tendered before the increase. In addition, Rule 10b–13 provides that during the pendency of tender offer, the bidder cannot purchase securities that are subject to the tender offer except under the tender offer—that is, the bidder cannot make private purchases during the duration of the tender offer.

(iv) *Withdrawal rights.* Under section 14(d)(5) of the Williams Act, a tendering shareholder can withdraw tendered but unaccepted shares at any time after sixty days from the date the tender offer was disseminated. Under Rule 14d–7, a tendering shareholder can withdraw tendered shares during the entire duration of the offer and any extension of the offer.

(v) *Proration.* Under Rule 14d–8, if a bidder makes a partial tender offer—that is, an offer for less than 100% of the target's securities—and more securities are tendered during the duration of the tender offer than the bidder has offered to accept, the bidder must accept all tendered securities, up to the stated percentage, on a pro rata basis.

5. *Obligations of the Target's Management.* Rule 14e–2 requires that no later than ten business days from the date the tender offer is first published, the target corporation (really, the target's board) must notify shareholders that the target takes one of the following positions: (A) Recommends acceptance of the tender offer. (B) Recommends rejection of the tender offer. (C) Expresses no opinion and is remaining neutral toward the tender offer. (D) Is unable to take a position with respect to the tender offer. The statement must also describe the reasons for target's position.

Under Rule 14d–9, any person who solicits or makes a recommendation to shareholders in respect of a tender offer (as opposed to making a tender offer) must file a Schedule 14D–9. This Schedule requires disclosure of the nature of, and the reasons for, the solicitation or recommendation; conflicts of interest of the person filing the statement; and any negotiation or transaction being undertaken that relates to either an extraordinary transaction (such as a merger) involving the target, a purchase or sale of a material amount of assets by the target, an acquisition of securities by the target, or a material change in the target's capitalization or in its dividend policy. Under Rule 14d–9(f), the statement that a target is required to make concerning its position on the tender offer is a solicitation or recommendation to shareholders within the meaning of Rule 14d–9. Accordingly, as a practical matter a target corporation must make the disclosures required by Schedule 14D–9.

6. *Tender Offers by Issuers.* Under section 13(e) of the Securities Exchange Act and Rule 13e, corporations that tender for their own stock ("issuer" or "self" tenders) are subject to obligations similar to those imposed on outside bidders under rules 14d and 14e.

7. *Anti-Fraud Provision.* Section 14(e) of the Securities Exchange Act prohibits material misstatements, misleading omissions,

and fraudulent or manipulative acts, in connection with a tender offer, or any solicitation in favor of or in opposition to a tender offer. Section 14(e) is closely comparable to Rule 10b–5, except that it does not contain the limiting language, "in connection with the purchase or sale" of securities, found in Rule 10b–5. It has been held that a plaintiff who brings suit for damages under section 14(e) must establish scienter. See Connecticut National Bank v. Fluor Corp., 808 F.2d 957 (2d Cir.1987).

8. *Standing.* A bidder does not have standing to sue for damages under the Williams Act, on the theory that the purpose of the Act is to protect the target's shareholders. Piper v. Chris–Craft Industries, Inc., 430 U.S. 1, 97 S.Ct. 926, 51 L.Ed.2d 124 (1977). The target's shareholders have standing to sue for damages under sections 14(d)(6) (the pro rata requirement), 14(d)(7) (the equal-consideration requirement), and 14(e) (the anti-fraud requirement), and, in appropriate cases, may sue for injunctive relief, under the anti-fraud provision, if they can show causation, because section 14(e) does not contain the purchase-or-sale requirement of Rule 10b–5. The target corporation can also sue for an injunction against the bidder for violation of the anti-fraud provision of section 14(e), because such an injunction will protect the interests of the target's shareholders. Gearhart Industries, Inc. v. Smith International, Inc., 741 F.2d 707 (5th Cir.1984).

In general, the courts have also given standing to shareholders of a target corporation to seek injunctive relief against continuing violations of § 13(d) (the 5% reporting requirement), including violations caused by false or misleading filings. The target corporation also has a private right of action to seek injunctive relief against continuing violations of § 13(d). The courts are divided on whether a shareholder of the target has an implied private right of action for damages under § 13(d). However, the majority rule is that corporations do not have standing to sue for damages under section 13(d). See Hallwood Realty Partners, L.P. v. Gotham Partners, L.P., 286 F.3d 613 (2d Cir. 2002).

Rival bidders cannot seek damages under the Williams Act against each other resulting from the lost opportunity to gain control, even when they own a nominal amount of shares in the target company. Id. at 35; Kalmanovitz v. G. Heileman Brewing Co., 595 F.Supp. 1385, 1393 (D. Del. 1984). However, courts have allowed a rival bidder to seek injunctive relief by concluding that an injunctive remedy would better protect the target's shareholders interests than providing damages to shareholders after the transaction is complete. Mobil Corp. v. Marathon Oil Co., 669 F.2d 366, 371–72 (6th Cir. 1981); Humana, Inc. v. American Medicorp, Inc., 445 F.Supp. 613, 614–15 (S.D.N.Y. 1977).

Unocal Corp. v. Mesa Petroleum Co.

Supreme Court of Delaware, 1985.
493 A.2d 946.

■ Before MCNEILLY and MOORE, JJ., and TAYLOR, JUDGE (Sitting by designation pursuant to Del.Const. Art. 4, § 12.)

■ MOORE, JUSTICE.

We confront an issue of first impression in Delaware—the validity of a corporation's self-tender for its own shares which excludes from participation a stockholder making a hostile tender offer for the company's stock.

The Court of Chancery granted a preliminary injunction to the plaintiffs, Mesa Petroleum Co., Mesa Asset Co., Mesa Partners II, and Mesa Eastern, Inc. (collectively "Mesa")[1], enjoining an exchange offer of the defendant, Unocal Corporation (Unocal) for its own stock. The trial court concluded that a selective exchange offer, excluding Mesa, was legally impermissible. We cannot agree with such a blanket rule. The factual findings of the Vice Chancellor, fully supported by the record, establish that Unocal's board, consisting of a majority of independent directors, acted in good faith, and after reasonable investigation found that Mesa's tender offer was both inadequate and coercive. Under the circumstances the board had both the power and duty to oppose a bid it perceived to be harmful to the corporate enterprise. On this record we are satisfied that the device Unocal adopted is reasonable in relation to the threat posed, and that the board acted in the proper exercise of sound business judgment. We will not substitute our views for those of the board if the latter's decision can be "attributed to any rational business purpose." Sinclair Oil Corp. v. Levien, Del.Supr., 280 A.2d 717, 720 (1971). Accordingly, we reverse the decision of the Court of Chancery and order the preliminary injunction vacated.

I.

The factual background of this matter bears a significant relationship to its ultimate outcome.

On April 8, 1985, Mesa, the owner of approximately 13% of Unocal's stock, commenced a two-tier "front loaded" cash tender offer for 64 million shares, or approximately 37%, of Unocal's outstanding stock at a price of $54 per share. The "back-end" was designed to eliminate the remaining publicly held shares by an exchange of securities purportedly worth $54 per share. However, pursuant to an order entered by the United States District Court for the Central District of California on April 26, 1985, Mesa issued a supplemental proxy statement to Unocal's stockholders disclosing that the securities offered in the second-step merger would be highly subordinated, and that Unocal's capitalization would differ significantly from its present structure. Unocal has rather aptly termed such securities "junk bonds".[2]

1. T. Boone Pickens, Jr., is President and Chairman of the Board of Mesa Petroleum and President of Mesa Asset and controls the related Mesa entities.

2. Mesa's May 3, 1985 supplement to its proxy statement states:

(i) following the Offer, the Purchasers would seek to effect a merger of Unocal and Mesa Eastern or an affiliate of Mesa Eastern (the "Merger") in which the remaining Shares would be acquired for a combination of subordinated debt securities and preferred stock; (ii) the securities to be received by Unocal share-

Unocal's board consists of eight independent outside directors and six insiders. It met on April 13, 1985, to consider the Mesa tender offer. Thirteen directors were present, and the meeting lasted nine and one-half hours. The directors were given no agenda or written materials prior to the session. However, detailed presentations were made by legal counsel regarding the board's obligations under both Delaware corporate law and the federal securities laws. The board then received a presentation from Peter Sachs on behalf of Goldman Sachs Co. (Goldman Sachs) and Dillon, Read Co. (Dillon Read) discussing the bases for their opinions that the Mesa proposal was wholly inadequate. Mr. Sachs opined that the minimum cash value that could be expected from a sale or orderly liquidation for 100% of Unocal's stock was in excess of $60 per share. In making his presentation, Mr. Sachs showed slides outlining the valuation techniques used by the financial advisors, and others, depicting recent business combinations in the oil and gas industry. The Court of Chancery found that the Sachs presentation was designed to apprise the directors of the scope of the analyses performed rather than the facts and numbers used in reaching the conclusion that Mesa's tender offer price was inadequate.

Mr. Sachs also presented various defensive strategies available to the board if it concluded that Mesa's two-step tender offer was inadequate and should be opposed. One of the devices outlined was a self-tender by Unocal for its own stock with a reasonable price range of $70 to $75 per share. The cost of such a proposal would cause the company to incur $6.1–6.5 billion of additional debt, and a presentation was made informing the board of Unocal's ability to handle it. The directors were told that the primary effect of this obligation would be to reduce exploratory drilling, but that the company would nonetheless remain a viable entity.

The eight outside directors, comprising a clear majority of the thirteen members present, then met separately with Unocal's financial advisors and attorneys. Thereafter, they unanimously agreed to advise the board that it should reject Mesa's tender offer as inadequate, and that Unocal should pursue a self-tender to provide the stockholders with a fairly priced alternative to the Mesa proposal. The board then reconvened and unanimously adopted a resolution rejecting as grossly

holders in the Merger would be subordinated to $2,400 million of debt securities of Mesa Eastern, indebtedness incurred to refinance up to $1,000 million of bank debt which was incurred by affiliates of Mesa Partners II to purchase Shares and to pay related interest and expenses and all then-existing debt of Unocal; (iii) the corporation surviving the Merger would be responsible for the payment of all securities of Mesa Eastern (including any such securities issued pursuant to the Merger) and the indebtedness referred to in item (ii) above, and such securities and indebtedness would be repaid out of funds generated by the operations of Unocal; (iv) the indebtedness incurred in the Offer and the Merger would result in Unocal being much more highly leveraged, and the capitalization of the corporation surviving the Merger would differ significantly from that of Unocal at present; and (v) in their analyses of cash flows provided by operations of Unocal which would be available to service and repay securities and other obligations of the corporation surviving the Merger, the Purchasers assumed that the capital expenditures and expenditures for exploration of such corporation would be significantly reduced.

inadequate Mesa's tender offer. Despite the nine and one-half hour length of the meeting, no formal decision was made on the proposed defensive self-tender.

On April 15, the board met again with four of the directors present by telephone and one member still absent. This session lasted two hours. Unocal's Vice President of Finance and its Assistant General Counsel made a detailed presentation of the proposed terms of the exchange offer. A price range between $70 and $80 per share was considered, and ultimately the directors agreed upon $72. The board was also advised about the debt securities that would be issued, and the necessity of placing restrictive covenants upon certain corporate activities until the obligations were paid. The board's decisions were made in reliance on the advice of its investment bankers, including the terms and conditions upon which the securities were to be issued. Based upon this advice, and the board's own deliberations, the directors unanimously approved the exchange offer. Their resolution provided that if Mesa acquired 64 million shares of Unocal stock through its own offer (the Mesa Purchase Condition), Unocal would buy the remaining 49% outstanding for an exchange of debt securities having an aggregate par value of $72 per share. The board resolution also stated that the offer would be subject to other conditions that had been described to the board at the meeting, or which were deemed necessary by Unocal's officers, including the exclusion of Mesa from the proposal (the Mesa exclusion). Any such conditions were required to be in accordance with the "purport and intent" of the offer.

Unocal's exchange offer was commenced on April 17, 1985, and Mesa promptly challenged it by filing this suit in the Court of Chancery. On April 22, the Unocal board met again and was advised by Goldman Sachs and Dillon Read to waive the Mesa Purchase Condition as to 50 million shares. This recommendation was in response to a perceived concern of the shareholders that, if shares were tendered to Unocal, no shares would be purchased by either offeror. The directors were also advised that they should tender their own Unocal stock into the exchange offer as a mark of their confidence in it.

Another focus of the board was the Mesa exclusion. Legal counsel advised that under Delaware law Mesa could only be excluded for what the directors reasonably believed to be a valid corporate purpose. The directors' discussion centered on the objective of adequately compensating shareholders at the "back-end" of Mesa's proposal, which the latter would finance with "junk bonds". To include Mesa would defeat that goal, because under the proration aspect of the exchange offer (49%) every Mesa share accepted by Unocal would displace one held by another stockholder. Further, if Mesa were permitted to tender to Unocal, the latter would in effect be financing Mesa's own inadequate proposal.

On April 24, 1985 Unocal issued a supplement to the exchange offer describing the partial waiver of the Mesa Purchase Condition. On May 1, 1985, in another supplement, Unocal extended the withdrawal, proration and expiration dates of its exchange offer to May 17, 1985.

Meanwhile, on April 22, 1985, Mesa amended its complaint in this action to challenge the Mesa exclusion. . . .

. . . [T]he Vice Chancellor granted Mesa a preliminary injunction. . . .

On May 13, 1985 the Court of Chancery certified this interlocutory appeal to us as a question of first impression, and we accepted it on May 14. The entire matter was scheduled on an expedited basis.

II.

The issues we address involve these fundamental questions: Did the Unocal board have the power and duty to oppose a takeover threat it reasonably perceived to be harmful to the corporate enterprise, and if so, is its action here entitled to the protection of the business judgment rule?

Mesa contends that the discriminatory exchange offer violates the fiduciary duties Unocal owes it. Mesa argues that because of the Mesa exclusion the business judgment rule is inapplicable, because the directors by tendering their own shares will derive a financial benefit that is not available to *all* Unocal stockholders. Thus, it is Mesa's ultimate contention that Unocal cannot establish that the exchange offer is fair to *all* shareholders, and argues that the Court of Chancery was correct in concluding that Unocal was unable to meet this burden.

Unocal answers that it does not owe a duty of "fairness" to Mesa, given the facts here. Specifically, Unocal contends that its board of directors reasonably and in good faith concluded that Mesa's $54 two-tier tender offer was coercive and inadequate, and that Mesa sought selective treatment for itself. Furthermore, Unocal argues that the board's approval of the exchange offer was made in good faith, on an informed basis, and in the exercise of due care. Under these circumstances, Unocal contends that its directors properly employed this device to protect the company and its stockholders from Mesa's harmful tactics.

III.

We begin with the basic issue of the power of a board of directors of a Delaware corporation to adopt a defensive measure of this type. Absent such authority, all other questions are moot. Neither issues of fairness nor business judgment are pertinent without the basic underpinning of a board's legal power to act.

The board has a large reservoir of authority upon which to draw. Its duties and responsibilities proceed from the inherent powers conferred by 8 Del.C. § 141(a), respecting management of the corporation's "business and affairs". Additionally, the powers here being exercised derive from 8 Del.C. § 160(a), conferring broad authority upon a corporation to deal in its own stock. From this it is now well established that in the acquisition of its shares a Delaware corporation may deal selectively with its stockholders, provided the directors have not acted out of a sole or primary purpose to entrench themselves in office. Cheff v. Mathes, Del.Supr., 199 A.2d 548, 554 (1964); Bennett v. Propp, Del.Supr., 187 A.2d 405, 408 (1962); Martin v. American Potash & Chemical Corporation, Del.Supr., 92 A.2d 295, 302 (1952); Kaplan v. Goldsamt, Del.Ch., 380 A.2d 556, 568–569 (1977); Kors v. Carey, Del.Ch., 158 A.2d 136, 140–141 (1960).

Finally, the board's power to act derives from its fundamental duty and obligation to protect the corporate enterprise, which includes stockholders, from harm reasonably perceived, irrespective of its source. See e.g. . . . Cheff v. Mathes, 199 A.2d at 556; Martin v. American Potash & Chemical Corp., 92 A.2d at 302; Kaplan v. Goldsamt, 380 A.2d at 568–69; Kors v. Carey, 158 A.2d at 141 . . . Thus, we are satisfied that in the broad context of corporate governance, including issues of fundamental corporate change, a board of directors is not a passive instrumentality.[8]

Given the foregoing principles, we turn to the standards by which director action is to be measured. In Pogostin v. Rice, Del.Supr., 480 A.2d 619 (1984), we held that the business judgment rule, including the standards by which director conduct is judged, is applicable in the context of a takeover. Id. at 627. The business judgment rule is a "presumption that in making a business decision the directors of a corporation acted on an informed basis, in good faith and in the honest belief that the action taken was in the best interests of the company." Aronson v. Lewis, Del.Supr., 473 A.2d 805, 812 (1984) (citations omitted). A hallmark of the business judgment rule is that a court will not substitute its judgment for that of the board if the latter's decision can be "attributed to any rational business purpose." Sinclair Oil Corp. v. Levien, Del.Supr., 280 A.2d 717, 720 (1971).

When a board addresses a pending takeover bid it has an obligation to determine whether the offer is in the best interests of the corporation and its shareholders. In that respect a board's duty is no different from any other responsibility it shoulders, and its decision should be no less entitled to the respect they otherwise would be accorded in the realm of business judgment. See also Johnson v. Trueblood, 629 F.2d 287, 292–293 (3d Cir.1980). There are, however, certain caveats to a proper exercise of this function. Because of the omnipresent specter that a board may be acting primarily in its own interests, rather than those of the corporation and its shareholders, there is an enhanced duty which calls for judicial examination at the threshold before the protections of the business judgment rule may be conferred.

This Court has long recognized that:

We must bear in mind the inherent danger in the purchase of shares with corporate funds to remove a threat to corporate policy when a threat to control is involved. The directors are of

---

8. Even in the traditional areas of fundamental corporate change, i.e., charter amendments [8 Del.C. § 242(b)], mergers [8 Del.C. §§ 251(b), 252(c), 253(a), and 254(d)], sale of assets [8 Del.C. § 271(a)], and dissolution [8 Del.C. § 275(a)], director action is a prerequisite to the ultimate disposition of such matters. See also, Smith v. Van Gorkom, Del.Supr., 488 A.2d 858, 888 (1985).

necessity confronted with a conflict of interest, and an objective decision is difficult.

Bennett v. Propp, Del.Supr., 187 A.2d 405, 409 (1962). In the face of this inherent conflict directors must show that they had reasonable grounds for believing that a danger to corporate policy and effectiveness existed because of another person's stock ownership. Cheff v. Mathes, 199 A.2d at 554–55. However, they satisfy that burden "by showing good faith and reasonable investigation...." Id. at 555. Furthermore, such proof is materially enhanced, as here, by the approval of a board comprised of a majority of outside independent directors who have acted in accordance with the foregoing standards. See Aronson v. Lewis, 473 A.2d at 812, 815; Puma v. Marriott, Del.Ch., 283 A.2d 693, 695 (1971); Panter v. Marshall Field Co., 646 F.2d 271, 295 (7th Cir.1981).

IV.

A.

In the board's exercise of corporate power to forestall a takeover bid our analysis begins with the basic principle that corporate directors have a fiduciary duty to act in the best interests of the corporation's stockholders. Guth v. Loft, Inc., Del.Supr., 5 A.2d 503, 510 (1939). As we have noted, their duty of care extends to protecting the corporation and its owners from perceived harm whether a threat originates from third parties or other shareholders. But such powers are not absolute. A corporation does not have unbridled discretion to defeat any perceived threat by any Draconian means available.

The restriction placed upon a selective stock repurchase is that the directors may not have acted solely or primarily out of a desire to perpetuate themselves in office. See Cheff v. Mathes, 199 A.2d at 556; Kors v. Carey, 158 A.2d at 140. Of course, to this is added the further caveat that inequitable action may not be taken under the guise of law. Schnell v. Chris–Craft Industries, Inc., Del.Supr. 285 A.2d 437, 439 (1971). The standard of proof established in Cheff v. Mathes ... is designed to ensure that a defensive measure to thwart or impede a takeover is indeed motivated by a good faith concern for the welfare of the corporation and its stockholders, which in all circumstances must be free of any fraud or other misconduct. Cheff v. Mathes, 199 A.2d at 554–55. However, this does not end the inquiry.

B.

A further aspect is the element of balance. If a defensive measure is to come within the ambit of the business judgment rule, it must be reasonable in relation to the threat posed. This entails an analysis by the directors of the nature of the takeover bid and its effect on the corporate enterprise. Examples of such concerns may include: inadequacy of the price offered, nature and timing of the offer, questions of illegality, the impact on "constituencies" other than shareholders (i.e., creditors, customers, employees, and perhaps even the community generally), the risk of nonconsummation, and the quality of securities being offered in the exchange. See Lipton and Brownstein, Takeover Responses and Directors' Responsibilities: An Update, p. 7, ABA National Institute on the Dynamics of Corporate Control (December 8, 1983). While not a controlling factor, it also seems to us that a board may reasonably consider the basic stockholder interests at stake, including those of short term speculators, whose actions may have fueled the coercive aspect of the offer at the expense of the long term investor.[9] Here, the threat posed was viewed by the Unocal board as a grossly inadequate two-tier coercive tender offer coupled with the threat of greenmail.

Specifically, the Unocal directors had concluded that the value of Unocal was substantially above the $54 per share offered in cash at the front end. Furthermore, they determined that the subordinated securities to be exchanged in Mesa's announced squeeze out of the remaining shareholders in the "back-end" merger were "junk bonds" worth far less than $54. It is now well recognized that such offers are a classic coercive measure designed to stampede shareholders into tendering at the first tier, even if the price is inadequate, out of fear of what they will receive at the back end of the transaction. Wholly beyond the coercive aspect of an inadequate two-tier tender offer, the threat was posed by a corporate raider with a national reputation as a "greenmailer".[13]

In adopting the selective exchange offer, the board stated that its objective was either to defeat the inadequate Mesa offer or, should the offer still succeed, provide the 49% of its stockholders, who would otherwise be forced to accept "junk bonds", with $72 worth of senior debt. We find that both purposes are valid.

However, such efforts would have been thwarted by Mesa's participation in the exchange offer. First, if Mesa could tender its shares, Unocal would effectively be subsidizing the former's continuing effort to buy Unocal stock at $54 per share. Second, Mesa could not, by

9. There has been much debate respecting such stockholder interests. One rather impressive study indicates that the stock of over 50 percent of target companies, who resisted hostile takeovers, later traded at higher market prices than the rejected offer price, or were acquired after the tender offer was defeated by another company at a price higher than the offer price. See Lipton, supra 35 Bus.Law. at 106–109, 132–133. Moreover, an update by Kidder Peabody & Company of this study, involving the stock prices of target companies that have defeated hostile tender offers during the period from 1973 to 1982 demonstrates that in a majority of cases the target's shareholders benefited from the defeat. The stock of 81% of the targets studied has, since the tender offer, sold at prices higher than the tender offer price. When adjusted for the time value of money, the figure is 64%. See Lipton & Brownstein, su-

pra ABA Institute at 10. The thesis being that this strongly supports application of the business judgment rule in response to takeover threats. There is, however, a rather vehement contrary view. See Easterbrook & Fischel, supra 36 Bus.Law. at 1739–1745.

13. The term "greenmail" refers to the practice of buying out a takeover bidder's stock at a premium that is not available to other shareholders in order to prevent the takeover. The Chancery Court noted that "Mesa has made tremendous profits from its takeover activities although in the past few years it has not been successful in acquiring any of the target companies on an unfriendly basis." Moreover, the trial court specifically found that the actions of the Unocal board were taken in good faith to eliminate both the inadequacies of the tender offer and to forestall the payment of "greenmail".

definition, fit within the class of shareholders being protected from its own coercive and inadequate tender offer.

Thus, we are satisfied that the selective exchange offer is reasonably related to the threats posed. It is consistent with the principle that "the minority stockholder shall receive the substantial equivalent in value of what he had before." Sterling v. Mayflower Hotel Corp., Del.Supr., 93 A.2d 107, 114 (1952). See also Rosenblatt v. Getty Oil Co., Del.Supr., 493 A.2d 929, 940 (1985). This concept of fairness, while stated in the merger context, is also relevant in the area of tender offer law. Thus, the board's decision to offer what it determined to be the fair value of the corporation to the 49% of its shareholders, who would otherwise be forced to accept highly subordinated "junk bonds", is reasonable and consistent with the directors' duty to ensure that the minority stockholders receive equal value for their shares.

V.

Mesa contends that it is unlawful, and the trial court agreed, for a corporation to discriminate in this fashion against one shareholder. It argues correctly that no case has ever sanctioned a device that precludes a raider from sharing in a benefit available to all other stockholders. However, as we have noted earlier, the principle of selective stock repurchases by a Delaware corporation is neither unknown nor unauthorized. Cheff v. Mathes, 199 A.2d at 554; Bennett v. Propp, 187 A.2d at 408; Martin v. American Potash & Chemical Corporation, 92 A.2d at 302; Kaplan v. Goldsamt, 380 A.2d 556–569; Kors v. Carey, 158 A.2d at 140–141; 8 Del.C. § 160. The only difference is that heretofore the approved transaction was the payment of "greenmail" to a raider or dissident posing a threat to the corporate enterprise. All other stockholders were denied such favored treatment, and given Mesa's past history of greenmail, its claims here are rather ironic.

However, our corporate law is not static. It must grow and develop in response to, indeed in anticipation of, evolving concepts and needs. Merely because the General Corporation Law is silent as to a specific matter does not mean that it is prohibited. See Providence & Worcester Co. v. Baker, Del.Supr., 378 A.2d 121, 123–124 (1977). In the days when *Cheff, Bennett, Martin* and *Kors* were decided, the tender offer, while not an unknown device, was virtually unused, and little was known of such methods as two-tier "front-end" loaded offers with their coercive effects. Then, the favored attack of a raider was stock acquisition followed by a proxy contest. Various defensive tactics, which provided no benefit whatever to the raider, evolved. Thus, the use of corporate funds by management to counter a proxy battle was approved. Hall v. Trans–Lux Daylight Picture Screen Corp., Del. Supr., 171 A. 226 (1934); Hibbert v. Hollywood Park, Inc., Del.Supr., 457 A.2d 339 (1983). Litigation, supported by corporate funds, aimed at the raider has long been a popular device.

More recently, as the sophistication of both raiders and targets has developed, a host of other defensive measures to counter such ever mounting threats has evolved and received judicial sanction. These include defensive charter amendments and other devices bearing some rather exotic, but apt, names: Crown Jewel, White Knight, Pac Man, and Golden Parachute. Each has highly selective features, the object of which is to deter or defeat the raider.

Thus, while the exchange offer is a form of selective treatment, given the nature of the threat posed here the response is neither unlawful nor unreasonable. If the board of directors is disinterested, has acted in good faith and with due care, its decision in the absence of an abuse of discretion will be upheld as a proper exercise of business judgment.

To this Mesa responds that the board is not disinterested, because the directors are receiving a benefit from the tender of their own shares, which because of the Mesa exclusion, does not devolve upon *all* stockholders equally. See Aronson v. Lewis, Del.Supr., 473 A.2d 805, 812 (1984). However, Mesa concedes that if the exclusion is valid, then the directors and all other stockholders share the same benefit. The answer of course is that the exclusion is valid, and the directors' participation in the exchange offer does not rise to the level of a disqualifying interest. . . .

Nor does this become an "interested" director transaction merely because certain board members are large stockholders. As this Court has previously noted, that fact alone does not create a disqualifying "personal pecuniary interest" to defeat the operation of the business judgment rule. Cheff v. Mathes, 199 A.2d at 554.

Mesa also argues that the exclusion permits the directors to abdicate the fiduciary duties they owe it. However, that is not so. The board continues to owe Mesa the duties of due care and loyalty. But in the face of the destructive threat Mesa's tender offer was perceived to pose, the board had a supervening duty to protect the corporate enterprise, which includes the other shareholders, from threatened harm.

Mesa contends that the basis of this action is punitive, and solely in response to the exercise of its rights of corporate democracy. Nothing precludes Mesa, as a stockholder, from acting in its own self-interest. See e.g., DuPont v. DuPont, 251 Fed. 937 (D.Del.1918), aff'd 256 Fed. 129 (3d Cir.1919); Ringling Bros.–Barnum & Bailey Combined Shows, Inc. v. Ringling, Del.Supr., 53 A.2d 441, 447 (1947); Heil v. Standard Gas & Electric Co., Del.Ch., 151 A. 303, 304 (1930). But see, Allied Chemical & Dye Corp. v. Steel & Tube Co. of America, Del.Ch., 120 A. 486, 491 (1923) (majority shareholder owes a fiduciary duty to the minority shareholders). However, Mesa, while pursuing its own interests, has acted in a manner which a board consisting of a majority of independent directors has reasonably determined to be contrary to the best interests of Unocal and its other shareholders. In this situation, there is no support in Delaware law for the proposition that, when responding to a perceived harm, a corporation must guarantee a benefit to a stockholder who is deliberately provoking the danger being addressed. There is no obligation of self-sacrifice by a corporation and its shareholders in the face of such a challenge.

Here, the Court of Chancery specifically found that the "directors' decision [to oppose the Mesa tender offer] was made in the good faith belief that the Mesa tender offer is inadequate." Given our standard of review under Levitt v. Bouvier, Del.Supr., 287 A.2d 671, 673 (1972), and Application of Delaware Racing Association, Del.Supr., 213 A.2d 203, 207 (1965), we are satisfied that Unocal's board has met its burden of proof. Cheff v. Mathes, 199 A.2d at 555.

VI.

In conclusion, there was directorial power to oppose the Mesa tender offer, and to undertake a selective stock exchange made in good faith and upon a reasonable investigation pursuant to a clear duty to protect the corporate enterprise. Further, the selective stock repurchase plan chosen by Unocal is reasonable in relation to the threat that the board rationally and reasonably believed was posed by Mesa's inadequate and coercive two-tier tender offer. Under those circumstances the board's action is entitled to be measured by the standards of the business judgment rule. Thus, unless it is shown by a preponderance of the evidence that the directors' decisions were primarily based on perpetuating themselves in office, or some other breach of fiduciary duty such as fraud, overreaching, lack of good faith, or being uninformed, a Court will not substitute its judgment for that of the board.

In this case that protection is not lost merely because Unocal's directors have tendered their shares in the exchange offer. Given the validity of the Mesa exclusion, they are receiving a benefit shared generally by all other stockholders except Mesa. In this circumstance the test of Aronson v. Lewis, 473 A.2d at 812, is satisfied. See also Cheff v. Mathes, 199 A.2d at 554. If the stockholders are displeased with the action of their elected representatives, the powers of corporate democracy are at their disposal to turn the board out. Aronson v. Lewis, Del.Supr., 473 A.2d 805, 811 (1984). See also 8 Del.C. §§ 141(k) and 211(b).

With the Court of Chancery's findings that the exchange offer was based on the board's good faith belief that the Mesa offer was inadequate, that the board's action was informed and taken with due care, that Mesa's prior activities justify a reasonable inference that its principle objective was greenmail, and implicitly, that the substance of the offer itself was reasonable and fair to the corporation and its stockholders if Mesa were included, we cannot say that the Unocal directors have acted in such a manner as to have passed an "unintelligent and unadvised judgment". Mitchell v. Highland–Western Glass Co., Del.Ch., 167 A. 831, 833 (1933). The decision of the Court of Chancery is therefore REVERSED, and the preliminary injunction is VACATED.*

---

* Accord: Burcham v. Bunten, 276 Kan. 393, 77 P.2d 130 (2003).

NOTE ON UNOCAL

The specific outcome in *Unocal*, allowing an exclusionary (discriminatory) tender offer, has been superseded by the all-holders rule under the Williams Act, which ousts Delaware law under the Supremacy Clause of the Constitution. However, the basic standard of review of defensive tactics adopted in the *Unocal* decision has survived, with some glosses, as the central rule governing takeovers under Delaware law.

NOTE ON UNITRIN, INC. v. AMERICAN GENERAL CORP.

In Unitrin, Inc. v. American General Corp., 651 A.2d 1361 (1995), American General Corporation announced a tender offer to purchase all of the stock of Unitrin, Inc. at $50⅜ per share. Unitrin's board responded by taking several defensive measures, including the adoption of a poison pill and a program to repurchase up to 10 million of Unitrin's 51.8 million shares on the open market at $50⅜. Unitrin's certificate of incorporation provided that a business combination with a more-than-15% shareholder had to be approved by a majority of continuing directors or by a 75% shareholder vote. Unitrin's directors collectively held 23% of Unitrin's stock prior to adoption of the repurchase program. The directors did not intend to sell their stock to Unitrin under the repurchase program.

American General brought an action in Delaware Chancery court to enjoin Unitrin from completing its repurchase program. The Chancery court issued a preliminary injunction against Unitrin, at a point when Unitrin had purchased nearly 5 million shares of its stock, partly on the ground that since the director-shareholders were not selling their stock, the effect of the repurchase program would be to increase their stock ownership from 23% to over 25%, thereby giving them a veto under the 75% supermajority voting provision. The Delaware Supreme Court reversed, and remanded for a decision by Chancery under the standards it set out. The Supreme Court's opinion provides an important gloss on *Unocal*:

> . . . [T]he Court of Chancery erred in applying the proportionality review *Unocal* requires by focusing upon whether the Repurchase Program was an "unnecessary" defensive response. See Paramount Communications, Inc. v. QVC Network, Inc., 637 A.2d at 45–46. The Court of Chancery should have directed its enhanced scrutiny: first, upon whether the Repurchase Program the Unitrin Board implemented was draconian, by being either preclusive or coercive and; second, if it was not draconian, upon whether it was within a range of reasonable responses to the threat American General's Offer posed. Consequently, the interlocutory preliminary injunctive judgment of the Court of Chancery is reversed. . . .

The first aspect of the *Unocal* burden, the reasonableness test, required the Unitrin Board to demonstrate that, after a reasonable investigation, it determined in good faith, that American General's Offer presented a threat to Unitrin that warranted a defensive response....

... The Court of Chancery determined ... that the Board reasonably believed that the American General Offer was inadequate and also reasonably concluded that the Offer was a threat to Unitrin's uninformed stockholders....

The second aspect or proportionality test of the initial *Unocal* burden required the Unitrin Board to demonstrate the proportionality of its response to the threat American General's Offer posed....

This Court has been and remains assiduous in its concern about defensive actions designed to thwart the essence of corporate democracy by disenfranchising shareholders....

Nevertheless, this Court has upheld the propriety of adopting poison pills in given defensive circumstances. Keeping a poison pill in place may be inappropriate, however, when those circumstances change dramatically....

The Court of Chancery and all parties agree that proxy contests do not generate 100% shareholder participation. The shareholder plaintiffs argue that 80–85% may be a usual turnout. Therefore, *without* the Repurchase Program, the director shareholders' absolute voting power of 23% would already constitute *actual voting power greater than* 25% in a proxy contest with normal shareholder participation below 100%....

This Court has recognized "the prerogative of a board of directors to resist a third party's unsolicited acquisition proposal or offer." *Paramount Communications, Inc. v. QVC Network, Inc.,* Del.Supr., 637 A.2d 34, 43 n. 13 (1994). The Unitrin Board did not have unlimited discretion to defeat the threat it perceived from the American General Offer by any draconian means available. *See Unocal,* 493 A.2d at 955. Pursuant to the *Unocal* proportionality test, the nature of the threat associated with a particular hostile offer sets the parameters for the range of permissible defensive tactics. Accordingly, the purpose of enhanced judicial scrutiny is to determine whether the Board acted reasonably in "relation ... to the threat which a particular bid allegedly poses to stockholder interests." *Mills Acquisition Co. v. Macmillan, Inc.,* Del.Supr., 559 A.2d 1261, 1288 (1989).

... Courts, commentators and litigators have attempted to catalogue the threats posed by hostile tender offers.... Commentators have categorized three types of threats:

(i) *opportunity loss* ... [where] a hostile offer might deprive target shareholders of the opportunity to select a superior alternative offered by target management [or, we would add, offered by another bidder]; (ii) *structural coercion,* ... the risk that disparate treatment of non-tendering shareholders might distort shareholders' tender decisions; and (iii) *substantive coercion,* ... the risk that shareholders will mistakenly accept an underpriced offer because they disbelieve management's representations of intrinsic value....*

The record reflects that the Unitrin Board perceived the threat from American General's Offer to be a form of substantive coercion....

The record appears to support Unitrin's argument that the Board's justification for adopting the Repurchase Program was its reasonably perceived risk of substantive coercion, *i.e.,* that Unitrin's shareholders might accept American General's inadequate Offer because of "ignorance or mistaken belief" regarding the Board's assessment of the long-term value of Unitrin's stock. *See Shamrock Holdings, Inc. v. Polaroid Corp.,* Del.Ch., 559 A.2d 278, 290 (1989).... The adoption of the Repurchase Program also appears to be consistent with this Court's holding that economic inadequacy is not the only threat presented by an all cash for all shares hostile bid, because the threat of such a hostile bid could be exacerbated by shareholder "ignorance or ... mistaken belief." *Paramount Communications, Inc. v. Time, Inc.,* 571 A.2d at 1153....

An examination of the cases applying *Unocal* reveals a direct correlation between findings of proportionality or disproportionality and the judicial determination of whether a defensive response was draconian because it was either coercive or preclusive in character. In *Time,* for example, this Court concluded that the Time board's defensive response was reasonable and proportionate since it was not aimed at "cramming down" on its shareholders a management-sponsored alternative, *i.e.,* was not coercive, and because it did not preclude Paramount from making an offer for the combined Time–Warner company, *i.e.,* was not preclusive....

... As common law applications of *Unocal's* proportionality standard have evolved, at least two characteristics of draconian defensive measures taken by a board of directors in responding to a threat have been brought into focus through enhanced judicial scrutiny. In the modern takeover lexicon, it is now clear that since *Unocal,* this Court has consistently recognized that defensive measures which are either preclusive or coercive are included within the common law definition of draconian.

If a defensive measure is not draconian, however, because it is not either coercive or preclusive, the *Unocal* proportionality test requires the focus of enhanced judicial scrutiny to shift to "the range of reasonableness." *Paramount Communications, Inc.*

---

* See Paramount Communications, Inc.
v. Time Inc., n. 17, pp. 1270–1271, supra.
(Footnote by ed.)

v. QVC Network, Inc., Del.Supr., 637 A.2d 34, 45–46 (1994). Proper and proportionate defensive responses are intended and permitted to thwart perceived threats. When a corporation is not for sale, the board of directors is the defender of the metaphorical medieval corporate bastion and the protector of the corporation's shareholders. The fact that a defensive action must not be coercive or preclusive does not prevent a board from responding defensively before a bidder is at the corporate bastion's gate....

The Court of Chancery found that the Unitrin Board reasonably believed that American General's Offer was inadequate.... Upon remand, in applying the correct legal standard to the factual circumstances of this case, the Court of Chancery may conclude that the implementation of the limited Repurchase Program was also within a range of reasonable additional defensive responses available to the Unitrin Board. In considering whether the Repurchase Program was within a range of reasonableness the Court of Chancery should take into consideration whether: (1) it is a statutorily authorized form of business decision which a board of directors may routinely make in a non-takeover context; (2) as a defensive response to American General's Offer it was limited and corresponded in degree or magnitude to the degree or magnitude of the threat, (*i.e.,* assuming the threat was relatively mild, was the response relatively "mild"?); (3) with the Repurchase Program, the Unitrin Board properly recognized that all shareholders are not alike, and provided immediate liquidity to those shareholders who wanted it....

――――――

ALI, PRINCIPLES OF CORPORATE GOVERNANCE § 6.02

[See Statutory Supplement]

――――――

Moran v. Household International, Inc.

Supreme Court of Delaware, 1985.
500 A.2d 1346.

■ Before CHRISTIE, CHIEF JUSTICE, and MCNEILLY and MOORE, JJ.

■ MCNEILLY, JUSTICE:

This case presents to this Court for review the most recent defensive mechanism in the arsenal of corporate takeover weaponry—the Preferred Share Purchase Rights Plan ("Rights Plan" or "Plan"). The validity of this mechanism has attracted national attention. *Amici curiae* briefs have been filed in support of appellants by the Security and Exchange Commission ("SEC") and the Investment Company Institute. An *amicus curiae* brief has been filed in support of appellees ("Household") by the United Food and Commercial Workers International Union.

In a detailed opinion, the Court of Chancery upheld the Rights Plan as a legitimate exercise of business judgment by Household. Moran v. Household International, Inc., Del.Ch., 490 A.2d 1059 (1985). We agree, and therefore, affirm the judgment below.

I

The facts giving rise to this case have been carefully delineated in the Court of Chancery's opinion. Id. at 1064–69. A review of the basic facts is necessary for a complete understanding of the issues.

On August 14, 1984, the Board of Directors of Household International, Inc. adopted the Rights Plan by a fourteen to two vote.[2] The intricacies of the Rights Plan are contained in a 48-page document entitled "Rights Agreement". Basically, the Plan provides that Household common stockholders are entitled to the issuance of one Right per common share under certain triggering conditions. There are two triggering events that can activate the Rights. The first is the announcement of a tender offer for 30 percent of Household's shares ("30% trigger") and the second is the acquisition of 20 percent of Household's shares by any single entity or group ("20% trigger").

If an announcement of a tender offer for 30 percent of Household's shares is made, the Rights are issued and are immediately exercisable to purchase $\frac{1}{100}$ share of new preferred stock for $100 and are redeemable by the Board for $.50 per Right. If 20 percent of Household's shares are acquired by anyone, the Rights are issued and become non-redeemable and are exercisable to purchase $\frac{1}{100}$ of a share of preferred. If a Right is not exercised for preferred, and thereafter, a merger or consolidation occurs, the Rights holder can exercise each Right to purchase $200 of the common stock of the tender offeror for $100. This "flip-over" provision of the Rights Plan is at the heart of this controversy.

Household is a diversified holding company with its principal subsidiaries engaged in financial services, transportation and merchandising. HFC, National Car Rental and Vons Grocery are three of its wholly-owned entities.

Household did not adopt its Rights Plan during a battle with a corporate raider, but as a preventive mechanism to ward off future advances. The Vice–Chancellor found that as early as February 1984, Household's management became concerned about the company's vulnerability as a takeover target and began considering amending its charter to render a takeover more difficult. After considering the matter, Household decided not to pursue a fair price amendment.[3]

---

2. Household's Board has ten outside directors and six who are members of management. Messrs. Moran (appellant) and Whitehead voted against the Plan. The record reflects that Whitehead voted against the Plan not on its substance but because he thought it was novel and would bring unwanted publicity to Household.

3. A fair price amendment to a corporate charter generally requires supermajority approval for certain business combinations and sets minimum price criteria for mergers. Moran, 490 A.2d at 1064, n. 1.

In the meantime, appellant Moran, one of Household's own Directors and also Chairman of the Dyson-Kissner-Moran Corporation, ("D–K–M") which is the largest single stockholder of Household, began discussions concerning a possible leveraged buy-out of Household by D–K–M. D–K–M's financial studies showed that Household's stock was significantly undervalued in relation to the company's break-up value. It is uncontradicted that Moran's suggestion of a leveraged buy-out never progressed beyond the discussion stage.

Concerned about Household's vulnerability to a raider in light of the current takeover climate, Household secured the services of Wachtell, Lipton, Rosen and Katz ("Wachtell, Lipton") and Goldman, Sachs & Co. ("Goldman, Sachs") to formulate a takeover policy for recommendation to the Household Board at its August 14 meeting. After a July 31 meeting with a Household Board member and a pre-meeting distribution of material on the potential takeover problem and the proposed Rights Plan, the Board met on August 14, 1984.

Representatives of Wachtell, Lipton and Goldman, Sachs attended the August 14 meeting. The minutes reflect that Mr. Lipton explained to the Board that his recommendation of the Plan was based on his understanding that the Board was concerned about the increasing frequency of "bust-up"[4] takeovers, the increasing takeover activity in the financial service industry, such as Leucadia's attempt to take over Arco, and the possible adverse effect this type of activity could have on employees and others concerned with and vital to the continuing successful operation of Household even in the absence of any actual bust-up takeover attempt. Against this factual background, the Plan was approved.

Thereafter, Moran and the company of which he is Chairman, D–K–M, filed this suit. On the eve of trial, Gretl Golter, the holder of 500 shares of Household, was permitted to intervene as an additional plaintiff. The trial was held, and the Court of Chancery ruled in favor of Household. Appellants now appeal from that ruling to this Court.

II

The primary issue here is the applicability of the business judgment rule as the standard by which the adoption of the Rights Plan should be reviewed. Much of this issue has been decided by our recent decision in Unocal Corp. v. Mesa Petroleum Co., Del.Supr., 493 A.2d 946 (1985). In *Unocal,* we applied the business judgment rule to analyze Unocal's discriminatory self-tender. We explained:

> When a board addresses a pending takeover bid it has an obligation to determine whether the offer is in the best interests of the corporation and its shareholders. In that respect a board's duty is no different from any other responsibility it shoulders, and its decisions should be no less entitled to the respect they otherwise would be accorded in the realm of business judgment.

4. "Bust-up" takeover generally refers to a situation in which one seeks to finance an acquisition by selling off pieces of the acquired company.

Id. at 954 (citation and footnote omitted).

Other jurisdictions have also applied the business judgment rule to actions by which target companies have sought to forestall takeover activity they considered undesirable....

This case is distinguishable from the ones cited, since here we have a defensive mechanism adopted to ward off possible future advances and not a mechanism adopted in reaction to a specific threat. This distinguishing factor does not result in the Directors losing the protection of the business judgment rule. To the contrary, pre-planning, for the contingency of a hostile takeover might reduce the risk that, under the pressure of a takeover bid, management will fail to exercise reasonable judgment. Therefore, in reviewing a pre-planned defensive mechanism it seems even more appropriate to apply the business judgment rule. See Warner Communications v. Murdoch, D.Del., 581 F.Supp. 1482, 1491 (1984).

Of course, the business judgment rule can only sustain corporate decision making or transactions that are within the power or authority of the Board. Therefore, before the business judgment rule can be applied it must be determined whether the Directors were authorized to adopt the Rights Plan.

III

Appellants vehemently contend that the Board of Directors was unauthorized to adopt the Rights Plan. First, appellants contend that no provision of the Delaware General Corporation Law authorizes the issuance of such Rights. Secondly, appellants, along with the SEC, contend that the Board is unauthorized to usurp stockholders' rights to receive hostile tender offers. Third, appellants and the SEC also contend that the Board is unauthorized to fundamentally restrict stockholders' rights to conduct a proxy contest. We address each of these contentions in turn.

A.

While appellants contend that no provision of the Delaware General Corporation Law authorizes the Rights Plan, Household contends that the Rights Plan was issued pursuant to 8 Del.C. §§ 151(g) and 157. It explains that the Rights are authorized by § 157[5] and the issue of preferred stock underlying the Rights is authorized by § 151.[6]

---

5. The power to issue rights to purchase shares is conferred by 8 Del.C. § 157 which provides in relevant part:

Subject to any provisions in the certificate of incorporation, every corporation may create and issue, whether or not in connection with the issue and sale of any shares of stock or other securities of the corporation, rights or options entitling the holders thereof to purchase from the corporation any shares of its capital stock of any class or classes, such rights or options to be evidenced by or

in such instrument or instruments as shall be approved by the board of directors.

6. 8 Del.C. § 151(g) provides in relevant part:

When any corporation desires to issue any shares of stock of any class or of any series of any class of which the voting powers, designations, preferences and relative, participating, optional or other rights, if any, or the qualifications, limitations or restrictions thereof, if any, shall not have been set forth in the certificate of incorporation or in

Appellants respond by making several attacks upon the authority to issue the Rights pursuant to § 157.

Appellants begin by contending that § 157 cannot authorize the Rights Plan since § 157 has never served the purpose of authorizing a takeover defense. Appellants contend that § 157 is a corporate financing statute, and that nothing in its legislative history suggests a purpose that has anything to do with corporate control or a takeover defense. Appellants are unable to demonstrate that the legislature, in its adoption of § 157, meant to limit the applicability of 157 to only the issuance of Rights for the purposes of corporate financing. Without such affirmative evidence, we decline to impose such a limitation upon the section that the legislature has not. . . .

As we noted in *Unocal:*

> [O]ur corporate law is not static. It must grow and develop in response to, indeed in anticipation of, evolving concepts and needs. Merely because the General Corporation Law is silent as to a specific matter does not mean that it is prohibited.

493 A.2d at 957. See also Cheff v. Mathes, Del.Supr., 199 A.2d 548 (1964).

Secondly, appellants contend that § 157 does not authorize the issuance of sham rights such as the Rights Plan. They contend that the Rights were designed never to be exercised, and that the Plan has no economic value. In addition, they contend the preferred stock made subject to the Rights is also illusory, citing Telvest, Inc. v. Olson, Del.Ch., C.A. No. 5798, Brown, V.C. (March 8, 1979).

Appellants' sham contention fails in both regards. As to the Rights, they can and will be exercised upon the happening of a triggering mechanism, as we have observed during the current struggle of Sir James Goldsmith to take control of Crown Zellerbach. See Wall Street Journal, July 26, 1985, at 3, 12. As to the preferred shares, we agree with the Court of Chancery that they are distinguishable from sham securities invalidated in *Telvest,* supra. The Household preferred, issuable upon the happening of a triggering event, have superior dividend and liquidation rights.

Third, appellants contend that § 157 authorizes the issuance of Rights "entitling holders thereof to purchase from the corporation any shares of *its* capital stock of any class . . ." (emphasis added). Therefore, their contention continues, the plain language of the statute does not authorize Household to issue rights to purchase another's capital stock upon a merger of consolidation.

Household contends, *inter alia,* that the Rights Plan is analogous to "anti-destruction" or "anti-dilution" provisions which are custom-

---

any amendment thereto but shall be provided for in a resolution or resolutions adopted by the board of directors pursuant to authority expressly vested in it by the provisions of the certificate of incorporation or any amendment thereto, a certificate setting forth a copy of such resolution or resolutions and the number of shares of stock of such class or series shall be executed, acknowledged, filed, recorded, and shall become effective, in accordance with § 103 of this title.

ary features of a wide variety of corporate securities. While appellants seem to concede that "anti-destruction" provisions are valid under Delaware corporate law, they seek to distinguish the Rights Plan as not being incidental, as are most "anti-destruction" provisions, to a corporation's statutory power to finance itself. We find no merit to such a distinction. We have already rejected appellants' similar contention that § 157 could only be used for financing purposes. We also reject that distinction here.

"Anti-destruction" clauses generally ensure holders of certain securities of the protection of their right of conversion in the event of a merger by giving them the right to convert their securities into whatever securities are to replace the stock of their company. See *Broad v. Rockwell International Corp.*, 5th Cir., 642 F.2d 929, 946, cert. denied, 454 U.S. 965, 102 S.Ct. 506, 70 L.Ed.2d 380 (1981); *Wood v. Coastal States Gas Corp.*, Del.Supr., 401 A.2d 932, 937–39 (1979); *B.S.F. Co. v. Philadelphia National Bank*, Del.Supr., 204 A.2d 746, 750–51 (1964). The fact that the rights here have as their purpose the prevention of coercive two-tier tender offers does not invalidate them. . . .

Having concluded that sufficient authority for the Rights Plan exists in 8 Del.C. § 157, we note the inherent powers of the Board conferred by 8 Del.C. § 141(a), concerning the management of the corporation's "business and *affairs*" (emphasis added), also provides the Board additional authority upon which to enact the Rights Plan. *Unocal*, 493 A.2d at 953.

B.

Appellants contend that the Board is unauthorized to usurp stockholders' rights to receive tender offers by changing Household's fundamental structure. We conclude that the Rights Plan does not prevent stockholders from receiving tender offers, and that the change of Household's structure was less than that which results from the implementation of other defensive mechanisms upheld by various courts.

Appellants' contention that stockholders will lose their right to receive and accept tender offers seems to be premised upon an understanding of the Rights Plan which is illustrated by the SEC *amicus* brief which states: "The Chancery Court's decision seriously understates the impact of this plan. In fact, as we discuss below, the Rights Plan will deter not only two-tier offers, but virtually all hostile tender offers."

The fallacy of that contention is apparent when we look at the recent takeover of Crown Zellerbach, which has a similar Rights Plan, by Sir James Goldsmith. Wall Street Journal, July 26, 1985, at 3, 12. The evidence at trial also evidenced many methods around the Plan ranging from tendering with a condition that the Board redeem the Rights, tendering with a high minimum condition of shares and Rights, tendering and soliciting consents to remove the Board and redeem the Rights, to acquiring 50% of the shares and causing Household to self-tender for the Rights. One could also form a group of up to 19.9% and solicit proxies for consents to remove the Board and redeem the Rights. These are but a few of the methods by which Household can still be acquired by a hostile tender offer.

In addition, the Rights Plan is not absolute. When the Household Board of Directors is faced with a tender offer and a request to redeem the Rights, they will not be able to arbitrarily reject the offer. They will be held to the same fiduciary standards any other board of directors would be held to in deciding to adopt a defensive mechanism, the same standard as they were held to in originally approving the Rights Plan. See *Unocal*, 493 A.2d at 954–55, 958.

In addition, appellants contend that the deterrence of tender offers will be accomplished by what they label "a fundamental transfer of power from the stockholders to the directors." They contend that this transfer of power, in itself, is unauthorized.

The Rights Plan will result in no more of a structural change than any other defensive mechanism adopted by a board of directors. The Rights Plan does not destroy the assets of the corporation. The implementation of the Plan neither results in any outflow of money from the corporation nor impairs its financial flexibility. It does not dilute earnings per share and does not have any adverse tax consequences for the corporation or its stockholders. The Plan has not adversely affected the market price of Household's stock.

Comparing the Rights Plan with other defensive mechanisms, it does less harm to the value structure of the corporation than do the other mechanisms. Other mechanisms result in increased debt of the corporation. See Whittaker Corp. v. Edgar, supra (sale of "prize asset"), Cheff v. Mathes, supra, (paying greenmail to eliminate a threat), Unocal Corp. v. Mesa Petroleum Co., supra, (discriminatory self-tender).

There is little change in the governance structure as a result of the adoption of the Rights Plan. The Board does not now have unfettered discretion in refusing to redeem the Rights. The Board has no more discretion in refusing to redeem the Rights than it does in enacting any defensive mechanism.

The contention that the Rights Plan alters the structure more than do other defensive mechanisms because it is so effective as to make the corporation completely safe from hostile tender offers is likewise without merit. As explained above, there are numerous methods to successfully launch a hostile tender offer.

C.

Appellant's third contention is that the Board was unauthorized to fundamentally restrict stockholders' rights to conduct a proxy contest. Appellants contend that the "20% trigger" effectively prevents any stockholder from first acquiring 20% or more shares before conducting a proxy contest and further, it prevents stockholders from banding together into a group to solicit proxies if, collectively, they own 20%

or more of the stock.[12] In addition, at trial, appellants contended that read literally, the Rights Agreement triggers the Rights upon the mere acquisition of the right to vote 20% or more of the shares through a proxy solicitation, and thereby precludes any proxy contest from being waged.[13]

Appellants seem to have conceded this last contention in light of Household's response that the receipt of a proxy does not make the recipient the "beneficial owner" of the shares involved which would trigger the Rights. In essence, the Rights Agreement provides that the Rights are triggered when someone becomes the "beneficial owner" of 20% or more of Household stock. Although a literal reading of the Rights Agreement definition of "beneficial owner" would seem to include those shares which one has the right to vote, it has long been recognized that the relationship between grantor and recipient of a proxy is one of agency, and the agency is revocable by the grantor at any time. Henn, Corporations § 196, at 518. Therefore, the holder of a proxy is not the "beneficial owner" of the stock. As a result, the mere acquisition of the right to vote 20% of the shares does not trigger the Rights.

The issue, then, is whether the restriction upon individuals or groups from first acquiring 20% of shares before waging a proxy contest fundamentally restricts stockholders' right to conduct a proxy contest. Regarding this issue the Court of Chancery found:

> Thus, while the Rights Plan does deter the formation of proxy efforts of a certain magnitude, it does not limit the voting power of individual shares. On the evidence presented it is highly conjectural to assume that a particular effort to assert shareholder views in the election of directors or revisions of corporate policy will be frustrated by the proxy feature of the Plan. Household's witnesses, Troubh and Higgins described recent corporate take-over battles in which insurgents holding less than 10% stock ownership were able to secure corporate control through a proxy contest or the threat of one.

Moran, 490 A.2d at 1080.

We conclude that there was sufficient evidence at trial to support the Vice-Chancellor's finding that the effect upon proxy contests will be minimal. Evidence at trial established that many proxy contests are won with an insurgent ownership of less than 20%, and that very large holdings are no guarantee of success. There was also testimony that the key variable in proxy contest success is the merit of an insurgent's issues, not the size of his holdings.

---

12. Appellants explain that the acquisition of 20% of the shares trigger the Rights, making them non-redeemable, and thereby would prevent even a future friendly offer for the ten-year life of the Rights.

13. The SEC still contends that the mere acquisition of the right to vote 20% of the shares through a proxy solicitation triggers the rights. We do not interpret the Rights Agreement in that manner.

IV

Having concluded that the adoption of the Rights Plan was within the authority of the Directors, we now look to whether the Directors have met their burden under the business judgment rule.

The business judgment rule is a "presumption that in making a business decision the directors of a corporation acted on an informed basis, in good faith and in the honest belief that the action taken was in the best interests of the company." Aronson v. Lewis, Del.Supr., 473 A.2d 805, 812 (1984) (citations omitted). Notwithstanding, in *Unocal* we held that when the business judgment rule applies to adoption of a defensive mechanism, the initial burden will lie with the directors. The "directors must show that they had reasonable grounds for believing that a danger to corporate policy and effectiveness existed.... [T]hey satisfy that burden 'by showing good faith and reasonable investigation....'" *Unocal,* 493 A.2d at 955 (citing Cheff v. Mathes, 199 A.2d at 55455). In addition, the directors must show that the defensive mechanism was reasonable in relation to the threat posed. *Unocal,* 493 A.2d at 955. Moreover, that proof is materially enhanced, as we noted in *Unocal,* where, as here, a majority of the board favoring the proposal consisted of outside independent directors who have acted in accordance with the foregoing standards. *Unocal,* 493 A.2d at 955; *Aronson,* 473 A.2d at 815. Then, the burden shifts back to the plaintiffs who have the ultimate burden of persuasion to show a breach of the directors' fiduciary duties. *Unocal,* 493 A.2d at 958.

There are no allegations here of any bad faith on the part of the Directors' action in the adoption of the Rights Plan. There is no allegation that the Directors' action was taken for entrenchment purposes. Household has adequately demonstrated, as explained above, that the adoption of the Rights Plan was in reaction to what it perceived to be the threat in the market place of coercive two-tier tender offers. Appellants do contend, however, that the Board did not exercise informed business judgment in its adoption of the Plan.

Appellants contend that the Household Board was uninformed since they were, *inter alia,* told the Plan would not inhibit a proxy contest, were not told the plan would preclude all hostile acquisitions of Household, and were told that Delaware counsel opined that the plan was within the business judgment of the Board.

As to the first two contentions, as we explained above, the Rights Plan will not have a severe impact upon proxy contests and it will not preclude all hostile acquisitions of Household. Therefore, the Directors were not misinformed or uninformed on these facts.

Appellants contend the Delaware counsel did not express an opinion on the flip-over provision of the Rights, rather only that the Rights would constitute validly issued and outstanding rights to subscribe to the preferred stock of the company.

To determine whether a business judgment reached by a board of directors was an informed one, we determine whether the directors were grossly negligent. Smith v. Van Gorkom, Del.Supr., 488 A.2d 858,

873 (1985). Upon a review of this record, we conclude the Directors were not grossly negligent. The information supplied to the Board on August 14 provided the essentials of the Plan. The Directors were given beforehand a notebook which included a three-page summary of the Plan along with articles on the current takeover environment. The extended discussion between the Board and representatives of Wachtell, Lipton and Goldman, Sachs before approval of the Plan reflected a full and candid evaluation of the Plan. Moran's expression of his views at the meeting served to place before the Board a knowledgeable critique of the Plan. The factual happenings here are clearly distinguishable from the actions of the directors of Trans Union Corporation who displayed gross negligence in approving a cash-out merger. Id.

In addition, to meet their burden, the Directors must show that the defensive mechanism was "reasonable in relation to the threat posed". The record reflects a concern on the part of the Directors over the increasing frequency in the financial services industry of "bootstrap" and "bust-up" takeovers. The Directors were also concerned that such takeovers may take the form of two-tier offers.[14] In addition, on August 14, the Household Board was aware of Moran's overture on behalf of D–K–M. In sum, the Directors reasonably believed Household was vulnerable to coercive acquisition techniques and adopted a reasonable defensive mechanism to protect itself.

V

In conclusion, the Household Directors receive the benefit of the business judgment rule in their adoption of the Rights Plan.

The Directors adopted the Plan pursuant to statutory authority in 8 Del.C. §§ 141, 151, 157. We reject appellants' contentions that the Rights Plan strips stockholders of their rights to receive tender offers, and that the Rights Plan fundamentally restricts proxy contests.

The Directors adopted the Plan in the good faith belief that it was necessary to protect Household from coercive acquisition techniques. The Board was informed as to the details of the Plan. In addition, Household has demonstrated that the Plan is reasonable in relation to the threat posed. Appellants, on the other hand, have failed to convince us that the Directors breached any fiduciary duty in their adoption of the Rights Plan.

While we conclude for present purposes that the Household Directors are protected by the business judgment rule, that does not end the matter. The ultimate response to an actual takeover bid must be judged by the Directors' actions at that time, and nothing we say here relieves them of their basic fundamental duties to the corporation and its stockholders. *Unocal,* 493 A.2d at 954–55, 958; Smith v. Van Gorkom, 488 A.2d at 87273; *Aronson,* 473 A.2d at 812–13; Pogostin v.

---

14. We have discussed the coercive nature of two-tier tender offers in *Unocal,* 493 A.2d at 956, n. 12. We explained in *Unocal* that a discriminatory self-tender was reasonably related to the threat of two-tier tender offers and possible greenmail.

Rice, Del.Supr., 480 A.2d 619, 627 (1984). Their use of the Plan will be evaluated when and if the issue arises.

* * *

AFFIRMED.*

NOTE ON CARMODY v. TOLL BROTHERS, INC.

The facts of the next principal case, *Quickturn Design Systems, Inc. v. Shapiro*, decided by the Delaware Supreme Court, can best be understood against the background of an earlier case decided by the Delaware Chancery Court, Carmody v. Toll Brothers, Inc., 723 A.2d 1180 (Del.Ch.1998). *Carmody* concerned the validity of a "dead hand" poison pill adopted by Toll Brothers, Inc. As described by Vice Chancellor Jacobs:

> A "dead hand" rights plan is one that cannot be redeemed except by the incumbent directors who adopted the plan or their designated successors.

> In substance, the "dead hand" provision operates to prevent any directors of Toll Brothers, except those who were in office as of the date of the Rights Plan's adoption (June 12, 1997) or their designated successors, from redeeming the Rights until they expire on June 12, 2007. That consequence flows directly from the Rights Agreement's [provision that] only "Continuing Directors" could redeem the Rights, and from its definition of a "Continuing Director," which is:

>> (i) any member of the Board of Directors of the Company, while such person is a member of the Board, who is not an Acquiring Person, or an Affiliate [as defined] or Associate [as defined] of an Acquiring Person, or a representative or nominee of an Acquiring Person or of any such Affiliate or Associate, and was a member of the Board prior to the date of this agreement, or (ii) any Person who subsequently becomes a member of the Board, while such Person is a member of the Board, who is not an Acquiring Person, or an Affiliate [as defined] or Associate [as defined] of an Acquiring Person, or a representative or nominee of an Acquiring Person or of any such Affiliate or Associate, if such Person's nomination for election or election to the Board is recommended or approved by a majority of the Continuing Directors.

Vice Chancellor Jacobs explained the genesis of dead hand pills as follows:

> For our purposes, the relevant history begins in the early 1980s with the advent of the "poison pill" as an antitakeover

---

Moran was reaffirmed in Account v. Hilton Hotels Corp., 780 A.2d 245 (2001).

measure. That innovation generated litigation focused upon the issue of whether any poison pill rights plan could validly be adopted under state corporation law. The seminal case, Moran v. Household International, Inc., answered that question in the affirmative.

In *Moran*, this Court and the Supreme Court upheld the "flip over" rights plan in issue there based on three distinct factual findings. The first was that the poison pill would not erode fundamental shareholder rights, because the target board would not have unfettered discretion arbitrarily to reject a hostile offer or to refuse to redeem the pill. Rather, the board's judgment not to redeem the pill would be subject to judicially enforceable fiduciary standards. The second finding was that even if the board refused to redeem the pill (thereby preventing the shareholders from receiving the unsolicited offer), that would not preclude the acquiror from gaining control of the target company, because the offeror could "form a group of up to 19.9% and solicit proxies for consents to remove the Board and redeem the Rights." Third, even if the hostile offer was precluded, the target company's stockholders could always exercise their ultimate prerogative— wage a proxy contest to remove the board. On this basis, the Supreme Court concluded that "the Rights Plan will not have a severe impact upon proxy contests and it will not preclude all hostile acquisitions of Household."

It being settled that a corporate board could permissibly adopt a poison pill, the next litigated question became: under what circumstances would the directors' fiduciary duties require the board to redeem the rights in the face of a hostile takeover proposal? That issue was litigated, in Delaware and elsewhere, during the second half of the 1980s. The lesson taught by that experience was that courts were extremely reluctant to order the redemption of poison pills on fiduciary grounds. The reason was the prudent deployment of the pill proved to be largely beneficial to shareholder interests: it often resulted in a bidding contest that culminated in an acquisition on terms superior to the initial hostile offer.

Once it became clear that the prospects were unlikely for obtaining judicial relief mandating a redemption of the poison pill, a different response to the pill was needed. That response, which echoed the Supreme Court's suggestion in Moran, was the foreseeable next step in the evolution of takeover strategy: a tender offer coupled with a solicitation for shareholder proxies to remove and replace the incumbent board with the acquiror's nominees who, upon assuming office, would redeem the pill. Because that strategy, if unopposed, would enable hostile offerors to effect an "end run" around the poison pill, it again was predictable and only a matter of time that target company boards would develop counter-strategies. With one exception—the "dead hand" pill—these counter-strategies proved "successful" only in cases where the purpose was to delay the process to enable the board to develop alternatives to the hostile offer. The counter-strategies were largely unsuccessful, however, where the goal was to stop the proxy contest (and as a consequence, the hostile offer) altogether.

For example, in cases where the target board's response was either to (i) amend the by-laws to delay a shareholders meeting to elect directors, or (ii) delay an annual meeting to a later date permitted under the bylaws, so that the board and management would be able to explore alternatives to the hostile offer (but not entrench themselves), those responses were upheld. On the other hand, where the target board's response to a proxy contest (coupled with a hostile offer) was (i) to move the shareholders meeting to a later date to enable the incumbent board to solicit revocations of proxies to defeat the apparently victorious dissident group, or (ii) to expand the size of the board, and then fill the newly created positions so the incumbents would retain control of the board irrespective of the outcome of the proxy contest, those responses were declared invalid.

This litigation experience taught that a target board, facing a proxy contest joined with a hostile tender offer, could, in good faith, employ non-preclusive defensive measures to give the board time to explore transactional alternatives. The target board could not, however, erect defenses that would either preclude a proxy contest altogether or improperly bend the rules to favor the board's continued incumbency.

In this environment, the only defensive measure that promised to be a "show stopper" (i.e., had the potential to deter a proxy contest altogether) was a poison pill with a dead hand feature. The reason is that if only the incumbent directors or their designated successors could redeem the pill, it would make little sense for shareholders or the hostile bidder to wage a proxy contest to replace the incumbent board. Doing that would eliminate from the scene the only group of persons having the power to give the hostile bidder and target company shareholders what they desired: control of the target company (in the case of the hostile bidder) and the opportunity to obtain an attractive price for their shares (in the case of the target company stockholders). It is against that backdrop that the legal issues presented here, which concern the validity of the "dead hand" feature, attain significance.

Vice Chancellor Jacobs concluded that the plaintiff's complaint stated a legally cognizable claim that a dead hand plan is invalid, on several grounds:

First, a dead hand pill violates the Delaware statute by impermissibly creating voting-power distinctions among directors without authorization in the certificate of incorporation, and by interfering with the directors' statutory power to manage the business and affairs of the corporation.

Second, a dead hand pill is unlawful under *Blasius* (See Chapter 4, supra), because it purposefully interferes with the shareholder voting franchise without any compelling justification.

Third, a dead hand pill is a "disproportionate" defensive measure under *Unocal/Unitrin*, because it either precludes or materially abridges the shareholders' rights to receive tender offers and to wage a proxy contest to replace the board.

In contrast to *Carmody*, a dead hand pill was upheld by a federal district court under Georgia law in *Invacare Corp. v. Healthdyne Technologies, Inc.*, 968 F.Supp. 1578 (N.D. Ga. 1997), although the result in that case was driven at least in part by an interpretation of language in the Georgia statute.

Quickturn Design Systems, Inc. v. Shapiro

Supreme Court of Delaware, 1998.
721 A.2d 1281.

■ Before WALSH, HOLLAND and HARTNETT, JUSTICES.

■ HOLLAND, JUSTICE:

The Quickturn case is an expedited appeal from a final judgment entered by the Court of Chancery. The dispute arises out of an ongoing effort by Mentor Graphics Corporation ("Mentor"), a hostile bidder, to acquire Quickturn Design Systems, Inc. ("Quickturn"), the target company. The plaintiffs-appellees are Mentor and an unaffiliated stockholder of Quickturn. The named defendants-appellants are Quickturn and its directors.

In response to Mentor's tender offer and proxy contest to replace the Quickturn board of directors, as part of Mentor's effort to acquire Quickturn, the Quickturn board enacted two defensive measures. First, it amended the Quickturn shareholder rights plan ("Rights Plan") by adopting a "no hand" feature of limited duration (the "Delayed Redemption Provision" or "DRP"). Second, the Quickturn board amended the corporation's by-laws to delay the holding of any special stockholders meeting requested by stockholders for 90 to 100 days after the validity of the request is determined (the "Amendment" or "By–Law Amendment").

Mentor filed actions for declaratory and injunctive relief in the Court of Chancery challenging the legality of both defensive responses by Quickturn's board. The Court of Chancery conducted a trial on the merits. It determined that the By–Law Amendment is valid. It also concluded, however, that the DRP is invalid on fiduciary duty grounds.

In this appeal, Quickturn argues that the Court of Chancery erred in finding that Quickturn's directors breached their fiduciary duty by adopting the Delayed Redemption Provision. We have concluded that, as a matter of Delaware law, the Delayed Redemption Provision was invalid. Therefore, on that alternative basis, the judgment of the Court of Chancery is affirmed.

STATEMENT OF FACTS

The Parties

Mentor (the hostile bidder) is an Oregon corporation, headquartered in Wilsonville, Oregon, whose shares are publicly traded on the NASDAQ national market system. Mentor manufactures, markets, and supports electronic design automation ("EDA") software and hardware. It also provides related services that enable engineers to design, analyze, simulate, model, implement, and verify the components of electronic systems. Mentor markets its products primarily for large firms in the communications, computer, semiconductor, consumer electronics, aerospace, and transportation industries.

Quickturn, the target company, is a Delaware corporation, headquartered in San Jose, California. Quickturn has 17,922,518 outstanding shares of common stock that are publicly traded on the NASDAQ national market system. Quickturn invented, and was the first company to successfully market, logic emulation technology, which is used to verify the design of complex silicon chips and electronics systems. Quickturn is currently the market leader in the emulation business, controlling an estimated 60% of the worldwide emulation market and an even higher percentage of the United States market. Quickturn maintains the largest intellectual property portfolio in the industry, which includes approximately twenty-nine logic emulation patents issued in the United States, and numerous other patents issued in foreign jurisdictions. Quickturn's customers include the world's leading technology companies, among them Intel, IBM, Sun Microsystems, Texas Instruments, Hitachi, Fujitsu, Siemens, and NEC.

Quickturn's board of directors consists of eight members, all but one of whom are outside, independent directors.[4] All have distinguished careers and significant technological experience. Collectively, the board has more than 30 years of experience in the EDA industry

---

4. The Quickturn board includes Messrs. Glen Antle (President and Chairman of Quickturn's board of directors); Michael D'Amour (Quickturn's founding CEO and chairman through 1993, and Executive Vice President for research and development and head of international sales until he left Quickturn management in 1995); Dean William A. Hasler (a former Vice Chairman and partner of KPMG Peat Marwick; a former Dean of the Haas Graduate School of Business at the University of California, Berkeley, a position he held until 1998; and currently a technology and business advisor); Keith Lobo (Quickturn's President and CEO); Charles D. Kissner (currently CEO and Chairman of the Board of Digital Microwave Corporation, a telecommunications company, and a former President, CEO, and director for Aristacom International, Inc.; also a former AT & T executive); Richard Alberding (a management consultant for high technology companies; and who currently serves on the board of directors of several technology companies); Dr. David Lam (former Vice President at Wyse Technology, former President and CEO of Expert Edge, Inc., and currently a technology and business advisor in the semiconductor equipment industry and Chairman of the David Lam Group); Dr. Yen–Son (Paul) Huang (a co-founder and President of PiE and, following PiE's merger with Quickturn in 1993, Executive Vice President of Quickturn until June 1997. Since then, Dr. Huang has served Quickturn only as a director).

and owns one million shares (about 5%) of Quickturn's common stock.

Since 1989, Quickturn has historically been a growth company, having experienced increases in earnings and revenues during the past seven years. Those favorable trends were reflected in Quickturn's stock prices, which reached a high of $15.75 during the first quarter of 1998, and generally traded in the $15.875 to $21.25 range during the year preceding Mentor's hostile bid.

Since the spring of 1998, Quickturn's earnings, revenue growth, and stock price levels have declined, largely because of the downturn in the semiconductor industry and more specifically in the Asian semiconductor market. Historically, 30%–35% of Quickturn's annual sales (approximately $35 million) had come from Asia, but in 1998, Quickturn's Asian sales declined dramatically with the downturn of the Asian market.[5] Management has projected that the negative impact of the Asian market upon Quickturn's sales should begin reversing itself sometime between the second half of 1998 and early 1999.

Quickturn–Mentor Patent Litigation

Since 1996, Mentor and Quickturn have been engaged in patent litigation that has resulted in Mentor being barred from competing in the United States emulation market. Because its products have been adjudicated to infringe upon Quickturn's patents, Mentor currently stands enjoined from selling, manufacturing, or marketing its emulation products in the United States. Thus, Mentor is excluded from an unquestionably significant market for emulation products.

The origin of the patent controversy was Mentor's sale of its hardware emulation assets, including its patents, to Quickturn in 1992. Later, Mentor reentered the emulation business when it acquired a French company called Meta Systems ("Meta") and began to market Meta's products in the United States in December 1995. Quickturn reacted by commencing a proceeding before the International Trade Commission ("ITC") claiming that Meta and Mentor were infringing Quickturn's patents. In August 1996, the ITC issued an order prohibiting Mentor from importing, selling, distributing, advertising, or soliciting in the United States, any products manufactured by Meta. That preliminary order was affirmed by the Federal Circuit Court of Appeals in August 1997. In December 1997, the ITC issued a Permanent Exclusion Order prohibiting Mentor from importing, selling, marketing, advertising, or soliciting in the United States, until at least April 28, 2009, any of the emulation products manufactured by Meta outside the United States.

At present, the only remaining patent litigation is pending in the Oregon Federal District Court. Quickturn is asserting a patent infringement damage claim that, Quickturn contends, is worth approximately

---

5. By the summer of 1998, Quickturn's stock price had declined to $6 per share. On August 11, 1998, the closing price was $8.00 It was in this trough period that Mentor, which had designs upon Quickturn since the fall of 1997, saw an opportunity to acquire Quickturn for an advantageous price.

$225 million. Mentor contends that Quickturn's claim is worth only $5.2 million or even less.

Mentor's Interest in Acquiring Quickturn

Mentor began exploring the possibility of acquiring Quickturn. If Mentor owned Quickturn, it would also own the patents, and would be in a position to "unenforce" them by seeking to vacate Quickturn's injunctive orders against Mentor in the patent litigation. The exploration process began when Mr. Bernd Braune, a Mentor senior executive, retained Arthur Andersen ("Andersen") to advise Mentor how it could successfully compete in the emulation market. The result was a report Andersen issued in October 1997, entitled "PROJECT VELOCITY" and "Strategic Alternatives Analysis." The Andersen report identified several advantages and benefits Mentor would enjoy if it acquired Quickturn.[10]

In December 1997, Mentor retained Salomon Smith Barney ("Salomon") to act as its financial advisor in connection with a possible acquisition of Quickturn. Salomon prepared an extensive study which it reviewed with Mentor's senior executives in early 1998. The Salomon study concluded that although a Quickturn acquisition could provide substantial value for Mentor, Mentor could not afford to acquire Quickturn at the then-prevailing market price levels. Ultimately, Mentor decided not to attempt an acquisition of Quickturn during the first half of 1998.

After Quickturn's stock price began to decline in May 1998, however, Gregory Hinckley, Mentor's Executive Vice President, told Dr. Walden Rhines, Mentor's Chairman, that "the market outlook being very weak due to the Asian crisis made it a good opportunity" to try acquiring Quickturn for a cheap price. Mr. Hinckley then assembled Mentor's financial and legal advisors, proxy solicitors, and others, and began a three month process that culminated in Mentor's August 12, 1998 tender offer.

Mentor Tender Offer and Proxy Contest

On August 12, 1998, Mentor announced an unsolicited cash tender offer for all outstanding common shares of Quickturn at $12.125 per share, a price representing an approximate 50% premium over Quickturn's immediate pre-offer price, and a 20% discount from Quickturn's February 1998 stock price levels. Mentor's tender offer, once consummated, would be followed by a second step merger in which Quickturn's nontendering stockholders would receive, in cash, the same $12.125 per share tender offer price.

---

10. These included: (i) eliminating the time and expense associated with litigation; (ii) creating synergy from combining two companies with complementary core competencies; (iii) reducing customer confusion over product availability, which in turn would accelerate sales; and (iv) eliminating the threat of a large competitor moving into the emulation market. Mentor has utilized these reasons in public statements in which it attempted to explain why its bid made sense.

Mentor also announced its intent to solicit proxies to replace the board at a special meeting. Relying upon Quickturn's then-applicable by-law provision governing the call of special stockholders meetings, Mentor began soliciting agent designations from Quickturn stockholders to satisfy the by-law's stock ownership requirements to call such a meeting.[11]

Quickturn Board Meetings

Under the Williams Act, Quickturn was required to inform its shareholders of its response to Mentor's offer no later than ten business days after the offer was commenced. During that ten day period, the Quickturn board met three times, on August 13, 17, and 21, 1998. During each of those meetings, it considered Mentor's offer and ultimately decided how to respond.

The Quickturn board first met on August 13, 1998, the day after Mentor publicly announced its bid. All board members attended the meeting, for the purpose of evaluating Mentor's tender offer. The meeting lasted for several hours. Before or during the meeting, each board member received a package that included (i) Mentor's press release announcing the unsolicited offer; (ii) Quickturn's press release announcing its board's review of Mentor's offer; (iii) Dr. Rhines's August 11 letter to Mr. Antle [Quickturn's president]; (iv) ... complaints filed by Mentor against Quickturn and its directors; and (v) copies of Quickturn's then-current Rights Plan and by-laws.

The Quickturn board first discussed retaining a team of financial advisors to assist it in evaluating Mentor's offer and the company's strategic alternatives. The board discussed the importance of selecting a qualified investment bank, and considered several investment banking firms. Aside from Hambrecht Quist ("H & Q"), Quickturn's long-time investment banker, other firms that the board considered included Goldman Sachs Co. and Morgan Stanley Dean Witter. Ultimately, the board selected H & Q, because the board believed that H & Q had the most experience with the EDA industry in general and with Quickturn in particular.[12]

During the balance of the meeting, the board discussed for approximately one or two hours (a) the status, terms, and conditions of Mentor's offer; (b) the status of Quickturn's patent litigation with Mentor; (c) the applicable rules and regulations that would govern the board's response to the offer required by the Securities Exchange Act of 1934 (the "34 Act"); (d) the board's fiduciary duties to Quickturn

---

11. The applicable by-law (Article II, § 2.3) authorized a call of a special stockholders meeting by shareholders holding at least 10% of Quickturn's shares. In their agent solicitation, Mentor informed Quickturn stockholders that Mentor intended to call a special meeting approximately 45 days after it received sufficient agent designations to satisfy the 10% requirement under the original by-law. The solicitation also disclosed Mentor's intent to set the date for the special meeting, and to set the record date and give formal notice of that meeting.

12. Apparently, the board had already decided to retain Quickturn's outside counsel, Wilson, Sonsini, Goodrich & Rosati, as its legal advisors. Larry Sonsini, Esquire, a senior partner of that firm, is shown on the minutes of all three board meetings as "Secretary of the Meeting," and appears to have authored those minutes in that capacity.

and its shareholders in a tender offer context; (e) the scope of defensive measures available to the corporation if the board decided that the offer was not in the best interests of the company or its stockholders; (f) Quickturn's then-current Rights Plan and special stockholders meeting by-law provisions; (g) the need for a federal antitrust filing; and (h) the potential effect of Mentor's offer on Quickturn's employees. The board also instructed management and H & Q to prepare analyses to assist the directors in evaluating Mentor's offer, and scheduled two board meetings, August 17, and August 21, 1998.

The Quickturn board next met on August 17, 1998. That meeting centered around financial presentations by management and by H & Q. Mr. Keith Lobo, Quickturn's President and CEO, presented a Medium Term Strategic Plan, which was a "top down" estimate detailing the economic outlook and the company's future sales, income prospects and future plans (the "Medium Term Plan"). The Medium Term Plan contained an optimistic (30%) revenue growth projection for the period 1998–2000.[13] After management made its presentation, H & Q supplied its valuation of Quickturn, which relied upon a "base case" that assumed management's 30% revenue growth projection. On that basis, H & Q presented various "standalone" valuations based on various techniques, including a discounted cash flow ("DCF") analysis. Finally, the directors discussed possible defensive measures, but took no action at that time.

The Quickturn board held its third and final meeting in response to Mentor's offer on August 21, 1998. Again, the directors received extensive materials and a further detailed analysis performed by H & Q. The focal point of that analysis was a chart entitled "Summary of Implied Valuation." That chart compared Mentor's tender offer price to the Quickturn valuation ranges generated by H & Q's application of five different methodologies.[14] The chart showed that Quickturn's value under all but one of those methodologies was higher than Mentor's $12.125 tender offer price.

Quickturn's Board Rejects Mentor's Offer as Inadequate

After hearing the presentations, the Quickturn board concluded that Mentor's offer was inadequate, and decided to recommend that Quickturn shareholders reject Mentor's offer. The directors based their decision upon: (a) H & Q's report; (b) the fact that Quickturn was experiencing a temporary trough in its business, which was reflected in its stock price; (c) the company's leadership in technology and patents and resulting market share; (d) the likely growth in Quickturn's markets (most notably, the Asian market) and the strength of

---

13. The Court of Chancery concluded that the Quickturn board had grounds to anticipate that the company could "turn around" in a year and perform at the projected revenue levels.

14. The five methodologies and the respective price ranges were: Historical Trading Range ($6.13–$21.63); Comparable Public Companies ($2.55–$15.61); Comparable M & A Transactions ($6.00–$31.36); Comparable Premiums Paid ($9.54–$10.72); and Discounted Cash Flow Analysis ($11.88–$57.87).

Quickturn's new products (specifically, its Mercury product); (e) the potential value of the patent litigation with Mentor; and (f) the problems for Quickturn's customers, employees, and technology if the two companies were combined as the result of a hostile takeover.

Quickturn's Defensive Measures

At the August 21 board meeting, the Quickturn board adopted two defensive measures in response to Mentor's hostile takeover bid. First, the board amended Article II, § 2.3 of Quickturn's by-laws, which permitted stockholders holding 10% or more of Quickturn's stock to call a special stockholders meeting. The By–Law Amendment provides that if any such special meeting is requested by shareholders, the corporation (Quickturn) would fix the record date for, and determine the time and place of, that special meeting, which must take place not less than 90 days nor more than 100 days after the receipt and determination of the validity of the shareholders' request.

Second, the board amended Quickturn's shareholder Rights Plan by eliminating its "dead hand" feature and replacing it with the Deferred Redemption Provision, under which no newly elected board could redeem the Rights Plan for six months after taking office, if the purpose or effect of the redemption would be to facilitate a transaction with an "Interested Person" (one who proposed, nominated or financially supported the election of the new directors to the board).[15] Mentor would be an Interested Person.

The effect of the By–Law Amendment would be to delay a shareholder-called special meeting for at least three months. The effect of the DRP would be to delay the ability of a newly-elected, Mentor-nominated board to redeem the Rights Plan or "poison pill" for six months, in any transaction with an Interested Person. Thus, the combined effect of the two defensive measures would be to delay any acquisition of Quickturn by Mentor for at least nine months.

PROCEDURAL HISTORY

Mentor filed this action in the Court of Chancery on August 12, 1998, seeking a declaratory judgment that Quickturn's newly adopted takeover defenses are invalid and an injunction requiring the Quickturn board to dismantle those defenses. After expedited briefing and oral argument, the Court of Chancery denied Quickturn's case dispositive pre-trial motion on October 9, 1998. A trial was held on October

---

15. The amended Rights Plan pertinently provides that: "[I]n the event that a majority of the Board of Directors of the Company is elected by stockholder action at an annual or special meeting of stockholders, then until the 180th day following the effectiveness of such election (including any postponement or adjournment thereof), the Rights shall not be redeemed if such redemption is reasonably likely to have the purpose or effect of facilitating a Transaction with an Interested Person."

An "Interested Person" is defined under the amended Rights Plan as "any Person who (i) is or will become an Acquiring Person if such Transaction were to be consummated or an Affiliate or Associate of such a Person, and (ii) is, or directly or indirectly proposed, nominated or financially supported, a director of [Quickturn] in office at the time of consideration of such Transaction who was elected at an annual or special meeting of stockholders."

19, 20, 23, 26 and 28, 1998. Thereafter, the parties submitted post-trial briefs on an expedited schedule.

During the course of the litigation in the Court of Chancery, the Quickturn board, relying upon the By–Law Amendment, noticed the special meeting requested by Mentor for January 8, 1999—71 days after the October 1, 1998 meeting date originally noticed by Mentor.[17] After the trial, Mentor announced in Amendments to its Schedule 14A–1 that were filed with the Securities and Exchange Commission, that it had received tenders of Quickturn shares which, together with the shares that Mentor already owned, represented over 51 of Quickturn's outstanding stock.

QUICKTURN BY–LAW AMENDMENT

At the time Mentor commenced its tender offer and proxy contest, Quickturn's by-laws authorized shareholders holding at least 10% of Quickturn's voting stock to call a special meeting of stockholders. The then-applicable by-law, Article II, § 2.3, read thusly:

> A special meeting of the stockholders may be called at any time by (i) the board of directors, (ii) the chairman of the board, (iii) the president, (iv) the chief executive officer or (v) one or more shareholders holding shares in the aggregate entitled to cast not less than ten percent (10%) of the votes at that meeting.

At the August 21, 1998 board meeting, the Quickturn board amended § 2.3 in response to the Mentor bid, to read as follows:

> A special meeting of the stockholders may be called at any time by (i) the board of directors, (ii) the chairman of the board, (iii) the president, (iv) the chief executive officer or (v) subject to the procedures set forth in this Section 2.3, one or more stockholders holding shares in the aggregate entitled to cast not less than ten percent (10%) of the votes at that meeting.
>
> Upon request in writing sent by registered mail to the president or chief executive officer by any stockholder or stockholders entitled to call a special meeting of stockholders pursuant to this Section 2.3, the board of directors shall determine a place and time for such meeting, which time shall be not less than ninety (90) nor more than one hundred (100) days after the receipt and determination of the validity of such request, and a record date for the determination of stockholders entitled to vote at such meeting in the manner set forth in Section 2.12 hereof. Following such receipt and determination, it shall be the duty of the secretary to cause notice to be given to the stockholders entitled to vote at such meeting, in the manner set forth in Section 2.4 hereof, that a meeting will be held at the time and place so determined.

17. Mentor later renoticed the special meeting date to November 24, 1998, anticipating that the Court of Chancery would issue its decision before that time. After the Court of Chancery informed the parties that it would be unable to issue a decision by November 24, Mentor agreed that its meeting would be convened and then immediately adjourned to a later date.

The Court of Chancery found that the Quickturn board amended the By–Law because (i) the original § 2.3 was incomplete: it did not explicitly state who would be responsible for determining the time, place, and record date for the meeting and (ii) the original by-law language arguably would have allowed a hostile bidder holding the requisite percentage of shares to call a special stockholders meeting on minimal notice and stampede the shareholders into making a decision without time to become adequately informed.

The Court of Chancery concluded that the By–Law Amendment responded to those concerns by explicitly making the Quickturn board responsible for fixing the time, place, record date and notice of the special meeting and by mandating a 90 to 100 day period of delay for holding the meeting after the validity of the shareholder's meeting request is determined. That specific delay period was chosen to make § 2.3 parallel to, and congruent with, Quickturn's "advance notice" by-law, which contained a similar 90 to 100 day minimum advance notice period.

The only By–Law Amendment-related issue that the Court of Chancery decided was whether the Amendment, standing alone, fell outside any range of potentially reasonable responses and, therefore, constituted a disproportionate response to the threat posed by the Mentor tender offer and proxy contest. Among the factors the Court of Chancery considered were whether the challenged defensive response "is a statutorily authorized form of business decision that a board of directors may routinely make in a non-takeover context,"[18] and whether the response was limited and corresponded in degree or magnitude to the degree or magnitude of the threat.[19]

The Court of Chancery concluded that the Quickturn board's adoption of the By–Law Amendment did not violate the fiduciary principles embodied in Unocal and its progeny. Although the Delayed Redemption Provision and the By–Law Amendment were enacted as a concerted defensive response to Mentor's hostile takeover efforts, Mentor did not file a cross-appeal challenging the Court of Chancery's decision upholding the validity of Quickturn's amendment to its by-laws. Consequently, the Court of Chancery's ruling on the By–Law Amendment is not at issue in this appeal and has become final.

QUICKTURN'S DELAYED REDEMPTION PROVISION

At the time Mentor commenced its bid, Quickturn had in place a Rights Plan that contained a so-called "dead hand" provision. That provision had a limited "continuing director" feature that became operative only if an insurgent that owned more than 15% of Quickturn's common stock successfully waged a proxy contest to replace a majority of the board. In that event, only the "continuing directors"

---

18. Unitrin, Inc. v. American General Corp., Del.Supr., 651 A.2d 1361, 1389 (1995); Unocal Corp. v. Mesa Petroleum Co., Del. Supr., 493 A.2d 946, 958 (1985); Cheff v. Mathes, Del.Supr., 199 A.2d 548, 554 (1964).

19. Unitrin, Inc. v. American General Corp., 651 A.2d at 1389.

(those directors in office at the time the poison pill was adopted) could redeem the rights.

During the same August 21, 1998 meeting at which it amended the special meeting by-law, the Quickturn board also amended the Rights Plan to eliminate its "continuing director" feature, and to substitute a "no hand" or "delayed redemption provision" into its Rights Plan. The Delayed Redemption Provision provides that, if a majority of the directors are replaced by stockholder action, the newly elected board cannot redeem the rights for six months if the purpose or effect of the redemption would be to facilitate a transaction with an "Interested Person."[21]

It is undisputed that the DRP would prevent Mentor's slate, if elected as the new board majority, from redeeming the Rights Plan for six months following their election, because a redemption would be "reasonably likely to have the purpose or effect of facilitating a Transaction" with Mentor, a party that "directly or indirectly proposed, nominated or financially supported" the election of the new board. Consequently, by adopting the DRP, the Quickturn board built into the process a six month delay period in addition to the 90 to 100 day delay mandated by the By–Law Amendment.

COURT OF CHANCERY INVALIDATES DELAYED REDEMPTION PROVISION

When the board of a Delaware corporation takes action to resist a hostile bid for control, the board of directors' defensive actions are subjected to "enhanced" judicial scrutiny.[22] For a target board's actions to be entitled to business judgment rule protection, the target board must first establish that it had reasonable grounds to believe that the hostile bid constituted a threat to corporate policy and effectiveness; and second, that the defensive measures adopted were "proportionate," that is, reasonable in relation to the threat that the board reasonably perceived. The Delayed Redemption Provision was reviewed by the Court of Chancery pursuant to that standard.

The Court of Chancery found: "the evidence, viewed as a whole, shows that the perceived threat that led the Quickturn board to adopt the DRP, was the concern that Quickturn shareholders might mistakenly, in ignorance of Quickturn's true value, accept Mentor's inadequate offer, and elect a new board that would prematurely sell the company before the new board could adequately inform itself of Quickturn's fair value and before the shareholders could consider

---

21. The "no hand" or Delayed Redemption Provision is found in a new Section 23(b) of the Rights Plan, which states: (b) Notwithstanding the provisions of Section 23(a), in the event that a majority of the Board of Directors of the Company is elected by stockholder action at an annual or special meeting of stockholders, then until the 180th day following the effectiveness of such election (including any postponement or adjournment thereof), the Rights shall not be redeemed if such redemption is reasonably likely to have the purpose or effect of facilitating a Transaction with an Interested Person.

Substantially similar provisions were added to Sections 24 ("Exchange") and 27 ("Supplements and Amendments") of the Rights Plan.

22. Unocal Corp. v. Mesa Petroleum Co., Del.Supr., 493 A.2d 946, 955 (1985).

other options." The Court of Chancery concluded that Mentor's combined tender offer and proxy contest amounted to substantive coercion.[25] Having concluded that the Quickturn board reasonably perceived a cognizable threat, the Court of Chancery then examined whether the board's response—the Delayed Redemption Provision— was proportionate in relation to that threat.

In assessing a challenge to defensive measures taken by a target board in response to an attempted hostile takeover, enhanced judicial scrutiny requires an evaluation of the board's justification for each contested defensive measure and its concomitant results. The Court of Chancery found that the Quickturn board's "justification or rationale for adopting the Delayed Redemption Provision was to force any newly elected board to take sufficient time to become familiar with Quickturn and its value, and to provide shareholders the opportunity to consider alternatives, before selling Quickturn to any acquiror." The Court of Chancery concluded that the Delayed Redemption Provision could not pass the proportionality test. Therefore, the Court of Chancery held that "the DRP cannot survive scrutiny under Unocal and must be declared invalid."

DELAYED REDEMPTION PROVISION VIOLATES FUNDAMENTAL DELAWARE LAW

In this appeal, Mentor argues that the judgment of the Court of Chancery should be affirmed because the Delayed Redemption Provision is invalid as a matter of Delaware law. According to Mentor, the Delayed Redemption Provision, like the "dead hand" feature in the Rights Plan that was held to be invalid in *Toll Brothers*,[29] will impermissibly deprive any newly elected board of both its statutory authority to manage the corporation under 8 Del.C. § 141(a) and its concomitant fiduciary duty pursuant to that statutory mandate. We agree.

Our analysis of the Delayed Redemption Provision in the Quickturn Rights Plan is guided by the prior precedents of this Court with regard to a board of directors authority to adopt a Rights Plan or "poison pill." In *Moran*, this Court held that the inherent powers of the Board conferred by 8 Del.C. § 141(a) concerning the management of the corporation's "business and affairs" provides the Board additional authority upon which to enact the Rights Plan.[30] Consequently,

25. Unitrin, Inc. v. American General Corp., 651 A.2d at 1387.

29. Carmody v. Toll Brothers, Inc., Del. Ch., C.A. No. 15983, Jacobs, V.C., 1998 WL 418896 (July 24, 1998) ("Toll Brothers"). See Bank of New York Co., Inc. v. Irving Bank Corp., N.Y.Sup.Ct., 139 Misc.2d 665, 528 N.Y.S.2d 482 (1988). See also Shawn C. Lese, Note: Preventing Control From the Grave: A Proposal for Judicial Treatment of Dead Hand Provisions in Poison Pills, 96 Colum.L.Rev. 2175 (1996); Jeffrey N. Gordon, "Just Say Never?" Poison Pills, Dead Hand Pills, and Shareholder Adopted By–Laws: An Essay for Warren Buffett, 19 Cardozo L.Rev.

511 (1997). Cf. Invacare Corp. v. Healthdyne Technologies, Inc., N.D.Ga., 968 F.Supp. 1578 (1997) (applying Georgia law).

30. Moran v. Household International, Inc., Del.Supr., 500 A.2d 1346, 1353 (1985), citing Unocal Corp. v. Mesa Petroleum Co., Del.Supr., 493 A.2d 946, 953 (1985).

When the Household Board of Directors is faced with a tender offer and a request to redeem the Rights [Plan], they will not be able to arbitrarily reject the offer. They will be held to the same fiduciary standards any other board of directors would be held to in deciding to adopt a defensive mechanism, the this Court upheld the adoption of the Rights Plan in *Moran* as a legitimate exercise of business judgment by the board of directors. In doing so, however, this Court also held the rights plan is not absolute:

In *Moran*, this Court held that the "ultimate response to an actual takeover bid must be judged by the Directors' actions at the time and nothing we say relieves them of their fundamental duties to the corporation and its shareholders." Consequently, we concluded that the use of the Rights Plan would be evaluated when and if the issue arises.

One of the most basic tenets of Delaware corporate law is that the board of directors has the ultimate responsibility for managing the business and affairs of a corporation.[36] Section 141(a) requires that any limitation on the board's authority be set out in the certificate of incorporation.[37] The Quickturn certificate of incorporation contains no provision purporting to limit the authority of the board in any way. The Delayed Redemption Provision, however, would prevent a newly elected board of directors from completely discharging its fundamental management duties to the corporation and its stockholders for six months. While the Delayed Redemption Provision limits the board of directors' authority in only one respect, the suspension of the Rights Plan, it nonetheless restricts the board's power in an area of fundamental importance to the shareholders negotiating a possible sale of the corporation. Therefore, we hold that the Delayed Redemption Provision is invalid under Section 141(a), which confers upon any newly elected board of directors full power to manage and direct the business and affairs of a Delaware corporation.

In discharging the statutory mandate of Section 141(a), the directors have a fiduciary duty to the corporation and its shareholders. This unremitting obligation extends equally to board conduct in a contest for corporate control. The Delayed Redemption Provision prevents a newly elected board of directors from completely discharging its fiduciary duties to protect fully the interests of Quickturn and its stockholders.[41]

This Court has recently observed that "although the fiduciary duty of a Delaware director is unremitting, the exact course of conduct that must be charted to properly discharge that responsibility will change in the specific context of the action the director is taking with regard to either the corporation or its shareholders."[42] This Court has held "[t]o the extent that a contract, or a provision thereof, purports to require a board to act or not act in such a fashion as to limit the

---

same standards as they were held to in originally approving the Rights Plan.

36. 8 Del.C. § 141(a). See Mills Acquisition Co. v. Macmillan, Inc., Del.Supr., 559 A.2d 1261, 1280 (1989).

37. 8 Del.C. § 141(a) states: "The business and affairs of every corporation organized under this chapter shall be managed by or under the direction of a board of directors, except as may be otherwise provided in this chapter or in its certificate of incorporation. If any such provision is made in the certifi-

cate of incorporation, the powers and duties conferred or imposed upon the board of directors by this chapter shall be exercised or performed to such extent and by such person or persons as shall be provided in the certificate of incorporation."

41. See Moran v. Household International, Inc., 500 A.2d at 1354.

42. Malone v. Brincat, Del.Supr., 722 A.2d 5 (1998).

exercise of fiduciary duties, it is invalid and unenforceable."[43] The Delayed Redemption Provision "tends to limit in a substantial way the freedom of [newly elected] directors' decisions on matters of management policy."[44] Therefore, "it violates the duty of each [newly elected] director to exercise his own best judgment on matters coming before the board."[45]

In this case, the Quickturn board was confronted by a determined bidder that sought to acquire the company at a price the Quickturn board concluded was inadequate. Such situations are common in corporate takeover efforts.[46] In Revlon, this Court held that no defensive measure can be sustained when it represents a breach of the directors' fiduciary duty. A fortiori, no defensive measure can be sustained which would require a new board of directors to breach its fiduciary duty. In that regard, we note Mentor has properly acknowledged that in the event its slate of directors are elected, those newly elected directors will be required to discharge their unremitting fiduciary duty to manage the corporation for the benefit of Quickturn and its stockholders.[47]

Conclusion

The Delayed Redemption Provision would prevent a new Quickturn board of directors from managing the corporation by redeeming the Rights Plan to facilitate a transaction that would serve the stockholders' best interests, even under circumstances where the board would be required to do so because of its fiduciary duty to the Quickturn stockholders. Because the Delayed Redemption Provision impermissibly circumscribes the board's statutory power under Section 141(a) and the directors' ability to fulfill their concomitant fiduciary duties, we hold that the Delayed Redemption Provision is invalid. On that alternative basis, the judgment of the Court of Chancery is AFFIRMED.

Revlon, Inc. v. MacAndrews & Forbes Holdings, Inc.

Supreme Court of Delaware, 1985.
506 A.2d 173.

In this battle for corporate control of Revlon, Inc. (Revlon), the Court of Chancery enjoined certain transactions designed to thwart

43. See Paramount Communications, Inc. v. QVC Network, Inc., 637 A.2d at 51 (emphasis added). See, e.g., Mills Acquisition Co. v. Macmillan, Inc., 559 A.2d at 1281 (holding that a "board of directors ... may not avoid its active and direct duty of oversight in a matter as significant as the sale of corporate control"); Grimes v. Donald, Del. Ch., C.A. No. 13358, slip op. at 17, Allen, C., 1995 WL 54441 (Jan. 11, 1995, revised Jan. 19, 1995), aff'd, Del.Supr., 673 A.2d 1207 (1996) ("[t]he board may not either formally or effectively abdicate its statutory power and

its fiduciary duty to manage or direct the management of the business and affairs of this corporation").

44. Abercrombie v. Davies, Del.Ch., 123 A.2d 893, 899 (1956), rev'd on other grounds, Del.Supr., 130 A.2d 338 (1957).

45. Id.

46. Revlon, Inc. v. MacAndrews Forbes Holdings, Inc., 506 A.2d at 185.

47. Malone v. Brincat, Del.Supr., 722 A.2d 5 (1998).

the efforts of Pantry Pride, Inc. (Pantry Pride) to acquire Revlon. The defendants are Revlon, its board of directors, and Forstmann Little Co. and the latter's affiliated limited partnership (collectively, Forstmann). The injunction barred consummation of an option granted Forstmann to purchase certain Revlon assets (the lock-up option), a promise by Revlon to deal exclusively with Forstmann in the face of a takeover (the no-shop provision), and the payment of a $25 million cancellation fee to Forstmann if the transaction was aborted. The Court of Chancery found that the Revlon directors had breached their duty of care by entering into the foregoing transactions and effectively ending an active auction for the company. The trial court ruled that such arrangements are not illegal *per se* under Delaware law, but that their use under the circumstances here was impermissible. We agree. See MacAndrews Forbes Holdings, Inc. v. Revlon, Inc., Del.Ch., 501 A.2d 1239 (1985). Thus, we granted this expedited interlocutory appeal to consider for the first time the validity of such defensive measures in the face of an active bidding contest for corporate control. Additionally, we address for the first time the extent to which a corporation may consider the impact of a takeover threat on constituencies other than shareholders. See Unocal Corp. v. Mesa Petroleum Co., 493 A.2d 946, 955 (1985).

In our view, lock-ups and related agreements are permitted under Delaware law where their adoption is untainted by director interest or other breaches of fiduciary duty. The actions taken by the Revlon directors, however, did not meet this standard. Moreover, while concern for various corporate constituencies is proper when addressing a takeover threat, that principle is limited by the requirement that there be some rationally related benefit accruing to the stockholders. We find no such benefit here.

Thus, under all the circumstances we must agree with the Court of Chancery that the enjoined Revlon defensive measures were inconsistent with the directors' duties to the stockholders. Accordingly, we affirm.

I.

The somewhat complex maneuvers of the parties necessitate a rather detailed examination of the facts. The prelude to this controversy began in June 1985, when Ronald O. Perelman, chairman of the board and chief executive officer of Pantry Pride, met with his counterpart at Revlon, Michel C. Bergerac, to discuss a friendly acquisition of Revlon by Pantry Pride. Perelman suggested a price in the range of $4050 per share, but the meeting ended with Bergerac dismissing those figures as considerably below Revlon's intrinsic value. All subsequent Pantry Pride overtures were rebuffed, perhaps in part based on Mr. Bergerac's strong personal antipathy to Mr. Perelman.

Thus, on August 14, Pantry Pride's board authorized Perelman to acquire Revlon, either through negotiation in the $42–$43 per share range, or by making a hostile tender offer at $45. Perelman then met with Bergerac and outlined Pantry Pride's alternate approaches. Bergerac remained adamantly opposed to such schemes and conditioned any further discussions of the matter on Pantry Pride executing a standstill agreement prohibiting it from acquiring Revlon without the latter's prior approval.

On August 19, the Revlon board met specially to consider the impending threat of a hostile bid by Pantry Pride.[3] At the meeting, Lazard Freres, Revlon's investment banker, advised the directors that $45 per share was a grossly inadequate price for the company. Felix Rohatyn and William Loomis of Lazard Freres explained to the board that Pantry Pride's financial strategy for acquiring Revlon would be through "junk bond" financing followed by a break-up of Revlon and the disposition of its assets. With proper timing, according to the experts, such transactions could produce a return to Pantry Pride of $60 to $70 per share, while a sale of the company as a whole would be in the "mid 50" dollar range. Martin Lipton, special counsel for Revlon, recommended two defensive measures: first, that the company repurchase up to 5 million of its nearly 30 million outstanding shares; and second, that it adopt a Note Purchase Rights Plan. Under this plan, each Revlon shareholder would receive as a dividend one Note Purchase Right (the Rights) for each share of common stock, with the Rights entitling the holder to exchange one common share for a $65 principal Revlon note at 12% interest with a one-year maturity. The Rights would become effective whenever anyone acquired beneficial ownership of 20% or more of Revlon's shares, unless the purchaser acquired all the company's stock for cash at $65 or more per share. In addition, the Rights would not be available to the acquiror, and prior to the 20% triggering event the Revlon board could redeem the rights for 10 cents each. Both proposals were unanimously adopted.

Pantry Pride made its first hostile move on August 23, with a cash tender offer for any and all shares of Revlon at $47.50 per common share and $26.67 per preferred share, subject to (1) Pantry Pride's obtaining financing for the purchase, and (2) the Rights being redeemed, rescinded or voided.

The Revlon board met again on August 26. The directors advised the stockholders to reject the offer. Further defensive measures also were planned. On August 29, Revlon commenced its own offer for up to 10 million shares, exchanging for each share of common stock tendered one Senior Subordinated Note (the Notes) of $47.50 principal at 11.75% interest, due 1995, and one-tenth of a share of $9.00 Cumulative Convertible Exchangeable Preferred Stock valued at $100 per share. Lazard Freres opined that the notes would trade at their face value on a fully distributed basis. Revlon stockholders tendered 87 percent of the outstanding shares (approximately 33 million), and the

---

3. There were 14 directors on the Revlon board. Six of them held senior management positions with the company, and two others held significant blocks of its stock. Four of the remaining six directors were associated at some point with entities that had various business relationships with Revlon.

On the basis of this limited record, however, we cannot conclude that this board is entitled to certain presumptions that generally attach to the decisions of a board whose majority consists of truly outside independent directors....

company accepted the full 10 million shares on a pro rata basis. The new Notes contained covenants which limited Revlon's ability to incur additional debt, sell assets, or pay dividends unless otherwise approved by the independent (non-management) members of the board.

At this point, both the Rights and the Note covenants stymied Pantry Pride's attempted takeover. The next move came on September 16, when Pantry Pride announced a new tender offer at $42 per share, conditioned upon receiving at least 90% of the outstanding stock. Pantry Pride also indicated that it would consider buying less than 90%, and at an increased price, if Revlon removed the impeding Rights. While this offer was lower on its face than the earlier $47.50 proposal, Revlon's investment banker, Lazard Freres, described the two bids as essentially equal in view of the completed exchange offer.

The Revlon board held a regularly scheduled meeting on September 24. The directors rejected the latest Pantry Pride offer and authorized management to negotiate with other parties interested in acquiring Revlon. Pantry Pride remained determined in its efforts and continued to make cash bids for the company, offering $50 per share on September 27, and raising its bid to $53 on October 1, and then to $56.25 on October 7.

In the meantime, Revlon's negotiations with Forstmann and the investment group Adler & Shaykin had produced results. The Revlon directors met on October 3, to consider Pantry Pride's $53 bid and to examine possible alternatives to the offer. Both Forstmann and Adler & Shaykin made certain proposals to the board. As a result, the directors unanimously agreed to a leveraged buyout by Forstmann. The terms of this accord were as follows: each stockholder would get $56 cash per share; management would purchase stock in the new company by the exercise of their Revlon "golden parachutes";[4] Forstmann would assume Revlon's $475 million debt incurred by the issuance of the Notes; and Revlon would redeem the Rights and waive the Notes covenants for Forstmann or in connection with any other offer superior to Forstmann's. The board did not actually remove the covenants at the October 3, meeting, because Forstmann then lacked a firm commitment on its financing, but accepted the Forstmann capital structure, and indicated that the outside directors would waive the covenants in due course. Part of Forstmann's plan was to sell Revlon's Norcliff Thayer and Reheis divisions to American Home Products for $335 million. Before the merger, Revlon was to sell its cosmetics and fragrance division to Adler Shaykin for $905 million. These transactions would facilitate the purchase by Forstmann or any other acquiror of Revlon.

When the merger, and thus the waiver of the Notes covenants, was announced, the market value of these securities began to fall. The Notes, which originally traded near par, around 100, dropped to 87.50 by October 8. One director later reported (at the October 12 meeting)

---

4. In the takeover context "golden parachutes" generally are understood to be termination agreements providing substantial bonuses and other benefits for managers and certain directors upon a change in control of a company.

a "deluge" of telephone calls from irate noteholders, and on October 10 the Wall Street Journal reported threats of litigation by these creditors.

Pantry Pride countered with a new proposal on October 7, raising its $53 offer to $56.25, subject to nullification of the Rights, a waiver of the Notes covenants, and the election of three Pantry Pride directors to the Revlon board. On October 9, representatives of Pantry Pride, Forstmann and Revlon conferred in an attempt to negotiate the fate of Revlon, but could not reach agreement. At this meeting Pantry Pride announced that it would engage in fractional bidding and top any Forstmann offer by a slightly higher one. It is also significant that Forstmann, to Pantry Pride's exclusion, had been made privy to certain Revlon financial data. Thus, the parties were not negotiating on equal terms.

Again privately armed with Revlon data, Forstmann met on October 11 with Revlon's special counsel and investment banker. On October 12, Forstmann made a new $57.25 per share offer, based on several conditions.[5] The principal demand was a lock-up option to purchase Revlon's Vision Care and National Health Laboratories divisions for $525 million, some $100–$175 million below the value ascribed to them by Lazard Freres, if another acquiror got 40% of Revlon's shares. Revlon also was required to accept a no-shop provision. The Rights and Notes covenants had to be removed as in the October 3 agreement. There would be a $25 million cancellation fee to be placed in escrow, and released to Forstmann if the new agreement terminated or if another acquiror got more than 19.9% of Revlon's stock. Finally, there would be no participation by Revlon management in the merger. In return, Forstmann agreed to support the par value of the Notes, which had faltered in the market, by an exchange of new notes. Forstmann also demanded immediate acceptance of its offer, or it would be withdrawn. The board unanimously approved Forstmann's proposal because: (1) it was for a higher price than the Pantry Pride bid, (2) it protected the noteholders, and (3) Forstmann's financing was firmly in place.[6] The board further agreed to redeem the rights and waive the covenants on the preferred stock in response to any offer above $57 cash per share. The covenants were waived, contingent upon receipt of an investment banking opinion that the Notes would trade near par value once the offer was consummated.

---

5. Forstmann's $57.25 offer ostensibly is worth $1 more than Pantry Pride's $56.25 bid. However, the Pantry Pride offer was immediate, while the Forstmann proposal must be discounted for the time value of money because of the delay in approving the merger and consummating the transaction. The exact difference between the two bids was an unsettled point of contention even at oral argument.

6. Actually, at this time about $400 million of Forstmann's funding was still sub-ject to two investment banks using their "best effort" to organize a syndicate to provide the balance. Pantry Pride's entire financing was not firmly committed at this point either, although Pantry Pride represented in an October 11 letter to Lazard Freres that its investment banker, Drexel Burnham Lambert, was highly confident of its ability to raise the balance of $350 million. Drexel Burnham had a firm commitment for this sum by October 18.

Pantry Pride, which had initially sought injunctive relief from the Rights plan on August 22, filed an amended complaint on October 14 challenging the lock-up, the cancellation fee, and the exercise of the Rights and the Notes covenants. Pantry Pride also sought a temporary restraining order to prevent Revlon from placing any assets in escrow or transferring them to Forstmann. Moreover, on October 22, Pantry Pride again raised its bid, with a cash offer of $58 per share conditioned upon nullification of the Rights, waiver of the covenants, and an injunction of the Forstmann lock-up.

On October 15, the Court of Chancery prohibited the further transfer of assets, and eight days later enjoined the lock-up, no-shop, and cancellation fee provisions of the agreement. The trial court concluded that the Revlon directors had breached their duty of loyalty by making concessions to Forstmann, out of concern for their liability to the noteholders, rather than maximizing the sale price of the company for the stockholders' benefit. MacAndrews & Forbes Holdings, Inc. v. Revlon, Inc., 501 A.2d at 1249–50.

II.

To obtain a preliminary injunction, a plaintiff must demonstrate both a reasonable probability of success on the merits and some irreparable harm which will occur absent the injunction. Gimbel v. Signal Companies, Del.Ch., 316 A.2d 599, 602 (1974), aff'd, Del.Supr., 316 A.2d 619 (1974). Additionally, the Court shall balance the conveniences of and possible injuries to the parties. Id.

A.

We turn first to Pantry Pride's probability of success on the merits. The ultimate responsibility for managing the business and affairs of a corporation falls on its board of directors. 8 Del.C. § 141(a). In discharging this function the directors owe fiduciary duties of care and loyalty to the corporation and its shareholders. Guth v. Loft, Inc., 23 Del.Supr. 255, 5 A.2d 503, 510 (1939); Aronson v. Lewis, Del.Supr., 473 A.2d 805, 811 (1984). These principles apply with equal force when a board approves a corporate merger pursuant to 8 Del.C. § 251(b);[9] Smith v. Van Gorkom, Del.Supr., 488 A.2d 858, 873 (1985); and of course they are the bedrock of our law regarding corporate takeover issues. Pogostin v. Rice, Del.Supr., 480 A.2d 619, 624 (1984); Unocal Corp. v. Mesa Petroleum Co., Del.Supr., 493 A.2d 946, 953, 955 (1985); Moran v. Household International, Inc., Del.Supr., 500 A.2d 1346, 1350 (1985). While the business judgment rule may be applicable to the actions of corporate directors responding to takeover threats, the principles upon which it is founded—care, loyalty and independence—must first be satisfied. Aronson v. Lewis, 473 A.2d at 812.

9. The statute provides in pertinent part:

(b) The board of directors of each corporation which desires to merge or consolidate shall adopt a resolution approving an agreement of merger or consolidation. 8 Del.C. § 251(b).

If the business judgment rule applies, there is a "presumption that in making a business decision the directors of a corporation acted on an informed basis, in good faith and in the honest belief that the action taken was in the best interests of the company." Aronson v. Lewis, 473 A.2d at 812. However, when a board implements antitakeover measures there arises "the omnipresent specter that a board may be acting primarily in its own interests, rather than those of the corporation and its shareholders . . ." Unocal Corp. v. Mesa Petroleum Co., 493 A.2d at 954. This potential for conflict places upon the directors the burden of proving that they had reasonable grounds for believing there was a danger to corporate policy and effectiveness, a burden satisfied by a showing of good faith and reasonable investigation. Id. at 955. In addition, the directors must analyze the nature of the takeover and its effect on the corporation in order to ensure balance—that the responsive action taken is reasonable in relation to the threat posed. Id.

B.

The first relevant defensive measure adopted by the Revlon board was the Rights Plan, which would be considered a "poison pill" in the current language of corporate takeovers—a plan by which shareholders receive the right to be bought out by the corporation at a substantial premium on the occurrence of a stated triggering event. See generally Moran v. Household International, Inc., Del.Supr., 500 A.2d 1346 (1985). By 8 Del.C. §§ 141 and 157,[10] the board clearly had the power to adopt the measure. Moran v. Household International, Inc., 500 A.2d at 1351. Thus, the focus becomes one of reasonableness and purpose.

The Revlon board approved the Rights Plan in the face of an impending hostile takeover bid by Pantry Pride at $45 per share, a price which Revlon reasonably concluded was grossly inadequate. Lazard Freres had so advised the directors, and had also informed them that Pantry Pride was a small, highly leveraged company bent on a "bust-up" takeover by using "junk bond" financing to buy Revlon cheaply, sell the acquired assets to pay the debts incurred, and retain the profit for itself.[11] In adopting the Plan, the board protected the shareholders from a hostile takeover at a price below the company's intrinsic value, while retaining sufficient flexibility to address any proposal deemed to be in the stockholders' best interests.

To that extent the board acted in good faith and upon reasonable investigation. Under the circumstances it cannot be said that the Rights

---

10. The relevant provision of Section 122 is:

Every corporation created under this chapter shall have power to:

(13) Make contracts, including contracts of guaranty and suretyship, incur liabilities, borrow money at such rates of interest as the corporation may determine, issue its notes, bonds and other obligations, and secure any of its obligations by mortgage, pledge or oth-er encumbrance of all or any of its property, franchises and income,. . . . 8 Del.C. § 122(13). . . .

11. As we noted in *Moran,* a "bust-up" takeover generally refers to a situation in which one seeks to finance an acquisition by selling off pieces of the acquired company, presumably at a substantial profit. See *Moran,* 500 A.2d at 1349, n. 4.

Plan as employed was unreasonable, considering the threat posed. Indeed, the Plan was a factor in causing Pantry Pride to raise its bids from a low of $42 to an eventual high of $58. At the time of its adoption the Rights Plan afforded a measure of protection consistent with the directors' fiduciary duty in facing a takeover threat perceived as detrimental to corporate interests. *Unocal*, 493 A.2d at 954–55. Far from being a "show-stopper," as the plaintiffs had contended in *Moran*, the measure spurred the bidding to new heights, a proper result of its implementation. See *Moran*, 500 A.2d at 1354, 1356–67.

Although we consider adoption of the Plan to have been valid under the circumstances, its continued usefulness was rendered moot by the directors' actions on October 3 and October 12. At the October 3 meeting the board redeemed the Rights conditioned upon consummation of a merger with Forstmann, but further acknowledged that they would also be redeemed to facilitate any more favorable offer. On October 12, the board unanimously passed a resolution redeeming the Rights in connection with any cash proposal of $57.25 or more per share. Because all the pertinent offers eventually equalled or surpassed that amount, the Rights clearly were no longer any impediment in the contest for Revlon. This mooted any question of their propriety under *Moran* or *Unocal*.

C.

The second defensive measure adopted by Revlon to thwart a Pantry Pride takeover was the company's own exchange offer for 10 million of its shares. The directors' general broad powers to manage the business and affairs of the corporation are augmented by the specific authority conferred under 8 Del.C. § 160(a), permitting the company to deal in its own stock. *Unocal*, 493 A.2d at 953–54; Cheff v. Mathes, 41 Del.Supr. 494, 199 A.2d 548, 554 (1964); Kors v. Carey, 39 Del.Ch. 47, 158 A.2d 136, 140 (1960). However, when exercising that power in an effort to forestall a hostile takeover, the board's actions are strictly held to the fiduciary standards outlined in *Unocal*. These standards require the directors to determine the best interests of the corporation and its stockholders, and impose an enhanced duty to abjure any action that is motivated by considerations other than a good faith concern for such interests. *Unocal*, 493 A.2d at 954–55; see Bennett v. Propp, 41 Del.Supr. 14, 187 A.2d 405, 409 (1962).

The Revlon directors concluded that Pantry Pride's $47.50 offer was grossly inadequate. In that regard the board acted in good faith, and on an informed basis, with reasonable grounds to believe that there existed a harmful threat to the corporate enterprise. The adoption of a defensive measure, reasonable in relation to the threat posed, was proper and fully accorded with the powers, duties, and responsibilities conferred upon directors under our law. *Unocal*, 493 A.2d at 954; Pogostin v. Rice, 480 A.2d at 627.

D.

However, when Pantry Pride increased its offer to $50 per share, and then to $53, it became apparent to all that the break-up of the company was inevitable. The Revlon board's authorization permitting management to negotiate a merger or buyout with a third party was a recognition that the company was for sale. The duty of the board had thus changed from the preservation of Revlon as a corporate entity to the maximization of the company's value at a sale for the stockholders' benefit. This significantly altered the board's responsibilities under the *Unocal* standards. It no longer faced threats to corporate policy and effectiveness, or to the stockholders' interests, from a grossly inadequate bid. The whole question of defensive measures became moot. The directors' role changed from defenders of the corporate bastion to auctioneers charged with getting the best price for the stockholders at a sale of the company.

III.

This brings us to the lock-up with Forstmann and its emphasis on shoring up the sagging market value of the Notes in the face of threatened litigation by their holders. Such a focus was inconsistent with the changed concept of the directors' responsibilities at this stage of the developments. The impending waiver of the Notes covenants had caused the value of the Notes to fall, and the board was aware of the noteholders' ire as well as their subsequent threats of suit. The directors thus made support of the Notes an integral part of the company's dealings with Forstmann, even though their primary responsibility at this stage was to the equity owners.

The original threat posed by Pantry Pride—the break-up of the company—had become a reality which even the directors embraced. Selective dealing to fend off a hostile but determined bidder was no longer a proper objective. Instead, obtaining the highest price for the benefit of the stockholders should have been the central theme guiding director action. Thus, the Revlon board could not make the requisite showing of good faith by preferring the noteholders and ignoring its duty of loyalty to the shareholders. The rights of the former already were fixed by contract. Wolfensohn v. Madison Fund, Inc., Del.Supr., 253 A.2d 72, 75 (1969); Harff v. Kerkorian, Del.Ch., 324 A.2d 215 (1974). The noteholders required no further protection, and when the Revlon board entered into an auction-ending lock-up agreement with Forstmann on the basis of impermissible considerations at the expense of the shareholders, the directors breached their primary duty of loyalty.

The Revlon board argued that it acted in good faith in protecting the noteholders because *Unocal* permits consideration of other corporate constituencies. Although such considerations may be permissible, there are fundamental limitations upon that prerogative. A board may have regard for various constituencies in discharging its responsibilities, provided there are rationally related benefits accruing to the stockholders. *Unocal*, 493 A.2d at 955. However, such concern for non-stockholder interests is inappropriate when an auction among active bidders is in progress, and the object no longer is to protect or maintain the corporate enterprise but to sell it to the highest bidder.

Revlon also contended that by Gilbert v. El Paso Co., Del.Ch., 490 A.2d 1050, 1054–55 (1984), it had contractual and good faith obligations to consider the noteholders. However, any such duties are limited to the principle that one may not interfere with contractual relationships by improper actions. Here, the rights of the noteholders were fixed by agreement, and there is nothing of substance to suggest that any of those terms were violated. The Notes covenants specifically contemplated a waiver to permit sale of the company at a fair price. The Notes were accepted by the holders on that basis, including the risk of an adverse market effect stemming from a waiver. Thus, nothing remained for Revlon to legitimately protect, and no rationally related benefit thereby accrued to the stockholders. Under such circumstances we must conclude that the merger agreement with Forstmann was unreasonable in relation to the threat posed.

A lock-up is not *per se* illegal under Delaware law. Its use has been approved in an earlier case. Thompson v. Enstar Corp., Del.Ch. (1984). Such options can entice other bidders to enter a contest for control of the corporation, creating an auction for the company and maximizing shareholder profit. Current economic conditions in the takeover market are such that a "white knight" like Forstmann might only enter the bidding for the target company if it receives some form of compensation to cover the risks and costs involved. Note, Corporations—Mergers—"Lock-up" Enjoined Under Section 14(e) of Securities Exchange Act—Mobil Corp. v. Marathon Oil Co., 669 F.2d 366 (6th Cir.1981), 12 Seton Hall L.Rev. 881, 892 (1982). However, while those lock-ups which draw bidders into the battle benefit shareholders, similar measures which end an active auction and foreclose further bidding operate to the shareholders' detriment. Note, Lock-up Options: Toward a State Law Standard, 96 Harv.L.Rev. 1068, 1081 (1983). . . .

The Forstmann option had a . . . destructive effect on the auction process. Forstmann had already been drawn into the contest on a preferred basis, so the result of the lock-up was not to foster bidding, but to destroy it. The board's stated reasons for approving the transaction were: (1) better financing, (2) noteholder protection, and (3) higher price. As the Court of Chancery found, and we agree, any distinctions between the rival bidders' methods of financing the proposal were nominal at best, and such a consideration has little or no significance in a cash offer for any and all shares. The principal object, contrary to the board's duty of care, appears to have been protection of the noteholders over the shareholders' interests.

While Forstmann's $57.25 offer was objectively higher than Pantry Pride's $56.25 bid, the margin of superiority is less when the Forstmann price is adjusted for the time value of money. In reality, the Revlon board ended the auction in return for very little actual improvement in the final bid. The principal benefit went to the directors, who avoided personal liability to a class of creditors to whom the board owed no further duty under the circumstances. Thus, when a board ends an intense bidding contest on an insubstantial basis, and where a significant by-product of that action is to protect the directors against a perceived threat of personal liability for consequences stemming from the adoption of previous defensive measures, the action cannot withstand the enhanced scrutiny which *Unocal* requires of director conduct. See *Unocal,* 493 A.2d at 954–55.

In addition to the lock-up option, the Court of Chancery enjoined the no-shop provision as part of the attempt to foreclose further bidding by Pantry Pride. MacAndrews & Forbes Holdings, Inc. v. Revlon, Inc., 501 A.2d at 1251. The no-shop provision, like the lock-up option, while not *per se* illegal, is impermissible under the *Unocal* standards when a board's primary duty becomes that of an auctioneer responsible for selling the company to the highest bidder. The agreement to negotiate only with Forstmann ended rather than intensified the board's involvement in the bidding contest.

It is ironic that the parties even considered a no-shop agreement when Revlon had dealt preferentially, and almost exclusively, with Forstmann throughout the contest. After the directors authorized management to negotiate with other parties, Forstmann was given every negotiating advantage that Pantry Pride had been denied: cooperation from management, access to financial data, and the exclusive opportunity to present merger proposals directly to the board of directors. Favoritism for a white knight to the total exclusion of a hostile bidder might be justifiable when the latter's offer adversely affects shareholder interests, but when bidders make relatively similar offers, or dissolution of the company becomes inevitable, the directors cannot fulfill their enhanced *Unocal* duties by playing favorites with the contending factions. Market forces must be allowed to operate freely to bring the target's shareholders the best price available for their equity.[14] Thus, as the trial court ruled, the shareholders' interests necessitated that the board remain free to negotiate in the fulfillment of that duty.

The court below similarly enjoined the payment of the cancellation fee, pending a resolution of the merits, because the fee was part of the overall plan to thwart Pantry Pride's efforts. We find no abuse of discretion in that ruling.

IV.

Having concluded that Pantry Pride has shown a reasonable probability of success on the merits, we address the issue of irreparable harm. The Court of Chancery ruled that unless the lock-up and other aspects of the agreement were enjoined, Pantry Pride's opportunity to bid for Revlon was lost. The court also held that the need for both bidders to compete in the marketplace outweighed any injury to Forstmann. Given the complexity of the proposed transaction between Revlon and Forstmann, the obstacles to Pantry Pride obtaining a

---

14. By this we do not embrace the passivity thesis rejected in *Unocal.* See 493 A.2d at 954–55, nn. 8–10. The directors' role remains an active one, changed only in the respect that they are charged with the duty of selling the company at the highest price attainable for the stockholders' benefit.

meaningful legal remedy are immense. We are satisfied that the plaintiff has shown the need for an injunction to protect it from irreparable harm, which need outweighs any harm to the defendants.

V.

In conclusion, the Revlon board was confronted with a situation not uncommon in the current wave of corporate takeovers. A hostile and determined bidder sought the company at a price the board was convinced was inadequate. The initial defensive tactics worked to the benefit of the shareholders, and thus the board was able to sustain its *Unocal* burdens in justifying those measures. However, in granting an asset option lock-up to Forstmann, we must conclude that under all the circumstances the directors allowed considerations other than the maximization of shareholder profit to affect their judgment, and followed a course that ended the auction for Revlon, absent court intervention, to the ultimate detriment of its shareholders. No such defensive measure can be sustained when it represents a breach of the directors' fundamental duty of care. See Smith v. Van Gorkom, Del. Supr., 488 A.2d 858, 874 (1985). In that context the board's action is not entitled to the deference accorded it by the business judgment rule. The measures were properly enjoined. The decision of the Court of Chancery, therefore, is

AFFIRMED.

NOTE ON REVLON

Unlike the defensive action in *Unocal,* which occurred after the tender offer was made, the Rights Plan (or "poison pill") in *Revlon* was adopted as a planning device to forestall a tender offer, or at least to give the board additional power to deal with a tender offer if one was made. Another type of pre-tender offer action that has this effect is the issuance of weighted-voting or non-voting stock. See the materials on such stock in Chapter 4. Supra.

BARKAN v. AMSTED INDUSTRIES, INC., 567 A.2d 1279 (Del. Supr.1989). "There is some dispute among the parties as to the meaning of *Revlon,* as well as its relevance to the outcome of this case. We believe that the general principles announced in *Revlon,* in *Unocal Corp. v. Mesa Petroleum Co.,* 493 A.2d 946 (Del.Supr.1985), and in *Moran v. Household International, Inc.,* 500 A.2d 1346 (Del. Supr.1985) govern this case and every case in which a fundamental change of corporate control occurs or is contemplated. However, the basic teaching of these precedents is simply that the directors must act in accordance with their fundamental duties of care and loyalty. *Unocal,* 493 A.2d at 95455; *Revlon,* 506 A.2d at 180. It is true that a court evaluating the propriety of a change of control or a takeover defense must be mindful of 'the omnipresent specter that a board may be acting primarily in its own interests, rather than those of the corporation and its shareholders.' *Unocal,* 493 A.2d at 954. Nevertheless, there is no single blueprint that a board must follow to fulfill its duties. A stereotypical approach to the sale and acquisition of corporate control is not to be expected in the face of the evolving techniques and financing devices employed in today's corporate environment. *Mills Acquisition Co. v. Macmillan, Inc.,* 559 A.2d 1261, 128688 (Del.Supr.1989). Rather, a board's actions must be evaluated in light of relevant circumstances to determine if they were undertaken with due diligence and in good faith. If no breach of duty is found, the board's actions are entitled to the protections of the business judgment rule. *Id.* at 954–55.

"This Court has found that certain fact patterns demand certain responses from the directors. Notably, in *Revlon* we held that when several suitors are actively bidding for control of a corporation, the directors may not use defensive tactics that destroy the auction process. *Revlon,* 506 A.2d at 182–85. When it becomes clear that the auction will result in a change of corporate control, the board must act in a neutral manner to encourage the highest possible price for shareholders. *Id.* However, *Revlon* does not demand that every change in the control of a Delaware corporation be preceded by a heated bidding contest. *Revlon* is merely one of an unbroken line of cases that seek to prevent the conflicts of interest that arise in the field of mergers and acquisitions by demanding that directors act with scrupulous concern for fairness to shareholders. When multiple bidders are competing for control, this concern for fairness forbids directors from using defensive mechanisms to thwart an auction or to favor one bidder over another. *Id.* When the board is considering a single offer and has no reliable grounds upon which to judge its adequacy, this concern for fairness demands a canvas of the market to determine if higher bids may be elicited. *In re Fort Howard Corp. Shareholders Litig.,* C.A. No. 9991, 1988 WL 83147 (Del.Ch.1988). When, however, the directors possess a body of reliable evidence with which to evaluate the fairness of a transaction, they may approve that transaction without conducting an active survey of the market. As the Chancellor recognized, the circumstances in which this passive approach is acceptable are limited. 'A decent respect for reality forces one to admit that . . . advice [of an investment banker] is frequently a pale substitute for the dependable information that a canvas of the relevant market can provide.' *In re Amsted Indus. Litig.,* letter op. at 19–20. The need for adequate information is central to the enlightened evaluation of a transaction that a board must make. Nevertheless, there is no single method that a board must employ to acquire such information. Here, the Chancellor found that the advice of the Special Committee's investment bankers, when coupled with the special circumstances surrounding the negotiation and consummation of the MBO, supported a finding that Amsted's directors had acted in good faith to arrange the best possible transaction for shareholders. Our own review of the record leads us to rule that the Chancellor's finding was well within the scope of his discretion."

Paramount Communications Inc. v. QVC Network

Supreme Court of Delaware, 1994.
637 A.2d 34.

■ Before VEASEY, CHIEF JUSTICE, MOORE and HOLLAND, JUSTICES.

Upon appeal from the Court of Chancery. AFFIRMED.

■ VEASEY, CHIEF JUSTICE.

In this appeal we review an order of the Court of Chancery dated November 24, 1993 (the "November 24 Order"), preliminarily enjoining certain defensive measures designed to facilitate a so-called strategic alliance between Viacom Inc. ("Viacom") and Paramount Communications Inc. ("Paramount") approved by the board of directors of Paramount (the "Paramount Board" or the "Paramount directors") and to thwart an unsolicited, more valuable, tender offer by QVC Network Inc. ("QVC"). In affirming, we hold that the sale of control in this case, which is at the heart of the proposed strategic alliance, implicates enhanced judicial scrutiny of the conduct of the Paramount Board under Unocal Corp. v. Mesa Petroleum Co., Del.Supr., 493 A.2d 946 (1985), and Revlon, Inc. v. MacAndrews & Forbes Holdings, Inc., Del.Supr., 506 A.2d 173 (1985). We further hold that the conduct of the Paramount Board was not reasonable as to process or result.

QVC and certain stockholders of Paramount commenced separate actions (later consolidated) in the Court of Chancery seeking preliminary and permanent injunctive relief against Paramount, certain members of the Paramount Board, and Viacom. This action arises out of a proposed acquisition of Paramount by Viacom through a tender offer followed by a second-step merger (the "Paramount–Viacom transaction"), and a competing unsolicited tender offer by QVC. The Court of Chancery granted a preliminary injunction. QVC Network, Inc. v. Paramount Communications Inc., Del.Ch., 635 A.2d 1245, Jacobs, V.C. (1993) (the "Court of Chancery Opinion"). We affirmed by order dated December 9, 1993, Paramount Communications Inc. v. QVC Network Inc., Del.Supr., Nos. 427 and 428, 1993, 637 A.2d 828, Veasey, C.J. (Dec. 9, 1993) (the "December 9 Order").

The Court of Chancery found that the Paramount directors violated their fiduciary duties by favoring the Paramount–Viacom transaction over the more valuable unsolicited offer of QVC. The Court of Chancery preliminarily enjoined Paramount and the individual defendants (the "Paramount defendants") from amending or modifying Paramount's stockholder rights agreement (the "Rights Agreement"), including the redemption of the Rights, or taking other action to facilitate the consummation of the pending tender offer by Viacom or any proposed second-step merger, including the Merger Agreement between Paramount and Viacom dated September 12, 1993 (the

"Original Merger Agreement"), as amended on October 24, 1993 (the "Amended Merger Agreement"). Viacom and the Paramount defendants were enjoined from taking any action to exercise any provision of the Stock Option Agreement between Paramount and Viacom dated September 12, 1993 (the "Stock Option Agreement"), as amended on October 24, 1993. The Court of Chancery did not grant preliminary injunctive relief as to the termination fee provided for the benefit of Viacom in Section 8.05 of the Original Merger Agreement and the Amended Merger Agreement (the "Termination Fee").

Under the circumstances of this case, the pending sale of control implicated in the Paramount–Viacom transaction required the Paramount Board to act on an informed basis to secure the best value reasonably available to the stockholders. Since we agree with the Court of Chancery that the Paramount directors violated their fiduciary duties, we have AFFIRMED the entry of the order of the Vice Chancellor granting the preliminary injunction and have REMANDED these proceedings to the Court of Chancery for proceedings consistent herewith....

I. FACTS ...

Paramount is a Delaware corporation with its principal offices in New York City. Approximately 118 million shares of Paramount's common stock are outstanding and traded on the New York Stock Exchange. The majority of Paramount's stock is publicly held by numerous unaffiliated investors. Paramount owns and operates a diverse group of entertainment businesses, including motion picture and television studios, book publishers, professional sports teams, and amusement parks.

There are 15 persons serving on the Paramount Board. Four directors are officer-employees of Paramount: Martin S. Davis ("Davis"), Paramount's Chairman and Chief Executive Officer since 1983; Donald Oresman ("Oresman"), Executive Vice–President, Chief Administrative Officer, and General Counsel; Stanley R. Jaffe, President and Chief Operating Officer; and Ronald L. Nelson, Executive Vice President and Chief Financial Officer. Paramount's 11 outside directors are distinguished and experienced business persons who are present or former senior executives of public corporations or financial institutions.

Viacom is a Delaware corporation with its headquarters in Massachusetts. Viacom is controlled by Sumner M. Redstone ("Redstone"), its Chairman and Chief Executive Officer, who owns indirectly approximately 85.2 percent of Viacom's voting Class A stock and approximately 69.2 percent of Viacom's nonvoting Class B stock through National Amusements, Inc. ("NAI"), an entity 91.7 percent owned by Redstone. Viacom has a wide range of entertainment operations, including a number of well-known cable television channels such as MTV, Nickelodeon, Showtime, and The Movie Channel. Viacom's equity co-investors in the Paramount–Viacom transaction include NYNEX Corporation and Blockbuster Entertainment Corporation.

QVC is a Delaware corporation with its headquarters in West Chester, Pennsylvania. QVC has several large stockholders, including Liberty Media Corporation, Comcast Corporation, Advance Publications, Inc., and Cox Enterprises Inc. Barry Diller ("Diller"), the Chairman and Chief Executive Officer of QVC, is also a substantial stockholder. QVC sells a variety of merchandise through a televised shopping channel. QVC has several equity co-investors in its proposed combination with Paramount including BellSouth Corporation and Comcast Corporation.

Beginning in the late 1980s, Paramount investigated the possibility of acquiring or merging with other companies in the entertainment, media, or communications industry. Paramount considered such transactions to be desirable, and perhaps necessary, in order to keep pace with competitors in the rapidly evolving field of entertainment and communications. Consistent with its goal of strategic expansion, Paramount made a tender offer for Time Inc. in 1989, but was ultimately unsuccessful. See Paramount Communications, Inc. v. Time Inc., Del. Supr., 571 A.2d 1140 (1989) (*"Time–Warner"*).

Although Paramount had considered a possible combination of Paramount and Viacom as early as 1990, recent efforts to explore such a transaction began at a dinner meeting between Redstone and Davis on April 20, 1993. Robert Greenhill ("Greenhill"), Chairman of Smith Barney Shearson Inc. ("Smith Barney"), attended and helped facilitate this meeting. After several more meetings between Redstone and Davis, serious negotiations began taking place in early July.

It was tentatively agreed that Davis would be the chief executive officer and Redstone would be the controlling stockholder of the combined company, but the parties could not reach agreement on the merger price and the terms of a stock option to be granted to Viacom. With respect to price, Viacom offered a package of cash and stock (primarily Viacom Class B nonvoting stock) with a market value of approximately $61 per share, but Paramount wanted at least $70 per share.

Shortly after negotiations broke down in July 1993, two notable events occurred. First, Davis apparently learned of QVC's potential interest in Paramount, and told Diller over lunch on July 21, 1993, that Paramount was not for sale. Second, the market value of Viacom's Class B nonvoting stock increased from $46.875 on July 6 to $57.25 on August 20. QVC claims (and Viacom disputes) that this price increase was caused by open market purchases of such stock by Redstone or entities controlled by him.

On August 20, 1993, discussions between Paramount and Viacom resumed when Greenhill arranged another meeting between Davis and Redstone. After a short hiatus, the parties negotiated in earnest in early September, and performed due diligence with the assistance of their financial advisors, Lazard Freres & Co. ("Lazard") for Paramount and Smith Barney for Viacom. On September 9, 1993, the Paramount Board was informed about the status of the negotiations and was provided information by Lazard, including an analysis of the proposed transaction.

On September 12, 1993, the Paramount Board met again and unanimously approved the Original Merger Agreement whereby Paramount would merge with and into Viacom. The terms of the merger provided that each share of Paramount common stock would be converted into 0.10 shares of Viacom Class A voting stock, 0.90 shares of Viacom Class B nonvoting stock, and $9.10 in cash. In addition, the Paramount Board agreed to amend its "poison pill" Rights Agreement to exempt the proposed merger with Viacom. The Original Merger Agreement also contained several provisions designed to make it more difficult for a potential competing bid to succeed. We focus, as did the Court of Chancery, on three of these defensive provisions: a "no-shop" provision (the "No–Shop Provision"), the Termination Fee, and the Stock Option Agreement.

First, under the No–Shop Provision, the Paramount Board agreed that Paramount would not solicit, encourage, discuss, negotiate, or endorse any competing transaction unless: (a) a third party "makes an unsolicited written, bona fide proposal, which is not subject to any material contingencies relating to financing"; and (b) the Paramount Board determines that discussions or negotiations with the third party are necessary for the Paramount Board to comply with its fiduciary duties.

Second, under the Termination Fee provision, Viacom would receive a $100 million termination fee if: (a) Paramount terminated the Original Merger Agreement because of a competing transaction; (b) Paramount's stockholders did not approve the merger; or (c) the Paramount Board recommended a competing transaction.

The third and most significant deterrent device was the Stock Option Agreement, which granted to Viacom an option to purchase approximately 19.9 percent (23,699,000 shares) of Paramount's outstanding common stock at $69.14 per share if any of the triggering events for the Termination Fee occurred. In addition to the customary terms that are normally associated with a stock option, the Stock Option Agreement contained two provisions that were both unusual and highly beneficial to Viacom: (a) Viacom was permitted to pay for the shares with a senior subordinated note of questionable marketability instead of cash, thereby avoiding the need to raise the $1.6 billion purchase price (the "Note Feature"); and (b) Viacom could elect to require Paramount to pay Viacom in cash a sum equal to the difference between the purchase price and the market price of Paramount's stock (the "Put Feature"). Because the Stock Option Agreement was not "capped" to limit its maximum dollar value, it had the potential to reach (and in this case did reach) unreasonable levels.

After the execution of the Original Merger Agreement and the Stock Option Agreement on September 12, 1993, Paramount and Viacom announced their proposed merger. In a number of public statements, the parties indicated that the pending transaction was a virtual certainty. Redstone described it as a "marriage" that would "never be torn asunder" and stated that only a "nuclear attack" could break the deal. Redstone also called Diller and John Malone of Tele–Communications Inc., a major stockholder of QVC, to dissuade them from making a competing bid.

Despite these attempts to discourage a competing bid, Diller sent a letter to Davis on September 20, 1993, proposing a merger in which QVC would acquire Paramount for approximately $80 per share, consisting of 0.893 shares of QVC common stock and $30 in cash. QVC also expressed its eagerness to meet with Paramount to negotiate the details of a transaction. When the Paramount Board met on September 27, it was advised by Davis that the Original Merger Agreement prohibited Paramount from having discussions with QVC (or anyone else) unless certain conditions were satisfied. In particular, QVC had to supply evidence that its proposal was not subject to financing contingencies. The Paramount Board was also provided information from Lazard describing QVC and its proposal.

On October 5, 1993, QVC provided Paramount with evidence of QVC's financing. The Paramount Board then held another meeting on October 11, and decided to authorize management to meet with QVC. Davis also informed the Paramount Board that Booz–Allen Hamilton ("Booz–Allen"), a management consulting firm, had been retained to assess, *inter alia*, the incremental earnings potential from a Paramount–Viacom merger and a Paramount–QVC merger. Discussions proceeded slowly, however, due to a delay in Paramount signing a confidentiality agreement. In response to Paramount's request for information, QVC provided two binders of documents to Paramount on October 20.

On October 21, 1993, QVC filed this action and publicly announced an $80 cash tender offer for 51 percent of Paramount's outstanding shares (the "QVC tender offer"). Each remaining share of Paramount common stock would be converted into 1.42857 shares of QVC common stock in a second-step merger. The tender offer was conditioned on, among other things, the invalidation of the Stock Option Agreement, which was worth over $200 million by that point.[5] QVC contends that it had to commence a tender offer because of the slow pace of the merger discussions and the need to begin seeking clearance under federal antitrust laws.

Confronted by QVC's hostile bid, which on its face offered over $10 per share more than the consideration provided by the Original Merger Agreement, Viacom realized that it would need to raise its bid in order to remain competitive. Within hours after QVC's tender offer was announced, Viacom entered into discussions with Paramount concerning a revised transaction. These discussions led to serious negotiations concerning a comprehensive amendment to the original Paramount–Viacom transaction. In effect, the opportunity for a "new deal" with Viacom was at hand for the Paramount Board. With the

---

5. By November 15, 1993, the value of the Stock Option Agreement had increased to nearly $500 million based on the $90 QVC bid. See Court of Chancery Opinion, 635 A.2d 1245, 1271.

QVC hostile bid offering greater value to the Paramount stockholders, the Paramount Board had considerable leverage with Viacom.

At a special meeting on October 24, 1993, the Paramount Board approved the Amended Merger Agreement and an amendment to the Stock Option Agreement. The Amended Merger Agreement was, however, essentially the same as the Original Merger Agreement, except that it included a few new provisions. One provision related to an $80 per share cash tender offer by Viacom for 51 percent of Paramount's stock, and another changed the merger consideration so that each share of Paramount would be converted into 0.20408 shares of Viacom Class A voting stock, 1.08317 shares of Viacom Class B nonvoting stock, and 0.20408 shares of a new series of Viacom convertible preferred stock. The Amended Merger Agreement also added a provision giving Paramount the right not to amend its Rights Agreement to exempt Viacom if the Paramount Board determined that such an amendment would be inconsistent with its fiduciary duties because another offer constituted a "better alternative."[6] Finally, the Paramount Board was given the power to terminate the Amended Merger Agreement if it withdrew its recommendation of the Viacom transaction or recommended a competing transaction.

Although the Amended Merger Agreement offered more consideration to the Paramount stockholders and somewhat more flexibility to the Paramount Board than did the Original Merger Agreement, the defensive measures designed to make a competing bid more difficult were not removed or modified. In particular, there is no evidence in the record that Paramount sought to use its newly-acquired leverage to eliminate or modify the No–Shop Provision, the Termination Fee, or the Stock Option Agreement when the subject of amending the Original Merger Agreement was on the table.

Viacom's tender offer commenced on October 25, 1993, and QVC's tender offer was formally launched on October 27, 1993. Diller sent a letter to the Paramount Board on October 28 requesting an opportunity to negotiate with Paramount, and Oresman responded the following day by agreeing to meet. The meeting, held on November 1, was not very fruitful, however, after QVC's proposed guidelines for a "fair bidding process" were rejected by Paramount on the ground that auction procedures were inappropriate and contrary to Paramount's contractual obligations to Viacom.

On November 6, 1993, Viacom unilaterally raised its tender offer price to $85 per share in cash and offered a comparable increase in the value of the securities being proposed in the second-step merger. At a telephonic meeting held later that day, the Paramount Board agreed to recommend Viacom's higher bid to Paramount's stockholders.

---

6. Under the Amended Merger Agreement and the Paramount Board's resolutions approving it, no further action of the Paramount Board would be required in order for Paramount's Rights Agreement to be amended. As a result, the proper officers of the company were authorized to implement the amendment unless they were instructed otherwise by the Paramount Board.

QVC responded to Viacom's higher bid on November 12 by increasing its tender offer to $90 per share and by increasing the securities for its second-step merger by a similar amount. In response to QVC's latest offer, the Paramount Board scheduled a meeting for November 15, 1993. Prior to the meeting, Oresman sent the members of the Paramount Board a document summarizing the "conditions and uncertainties" of QVC's offer. One director testified that this document gave him a very negative impression of the QVC bid.

At its meeting on November 15, 1993, the Paramount Board determined that the new QVC offer was not in the best interests of the stockholders. The purported basis for this conclusion was that QVC's bid was excessively conditional. The Paramount Board did not communicate with QVC regarding the status of the conditions because it believed that the No–Shop Provision prevented such communication in the absence of firm financing. Several Paramount directors also testified that they believed the Viacom transaction would be more advantageous to Paramount's future business prospects than a QVC transaction.[7] Although a number of materials were distributed to the Paramount Board describing the Viacom and QVC transactions, the only quantitative analysis of the consideration to be received by the stockholders under each proposal was based on then-current market prices of the securities involved, not on the anticipated value of such securities at the time when the stockholders would receive them.[8]

The preliminary injunction hearing in this case took place on November 16, 1993. On November 19, Diller wrote to the Paramount Board to inform it that QVC had obtained financing commitments for its tender offer and that there was no antitrust obstacle to the offer. On November 24, 1993, the Court of Chancery issued its decision granting a preliminary injunction in favor of QVC and the plaintiff stockholders. This appeal followed.

II. APPLICABLE PRINCIPLES OF ESTABLISHED DELAWARE LAW

The General Corporation Law of the State of Delaware (the "General Corporation Law") and the decisions of this Court have repeatedly recognized the fundamental principle that the management of the business and affairs of a Delaware corporation is entrusted to its directors, who are the duly elected and authorized representatives of the stockholders. 8 Del.C. § 141(a); Aronson v. Lewis, Del.Supr., 473 A.2d 805, 811–12 (1984); Pogostin v. Rice, Del.Supr., 480 A.2d 619, 624 (1984). Under normal circumstances, neither the courts nor the stockholders should interfere with the managerial decisions of the

7. This belief may have been based on a report prepared by BoozAllen and distributed to the Paramount Board at its October 24 meeting. The report, which relied on public information regarding QVC, concluded that the synergies of a Paramount–Viacom merger were significantly superior to those of a Paramount–QVC merger. QVC has labelled the Booz–Allen report as a joke.

8. The market prices of Viacom's and QVC's stock were poor measures of their actual values because such prices constantly fluctuated depending upon which company was perceived to be the more likely to acquire Paramount.

directors. The business judgment rule embodies the deference to which such decisions are entitled. *Aronson,* 473 A.2d at 812.

Nevertheless, there are rare situations which mandate that a court take a more direct and active role in overseeing the decisions made and actions taken by directors. In these situations, a court subjects the directors' conduct to enhanced scrutiny to ensure that it is reasonable.[9] The decisions of this Court have clearly established the circumstances where such enhanced scrutiny will be applied. E.g., *Unocal,* 493 A.2d 946; Moran v. Household Int'l, Inc., Del.Supr., 500 A.2d 1346 (1985); *Revlon,* 506 A.2d 173. . . . The case at bar implicates two such circumstances: (1) the approval of a transaction resulting in a sale of control, and (2) the adoption of defensive measures in response to a threat to corporate control.

A. The Significance of a Sale or Change[10] of Control

When a majority of a corporation's voting shares are acquired by a single person or entity, or by a cohesive group acting together, there is a significant diminution in the voting power of those who thereby become minority stockholders. Under the statutory framework of the General Corporation Law, many of the most fundamental corporate changes can be implemented only if they are approved by a majority vote of the stockholders. Such actions include elections of directors, amendments to the certificate of incorporation, mergers, consolidations, sales of all or substantially all of the assets of the corporation, and dissolution. 8 Del.C. §§ 211, 242, 251258, 263, 271, 275. Because of the overriding importance of voting rights, this Court and the Court of Chancery have consistently acted to protect stockholders from unwarranted interference with such rights.[11]

In the absence of devices protecting the minority stockholders,[12] stockholder votes are likely to become mere formalities where there is

---

9. Where actual self-interest is present and affects a majority of the directors approving a transaction, a court will apply even more exacting scrutiny to determine whether the transaction is entirely fair to the stockholders. E.g., Weinberger v. UOP, Inc., Del. Supr., 457 A.2d 701, 71011 (1983); Nixon v. Blackwell, Del.Supr., 626 A.2d 1366, 1376 (1993).

10. For purposes of our December 9 Order and this Opinion, we have used the terms sale of control and change of control interchangeably without intending any doctrinal distinction.

11. See Schnell v. Chris–Craft Industries Inc., Del.Supr., 285 A.2d 437, 439 (1971) (holding that actions taken by management to manipulate corporate machinery "for the purpose of obstructing the legitimate efforts of dissident stockholders in the exercise of their rights to undertake a proxy contest against management" were "contrary to established principles of corporate democracy" and therefore invalid); Giuricich v. Emtrol Corp., Del.Supr., 449 A.2d 232, 239 (1982)

(holding that "careful judicial scrutiny will be given a situation in which the right to vote for the election of successor directors has been effectively frustrated"); . . . Stroud v. Grace, Del.Supr., 606 A.2d 75, 84 (1992) (directors' duty of disclosure is premised on the importance of stockholders being fully informed when voting on a specific matter); Blasius Indus., Inc. v. Atlas Corp., Del.Ch., 564 A.2d 651, 659 n. 2 (1988) ("Delaware courts have long exercised a most sensitive and protective regard for the free and effective exercise of voting rights.").

12. Examples of such protective provisions are supermajority voting provisions, majority of the minority requirements, etc. Although we express no opinion on what effect the inclusion of any such stockholder protective devices would have had in this case, we note that this Court has upheld, under different circumstances, the reasonableness of a standstill agreement which limited a 49.9 percent stockholder to 40 percent board representation. *Ivanhoe,* 535 A.2d at 1343.

a majority stockholder. For example, minority stockholders can be deprived of a continuing equity interest in their corporation by means of a cash-out merger. *Weinberger*, 457 A.2d at 703. Absent effective protective provisions, minority stockholders must rely for protection solely on the fiduciary duties owed to them by the directors and the majority stockholder, since the minority stockholders have lost the power to influence corporate direction through the ballot. The acquisition of majority status and the consequent privilege of exerting the powers of majority ownership come at a price. That price is usually a control premium which recognizes not only the value of a control block of shares, but also compensates the minority stockholders for their resulting loss of voting power.

In the case before us, the public stockholders (in the aggregate) currently own a majority of Paramount's voting stock. Control of the corporation is not vested in a single person, entity, or group, but vested in the fluid aggregation of unaffiliated stockholders. In the event the Paramount–Viacom transaction is consummated, the public stockholders will receive cash and a minority equity voting position in the surviving corporation. Following such consummation, there will be a controlling stockholder who will have the voting power to: (a) elect directors; (b) cause a break-up of the corporation; (c) merge it with another company; (d) cash-out the public stockholders; (e) amend the certificate of incorporation; (f) sell all or substantially all of the corporate assets; or (g) otherwise alter materially the nature of the corporation and the public stockholders' interests. Irrespective of the present Paramount Board's vision of a long-term strategic alliance with Viacom, the proposed sale of control would provide the new controlling stockholder with the power to alter that vision.

Because of the intended sale of control, the Paramount–Viacom transaction has economic consequences of considerable significance to the Paramount stockholders. Once control has shifted, the current Paramount stockholders will have no leverage in the future to demand another control premium. As a result, the Paramount stockholders are entitled to receive, and should receive, a control premium and/or protective devices of significant value. There being no such protective provisions in the Viacom–Paramount transaction, the Paramount directors had an obligation to take the maximum advantage of the current opportunity to realize for the stockholders the best value reasonably available.

B. The Obligations of Directors in a Sale or Change of Control Transaction

The consequences of a sale of control impose special obligations on the directors of a corporation. In particular, they have the obligation of acting reasonably to seek the transaction offering the best value reasonably available to the stockholders. The courts will apply enhanced scrutiny to ensure that the directors have acted reasonably. The obligations of the directors and the enhanced scrutiny of the courts are well-established by the decisions of this Court. The directors' fiduciary duties in a sale of control context are those which generally attach. In short, "the directors must act in accordance with their fundamental duties of care and loyalty." Barkan v. Amsted Indus., Inc., Del.Supr., 567 A.2d 1279, 1286 (1989). As we held in *Macmillan:*

> It is basic to our law that the board of directors has the ultimate responsibility for managing the business and affairs of a corporation. In discharging this function, the directors owe fiduciary duties of care and loyalty to the corporation and its shareholders. **This unremitting obligation extends equally to board conduct in a sale of corporate control.**

559 A.2d at 1280 (emphasis supplied) (citations omitted).

In the sale of control context, the directors must focus on one primary objective—to secure the transaction offering the best value reasonably available for the stockholders—and they must exercise their fiduciary duties to further that end. The decisions of this Court have consistently emphasized this goal. *Revlon,* 506 A.2d at 182 ("The duty of the board . . . [is] the maximization of the company's value at a sale for the stockholders' benefit.") . . . .

In pursuing this objective, the directors must be especially diligent. See Citron v. Fairchild Camera and Instrument Corp., Del.Supr., 569 A.2d 53, 66 (1989) (discussing "a board's active and direct role in the sale process"). In particular, this Court has stressed the importance of the board being adequately informed in negotiating a sale of control: "The need for adequate information is central to the enlightened evaluation of a transaction that a board must make." *Barkan,* 567 A.2d at 1287. This requirement is consistent with the general principle that "directors have a duty to inform themselves, prior to making a business decision, of all material information reasonably available to them." *Aronson,* 473 A.2d at 812. See also Cede & Co. v. Technicolor, Inc., Del.Supr., 634 A.2d 345, 367 (1993); Smith v. Van Gorkom, Del.Supr., 488 A.2d 858, 872 (1985). Moreover, the role of outside, independent directors becomes particularly important because of the magnitude of a sale of control transaction and the possibility, in certain cases, that management may not necessarily be impartial. See *Macmillan,* 559 A.2d at 1285 (requiring "the intense scrutiny and participation of the independent directors").

Barkan teaches some of the methods by which a board can fulfill its obligation to seek the best value reasonably available to the stockholders. 567 A.2d at 1286–87. These methods are designed to determine the existence and viability of possible alternatives. They include conducting an auction, canvassing the market, etc. Delaware law recognizes that there is no single blueprint that directors must follow. Id. at 1286–87; *Citron,* 569 A.2d at 68; *Macmillan,* 559 A.2d at 1287.

In determining which alternative provides the best value for the stockholders, a board of directors is not limited to considering only the amount of cash involved, and is not required to ignore totally its view of the future value of a strategic alliance. See *Macmillan,* 559 A.2d at 1282 n. 29. Instead, the directors should analyze the entire situation and evaluate in a disciplined manner the consideration being offered. Where stock or other non-cash consideration is involved, the board should try to quantify its value, if feasible, to achieve an objective comparison of the alternatives.[13] In addition, the board may assess a variety of practical considerations relating to each alternative, including:

> [an offer's] fairness and feasibility; the proposed or actual financing for the offer, and the consequences of that financing; questions of illegality; . . . the risk of non-consum[m]ation; . . . the bidder's identity, prior background and other business venture experiences; and the bidder's business plans for the corporation and their effects on stockholder interests.

Macmillan, 559 A.2d at 1282 n. 29. These considerations are important because the selection of one alternative may permanently foreclose other opportunities. While the assessment of these factors may be complex, the board's goal is straightforward: having informed themselves of all material information reasonably available, the directors must decide which alternative is most likely to offer the best value reasonably available to the stockholders.

C. Enhanced Judicial Scrutiny of a Sale or Change of Control Transaction

Board action in the circumstances presented here is subject to enhanced scrutiny. Such scrutiny is mandated by: (a) the threatened diminution of the current stockholders' voting power; (b) the fact that an asset belonging to public stockholders (a control premium) is being sold and may never be available again; and (c) the traditional concern of Delaware courts for actions which impair or impede stockholder voting rights (see supra note 11). In *Macmillan,* this Court held:

> When *Revlon* duties devolve upon directors, this Court will continue to exact an enhanced judicial scrutiny at the threshold, as in *Unocal,* before the normal presumptions of the business judgment rule will apply.[14]

559 A.2d at 1288. The *Macmillan* decision articulates a specific two-part test for analyzing board action where competing bidders are not treated equally:[15]

> In the face of disparate treatment, the trial court must first examine whether the directors properly perceived that sharehold-

---

13. When assessing the value of non-cash consideration, a board should focus on its value as of the date it will be received by the stockholders. Normally, such value will be determined with the assistance of experts using generally accepted methods of valuation. See In re RJR Nabisco, Inc. Shareholders Litig., Del.Ch., C.A. No. 10389, Allen, C. (Jan. 31, 1989), reprinted at 14 Del.J.Corp.L. 1132, 1161.

14. Because the Paramount Board acted unreasonably as to process and result in this sale of control situation, the business judgment rule did not become operative.

15. Before this test is invoked, "the plaintiff must show, and the trial court must find, that the directors of the target company treated one or more of the respective bidders on unequal terms." *Macmillan,* 559 A.2d at 1288.

er interests were enhanced. In any event the board's action must be reasonable in relation to the advantage sought to be achieved, or conversely, to the threat which a particular bid allegedly poses to stockholder interests.

Id. See also Roberts v. General Instrument Corp., Del.Ch., C.A. No. 11639, Allen, C. (Aug. 13, 1990), reprinted at 16 Del.J.Corp.L. 1540, 1554 ("This enhanced test requires a judicial judgment of reasonableness in the circumstances.").

The key features of an enhanced scrutiny test are: (a) a judicial determination regarding the adequacy of the decisionmaking process employed by the directors, including the information on which the directors based their decision; and (b) a judicial examination of the reasonableness of the directors' action in light of the circumstances then existing. The directors have the burden of proving that they were adequately informed and acted reasonably.

Although an enhanced scrutiny test involves a review of the reasonableness of the substantive merits of a board's actions,[16] a court should not ignore the complexity of the directors' task in a sale of control. There are many business and financial considerations implicated in investigating and selecting the best value reasonably available. The board of directors is the corporate decisionmaking body best equipped to make these judgments. Accordingly, a court applying enhanced judicial scrutiny should be deciding whether the directors made a **reasonable** decision, not a **perfect** decision. If a board selected one of several reasonable alternatives, a court should not second-guess that choice even though it might have decided otherwise or subsequent events may have cast doubt on the board's determination. Thus, courts will not substitute their business judgment for that of the directors, but will determine if the directors' decision was, on balance, within a range of reasonableness. See *Unocal*, 493 A.2d at 955–56; *Macmillan*, 559 A.2d at 1288; Nixon, 626 A.2d at 1378.

D. *Revlon* and *Time–Warner* Distinguished

The Paramount defendants and Viacom assert that the fiduciary obligations and the enhanced judicial scrutiny discussed above are not implicated in this case in the absence of a "break-up" of the corporation, and that the order granting the preliminary injunction should be reversed. This argument is based on their erroneous interpretation of our decisions in *Revlon* and *Time–Warner*.

In *Revlon*, we reviewed the actions of the board of directors of Revlon, Inc. ("Revlon"), which had rebuffed the overtures of Pantry Pride, Inc. and had instead entered into an agreement with Forstmann

---

16. It is to be remembered that, in cases where the traditional business judgment rule is applicable and the board acted with due care, in good faith, and in the honest belief that they are acting in the best interests of the stockholders (which is not this case), the Court gives great deference to the substance of the directors' decision and will not invalidate the decision, will not examine its reasonableness, and "will not substitute our views for those of the board if the latter's decision can be 'attributed to any rational business purpose.'" *Unocal*, 493 A.2d at 949 (quoting Sinclair Oil Corp. v. Levien, Del.Supr., 280 A.2d 717, 720 (1971)). See *Aronson*, 473 A.2d at 812.

Little & Co. ("Forstmann") providing for the acquisition of 100 percent of Revlon's outstanding stock by Forstmann and the subsequent breakup of Revlon. Based on the facts and circumstances present in *Revlon*, we held that "[t]he directors' role changed from defenders of the corporate bastion to auctioneers charged with getting the best price for the stockholders at a sale of the company." 506 A.2d at 182. We further held that "when a board ends an intense bidding contest on an insubstantial basis, . . . [that] action cannot withstand the enhanced scrutiny which *Unocal* requires of director conduct." Id. at 184.

It is true that one of the circumstances bearing on these holdings was the fact that "the break-up of the company . . . had become a reality which even the directors embraced." Id. at 182. It does not follow, however, that a "break-up" must be present and "inevitable" before directors are subject to enhanced judicial scrutiny and are required to pursue a transaction that is calculated to produce the best value reasonably available to the stockholders. In fact, we stated in *Revlon* that "when bidders make relatively similar offers, or dissolution of the company becomes inevitable, the directors cannot fulfill their enhanced *Unocal* duties by playing favorites with the contending factions." Id. at 184 (emphasis added). *Revlon* thus does not hold that an inevitable dissolution or break-up is necessary.

The decisions of this Court following *Revlon* reinforced the applicability of enhanced scrutiny and the directors' obligation to seek the best value reasonably available for the stockholders where there is a pending sale of control, regardless of whether or not there is to be a break-up of the corporation. In *Macmillan*, this Court held:

> We stated in *Revlon*, and again here, that **in a sale of corporate control** the responsibility of the directors is to get the highest value reasonably attainable for the shareholders.

559 A.2d at 1288 (emphasis added). In *Barkan*, we observed further:

> We believe that the general principles announced in *Revlon*, in Unocal Corp. v. Mesa Petroleum Co., Del.Supr., 493 A.2d 946 (1985), and in Moran v. Household International, Inc., Del.Supr., 500 A.2d 1346 (1985) govern this case and every case in which a **fundamental change of corporate control** occurs or is contemplated.

567 A.2d at 1286 (emphasis added).

Although *Macmillan* and *Barkan* are clear in holding that a change of control imposes on directors the obligation to obtain the best value reasonably available to the stockholders, the Paramount defendants have interpreted our decision in *Time–Warner* as requiring a corporate break-up in order for that obligation to apply. The facts in *Time–Warner*, however, were quite different from the facts of this case, and refute Paramount's position here. In *Time–Warner*, the Chancellor held that there was no change of control in the original stock-for-stock merger between Time and Warner because Time would be owned by a fluid aggregation of unaffiliated stockholders both before and after the merger:

> If the appropriate inquiry is whether a change in control is contemplated, the answer must be sought in the specific circumstances surrounding the transaction. Surely under some circumstances a stock for stock merger could reflect a transfer of corporate control. That would, for example, plainly be the case here if Warner were a private company. But where, as here, the shares of both constituent corporations are widely held, corporate control can be expected to remain unaffected by a stock for stock merger. This in my judgment was the situation with respect to the original merger agreement. When the specifics of that situation are reviewed, it is seen that, aside from legal technicalities and aside from arrangements thought to enhance the prospect for the ultimate succession of [Nicholas J. Nicholas, Jr., president of Time], neither corporation could be said to be acquiring the other. **Control of both remained in a large, fluid, changeable and changing market.**
>
> The existence of a control block of stock in the hands of a single shareholder or a group with loyalty to each other does have real consequences to the financial value of "minority" stock. The law offers some protection to such shares through the imposition of a fiduciary duty upon controlling shareholders. **But here, effectuation of the merger would not have subjected Time shareholders to the risks and consequences of holders of minority shares. This is a reflection of the fact that no control passed to anyone in the transaction contemplated.** The shareholders of Time would have "suffered" dilution, of course, but they would suffer the same type of dilution upon the public distribution of new stock.

Paramount Communications, Inc. v. Time Inc., Del.Ch., No. 10866, Allen, C. (July 17, 1989), reprinted at 15 Del.J.Corp.L. 700, 739 (emphasis added). Moreover, the transaction actually consummated in *Time–Warner* was not a merger, as originally planned, but a sale of Warner's stock to Time.

In our affirmance of the Court of Chancery's well-reasoned decision, this Court held that "The Chancellor's findings of fact are supported by the record and **his conclusion is correct as a matter of law.**" 571 A.2d at 1150 (emphasis added). Nevertheless, the Paramount defendants here have argued that a break-up is a requirement and have focused on the following language in our *Time–Warner* decision:

> However, we premise our rejection of plaintiffs' *Revlon* claim on different grounds, namely, the absence of any substantial evidence to conclude that Time's board, in negotiating with Warner, made the dissolution or break-up of the corporate entity inevitable, as was the case in *Revlon.*

Under Delaware law there are, generally speaking and **without excluding other possibilities,** two circumstances which may implicate *Revlon* duties. The first, and clearer one, is when a corporation **initiates an active bidding process seeking to sell itself** or to effect a business reorganization involving a clear break-up of the company. However, *Revlon* duties may also be triggered where, in response to a bidder's offer, a target abandons its long-term strategy and seeks an alternative transaction involving the breakup of the company.

Id. at 1150 (emphasis added) (citation and footnote omitted).

The Paramount defendants have misread the holding of *Time–Warner.* Contrary to their argument, our decision in *Time–Warner* expressly states that the two general scenarios discussed in the above-quoted paragraph are not the only instances where "*Revlon* duties" may be implicated. The Paramount defendants' argument totally ignores the phrase "without excluding other possibilities." Moreover, the instant case is clearly within the first general scenario set forth in *Time–Warner.* The Paramount Board, albeit unintentionally, had "initiate[d] an active bidding process seeking to sell itself" by agreeing to sell control of the corporation to Viacom in circumstances where another potential acquiror (QVC) was equally interested in being a bidder.

The Paramount defendants' position that both a change of control and a break-up are required must be rejected. Such a holding would unduly restrict the application of *Revlon,* is inconsistent with this Court's decisions in *Barkan* and *Macmillan,* and has no basis in policy. There are few events that have a more significant impact on the stockholders than a sale of control or a corporate break-up. Each event represents a fundamental (and perhaps irrevocable) change in the nature of the corporate enterprise from a practical standpoint. It is the significance of **each** of these events that justifies: (a) focusing on the directors' obligation to seek the best value reasonably available to the stockholders; and (b) requiring a close scrutiny of board action which could be contrary to the stockholders' interests.

Accordingly, when a corporation undertakes a transaction which will cause: (a) a change in corporate control; or (b) a break-up of the corporate entity, the directors' obligation is to seek the best value reasonably available to the stockholders. This obligation arises because the effect of the Viacom–Paramount transaction, if consummated, is to shift control of Paramount from the public stockholders to a controlling stockholder, Viacom. Neither *Time–Warner* nor any other decision of this Court holds that a "break-up" of the company is essential to give rise to this obligation where there is a sale of control.

III. BREACH OF FIDUCIARY DUTIES BY PARAMOUNT BOARD

We now turn to duties of the Paramount Board under the facts of this case and our conclusions as to the breaches of those duties which warrant injunctive relief.

A.   The Specific Obligations of the Paramount Board

Under the facts of this case, the Paramount directors had the obligation: (a) to be diligent and vigilant in examining critically the Paramount–Viacom transaction and the QVC tender offers; (b) to act in good faith; (c) to obtain, and act with due care on, all material information reasonably available, including information necessary to compare the two offers to determine which of these transactions, or an alternative course of action, would provide the best value reasonably available to the stockholders; and (d) to negotiate actively and in good faith with both Viacom and QVC to that end.

Having decided to sell control of the corporation, the Paramount directors were required to evaluate critically whether or not all material aspects of the Paramount–Viacom transaction (separately and in the aggregate) were reasonable and in the best interests of the Paramount stockholders in light of current circumstances, including: the change of control premium, the Stock Option Agreement, the Termination Fee, the coercive nature of both the Viacom and QVC tender offers,[17] the No–Shop Provision, and the proposed disparate use of the Rights Agreement as to the Viacom and QVC tender offers, respectively.

These obligations necessarily implicated various issues, including the questions of whether or not those provisions and other aspects of the Paramount–Viacom transaction (separately and in the aggregate): (a) adversely affected the value provided to the Paramount stockholders; (b) inhibited or encouraged alternative bids; (c) were enforceable contractual obligations in light of the directors' fiduciary duties; and (d) in the end would advance or retard the Paramount directors' obligation to secure for the Paramount stockholders the best value reasonably available under the circumstances.

The Paramount defendants contend that they were precluded by certain contractual provisions, including the No–Shop Provision, from negotiating with QVC or seeking alternatives. Such provisions, whether or not they are presumptively valid in the abstract, may not, validly define or limit the directors' fiduciary duties under Delaware law or prevent the Paramount directors from carrying out their fiduciary duties under Delaware law. To the extent such provisions are inconsistent with those duties, they are invalid and unenforceable. See *Revlon*, 506 A.2d at 184–85.

Since the Paramount directors had already decided to sell control, they had an obligation to continue their search for the best value reasonably available to the stockholders. This continuing obligation included the responsibility, at the October 24 board meeting and thereafter, to evaluate critically both the QVC tender offers and the Paramount–Viacom transaction to determine if: (a) the QVC tender

---

17. Both the Viacom and the QVC tender offers were for 51 percent cash and a "back-end" of various securities, the value of each of which depended on the fluctuating value of Viacom and QVC stock at any given time. Thus, both tender offers were two-tiered, front-end loaded, and coercive. Such coercive offers are inherently problematic and should be expected to receive particularly careful analysis by a target board. See *Unocal*, 493 A.2d at 956.

offer was, or would continue to be, conditional; (b) the QVC tender offer could be improved; (c) the Viacom tender offer or other aspects of the Paramount–Viacom transaction could be improved; (d) each of the respective offers would be reasonably likely to come to closure, and under what circumstances; (e) other material information was reasonably available for consideration by the Paramount directors; (f) there were viable and realistic alternative courses of action; and (g) the timing constraints could be managed so the directors could consider these matters carefully and deliberately.

B. The Breaches of Fiduciary Duty by the Paramount Board

The Paramount directors made the decision on September 12, 1993, that, in their judgment, a strategic merger with Viacom on the economic terms of the Original Merger Agreement was in the best interests of Paramount and its stockholders. Those terms provided a modest change of control premium to the stockholders. The directors also decided at that time that it was appropriate to agree to certain defensive measures (the Stock Option Agreement, the Termination Fee, and the No–Shop Provision) insisted upon by Viacom as part of that economic transaction. Those defensive measures, coupled with the sale of control and subsequent disparate treatment of competing bidders, implicated the judicial scrutiny of *Unocal, Revlon, Macmillan,* and their progeny. We conclude that the Paramount directors' process was not reasonable, and the result achieved for the stockholders was not reasonable under the circumstances.

When entering into the Original Merger Agreement, and thereafter, the Paramount Board clearly gave insufficient attention to the potential consequences of the defensive measures demanded by Viacom. The Stock Option Agreement had a number of unusual and potentially "draconian"[18] provisions, including the Note Feature and the Put Feature. Furthermore, the Termination Fee, whether or not unreasonable by itself, clearly made Paramount less attractive to other bidders, when coupled with the Stock Option Agreement. Finally, the No–Shop Provision inhibited the Paramount Board's ability to negotiate with other potential bidders, particularly QVC which had already expressed an interest in Paramount.[19]

---

18. The Vice Chancellor so characterized the Stock Option Agreement. Court of Chancery Opinion, 635 A.2d 1245, 1272. We express no opinion whether a stock option agreement of essentially this magnitude, but with a reasonable cap and without the Note and Put Features, would be valid or invalid under other circumstances. See Hecco Ventures v. Sea–Land Corp., Del.Ch., C.A. No. 8486, Jacobs, V.C. (May 19, 1986) (21.7 percent stock option); In re Vitalink Communications Corp. Shareholders Litig., Del.Ch., C.A. No. 12085, Chandler, V.C. (May 16, 1990) (19.9 percent stock option).

19. We express no opinion whether certain aspects of the No–Shop Provision here

could be valid in another context. Whether or not it could validly have operated here at an early stage solely to prevent Paramount from actively "shopping" the company, it could not prevent the Paramount directors from carrying out their fiduciary duties in considering unsolicited bids or in negotiating for the best value reasonably available to the stockholders. *Macmillan,* 559 A.2d at 1287. As we said in *Barkan:* "Where a board has no reasonable basis upon which to judge the adequacy of a contemplated transaction, a no-shop restriction gives rise to the inference that the board seeks to forestall competing bids." 567 A.2d at 1288. See also *Revlon,* 506 A.2d at 184 (holding that "[t]he no-shop provision, like the lock-up option, while not *per*

Throughout the applicable time period, and especially from the first QVC merger proposal on September 20 through the Paramount Board meeting on November 15, QVC's interest in Paramount provided the **opportunity** for the Paramount Board to seek significantly higher value for the Paramount stockholders than that being offered by Viacom. QVC persistently demonstrated its intention to meet and exceed the Viacom offers, and frequently expressed its willingness to negotiate possible further increases.

The Paramount directors had the opportunity in the October 23–24 time frame, when the Original Merger Agreement was renegotiated, to take appropriate action to modify the improper defensive measures as well as to improve the economic terms of the Paramount–Viacom transaction. Under the circumstances existing at that time, it should have been clear to the Paramount Board that the Stock Option Agreement, coupled with the Termination Fee and the No–Shop Clause, were impeding the realization of the best value reasonably available to the Paramount stockholders. Nevertheless, the Paramount Board made no effort to eliminate or modify these counterproductive devices, and instead continued to cling to its vision of a strategic alliance with Viacom. Moreover, based on advice from the Paramount management, the Paramount directors considered the QVC offer to be "conditional" and asserted that they were precluded by the No–Shop Provision from seeking more information from, or negotiating with, QVC.

By November 12, 1993, the value of the revised QVC offer on its face exceeded that of the Viacom offer by over $1 billion at then current values. This significant disparity of value cannot be justified on the basis of the directors' vision of future strategy, primarily because the change of control would supplant the authority of the current Paramount Board to continue to hold and implement their strategic vision in any meaningful way. Moreover, their uninformed process had deprived their strategic vision of much of its credibility. See *Van Gorkom,* 488 A.2d at 872; Cede v. Technicolor, 634 A.2d at 367; Hanson Trust PLC v. ML SCM Acquisition Inc., 2d Cir., 781 F.2d 264, 274 (1986).

When the Paramount directors met on November 15 to consider QVC's increased tender offer, they remained prisoners of their own misconceptions and missed opportunities to eliminate the restrictions they had imposed on themselves. Yet, it was not "too late" to reconsider negotiating with QVC. The circumstances existing on November 15 made it clear that the defensive measures, taken as a whole, were problematic: (a) the No–Shop Provision could not define or limit their fiduciary duties; (b) the Stock Option Agreement had become "draconian"; and (c) the Termination Fee, in context with all the circumstances, was similarly deterring the realization of possibly higher bids. Nevertheless, the Paramount directors remained paralyzed by their uninformed belief that the QVC offer was "illusory." This final

se illegal, is impermissible under the *Unocal* standards when a board's primary duty becomes that of an auctioneer responsible for selling the company to the highest bidder").

opportunity to negotiate on the stockholders' behalf and to fulfill their obligation to seek the best value reasonably available was thereby squandered.[20]

IV. VIACOM'S CLAIM OF VESTED CONTRACT RIGHTS

Viacom argues that it had certain "vested" contract rights with respect to the No–Shop Provision and the Stock Option Agreement.[21] In effect, Viacom's argument is that the Paramount directors could enter into an agreement in violation of their fiduciary duties and then render Paramount, and ultimately its stockholders, liable for failing to carry out an agreement in violation of those duties. Viacom's protestations about vested rights are without merit. This Court has found that those defensive measures were improperly designed to deter potential bidders, and that such measures do not meet the reasonableness test to which they must be subjected. They are consequently invalid and unenforceable under the facts of this case.

The No–Shop Provision could not validly define or limit the fiduciary duties of the Paramount directors. To the extent that a contract, or a provision thereof, purports to require a board to act or not act in such a fashion as to limit the exercise of fiduciary duties, it is invalid and unenforceable. Cf. Wilmington Trust v. Coulter, 200 A.2d at 452–54. Despite the arguments of Paramount and Viacom to the contrary, the Paramount directors could not contract away their fiduciary obligations. Since the No–Shop Provision was invalid, Viacom never had any vested contract rights in the provision.

As discussed previously, the Stock Option Agreement contained several "draconian" aspects, including the Note Feature and the Put Feature. While we have held that lock-up options are not *per se* illegal, see *Revlon,* 506 A.2d at 183, no options with similar features have ever been upheld by this Court. Under the circumstances of this case, the Stock Option Agreement clearly is invalid. Accordingly, Viacom never had any vested contract rights in that Agreement.

Viacom, a sophisticated party with experienced legal and financial advisors, knew of (and in fact demanded) the unreasonable features of the Stock Option Agreement. It cannot be now heard to argue that it obtained vested contract rights by negotiating and obtaining contractual provisions from a board acting in violation of its fiduciary duties. As

---

20. The Paramount defendants argue that the Court of Chancery erred by assuming that the Rights Agreement was pulled at the November 15 meeting of the Paramount Board. The problem with this argument is that, under the Amended Merger Agreement and the resolutions of the Paramount Board related thereto, Viacom would be exempted from the Rights Agreement in the absence of further action of the Paramount Board and no further meeting had been scheduled or even contemplated prior to the closing of the Viacom tender offer. This failure to schedule and hold a meeting shortly before the closing date in order to make a final decision, based on all of the information and circumstances then existing, whether to exempt Viacom from the Rights Agreement was inconsistent with the Paramount Board's responsibilities and does not provide a basis to challenge the Court of Chancery's decision.

21. Presumably this argument would have included the Termination Fee had the Vice Chancellor invalidated that provision or if appellees had cross-appealed from the Vice Chancellor's refusal to invalidate that provision.

the Nebraska Supreme Court said in rejecting a similar argument in ConAgra, Inc. v. Cargill, Inc., Neb.Supr., 382 N.W.2d 576, 587–88 (1986), "To so hold, it would seem, would be to get the shareholders coming and going." Likewise, we reject Viacom's arguments and hold that its fate must rise and fall, and in this instance fall, with the determination that the actions of the Paramount Board were invalid.

V. CONCLUSION

The realization of the best value reasonably available to the stockholders became the Paramount directors' primary obligation under these facts in light of the change of control. That obligation was not satisfied, and the Paramount Board's process was deficient. The directors' initial hope and expectation for a strategic alliance with Viacom was allowed to dominate their decisionmaking process to the point where the arsenal of defensive measures established at the outset was perpetuated (not modified or eliminated) when the situation was dramatically altered. QVC's unsolicited bid presented the opportunity for significantly greater value for the stockholders and enhanced negotiating leverage for the directors. Rather than seizing those opportunities, the Paramount directors chose to wall themselves off from material information which was reasonably available and to hide behind the defensive measures as a rationalization for refusing to negotiate with QVC or seeking other alternatives. Their view of the strategic alliance likewise became an empty rationalization as the opportunities for higher value for the stockholders continued to develop.

It is the nature of the judicial process that we decide only the case before us—a case which, on its facts, is clearly controlled by established Delaware law. Here, the proposed change of control and the implications thereof were crystal clear. In other cases they may be less clear. The holding of this case on its facts, coupled with the holdings of the principal cases discussed herein where the issue of sale of control is implicated, should provide a workable precedent against which to measure future cases.

For the reasons set forth herein, the November 24, 1993, Order of the Court of Chancery has been AFFIRMED, and this matter has been REMANDED for proceedings consistent herewith, as set forth in the December 9, 1993, Order of this Court.

———

ARNOLD v. SOCIETY FOR SAVINGS BANCORP, INC., 650 A.2d 1270 (Del.1994). In considering a claim that a corporation's directors were subject to *Revlon* duties, the Delaware Supreme Court stated:

> ... The directors of a corporation have the obligation of acting reasonably to seek the transaction offering the best value reasonably available to the stockholders, *Paramount Communications, Inc. v. QVC Network, Inc.*, Del.Supr., 637 A.2d 34, 43 (1994), in at least the following three scenarios: (1) "when a

corporation initiates an active bidding process seeking to sell itself or to effect a business reorganization involving a clear break-up of the company," *Paramount Communications, Inc. v. Time Inc.,* Del.Supr., 571 A.2d 1140, 1150 (1989) [*Time–Warner*]; (2) "where, in response to a bidder's offer, a target abandons its long-term strategy and seeks an alternative transaction involving the break-up of the company," *id.;* or (3) when approval of a transaction results in a "sale or change of control," *QVC*, 637 A.2d at 42– 43, 47. In the latter situation, there is no "sale or change in control" when " '[c]ontrol of both [companies] remain[s] in a large, fluid, changeable and changing market.' " *Id.* at 47....

Hilton Hotels Corporation v. ITT Corporation

United States District Court, District of Nevada, 1997.
978 F.Supp. 1342.

■ PHILIP M. PRO, UNITED STATES DISTRICT JUDGE.

Before the Court for consideration is the ... Motion for Injunctive and Declaratory Relief ... filed ... on behalf of Hilton Hotels Corporation and HLT Corporation (collectively "Hilton")....

I. FACTS

On January 27, 1997, Hilton announced a $55.00 per share tender offer for the stock of ITT, and announced plans for a proxy contest at ITT's 1997 annual meeting....

On February 11, 1997, ITT formally rejected Hilton's tender offer. ITT proceeded to sell several of its non-core assets and opposed Hilton's takeover attempt before gaming regulatory bodies in Nevada, New Jersey and Mississippi.

When it became apparent that ITT would not conduct its annual meeting in May 1997, as it had customarily done in preceding years, Hilton filed a motion for a mandatory injunction to compel ITT to conduct the annual meeting in May. On April 21, 1997, this Court denied Hilton's Motion, finding that Nevada law and ITT's by-laws did not require that ITT conduct its annual meeting within twelve months of the prior meeting, but rather that ITT had eighteen months within which to do so. *Hilton Hotels Corp. and HLT v. ITT Corp., 962 F. Supp. 1309 (D. Nev. 1997),* aff'd, *116 F.3d 1483 (9th Cir. 1997).*

On July 15, 1997, ITT announced a Comprehensive Plan which, among other things, proposed to split ITT into three new entities, the largest of which would become ITT Destinations. ITT Destinations would be comprised of the current ITT's hotel and gaming business which account for approximately 93% of ITT's current assets. A second entity, ITT Educational Services, would consist of the current ITT's technical schools, and ITT's European Yellow Pages Division would remain with the current ITT as ITT World Directories.

Most significantly, under the Comprehensive Plan, the board of directors of the new ITT Destinations would be comprised of the members of ITT's current board with one important distinction. The new board would be a "classified" or "staggered" board divided into three classes with each class of directors serving for a term of three years, and with one class to be elected each year. Moreover, a shareholder vote of 80% would be required to remove directors without cause, and 80% shareholder vote would also be required to repeal the classified board provision or the 80% requirement to remove directors without cause.

Additionally, the record fairly supports Hilton's contention that the Comprehensive Plan contains a "poison pill" resulting in a $1.4 billion tax liability which would be triggered if Hilton successfully acquired more than 50% of ITT Destinations and that Hilton would be liable for 90% of the tax bill.

Finally, and critical to this Court's analysis, ITT seeks to implement the Comprehensive Plan prior to ITT's 1997 annual meeting and without obtaining shareholder approval.

II. THE PARTIES' CONTENTIONS AND APPLICABLE LEGAL STANDARDS ...

Shortly after ITT's announcement of its Comprehensive Plan, Hilton announced an amended tender offer of $70.00 per share which was rejected by ITT. On August 26, 1997, Hilton filed its Motion for Injunctive and Declaratory Relief ... seeking:

    1. A preliminary and permanent injunction enjoining ITT from proceeding with its Comprehensive Plan;

    2. Declaring that by adopting the Comprehensive Plan, ITT's directors had breached their fiduciary duties to ITT and its shareholders;

    3. Declaring that ITT may not implement its Comprehensive Plan without obtaining a shareholder vote; and

    4. Requiring ITT to conduct its 1997 annual meeting for the election of directors not later than November 14, 1997. ...

III. DISCUSSION

This case involves consideration of the powers and duties of the board of directors of a Nevada corporation in responding to a hostile takeover attempt, and the importance of protecting the franchise of the shareholders of the corporation in the process.

Many courts have grappled with legal issues presented by the strategies employed by hostile bidders, such as Hilton, and the concomitant anti-takeover defensive measures utilized by target companies, such as ITT. Coupling an unsolicited tender offer with a proxy contest to replace the incumbent board is a favored strategy of would-be acquirors. A variety of sophisticated defensive measures, including "poison pill" plans have also evolved to frustrate a host of takeover attempts. As a result, "replacing the incumbent directors of the target corporation is viewed as an efficient way to eliminate the target company's ability to utilize these anti-takeover defenses." *Kidsco v. Dinsmore III, 674 A.2d 483, 490 (Del. Ch. 1995).* See also *Unitrin, Inc. v. American Gen. Corp., 651 A.2d 1361, 1379 (Del. 1995).*

Nevada state case law is virtually silent on the subject. However, provisions of Chapter 78 of the Nevada Revised Statutes ("N.R.S.") speak to the respective rights and duties of directors and officers of corporations, and the rights of corporate stockholders. Nevada's statutory scheme does not, however, provide clear guidance in this case. While N.R.S. § 78.138 addresses several powers of a corporate board in undertaking defensive measures to resist a hostile takeover, nothing in the Nevada statutes, or elsewhere in the law of Nevada, authorizes the incumbent board of a corporation to entrench itself by effectively removing the right of the corporation's shareholders to vote on who may serve on the board of the corporation in which they own a share. Whether a target corporation such as ITT can do so in the face of a hostile takeover attempt by Hilton is the dispositive issue presented in this case.

Where, as here, there is no Nevada statutory or case law on point for an issue of corporate law, this Court finds persuasive authority in Delaware case law. *Shoen v. AMERCO, 885 F. Supp. 1332, 1341 n.20 (D. Nev. 1994).*

    ... *Legal Framework for Board Action in Response to a Proxy Contest and Tender Offer.*

As this case involves both a tender offer and a proxy contest by Hilton, the proper legal standard is a Unocal/Blasius analysis as articulated in *Stroud v. Grace, 606 A.2d 75, 92 n.3 (Del. 1992),* and *Unitrin, 651 A.2d 1361 at 1379.*

> In assessing a challenge to defensive actions by a target corporation's board of directors in a takeover context, this Court has held that the Court of Chancery should evaluate the board's overall response, including the justification for each contested defensive measure, and the results achieved thereby. Where all of the target board's defensive actions are inextricably related, the principles of *Unocal* require that such actions be scrutinized collectively as a unitary response to the perceived threat.

Unitrin, 651 A.2d at 1386–87 (emphasis supplied).

> Where an acquiror launches both a proxy fight and a tender offer, it "necessarily invoke[s] both *Unocal* and *Blasius*" because "both [tests] recognize the inherent conflicts of interest that arise when shareholders are not permitted free exercise of their franchise.... In certain circumstances, [the judiciary] must recognize the special import of protecting the shareholders' franchise within Unocal's requirement that any defensive measure be proportionate and 'reasonable in relation to the threat posed.'"

Unitrin, 651 A.2d at 1379 (quoting *Stroud, 606 A.2d 75 at 92 n.3*).

A board's unilateral decision to adopt a defensive measure touching "upon issues of control" that purposefully disenfranchises its shareholders is strongly suspect under *Unocal*, and cannot be sustained without a "compelling justification."

Stroud, 606 A.2d at 92 n.3.

These cases have drawn a distinction between the exercise of two types of corporate power: 1) power over the assets of the corporation and 2) the power relationship between the board (management) and the shareholders. Actions involving the first type of power invoke the business judgment rule, or *Unocal* if an action is in response to a reasonably perceived threat to the corporation. Actions involving the second power invoke a *Blasius* analysis. The issues raised in this case require the Court to focus on the power relationship between ITT's board and ITT shareholders, not on the ITT board's actions relating to corporate assets.

Several amicus briefs have been filed on behalf of ITT shareholders, urging that they be allowed to vote on the Comprehensive Plan and the board of directors at the 1997 annual meeting. This Court has found no legal basis mandating a shareholder vote on the adoption of ITT's Comprehensive Plan in its entirety. However, as the Court finds that the Comprehensive Plan would violate the power relationship between ITT's board and ITT's shareholders by impermissibly infringing on the shareholders' right to vote on members of the board of directors, it must be enjoined. . . .

. . . Delaware precedent establishes that a board has power over the management and assets of a corporation, but that power is not unbridled. That *power* is limited by the right of shareholders to vote for the members of the board. As articulated in *Shoen*, this right underlies the concept of corporate democracy. This Court fully endorses the reasoning in *Shoen* and *Blasius* regarding the importance of the shareholder franchise to the entire scheme of corporate governance. This Court will, therefore, examine ITT's Comprehensive Plan under the Unocal/Blasius analysis.

Unocal requires the Court to consider the following two questions: 1) Does ITT have reasonable grounds for believing a danger to corporate policy and effectiveness exists? 2) Is the response reasonable in relation to the threat? If it is a defensive measure touching on issues of control, the court must examine whether the board purposefully disenfranchised its shareholders, an action that cannot be sustained without a compelling justification. *Stroud, 606 A.2d at 92 n.3.*

1. *The Classified Board for ITT Destinations*

The first defensive action this Court will analyze under the *Unocal* standard is the provision in the Comprehensive Plan for a classified board for ITT Destinations.

a. *Reasonable grounds for believing a threat to corporate policy and effectiveness exists.*

Nine of ITT's eleven directors are outside directors. Under *Unocal*, such a majority materially enhances evidence that a hostile offer presents a threat warranting a defensive response. *Unitrin, 651 A.2d at 1375.*

ITT argues strenuously that the Comprehensive Plan is better than Hilton's offer. This is not for the Court to decide, and it is not determinative under its analysis. Under *Unocal*, a court must first determine if there is a threat to corporate policy and effectiveness. ITT has failed to demonstrate such a threat.

ITT has made no showing that Hilton will pursue a different corporate policy than ITT seeks to implement through its Comprehensive Plan. In fact, over the past few months, ITT has to a large extent adopted Hilton's proposed strategy of how it says it will govern ITT if its slate of directors is elected. There has also been no showing of Hilton's inability or ineffectiveness to run ITT if it does succeed in its takeover attempt. ITT cites to the fact that some Sheraton franchise owners will be unhappy if Hilton enters into certain management contracts, but this is not fundamental or pervasive enough to constitute a "threat" to ITT's corporate policy or effectiveness.

The ITT board has also failed to meet its burden of showing "good faith and reasonable investigation" of a threat to corporate policy or effectiveness which would meet the burden placed on the board under the first prong of the Unocal test. Since Hilton's tender offer was announced, the ITT board has not met with Hilton to discuss the offer. Moreover, the overwhelming majority of ITT's evidence of good faith relates to its approval of the Comprehensive Plan, not to the inadequacy of Hilton's offer.

The sole "threat" ITT points to is that Hilton's offer of $70 a share is inadequate, primarily because this price does not contain a control premium. However, at the August 14, 1997, ITT board meeting, Goldman Sachs told the ITT board that the market valued ITT's plan at $62 to $64 dollars a share. This contradicts ITT's argument that there is no control premium over market price contained in Hilton's offer. That ITT itself was offering to buy back roughly 26% of its stock at $70 a share does not nullify this fact.

The only attempt ITT has made to satisfy the first prong of the *Unocal* analysis is to argue that Hilton's price is inadequate. However, while inadequacy of an offer is a legally cognizable threat, *Paramount Communications, Inc. v. Time, Inc., 571 A.2d 1140, 1153 (Del. 1989),* ITT has shown no real harm to corporate policy or effectiveness.... As ITT itself is offering only $70 a share, and the Comprehensive Plan involves greatly increasing the leveraging of ITT, its claim that Hilton's offer of $70 a share is a threat to policy or effectiveness is unpersuasive. In light of these facts, the alleged inadequacy of Hilton's offer is not a severe threat to ITT. Under the proportionality requirement, the nature of Hilton's threat will set the parameters for the range of permissible defensive tactics under the second prong of the *Unocal* test. *Unitrin, 651 A.2d 1361 at 1384.*

b. *ITT's Response was Preclusive*

Assuming Hilton's offer constitutes a cognizable threat under *Unocal*, ITT's response cannot be preclusive or coercive, and it must be within the range of reasonableness. As articulated in *Unitrin*, a board cannot "cram down" on shareholders a management sponsored alternative. *Unitrin, 651 A.2d at 1387.* The installation of a classified board for ITT Destinations, a company which will encompass 93% of the current ITT's assets and 87% of its revenues, is clearly preclusive and coercive under Unitrin. The classified board provision for ITT Destinations will preclude current ITT shareholders from exercising a right they currently possess—to determine the membership of the board of ITT. At the very minimum, ITT shareholders will have no choice but to accept the Comprehensive Plan and a majority of ITT's incumbent board members for another year. Therefore, the Comprehensive Plan is preclusive.

c. *The Primary Purpose of the Comprehensive Plan is to Interfere with Shareholder Franchise*

ITT's response to Hilton's tender offer touches upon issues of control, and this Court must determine whether the response purposefully disenfranchises ITT's shareholders. If so, under the analysis of *Stroud* and *Unitrin*, it is not a reasonable response unless a "compelling justification" exists. It is important to note that in *Blasius*, the board did something that normally would be entirely permissible under Delaware law and its own by-laws: it expanded the board from seven to nine individuals. It did this in the face of a hostile takeover by a company financed through "junk bonds" and two individuals who sought to substantially "cash out" many of the target corporation's assets. *Blasius, 564 A.2d at 653–54.* Still, while the board in *Blasius* had a good faith reason to act as it did, and it acted with appropriate care, the board could not lawfully prevent the shareholders from electing a majority of new directors.

Blasius' factual scenario is strikingly similar to the circumstances surrounding ITT's actions. Normally, a corporation is free to adopt a classified board structure. In fact many companies, including Hilton, have classified boards. As long as the classified board is adopted in the proper manner, whether through charter amendment, changes in the by-laws of a company or through shareholder vote, it is permissible. However, *Blasius* illustrates that even if an action is normally permissible, and the board adopts it in good faith and with proper care, a board cannot undertake such action if the primary purpose is to disenfranchise the shareholders in light of a proxy contest. *Blasius, 564 A.2d at 652.* Thus, while ITT could normally adopt a classified board or issue a dividend of shares creating ITT Destinations, it cannot undertake these actions if the primary purpose is to disenfranchise ITT shareholders in light of Hilton's tender offer and proxy contest.

As a board would likely never concede that its primary purpose was to entrench itself, this Court must look to circumstantial evidence to determine the primary purpose of ITT's action touching upon issues of control. While none of the following factors are dispositive, collectively they eliminate all questions of material fact, and demonstrate that the primary purpose of ITT's Comprehensive Plan was to disenfranchise its shareholders.

i.   *Timing*

The intent evidenced by the timing of the Comprehensive Plan is transparent. Although ITT claims that a spin-off or sale was contemplated before Hilton's tender offer, it makes no mention of when the board determined to move from an annually elected board to a classified board. Moreover, all aspects of ITT's Comprehensive Plan were formulated against the backdrop of Hilton's tender offer and proxy contest, and the Plan was not announced until well after Hilton's initial tender offer. Finally, this major restructuring of ITT was announced and to be implemented in a little over two months, and designed to take effect less than two months before the annual meeting was to be held at which shareholders would have the opportunity to vote on an annually elected rather than a classified board.

ii.   *Entrenchment*

The ITT directors who are approving the Comprehensive Plan are the same directors who will fill the classified board positions of ITT Destinations. ITT and its advisors recognized from the outset that they were vulnerable because they did not have a staggered board of directors. The members of ITT's board are appointing themselves to new, more insulated positions, and at least seven of the eleven directors are avoiding the shareholder vote that would otherwise occur at ITT's 1997 annual meeting. While companies may convert from annual to classified boards, as Blasius illustrates, the rub is in the details. It is the manner of adopting the Comprehensive Plan with its provision for a new certified board comprised of incumbent ITT directors which supports the conclusion that ITT's Plan is primarily designed to entrench the incumbent board.

iii.   *ITT's Stated Purpose*

ITT has offered no credible justification for not seeking shareholder approval of the Comprehensive Plan. ITT simply claims that it wants to "avoid market risks and other business problems." (pp. 10–11 of ITT's Opposition). Such vague generalizations do not approach the required showing of a reasonable justification other than entrenchment for the board's action. Simply stating that its "advisors" suggested a rapid implementation of the Comprehensive Plan, without pointing to a specific risk or problem, is insufficient to meet ITT's burden.

iv.   *Benefits of Comprehensive Plan*

ITT argues that there are economic benefits to the Comprehensive Plan, and general benefits of the classified board provision for ITT Destinations. That may be true, but the additional benefits of a plan infringing on shareholder voting rights do not remedy the fundamental flaw of board entrenchment.

v. *Effect of Classified Board*

The classified board provision for ITT Destinations under ITT's Comprehensive Plan ensures that ITT shareholders will be absolutely precluded from electing a majority of the directors nominated under Hilton's proxy contest at the 1997 annual meeting. Such a Plan, coupled with ITT's vehement opposition to Hilton's tender offer, is inconsistent with ITT's earlier argument that a delay of the 1997 annual meeting from May to November would afford shareholders additional time to inform themselves and more fully consider the implications of their vote for directors at the 1997 annual meeting.

ITT's position is particularly anomalous given the fact that when ITT previously split the company in 1995, it sought shareholder approval. While shareholder approval may not be absolutely required to split ITT now anymore than it was in 1995, the fact that the ITT board decided to subject the 1995 split of the company to a shareholder vote is strong evidence that the primary purpose of its attempts to implement the Comprehensive Plan prior to the 1997 annual meeting is to entrench the incumbent ITT board.

vi. *Failure to Obtain an IRS Opinion as
to Effects of the Comprehensive Plan*

ITT is not seeking an Internal Revenue Service opinion regarding the tax consequences of the three-way split of ITT under the Comprehensive Plan. It is doubtful that an Internal Revenue Service opinion on the matter could be obtained before ITT's 1997 annual meeting. Furthermore, there are serious questions as to the extent to which implementation of the Comprehensive Plan will constitute a taxable event to ITT and its shareholders, or the extent to which Hilton would incur adverse tax consequences if it attempted to take over ITT Destinations once the Comprehensive Plan is implemented. ITT dismisses these concerns by arguing that its attorneys advise that there are no adverse tax consequences under the Comprehensive Plan. However, the record demonstrates otherwise. ITT's counsel conceded that there is no binding precedent on point and that the issue was not free from doubt. While obtaining a tax opinion from the Internal Revenue Service may not be mandatory, ITT's failure to seriously consider obtaining such an opinion provides additional evidence that ITT's primary intention in implementing the Comprehensive Plan at this time was to impede the shareholder franchise.

2. *Other Provisions of the Comprehensive Plan*

This Court's analysis regarding the threat to ITT under the first prong of Unocal is equally applicable to the remaining elements of the Comprehensive Plan. Whether the other aspects of ITT's Comprehensive Plan violate the second step of the Unocal analysis, that is whether they are preclusive or coercive, is problematic. Certainly the record before the Court supports Hilton's contention that the "tax poison pill" relating to its potential purchase of ITT Destinations is preclusive and coercive. Hilton also argues that ITT's Plan is coercive because ITT is offering $70.00 a share for only 26% of the stock. Since the trading value of the stock is $62.00 to $64.00 per share, shareholders will have to tender their shares immediately to avoid a financial loss. These arguments create serious questions as to whether the other elements of the Comprehensive Plan are preclusive and coercive.

The *Unocal* test is also referred to as a "proportionality test." see, e.g., *Unitrin, 651 A.2d at 1384*. Serious questions remain as to whether the Comprehensive Plan is reasonable in relation to the threat posed by Hilton's offer. The Comprehensive Plan entails a split-up of ITT and spin-off of 93% of the company's assets without a shareholder vote. There are important tax considerations, both the "tax poison pill" discussed above and the relative tax burdens of spinning off World Directories as opposed to one of the smaller entities. Additionally, other aspects of the financial restructuring involved in the Comprehensive Plan illustrate that the plan is extremely complex, and that the three ITTs emerging from the plan will be fundamentally different companies.

Serious questions exist as to whether the remaining provisions of the Comprehensive Plan are preclusive or coercive, or reasonable responses under *Unocal*. This Court finds it unnecessary, however, to undertake an exhaustive analysis of the laundry list of issues presented by both parties. The different provisions of the Comprehensive Plan are inextricably related, and this Court has already concluded that the staggered board provision is preclusive and was enacted for the primary purpose of entrenching the current board. Therefore, the entire Comprehensive Plan must be enjoined. . . .

IV.   CONCLUSION

Earlier in this litigation, the Court fully embraced pertinent language in Shoen and Blasius regarding the importance of the shareholder franchise. *Hilton, 962 F. Supp. at 1310*. Those principles encompass fundamental concepts of corporate governance and bear repetition.

Shareholders do not exercise day-to-day business judgments regarding the operation of a corporation—those are matters left to the reasonable discretion of directors, officers and the corporation's management team. Corporate boards have great latitude in exercising their business judgments as they should. As a result, shareholders generally have only two protections against perceived inadequate business performance. They may sell their stock or vote to replace incumbent board members. For this reason, interference with the shareholder franchise is especially serious. It is not to be left to the board's business judgment, precisely because it undercuts a primary justification for allowing directors to rely on their business judgment in almost every other context. Indeed, as the court in Shoen noted, "one of the justifications for the business judgment rule's insulation of directors from liability for almost all of their decisions is that unhappy shareholders can always vote the directors out of office." *Shoen, 885 F. Supp. at 1340*.

As this Court has noted previously, " 'inquiries concerning fiducia-ry duties are inherently particularized and contextual. It is probably not possible to work out rules that will be perfectly predictive of future cases involving claimed impediments to the shareholder vote. It is sufficient to express a reasoned judgment on the facts presented.' " *Hilton, 962 F. Supp. at 1311* (quoting *Stahl v. Apple Bancorp, Inc., 579 A.2d 1115 at 1125).*

ITT strongly argues that its Comprehensive Plan is superior to Hilton's alternative tender offer. This argument should be directed to ITT's shareholders, not this Court.

ITT also claims that it has properly considered other constituen-cies in responding to Hilton's offer, as it is expressly allowed to do under N.R.S. § 78.138. ITT is correct. Other constituencies may be considered under that provision, but nothing in that statute suggests that the interests of third parties are as important as the right of shareholder franchise. While the two interests are not exclusive, neither are they equal. The right of shareholders to vote on directors at an annual meeting is a fundamental principle of corporate law, and it is not outweighed by the interests listed in N.R.S. § 78.138.

Likewise, the good faith of the ITT board in implementing the Comprehensive Plan does not change this Court's analysis.... Simply put, there is no compelling justification for infringement of the shareholder franchise as proposed by the implementation of ITT's Comprehensive Plan before the 1997 annual meeting.

The ultimate outcome of the election of directors at ITT's 1997 annual meeting is not a relevant inquiry for this Court. That is something for the shareholders who own ITT to decide when they select the board who will lead the corporation. If a majority of the incumbent ITT board is re-elected after a fully-informed and fair shareholder vote, that board will be free to implement any business plan it chooses so long as that plan is consistent with ITT's charter and by-laws, and governing law.

This Court concludes that the structure and timing of ITT's Comprehensive Plan with its classified board provision for ITT Desti-nations, is preclusive and leaves no doubt that the primary purpose for ITT's proposed implementation of the Comprehensive Plan before the 1997 annual meeting is to impermissibly impede the exercise of the shareholder franchise by depriving shareholders of the opportunity to vote to re-elect or to oust all or as many of the incumbent ITT directors as they may choose at the upcoming annual meeting. It has as its primary purpose the entrenchment of the incumbent ITT board. As a result, the Court concludes that Hilton has prevailed on the merits of its claim for permanent injunctive relief.

IT IS THEREFORE ORDERED that Hilton's Motion for Permanent Injunctive Relief is granted to the extent that ITT is hereby enjoined from implementing its Comprehensive Plan announced July 15, 1997.

IT IS FURTHER ORDERED that ITT's annual meeting shall be held no later than November 14, 1997. . . .

. . .

Omnicare, Inc. v. NCS Healthcare, Inc.

Supreme Court of Delaware 2003.
818 A.2d 914.

■ Before: VEASEY, CHIEF JUSTICE, WALSH, HOLLAND, BERGER and STEELE, JUSTICES, constituting the Court en Banc.

■ HOLLAND, JUSTICE, for the majority: . . .

NCS Healthcare, Inc. ("NCS"), a Delaware corporation, was the object of competing acquisition bids, one by Genesis Health Ventures, Inc., ("Genesis"), a Pennsylvania Corporation, and the other by Omnicare, Inc. ("Omnicare"), a Delaware corporation. . . .

NCS, is a Delaware corporation headquartered in Beachwood, Ohio. NCS is a leading independent provider of pharmacy services to long-term care institutions including skilled nursing facilities, assisted living facilities and other institutional healthcare facilities. NCS common stock consists of Class A shares and Class B shares. The Class B shares are entitled to ten votes per share and the Class A shares are entitled to one vote per share. The shares are virtually identical in every other respect.

The defendant Jon H. Outcalt is Chairman of the NCS board of directors. Outcalt owns 202,063 shares of NCS Class A common stock and 3,476,086 shares of Class B common stock. The defendant Kevin B. Shaw is President, CEO and a director of NCS. At the time the merger agreement at issue in this dispute was executed with Genesis, Shaw owned 28,905 shares of NCS Class A common stock and 1,141,134 shares of Class B common stock.

The NCS board has two other members, defendants Boake A. Sells and Richard L. Osborne. Sells is a graduate of the Harvard Business School. He was Chairman and CEO at Revco Drugstores in Cleveland, Ohio from 1987 to 1992, when he was replaced by new owners. Sells currently sits on the boards of both public and private companies. Osborne is a full-time professor at the Weatherhead School of Management at Case Western Reserve University. He has been at the university for over thirty years. Osborne currently sits on at least seven corporate boards other than NCS.

The defendant Genesis is a Pennsylvania corporation with its principal place of business in Kennett Square, Pennsylvania. It is a leading provider of healthcare and support services to the elderly. . . .

The plaintiffs in the class action own an unspecified number of shares of NCS Class A common stock. They represent a class consisting of all holders of Class A common stock. As of July 28, 2002, NCS had 18,461,599 Class A shares and 5,255,210 Class B shares outstanding.

Omnicare is a Delaware corporation with its principal place of business in Covington, Kentucky. Omnicare is in the institutional pharmacy business, with annual sales in excess of $2.1 billion during its last fiscal year. . . .

FACTUAL BACKGROUND . . .

NCS Seeks Restructuring Alternatives

Beginning in late 1999, changes in the timing and level of reimbursements by government and third-party providers adversely affected market conditions in the health care industry. As a result, NCS began to experience greater difficulty in collecting accounts receivables, which led to a precipitous decline in the market value of its stock. NCS common shares that traded above $20 in January 1999 were worth as little as $5 at the end of that year. By early 2001, NCS was in default on approximately $350 million in debt, including $206 million in senior bank debt and $102 million of its 5 3/4% Convertible Subordinated Debentures (the "Notes"). After these defaults, NCS common stock traded in a range of $0.09 to $0.50 per share until days before the announcement of the transaction at issue in this case.

NCS began to explore strategic alternatives that might address the problems it was confronting. . . .

Omnicare's Initial Negotiations

In the summer of 2001, NCS invited Omnicare, Inc. to begin discussions with Brown Gibbons [NCS's investment banker] regarding a possible transaction. On July 20, Joel Gemunder, Omnicare's President and CEO, sent Shaw [NCS's CEO] a written proposal to acquire NCS in a bankruptcy sale under Section 363 of the Bankruptcy Code. This proposal was for $225 million subject to satisfactory completion of due diligence. . . .

NCS Financial Improvement

. . . In March 2002, NCS decided to form an independent committee of board members who were neither NCS employees nor major NCS stockholders (the "Independent Committee") [to consider transactions that would provide some value for NCS's stockholders]. The NCS board thought this was necessary because, due to NCS's precarious financial condition, it felt that fiduciary duties were owed to the enterprise as a whole rather than solely to NCS stockholders.

Sells and Osborne were selected as the members of the committee, and given authority to consider and negotiate possible transactions for NCS. The entire four member NCS board, however, retained authority to approve any transaction. The Independent Committee retained the same legal and financial counsel as the NCS board.

The Independent Committee met for the first time on May 14, 2002. At that meeting Pollack suggested that NCS seek a "stalking-horse merger partner" to obtain the highest possible value in any transaction. The Independent Committee agreed with the suggestion.

Genesis Initial Proposal

Two days later, on May 16, 2002, Scott Berlin of Brown Gibbons, Glen Pollack [also of Brown Gibbons] and Boake Sells [a member of NCS's independent committee] met with George Hager, CFO of Genesis, and Michael Walker, who was Genesis's CEO. At that meeting, Genesis made it clear that if it were going to engage in any negotiations with NCS, it would not do so as a stalking horse. As one of its advisors testified, "We didn't want to be someone who set forth a valuation for NCS which would only result in that valuation ... being publicly disclosed, and thereby creating an environment where Omnicare felt to maintain its competitive monopolistic positions, that they had to match and exceed that level." Thus, Genesis "wanted a degree of certainty that to the extent [it] w[as] willing to pursue a negotiated merger agreement ..., [it] would be able to consummate the transaction [it] negotiated and executed."

In June 2002, Genesis proposed a transaction for the acquisition of NCS.... As discussions continued, the terms proposed by Genesis continued to improve....

Genesis Exclusivity Agreement

NCS's financial advisors and legal counsel met again with Genesis and its legal counsel on June 26, 2002, to discuss a number of transaction-related issues....

At the June 26 meeting, Genesis's representatives demanded that, before any further negotiations take place, NCS agree to enter into an exclusivity agreement with it. As Hager from Genesis explained it: "[I]f they wished us to continue to try to move this process to a definitive agreement, that they would need to do it on an exclusive basis with us. We were going to, and already had incurred significant expense, but we would incur additional expenses ..., both internal and external, to bring this transaction to a definitive signing. We wanted them to work with us on an exclusive basis for a short period of time to see if we could reach agreement." On June 27, 2002, Genesis's legal counsel delivered a draft form of exclusivity agreement for review and consideration by NCS's legal counsel.

The Independent Committee met on July 3, 2002, to consider the proposed exclusivity agreement. Pollack presented a summary of the terms of a possible Genesis merger, which had continued to improve. The then-current Genesis proposal included (1) repayment of the NCS senior debt in full, (2) payment of par value for the Notes (without accrued interest) in the form of a combination of cash and Genesis stock, (3) payment to NCS stockholders in the form of $24 million in Genesis stock, plus (4) the assumption, because the transaction was to be structured as a merger, of additional liabilities to trade and other unsecured creditors.

NCS director Sells testified [that] Pollack told the Independent Committee at a July 3, 2002 meeting that Genesis wanted the Exclusivity Agreement to be the first step towards a completely locked up transaction that would preclude a higher bid from Omnicare:

A. [Pollack] explained that Genesis felt that they had suffered at the hands of Omnicare and others. I guess maybe just Omnicare. I don't know much about Genesis [sic] acquisition history. But they had suffered before at the 11:59:59 and that they wanted to have a pretty much bulletproof deal or they were not going to go forward.

Q. When you say they suffered at the hands of Omnicare, what do you mean?

A. Well, my expression is that that was related to—a deal that was related to me or explained to me that they, Genesis, had tried to acquire, I suppose, an institutional pharmacy, I don't remember the name of it. Thought they had a deal and then at the last minute, Omnicare outbid them for the company in a like 11:59 kind of thing, and that they were unhappy about that. And once burned, twice shy.

After NCS executed the exclusivity agreement, Genesis provided NCS with a draft merger agreement, a draft Noteholders' support agreement, and draft voting agreements for Outcalt and Shaw, who together held a majority of the voting power of the NCS common stock. Genesis and NCS negotiated the terms of the merger agreement over the next three weeks. During those negotiations, the Independent Committee and [an Ad Hoc Committee that had been formed to represent the Noteholders] persuaded Genesis to improve the terms of its merger. . . .

Omnicare Proposes Negotiations . . .

On the afternoon of July 26, 2002, Omnicare faxed to NCS a letter outlining a proposed acquisition. . . . Omnicare's proposal, however, was expressly conditioned on negotiating a merger agreement, obtaining certain third party consents, and completing its due diligence. . . .

Late in the afternoon of July 26, 2002, NCS representatives received voicemail messages from Omnicare asking to discuss the letter. The exclusivity agreement prevented NCS from returning those calls. In relevant part, that agreement precluded NCS from "engag[ing] or particpat[ing] in any discussions or negotiations with respect to a Competing Transaction or a proposal for one." The July 26 letter from Omnicare met the definition of a "Competing Transaction."

. . . Nevertheless, the Independent Committee [decided] to use Omnicare's letter to negotiate for improved terms with Genesis.

Genesis Merger Agreement and Voting Agreements

Genesis responded to the NCS request to improve its offer as a result of the Omnicare fax the next day. On July 27, Genesis proposed substantially improved terms. . . . In return for [its] concessions, Genesis stipulated that the transaction had to be approved by midnight the next day, July 28, or else Genesis would terminate discussions and withdraw its offer. . . .

. . . [The NCS board met on July 28.] After receiving similar reports and advice from its legal and financial advisors, the board concluded that "balancing the potential loss of the Genesis deal against the uncertainty of Omnicare's letter, results in the conclusion that the only reasonable alternative for the Board of Directors is to approve the Genesis transaction." The board first voted to authorize the voting agreements [described below] with Outcalt and Shaw, for purposes of Section 203 of the Delaware General Corporation Law ("DGCL"). The board was advised by its legal counsel that "under the terms of the merger agreement and because NCS shareholders representing in excess of 50% of the outstanding voting power would be required by Genesis to enter into stockholder voting agreements contemporaneously with the signing of the merger agreement, and would agree to vote their shares in favor of the merger agreement, shareholder approval of the merger would be assured even if the NCS Board were to withdraw or change its recommendation. *These facts would prevent NCS from engaging in any alternative or superior transaction in the future.*" (emphasis added).

After listening to a summary of the merger terms, the board then resolved that the merger agreement and the transactions contemplated thereby were advisable and fair and in the best interests of all the NCS stakeholders. The NCS board further resolved to recommend the transactions to the stockholders for their approval and adoption. A definitive merger agreement between NCS and Genesis and the stockholder voting agreements were executed later that day. . . .

NCS/Genesis Merger Agreement

Among other things, the NCS/Genesis merger agreement provided the following:

- NCS stockholders would receive 1 share of Genesis common stock in exchange for every 10 shares of NCS common stock held;

- NCS stockholders could exercise appraisal rights under 8 Del.C. § 262;

- NCS would redeem NCS's Notes in accordance with their terms;

- NCS would submit the merger agreement to NCS stockholders regardless of whether the NCS board continued to recommend the merger;

- NCS would not enter into discussions with third parties concerning an alternative acquisition of NCS, or provide non-public information to such parties, unless (1) the third party provided an unsolicited, bona fide written proposal documenting the terms of the acquisition; (2) the NCS board believed in good faith that the proposal was or was likely to result in an acquisition on terms superior to those contemplated by the NCS/Genesis merger agreement; and (3) before providing non-public information to that third party, the third party would execute a confidentiality agreement at least as restrictive as the one in place between NCS and Genesis; and

• If the merger agreement were to be terminated, under certain circumstances NCS would be required to pay Genesis a $6 million termination fee and/or Genesis's documented expenses, up to $5 million.

[The merger agreement did not include a fiduciary out. A fiduciary out is a term in a merger agreement that provides that *another* term (or terms) in the agreement, which restricts in a certain way the discretion of the board of the corporation that is to be acquired, does not apply if the restriction would result in a breach of the board's fiduciary duties to the corporation and its shareholders. Among the kinds of terms to which a fiduciary out may apply are no-talk clauses, which prohibit the Board from discussing a merger of the Corporation into a third party, and provisions, like the one in *Omnicare*, that require the Board to submit the merger to the shareholders for their approval.]

Voting Agreements

[Contemporaneously with, and as required by, the merger agreement,] Outcalt and Shaw, in their capacity as NCS stockholders, entered into voting agreements with Genesis. NCS was also required to be a party to the voting agreements by Genesis. Those agreements provided, among other things, that:

• Outcalt and Shaw were acting in their capacity as NCS stockholders in executing the agreements, not in their capacity as NCS directors or officers;

• Neither Outcalt nor Shaw would transfer their shares prior to the stockholder vote on the merger agreement;

• Outcalt and Shaw agreed to vote all of their shares in favor of the merger agreement; and

• Outcalt and Shaw granted to Genesis an irrevocable proxy to vote their shares in favor of the merger agreement.

• The voting agreement was specifically enforceable by Genesis.

The merger agreement further provided that if either Outcalt or Shaw breached the terms of the voting agreements, Genesis would be entitled to terminate the merger agreement and potentially receive a $6 million termination fee from NCS. Such a breach was impossible since Section 6 provided that the voting agreements were specifically enforceable by Genesis.

Omnicare's Superior Proposal ...

On October 6, 2002, Omnicare irrevocably committed itself to a transaction with NCS. Pursuant to the terms of its proposal, Omnicare agreed to acquire all the outstanding NCS Class A and Class B shares [through a tender offer] at a price of $3.50 per share in cash. [The Omnicare bid offered the NCS stockholders cash equal to more than twice the then-current market value of the shares to be received in the Genesis merger. The transaction offered by Omnicare also treated NCS's other stakeholders on equal terms with the Genesis agreement.]

The merger agreement between Genesis and NCS contained a provision authorized by Section 251(c) of Delaware's corporation law. It required that the Genesis agreement be placed before the corporation's stockholders for a vote, even if the NCS board of directors no longer recommended it. At the insistence of Genesis, the NCS board also agreed to omit any effective fiduciary clause from the merger agreement. In connection with the Genesis merger agreement, two stockholders of NCS, who held a majority of the voting power, agreed unconditionally to vote all of their shares in favor of the Genesis merger. Thus, the combined terms of the voting agreements and merger agreement guaranteed, ab initio, that the transaction proposed by Genesis would obtain NCS stockholder's approval. As a result of this irrevocable offer, on October 21, 2002, the NCS board withdrew its recommendation that the stockholders vote in favor of the NCS/Genesis merger agreement. NCS's financial advisor withdrew its fairness opinion of the NCS/Genesis merger agreement as well. . . .

LEGAL ANALYSIS . . .

Deal Protection Devices Require Enhanced Scrutiny

The dispositive issues in this appeal involve the defensive devices that protected the Genesis merger agreement. The Delaware corporation statute provides that the board's management decision to enter into and recommend a merger transaction can become final only when ownership action is taken by a vote of the stockholders. Thus, the Delaware corporation law expressly provides for a balance of power between boards and stockholders which makes merger transactions a shared enterprise and ownership decision. Consequently, a board of directors' decision to adopt defensive devices to protect a merger agreement may implicate the stockholders' right to effectively vote contrary to the initial recommendation of the board in favor of the transaction.

It is well established that conflicts of interest arise when a board of directors acts to prevent stockholders from effectively exercising their right to vote contrary to the will of the board. The "omnipresent specter" of such conflict may be present whenever a board adopts defensive devices to protect a merger agreement. The stockholders' ability to effectively reject a merger agreement is likely to bear an inversely proportionate relationship to the structural and economic devices that the board has approved to protect the transaction. . . .

There are inherent conflicts between a board's interest in protecting a merger transaction it has approved, the stockholders' statutory right to make the final decision to either approve or not approve a merger, and the board's continuing responsibility to effectively exercise its fiduciary duties at all times after the merger agreement is executed. These competing considerations require a threshold determination that board-approved defensive devices protecting a merger transaction are within the limitations of its statutory authority and consistent with the directors' fiduciary duties. Accordingly, in *Paramount v. Time*, we held that the business judgment rule applied to the Time board's original decision to merge with Warner.[105] We further held, however, that defensive devices adopted by the board to protect the original merger transaction must withstand enhanced judicial scrutiny under the *Unocal* standard of review, even when that merger transaction does not result in a change of control.[106]

Enhanced Scrutiny Generally ...

A board's decision to protect its decision to enter a merger agreement with defensive devices against uninvited competing transactions that may emerge is analogous to a board's decision to protect against dangers to corporate policy and effectiveness when it adopts defensive measures in a hostile takeover contest. In applying *Unocal's* enhanced judicial scrutiny in assessing a challenge to defensive actions taken by a target corporation's board of directors in a takeover context, this Court held that the board "does not have unbridled discretion to defeat perceived threats by any draconian means available."[107] Similarly, just as a board's statutory power with regard to a merger decision is not absolute, a board does not have unbridled discretion to defeat any perceived threat to a merger by protecting it with any draconian means available.

Since *Unocal*, "this Court has consistently recognized that defensive measures which are either preclusive or coercive are included within the common law definition of draconian." ...

Therefore, in applying enhanced judicial scrutiny to defensive devices designed to protect a merger agreement, a court must first determine that those measures are not preclusive or coercive *before* its focus shifts to the "range of reasonableness" in making a proportionality determination....

Deal Protection Devices

Defensive devices, as that term is used in this opinion, is a synonym for what are frequently referred to as "deal protection devices." Both terms are used interchangeably to describe any measure or combination of measures that are intended to protect the consummation of a merger transaction. Defensive devices can be economic, structural, or both.

Deal protection devices need not all be in the merger agreement itself. In this case, for example, the Section 251(c) provision in the merger agreement was combined with the separate voting agreements to provide a structural defense for the Genesis merger agreement against any subsequent superior transaction. Genesis made the NCS

---

105. *Paramount Communications, Inc. v. Time Inc.*, 571 A.2d at 1152.

106. Id. at 115–155; *Unocal Corp. v. Mesa Petroleum Co.*, 493 A.2d 946 (Del.1985);

see *In re Santa Fe Pacific Corp. Shareholder Litigation*, 669 A.2d 59 (Del.1995).

107. *Unocal Corp. v. Mesa Petroleum Co.*, 493 A.2d at 955.

board's defense of its transaction absolute by insisting on the omission of any effective fiduciary out clause in the NCS merger agreement. . . .

In this case, the stockholder voting agreements were inextricably intertwined with the defensive aspects of the Genesis merger agreement. In fact, the voting agreements with Shaw and Outcalt were the linchpin of Genesis' proposed tripartite defense. Therefore, Genesis made the execution of those voting agreements a non-negotiable condition precedent to its execution of the merger agreement. In the case before us, the Court of Chancery held that the acts which locked-up the Genesis transaction were the Section 251(c) provision and "the execution of the voting agreement by Outcalt and Shaw."

With the assurance that Outcalt and Shaw would irrevocably agree to exercise their majority voting power in favor of its transaction, Genesis insisted that the merger agreement reflect the other two aspects of its concerted defense, i.e., the inclusion of a Section 251(c) provision and the omission of any effective fiduciary out clause. Those dual aspects of the merger agreement would not have provided Genesis with a complete defense in the absence of the voting agreements with Shaw and Outcalt.

These Deal Protection Devices Unenforceable

In this case, the Court of Chancery correctly held that the NCS directors' decision to adopt defensive devices to completely "lock up" the Genesis merger mandated "special scrutiny" under the two-part test set forth in *Unocal*.[108] That conclusion is consistent with our holding in *Paramount v. Time* that safety devices adopted to protect a transaction that did not result in a change of control are subject to enhanced judicial scrutiny under a *Unocal* analysis.[109] . . . .

Pursuant to the judicial scrutiny required under *Unocal*'s two-stage analysis, the NCS directors must first demonstrate "that they had reasonable grounds for believing that a danger to corporate policy and effectiveness existed. . . ." To satisfy that burden, the NCS directors are required to show they acted in good faith after conducting a reasonable investigation. The threat identified by the NCS board was the possibility of losing the Genesis offer and being left with no comparable alternative transaction.

The second stage of the *Unocal* test requires the NCS directors to demonstrate that their defensive response was "reasonable in relation to the threat posed." This inquiry involves a two-step analysis. The NCS directors must first establish that the merger deal protection devices adopted in response to the threat were not "coercive" or "preclusive," and then demonstrate that their response was within a "range of reasonable responses" to the threat perceived. In *Unitrin*, we stated:

---

108. *In re NCS Healthcare, Inc.*, 2002 WL 31720732, at *16 (Del.Ch. Nov.22, 2002). See *Unocal Corp. v. Mesa Petroleum Co.*, 493 A.2d 946, 955 (Del.1985).

109. See *Paramount Communications, Inc. v. Time Inc.*, 571 A.2d 1140, 1151 (Del. 1989) ("holding that structural safety devices" in a merger agreement are properly subject to a *Unocal* analysis).

- A response is "coercive" if it is aimed at forcing upon stockholders a management-sponsored alternative to a hostile offer.

- A response is "preclusive" if it deprives stockholders of the right to receive all tender offers or precludes a bidder from seeking control by fundamentally restricting proxy contests or otherwise.

This aspect of the *Unocal* standard provides for a disjunctive analysis. If defensive measures are either preclusive or coercive they are draconian and impermissible. In this case, the deal protection devices of the NCS board were both preclusive and coercive.

This Court enunciated the standard for determining stockholder coercion in the case of *Williams v. Geier*.[110] A stockholder vote may be nullified by wrongful coercion "where the board or some other party takes actions which have the effect of causing the stockholders to vote in favor of the proposed transaction for some reason other than the merits of that transaction." ...

... [A]ny stockholder vote [in this case] would have been robbed of its effectiveness by the impermissible coercion that predetermined the outcome of the merger without regard to the merits of the Genesis transaction at the time the vote was scheduled to be taken. Deal protection devices that result in such coercion cannot withstand *Unocal*'s enhanced judicial scrutiny standard of review because they are not within the range of reasonableness.

Although the minority stockholders were not forced to vote for the Genesis merger, they were required to accept it because it was a fait accompli. The record reflects that the defensive devices employed by the NCS board are preclusive and coercive in the sense that they accomplished a fait accompli. In this case, despite the fact that the NCS board has withdrawn its recommendation for the Genesis transaction and recommended its rejection by the stockholders, the deal protection devices approved by the NCS board operated in concert to have a preclusive and coercive effect. Those tripartite defensive measures—the Section 251(c) provision, the voting agreements, and the absence of an effective fiduciary out clause—made it "mathematically impossible" and "realistically unattainable" for the Omnicare transaction or any other proposal to succeed, no matter how superior the proposal.[111]

The deal protection devices adopted by the NCS board were designed to coerce the consummation of the Genesis merger and preclude the consideration of any superior transaction. The NCS directors' defensive devices are not within a reasonable range of responses to the perceived threat of losing the Genesis offer because they are preclusive and coercive. Accordingly, we hold that those deal protection devices are unenforceable.

---

110. *Williams v. Geier*, 671 A.2d 1368 (Del.1996).

111. See *Unitrin, Inc. v. Am. Gen. Corp.*, 651 A.2d at 1388–89; see also *Carmody v. Toll Bros., Inc.*, 723 A.2d 1180, 1195 (Del. Ch.1998) (citations omitted).

Effective Fiduciary Out Required

The defensive measures that protected the merger transaction are unenforceable not only because they are preclusive and coercive but, alternatively, they are unenforceable because they are invalid as they operate in this case. Given the specifically enforceable irrevocable voting agreements, the provision in the merger agreement requiring the board to submit the transaction for a stockholder vote and the omission of a fiduciary out clause in the merger agreement completely prevented the board from discharging its fiduciary responsibilities to the minority stockholders when Omnicare presented its superior transaction. "To the extent that a [merger] contract, or a provision thereof, purports to require a board to act or not act in such a fashion as to limit the exercise of fiduciary duties, it is invalid and unenforceable."[112] . . .

Under the circumstances presented in this case, where a cohesive group of stockholders with majority voting power was irrevocably committed to the merger transaction, "[e]ffective representation of the financial interests of the minority shareholders imposed upon the [NCS board] an affirmative responsibility to protect those minority shareholders' interests."[113] The NCS board could not abdicate its fiduciary duties to the minority by leaving it to the stockholders alone to approve or disapprove the merger agreement because two stockholders had already combined to establish a majority of the voting power that made the outcome of the stockholder vote a foregone conclusion. . . .

Taking action that is otherwise legally possible . . . does not ipso facto comport with the fiduciary responsibilities of directors in all circumstances.[114] The synopsis to the amendments that resulted in the enactment of Section 251(c) in the Delaware corporation law statute specifically provides: "the amendments are not intended to address the question of whether such a submission requirement is appropriate in any particular set of factual circumstances." Section 251 provisions, like the no-shop provision examined in *QVC*, are "presumptively valid in the abstract."[115] Such provisions in a merger agreement may not, however, "validly define or limit the directors' fiduciary duties under Delaware law or prevent the [NCS] directors from carrying out their fiduciary duties under Delaware law."[116]

Genesis admits that when the NCS board agreed to its merger conditions, the NCS board was seeking to assure that the NCS credi-

---

112. *Paramount Communications Inc. v. QVC Network Inc.*, 637 A.2d 34, 51 (Del. 1993) (citation omitted). Restatement (Second) of Contracts § 193 explicitly provides that a "promise by a fiduciary to violate his fiduciary duty or a promise that tends to induce such a violation is unenforceable on grounds of public policy." The comments to that section indicate that "[d]irectors and other officials of a corporation act in a fiduciary capacity and are subject to the rule stated in this Section." Restatement (Second) of Contracts § 193 (1981) (emphasis added).

113. *McMullin v. Beran*, 765 A.2d 910, 920 (Del.2000).

114. *MM Companies v. Liquid Audio, Inc.*, 813 A.2d 1118, 1132 (Del.2003) (citation omitted).

115. *Paramount Communications Inc. v. QVC Network Inc.*, 637 A.2d at 48.

116. Id.

tors were paid in full and that the NCS stockholders received the highest value available for their stock. In fact, Genesis defends its "bulletproof" merger agreement on that basis. We hold that the NCS board did not have authority to accede to the Genesis demand for an absolute "lock-up."

The directors of a Delaware corporation have a continuing obligation to discharge their fiduciary responsibilities, as future circumstances develop, after a merger agreement is announced. Genesis anticipated the likelihood of a superior offer after its merger agreement was announced and demanded defensive measures from the NCS board that completely protected its transaction.[117] Instead of agreeing to the absolute defense of the Genesis merger from a superior offer, however, the NCS board was required to negotiate a fiduciary out clause to protect the NCS stockholders if the Genesis transaction became an inferior offer. By acceding to Genesis' ultimatum for complete protection in futuro, the NCS board disabled itself from exercising its own fiduciary obligations at a time when the board's own judgment is most important,[118] i.e. receipt of a subsequent superior offer.

Any board has authority to give the proponent of a recommended merger agreement reasonable structural and economic defenses, incentives, and fair compensation if the transaction is not completed. To the extent that defensive measures are economic and reasonable, they may become an increased cost to the proponent of any subsequent transaction. Just as defensive measures cannot be draconian, however, they cannot limit or circumscribe the directors' fiduciary duties. Notwithstanding the corporation's insolvent condition, the NCS board had no authority to execute a merger agreement that subsequently prevented it from effectively discharging its ongoing fiduciary responsibilities.

The stockholders of a Delaware corporation are entitled to rely upon the board to discharge its fiduciary duties at all times.[119] The fiduciary duties of a director are unremitting and must be effectively discharged in the specific context of the actions that are required with regard to the corporation or its stockholders as circumstances change.[120] The stockholders with majority voting power, Shaw and Outcalt, had an absolute right to sell or exchange their shares with a third party at any price. This right was not only known to the other directors of NCS, it became an integral part of the Genesis agreement. In its answering brief, Genesis candidly states that its offer "came with a condition—Genesis would not be a stalking horse and would not

---

117. The marked improvements in NCS's financial situation during the negotiations with Genesis strongly suggests that the NCS board should have been alert to the prospect of competing offers or, as eventually occurred, a bidding contest.

118. See *Malone v. Brincat*, 722 A.2d 5, 10 (Del.1998) (directors' fiduciary duties do not operate intermittently). See also *Moran v. Household Int'l, Inc.*, 500 A.2d 1346 (Del. 1985).

119. *Malone v. Brincat*, 722 A.2d at 10.

120. Id.; *Moran v. Household Int'l, Inc.*, 500 A.2d at 1357 (use of defense evaluated if and when the issue arises).

agree to a transaction to which NCS's controlling shareholders were not committed."

The NCS board was required to contract for an effective fiduciary out clause to exercise its continuing fiduciary responsibilities to the minority stockholders.[121] The issues in this appeal do not involve the general validity of either stockholder voting agreements or the authority of directors to insert a Section 251(c) provision in a merger agreement. In this case, the NCS board combined those two otherwise valid actions and caused them to operate in concert as an absolute lock up, in the absence of an effective fiduciary out clause in the Genesis merger agreement.

In the context of this preclusive and coercive lock up case, the protection of Genesis' contractual expectations must yield to the supervening responsibility of the directors to discharge their fiduciary duties on a continuing basis. The merger agreement and voting agreements, as they were combined to operate in concert in this case, are inconsistent with the NCS directors' fiduciary duties. To that extent, we hold that they are invalid and unenforceable.[122] ...

■ VEASEY, CHIEF JUSTICE, with whom STEELE, JUSTICE, joins dissenting. . . .

. . . [T]he Majority has removed from their proper context the contractual merger protection provisions. The lock-ups here cannot be reviewed in a vacuum. A court should review the entire bidding process to determine whether the independent board's actions permitted the directors to inform themselves of their available options and whether they acted in good faith.

Going into negotiations with Genesis, the NCS directors knew that, up until that time, NCS had found only one potential bidder, Omnicare. Omnicare had refused to buy NCS except at a fire sale price through an asset sale in bankruptcy. Omnicare's best proposal at that stage would not have paid off all creditors and would have provided nothing for stockholders. The Noteholders, represented by the Ad Hoc Committee, were willing to oblige Omnicare and force NCS into bankruptcy if Omnicare would pay in full the NCS debt. Through the NCS board's efforts, Genesis expressed interest that became increasingly attractive. Negotiations with Genesis led to an offer paying creditors off and conferring on NCS stockholders $24 million—an amount infinitely superior to the prior Omnicare proposals.

But there was, understandably, a sine qua non. In exchange for offering the NCS stockholders a return on their equity and creditor payment, Genesis demanded certainty that the merger would close. If the NCS board would not have acceded to the Section 251(c) provision, if Outcalt and Shaw had not agreed to the voting agreements and

121. See *Paramount Communications Inc. v. QVC Network Inc.*, 637 A.2d at 42–43. Merger agreements involve an ownership decision and, therefore, cannot become final without stockholder approval. Other contracts do not require a fiduciary out clause because they involve business judgments that are within the exclusive province of the board of directors' power to manage the affairs of the corporation. See *Grimes v. Donald*, 673 A.2d 1207, 1214–15 (Del.1996).

122. *Paramount Communications, Inc. v. QVC Network, Inc.*, 637 A.2d at 51.

if NCS had insisted on a fiduciary out, there would have been no Genesis deal! Thus, the only value-enhancing transaction available would have disappeared. NCS knew that Omnicare had spoiled a Genesis acquisition in the past, and it is not disputed by the Majority that the NCS directors made a reasoned decision to accept as real the Genesis threat to walk away.

When Omnicare submitted its conditional eleventh-hour bid, the NCS board had to weigh the economic terms of the proposal against the uncertainty of completing a deal with Omnicare. Importantly, because Omnicare's bid was conditioned on its satisfactorily completing its due diligence review of NCS, the NCS board saw this as a crippling condition, as did the Ad Hoc Committee. As a matter of business judgment, the risk of negotiating with Omnicare and losing Genesis at that point outweighed the possible benefits. The lock-up was indisputably a sine qua non to any deal with Genesis.

A lock-up permits a target board and a bidder to "exchange certainties."[123] Certainty itself has value. The acquirer may pay a higher price for the target if the acquirer is assured consummation of the transaction. The target company also benefits from the certainty of completing a transaction with a bidder because losing an acquirer creates the perception that a target is damaged goods, thus reducing its value. . . .

The Majority invalidates the NCS board's action by announcing a new rule that represents an extension of our jurisprudence. That new rule can be narrowly stated as follows: A merger agreement entered into after a market search, before any prospect of a topping bid has emerged, which locks up stockholder approval and does not contain a "fiduciary out" provision, is per se invalid when a later significant topping bid emerges. As we have noted, this bright-line, per se rule would apply regardless of (1) the circumstances leading up to the agreement and (2) the fact that stockholders who control voting power had irrevocably committed themselves, as stockholders, to vote for the merger. Narrowly stated, this new rule is a judicially-created "third rail" that now becomes one of the given "rules of the game," to be taken into account by the negotiators and drafters of merger agreements. In our view, this new rule is an unwise extension of existing precedent. . . .

The very measures the Majority cites as "coercive" were approved by Shaw and Outcalt through the lens of their independent assessment of the merits of the transaction. The proper inquiry in this case is whether the NCS board had taken actions that "have the effect of causing the stockholders to vote in favor of the proposed transaction for some reason other than the merits of that transaction."[124] Like the termination fee upheld as a valid liquidated damages clause against a claim of coercion in *Brazen v. Bell Atlantic Corp.*, the deal protection measures at issue here were an "integral part of the merits of the

123. See *Rand v. Western Air Lines*, 1994 WL 89006 at *6 (Del.Ch.).

124. *Geier*, 671 A.2d at 1382–83 (citations omitted).

transaction" as the NCS board struggled to secure and did secure—the only deal available.[125]

Outcalt and Shaw were fully informed stockholders. As the NCS controlling stockholders, they made an informed choice to commit their voting power to the merger. The minority stockholders were deemed to know that when controlling stockholders have 65% of the vote they can approve a merger without the need for the minority votes. Moreover, to the extent a minority stockholder may have felt "coerced" to vote for the merger, which was already a fait accompli, it was a meaningless coercion—or no coercion at all—because the controlling votes, those of Outcalt and Shaw, were already "cast." Although the fact that the controlling votes were committed to the merger "precluded" an overriding vote against the merger by the Class A stockholders, the "pejorative" preclusive label applicable in a *Unitrin* fact situation has no application here. Therefore, there was no meaningful minority stockholder voting decision to coerce.

In applying *Unocal* scrutiny, we believe the Majority incorrectly preempted the proportionality inquiry. In our view, the proportionality inquiry must account for the reality that the contractual measures protecting this merger agreement were necessary to obtain the Genesis deal. The Majority has not demonstrated that the director action was a disproportionate response to the threat posed. Indeed, it is clear to us that the board action to negotiate the best deal reasonably available with the only viable merger partner (Genesis) who could satisfy the creditors and benefit the stockholders, was reasonable in relation to the threat, by any practical yardstick.

An Absolute Lock-up is Not a Per Se Violation of Fiduciary Duty

We respectfully disagree with the Majority's conclusion that the NCS board breached its fiduciary duties to the Class A stockholders by failing to negotiate a "fiduciary out" in the Genesis merger agreement. What is the practical import of a "fiduciary out?" It is a contractual provision, articulated in a manner to be negotiated, that would permit the board of the corporation being acquired to exit without breaching the merger agreement in the event of a superior offer.

In this case, Genesis made it abundantly clear early on that it was willing to negotiate a deal with NCS but only on the condition that it would not be a "stalking horse." Thus, it wanted to be certain that a third party could not use its deal with NCS as a floor against which to begin a bidding war. As a result of this negotiating position, a "fiduciary out" was not acceptable to Genesis. The Majority Opinion holds that such a negotiating position, if implemented in the agreement, is invalid per se where there is an absolute lock-up. We know of no authority in our jurisprudence supporting this new rule, and we believe it is unwise and unwarranted....

Conclusion

It is regrettable that the Court is split in this important case. One hopes that the Majority rule announced here—though clearly errone-

125. 695 A.2d 43, 50 (Del.1997).

ous in our view—will be interpreted narrowly and will be seen as sui generis. By deterring bidders from engaging in negotiations like those present here and requiring that there must always be a fiduciary out, the universe of potential bidders who could reasonably be expected to benefit stockholders could shrink or disappear. Nevertheless, if the holding is confined to these unique facts, negotiators may be able to navigate around this new hazard.

Accordingly, we respectfully dissent.

[The separate dissenting opinion of Justice Steele is omitted.]

———

NOTE ON STATE TAKEOVER STATUTES

Most states now have statutes regulating takeover bids. These statutes tend to fall into several patterns, although they are highly variable within those patterns. This Note will canvass the major patterns, generally by discussing one statute within each pattern. However, it should be borne in mind that even statutes that fall into a given pattern often diverge in material respects. Furthermore, because the statutes are highly complex, only their main features will be discussed.

State takeover statutes have evolved over time. Conventionally, they are categorized as first-, second-, and third-generation statutes.

1. *First-Generation Statutes*. The *first-generation* statutes tended to impose very stringent requirements on takeover bids, including fairness reviews by state agencies. Moreover, generally speaking the application of the statutes was not limited to corporations incorporated in the relevant state. In Edgar v. MITE Corp., 457 U.S. 624, 102 S.Ct. 2629, 73 L.Ed.2d 269 (1982), the Supreme Court held one such statute, the Illinois Takeover Act, unconstitutional. Six justices addressed the merits of the case. All six justices held that the Illinois Act violated the Commerce Clause in two ways. First, the Act unconstitutionally regulated commerce taking place across state lines, because the Act applied to prevent an offeror from making an offer even to non-Illinois shareholders. Second, the Act imposed an excessive burden on interstate commerce, because the Act permitted the Illinois secretary of state to block a nationwide tender offer. Three of the justices also held that the Illinois statute was unconstitutional under the Supremacy Clause, on the ground that a major objective of the Williams Act was to maintain a neutral balance between management and the bidder, and the Illinois Act violated this balance.

2. *Second-Generation Statutes.* After the decision in Edgar v. MITE Corp., a number of states adopted *second-generation* takeover statutes. These statutes fall into two major patterns: control-share-acquisition statutes and fair-price statutes.

a. *Control-share-acquisition statutes. Control-share-acquisition statutes* provide that if an acquiring shareholder crosses a designated threshold of stock ownership, the shareholder is prohibited from voting the acquired shares unless he obtains approval to do so by vote of a majority of the corporation's disinterested shareholders, that is, shareholders other than the acquiror and the corporation's management.

In CTS Corp. v. Dynamics Corp. of America, 481 U.S. 69, 107 S.Ct. 1637, 95 L.Ed.2d 67 (1987), the Supreme Court upheld the constitutionality of Indiana's control-share-acquisition statute. That statute applied whenever a person acquired shares that, but for the operation of the statute, would bring the person's voting power in the corporation to or above 20%, 33 1/3%, or 50% of total voting power. An acquiror that crossed one of these thresholds could not vote the acquired stock unless voting rights were approved by a majority of all disinterested shareholders voting at the next regularly scheduled meeting of the shareholders or at a specially scheduled meeting. The statute was limited to target corporations incorporated in Indiana. The Court concluded that the Indiana statute did not violate the Commerce Clause, because it did not discriminate against interstate commerce, and did not subject activities to inconsistent regulation. The statute applied only to Indiana corporations, and a state has authority to regulate domestic corporations, including the authority to define the voting rights of shareholders.

The Court also held that the Indiana statute was not preempted by the Williams Act. In this regard, the Court contrasted the Indiana statute with the Illinois statute that was found unconstitutional in *MITE*.

First, the Illinois statute provided for a twenty-day precommencement period. During this time, management could disseminate its views on the upcoming tender offer to shareholders, but bidders could not publish their offers. This conflicted with the Williams Act, because Congress had deleted precommencement-notice provisions from the Williams Act. In contrast, the Indiana statute did not give either management or the would-be acquiror an advantage in communicating with shareholders about an impending tender offer.

Second, the Illinois statute provided for a review of the fairness of tender offers by the Illinois Secretary of State. This conflicted with the Williams Act, because Congress intended shareholders to be free to make their own decisions. In contrast, the Indiana statute did not allow the state government to interpose its views of fairness between willing buyers and sellers of shares of the target company. Rather, the statute allowed shareholders to collectively evaluate the fairness of the offer.

Third, the Illinois statute set no deadline for the state-agency hearing on a tender offer, so that management could indefinitely stymie a takeover. This conflicted with the Williams Act, because Congress anticipated that bidders would be free to go forward without unreasonable delay. In contrast, the Indiana statute did not impose an indefinite delay on tender offers. Nothing in the Indiana statute prohibited an offeror from consummating an offer on the twentieth business day, the earliest day permitted under federal law, and full voting rights would be vested or denied within fifty days after commencement of the tender offer.

b. *Fair-price statutes*. *Fair-price statutes* essentially require that if a winning bidder makes a two-tier tender offer, it must pay nontendering shareholders the highest price it has paid for target shares within a specified recent period (typically, two years) if, after having acquired control of the target, the bidder seeks to engage in a business combination, or one of certain other defined transactions, with the target. There is an exception if the transaction is approved by (typically) 80 percent of all shares and two-thirds of the shares not owned by the bidder.

3. *Third-Generation Statutes.*

a. *Waiting-period statutes*. *Waiting-period statutes* prohibit a corporation, B, who acquires more than a specific percentage of another corporation, T, from merging with T, or engaging in certain other transactions with T, for a designated waiting period, unless certain conditions are satisfied. The idea is that in many cases a prospective bidder (B) expects to finance a tender offer for the stock of the target (T) partly by using T's assets as collateral. If B cannot expect to merge with T shortly after the tender offer succeeds, that kind of financing will be difficult or impossible to obtain. In addition, B may have various business reasons for wanting to merge with T after a tender offer, rather than running T as a partly owned subsidiary. These purposes are also frustrated by waiting-period statutes.

The New York statute, N.Y. Bus.Corp.Law § 912, provides for a five-year delay in effecting specified transactions, even if the transaction is not self-interested, unless the transaction is approved by T's board of directors prior to B's acquisition of the designated percentage of T's stock. The less stringent Delaware statute, Del.G.C.L. § 203, prohibits business combinations and other designated transactions between B and T for a period of three years unless B acquires 85% of T's shares in the initial tender offer, or the transaction is approved by 85% of T's shares other than the shares held by B.

b. *Amanda*. In Amanda Acquisition Corp. v. Universal Foods Corp., 877 F.2d 496, cert. denied, 493 U.S. 955, 110 S.Ct. 367, 107 L.Ed.2d 353 (1989), the Seventh Circuit held that the Wisconsin waiting-period statute was constitutional:

> [Arguments against state anti-takeover statutes based on preemption have] not won easy acceptance among the Justices for several reasons. First there is§ 28(a) of the '34 Act, 14 U.S.C. § 78bb(a), which provides that "[n]othing in this chapter shall affect the jurisdiction of the securities commission . . . of any State over any security or any person insofar as it does not conflict with the provisions of this chapter or the rules and regulations thereunder." . . . [T]he SEC has not drafted regulations concerning mergers with controlling shareholders, and the Act itself does not address the subject. . . .
>
> . . . [T]he best argument for preemption is the Williams Act's "neutrality" between bidder and management, a balance designed to leave investors free to choose. This is not a confident jumping-off point, though . . . .

There is a big difference between what congress *enacts* and what it *supposes* will ensue. Expectations about the consequences of a law are not themselves law. To say that Congress wanted to be neutral between bidder and target . . . is not to say that it also forbade the states to favor one of these sides. . . .

Any bidder complying with federal law is free to acquire shares of Wisconsin firms on schedule. Delay in completing a second-stage merger may make the target less attractive, and thus depress the price offered or even lead to an absence of bids; it does not, however, alter any of the procedures governed by federal regulation. . . .

. . . It is not attractive [under the statute] to put bids on the table for Wisconsin corporations, but because Wisconsin leaves the process alone once a bidder appears, its law may co-exist with the Williams Act. . . .

The Commerce Clause, Art. I, § 8 cl. 3 of the Constitution, grants Congress the power "[t]o regulate Commerce . . . among the several States". . . .

When state law discriminates against interstate commerce expressly—for example, when Wisconsin closes its border to butter from Minnesota—the [anti-discrimination aspect of the] Commerce Clause steps in. The law before us is not of this type; it is neutral between inter-state and intra-state commerce. Amanda therefore presses on us the broader, all-weather, be-reasonable vision of the Constitution. Wisconsin has passed a law that unreasonably injures investors, most of whom live outside of Wisconsin, and therefore it has to be unconstitutional, as Amanda sees things. . . . [However, the Supreme] Court has looked for discrimination rather than for baleful effects. . . .

. . . The Commerce clause does not demand that states leave bidders a "meaningful opportunity for success."

c. *Other third-generation statutes. Amanda*, and perhaps other factors, emboldened some states to adopt other, extremely exotic, and in some cases draconian, third-generation statutes. For example, the Pennsylvania statute provides, among many other things, that persons who own, offer to acquire, or publicly announce an intention to acquire, 20% of the stock of a publicly traded Pennsylvania corporation must disgorge any profits they realize from the disposition of that corporation's stock within a defined period. The Massachusetts statute requires every publicly held Massachusetts corporation to have a classified board.

d. *Constituency statutes.* A number of states have also adopted *constituency statutes*, which allow a board to consider the interests of groups ("constituencies") other than shareholders in making decisions, including decisions to resist takeovers. These statutes give the board increased leeway to resist a takeover, because often these other constituencies—for example, labor and the local community—are opposed to takeovers.

CHAPTER XIII

DISTRIBUTIONS TO SHAREHOLDERS

INTRODUCTION

Corporations normally can distribute funds to shareholders in one of four ways:

(1) As dividends, that is, by making pro rata distributions of cash, securities, or interests in other kinds of property.

(2) By repurchasing shares.

(3) By paying shareholder-employees inflated salaries. This technique is most commonly used in close corporations, for tax reasons: In calculating taxable income, a corporation can deduct salaries, but cannot deduct dividends.

(4) On liquidation, by paying each shareholder her pro rata share of corporate assets remaining after the claim of creditors have been satisfied or provided for.

This Chapter will concern the first two kinds of distributions—dividends and stock repurchases. Inflated salaries are considered in Chapters 6 (Close Corporations) and 9 (Duty of Loyalty), supra. Distributions in liquidation only infrequently raise significant legal problems if creditors have been either paid or provided for.

The architecture of this Chapter is as follows: Dividend policy is considered in Section 1. Limitations on dividends under creditors' rights law are considered in Section 2. Limitations on dividends under traditional corporate statutes are considered in Section 3. Contractual limitations on dividends are considered in Section 4. Limitations on dividends under the modern dividend statutes are considered in Section 5. The liability of directors and shareholders for improper dividends is considered in Sections 6 and 7. The repurchase by a corporation of its own stock is considered in Section 8. An issue related to dividends, liability for watered stock, is considered in section 9.

SECTION 1. DIVIDEND POLICY

Dividend policy raises two very different kinds of issues. The first issue is how a corporation should determine the level of dividends it should pay. The materials in Section 1(a) address that issue. Although dividend policy is largely an issue of efficiency, it spills over into law when shareholders bring a suit to force a corporation to pay dividends. That issue will be considered in Section 1(b).

————

(a) THE ELEMENTS OF DIVIDEND POLICY

————

Richard A. Brealey & Stewart C. Myers & Franklin Allen, Principles of Corporate Finance

Eighth ed., 2006.

In the mid–1950s John Lintner conducted a classic series of interviews with corporate managers about their dividend policies. His conclusions can be summarized in four stylized facts:

1.   Firms have long-run target dividend payout ratios. Mature companies with stable earnings generally pay out a high proportion of earnings; growth companies have low payouts (if they pay any dividends at all).

2.   Managers focus more on dividend changes than on absolute levels. Thus, paying a $2.00 dividend is an important financial decision if last year's dividend was $1.00, but no big deal if last year's dividend was $2.00.

3.   Dividend changes follow shifts in long-run, sustainable earnings. Managers "smooth" dividends. Transitory earnings changes are unlikely to affect dividend payouts.

4.   Managers are reluctant to make dividend changes that might have to be reversed. They are particularly worried about having to rescind a dividend increase. . . .

When Lintner conducted his interviews, dividends were effectively the only means of distributing cash. More recent work on payout policy since the dramatic increase in repurchases suggests a fifth stylized fact.

5.   Firms repurchase stock when they have accumulated a large amount of unwanted cash or wish to change their capital structure by replacing equity with debt.

THE INFORMATION IN DIVIDENDS AND STOCK REPURCHASES

In some countries you cannot rely on the information that companies provide. Passion for secrecy and a tendency to construct multilayered corporate organizations produce asset and earnings figures that are next to meaningless. Some people say that, thanks to creative accounting, the situation is little better for some companies in the United States.

How does an investor in such a world separate marginally profitable firms from the real money makers? One clue is dividends. Investors can't read managers' minds, but they can learn from managers' actions. They know that a firm which reports good earnings and pays a generous dividend is putting its money where its mouth is. We can understand, therefore, why investors would value the information content of dividends and would refuse to believe a firm's reported earnings unless they were backed up by an appropriate dividend policy.

Of course, firms can cheat in the short run by overstating earnings and scraping up cash to pay a generous dividend. But it is hard to cheat in the long run, for a firm that is not making enough money will not have enough cash to pay out. If a firm chooses a high dividend payout without the cash flow to back it up, that firm will ultimately have to reduce its investment plans or turn to investors for additional debt or equity financing. All of these consequences are costly. Therefore, most managers don't increase dividends until they are confident that sufficient cash will flow in to pay them.

Researchers, who have attempted to measure the information in dividend changes, have come up with mixed evidence. Some have found that dividend changes have little or no ability to predict future earnings. However, Healey and Palepu, who focus on companies that paid a dividend for the first time, find that on average earnings jumped 43 percent in the year a dividend was paid. If managers thought that this was a temporary windfall, they might have been cautious about committing themselves to paying out cash. But it looks as if these managers had good reason to be confident about prospects, for earnings continued to rise in the following years.[1]

THE PAYOUT CONTROVERSY

We have seen that a change in payout may provide information about management's confidence in the future and so affect the stock price. But eventually this change in the stock price would happen anyway as information about future earnings seeps out through other channels. But does the payout policy *change* the value of the stock, rather than simply providing a signal of its value?

On this issue, economists fall into three groups. On the right, there is a conservative group which believes that an increase in the dividend payout increases firm value. On the left, there is a radical group which believes that a higher dividend payout reduces value. And in the center, there is a middle-of-the-road party which claims that payout policy makes no difference.

The middle-of-the-road party was founded in 1961 by Miller and Modigliani (always referred to as "MM" or "M and M"), when they published a theoretical paper showing the irrelevance of dividend policy in a world without taxes, transaction costs, or other market imperfections.[12] . . .

1. See P. Healey and K. Palepu, "Earnings Information Conveyed by Dividend Initiations and Omissions," Journal of Financial Economics 21 (1988), pp. 149–175.

12. M.H. Miller and F. Modigliani: "Dividend Policy, Growth and the Valuation of Shares," *Journal of Business,* 34: 411–433 (October 1961).

In their classic 1961 article MM argued as follows: Suppose your firm has settled on its investment program. You have worked out how much of this program can be financed from borrowing, and you plan to meet the remaining funds requirement from retained earnings. Any surplus money is to be paid out as dividends.

Now think what happens if you want to increase the dividend payment without changing the investment and borrowing policy. The extra money must come from somewhere. If the firm fixes its borrowing, the only way it can finance the extra dividend is to print some more shares and sell them. The new stockholders are going to part with their money only if you can offer them shares that are worth as much as they cost. But how can the firm do this when its assets, earnings, investment opportunities and, therefore, market value are all unchanged? The answer is that there must be a *transfer of value* from the old to the new stockholders. The new ones get the newly printed shares, each one worth less than before the dividend change was announced, and the old ones suffer a capital loss on their shares. The capital loss borne by the old shareholders just offsets the extra cash dividend they receive. . . .

Does it make any difference to the old stockholders that they receive an extra dividend payment plus an offsetting capital loss? It might if that were the only way they could get their hands on cash. But as long as there are efficient capital markets, they can raise the cash by selling shares. Thus the old shareholders can "cash in" either by persuading the management to pay a higher dividend or by selling some of their shares. In either case there will be a transfer of value from old to new shareholders. The only difference is that in the former case this transfer is caused by a dilution in the value of each of the firm's shares, and in the latter case it is caused by a reduction in the number of shares held by the old shareholders. . . .

Because investors do not need dividends to get their hands on cash, they will not pay higher prices for the shares of firms with high payouts. Therefore firms ought not to worry about dividend policy. They can let dividends fluctuate as a by-product of their investment and financing decisions. [This conclusion is known as the MM dividend-irrelevance proposition.] . . .

[One reason that some or many corporations may pay high dividends in the real world is that there] is a natural clientele for high-payout stocks. Trusts and endowment funds may prefer high-dividend stocks because dividends are regarded as spendable "income," whereas capital gains are "additions to principal."

There is also a natural clientele of investors who look to their stock portfolios for a steady source of cash to live on. In principle this cash could be easily generated from stocks paying no dividends at all; the investor could just sell off a small fraction of his or her holdings from time to time. But it is simpler and cheaper for AT & T to send a quarterly check than for its stockholders to sell, say, one share every 3 months. AT & T's regular dividends relieve many of its shareholders of transaction costs and considerable inconvenience. . . .

There is another reason that shareholders often clamor for more generous payouts. Suppose a company has plenty of free cash flow but few profitable investment opportunities. Shareholders may not trust the managers to spend retained earnings wisely and may fear that the money will be plowed back into building a larger empire rather than a more profitable one. In such cases investors may clamor for higher dividends or a stock repurchase not because these are valuable in themselves, but because they encourage a more careful, value-oriented investment policy.

Alon Brav, John R. Graham, Campbell R. Harvey & Roni Michaely

PAYOUT POLICY IN THE 21ST CENTURY

Tuck Contemporary Corporate Finance Issues III Conference Paper, June 14, 2004.

... In 1956, John Lintner laid the foundation for the modern understanding of dividend policy. Lintner (1956) interviewed managers from 28 companies and concluded that dividends are sticky, tied to long-term sustainable earnings, paid by mature companies, smoothed from year to year, and that managers target a long-term payout ratio when determining dividend policy. In this paper, we survey and interview financial executives at the start of the 21st century to learn how dividend and repurchase policies are currently determined. We shed light on managers' motives as well as on payout theories....

Our analysis indicates that maintaining the dividend level is a priority on a par with investment decisions. Managers express a strong desire to avoid dividend cuts, except in extraordinary circumstances. However, beyond maintaining a level of dividends per share, payout policy is a second-order concern—increases in dividends are considered only after investment and liquidity needs are met. In contrast to Lintner's era, we find that the target payout ratio is no longer the preeminent decision variable affecting payout decisions. In terms of when nonpayers might initiate dividend payments, two reasons dominate: a sustainable increase in earnings, and demand by institutional investors.

Several factors stand out as influencing [corporation's policy concerning distributions through the repurchase of stock as opposed to dividends]. Consistent with a Miller and Modigliani irrelevance theorem, and in contrast to decisions about preserving the level of the dividend, managers make repurchase decisions after investment decisions. Many executives view share repurchases as being more flexible than dividends, and they use this flexibility in an attempt to time the market by accelerating repurchases when they believe their stock price is low. CFOs are also very conscious of how repurchases affect earnings per share.... Companies are likely to repurchase when good investments are hard to find, when their stock's float is adequate, and to offset option dilution.

Executives believe that dividend and repurchase decisions convey information to investors. However, this information conveyance does not appear to be consciously related to signaling in the academic sense. Managers reject the notion that they pay dividends as a costly signal to convey their firm's true worth or to purposefully separate their firm from competitors. Overall, we find little support for both the assumptions and resulting predictions of academic signaling theories that are designed to predict payout policy decisions, at least not in terms of conscious decisions that executives make about payout. . . .

Executives indicate that taxes are a second-order payout policy concern. Most say that tax considerations are not a dominant factor in their decision about whether to pay dividends, to increase dividends, or in their choice between payout in the form of repurchases or dividends. A follow-up survey conducted in June 2003, after tax legislation passed that reduced dividend taxation, reinforces the second-order importance of taxation. More than two-thirds of the executives in that survey say that the dividend tax reduction would definitely not or probably not affect their dividend decisions. . . .

———

(b) JUDICIAL REVIEW OF DIVIDEND POLICY

———

(1) PUBLICLY HELD CORPORATIONS WITH A CONTROLLING SHAREHOLDER

———

SINCLAIR OIL CORP. v. LEVIEN

[See Chapter 9, supra]

———

See also Gabelli & Co. v. Liggett Group Inc., 479 A.2d 276 (Del.Supr.1984); Berwald v. Mission Development Co., 40 Del.Ch. 509, 185 A.2d 480 (Del.Supr.1962).

———

(2) CLOSE CORPORATIONS

———

SMITH v. ATLANTIC PROPERTIES, INC.

[See Chapter 6, supra]

———

DODGE v. FORD

[See Chapter 4, supra]

————

NOTE ON COMPELLING DIVIDENDS IN CLOSE CORPORATIONS

It is hard to imagine a real-life scenario today in which the courts would order a publicly held corporation to pay a dividend. Indeed, traditionally the courts have been reluctant to order the declaration of dividends even in the close-corporation context. See, e.g., Gottfried v. Gottfried, 73 N.Y.S.2d 692 (1947). There are signs of a shift in this area, accompanying the courts' increased understanding of close-corporation dynamics. For example, in Miller v. Magline, Inc., 76 Mich.App. 284, 256 N.W.2d 761 (1977), Magline's stock was owned by eight shareholders—most or all of whom were officers and employees—and their relatives. The principal shareholders and officers were Miller, Thorpe, and Law. In 1950 these three adopted a policy under which corporate managers were compensated by a low base salary coupled with an incentive bonus based on a percentage of earnings. The remaining profits were retained for working capital, and apparently no dividends were paid.

This policy was satisfactory to all concerned until 1962, when Miller ceased his active role in corporate management as a result of a serious injury, and Thorpe resigned as vice-president. The board then adopted resolutions confirming Law and other shareholders in their respective offices, and fixing the incentive bonuses at an aggregate of 23% of net earnings before taxes. The employment resolutions remained in effect until 1966, when the board reduced the incentive bonuses to an aggregate of 14½% of net earnings before taxes, but raised base salaries. During 1963–1968, corporate earnings—and hence incentive bonuses—increased dramatically, due to Viet Nam defense procurement contracts. Thus while Law received compensation of $10,016 in 1962, from 1963 to 1968 his compensation was $22,664, $92,419, $137,558, $75,402, $120,183, and $107,887, respectively. Meanwhile, Magline's earned surplus during this period increased from $459,710 to $2,492,156. Miller and Thorpe, who were no longer actively employed, brought suit to compel the corporation to pay dividends. The Chancellor ordered the corporation to pay a dividend of $75 per share for the period July 1, 1963 to June 30, 1968:

It is our opinion ... that the directors of the management group were placed in the impossible situation of trying to give an impartial answer to the determination as to whether dividends should be granted. They already were taking a profit distribution via a percentile of profits before taxes. Therefore, we deem it an untenable position to argue that nonpayment of dividends is justified on the basis that such a concept of profit distribution would imperil the continued well being of the corporation. If such retention of profits were indicated they should have been more diligent in seeing that distributions based upon percentage of profits also should be curtailed....

... To the extent that the management group, as directors, has adopted a nondividend policy, we are of the opinion that it has defeated one of the major purposes of a profit corporation, that is, to accumulate profits and divide them amongst the corporate owners when that is reasonable and proper.

The Michigan Court of Appeals affirmed:

... In the landmark case on court-compelled dividends for closed corporations, Dodge v. Ford Motor Co., 204 Mich. 459, 500, 170 N.W. 668, 682, 3 A.L.R. 413 (1919), the Court adopted the following statements:

... The discretion of the directors will not be interfered with by the courts, unless there has been bad faith, wilful neglect, or abuse of discretion. (Emphasis added.)

Defendant contends that under the business judgment rule a court may not compel a dividend in the absence of clear and convincing proof of fraud, conspiracy, waste, or gross abuse of discretion by the board of directors. In so arguing, defendant carefully elides the statement in the rules above quoted that a court may compel a dividend when the board's refusal to declare one would constitute a "breach of that good faith which they are bound to exercise towards the stockholders." Dodge v. Ford Motor Co., supra, at 500, 170 N.W. at 682, quoting Hunter v. Roberts, Throp & Co., 83 Mich. 63, 71, 47 N.W. 131 (1890). Breach of this fiduciary duty amounts to a breach of trust, and has consistently been recognized in Michigan as a ground for court intervention. Under the circumstances here, their participating in a distribution to them of those profits and a squirreling away of the balance to meet future needs is, in our opinion, inequitable in not giving consideration properly to the needs and requirements of all of the stockholders of the corporation.

In the course of its opinion, the court analyzed and rejected arguments that a dividend was inappropriate on the grounds that Magline had working-capital shortages, Magline might be subject to government-contract-renegotiation liability, Magline's plant was becoming outmoded and would require extensive renovation, Magline's business was cyclical and highly competitive, and losses were predicted for the upcoming fiscal year ending 1970.

See also, e.g., Cole Real Estate Corp. v. Peoples Bank & Trust Co., 160 Ind.App. 88, 310 N.E.2d 275 (1974).

Where a close corporation pays salaries to some shareholders, while not declaring dividends, as an alternative to ordering the payment of dividends the court may order dissolution or a mandatory buyout on the ground of oppression. See Chapter 6, supra.

SECTION 2.   LIMITATIONS ON DIVIDENDS UNDER CREDITORS' RIGHTS LAW

Traditionally, dividends have been regulated by two very different, overlapping, sets of legal rules. The first set of rules is located in creditor's rights (or fraudulent-conveyance) law. These rules center on, but are not limited to, the concept of insolvency, and emphasize the liability of *shareholders* for the *receipt* of improper dividends. The second set of rules is located in state corporation law. These rules emphasize the liability of *directors* for the *payment* of improper dividends. Limitations on dividends under the law of creditor's rights will be considered in this Section. Limitations on dividends under corporation law will be considered in Section 3.

N.Y. BUS. CORP. LAW §§ 102(a)(8), 510(a), (b)

[See Statutory Supplement]

UNIFORM FRAUDULENT TRANSFER ACT §§ 1, 2, 4, 5

[See Statutory Supplement]

BANKRUPTCY CODE §§ 101(32), 548(a)

[See Statutory Supplement]

BACKGROUND NOTE ON THE LAW OF CREDITORS' RIGHTS

1. *Definition.* Creditors' rights law imposes several limitations on transfers of assets without adequate consideration. The most prominent limits turns on the concept of insolvency. Insolvency limits on transfers are based on the transferor's financial condition in terms of either (i) its inability to pay its debts as they become due, or (ii) whether its liabilities exceed its assets. Accordingly, there are two broad definitions of the term *insolvency*.

The first definition—inability to pay debts as they become due—is embodied in most corporate dividend statutes, such as N.Y.Bus.Corp. Law § 102(a)(8). This is known as the *equity meaning* of insolvency, because it was the test generally applied by the equity courts, which had jurisdiction over insolvent estates before the enactment of the federal bankruptcy statute.

The second definition of insolvency—liabilities in excess of assets—is embodied in the Bankruptcy Code and the Uniform Fraudulent Transfer Act ("UFTA"). This second definition is known as the *bankruptcy meaning* of insolvency.[1]

The difference between these two conceptions can be very great. The equity insolvency test is concerned with current liquidity of the going enterprise; the emphasis of the bankruptcy sense of insolvency is upon liquidation of the enterprise. It is easily possible for an enterprise to be short of cash and other liquid means of payment while at the same time holding illiquid assets of great value; such an enterprise may well fail the equity insolvency test. It is also a quite possible occurrence for an enterprise to have a large current cash flow while steadily operating at a loss and suffering a continuing erosion of its asset base; in time, such an enterprise will fail to meet the bankruptcy test of insolvency.

Those with any familiarity with accounting will recognizes that the equity insolvency test is concerned with the income and cash flow statements of the enterprise while the bankruptcy insolvency test is focused on the balance sheet of the enterprise. For this reason, the bankruptcy insolvency test is frequently referred to as the "balance sheet" or "net worth" test.

B. Manning & J. Hanks, Legal Capital 64 (3d ed. 1990).

2. *Application of Fraudulent Conveyance Laws to Dividends.* There is some academic controversy concerning whether fraudulent-conveyance laws are applicable to dividends. However, the cases, while few, uniformly hold that dividends are subject to those laws. See Barbara Black, Corporate Dividends and Stock Repurchases § 4.05[6][b] (1998).

3. *Insolvency Under the Dividend Statutes.* Many corporate-law dividend statutes explicitly incorporate an insolvency limitation on the payment of dividends. See, e.g., N.Y.Bus.Corp.Law § 510. Others do not, although they may embody parallel concepts. The Official Comment to Model Act § 6.40 states that "[t]he Revised Model Business Corporation Act establishes the validity of distributions from the corporate law standpoint under section 6.40 and determines the potential liability of directors for improper distributions under sections 8.30 and 8.33. The federal Bankruptcy Act and state fraudulent conveyance statutes, on the other hand, are designed to enable the trustee or other representative to recapture for the benefit of creditors funds distributed to others in some circumstances. In light of these diverse purposes, it was not thought necessary to make the tests of

---

1. Under the Bankruptcy Code, the test for whether a debtor can be put into involuntary bankruptcy turns principally on whether the debtor is insolvent in the equity sense. See 11 U.S.C.A. § 303(h). However, once a debtor has been put into bankruptcy, the bankruptcy trustee's right to avoid a pre-bankruptcy transfer turns in large part on whether at the time of the transfer the debtor was insolvent in the bankruptcy sense. See 11 U.S.C.A. §§ 101(32), 548.

The bankruptcy meaning of insolvency is itself susceptible to different nuances, as may be seen by comparing 11 U.S.C.A. § 101(32) with UFTA § 2(a).

section 6.40 identical to the tests for insolvency under these various statutes." Cal.Corp.Code § 506(d), which governs the liability of shareholders who have received improper dividends, provides that "[n]othing contained in this section affects any liability which any shareholder may have under [the Uniform Fraudulent Transfer Act]."

4. *Unreasonably Small Capital.* Another important limitation on transfer under the UFTA and cognate Acts is that a transfer without adequate consideration is prohibited if it would leave the transferor with unreasonably small capital.

―――――

MARKELL, TOWARD TRUE AND PLAIN DEALING: A THEORY OF FRAUDULENT TRANSFERS INVOLVING UNREASONABLY SMALL CAPITAL, 21 Ind.L.Rev. 469, 487 (1988). "After the promulgation of the [Uniform Fraudulent Conveyance Act,] section 5 [the predecessor of UFTA § 4] received little independent notice. The case law that did develop, however, did little to illuminate the basic question: what is the scope of the unreasonably small capital provision? . . . The main view, to the extent that one developed, focused on the transferor's ability to marshall sufficient cash, either from operations, equity infusions, new loans or some combination of these, to pay expected creditors. These cases took a forward looking view, comparing anticipated cash flow against anticipated debt incurrence."

SECTION 3.   LIMITATIONS ON DIVIDENDS UNDER THE CORPORATE STATUTES

―――――

(a) INTRODUCTION

1. *In General.* In addition to limitations placed on dividends under the law of creditors' rights, corporate law also governs the power to declare and pay dividends. Cases like Dodge v. Ford, supra, concern the issue, when may a corporation be *compelled* to pay dividends. Most of the law of dividends, however, centers on *limitations* on a corporation's power to pay dividends. These limitations may be thought of as financial, in the narrow sense that they are not based on judicial determinations of sound dividend policy, but instead turn on quantified objective tests. Under traditional statutes, however, the limitations involve concepts that are typically of little or no relevance under modern financial theory.

2. *Who Does Corporate Dividend Law Protect?* A preliminary issue raised by the corporate law of dividends is, who does this body of law protect? The class of persons protected by creditors' rights law is clear—creditors. The classes of persons protected by the corporate dividend statutes has not always been clear.

Obviously, one group of persons who could be protected by these statutes is creditors. As stated in D. Kehl, Corporate Dividends (1941), "With the liability of corporate stockholders . . . limited to the amount of capital subscribed . . . it soon became apparent that the original capital should be permanently devoted to the needs of the corporation as at least a partial substitute for the unlimited personal liability existing in individual enterprise." But then, "If the creation of a capital fund was not to defeat its purpose, safeguards against its withdrawal by repayment to shareholders in the guise of dividends, or otherwise, were indispensable. Historically, the principal objective of dividend law has therefore been the preservation of a minimum of assets as a safeguard in assuring the payment of creditors' claims."

In addition to creditors, some of the corporate dividend statutes are also designed to protect the preferences of preferred shareholders.

Finally, at one time it was thought that the corporate dividend statutes were intended to protect common shareholders, partly on the ground that excessive dividends might injure the corporate enterprise, and partly on the ground that dividends out of capital might mislead shareholders into thinking that the corporation was earning money when in fact it wasn't.

Today, the concept that the corporate dividend statutes protect common shareholders is not generally accepted. Furthermore, although the protection that the statutes give to preferred shareholders may sometimes be significant, many corporations have no preferred shareholders. That leaves the protection of creditors. As the following materials will show, however, in fact creditors get very little protection from the traditional dividend statutes.

3. *Traditional and modern dividend statutes.* The dividend statutes can be divided into traditional and modern statutes. The traditional statutes, in turn, can be divided into two subcategories. Most of the traditional statutes center on a *capital-impairment* (or a *capital-and-surplus* or *balance-sheet*) test. A few center on an *earned-surplus* (or *income-statement* test). The following sections will discuss the traditional capital-impairment statutes, the traditional earned-surplus statutes, and the modern statutes, respectively.

(b) TRADITIONAL STATUTES—PART I: BALANCE-SHEET OR CAPITAL-IMPAIRMENT STATUTES

(1) THE CAPITAL–IMPAIRMENT TEST AND ITS MEANING

DEL. GEN. CORP. LAW §§ 141(e), 154, 170

[See Statutory Supplement]

N.Y. BUS. CORP. LAW §§ 102(a)(9), (12), (13), 506, 510

[See Statutory Supplement]

INTRODUCTORY NOTE

1. *Legal Capital and Par Value*. Most of the traditional statutes turn on the concept of *legal capital*. That concept, in turn, can only be understood against the background of a concept known as *par* or *par value*.

a. *Par value*. Originally, the par value of a share was the price at which it was expected that the share would be issued (sold) by the corporation. Thus in the paradigm case, a share that carried a $100 par value would be issued for $100. Eventually, a practice emerged under which the par value of stock was not the price at which the stock was to be issued, but a purely nominal amount. For example, stock that was to be issued at $100 might carry a par value of only $1, or even less. Such stock is known as *low-par value* stock. Still later, the statutes were amended to allow the issuance of *no-par value* stock—that is, stock that did not carry any par value at all.

b. *Legal capital*. *Legal capital* is the sum of (i) the par value of all par-value stock, and (ii) such additional amounts as the board assigns to capital, either in connection with the issuance of low-par or no-par stock, or thereafter. Legal capital (or *stated capital*) is a legal construct, with little or no economic reality. *Economic capital* is the amount that the owners of an enterprise have invested in the enterprise, directly or indirectly. When stock was issued at its par value, the concepts of economic and legal capital were tied together. The advent of low-par and no-par stock severed that tie. Because the concept of legal capital is tied to par value, it has become artificial. Nevertheless, the concept still remains important under the traditional dividend statutes.

2. *Structure of the Traditional Statutes*. Most traditional corporate dividend statutes begin with an insolvency test. There are three possible reasons why these statutes employ an insolvency test, which would be applicable in any event under creditors' rights law. First, it has not always been entirely clear whether creditors' rights law applies to dividends. Second, creditors' rights law emphasize the liability of transferees (in the case of corporations, shareholders) for improper distributions. In contrast, the corporate dividend statutes emphasize the liability of directors. Third, the basic creditors' rights laws—the Bankruptcy Code and the Uniform Fraudulent Transfer Act, and cognate statutes—turn on the bankruptcy meaning of insolvency. In contrast, a dividend statute may employ either the equity meaning of insolvency or both the bankruptcy and the equity meanings.

After beginning with an insolvency test, the traditional dividend statutes add a second basic test, which is frequently subject to important exceptions. The most common second basic test is a capital-impairment or balance-sheet test. The capital-impairment statutes center on whether the corporation's assets exceed its liabilities plus its capital. Under this test, a dividend cannot be paid if, before or after payment of the dividend, the corporation's assets are or would be less than the sum of its liabilities plus its capital or, in some cases, the sum of liabilities, capital, and liquidation preferences. (In contrast, under the bankruptcy meaning of the insolvency test, a dividend may be paid as long as after the payment the corporation's assets will exceed its liabilities.) Capital-impairment statutes can be conceptualized in two, functionally identical ways: as prohibiting dividends out of capital, or as permitting dividends only out of surplus.

————

Klang v. Smith's Food & Drug Centers, Inc.

Supreme Court of Delaware, 1997.
702 A.2d 150.

■ Before Veasey, C.J., Walsh, Holland, Hartnett and Berger, JJ., constituting the Court en Banc.

■ Veasey, Chief Justice:

This appeal calls into question the actions of a corporate board in carrying out a merger and self-tender offer. Plaintiff in this purported class action alleges that a corporation's repurchase of shares violated the statutory prohibition against the impairment of capital. . . .

No corporation may repurchase or redeem its own shares except out of "surplus," as statutorily defined, or except as expressly authorized by provisions of the statute not relevant here. Balance sheets are not, however, conclusive indicators of surplus or a lack thereof. Corporations may revalue assets to show surplus, but perfection in that process is not required. Directors have reasonable latitude to depart from the balance sheet to calculate surplus, so long as they evaluate assets and liabilities in good faith, on the basis of acceptable data, by methods that they reasonably believe reflect present values, and arrive at a determination of the surplus that is not so far off the mark as to constitute actual or constructive fraud.

We hold that, on this record, the Court of Chancery was correct in finding that there was no impairment of capital and there were no disclosure violations. Accordingly, we affirm.

Facts

Smith's Food & Drug Centers, Inc. ("SFD") is a Delaware corporation that owns and operates a chain of supermarkets in the Southwestern United States. Slightly more than three years ago, Jeffrey P. Smith, SFD's Chief Executive Officer, began to entertain suitors with an interest in acquiring SFD. At the time, and until the transactions at issue, Mr. Smith and his family held common and preferred stock constituting 62.1% voting control of SFD. Plaintiff and the class he purports to represent are holders of common stock in SFD.

On January 29, 1996, SFD entered into an agreement with The Yucaipa Companies ("Yucaipa"), a California partnership also active in the supermarket industry. Under the agreement, the following would take place:

(1) Smitty's Supermarkets, Inc. ("Smitty's"), a wholly-owned subsidiary of Yucaipa that operated a supermarket chain in Arizona, was to merge into Cactus Acquisition, Inc. ("Cactus"), a subsidiary of SFD, in exchange for which SFD would deliver to Yucaipa slightly over 3 million newly-issued shares of SFD common stock;

(2) SFD was to undertake a recapitalization, in the course of which SFD would assume a sizable amount of new debt, retire old debt, and offer to repurchase up to fifty percent of its outstanding shares (other than those issued to Yucaipa) for $36 per share; and

(3) SFD was to repurchase 3 million shares of preferred stock from Jeffrey Smith and his family.

SFD hired the investment firm of Houlihan Lokey Howard & Zukin ("Houlihan") to examine the transactions and render a solvency opinion. Houlihan eventually issued a report to the SFD Board replete with assurances that the transactions would not endanger SFD's solvency, and would not impair SFD's capital in violation of 8 *Del.C.* § 160. On May 17, 1996, in reliance on the Houlihan opinion, SFD's Board determined that there existed sufficient surplus to consummate the transactions, and enacted a resolution proclaiming as much. On May 23, 1996, SFD's stockholders voted to approve the transactions, which closed on that day. The self-tender offer was over-subscribed, so SFD repurchased fully fifty percent of its shares at the offering price of $36 per share.

Disposition in the Court of Chancery

This appeal came to us after an odd sequence of events in the Court of Chancery. On May 22, 1996, the day before the transactions closed, plaintiff Larry F. Klang filed a purported class action in the Court of Chancery against Jeffrey Smith and his family, various members of the SFD Board, Yucaipa, Yucaipa's managing general partner Ronald W. Burkle, Smitty's and Cactus.... [Plaintiff] contended that the stock repurchases violated 8 *Del.C.* § 160[2] by impairing SFD's capital....

2. Section 160(a) provides:

(a) Every corporation may purchase, redeem, receive, take or otherwise acquire, own and hold, sell, lend exchange, transfer or otherwise dispose of, pledge, use and otherwise deal in and with its own shares; provided, however, that no corporation shall:

(1) Purchase or redeem its own shares of capital stock for cash or other property when the capital of the corporation is impaired or when such purchase or redemption would cause any impairment of the capital of the corporation, except that a corporation may purchase or redeem out of capital any of its own shares which are entitled upon any distribution of its assets, whether by dividend or in liquidation, to a preference over another class or series of its stock, or, if no shares entitled to such a preference are outstanding, any of its own shares, if such shares will be retired upon their acquisition and the capital of the corporation reduced in accordance with §§ 243 and 244 of this title.

After defendants answered the amended complaint, plaintiff took full discovery. The Court of Chancery heard plaintiff's motion to have the transactions rescinded, and released a Memorandum Opinion dismissing plaintiff's claims in full.

Plaintiff's Capital–Impairment Claim

A corporation may not repurchase its shares if, in so doing, it would cause an impairment of capital, unless expressly authorized by Section 160. A repurchase impairs capital if the funds used in the repurchase exceed the amount of the corporation's "surplus," defined by 8 *Del.C.* § 154 to mean the excess of net assets over the par value of the corporation's issued stock.[5]

Plaintiff asked the Court of Chancery to rescind the transactions in question as violative of Section 160. As we understand it, plaintiff's position breaks down into two analytically distinct arguments. First, he contends that SFD's balance sheets constitute conclusive evidence of capital impairment. He argues that the negative net worth that appeared on SFD's books following the repurchase compels us to find a violation of Section 160. Second, he suggests that even allowing the Board to "go behind the balance sheet" to calculate surplus does not save the transactions from violating Section 160. In connection with this claim, he attacks the SFD Board's off-balance-sheet method of calculating surplus on the theory that it does not adequately take into account all of SFD's assets and liabilities. Moreover, he argues that the May 17, 1996 resolution of the SFD Board conclusively refutes the Board's claim that revaluing the corporation's assets gives rise to the required surplus. We hold that each of these claims is without merit.

SFD's balance sheets do not establish a violation of 8 *Del.C.* § 160

In an April 25, 1996 proxy statement, the SFD Board released a pro forma balance sheet showing that the merger and self-tender offer would result in a deficit to surplus on SFD's books of more than $100 million. A balance sheet the SFD Board issued shortly after the transactions confirmed this result. Plaintiff asks us to adopt an interpretation of 8 *Del.C.* § 160 whereby balance-sheet net worth is controlling for purposes of determining compliance with the statute.[6] Defendants do not dispute that SFD's books showed a negative net worth in the wake of its transactions with Yucaipa, but argue that corporations should have the presumptive right to revalue assets and liabilities to comply with Section 160.

5. Section 154 provides, "Any corporation may, by resolution of its board of directors, determine that only a part of the consideration . . . received by the corporation for . . . its capital stock . . . shall be capital. . . . The excess . . . of the net assets of the corporation over the amount so determined to be capital shall be surplus. Net assets means the amount by which total assets exceed total liabilities. Capital and surplus are not liabilities for this purpose."

6. *See, e.g., Wright v. Heizer Corp.,* N.D.Ill., 503 F.Supp. 802, 810 (1980); *In re Kettle of Fried Chicken of America, Inc.,* 513 F.2d 807, 811 (6th Cir.1975).

Plaintiff advances an erroneous interpretation of Section 160. We understand that the books of a corporation do not necessarily reflect the current values of its assets and liabilities. Among other factors, unrealized appreciation or depreciation can render book numbers inaccurate. It is unrealistic to hold that a corporation is bound by its balance sheets for purposes of determining compliance with Section 160. Accordingly, we adhere to the principles of *Morris v. Standard Gas & Electric Co.*[7] allowing corporations to revalue properly its assets and liabilities to show a surplus and thus conform to the statute.

It is helpful to recall the purpose behind Section 160. The General Assembly enacted the statute to prevent boards from draining corporations of assets to the detriment of creditors and the long-term health of the corporation.[8] That a corporation has not yet realized or reflected on its balance sheet the appreciation of assets is irrelevant to this concern. Regardless of what a balance sheet that has not been updated may show, an actual, though unrealized, appreciation reflects real economic value that the corporation may borrow against or that creditors may claim or levy upon. Allowing corporations to revalue assets and liabilities to reflect current realities complies with the statute and serves well the policies behind this statute.

The SFD Board appropriately revalued corporate assets to comply with 8 *Del.C.* § 160.

Plaintiff contends that SFD's repurchase of shares violated Section 160 even without regard to the corporation's balance sheets. Plaintiff claims that the SFD Board was not entitled to rely on the solvency opinion of Houlihan, which showed that the transactions would not impair SFD's capital given a revaluation of corporate assets. The argument is that the methods that underlay the solvency opinion were inappropriate as a matter of law because they failed to take into account all of SFD's assets and liabilities. In addition, plaintiff suggests that the SFD Board's resolution of May 17, 1996 itself shows that the transactions impaired SFD's capital, and that therefore we must find a violation of 8 *Del.C.* § 160. We disagree, and hold that the SFD Board revalued the corporate assets under appropriate methods. Therefore the self-tender offer complied with Section 160, notwithstanding errors that took place in the drafting of the resolution.

On May 17, 1996, Houlihan released its solvency opinion to the SFD Board, expressing its judgment that the merger and self-tender offer would not impair SFD's capital. Houlihan reached this conclusion by comparing SFD's "Total Invested Capital" of $1.8 billion—a figure Houlihan arrived at by valuing SFD's assets under the "market multiple" approach—with SFD's long-term debt of $1.46 billion. This comparison yielded an approximation of SFD's "concluded equity value" equal to $346 million, a figure clearly in excess of the outstanding par value of SFD's stock. Thus, Houlihan concluded, the transactions would not violate 8 *Del.C.* § 160.

7. *Morris v. Standard Gas & Electric Co.*, Del.Ch., 63 A.2d 577 (1949).

8. *See Pasotti v. United States Guardian Corp.*, 156 A. 255, at 257 (Del.Ch.1931).

Plaintiff contends that Houlihan's analysis relied on inappropriate methods to mask a violation of Section 160. Noting that 8 *Del.C.* § 154 defines "net assets" as "the amount by which total assets exceeds total liabilities," plaintiff argues that Houlihan's analysis is erroneous as a matter of law because of its failure to calculate "total assets" and "total liabilities" as separate variables. In a related argument, plaintiff claims that the analysis failed to take into account all of SFD's liabilities, *i.e.*, that Houlihan neglected to consider current liabilities in its comparison of SFD's "Total Invested Capital" and long-term debt. Plaintiff contends that the SFD Board's resolution proves that adding current liabilities into the mix shows a violation of Section 160. The resolution declared the value of SFD's assets to be $1.8 billion, and stated that its "total liabilities" would not exceed $1.46 billion after the transactions with Yucaipa. As noted, the $1.46 billion figure described only the value of SFD's long-term debt. Adding in SFD's $372 million in current liabilities, plaintiff argues, shows that the transactions impaired SFD's capital.

We believe that plaintiff reads too much into Section 154. The statute simply defines "net assets" in the course of defining "surplus." It does not mandate a "facts and figures balancing of assets and liabilities" to determine by what amount, if any, total assets exceeds total liabilities.[9] The statute is merely definitional. It does not require any particular method of calculating surplus, but simply prescribes factors that any such calculation must include. Although courts may not determine compliance with Section 160 except by methods that fully take into account the assets and liabilities of the corporation, Houlihan's methods were not erroneous as a matter of law simply because they used Total Invested Capital and long-term debt as analytical categories rather than "total assets" and "total liabilities."

We are satisfied that the Houlihan opinion adequately took into account all of SFD's assets and liabilities. Plaintiff points out that the $1.46 billion figure that approximated SFD's long-term debt failed to include $372 million in current liabilities, and argues that including the latter in the calculations dissipates the surplus. In fact, plaintiff has misunderstood Houlihan's methods. The record shows that Houlihan's calculation of SFD's Total Invested Capital is already net of current liabilities. Thus, subtracting long-term debt from Total Invested Capital does, in fact, yield an accurate measure of a corporation's net assets.

The record contains, in the form of the Houlihan opinion, substantial evidence that the transactions complied with Section 160. Plaintiff has provided no reason to distrust Houlihan's analysis. In cases alleging impairment of capital under Section 160, the trial court may defer to the board's measurement of surplus unless a plaintiff can show that the directors "failed to fulfill their duty to evaluate the assets on the basis of acceptable data and by standards which they are entitled to believe reasonably reflect present values."[10] In the absence

9. *See Farland v. Wills*, Del.Ch., 1 Del. J.Corp.L. 467, 475 (1975).

10. *Morris*, 63 A.2d at 582.

of bad faith or fraud on the part of the board, courts will not "substitute [our] concepts of wisdom for that of the directors."[11] Here, plaintiff does not argue that the SFD Board acted in bad faith. Nor has he met his burden of showing that the methods and data that underlay the board's analysis are unreliable or that its determination of surplus is so far off the mark as to constitute actual or constructive fraud.[12] Therefore, we defer to the board's determination of surplus, and hold that SFD's self-tender offer did not violate 8 *Del.C.* § 160.

On a final note, we hold that the SFD Board's resolution of May 17, 1996 has no bearing on whether the transactions conformed to Section 160. The record shows that the SFD Board committed a serious error in drafting the resolution: the resolution states that, following the transactions, SFD's "total liabilities" would be no more than $1.46 billion. In fact, that figure reflects only the value of SFD's long-term debt. Although the SFD Board was guilty of sloppy work, and did not follow good corporate practices, it does not follow that Section 160 was violated. The statute requires only that there exist a surplus after a repurchase, not that the board memorialize the surplus in a resolution. The statute carves out a class of transactions that directors have no authority to execute, but does not, in fact, require any affirmative act on the part of the board. The SFD repurchase would be valid in the absence of any board resolution. A mistake in documenting the surplus will not negate the substance of the action, which complies with the statutory scheme....

The judgment of the Court of Chancery is affirmed.

———

NOTE ON KLANG v. SMITH'S FOOD & DRUG CENTERS, INC.

1. *Applicability of Klang to Dividends. Klang* concerned a repurchase of the corporation's stock, rather than a dividend. Although certain problems are unique to repurchases—see Section 8, infra—under almost every dividend statute the test for the legality of a repurchase is substantially the same as the test for the legality of a dividend. Accordingly, *Klang* governs the payment of dividends under the Delaware statute as well as the repurchase of stock.

2. *The Scholarly Debate.* Beginning in the 1940s, there was a long debate in the scholarly literature on whether a capital-impairment test permitted the payment of dividends up to the difference between the *actual value* of the corporation's assets and its liabilities and capital, or only up to the difference between the corporation's assets and its liabilities and capital *as shown on the corporation's balance sheet*. The debate was largely triggered by the leading case of Randall

11. *Id.* at 583.

12. We interpret 8 *Del.C.* § 172 to entitle boards to rely on experts such as Houlihan to determine compliance with 8 *Del.C.* § 160. Plaintiff has not alleged that the SFD Board failed to exercise reasonable care in selecting Houlihan, nor that rendering a solvency opinion is outside Houlihan's realm of competence. Compare 8 *Del.C.* § 141(e) (providing that directors may rely in good faith on records, reports, experts, etc.).

v. Bailey, 23 N.Y.S.2d 173 (Sup.Ct. 1940), aff'd, 288 N.Y. 280, 43 N.E.2d 43 (1942), in which the New York courts took essentially the same position as that later taken by *Klang*. Despite the post-Randall v. Bailey debate, the weight of authority favored the rule of Randall v. Bailey. *Klang* probably puts the debate to rest for practical purposes.

––––––––

NOTE ON BALANCE–SHEET ACCOUNTING FOR CORPORATE EQUITY

Corporate balance-sheet accounting has traditionally differed from accounting for proprietorships and partnerships in the way that equity (ownership interests) is treated. In the sole proprietorship and the partnership, equity as it appears on the balance sheet is normally a fairly straightforward account. In the corporation, however, equity has traditionally been divided into Stated Capital and Surplus. Surplus, in turn, has been redivided into a number of further subaccounts.

To begin with, *Stated Capital* (or Capital Stock) consists of the total par value of issued stock that has par value, plus any other amounts allocated to capital by the board. The two most important *Surplus* accounts are Earned Surplus and Capital Surplus.

Broadly speaking, capital surplus is that portion of surplus that is derived from sources other than earnings, such as amounts paid for stock in excess of the stock's par value. In theory, the permissibility of dividends out of capital surplus marks the major difference between the balance-sheet and earned-surplus tests: Under a balance-sheet test, dividends can be paid out of capital surplus unless specifically prohibited, because such dividends do not impair capital. In contrast, under an earned-surplus test, dividends can be paid out of capital surplus only if specifically permitted, because capital surplus is not earned surplus. In practice, however, as will be seen, the two tests converge.

Two of the most important types of capital surplus are *paid-in surplus* and *reduction surplus*.

1. *Paid-in Surplus.* Paid-in surplus is the excess of (i) the total sale price of newly issued stock, over (ii) that portion of the sale price that constitutes par value or is otherwise allocated by the board to stated capital. This type of surplus is a byproduct of the low-par and no-par phenomena, because it does not arise if stock is issued at par value. In an economic sense, paid-in surplus constitutes capital, because it is part of the shareholders' initial equity investment. Nevertheless, the capital-impairment statutes routinely permit dividends out of paid-in surplus.

2. *Reduction Surplus.* Reduction surplus is the amount by which stated capital is reduced through corporate action pursuant to statutory authority. There are a number of techniques for reducing capital and thereby creating reduction surplus. The most significant of these techniques is to amend the certificate of incorporation to reduce the par value of the corporation's stock. Such a reduction creates a new

surplus fund equal to the amount by which stated capital has been reduced. This fund is called reduction surplus, and is a subcategory of capital surplus.

In recent years, accountants have tended to substitute descriptive nomenclature for the traditional Surplus terminology. For example, Earned Surplus is given a title such as Retained Income, Retained Earnings, or Accumulated Earnings. Paid-in Surplus is given a title such as Capital Contributed for Shares in Excess of Par or Stated Value. However, the new titles do not work a difference in substance, and courts, legislators, and lawyers have continued to use the old terminology.

As will be shown later in this Chapter, Capital and Surplus accounts, and their modern counterparts like Retained Earnings, have become irrelevant under many of the newer dividend statutes. However, the terms are likely to continue in use on financial statements, both because many statutes (including those of important corporate states like Delaware and New York) still turn on capital-and-surplus concepts, and because accountants are unlikely to quickly drop long-established practices.

(2) EXCEPTIONS TO THE BASIC CAPITAL–IMPAIRMENT TEST

(A) *The Current–Earnings Test; Nimble Dividends*

DEL. GEN. CORP. LAW § 170

[See Statutory Supplement]

Under a few statutes, like that of Delaware, dividends can be paid out of current profits even if capital is or would be impaired. Such dividends are known as *nimble dividends*. The term "nimble" is used to describe such dividends because under the statutes the dividend can be paid only out of *current* profits, so that directors must be sufficiently nimble to declare the dividends before the close of the current period or within a short time thereafter.

One justification that has been put forward for permitting dividends out of current profits, even when capital is impaired, is that this technique allows the corporation to continue regular dividends on its preferred stock. Another is that a corporation that has suffered heavy losses may need to attract new capital to remain viable, and may be unable to attract new capital if it cannot pay dividends.

Both justifications are thin. Essentially, the ability to pay nimble dividends, in states that permit such dividends, seems to be an erosion—one of many—in the idea that capital should be preserved to protect creditors.

———

(B) Wasting–Asset Corporations

———

NOTE ON WASTING–ASSET CORPORATIONS

Normally, in determining profits—and therefore surplus—a corporation must subtract from its gross revenues an appropriate amount for depreciation or depletion. However, some statutes, like N.Y.Bus. Corp.Law § 510(b) and Del.Gen.Corp.Law § 170(b), provide that in the case of a wasting-asset corporation, profits can be calculated for dividend purposes without regard to depreciation or depletion, subject to certain limitations. A *wasting-asset* corporation is a corporation that is in the business of exploiting a non-replenishable asset, like a coal mine, an oil well, a rock quarry, or a patent.

The justification sometimes given for permitting dividends without regard to an allowance for depletion of a wasting asset is that all concerned parties expect that the corporation's lifetime will be limited to the lifetime of the wasting asset, so that there is no reason to preserve the corporation's capital beyond the lifetime of that asset. This justification, like the justification for nimble dividends, is thin, because many corporations with wasting assets either hold nonwasting assets as well, hold a portfolio of wasting assets that is continually refreshed, or both.

———

(C) Dividends out of Capital Surplus

———

N.Y. BUS. CORP. LAW §§ 102(a)(9), (13), (14), 510, 516, 520
[See Statutory Supplement]

———

DEL. GEN. CORP. LAW §§ 154, 170, 242(a)(3), 244
[See Statutory Supplement]

———

NOTE ON DIVIDENDS OUT OF CAPITAL SURPLUS

The capital-impairment statutes routinely permit dividends out of both paid-in and reduction surplus, with no significant safeguards for creditors beyond those imposed by the insolvency test. The payment of dividends out of capital surplus seems anomalous under a capital-impairment statute, in which the emphasis is placed on preservation of capital. The power of the corporation to reduce capital, and pay dividends out of the resulting reduction surplus, creates a gaping breach in the purported wall set up by dividend law to protect the interests of creditors.

_____

(c) TRADITIONAL STATUTES—PART II: EARNED-SURPLUS STATUTES

_____

NOTE ON THE EARNED-SURPLUS TEST

At one time, the Model Act employed a test for dividends that centered on whether a corporation had *earned surplus*. Earned surplus was defined as "the portion of ... surplus ... equal to the balance of ... net profits, income, gains and losses from the date of incorporation ... after deducting subsequent distributions to shareholders and transfers to stated capital and capital surplus made out of earned surplus." William Hackney commented as follows:

> In attempting to formulate statutory language limiting dividends to income, two distinct approaches were found possible.
>
> One is, like the capital-impairment restriction, a balance-sheet test. The surplus of net assets in excess of capital is obtained and then analyzed and any which is not paid-in or other capital surplus is deemed accumulated income.
>
> The second approach ... is to take the balance of all the corporate income statements to date and deduct dividends and other transfers therefrom, with the remainder being earned surplus.
>
> The Model Act definition, it seems, utilizes the aggregate-income-statement method of arriving at earned surplus. It does not use the balance sheet as a source of reference but directs one to take the balance of net profits, income, gains and losses over a period of time.[1]

Despite the focus on earned surplus, the prior version of the Model Act, and the statutes that adopted the Act, also permitted dividends out of capital surplus if the dividend was permitted by the articles of incorporation or approved by the shareholders and was identified as a distribution from capital; there were no accrued dividends on an issue of cumulative preferred stock; and the dividend did not impair the liquidation preference of preferred stock. In practice, therefore, the earned surplus test tended to converge with the capital-impairment test.

---

1. Hackney, The Financial Provisions of the Model Business Corporations Act, 70 Harv.L.Rev. 1357, 1365–66 (1957).

As Hackney pointed out, "The net result [of earned-surplus statutes based on the old Model Act] is an apparent limitation of the funds available for dividends to earned surplus, but actually, in so far as real protection to creditors or preferred stockholders is concerned, there is a complete eradication of the concept of common capital as a cushion protecting the senior interests." Hackney, The Financial Provisions of the Model Business Corporation Act, 70 Harv.L.Rev. 1357, 1389 (1957).

The current version of the Model Act has dropped the earned-surplus approach. That approach is now followed by only a few statutes.

SECTION 4. CONTRACTUAL RESTRICTIONS ON THE PAYMENT OF DIVIDENDS

_____

BACKGROUND NOTE

It should be obvious by now that the traditional dividend statutes provide little protection to creditors beyond that already afforded by the law of creditors' rights. These statutes are so liberal in allowing capital surplus to be created, either through the use of no-par or low-par capitalization when stock is originally issued, or thereafter through a reduction of capital, that corporations can usually make routine distributions out of economic (although not "legal") capital, even in the absence of retained earnings.

Involuntary creditors, trade creditors, and short-term lenders must normally take the protection of dividend law as they find it. Institutional lenders, however, who provide large amounts of money over a long period of time, have the power to impose contractual restrictions on dividends beyond the weak limits imposed by corporation law, and often do so. Similar restrictions are often extracted by underwriters in connection with bonds and preferred stock issued to the public. Indeed, as a practical matter, it may be said that much of the modern law of dividends is contractual rather than statutory. The practical question is usually not whether a dividend is prohibited by statute, but whether it is prohibited by arrangements with lending institutions or provisions agreed upon in connection with bond or preferred-stock financing.

_____

FORM OF BOND INDENTURE PROVISION RESTRICTING DIVIDENDS

[See Statutory Supplement]

_____

SECTION 5.   THE MODERN DIVIDEND STATUTES

———

CAL. CORP. CODE §§ 114, 166, 500–503, 507

[See Statutory Supplement]

———

MODEL BUS. CORP. ACT §§ 1.40(6), 6.40

[See Statutory Supplement]

———

NOTE ON THE MODERN DIVIDEND STATUTES

California's dividend provisions, enacted in 1977, marked a sweeping break with traditional dividend statutes. Until that time, the foundation of most statutes was a legal concept—stated capital. In contrast, the foundation of the California statute is a set of economic realities: retained earnings, asset-liability ratios, liquidation preferences, and an insolvency test. The Model Business Corporation Act followed suit in breaking with the traditional statutes, although it employed a much different approach than the California statute. Among other things, these statutes eliminate the concept of par value for all practical purposes.

———

KUMMERT, STATE STATUTORY RESTRICTIONS ON FINANCIAL DISTRIBUTIONS BY CORPORATIONS TO SHAREHOLDERS (pt. II), 59 Wash.L.Rev. 185, 282–84 (1984). "[The California and Model Business Corporation Act approaches] have some remarkable similarities. [Both] proceed from a common assessment of the inadequacies of the concept of legal capital to abolish not only the statutory underpinnings of the concept (the notion of par value and accounting rules for consideration received for shares), but also the series of exceptions (nimble dividends, depletion dividends, and special repurchases of shares) and fictions (treasury shares) erected because of the existence of the concept. [Both] subject transfers of cash or property, or incurrences of indebtedness, by a corporation without consideration to its shareholders to a single set of restrictions, regardless of the form in which the transfer, or incurrence, occurs. [Both] address applications of the restrictions to such transfers, or incurrences, where the transferor, or obligor, is either the parent, or the subsidiary, of another corporation. Finally, drafters of each of the systems based their efforts on the premise that statutory systems founded on legal capital were essentially misleading insofar as they led creditors and senior security holders to believe that such systems operated to protect their interests.

"[D]espite these similarities, the [California and Model Act] systems can be clearly distinguished on the basis of their respective responses to that possible misrepresentation. The California series attempts to rectify the misrepresentation by promulgating rules that will provide creditors and senior shareholders with the type of protection they *thought* they were getting from the legal capital system. On the other hand, the Amended Model Act [attempts] to rectify the misrepresentation by promulgating rules that will provide creditors and senior shareholders with the level of protection that the drafters perceived such groups *actually received* from the legal capital system. This variance in fundamental goals in turn produces the significant differences between the Acts on such issues as the relative freedom directors have and the status in the event of financial difficulty of debt issued on repurchase of shares."

———

Another difference between the California and Model Act approaches is that the California statute is in effect an economic counterpart of the earned-surplus test, while the Model Act is in effect an economic counterpart of the capital-impairment test.

———

SECTION 6.   LIABILITY OF DIRECTORS FOR IMPROPER DIVIDENDS

Liability for an improper dividend is governed by two bodies of law: corporation law, and the law of creditors' rights. Liability may be imposed on the directors who authorize the dividend, on the shareholders who receive it, or both. In general, corporation law tends to emphasize the liability of directors, while creditors' rights law tends to emphasize the liability of shareholders.

Subject to certain exceptions, liability for an improper repurchase of a corporation's own stock is treated the same way as liability for an improper dividend.

———

N.Y. BUS. CORP. LAW § 719

[See Statutory Supplement]

———

MODEL BUS. CORP. ACT § 8.33

[See Statutory Supplement]

———

DEL. GEN. CORP. LAW §§ 172, 174

[See Statutory Supplement]

———

NOTE ON LIABILITY OF DIRECTORS FOR IMPROPER DIVIDENDS

The liability of directors for improper dividends is governed in the first instance by state corporation law. Most statutes do not leave the issue of directors' liability for the improper declaration of dividends to the general duty of care, but instead include special provisions concerning such liability. Typically, the statutes either permit directors to raise a defense of good-faith reliance on defined financial statements; condition directors' liability on bad faith or lack of due care; or both. The measure of recovery may be either the full amount of an improper dividend, or the injury suffered by creditors or shareholders up to the amount of the distribution, depending on the statute.

Many statutes provide that a director who is held liable for an improper distribution is entitled to contribution from other directors who voted for or assented to the distribution without complying with the applicable standard of conduct. See, e.g., Del.Gen.Corp.Law § 174(b).

A director who is held liable for an improper dividend may also be entitled to reimbursement from shareholders who received the dividend with knowledge of its illegality, or with knowledge of facts that indicated that the dividend was illegal, again depending on the statute.

SECTION 7. LIABILITY OF SHAREHOLDERS FOR IMPROPER DIVIDENDS

———

DEL. GEN. CORP. LAW § 174(c)

[See Statutory Supplement]

———

MODEL BUS. CORP. ACT § 8.33(b)

[See Statutory Supplement]

———

N.Y. BUS. CORP. LAW § 719(d)

[See Statutory Supplement]

———

CAL. CORP. CODE § 506

[See Statutory Supplement]

UNIFORM FRAUDULENT TRANSFER ACT § 7

[See Statutory Supplement]

NOTE ON SHAREHOLDER LIABILITY FOR IMPROPER DIVIDENDS

The liability of shareholders who receive an improper dividend reflects both corporation law and the law of creditors' rights. Because the corporate statutes are often not well developed in this area, the common law—that is, the law governing shareholder liability for receipt of improper dividends in the absence of a statutory provision concerning such liability—remains highly significant.

1. *Common Law Rules.*

a. *Insolvency.* At common law, if a dividend either resulted in insolvency or was paid when the corporation was already insolvent, a shareholder was liable for the amount of the dividend that he received, on the theory that it constituted a fraudulent conveyance. The fact that the shareholder acted in good faith—that is, did not know of the insolvency—was deemed irrelevant. See Fuld, Recovery of Illegal and Partial Liquidating Dividends from Stockholders, 28 Va.L.Rev. 50, 51 (1941).

b. *Improper dividends not involving insolvency.* The position at common law was more complex where the corporation was not insolvent, but the dividend was improper under a corporate dividend statute. If the shareholder was on notice that the dividend was improper, she was liable either on a theory of unjust enrichment or on the theory that she was privy to the directors' wrong and had no equities in her favor. See Alfred J. Brown Seed Co. v. Brown, 240 Mich. 569, 215 N.W. 772 (1927). However, if the corporation was solvent at the time of the dividend, and the shareholder received the dividend in good faith, she was not liable under the corporate statutes. See McDonald v. Williams, 174 U.S. 397, 19 S.Ct. 743, 43 L.Ed. 1022 (1899). See generally Fuld, Recovery of Illegal and Partial Liquidating Dividends from Stockholders, 28 Va.L.Rev. 50 (1941); Briggs, Stockholders' Liability for Unlawful Dividends, 8 Temple L.Q. 145 (1934).

c. *Wood v. National City.* The common law position on shareholder's liability for improper dividends was summed up by Judge Learned Hand in Wood v. National City Bank, 24 F.2d 661 (2d Cir.1928). The receiver of the Stanton Oil Company brought suit to recover dividends from Stanton's shareholders. The court said it was impossible to determine whether the plaintiff alleged the dividends were improper because they impaired capital or because the corporation was insolvent in the bankruptcy sense, but the complaint was at least susceptible of the latter interpretation. The court continued:

> Such being a permissible construction of the complaint, the question of its sufficiency depends upon the law of stockholders' liability. We have not to do with the liability commonly imposed by statute, because, whatever that may be in Delaware, the plaintiff does not invoke it here. He depends upon the fact that the directors have paid, and the defendants received, dividends when the corporation was insolvent. Merely because [a dividend] impairs the capital stock, it is commonly regarded as a wrong to creditors on the directors' part, and it is often made such by statute. We may, without discussion, assume that it would be a wrong in the case at bar. Even so, it is primarily only the wrong of those who commit it, like any other tort, and innocent participants are not accomplices to its commission. Hence it has been settled, at least for us, that, when the liability is based merely on the depletion of the capital, a stockholder must be charged with notice of that fact. McDonald v. Williams, 174 U.S. 397, 19 S.Ct. 743, 43 L.Ed. 1022. . . .

> However, there is quite another theory, and quite another liability, if the payments not only impair the capital, but are taken out of assets already too small to pay the existing debts. The situation then strictly is not peculiar to corporation law, but merely an instance of a payment from an insolvent estate. Since, as we have said, a stockholder is a donee, he receives such payments charged with whatever trust they were subject to in the hands of the corporation. In that situation it can indeed be said with some truth that the corporate assets have become a "trust fund." Wabash etc. Ry. v. Ham, 114 U.S. 587, 594, 5 S.Ct. 1081, 29 L.Ed. 235. Hence it has never been doubted, so far as we can find, at least in any federal court, that if the dividends are paid in fraud of creditors the stockholder is so liable. . . .

2. *Statutory Rules.* Overlaying the common law rules governing the liability of shareholders for improper distributions are modern statutory rules that specifically govern such liability.

a. *Corporate statutes.* The corporate statutes frequently contain provisions under which a shareholder may be obliged to disgorge an improper dividend. Some statutes make shareholders directly liable to the corporation. For example, Cal.Corp.Code § 506(a) provides that a shareholder who receives a distribution prohibited by the statute, with knowledge of facts indicating the impropriety, is liable to the corporation for the benefit of prior creditors or senior shareholders. The liability is "for the amount so received by such shareholder . . . but not exceeding the liabilities of the corporation owed to nonconsenting creditors at the time of the violation and the injury suffered by nonconsenting shareholders, as the case may be." More commonly, the statutes impose liability only on directors, but confer upon directors who have been held liable a right to contribution from shareholders who received a dividend with knowledge of facts indicating its impropriety, or with knowledge of the illegality, depending on the statute. See, e.g., N.Y.Bus.Corp.Law § 719(d); Rev.Model Bus. Corp.Act § 8.33(b).

b. *Uniform Fraudulent Transfer Act.* Uniform Fraudulent Transfer Act (UFTA) § 5 renders fraudulent a transfer without a reasonably equivalent exchange when the transferor was or thereby became insolvent. UFTA § 4 renders fraudulent a transfer without a reasonably equivalent exchange when the transferor was engaged or about to engage in a business or transaction for which its remaining assets were unreasonably small. Under UFTA § 7, a creditor can avoid a fraudulent transfer to the extent necessary to satisfy his claim, and may obtain an attachment or other provisional remedy against the asset transferred or other property of the transferee.

c. *Bankruptcy law.* Three provisions of the Bankruptcy Code are applicable to the liability of shareholders for improper distributions:

(i) 11 U.S.C.A. § 544(b) provides that a trustee in bankruptcy can avoid any transfer by the bankrupt that is "voidable under applicable law by a creditor holding an unsecured claim" that is allowable under the Bankruptcy Code. This allows the trustee to recover an improper distribution from the shareholders if a creditor could have avoided the distribution under either the UFTA, a local statutory counterpart of the UFTA, or the common law.

(ii) 11 U.S.C.A. § 548 in effect adopts counterparts of UFTA §§ 4 and 5, supra, as part of the bankruptcy statute itself. Accordingly, the trustee can normally bring suit under § 548 whenever counterparts of the standards set forth in UFTA §§ 4 and 5 are violated, even if the UFTA or a cognate statute has not been adopted in the relevant state. Under the Supremacy Clause, the provisions of 11 U.S.C.A. § 548 cannot be overridden by state corporation law.

(iii) 11 U.S.C.A. § 541(a) vests the bankruptcy estate with all of the debtor's causes of action. Therefore, if the corporation could have sued the shareholder under state law for return of an improper dividend, the trustee can bring suit under § 541(a).

SECTION 8. REPURCHASE BY A CORPORATION OF ITS OWN STOCK

A repurchase by a corporation of its own stock may implicate a variety of legal rules. Some of the relevant legal rules are financial. These rules are the subject of Subsection (a). Other rules are designed to deal with problems like unfairness and manipulation. Some of those rules will be briefly considered in Subsection (b).

(a) FINANCIAL LIMITATIONS ON STOCK REPURCHASES

N.Y. BUS. CORP. LAW §§ 513, 515

[See Statutory Supplement]

DEL. GEN. CORP. LAW § 160(a)

[See Statutory Supplement]

MODEL BUS. CORP. ACT §§ 1.40(6), 6.40

[See Statutory Supplement]

CAL. CORP. CODE § 510(a)

[See Statutory Supplement]

NOTE ON FINANCIAL LIMITATIONS ON A REPURCHASE BY A CORPORATION OF ITS OWN STOCK

1. *General Rule.* When a corporation purchases shares of its own stock, corporate assets flow out to shareholders. Accordingly, from the perspective of creditors a repurchase of stock is economically indistinguishable from a dividend. Ideally, therefore, the financial limitations on repurchases should generally be the same as those for dividends. Thus the California statute and the Model Act treat repurchases and dividends together under the heading, "distributions." Most other statutes provide that, with specified exceptions, a corporation can expend funds to purchase its own stock only if it could pay a dividend in the same amount.

2. *Exceptions.* Despite the general parity in the treatment of dividends and repurchases, most of the traditional statutes permit a corporation to purchase its own stock out of capital for certain specified purposes. The most common such purposes are (i) eliminating fractional shares, (ii) collecting or compromising a shareholder's indebtedness to the corporation, (iii) paying dissenting shareholders for their shares pursuant to the exercise of appraisal rights, and (iv) redeeming or purchasing redeemable stock. See, e.g., Del.Gen.Corp. Law § 160(a)(1); N.Y.Bus.Corp.Law § 513(b), (c). The last of these exceptions, which is probably the most important, is usually supported on the grounds that redeemable stock is temporary by the

terms of its creation, so that senior interests will not rely on the cushion provided by the capital such shares have contributed; that the exception facilitates refunding of higher-dividend-rate preferred with lower-dividend-rate preferred (redeemable stock is almost invariably preferred); and that abuse is unlikely because the board, which must make a decision to redeem, normally represents the interests of common, not preferred.

3. *Installment Payments*. Dividends are normally made payable shortly after being declared. In contrast, payment for repurchased stock is sometimes made in installments over a period of years. This raises the issue whether the permissibility of a repurchase under an installment contract should be determined: (i) at the time the original contract is made, based on the effect of paying the full amount of the contract price; (ii) at the time each installment is scheduled to be paid, based on the effect of paying the installment at that time; or (iii) both. "Most courts have held that [in the case of an installment contract to repurchase stock] the corporation must pass the equitable insolvency test, initially at the time of contract, with respect to the entire purchase price, and subsequently, at the time of each payment, with respect to the amount of the installment.... While there is less consensus on the proper application of the surplus test, currently the favored view is that the surplus limitation is applied only once, when the contract is entered into, with respect to the entire purchase price." Barbara Black, Corporate Dividends and Share Repurchases § 6:19 (2003).

MODEL BUS. CORP. ACT § 6.40(e)

[See Statutory Supplement]

CAL. CORP. CODE § 166

[See Statutory Supplement]

NOTE ON LIABILITY FOR REPURCHASES IN VIOLATION OF STATUTORY FINANCIAL PROVISIONS

In general, liability for payments made by a corporation to purchase its own stock in violation of statutory financial provisions is governed by the rules that apply to liability for improper dividends. In re Burnet–Clark, Ltd., 56 F.2d 744 (2d Cir.1932); Precision Extrusions, Inc. v. Stewart, 36 Ill.App.2d 30, 183 N.E.2d 547 (1962). As regards shareholder liability, however, there are several potential differences between the two situations. In In re Kettle Fried Chicken of America, Inc., 513 F.2d 807 (6th Cir.1975), a repurchase had violated Del. § 160 because the corporation's capital was impaired when the stock was repurchased. The trustee in bankruptcy sued several shareholders to recover amounts the corporation had paid for their stock. The referee found that "defendants were not aware of the pall of illegality surrounding this transaction." Defendants argued that shareholders who have resold their stock to a solvent corporation without knowledge that capital was impaired should not be liable for amounts received, relying by analogy on a line of dividend cases. The court rejected this argument, on the ground that "the purchase of its own stock by a corporation is not its usual or ordinary course of business and in no sense is comparable to the declaration of a corporate dividend." See also Kleinberg v. Schwartz, 87 N.J.Super. 216, 208 A.2d 803 (1965), aff'd on opinion below 46 N.J. 2, 214 A.2d 313. But see Palmer v. Justice, 322 F.Supp. 892 (N.D.Tex.1971), aff'd on other grounds 451 F.2d 371 (5th Cir.).

Another distinction between shareholder liability based on (i) the receipt of improper dividends and (ii) improper payments for stock, is that a shareholder who receives a dividend knows it has been paid by the corporation, while a shareholder who sells his stock may not know the corporation is the buyer, if the corporation acted through an agent or purchased the stock on an open market. See Kleinberg v. Schwartz, supra.

(b) NONFINANCIAL RULES CONCERNING STOCK REPURCHASES

SECURITIES EXCHANGE ACT § 9(a)(2) AND RULES 10b–5, 10b–6, AND 10b–18

[See Statutory Supplement]

NOTE ON NONFINANCIAL LIMITATIONS ON STOCK REPURCHASES

1. *Differences Between Dividends and Repurchases.* Although a repurchase by a corporation of its own stock can and normally should be treated like a dividend for purposes of financial limitations on distributions under corporate law, there are several important economic differences between a dividend and a repurchase. Among the most important are as follows: (i) A dividend is pro rata, while a repurchase may not be. Accordingly, in the case of a dividend all shareholders are treated equally, while in the case of a repurchase, they may not be. (ii) In the case of a dividend, the shareholder gives up nothing. In the case of a non-pro-rata repurchase, the shareholder gives up part of all of his relative share in the corporation's equity. (iii) A dividend usually involves a relatively small fraction of a corporation's assets. A repurchase may involve a very significant fraction of a

corporation's assets, particularly in a close corporation, and often even in a publicly held corporation.

2. *Modes of Repurchases*. Repurchases by a corporation of its own stock may be made through tender offers (*self-tenders*), through purchases on the market (*open-market purchases*), or through negotiated purchases from one or more individual shareholders *(targeted or selective repurchases)*. Self-tenders are usually made for a short period at a fixed price that is open to all shareholders. Open-market purchases may be made over a long period of time at the prices prevailing when each purchase is made. Like self-tenders, open-market repurchases are effectively open to all shareholders, because any shareholder can sell into the market. Negotiated purchases from individual shareholders are by definition not open to all shareholders, and are therefore subject to various kinds of abuse—in particular, paying a price to the selling shareholder that is higher than the price available to other shareholders, or providing liquidity to the selling shareholder that is unavailable to other shareholders.

3. *Nonfinancial Rules*. The differences between dividends and repurchases, and the resulting possibilities for unfairness and manipulation that may result from the different modes of effecting repurchases, have led to a variety of nonfinancial rules governing repurchases. Some of the relevant issues and rules will be briefly considered in the remainder of this Note.

4. *Discrimination Among Shareholders in a Close Corporation*. Especially in close corporations, a selective repurchase of a corporation's own stock can be used as an instrument to discriminate among shareholders, by getting cash into the hands of one shareholder or one fraction without distributing cash to other shareholders or factions. This issue is considered in Chapter 6 (Close Corporations), supra.

5. *Selective Repurchases and Greenmail in Publicly Held Corporations*. A corporation may repurchase its own stock to get rid of, or buy off, a shareholder who is at odds with the corporation or, more usually, with the corporation's management. Typically in such cases the corporation pays the shareholder a price higher than the market price of the stock. Selective repurchases for this purpose have been permitted by the courts within broad limits, unless it is shown that the repurchase was for entrenchment purposes. See, e.g., Cheff v. Mathes, 41 Del.Ch. 494, 199 A.2d 548 (Sup.Ct.1964); Bennett v. Propp, 41 Del.Ch. 14, 187 A.2d 405 (Sup.Ct.1962); Kahn v. Roberts, 679 A.2d 460 (Del.1996).

Where, in the case of a selective repurchase, the very purpose of the shareholder's original acquisition of the stock was to induce the corporation to buy him out at a profit so as to get rid of him as a shareholder, the transaction is known as *greenmail*. Often, if not usually, greenmail is a means by which managers improperly use corporate assets—the funds used to buy off the greenmailer—to preserve themselves in office. See Heckmann v. Ahmanson, 168 Cal. App.3d 119, 214 Cal.Rptr. 177 (1985) (greenmailer may be forced to disgorge profits). But see Kamerman v. Steinberg, 891 F.2d 424 (2d

Cir.1989). Several states have statutes that regulate greenmail. For example, N.Y.B.C.L. § 513(c) provides that a corporation may not make a targeted repurchase of more than 10% of its stock for a price above market value, unless the stock has been held for more than two years or the transaction is approved by both the board and a majority of the outstanding shares.

The prospect of greenmail has also been diminished by the tax laws. Internal Revenue Code § 5881 imposes a penalty, in the form of a 50% excise tax, on the profit realized by a greenmailer from the receipt of greenmail. Because the greenmailer's profit is taxable, while the excise tax is not deductible, if the greenmailer is a corporation in the 34% bracket the effect of § 5881 is to impose an 84% effective tax rate on the profits from greenmail. Moreover, neither the amount of the payment to the greenmailer nor the expenses connected to that payment are deductible by the corporation.

A payment must meet three conditions to be considered greenmail under section 5881(b). First, the bidder must have held the target's stock for less than two years before entering into the agreement to sell the stock to the corporation. IRC § 5881(b)(1). Second, during the two-year period the bidder (or a related party or a person acting in concert with the bidder) must have "made or threatened to make a public tender offer for stock of such corporation." IRC § 5881(b)(2). Third, the repurchase by the corporation must be pursuant to an offer containing terms not made available to all shareholders. IRC § 5881(b)(3). If the repurchase does not meet these requirements, the bidder will not be subject to the excise tax. This can be accomplished, for example, by not making or threatening a tender offer or, perhaps, by making only an implicit threat.

6. *Self-Tenders.* A publicly held corporation may offer to repurchase a significant portion of its shares through a self-tender for its own stock. Such self-tenders are governed by the Williams Act and the rules thereunder. See Chapter 12, supra.

7. *Going Private.* A publicly held corporation may repurchase the shares held by its public shareholders (as opposed to the shares held by its managers or controlling shareholders) for the purpose of eliminating public ownership. Such a *going-private* transaction may be engaged in to increase corporate efficiency, to shift wealth from unknowledgeable outsiders to knowledgeable insiders, or both. Going-private transactions are considered in Chapter 12, supra.

8. *Section 9(a)(2) and Rule 10b–18.* Repurchases by a corporation of its own stock frequently have the side effect, or the intended effect, of maintaining or increasing the market price of the stock. A repurchase for manipulative purposes is subject to the general anti-manipulative provisions of the securities acts, particularly § 9(a)(2) of the Securities Exchange Act and Rule 10b–5 under that Act. However, Rule 10b–18 under the Securities Exchange Act provides a safe harbor against violation of those provisions. Under Rule 10b–18, a corporation will not be deemed to have violated § 9(a)(2) or Rule 10b–5 solely by reason of the manner, timing, price, and volume of its

repurchases if it repurchases its common stock in the market in accordance with conditions concerning manner, timing, price, and volume that are set out in that section. A repurchase that does not qualify for the safe-harbor protection of Rule 10b–18 is not by reason of that fact deemed to have violated § 9(a)(2) or Rule 10(b)(5).

SECTION 9. LIABILITY FOR WATERED STOCK, AND RELATED ISSUES

NOTE ON WATERED STOCK AND RELATED ISSUES

1. *Liability for Watered Stock.* In early days, when stock typically had high par value, shares were often issued at less than par. Sometimes shares could not be issued at par because the real value of the shares was less than their par value. Sometimes shares were issued in exchange for property that was supposed to be worth the aggregate par value of the shares, but was not, because the property was overvalued.

These and other reasons gave rise to a large and complicated body of law, which centered on "bonus," "discount" and "watered" stock. " 'Bonus' shares are shares issued without payment of any amount, perhaps as a 'bonus' for the purchase of another class of security.... 'Discount' shares are shares issued for an amount less than par; e.g., $10 par stock issued for a $7 cash payment.... 'Watered shares' . . . are shares issued for non-liquid property which is worth less than par although asserted to be worth at least par." T. Fiflis, Accounting Issues for Lawyers 366, note h (4th ed. 1991). The term *watered stock* is commonly used to describe bonus and discount stock as well. The term "is a pun derived from the practice of certain ranchers or traders who watered their livestock before weighing at sale points." Id. at 366.

A shareholder to whom watered stock had been issued would not be liable to make any further payment solely as a matter of contract, because he would have paid all that he agreed to pay. Under corporation law, however, a holder of watered stock was often subject to liability to the corporation, or more usually to its creditors, in the amount of the difference between the par value of the stock and either (i) the money price the shareholder paid, or (ii) the value of property the shareholder exchanged for the stock. This liability was grounded on various theories.

At first, the liability was grounded on the "trust fund" theory, associated with Wood v. Dummer, 30 Fed.Cas. 435, 436 (C.C.Me. 1824). This case involved a suit by creditors against shareholders to whom an allegedly improper dividend had been paid. In the following famous passage, Judge Story established the trust-fund theory of capital and dividends:

It appears to me very clear upon general principles ... that the capital stock of banks is to be deemed a pledge or trust fund for the payment of the debts contracted by the bank. The public, as well as the legislature, have always supposed this to be a fund appropriated for such purpose. The individual stockholders are not liable for the debts of the bank in their private capacities. The charter relieves them from personal responsibility, and substitutes the capital stock in its stead. Credit is universally given to this fund by the public, as the only means of repayment. During the existence of the corporation it is the sole property of the corporation, and can be applied only according to its charter, that is, as a fund for payment of its debts, upon the security of which it may discount and circulate notes. Why, otherwise, is any capital stock required by our charters? If the stock may, the next day after it is paid in, be withdrawn by the stockholders without payment of the debts of the corporation, why is its amount so studiously provided for, and its payment by the stockholders so diligently required? To me this point appears so plain upon principles of law, as well as common sense, that I cannot be brought into any doubt, that the charters of our banks make the capital stock a trust fund for the payment of all the debts of the corporation. The bill-holders and other creditors have the first claims upon it; and the stockholders have no rights, until all the other creditors are satisfied. They have the full benefit of all the profits made by the establishment, and cannot take any portion of the fund, until all the other claims on it are extinguished. Their rights are not to the capital stock, but to the residuum after all demands on it are paid.

In Hospes v. Northwestern Mfg. & Car Co., 48 Minn. 174, 50 N.W. 1117 (1892), the Minnesota court showed that the trust-fund theory for liability on watered stock didn't make sense, and was riddled with exceptions. *Hospes* substituted a new theory, known as the constructive-fraud, misrepresentation, or holding-out theory. The basis of the theory was that:

The capital of a corporation is the basis of its credit. It is a substitute for the individual liability of those who own its stock. People deal with it and give it credit on the faith of it. They have a right to assume that it has paid-in capital to the amount which it represents itself as having; and if they give it credit on the faith of that representation, and if the representation is false, it is a fraud upon them; and, in case the corporation becomes insolvent, the law, upon the plainest principles of common justice, says to the delinquent stockholder, "Make that representation good by paying for your stock."

The difference between the trust-fund and constructive-fraud theories was that "the trust fund theory purported to hold the shareholder liable in all events to make up this difference for the benefit of creditors, although certain exceptions were later made by the courts following this theory; whereas, the fraud theory made certain exceptions in cases where the particular creditor plaintiff could not have relied on the full amount of the par value of the stock having been paid in, for example, if his debt arose before the transaction in which the stock was issued." 2 H. Marsh & R. Finkle, Marsh's California Corporations Law § 16.04 (4th ed. 2000).

The constructive-fraud theory had two basic corollaries: (1) Suit could only be brought by creditors who had extended credit after the watered stock was issued. (2) Suit could only be brought by creditors who had relied on the corporation's capital. However, reliance was normally presumed, either conclusively or subject to rebuttal. See Bing Crosby Minute Maid Corp. v. Eaton, 46 Cal.2d 484, 297 P.2d 5 (1956).

After *Hospes,* the trust-fund theory was largely abandoned, usually in favor of the constructive-fraud theory. That theory, however, was also criticized, see Ballantine, Stockholders' Liability in Minnesota, 7 Minn.L.Rev. 79, at 89 (1923), and some courts adopted the "statutory liability" theory, under which liability for watered stock was rested on a provision of the relevant statute, such as a provision that shareholders shall be liable for the consideration for which the shares were authorized to be issued. Under this theory, the time at which the creditor had extended credit was irrelevant, as was the creditor's reliance.

Low-par stock made watered-stock liability unimportant, because such stock is almost invariably issued for cash or property worth at least the par value of the stock. In addition, people began to care less about the whole problem, because modern disclosure requirements and fiduciary obligations obviated the problems that gave rise to watered-stock liability. Nevertheless, shareholder liability based on the purchase of stock is not completely a dead letter. Many or most statutes still make provision for par value, and in such states watered-stock liability may arise where, as a result of bad planning or other factors, the corporation uses a high-par-value stock. See, e.g., Hanewald v. Bryan's Inc., 429 N.W.2d 414 (N.D.1988).

2. *Liability for Unpaid Subscriptions.* Wholly without regard to the concept of par value, a shareholder is liable for the unpaid balance of the amount he agreed to pay for his stock. This liability can often be enforced directly by creditors. See, e.g., Del.Gen.Corp.Law §§ 162, 325; Model Act § 6.20(d).

3. *Related Issues.* The law governing watered stock involved several issues that were related to, but separate from, the problem of liability for watered stock. One of these issues concerned the weight to be given to the board's valuation of the consideration for which stock was issued, where the consideration consisted of property or services rather than cash. This issue has been resolved by modern statutes, which makes the board's valuation conclusive in the absence of fraud or bad faith. A second issue involved the types of consideration for which stock could be issued when, as was commonly the case, the statutes restricted such consideration. A recurring question of this kind was whether stock could be issued for future services to be performed by the purchaser. Originally, the answer was no. See, e.g., Brown v. Watson, 285 App.Div. 587, 139 N.Y.S.2d 628 (1955); United Steel Industries, Inc. v. Manhart, 405 S.W.2d 231 (Tex.Civ.App.1966). However, most modern statutes now permit stock to be issued in exchange for a contract to perform services.

CHAPTER XIV

THE PUBLIC DISTRIBUTION OF SECURITIES

SECTION 1. INTRODUCTION

The law governing the public distribution of securities is extremely intricate. The purpose of this Chapter is to examine the structure of the Securities Act, and the most important concepts and rules in this area. Many details and qualifications are left to coverage in Securities Regulation courses.

(a) AN OVERVIEW OF THE SECURITIES MARKETS

ROSS, WESTERFIELD, & JORDAN, FUNDAMENTALS OF CORPORATE FINANCE

See Chapter 5, supra.

(b) AN OVERVIEW OF THE SECURITIES ACT

Securities and Exchange Commission, The Investor's Advocate: How the SEC Protects Investors and Maintains Market Integrity

(2005 rev.)

Often referred to as the "truth in securities" law, the Securities Act of 1933 has two basic objectives:

- require that investors receive financial and other significant information concerning securities being offered for public sale; and

- prohibit deceit, misrepresentations, and other fraud in the sale of securities. . . .

Purpose of Registration

A primary means of accomplishing these goals is the disclosure of important financial information through the registration of securities. This information enables investors, not the government, to make informed judgments about whether to purchase a company's securities. While the SEC requires that the information provided be accurate, it does not guarantee it. Investors who purchase securities and suffer losses have important recovery rights if they can prove that there was incomplete or inaccurate disclosure of important information.

The Registration Process

In general, securities sold in the U.S. must be registered. The registration forms companies file provide essential facts while minimizing the burden and expense of complying with the law. In general, registration forms call for:

- a description of the company's properties and business;
- a description of the security to be offered for sale;
- information about the management of the company; and
- financial statements certified by independent accountants.

All companies, both domestic and foreign, must file their registration statements electronically. These statements and the accompanying prospectuses become public shortly after filing, and investors can access them [electronically]. Registration statements are subject to examination for compliance with disclosure requirements.

Not all offerings of securities must be registered with the Commission. Some exemptions from the registration requirement include:

- private offerings to a limited number of persons or institutions;
- offerings of limited size;
- intrastate offerings; and
- securities of municipal, state, and federal governments.

By exempting many small offerings from the registration process, the SEC seeks to foster capital formation by lowering the cost of offering securities to the public.

SEC, Q & A: Small Business and The SEC

(2004 rev.)

How Does My Small Business Register a Public Offender?

If you decide on a registered public offering, the Securities Act requires your company to file a registration statement with the SEC before the company can offer its securities for sale. You cannot actually sell the securities covered by the registration statement until the SEC staff declares it "effective," even though registration statements become public immediately upon filing.

Registration statements have two principal parts:

- Part I is the prospectus, the legal offering or "selling" document. Your company—the "issuer" of the securities—must describe in the prospectus the important facts about its business operations, financial condition, and management. Everyone who buys the new issue, as well as anyone who is made an offer to purchase the securities, must have access to the prospectus.

- Part II contains additional information that the company does not have to deliver to investors. Anyone can see this information by requesting it from one of the SEC's public reference rooms or by looking it up on the SEC Web site.

The Basic Registration Form—Form S–1

All companies can use Form S–1 to register their securities offerings. You should not prepare a registration statement as a fill-in-the-blank form, like a tax return. It should be similar to a brochure, providing readable information. If you file this form, your company must describe each of the following in the prospectus:

- its business;
- its properties;
- its competition;
- the identity of its officers and directors and their compensation;
- material transactions between the company and its officers and directors;
- material legal proceedings involving the company or its officers and directors;
- the plan for distributing the securities; and the intended use of the proceeds of the offering.

Information about how to describe these items is set out in SEC rules. Registration statements also must include financial statements audited by an independent certified public accountant.

In addition to the information expressly required by the form, your company must also provide any other information that is necessary to make your disclosure complete and not misleading. You also must clearly describe any risks prominently in the prospectus, usually at the beginning. Examples of these risk factors are:

- lack of business operating history;
- adverse economic conditions in a particular industry;
- lack of a market for the securities offered; and
- dependence upon key personnel. . . .

Staff Review of Registration Statements

SEC staff examines registration statements for compliance with disclosure requirements. If a filing appears incomplete or inaccurate, the staff usually informs the company by letter. The company may file correcting or clarifying amendments. Once the company has satisfied the disclosure requirements, the staff declares the registration statement effective. The company may then begin to sell its securities. The SEC can refuse or suspend the effectiveness of any registration statement if it concludes that the document is misleading, inaccurate, or incomplete.

(c) AN OVERVIEW OF THE UNDERWRITING PROCESS

L. Loss & J. Seligman, Fundamentals of Securities Regulation 73–86

4th ed. 2004.

. . . DISTRIBUTION TECHNIQUES

The registration and prospectus provisions of the Securities Act of 1933 can be understood—and their effectiveness evaluated—only on the background of the techniques by which securities are distributed in the United States. [Among these are strict or "old-fashioned" underwriting, firm-commitment underwriting, and best-efforts underwriting.] . . . .

1.   Strict or "Old–Fashioned" Underwriting

Under the traditional English system of distribution—which is no longer common in that country—the issuer did not sell to an investment banking house for resale to the public, either directly or through a group of dealers. Instead a designated "issuing house" advertised the issue and received applications and subscriptions from the public on the issuer's behalf after an announced date. When sufficient applications had been received, an announcement was made that "the lists are closed," and the issuer proceeded to allot the securities directly to the applicants or subscribers, using various methods of proration in the event of an oversubscription. Securities firms normally subscribed to new issues not for their own accounts with a view to resale at a profit, but only as brokers for the accounts of their customers. Before the public offering was thus made, the issue was "underwritten" in order to ensure that the company would obtain the amount of funds it required.

This was underwriting in the strict insurance sense. For a fee or premium, the underwriter agreed to take up whatever portion of the issue was not purchased by the public within a specified time. . . .

This method of distribution is called in the United States "strict" or "old-fashioned" or "standby" underwriting. It is seldom if ever used here except in connection with offerings to existing stockholders by means of warrants or rights. . . .

2. Firm–Commitment Underwriting

For some time, the most prevalent type of underwriting has been the "firm-commitment" variety. It is not, technically, underwriting in the classic insurance sense. But its purpose and effect are much the same in that it assures the issuer of a specified amount of money at a certain time (subject frequently to specified conditions precedent in the underwriting contract) and shifts the risk of the market (at least in part) to the investment bankers. The issuer typically sells the entire issue outright to a group of securities firms, represented by one or several "managers" or "principal underwriters" or "representatives." They, in turn, sometimes sell at a differential to a "selling group" of dealers, [who] sell at another differential to the public. In a very limited sense the process is comparable to the merchandising of beans or automobiles or baby rattles. The issuer is the manufacturer of the securities; the members of the underwriting group are the wholesalers; and the members of the selling group are the retailers. But it is not quite so simple. In most firm-commitment underwritings, securities of particular issuers are distributed not continually but once in a long time, and then in a large batch. And the securities market is quite a different animal from the market for canned beans. . . .

. . . By the turn of the century, it was common in the case of large offerings for a single investment banker to do the "origination"—that is, carry on the preliminary negotiations with the issuer, make the investigations deemed necessary, and then purchase the issue from the issuer. The banker was chosen on the basis of his past relationships with the issuer and his past performance. The "origination" stage was followed by the process of "syndication": In order to spread the commitment, the originating banker would immediately sell the issue to a small "original purchase group." That group would in turn sell to a larger "banking group" . . . The originating banker would become a member of the purchase group; the members of that group would likewise become members of the banking group; and the originating banker would manage both groups. . . . [T]hese groups were not designed primarily to do the actual distributing; often the members of the groups were not organized for retailing purposes. The public sale would be effected, for the account of whichever group last bought the issue, by the manager (the originating banker) through an organization of employees and agents, which would sometimes include those members of the purchase and banking groups who were geared for retail distribution.

With the increase in the number and size of securities issues during the First World War, as well as the development of coast-to-coast telephone and wire systems, both groups tended to grow in membership and, in order to facilitate the actual mechanics of distribution, it became customary to add still another step to the elaborate process: Instead of the originating banker's selling through agents and employees, a much larger and more dispersed "selling group" or "selling syndicate" would take the issue from the banking group; those members of the earlier group or groups with distributive facilities would join this new group; and it, too, would be managed by the originating banker. . . .

The passage of the Securities Act of 1933 made for a simplification of this system. Under the statute only negotiations between the issuer and "underwriters" are permitted before the filing of the registration statement. Until then, the securities may not be offered to the public or even to dealers who are not "underwriters" within the statutory definition. And until the actual effective date of the registration statement, no sales or contracts may be made except with underwriters. This, in practice, means that there is usually a short period (a few hours at most) between the signing of the underwriting contract and the effective date of the registration statement during which whoever is committed to purchase at a fixed price cannot legally shift his or her liability against a possible market decline. To protect the underwriter until the closing (usually one week later) the "market out" clause in the underwriting contract was developed.

Although the use of this clause is by no means universal, it is not considered "cricket" to take advantage of it; it typically provides that the manager of the underwriting group (or the representatives of the group) may terminate the agreement if before the date of public offering (or before the date of the closing or settlement between underwriters and issuer) the issuer or any subsidiary sustains a material adverse change, trading in the securities is suspended, minimum or maximum prices or government restrictions on securities trading are put into effect, a general banking moratorium is declared, or, in the judgment of the managing underwriter (or, alternatively, the representatives of the underwriters or a majority in interests of the several underwriters), material changes in "general economic, political or financial conditions" or the effect of international conditions on financial markets in the United States makes it impracticable or inadvisable to market the securities at specified public offering price. This clause is much broader than the traditional *force majeure* provision. Another result of the Securities Act and the stock transfer taxes enforced until 1965 was a tendency to reduce the number of transfers between groups and to enlarge the number of "underwriters" who bear the initial risk. In effect, the originating banker and the purchase and banking groups have all been combined into a single "underwriting syndicate or group." . . .

3. Best–Efforts Underwriting

Companies that are not well established are not apt to find an underwriter that will give a firm commitment and assume the risk of distribution. Of necessity, therefore, they customarily distribute their securities through firms that merely undertake to use their best efforts. Paradoxically, this type of distribution is also preferred on occasion by companies that are so well established that they can do without any underwriting commitment, thus saving on the cost of distribution. The securities house, instead of buying the issue from the company and reselling it as principal, sells it for the company as agent; and its compensation takes the form of an agent's commission rather than a merchant's or dealer's profit. There may still be a selling group to help in the merchandising. But its members likewise do not buy from the issuer; they are subagents. This, of course, is not really underwriting; it is simply merchandising....

––––––

Coffee & Seligman, Securities Regulation—Cases and Materials 93–94

9th ed. 2004.

... A selling group member gets compensated in the form of a selling concession, which typically amounts to 50–60% of the gross spread between the public offering price and the net amount received by the issuer.

This "gross spread" is the difference between the price to the issuer and the public offering price. It represents the compensation which is distributed among the managing underwriter, members of the underwriting syndicate and the members of the selling group—the "underwriting discounts and commissions" shown on the cover page of the prospectus or offering circular. The issuer sells the securities to the underwriting syndicate at a discount from the public offering price. In an initial public offering, this discount has long been in the range of 7 to 7 ½%.... The discount is considerably less for seasoned equity offerings by already public corporations and even less for debt offerings. Simply to illustrate the allocation of this discount within the underwriting group, let us assume that the issue is to be sold to the public for $10, with $9 going to the issuer. On this basis, the compensation might be sliced up as follows. First, the lead underwriter will receive a management fee of 20 cents per share for finding and packaging the issue, and to compensate it for managing the offering and in "running the books." The next slice would be a fee of about 30 cents a share which is called the "gross underwriting fee." This fee provides compensation to the underwriting group for their expenses, such as underwriters' counsel, "tombstone" advertising and stabilizing expenses.... [and] compensation for the use of capital and for assuming the risk in the underwriting. The remaining 50 cents of the spread goes to the underwriting firm or the selling group member that actually sells the stock at retail.

––––––

SECTION 2. WHAT CONSTITUTES A "SECURITY"

––––––

SECURITIES ACT § 2(1)

[See Statutory Supplement]

––––––

McGinty, What is a Security?

1993 Wisc.L.Rev. 1033, 1037–39.

In drafting the definition of security, Congress faced two opposing problems. On the one hand, if it defined "security" to include only arrangements with the same names as instruments traded on securities exchanges (like "stock" and "bonds"), shady promoters could escape the securities laws simply by labeling their investment schemes with unusual names. On the other hand, if Congress defined "security" overbroadly (for example, to include "any . . . evidence of indebtedness"), the securities laws could apply to I.O.U.s given between friends or to notes given by parents to a private school for the duration of their child's enrollment. The former approach would exclude arrangements that should be included, thus frustrating Congress's purpose of protecting investors. The latter approach would include arrangements that should not be included, impose significant unnecessary transaction costs, burden the federal judiciary and federalize numerous issues better left to state law. Congress, for its part, drafted the definition of "security" broadly enough to sweep in devious investment schemes bearing innocuous titles. The courts, for their part, have attempted to construe "security" broadly enough to include such schemes, and yet narrowly enough to exclude arrangements whose names fortuitously suggest a security but whose economic realities do not. . . .

Some of the terms that Congress used to define security—such as "investment contract"—lack an established meaning outside judicial opinions and so create elasticity. Other more standard terms such as "stock" or "notes" have accepted meanings within the securities industry, but can also be used in circumstances where one would rationally think no security exists. Because the definitional paragraph begins with the proclamation, "The term 'security' means *any* note, stock . . ." and the other included instruments, the unqualified "any" suggests that all instruments bearing a name listed in the definitional paragraph should be covered, even a note given by one neighbor to another.

Some courts and commentators have argued that the context clause [that is, the introductory clause to Section 2, which provides that "unless the context otherwise requires" the terms in Section 2 have the meanings given in that Section] permits courts to exclude arrangements that possess the standard names but that are not really securities. Yet the statute nowhere defines or even suggests the scope of the context clause's qualification. Thus, construing the definitional section presents two unappetizing choices. If courts restrict the definitional section to the definitional paragraph alone, the logical result is over-inclusiveness and mindless literalism. If the definitional section includes the context clause, the statute is threatened with unbounded judicial discretion. . . .

———

NOTE ON THE MEANING OF "SECURITY"

As Professor McGinty points out, the definition of "security" in section 2(1) is extremely broad. In particular, the term "investment contract" has been viewed by the courts as a "catch-all" phrase designed to encompass novel devices that serve the same purposes as a security.

The first major case dealing with the scope of Section 2(1) was SEC v. C.M. Joiner Leasing Corp., 320 U.S. 344, 64 S.Ct. 120, 88 L.Ed. 88 (1943). In pursuance of a plan to finance the drilling of oil wells, lessees of large tracts engaged in a campaign to sell assignments of leaseholds, and represented to potential purchasers that test oil wells would be drilled. The promotional literature emphasized the potential return to the purchaser upon the drilling of a successful well. The Supreme Court held that the transactions involved securities within the meaning of Section 2(1), even though under Texas law the leaseholds conveyed interests in land:

> In the Securities Act the term "security" was defined to include by name or description many documents in which there is common trading for speculation or investment. Some, such as notes, bonds, and stocks, are pretty much standardized and the name alone carries well-settled meaning. Others are of more variable character and were necessarily designated by more descriptive terms, such as "transferable share," "investment contract," and "in general any interest or instrument commonly known as a security." We cannot read out of the statute these general descriptive designations merely because more specific ones have been used to reach some kinds of documents. Instruments may be included within any of these definitions, as a matter of law, if on their face they answer to the name or description. However, the reach of the Act does not stop with the obvious and commonplace. Novel, uncommon, or irregular devices, whatever they appear to be, are also reached if it be proved as matter of fact that they were widely offered or dealt in under terms or courses of dealing which established their character in commerce as "investment contracts," or as "any interest or instrument commonly known as a 'security.' "

320 U.S. at 351, 64 S.Ct. at 123.

Three years later, in SEC v. W.J. Howey Co., 328 U.S. 293, 66 S.Ct. 1100, 90 L.Ed. 1244 (1946), the Supreme Court clarified the *Joiner* holding. In *Howey,* a Florida corporation that owned a large citrus orchard offered land-sale contracts for small parcels of the orchard land, along with service contracts for harvesting and marketing the citrus fruit. The purchasers' tracts were jointly cultivated, and the corporation sold the fruit, distributing to the purchasers of the land-sale contracts a pro rata portion of the profits based on the acreage they owned. The purchasers had no legal right of entry on the land to market the crop, and had no right to specific fruit. Against this background, the Court established a definition of "investment contract" that has come to be generally accepted:

> [A]n investment contract for purposes of the Securities Act means a contract, transaction or scheme whereby a person invests his money in a common enterprise and is led to expect profits solely from the efforts of the promoter or a third party. . . .

Id. at 298–99, 66 S.Ct. at 1103, 90 L.Ed. at 1249.

The Court then held that the transactions in effect involved the offering of an opportunity to contribute money and share in the profits of a large citrus-fruit enterprise managed and partly owned by W.J. Howey Co. The land-sales contracts served as a convenient method of determining the investors' allocable shares of the profits, but the resulting transfers of rights in land were viewed by the Court as "purely incidental" to the profit-seeking business venture:

> . . . The investors provide the capital and share in the earnings and profits; the promoters manage, control and operate the enterprise. It follows that the arrangements whereby the investors' interests are made manifest involve investment contracts, regardless of the legal terminology in which such contracts are clothed. . . .

Id. at 300.

Subsequent cases have generally relied on the *Howey* characterization of an "investment contract." However, more recent decisions added important refinements to the *Howey* test.

SEC v. Glenn W. Turner Enterprises, Inc., 474 F.2d 476 (9th Cir.1973), cert. denied 414 U.S. 821, 94 S.Ct. 117, 38 L.Ed.2d 53, concerned a pyramid selling scheme. The scheme involved the sale of self-improvement contracts by Dare to be Great, Inc., which offered buyers the opportunity of earning commissions on the sale of such contracts to others. The defendants' main contention was that the buyers of the self-improvement contracts did not expect profits "*solely* from the efforts of others," within the meaning of *Howey*, but instead were required to exert some efforts of their own to realize a return on their initial cash outlay.

The court concluded that literal adherence to the *Howey* test could allow circumvention of the Act, by a requirement that the buyer contribute a modicum of effort. Accordingly, the court looked to a realistic test, focusing on "whether the efforts made by those other than the investor are the undeniably significant ones, those essential managerial efforts which affect the failure or success of the enterprise." Because the buyers in *Glenn W. Turner* were in essence obtaining shares in the proceeds of the selling efforts of Dare, and the success of the enterprise was dependent upon the "essential managerial efforts" of Dare, the court found that the *Howey* test had been satisfied:

> For purposes of the present case, the sticking point in the *Howey* definition is the word "solely", a qualification which of course exactly fitted the circumstances in *Howey*. All the other

elements of the *Howey* test have been met here. There is an investment of money, a common enterprise,[1] and the expectation of profits to come from the efforts of others....

We hold, however, that in light of the remedial nature of the legislation, the statutory policy of affording broad protection to the public, and the Supreme Court's admonitions that the definition of securities should be a flexible one, the word "solely" should not be read as a strict or literal limitation on the definition of an investment contract, but rather must be construed realistically, so as to include within the definition those schemes which involve in substance, if not form, securities.

Id. at 481–82.

Turner also expanded on the meaning of the *Howey* requirement of a "common enterprise." *Turner* itself focused on the commonality of enterprise between the investors and the promoter. See also *SEC v. Koscot Interplanetary, Inc.*, 497 F.2d 473 (5th Cir.1974). This kind of commonality is sometimes known as *vertical commonality*. Vertical commonality has been interpreted in two different ways. Under one approach, known as *broad vertical commonality*, the common enterprise test is satisfied if the promoter's *efforts* are the dominant factor in the success of the investments. *Turner* essentially followed this approach. Under a second approach, sometimes known as *strict vertical commonality*, the fortunes of investors must be tied not only to the efforts of the promoter, but to the *fortunes* of the promoter. See, e.g., Revak v. SEC Realty Corp., 18 F.3d 81 (2d Cir.1994). Furthermore, some courts held that the common-enterprise test will be satisfied only if there is a pooling of investment funds accompanied by pro rata interests in profits among the investors. See Wals v. Fox Hills Development Corp., 24 F.3d 1016 (7th Cir. 1994).

Two subsequent Supreme Court cases, International Brotherhood of Teamsters v. Daniel and Marine Bank v. Weaver, indicate some outer limits of the definition of a security.

In International Brotherhood of Teamsters v. Daniel, 439 U.S. 551, 99 S.Ct. 790, 58 L.Ed.2d 808 (1979), the Court held that an employee's interest in a noncontributory compulsory pension plan did not constitute a security. The Teamsters' pension plan required twenty years of continuous service in order to be eligible for pension benefits, and a member of the Teamsters had been denied pension benefits because of a seven-month hiatus in his work record. The employee sued the Teamsters, his union local, and a trustee of the fund, alleging violations of § 10(b) and Rule 10b–5 of the 1934 Act and § 17(a) of the 1933 Act.

The Court began its analysis by examining the statutory language of the two Securities Act and the Securities Exchange Act, noting that neither Act's definition of "security" referred to pension plans of any

1. A common enterprise is one in which the fortunes of the investor are interwoven with and dependent upon the efforts and success of those seeking the investment or of third parties.

type. The Court then turned to the claim that an employee's interest in a plan was an "investment contract." The Court reiterated the *Howey* definition of an investment contract, and proceeded to analyze the Teamster pension plan at issue to determine whether it involved an "investment of money" and an "expectation of profit from a common enterprise." The Court first held that the investment test was not satisfied. Under the pension plan, the employees made no contributions themselves. The Court stated that any "investment" made in the plan by an employee through permitting part of his compensation to take the form of a deferred pension benefit was "a relatively insignificant part of an employee's total and indivisible compensation package." The Court said that since an employee surrenders his labor "as a whole," it was "only in the most abstract sense" that an employee exchanged part of his labor in return for the possible benefits. The Court concluded, "Looking at the economic realities, it seems clear that an employee is selling his labor to obtain a livelihood, not making an investment" for the future.

Turning to the second element of the *Howey* definition, the Court found that the plan involved no expectation of profits from a common enterprise. Although the pension fund depended to some extent on earnings from its assets, which in turn depended upon the efforts of the pension fund's managers, the Court said that a far larger portion of a pension fund's income came from employer contributions, an income source that did not depend on the skill or efforts of the fund's managers.

In Marine Bank v. Weaver, 455 U.S. 551, 102 S.Ct. 1220, 71 L.Ed.2d 409 (1982), the Court held that a bank certificate of deposit was not a "security" under section 3(a)(10) of the 1934 Act, because extensive banking regulation, together with federal insurance, virtually eliminated any risk to the holder of such a certificate:

> ... It is unnecessary to subject issuers of bank certificates of deposit to liability under the antifraud provisions of the federal securities laws since the holders of bank certificates of deposit are abundantly protected under the federal banking laws....

The *Howey* test applies only to the residual category of "investment contracts," not to garden-variety securities, like stock. However, even interests that carry the *name* of a garden-variety security may not constitute a security for purposes of the 1933 Act. Just as *Howey* and *Turner* gave a functional meaning to the exotic term *investment contract*, several important cases have given a functional meaning to garden-variety terms like *stock*. For example, United Housing Foundation, Inc. v. Forman, 421 U.S. 837, 95 S.Ct. 2051, 44 L.Ed.2d 621 (1975), involved the purchase, by tenants, of shares of stock in Co-op City, a nonprofit cooperative housing corporation, in order to obtain the right to lease apartments in Co-op City. Each tenant was required to buy shares of stock in the cooperative to get that right, and to offer his stock back to the cooperative at the initial selling price upon termination of his occupancy. Accordingly, the stock was tied inextricably to the apartment, and no profit could be realized upon resale of the stock. The Supreme Court noted that the basic principle that had guided all of the Court's decisions concerning the scope of the definition of "security" was that " 'form should be disregarded for substance and the emphasis should be on economic reality,' " Although the shares in Co-op City were called "stock," the shares did not have any of the characteristics "that in our commercial world fall within the ordinary concept of a security," especially in that the shares lacked "the most common feature of stock: the right to receive 'dividends contingent upon an apportionment of profits.' " The Court held that such shares of stock therefore were not securities within the meaning of the 1933 Act, but in effect only a recoverable deposit.

NOTE ON LANDRETH TIMBER CO. v. LANDRETH

In Landreth Timber Co. v. Landreth, 471 U.S. 681, 105 S.Ct. 2297, 85 L.Ed.2d 692 (1985), the plaintiffs had purchased all the outstanding stock of Landreth Timber from members of the Landreth family, who had offered the stock for sale through local and out-of-state brokers. Subsequently, the plaintiffs brought suit against the sellers on the grounds that the sellers had violated the Securities Act by widely offering the stock, and then selling it, without registration; and had violated the Securities Exchange Act by making misrepresentations and failing to state material facts. The Ninth Circuit interpreted *Howey* to require the courts to determine in every case whether economic realities indicated that the Acts applied. Within that framework, the Ninth Circuit followed a doctrine, developed by some courts, that the federal securities laws did not apply to a sale of all of a corporation's stock, because the economic realities were that such a transaction involved the sale of a business, not the sale of "securities" within the meaning of the Acts. The Supreme Court reversed:

> As we ... recognized in *Forman,* the fact that instruments bear the label "stock" is not of itself sufficient to invoke the coverage of the Acts. Rather, we concluded that we must also determine whether those instruments possess "some of the significant characteristics typically associated with" stock, *id.,* at 851, 95 S.Ct., at 2060, recognizing that when an instrument is both called "stock" and bears stock's usual characteristics, "a purchaser justifiably [may] assume that the federal securities laws apply," *id.,* at 850, 95 S.Ct., at 2059. We identified those characteristics usually associated with common stock as (i) the right to receive dividends contingent upon an apportionment of profits; (ii) negotiability; (iii) the ability to be pledged or hypothecated; (iv) the conferring of voting rights in proportion to the number of shares owned; and (v) the capacity to appreciate in value.[2] *Id.,* at 851, 95 S.Ct., at 2060.

---

2. Although we did not so specify in *Forman,* we wish to make clear here that these characteristics are those usually associated with common stock, the kind of stock often at issue in cases involving the sale of a business. Various types of preferred stock may have different characteristics and still be covered by the Acts.

Under the facts of *Forman,* we concluded that the instruments at issue there were not "securities" within the meaning of the Acts. That case involved the sale of shares of stock entitling the purchaser to lease an apartment in a housing cooperative. The stock bore none of the characteristics listed above that are usually associated with traditional stock. Moreover, we concluded that under the circumstances, there was no likelihood that the purchasers had been misled by use of the word "stock" into thinking that the federal securities laws governed their purchases. The purchasers had intended to acquire low-cost subsidized living space for their personal use; no one was likely to have believed that he was purchasing investment securities. *Ibid.*

In contrast, it is undisputed that the stock involved here possesses all of the characteristics we identified in *Forman* as traditionally associated with common stock. Indeed, the District Court so found. App. to Pet. for Cert. 13a. Moreover, unlike in *Forman,* the context of the transaction involved here—the sale of stock in a corporation—is typical of the kind of context to which the Acts normally apply. It is thus much more likely here than in *Forman* that an investor would believe he was covered by the federal securities laws. Under the circumstances of this case, the plain meaning of the statutory definition mandates that the stock be treated as "securities" subject to the coverage of the Acts.

Reading the securities laws to apply to the sale of stock at issue here comports with Congress' remedial purpose in enacting the legislation to protect investors by "compelling full and fair disclosure relative to the issuance of 'the many types of instruments that in our commercial world fall within the ordinary concept of a security.'" *SEC v. W.J. Howey Co.,* 328 U.S., at 299, 66 S.Ct., at 1103 (quoting H.R.Rep. No. 85, 73d Cong., 1st Sess., 11 (1933)). Although we recognize that Congress did not intend to provide a comprehensive federal remedy for all fraud, *Marine Bank v. Weaver,* 455 U.S. 551, 556, 102 S.Ct. 1220, 1223, 71 L.Ed.2d 409 (1982), we think it would improperly narrow Congress' broad definition of "security" to hold that the traditional stock at issue here falls outside the Acts' coverage....

It is fair to say that our cases have not been entirely clear on the proper method of analysis for determining when an instrument is a "security." This Court has decided a number of cases in which it looked to the economic substance of the transaction, rather than just to its form, to determine whether the Acts applied....

Respondents contend that *Forman* and the cases on which it was based require us to reject the view that the shares of stock at issue here may be considered "securities" because of their name and characteristics. Instead, they argue that our cases require us in every instance to look to the economic substance of the transaction to determine whether the *Howey* test has been met. According to respondents, it is clear that petitioner sought not to earn profits from the efforts of others, but to buy a company that it could manage and control. Petitioner was not a passive investor of the kind Congress intended the Acts to protect, but an active entrepreneur, who sought to "use or consume" the business purchased just as the purchasers in *Forman* sought to use the apartments they acquired after purchasing shares of stock. Thus, respondents urge that the Acts do not apply.

We disagree with respondents' interpretation of our cases. First, it is important to understand the contexts within which these cases were decided. All of the cases on which respondents rely involved unusual instruments not easily characterized as "securities." Thus, if the Acts were to apply in those cases at all, it would have to have been because the economic reality underlying the transactions indicated that the instruments were actually of a type that falls within the usual concept of a security. In the case at bar, in contrast, the instrument involved is traditional stock, plainly within the statutory definition. There is no need here, as there was in the prior cases, to look beyond the characteristics of the instrument to determine whether the Acts apply.

. . . Respondents are correct that in *Forman* we eschewed a "literal" approach that would invoke the Acts' coverage simply because the instrument carried the label "stock." *Forman* does not, however, eliminate the Court's ability to hold that an instrument is covered when its characteristics bear out the label. See *supra,* at 2302–2303.

[W]e would note that the *Howey* economic reality test was designed to determine whether a particular instrument is an "investment contract," not whether it fits within *any* of the examples listed in the statutory definition of "security." . . .

––––––

REVES v. ERNST & YOUNG, 494 U.S. 56 (1990). This case presented the question whether demand notes issued by an agricultural Co–Op were "securities" within the meaning of § 3(a)(10) of the Securities Exchange Act of 1934. To raise money to support its general business operations, the Co–Op had sold promissory notes, payable on demand by the holder. The notes were uncollateralized and uninsured, and paid a variable rate of interest that was adjusted monthly to keep it higher than the rate paid by local financial institutions. The Co–Op offered the notes to its 23,000 members and also to nonmembers, and marketed the scheme as an "Investment Program." Advertisements for the notes, which appeared in each Co–Op newsletter, read in part: "YOUR CO–OP has more than $11,000,000 in assets to stand behind your investments. The Investment is not [Federally] insured but it is . . . Safe . . . Secure . . . and available when you need it."

Subsequently, the Co–Op filed for bankruptcy. Plaintiffs, a class of note holders, then sued Arthur Young & Co., the Co–Op's outside auditor, under the antifraud provisions of the Securities Exchange Act. The basis of the complaint was that Arthur Young had intentionally failed to apply generally accepted accounting principles in an effort inflate the value of Co–Op's assets and net worth, and that except for Arthur Young's actions, the plaintiffs would not have purchased the notes. Arthur Young argued that the plaintiffs could not bring suit under the Securities Exchange Act, because the notes were not securities within the meaning of the Act. The Supreme Court held that the notes did constitute securities:

> The fundamental purpose undergirding the Securities Acts is "to eliminate serious abuses in a largely unregulated securities market." United Housing Foundation, Inc. v. Forman, 421 U.S. 837, 849, 95 S.Ct. 2051, 2059, 44 L.Ed.2d 621 (1975)....

> Congress did not, however, "intend to provide a broad federal remedy for all fraud." Marine Bank v. Weaver, 455 U.S. 551, 556, 102 S.Ct. 1220, 1223, 71 L.Ed.2d 409 (1982).... Congress' purpose in enacting the securities laws was to regulate *investments,* in whatever form they are made and by whatever name they are called.

> A commitment to an examination of the economic realities of a transaction does not necessarily entail a case-by-case analysis of every instrument, however. Some instruments are obviously within the class Congress intended to regulate because they are by their nature investments. In Landreth Timber Co. v. Landreth, 471 U.S. 681, 105 S.Ct. 2297, 85 L.Ed.2d 692 (1985), we held that an instrument bearing the name "stock" that, among other things, is negotiable, offers the possibility of capital appreciation, and carries the right to dividends contingent on the profits of a business enterprise is plainly within the class of instruments Congress intended the securities laws to cover....

> We made clear in *Landreth Timber* that stock was a special case, explicitly limiting our holding to that sort of instrument. Id., at 694, 105 S.Ct., at 2304....

> Because the *Landreth Timber* formula cannot sensibly be applied to notes, some other principle must be developed to define the term "note." ...

> The [Second Circuit has adopted a] "family resemblance" approach [that] begins with a presumption that *any* note with a term of more than nine months is a "security." See, e.g., Exchange Nat'l Bank of Chicago v. Touche Ross & Co., 544 F.2d 1126, 1137 (C.A.2 1976). Recognizing that not all notes are securities, however, the Second Circuit has also devised a list of notes that it has decided are obviously not securities. Accordingly, the "family resemblance" test permits an issuer to rebut the presumption that a note is a security if it can show that the note in question "bear[s] a strong family resemblance" to an item on

the judicially crafted list of exceptions, id., at 1137–1138, or convinces the court to add a new instrument to the list. See, e.g., Chemical Bank v. Arthur Andersen & Co., 726 F.2d 930, 939 (C.A.2 1984) . . . .

[We adopt the "family resemblance" test.] The test begins with the language of the statute; because the Securities Acts define "security" to include "any note," we begin with a presumption that every note is a security. We nonetheless recognize that this presumption cannot be irrebuttable. As we have said . . . Congress was concerned with regulating the investment market, not with creating a general federal cause of action for fraud. In an attempt to give more content to that dividing line, the Second Circuit has identified a list of instruments commonly denominated "notes" that nonetheless fall without the "security" category. See *Exchange Nat. Bank*, supra, at 1138 (types of notes that are not "securities" include "the note delivered in consumer financing, the note secured by a mortgage on a home, the short-term note secured by a lien on a small business or some of its assets, the note evidencing a 'character' loan to a bank customer, short-term notes secured by an assignment of accounts receivable, or a note which simply formalizes an open-account debt incurred in the ordinary course of business. . . .

We agree that the items identified by the Second Circuit are not properly viewed as "securities." More guidance, though, is needed. It is impossible to make any meaningful inquiry into whether an instrument bears a "resemblance" to one of the instruments identified by the Second Circuit without specifying what it is about *those* instruments that makes *them* non-"securities." Moreover, as the Second Circuit itself has noted, its list is "not graven in stone," ibid., and is therefore capable of expansion. Thus, some standards must be developed for determining when an item should be added to the list.

An examination of the list itself makes clear what those standards should be. In creating its list, the Second Circuit was applying the same factors that this Court has held apply in deciding whether a transaction involves a "security." First, we examine the transaction to assess the motivations that would prompt a reasonable seller and buyer to enter into it. If the seller's purpose is to raise money for the general use of a business enterprise or to finance substantial investments and the buyer is interested primarily in the profit the note is expected to generate, the instrument is likely to be a "security." If the note is exchanged to facilitate the purchase and sale of a minor asset or consumer good, to correct for the seller's cash-flow difficulties, or to advance some other commercial or consumer purpose, on the other hand, the note is less sensibly described as a "security." See, e.g., Forman, 421 U.S., at 851, 95 S.Ct., at 2060 (share of "stock" carrying a right to subsidized housing not a security because "the inducement to purchase was solely to acquire subsidized low-cost living space; it was not to invest for profit"). Second, we examine the "plan of distribution" of the instrument, SEC v. C.M. Joiner Leasing Corp., 320 U.S. 344, 353, 64 S.Ct. 120, 124, 88 L.Ed. 88 (1943), to determine whether it is an instrument in which there is "common trading for speculation or investment," id., at 351, 64 S.Ct., at 123. Third, we examine the reasonable expectations of the investing public: The Court will consider instruments to be "securities" on the basis of such public expectations, even where an economic analysis of the circumstances of the particular transaction might suggest that the instruments are not "securities" as used in that transaction.... Finally, we examine whether some factor such as the existence of another regulatory scheme significantly reduces the risk of the instrument, thereby rendering application of the Securities Acts unnecessary. See, e.g., Marine Bank, 455 U.S., at 557–559, and n. 7, 102 S.Ct., at 1224–1225, and n. 7.

We conclude, then, that in determining whether an instrument denominated a "note" is a "security," courts are to apply the version of the "family resemblance" test that we have articulated here: a note is presumed to be a "security," and that presumption may be rebutted only by a showing that the note bears a strong resemblance (in terms of the four factors we have identified) to one of the enumerated categories of instrument. If an instrument is not sufficiently similar to an item on the list, the decision whether another category should be added is to be made by examining the same factors.

Applying this family resemblance test to Co–Op's notes, the Court had "little difficulty in concluding that the notes at issue were 'securities.'" The Co–Op sold the notes to raise capital for its business operations; the purchasers bought the notes to earn a profit in the form of interest; the notes were offered to more than 23,000 Co–Op members as well as to non-members; the notes were advertised as "investments"; and there was no risk-reducing factor, such as collateralization or insurance, to suggest that the notes were not securities.

Securities and Exchange Commission v. Edwards

United States Supreme Court, 2004.
540 U.S. 389, 124 S.Ct. 892.

■ JUSTICE O'CONNOR delivered the opinion of [a unanimous] Court.

"Opportunity doesn't always knock ... sometimes it rings." App. 113 (ETS Payphones promotional brochure). And sometimes it hangs up. So it did for the 10,000 people who invested a total of $300 million in the payphone sale-and-leaseback arrangements touted by respondent under that slogan. The Securities and Exchange Commission (SEC) argues that the arrangements were investment contracts, and thus were subject to regulation under the federal securities laws. In this case, we must decide whether a moneymaking scheme is excluded from the term "investment contract" simply because the scheme offered a contractual entitlement to a fixed, rather than a variable, return.

I

Respondent Charles Edwards was the chairman, chief executive officer, and sole shareholder of ETS Payphones, Inc. (ETS).* ETS, acting partly through a subsidiary also controlled by respondent, sold payphones to the public via independent distributors. The payphones were offered packaged with a site lease, a 5–year leaseback and management agreement, and a buyback agreement. All but a tiny fraction of purchasers chose this package, although other management options were offered. The purchase price for the payphone packages was approximately $7,000. Under the leaseback and management agreement, purchasers received $82 per month, a 14% annual return. Purchasers were not involved in the day-to-day operation of the payphones they owned. ETS selected the site for the phone, installed the equipment, arranged for connection and long-distance service, collected coin revenues, and maintained and repaired the phones. Under the buyback agreement, ETS promised to refund the full purchase price of the package at the end of the lease or within 180 days of a purchaser's request.

In its marketing materials and on its website, ETS trumpeted the "incomparable pay phone" as "an exciting business opportunity," in which recent deregulation had "open[ed] the door for profits for individual pay phone owners and operators." According to ETS, "[v]ery few business opportunities can offer the potential for ongoing revenue generation that is available in today's pay telephone industry." App. 114–115 (ETS brochure); *id.*, at 227 (ETS website); see *id.*, at 13 (Complaint §§ 37–38).

The payphones did not generate enough revenue for ETS to make the payments required by the leaseback agreements, so the company depended on funds from new investors to meet its obligations. In September 2000, ETS filed for bankruptcy protection. The SEC brought this civil enforcement action the same month. It alleged that respondent and ETS had violated the registration requirements of §§ 5(a) and (c) of the Securities Act of 1933, 68 Stat. 684, 15 U.S.C. §§ 77e(a), (c), the antifraud provisions of both § 17(a) of the Securities Act of 1933, 114 Stat. 2763A–452, 15 U.S.C. § 77q(a), and § 10(b) of the Securities Exchange Act of 1934, 48 Stat. 891, as amended 114 Stat. 2763A–454, 15 U.S.C. § 78j(b), and Rule 10b–5 thereunder, 17 CFR § 240.10b–5 (2003). The District Court concluded that the payphone sale-and-leaseback arrangement was an investment contract within the meaning of, and therefore was subject to, the federal securities laws. *SEC v. ETS Payphones, Inc.,* 123 F.Supp.2d 1349

---

* Because the Court of Appeals ordered the complaint dismissed, we treat the case as we would an appeal from a successful motion to dismiss and accept as true the allegations in the complaint. *SEC v. Zandford,* 535 U.S. 813, 818, 122 S.Ct. 1899, 153 L.Ed.2d 1 (2002); *Saudi Arabia v. Nelson,* 507 U.S. 349, 351, 354, 113 S.Ct. 1471, 123 L.Ed.2d 47 (1993).

(N.D.Ga.2000). The Court of Appeals reversed. 300 F.3d 1281 (C.A.11 2002) *(per curiam)*. It held that respondent's scheme was not an investment contract, on two grounds. First, it read this Court's opinions to require that an investment contract offer either capital appreciation or a participation in the earnings of the enterprise, and thus to exclude schemes, such as respondent's, offering a fixed rate of return. *Id.,* at 1284–1285. Second, it held that our opinions' requirement that the return on the investment be "derived solely from the efforts of others" was not satisfied when the purchasers had a contractual entitlement to the return. *Id.,* at 1285. We conclude that it erred on both grounds.

II

"Congress' purpose in enacting the securities laws was to regulate *investments,* in whatever form they are made and by whatever name they are called." *Reves v. Ernst & Young,* 494 U.S. 56, 61, 110 S.Ct. 945, 108 L.Ed.2d 47 (1990). To that end, it enacted a broad definition of "security," sufficient "to encompass virtually any instrument that might be sold as an investment." *Ibid.* Section 2(a)(1) of the 1933 Act, 15 U.S.C. § 77b(a)(1), and § 3(a)(10) of the 1934 Act, 15 U.S.C. § 78c(a)(10), in slightly different formulations which we have treated as essentially identical in meaning, *Reves, supra,* at 61, n. 1, 110 S.Ct. 945, define "security" to include "any note, stock, treasury stock, security future, bond, debenture, . . . investment contract, . . . [or any] instrument commonly known as a 'security'. "Investment contract" is not itself defined.

The test for whether a particular scheme is an investment contract was established in our decision in *SEC v. W.J. Howey Co.,* 328 U.S. 293, 66 S.Ct. 1100, 90 L.Ed. 1244 (1946). We look to "whether the scheme involves an investment of money in a common enterprise with profits to come solely from the efforts of others." *Id.,* at 301, 66 S.Ct. 1100. This definition "embodies a flexible rather than a static principle, one that is capable of adaptation to meet the countless and variable schemes devised by those who seek the use of the money of others on the promise of profits." *Id.,* at 299, 66 S.Ct. 1100.

In reaching that result, we first observed that when Congress included "investment contract" in the definition of security, it "was using a term the meaning of which had been crystallized" by the state courts' interpretation of their " 'blue sky' " laws. *Id.,* at 298, 66 S.Ct. 1100. (Those laws were the precursors to federal securities regulation and were so named, it seems, because they were "aimed at promoters who 'would sell building lots in the blue sky in fee simple.' " 1 L. Loss & J. Seligman, Securities Regulation 36, 31–43 (3d ed.1998) (quoting Mulvey, Blue Sky Law, 36 Can. L. Times 37 (1916)).) The state courts had defined an investment contract as "a contract or scheme for 'the placing of capital or laying out of money in a way intended to secure income or profit from its employment,' " and had "uniformly applied" that definition to "a variety of situations where individuals were led to invest money in a common enterprise with the expectation that they would earn a profit solely through the efforts of the promoter or [a third party]." *Howey, supra,* at 298, 66 S.Ct. 1100 (quoting *State v. Gopher Tire & Rubber Co.,* 146 Minn. 52, 56, 177 N.W. 937, 938 (1920)). Thus, when we held that "profits" must "come solely from the efforts of others," we were speaking of the profits that investors seek on their investment, not the profits of the scheme in which they invest. We used "profits" in the sense of income or return, to include, for example, dividends, other periodic payments, or the increased value of the investment.

There is no reason to distinguish between promises of fixed returns and promises of variable returns for purposes of the test, so understood. In both cases, the investing public is attracted by representations of investment income, as purchasers were in this case by ETS' invitation to " 'watch the profits add up.' " App. 13 (Complaint § 38). Moreover, investments pitched as low-risk (such as those offering a "guaranteed" fixed return) are particularly attractive to individuals more vulnerable to investment fraud, including older and less sophisticated investors. See S.Rep. No. 102–261, Vol. 2, App., p. 326 (1992) (Staff Summary of Federal Trade Commission Activities Affecting Older Consumers). Under the reading respondent advances, unscrupulous marketers of investments could evade the securities laws by picking a rate of return to promise. We will not read into the securities laws a limitation not compelled by the language that would so undermine the laws' purposes.

Respondent protests that including investment schemes promising a fixed return among investment contracts conflicts with our precedent. We disagree. No distinction between fixed and variable returns was drawn in the blue sky law cases that the *Howey* Court used, in formulating the test, as its evidence of Congress' understanding of the term. *Howey, supra,* at 298, and n. 4, 66 S.Ct. 1100. Indeed, two of those cases involved an investment contract in which a fixed return was promised. *People v. White,* 124 Cal.App. 548, 550–551, 12 P.2d 1078, 1079 (1932) (agreement between defendant and investors stated that investor would give defendant $5,000, and would receive $7,500 from defendant one year later); *Stevens v. Liberty Packing Corp.,* 111 N.J.Eq. 61, 62–63, 161 A. 193, 193–194 (1932) ("ironclad contract" offered by defendant to investors entitled investors to $56 per year for 10 years on initial investment of $175, ostensibly in sale-and-leaseback of breeding rabbits).

None of our post-*Howey* decisions is to the contrary. In *United Housing Foundation, Inc. v. Forman,* 421 U.S. 837, 95 S.Ct. 2051, 44 L.Ed.2d 621 (1975), we considered whether "shares" in a nonprofit housing cooperative were investment contracts under the securities laws. We identified the "touchstone" of an investment contract as "the presence of an investment in a common venture premised on a reasonable expectation of profits to be derived from the entrepreneurial or managerial efforts of others," and then laid out two examples of investor interests that we had previously found to be "profits." *Id.,* at 852, 95 S.Ct. 2051. Those were "capital appreciation resulting from the development of the initial investment" and "participation in earnings resulting from the use of investors' funds." *Ibid.* We contrasted those examples, in which "the investor is 'attracted solely by the prospects of a return' " on the investment, with housing cooperative shares, regarding which the purchaser "is motivated by a desire to use or consume the item purchased." *Id.,* at 852–853, 95 S.Ct. 2051 (quoting *Howey, supra,* at 300, 66 S.Ct. 1100). Thus, *Forman* supports the commonsense understanding of "profits" in the *Howey* test as simply "financial returns on . . . investments." 421 U.S., at 853, 95 S.Ct. 2051. . . .

Given that respondent's position is supported neither by the purposes of the securities laws nor by our precedents, it is no surprise that the SEC has consistently taken the opposite position, and maintained that a promise of a fixed return does not preclude a scheme from being an investment contract. It has done so in formal adjudications, *e.g., In re Abbett, Sommer & Co.,* 44 S.E.C. 104, 1969 WL 95359 (1969) (holding that mortgage notes, sold with a package of management services and a promise to repurchase the notes in the event of default, were investment contracts); see also *In re Union Home Loans* (Dec. 16, 1982), 26 S.E.C. Docket 1517 (report and order regarding settlement, stating that sale of promissory notes secured by deeds of trust, coupled with management services and providing investors "a specified percentage return on their investment," were investment contracts), and in enforcement actions, *e.g., SEC v. Universal Service Assn.,* 106 F.2d 232, 234, 237 (C.A.7 1939) (accepting SEC's position that an investment scheme promising "assured profit of 30% per annum with no chance of risk or loss to the contributor" was a security because it satisfied the pertinent substance of the *Howey* test, "[t]he investment of money with the expectation of profit through the efforts of other persons"); see also *SEC v. American Trailer Rentals Co.,* 379 U.S. 594, 598, 85 S.Ct. 513, 13 L.Ed.2d 510 (1965) (noting that "the SEC advised" the respondent that its "sale and lease-back arrangements," in which investors received "a set 2% of their investment per month for 10 years," "were investment contracts and therefore securities" under the 1933 Act).

The Eleventh Circuit's perfunctory alternative holding, that respondent's scheme falls outside the definition because purchasers had a contractual entitlement to a return, is incorrect and inconsistent with our precedent. We are considering investment *contracts.* The fact that investors have bargained for a return on their investment does not mean that the return is not also expected to come solely from the efforts of others. Any other conclusion would conflict with our holding that an investment contract was offered in *Howey* itself. 328 U.S., at 295–296, 66 S.Ct. 1100 (service contract entitled investors to allocation of net profits).

We hold that an investment scheme promising a fixed rate of return can be an "investment contract" and thus a "security" subject to the federal securities laws. The judgment of the United States Court of Appeals for the Eleventh Circuit is reversed, and the case is remanded for further proceedings consistent with this opinion.

It is so ordered.

SECTION 3.   WHAT CONSTITUTES A "SALE" AND AN "OFFER TO SELL"

––––––

SECURITIES ACT §§ 2(a)(3), 3(a)(9); SECURITIES ACT RULE 145

[See Statutory Supplement]

––––––

NOTE ON THE MEANING OF "SALE" AND "OFFER TO SELL"

The term "sale" or "sell" is defined in section 2(a)(3) of the Securities Act to include "every contract of sale or disposition of a security or interest in a security, for value." The term "offer to sell," "offer for sale," or "offer" is defined to include "every attempt or offer to dispose of, or solicitation of an offer to buy, a security or interest in a security, for value." The use of the word "includes" rather than "means" emphasizes the breadth of these definitions, and the courts have also interpreted the terms broadly "to include ingenious methods employed to obtain money from members of the public to finance ventures." S.E.C. v. Addison, 194 F.Supp. 709, 722 (N.D.Tex.1961).

Under Rubin v. United States, 449 U.S. 424, 101 S.Ct. 698, 66 L.Ed.2d 633 (1981), a pledge is an offer or a sale for purposes of the 1933 Act.

SECTION 4.   THE REQUIREMENT OF REGISTRATION

(a) THE BROAD SWEEP OF SECTION 5

––––––

SECURITIES ACT §§ 2(10), 5

[See Statutory Supplement]

––––––

NOTE ON SECTION 5

The structure of the Securities Act is exceptionally intricate. The key provision is section 5. Section 5(a) provides:

> Unless a registration statement is in effect as to a security, it shall be unlawful for any person, directly or indirectly—
>
> (1) to make use of any means or instruments of transportation or communication in interstate commerce or of the mails to sell such security through the use or medium of any prospectus or otherwise; or
>
> (2) to carry or cause to be carried through the mails or in interstate commerce, by any means or instruments of transportation, any such security for the purpose of sale or for delivery after sale.

Section 5(c) provides:

> It shall be unlawful for any person, directly or indirectly, to make use of any means or instruments of transportation or communication in interstate commerce or of the mails to offer to sell or offer to buy through the use or medium of any prospectus or otherwise any security, unless a registration statement has been filed as to such security. . . .

Section 2(10) defines a "prospectus" to mean "any prospectus, notice, circular, advertisement, letter, or communication, written or by radio or television, which offers any security for sale or confirms the sale of any security," subject to certain exceptions.

Putting section 2(10) together with section 5(a) and (c), if any person sells, or offers to sell or buy, a security by any means of transportation or communication in interstate commerce or by mail, or sends a security through the mail or in interstate commerce for purposes of sale or delivery after sale, the security must be registered, unless an exemption applies. Therefore, section 5 prohibits virtually every sale or offer to sell a security, no matter how trivial, and no matter who the seller, unless the security is registered under the Act or an exemption applies. Other provisions of the Act then carve out a variety of exemptions for large classes of securities and transactions. By virtue of the exemptions, these securities and transactions do not require registration, despite the sweeping language of section 5. The balance of this Section will consider exemptions based on (1) the number and character of the offerees, (2) the size of the offering, (3) the intrastate nature of an offering, and (4) the absence of an issuer, underwriter, or dealer.

(b) PRIVATE PLACEMENTS

———

SECURITIES ACT § 4(2)

[See Statutory Supplement]

———

S.E.C. v. Ralston Purina Co.

Supreme Court of the United States, 1953.
346 U.S. 119, 73 S.Ct. 981, 97 L.Ed. 1494.

■ MR. JUSTICE CLARK delivered the opinion of the Court.

Section 4(1) of the Securities Act of 1933 exempts "transactions by an issuer not involving any public offering"[1] from the registration requirements of § 5. We must decide whether Ralston Purina's offerings of treasury stock to its "key employees" are within this exemption. On a complaint brought by the Commission under § 20(b) of the Act seeking to enjoin respondent's unregistered offerings, the District Court held the exemption applicable and dismissed the suit. The Court of Appeals affirmed. The question has arisen many times since the Act was passed; an apparent need to define the scope of the private offering exemption prompted certiorari. 345 U.S. 903, 73 S.Ct. 643.

Ralston Purina manufactures and distributes various feed and cereal products. Its processing and distribution facilities are scattered throughout the United States and Canada, staffed by some 7,000 employees. At least since 1911 the company has had a policy of encouraging stock ownership among its employees; more particularly, since 1942 it has made authorized but unissued common shares available to some of them. Between 1947 and 1951, the period covered by the record in this case, Ralston Purina sold nearly $2,000,000 of stock to employees without registration and in so doing made use of the mails.

In each of these years, a corporate resolution authorized the sale of common stock "to employees ... who shall, without any solicitation by the Company or its officers or employees, inquire of any of them as to how to purchase common stock of Ralston Purina Company." A memorandum sent to branch and store managers after the resolution was adopted, advised that "The only employees to whom this stock will be available will be those who take the initiative and are interested in buying stock at present market prices." Among those responding to these offers were employees with the duties of artist, bakeshop foreman, chow loading foreman, clerical assistant, copywriter, electrician, stock clerk, mill office clerk, order credit trainee, production trainee, stenographer, and veterinarian. The buyers lived in over fifty widely separated communities scattered from Garland, Texas, to Nashua, New Hampshire and Visalia, California. The lowest salary bracket of those purchasing was $2,700 in 1949, $2,435 in 1950 and $3,107 in 1951. The record shows that in 1947, 243 employees bought stock, 20 in 1948, 414 in 1949, 411 in 1950, and the 1951 offer, interrupted by this litigation, produced 165 applications to purchase. No records were kept of those to whom the offers were made; the estimated number in 1951 was 500.

---

1. 48 Stat. 77, as amended, 48 Stat.   This is now § 4(2).]
906, 15 U.S.C. § 77d, 15 U.S.C.A. § 77d. [Ed.

The company bottoms its exemption claim on the classification of all offerees as "key employees" in its organization. Its position on trial was that "A key employee . . . is not confined to an organization chart. It would include an individual who is eligible for promotion, an individual who especially influences others or who advises others, a person whom the employees look to in some special way, an individual, of course, who carries some special responsibility, who is sympathetic to management and who is ambitious and who the management feels is likely to be promoted to a greater responsibility." That an offering to all of its employees would be public is conceded.

The Securities Act nowhere defines the scope of § 4(1)'s private offering exemption. Nor is the legislative history of much help in staking out its boundaries. The problem was first dealt with in § 4(1) of the House Bill, H.R. 5480, 73d Cong., 1st Sess., which exempted "transactions by an issuer not with or through an underwriter; . . ." The bill, as reported by the House Committee, added "and not involving any public offering." H.R.Rep. No. 85, 73d Cong., 1st Sess. 1. This was thought to be one of those transactions "where there is no practical need for [the bill's] application or where the public benefits are too remote." Id., at 5.[5] The exemption as thus delimited became law.[6] It assumed its present shape with the deletion of "not with or through an underwriter" by § 203(a) of the Securities Exchange Act of 1934, 48 Stat. 906, a change regarded as the elimination of superfluous language. H.R.Rep. No. 1838, 73d Cong., 2d Sess. 41.

Decisions under comparable exemptions in the English Companies Acts and state "blue sky" laws, the statutory antecedents of federal securities legislation, have made one thing clear—to be public, an offer need not be open to the whole world. In Securities and Exchange Comm'n v. Sunbeam Gold Mines Co., 95 F.2d 699 (9th Cir.1938), this point was made in dealing with an offering to the stockholders of two corporations about to be merged. Judge Denman observed that:

> "In its broadest meaning the term 'public' distinguishes the populace at large from groups of individual members of the public segregated because of some common interest or characteristic. Yet such a distinction is inadequate for practical purposes; manifestly, an offering of securities to all redheaded men, to all residents of Chicago or San Francisco, to all existing stockholders of the General Motors Corporation or the American Telephone & Telegraph Company, is no less 'public', in every realistic sense of

---

5. " * * * the bill does not affect transactions beyond the need of public protection in order to prevent recurrences of demonstrated abuses." Id., at 7. In a somewhat different tenor, the report spoke of this as an exemption of "transactions by an issuer unless made by or through an underwriter so as to permit an issuer to make a specific or an isolated sale of its securities to a particular person, but insisting that if a sale of the issuer's securities should be made generally to the public that that transaction shall come within the purview of the Act." Id., at 15, 16.

6. The only subsequent reference was an oblique one in the statement of the House Managers on the Conference Report: "Sales of stock to stockholders become subject to the act unless the stockholders are so small in number that the sale to them does not constitute a public offering." H.R.Rep. No. 152, 73d Cong., 1st Sess. 25.

the word, than an unrestricted offering to the world at large. Such an offering, though not open to everyone who may choose to apply, is none the less 'public' in character, for the means used to select the particular individuals to whom the offering is to be made bear no sensible relation to the purposes for which the selection is made.... To determine the distinction between 'public' and 'private' in any particular context, it is essential to examine the circumstances under which the distinction is sought to be established and to consider the purposes sought to be achieved by such distinction." 95 F.2d at 701.

The courts below purported to apply this test. The District Court held, in the language of the *Sunbeam* decision, that "The purpose of the selection bears a 'sensible relation' to the class chosen," finding that "The sole purpose of the 'selection' is to keep part stock ownership of the business within the operating personnel of the business and to spread ownership throughout all departments and activities of the business." The Court of Appeals treated the case as involving "an offering, without solicitation, of common stock to a selected group of key employees of the issuer, most of whom are already stockholders when the offering is made, with the sole purpose of enabling them to secure a proprietary interest in the company or to increase the interest already held by them."

Exemption from the registration requirements of the Securities Act is the question. The design of the statute is to protect investors by promoting full disclosure of information thought necessary to informed investment decisions. The natural way to interpret the private offering exemption is in light of the statutory purpose. Since exempt transactions are those as to which "there is no practical need for [the bill's] application," the applicability of § 4(1) should turn on whether the particular class of persons affected need the protection of the Act. An offering to those who are shown to be able to fend for themselves is a transaction "not involving any public offering."

The Commission would have us go one step further and hold that "an offering to a substantial number of the public" is not exempt under § 4(1). We are advised that "whatever the special circumstances, the Commission has consistently interpreted the exemption as being inapplicable when a large number of offerees is involved." But the statute would seem to apply to a "public offering" whether to few or many.[11] It may well be that offerings to a substantial number of persons would rarely be exempt. Indeed nothing prevents the commission, in enforcing the statute, from using some kind of numerical test in deciding when to investigate particular exemption claims. But there is no warrant for superimposing a quantity limit on private offerings as a matter of statutory interpretation.

11. See Viscount Sumner's frequently quoted dictum in Nash v. Lynde, " 'The public' ... is of course a general word. No particular numbers are prescribed. Anything from two to infinity may serve: perhaps even one, if he is intended to be the first of a series of subscribers, but makes further proceedings needless by himself subscribing the whole." [1929] A.C. 158, 169.

The exemption, as we construe it, does not deprive corporate employees, as a class, of the safeguards of the Act. We agree that some employee offerings may come within § 4(1), e.g., one made to executive personnel who because of their position have access to the same kind of information that the act would make available in the form of a registration statement. Absent such a showing of special circumstances, employees are just as much members of the investing "public" as any of their neighbors in the community. Although we do not rely on it, the rejection in 1934 of an amendment which would have specifically exempted employee stock offerings supports this conclusion. The House Managers, commenting on the Conference Report, said that "the participants in employee" stock-investment plans may be in as great need of the protection afforded by availability of information concerning the issuer for which they work as are most other members of the public. H.R.Rep. No. 1838, 73d Cong., 2d Sess. 41.

Keeping in mind the broadly remedial purposes of federal securities legislation, imposition of the burden of proof on an issuer who would plead the exemption seems to us fair and reasonable. Schlemmer v. Buffalo, R. & P.R. Co., 1907, 205 U.S. 1, 10, 27 S.Ct. 407, 408, 51 L.Ed. 681. Agreeing, the court below thought the burden met primarily because of the respondent's purpose in singling out its key employees for stock offerings. But once it is seen that the exemption question turns on the knowledge of the offerees, the issuer's motives, laudable though they may be, fade into irrelevance. The focus of inquiry should be on the need of the offerees for the protections afforded by registration. The employees here were not shown to have access to the kind of information which registration would disclose. The obvious opportunities for pressure and imposition make it advisable that they be entitled to compliance with § 5.

Reversed.

■ THE CHIEF JUSTICE and MR. JUSTICE BURTON dissent.

■ MR. JUSTICE JACKSON took no part in the consideration or decision of this case.

————

NOTE ON DORAN v. PETROLEUM MANAGEMENT CORP.

Doran v. Petroleum Management Corp., 545 F.2d 893 (5th Cir. 1977) provides a useful gloss on *Ralston Purina,* and a picture of the present state of the law:

This court has in the past identified four factors relevant to whether an offering qualifies for the [private placement] exemption. The consideration of these factors, along with the policies embodied in the 1933 Act, structure the inquiry. . . . The relevant factors include the number of offerees and their relationship to each other and the issuer, the number of units offered, the size of the offering, and the manner of the offering. Consideration of these factors need not exhaust the inquiry, nor is one factor's weighing heavily in favor of the private status of the offering sufficient to ensure the availability of the exemption. Rather, these factors serve as guideposts to the court in attempting to determine whether subjecting the offering to registration requirements would further the purposes of the 1933 Act. . . .

A. *The Number of Offerees*

Establishing the number of persons involved in an offering is important both in order to ascertain the magnitude of the offering and in order to determine the characteristics and knowledge of the persons thus identified.

The number of offerees, not the number of purchasers, is the relevant figure in considering the number of persons involved in an offering . . . A private placement claimant's failure to adduce any evidence regarding the number of offerees will be fatal to the claim. . . . The number of offerees is not itself a decisive factor in determining the availability of the private offering exemption. Just as an offering to few may be public, so an offering to many may be private. *SEC v. Ralston Purina Co., supra,* 346 U.S. at 125, 73 S.Ct. at 984–85. Nevertheless, "the more offerees, the more likelihood that the offering is public." *Hill York Corp. v. American International Franchises, Inc., supra,* 448 F.2d 680 at 688. . . .

B. *The Offerees' Relationship to the Issuer*

Since *SEC v. Ralston,* . . . courts have sought to determine the need of offerees for the protections afforded by registration by focusing on the relationship between offerees and issuer and more particularly on the information available to the offerees. . . . Once the offerees have been identified, it is possible to investigate their relationship to the issuer. . . .

1. *The role of investment sophistication* . . .

. . . [Evidence] of a high degree of business or legal sophistication on the part of all offerees does not suffice to bring the offering within the private placement exemption. We clearly established that proposition in *Hill York Corp. v. American International Franchises, Inc., supra,* 448 F.2d at 690. We reasoned that "if the plaintiffs did not possess the information requisite for a registration statement, they could not bring their sophisticated knowledge of business affairs to bear in deciding whether or not to invest. . . ." . . .

In short, there must be sufficient basis of accurate information upon which the sophisticated investor may exercise his skills. Just as a scientist cannot be without his specimens, so the shrewdest investor's acuity will be blunted without specifications about the issuer. For an investor to be invested with exemptive status he must have the required data for judgment.

2. *The requirement of available information*

The interplay between two factors, the relationship between offerees and issuer and the offerees' access to information that registration would disclose, has been a matter of some conceptual and terminological difficulty. For purposes of this discussion, we shall adopt the following conventions: We shall refer to offerees who have not been furnished registration information directly, but who are in a position relative to the issuer to obtain the information registration would provide, as having "access" to such information. By a position of access we mean a relationship based on factors such as employment, family, or economic bargaining power that enables the offeree effectively to obtain such information. See SEC Rule 146(e), 17 C.F.R. § 280.146(e) (1976). When offerees, regardless of whether they occupy a position of access, have been furnished with the information a registration statement would provide, we shall say merely that such information has been disclosed. When the offerees have access to or there has been disclosure of the information registration would provide, we shall say that such information was available.

The requirement that all offerees have available the information registration would provide has been firmly established by this court as a necessary condition of gaining the private offering exemption. . . .

More specifically, we shall require on remand that the defendants demonstrate that all offerees, whatever their expertise, had available the information a registration statement would have afforded a prospective investor in a public offering. Such a showing is not independently sufficient to establish that the offering qualified for the private placement exemption, but it is necessary to gain the exemption and is to be weighed along with the sophistication and number of the offerees, the number of units offered, and the size and manner of the offering. . . .

C. *On Remand: The Issuer–Offeree Relationship*

In determining on remand the extent of the information available to the offerees, the district court must keep in mind that the "availability" of information means either disclosure of or effective access to the relevant information. The relationship between issuer and offeree is most critical when the issuer relies on the latter route.

To begin with, if the defendants could prove that all offerees were actually furnished the information a registration statement would have provided, whether the offerees occupied a position of access pre-existing such disclosure would not be dispositive of the status of the offering. If disclosure were proved and if, as here, the remaining factors such as the manner of the offering and the investment sophistication of the offerees weigh heavily in favor of the private status of the offering, the absence of a privileged relationship between offeree and issuer would not preclude a finding that the offering was private. Any other conclusion would tear out of context this court's earlier discussions of the § 4(2) exemption and would conflict with the policies of the exemption.

Alternatively it might be shown that the offeree had access to the files and [records] of the company that contained the relevant information. Such access might be afforded merely by the position of the offeree or by the issuer's promise to open appropriate files and records to the offeree as well as to answer inquiries regarding material information. In either case, the relationship between offeree and issuer now becomes critical, for it must be shown that the offeree could realistically have been expected to take advantage of his access to ascertain the relevant information. Similarly the investment sophistication of the offeree assumes added importance, for it is important that he could have been expected to ask the right questions and seek out the relevant information. . . .

———

SEC, Q & A: Small Business and the SEC

(2004 rev.)

. . . Private Offering Exemption

Section 4(2) of the Securities Act provides exemption from registration for "transactions by an issuer not involving any public offering." There has been much uncertainty as to the precise limits of this private offering exemption. Generally, sales to persons who have access to information about the company and are able to fend for themselves (such as those directly managing the business) fall within the intended scope of the exemption. These are known as "sophisticated investors." As the number of purchasers increase and their relationship to the company and its management becomes more remote, however, it becomes more difficult for an issuer to demonstrate that the transaction does, in fact, qualify for the exemption.

To qualify the offering under this exemption, it is necessary that the persons to whom your company sells the security:

- have sufficient knowledge and experience in financial and business matters that they are capable of evaluating the risks and merits of the investment (the "sophisticated investor"), or are able to bear the economic risk of the investment;

- have access to the type of information normally provided in a prospectus; and

- agree not to resell or distribute the securities.

In addition, you may not use any form of public solicitation or general advertising in connection with the offering.

The precise limits of this private offering exemption are uncertain. As the number of purchasers increases and their relationship to the company and its management becomes more remote, it is more difficult to show that the transaction qualifies for the exemption. You should know that if you offer securities to even one person who does not meet the necessary conditions, the entire offering may be in violation of the Securities Act.

Rule 506, another "safe harbor" rule, provides objective standards that you can rely on to meet the requirements of this exemption. . . .

(c) LIMITED OFFERINGS

SECURITIES ACT §§ 2(15), 3(b), 4(2), 4(6)
[See Statutory Supplement]

SECURITIES ACT RULE 215; REGULATION D (RULES 501–508)
[See Statutory Supplement]

Ratner & Hazen, Securities Regulation in a Nutshell 59–60
7th ed. 2002.

[Securities Act] § 3(b) authorizes the SEC, "by rules and regulations," to exempt offerings, not exceeding a specified dollar amount, when it finds that registration is not necessary "by reason of the small amount involved or the limited character of the public offering." The dollar limit has been periodically raised by Congress from its initial level of $100,000, the most recent increase coming in 1980 and raising the limit from $2 million to the present level of $5 million. Under this authority, the Commission has adopted a number of rules providing exemptions for certain specialized kinds of offerings, as well as the general exemption in Regulation A. . . .

. . . Also in 1980, Congress added a new § 4(6) to the 1933 Act, exempting any offering of not more than $5 million made solely to "accredited investors" (defined to include specified types of institutions and other classes of investors that the SEC might specify by rule).

These developments set the stage for the coordination of the private offering and small offering exemptions in a new Regulation D.

SEC, Q & A: Small Business and the SEC
2004 rev.

. . . Regulation D

Regulation D establishes three exemptions from Securities Act registration. Let's address each one separately.

Rule 504

Rule 504 provides an exemption for the offer and sale of up to $1,000,000 of securities in a 12-month period. Your company may use this exemption so long as it is ... not subject to Exchange Act reporting requirements. Like the other Regulation D exemptions, in general you may not use public solicitation or advertising to market the securities and purchasers [must] receive "restricted" securities, meaning that they may not sell the securities without registration or an applicable exemption. However, you can use this exemption for a public offering of your securities and investors will receive freely tradable securities under the following circumstances:

- You register the offering exclusively in one or more states that require a publicly filed registration statement and delivery of a substantive disclosure document to investors;

- You register and sell in a state that requires registration and disclosure delivery and also sell in a state without those requirements, so long as you deliver the disclosure documents mandated by the state in which you registered to all purchasers; or,

- You sell exclusively according to state law exemptions that permit general solicitation and advertising, so long as you sell only to "accredited investors," a term we describe in more detail below in connection with Rule 505 and Rule 506 offerings.

Even if you make a private sale where there are no specific disclosure delivery requirements, you should take care to provide sufficient information to investors to avoid violating the antifraud provisions of the securities laws. This means that any information you provide to investors must be free from false or misleading statements. Similarly, you should not exclude any information if the omission makes what you do provide investors false or misleading.

Rule 505

Rule 505 provides an exemption for offers and sales of securities totaling up to $5 million in any 12-month period. Under this exemption, you may sell to an unlimited number of "accredited investors" and up to 35 other persons who do not need to satisfy the sophistication or wealth standards associated with other exemptions. Purchasers must buy for investment only, and not for resale. The issued securities are "restricted." Consequently, you must inform investors that they may not sell for at least a year without registering the transaction. You may not use general solicitation or advertising to sell the securities.

An "accreditied investor" is:

- a bank, insurance company, registered investment company, business development company, or small business investment company;

- an employee benefit plan, within the meaning of the Employee Retirement Income Security Act, if a bank, insurance company, or registered investment adviser makes the investment decisions, or if the plan has total assets in excess of $5 million;

- a charitable organization, corporation or partnership with assets exceeding $5 million;

- a director, executive officer, or general partner of the company selling the securities;

- a business in which all the equity owners are accredited investors;

- a natural person with a net worth of at least $1 million;

- a natural person with income exceeding $200,000 in each of the two most recent years or joint income with a spouse exceeding $300,000 for those years and a reasonable expectation of the same income level in the current year; or

- a trust with assets of at least $5 million, not formed to acquire the securities offered, and whose purchases are directed by a sophisticated person.

It is up to you to decide what information you give to accredited investors, so long as it does not violate the antifraud prohibitions. But you must give non-accredited investors disclosure documents that generally are the same as those used in registered offerings. If you provide information to accredited investors, you must make this information available to the non-accredited investors as well. You must also be available to answer questions by prospective purchasers.

Here are some specifics about the financial statement requirements applicable to this type of offering:

- Financial statements need to be certified by an independent public accountant;

- If a company other than a limited partnership cannot obtain audited financial statements without unreasonable effort or expense, only the company's balance sheet, to be dated within 120 days of the start of the offering, must be audited; and

- Limited partnerships unable to obtain required financial statements without unreasonable effort or expense may furnish audited financial statements prepared under the federal income tax laws.

Rule 506

. . . Rule 506 is a "safe harbor" for the private offering exemption. If your company satisfies the following standards, you can be assured that you are within the Section 4(2) exemption:

- You can raise an unlimited amount of capital;

- You cannot use general solicitation or advertising to market the securities;

- You can sell securities to an unlimited number of accredited investors (the same group we identified in the Rule 505 discussion) and up to 35 other purchasers. Unlike Rule 505, all non-accredited investors, either alone or with a purchaser representative, must be sophisticated—that is, they must have sufficient knowledge and experience in financial and business matters to make them capable of evaluating the merits and risks of the prospective investment;

- It is up to you to decide what information you give to accredited investors, so long as it does not violate the antifraud prohibitions. But you must give non-accredited investors disclosure documents that generally are the same as those used in registered offerings. If you provide information to accredited investors, you must make this information available to the non-accredited investors as well;

- You must be available to answer questions by prospective purchasers;

- Financial statement requirements are the same as for Rule 505; and

- Purchasers receive "restricted" securities. Consequently, purchasers may not freely trade the securities in the secondary market after the offering.

. . . Accredited Investor Exemption—Section 4(6)

Section 4(6) of the Securities Act exempts from registration offers and sales of securities to accredited investors when the total offering price is less than $5 million. The definition of accredited investors is the same as that used in Regulation D. Like the exemptions in Rule 505 and 506, this exemption does not permit any form of advertising or public solicitation. There are no document delivery requirements. Of course, all transactions are subject to the antifraud provisions of the securities laws.

———

RATNER & HAZEN, SECURITIES REGULATION IN A NUT-SHELL 64 (7th ed. 2002). "Offerings complying with the terms of . . . Rule 504 or 505 are deemed to be exempt under [Securities Act] § 3(b); offerings pursuant to . . . Rule 506, since they may exceed $5 million, cannot be exempt under § 3(b) and are considered to be non-public offerings under . . . § 4(2). Rule 506 is not the exclusive means of making a non-public offering; the Preliminary Note to Regulation D states specifically that failure to satisfy all the terms and conditions of . . . Rule 506 shall not raise any presumption that the exemption provided by § 4(2) is not available."

———

NOTE ON THE SIGNIFICANCE OF EXEMPTIONS

It's important to keep in mind that a provision exempting securities from registration under Section 5 does not necessarily mean that a seller or offeror of those securities is not required to provide the buyers with information. Some exemptions explicitly require the seller to provide information very much like that required in a registration statement. For example, Regulation A (discussed below) requires an elaborate Offering Circular, and Regulation D requires the provision of registration-like information in certain cases. Other exemptions implicitly require the provision of information. For example, a distribution is unlikely to qualify as a private placement unless the offerees have had access to the kind of information that would have been disclosed under a registration statement. Accordingly, when sales are made under Section 4(2) or Rule 506 through investment bankers, the issuer typically supplies an information statement that provides prospectus-like disclosure. See Note on Doran v. Petroleum Management Corp., supra.

If an offeror of securities has to provide information comparable to that in a registration statement, what is the benefit of an exemption? First, *comparable* information may cost less to assemble and provide than the full information required in a registration statement. Second, an information statement may not require clearance by the SEC, as does a registration statement. Third, certain liability provisions of the Securities Act are keyed into registration, and therefore do not apply to an information statement. See Section 7, infra.

———

(d) REGULATION A

———

SECURITIES ACT § 3(b); SECURITIES ACT REG. A [RULES 251–263]

[See Statutory Supplement]

———

SEC, Q & A: Small Business and the SEC

(2004 rev.)

... Regulation A

... Section 3(b) of the Securities Act authorizes the SEC to exempt from registration small securities offerings. By this authority, we created Regulation A, an exemption for public offerings not exceeding $5 million in any 12–month period. If you choose to rely on this exemption, your company must file an offering statement, consisting of a notification, offering circular, and exhibits, with the SEC for review.

Regulation A offerings share many characteristics with registered offerings. For example, you must provide purchasers with an offering circular that is similar in content to a prospectus. Like registered offerings, the securities can be offered publicly and are not "restricted," meaning they are freely tradeable in the secondary market after the offering. The principal advantages of Regulation A offerings, as opposed to full registration, are:

- The financial statements are simpler and don't need to be audited;
- There are no Exchange Act reporting obligations after the offering unless the company has more than $10 million in total assets and more than 500 shareholders;
- Companies may choose among three formats to prepare the offering circular, one of which is a simplified question-and-answer document; and
- You may "test the waters" to determine if there is adequate interest in your securities before going through the expense of filing with the SEC.

All types of companies which do not report under the Exchange Act may use Regulation A, except "blank check" companies, those with an unspecified business, and investment companies registered or required to be registered under the Investment Company Act of 1940. In most cases, shareholders may use Regulation A to resell up to $1.5 million of securities.

If you "test the waters," you can use general solicitation and advertising prior to filing an offering statement with the SEC, giving you the advantage of determining whether there is enough market interest in your securities before you incur the full range of legal, accounting, and other costs associated with filing an offering statement. You may not, however, solicit or accept money until the SEC staff completes its review of the filed offering statement and you deliver prescribed offering materials to investors.

Larry Sonsini, Regulation A

16 Review Sec. Reg. 781
1983.

. . . Regulation A is the body of rules the SEC designed pursuant to section 3(b) to provide a general exemption for [small] issuances. . . .

GENERAL PROCEDURE

Documents to Be Filed. The regulation A process is initiated by the filing of a single document, designated the "Offering Statement," on form I–A. The Offering Statement, consisting of three parts, is the basic form to be used for every offering made under the exemption.

1.   Part I of the Offering Statement is the "Notification." The purpose of the notification is to present information necessary to determine the availability of the exemption. . . .

2.   Part II of the Offering Statement consists of the Offering Circular, which must be distributed to investors. The general instructions to part II indicate the items to which a particular issuer must respond. The disclosure requirements of the Offering Circular are derived from schedule I under the Securities Act, the basic schedule for registration statement disclosure. The disclosures of part II emphasize information on the business of the issuer, the quality of its management, potential conflicts of interest, and the use of proceeds. . . .

3.   Part III of the offering statement requires a listing of exhibits. . . .

PRACTICAL ASPECTS OF REGULATION A

The most practical use of regulation A is for the offer and sale of securities by nonreporting ("privately held") issuers. Such offerings usually occur under employee stock option and purchase plans. These plans typically provide for a rather broad distribution of securities among the employee group. Because the plans usually involve a continuing offering, i.e., the continuous grant of stock options or the sale of shares under stock purchase plans, sooner or later the issuer faces a greater difficulty in perfecting an exemption under the Securities Act for the transactions. As the employee group broadens and deepens within the organization to middle and lower management personnel, the issuer can no longer rely on many of the conditions that must be satisfied under the private placement exemptions. Similarly, because many employees will reside in jurisdictions other than those where the issuer is incorporated and doing business, the intrastate offering exemption under section 3(a)(11) and rule 147 of the Securities Act will be unavailable. Also, privately held issuers will often find it inappropriate to file a registration statement under the Securities Act to cover its transactions under employee stock benefit plans. The cost of registration may be high, and the issuer may not be able to satisfy certain disclosure requirements, such as those regarding financial statements. Therefore, the exemption offered by regulation A may prove most beneficial in these employee stock benefit plans. The burden of disclosure is less than under the standard registration statement forms, particularly with respect to certified financial statements. . . . The cost of perfecting the exemption under the regulation will usually be less than for the preparation, filing, and policing of a registration statement. In addition, the scope of the required disclosure under the offering circular may be well suited for an offering of securities to an employee group who, by definition, are familiar with the business of the issuer.

It should be noted, however, that there is no exemption from compliance with the antifraud provisions of the Securities Acts. Accordingly, notwithstanding the required disclosure under the regulation, the issuer must give consideration to the disclosure of all material information, whether or not specifically covered by an item of the notification. Therefore an issuer should refer to the disclosure items required under a registration statement to determine additional areas of materiality.

The use of regulation A for public offerings of securities other than pursuant to employee stock programs is ... more limited. Although the amendments to the regulation that now allow the use of a preliminary offering circular have made the regulation more appropriate for a public offering, there is still concern, particularly among many underwriters, that the advantages of the limited disclosure requirements of the regulation may not be suited to a public offering of broad distribution.

The burden of establishing exemption from the registration requirements of the Securities Act rests solely on the issuer or person claiming the exemption. As a result, with respect to regulation A, the issuer must be prepared to establish that the offering comes within the regulation and that all the conditions are satisfied.

The civil liability provisions of section 11 of the Securities Act do not apply to use of the regulation, because section 11 only applies to a registration statement filed under the Securities Act. However, the provisions of section 12 of the Securities Act apply to an offering and sale of securities under regulation A.

————

Securities Act Release No. 33–6949 (1992)

[Small Business Initiatives] ...

A. *Regulation A*

As adopted, the dollar ceiling for a Regulation A offering is now $5 million in any 12–month period, including no more than $1.5 million in non-issuer resales....

B. *"Testing the Waters"*

As discussed in the [Proposing] Release, one of the major impediments to a Regulation A financing for a small start-up or developing company with no established market for its securities, is the cost of preparing the mandated offering statement. The full costs of compliance would be incurred without knowing whether there will be any investor interest in the company.

To remedy this situation, the Commission proposed for the first time to permit companies relying on the Regulation A exemption to "test the waters" for potential interest in the company prior to filing and delivery of the mandated offering statement. All test the water documents are required to be submitted to the Commission at the time of first use. The proposal was enthusiastically endorsed by private sector commenters as a necessary and appropriate solution to a significant regulatory impediment to small business financing, and, as drafted, is consistent with investor protection interests.

A number of refinements have been included in the test the water provisions in response to public comment. First, while the Regulation continues to require that the "testing of the waters" begin with a written solicitation of interest submitted to the Commission at the time of first use, the rules have been revised to make clear that submission of the document is not a condition to the exemption. Failure to comply with the requirement is a grounds for Commission suspension of the exemption.

As proposed, the written test the water document was a free writing subject to the inclusion of two mandated statements—first, that no funds were being solicited or would be accepted, and secondly that a detailed offering document would follow. Some commenters suggested that even these few items should be deleted, while others suggested additional requirements or specific prescription of the content.

The rule as adopted continues to provide for free writing with the inclusion of the following items:

1. a statement that no money is being solicited, or will be accepted; that no sales can be made until delivery and qualification of the offering circular, and that indications of interest involve no obligation or commitment of any kind; and

2. a brief, general identification of the company's business, products and chief executive officer.

The rule has been revised to make clear that inclusion of these statements in the soliciting document is not a condition to the exemption, but failure to include the statements is a basis for Commission suspension of the exemption. . . .

Once the offering statement required by Regulation A is filed with the Commission, the issuer may not continue to use its written "test the waters" solicitation materials. The rule requires that at least 20 calendar days elapse between the last use of the solicitation of interest document or broadcast and any sale of securities in the Regulation A offering. Compliance with the rules limiting the use of the test the water documents after filing of the offering statement is not a condition to the exemption, but [noncompliance] is a violation of the rule and is a basis for Commission suspension of the exemption. . . .

———

(e) THE INTRASTATE EXEMPTION

———

SECURITIES ACT § 3(a)(11); SECURITIES ACT RULE 147

[See Statutory Supplement]

———

Securities Act Release No. 4434 (1961)

[SECTION 3(a)(11) EXEMPTIONS FOR LOCAL OFFERINGS]

General Nature of Exemption

Section 3(a)(11), as amended in 1954, exempts from the registration and prospectus requirements of the Act:

> Any security which is a part of an issue offered and sold only to persons resident within a single State or Territory, where the issuer of such security is a person resident and doing business within, or, if a corporation, incorporated by and doing business within, such State or Territory.

The legislative history of the Securities Act clearly shows that this exemption was designed to apply only to local financing that may practicably be consummated in its entirety within the state or territory in which the issuer is both incorporated and doing business. As appears from the legislative history, by amendment to the Act in 1934, this exemption was removed from section 5(c) and inserted in section 3, relating to "Exempted Securities," in order to relieve dealers of an unintended restriction on trading activity. This amendment was not intended to detract from its essential character as a transaction exemption.

"Issue" Concept

A basic condition of the exemption is that the *entire issue* of securities be offered and sold exclusively to residents of the state in question. Consequently, an offer to a nonresident which is considered a part of the intrastate issue will render the exemption unavailable to the entire offering.

Whether an offering is "a part of an issue," that is, whether it is an integrated part of an offering previously made or proposed to be made, is a question of fact and depends essentially upon whether the offerings are a related part of a plan or program. Unity Gold Corporation, 3 S.E.C. 618, 625 (1938); Peoples Securities Company, Securities Exchange Act Release No. 6176, Feb. 10, 1960. Thus, the exemption should not be relied upon in combination with another exemption for the different parts of a single issue where a part is offered or sold to nonresidents.

The determination of what constitutes an "issue" is not governed by state law. Shaw v. U.S., 131 F.2d 476, 480 (9th Cir.1942). Any one or more of the following factors may be determinative of the question of integration: (1) are the offerings part of a single plan of financing; (2) do the offerings involve issuance of the same class of security; (3) are the offerings made at or about the same time; (4) is the same type of consideration to be received, and (5) are the offerings made for the same general purpose.

Moreover, since the exemption is designed to cover only those security distributions, which, as a whole, are essentially local in character, it is clear that the phrase "sold only to persons resident" as used in section 3(a)(11) cannot refer merely to the initial sales by the issuing corporation to its underwriters, or even the subsequent resales by the underwriters to distributing dealers. To give effect to the fundamental purpose of the exemption, it is necessary that the entire issue of securities shall be offered and sold to, and come to rest only in the hands of residents within the state. If any part of the issue is offered or sold to a nonresident, the exemption is unavailable not only for the securities so sold, but for all securities forming a part of the issue, including those sold to residents.... It is incumbent upon the issuer, underwriter, dealers and other persons connected with the offering to make sure that it does not become an interstate distribution through resales. It is understood to be customary for such persons to obtain assurances that purchases are not made with a view to resale to nonresidents.

Doing Business Within the State

In view of the local character of the section 3(a)(11) exemption, the requirement that the issuer be doing business in the state can only be satisfied by the performance of substantial operational activities in the state of incorporation. The doing business requirement is not met by functions in the particular state such as bookkeeping, stock record and similar activities or by offering securities in the state....

Residence Within the State

Section 3(a)(11) requires that the entire issue be confined to a single state in which the issuer, the offerees and the purchasers are residents. Mere presence in the state is not sufficient to constitute residence as in the case of military personnel at a military post. S.E.C. v. Capital Funds, Inc. No. A46–60, D.Alaska, 1960. The mere obtaining of formal representations of residence and agreements not to resell to nonresidents or agreements that sales are void if the purchaser is a nonresident should not be relied upon without more as establishing the availability of the exemption....

Resales

From these general principles it follows that if during the course of distribution any underwriter, any distributing dealer (whether or not a member of the formal selling or distributing group), or any dealer or other person purchasing securities from a distributing dealer for resale were to offer or sell such securities to a nonresident, the exemption would be defeated. In other words, section 3(a)(11) contemplates that the exemption is applicable only if the entire issue is distributed pursuant to the statutory conditions. Consequently, any offers or sales to a nonresident in connection with the distribution of the issue would destroy the exemption as to all securities which are a part of that issue, including those sold to residents regardless of whether such sales are made directly to nonresidents or indirectly through residents who as part of the distribution thereafter sell to nonresidents. It would furthermore be immaterial that sales to nonresidents are made without use of the mails or instruments of interstate commerce. Any such sales of part of the issue to nonresidents, however few, would not be in compliance with the conditions of section 3(a)(11), and would render the exemption unavailable for the entire offering including the sales to residents. . . .

This is not to suggest, however, that securities which have actually come to rest in the hands of resident investors, such as persons purchasing without a view to further distribution or resale to nonresidents, may not in due course be resold by such persons, whether directly or through dealers or brokers, to nonresidents without in any way affecting the exemption. The relevance of any such resales consists only of the evidentiary light which they might cast upon the factual question whether the securities had in fact come to rest in the hands of resident investors. If the securities are resold but a short time after their acquisition to a nonresident this fact, although not conclusive, might support an inference that the original offering had not come to rest in the state, and that the resale therefore constituted a part of the process of primary distribution; a stronger inference would arise if the purchaser involved were a security dealer. It may be noted that the nonresidence of the underwriter or dealer is not pertinent so long as the ultimate distribution is solely to residents of the state. . . .

———

SECURITIES ACT RELEASE NO. 5450 (1974)

[Rule 147]

The Securities and Exchange Commission today adopted Rule 147 which defines certain terms in, and clarifies certain conditions of, section 3(a)(11) of the Securities Act of 1933 ("the Act"). . . .

Background and Purpose . . .

Certain basic questions have arisen in connection with interpreting Section 3(a)(11). They are:

1. what transactions does the Section cover;

2. what is "part of an issue" for purposes of the Section;

3. when is a person "resident within" a state or territory for purposes of the Section; and

4. what does "doing business within" mean in the context of the Section?

The courts and the Commission have addressed themselves to these questions in the context of different fact situations, and some general guidelines have been developed. Certain guidelines were set forth by the Commission in Securities Act Release No. 4434 and, in part, are reflected in Rule 147. However, in certain respects, as pointed out below, the rule differs from past interpretations.

The Transaction Concept

Although the intrastate offering exemption is contained in Section 3 of the Act, which Section is phrased in terms of exempt "securities" rather than "transactions", the legislative history and Commission and judicial interpretations indicate that the exemption covers only specific transactions and not the securities themselves. Rule 147 reflects this interpretation. . . .

The "Person Resident Within" Concept

The object of the Section 3(a)(11) exemption, i.e., to restrict the offering to persons within the same locality as the issuer who are, by reason of their proximity, likely to be familiar with the issuer and protected by the state law governing the issuer, is best served by interpreting the residence requirement narrowly. In addition, the determination of whether all parts of the issue have been sold only to residents can be made only after the securities have "come to rest" within the state or territory. Rule 147 retains these concepts, but provides more objective standards for determining when a person is considered a resident within a state for purposes of the rule and when securities have come to rest within a state.

The "Doing Business Within" Requirement

Because the primary purpose of the intrastate exemption was to allow an essentially local business to raise money within the state where the investors would be likely to be familiar with the business and with the management, the doing business requirement has traditionally been viewed strictly. First, not only should the business be located within the state, but the principal or predominant business must be carried on there. Second, substantially all of the proceeds of the offering must be put to use within the local area.

Rule 147 reinforces these requirements by providing specific percentage amounts of business that must be conducted within the state, and of proceeds from the offering that must be spent in connection with such business. In addition, the rule requires that the principal office of the issuer be within the state.

SEC, Q & A: Small Business and The SEC

(2004 rev.)

Intrastate Offering Exemption

Section 3(a)(11) of the Securities Act is generally known as the "intrastate offering exemption." This exemption facilitates the financing of local business operations. To qualify for the intrastate offering exemption, your company must:

- be incorporated in the state where it is offering the securities;
- carry out a significant amount of its business in that state; and

● make offers and sales only to residents of that state.

There is no fixed limit on the size of the offering or the number of purchasers. Your company must determine the residence of each purchaser. If any of the securities are offered or sold to even one out-of-state person, the exemption may be lost. Without the exemption, the company could be in violation of the Securities Act registration requirements. If a purchaser resells any of the securities to a person who resides outside the state within a short period of time after the company's offering is complete (the usual test is nine months), the entire transaction, including the original sales, might violate the Securities Act. Since secondary markets for these securities rarely develop, companies often must sell securities in these offerings at a discount.

It will be difficult for your company to rely on the intrastate exemption unless you know the purchasers and the sale is directly negotiated with them. If your company holds some of its assets outside the state, or derives a substantial portion of its revenues outside the state where it proposes to offer its securities, it will probably have a difficult time qualifying for the exemption.

You may follow Rule 147, a "safe harbor" rule, to ensure that you meet the requirements for this exemption. It is possible, however, that transactions not meeting all requirements of Rule 147 may still qualify for the exemption.

———

NOTE ON THE INTEGRATION OF SECURITIES ISSUES

In general, an issue of securities cannot be artificially segregated into parts for the purpose of qualifying one part for an exemption when the issue taken as a whole would not qualify.

> The determination whether securities are being offered as part of a single "issue" will depend upon a consideration of various factors concerning the methods of sale and distribution employed to effect the offerings and the disposition of the proceeds. If the offerings may be segregated into separate blocks, as evidenced by material differences in the use of the proceeds, in the manner and terms of distribution, and in similar related details, each offering will be a separate "issue." In the main, of course, each case must be determined upon the basis of its own facts.

In the Matter of Unity Gold Corp., 3 S.E.C. 618, 625 (1938). See also Securities Act Release No. 1459 (1937); Securities Act Release No. 2029 (1939). Securities Act Release No. 4434 (1961) adds:

> Any one or more of the following factors may be determinative of the question of integration: (1) are the offerings part of a single plan of financing; (2) do the offerings involve issuance of the same class of security; (3) are the offerings made at or about the

same time; (4) is the same type of consideration to be received, and (5) are the offerings made for the same general purpose.

_____

(f) TRANSACTIONS NOT INVOLVING AN ISSUER, UNDERWRITER, OR DEALER

_____

SECURITIES ACT §§ 2(11), 4(1), 4(3)

[See Statutory Supplement]

_____

INTRODUCTORY NOTE

Securities Act section 5 broadly prohibits the sale of unregistered securities by any person, subject to the various exemptions under the Act. However, section 4(1) of the Act exempts, from section 5's prohibition, transactions by any person other than an issuer, underwriter, or dealer. In effect, therefore, despite its broad language section 5 is applicable only to sales by an issuer, a dealer, or an underwriter.

Section 2(a)(4) defines an *issuer* as "every person who issues or proposes to issue any security."

Section 2(a)(12) defines a *dealer* as "any person who engages either for all or part of his time, directly or indirectly, as agent, broker, or principal, in the business of offering, buying, selling, or otherwise dealing or trading in securities issued by another person." However, section 4(3) exempts most transactions by dealers from the registration requirement.

Since the definition of issuer is fairly straightforward, and since most transactions by dealers are empted under section 4(3), the difficult problems in applying section 4(1) concern the meaning of "underwriters" for purposes of that section. Persons who are underwriters for this purpose are known as *statutory underwriters*. The paradigm case of a statutory underwriter is an investment professional who distributes stock on behalf of an issuer. However, section 2(a)(11) defines "underwriter" so as to pick up transactions that don't look anything like that paradigm:

> The term "underwriter" means any person who has purchased from an issuer with a view to, or offers or sells for an issuer in connection with, the distribution of any security, or participates or has a direct or indirect participation in any such undertaking, or participates or has a participation in the direct or indirect underwriting of any such undertaking; but such term shall not include a person whose interest is limited to a commission from

an underwriter or dealer not in excess of the usual and customary distributors' or sellers' commission. As used in this paragraph the term "issuer" shall include, in addition to an issuer, any person directly or indirectly controlling or controlled by the issuer, or any person under direct or indirect common control with the issuer.

The balance of the present Section will explicate Section 2(a)(11) of the Securities Act by considering: (1) The meaning and implications of the terms, "offers or sells for an issuer in connection with . . . the distribution of any security" and "purchased from an issuer with a view to . . . the distribution of any security." (2) The meaning and implications of the terms, "any person directly or indirectly controlling . . . the issuer." (3) Rules 144 and 144A.

---

(1) WHO IS A STATUTORY UNDERWRITER

NOTE ON THE MEANING OF TERM "OFFERS OR SELLS FOR AN ISSUER IN CONNECTION WITH . . . THE DISTRIBUTION OF ANY SECURITY"

The language in section 2(a)(11), "offers or sells for an issuer in connection with . . . the distribution of any security," has been construed very broadly. Perhaps the most notable case is SEC v. Chinese Consolidated Benevolent Ass'n., 120 F.2d 738 (2d Cir.1941), cert. denied 314 U.S. 618, 62 S.Ct. 106, 86 L.Ed. 497. The defendant had sold unregistered Chinese government bonds in the United States at the beginning of World War II. The defendant claimed it was not an underwriter within the meaning of then-section 2(11) because it had no agreement with the Chinese government to sell the bonds, and was not compensated for selling the bonds, but instead acted out of loyalty to China. Held, the defendant was nevertheless an underwriter:

> Under section 4(1) the defendant is not exempt from registration requirements if it is "an underwriter". The court below reasons that [the defendant] is not to be regarded as an underwriter since it does not sell or solicit offers to buy "for an issuer in connection with, the distribution" of securities. In other words, it seems to have been held that only solicitation authorized by the issuer in connection with the distribution of the Chinese bonds would satisfy the definition of underwriter contained in Section 2(11) and that defendant's activities were never for the Chinese government but only for the purchasers of the bonds. Though the defendant solicited the orders, obtained the cash from the purchasers and caused both to be forwarded so as to procure the bonds, it is nevertheless contended that its acts could not have been for the Chinese government because it had no contractual arrangement or even understanding with the latter. But the aim of the Securities Act is to have information available for investors.

This objective will be defeated if buying orders can be solicited which result in uninformed and improvident purchasers. It can make no difference as regards the policy of the act whether an issuer has solicited orders through an agent, or has merely taken advantage of the services of a person interested for patriotic reasons in securing offers to buy. The aim of the issuer is to promote the distribution of the securities, and of the Securities Act is to protect the public by requiring that it be furnished with adequate information upon which to make investments. Accordingly the words "[sell] for an issuer in connection with the distribution of any security" ought to be read as covering continual solicitations, such as the defendant was engaged in, which normally would result in a distribution of issues of unregistered securities within the United States. Here a series of events were set in motion by the solicitation of offers to buy which culminated in a distribution that was initiated by the defendant. We hold that the defendant acted as an underwriter.

120 F.2d at 740–41.

NOTE ON THE MEANING OF THE TERM "ANY PERSON WHO HAS PURCHASED FROM AN ISSUER WITH A VIEW TO . . . DISTRIBUTION"

Section 2(a)(11) also includes within the term "underwriter," for purposes of that section, a person "who has purchased from an issuer with a view to . . . distribution." Even a person who is not an underwriter in the normal usage of that term may be a statutory underwriter under this provision. Assume that P has purchased securities from an issuer in a private placement. If P purchased the securities with the intent to offer or resell them through a distribution—as opposed to having purchased with an "investment intent"—he is an underwriter under section 2(a)(11). The classic case is that in which P has purchased unregistered securities under the private-placement exemption, and then quickly turned around and re-offered the securities to a number of buyers.

In Gilligan, Will & Co. v. S.E.C., 267 F.2d 461 (2d Cir.1959), cert. denied 361 U.S. 896, 80 S.Ct. 200, 4 L.Ed.2d 152, Gilligan, a partner in Gilligan Will, purchased $100,000 of a $3,000,000 private placement of Crowell–Collier convertible debentures for his own account, representing that he purchased for investment. Notwithstanding these representations, Gilligan quickly sold $45,000 of the debentures to Louis Alter; made offers to two other potential purchasers (selling $5,000 of debentures to one of them); and placed the remaining debentures in a Gilligan Will trading account. Ten months later, Gilligan, Alter, and the Gilligan Will firm converted their debentures into common stock and sold the stock at a profit on the American Stock Exchange. Gilligan and Alter later subscribed to an additional $200,000 of debentures, which they similarly converted to common stock. Gilligan Will also was active in selling $200,000 of the debentures to a mutual fund, and as a result of this transaction other parties received warrants to purchase Crowell–Collier stock.

Gilligan and Gilligan Will argued that since the conversion and sales occurred more than ten months after the purchase of the debentures, the Commission was bound to find that the debentures so converted had been held for investment, and were not purchased with a view to distribution. The court rejected this contention:

> ... Petitioners concede that if such sales were intended at the time of purchase, the debentures would not then have been held as investments; but [they argue] that the stipulation reveals that the sales were undertaken only after a change of the issuer's circumstances as a result of which petitioners, acting as prudent investors, thought it wise to sell. The catalytic circumstances were the failure, noted by Gilligan, of Crowell–Collier to increase its advertising space as he had anticipated it would. We agree with the Commission that in the circumstances here presented the intention to retain the debentures only if Crowell–Collier continued to operate profitably was equivalent to a "purchase ... with a view to ... distribution" within the statutory definition of underwriters in § 2(11). To hold otherwise would be to permit a dealer who speculatively purchases an unregistered security in the hope that the financially weak issuer had, as is stipulated here, "turned the corner," to unload on the unadvised public what he later determines to be an unsound investment without the disclosure sought by the securities laws, although it is in precisely such circumstances that disclosure is most necessary and desirable....

RATNER & HAZEN, SECURITIES REGULATION IN A NUTSHELL 73–74 (7th ed. 2002). "One unresolved question is whether a person who has purchased securities from the issuer in a non-public transaction can resell those securities in another *private* transaction, and, if so, what limitations apply to such resales. Since this situation is not technically covered by either § 4(1) or § 4(2), it is sometimes said to be covered by the '§ 4(1½) exemption.'

"In response to requests for codification of the '§ 4(1½)' exemption, the SEC in 1990 adopted ... Rule 144A.... Rule 144A, however, does not deal with the question of the resale by an individual purchaser to another individual who might have qualified as a purchaser in the original offering. What the rule does is to permit unlimited resales of securities that have never been registered under the 1933 Act, as long as all such sales are made to a specified class of 'qualified institutional buyers,' defined generally as including any institution with more that $100 million of investments. The exemption is available only for securities of a class that is *not* traded on any U.S. securities exchange or in the NASDAQ system. It does not require the institutions to deal directly with one another; it permits securities firms to participate in the transactions, either as agent or principal, and in fact permits an active trading market in these securities, a substantial proportion of which are securities of foreign issuers who are unwilling to subject themselves to U.S. disclosure requirements."

---

(2) SALES BY CONTROLLING PERSONS

NOTE ON OFFERS OR SALES CONTROLLING PERSONS

A distribution of unregistered securities by a person who is in control of an issuer is comparable in many respects to a sale by the issuer itself. Accordingly, distributions by controlling persons are not exempt under section 4(1). This result is reached circuitously. Under the last sentence of Section 2(a)(11), a person is an underwriter if he offers or sells securities for a person who *controls* the issuer, "in connection with ... the distribution of any security." (Under Securities Act Rule 405, "[t]he term 'control' ... means the possession, direct or indirect, of the power to direct or cause the direction of the management and policies of a person, whether through the ownership of voting securities, by contract, or otherwise.")

The applicability of the principle that a distribution on behalf of a controlling person is not exempt from section 5 is often complicated by two issues: whether a particular sale on behalf of a controlling person constitutes a "distribution," and whether the sale comes within the exemption in section 4(4) for "brokers' transactions executed upon customers' orders on any exchange or in the over-the-counter market but not the solicitation of such orders."

The Distribution Question: Section 4(1). In In the Matter of Ira Haupt & Co., 23 S.E.C. 589 (1946), Ira Haupt & Company, a brokerage firm, sold approximately 93,000 shares of the unregistered common stock of Park & Tilford, Inc. for the accounts of David A. Schulte and a corporation and trust controlled by Schulte. The sales were made in small lots over the course of approximately six months, pursuant to Schulte's instructions to sell 200–share blocks from his personal holdings at "59 and every quarter up," and up to 73,000 shares for the trust "at $80 per share or better." The price of the stock rose sharply from $57 to $98 per share during this period, because of the announcement that a whiskey dividend would be distributed in kind to the shareholders of Park & Tilford. (A dividend in liquor was especially welcome during the wartime shortage.) Schulte was aware of the planned dividend at the time he placed his sell order with Ira Haupt.

The Schulte interests initially held over 90 percent of the common stock of Park & Tilford, and it was therefore conceded that they controlled Park & Tilford. Accordingly, it was clear that Ira Haupt was selling the securities for a person "controlling the issuer" as contemplated by the last sentence of then section 2(11). Ira Haupt nevertheless denied that it was a statutory underwriter for purposes of the transactions because the sales were not effected "in connection with . . . the distribution of any security."

At the outset, the Commission noted that although the term "distribution" is not defined in the Act, it had previously been held to comprise "the entire process by which in the course of a public offering the block of securities is dispersed and ultimately comes to rest in the hands of the investing public." The Commission further remarked:

> We find no validity in the argument that a predetermination of the precise number of shares which are to be publicly dispersed is an essential element of a distribution. Nor do we think that a "distribution" loses its character as such merely because the extent of the offering may depend on certain conditions such as the market price. . . . Such offerings are not any less a "distribution" merely because their precise extent cannot be predetermined. . . .

The Commission concluded that

> . . . [Ira Haupt] was selling for the Schulte interests, controlling shareholders of Park & Tilford, in connection with the distribution of their holdings in the stock and was, therefore, an "underwriter" within the meaning of the Act.

Thus, the exemption of section 4(1) was not applicable to the transactions.

Brokers' Transactions: Section 4(4). Ira Haupt also claimed that the transactions fell within section 4(4) (then 4(2)), which exempts "brokers' transactions executed upon customers' orders on any exchange or in the over-the-counter market but not the solicitation of such orders." The S.E.C. rejected this defense as well:

> What we must determine is whether the broad provisions which by their terms plainly require registration and the disclosure of pertinent information to prospective investors in the case of public distributions by controlling persons, through underwriters, are so limited by the general language of section [4(4)] as to withdraw the basic protection afforded by the Act where the securities are offered to the public in an avid market by a method which we will assume, *arguendo,* foregoes the sales effort usually considered necessary to accomplish similar distributions. . . .
>
> We find nothing in the language or legislative history of section [4(4)] to compel the exemption of this type of secondary distribution and the consequent overriding of the general objectives and policy of the Act. On the contrary, there are affirmative indications that section [4(4)] was meant to preserve the distinction between the "trading" and "distribution" of securities which separates the exempt and non-exempt transactions under section 4(1) . . . .

From the [legislative history], it is apparent that transactions by an issuer or underwriter and transactions by a dealer during the period of *distribution* ... must be preceded by registration and the use of a prospectus. It is likewise apparent that Congress intended that, during this period, persons other than an issuer, underwriter, or dealer should be able to *trade* in the security without use of a prospectus. Since such persons would carry on their trading largely through the use of brokers (who are included in the general definition of dealers), such trading through brokers without the use of a prospectus could be permitted during the first year after the initial offering only if there were a special exemption for dealers acting as brokers. The importance of this special exemption is emphasized in the case where a stop order might be entered against a registration statement. For, although such a stop order was intended to and would operate to stop all *distribution* activities, it would also result in stopping all *trading* by individuals through dealers acting as brokers unless a special exemption were provided for brokers. It was in recognition of this fact and to permit a dealer to act as a broker for an individual's trading transactions, while the security is being distributed and during the period of a stop order, that section [4(4)] was enacted. . . .

Similarly, in United States v. Wolfson, 405 F.2d 779 (2d Cir.1968), cert. denied 394 U.S. 946, 89 S.Ct. 1275, 22 L.Ed.2d 479 (1969), the court upheld the conviction of a controlling shareholder for failing to register shares distributed through brokers. The court gave short shrift to the argument that the broker's exemption protected a controlling shareholder:

... [T]he appellants contend that the brokers in this case cannot be classified as underwriters because their part in the sales transactions came within § 4(4), 15 U.S.C.A. § 77d(4), which exempts "brokers' transactions executed upon customers' orders on any exchange or in the over-the-counter market but not the solicitation of such orders." The answer to this contention is that § 4(4) was designed only to exempt the brokers' part in security transactions. Stadia Oil & Uranium Co. v. Wheelis, 251 F.2d 269, 275 (C.A.10, 1957). Control persons must find their own exemptions.

There is nothing inherently unreasonable for a broker to claim the exemption of § 4(4) ... when he is unaware that his customer's part in the transaction is not exempt. . . .

Certainly if the appellants' sales, which clearly amounted to a distribution ... had been made through a broker or brokers with knowledge of the circumstances, the brokers would not be entitled to the exemption. It will hardly do for the appellants to say that because they kept the true facts from the brokers they can take advantage of the exemption the brokers gained thereby.

(3) RULES 144 AND 144A

SECURITIES ACT RULE 144

[See Statutory Supplement]

The wide ambit given to the meaning of the term underwriter, together with the coverage of sales by controlling persons, made it difficult for controlling persons, and persons holding restricted securities, to know when they could safely trade unregistered shares. The SEC has sought to meet this problem by providing safe harbors for certain such sales under Rules 144 and 144A.

SECURITIES ACT RELEASE NO. 5223 (1973) [NOTICE OF ADOPTION OF RULE 144]....

... [T]he Commission is of the view that "distribution" is the significant concept in interpreting the statutory term "underwriter." In determining when a person is deemed not to be engaged in a distribution several factors must be considered.

First, the purpose and underlying policy of the Act to protect investors requires, in the Commission's opinion, that there be adequate current information concerning the issuer, whether the resales of securities by persons result in a distribution or are effected in trading transactions. Accordingly, the availability of the rule is conditioned on the existence of adequate current public information.

Secondly, a holding period prior to resale is essential, among other reasons, to assure that those persons who buy under a claim of a Section 4(2) exemption have assumed the economic risks of investment, and therefore, are not acting as conduits for sale to the public of unregistered securities, directly or indirectly, on behalf of an issuer. It should be noted that there is nothing in Section 2(11) which places a time limit on a person's status as an underwriter. The public has the same need for protection afforded by registration whether the securities are distributed shortly after their purchase or after a considerable length of time.

A third factor, which must be considered in determining what is deemed not to constitute a "distribution," is the impact of the particular transaction or transactions on the trading markets. It is consistent with the rationale of the Act that Section 4(1) be interpreted to permit only routine trading transactions as distinguished from distributions. Therefore, a person reselling securities under Section 4(1) of the Act must sell the securities in such limited quantities and in such a manner so as not to disrupt the trading markets. The larger the amount of securities involved, the more likely it is that such resales may involve methods of offering and amounts of compensation usually associated with a distribution rather than routine trading transactions. Thus, solicitation of buy orders or the payment of extra compensation are not permitted by the rule.

In summary, if the sale in question is made in accordance with all the provisions of the rule, . . . any person who sells restricted securities shall be deemed not to be engaged in a distribution of such securities and therefore not an underwriter thereof. The rule also provides that any person who sells restricted or other securities on behalf of a person in a control relationship with the issuer shall be deemed not to be engaged in a distribution of such securities and therefore not to be an underwriter thereof, if the sale is made in accordance with all the conditions of the rule.

SECURITIES ACT RULE 144A

[See Statutory Supplement]

SECURITIES ACT RELEASE NO. 6862 (1990)

[RESALE OF RESTRICTED SECURITIES; CHANGES TO METHOD OF DETER-MINING HOLDING PERIOD OF RESTRICTED SECURITIES UNDER RULES 144 AND 145.]

. . . NEW RULE 144A

. . . Rule 144A . . . [is] the first step toward achieving a more liquid and efficient institutional resale market for unregistered securities. The Commission intends to monitor the evolution of this market and to revisit the Rule with a view to making any appropriate changes. . . .

A. General

Rule 144A sets forth a non-exclusive safe harbor from the registration requirements of Section 5 of the Securities Act for the resale of restricted securities to specified institutions by persons other than the issuer of such securities. The transactions covered by the safe harbor are private transactions that, on the basis of a few objective standards, can be defined as outside the purview of Section 5, without the necessity of undertaking the more usual analysis under Sections 4(1) and 4(3) of the Securities Act.

By providing that transactions meeting its terms are not "distributions," the Rule essentially confirms that such transactions are not subject to the registration provisions of the Securities Act. In the case of persons other than issuers or dealers, the rule does this by providing that any such person who offers and sells securities in accordance with the Rule will be deemed not to be engaged in a distribution and therefore not to be an underwriter within the meanings of Sections 2(11)and 4(1) of the Securities Act. Such persons therefore may rely on the exemption from registration provided by Section 4(1) for transactions by persons other than issuers, underwriters or dealers. Dealers have the benefit of an exemption from registration under Section 4(3) of the Securities Act, except when they are participants in a distribution or within a specified period after the securities have been offered to the public. The Rule provides that, if the conditions of the Rule are met, a dealer will be deemed not to be a participant in a distribution of securities within the meaning of Section 4(3)(C) of the Act and not to be an underwriter of such securities within the meaning of Section 2(11) of the Act, and the securities will be deemed not to have been offered to the public within the meaning of Section 4(3)(A) of the Act. . . .

B. Eligible Securities

Rule 144A would not extend to the offer or sale of securities that, when issued, were of the same class as securities listed on a national securities exchange registered under Section 6 of the Exchange Act or quoted in an automated inter-dealer quotation system. Accordingly, privately-placed securities that, at the time of their issuance, were fungible with securities trading on a U.S. exchange or quoted in NASDAQ would not be eligible for resale under the Rule. . . .

C. Eligible Purchasers

1. Types of Institutions Covered

. . . [E]xcept for registered broker-dealers, to be a "qualified institutional buyer" an institution must in the aggregate own and invest on a discretionary basis at least $100 million in securities of issuers that are not affiliated with the institution. . . .

D. Information Requirement . . .

As adopted, availability of the Rule is conditioned upon the holder and a prospective purchaser designated by the holder having the right to obtain from the issuer, upon the holder's request to the issuer, certain basic financial information, and upon such prospective purchaser having received such information at or prior to the time of sale, upon such purchaser's request to the holder or the issuer. This information is required only where the issuer does not file periodic reports under the Exchange Act, . . . and does not furnish home country information to the Commission pursuant to Rule 12g3–2(b). . . .

The Commission does not believe that the limited information requirement should impose a significant burden on those issuers subject to the requirement. Many foreign issuers that will be subject to the requirement, which were the focus of the commenters' concern, will have securities traded in established offshore markets, and already will have made the required information publicly available in such markets. Even for domestic issuers, the required information represents only a portion of that which would be necessary before a U.S. broker or dealer could submit for publication a quotation for the securities of such an issuer in a quotation medium in the United

States.... The Commission expects that the kinds of information commonly furnished under Rule 12g3–2(b) by foreign private issuers almost invariably would satisfy the information requirement and that foreign private issuers who wish their securities to be Rule 144A– eligible will simply obtain a Rule 12g3–2(b) exemption on a voluntary basis. Financial statements meeting the timing requirements of the issuer's home country or principal trading markets would be considered sufficiently current for purposes of the information requirement of the Rule....

NOTE ON EXEMPTED SECURITIES

The exemptions considered in this Section relate to types of *transactions,* and for the most part provide an exemption only from *section 5.* The Securities Act also exempts certain types of *securities* from the provisions of *the entire Act.* These exemptions are to be found in sections 3(a)(1)–(a)(8). They include U.S. government, state, and municipal securities (section 3(a)(2)), certain short-term paper (section 3(a)(3)), and bankruptcy trustee certificates (section 3(a)(7)).

SECTION 5.   MECHANICS OF REGISTRATION

SECURITIES ACT FORMS S–1, S–2, AND S–3

[See Statutory Supplement]

NOTE ON THE MECHANICS OF REGISTRATION

Assuming that an issue of securities must be registered, the registration process is begun by filing with the SEC a registration statement on the applicable form. The basic forms are S–1, S–2, and S–3, but there are many other forms for special situations.

In general, the registration statement must describe such matters as the characteristics of the securities; the character and size of the business enterprise; its capital structure, financial history, and earnings; underwriters' commissions; the names of persons who participate in the direction, management, or control of the business; their security holdings and remuneration, including options; payments to promoters made within two years or intended to be made in the near future; acquisitions of property not in the ordinary course of business, and the interests of directors, officers, and principal stockholders therein; pending or threatened legal proceedings; and the purpose to which the proceeds of the offering are to be applied. The registration statement must include the issuer's financial statements, certified by independent accountants.

The Commission is empowered to prevent the sale of securities to the public on the basis of registration statements that contain inaccurate or incomplete information. The Staff of the Division of Corporate Finance usually notifies the registrant, by an informal letter of comment, of respects in which the registration statement apparently fails to conform to these requirements. The registrant is afforded an opportunity to file an amendment before the statement becomes effective. However, in certain cases, such as where the deficiencies in a registration statement appear to stem from careless disregard of applicable requirements or a deliberate attempt to conceal or mislead, the Commission either institutes an investigation to determine whether "stop-order" proceedings should be instituted, or immediately issues such an order.

The minimum waiting period between the time of filing the registration statement and the time it may become effective is twenty days. This waiting period is designed to provide investors with an opportunity to become familiar with the proposed offering. Information disclosed in the registration statement is disseminated during the waiting period by means of the preliminary prospectus, which presents in summary form the more important of the required disclosures.

NOTE ON THE INTEGRATION OF DISCLOSURE UNDER THE 1933 AND 1934 ACTS

Within recent years, the content of the registration forms has been dramatically affected by the concept of integration. The Securities Exchange Act of 1934 requires *periodic disclosure* by issuers whose stock is registered under that Act. For example, such issuers must file an annual 10–K report, which includes financial statements and various other information; must annually distribute a proxy statement, or the equivalent, containing information on such matters as remuneration of directors and officers and conflict-of-interest transactions; and must file timely 8–K reports whenever certain material events have occurred. In contrast, the Securities Act of 1933 requires only *transactional disclosure*—that is, disclosure only in connection with specific public distributions. Until the late 1970s, the disclosure schemes of the two Acts proceeded on separate tracks. At that time, the Commission undertook a program of integrating the two disclosure schemes. Partly, this was accomplished by a uniform Regulation, S–K, which provides equivalent definitions and disclosure requirements under the two Acts. Partly, it was accomplished by stratifying issuers into three classes, and reducing the amount of disclosure required in registration statements under the 1933 Act filed for issuers that are already making periodic disclosure under the 1934 Act, and for issuers as to whom a great deal of information is likely to be publicly available even apart from the 1934 Act's disclosure requirements.

———

Securities Act Release No. 6331 (1981)

[REGISTRATION FORMS]

... II. Overview

Under the proposed registration statement framework, registrants would be classified into three categories: (1) companies which are widely followed by professional analysts; (2) companies which have been subject to the periodic reporting system of the Exchange Act for three or more years, but which are not widely followed; and (3) companies which have been in the Exchange Act reporting system for less than three years. The first category would be eligible to use proposed Form S–3, which relies on incorporation by reference of Exchange Act reports and contains minimal disclosure in the prospectus. This form is predicated on the Commission's belief that the market operates efficiently for these companies, i.e., that the disclosure in Exchange Act reports and other communications by the registrant, such as press releases, has already been disseminated and accounted for by the market place. The second category would be eligible for Form S–2, which represents a combination of incorporation by reference of Exchange Act reports and presentation in the prospectus or in an annual report to security holders of certain information. The third category would use Form S–1, which requires complete disclosure of information in the prospectus and does not permit incorporation by reference. . . .

Proposed Form S–3 recognizes the applicability of the efficient market theory to the registration statement framework with respect to those registrants which usually provide high quality corporate reports, including Exchange Act reports, and whose corporate information is broadly disseminated, because such companies are widely followed by professional analysts and investors in the market place. Because these registrants are widely followed, the disclosure set forth in the prospectus may appropriately be limited, without the loss of investor protection, to information concerning the offering and material facts which have not been disclosed previously. The abbreviated disclosure is made possible by the use of incorporation by reference of the registrant's Exchange Act information into the prospectus. Because of the abbreviated disclosure, the utility of proposed Form S–3 is limited to widely followed companies. . . . The proposed float requirement is designed to correlate the use of abbreviated Form S–3 to widely followed registrants.

... [P]roposed Form S–2 is designed for improved readability by streamlining disclosure requirements and allowing certain disclosure obligations to be satisfied either through the delivery of the annual report to security holders or by presentation of comparable updated information in the prospectus. More specifically, the financial statements, management's discussion and analysis and the brief business description required by proposed Form S–2 are identical to those already presented in the annual report to security holders. . . .

Finally, proposed Form S–1 . . . would be used to register securities when no other form is authorized or prescribed and would be used by companies in the Exchange Act reporting system for less than three years, such as new issuers. To ensure that adequate information concerning these registrants is readily available to investors, proposed Form S–1 requires delivery of a more lengthy and comprehensive prospectus than either proposed Form S–2 or Form S–3. . . .

III. Synopsis . . .

A. *Eligibility Rules for Use of Forms S–3, S–2 and S–1* . . .

1. *Form S–3*

The eligibility requirements for use of Form S–3 are broken down into two classifications, "Registrant Requirements" and "Transaction Requirements." A registrant first must meet the Registrant Requirements (which are identical for Forms S–3 and S–2) and then must meet at least one of the Transaction Requirements before it can use Form S–3. . . .

2. *Form S–2*

. . . [T]he Registrant Requirements of Form S–3 also constitute virtually the entire eligibility requirements for the use of Form S–2. . . .

3. *Form S–1*

. . . [T]his more comprehensive form must be used by first time filers and others who have only been filing reports for a short period of time. . . .

c. *Disclosure Provisions*

In proposed Forms S–1, S–2 and S–3, the Commission has developed a Securities Act registration system which identifies the information material to investment decisions in the context of all public offerings and then determines in what form and to whom issuers must disseminate such information. The material information will be required to be part of all Securities Act registration statements, regardless of the form used, through incorporation by reference in some cases. Differences among the forms primarily involve dissemination, i.e., the extent to which the required information must be presented in the prospectus, or may be presented in other documents delivered with the prospectus and incorporated by reference, or may be simply incorporated by reference from information contained in the Exchange Act continuous reporting system.

Generally, it is the issuer-oriented part of the information material to a public offering, as opposed to the transaction-specific information, which, depending on the form available, may be satisfied otherwise than through full prospectus presentation. This information includes the basic package of information about the issuer which the Commission believes is material to investment decisions in all contexts and thus is also required to be presented in annual reports to the Commission on Form 10–K and in annual reports to security holders. Information about the offering will not have been reported on in any other disclosure document or otherwise have been publicly disseminated and thus will be required to be presented in all cases. . . .

2. *Incorporation by Reference*

The technique of incorporation by reference of Exchange Act disclosure documents is central to the integrated Securities Act registration system represented by proposed Forms S–1, S–2 and S–3. Proposed Form S–3 relies on incorporation by reference to replace prospectus presentation of information about the issuer of the securities being registered. Proposed Form S–2 uses incorporation by reference to allow streamlining of the prospectus presentation of issuer-specific information. Proposed Form S–1 uses no incorporation by reference and instead requires full disclosure about the issuer of the securities to be presented in the prospectus. . . .

3. *Disclosure Requirements by Form*

a. *Form S–3*

Proposed Form S–3 provides the shortest form for Securities Act registration. The prospectus would be required to present [certain] items calling for information about the offering. . . .

Information concerning the registrant would be incorporated by reference from Exchange Act reports, which would be available to investors on request. The documents required to be incorporated are the latest annual report on Form 10–K and all other reports filed pursuant to Section 13(a) or 15(d) of the Exchange Act since the end of the fiscal year covered by the Form 10–K, including all Section 13(d) or 15(d) reports filed subsequent to effectiveness of the registration statement and prior to termination of the offering. Unless there has been a material change in the registrant's affairs which has not been reported in an Exchange Act filing, the prospectus would not be required to present any information concerning the registrant. . . .

b. *Form S–2*

Proposed Form S–2 provides a simplified form for registration by certain registrants. While it requires delivery of information about the registrant in addition to delivery of the same information about the offering as required by Form S–3, proposed Form S–2 significantly streamlines the registrant-specific disclosure by making the required level of disclosure delivered to investors that of the annual report to security holders pursuant to Rule 14a–3 rather than that of the annual report on Form 10–K. Required information about the registrant includes the basic information package components (market price and dividend data, selected financial data, financial statements and management's discussion and analysis) and such other items (brief descriptions of business, segments, supplementary financial information) as are required to be included in the annual report to security holders pursuant to Rule 14a–3. Moreover, registrants are granted the option of providing this information either by presenting it in the prospectus or by delivering the latest annual report to security holders along with the prospectus. Finally, the registrant's latest annual report on Form 10–K and periodic reports on Form 10–Q and Form 8–K must be incorporated by reference into the prospectus, and made available upon request, to round out the information provided about the registrant....

If the Form S–2 registrant elects the alternative of delivering its annual report, it must incorporate certain information in that document by reference and describe in the prospectus any material changes in its affairs since the end of the latest fiscal year reported in the delivered annual report. In addition, it must provide updating information but may avoid duplication of previously reported quarterly information because updating may be accomplished by any one of three means: (1) including in the prospectus such financial and other information as would be required to be reported in a report on Form 10–Q; (2) delivering a copy of the latest Form 10–Q with the prospectus and annual report; (3) delivering a copy of the latest informal quarterly report to shareholders if such report contained the same required information....

c. *Form S–1*

Proposed Form S–1 presents a simple format. Full disclosure of all material information about the offering and the registrant is required to be presented in the prospectus itself. No incorporation by reference to any Exchange Act documents is allowed. Proposed Form S–1 looks entirely to Regulation S–K for its non-financial substantive disclosure provisions. First, like proposed Forms S–2 and S–3, proposed Form S–1 requires prospectus presentation of the offering-oriented items of § 229.500 of Regulation S–K and the description of securities (proposed Item 202 of Regulation S–K). In addition, the proposed Form S–1 prospectus must include the same information about the registrant as is required to be reported in an annual report on Form 10–K. This information includes, in addition to the basic information package with respect to the registrant, the full Regulation S–K descriptions of business, properties and legal proceedings as well as the Regulation S–K disclosures with respect to management and security holders....

SECURITIES ACT RULES § 176, 415

[See Statutory Supplement]

Securities Act Release No. 6276 (1981) [Shelf Registration]

... The last sentence of Section 6(a) of the Securities Act provides: "A registration statement shall be deemed effective only as to the securities specified therein as proposed to be offered." ... [The Commission has interpreted] that sentence to prohibit the registration of securities for a delayed or postponed offering, commonly referred to as "shelf" offering or registration.

In the absence of any specific legislative comment upon the meaning of the last sentence of Section 6(a) of the Securities Act, as enacted by Congress in 1933, early opinions of the Commission and its staff interpreted the provision as requiring that a registration statement be effective only as to those securities proposed to be offered "in the proximate future".... This general prohibition against shelf registration was designed to effectuate the clear policy underlying the last sentence of Section 6(a) that "the registration statements and prospectuses on which they rely, so far as is reasonably possible, provide current information." This interpretation was, in turn, premised upon the assumption that the registration of securities which are to be offered at "some remote future time" gives "the appearance of a registered status" without providing its true substance—accurate and current information.

In practice, the Commission has never adhered to such an absolute prohibition [and].... such registration has been permitted for several types of offerings....

After substantial experience with [several] types of shelf registration, the Commission is not aware of major abuses that have harmed investors. In addition, the integration of the Securities Act and Exchange Act disclosure systems provides an increasingly efficient basis for updating disclosure in securities offerings. Shelf registrations can utilize integration effectively thereby facilitating the development of important new capital raising techniques. Accordingly, the Commission believes that a restrictive policy on shelf registration is not appropriate or necessary for the protection of investors. The Commission is proposing ... that its stated prohibition of shelf registration be replaced with proposed Rule [415]....

Securities Act Release No. 6383 (1982) [Shelf Registration]

... Rule 415 permits shelf registration of "at the market offerings" of equity securities directly by or on behalf of the registrant. Because such offerings raise concerns for the public and for the marketplace, the [original] Shelf Release proposed the imposition of two conditions. First, the Commission proposed that those securities must be sold through an underwriter or underwriters, acting as principal(s) or agent(s) for the registrant, and that such underwriter(s) must be named in the prospectus which is part of the registration statement. Second, the Commission proposed to define an "at the market offering" as an offering of securities into an existing trading market for outstanding shares of the same class of securities at other than a fixed price on or through the facilities of a national securities exchange or to a market maker otherwise than on an exchange.

A number of commentators agreed with the Commission that it should impose conditions upon the availability of shelf registration for an at the market offering. The Commission has determined to adopt the conditions proposed and to adopt two further conditions: (1) that the registrant must meet the registrant requirements and applicable transaction requirements of Form S–3 and (2) that the amount of securities registered must not exceed ten percent of the registrant's non-affiliate float. The Commission is conditioning primary equity offerings at the market on Form S–3 availability and is limiting such offerings to ten percent of a registrant's float in view of the experimental nature of the temporary rule.

The Commission is adopting the requirement for a named underwriter because it believes that the direct involvement of an underwriter can provide a desirable discipline upon such offerings of equity securities into an existing trading market and that the presence of an underwriter helps to ensure that accurate and current disclosure is made to investors in the prospectus and that the prospectus delivery requirements of the Securities Act are met....

Securities Act Release No. 6499 (1983) [Shelf Registration]

... During the eighteen months [Rule 415] has been in effect, it has worked well and has provided registrants with substantial benefits in their financings.... On the other hand, the Commission believes that concerns raised about the quality and timing of disclosure and due diligence are important to address because they relate to the adequacy of disclosure investors receive in connection with public offerings. Having weighed all considerations, the Commission is modifying Rule 415 to strike an appropriate balance by making it available for offerings eligible to be registered on Form S–3 ... and for traditional shelf offerings....

For registrants not eligible to use short form registration, however, the Commission believes that concerns about disclosure and due diligence outweigh the benefits of Rule 415. The Commission also notes that shelf registration may not be as advantageous for such registrants because they cannot rely on subsequently filed Exchange Act reports for certain updating of the information in the shelf registration statement. Such updating requires the filing of post-effective amendments. Indeed, few non–S–3 ... registrants have used Rule 415 for other than traditional shelf offerings....

Securities Act Release No. 6964 [Simplification of Registration Procedures for Primary Offerings]

1992.

. . . Today's initiatives recognize and build on the success of the integrated disclosure system and shelf registration process adopted 10 years ago. Form S–3, the short-form registration statement that permits maximum reliance upon Exchange Act reports filed by issuers, will now be available to a larger class of issuers and transactions, including issuers of investment grade asset-backed securities. The Commission's shelf registration procedures also are extended to these newly eligible issuers, thereby allowing significantly greater numbers of issuers the flexibility to access the public securities markets on demand without having to obtain additional clearance from the Commission's staff. These changes remove unnecessary regulatory obstacles to capital raising and should reduce the costs of securitizing a variety of financial assets, including pools of small business loans.

Three principal changes to the Form S–3 eligibility requirements have been made. First, the reporting history necessary to register on Form S–3 has been reduced from 36 to 12 months for most issuers. Second, the aggregate market value of the issuer's voting stock held by non-affiliates (referred to as the "public float") qualifying an issuer for use of Form S–3 for any of its securities has been reduced from $150 million to $75 million, and the 3 million share trading volume test has been eliminated. Third, Form S–3 has been amended to specifically permit registration of investment grade asset-backed securities without regard to whether the issuer or registrant has a reporting history.

Because shelf registration is available for offerings registered, or eligible to be registered, on Form S–3, these changes to Form S–3 also extend shelf registration to these newly eligible issuers and offerings. Thus, Rule 415 shelf registration will be available for offerings of investment grade asset-backed securities. . . .

To provide additional flexibility and facilitate the use of shelf registration for delayed offerings of common stock, Form S–3 has been revised as proposed to permit Form S–3 eligible companies to register debt, equity and other securities on a single shelf registration statement, without having to specify in the registration statement the amount of each class of securities to be offered. Prospectus supplements filed after effectiveness will disclose the amount of the particular security being offered to investors, thereby insuring that investors receive the same information currently provided. . . .

SECTION 6. DUTIES AND PROHIBITIONS WHEN A SECURITY IS IN REGISTRATION

INTRODUCTORY NOTE

Assuming that a registration statement must be filed, the issuer, underwriter, and broker-dealers come under a variety of duties and prohibitions. To analyze these duties and prohibitions, it is necessary to separately consider three time periods. The first is the period before registration (the "prefiling period"). The second is the period between the time the registration statement is filed and the time it becomes effective (the "waiting period"). The third is the period after the registration statement becomes effective (the "post-effective period").

Note that the term "in registration" is used to mean "the entire process of registration, at least from the time an issuer reaches an understanding with the broker-dealer which is to act as managing underwriter prior to the filing of a registration statement and the period of 40 to 90 days during which dealers must deliver a prospectus." Securities Act Release No. 5180 n. 1 (1971).

––––––

(a) OVERVIEW

––––––

Securities Act Release No. 4697 (1964) [Offers and Sales of Securities by Underwriters and Dealers]

In view of recent comments in the press concerning the rights and obligations of, and limitations on, dealers in connection with distributions of registered securities, the Commission takes this opportunity to explain the operation of section 5 of the Securities Act of 1933 with particular reference to the limitations upon, and responsibilities of, underwriters and dealers in the offer and sale of an issue of securities prior to and after the filing of a registration statement.

The discussion below assumes that the offering is not exempt from the registration requirements of the Act and, unless otherwise stated, that the mails or facilities of interstate or foreign commerce are used.

The Period Before the Filing of a Registration Statement

Section 5 of the Securities Act prohibits both offers to sell and offers to buy a security before a registration statement is filed. Section 2(3) of the Act, however, exempts preliminary negotiations or agreements between the issuer or other person on whose behalf the distribution is to be made and any underwriter or among underwriters. Thus, negotiation of the financing can proceed during this period but neither the issuer nor the underwriter may offer the security either to investors or to dealers, and dealers are prohibited from offering to buy the securities during this period.[1] Consequently, not only may no steps be taken to form a selling group but also dealers may not seek inclusion in the selling group prior to the filing.

It should be borne in mind that publicity about an issuer, its securities or the proposed offering prior to the filing of a registration statement may constitute an illegal offer to sell. Thus, announcement of the underwriter's identity should be avoided during this period. Experience shows that such announcements are very likely to lead to illegal offers to buy. This subject will not be further discussed in this release since it has been extensively considered elsewhere.[2]

These principles, however, are not intended to restrict the normal communications between an issuer and its stockholders or the announcement to the public generally of information with respect to important business and financial developments. Such announcements are required in the listing agreements used by stock exchanges, and the Commission is sensitive to the importance of encouraging this type of communication. In recognition of this requirement of certain stock exchanges, the Commission adopted Rule 135, which permits a brief announcement of proposed rights offerings, proposed exchange offerings, and proposed offerings to employees as not constituting an offer of a security for the purposes of section 5 of the Act.

The Period After the Filing and Before the Effective Date

After the registration statement is filed, and before its effective date, offers to sell the securities are permitted but no written offer may be made except by means of a statutory prospectus. For this purpose the statutory prospectus includes the preliminary prospectus provided for in Rule 433 as well as the summary prospectus provided for in Rules 434 and 434A. In addition the so-called "tombstone" advertisement permitted by Rule 134 may be used.

During the period after the filing of a registration statement, the freedom of an underwriter or dealer expecting to participate in the distribution, to communicate with his customers is limited only by the antifraud provisions of the Securities Act and the Securities Exchange Act, and by the fact that written offering material other than a statutory prospectus or tombstone advertisement may not be used. In other words, during this period "free writing" is illegal. The dealer, therefore, can orally solicit indications of interest or offers to buy and may discuss the securities with his customers and advise them whether or not in his opinion the securities are desirable or suitable for them. In this connection a dealer proposing to discuss an issue of securities with his customers should obtain copies of the preliminary prospectus

---

1. The reason for this provision was stated in the House Report on the bill as originally enacted as follows:

"... Otherwise, the underwriter ... could accept them in the order of their priority and thus bring pressure upon dealers, who wish to avail themselves of a particular security offering, to rush their orders to buy without adequate consideration of the nature of the security being offered." H.R.Report No. 85, 73rd Cong., 1st Sess. (1933), p. 11.

2. See Securities Act Release No. 3844 (1957); Carl M. Loeb, Rhoades & Co., 38 S.E.C. 843 (1959); First Maine Corporation, 38 S.E.C. 882 (1959).

in order to have a reliable source of information. This is particularly important where he proposes to recommend the securities, or where information concerning them has not been generally available. The corollary of the dealer's obligation to secure the copy is the obligation of the issuer and managing underwriters to make it readily available. Rule 460 provides that as a condition to acceleration of the effective date of a registration statement, the Commission will consider whether the persons making the offering have taken reasonable steps to make the information contained in the registration statement available to dealers who may participate in the distribution.

It is a principal purpose of the so-called "waiting period" between the filing date and the effective date to enable dealers and, through them, investors to become acquainted with the information contained in the registration statement and to arrive at an unhurried decision concerning the merits of the securities. Consistently with this purpose, no contracts of sale can be made during this period, the purchase price may not be paid or received and offers to buy may be cancelled.

The Period After the Effective Date

When the registration statement becomes effective oral offerings may continue and sales may be made and consummated. A copy of the final statutory prospectus must be delivered in connection with any written offer or confirmation or upon delivery of the security, whichever first occurs. Supplemental sales literature ("free writing") may be used if it is accompanied or preceded by a prospectus. However, care must be taken to see that all such material is at the time of use not false or misleading under the standards of section 17(a) of the Act. If the offering continues over an extended period, the prospectus should be current under the standards of section 10(a)(3). All dealers trading in the registered security must continue to employ the prospectus for the period referred to in section 4.

———

(b) THE PRE-FILING PERIOD

———

SECURITIES ACT §§ 2(a)(3), 5

[See Statutory Supplement]

———

NOTE ON THE PRE-FILING PERIOD

Section 5(a) of the 1933 Act provides that:

> Unless a registration statement is in effect as to a security, it shall be unlawful for any person, directly or indirectly—(1) to make use of any means or instruments of transportation or communication in interstate commerce or of the mails to sell such security

through the use or medium of any prospectus or otherwise; or (2) to carry or cause to be carried through the mails or in interstate commerce, by any means or instruments of transportation, any such security for the purpose of sale or for delivery after sale.

Section 5(a)(c) provides that:

It shall be unlawful for any person, directly or indirectly, to make use of any means or instruments of transportation or communication in interstate commerce or of the mails to offer to sell or offer to buy through the use or medium of any prospectus or otherwise any security, unless a registration statement has been filed as to such security. . . .

Section 2(a)(3) provides that:

The term "sale" or "sell" shall include every contract of sale or disposition of a security or interest in a security, for value. The term "offer to sell", "offer for sale", or "offer" shall include every attempt or offer to dispose of, or solicitation of an offer to buy, a security or interest in a security, for value.

There is an important exception to section 2(a)(3):

The terms defined in [§ 2(a)(3)] and the term "offer to buy" as used in subsection (c) of section 5 shall not include preliminary negotiations or agreements between an issuer . . . and any underwriter or among underwriters who are or are to be in privity of contract with an issuer. . . .

Putting together §§ 5(a), 5(c), and 2(a)(3), neither a sale of securities, nor an oral or written offer to sell securities, that are to be registered, may be made during the prefiling period, except for preliminary negotiations between the issuer and the underwriter and between underwriters. The prohibition against offers in the prefiling period extends not only to formal offers, but to "gun-jumping"— unusual publicity by the issuer or a prospective underwriter that in effect is a preliminary step in the selling effort. On the other hand, if a corporation is already publicly held, blocking the normal flow of information would adversely affect the integrity of the market for the securities that are already outstanding. The cases and rules governing the prefiling period attempt to reconcile the undesirability of gun-jumping with the desirability of maintaining the normal flow of information concerning corporations that are already publicly held.

SECURITIES ACT RULES 135, 137, 139

[See Statutory Supplement]

NOTE ON IN THE MATTER OF CARL M. LOEB, RHOADES & CO. AND CHRIS–CRAFT INDUSTRIES v. BANGOR PUNTA CORP.

1. In In the Matter of Carl M. Loeb, Rhoades & Co., 38 S.E.C. 843 (1959), Davis had formed Arvida Corporation and transferred land

to it. He then proposed that Arvida engage in a public offering of stock. A press release, issued under the name of Loeb, Rhoades, as underwriter, stated the Davis had transferred to Arvida his holdings of over 100,000 acres in an area of the Florida Gold Coast, and that part of the land was to be developed immediately into residential communities. The press release said that Arvida would have assets of over 100 million dollars, derived from Davis's investment and sales of stock that would begin within 60 days. The substance of the release appeared in three New York papers and in numerous other news sources across the country. The probable price of the securities was disclosed at a news conference held the day the release was issued.

The announcement and publicity generated buying interest in Arvida stock of at least $500,000. One hundred securities firms expressed an interest in participating in the underwriting. Loeb, Rhoades received at least 58 expressions of interest from the public, including at least 17 specific offers to buy.

Subsequently, Arvida filed a registration statement covering its planned offering of securities. The statement disclosed that Arvida's properties were subject to a mortgage of about $31 million, of which about $21 million would be due within five years. This indicated that a large part of the offering would probably be used to meet the mortgage obligations rather than to improve the land, and in fact only $2.8 million was budgeted for development of the land in the first year. Furthermore, about sixty-one percent of Arvida land was located in rural areas, away from existing urban development. Much of the land was accessible only by unpaved roads, and some was entirely inaccessible by automobile. About fifty percent of the land was below flood criteria established by local governments and below the minimum elevation at which land could be developed. The SEC concluded that Arvida had violated Section 5(c):

> [P]ublicity, prior to the filing of a registration statement by means of public media of communication, with respect to an issuer or it[s] securities, emanating from broker-dealer firms who as underwriters or prospective underwriters have negotiated or are negotiating for a public offering of the securities of such issuer, must be presumed to set in motion or to be a part of the distribution process and therefore to involve an offer to sell or a solicitation or an offer to buy such securities prohibited by Section 5(c).

38 S.E.C. at 851. In dealing with the defendants' argument that the information in the release constituted news, the Commission said that the registration requirements were

> equally applicable whether or not the issuer or the surrounding circumstances have, or by astute public relations activities may be made to appear to have, news value.... In the normal conduct of its business a corporation may continue to advertise its products and services without interruption, it may send out its customary quarterly, annual and other periodic reports to security holders, and it may publish its proxy statements, send out its dividend notices and make routine announcements to the press. This flow

of normal corporate news, unrelated to a selling effort for an issue of securities, is natural, desirable and entirely consistent with the objective of disclosure to the public which underlies the federal securities laws. However, an issuer who is party to or collaborates with underwriters or prospective underwriters in initiating or securing publicity must be regarded as participating directly or indirectly in an offer to sell or a solicitation of an offer to buy prohibited by section 5(c).

38 S.E.C. at 852–53.

2.   Chris–Craft Industries, Inc. v. Bangor Punta Corp., 426 F.2d 569 (2d Cir.1970) involved a bitter contest for the control of Piper Aircraft Corporation. Bangor proposed to make an exchange offer of its securities for Piper securities. Since the exchange offer constituted a public offering of Bangor securities, Bangor had to file a registration statement. While Bangor was in the process of preparing the registration statement, it issued a press release stating that it had agreed to exchange a package of Bangor securities "having a value, in the written opinion of The First Boston Corporation, of $80 or more" per Piper share. Held, Bangor had violated § 5(c):

> Chris–Craft argues, and the argument is supported by the SEC, both in its action filed May 26 against Bangor Punta and in its *amicus curiae* brief in this court, that the categories of information privileged under [Rule 135] are exclusive. In view of this exclusivity they contend that as the rule does not mention disclosure of the value of the securities to be offered, Bangor Punta's and Piper's announcements that the package of securities offered by Bangor Punta would be valued at $80 oversteps the exemption and makes the press release an offer to sell.

> We agree with this contention. When it is announced that securities will be sold at some date in the future and, in addition, an attractive description of these securities and of the issuer is furnished, it seems clear that such an announcement provides much the same kind of information as that contained in a prospectus. See S.E.C. v. Arvida Corp., 169 F.Supp. 211 (S.D.N.Y. 1958). Doubtless the line drawn between an announcement containing sufficient information to constitute an offer and one which does not must be to some extent arbitrary. A checklist of features that may be included in an announcement which does not also constitute an offer to sell serves to guide the financial community and the courts far better than any judicially formulated "rule of reason" as to what is or is not an offer. Rule 135 provides just such a checklist, and if the Rule is not construed as setting forth an exclusive list, then much of its value as a guide is lost.

> Moreover, it is reasonable to conclude that the assigning of a value to offered shares constitutes an offer to sell. One of the evils of a premature offer is its tendency to encourage the formation by

the offeree of an opinion of the value of the securities before a registration statement and prospectus are filed.

———

Securities Act Release No. 5180 (1971)

[GUIDELINES FOR THE RELEASE OF INFORMATION BY ISSUERS WHOSE SECURITIES ARE IN REGISTRATION]

The Commission today took note of situations when issuers whose securities are "in registration" may have refused to answer legitimate inquiries from stockholders, financial analysts, the press or other persons concerning the company or some aspect of its business. The Commission hereby emphasizes that there is no basis in the securities acts or in any policy of the Commission which would justify the practice of non-disclosure of *factual* information by a publicly held company on the grounds that it has securities in registration under the Securities Act of 1933 ("Act"). Neither a company in registration nor its representatives should instigate publicity for the purpose of facilitating the sale of securities in a proposed offering. . . .

. . . It has been asserted that the increasing obligations and incentives of corporations to make timely disclosures concerning their affairs creates a possible conflict with statutory restrictions on publication of information concerning a company which has securities in registration. As the Commission has stated in previously issued releases this conflict may be more apparent than real. Disclosure of factual information in response to inquiries or resulting from a duty to make prompt disclosure under the antifraud provisions of the securities acts or the timely disclosure policies of self-regulatory organizations, at a time when a registered offering of securities is contemplated or in process, can and should be effected in a manner which will not unduly influence the proposed offering.

Statutory Requirements

In order for issuers and their representatives to avoid problems in responding to inquiries, it is essential that such persons be familiar with the statutory requirements governing this area. Generally speaking, Section 5(c) of the Act makes it unlawful for any person directly or indirectly to make use of any means or instruments of interstate commerce or of the mails *to offer to sell* a security unless a registration statement has been filed with the Commission as to such security. Questions arise from time to time because many persons do not realize that the phrase "offer to sell" is broadly defined by the Act and has been liberally construed by the courts and Commission. For example, the publication of information and statements, and publicity efforts, made in advance of a proposed financing which have the effect of conditioning the public mind or arousing public interest in the issuer or in its securities constitutes an offer in violation of the Act. The same holds true with respect to publication of information which is part of a selling effort between the filing date and the effective date of a registration statement. . . .

Guidelines

The Commission strongly suggests that all issuers establish internal procedures designed to avoid problems relating to the release of corporate information when in registration. As stated above, issuers and their representatives should not initiate publicity when in registration, but should nevertheless respond to legitimate inquiries for factual information about the company's financial condition and business operations. Further, care should be exercised so that, for example, predictions, projections, forecasts, estimates and opinions concerning value are not given with respect to such things, among other, as sales and earnings and value of the issuer's securities.

It has been suggested that the Commission promulgate an all inclusive list of permissible and prohibited activities in this area. This is not feasible for the reason that determinations are based upon the particular facts of each case. However, the Commission as a matter of policy encourages the flow of factual information to shareholders and the investing public. Issuers in this regard should:

1.   Continue to advertise products and services.

2.   Continue to send out customary quarterly, annual and other periodic reports to stockholders.

3.   Continue to publish proxy statements and send out dividend notices.

4.   Continue to make announcements to the press with respect to factual business and financial developments; *i.e.,* receipt of a contract, the settlement of a strike, the opening of a plant, or similar events of interest to the community in which the business operates.

5.   Answer unsolicited telephone inquiries from stockholders, financial analysts, the press and others concerning factual information.

6.   Observe an "open door" policy in responding to unsolicited inquiries concerning factual matters from securities analysts, financial analysts, security holders, and participants in the communications field who have a legitimate interest in the corporation's affairs.

7.   Continue to hold stockholder meetings as scheduled and to answer shareholders' inquiries at stockholder meetings relating to factual matters.

In order to curtail problems in this area, issuers in this regard should avoid:

1.   Issuance of forecasts, projections, or predictions relating but not limited to revenues, income, or earnings per share.

2.   Publishing opinions concerning values.

In the event a company publicly releases material information concerning new corporate developments during the period that a registration statement is pending, the registration statement should be amended at or prior to the time the information is released. If this is not done and such information is publicly released through inadvertence, the pending registration statement should be promptly amended to reflect such information. . . .

———

(c) THE WAITING PERIOD

———

SECURITIES ACT §§ 2(a)(10), 5, 8, 10; SECURITIES ACT RULES 134, 152c–8, 430, 431, 460

[See Statutory Supplement]

———

NOTE ON THE WAITING PERIOD

1.   Section 8 of the 1933 Act provides that "Except as hereinafter provided, the effective date of a registration statement shall be the twentieth day after the filing thereof or such earlier date as the Commission may determine. . . ."

Accordingly, there is always a waiting period between the time at which a registration statement is filed and the time at which it is effective. Section 5(a) prohibits *sales* unless a registration is effective, thereby prohibiting sales during the waiting period. Section 5(c) prohibits offers "[making] use of any means of interstate commerce to offer to sell ... through the use or medium of any prospectus or otherwise any security, unless a registration statement has been filed," but does not prohibit offers, as such, during the waiting period. However, section 5(b) prohibits the transmission of "any prospectus relating to any securities with respect to which a registration statement has been filed ... unless such prospectus meets the requirements of section 10." Section 2(a)(10) defines "prospectus" very broadly to mean "any prospectus, notice, circular, advertisement, letter, or communication, written or by radio or television, which offers any security for sale or confirms the sale of any security."

The combined effect of sections 5 and 2(a)(10) on issuers, underwriters and dealers, is that during the waiting period: (1) *sales* are not permissible; (2) *oral offers* are permissible, and (3) writings relating to the securities are permissible only if they specifically permitted by statute or rule.

2.   What writings *are* permitted during the waiting period?

In theory, a *final prospectus* (also sometimes known as a *section 10(a) prospectus* or a *statutory prospectus*) is permissible. In practice, however, use of a final prospectus during this period is impossible, because a final prospectus must include certain information that is usually not decided upon until the waiting period is over.

However, certain other writings are permissible.

(a) *Preliminary prospectus.* Section 10(b) of the Securities Act provides that:

> In addition to the prospectus permitted or required in sub-section (a), the Commission shall by rules or regulations deemed necessary or appropriate in the public interest or for the protection of investors permit the use of a prospectus for the purposes of subsection (b)(1) of section 5 which omits in part or summarizes information in the prospectus specified in subsection (a).

Pursuant to section 10(b), the Commission has promulgated Rule 430, which provides that

> A form of prospectus filed as a part of the registration statement shall be deemed to meet the requirements of section 10 of the Act for the purpose of section 5(b)(1) thereof prior to the effective date of the registration statement, provided such form of prospectus contains substantially the information required by the Act and the rules and regulations thereunder to be included in a prospectus meeting the requirements of section 10(a) of the Act for the securities being registered, or contains substantially that information except for the omission of information with respect to the offering price, underwriting discounts or commissions, discounts or commissions to dealers, amount of proceeds, conversion rates, call prices, or other matters dependent upon the offering price.

The writing permitted under section 10(b) and Rule 430 is known as a *preliminary prospectus* or *red herring* (so-called because of a red legend that appears on the cover page).

(b) *Summary prospectus.* Under Rule 431, certain issuers can use a *summary prospectus* during the waiting period. Under that Rule:

> . . . A summary prospectus shall contain the information specified in the instructions as to summary prospectuses in the form used for registration of the securities to be offered. Such prospectus may include any other information the substance of which is contained in the registration statement except as otherwise specifically provided in the instructions as to summary prospectuses in the form used for registration.

(c) *Tombstone ads.* Under section 2(a)(10)(b), an ad can be used during the waiting period, if the ad states only from whom a written prospectus, meeting the requirements of section 10, may be obtained, and does no more than identify the security, state the price, state by whom orders will be executed, and contain such other information as the Commission may prescribe. Such an ad is known as a *tombstone ad*, because of its spare nature and typical black border.

(d) *Identifying statement.* Under section 2(a)(10)(b) and Rule 134, an *identifying statement*—in effect, an expanded tombstone ad—can be used during the waiting period. Under Rule 134, certain information, in addition to that specified in section 2(a)(10)(b) for tombstone ads, may be included in an identifying statement.

In short, during the waiting period, issuers, underwriters, and dealers can reach potential customers in writing only by a preliminary prospectus, a summary prospectus, a tombstone ad, or an identifying statement. Any other kind of writing—known as *free writing*—is prohibited.

_____

(d) The Post-Effective Period

_____

SECURITIES ACT §§ 2(3), 2(10), 4(3), 5, 10; SECURITIES ACT RULES 153, 174, 427

[See Statutory Supplement]

_____

NOTE ON THE POST–EFFECTIVE PERIOD

After the registration statement has become effective there is no prohibition on either offers or sales, as such. Accordingly, *free writings*—writings other than those permitted during the waiting period—are permitted, with an important limitation. The limitation is that under sections 2(10) and 5(b)(1), no writings may be distributed concerning a security as to which a registration is in effect unless prior to, or at the same time, a section 10 prospectus has been delivered.

Furthermore, under section 5(b)(2) if a registration statement is in effect as to a security, a section 10 prospectus must precede or accompany any securities sold. A section 10 prospectus must also precede or accompany any confirmation of a sale of registered securities, so that a sale cannot be effectively closed without delivery of a section 10 prospectus.

How long do these restrictions last?

Sales of registered securities by an *issuer* must always be accompanied by a section 10 prospectus.

All *underwriters* of an offering, and all *dealers* who were participants in the distribution, are subject to the prospectus-delivery requirement as long as they are offering an unsold allotment of the original public offering. Dealers are also subject to the prospectus-delivery requirement, whether or not they are selling an unsold allotment, during a specified period after commencement of the offering.

However, section 4(4) of the Securities Act provides that "broker's transactions executed upon customers' orders on any exchange or in the over-the-counter market" are exempted from the prospectus-delivery requirement. This exemption "permits individuals to sell their securities through a broker in an ordinary brokerage transaction, during the period of distribution or while a stop order is in effect, without regard to the registration and prospectus requirements of section 5." In the Matter of Ira Haupt & Co., 23 S.E.C. 589 (1946).

SECTION 7.   LIABILITIES UNDER THE SECURITIES ACT

SECURITIES ACT §§ 11, 12, 17, 21d(g), 27A; SECURITIES ACT RULES 175, 176

[See Statutory Supplement]

NOTE ON LIABILITIES UNDER THE SECURITIES ACT

The Securities Act contains four basic liability provisions: Sections 11, 12(a)(1), 12(a)(2), and 17(a).

1. *Section 17(a).* Section 17(a) is a general antifraud provision, whose applicability does not turn on whether there has been a violation of section 5, the registration provision. Section 17(a) is highly comparable to rule 10b–5, because rule 10b–5 was modeled on section 17(a). However, rule 10b–5 regulates both sellers and buyers, while section 17(a) regulates only sellers. On the other hand, section 17(a) applies to "offers" while rule 10b–5 does not.

Scienter is a necessary element of a violation of section 17(a)(1), but not of sections 17(a)(2) or 17(a)(3). Aaron v. S.E.C., 446 U.S. 680, 100 S.Ct. 1945, 64 L.Ed.2d 611 (1980).

There is no private right of action under section 17(a). See, e.g., Finkel v. Stratton Corp., 962 F.2d 169, 174–75 (2d Cir.1992).

2. *Section 12(a)(2).* Section 12(a)(2) provides that, subject to certain conditions, any person who offers or sells a security by means of a prospectus or oral communication is liable to the purchaser for rescission or damages, if the prospectus or oral communication includes a material misstatement or has a material omission. Thus section 12(a)(2), like section 17(a), is an antifraud provision. Unlike section 17(a), section 12(a)(2) explicitly gives buyers a private right of action. Gustafson v. Alloyd Co., 513 U.S. 561, 115 S.Ct. 1061, 131 L.Ed.2d 1 (1995). However section 12(a)(2) applies only to securities sold in public offerings by issuers or their controlling shareholders. *Gustafson,* supra.

The principal conditions to the seller's liability under section 12(a)(2) are as follows: (1) The buyer must not have known the truth. (2) If the misstatement involves a forward-looking statement, the buyer has available the safe harbor provided by section 27A and rule 175. (3) The seller is not liable if and to the extent he proves that any or all of the amount that the buyer could otherwise have recovered arose from factors other than the misstatement or omission. (This reflects the concept of "loss causation," discussed in Chapter 10.)

The buyer's recovery is limited to the return of the purchase price (plus interest, but minus the amount of any income received), unless he has resold the security. If the buyer has resold the security, he is entitled to the difference between the price he paid for the security and the price at which he resold the security.

To obtain relief under section 12(a)(2) the buyer must show a false statement or material omission. There is no requirement that the plaintiff relied on the misstatement or omission. He need only show that he did not know the truth. Once the buyer shows that an omission was material, or that a material statement was false, the seller has the burden of showing that he did not know and "in the exercise of reasonable care could not have known" of the untruth or omission. In effect, therefore, section 12(a)(2) makes the seller liable for negligence in connection with a misrepresentation or omission, and puts the burden of proof on the seller to show that he was not negligent.

3. *Section 12(a)(1)*. Section 12(a)(1) gives buyers a private right of action against sellers who violate section 5 of the 1933 Act—that is, for the most part, against sellers who either (1) sell securities that are required to be, but are not, registered, or (2) sell securities without delivering a required section 10 prospectus or deliver a prospectus that does not satisfy section 10. A seller's liability under section 12(a)(1) is strict. The buyer does not need to show fraud or even a material misstatement or omission in the registration statement. However, the remedy under section 12(a)(1) is limited to buyers who are in privity with—that is, who purchased directly from—the seller in question.

The basic remedy under section 12(a)(1) is rescission. However, a buyer who sold the stock before she brought suit can sue for the difference between the price that she paid for the stock and the price at which she sold it.

The term "seller" in section 12(a)(1) is broadly construed to mean any person who successfully solicits a purchase and who is motivated at least in part by a desire to serve his own financial interests or those of the owner of the securities. Pinter v. Dahl, 486 U.S. 622, 108 S.Ct. 2063, 100 L.Ed.2d 658 (1988).

4. *Section 11*. Section 11 gives buyers a private right of action for material misstatements or omissions in a registration statement, subject to certain conditions and defenses. A variety of persons may be potentially liable under section 11, including the issuer, the directors and certain officers of the issuer, the underwriters, and experts (such as accountants) who have taken responsibility for some portion of the registration statement.

Section 11 does not require privity: any person who has purchased the security in question, either in the original distribution or later in the aftermarket, can bring suit. However, liability under section 11 extends only to the securities issued under the registration statement. Accordingly, a buyer who purchased the same class of securities as those registered, but cannot trace the securities she purchased back to the registration statement, cannot bring suit under section 11 even though the securities she purchased were economically identical to the securities issued under the registration statement. Barnes v. Osofsky, 373 F.2d 269 (2d Cir.1967). (However, such a buyer might be able to bring suit under Rule 10b–5.)

Section 11 does not require the buyer to show reliance or causation. However, it is defense that the buyer knew the truth at the time he acquired the security. Under section 27A of the 1933 Act, under certain circumstances there is no liability under section 11 for forward-looking statements.

Damages under section 11 are limited to the difference between the original offering price and the value of the securities at the time of suit. Furthermore, under a proviso to section 11(e), if the defendant proves that any portion (or all) of the damages is based on factors other than the relevant misstatement or omission, that portion of the damages cannot be recovered. This proviso is sometimes referred to as "negative causation." Essentially, it is a form of loss causation, with the burden of proof on the defendant.

An issuer is strictly liable under section 11. Persons other than the issuer (such as directors of the issuer, or experts) can escape liability by establishing what is known as the *due diligence defense*. Under this defense a non-expert, as to the nonexpertised portions of the registration statement, and an expert, as to the expertised portions, will not be liable if "he had, after reasonable investigation, reasonable ground to believe" that the relevant statements were true and that there were no material omissions. As to the expertised portions of the registration statement, a nonexpert will not be liable if "he had no reasonable ground to believe" that the statements made by the expert were untrue or contained material omissions.

Thus section 11, like section 12(a)(2), adopts a negligence standard, with the burden of proof on the defendants to show that they were not negligent. There is a difference in the formulations of the negligence standards in sections 11 and 12(a)(2), and it is not clear whether this means that there are differences in the investigation required to satisfy the defendant's burden of proof under the two sections. See Sanders v. John Nuveen & Co., Inc., 619 F.2d 1222 (7th Cir.1980), cert. denied 450 U.S. 1005, 101 S.Ct. 1719, 68 L.Ed.2d 210 (1981) (opinion of Justice Powell, dissenting from denial of certiorari).

Escott v. BarChris Constr. Corp.

United States District Court, Southern District, New York, 1968.
283 F.Supp. 643.

OPINION

■ McLean, District Judge.

This is an action by purchasers of 5½ per cent convertible subordinated fifteen year debentures of BarChris Construction Corporation

(BarChris). Plaintiffs purport to sue on their own behalf and "on behalf of all other and present and former holders" of the debentures. When the action was begun on October 25, 1962, there were nine plaintiffs. Others were subsequently permitted to intervene. At the time of the trial, there were over sixty.

The action is brought under Section 11 of the Securities Act of 1933 (15 U.S.C.A. § 77k). Plaintiffs allege that the registration statement with respect to these debentures filed with the Securities and Exchange Commission, which became effective on May 16, 1961, contained material false statements and material omissions.

Defendants fall into three categories: (1) the persons who signed the registration statement; (2) the underwriters, consisting of eight investment banking firms, led by Drexel & Co. (Drexel); and (3) BarChris's auditors, Peat, Marwick, Mitchell & Co. (Peat, Marwick).

The signers, in addition to BarChris itself, were the nine directors of BarChris, plus its controller, defendant Trilling, who was not a director. Of the nine directors, five were officers of BarChris, i.e., defendants Vitolo, president; Russo, executive vice president; Pugliese, vice president; Kircher, treasurer; and Birnbaum, secretary. Of the remaining four, defendant Grant was a member of the firm of Perkins, Daniels, McCormack & Collins, BarChris's attorneys. He became a director in October 1960. Defendant Coleman, a partner in Drexel, became a director on April 17, 1961, as did the other two, Auslander and Rose, who were not otherwise connected with BarChris.

Defendants, in addition to denying that the registration statement was false, have pleaded the defenses open to them under Section 11 of the Act, plus certain additional defenses, including the statute of limitations. Defendants have also asserted cross-claims against each other, seeking to hold one another liable for any sums for which the respective defendants may be held liable to plaintiffs.

This opinion will not concern itself with the cross-claims or with issues peculiar to any particular plaintiff. These matters are reserved for later decision. On the main issue of liability, the questions to be decided are (1) did the registration statement contain false statements of fact, or did it omit to state facts which should have been stated in order to prevent it from being misleading; (2) if so, were the facts which were falsely stated or omitted "material" within the meaning of the Act; (3) if so, have defendants established their affirmative defenses?

Before discussing these questions, some background facts should be mentioned. At the time relevant here, BarChris was engaged primarily in the construction of bowling alleys, somewhat euphemistically referred to as "bowling centers." These were rather elaborate affairs. They contained not only a number of alleys or "lanes," but also, in most cases, bar and restaurant facilities.

BarChris was an outgrowth of a business started as a partnership by Vitolo and Pugliese in 1946. The business was incorporated in New York in 1955 under the name of B & C Bowling Alley Builders, Inc. Its name was subsequently changed to BarChris Construction Corporation.

The introduction of automatic pin setting machines in 1952 gave a marked stimulus to bowling. It rapidly became a popular sport, with the result that "bowling centers" began to appear throughout the country in rapidly increasing numbers. BarChris benefited from this increased interest in bowling. Its construction operations expanded rapidly. It is estimated that in 1960 BarChris installed approximately three per cent of all lanes built in the United States. It was thus a significant factor in the industry, although two large established companies, American Machine & Foundry Company and Brunswick, were much larger factors. These two companies manufactured bowling equipment, which BarChris did not. They also built most of the bowling alleys, 97 per cent of the total, according to some of the testimony.

BarChris's sales increased dramatically from 1956 to 1960. According to the prospectus, net sales, in round figures, in 1956 were some $800,000, in 1957 $1,300,000, in 1958 $1,700,000. In 1959 they increased to over $3,300,000, and by 1960 they had leaped to over $9,165,000.

For some years the business had exceeded the managerial capacity of its founders. Vitolo and Pugliese are each men of limited education. Vitolo did not get beyond high school. Pugliese ended his schooling in seventh grade. Pugliese devoted his time to supervising the actual construction work. Vitolo was concerned primarily with obtaining new business. Neither was equipped to handle financial matters....

In general, BarChris's method of operation was to enter into a contract with a customer, receive from him at that time a comparatively small down payment on the purchase price, and proceed to construct and equip the bowling alley. When the work was finished and the building delivered, the customer paid the balance of the contract price in notes, payable in installments over a period of years. BarChris discounted these notes with a factor and received part of their face amount in cash. The factor held back part as a reserve.

In 1960 BarChris began a practice which has been referred to throughout this case as the "alternative method of financing." In substance this was a sale and leaseback arrangement. It involved a distinction between the "interior" of a building and the building itself, i.e., the outer shell. In instances in which this method applied, BarChris would build and install what it referred to as the "interior package." Actually this amounted to constructing and installing the equipment in a building. When it was completed, it would sell the interior to a factor, James Talcott Inc. (Talcott), who would pay BarChris the full contract price therefor. The factor then proceeded to lease the interior either directly to BarChris's customer or back to a subsidiary of BarChris. In the latter case, the subsidiary in turn would lease it to the customer.

Under either financing method, BarChris was compelled to expend considerable sums in defraying the cost of construction before it received reimbursement. As a consequence, BarChris was in constant need of cash to finance its operations, a need which grew more pressing as operations expanded.

In December 1959, BarChris sold 560,000 shares of common stock to the public at $3.00 per share. This issue was underwritten by Peter Morgan & Company, one of the present defendants.

By early 1961, BarChris needed additional working capital. The proceeds of the sale of the debentures involved in this action were to be devoted, in part at least, to fill that need.

The registration statement of the debentures, in preliminary form, was filed with the Securities and Exchange Commission on March 30, 1961. A first amendment was filed on May 11 and a second on May 16. The registration statement became effective on May 16. The closing of the financing took place on May 24. On that day BarChris received the net proceeds of the financing.

By that time BarChris was experiencing difficulties in collecting amounts due from some of its customers. Some of them were in arrears in payments due to factors on their discounted notes. As time went on those difficulties increased. Although BarChris continued to build alleys in 1961 and 1962, it became increasingly apparent that the industry was overbuilt. Operators of alleys, often inadequately financed, began to fail. Precisely when the tide turned is a matter of dispute, but at any rate, it was painfully apparent in 1962.

In May of that year BarChris made an abortive attempt to raise more money by the sale of common stock. It filed with the Securities and Exchange Commission a registration statement for the stock issue which it later withdrew. In October 1962 BarChris came to the end of the road. On October 29, 1962, it filed in this court a petition for an arrangement under Chapter XI of the Bankruptcy Act. BarChris defaulted in the payment of the interest due on November 1, 1962 on the debentures.

[The court continued with a lengthy description of BarChris's registration statement for the 1961 debentures.] . . .

For convenience, the various falsities and omissions [in the 1961 debenture registration statement] which I have discussed in the preceding pages are recapitulated here. They were as follows:

1. 1960 Earnings
   (a) Sales
As per prospectus	$9,165,320
Correct figure	8,511,420
Overstatement	$ 653,900

   (b) Net Operating Income
As per prospectus	$1,742,801

Correct figure		1,496,196
Overstatement		$ 246,605

(c) Earnings per Share

As per prospectus		$ .75
Correct figure		.65
Overstatement		$ .10

2. 1960 Balance Sheet Current Assets

As per prospectus	$4,524,021
Correct figure	3,914,332
Overstatement	$ 609,689

3. Contingent Liabilities as of December 31, 1960 on Alternative Method of Financing

As per prospectus	$ 750,000
Correct figure	1,125,795
Understatement	$ 375,795
Capitol Lanes should have been shown as a direct liability	$ 325,000

4. Contingent Liabilities as of April 30, 1961

As per prospectus	$ 825,000
Correct figure	1,443,853
Understatement	$ 618,853
Capitol Lanes should have been shown as a direct liability	$ 314,166

5. Earnings Figures for Quarter ending March 31, 1961

(a) Sales

As per prospectus	$2,138,455
Correct figure	1,618,645
Overstatement	$ 519,810

(b) Gross Profit

As per prospectus	$ 483,121
Correct figure	252,366
Overstatement	$ 230,755

6. Backlog as of March 31, 1961

As per prospectus	$6,905,000
Correct figure	2,415,000
Overstatement	$4,490,000

7. Failure to Disclose Officers' Loans Outstanding and Unpaid on May 16, 1961 — $ 386,615

8. Failure to Disclose Use of Proceeds in Manner not Revealed in Prospectus

Approximately — $1,160,000

9. Failure to Disclose Customers' Delinquencies in May 1961 and BarChris's Potential Liability with Respect Thereto

Over $1,350,000

10. Failure to Disclose the Fact that BarChris was Already Engaged, and was about to be More Heavily Engaged, in the Operation of Bowling Alleys

Materiality

It is a prerequisite to liability under Section 11 of the Act that the fact which is falsely stated in a registration statement, or the fact that is omitted when it should have been stated to avoid misleading, be "material." [The court found that several misstatements and omissions were material within the meaning of the Act.] . . . .

The "Due Diligence" Defenses

Section 11(b) of the Act provides that:

" * * * no person, other than the issuer, shall be liable * * * who shall sustain the burden of proof—

* * *

(3) that (A) as regards any part of the registration statement not purporting to be made on the authority of an expert * * * he had, after reasonable investigation, reasonable ground to believe and did believe, at the time such part of the registration statement became effective, that the statements therein were true and that there was no omission to state a material fact required to be stated therein or necessary to make the statements therein not misleading; * * * "

* * *

Section 11(c) defines "reasonable investigation" as follows:

"In determining, for the purpose of paragraph (3) of subsection (b) of this section, what constitutes reasonable investigation and reasonable ground for belief, the standard of reasonableness shall be that required of a prudent man in the management of his own property."

Every defendant, except BarChris itself, to whom, as the issuer, these defenses are not available, and except Peat, Marwick, whose position rests on a different statutory provision, has pleaded these affirmative defenses. Each claims that (1) as to the part of the registration statement purporting to be made on the authority of an expert (which, for convenience, I shall refer to as the "expertised portion"), he had no reasonable ground to believe and did not believe that there were any untrue statements or material omissions, and (2) as to the other parts of the registration statement, he made a reasonable investigation, as a result of which he had reasonable ground to believe and did believe that the registration statement was true and that no material fact was omitted. As to each defendant, the question is whether he has sustained the burden of proving these defenses. Surprising enough, there is little or no judicial authority on this question. No decisions directly in point under Section 11 have been found.

Before considering the evidence, a preliminary matter should be disposed of. The defendants do not agree among themselves as to who the "experts" were or as to the parts of the registration statement which were expertised. Some defendants say that Peat, Marwick was the expert, others say that BarChris's attorneys, Perkins, Daniels, McCormack & Collins, and the underwriters' attorneys, Drinker, Biddle & Reath, were also the experts. On the first view, only those portions of the registration statement purporting to be made on Peat, Marwick's authority were expertised portions. On the other view, everything in the registration statement was within this category, because the two law firms were responsible for the entire document.

The first view is the correct one. To say that the entire registration statement is expertised because some lawyer prepared it would be an unreasonable construction of the statute. Neither the lawyer for the company nor the lawyer for the underwriters is an expert within the meaning of Section 11. The only expert, in the statutory sense, was Peat, Marwick, and the only parts of the registration statement which purported to be made upon the authority of an expert were the portions which purported to be made on Peat, Marwick's authority.

The parties also disagree as to what those portions were. Some defendants say that it was only the 1960 figures (and the figures for prior years, which are not in controversy here). Others say in substance that it was every figure in the prospectus. The plaintiffs take a somewhat intermediate view. They do not claim that Peat, Marwick expertised every figure, but they do maintain that Peat, Marwick is responsible for a portion of the text of the prospectus, i.e., that pertaining to "Methods of Operation," because a reference to it was made in footnote 9 to the balance sheet.

Here again, the more narrow view is the correct one. The registration statement contains a report of Peat, Marwick as independent public accountants dated February 23, 1961. This relates only to the consolidated balance sheet of BarChris and consolidated subsidiaries as of December 31, 1960, and the related statement of earnings and retained earnings for the five years then ended. This is all that Peat, Marwick purported to certify. It is perfectly clear that it did not purport to certify the 1961 figures, some of which are expressly stated in the prospectus to have been unaudited.

Moreover, plaintiffs' intermediate view is also incorrect. The cross reference in footnote 9 to the "Methods of Operation" passage in the prospectus was inserted merely for the convenience of the reader. It is not a fair construction to say that it thereby imported into the balance sheet everything in that portion of the text, much of which had nothing to do with the figures in the balance sheet.

I turn now to the question of whether defendants have proved their due diligence defenses. The position of each defendant will be separately considered.

Russo

Russo was, to all intents and purposes, the chief executive officer of BarChris. He was a member of the executive committee. He was familiar with all aspects of the business. He was personally in charge of dealings with the factors. He acted on BarChris's behalf in making the financing agreements with Talcott and he handled the negotiations with Talcott in the spring of 1961. He talked with customers about their delinquencies.

Russo prepared the list of jobs which went into the backlog figure. He knew the status of those jobs. In addition to being chief executive officer of BarChris, he was a director of T–Bowl International, Inc., and the principals in St. Ann's were his friends.

It was Russo who arranged for the temporary increase in Bar-Chris's cash in banks on December 31, 1960, a transaction which borders on the fraudulent. He was thoroughly aware of BarChris's stringent financial condition in May 1961. He had personally advanced large sums to BarChris of which $175,000 remained unpaid as of May 16.

In short, Russo knew all the relevant facts. He could not have believed that there were no untrue statements or material omissions in the prospectus. Russo has no due diligence defenses.

Vitolo and Pugliese

They were the founders of the business who stuck with it to the end. Vitolo was president and Pugliese was vice president. Despite their titles, their field of responsibility in the administration of Bar-Chris's affairs during the period in question seems to have been less all-embracing than Russo's. Pugliese in particular appears to have limited his activities to supervising the actual construction work.

Vitolo and Pugliese are each men of limited education. It is not hard to believe that for them the prospectus was difficult reading, if indeed they read it at all.

But whether it was or not is irrelevant. The liability of a director who signs a registration statement does not depend upon whether or not he read it or, if he did, whether or not he understood what he was reading.

And in any case, Vitolo and Pugliese were not as naive as they claim to be. They were members of BarChris's executive committee. At meetings of that committee BarChris's affairs were discussed at length. They must have known what was going on. Certainly they knew of the inadequacy of cash in 1961. They knew of their own large advances to the company which remained unpaid. They knew that they had agreed not to deposit their checks until the financing proceeds were received. They knew and intended that part of the proceeds were to be used to pay their own loans.

All in all, the position of Vitolo and Pugliese is not significantly different, for present purposes, from Russo's. They could not have believed that the registration statement was wholly true and that no material facts had been omitted. And in any case, there is nothing to show that they made any investigation of anything which they may not have known about or understood. They have not proved their due diligence defenses.

Kircher

Kircher was treasurer of BarChris and its chief financial officer. He is a certified public accountant and an intelligent man. He was thoroughly familiar with BarChris's financial affairs. He knew the terms of BarChris's agreements with Talcott. He knew of the customers' delinquency problem. He participated actively with Russo in May 1961 in the successful effort to hold Talcott off until the financing proceeds came in. He knew how the financing proceeds were to be applied and he saw to it that they were so applied. He arranged the officers' loans and he knew all the facts concerning them.

Moreover, as a member of the executive committee, Kircher was kept informed as to those branches of the business of which he did not have direct charge. He knew about the operation of alleys, present and prospective. He knew that Capitol was included in 1960 sales and that Bridge and Yonkers were included in first quarter 1961 sales despite the fact that they were not sold. Kircher knew of the infirmities in customers' contracts included in the backlog figure. Indeed, at a later date, he specifically criticized Russo's handling of the T–Bowl situation. In brief, Kircher knew all the relevant facts.

Kircher worked on the preparation of the registration statement. He conferred with Grant and on occasion with Ballard. He supplied information to them about the company's business. He read the prospectus and understood it. He knew what it said and what it did not say.

Kircher's contention is that he had never before dealt with a registration statement, that he did not know what it should contain, and that he relied wholly on Grant, Ballard and Peat, Marwick to guide him. He claims that it was their fault, not his, if there was anything wrong with it. He says that all the facts were recorded in BarChris's books where these "experts" could have seen them if they had looked. He says that he truthfully answered all their questions. In effect, he says that if they did not know enough to ask the right questions and to give him the proper instructions, that is not his responsibility.

There is an issue of credibility here. In fact, Kircher was not frank in dealing with Grant and Ballard. He withheld information from them. But even if he had told them all the facts, this would not have constituted the due diligence contemplated by the statute. Knowing the facts, Kircher had reason to believe that the expertised portion of the prospectus, i.e., the 1960 figures, was in part incorrect. He could not shut his eyes to the facts and rely on Peat, Marwick for that portion.

As to the rest of the prospectus, knowing the facts, he did not have a reasonable ground to believe it to be true. On the contrary, he must have known that in part it was untrue. Under these circumstances, he was not entitled to sit back and place the blame on the lawyers for not advising him about it.

Kircher has not proved his due diligence defenses. . . .

Auslander

Auslander was an "outside" director, i.e., one who was not an officer of BarChris. He was chairman of the board of Valley Stream National Bank in Valley Stream, Long Island. In February 1961 Vitolo asked him to become a director of BarChris. Vitolo gave him an enthusiastic account of BarChris's progress and prospects. As an inducement, Vitolo said that when BarChris received the proceeds of a forthcoming issue of securities, it would deposit $1,000,000 in Auslander's bank.[18]

In February and early March 1961, before accepting Vitolo's invitation, Auslander made some investigation of BarChris. He obtained Dun & Bradstreet reports which contained sales and earnings figures for periods earlier than December 31, 1960. He caused inquiry to be made of certain of BarChris's banks and was advised that they regarded BarChris favorably. He was informed that inquiry of Talcott had also produced a favorable response.

On March 3, 1961, Auslander indicated his willingness to accept a place on the board. Shortly thereafter, on March 14, Kircher sent him a copy of BarChris's annual report for 1960. Auslander observed that BarChris's auditors were Peat, Marwick. They were also the auditors for the Valley Stream National Bank. He thought well of them.

Auslander was elected a director on April 17, 1961. The registration statement in its original form had already been filed, of course without his signature. On May 10, 1961, he signed a signature page for the first amendment to the registration statement which was filed on May 11, 1961. This was a separate sheet without any document attached. Auslander did not know that it was a signature page for a registration statement. He vaguely understood that it was something "for the SEC."

Auslander attended a meeting of BarChris's directors on May 15, 1961. At that meeting he, along with the other directors, signed the signature sheet for the second amendment which constituted the registration statement in its final form. Again, this was only a separate sheet without any document attached. Auslander never saw a copy of the registration statement in its final form.

At the May 15 directors' meeting, however, Auslander did realize that what he was signing was a signature sheet to a registration statement. This was the first time that he had appreciated that fact. A copy of the registration statement in its earlier form as amended on May 11, 1961 was passed around at the meeting. Auslander glanced at it briefly. He did not read it thoroughly.

At the May 15 meeting, Russo and Vitolo stated that everything was in order and that the prospectus was correct. Auslander believed this statement.

---

18. After BarChris received the financing proceeds, it deposited in the Valley Stream National Bank not $1,000,000, but $150,000 in a checking account and $150,000 in a six-months' time deposit. The checking account was reduced to approximately $12,000 within a few weeks.

In considering Auslander's due diligence defenses, a distinction is to be drawn between the expertised and non-expertised portions of the prospectus. As to the former, Auslander knew that Peat, Marwick had audited the 1960 figures. He believed them to be correct because he had confidence in Peat, Marwick. He had no reasonable ground to believe otherwise.

As to the non-expertised portions, however, Auslander is in a different position. He seems to have been under the impression that Peat, Marwick was responsible for all the figures. This impression was not correct, as he would have realized if he had read the prospectus carefully. Auslander made no investigation of the accuracy of the prospectus. He relied on the assurance of Vitolo and Russo, and upon the information he had received in answer to his inquiries back in February and early March. These inquiries were general ones, in the nature of a credit check. The information which he received in answer to them was also general, without specific reference to the statements in the prospectus, which was not prepared until some time thereafter.

It is true that Auslander became a director on the eve of the financing. He had little opportunity to familiarize himself with the company's affairs. The question is whether, under such circumstances, Auslander did enough to establish his due diligence defense with respect to the non-expertised portions of the prospectus.

Although there is a dearth of authority under Section 11 on this point, an English case under the analogous Companies Act is of some value. In Adams v. Thrift, [1915] 1 Ch. 557, aff'd, [1915] 2 Ch. 21, it was held that a director who knew nothing about the prospectus and did not even read it, but who relied on the statement of the company's managing director that it was "all right," was liable for its untrue statements. See also In the Matter of Interstate Hosiery Mills, Inc., 4 S.E.C. 706 (1939).

Section 11 imposes liability in the first instance upon a director, no matter how new he is. He is presumed to know his responsibility when he becomes a director. He can escape liability only by using that reasonable care to investigate the facts which a prudent man would employ in the management of his own property. In my opinion, a prudent man would not act in an important matter without any knowledge of the relevant facts, in sole reliance upon representations of persons who are comparative strangers and upon general information which does not purport to cover the particular case. To say that such minimal conduct measures up to the statutory standard would, to all intents and purposes, absolve new directors from responsibility merely because they are new. This is not a sensible construction of Section 11, when one bears in mind its fundamental purpose of requiring full and truthful disclosure for the protection of investors.

I find and conclude that Auslander has not established his due diligence defense with respect to the misstatements and omissions in those portions of the prospectus other than the audited 1960 figures. . . .

Grant

Grant became a director of BarChris in October 1960. His law firm was counsel to BarChris in matters pertaining to the registration of securities. Grant drafted the registration statement for the stock issue in 1959 and for the warrants in January 1961. He also drafted the registration statement for the debentures. In the preliminary division of work between him and Ballard, the underwriters' counsel, Grant took initial responsibility for preparing the registration statement, while Ballard devoted his efforts in the first instance to preparing the indenture.

Grant is sued as a director and as a signer of the registration statement. This is not an action against him for malpractice in his capacity as a lawyer. Nevertheless, in considering Grant's due diligence defenses, the unique position which he occupied cannot be disregarded. As the director most directly concerned with writing the registration statement and assuring its accuracy, more was required of him in the way of reasonable investigation than could fairly be expected of a director who had no connection with this work.

There is no valid basis for plaintiffs' accusation that Grant knew that the prospectus was false in some respects and incomplete and misleading in others. Having seen him testify at length, I am satisfied as to his integrity. I find that Grant honestly believed that the registration statement was true and that no material facts had been omitted from it.

In this belief he was mistaken, and the fact is that for all his work, he never discovered any of the errors or omissions which have been recounted at length in this opinion, with the single exception of Capitol Lanes. He knew that BarChris had not sold this alley and intended to operate it, but he appears to have been under the erroneous impression that Peat, Marwick had knowingly sanctioned its inclusion in sales because of the allegedly temporary nature of the operation.

Grant contends that a finding that he did not make a reasonable investigation would be equivalent to a holding that a lawyer for an issuing company, in order to show due diligence, must make an independent audit of the figures supplied to him by his client. I do not consider this to be a realistic statement of the issue. There were errors and omissions here which could have been detected without an audit. The question is whether, despite his failure to detect them, Grant made a reasonable effort to that end.

Much of this registration statement is a scissors and paste-pot job. Grant lifted large portions from the earlier prospectuses, modifying them in some instances to the extent that he considered necessary. But BarChris's affairs had changed for the worse by May 1961. Statements that were accurate in January were no longer accurate in May. Grant never discovered this. He accepted the assurances of Kircher and Russo that any change which might have occurred had been for the better, rather than the contrary.

It is claimed that a lawyer is entitled to rely on the statements of his client and that to require him to verify their accuracy would set an unreasonably high standard. This is too broad a generalization. It is all a matter of degree. To require an audit would obviously be unreasonable. On the other hand, to require a check of matters easily verifiable is not unreasonable. Even honest clients can make mistakes. The statute imposes liability for untrue statements regardless of whether they are intentionally untrue. The way to prevent mistakes is to test oral information by examining the original written record.

There were things which Grant could readily have checked which he did not check. For example, he was unaware of the provisions of the agreements between BarChris and Talcott. He never read them. Thus, he did not know, although he readily could have ascertained, that BarChris's contingent liability on Type B leaseback arrangements was 100 per cent, not 25 per cent. He did not appreciate that if BarChris defaulted in repurchasing delinquent customers' notes upon Talcott's demand, Talcott could accelerate all the customer paper in its hands, which amounted to over $3,000,000.

As to the backlog figure, Grant appreciated that scheduled unfilled orders on the company's books meant firm commitments, but he never asked to see the contracts which, according to the prospectus, added up to $6,905,000. Thus, he did not know that this figure was overstated by some $4,490,000.

Grant was unaware of the fact that BarChris was about to operate Bridge and Yonkers. He did not read the minutes of those subsidiaries which would have revealed that fact to him. On the subject of minutes, Grant knew that minutes of certain meetings of the BarChris executive committee held in 1961 had not been written up. Kircher, who had acted as secretary at those meetings, had complete notes of them. Kircher told Grant that there was no point in writing up the minutes because the matters discussed at those meetings were purely routine. Grant did not insist that the minutes be written up, nor did he look at Kircher's notes. If he had, he would have learned that on February 27, 1961 there was an extended discussion in the executive committee meeting about customers' delinquencies, that on March 8, 1961 the committee had discussed the pros and cons of alley operation by BarChris, that on March 18, 1961 the committee was informed that BarChris was constructing or about to begin constructing twelve alleys for which it had no contracts, and that on May 13, 1961 Dreyfuss, one of the worst delinquents, had filed a petition in Chapter X.

Grant knew that there had been loans from officers to BarChris in the past because that subject had been mentioned in the 1959 and January 1961 prospectuses. In March Grant prepared a questionnaire to be answered by officers and directors for the purpose of obtaining information to be used in the prospectus. The questionnaire did not inquire expressly about the existence of officers' loans. At approximately the same time, Grant prepared another questionnaire in order to obtain information on proxy statements for the annual stockholders' meeting. This questionnaire asked each officer to state whether he was indebted to BarChris, but it did not ask whether BarChris was indebted to him.

Despite the inadequacy of these written questionnaires, Grant did, on March 16, 1961, orally inquire as to whether any officers' loans were outstanding. He was assured by Russo, Vitolo and Pugliese that all such loans had been repaid. Grant did not ask again. He was unaware of the new loans in April. He did know, however, that, at Kircher's request, a provision was inserted in the indenture which gave loans from individuals priority over the debentures. Kircher's insistence on this clause did not arouse his suspicions.

It is only fair to say that Grant was given to understand by Kircher that there were no new officers' loans and that there would not be any before May 16. It is still a close question, however, whether, under all the circumstances, Grant should have investigated further, perhaps by asking Peat, Marwick, in the course of its S–1 review, to look at the books on this particular point. I believe that a careful man would have checked.

There is more to the subject of due diligence than this, particularly with respect to the application of proceeds and customers' delinquencies.

The application of proceeds language in the prospectus was drafted by Kircher back in January. It may well have expressed his intent at that time, but his intent, and that of the other principal officers of BarChris, was very different in May. Grant did not appreciate that the earlier language was no longer appropriate. He never learned of the situation which the company faced in May. He knew that BarChris was short of cash, but he had no idea how short. He did not know that BarChris was withholding delivery of checks already drawn and signed because there was not enough money in the bank to pay them. He did not know that the officers of the company intended to use immediately approximately one-third of the financing proceeds in a manner not disclosed in the prospectus, including approximately $1,000,000 in paying old debts.

In this connection, mention should be made of a fact which has previously been referred to only in passing. The "negative cash balance" in BarChris's Lafayette National Bank account in May 1961 included a check dated April 10, 1961 to the order of Grant's firm, Perkins, Daniels, McCormack & Collins, in the amount of $8,711. This check was not deposited by Perkins, Daniels until June 1, after the financing proceeds had been received by BarChris. Of course, if Grant had knowingly withheld deposit of this check until that time, he would be in a position similar to Russo, Vitolo and Pugliese. I do not believe, however, that that was the case. I find that the check was not delivered by BarChris to Perkins, Daniels until shortly before June 1.

This incident is worthy of mention, however, for another reason. The prospectus stated on page 10 that Perkins, Daniels had "received fees aggregating $13,000" from BarChris. This check for $8,711 was one of those fees. It had not been received by Perkins, Daniels prior to

May 16. Grant was unaware of this. In approving this erroneous statement in the prospectus, he did not consult his own bookkeeper to ascertain whether it was correct. Kircher told him that the bill had been paid and Grant took his word for it. If he had inquired and had found that this representation was untrue, this discovery might well have led him to a realization of the true state of BarChris's finances in May 1961.

As far as customers' delinquencies are concerned, although Grant discussed this with Kircher, he again accepted the assurances of Kircher and Russo that no serious problem existed. He did not examine the records as to delinquencies, although BarChris maintained such a record. Any inquiry on his part of Talcott or an examination of BarChris's correspondence with Talcott in April and May 1961 would have apprised him of the true facts. It would have led him to appreciate that the statement in this prospectus, carried over from earlier prospectuses, to the effect that since 1955 BarChris had been required to repurchase less than one-half of one per cent of discounted customers' notes could no longer properly be made without further explanation.

Grant was entitled to rely on Peat, Marwick for the 1960 figures. He had no reasonable ground to believe them to be inaccurate. But the matters which I have mentioned were not within the expertised portion of the prospectus. As to this, Grant, was obliged to make a reasonable investigation. I am forced to find that he did not make one. After making all due allowances for the fact that BarChris's officers misled him, there are too many instances in which Grant failed to make an inquiry which he could easily have made which, if pursued, would have put him on his guard. In my opinion, this finding on the evidence in this case does not establish an unreasonably high standard in other cases for company counsel who are also directors. Each case must rest on its own facts. I conclude that Grant has not established his due diligence defenses except as to the audited 1960 figures.

The Underwriters and Coleman

The underwriters other than Drexel made no investigation of the accuracy of the prospectus. One of them, Peter Morgan, had underwritten the 1959 stock issue and had been a director of BarChris. He thus had some general familiarity with its affairs, but he knew no more than the other underwriters about the debenture prospectus. They all relied upon Drexel as the "lead" underwriter.

Drexel did make an investigation. The work was in charge of Coleman, a partner of the firm, assisted by Casperson, an associate. Drexel's attorneys acted as attorneys for the entire group of underwriters. Ballard did the work, assisted by Stanton.

On April 17, 1961 Coleman became a director of BarChris. He signed the first amendment to the registration statement filed on May 11 and the second amendment, constituting the registration statement in its final form, filed on May 16. He thereby assumed a responsibility as a director and signer in addition to his responsibility as an underwriter.

The facts as to the extent of the investigation that Coleman made may be briefly summarized. He was first introduced to BarChris on September 15, 1960. Thereafter he familiarized himself with general conditions in the industry, primarily by reading reports and prospectuses of the two leading bowling alley builders, American Machine & Foundry Company and Brunswick. These indicated that the industry was still growing. He also acquired general information on BarChris by reading the 1959 stock prospectus, annual reports for prior years, and an unaudited statement for the first half of 1960. He inquired about BarChris of certain of its banks and of Talcott and received favorable replies.

The purpose of this preliminary investigation was to enable Coleman to decide whether Drexel would undertake the financing. It did not have direct reference to any specific registration statement for at that time, of course, none had been prepared. Coleman was sufficiently optimistic about BarChris's prospects to buy 1,000 shares of its stock, which he did in December 1960.

On January 24, 1961, Coleman held a meeting with Ballard, Grant and Kircher, among others. By that time Coleman had about decided to go ahead with the financing, although Drexel's formal letter of intent was not delivered until February 9, 1961 (subsequently revised on March 7, 1961). At this meeting Coleman asked Kircher how BarChris intended to use the proceeds of the financing. In reply to this inquiry, Kircher wrote a letter to Coleman dated January 30, 1961 outlining BarChris's plans. This eventually formed the basis of the application of proceeds section in the prospectus.

Coleman continued his general investigation. He obtained a Dun & Bradstreet report on BarChris on March 16, 1961. He read BarChris's annual report for 1960 which was available in March.

By mid-March, Coleman was in a position to make more specific inquiries. By that time Grant had prepared a first draft of the prospectus, consisting of a marked-up copy of the January 1961 warrant prospectus. Coleman attended three meetings to discuss the prospectus with BarChris's representatives. The meetings were held at Perkins, Daniels' office on March 20, March 23 and March 24, 1961. Those present included Grant or his partner McCormack and Kircher for the company, and Coleman, Casperson and Ballard for the underwriters. Logan, Peat, Marwick's manager of the 1960 audit, was present at one of the meetings.

At these discussions, which were extensive, successive proofs of the prospectus were considered and revised. At this point the 1961 figures were not available. They were put in the prospectus in May.

Coleman and Ballard asked pertinent questions and received answers which satisfied them. Among other things, the following transpired.

Logan explained some of the 1960 figures, including the reserve for bad debts, which he considered adequate.

There was a discussion of the application of proceeds section. It was not changed in any respect material here.

As to the backlog of orders on hand, Ballard said that the figure, not then available, must be "hard and fast," not "puffy." Grant and Kircher "concurred."

There was talk about the 15 to 25 per cent down payment figure. Kircher said that this was accurate.

More important for our purposes, there was a discussion of the one-half of one per cent figure with respect to BarChris's past experience in repurchasing discounted customers' notes. Kircher said that this figure was "conservative." Ballard inquired whether, regardless of what past experience had been, there was "any real chance that you see of being forced to take any [alleys] back in the future?" Kircher's answer was "negative."

The alternative method of financing was explained. Kircher said that BarChris's contingent liability was only 25 per cent.

There was talk about operating alleys. Kircher said that BarChris did not operate any. Coleman and Ballard inquired whether BarChris built alleys on speculation, i.e., without any customer's contract for them. Kircher said BarChris did not.

There was discussion of officers' loans. Kircher said that the $155,000 had been repaid and that no further officers' loans were contemplated. Coleman said that this was wise, for loans from officers "indicated financial instability of the company."

Coleman did not participate personally in any further meetings of this sort. Casperson attended some and reported to Coleman. Ballard advised Coleman as to what he was doing.

After Coleman was elected a director on April 17, 1961, he made no further independent investigation of the accuracy of the prospectus. He assumed that Ballard was taking care of this on his behalf as well as on behalf of the underwriters.

In April 1961 Ballard instructed Stanton to examine BarChris's minutes for the past five years and also to look at "the major contracts of the company."[23] Stanton went to BarChris's office for that purpose on April 24. He asked Birnbaum for the minute books. He read the minutes of the board of directors and discovered interleaved in them a few minutes of executive committee meetings in 1960. He asked Kircher if there were any others. Kircher said that there had been other executive committee meetings but that the minutes had not been written up.

---

23. Stanton was a very junior associate. He had been admitted to the bar in January 1961, some three months before. This was the first registration statement he had ever worked on.

Stanton read the minutes of a few BarChris subsidiaries. His testimony was vague as to which ones. He had no recollection of seeing the minutes of Capitol Lanes, Inc. or Biel or Parkway Lanes, Inc. He did not discover that BarChris was operating Capitol or that it planned to operate Bridge and Yonkers.

As to the "major contracts," all that Stanton could remember seeing was an insurance policy. Birnbaum told him that there was no file of major contracts. Stanton did not examine the agreements with Talcott. He did not examine the contracts with customers. He did not look to see what contracts comprised the backlog figure. Stanton examined no accounting records of BarChris. His visit, which lasted one day, was devoted primarily to reading the directors' minutes.

On April 25 Ballard wrote to Grant about certain matters which Stanton had noted on his visit to BarChris the day before, none of which Ballard considered "very earth shaking." As far as relevant here, these were (1) Russo's remark as recorded in the executive committee minutes of November 3, 1960 to the effect that because of customers' defaults, BarChris might find itself in the business of operating alleys; (2) the fact that the minutes of Sanpark Realty Corporation were incomplete; and (3) the fact that minutes of the executive committee were missing.

On May 9, 1961, Ballard came to New York and conferred with Grant and Kircher. They discussed the Securities and Exchange Commission's deficiency letter of May 4, 1961 which required the inclusion in the prospectus of certain additional information, notably net sales, gross profits and net earnings figures for the first quarter of 1961. They also discussed the points raised in Ballard's letter to Grant of April 25. As to the latter, most of the conversation related to what Russo had meant by his remark on November 3, 1960. Kircher said that the delinquency problem was less severe now than it had been back in November 1960, that no alleys had been repossessed, and that although he was "worried about one alley in Harlem" (Dreyfuss), that was a "special situation." Grant reported that Russo had told him that his statement on November 3, 1960 was "merely hypothetical." On the strength of this conversation Ballard was satisfied that the one-half of one per cent figure in the prospectus did not need qualification or elaboration.

As to the missing minutes, Kircher said that those of Sanpark were not significant and that the executive committee meetings for which there were no written minutes were concerned only with "routine matters."

It must be remembered that this conference took place only one week before the registration statement became effective. Ballard did nothing else in the way of checking during that intervening week.

Ballard did not insist that the executive committee minutes be written up so that he could inspect them, although he testified that he knew from experience that executive committee minutes may be extremely important. If he had insisted, he would have found the minutes highly informative, as has previously been pointed out.... Ballard did not ask to see BarChris's schedule of delinquencies or Talcott's notices of delinquencies, or BarChris's correspondence with Talcott.

Ballard did not examine BarChris's contracts with Talcott. He did not appreciate what Talcott's rights were under those financing agreements or how serious the effect would be upon BarChris of any exercise of those rights.

Ballard did not investigate the composition of the backlog figure to be sure that it was not "puffy." He made no inquiry after March about any new officers' loans, although he knew that Kircher had insisted on a provision in the indenture which gave loans from individuals priority over the debentures. He was unaware of the seriousness of BarChris's cash position and of how BarChris's officers intended to use a large part of the proceeds. He did not know that BarChris was operating Capitol Lanes.

Like Grant, Ballard, without checking, relied on the information which he got from Kircher. He also relied on Grant who, as company counsel, presumably was familiar with its affairs.

The formal opinion which Ballard's firm rendered to the underwriters at the closing on May 24, 1961 made clear that this is what he had done. The opinion stated (underscoring supplied):

> "In the course of the preparation of the Registration Statement and Prospectus by the Company, we have had numerous conferences with representatives of and counsel for the Company and with its auditors and we have raised many questions regarding the business of the Company. Satisfactory answers to such questions were in each case given us, and all other information and documents we requested have been supplied. We are of the opinion that the *data presented* to us are accurately reflected in the Registration Statement and Prospectus and that there has been omitted from the Registration Statement no material facts *included in such data.* Although *we have not otherwise verified* the completeness or accuracy of the information furnished to us, on the basis of the foregoing and with the exception of the financial statements and schedules (which this opinion does not pass upon), we have no reason to believe that the Registration Statement or Prospectus contains any untrue statement of any material fact or omits to state a material fact required to be stated therein or necessary in order to make the statements therein not misleading."

Coleman testified that Drexel had an understanding with its attorneys that "we expect them to inspect on our behalf the corporate records of the company including, but not limited to, the minutes of the corporation, the stockholders and the committees of the board authorized to act for the board." Ballard manifested his awareness of this understanding by sending Stanton to read the minutes and the major contracts. It is difficult to square this understanding with the formal opinion of Ballard's firm which expressly disclaimed any attempt to verify information supplied by the company and its counsel.

In any event, it is clear that no effectual attempt at verification was made. The question is whether due diligence required that it be made. Stated another way, it is sufficient to ask questions, to obtain answers which, if true, would be thought satisfactory, and to let it go at that, without seeking to ascertain from the records whether the answers in fact are true and complete?

I have already held that this procedure is not sufficient in Grant's case. Are underwriters in a different position, as far as due diligence is concerned?

The underwriters say that the prospectus is the company's prospectus, not theirs. Doubtless this is the way they customarily regard it. But the Securities Act makes no such distinction. The underwriters are just as responsible as the company if the prospectus is false. And prospective investors rely upon the reputation of the underwriters in deciding whether to purchase the securities.

There is no direct authority on this question, no judicial decision defining the degree of diligence which underwriters must exercise to establish their defense under Section 11.[25]

There is some authority in New York for the proposition that a director of a corporation may rely upon information furnished him by the officers without independently verifying it. See Litwin v. Allen, 25 N.Y.S.2d 667 (Sup.Ct.1940).

In support of that principle, the court in Litwin (25 N.Y.S.2d at 719) quoted from the opinion of Lord Halsbury in Dovey v. Cory, [1901] App.Cas. 477, 486, in which he said:

> "The business of life could not go on if people could not trust those who are put into a position of trust for the express purpose of attending to details of management."

Of course, New York law does not govern this case. The construction of the Securities Act is a matter of federal law. But the underwriters argue that Litwin is still in point, for they say that it establishes a standard of reasonableness for the reasonably prudent director which should be the same as the standard for the reasonably prudent underwriter under the Securities Act.

In my opinion the two situations are not analogous. An underwriter has not put the company's officers "into a position of trust for the express purpose of attending to details of management." The underwriters did not select them. In a sense, the positions of the underwriter and the company's officers are adverse. It is not unlikely that statements made by company officers to an underwriter to induce him

---

25. There are at least two decisions of the Securities and Exchange Commission which indicate that it is the Commission's view that an underwriter must go beyond and behind the representations of management. Matter of Richmond Corp., [1962–1964 Decisions] CCH Sec.L.Rep. § 76,904 (1963); Matter of Charles E. Bailey & Co., 35 S.E.C. 33 (1953).

to underwrite may be self-serving. They may be unduly enthusiastic. As in this case, they may, on occasion, be deliberately false.

The purpose of Section 11 is to protect investors. To that end the underwriters are made responsible for the truth of the prospectus. If they may escape that responsibility by taking at face value representations made to them by the company's management, then the inclusion of underwriters among those liable under Section 11 affords the investors no additional protection. To effectuate the statute's purpose, the phrase "reasonable investigation" must be construed to require more effort on the part of the underwriters than the mere accurate reporting in the prospectus of "data presented" to them by the company. It should make no difference that this data is elicited by questions addressed to the company officers by the underwriters, or that the underwriters at the time believe that the company's officers are truthful and reliable. In order to make the underwriters' participation in this enterprise of any value to the investors, the underwriters must make some reasonable attempt to verify the data submitted to them. They may not rely solely on the company's officers or on the company's counsel. A prudent man in the management of his own property would not rely on them.

It is impossible to lay down a rigid rule suitable for every case defining the extent to which such verification must go. It is a question of degree, a matter of judgment in each case. In the present case, the underwriters' counsel made almost no attempt to verify management's representations. I hold that that was insufficient.

On the evidence in this case, I find that the underwriters' counsel did not make a reasonable investigation of the truth of those portions of the prospectus which were not made on the authority of Peat, Marwick as an expert. Drexel is bound by their failure. It is not a matter of relying upon counsel for legal advice. Here the attorneys were dealing with matters of fact. Drexel delegated to them, as its agent, the business of examining the corporate minutes and contracts. It must bear the consequences of their failure to make an adequate examination.

The other underwriters, who did nothing and relied solely on Drexel and on the lawyers, are also bound by it. It follows that although Drexel and the other underwriters believed that those portions of the prospectus were true, they had no reasonable ground for that belief, within the meaning of the statute. Hence, they have not established their due diligence defense, except as to the 1960 audited figures.[26]

The same conclusion must apply to Coleman. Although he participated quite actively in the earlier stages of the preparation of the prospectus, and contributed questions and warnings of his own, in addition to the questions of counsel, the fact is that he stopped his

26. In view of this conclusion, it becomes unnecessary to decide whether the underwriters other than Drexel would have been protected if Drexel had established that as lead underwriter, it made a reasonable investigation.

participation toward the end of March 1961. He made no investigation after he became a director. When it came to verification, he relied upon his counsel to do it for him. Since counsel failed to do it, Coleman is bound by that failure. Consequently, in his case also, he has not established his due diligence defense except as to the audited 1960 figures.

Peat, Marwick

Section 11(b) provides:

"Notwithstanding the provisions of subsection (a) no person * * * shall be liable as provided therein who shall sustain the burden of proof—

* * *

"(3) that * * * (B) as regards any part of the registration statement purporting to be made upon his authority as an expert * * * (i) he had, after reasonable investigation, reasonable ground to believe and did believe, at the time such part of the registration statement became effective, that the statements therein were true and that there was no omission to state a material fact required to be stated therein or necessary to make the statements therein not misleading * * *."

This defines the due diligence defense for an expert. Peat, Marwick has pleaded it.

The part of the registration statement purporting to be made upon the authority of Peat, Marwick as an expert was, as we have seen, the 1960 figures. But because the statute requires the court to determine Peat, Marwick's belief, and the grounds thereof, "at the time such part of the registration statement became effective," for the purposes of this affirmative defense, the matter must be viewed as of May 16, 1961, and the question is whether at that time Peat, Marwick, after reasonable investigation, had reasonable ground to believe and did believe that the 1960 figures were true and that no material fact had been omitted from the registration statement which should have been included in order to make the 1960 figures not misleading. In deciding this issue, the court must consider not only what Peat, Marwick did in its 1960 audit, but also what it did in its subsequent "S–1 review." The proper scope of that review must also be determined.

It may be noted that we are concerned at this point only with the question of Peat, Marwick's liability to plaintiffs. At the closing on May 24, 1961, Peat, Marwick delivered a so-called "comfort letter" to the underwriters. This letter stated:

"It is understood that this letter is for the information of the underwriters and is not to be quoted or referred to, in whole or in part, in the Registration Statement or Prospectus or in any literature used in connection with the sale of securities."

Plaintiffs may not take advantage of any undertakings or representations in this letter. If they exceeded the normal scope of an S–1 review (a question which I do not now decide) that is a matter which relates only to the crossclaims which defendants have asserted against each other and which I have postponed for determination at a later date.

The 1960 Audit

Peat, Marwick's work was in general charge of a member of the firm, Cummings, and more immediately in charge of Peat, Marwick's manager, Logan. Most of the actual work was performed by a senior accountant, Berardi, who had junior assistants, one of whom was Kennedy.

Berardi was then about thirty years old. He was not yet a C.P.A. He had had no previous experience with the bowling industry. This was his first job as a senior accountant. He could hardly have been given a more difficult assignment.

After obtaining a little background information on BarChris by talking to Logan and reviewing Peat, Marwick's work papers on its 1959 audit, Berardi examined the results of test checks of BarChris's accounting procedures which one of the junior accountants had made, and he prepared an "internal control questionnaire" and an "audit program." Thereafter, for a few days subsequent to December 30, 1960, he inspected BarChris's inventories and examined certain alley construction. Finally, on January 13, 1961, he began his auditing work which he carried on substantially continuously until it was completed on February 24, 1961. Toward the close of the work, Logan reviewed it and made various comments and suggestions to Berardi.

It is unnecessary to recount everything that Berardi did in the course of the audit. We are concerned only with the evidence relating to what Berardi did or did not do with respect to those items which I have found to have been incorrectly reported in the 1960 figures in the prospectus. More narrowly, we are directly concerned only with such of those items as I have found to be material.

Capitol Lanes

First, and foremost is Berardi's failure to discover that Capitol Lanes had not been sold. This error affected both the sales figure and the liability side of the balance sheet. Fundamentally, the error stemmed from the fact that Berardi never realized that Heavenly Lanes and Capitol were two different names for the same alley. In the course of his audit, Berardi was shown BarChris's contract file. He examined the contracts in the file and made a list of them. The file must have included a contract with an outside purchaser for Heavenly Lanes, although no such contract was ever produced at the trial, for Berardi included Heavenly on his list. Apparently there was no contract in the file for a lane name Capitol because that name did not appear on Berardi's list.

Kircher also made a list of jobs. Heavenly was on his list. Capitol was not. Berardi compared the two lists and satisfied himself that he had the proper jobs to be taken into account. Berardi assumed that Heavenly was to be treated like any other completed job. He included it in all his computations.

The evidence is conflicting as to whether BarChris's officers expressly informed Berardi that Heavenly and Capitol were the same thing and that BarChris was operating Capitol and had not sold it. I find that they did not so inform him.

Berardi did become aware that there were references here and there in BarChris's records to something called Capitol Lanes. He also knew that there were indications that at some time BarChris might operate an alley of that name. He read the minutes of the board of directors' meeting of November 22, 1960 which recited that:

> "* * * the Chairman recommended that the Corporation operate Capitol Lanes, 271 Main Street, East Haven, Connecticut, through a corporation which would be a subsidiary of Sanpark Realty Corp."

The minutes further recorded that:

> "* * * it was unanimously agreed that the officers of the Corporation exercise their discretion as to operating Capitol Lanes through the aforesaid subsidiary on an experimental basis."

The junior accountant, Kennedy, read the minute book of Capitol Lanes, Inc., a Connecticut corporation organized in December 1960. The book contained a certificate of incorporation which empowered the corporation, among many other things, to own and manage bowling alleys. There was no minute in the book, however, that indicated that the corporation actually did own or manage one.

Berardi knew from various BarChris records that Capitol Lanes, Inc. was paying rentals to Talcott. Also, a Peat, Marwick work paper bearing Kennedy's initials recorded that Capitol Lanes, Inc. held certain insurance policies, including a fire insurance policy on "contents," a workmen's compensation and a public liability policy. Another Peat, Marwick work paper also bearing Kennedy's initials recorded that Capitol Lanes, Inc. had $1,000 in a fund in Connecticut. A note on this paper read:

> "Traced to disbursements book—advanced for operation of alley—not expensed at 12/31/60."

Logan's written comments upon the audit contained an entry reading as follows:

> "When talking to Ted Kircher in latter part of '60 he indicated one subsidiary is leasing alley built by BarChris—the profit on this job should be eliminated as its ownership is within the affiliated group."

Opposite this note is an entry by Berardi reading as follows:

"Properties sold to others by affiliates. Capitol Lanes is paying currently lease rentals which amount to a lease purchase plan."

This note is somewhat ambiguous. If by "others" Berardi meant outside buyers, then it would seem that he should have accounted in some way for this sale, which he did not do. Presumably, by "others" he meant "other affiliates." Hence, he regarded the transaction, whatever he thought it to have been, as an intercompany one. Apparently Logan so understood Berardi's explanation.

Berardi testified that he inquired of Russo about Capitol Lanes and that Russo told him that Capitol Lanes, Inc. was going to operate an alley some day but as yet it had no alley. Berardi testified that he understood that the alley had not been built and that he believed that the rental payments were on vacant land.

I am not satisfied with this testimony. If Berardi did hold this belief, he should not have held it. The entries as to insurance and as to "operation of alley" should have alerted him to the fact that an alley existed. He should have made further inquiry on the subject. It is apparent that Berardi did not understand this transaction.

In any case, he never identified this mysterious Capitol with the Heavenly Lanes which he had included in his sales and profit figures. The vital question is whether he failed to make a reasonable investigation which, if he had made it, would have revealed the truth.

Certain accounting records of BarChris, which Berardi testified he did not see, would have put him on inquiry. One was a job cost ledger card for job no. 6036, the job number which Berardi put on his own work sheet for Heavenly Lanes. This card read "Capital Theatre (Heavenly)." In addition, two accounts receivable cards each showed both names on the same card, Capitol and Heavenly. Berardi testified that he looked at the accounts receivable records but that he did not see these particular cards. He testified that he did not look on the job cost ledger cards because he took the costs from another record, the costs register.

The burden of proof on this issue is on Peat, Marwick. Although the question is a rather close one, I find that Peat, Marwick has not sustained that burden. Peat, Marwick has not proved that Berardi made a reasonable investigation as far as Capitol Lanes was concerned and that his ignorance of the true facts was justified.

Howard Lanes Annex

Berardi also failed to discover that this alley was not sold. Here the evidence is much scantier. Berardi saw a contract for this alley in the contract file. No one told him that it was to be leased rather than sold. There is no evidence to indicate that any record existed which would have put him on notice. I find that his investigation was reasonable as to this item.

* * *

This disposes of the inaccuracies in the 1960 sales figures. I turn now to the errors in the current assets which involve four items: cash, reserve for Federal Lanes, factors' reserves and Howard Lanes Annex, which latter I have already covered.

As to cash, Berardi properly obtained a confirmation from the bank as to BarChris's cash balance on December 31, 1960. He did not know that part of this balance had been temporarily increased by the deposit of reserves returned by Talcott to BarChris conditionally for a limited time. I do not believe that Berardi reasonably should have known this. Although Peat, Marwick's work papers record the fact that these reserves were returned, there was nothing to indicate that the payment was conditional. Russo obviously did not reveal this fact. It would not be reasonable to require Berardi to examine all of Bar-Chris's correspondence files when he had no reason to suspect any irregularity.

As to the reserve on Federal Lanes, there is little to add to the earlier discussion of this subject in this opinion. I appreciate that in that instance the court has substituted its judgment for that of Russo and Berardi. For the reasons previously mentioned, I believe that their judgment was clearly wrong.

As to factors' reserves, it is hard to understand how Berardi could have treated this item as entirely a current asset when it was obvious that most of the reserves would not be released within one year. If Berardi was unaware of that fact, he should have been aware of it.

The net result, as far as current assets are concerned, is that Peat, Marwick is responsible for the errors as to reserves but not for those involving the cash item and the receivable from Howard Lanes Annex.

Contingent Liabilities

Berardi erred in computing the contingent liability on Type B leaseback transactions at 25 per cent. He testified that he was shown an agreement with Talcott which fixed the contingent liability at that amount. In this testimony he was mistaken. No such document is contained in Peat, Marwick's work papers. The evidence indicates that it never existed. Berardi did not examine the documents which are in evidence which establish that BarChris's contingent liability on this type of transaction was in fact 100 per cent. Berardi did not make a reasonable investigation in this instance. Although I have found that the error in understanding contingent liabilities as of December 31, 1960 would not have deterred a prospective purchaser, the error is nevertheless of some importance because it apparently led Trilling into making a larger error in computing the contingent liability figure as of April 30, 1961.

The S–1 Review

The purpose of reviewing events subsequent to the date of a certified balance sheet (referred to as an S–1 review when made with reference to a registration statement) is to ascertain whether any material change has occurred in the company's financial position which should be disclosed in order to prevent the balance sheet figures from being misleading. The scope of such a review, under generally accepted auditing standards, is limited. It does not amount to a complete audit.

Peat, Marwick prepared a written program for such a review. I find that this program conformed to generally accepted auditing standards. Among other things, it required the following:

"1. Review minutes of stockholders, directors and committees. * * *

"2. Review latest interim financial statements and compare with corresponding statements of preceding year. Inquire regarding significant variations and changes.

* * *

"4. Review the more important financial records and inquire regarding material transactions not in the ordinary course of business and any other significant items.

* * *

"6. Inquire as to changes in material contracts * * *.

* * *

"10. Inquire as to any significant bad debts or accounts in dispute for which provision has not been made.

* * *

"14. Inquire as to * * * newly discovered liabilities, direct or contingent * * *."

Berardi made the S–1 review in May 1961. He devoted a little over two days to it, a total of 20½ hours. He did not discover any of the errors or omissions pertaining to the state of affairs in 1961 which I have previously discussed at length, all of which were material. The question is whether, despite his failure to find out anything, his investigation was reasonable within the meaning of the statute.

What Berardi did was to look at a consolidating trial balance as of March 31, 1961 which had been prepared by BarChris, compare it with the audited December 31, 1960 figures, discuss with Trilling certain unfavorable developments which the comparison disclosed, and read certain minutes. He did not examine any "important financial records" other than the trial balance. As to minutes, he read only what minutes Birnbaum gave him, which consisted only of the board of directors' minutes of BarChris. He did not read such minutes as there were of the executive committee. He did not know that there was an executive committee, hence he did not discover that Kircher had notes of executive committee minutes which had not been written up. He did not read the minutes of any subsidiary.

In substance, what Berardi did is similar to what Grant and Ballard did. He asked questions, he got answers which he considered satisfactory, and he did nothing to verify them. For example, he obtained from Trilling a list of contracts. The list included Yonkers and Bridge. Since Berardi did not read the minutes of subsidiaries, he did not learn that Yonkers and Bridge were intercompany sales. The list also included Woonsocket and the six T–Bowl jobs, Moravia Road, Milford, Groton, North Attleboro, Odenton and Severna Park. Since Berardi did not look at any contract documents, and since he was unaware of the executive committee minutes of March 18, 1961 (at that time embodied only in Kircher's notes), he did not learn that BarChris had no contracts for these jobs. Trilling's list did not set forth contract prices for them, although it did for Yonkers, Bridge and certain others. This did not arouse Berardi's suspicion.

Berardi noticed that there had been an increase in notes payable by BarChris. Trilling admitted to him that BarChris was "a bit slow" in paying its bills. Berardi recorded in his notes of his review that BarChris was in a "tight cash position." Trilling's explanation was that BarChris was experiencing "some temporary difficulty."

Berardi had no conception of how tight the cash position was. He did not discover that BarChris was holding up checks in substantial amounts because there was no money in the bank to cover them. He did not know of the loan from Manufacturers Trust Company or of the officers' loans. Since he never read the prospectus, he was not even aware that there had ever been any problem about loans from officers.

During the 1960 audit Berardi had obtained some information from factors, not sufficiently detailed even then, as to delinquent notes. He made no inquiry of factors about this in his S–1 review. Since he knew nothing about Kircher's notes of the executive committee meetings, he did not learn that the delinquency situation had grown worse. He was content with Trilling's assurance that no liability theretofore contingent had become direct.

Apparently the only BarChris officer with whom Berardi communicated was Trilling. He could not recall making any inquiries of Russo, Vitolo or Pugliese. As to Kircher, Berardi's testimony was self-contradictory. At one point he said that he had inquired of Kircher and at another he said that he could not recall making any such inquiry.

There had been a material change for the worse in BarChris's financial position. That change was sufficiently serious so that the failure to disclose it made the 1960 figures misleading. Berardi did not discover it. As far as results were concerned, his S–1 review was useless.

Accountants should not be held to a standard higher than that recognized in their profession. I do not do so here. Berardi's review did not come up to that standard. He did not take some of the steps which Peat, Marwick's written program prescribed. He did not spend an adequate amount of time on a task of this magnitude. Most important of all, he was too easily satisfied with glib answers to his inquiries.

This is not to say that he should have made a complete audit. But there were enough danger signals in the materials which he did examine to require some further investigation on his part. Generally accepted accounting standards required such further investigation under these circumstances. It is not always sufficient merely to ask questions.

Here again, the burden of proof is on Peat, Marwick. I find that that burden has not been satisfied. I conclude that Peat, Marwick has not established its due diligence defense. . . .

Defendants' motions to dismiss this action, upon which decision was reserved at the trial, are denied. Motions made at various times during the trial to strike certain testimony are also denied, except in so far as such motions pertain to evidence relating to the issues still undecided.

Pursuant to Rule 52(a), this opinion constitutes the court's findings of fact and conclusions of law with respect to the issues determined herein.

So ordered.

SECTION 8.   BLUE SKY LAWS

NOTE ON BLUE SKY LAWS

Prior to the entry of the federal government into the field of securities regulation in 1933, almost all of the states had adopted statutes designed to protect the public from "speculative schemes which have no more basis than so many feet of 'blue sky.'" Hall v. Geiger–Jones Co., 242 U.S. 539, 550, 37 S.Ct. 217, 220–21, 61 L.Ed. 480, 489 (1917).

At present, all states have blue-sky laws in effect. The blue-sky laws vary tremendously in coverage, approach and impact. Three basic methods of regulation are employed, which are sometimes referred to as the *fraud*, *dealer-registration*, and *securities-registration* methods. Most states have adopted all three methods to varying extents, but the methods are adopted in different forms, and the governing standards and procedures vary widely from state to state.

1. *The Fraud Method.* The fraud method simply makes certain practices, usually described by some form of the word "fraud," grounds for criminal prosecution, suspension of trading, or both. The blue-sky administrator normally has broad investigatory powers, but those powers are usually exercised only where there has been complaint or where there are suspicious circumstances. Probably for this reason, the fraud method is not thought to be sufficient in itself.

2. *The Dealer–Registration Method.* The dealer-registration method requires dealers (including issuers, brokers, and salesmen) to register as a prerequisite to trading in securities within a state's borders. The amount, detail, and nature of the information required to register varies widely. In a majority of states, registration may be denied or revoked for cause. The blue-sky administrator sometimes has considerable discretion in determining whether a dealer will be permitted to do business within the state.

3. *The Securities–Registration Method.* The securities-registration method prohibits dealing in an issue of securities until the issue has been qualified under a designated statutory standard, and in accordance with a designated statutory procedure. This method is sometimes referred to as *merit regulation*, because in contrast to registration under the Securities Act, the blue-sky administrator can deny registration on the ground that the securities issue lacks merit, even though full disclosure has been made. The standards and procedures vary considerably from state to state. In general, the standards and procedures are aimed at unseasoned speculative securities that are to be offered to the general public.

The securities-registration or merit-regulation method encompasses three basic approaches.

a. *The qualifying approach.* Under the *qualifying* approach, trading in an issue of non-exempt securities is permitted only if an affirmative administrative determination has been made that the issue meets a designated statutory standard, such as "fair, just and equitable." More specific standards are usually imposed on issues of particularly unsafe kinds.

b. *The Notification approach.* Under the *notification* approach, which is often available for seasoned securities, registration becomes effective after a designated period following notice to the blue-sky administrator of the proposed new issuance, unless the administrator moves to block it.

c. *The Coordination approach.* The *coordination* approach is similar to the notification approach, but is available only for issues registered under the federal Securities Act. The information submitted to the blue-sky administrator basically consists of copies of the material filed with the SEC. In the absence of adverse action by the administrator, the state registration becomes effective at the moment the federal registration statement becomes effective.

4. *Federal Preemption.* In 1996, section 18 of the Securities Act was amended to preclude states from requiring blue-sky-law registration of securities that are designated in section 18 as "covered securities." Covered securities, which section 18 exempts from state registration requirements, include (i) Securities listed on the New York Stock Exchange, the American Stock Exchange, and the Nasdaq's National Market System. (ii) Securities offered only to "qualified purchasers," as defined by the SEC. (iii) Certain securities whose sale is exempt from registration under the Securities Act.

Under section 18, therefore, the reach of the blue-sky laws has been substantially reduced. The states now can only apply merit-regulation registration requirements to securities that are not "covered securities" under section 18. The states can, however, continue to bring fraud proceedings, and to require filing, even in respect to covered securities, solely for purposes of notice, coordination, and—most significantly—filing-fee charges.

APPENDIX

NOTE ON THE SARBANES–OXLEY ACT

The Sarbanes–Oxley Act of 2002 ("Sarbanes–Oxley" or "the Act") was adopted against the background of, and in response to, several major corporate scandals in the United States. The most well-known concerned Enron and WorldCom. Enron was the leader in its business sector of energy trading, and was the seventh largest corporation in the *Fortune 500*. WorldCom was a leader in the telecom sector, and the forty-second largest corporation in the *Fortune 500*. Both corporations were discovered to have systematically and massively distorted their financial condition—income, expenses, assets, and liabilities. Soon after that discovery, both corporations filed for protection under Chapter 11 of the Bankruptcy Code. Among other major corporations that are known to have or seem to have engaged in massive financial fraud were Adelphia Communications Corporation, Global Crossing Ltd., HealthSouth Corp., Rite Aid Corp., and Xerox Corp. Adelphia and Global Crossing also filed for protection under the Bankruptcy Code.

It quickly became apparent that many other American corporations had also systematically distorted their financial condition, although in most of the other cases the impact was not as grave as it was in the case of Enron and WorldCom. It also became apparent that there were two related underlying reasons that led to these severe problems. One reason concerned executive compensation. The other reason concerned the accounting profession.

A. *Executive Compensation*

Beginning around fifteen years ago, many observers came to believe that there was very little relation between executive pay and corporate performance. Accordingly, institutional investors and others began pressing for a closer link between pay and performance.

The corporate response to this pressure was to award very large amounts of executive stock options as compensation. The theory was that stock options effected a link between pay and performance, because executives would profit from the options if and only if their corporations performed well and the value of the options therefore increased, and because stock options would align the interests of the executives with the interests of shareholders. Thus in 1990, only 8% of the pay package of the typical CEO was in equity. In contrast, in 2001, 66% of the pay package of the typical CEO was in equity.

Executive stock options have long been common in the United States. What changed was the massive scale on which such options came to be awarded. For example, in 1999 alone Michael Eisner's compensation as CEO of Disney was $576 million, and Sandy Weill's compensation as CEO of Citigroup was $167 million—in each case mostly attributable to the exercise of stock options. (Michael Eisner's total stock-option compensation was probably close to $2 billion).

Two elements of executive stock options stand out for present purposes—lack of expensing and lack of indexing.

1. *Lack of expensing.* In the past, generally accepted accounting principles in the United States have not required that the value of executive stock options be *expensed*, that is, deducted from income. Accordingly, executive compensation that takes the form of stock options has been somewhat opaque, and has not affected the corporation's reported income. Partly for these reasons, there has proved to be little if any constraint on this form of compensation.

2. *Lack of indexing.* The value of a corporation's stock can increase even if the corporation performs poorly in relation to the general market, the business sector that the corporation is in, or both. This may occur because, for example, the economy goes from recession to growth, so that the value of all stocks rise, or because there is an increase in the value of stocks in the sector in which the corporation does business due to exogenous conditions, such as change in oil prices or in tariffs. However, executive stock options are seldom if ever indexed to either the general stock market or to stocks in the corporation's business sector. Accordingly, the value of executive stock options may, and undoubtedly does, frequently go up even if the corporation underperforms the market, the corporation's business sector, or both.

The direct effect of the surge in executive stock options has been to shift some corporate wealth from shareholders to managers. The indirect and perhaps more important effect was to give managers a powerful incentive to manipulate the corporation's apparent financial condition, so as to drive up the price of the corporation's stock and therefore the value of their options.

B.   The Accounting Profession

At the same time as the number and value of executive stock options was going sky high, there were also significant changes in the economics of the accounting profession and the manner in which that profession was regulated. The basic function of accountants is to audit, that is, to perform appropriate sampling tests to ensure that the financial data of a client is accurate, and to apply generally accepted principles to ensure that the way in which financial statements are presented reflects the corporation's underlying financial realities. In performing this function, accountants serve as *gatekeepers*, that is, they serve or should serve to fence out improper financial statements. The change in the economics of the profession involved the growth of *consulting*, as opposed to *audit*, services. Prior to the 1990s, accountants traditionally had given tax advice as well as performing audits, and had also developed other consulting activities, such as management consulting and computer consulting. Until the 1990s, however, accounting firms had for the most part not put major emphasis on selling consulting services to their own audit clients. That changed dramatically in the mid–1990s. Partly this change resulted from the fact that auditing had become commodified—that is, the auditing services of the various accounting firms had begun to look fairly indistinguishable. As a result of this commodification, corporations put downward pressure on auditing fees, and the profit margins on auditing became relatively low. In contrast, consulting was not commodified, and profit margins were very high. Moreover, an accounting firm that provided audit services to a corporation was in a very good position to get consulting contracts from the client corporation as a result of the knowledge about the corporation's business that the accountant derived from auditing. Accordingly, the volume of non-audit services that accountants provided to their audit clients began to markedly increase. Furthermore, it became common for accounting firms to push their lead auditors (the members of the firm who led the auditing teams) to increase the accounting firm's consulting revenues from the audit clients, and to compensate lead auditors in significant part based on the amount of consulting business they developed from their audit clients.

This massive provision of non-audit services by accounting firms seriously threatened the integrity of the accountants' gatekeeping function. There has always been a tension between the duties and the interests of accounting firms. The *duties* of accounting firms are to ensure that their audit clients' financial statements present fairly the clients' financial condition. The *interests* of accounting firms are to make profits. These duties and interests conflict when the client wants to present its financial condition—income, expenses, assets, and liabilities—in an improper way. In such cases, the client can bring to bear two sorts of pressure on its accountant to go along with the impropriety. The first kind of pressure is a threat to discharge the accountant. The second kind of pressure is a threat to force the reassignment of the lead auditor. If a client pushes an accounting firm to reassign the partner who is serving as the client's lead auditor, that partner may suffer financially and in other ways.

The pressure that a corporate client could put on its accounting firms, and lead auditor, to acquiesce in an improper presentation of the client's financial condition, was enormously accentuated by the growth of non-audit services, because clients who were displeased with an accounting firm's audit services could punish the firm by not renewing existing contracts, or by withholding new contracts, for these highly profitable services. This pressure was further intensified by the fact it is difficult for a corporation to discharge an accounting firm as its outside auditor, but easy to not renew an accounting firm's consulting contracts, or to not award further consulting contracts.

In short, in the 1990s the economics of the accounting profession had developed in a way that made it extremely attractive for accounting firms to abdicate their gatekeeper function by bending to their client's financial improprieties. At the same time, there were important changes in the law that reduced the risks to an accounting firm for such an abdication. In the years prior to 1994, the Courts of Appeal had all held that an accountant who aided and abetted a client's fraudulent conduct violated SEC Rule 10b–5. In 1994, however, the Supreme Court overthrew this rule in *Central Bank of Denver v. First Interstate Bank of Denver*, 511 U.S. 164, and held that Rule 10b–5 did not impose aiding-and-abetting liability. Later, Congress adopted the Private Securities Litigation Act, which generally made securities-law litigation more difficult. Accordingly, just as accounting firms were coming under increasing economic pressure to aid and abet corporate fraud, the main sanction against aiding and abetting was removed. The result of these developments was disasters like Enron and WorldCom.

II. Sarbanes–Oxley

Sarbanes–Oxley was developed against the background of, and as a response to the developments. The major provisions of the Act can be divided into three overlapping categories: accounting, corporate governance, and disclosure. In many cases, the Act does not directly regulate given conduct, but instead directs the SEC to adopt rules to regulate the conduct. References in the balance of this Note to the Act should be understood to mean the Act as implemented by SEC rules.

A. Accounting

A large part of Sarbanes–Oxley is directed to the adoption of institutions and mechanisms designed to reinstate the integrity of the accounting process and improve the efficacy of financial reporting. The Act addresses those issues in four ways. First, the Act creates a new Board to supervise accounting firms. Second, the Act regulates the provision of non-audit services by accountants to their auditing clients. Third, the Act strengthens the role of the corporate audit committee. Fourth, the Act requires the CEO and the chief financial officer (CFO) to certify the corporation's financial statements.

1. *Supervision of accountants.* Prior to Sarbanes–Oxley, there was no institutional mechanism to provide general supervision of accounting firms. Sarbanes–Oxley changed this by creating the Public Company Accounting Oversight Board ("the Board"), and requiring all accounting firms that prepare audit reports for public companies to become "registered public accountants" by registering with the Board. (In the balance of this Note, the terms *accounting firms*, *accountants*, and *outside auditors* will be used to mean registered public accountants, and the terms *corporations* and *audit clients* will be used to mean publicly held corporations and other publicly held entities that are regulated under Sarbanes–Oxley.*)

The Act gives the Board large powers with respect to auditing and attestation standards, quality-control standards, ethical standards to govern the preparation of audit reports, standards of independence, and other standards relating to the preparation and issuance of audit

---

* Different sections of Sarbanes–Oxley regulate slightly different groups of publicly held corporations. Furthermore, some regulation under Sarbanes–Oxley is direct and some is indirect. For further simplicity of exposi-tion, this Note does not distinguish either between slightly different groups of publicly held corporations under the Act, or between direct and indirect regulation under the Act.

reports. In addition, certain standards are specified by the Act. (For example, a partner of an accounting firm other than the lead auditor must review and approve audit reports, and lead auditors must be rotated at least every five years.) The Act also directs the Board to conduct regular compliance inspections, and authorizes the Board to discipline accounting firms that violate the Act, the rules issued by the Board, securities laws relating to the preparation and issuance of audit reports, or professional standards.

2. *Non-audit services.* Sarbanes–Oxley also regulates the provision of non-audit (consulting) services by accounting firms to their audit clients. This regulation takes two forms.

a. *Prohibited Services.* First, accounting firms are prohibited from rendering certain non-audit services to their audit clients. These prohibited services include: (1) Bookkeeping or other services related to the corporation's accounting records or financial statements. (2) The design and information of financial-information services. (3) Appraisal or valuation services, and fairness opinions. (4) Actuarial services. (5) Internal-audit outsourcing services. (6) Management-function services. (7) Human-resource (personnel) services. (8) Broker-dealer services. (9) Investment-adviser services. (10) Investment-banker services. (11) Legal services. Notably, the provision of tax-consulting services is not prohibited.

b. *Permitted Non–Audit Services.* Accountants are not prohibited from rendering other non-audit services to their audit clients. However, the rendition of such services (including, for example, tax consulting) must be approved in advance by the corporation's audit committee, and disclosed to investors in the corporation's periodic reports.

3. *Audit Committee.* Sarbanes–Oxley dramatically enhances the role of the audit committee in controlling the relationship between corporations and accounting firms. A corporation's accountant—its outside auditor—audits the financial results achieved by the corporation's senior executives. Therefore, there is a serious conflict of interest if power over the appointment and retention of the outside auditor, and oversight of the outside auditor, is vested in the very executives whose results are being audited. Vesting that power in the board, rather than the executives, would also be insufficient. Often the board is effectively dominated by the CEO, and in any event a board has so many issues to deal with that it cannot effectively oversee the accounting process. Accordingly, there has been a long-term trend to vest the power to retain, dismiss, and oversee the corporation's accountant in the audit committee. Sarbanes–Oxley carries this trend forward in two critical respects.

First, the Act effectively requires corporations to have an audit committee, and requires the committee to be composed entirely of independent directors. In addition, a corporation must disclose annually whether the audit committee includes at least one financial expert, and if so, the name of the expert. A corporation that does not have an audit-committee financial expert will be required to disclose this fact and explain why it has no such expert.

Second, the Act makes the audit committee—not the senior executives, the board, or the shareholders—directly responsible for the appointment, compensation, and oversight of the independent outside auditor, and requires the outside auditor to report to the audit committee. The audit committee is also empowered to engage independent counsel and other advisers at the corporation's expense, and is required to establish procedures for receiving and evaluating anonymous submissions by employees regarding questionable accounting or auditing matters.

4. *Certifications*. In addition to the controls over accounting firms, Sarbanes–Oxley and the rules thereunder require the CEO and the CFO to certify, in connection with the filing of their company's periodic reports, that they have reviewed the report, and that based on their knowledge: (1) The report does not contain any material misstatement or omission; and (2) "the financial statements, and other financial information included in the report, fairly present in all material respects the financial condition and results of operations of the [corporation] as of, and for, the periods presented in the report."

The critical point here is this: Under American accounting practice, the accountant normally certifies that the corporation's financial statements present fairly, in all material respects, the financial condition of the corporation, and the results of its operations and cash flows, in accordance with generally accepted accounting principles (GAAP). However, there may be cases where the corporation's financial statement present fairly the corporation's financial condition in accordance with GAAP, but do not present fairly the corporation's financial condition. This may occur, for example, because several different principles could be used to account for a particular item under GAAP; or because the spirit of GAAP can be evaded by a technicality; or simply because particular GAAP principles are bad principles that are kept in place by as a result of pressure exerted on the authority that sets GAAP. In contrast, under Sarbanes–Oxley the CEO and CFO must certify that the corporation's financial statements fairly present the corporation's financial condition, rather than present the corporation's financial position fairly in accordance with GAAP. Accordingly, when the CEO or CFO has reason to know that financial statements that comply with GAAP nevertheless fail to fairly present the corporation's financial condition, they cannot give the certification required by Sarbanes–Oxley.

B.   *Corporate Governance*

Sarbanes–Oxley affects corporate governance directly and indirectly. Indirectly, the Act affects corporate governance through regulation of the corporation's outside auditor (Part A, supra) and through disclosure requirements (Part C, infra). The Act has a more direct effect on governance in four areas: the audit committee, internal control, codes of ethics, and loans to officers and directors.

1. *Audit committee*. The extensive regulation of audit committees under Sarbanes–Oxley has been discussed above. A significant aspect of this regulation is that it overrides state corporation law,

rather than supplementing state corporation law through disclosure requirements and the like. Under state corporation law, the creation and composition of all board committees is a board decision, and all board committees operate subject to board control. In contrast, Sarbanes–Oxley requires corporations to have audit committees, regulates the composition of audit committees, and makes the audit committee, rather than the board, responsible for the appointment, compensation, and oversight of the corporation's outside auditor.

2. *Internal control.* Sarbanes–Oxley requires corporations to file an internal control report. This report must be set forth in each annual report, and must state management's responsibility for establishing and maintaining an adequate control structure and procedures for financial reporting. This report must also contain management's assessment of the effectiveness of the internal control structure and the corporation's procedures for financial reporting. The outside auditor must attest to, and report on, this report.

In addition, the CEO and the CFO must certify, in connection with the filing of a company's periodic reports, that:

(1) They are responsible for establishing and maintaining internal controls.

(2) They have designed such internal controls as are necessary to ensure that material information relating to the corporation is made known to them during the reporting period.

(3) They have evaluated the effectiveness of the corporation's internal controls within the past 90 days, and have presented, in the report, their conclusions about the effectiveness of their internal controls as of that date.

(4) They have disclosed to the outside auditor, and to the corporation's audit committee, all significant deficiencies in the design or operation of internal controls, and any fraud, whether or not material, that involves management or other employees who have a significant role in the corporation's internal controls.

(5) They have indicated in the report whether there were significant changes in internal controls, or other factors, after the date of their evaluation, that could significantly affect those controls.

3. *Codes of Ethics.* Voluntarily adopted codes of ethics, or some counterpart instruments, have become a common instrument of internal governance. Such codes normally state principles on such matters as conflicts of interest and law compliance; include educational material concerning those matters; set out mechanisms to ensure compliance with the provisions of the code; and require employees to periodically attest that they have read and understand the code. Sarbanes–Oxley strengthens this instrument. The Act requires corporations to disclose whether they have adopted a code of ethics for the executive officer, the principal financial officer, and the comptroller or principal accounting officer, or if not, why not. Changes in, or waivers of, the code must be promptly disclosed. The Act defines "code of ethics" to mean standards that are reasonably necessary to promote honest and

ethical conduct, including the ethical handling of actual or apparent conflicts of interest between personal and professional relationships, full and fair disclosure, and compliance with applicable governmental rules and regulations.

4. *Loans to Directors and Officers.* Traditionally, many state corporation statutes included provisions that prohibited or regulated loans to directors and officers. The premise of these statutory provisions was that such loans can be a source of special problems, because they may be inadequately secured, unduly risky, or carry an inadequate rate of interest, as compared to loans made at arm's length, and these shortfalls may be opaque to shareholders. Most, perhaps all, state statutes have dropped these provisions. However, the concept has been reinstated by Sarbanes–Oxley, which provides that publicly held corporations may not directly or indirectly extend or maintain credit, arrange for an extension of credit, or renew an extension of credit, in the form of a personal loan, to or for any director or executive officer.

C. Disclosure

In addition to the disclosure rules discussed above, Sarbanes–Oxley amended Section 16 of the Exchange Act to require that principal stockholders, officers, and directors report to the SEC all changes in their ownership of securities within two business days of the transaction, instead of the following month, as was previously required. These reports must be filed electronically, and must be made public through the SEC's website and the corporation's website within one business day of filing. The filing deadlines for quarterly and annual periodic reports have also been accelerated.*

---

* The Act also includes provisions concerning the role of a corporation's attorneys. Implementation of those provisions is still ongoing.

INDEX

References are to Pages

1379

DIVIDENDS AND DISTRIBUTIONS
Bad faith, close corporations, 327 et seq.
Balance-sheet accounting for corporate equity, 1183
Capital impairment statutes
    Generally, 1175 et seq.
    Current earnings test, 1184
    Earned surplus statutes, 1186
    Exceptions, 1184 et seq.
    Nimble dividends, 1184
    Wasting assets corporations, 1184
Capital surplus, dividends from, 1185
Capitalization requirements and fraudulent transfer restrictions, 1174
Close corporations
    Bad faith, 327 et seq.
    Repurchase of shares, 1188
Compensation characterized as
    Generally, 640
    See also Compensation, this index
Current earnings test, capital impairment statutes and, 1184
Dividend record, consideration of in valuation of corporation, 396
Earned surplus
    Generally, 1185
    Statutes, 1175
Fraudulent transfers, 255
Freezeouts of minority shareholders, 327 et seq.
Inadequate capitalization and piercing of corporate veil, 241, 247
Legal capital restrictions, 1175
Limited liability companies
    Generally, 462
    Wages distinguished, 464
Nimble dividends, 1184
Paid-in surplus, 1185
Par value and dividends, 1175
Piercing doctrine and unlimited distributions, 240
Reduction surplus, 1185
Refusal to declare dividends, tax implications, 382
Repurchase of shares
    Capital impairment statutes, 1182
    Close corporations, 1188
    Dividends distinguished, 1177, 1187
    Greenmail transactions, 1188
    Manipulative transactions, 1187
    Modes of, 1187
    Selective repurchase of shares, 1188
    Self-tenders, 1189
Selective repurchase of shares, 1188
Social responsibility and maximization of profits, 134 et seq.
Statutory limitations on dividends, 1174 et seq.
Surplus
    Generally, 1185
    Requirement that dividend by paid from, 511
Tax implications of refusal to declare dividends, 382
Value of corporation, consideration of dividend record in determining, 396

DIVIDENDS AND DISTRIBUTIONS —Cont'd
Waste of assets, distribution attacked as, 507 et seq.
Wasting assets corporations, 1184

DUTIES
Care, Duty of, this index
Disclosure, Duty of, this index
Fiduciary Duties, this index
Law, Duty to Obey, this index
Legal compliance, 553
Loyalty, Duty of, this index

EFFICIENT CAPITAL MARKETS HYPOTHESIS (ECMH)
See Markets, this index

EMPLOYEE STOCK OWNERSHIP PLANS (ESOP)
Generally, 334
Repurchase plans, 335

ENTERPRISE LIABILITY
Generally, 7
Limited liability and, 232

ENTITY STATUS
Characteristics of corporate form, 106

EQUITABLE SUBROGATION
Shareholder claims, 252 et seq.

ESTOPPEL
Agency by, 10
Ultra vires and, 123

EXECUTIVE COMPENSATION
See Compensation, this index

FIDUCIARY DUTIES
See also Loyalty, Duty of, this index
Agency Relationships, this index
Close corporation shareholders, 374 et seq.
Employee shareholders fiduciary obligations to, 374 et seq., 386

FINANCIAL STATEMENTS
Generally, 25 et seq.
Accounting equation, 29
Balance sheets
    Generally, 26
    Corporate equity, treatment of, 1183
    Earned surplus, 1183
    Paid-in surplus, 1183
Capital accounts, partnership, 51 et seq.
Depreciation, 30
Double entry bookkeeping, 29
Expected return, 511
Income statements, 27
Net worth, 29
Owner's equity, 29
Partnership capital accounts, 51 et seq.
Present value, 128
Risk, accounting for, 512
Shareholders' rights to receive, 270

FRANCHISE TAXES
Incorporation choices and, 107

†